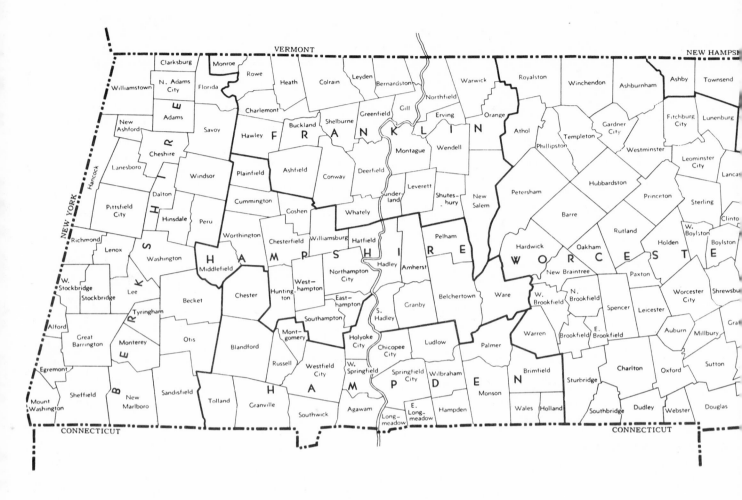

OUTLINE MAP
OF
MASSACHUSETTS

Published by
THE NATIONAL SURVEY
CHESTER, VERMONT

SCALE OF MILES

Copyright, THE NATIONAL SURVEY, Chester, Vt.

ATLANTIC

OCEAN

Massachusetts

A Bibliography of Its History

Massachusetts
A Bibliography of Its History

Volume One of Bibliographies of New England History

Prepared by the

COMMITTEE FOR A NEW ENGLAND BIBLIOGRAPHY

JOHN BORDEN ARMSTRONG
Boston University
Chairman

Edited by
JOHN D. HASKELL, JR.

UNIVERSITY PRESS OF NEW ENGLAND
Hanover and London

University Press of New England
Brandeis University
Brown University
Clark University
Dartmouth College
University of New Hampshire
University of Rhode Island
Tufts University
University of Vermont

*This volume has been
made possible in part by a grant
from the Research Materials
Program of the National Endowment
for the Humanities.*

With the exception of minor corrections in the front matter, this volume, originally published by G. K. Hall in 1976, is reprinted by the University Press of New England with no revisions.

Printed in the United States of America on permanent/durable acid-free paper.

LIBRARY OF CONGRESS CATALOGING IN PUBLICATION DATA

Haskell, John D. (John Duncan)
   Massachusetts, a bibliography of its history.

   Reprint. Originally published: Boston: G. K. Hall, 1976.
(Bibliographies of New England history; v. 1) With minor corrections in the front matter.
   Includes index.
   1. Massachusetts—History—Bibliography—Union lists.
2. Catalogs, Union—United States. I. Committee for a New England Bibliography. II. Title. III. Series: Bibliographies of New England history; v. 1.
Z1295.H24 1983 [F64] 016.9744 83-19872
ISBN 0-87451-282-4

Sponsors

American Antiquarian Society
Amherst College Library
Bangor Public Library
Bay State Historical League
Boston Athenaeum
Boston College
Boston Public Library
Boston University
Bowdoin College
Brown University Library
Colonial Society of Massachusetts
Connecticut Historical Society
Connecticut Library Association
Fred Harris Daniels Foundation, Inc.
Dartmouth College Library
Essex Institute
Faust and Louisa Fiore Memorial
Maine Historical Society
Maine State Archives
Massachusetts Historical Society
Mount Holyoke College
New England Historic Genealogical Society
New England Library Association
New Hampshire Historical Society
Old Sturbridge Village
Providence Public Library
Putnam Foundation
Rhode Island Historical Society

Smith College
Society of Colonial Wars in Massachusetts
Trinity College Library
University of Connecticut Foundation
University of Maine
University of Massachusetts
University of New Hampshire
University of Rhode Island Library
University of Vermont Library
Vermont Department of Libraries
Vermont Historical Society
Warren Brothers Company
Wellesley College Library
Wesleyan University
Williams College

Officers

Committee for a New England Bibliography

John Borden Armstrong   *Chairman*
Boston University

Albert T. Klyberg   *First Vice Chairman*
Rhode Island Historical Society

Mary L. Fisher   *Editorial Vice Chairman*
General Electric Company

Barnes Riznik   *Financial Vice Chairman*
Old Sturbridge Village

Marcus A. McCorison   *Treasurer*
American Antiquarian Society

Bryant F. Tolles, Jr.   *Clerk*
Essex Institute

Contents

Preface

USERS OF THIS bibliography may find a brief account of its origins interesting and even instructive for, emanating as it does from the land of the Puritans, this is a bibliography with a moral. Scholars, librarians, teachers, and others concerned with the history of New England have long been painfully aware of the lack of any adequate bibliographical control over the vast historical resources of the region. Individual efforts to solve the problem were understandably discouraged by its size and complexity. Nonetheless, in recent years, the work of a growing number of scholars has emphasized the need for such control even as their writings made the problem larger. A series of conferences sponsored by the American Association of University Presses and the New England Library Association in 1968 and 1969 brought together people who agreed that a bibliography of New England history was needed and feasible, that there would be no better time for it than during the nation's Bicentennial, and, most significantly, that they should assume responsibility for the project.

The Committee for a New England Bibliography was formed in 1969 by a group of about twenty historians, librarians, and historical society personnel; the next year it was incorporated under the laws of the Commonwealth of Massachusetts as a non-profit, tax-exempt organization. After an extended debate, the committee produced a general plan for the bibliography, which appeared in summary form as an announcement in the September 1970 issue of the *New England Quarterly*.

Recognizing that the possible scope of the work was practically limitless, the committee developed discrete guidelines to encompass a significant portion of the region's historical materials. Priority was given to printed materials over manuscripts and contemporaneously printed of-ficial documents. It is hoped that the success of the current project may pave the way for guides to these materials. An additional criterion for inclusion was that the work be consciously written as history, or contain a dimension of time. Experts may differ on the wisdom of particular inclusions or exclusions, but I believe the user will appreciate the breadth of coverage, for the bibliography goes far beyond a listing of monographs in regional, local, or political history. Herein will be found entries for articles in national and local periodicals, foreign language publications, edited series of government publications, collected biography, plus gazetteers, diaries, and travel accounts, from the earliest time to the present. Categories that clearly did not meet our criteria were, of course, excluded. It was decided that individual volumes in the series would be devoted to one or more states, depending on the number of entries, and there would be a final, general volume for the region. First attention was given to the state with the most material, and hence the most bibliographical problems, Massachusetts. In this fashion, while trying to recognize limitations of time and cost, the committee sought to compile a bibliography with a clear identity and one which would be comprehensive within that definition.

For this undertaking, the committee contained in its membership a wealth of talent and experience, although the same was already heavily mortgaged to other commitments and was scattered throughout New England. A careful delegation of responsibility for various parts of the project, and regular meetings and communication, enabled the committee to utilize the ability and dedication of those involved. Matters of organization and policy were primarily the responsibility of the committee's officers. The task of transforming the original general plan for the bibliography into sound and detailed guidelines was mainly the work of a small editorial board.

Financial support for the project was first sought from, and demonstrated by, the libraries and the academic and historical institutions of New England. Once this basis was established, the search for support was directed towards local foundations and private enterprise. A contribution of five hundred dollars or more formally qualified the donor as a "sponsor" of the bibliography. The project's sponsors now number forty-three, and they are listed herein. Some sponsors made more than one contribution, and other organizations and individuals made smaller contributions. All helped to demonstrate support for the idea of the bibliography, and thereby assist the committee's efforts in finding major foundation support.

With this basis of matching funds, the committee in 1972 was awarded an initial two-year grant from the National Endowment for the Humanities, and the grant has been renewed subsequently on the basis of the committee's continuing to raise matching funds. It is my pleasure to express here the committee's gratitude to the Endowment for its support, which has been crucial to the project, and for the guidance and counsel provided by the Endowment's staff during the last several years.

Other essentials for the project then began to fall into place. A national search for an editor was successfully concluded with the appointment of John Duncan Haskell, Jr., who commenced his work in November 1972. Boston University provided the editor and his assistant with an office and other benefits and courtesies. From the beginning of the undertaking, Herbert Brown of the *New England Quarterly* has provided us with the means of bringing the project to the attention of the public. Several committee members contrib-

uted manuscript bibliographies relating to New England. T. D. Seymour Bassett, of the University of Vermont, made a detailed survey of existing bibliographies of New England, which served to demonstrate the inadequacy of existing guides to the history of the region. This appeared in the June 1971 issue of the *New England Quarterly*. In short, the work of many individuals moved the project forward.

Although it is impossible to give their names, I want to express my gratitude to the many individuals who have advised and aided me on so many aspects of this enterprise, and particularly to my fellow committee members who educated me about details of compiling and publishing a bibliography of which I had been completely and blissfully ignorant. Such aid and encouragement repeatedly prevented my miring in the slough of despond. More positively, as an unanticipated personal benefit of this experience, I have gained valued friendships.

Much remains to be done to complete the Bibliographies of New England History. Fund raising will be a major concern as long as the project lasts, and it may be doubted that the times are ever really favorable for raising money for a bibliography. Different state volumes will present different problems. Nonetheless, as the first volume goes to the publisher, and the editorial machinery is redirected "down east," I believe that the committee has reached an important turning point, and that we have demonstrated that even in times of social disorder and economic distress, scholarly projects of merit but with no special allure or modishness can still be accomplished. And that, dear reader, seems to me to be the moral, the value beyond the value of such a bibliography. It may serve as an instructive example of what can be accomplished by the voluntary, cooperative efforts of individuals and institutions.

John Borden Armstrong
Associate Professor of History
Boston University

21 May 1975

Introduction

THE ARRANGEMENT of this volume follows the guidelines established by the Committee for a New England Bibliography for the Bibliographies of New England History series. It includes works of political, economic, social, and intellectual history. December 1972 was established as the terminal date for making entries, but it has been possible to include a number of titles published since then.

Geographically, Massachusetts has been considered in terms of its present boundaries. Although parts of all of the adjacent states were at one time administered or claimed by Massachusetts, no attempt has been made to include herein works relating to places which are no longer in the state. For example, although Maine was part of Massachusetts until 1820, works pertaining to Maine alone will appear in the Maine volume. However, works relating to the separation of Maine from Massachusetts appear herein and will be included also in the Maine volume.

Entries are alphabetical within a geographical framework. Works relating to the state as a whole or to several counties appear first, followed by references to individual counties, followed by the three hundred and fifty-one cities and towns. Works relating to more than one place, all of which are in the same county, appear under the county. Works pertaining to several cities or towns in different counties are found under the first named city or town.

Complete bibliographic reference is given once only. Analytics have not been made for county histories. The reader is urged to consult the index, if he wishes to locate all the entries relating to a particular place. Spelling follows that adopted by *Historical Data Relating to Counties, Cities, and Towns in Massachusetts* (entry 1165).

The bibliography is comprised of both monographs and periodical articles. Included are edited series of published archival documents and vital records, published diaries, personal papers, journals, account books, travel narratives, collected biography, natural history, literary history, historical archaeology, and military history, but only insofar as they relate to the history of a Massachusetts locale. Bibliographies relating to Massachusetts subjects and places, and histories of institutions, firms, associations, and industries are also cited.

Although the editorial search has been limited to American libraries and catalogs, the bibliography includes foreign-language titles.

Birth and death dates of authors have been given only when necessary to distinguish those persons from others of the same name who appear as authors or subjects in this bibliography. Pseudonymous works are entered under the author's autonym, with a cross reference from the pseudonym in the index. Authorships attributed by individuals or libraries other than the Library of Congress are noted.

Writings by the same author which appear consecutively are arranged alphabetically, regardless of whether they were written by the author alone or jointly. In those few entries where a multivolume work was written by several authors who did not write contemporaneously, this distinction has been noted. Title changes are indicated in a note. The latest edition is cited in full with the date of the first edition, if known, indicated in parentheses immediately following the title. Place of publication and dates supplied by the editor appear in square brackets. Variant imprints for multivolume works appear in a note. For broadsides, dimensions are given in inches, height before width.

A location is given only for those works which do not appear in the published catalogs of the Library of Congress or in the *National Union Catalog*.

The symbols are those used in the *National Union Catalog*, except for those supplied by the editor in square brackets for works in those libraries which do not have an assigned symbol. See page xxv for the key to symbols. Locations are not given for periodical articles. Users should refer to the *Union List of Serials*, *New Serial Titles*, or regional lists as available.

Index entries are given for authors, editors, compilers, subjects, and geographical places, including name changes and extinct places. Institutions appear in the index as authors only. Histories of such institutions are listed under collective subjects such as universities and colleges, historical societies, and insurance companies. It is to be stressed that since index references are to entry numbers, the reader can choose those entries under a subject which refer to a particular place by first referring to the inclusive numbers for that place in the table of contents. Entry numbers for bibliographies relating to a particular place or subject appear immediately after the heading for that place or subject, followed by a semicolon.

Beyond the published material which these volumes bring to notice, the serious student of a locale is urged to make a personal visit to the local library and/or historical society, since, by their very nature, local history materials are not widely distributed beyond the place to which they pertain. Often these institutions also have collections of mounted newspaper clippings, prints and photographs, scrap books, and typescripts prepared by members of the community. Inquiry should also be made of materials which may be yet uncataloged.

John D. Haskell, Jr.

Cities and Towns within Counties

Cities are designated by capital letters.

Barnstable County
Barnstable
Bourne
Brewster
Chatham
Dennis
Eastham
Falmouth
Harwich
Mashpee
Orleans
Provincetown
Sandwich
Truro
Wellfleet
Yarmouth

Berkshire County
Adams
Alford
Becket
Cheshire
Clarksburg
Dalton
Egremont
Florida
Great Barrington
Hancock
Hinsdale
Lanesborough
Lee
Lenox
Monterey
Mount Washington
New Ashford
New Marlborough
NORTH ADAMS
Otis
Peru
PITTSFIELD
Richmond
Sandisfield
Savoy
Sheffield
Stockbridge

Tyringham
Washington
West Stockbridge
Williamstown
Windsor

Bristol County
Acushnet
ATTLEBORO
Berkley
Dartmouth
Dighton
Easton
Fairhaven
FALL RIVER
Freetown
Mansfield
New Bedford
North Attleborough
Norton
Raynham
Rehoboth
Seekonk
Somerset
Swansea
Taunton
Westport

Dukes County
Chilmark
Edgartown
Gay Head
Gosnold
Oak Bluffs
Tisbury
West Tisbury

Essex County
Amesbury
Andover
BEVERLY
Boxford
Danvers

Essex
Georgetown
GLOUCESTER
Groveland
Hamilton
HAVERHILL
Ipswich
LAWRENCE
LYNN
Lynnfield
Manchester
Marblehead
Merrimac
Methuen
Middleton
Nahant
Newbury
NEWBURYPORT
North Andover
PEABODY
Rockport
Rowley
SALEM
Salisbury
Saugus
Swampscott
Topsfield
Wenham
West Newbury

Franklin County
Ashfield
Bernardston
Buckland
Charlemont
Colrain
Conway
Deerfield
Erving
Gill
Greenfield
Hawley
Heath
Leverett
Leyden

Monroe
Montague
New Salem
Northfield
Orange
Rowe
Shelburne
Shutesbury
Sunderland
Warwick
Wendell
Whately

Hampden County
Agawam
Blandford
Brimfield
Chester
CHICOPEE
East Longmeadow
Granville
Hampden
Holland
HOLYOKE
Longmeadow
Ludlow
Monson
Montgomery
Palmer
Russell
Southwick
SPRINGFIELD
Tolland
Wales
West Springfield
WESTFIELD
Wilbraham

Hampshire County
Amherst
Belchertown
Chesterfield
Cummington
Easthampton

Goshen
Granby
Hadley
Hatfield
Huntington
Middlefield
NORTHAMPTON
Pelham
Plainfield
South Hadley
Southampton
Ware
Westhampton
Williamsburg
Worthington

Middlesex County
Acton
Arlington
Ashby
Ashland
Ayer
Bedford
Belmont
Billerica
Boxborough
Burlington
CAMBRIDGE
Carlisle
Chelmsford
Concord
Dracut
Dunstable
EVERETT
Framingham
Groton
Holliston
Hopkinton
Hudson
Lexington
Lincoln
Littleton
LOWELL
MALDEN
MARLBOROUGH
Maynard
MEDFORD
MELROSE
Natick
NEWTON
North Reading

Pepperell
Reading
Sherborn
Shirley
SOMERVILLE
Stoneham
Stow
Sudbury
Tewksbury
Townsend
Tyngsborough
Wakefield
WALTHAM
Watertown
Wayland
Westford
Weston
Wilmington
Winchester
WOBURN

Nantucket County
Nantucket

Norfolk County
Avon
Bellingham
Braintree
Brookline
Canton
Cohasset
Dedham
Dover
Foxborough
Franklin
Holbrook
Medfield
Medway
Millis
Milton
Needham
Norfolk
Norwood
Plainville
QUINCY
Randolph
Sharon
Stoughton
Walpole
Wellesley

Westwood
Weymouth
Wrentham

Plymouth County
Abington
Bridgewater
BROCKTON
Carver
Duxbury
East Bridgewater
Halifax
Hanover
Hanson
Hingham
Hull
Kingston
Lakeville
Marion
Marshfield
Mattapoisett
Middleborough
Norwell
Pembroke
Plymouth
Plympton
Rochester
Rockland
Scituate
Wareham
West Bridgewater
Whitman

Suffolk County
BOSTON
CHELSEA
REVERE
Winthrop

Worcester County
Ashburnham
Athol
Auburn
Barre
Berlin
Blackstone
Bolton
Boylston
Brookfield

Charlton
Clinton
Douglas
Dudley
East Brookfield
FITCHBURG
GARDNER
Grafton
Hardwick
Harvard
Holden
Hopedale
Hubbardston
Lancaster
Leicester
LEOMINSTER
Lunenburg
Mendon
Milford
Millbury
Millville
New Braintree
North Brookfield
Northborough
Northbridge
Oakham
Oxford
Paxton
Petersham
Phillipston
Princeton
Royalston
Rutland
Shrewsbury
Southborough
Southbridge
Spencer
Sterling
Sturbridge
Sutton
Templeton
Upton
Uxbridge
Warren
Webster
West Boylston
West Brookfield
Westborough
Westminster
Winchendown
WORCESTER

Serial Abbreviations

*Only those titles for which abbreviations are used in this
volume are listed. This is not a complete list of serials searched or cited.*

AASP	*American Antiquarian Society. Proceedings*
ABAJ	*American Bar Association. Journal*
AgricHist	*Agricultural History*
AHI	*American History Illustrated*
AHR	*American Historical Review*
AIrHSJ	*American Irish Historical Society. Journal*
AJA	*American Jewish Archives*
AJHQ	*American Jewish Historical Quarterly*
AJHSP	*American Jewish Historical Society. Publications*
Am Heritage	*American Heritage*
AmHistRecord	*American Historical Record*
AmJLegalHist	*American Journal of Legal History*
AmJSoc	*American Journal of Sociology*
AmNep	*American Neptune*
AmPolSciRev	*American Political Science Review*
AmQ	*American Quarterly*
AmSocRev	*American Sociological Review*
Atlantic	*Atlantic Monthly*
BBHS	*Business Historical Society. Bulletin*
BBNL	*Bowen's Boston News-Letter and City Record*
Belmont HSN	*Belmont Historical Society Newsletter*
BHistMed	*Bulletin of the History of Medicine*
BHSSC	*Berkshire Historical and Scientific Society. Collections*
BJCH	*Bulletin from Johnny Cake Hill*
Blandford Mo	*Blandford Monthly*
BPLQ	*Boston Public Library Quarterly*
Brookline HPSP	*Brookline Historical Publication Society. Publications*
Brookline HSP	*Brookline Historical Society. Proceedings*
BSM	*Bay State Monthly*
BSProc	*Bostonian Society. Proceedings*
BSPub	*Bostonian Society. Publications*
BULRev	*Boston University Law Review*
BusHR	*Business History Review*
CaHSP	*Cambridge Historical Society. Publications*
CanJHist	*Canadian Journal of History*
CathHistRev	*Catholic Historical Review*
CCAPL	*Cape Cod and All the Pilgrim Land*
CCB	*Cape Cod Beacon*
CCC	*Cape Cod Compass*

CEAIA	*Chronicle of the Early American Industries Association*
Clinton HSHP	*Clinton Historical Society. Historical Papers*
ColumLRev	*Columbia Law Review*
CongQ	*Congregational Quarterly*
CottHR	*Cotton History Review*
CSMP	*Colonial Society of Massachusetts. Publications*
CVHSP	*Connecticut Valley Historical Society. Papers and Proceedings*
DanHC	*Danvers Historical Society. Historical Collections*
DCI	*Dukes County Intelligencer*
DedHR	*Dedham Historical Register*
ECHGR	*Essex-County Historical and Genealogical Register*
EconHistRev	*Economic History Review*
EEH	*Explorations in Entrepreneurial History (became Explorations in Economic History with second series, volume seven)*
EIB	*Essex Institute. Bulletin*
EIHC	*Essex Institute. Historical Collections*
EIP	*Essex Institute. Proceedings*
Essex Antiq	*Essex Antiquarian*
Fall River HSP	*Fall River Historical Society. Proceedings*
FHABull	*Friends' Historical Association. Bulletin*
FitchHSP	*Fitchburg Historical Society. Proceedings*
GeogRev	*Geographical Review*
Granite Mo	*Granite Monthly*
HarvLibBul	*Harvard Library Bulletin*
HarvLRev	*Harvard Law Review*
HistEdQ	*History of Education Quarterly*
HistMag	*Historical Magazine*
HistNan	*Historic Nantucket*
HJWM	*Historical Journal of Western Massachusetts*
HMPEC	*Historical Magazine of the Protestant Episcopal Church*
HPHR	*Hyde Park Historical Record*
JAH	*Journal of American History (1964–)*
JAmHist	*Journal of American History (1907–1935)*
JAS	*Journal of American Studies*
JEBH	*Journal of Economic and Business History*
JEconHist	*Journal of Economic History*
JHistMed	*Journal of the History of Medicine and Allied Sciences*
JLibHist	*Journal of Library History*
JNegroEd	*Journal of Negro Education*
JNegroHist	*Journal of Negro History*
JSocHist	*Journal of Social History*
LabHist	*Labor History*
LexHSP	*Lexington Historical Society. Proceedings*
Littleton HSP	*Littleton Historical Society. Proceedings*
LJ	*Library Journal*
Lowell HSC	*Lowell Historical Society. Contributions*
Lynn HSR	*Lynn Historical Society. Register*
MagAmHist	*Magazine of American History*
MagHist	*Magazine of History*
MalHR	*Malden Historical Society. Register*
MASB	*Massachusetts Archaeological Society. Bulletin*

Location Symbols

ICN	*Newberry Library, Chicago*
M	*Massachusetts State Library, Boston*
MAJ	*Jones Library, Amherst*
MB	*Boston Public Library*
MBaC	*Cape Cod Community College, Barnstable*
MBC	*American Congregational Association, Boston*
MBNEH	*New England Historic Genealogical Society, Boston*
MBo	*Jonathan Bourne Public Library, Bourne*
MBSpnea	*Society for the Preservation of New England Antiquities, Boston*
MBU	*Boston University*
MChaE	*Eldridge Public Library, Chatham*
MChaHi	*Chatham Historical Society*
MDeeH	*Historic Deerfield, Inc.*
MDeeP	*Pocumtuck Valley Memorial Association, Deerfield*
MeU	*University of Maine, Orono*
MFa	*Falmouth Public Library*
MFi	*Fitchburg Public Library*
MGreen	*Greenfield Public Library*
MH	*Harvard University, Cambridge*
MH-BA	*Harvard University, Graduate School of Business Administration, Boston*
MHarB	*Brooks Free Library, Harwich*
MHi	*Massachusetts Historical Society, Boston*
MHy	*Hyannis Public Library, Barnstable*
MNF	*Forbes Library, Northampton*
MNt	*Newton Free Library*
MOHi	*Orleans Historical Society*
MPB	*Berkshire Athenaeum, Pittsfield*
MRead	*Reading Public Library*
MS	*City Library, Springfield*
MSaE	*Essex Institute, Salem*
MWA	*American Antiquarian Society, Worcester*
MWalAJHi	*American Jewish Historical Society, Waltham*
MY	*Yarmouth Library Association*

Massachusetts
A Bibliography of Its History

MASSACHUSETTS

1 ABBATT, WILLIAM. "The practical work of the S.A.R.: the Massachusetts Society." MagHist, 7 (1908), 81-82.

2 ABBOTT, KATHARINE MIXER. South Shore trolley trips. Boston: Heintzemann Pr., 1898. Pp. 108.

3 _____. Trolley trips on a Bay State triangle for sixty sunny days. Lowell: Thompson & Hill, 1897. Pp. 86.
Essex and Middlesex Counties.

4 ABBOTT, RICHARD H. "Massachusetts and the recruitment of southern Negroes." Civil War History, 14 (1968), 197-210.

5 ABRAMS, RICHARD M. Conservatism in a progressive era: Massachusetts politics, 1900-1912. Cambridge: Harvard Univ. Pr., 1964. Pp. xiv, 327.

6 _____. "A paradox of progressivism: Massachusetts on the eve of insurgency." PolSciQ, 75 (1960), 379-399.

7 AN ACCOUNT of some of the bridges over the Charles River. Cambridge: Chronicle Pr., 1858. Pp. 45.

8 ADAMS, ALTON D. "Municipal gas and electric plants in Massachusetts." PolSciQ, 17 (1902), 247-255.
Street lighting, 1890.

9 ADAMS, BROOKS. The emancipation of Massachusetts: the dream and the reality. (1887) Rev. and enl. ed. Boston: Houghton Mifflin, 1919. Pp. vi, 534.

10 _____. "The embryo of a Commonwealth." Atlantic, 54 (1884), 610-619.

11 ADAMS, CHARLES FRANCIS, 1807-1886. Diary. Aïda DiPace Donald and David Donald, eds. Cambridge: Harvard Univ. Pr., 1964.

12 ADAMS, CHARLES FRANCIS, 1835-1915, ed. Antinomianism in the colony of Massachusetts Bay, 1636-1638. Boston: The Prince Society, 1894. Pp. 415.

13 _____, et al. "Genesis of the Massachusetts town and the origin of the town-meeting government." MHSP, 2 Ser., 7 (1891-1892), 172-263, 441-449.

14 _____. Massachusetts: its historians and its history; an object lesson. (1893) [3d. ed.] Boston: Houghton Mifflin, 1898. Pp. 110.

15 _____. "Old planters about Boston Harbor." MHSP, (1878), 194-206.

16 _____. Three episodes in Massachusetts history: the settlement of Boston Bay; the Antinomian controversy; a study of church and town government. (1892) 5th ed. Boston: Houghton Mifflin, 1896. 2v.

17 ADAMS, JAMES TRUSLOW. The Adams family. Boston: Little, Brown, 1930. Pp. vi, 364.

18 ADAMS, JOHN, 1735-1826. Diary and autobiography. L. H. Butterfield, ed., Leonard C. Faber and Wendell D. Garrett, assistant eds. Cambridge: Harvard Univ. Pr., 1961. 4v.

19 _____. The earliest diary of John Adams: June 1753-April 1754, September 1758-January 1759. L. H. Butterfield, ed., Wendell D. Garrett and Marc Friedlaender, associate eds. Cambridge: Harvard Univ. Pr., 1966. Pp. xx, 120.

20 _____. Legal papers of John Adams. L. Kinvin Wroth and Hiller B. Zobel, eds. Cambridge: Harvard Univ. Pr., 1965. 3v.

21 ADAMS, JOHN, 1875-1964. "Memories of an old man." MHSP, 72 (1957-1960), 294-299.
General reminiscences.

22 _____. "Random sketches over eighty years." MHSP, 72 (1957-1960), 300-308.
General reminiscences.

23 ADAMS, JOHN QUINCY. Memoirs of John Quincy Adams, comprising portions of his diary from 1795 to 1848. Charles Francis Adams, ed. Philadelphia: J. B. Lippincott, 1874-1877. 12v.

24 _____. The social compact, exemplified in the constitution of the Commonwealth of Massachusetts; with remarks on the theories of divine right of Hobbes and of Filmer, and the counter theories of Sidney, Locke, Montesquieu, and Rousseau, concerning the origin and nature of government: a lecture, delivered before the Franklin Lyceum, at Providence, R.I., November 25, 1842. Providence: Knowles and Vose, 1842. Pp. 32.

25 ADAMS, THOMAS BOYLSTON. "Bad news from Virginia." Virginia Magazine of History and Biography, 74 (1966), 131-140.
1623 attack on Massachusetts Indians by Plymouth settlers resulted from knowledge of a 1622 massacre in Virginia.

26 _____. The crime of the Pilgrims: an address delivered at Monticello on 14 April 1958. Charlottesville, Va.: Thomas Jefferson Memorial Foundation, 1958. Pp. 16.

27 ADAMS FAMILY. ARCHIVES. Adams family correspondence. L. H. Butterfield, ed., Wendell D. Garrett, associate ed., Marjorie E. Sprague, assistant ed. Cambridge: Harvard Univ. Pr., 1963-.

28 ADDISON, ALBERT CHRISTOPHER. The romantic story of the Mayflower Pilgrims, and its place in the life of to-day. (1911) New ed. Boston: Page Co., 1918. Pp. xxii, 192.

29 "ADDITIONAL notes on the Massachusetts laws concerning slavery and Negroes." HistMag, 8 (1864), 169-174.

30 ADLOW, ELIJAH. "Chief Justice Lemuel Shaw and the law of negligence." MassLQ, 42 (1957), 55-73.
1830-1860.

31 ____. "Lemuel Shaw and the judicial function." MassLQ, 45 (1960), 52-69.
1820s.

32 AIKEN, JOHN A. "The Mohawk Trail." MagHist, 11 (1910), 305-313; 12 (1910), 1-8.

33 ALBRO, JOHN ADAMS. The fathers of New England: A discourse delivered at Cambridge, December 22, 1844. Boston: C. C. Little and J. Brown, 1845. Pp. 40.

34 ALDEN, EBENEZER. "An account of the Massachusetts Medical Society with biographical notices of the founders." American Quarterly Register, 12 (1839-1840), 358-370; 13 (1840-1841), 75-86.

35 ____. "Biographical notices of deceased physicians in Massachusetts." NEHGR, 1 (1847), 60-64, 178-182.

36 ALDRICH, PELEG EMORY. "The criminal laws of Massachusetts." AASP, No. 65 (October 21, 1875), 65-78.

37 ____. "Massachusetts and Maine, their union and separation." AASP, No. 71 (April 24, 1878), 43-64.

38 ALEXANDER, ARTHUR F. "A footnote on Massachusetts' deserters who went to sea during the American Revolution." AmNep, 10 (1950), 43-51.

39 ALEXANDER, DONALD NELSON. The Diocese of Western Massachusetts, 1901-1951.... Springfield, [1951] Pp. 85.

40 ALFONSO, JOSÉ ANTONIO. Los peregrinos del Mayflower i su influencia americana: discurso pronunciado en el acto solemne celebrado en el Santiago college por algunos miembros de la colonia norteamericana, en conmemoración del tercer centenario de la llegada de los peregrinos del 'Mayflower' a las costas de la Nueva Inglaterra. Santiago de Chile: Imprenta Universitaria, 1921. Pp. 16.

41 ALLEN, GARDNER WELD. Massachusetts privateers of the Revolution. Boston: Massachusetts Historical Society, 1927. Pp. vi, 356.

42 ALLEN, MARY MOORE. Origin of names of Army and Air Corps posts, camps and stations in World War II in Massachusetts. Black Mountain, N.C., [1954?] 34 leaves.

43 ALLEN, VIRGINIA WARREN. "Winged skull and weeping willow." Antiques, 29 (1936), 250-253.
Funeral customs.

44 ALLEN, WALTER SPOONER. Street railways; development of street railways in the Commonwealth of Massachusetts. [New Bedford?, 1899?]. Pp. 26.

45 "ALONG the South Shore." Harper's Magazine, 57 (1878), 1-14.

46 AMERICAN ANTIQUARIAN SOCIETY, WORCESTER, MASS. The Bradford manuscript: account of the part taken by the American Antiquarian Society in the return of the Bradford manuscript to America. Worcester: C. Hamilton, 1898. Pp. 108.

47 ____. Paul Revere's engravings. Clarence S. Brigham, comp. Worcester, 1954. Pp. xvi, 181.

48 AMES, AZEL. The May-flower and her log, July 15, 1620-May 6, 1621, chiefly from original sources. Boston: Houghton Mifflin, 1901. Pp. xxii, 375.

49 AMES, FISHER. Works of Fisher Ames, with a selection from his speeches and correspondence. Seth Ames, ed. Boston: Little, Brown, 1854. 2v.

50 AMORY, THOMAS COFFIN. "Seals of Massachusetts." MHSP, (1867-1869), 94-104.

51 ANCIENT AND HONORABLE ARTILLERY COMPANY OF MASSACHUSETTS. Historical sketch of the Ancient and Honorable Artillery Company of Massachusetts...and a catalogue of the museum of the company. [Boston], 1909. Pp. 64. MB.

52 "ANCIENT Houses." NEHGR, 22 (1868), 64-65.

53 ANDERSON, R. C. "The Mayflower." Mariner's Mirror, 12 (1926), 260-263.

54 ANDREWS, CHARLES MCLEAN. "Historic doubts regarding early Massachusetts history." CSMP, 28 (1930-1933), 280-294.

55 ANDREWS, HENRY FRANKLIN. List of freemen, Massachusetts Bay Colony from 1630 to 1691, with the Freeman's Oath, the first paper printed in New England. [Exira, Iowa:] Exira printing, 1906. unpaged.

56 THE ANDROS tracts: being a collection of pamphlets and official papers issued during the period between the overthrow of the Andros government and the establishment of the second charter of Massachusetts. W. H. Whitmore, ed. Boston: The Prince Society, 1868-1874. 3v.
Reprinted from the original editions and manuscripts.

57 APPLEGATE, M. RICHARD. Massachusetts Forest and Park Association, a history, 1898-1973. Boston: Massachusetts Forest and Park Association, 1974. Pp. 75.

58 APPLETON, CHARLES SUMNER. "The loyal petitions of 1666." MHSP, 2 Ser., 6 (1890-1891), 469-477.

59   APPLETON, WILLIAM SUMNER. "The Whigs of
      Massachusetts." MHSP, 2 Ser., 11 (1896-
1897), 278-282.
      1840-1850.

60   ARBER, EDWARD, ed. The story of the Pilgrim
      Fathers, 1606-1623 A.D.; as told by themselves,
their friends, and their enemies. Boston: Houghton, Mifflin, 1897. Pp. x, 634.

61   ARCHER, GLEASON LEONARD. "How the Pilgrims
      built their houses." Americana, 29 (1935),
147-155.

62   _____. Mayflower heroes. New York: Century
      Co., 1931. Pp. xv, 346.

63   _____. With axe and musket at Plymouth. N.Y.:
American Historical Society, 1936. Pp. 305.
Plymouth Colony.

64   ARMSTRONG, WILBUR BOWMAN. The government in
      Massachusetts. South Lancaster: College Pr.,
1939. v.p.

65   ASHER, ROBERT. "Business and workers' welfare
      in the progressive era: workmen's compensa-
tion reform in Massachusetts, 1880-1911." BusHR,
43 (1969), 452-475.

66   ATKINSON, THOMAS E. "The development of the
      Massachusetts probate system." Michigan Law
Review, 42 (1943-1944), 425-452.

67   ATWOOD, WILLIAM FRANKLIN. The Pilgrim story,
      largely a compilation from the documents of
Governor Bradford and Governor Winslow, severally
and in collaboration; together with a list of Mayflower passengers. Plymouth: Memorial Pr., 1940.
Pp. 74.

68   AUSTIN, GEORGE LOWELL. The history of Massa-
      chusetts, from the landing of the Pilgrims to
the present time.... Boston: B. B. Russell, 1884.
Pp. xx, 598.

69   AUSTIN, JAMES TRECOTHICK, 1784-1870. The life
      of Elbridge Gerry, with contemporary letters
to the close of the American Revolution. Boston:
Wells and Lilly, 1828-1829. 2v.

70   "THE AUTOMOBILE industry." Industry, 2 (Jan-
      uary 1934) 9-14, 49.

71   AWFUL calamities: or, the shipwrecks of De-
      cember, 1839, being a full account of the
dreadful hurricanes of Dec. 15, 21 & 27, on the
coast of Massachusetts...comprising also a particular relation of the shipwreck of the following vessels: barque Lloyd, brigs Pocahontas, Rideout and
J. Palmer, and schs. Deposite, Catharine Nichols
and Miller; and also of the dreadful disasters at
Gloucester. 5th ed. Boston: J. Howe, 1840.
Pp. 24.

72   BABCOCK, MARY KENT DAVEY. "The constitutional
      convention, Diocese of Massachusetts, October
5. 1790." HMPEC, 9 (1940), 142-153.

73   BACHELLER, EDWARD FRANKLIN and CHARLES A. LAW-
      RENCE. Colonial landmarks of the old Bay
State. (1896) [2d. ed.]. Lynn: Souvenir Publishing, 1896. Pp. vi, 31.
      Historic houses.

74   BACON, EDWIN MUNROE. Historic pilgrimages in
      New England; among landmarks of Pilgrim and
Puritan days and of the provincial and revolutionary periods. N.Y.: Silver, Burdett, 1898. Pp.
xiv, 475.
      Limited to Massachusetts.

75   _____. Walks and rides in the country round
      about Boston: covering thirty-six cities and
towns, parks and public reservations, within a
radius of twelve miles from the State House. Boston: Houghton Mifflin, 1897. Pp. vi, 419.

76   BACON, LEONARD. An address before the New
      England Society of the City of New York, on
Forefathers' Day, December 22, 1838. N.Y.: E.
Collier, 1839. Pp. 46.
      Pilgrim Fathers.

77   _____. The genesis of the New England
      churches. N.Y.: Harper & Bros., 1874. Pp.
xiv, 485.

78   BAGG, ERNEST NEWTON. An architectural mono-
      graph: late eighteenth century architecture
in western Massachusetts. N.Y.: R. F. Whitehead,
1925. Pp. 23.

79   _____. "The psalms, tune books and music of
      the Forefathers." BSProc, (1904), 38-57.

80   BAILEY, DUDLEY P., JR. "The history of bank-
      ing in Massachusetts." Bankers Magazine, 11
(1876), 113-121, 207-216, 301-312.

81   BAILEY, EBENEZER. "The separation of Church
      and State in Massachusetts." FitchHSP, 4
(1900-1906), 19-34.

82   BAILEY, FREDERIC WILLIAM, comp. Early Massa-
      chusetts marriages prior to 1800.... New Ha-
ven: Bureau of American Ancestry, 1897-1914. 3v.

83   BAILEY, HENRY TURNER. Industrial drawing in
      the public schools of Massachusetts: a sketch
of its history. n.p., 1893. Pp. 8.

84   _____. A sketch of the history of public art
      instruction in Massachusetts. Boston: Wright
& Potter, 1900. Pp. 53.

85   BAILEY, HOLLIS RUSSELL. Attorneys and their
      admission to the bar in Massachusetts. Bos-
ton: W. J. Nagel, 1907. Pp. 167.

86   BAILEY, RICHARD BRIGGS. Pilgrim possessions
      as told by their wills and inventories.
[Weston?], 1951. 150 leaves.

87   BAILYN, BERNARD and LOTTE BAILYN. Massachu-
      setts shipping, 1697-1714: a statistical
study. Cambridge: Harvard Univ. Pr., 1959. Pp.
xi, 148.

88   BAIRD, E. G. "Business regulation in coloni-
      al Massachusetts (1620-1780)." Dakota Law
Review, 3 (1931), 227-256.

89   BAKER, DONALD I. "Competition and regulation: Charles River Bridge recrossed." Cornell Law Review, 60 (1974-1975), 159-182.

90   BAKER, EDWARD W. "The 'Old Worcester Turnpike.'" BrooklineHSP, (1907), 24-47.

91   BAKER, HENRY MOORE. The pilgrim Puritans, a lecture delivered in All Soul's Church, Washington, D.C., Sunday evening, December 22, 1889. Washington: Gibson Bros., 1890. Pp. 16.

92   BAKER, MARY ROYS. "Anglo-Massachusetts trade union roots, 1130-1790." LabHist, 14 (1973), 352-396.

93   BALDWIN, FOY SPENCER. "Early evolution of the public school in Massachusetts." NEM, New Ser., 34 (1906), 424-431.

94   BALL, BENJAMIN ABSALOM, ed. Government of the Commonwealth of Massachusetts, a souvenir; historical, descriptive, and biographical sketches by various authors. Boston: Ticknor, 1885. Pp. xv, 287.

95   BANKS, CHARLES EDWARD. The English ancestry and homes of the Pilgrim Fathers, who came to Plymouth on the "Mayflower" in 1620, the "Fortune" in 1621, and the "Anne" and the "Little James" in 1623. N.Y.: Grafton Pr., 1929. Pp. xi, 187.

96   _____. The planters of the Commonwealth; a study of the emigrants and emigration in colonial times: to which are added lists of passengers to Boston and to the Bay Colony; the ships which brought them; their English homes, and the places of their settlement in Massachusetts, 1620-1640. Boston: Houghton Mifflin, 1930. Pp. xiii, 231.

97   _____. The Winthrop fleet of 1630: an account of the vessels, the voyage, the passengers and their English homes, from original authorities. Boston: Houghton Mifflin, 1930. Pp. ix, 118.

98   BANKS, RONALD F. Maine becomes a state: the movement to separate Maine from Massachusetts, 1785-1820. Middletown, Conn.: Wesleyan Univ. Pr., 1970. Pp. xx, 425.

99   BANNER, JAMES M., JR. To the Hartford Convention: the Federalists and the origins of party politics in Massachusetts, 1789-1815. N.Y.: Knopf, 1970. Pp. xiii, 378.

100   BANVARD, JOSEPH. Plymouth and the Pilgrims; or, incidents of adventure in the history of the first settlers. (1851) New ed., rev. and enl. Chicago: Interstate Publishing, 1886. Pp. 303.

101   BAPTISTS. MASSACHUSETTS. FRAMINGHAM BAPTIST ASSOCIATION. Consolidated history of the fifteen churches of the Framingham Baptist Association, published by vote of the association and revised to January 1, 1901.... South Framingham: Framingham Tribune, 1902. Pp. 131.
      Middlesex, Norfolk and Worcester counties.

102   BARBER, ALANSON D. "The alleged persecution of Massachusetts, or justice to the Pilgrims." New Englander and Yale Review, 56 (1892), 255-266.

103   BARBER, JOHN WARNER. Historical collections, being a general collection of interesting facts, traditions, biographical sketches, anecdotes &c., relating to the history and antiquities of every town in Massachusetts, with geographical descriptions. Worcester: Dorr, Howland, 1839. Pp. viii, 624.

104   BARBER, LAURENCE LUTHER. "Grandmother clocks." Antiques, 31 (1937), 244-246.
      Joshua Wilder of Hingham and Simon Willard of Boston.

105   _____. "Massachusetts shelf clocks." Antiques, 32 (1937), 20-21.

106   BARBROOK, ALEC. God save the Commonwealth: an electoral history of Massachusetts. Amherst: Univ. of Massachusetts Pr., 1973. Pp. ix, 220.

107   BARDWELL, FRANCIS. "Public outdoor relief and the care of the aged in Massachusetts." Social Service Review, 4 (1930), 199-209.

108   BARRINGTON, WILLIAM WILDMAN BARRINGTON, 2d viscount. The Barrington-Bernard correspondence and illustrative matter, 1760-1770, drawn from the 'Papers of Sir Francis Bernard' (sometime governor of Massachusetts-Bay. Edward Channing and Archibald Cary Coolidge, eds. Cambridge: Harvard Univ. Pr., 1912. Pp. xxiii, 306.

109   BARRY, JOHN STETSON. The history of Massachusetts.... (1855-1857) 4th ed. Boston, 1856-1857. 3v.
      1492-1820.

110   BARTLETT, JOSIAH. "An historical sketch of the progress of medical science in Massachusetts....". MHSC, 2 Ser., 1 (1814), 105-139.

111   BARTLETT, ROBERT MERRILL. The Pilgrim way. Philadelphia: Pilgrim Pr., 1971. Pp. xi, 371.

112   BARTLETT, WILLIAM HENRY. The Pilgrim Fathers; or, the founders of New England in the reign of James the First. London: A. Hall, Virtue, 1853. Pp. xii, 240.
      Has been translated into Dutch.

113   BASILE, FRED C. Massachusetts Tree Wardens' and Foresters' Association...1913-1963. Haverhill, 1962. Pp. 61. M.

114   BATES, WILLIAM GELSTON. An address, delivered in the new court house, in Springfield, Hampden County, Massachusetts, at the dedication of the same, April 28, 1874, containing sketches of the early history of the old county of Hampshire and the county of Hampden, and of the members of the bar in those counties, with an appendix. Springfield: Clark W. Bryan, 1874. Pp. 96.

115   BATTIS, EMERY JOHN. Saints and sectaries: Anne Hutchinson and the Antinomian controversy in the Massachusetts Bay Colony. Chapel Hill: Univ. of North Carolina Pr., 1962. Pp. xv, 379.

116   BAXTER, SYLVESTER. "The great November storm of 1898." Scribner's Magazine, 26 (1899), 515-524.

117   ____. "Why Aberjona?" MalHR, No. 5 (1917-1918), 68-70.
An early name for the upper Mystic River.

118   BAYLIES, FRANCIS. An historical memoir of the colony of New Plymouth, from the flight of the Pilgrims into Holland in the year 1608, to the union of that colony with Massachusetts in 1692. (1830) Samuel G. Drake, ed. Boston: Wiggin & Lunt, 1866. 2v.

119   BEAN, WILLIAM G. "Puritan versus Celt, 1850-1860," NEQ, 7 (1934), 70-89.
Irish immigration.

120   BEARD, CHARLES AUSTIN. "Historians at work: Brooks and Henry Adams." Atlantic, 171 (1943), 87-93.

121   BEARDSLEY, FRANK GRENVILLE. The builders of a nation, a history of the Pilgrim Fathers. Boston: R. G. Badger, 1921. Pp. 356.

122   BECKER, GEORGE P. and CHARLES E. FISHER. "Boston and Albany locomotives, 1832-1930." RLHSB, No. 22 (1930), 9-33.

123   BECKER, GEORGE P. "Motive power of the Boston and Albany Railroad." Railroad Enthusiast, 9 (January, 1942), 5-9.

124   BEDFORD, HENRY F. Socialism and the workers in Massachusetts, 1889-1912. Amherst: Univ. Massachusetts Pr., 1966. Pp. xiii, 315.

125   BEECHER, LYMAN. The memory of our fathers, a sermon delivered at Plymouth, on the twenty-second of December, 1827. Boston: T. R. Marvin, 1828. Pp. 39.

126   BEISNER, ROBERT L. "Brooks Adams and Charles Francis Adams, Jr.: Historians of Massachusetts." NEQ, 35 (1962), 48-70.

127   BELL, HUGH F. "'A personal challenge' the Otis-Hutchinson currency controversy, 1761-1762." EIHC, 106 (1970), 297-323.

128   BELL, STOUGHTON. "Massachusetts and the unlawful practice of the law." MassLQ, 21 (April, 1936), 28-39.

129   BELLIVEAU, PIERRE. French neutrals in Massachusetts; the story of Acadians rounded up by soldiers from Massachusetts and their captivity in the Bay Province, 1755-1766. Boston: Kirk S. Giffen, 1972. Pp. xiv, 259.

130   BELZ, HERMAN J. "Currency reform in colonial Massachusetts, 1749-1750. EIHC, 103 (1967), 66-84.

131   ____. "Paper money in Colonial Massachusetts." EIHC, 101 (1965), 149-163.

132   BENNETT, EDMUND HATCH. Massachusetts digest of the reported decisions of the Supreme Judicial Court of the Commonwealth of Massachusetts from 1804 to 1879, with references to earlier cases, by Edmund H. Bennett, Russell Gray and Henry W. Swift.... Boston: Little, Brown, 1881. 3v.

133   BENNETT, FRANK PIERCE, JR. The story of mutual savings banks. Boston, 1924. Pp. 140. Drawn chiefly from Massachusetts banking history from 1816 to the 1920s.

134   BENSON, ALBERT EMERSON. History of the Massachusetts Society for Promoting Agriculture, 1892-1942. Boston: Meador, 1942. Pp. 122.

135   BENSON, GEORGE CHARLES SUMNER. The administration of the civil service in Massachusetts, with special reference to state control of civil service. Cambridge: Harvard Univ. Pr., 1935. Pp. xiv, 90.

136   BENTON, JOSIAH HENRY. Early census making in Massachusetts, 1643-1765, with a reproduction of the lost census of 1765 (recently found) and documents relating thereto. Boston: Charles E. Goodspeed, 1905. Pp. 104.

137   BERMAN, EDWARD. The Massachusetts system of savings-bank life insurance. Washington: Govt. Print. Off., 1935. Pp. viii, 113.

138   BERMAN, LOUIS M. Trends in the length of time incarcerated in Massachusetts correctional institutions: 1945-1966. [Boston?]: 1968. 15 leaves.

139   BERRY, JOSEPH BREED. History of the Diocese of Massachusetts, 1810-1872. Boston: The Diocesan Library, Diocese of Massachusetts, 1959. Pp. vi, 252.

140   BESSOM, JOSEPH H. "Early Massachusetts 'Tractarians.'" HMPEC, 37 (1968), 139-149. Edited by Lawrence L. Brown; High Church views two decades before the Oxford movement.

141   BICKNELL, THOMAS WILLIAMS. "Free common schools." MNEH, 2 (1892) 149-164.

142   ____. "John Myles: religious tolerance in Massachusetts." MNEH, 2 (1892), 213-242.

143   BIGELOW, MELVILLE MADISON. "Primogeniture in Massachusetts." MHSP, 45 (1911-1912), 34-35.

144   BILLIAS, GEORGE ATHAN. The Massachusetts land bankers of 1740. [Orono]: Univ. of Maine, 1959. Pp. x, 59.

145   BIOGRAPHICAL encyclopaedia of Massachusetts of the nineteenth century. N.Y.: Metropolitan Publishing and Engraving, 1879-1883. 2v. MHi.

146   BIOGRAPHICAL sketches of representative citizens of the Commonwealth of Massachusetts....
Boston: Graves & Steinbarger, 1901. Pp. 1092.

147   BIRCKHEAD, HUGH. The Puritan's contribution to to-day.... The eleventh annual sermon of the New England Society in the City of New York, preached at Saint George's Church on Forefathers' Sunday, December 18th, 1910. [New York?, 1910?]. Pp. 14.

148   BISBEE, JOHN HATCH. "The Mountain Association, Massachusetts." CongQ, 20 (1878), 573-576.
       A ministerial association in Berkshire and Hampshire counties, 1790-1837.

149   BISHOP, ROBERT ROBERTS. The Senate of Massachusetts: an historical sketch. Boston: G. H. Ellis, 1882. Pp. 49.

150   BISTRUP, FRANK V. "Industry's place in Massachusetts." Industry, 2 (November, 1936), 25-28.
       1920s and 1930s.

151   BLACK, FRANK SWETT. Address of Honorable Frank S. Black before the New England Society, New York, December 22, 1908. [New York?, 1908?]. Pp. 7.
       Pilgrim Fathers.

152   BLACK, S. BRUCE. "Workmen's compensation - 50 years of progress." Industry, 27 (August, 1962), 13-14, 46.

153   BLACKMON, JOAB L., JR. "Judge Samuel Sewall's efforts in behalf of the first Americans." Ethnohistory, 16 (1969), 165-176.
       Indians.

154   BLAKE, JOHN BALLARD. The early history of vital statistics in Massachusetts. BHistMed, 29 (1955), 46-68.
       1639-1850.

155   BLANCHARD, JONATHAN. Christ purifying His temple; or, the principle of the Puritans, a sermon preached in the Mount Vernon Church of Christ...Boston, Massachusetts, Sabbath, Dec. 24, 1865, 'Forefathers' Day'. Boston: Congregational Board of Publication, 1866. Pp. 29.
       Pilgrim Fathers.

156   BLAXLAND, GEORGE CUTHBERT. 'Mayflower' essays on the story of the Pilgrim Fathers as told in Governor Bradford's ms. history of the Plimoth Plantation, with a reproduction of Captain John Smith's map of New England. London: Ward & Downey, 1896. Pp. vi, 146.

157   BLISS, GEORGE, 1764-1830. An address to the members of the bar of the counties of Hampshire, Franklin and Hampden, at their annual meeting at Northampton, September, 1826. Springfield: Tannatt, 1827. Pp. 35.
       Lawyers.

158   BLISS, GEORGE, 1793-1873. Historical memoir of the Western Railroad. Springfield: S. Bowles, 1863. Pp. 190.

159   BLODGETT, GEOFFREY T. The gentle reformers: Massachusetts Democrats in the Cleveland era. Cambridge: Harvard Univ. Pr., 1966. Pp. xiii, 342.

160   BOARDMAN, WALDO ELIAS. Biographies of the founders, ex-presidents, prominent early members and others of the Massachusetts Dental Society. Boston: Massachusetts Dental Society, 1914. Pp. 224.

161   BOCHAT, KENNETH P. "The Pine Tree Shilling." AmHeritage, 4 (1952-1953), 10-11.

162   BODGE, GEORGE MADISON. Historical sketch of the Norfolk Conference of Unitarian and other Christian Churches; prepared for and read at the one hundredth session of the conference, held at Randolph, June 12, 1900, with brief sketches of the churches now belonging to the conference and lists of their ministers, to the present time.... [Randolph?], 1900. Pp. 48.
       Not limited to Norfolk County.

163   BOLTON, R. A. "Our nation's birthplace." Cape Cod Magazine, 8 (February-March, 1925), 19-24.
       Plymouth and Provincetown.

164   BONAZZI, TIZIANO. Il sacro esperimento, teologia e politica nell'America puritana. Bologna: Il. mulino, 1970. Pp. 515.

165   BOSTON (ARCHDIOCESE). A brief historical review of the Archdiocese of Boston, 1907-1923. Boston: Pilot Publishing, 1925. Pp. viii, 263.

166   BOSTON (ARCHDIOCESE). DEPARTMENT OF EDUCATION. A decade of progress, 1944-1954. [Boston?, 1955]. Pp. 23. M.

167   BOSTON, CLINTON, FITCHBURG AND NEW BEDFORD RAILROAD COMPANY. Detailed statement, giving its history, location, and the consolidations which have resulted in the formation of the present corporation; also statement showing the present financial condition of the consolidated company. Fitchburgh, 1876. Pp. 16.

168   BOSTON HERALD. Scenes and characters of the Massachusetts Bay Colony, 1630-1700. Boston: Old Colony Distributing, 1930. Unpaged.

169   BOSTON TRAVELER. Bay State notables in cartoon: being a series of cartoons of leading Massachusetts men published in the Boston Traveler and gathered together in this form as a permanent souvenir. Boston, 1907. Unpaged.
       Biography.

170   BOWDITCH, WILLIAM INGERSOLL. Taxation of women in Massachusetts. Cambridge: J. Wilson and Son, 1875. Pp. 71.

171   NO ENTRY

172   BOWEN, JAMES LORENZO. Massachusetts in the war, 1861-1865. (1889) 2d ed. Springfield: Bowen & Son, 1893. Pp. xv, 1029.
       Biographies.

173 BOWEN, RICHARD LE BARON. Massachusetts records; a handbook for genealogists, historians, lawyers, and other researchers. Rehoboth, 1957. Pp. 66.

174 _____. "The 1690 tax revolt of Plymouth Colony towns." NEHGR, 112 (1958), 4-14.

175 BOWMAN, GEORGE ERNEST. The Mayflower Compact and its signers, with facsimiles and a list of the Mayflower passengers, 1620-1920. Boston: Massachusetts Society of Mayflower Descendants, 1920. Pp. 19.

176 BOYDEN, ALBERT GARDNER. Brief historical sketch of the Massachusetts normal schools. Boston: N. Sawyer & Son, 1893. Pp. 8.

177 BOYER, PAUL S. "Borrowed rhetoric: the Massachusetts excise controversy of 1754." WMQ, 3 Ser., 21 (1964), 328-351.

178 BOYNTON, CHARLES BRANDON. Oration delivered before the New England Society of Cincinnati, on the anniversary of the landing of the Pilgrims, December 22d, 1847. Cincinnati: Collins & Van Wagner, 1848, Pp. 32.

179 BRADBURY, FRANK E. "Laws and courts of the Massachusetts Bay Colony." BSPub, 10 (1913), 129-159.

180 BRADFORD, ALDEN. History of Massachusetts.... Boston: Richardson and Lord, 1822-1829. 3v. 1764-1820; v. 2 published by Wells and Lilly; v. 3 published by the author.

181 _____. History of Massachusetts, for two hundred years: from the year 1620 to 1820. Boston: Hilliard, Gray, 1835. Pp. xii, 480.

182 _____. A sermon delivered at Plymouth, December 21st, 1804; the anniversary of the landing of our fathers in December, 1620. Boston: Gilbert & Dean, 1805. Pp. 24.

183 [_____], ed. Speeches of the governors of Massachusetts, from 1765 to 1775; and the answers of the House of Representatives, to the same; with their resolutions and addresses for that period. Boston: Russell and Gardner, 1818. Pp. 424.

184 BRADFORD, GAMALIEL, 1831-1911. "Historic evolution in Massachusetts." MHSP, 2 Ser., 16 (1902), 238-247.
     Politics and government.

185 BRADFORD, GERSHOM. In with the sea wind; the trials and triumphs of some Yankee sailors. Barre: Barre Gazette, 1962. Pp. 255.

186 BRADFORD, WILLIAM. Bradford's history of Plymouth Plantation, 1606-1646. William T. Davis, ed. N.Y.: C. Scribner's Sons, 1908. Pp. xv, 437.

187 _____. History of Plymouth Plantation.... Now first printed from the original manuscript, for the Massachusetts Historical Society.

Boston: Little, Brown, 1856. Pp. xix, 476. 1608-1646.

188 _____. History of Plymouth Plantation 1620-1647, Worthington C. Ford, ed. Boston: Houghton Mifflin, 1912. 2v.

189 _____. Of Plymouth Plantation, 1620-1647. Samuel Eliot Morison, ed. New ed. N.Y.: Knopf, 1952. v.p.

190 "BRADFORD'S letter to Winthrop, 1631." NEHGR, 2 (1848), 240-244.
     Edited.

191 BRADLEE, FRANCIS BOARDMAN CROWNINSHIELD. "The Boston, Revere Beach and Lynn narrow gauge railroad." EIHC, 57 (1921), 273-280.

192 BRADLEY, THOMAS D. A condensed history of the Ancient and Honorable Artillery Company, 1638 to 1888. Boston: A. Mudge & Son, 1889. Pp. 70.

193 BRADSTREET, ALVAH JUDSON. "The colonial Bradstreets." DanHC, 23 (1935), 58-64.

194 BRANDT, LILLIAN. "The Massachusetts slave trade." NEM, New Ser., 21 (1899-1900), 83-96.

195 BRAUER, KINLEY J. Cotton versus conscience; Massachusetts Whig politics and southwestern expansion, 1843-1848. Lexington: Univ. of Kentucky Pr., 1967. Pp. vi, 272.

196 _____. "The Massachusetts State Texas Committee: A last stand against the annexation of Texas." JAH, 51 (1964-1965), 214-231.
     Antislavery.

197 BRAYLEY, ARTHUR WELLINGTON. Bakers and baking in Massachusetts, including the flour, baking supply and kindred interests, from 1620 to 1909. Boston: Master Bakers' Association of Massachusetts, 1909. Pp. xx, 336.

198 _____. "The development of the shoe and leather trade in Massachusetts." Bostonian, 1 (1894-1895), 29-64, 150-172, 275-282, 398-407, 525-529, 651-656.

199 BREEN, TIMOTHY H. "Persistent localism: English social change and the shaping of New England institutions." WMQ, 3 Ser., 32 (1975), 3-28.

200 _____. and STEPHEN FOSTER. "The Puritans' greatest achievement: a study of social cohesion in seventeenth-century Massachusetts." JAH, 60 (1973-1974), 5-22.

201 BREEN, TIMOTHY H. "Who governs: the town franchise in seventeenth-century Massachusetts." WMQ, 3 Ser., 27 (1970), 460-474.

202 BRENNAN, ELLEN ELIZABETH. "The Massachusetts Council of the Magistrates." NEQ, 4 (1931), 54-93.
     Established in 1644.

203 ____. Plural office-holding in Massachusetts, 1760-1780, its relation to the 'separation' of departments of government. Chapel Hill: Univ. of North Carolina Pr., 1945. Pp. xiii, 227.

204 BRIDGMAN, ARTHUR MILNOR, ed. A souvenir of Massachusetts legislators.... Stoughton: A. M. Bridgman, 1892-1917. 24v.
Issued annually except 1912 and 1913: biographical sketches.

205 BRIDGMAN, RAYMOND LANDON. The Massachusetts Constitutional Convention of 1917; its causes, forces and factions; its conflicts and consequences, mention of every proposed amendment.... Boston: 1923. Pp. vi, 271.

206 ____. "A Massachusetts crisis." NEM, New Ser., 36 (1907), 63-70.
1896, annual vs. biennial elections of state officials.

207 ____. "The natural history of a state." NEM, New Ser., 23 (1900-1901), 116-122.
Political development.

208 ____. Ten years of Massachusetts. Boston: D. C. Heath, 1888. Pp. 127.
1878-1887.

209 BRIEF sketch of the character and sufferings of the Pilgrims who settled at Plymouth, Dec. 1620. Boston: John H. A. Frost, 1820. Pp. 8.

210 BRIGGS, LLOYD VERNON. Fifteen months' service on the old supervisory State Board of Insanity in Massachusetts, 1913-1914. Boston: Priv. Print., 1928. Pp. xiii, 437.

211 BRIGGS, ROSE THORNTON. "Books of the Pilgrims as recorded in their inventories and preserved in Pilgrim Hall." OTNE, 61 (1970-1971), 41-46.

212 BRIGHAM, ALBERT PERRY. "Cape Cod and the Old Colony." GeogRev, 10 (1900), 1-22.
Barnstable and Plymouth counties.

213 ____. Cape Cod and the Old Colony. N.Y.: G. P. Putnam's Sons, 1920. Pp. xi, 284.

214 BRIGHAM, CLARENCE SAUNDERS. "Paul Revere dismounted." Walpole Society Notebook, (1944), 12-14.

215 BRIGHAM, WILLIAM. The colony of New Plymouth, and its relations to Massachusetts: a lecture of a course by members of the Massachusetts Historical Society, delivered before the Lowell Institute, Jan. 19, 1869. Boston: J. Wilson and Son, 1869. Pp. 27.

216 BROCHES, SAMUEL. Jews in New England: Pt. I, historical study of the Jews in Massachusetts (1650-1750). N.Y.: Bloch Publishing, 1942. Pp. 68.

217 "THE BROOKFIELD Association." CongQ, 12 (1870), 274-290.
A ministerial association in Hampden and Worcester counties.

218 BROOKS, DEXTER M. Of Plymouth Plantation. Plymouth: Leyden Publishing, 1949. Unpaged.

219 BROOKS, ELAINE. "Massachusetts Anti-slavery Society." JNegroHist, 30 (1945), 311-330.

220 BROOKS, ELBRIDGE STREETER. Stories of the old Bay State. N.Y.: American Book Co., 1899. Pp. 284.

221 BROWN, ABBIE FARWELL. "Notable trees about Boston." NEM, New Ser., 22 (1900), 503-523.

222 BROWN, ABRAM ENGLISH. Beneath old roof trees. Boston: Lee and Shepard, 1896. Pp. xiii, 343.

223 ____. Beside old hearth-stones. Boston: Lee and Shepard, 1897.

224 BROWN, ARTHUR MARCH. "Labor questions in the courts of Massachusetts." American Law Review, 42 (1908), 706-734.

225 BROWN, B. KATHERINE. "Freemanship in Puritan Massachusetts." AHR, 59 (1953-1954), 865-883.

226 ____. "A note on the Puritan concept of aristocracy." MVHR, 41 (1954-1955), 105-112.
Suffrage.

227 BROWN, JOHN. The Pilgrim Fathers of New England and their Puritan successors. 4th ed. London: Religious Tract Society, 1920. Pp. 352.

228 BROWN, RICHARD D. "The emergence of urban society in rural Massachusetts, 1760-1820." JAH, 61 (1974), 29-51.

229 ____. "The emergence of voluntary associations in Massachusetts, 1760-1830." Journal of Voluntary Action Research, 2 (April, 1973), 64-73.

230 ____. "The Massachusetts Convention of Towns, 1768." WMQ, 3 Ser., 26 (1969), 94-104.

231 BROWN, ROBERT ELDON. "Democracy in colonial Massachusetts." NEQ, 25 (1952), 291-313.

232 ____. Middle-class democracy and the Revolution in Massachusetts, 1691-1780. Ithaca: Cornell Univ. Pr., 1955. Pp. ix, 458.

233 ____. "Restriction of representation in colonial Massachusetts." MVHR, 40 (1953-1954), 463-476.

234 BROWNE, WILLIAM BRADFORD. The Mohawk Trail; its history and course, with map and illustrations, together with an account of Fort Massachusetts and of the early turnpikes over Hoosac Mountain. Pittsfield: Sun Printing, 1920. Pp. 40.
Berkshire and Franklin counties.

235 ____. "A study in origins." PVMA, 7
(1921-1929), 23-47.
Chronology of settlements in Massachusetts.

236 BRUCE, JAMES F. Life and opinion in Massachusetts from 1630-1649. Sydney: W. A. Gul-
lick, 1912. Pp. 35.

237 BRUNET, MICHEL. "The secret ballot issue in
Massachusetts politics from 1851 to 1853."
NEQ, 25 (1952), 354-362.

238 BRUSH, JOHN WOOLMAN. Baptists in Massachusetts. Valley Forge, [Pa]: Judson Pr.,
1970. Pp. 78.

239 BRYAN, CLARK W. Carriage driving in and near
unto western Massachusetts.... Springfield,
1892. Pp. 162.

240 BUCHANAN, JOHN G. "Drumfire from the pulpit:
natural law in colonial election sermons of
Massachusetts." AmJLegalHist, 12 (1968), 232-244.

241 BUCK, EDWARD. Massachusetts ecclesiastical
law. Boston: Gould and Lincoln, 1866.
Pp. viii, 310.

242 BUCKINGHAM, EDGAR. "Morality, learning, and
religion, in Massachusetts in olden times."
PVMA, 2 (1880-1889), 8-27.

243 BUCKINGHAM, SAMUEL GILES. A memorial of the
Pilgrim Fathers. Springfield: S. Bowles,
1867. Pp. 52.

244 BUCKLY, JULIAN A. An architectural monograph
on domestic architecture in Massachusetts,
1750-1800. Saint Paul: White Pine Bureau, 1916.
Pp. 16.

245 BUENKER, JOHN D. "The Mahatma and progressive
reform: Martin Lomasney as lawmaker, 1911-
1917." NEQ, 44 (1971), 397-419.

246 BUFFINTON, ARTHUR H. "The isolationist policy of colonial Massachusetts." NEQ, 1 (1928),
158-179.

247 ____. "The Massachusetts experiment of
1630." CSMP, 32 (1933-1937), 308-320.

248 BUHLER, KATHRYN C. Massachusetts silver in
the Frank L. and Louise C. Harrington collection. Worcester: Barre, 1965. Pp. 121.

249 BULLARD, LEWIS H. "Memories of the Boston &
Albany." Railroad Enthusiast, 8 (May-June,
1941), 14-16.

250 BULLEN, HENRY LEWIS. "The printer leaders of
the Pilgrim Fathers." American Printer, 71
(December 20, 1920), 48-49.

251 BULLOCK, ALEXANDER HAMILTON. "The centennial
of the Massachusetts Constitution." AASP,
New Ser., 1 (1880-1881), 189-235.
Constitution of 1780.

252 BULLOCK, CHARLES JESSE. Historical sketch of
the finances and financial policy of Massachusetts from 1790 to 1905. N.Y.: Macmillan, 1907.
Pp. 144.

252A ____. "Taxation of property and income in
Massachusetts." QJEcon, 31 (1916), 1-61.

253 BURBANK, ALFRED STEVENS, comp. A brief history of the Pilgrims, comp. from the writings
of Governor Bradford and Governor Winslow, and
largely in their own words. Plymouth: A. S. Burbank, [1920?]. Pp. 57.

254 BURG, B. RICHARD. "The Bay Colony retaliates:
a taste of venom in Puritan debate." HMPEC,
38 (1969), 281-289.

255 BURNHAM, COLLINS G. "Olden time music in the
Connecticut Valley." NEM, New Ser., 24
(1901), 12-27.
Limited to Massachusetts.

256 BURRAGE, HENRY SWEETSER. "The contest for religious liberty in Massachusetts." American
Society for Church History. Papers, (1894), 149-
192.

257 BURRILL, ELLEN MUDGE. A monograph on the
charters and constitution of Massachusetts.
Lynn: T. P. Nichols & Son, 1932. Pp. 48.

258 ____. The Pilgrim tercentenary, a paper on
Governor William Bradford's History of Plimoth Plantation. [Lynn], 1920. Pp. 15.

259 ____. The State House, Boston, Massachusetts. (1901) 9th ed. Boston: Wright and
Potter, 1927. Pp. 190.

260 BUSH, GEORGE GARY. History of higher education in Massachusetts. Washington: Govt.
Print. Off., 1891. Pp. 445.

261 BUSHNELL, DAVID. "The treatment of the Indians in Plymouth Colony." NEQ, 26 (1953),
193-218.

262 BUSHNELL, HORACE. The fathers of New England:
an oration delivered before the New England
Society of New-York, December 21, 1849.... N.Y.:
G. P. Putnam, 1850. Pp. 44.

263 "A BUSINESS trait of the Pilgrims." CongQ,
12 (1870), 533-538.

264 BUTLER, MARTIN J. "The Nonquitt-Cuttyhunk
boats." Steamboat Bill, 23 (1966), 91-97.
Between Dartmouth and Gosnold.

265 CAHILL, ALICE MARIE. "Nineteenth century library innovation: the [Massachusetts] Division [of Library Extension] from 1890 to 1940."
Bay State Librarian, 55 (October, 1965), 7-12.

266 CAHILL, CHARLES T. 300th anniversary of the
Ancient and Honorable Artillery Company, June
6th, 1938. Historical sketch.... Boston: Geo. E.
Crosby, [1938?]. Unpaged. M.

267 CALLAHAN, JAMES W. Agricultural land use
     changes and population growth in six western
Massachusetts communities, 1940-1965. [Amherst]:
Experiment Station, College of Agriculture, Univ.
of Massachusetts, 1966. Pp. iii, 25.

268 _____. An analysis of municipal expenditures
     and revenue sources in 82 Massachusetts towns,·
1956-1964. Amherst: Massachusetts Cooperative Extension Service and the Massachusetts Agricultural
Experiment Station, 1968. Pp. 24.

269 CAMERON, KENNETH WALTER, comp. The Massachu-
     setts lyceum during the American renaissance;
materials for the study of the oral tradition in
American letters: Emerson, Thoreau, Hawthorne, and
other New-England lecturers. Hartford: Transcendental Books, 1969. 226 leaves.

270 CAMPBELL, COLIN. "The 71st Highlanders in
     Massachusetts, 1776-1780." NEHGR, 112 (1958),
200-213, 265-275; 113 (1959), 3-14, 84-94.
     British regiment.

271 CANDEE, RICHARD M. "A documentary history of
     Plymouth Colony architecture, 1620-1700."
OTNE, 59 (1968-1969), 59-71, 105-111; 60 (1969-
1970), 37-53.

272 "THE CANDY Industry." Industry, 1 (January,
     1936), 11-12, 40.

273 CARD, ANTHA E. "They knew they were Pil-
     grims." Eternity, (November, 1957), 12-13,
33-36.

274 CAREY, P. H. Massachusetts electric compan-
     ies. Financial analysis of the Boston &
Northern Street Railway Company, and the Old Colony
Street Railway Company, since their organization.
N.Y.: Poor, [1905]. Pp. 23.

275 CARLEVALE, JOSEPH WILLIAM. Leading Americans
     of Italian descent in Massachusetts. Plym-
outh: Memorial Pr., 1946. Pp. 861.

276 CARNEY, FRANCIS J., ALAN TOSTI and ALEX TUR-
     CHETTE. An analysis of convicted murderers
in Massachusetts, 1943-1966. [Boston]: Massachusetts Department of Correction, [1968?]. Pp. 12.
M.

277 CARPENTER, EDMUND JANES. The Mayflower Pil-
     grims. N.Y.: Abingdon Pr., 1918. Pp. 255.

278 _____. "Old Ironsides." NEM, New Ser., 17
     (1897-1898), 263-282.
     U.S.S. Constitution.

279 CARPENTER, WILLIAM HENRY. The history of
     Massachusetts, from its earliest settlement
to the present time. Philadelphia: Lippincott,
Grambo, 1853. Pp. 330.

280 CARTER, GEORGE E. Democrat in heaven--Whig
     on earth--the politics of Ralph Waldo Emer-
son. Historical New Hampshire, 27 (1972), 123-140.

281 CARTER, JAMES GORDON. Essays upon popular
     education, containing a particular examina-
tion of an institution for the education of

teachers. Boston: Bowles & Dearborn, 1826.
Pp. iv, 60.

282 _____ and WILLIAM H. BROOKS. A geography of
     Massachusetts; for families and schools. Em-
bracing 1. A topographical view of the towns of
each county.... 2. A general view of each county.
3. A general view of the state.... Boston: Hilliard, Gray, Little, and Wilkins, 1830. Pp. x, 224.
     Brief descriptions of towns and counties.

283 CARY, THOMAS GREAVES. Memoir of Thomas Hand-
     asyd Perkins; containing extracts from his
diaries and letters.... Boston: Little, Brown,
1856. Pp. 304.

284 CASS, LEWIS. Address delivered before the New
     England Society of Michigan, December 22,
1848. Detroit: F. P. Markham & Bros., 1849.
Pp. 47.

285 THE CATHOLIC MIRROR, SPRINGFIELD, MASS. A
     century of Catholicism in western Massachu-
setts; being a chronicle of the establishment, early
struggle, progress and achievements of the Catholic
Church in the five western counties of Worcester,
Hampden, Hampshire, Berkshire and Franklin, in the
Bay State, whose Catholic citizens have responded
nobly to every challenge of citizenship, whether it
be a call to the colors or to the highest civic
posts within the gift of Massachusetts. Springfield: Mirror Pr., 1931. Pp. 350, cxxxii.

286 CAVANAGH, WILLIAM HENRY. Colonial expansion,
     including the rise and fall of historic set-
tlements. Boston: R. G. Badger, 1924. Pp. 263.

287 CENTRAL MASSACHUSETTS REGIONAL PLANNING COM-
     MISSION. Historical highlights. Worcester,
1969. v.p.

288 CHACE, PAUL G. "Ceramics in Plymouth Colony,
     an analysis of estate inventories, 1631-1675."
OPOCS, No. 3 (December, 1972), 1-12.

289 CHADWICK, JOHN WHITE. "In western Massachu-
     setts." Harper's Magazine, 61 (1880), 873-
887.

290 CHAMBERLAIN, HENRY H. "The Boston and Worces-
     ter Turnpike and the bridge." Worcester
HSProc, (1897-1899), 197-198.
     Bridge at Long Pond, Worcester.

291 CHAMBERLAIN, MELLEN. "Governor Winthrop's es-
     tate." MHSP, 2 Ser., 7 (1891-1892), 127-143.

292 CHAMBERLAIN, NATHAN HENRY. Samuel Sewall and
     the world he lived in. Boston: De Wolfe,
Fiske, 1897. Pp. xv, 319.

293 CHANDLER, JOSEPH EVERETT. Colonial cottages.
     St. Paul, 1915. Pp. 16. MB.
     Latter half of seventeenth century.

294 CHANDLER, JOSEPH RIPLEY. 'The Pilgrims of the
     rock': an oration, delivered in the First
Congregational Church, before the Society of the
Sons of New England of Philadelphia, at their second
anniversary on the 22nd December, 1845.... Philadelphia: J. C. Clark, 1846. Pp. 31.

295   CHANDLER, PELEG W. "Witch-trials in Massa-
         chusetts." MHSP, 20 (1882-1883), 395-401.

296   CHAPIN, HOWARD MILLAR. Roger Williams and
         the King's colors; the documentary evidence.
Providence: E. L. Freeman, 1928. Pp. 26.

297   CHAPIN, STEPHEN. The duty of living for the
         good of posterity: a sermon, delivered at
North-Yarmouth, December 22, 1820, in commemoration
of the close of the second century from the landing
of the fore-fathers of New England. Portland: T.
Todd, 1821. Pp. 48.

298   CHAPMAN, HENRY. "Early movements to separate
         the District of Maine from Massachusetts and
the Brunswick Convention of 1816." Pejebscot Historical Society. Collections, 1 (1889), 1-20.

299   CHAPMAN, MARIA WESTON. Right and wrong in
         Massachusetts. Boston: Dow & Jackson's
Anti-slavery Pr., 1839. Pp. 177.
         Massachusetts Anti-slavery Society, 1837-1839.

300   CHAPPLE, WILLIAM DISMORE. "The public service
         of John Endecott in the Massachusetts Bay Col-
ony." EIHC, 65 (1929), 403-447.

301   CHARLTON, WARWICK. The second Mayflower ad-
         venture. Boston: Little, Brown, 1957.
Pp. 245.

302   CHASE, ELLEN. The beginnings of the American
         Revolution, based on contemporary letters,
and other documents. N.Y.: Baker and Taylor,
1910. 3v.

303   CHASE, LEVI BADGER. The Bay path and along
         the way. Norwood, 1919. Pp. xxii, 246.
         Indian trails.

304   CHASE, PHILIP PUTNAM. "The attitude of the
         Protestant clergy in Massachusetts during the
election of 1884." MHSP, 64 (1930-1932), 467-498.

305   _____. "A crucial juncture in the political
         careers of Lodge and Long." MHSP, 70 (1950-
1953), 102-127.
         Election of 1886.

306   CHASE MANHATTAN BANK, NEW YORK. Massachu-
         setts, the Bay State. N.Y., [1936]. Pp. 70.

307   CHESTER, JOHN. A sermon, in commemoration of
         the landing of the New-England Pilgrims. De-
livered in the 2d. Presbyterian Church, Albany, December 22nd, 1820: on the completion of the second
century, since that event. Albany: E. and E. Hosford, 1820. Pp. 31.

308   CHEVALLEY, LOUIS. Cotton Mather et la fin de
         la théocratie au Massachusetts, 1663-1728.
Angers: Imprimerie Cooperative Angevine, 1900.
Pp. ix, 197. MB.

309   CHICKERING, JESSE. "Progress of wealth in
         Massachusetts from 1790 to 1840." Merchants'
Magazine, 16 (1847), 435-444.

310   _____. A statistical view of the population
         of Massachusetts, from 1765 to 1840. Boston:
Charles Little and James Brown, 1846. Pp. 160.

311   "THE CHINESE of the eastern states.' Manches-
         ter, N.H.: L'Avenir National Publishing,
1925. Pp. 23.
         Protests against the epithet 'Chinese of the
east' first bestowed upon the French Canadi-
ans in the twelfth annual report of the Massachusetts Bureau of Statistics and Labor published in 1881.

312   CHRISTENSON, JAMES A. "Real estate acquisi-
         tions for metropolitan Boston's water supply
in the Swift River and Ware River watersheds." New
England Water Works Association. Journal, 54
(1940), 194-255.

313   CLARK, GEORGE FABER. History of the temper-
         ance reform in Massachusetts, 1813-1883. Bos-
ton: Clarke & Carruth, 1888. Pp. xi, 268.

314   CLARK, JOSEPH SYLVESTER. "Did the Pilgrims
         wrong the Indians?" CongQ, 1 (1859), 129-135.

315   _____. A historical sketch of the Congrega-
         tional churches in Massachusetts, from 1620
to 1858. Boston: Congregational Board of Publication, 1858. Pp. xii, 344.

316   _____. "How slavery was abolished in Massa-
         chusetts." CongQ, 2 (1860), 42-48.

317   CLARK, MARY. Biographical sketches of the
         fathers of New England, intended to acquaint
youth with the lives, characters and sufferings of
those who founded our civil and religious institutions. Concord [N.H.]: Marsh, Capen and Lyon,
1836. Pp. 180.

318   _____. A concise history of Massachusetts,
         from its first settlement. N.Y.: D. & G. F.
Cooledge, 1837. Pp. iv, 180.

319   [_____]. Conversations on the history of
         Massachusetts, from its settlement to the
present period; for the use of schools and families.
By a friend of youth. Boston: Munroe & Francis,
1831. Pp. 180.

320   CLARK, WALTER E. Quabbin Reservoir; memories
         of conditions that existed in the Swift and
Ware River Valleys while Quabbin Reservoir was be-
ing developed. N.Y.: Hobson Book Pr., 1946.
Pp. viii, 272.

321   CLARK, WILLIAM HORACE and DANIEL L. MARSH,
         comps. The story of Massachusetts. The
American Historical Society, 1938. 4v.

322   CLARKE, JULIUS L. History of the Massachu-
         setts Insurance Department: including a
sketch of the origin and progress of insurance, and
of the insurance legislation of the state, from
1780 to 1876. Boston: Wright & Potter, 1876.
Pp. 100.

323 CLASON, A. W. "The convention of Massachusetts." MagAmHist, 14 (1885), 529-545.
1788; U. S. Constitution.

324 CLUNE, MARY CATHERINE. "Joseph Hawley's criticism of the Constitution of Massachusetts."
SCSH, 3 (1917-1918), 5-56.

325 COBB, ALVAN. God's culture of his vineyard.
A sermon, delivered at Plymouth before the
Robinson congregation, on the 22d of December, 1831.
Taunton: E. Anthony, 1832. Pp. 24.

326 COBB, CHARLES WIGGINS. Notes on Massachusetts
manufacturing. [Amherst]: Amherst College,
1939-1948. v.p.
1869-1932; issued in 6 parts.

327 COCKSHOTT, WINNIFRED. The Pilgrim Fathers:
their church and colony. London: Methuen,
[1909]. Pp. xv, 348.

328 CODMAN, JOHN. The faith of the Pilgrims. A
sermon delivered at Plymouth, on the twenty-
second of December, 1831. Boston: Perkins, 1832.
Pp. 28.

329 NO ENTRY

330 COHEN, RONALD D. "Church and State in seventeenth-century Massachusetts: another look
at the Antinomian controversy." Journal of Church
and State, 12 (1970), 475-493.

331 _____. "New England and New France, 1632-
1651: external relations and internal dis-
agreements among the Puritans." EIHC, 108 (1972),
252-271.
Limited to Massachusetts.

332 COHEN STUART, MARTINUS. The Pilgrim Fathers'
first meeting for public worship in North
America. A brief historical sketch with an engraved illustration representing the same subject.
(1860) 2d. ed. Amsterdam: W. H. Kirberger, 1866.
Pp. 35.

333 COLBURN, JEREMIAH. Bibliography of the local
history of Massachusetts. Boston: W. P.
Lunt, 1871. Pp. 119.

334 COLE, WILLIAM ISAAC. Immigrant races in
Massachusetts: The Greeks. [Boston?, 1919?].
Unpaged.

335 COLEMAN, WILLIAM MACON. The history of the
primitive Yankees; or, The Pilgrim Fathers in
England and Holland. Washington: Columbia Publishing, 1881. Pp. 62.

336 COLONIAL SOCIETY OF MASSACHUSETTS. Handbook,
1892-1952. Boston, 1953. Pp. 98.
Contains historical sketch by Walter M. Whitehill.

337 COMBE, GEORGE. Notes on the new reformation
in Germany, and on national education and the
common schools of Massachusetts. Edinburgh: Mac-
lachlan, Stewart, 1845. Pp. 37.
Nineteenth century.

338 COMER, WILLIAM RUSSELL. Landmarks 'in the Old
Bay State.' Wellesley, 1911. Pp. x, 350.

339 COMLEY, WILLIAM J. Comley's history of Massachusetts, with portraits and biographies of
some of the old settlers, and many of her most prominent manufacturers, professional and business
men.... Boston: Comley Bros., 1879. Pp. vi, 462.

340 "THE COMMON school controversy in Massachusetts." New Englander, 5 (1847), 513-522.

341 "COMPLETE list of the Congregational and Presbyterian ministers in Massachusetts from the
settlement of the colonies of Plymouth and Massachusetts Bay to the present time." American Quarterly
Register, 7 (1834-1835), 28-38.
Suffolk and Berkshire counties only; gives information regarding birth, education, settlement, dismission and death.

342 COMSTOCK, HELEN. "Pilgrim chairs." Antiques,
68 (1955), 450-451.

343 COMSTOCK, WILLIAM OGILVIE. "Four mounted
messengers of the Revolution." Brookline HSP,
(1913), 17-28.
Paul Revere, William Dawes, Marinus Willett
and Thomas Lamb.

344 CONANT, SYLVANUS. An anniversary sermon
preached at Plymouth, December 23, 1776, in
grateful memory of the first landing of our worthy
ancestors in that place, An. Dom. 1620. Boston:
Thomas & John Fleet, 1777. Pp. 31.

345 "CONFISCATED estates." NEHGR, 12 (1858), 71-
73.
Confiscated loyalist estates after the Revolution.

346 "THE CONGREGATIONAL churches of Massachusetts." Spirit of the Pilgrims, 1 (1828), 57-
74, 113-140.

347 CONNECTICUT. Celebration as authorized by the
Connecticut legislature of 1919 in commemoration of the three hundredth anniversary of the landing of the Pilgrims at Plymouth Rock, 1620...Hart-
ford, Connecticut, December the twenty-first,
1920.... [Hartford, 1920]. Unpaged.

348 CONNECTICUT. COMMISSION ON THE CELEBRATION OF
THE THREE HUNDREDTH ANNIVERSARY OF THE LAND-
ING OF THE PILGRIMS AT PLYMOUTH ROCK. The
proceedings by the state of Connecticut in commemoration of the tercentenary anniversary of the landing of the Pilgrims on Plymouth Rock, 1620-1920.
[Hartford?, 1921?]. Pp. 35.

349 CONOVER, GEORGE STILLWELL. The Genesee Tract. Cessions between New York and Massachusetts. The Phelps and Gorham Purchase. Robert Morris. Captain Charles Williamson and the Pulteney Estate. Geneva, N.Y., 1889. Pp. 16.

350 CONRY, JOSEPH A. "Massachusetts in the Supreme Court of the United States and in the office of Attorney General." MassLQ, 21 (July, 1936), 29-37.

351 CONSUMERS' LEAGUE OF MASSACHUSETTS. [History, constitution, list of officers. Cambridge, 1898?]. Unpaged.

352 CONVENTION OF CONGREGATIONAL MINISTERS OF MASSACHUSETTS. An historical sketch of the Convention of the Congregational Ministers in Massachusetts; with an account of its funds; its connexion with the Massachusetts Congregational Charitable Society; and its rules and regulations.... Cambridge: Hilliard and Metcalf, 1821. Pp. 32.

353 CONWELL, RUSSELL HERMAN. "Massachusetts battlefields of the Revolution: a newspaperman describes Somerville, Charlestown, Concord, Lexington, and Salem in 1869." DAR, 100 (1966), 5-10, 98-101, 222-227, 346-349, 424, 437, 442.
  Edited by Joseph C. Carter.

354 COOK, ARTHUR MALCOLM. Lincolnshire links with the U.S.A. Lincoln [England]: The Subdeanery, 1956. Pp. 90.
  Pilgrims and the Massachusetts Bay Colony.

355 COOK, HAROLD OATMAN. Fifty years a forester. Boston: Massachusetts Forest and Park Association, 1961. Pp. 63.
  Development of state forests.

356 COOLEY, E. H. "Our oldest industry--fish." Industry, 1 (July, 1936), 12, 42-43.

357 ____. "This fishing industry of ours." Industry, 2 (July, 1937), 16-18.

358 COOLIDGE, CALVIN. "Massachusetts and its place in the life of the nation." National Geographic Magazine, 43 (1923), 337-352.

359 COOMBS, ZELOTES WOOD. "General Henry Knox and the Ticonderoga cannon." Worcester HSPub, New Ser., 1 (1928-1935), 3-20.
  Route in Massachusetts over which Knox brought captured guns and ammunition to colonial army at Cambridge, 1775-1776.

360 COPLEY, JOHN SINGLETON. Letters & papers of John Singleton Copley and Henry Pelham, 1739-1776. [Boston]: Massachusetts Historical Society, 1914. Pp. xxii, 384.

361 COPP, JOSEPH A. 'The old ways'--or the Pilgrims and their principles; a discourse on the anniversary of the landing of the Pilgrims, delivered in Broadway Church, Chelsea, Mass., December 21, 1858. Boston: T. R. Marvin, 1857. Pp. 24.

362 CORDNER, JOHN. The vision of the Pilgrim Fathers, an oration, spoken before the New

England Society of Montreal, in the American Presbyterian Church, on 22nd December, 1856. Montreal: H. Rose, 1857. Pp. 54.

363 CORNWALL, ANNA LLOYD. A century of service: Massachusetts Society for Aiding Discharged Prisoners, 1846-1946. [Boston]: The Society [1946]. Pp. 61.

364 THE COTTAGE city, or the season at Martha's Vineyard.... Lawrence: Merrill & Crocker, 1879. Pp. 36.
  Relates to both Dukes County and Nantucket.

365 COUGHLIN, MAGDALEN. "The entrance of the Massachusetts merchant into the Pacific." Southern California Quarterly, 48 (1966), 327-352.

366 COURTNEY, FREDERICK, GEORGE C. SHATTUCK and BENJAMIN H. PADDOCK. The commemorative discourses in observance of the centennial year of the church in the Diocese of Massachusetts. A.D. 1885. Boston: The Convention, 1885. Pp. xii, 128.

367 CRAFTS, WILLIAM. Address delivered before the New-England Society of South-Carolina on the 22nd December, 1820, being the two hundredth anniversary of the landing at Plymouth of the ancestors of New England. Charleston: T. B. Stephens, 1820. Pp. 16.

368 CRANDON, JOHN HOWLAND. "Colonial and Revolutionary social life." BSProc, (1905), 41-60.

369 CRANE, ELLERY BICKNELL. "The Boston and Worcester Turnpike." Worcester HSProc, 17 (1900-1901), 585-598.

370 ____. "The early militia system of Massachusetts." Worcester HSProc, (1888), 105-127.

371 ____. "Early paper mills in Massachusetts, especially Worcester County." Worcester HSProc, (1886), 115-130.

372 "SHAYS' Rebellion." Worcester HSProc, (1881), 61-111.

373 CRANE, JOHN CALVIN. "Fuse or flintlock--which?" Worcester HSProc, (1897-1899), 499-504.
  King Philip's War.

374 CRAWFORD, MARY CAROLINE. Famous families of Massachusetts. Boston: Little, Brown, 1930. 2v.

375 ____. In the days of the Pilgrim Fathers. Boston: Little, Brown, 1920. Pp. xiv, 331.

376 CRIPPEN, T. G. "The psalmody of the Pilgrims." Congregational Historical Society. Transactions, 8 (1920), 75-80.

377 CROCKER, GEORGE W. "The rural school of a half century ago." NEM, New Ser., 24 (1901), 583-587.

378 CULVER, RAYMOND BENJAMIN. Horace Mann and religion in the Massachusetts public schools. New Haven: Yale Univ. Pr., 1929. Pp. x, 301.

379 CUMMING, JAMES D. "Incidents of olden time." American Pioneer, 2 (1843), 372-374.
Shays' Rebellion.

380 CUMMINGS, ABBOTT LOWELL, ed. Rural household inventories, establishing the names, uses and furnishings of rooms in the colonial New England home, 1675-1775. Boston: Society for the Preservation of New England Antiquities, 1964. Pp. xi, 306.
Limited to Massachusetts; detailed index.

381 CUMMINGS, J. L. "Painted chests from the Connecticut Valley." Antiques, 34 (1938), 192-193.

382 CUMMINGS, OSMOND RICHARD. "The Bay State Street Railway." Transportation Bulletin, No. 64 (August-September, 1960) entire issue.

383 _____. "The trolley air line: a history of the Boston & Worcester Street Railway." Transportation, 8 (1954), 1-50.

384 CUNNINGHAM, W. J. "Millionaires in the making." History Today, 19 (1969), 382-387.
Francis Cabot Lowell, Patrick Tracy Jackson and Nathan Appleton.

385 CURRAN, WILLIAM J. "The struggle for equity jurisdiction in Massachusetts." BULRev, 31 (1951), 269-296.
1774-1877.

386 CURRIER, FESTUS CURTIS. Reminiscences and observations of the nineteenth century, more particularly relating to the first half. Fitchburg: Sentinel Printing, 1902. Pp. 106.

387 CURRIER, FREDERICK A. "The Massachusetts Canal." FitchHSP, 5 (1907-1913), 167-180.
Proposed in 1825 to run from the Charles to the Hudson; never constructed.

388 CUSHING, ABEL. Historical letters on the first charter of Massachusetts government. Boston: J. N. Bang, 1839. Pp. 204.
Constitution of 1629.

389 CUSHING, CHRISTOPHER. "The Brookfield Association." CongQ, 20 (1878), 528-572.
A ministerial association of Hampden and Worcester counties.

390 CUSHING, HARRY ALONZO. History of the transition from provincial to commonwealth government in Massachusetts. N.Y.:, 1896. Pp. vi, 281.

391 _____. "Political activity of Massachusetts towns during the Revolution." American Historical Association. Annual Report, (1895), 105-113.

392 CUSHING, JOHN DANIEL. "The Cushing court and the abolition of slavery in Massachusetts: more notes on the 'Quock Walker Case.'" AmJLegal Hist, 5 (1961), 118-144.

393 _____. "Notes on disestablishment in Massachusetts, 1780-1833." WMQ, 3 Ser., 26 (1969), 169-190.

394 CUTLER, FREDERICK MORSE. The old First Massachusetts Coast Artillery in war and peace. Boston: Pilgrim Pr., 1917. Pp. 180.
Founded in 1784.

395 CUTLER, URIEL WALDO. "Backward and forward along the Old Worcester Turnpike." Worcester HSPub, New Ser., 2 (1936-1943), 58-61.

396 _____. "Trail and pike: a study in highway development." Worcester HSPub, New Ser., 1 (1928-1935), 21-34.

397 CUTTER, R. AMMI. "A quarter century of Massachusetts compulsory automobile insurance - its rate making aspects." Insurance Law Review, (1953), 671-677.
1927-1952.

398 CUTTER, WILLIAM RICHARD and WILLIAM FREDERIC ADAMS. Genealogical and personal memoirs relating to the families of the state of Massachusetts. N.Y.: Lewis Historical Publishing, 1910. 4v.
Biographies.

399 CUTTER, WILLIAM RICHARD, ed. Memorial encyclopedia of the state of Massachusetts. N.Y.: American Historical Society, 1917. 3v.
Biographies.

400 DAME, LORIN L. "Historic trees." BSM 1 (1884), 84-88.

401 DANA, RICHARD HENRY, 1851. "Sir William Vernon Harcourt and the Australian ballot law." MHSP, 58 (1924-1925), 401-418.
1888.

402 DANIELS, BRUCE C. "Defining economic classes in colonial Massachusetts." AASP, 83 (1973), 251-259.

403 DANIELS, JOHN E. "Twenty-five years of Associated Industries of Massachusetts." Industry, 6 (October, 1940), 7-16, 50, 52, 54, 56, 58, 60, 62, 64, 66, 68, 70, 72, 74, 80A-80B, 80D.
Manufacturers' association.

404 DARLING, ARTHUR BURR. "Jacksonian democracy in Massachusetts, 1824-1848." AHR, 29, (1923-1924), 271-287.

405 _____. Political changes in Massachusetts, 1824-1848: a study of liberal movements in politics. New Haven: Yale Univ. Pr., 1925. Pp. xii, 392.

406 DAUGHTERS OF THE AMERICAN REVOLUTION, MASSACHUSETTS. History of the Massachusetts Daughters of the American Revolution. Catherine M. Warren, comp. [Boston], 1932. Pp. 425.

407 DAVENPORT, DONALD HILLS. The co-operative banks of Massachusetts. Boston: Harvard Univ. Graduate School of Business Administration, Bureau of Business Research, 1938. Pp. x, 53.
History, 1877-1937.

408 DAVIS, ANDREW MCFARLAND. "Alphabetical list of partners in the Land Bank of 1740." NEHGR, 50 (1896), 187-197, 308-317.
    Edited.

409 _____. "Certain additional notes touching upon the subjects of ignominious punishments and of the Massachusetts currency." AASP, New Ser., 13 (1899-1900), 67-73.

410 _____. "Certain considerations concerning the coinage of the Colony and the public bills of credit of the Province of Massachusetts Bay." American Academy of Arts and Sciences. Proceedings, 33 (1898), 190-211.

411 _____. Colonial currency reprints, 1682-1751. Boston: The Prince Society, 1910-1911. 4v.

412 _____. "The confiscation laws of Massachusetts." CSMP, 8 (1902-1904), 50-72.
    1770s and 1780s.

413 _____. "Corporations in the days of the Colony." CSMP, 1 (1892-1894), 183-214.

414 _____. "Curious features of some of the early notes or bills used as a circulating medium in Massachusetts." CSMP, 10 (1904-1906), 84-101.

415 _____. Currency and banking in the province of the Massachusetts Bay. N.Y.: Macmillan, 1901. 2v.

416 _____. "The currency and provincial politics." CSMP, 6 (1899-1900), 157-172.

417 _____. "Emergent treasury-supply in Massachusetts in early days." AASP, New Ser., 17 (1905-1906), 32-68.
    1645-1780.

418 _____. "Frost v. Leighton." CSMP, 3 (1895-1897), 246-264.
    1734; John Frost and William Leighton.

419 _____. "The General Court and quarrels between individuals arising from the Land Bank." AASP, New Ser., 11 (1896-1897), 351-368.
    1740.

420 _____. "Hints of contemporary life in the writings of Thomas Shepard." CSMP, 12 (1908-1909), 136-162.
    Seventeenth century social life and customs.

421 _____. "Historical work in Massachusetts." CSMP, 1 (1892-1894), 21-71.
    Historical sketches of historical societies.

422 _____. "The law of adultery and ignominious punishments - with especial reference to the penalty of wearing a letter affixed to the clothing." AASP, New Ser., 10 (1895), 97-126.

423 _____. "Lawful money, 1778 and 1779." NEHGR, 57 (1903), 163-167.

424 _____. "Legislation and litigation connected with the Land Bank of 1740." AASP, New Ser., 11 (1896-1897), 86-123.

425 _____. "The limitation of prices in Massachusetts, 1776-1779." CSMP, 10 (1904-1906), 119-134.

426 _____. "The Massachusetts Bay currency, 1690-1750: the plates." AASP, New Ser., 12 (1897-1898), 410-424.

427 _____. Provincial banks: land and silver. CSMP, 3 (1895-1897), 2-40.
    1740.

428 _____. "The Shays' Rebellion." AASP, New Ser., 21 (1911), 57-79.

429 _____. Tracts relating to the currency of the Massachusetts Bay, 1682-1720. Boston: Houghton Mifflin, 1902. Pp. x, 394.

430 DAVIS, BANCROFT G. "Fifty years of judicial reporting in Massachusetts." Bar Bulletin, No. 134 (March, 1938), 19-23.
    1888-1938.

431 DAVIS, DANIEL. "Proceedings of the two conventions held at Portland to consider the expediency of a separate government in the District of Maine." MHSC, 4 (1795), 25-40.

432 DAVIS, GARRET. Speech of Hon. Garrett Davis, of Kentucky, on the state of the Union; in which he gave a sketch of the political history of Massachusetts; delivered in the Senate of the United States, February 16 & 17, 1864. Washington: L. Towers, 1864. Pp. 39.

433 DAVIS, HARRISON MERRILL. "Local government under the first charter." EIHC, 66 (1930), 161-181.

434 DAVIS, JOHN, 1761-1847. A discourse before the Massachusetts Historical Society, Boston, December 22, 1813, at their anniversary commemoration of the first landing of our ancestors at Plymouth, in 1620. Boston: John Eliot, 1814. Pp. 31.

435 DAVIS, LANCE EDWIN. Sources of industrial finance: the American textile industry, a case study. EEH, 9 (1956-1957), 189-203.
    Massachusetts, 1827-1860.

436 DAVIS, WILLIAM THOMAS. Bench and bar of the Commonwealth of Massachusetts. Boston: Boston History Co., 1895. 2v.
    Biographies of lawyers.

437 _____. History of the judiciary of Massachusetts, including the Plymouth and Massachusetts colonies, the province of the Massachusetts Bay, and the Commonwealth. Boston: Boston Book Co., 1900. Pp. xxiv, 446.

438 DAWES, SARAH ELIZABETH. Colonial Massachusetts; stories of the old Bay State. N.Y.: Silver, Burdett, 1899. Pp. 187.

439 DAWSON, HENRY BARTON. Declaration of Independence by the colony of Massachusetts Bay, May 1, 1776. [N.Y., 1862]. Pp. 12.

440   DAY, CLIVE. Capitalistic and socialistic ten-
        dencies in the Puritan colonies. American
Historical Association. Annual Report, (1925), 223-
235.

441   DEAN, CHRISTOPHER C. A brief history of the
        Massachusetts Sabbath School Society, and of
the rise and progress of Sabbath schools in the
orthodox Congregational denomination in Massachusetts. Boston: Sabbath School Society, 1852.
Pp. 36.

442   DEANE, CHARLES. "The connection of Massachu-
        setts with slavery and the slave-trade."
AASP, New Ser. 4, (1885-1887), 191-222.

443   ____. and JOEL PARKER. "The forms in issuing
        letters patent by the crown of England [with
some remarks relating to the early history of the
Massachusetts charter of 4th Charles I]." MHSP,
(1869-1870), 166-196.

444   DEANE, CHARLES. "The Irish donation in 1676."
        NEHGR, 2 (1848), 245-249.
        Aid to Massachusetts after King Philip's War.

445   ____. "Judge Lowell and the Massachusetts
        Declaration of Rights." MHSP, (1873-1875),
299-304.
        State constitution, 1779-1780.

446   DE COSTA, BENJAMIN FRANKLIN. Footprints of
        Miles Standish. Charlestown: Re-printed from
the Church Monthly for private distribution, 1864.
Pp. 24.

447   DEEDY, JOHN G., ed. The Church in Worcester,
        New England: a modern diocese with an an-
cient name. Worcester: Designed by the Hawthorne
Pr. for the Guild of Our Lady of Providence, St.
Vincent Hospital, 1956. Unpaged.
        Roman Catholic Diocese of Worcester.

448   DEETZ, JAMES. "The reality of the Pilgrim
        Fathers." Natural History, 78 (November,
1969), 32-45.

449   DELABARRE, EDMUND BURKE. "A possible pre-
        Algonkian culture in southeastern Massachu-
setts." American Anthropologist, New Ser., 27
(1925), 359-369.

450   DEMOS, JOHN. A little commonwealth: family
        life in Plymouth Colony. N.Y.: Oxford Univ.
Pr., 1970.

451   ____. "Notes on life in Plymouth Colony."
        WMQ, 3 Ser., 22 (1965), 264-286.

452   DERBY, ELIAS HASKET. The history of paper
        money in the province of Massachusetts before
the Revolution, with an account of the Land Bank
and the Silver Bank, read before the American Statistical Association at Boston, May, 1874. Boston:
New England News Co., 1874. Pp. 16.

453   DERBY, JOHN BARTON. Political reminiscences,
        including a sketch of the origin and history
of the 'Statesman Party' of Boston. Boston: Homer
& Palmer, 1835. Pp. 172.
        Democratic Party.

454   DETHLEFSEN, EDWIN and JAMES DEETZ. "Death
        heads, cherubs, and willow trees: experimen-
tal archaeology in colonial cemeteries." American
Antiquity, 31 (1966), 502-510.
        Analysis of gravestone decorations in Massa-
        chusetts.

455   DEXTER, HENRY MARTYN. As to Roger Williams,
        and his 'banishment' from the Massachusetts
Plantation; with a few further words concerning the
Baptists, the Quakers, and religious liberty. Bos-
ton: Congregational Publishing Society, 1876.
Pp. vi, 146.

456   ____. Memoranda, historical, chronological,
        &c. prepared with the hope to aid those whose
interest in Pilgrim memorials, and history, is
freshened by this jubilee year, and who may not have
a large historical library at hand. Boston, 1870.
Pp. 39.

457   DEXTER, MORTON. "Differences between Plymouth
        and Jamestown." CSMP, 12 (1908-1909), 256-
270.

458   ____. The story of the Pilgrims. Boston:
        Congregational Sunday-School and Publishing
Society, 1894. Pp. ix, 363.

459   DIAZ, ABBY MORTON. "Massachusetts State Fed-
        eration of Women's Clubs." National Magazine,
4 (1896), 181-209.
        Brief sketches of individual clubs.

460   ____. "Old Plymouth schools." Bostonian, 1
        (1894-1895), 494-502.
        Plymouth Colony.

461   ____. "Women's clubs." Bostonian, 2 (1895),
        179-183, 288-292, 383-386, 516-519.

462   DICKINSON, RODOLPHUS. A geographical and
        statistical view of Massachusetts proper.
Greenfield: Denio and Phelps, 1813. Pp. 80.

463   DICKSON, JOHN. "Economic regulations and re-
        strictions on personal liberty in early Massa-
chusetts." PVMA 7 (1921-1929), 485-525.
        1630-1675.

464   DILLINGHAM, WILLIAM HENRY. An oration deliv-
        ered before the Society of the Sons of New
England of Philadelphia, December 22d, 1847, the
anniversary of the landing of the Pilgrims. Philadelphia: J. C. Clark, 1847. Pp. 38.

465   DIMOND, ALAN J. "Congestion in the Superior
        Court since its creation in 1859 and proposals
for relief." MassLQ, 38 (June, 1953), 95-125.

466   ____. The Superior Court of Massachusetts:
        its origin and development. Boston: Little,
Brown, 1960. Pp. 187.

467   DINCAUZE, DENA FERRAN. Cremation cemeteries
        in eastern Massachusetts. Cambridge: Peabody
Museum, 1968. Pp. vii, 103.

468   DINKIN, ROBERT J. "Seating the meeting house
        in early Massachusetts." NEQ, 43 (1970),
450-464.

469 DINMORE, HARRY C. "A comparison of the Pawtucket and Middlesex Canals and the Boston and Lowell Railroad." Towpath Topics, 9 (October, 1971), 7-11.

470 DINNEEN, JOSEPH FRANCIS. The Kennedy family. Boston: Little, Brown, 1960. Pp. 238.

471 DODD, EDWIN MERRICK. American business corporations until 1860, with special reference to Massachusetts. Cambridge: Harvard Univ. Pr., 1954. Pp. 524.

472 _____. "The evolution of limited liability in American industry: Massachusetts." HarvL Rev, 61 (1947-1948), 1351-1379.

473 _____. "The evolution of limited liability in Massachusetts." MHSP 68 (1944-1947), 228-256.

474 _____. "Statutory developments in business corporation law, 1886-1936." HarvLRev, 1 (1936), 27-59.

475 DOERING, CARL RUPP. "Death rate from diphtheria in Massachusetts for 51 years, 1875-1925." National Academy of Sciences. Proceedings, 13 (1927), 12-14.

476 DOHERTY, RICHARD POWERS. History of the Massachusetts Committee on Public Safety 1940-1945. [Boston], 1945. Pp. vii, 171.

477 DOHERTY, WILLIAM W. "The Republican Party in Massachusetts." NEM, 48 (1912-1913), 505-515; 49 (1913), 21-24, 33-35, 87-95.

478 DONHAM, S. AGNES. The Eastern Massachusetts Home Economics Association, formerly New England Home Economics Association: the first forty-three years, 1909-1952. [Boston?]: Eastern Massachusetts Home Economics Association, 1954. Pp. 90.

479 DONOVAN, GEORGE FRANCIS. The pre-revolutionary Irish in Massachusetts, 1620-1775. Menasha, Wis.: George Banta, 1932. Pp. 158.

480 DOOLITTLE, BENJAMIN. A short narrative of mischief done by the French and Indian enemy, on the western frontiers of the province of the Massachusetts-Bay; from the beginning of the French war, proclaimed by the King of France March 15th 1743, 4; and by the King of Great Britain March 29th 1744, to August 2d 1748.... Boston: S. Kneeland, 1750. Pp. 22.

481 DORLAND, ARTHUR GARRATT. The royal disallowance in Massachusetts. Kingston, Ontario: Jackson Pr., 1917. Pp. 33.

482 DOUGLAS, CHARLES HENRY JAMES. The financial history of Massachusetts, from the organization of the Massachusetts Bay Company to the American Revolution. N.Y., 1892. Pp. 148.

483 DOW, GEORGE FRANCIS, ed. "Building agreements in seventeenth-century Massachusetts." OTNE, 12 (1921-1922), 135-139; 13 (1922-1923), 28-32, 131-134.

484 _____. Every day life in the Massachusetts Bay Colony. Boston: Society for the Preservation of New England Antiquities, 1935. Pp. xii, 293.
    Social life and customs.

485 _____. "Notes on the use of pewter in Massachusetts during the seventeenth century." OTNE, 14 (1923-1924), 29-32.

486 DOWNES, WILLIAM HOWE. "The Charles River Basin." NEM, New Ser., 15 (1896), 193-211.

487 DRAKE, SAMUEL ADAMS. Our colonial homes. Boston: Lee and Shepard, 1894. Pp. 211.

488 DRAPER, ANDREW SLOAN. An address at Forefathers' convocation, Sunday, December 13, 1896. The Pilgrim and his share in American life. Champaign, Ill.: Gazette Print [1896]. Pp. 23.

489 DUBERMAN, MARTIN B. "Behind the scenes as the Massachusetts 'coalition' of 1851 divides the spoils." EIHC, 99 (1963), 152-160.

490 _____. "Some notes on the beginnings of the Republican Party in Massachusetts." NEQ, 34 (1961), 364-370.

491 DUBOFSKY, MELVYN. "Daniel Webster and the Whig theory of economic growth: 1828-1848." NEQ, 42 (1969), 551-572.

492 DUDLEY, DEAN, comp. Directory and history of Plymouth and Barnstable counties for 1873-1874, containing a history and register, and alphabetical list of the professions, trades and other business pursuits of each town.... Boston, 1873. v.p.

493 DUNIWAY, CLYDE AUGUSTUS. The development of freedom of the press in Massachusetts. N.Y.: Longmans, Green, 1906. Pp. xv, 202.

494 DUNKIN, BENJAMIN FANEUIL. Address, delivered before the members of the New-England Society, in Charleston, at their anniversary meeting, December 20th, 1819. Charleston: Courier Office, 1820. Pp. 8.

495 DUNTON, JOHN. John Dunton's letters from New-England. W. H. Whitmore, ed. Boston: For the [Prince] Society, 1867. Pp. xxiv, 340.

496 DURNIN, RICHARD BERRY. "Schooling and the Plymouth Colony." MayflowerQ, 38 (1972), 45-51.

497 DUTTON, SAMUEL WILLIAM SOUTHMAYD. The fathers of New England - religion their ruling motive in their emigration. A sermon preached on the Lord's day, December 22d, 1850, the two hundred and thirtieth anniversary of the landing of the Pilgrims. New Haven: A. H. Maltby, 1851. Pp. 17.

498 DWIGHT, THEODORE. History of the Hartford Convention with a review of the policy of the United States government which led to the War of 1812. N.Y.: N. & J. White, 1833. Pp. 447.

499   DYER, DAVID. A discourse, on the character-
          istics of the Puritans, delivered in Dorches-
ter, December 21, 1845. Boston: T. R. Marvin,
1846. Pp. 24.

500   DYER, WALTER A. "Embattled farmers." NEQ, 4
          (1931), 460-481.
          Shays' Rebellion.

501   EASTMAN, LUCIUS R., JR. "Sketch of the Nor-
          folk Association in Massachusetts." CongQ, 8
(1866), 17-28.
          A ministerial association; not limited to
Norfolk County.

502   EATON, ASA B. Executive and legislative de-
          partments of the state of Massachusetts, 1868.
Lowell: Stone & Huse, 1868. Pp. 35.
          Biographies.

503   EATON, JOSEPH GILES. The last exploit of
          Old Ironsides, or the action between the Con-
stitution and the Cyane and Levant. [Boston]: Military Historical Society of Massachusetts, 1901.
Pp. 18.

504   EATON, WILLIAM HARRISON. Historical sketch
          of the Massachusetts Baptist Missionary Soci-
ety and Convention, 1802-1902. Boston: Massachusetts Baptist Convention, 1903. Pp. x, 240.

505   EATON, WILLIAM LORENZO. An account of the
          movement in Massachusetts to close the rural
schools, and to transport their pupils, at public
expense, to the village schools. Boston: Nathan
Sawyer & Son, 1893. Pp. 8.

506   EDES, HARRY HERBERT. "Josiah Barker, and his
          connection with shipbuilding in Massachu-
setts." NEHGR, 24 (1870), 297-305.

507   EDMANDS, THOMAS F. "The Massachusetts mili-
          tia." NEM, New Ser., 11 (1894-1895), 770-783.

508   EDMONDS, JOHN HENRY. "How Massachusetts re-
          ceived the Declaration of Independence."
AASP, New Ser., 35 (1925), 227-252.

509   _____. "The Massachusetts archives." AASP,
New Ser., 31 (1921), 18-60.
          Chronological study of the development of the
collections.

510   EDWARDS, B. B. "Complete list of the Congre-
          gational ministers in the old county of Hamp-
shire, Ms. (including the present counties of
Hampshire, Franklin and Hampden) from the first
settlement to the present times." American Quarterly Register, 10 (1837-1838), 260-276, 379-407.
          Includes brief sketches of the towns.

511   EDWARDS, WILLIAM CHURCHILL. Ships of the
          United States Navy named for the Commonwealth
of Massachusetts. Quincy: Bethlehem Steel, 1941.
Pp. 24. MBNEH.

512   EELLS, JAMES. An address in recognition of
          six tablets erected to do honor to Governor
Henry Vane, Mistress Anne Hutchinson, Governor John
Leverett, Governor Simon Bradstreet, Mistress Anne
Bradstreet, Governor John Endecott; given in the

First Church in Boston on Forefathers' Day, December
twenty-first nineteen hundred and four. Boston:
Geo. H. Ellis, [1904?]. Pp. 32

513   ELDREDGE, DANIEL. Massachusetts co-operative
          banks, or building associations, a history of
their growth from 1877 to 1893. Boston: G. H. Ellis, 1893. Pp. 44.

514   ELDRIDGE, AZARIAH. An address delivered be-
          fore the New England Society, in Ann Arbor,
Mich., on Fore-fathers Day, December 22, 1860.
Ann Arbor: E. B. Pond, 1861. Pp. 15.
          Pilgrim Fathers.

515   ELIOT, CHARLES WILLIAM, b. 1834. Massachu-
          setts: an old and prosperous democracy and a
safe social order. Hingham: Village Pr., 1905.
Pp. 15.

516   ELIOT, CHARLES WILLIAM, II. "The Charles Riv-
          er Basin." CaHSP, 39 (1961-1963), 23-38.

517   ELIOT, CHRISTOPHER RHODES. "History of the
          Massachusetts Convention of Congregational
Ministers from 1887 to 1941." UHSP, 8, Pt. 1,
(1947), 17-36.

518   ELIOT, JOHN, 1604-1690. John Eliot and the
          Indians, 1652-1657, being letters addressed
to Rev. Jonathan Hammer of Barnstaple, England, reproduced from the original manuscripts in the possession of Theodore N. Vail. Wilberforce Eames, ed.
N.Y.: Adams & Grace Pr., 1915. 31 leaves.

519   ELIOT, JOHN, 1754-1813. "Ecclesiastical his-
          tory of Massachusetts." MHSC, 9 (1804), 1-49;
10 (1809), 1-37; 2 Ser., 1 (1814), 194-210.

520   _____. "Ecclesiastical history of Massachu-
          setts and the Old Colony of Plymouth." MHSC,
7 (1800), 262-280.
          Author attribution by the editor.

521   ELIOT, SAMUEL ATKINS, 1862-1950. Biographical
          history of Massachusetts; biographies and
autobiographies of the leading men in the state.
Boston: Massachusetts Biographical Society, 1909-
1918. 10v.

522   ELLIS, GEORGE EDWARD. I. The aims and pur-
          poses of the founders of Massachusetts. II.
Their treatment of intruders and dissentients. Two
lectures of a course by members of the Massachusetts
Historical Society, delivered before the Lowell In-
stitute on Jan. 8 and Jan. 12, 1869. Boston: J.
Wilson and Son, 1869. Pp. 100.
          Church and State.

523   _____. The church and the parish in Massachu-
          setts usage and law, address delivered at the
commemoration of the 250th anniversary of the gathering of the First Church in Dedham, Mass., as observed jointly by the First Parish and the First
Congregational Church, on Nov. 19, 1888. Boston,
1889. Pp. 37.

524   _____. A half-century of the Unitarian con-
        troversy, with particular reference to its
origin, its course, and its prominent subjects
among the Congregationalists of Massachusetts. Boston: Crosby, Nichols, 1857. Pp. xxiv, 511.

525   _____. The Puritan age and rule in the colony
        of the Massachusetts Bay, 1629-1685. Boston:
Houghton Mifflin, 1888. Pp. xix, 576.

526   ELLSWORTH, EDWARD W. Massachusetts in the
        Civil War. Vol. III: a year of crisis, 1862-
1863. Boston: Massachusetts Civil War Centennial
Commission, 1962. Pp. 48. M.

527   ELY, ALFRED. A sermon, delivered at Monson,
        Massachusetts, December 22, 1820; the second
centurial anniversary of the landing of the Fathers
of New-England, at Plymouth.... Hartford: Goodwin
& Sons, 1821. Pp. 27.
        Pilgrim Fathers.

528   EMBURY, AYMAR, II. "An architectural mono-
        graph: houses in southeastern Massachusetts."
WPSAM, 14 (1928), 147-168.

529   EMERSON, GEORGE BARRELL. Education in Massa-
        chusetts: early legislation and history, a
lecture of a course by members of the Massachusetts
Historical Society, delivered before the Lowell Institute, Feb. 16, 1869. Boston: Wilson and Son,
1869. Pp. 36.

530   EMERSON, RALPH WALDO. "Historic notes on life
        and letters in Massachusetts." Atlantic, 52
(1883), 529-543.
        Intellectual life.

531   EMMONS, NATHANAEL. A sermon, delivered Dec.
        31, 1820. The last Lord's day in the second
century since our forefathers first settled in
Plymouth. Dedham: H. & W. H. Mann, 1821. Pp. 24.

532   ENCYCLOPEDIA of Massachusetts, biographical-
        genealogical. William Richard Cutter, et al,
comps. N.Y.: American Historical Society, 1916.
5v.

533   ENDICOTT, CHARLES MOSES. Memoir of John Ende-
        cott, first governor of the colony of Massa-
chusetts Bay, being also a succinct account of the
rise and progress of the colony, from 1628 to
1665.... Salem: Observer Office, 1847. Pp. 116.

534   ENDICOTT, WILLIAM CROWNINSHIELD, 1826-1900.
        Address at the commemoration of the landing
of John Endicott, before the Essex Institute, Sept.
18, 1878. Salem: Salem Pr., 1879. Pp. 38.

535   ENDICOTT, WILLIAM CROWNINSHIELD, 1860-1936.
        John Endecott and John Winthrop; address by
William Crowninshield Endicott...at the tercentenary banquet at Salem, June 12, 1930, to commemorate
the arrival of Governor Winthrop with the charter.
Boston: Thomas Todd, 1930. Pp. 32.

536   ENO, JOEL N. "The expansion of Massachu-
        setts--chronological--based on the official
records." Americana, 24 (1930), 28-40.

537   _____. "The expansion of New England as begun
        in Plymouth." Americana, 23 (1929), 403-410.
Plymouth Colony.

538   ERIKSON, KAI T. Wayward Puritans; a study in
        the sociology of deviance. N.Y.: Wiley,
1966. Pp. xv, 228.

539   ESSEX INSTITUTE, SALEM, MASS. Report of the
        committee of the Essex Institute on the first
church of the Pilgrims. Rendered June 19, 1865.
[Salem, 1865]. Pp. 8.

540   ETULAIN, RICHARD. "John Cotton and the Anne
        Hutchinson controversy." Rendezvous, 2
(1967), 9-18.

541   EVANS, GEORGE HILL. Governor Winthrop's ship,
        The Blessing of the Bay: the story and the
records. Somerville, 1932. Pp. 11.

542   EVANS, LAWRENCE B. "The Constitutional Con-
        vention of Massachusetts." AmPolSciRev, 15
(1921), 214-232.
        1917-1919.

543   EVANS, PAUL D. "The Pulteney Purchase." New
        York State Historical Association. Quarterly
Journal, 3 (1922), 83-104.
        Boundary dispute with New York, 1786.

544   EVERETT, CHARLES CARROLL. A sermon preached
        Dec. 17th, 1865, the Sunday preceding the
anniversary of the landing of the Pilgrims. Bangor:
B. A. Burr, 1865. Pp. 10.
        Pilgrim Fathers.

545   EVERETT, EDWARD. An oration delivered at
        Plymouth, December 22, 1824. Boston: Cum-
mings, Hilliard, 1825. Pp. 46.
        Pilgrim Fathers.

546   EVERETT, ELIZABETH LOWELL. Ye governour and
        companie of Massachusetts Bay. Philadelphia:
Dorrance, 1931. Pp. 187.

547   EXCURSIONS in the bay, Boston to Cape Ann and
        Provincetown. Boston: Hall & Whiting, 1881.
Pp. 42.

548   EZELL, JOHN S. "When Massachusetts played the
        lottery." NEQ, 22 (1949), 316-335.
        Eighteenth and nineteenth centuries.

549   FAIRMAN, CHARLES G. "Saving a state's moun-
        tains, Massachusetts plan of public reserva-
tions." NEM, New Ser., 42 (1910), 406-416.

550   FALL RIVER LINE. The tip end of Yankee land.
        n.p., 1885. Pp. 64.

551   "THE FALL River Line steamboat express."
        RLHSB, No. 43 (1937), 77.
        Train from Boston to Fall River; 90th anniver-
sary.

552   FARNSWORTH, ALBERT. "Shays' Rebellion."
        MassLQ, 12 (1927), 29-42.

553 "THE FEDERAL Constitutional Convention in Massachusetts in 1788." MassLQ, 10 (February, 1925), 40-44.

554 FEDERAL WRITERS' PROJECT. MASSACHUSETTS. The Albanian struggle in the old world and new.... Boston: The Writer, Inc., 1939. Pp. ix, 168.

555 _____. The Armenians in Massachusetts.... Boston: Armenian Historical Society, 1937. Pp. 148.

556 _____. Massachusetts; a guide to the Pilgrim state, (1937), Ray Bearse, ed. 2d. ed., rev. and enl. Boston: Houghton Mifflin, 1971. Pp. xiv, 525.
First edition has title: Massachusetts: a guide to its places and people.

557 FEER, ROBERT A. "The devil and Daniel Shays." CaHSP, 40 (1964-1966), 7-22.
Shays' Rebellion.

558 _____. "Imprisonment for debt in Massachusetts before 1800." MVHR, 48 (1961-1962), 252-269.

559 _____. "Shays's Rebellion and the Constitution: a study in causation." NEQ, 42 (1969), 388-410.

560 FELT, JOSEPH BARLOW. An historical account of Massachusetts currency. Boston: Perkins & Marvin, 1839. Pp. 259.

561 _____. "Statistics of population in Massachusetts. American Statistical Association. Collections, 1 (1843-1847), 121-214.

562 _____. "Statistics of taxation in Massachusetts including valuation and population." American Statistical Association. Collections, 1 (1843-1847), 221-596.

563 _____. "Statistics of towns in Massachusetts." American Statistical Association. Collections, 1 (1843-1847), 9-100.

564 _____. Who was the first governor of Massachusetts? Boston: T. R. Marvin, 1853. Pp. 17.

565 FENN, WILLIAM WALLACE. "How the schism came." UHSP, 1, Pt. 1, (1925), 3-21.
Unitarianism.

566 FIELD, MAXWELL. "Footwear Association to enter second century determined to slow imports." Industry, 34 (July, 1969), 39-40, 43-44.
New England Footwear Association, Inc.

567 FIELD, PHINEAS. "Slavery in Massachusetts." PUMA, 1 (1870-1879), 480-486.

568 "THE FIFTIETH Anniversary of the Land Court of Massachusetts 1898-1948." MassLQ, 34 (January, 1949), entire issue.

569 "FIFTY years of university extension, 1915-1965." Massachusetts Department of Education. Division of University Extension. Bulletin, 50 (January 18, 1965), entire issue.

570 "FIFTY years of workmen's compensation in Massachusetts." Industry, 27 (May, 1962), 17, 53.

571 FINGERHUT, EUGENE R. "Were the Massachusetts Puritans Hebraic?" NEQ, 40 (1967), 521-531.

572 FINOTTI, J. M. "Chronology of Catholicity in Massachusetts." United States Catholic Historical Magazine, 1 (1887), 314-315.
1647-1791.

573 FIORE, JORDAN DOMENIC. Massachusetts in ferment: the coming of the American Revolution, a chronological survey, 1760-1775. Boston: Revolutionary War Bicentennial Commission, 1971. Unpaged. MB.

574 _____. Massachusetts in the Civil War. Vol. II: the year of trial and testing; 1861-1862. Boston: Massachusetts Civil War Centennial Commission, 1961. Pp. 48. M.

575 "THE FIRST coinage in America." HistMag, 1 (1857), 225-227.

576 "THE FIRST North American coins." HistMag, 3 (1859), 197-201, 316-318.

577 FISHER, CHARLES EBEN. "Locomotive performance of nearly one hundred years ago." RLHSB, No. 23 (1930), 9-21.
Boston and Worcester Railroad, 1835-1837.

578 _____. The story of the Old Colony Railroad. Taunton: C. A. Hack & Son, 1919. Pp. 196.

579 _____. "Whistler's railroad, the Western Railroad of Massachusetts." RLHSB, No. 69 (1947), entire issue.

580 FISHER, FRED W. "Trends in zoning in Massachusetts." BULRev, 36 (1956), 347-353.
Since 1920.

581 FISHER, HERBERT ALBERT LAURENS. The Bay Colony; a tercentenary address. Boston: Houghton Mifflin, 1930. Pp. viii, 52.

582 FISHER, HORACE N. "'The embattled farmers.'" MagHist, 10 (1909), 207-212.
Regiments of minute men throughout the colony.

583 FISHMAN, IRVING. "Employers' liability in Massachusetts for the negligence of his independent contractor." BULRev, 34 (1954), 195-204.
1855-1950.

584 FISKE, JOHN, 1842-1901. "The paper money craze of 1786 and the Shays' Rebellion." Atlantic, 58 (1886), 376-385.

585 FISKE, WILSON. "The Bay Path." MedHr, 30 (1927), 25-31.
A road which linked the Bay Colony with the settlements on the Connecticut River.

586 FITZ, REGINALD H. "The rise and fall of the licensed physician in Massachusetts, 1781-1860." American Association of Physicians. Transactions, 9 (1894), 1-18.

587 FLAGG, CHARLES ALLCOTT. A guide to Massachusetts local history; being a bibliographic index to the literature of the towns, cities and counties of the state, including books, pamphlets, articles in periodicals and collected works, books in preparation, historical manuscripts, newspaper clippings, etc. Salem: Salem Pr., 1907. Pp. ix, 256.

588 _____, comp. An index of pioneers from Massachusetts to the West, especially the state of Michigan. This list includes many sons and daughters of old Bay State families who removed to New York and states of the Middle West. Salem: Salem Pr., 1915. Pp. iii, 86.

589 FLEMING, THOMAS J. One small candle; the Pilgrims' first year in America. N.Y.: Norton, 1961. Pp. 222.

590 [FORBES, ABNER]. The rich men of Massachusetts: containing a statement of the reputed wealth of about two thousand persons, with brief sketches of nearly fifteen hundred characters. (1851) 2d. ed. Boston: Redding, 1852. Pp. vii, 224.

591 FORBES, ALLAN. "Early Myopia at Brookline, Dedham, Framingham, Southboro and Milton." EIHC, 78 (1942), 97-116.
Myopia Hunt Club.

592 _____. and RALPH M. EASTMAN. Town and city seals of Massachusetts; presenting the official seals of some of the towns and cities of Massachusetts, together with brief historical sketches and local anecdotes. Boston: State Street Trust Co., 1950-1951. 2v.

593 FORBES, ALLAN W. "Apprenticeship in Massachusetts, its early importance and later neglect." Worcester HSPub, New Ser., 2 (1936-1943), 5-25.

594 FORBES, HARRIETTE MERRIFIELD. "Early New England gravestones and the men who made them." PVMA, 7 (1921-1929), 331-342.
Limited to Massachusetts.

595 FORBES, HENRY A. CROSBY and HENRY LEE. Massachusetts help to Ireland during the great famine.... Milton: Captain Robert Bennet Forbes House, 1967. Pp. xxiv, 106.

596 FORD, WORTHINGTON CHAUNCEY. Address made at the general court of the Society of Colonial Wars in the State of Rhode Island and Providence Plantations, December 30, 1920. [Providence, 1921?]. Pp. 14.
Pilgrim Fathers.

597 _____. and ALBERT MATTHEWS. "Bibliography of the laws of the Massachusetts Bay, 1641-1776." CSMP, 4 (1910), 291-480.

598 FORD, WORTHINGTON CHAUNCEY. "Bibliography of the Massachusetts House Journals, 1715-1776." CSMP, 4 (1910), 201-289.

599 _____. Broadsides, ballads, &c. printed in Massachusetts 1639-1800. [Boston]: Massachusetts Historical Society, 1922. Pp. xvi, 483.

600 _____. "Franklin's accounts against Massachusetts." MHSP, 56 (1922-1923), 94-120. 1770-1775.

601 _____. "The governor and council of the province of Massachusetts Bay, August, 1714-March, 1715." MHSP, 2 Ser., 15 (1901-1902), 327-362.

602 _____. "Letters of Elbridge Gerry." NEHGR, 49 (1895), 430-441; 50 (1896), 21-30. 1784-1801.

603 FORMAN, BENNO M. "Mill sawing in seventeenth-century Massachusetts." OTNE, 60 (1969-1970), 110-130, 149.

604 FOSTER, STEPHEN. "The Massachusetts franchise in the seventeenth century." WMQ, 3 Ser., 24 (1967), 613-623.

605 FOUNTAIN, DAVID GUY. The 'Mayflower' Pilgrims and their pastor. Worthing, [England]: Walter, 1970. Pp. 80.

606 FOWLE, ISABEL PROCTOR. "Early colonial customs prior to 1730." Bostonian, 1 (1894-1895), 258-268.

607 FOWLER, WILLIAM CHAUNCEY. "Local law in Massachusetts, historically considered." NEHGR. 25 (1871), 274-284, 345-351; 26 (1872), 55-60, 284-293.

608 FOX, SANFORD J. Science and justice; the Massachusetts witchcraft trials. Baltimore: Johns Hopkins Pr., 1968. Pp. xix, 121.

609 NO ENTRY

610 FRANCIS, MAY E., comp. History of the Pilgrims. Waterloo, Iowa: W. B. Howell, 1915. Pp. 31.

611 FREEMAN, H. A. "The genesis of the Western R.R." RLHSB, No. 22 (1930), 5-8.

612 FREEMASONS. MASSACHUSETTS. GRAND LODGE. The constitutions of the Ancient and Honorable Fraternity of Free and Accepted Masons: containing their history, charges, addresses, &c...to which are added, the history of masonry in the Commonwealth of Massachusetts.... Worcester: Isaiah Thomas, 1792. Pp. xvi, 288.

613 _____. Proceedings at the Most Worshipful Grand Lodge of Ancient Free and Accepted Masons of the Commonwealth of Massachusetts in union with the Most Ancient and Honorable Grand Lodges in Europe and America, according to the old constitutions, 1792-1815. Cambridge: Caustic-Claflin, 1905. Pp. 685.

614 _____. Proceedings in masonry: St. John's Grand Lodge, 1733-1792; Massachusetts Grand Lodge, 1769-1792, with an appendix, containing copies of many ancient documents, and a table of lodges. Boston: Grand Lodge of Massachusetts, 1895. Pp. x, 521.

615 _____. The two hundredth anniversary of the Most Worshipful Grand Lodge of Ancient Free and Accepted Masons of the Commonwealth of Massachusetts, June 25, 26, 27, and 28, H. L. 5933. Boston, 1933. Pp. 173.

616 FREEMASONS. MASSACHUSETTS. PRINCE HALL GRAND LODGE. Proceedings of the one hundredth anniversary of the granting of warrant 459 to African Lodge, at Boston...Sept. 29th, 1884, under the auspices of the M. W. Prince Hall Grand Lodge F and A Masons.... Boston: Franklin Pr., 1885. Pp. 40.

617 FREEMASONS. MASSACHUSETTS. ROYAL AND SELECT MASTERS. The Cryptic Rite, origin and significance of Royal and Select Masters of Massachusetts. George Robert Hoskins, comp. Cambridge, [1926]. Pp. 12.

618 FREEMASONS. MASSACHUSETTS. ROYAL ARCH MASONS. GRAND CHAPTER. Centennial celebration of the formation of the Grand Royal Arch Chapter, Commonwealth of Massachusetts, held in Masonic Temple, Boston, Massachusetts. Boston: Parkhill, 1900. Pp. 104.

619 FREIBERG, MALCOLM. "Thomas Hutchinson and the province currency." NEQ, 30, (1957), 190-208.

620 _____. "An unknown Stamp Act letter. MHSP, 78 (1966), 138-142.

621 _____. "The Winthrops and their papers." MHSP, 80, (1968), 55-70.

622 FRIEDMAN, HARRY GEORGE. The taxation of corporations in Massachusetts. N.Y.: Columbia Univ. Pr., 1907. Pp. 177.

623 FRIEDMAN, LEE MAX. "Early Jewish residents in Massachusetts." AJHSP, 23 (1915), 79-90.

624 [FROST, JOHN EDWARD], comp. Immortal voyage... and Pilgrim parallels: problems, protests, patriotism, 1620-1970. Jack Frost, ed. North Scituate: Hawthorne Pr., 1970. Pp. 110.

625 FROTHINGHAM, LOUIS ADAMS. A brief history of the constitution and government of Massachusetts. Cambridge: Harvard Univ., 1916. Pp. v, 140.

626 FRUITS of the Mayflower, or, conversations respecting the Pilgrim Fathers. N.Y.: M. W. Dodd, 1849. Pp. 108.

627 FUESS, CLAUDE MOORE. A brief history of the American Legion in Massachusetts from its founding in 1919 to the election of officers for 1926. [Boston?, 1925]. Pp. 53.

628 FULLER, RAYMOND GARFIELD and MABEL A. STRONG. Child labor in Massachusetts; an inquiry under the auspices of the Massachusetts Child Labor Committee. Boston: Massachusetts Child Labor Committee, 1926. Pp. 170.

629 FURNESS, WILLIAM HENRY. The spirit of the Pilgrims. An oration delivered before the Society of the Sons of New England of Philadelphia December 22d, 1846, in commemoration of the landing of the Pilgrims ccxxvi years ago. Philadelphia: J. C. Clark, 1846. Pp. 22.

630 FUSSELL, G. E. "Social and agrarian backgrounds of the Pilgrim Fathers." AgricHist, 7 (1933), 183-202.

631 GALE, NAHUM. The Pilgrims' first year in New England. Boston: Massachusetts Sabbath School Society, [1857]. Pp. viii, 336.

632 GALVIN, GEORGE W. "Inhuman treatment of prisoners in Massachusetts." Arena, 32 (1904), 577-586.
1895-1904.

633 GANNETT, HENRY. A geographic dictionary of Massachusetts. Washington: Govt. Print. Off., 1894. Pp. 126.

634 GANNON, FREDERIC AUGUSTUS. A short history of American shoemaking. Salem: Newcomb & Gauss, 1912. Pp. 65.
Limited to Massachusetts.

635 GARDNER, FRANK A. "Colonel Asa Whitcomb's Regiment." MassMag, 7 (1914), 51-84.
Revolutionary; biography.

636 _____. "Colonel David Brewer's Regiment." MassMag, 10 (1917), 32-46, 167-178.
Revolutionary; biography.

637 _____. "Colonel Ephraim Doolittle's Regiment." MassMag, 2 (1909), 11-29.
Revolutionary; biography.

638 _____. "Colonel John Fellows's Regiment." MassMag, 2 (1909), 141-161.
Revolutionary, biography; Worcester, Hampshire and Berkshire counties.

639 _____. "Colonel John Nixon's Regiment." Mass Mag, 7 (1914), 99-123.
Revolutionary; biography.

640 _____. "Colonel Jonathan Brewer's Regiment." MassMag, 9 (1916), 137-153, 189-204.
Revolutionary; biography.

641 _____. "Colonel Joseph Read's Regiment. MassMag, 9 (1916), 87-106.
Revolutionary; biography.

642 _____. "Colonel Paul Dudley Sargent's Regiment." MassMag, 6 (1913), 82-94, 125-136.
Revolutionary; biography.

643 _____. "Colonel Ruggles Woodbridge's Regiment." MassMag, 4 (1911), 29-42, 82-95.
Revolutionary; biography.

644 ____. "Colonel Samuel Gerrish's Regiment." MassMag, 4 (1911), 221-243. Revolutionary; biography.

645 ____. "Colonel Thomas Gardner's Regiment." MassMag, 4 (1911), 153-173. Revolutionary; biography

646 ____. "Colonel William Heath's and Colonel John Greaton's Regiments." MassMag, 5 (1912), 15-28, 55-72. Revolutionary; biography.

647 ____. "The Founders of the Massachusetts Bay Colony." MassMag, 1 (1908), 27-37. Includes biographical sketches.

648 ____. "General Artemas Ward's and Colonel Jonathan Ward's Regiments." MassMag, 8 (1915), 123-152, 185-200. Revolutionary; biography.

649 GARDNER, GEORGE CLARENCE. An architectural monograph, Massachusetts Bay influence on Connecticut Valley colonial.... N.Y.: R. F. Whitehead, 1925. Pp. 20.

650 GARDNER, LUCIE M. "Settlers about Boston Bay prior to 1630." MassMag, 2 (1909), 115-117, 176-183. Biographies.

651 GARDNER, VIRGINIA ATKINSON, comp. A history of the Massachusetts Society of the Colonial Dames of America, 1893-1937. Boston: Thomas Todd, [1937?]. Pp. 26.

652 GARGAN, HELENA NORDHOFF. Pilgrim, Puritan and Papist in Massachusetts; read at the annual meeting of the [New England Catholic Historical] Society, June 5, 1902.... Boston: T. A. Whalen, 1902. Pp. 33.

653 GARLAND, JAMES SMITH. Massachusetts town law; a digest of statutes and decisions concerning towns and town officers; being the Massachusetts portion of Garland's "New England town law," reprinted with supplement containing later statutes and decisions. Boston: Boston Book Co., 1908. Pp. iv, 226.

654 GARRETT, EDMUND HENRY. "The coat of arms and Great Seal of Massachusetts." NEM, New Ser., 23 (1900-1901), 623-635.

655 ____. The Pilgrim shore. Boston: Little, Brown, 1900. Pp. 234. Norfolk and Plymouth counties.

656 GARRETT, WENDELL D. "The discovery of the Charles River by the Vikings according to the Book of Horsford." CaHSP, 40 (1964-1966), 94-109.

657 ____. "The papers of the Adams family: 'a natural resource' of history." Historical New Hampshire, 21 (1966), 28-37.

658 GATELL, FRANK OTTO. "Palfrey's vote, the conscience Whigs, and the election of Speaker Winthrop. NEQ, 31 (1958), 218-231. 1847-1848.

659 GAWALT, GERARD W. "Massachusetts legal education in transition, 1766-1840." AmJLegal Hist, 17 (1973), 27-50.

660 ____. "Sources of anti-lawyer sentiment in Massachusetts, 1740-1840." AmJLegalHist, 14 (1970), 283-307.

661 GAY, GEORGE E., comp. Origin and organization of the normal schools in Massachusetts. Boston: Wright & Potter, [1900]. Pp. 130.

662 GEOGHEGAN, WILLIAM EARLE. "The auxiliary steam packet 'Massachusetts.'" Steamboat Bill, 27 (1970), 26-33. Built at East Boston, 1845.

663 GETTEMY, CHARLES FERRIS. An historical survey of census taking in Massachusetts. Boston: Wright & Potter, 1919. Pp. 57. M.

664 GETTING, VLADO ANDREW and CLAIRE F. RYDER. "The theory and practice of public health." NEJMed, 249 (1953), 354-361. Massachusetts, 1901-1950.

665 GILBOY, ELIZABETH WATERMAN. Applicants for work relief; a study of Massachusetts families under the FERA and WPA. Cambridge: Harvard Univ. Pr., 1940. Pp. xviii, 273.

666 GILL, CRISPIN. Mayflower remembered; a history of the Plymouth Pilgrims. N.Y.: Taplinger, 1970. Pp. 206.

667 GILL, ELIZA M. "The Mayflower of the Pilgrims." MedHR, 30 (1927), 56-57.

668 GILL PUBLICATIONS, INC., BOSTON. Three hundred years of shoe & leather making in Massachusetts. Boston, 1930. Pp. 78.

669 GILMAN, ALFRED. "Rev. John Eliot (apostle to the Indians), Passaconaway, Wannalancet and Captain Samuel Mosely." ORHAL, 3 (1884-1887), 90-111.

670 GIPSON, LAWRENCE HENRY. "Aspects of the beginning of the American Revolution in Massachusetts Bay, 1760-1762." AASP, 67 (1957), 11-32.

671 ____. "Massachusetts Bay and American colonial union, 1754." AASP, 71 (1961), 63-92.

672 GIRAUDOUX, JEAN. Amica America. (1918) Paris: B. Grasset, [1938]. Pp. 216.

673 GLADDEN, WASHINGTON. From the Hub to the Hudson: with sketches of nature, history and industry in north-western Massachusetts. Boston: New England News, 1869. Pp. iv, 149.

674 GLIDDEN, CHARLES H. Republican Club of Massachusetts, a brief sketch of thirty years' activity. Boston, 1921. Pp. 42. MB.

675 GLUECK, SHELDON and ELEANOR T. GLUECK. 500 criminal careers. N.Y.: A. A. Knopf, 1930. Pp. xxvii, 365, xvi.

676 _____. and _____. Five hundred delinquent women. N.Y.: A. A. Knopf, 1934. Pp. xxiv, 539, x.

677 _____. and _____. Later criminal careers. N.Y.: The Commonwealth Fund, 1937. Pp. xi, 403.
Sequel to 500 Criminal Careers.

678 GODDARD, DELANO ALEXANDER. The Mathers weighed in the balances...and found not wanting. Boston: Daily Advertiser, 1870. Pp. 32.

679 GOEBEL, JULIUS. "King's law and local custom in seventeenth-century New England." Colum LR, 31 (1931), 416-448.
Plymouth Colony.

680 GOMES, PETER J. "What can we believe about the Pilgrims?" NEHGR, 124 (1970), 134-139.

681 GOODALE, GEORGE LINCOLN. British and colonial army surgeons on the 19th of April, 1775. An address delivered on the 19th of April, 1899, before the Middlesex South District Medical Society. [Cambridge?, 1899]. Pp. 26.
Massachusetts physicians at outbreak of the Revolution.

682 GOODELL, ABNER CHENEY, JR. An address delivered in the Old South Meeting-house in Boston, November 27, 1895 before the Society of Colonial Wars in the Commonwealth of Massachusetts, in commemoration of the six hundredth anniversary of the first summoning of citizens and burgesses to the Parliament of England, wherein the history of the House of Commons is sketched and a comparison made of the development of the legislatures of Great Britain and of the Commonwealth of Massachusetts. Boston: Rockwell and Churchill Pr., 1897. Pp. 36.

683 _____. "A brief review of the history of the Puritans and the Separatists from the Church of England: in which the difference between the nonconformists of Massachusetts Bay and the Separatists of Plymouth is discussed." EIHC, 4 (1862), 145-157.

684 _____. "Censorship of the press in Massachusetts." MHSP, 2 Ser., 8 (1892-1894), 271-274.

685 _____. A chronological sketch of the legislation from 1752 to 1884 on the subject of printing the acts and resolves of the province of Massachusetts Bay. Boston: 1889. Pp. 47.

686 _____. "Origin of towns in Massachusetts." MHSP, 2 Ser., 5 (1889-1890), 320-331.

687 _____. "Provincial seals in Massachusetts." MHSP, 20 (1882-1883), 157-170.

688 _____. "Sketch of the legislation of Massachusetts (the Provincial period)." EIB, 3 (1871), 157-160.
1692-1780.

689 _____. "The title 'Colony' and 'Province' as applied to Massachusetts." MHSP, 2 Ser., 1 (1884-1885), 192-199.

690 _____. The trial and execution, for petit treason, of Mark and Phillis, slaves of Capt. John Codman, who murdered their master as Charlestown, Mass., in 1755; for which the man was hanged and gibbeted, and the woman was burned to death. Including, also, some account of other punishments by burning in Massachusetts. Cambridge: J. Wilson and Son, 1883. Pp. 39.

691 _____. "Witch-trials in Massachusetts." MHSP, 20 (1882-1883), 280-326.

692 GOODMAN, ABRAM VORSEN. "Roots of America I: in Puritan Massachusetts." Menorah Journal, 28 (1940), 17-25.
Jews.

693 GOODMAN, PAUL. The Democratic-Republicans of Massachusetts; politics in a young republic. Cambridge: Harvard Univ. Pr., 1964. Pp. xiii, 281.

694 GOODWIN, HENRY MARTYN. The Pilgrim Fathers: a glance at their history, character and principles, in two memorial discourses, delivered in the First Congregational Church, Rockford, May 22, 1870. Rockford, Ill.: Bird, Conick, & Flint, 1870. Pp. 36.

695 GOODWIN, JOHN ABBOT. "Boston and Lowell Railroad." Towpath Topics, 5 (August, 1967), [6-8].

696 _____. The Pilgrim Fathers: oration delivered before the City Council and citizens of Lowell, December 22, 1876. Lowell: Penhallow Printing, 1877. Pp. 50.

697 _____. The Pilgrim republic; an historical review of the colony of New Plymouth, with sketches of the rise of other New England settlements, the history of Congregationalism, and the creeds of the period. Boston: Ticknor, 1888. Pp. xli, 662.

698 _____. The Puritan conspiracy against the Pilgrim Fathers and the Congregational Church, 1624. Boston: Cupples, Upham, 1883. Pp. 20.

699 GOOGINS, MARY SOULE. "Women of the 'Mayflower' and Plymouth Colony." MedHR, 26 (1923), 25-34.

700 GOOKIN, WARNER FOOTE. "Massasoit's domain: is 'Wampanoag' the correct designation?" MASB, 20 (1958-1959), 12-14.

701 _____. "The Pilgrims as archaeologists." MASB, 11 (1949-1950), 19-21.

702 _____. A voyage of discovery to the southern parts of Norumbega, including the places named Cape Cod, Martha's Vineyard and the Elizabeth Islands by their discoverer, Bartholomew Gosnold in the year 1602 A.D. Edgartown: Dukes County Historical Society, 1950. Pp. 20.

703 GORDON, GEORGE ANGIER. The genius of the
     Pilgrim. Pilgrim Pr., 1913. Pp. 31.

704 GOSS, ELBRIDGE HENRY. "Early bells of Massa-
     chusetts." NEHGR, 28 (1874), 176-184, 279-
288; 37 (1883), 46-52.

705 GOTTFRIED, MARION H. "The first depression in
     Massachusetts." NEQ, 9 (1936), 655-678.
     1640.

706 GRAND ARMY OF THE REPUBLIC. DEPARTMENT OF
     MASSACHUSETTS. Early history of the Depart-
ment of Massachusetts, G. A. R., from 1866 to 1880
inclusive. Boston: E. B. Stillings, 1895. Pp. iv,
453.

707 GRANT, SIDNEY S. and SAMUEL E. ANGOFF. "Mas-
     sachusetts and censorship." BULRev, 10
(1930), 36-60, 147-194.

708 GRAY, F. C. "Remarks on the early laws of
     Massachusetts Bay." MHSC, 3 Ser., 8 (1843),
191-215.

709 GREAT BRITAIN. SOVEREIGNS, ETC. Massachu-
     setts royal commissions, 1681-1774. Boston:
The [Colonial] Society [of Massachusetts], 1913.
Pp. xxxv, 409.

710 GREEN, SAMUEL ABBOTT. "The first census of
     Massachusetts." American Statistical Associ-
ation. Publications, New Ser., 2 (1890-1891), 182-
185.
     1765.

711 _____. History of medicine in Massachusetts:
     a centennial address delivered before the
Massachusetts Medical Society at Cambridge, June 7,
1881. Boston: A. Williams, 1881. Pp. 131.

712 [_____]. A letter said to have been written
     by Cotton Mather, shown to be a miserable
forgery. [Cambridge?, 1908?]. Pp. 3.
     Letter giving details of a scheme to capture
     and sell into slavery William Penn and his
     company, bears date Sept. 15, 1682. It was
     actually written by J. F. Shunk and published
     in the Easton, Pa., 'Argus,' 1870.

713 _____. "Old milestones leading from Boston."
     MHSP, 42 (1908-1909), 87-111.

714 _____. "Remarks on Otis's argument against
     the Writs of Assistance." MHSP, 2 Ser., 6
(1890-1891), 190-196.

715 _____. Remarks on the Boston Magazine, the
     Geographical gazetteer of Massachusetts, and
John Norman, engraver. Cambridge: J. Wilson and
Son, 1904. Pp. 7.

716 _____. "The use of prayers at funerals in
     Massachusetts." MHSP, 2 Ser., 5 (1889-1890),
331-332.

717 GREEN, SAMUEL SWETT. "Voluntary system in
     the maintenance of ministers." AASP, New
Ser., 4 (1885-1887), 86-126.
     Seventeenth century.

718 GREENE, EVARTS BOUTELL. The place of the
     Pilgrims in American history.... [Urbana]:
Univ. of Illinois Pr., 1921. Pp. 42.

719 [GREENLEAF, THOMAS]. Geographical gazetteer
     of the towns in the Commonwealth of Massachu-
setts. Boston: Greenleaf and Freeman, 1784-1785.
Pp. 98.
     Issued in parts, appended to the monthly num-
     bers of the 'Boston Magazine,' October, 1784-
     December, 1785. Includes only Suffolk County
     and part of Middlesex County.

720 GREENOUGH, CHESTER NOYES. "Algernon Sidney
     and the motto of the Commonwealth of Massachu-
setts." MHSP, 51 (1917-1918), 259-282.

721 GREENSLET, FERRIS. The Lowells and their sev-
     en worlds.... Boston: Houghton Mifflin,
1946. Pp. xi, 442.

722 GRIFFIS, WILLIAM ELIOT. The influence of the
     Netherlands in the making of the English com-
monwealth and the American republic, with notice of
what the Pilgrims learned in Holland, their treatment by the government and people, and answers to
criticisms made upon the proposed Delfshaven memorial. A paper read before the Boston Congregational
Club, Monday evening...Oct. 26, 1891. Boston: De
Wolfe, Fiske, [1891]. Pp. 40.

723 _____. Massachusetts: a typical American
     commonwealth. Cambridge: J. Wilson and Son,
1893. Pp. 38.

724 _____. The Pilgrims in their three homes,
     England, Holland, America. (1898) Rev. ed.
Boston: Houghton Mifflin, 1914. Pp. vii, 312.

725 GRINNELL, FRANK WASHBURN. "Constitutional
     history of the Supreme Judicial Court of Mas-
sachusetts from the Revolution to 1813." MassLQ, 2
(1917), 359-552, 559.

726 _____. "Continuous history of the 'Superior
     Court of Judicature, Court of Assize and Gen-
eral Jaol Delivery' and the 'Supreme Judicial Court'
of Massachusetts as told by the portraits of the
justices 1692 to 1920, also the portraits of the
justices of the Supreme Court of the United States
appointed from Massachusetts since 1789." MassLQ, 6
(1920), 1-8.

727 _____. "Court unification in the Bay State."
     American Judicature Society. Journal, 15
(1932), 170-173.
     Twentieth century.

728 _____. "The experimental development of early
     Massachusetts courts." MassLQ, 1 (1915-1916),
75-76.
     Nineteenth century.

729 _____. "The government of Massachusetts prior
     to the Federal Constitution." MassLQ, 10
(1924-1925), 175-232.

730 _____, ed. "The legal history of Massachu-
     setts, 1620-1953." MassLQ, 38 (August, 1953),
3-132.

731 _____. "Some early lawyers of Massachusetts and their present influence in the life of the nation." Maryland State Bar Association. Report of the Annual Meeting, 26 (1921), 175-199.

732 GROSVENOR, WILLIAM MERCER. The Puritan remnant...the twelfth annual sermon of the New England Society in the City of New York, preached at the Cathedral of Saint John the Divine on Forefathers' Sunday, December 17th, 1911. [N.Y., 1911]. Pp. 11.

733 GUILD, COURTENAY. "Musical steps." BSProc, (1929), 21-36.
Harvard Musical Association, Handel and Haydn Society and the Apollo Club.

734 GULICK, LUTHER HALSEY. Evolution of the budget in Massachusetts. N.Y.: Macmillan, 1920. Pp. xiv, 243.

735 GUMMERE, RICHARD M. "Thomas Hutchinson and Samuel Adams, a controversy in the classical tradition." BPLQ, 10 (1958), 119-130, 203-212.

736 GUSTAFSON, EVELINA. Ghost towns 'neath Quabbin Reservoir. Boston: Amity Pr., 1940. Pp. 125.

737 GUTMAN, ROBERT. "Birth and death registration in Massachusetts." Milbank Memorial Fund Quarterly 36 (1958), 58-74, 373-402; 37 (1959), 297-326, 386-417.

738 _____. "Birth statistics of Massachusetts during the nineteenth century." Population Studies, 10 (1956-1957), 69-94.

739 HADLEY, SAMUEL P. "Important events in the year 1840." Lowell HSC 2 (1921-1926), 314-322.

740 HAGUE, JOHN ALLEN. "The Massachusetts Constitutional Convention: 1917-1919." NEQ, 27 (1954), 147-167.

741 HALE, EDWARD EVERETT. Centennial of the Constitution. Boston: George H. Ellis, 1880. Pp. 12. M.
Massachusetts Constitution.

742 _____. Some recollections of the century. National Magazine, 6 (1897), 30-35, 124-130, 241-250, 341-349, 434-440, 533-540.

743 _____. The story of Massachusetts. Boston: D. Lothrop, 1891. Pp. 359.

744 HALE, RICHARD KINT. A brief history of the development of the Division of Waterways and Public Lands of the Massachusetts Department of Public Works. Boston Society of Civil Engineers. Journal, 13 (1926), 135-149.

745 HALES, JOHN GROVES. A survey of Boston and its vicinity; shewing the distance from the Old State House...to all the towns and villages not exceeding fifteen miles therefrom...together with a short topographical sketch of the country.... Boston: E. Lincoln, 1821. Pp. 156.

746 HALL, ALBERT HARRISON. "How Massachusetts grew, 1630-1642: a study of town boundaries." CaHSP, 21 (1930-1931), 19-49.

747 HALL, CHARLES WINSLOW, ed. Regiments and armories of Massachusetts; an historical narration of the Massachusetts Volunteer Militia, with portraits and biographies of officers past and present. Boston: W. W. Potter, 1899-1901. 2v.

748 HALL, DAVID D., comp. The Antinomian controversy, 1636-1638: a documentary history. Middletown, Conn.: Wesleyan Univ. Pr., 1968. Pp. viii, 447.

749 _____, comp. Puritanism in seventeenth-century Massachusetts. N.Y.: Holt, Rinehart and Winston, 1968.
Essays.

750 HALL, EDWARD A. "The Irish pioneers of the Connecticut Valley". AIrHSJ, 4 (1904), 43-54.
Limited to Massachusetts.

751 HALL, GEORGE D., COMPANY, BOSTON. Official chronicle and tribute book; containing a record of the establishment of the Massachusetts Bay Colony in New England by the Puritans, and the setting up of independent government in America; a chronicle of three hundred years outstanding events in the history of the Commonwealth; together with a tribute section which shall be an enduring memorial of its present men and women, companies, organizations, cities and towns listed herein who have been pre-eminent in making the proud history of Massachusetts. Boston, 1930. Pp. 448.

752 _____. Official program of the city of Boston tercentenary celebration and records of the individuals, firms, and institutions whose own history makes part of the history of the city. Boston, 1930. Pp. 208.

753 HALL, JOHN PHILIP. "Knights of St. Crispin in Massachusetts, 1869-1878." JEconHist, 18 (1958), 161-175.
Labor.

754 HALL, JOHN W. D. "Reminiscences of Shay's [sic] Insurrection." Old Colony HSC, No. 4 (1889), 79-87.

755 HALL, JONATHAN PRESCOTT. A discourse delivered before the New England Society, in the City of New York, December 22, 1847. N.Y.: G. F. Nesbitt, 1848. Pp. 77.
Pilgrim Fathers.

756 HALL, MICHAEL G. "Randolph, Dudley, and the Massachusetts moderates in 1683." NEQ, 29 (1956), 513-516.
Edward Randolph and Joseph Dudley.

757 HALL, ROBERT. Maine's admission to the Union. Sprague's Journal of Maine History, 8 (1920), 8-18.

758 HALL, VAN BECK. Politics without parties: Massachusetts, 1780-1791. Pittsburgh: Univ. of Pittsburgh Pr., 1972. Pp. xvii, 375.

759 HALLEY, ROBERT. Lecture on the Pilgrim Fathers. Manchester, [England]: Thomas Agnew and Sons, 1854. Pp. 35.

760 HALLOWELL, JAMES MOTT. The taxation of domestic manufacturing corporations in Massachusetts.... [Boston? 1908]. Pp. 61
1776-1908.

761 HALLOWELL, RICHARD PRICE. The Quaker invasion of Massachusetts. (1883) 3d ed. Boston: Houghton Mifflin, 1884. Pp. vi, 227.

762 HAMILTON, EDWARD PIERCE. "Early industry of the Neponset and the Charles." MHSP, 71 (1953-1957), 108-123.
1650-1812.

763 HAMMOND, JOHN C. "The Great and General Court of Massachusetts Bay Colony." Massachusetts Bar Association. Annual Report and...Proceedings, 4 (1914), 42-63.

764 HANDLIN, OSCAR and MARY FLUG HANDLIN. Commonwealth; a study of the role of government in the American economy: Massachusetts, 1774-1861. N.Y.: New York Univ. Pr., 1947.

765 HANDLIN, OSCAR. "Laissez-faire thought in Massachusetts, 1790-1880." JEconHist, 3, Supplement (December, 1943), 55-65.

766 _____. and MARY FLUG HANDLIN, eds. The popular sources of political authority; documents on the Massachusetts Constitution of 1780. Cambridge: Harvard Univ. Pr., 1966. Pp. xi, 962.

767 _____. and _____. "Radicals and conservatives in Massachusetts after independence." NEQ, 17 (1944), 343-355.

768 _____. and _____. "Revolutionary economic policy in Massachusetts." WMQ, 3 Ser., 4 (1947), 3-26.

769 HANKS, CHARLES STEDMAN. Our Plymouth forefathers, the real founders of our republic. Boston: D. Estes, 1908. Pp. 339.

770 HANNAH, SAMUEL D. 'Cast-up' lands. Yarmouthport, 1927. Pp. 4.

771 _____. Permissive uses of the common lands of proprietary plantations. Yarmouthport, 1927. Pp. 4.

772 HANSEN, ANN N. "Ships of the Puritan migration to Massachusetts Bay." AmNep, 23 (1963), 62-66.

773 HANSEN, HARRY. Old Ironsides, the fighting 'Constitution.' N.Y.: Random House, 1955. Pp. 180.

774 HANSEN, MILLARD WINCHESTER. "The significance of Shays' Rebellion." South Atlantic Quarterly, 39 (1940), 305-317.

775 HARDING, SAMUEL BANNISTER. The contest over the ratification of the Federal Constitution in the state of Massachusetts. N.Y.: Longmans, Green, 1896. Pp. 194.

776 HARLING, FREDERICK F. "The Indians of eastern Massachusetts 1620-1645." HJWM, 1 (Spring 1972), 28-36.

777 HARLOW, LOUIS KINNEY. At Gray Gables and walks along the shore of Buzzard's Bay...with an historical and descriptive sketch of Buzzard's Bay.... N.Y.: R. Tuck & Sons, 1895. Pp. 15.

778 HARLOW, RALPH VOLNEY. "Economic conditions in Massachusetts during the American Revolution." CSMP, 20 (1917-1919), 163-190.

779 HARMOND, RICHARD. "Troubles of Massachusetts Republicans during the 1880s." Mid-America, 56 (1974), 85-99.

780 HARRINGTON, C. S. "A historic railroad." National Magazine, 18 (1903), 269-275.
Boston and Albany.

781 HARRINGTON, FRED HARVEY. "Nathaniel Prentiss Banks, a study in anti-slavery politics." NEQ, 9 (1936), 626-654.
1840s and 1850s.

782 HARRINGTON, LAURENCE P. History of unemployment insurance in Massachusetts. n.p., 1939. 5 leaves. M.

783 [HARRIS, CHARLES]. The state sovereignty record of Massachusetts. By a Son of Norfolk. Norfolk, Va.: Fatherly, 1872. Pp. 28.
Author attribution by the Newberry Library.

784 HARRIS, CHARLES NATHAN. Massachusetts digest supplement; a digest of the reported decisions of the Supreme Judicial Court of the Commonwealth of Massachusetts from 1879 to [1901]...contained in the Massachusetts Reports (vols. 128 to [177]...inclusive). Boston: Little, Brown, 1895-1902. 2v.

785 HARRIS, JAMES RENDEL. The finding of the 'Mayflower.' London: Longmans, Green, 1920. Pp. v, 58.

786 _____. The last of the 'Mayflower.' Manchester, [England]: Univ. Pr., 1920. Pp. 122.

787 _____. The return of the 'Mayflower'.... Manchester, [England]: Univ. Pr., 1919. Pp. vi, 35.

788 _____. Three letters of John Eliot and a bill of lading of the 'Mayflower.' John Rylands Library. Bulletin, 5 (1918-1920), 102-110.

789 HARRISON, LOWELL. "Early Massachusetts school system." EIHC, 86 (1950), 380-388.

790 NO ENTRY

791 HART, ALBERT BUSHNELL, ed. Commonwealth history of Massachusetts, colony, province and state. N.Y.: The States History Co., 1927-1930. 5v.
An unnumbered "Biographical Volume," uniform in format with rest of the set, was later (not after February, 1936) published by the

(HART, ALBERT BUSHNELL, ed.)
Lewis Historical Publishing Co. of New York.
(Pp. 347). A copy is at MBNEH.

792 HART, CHARLES H. Paul Revere's first ride,
December 17-27, 1773." MHSP, 2 Ser., 20
(1906-1907), 560-563.
Carried news of the Boston Tea Party to New
York.

793 HARTWELL, EDWARD MUSSEY. "Primary elections
in Massachusetts, 1640-1694." American Political Science Association. Proceedings, (1910),
210-224.

794 HASKINS, GEORGE LEE. "The beginning of the
recording system in Massachusetts." BULRev,
21 (1941), 281-304.
Recording of deeds, mortgages, leases, etc.

795 _____. "Codification of the law in colonial
Massachusetts: a study of comparative law."
Indiana Law Journal, 30 (1954), 1-17.
Code of 1648.

796 _____. "Ecclesiastical antecedents of criminal punishment in Massachusetts." MHSP, 72
(1957-1960), 21-35.
Seventeenth century.

797 _____. "Gavelkind and the charter of Massachusetts Bay. CSMP, 34 (1937-1942), 483-498.

798 _____. Law and authority in early Massachusetts: a study in tradition and design.
N.Y.: Macmillan, 1960. Pp. 298.

799 _____. "The legacy of Plymouth." Mayflower
Q, 27 (August, 1962), 12-19.
Plymouth Colony.

800 _____. Of law and liberty in colonial Massachusetts, 1630-1650; an address delivered before the annual meeting of the Society of Colonial
Wars in the Commonwealth of Pennsylvania, held at
the Philadelphia Club, March 13, 1958. Philadelphia: The Society, 1958. Pp. 11.

801 _____. "A problem in the reception of the
common law in the colonial period." UPaLRev,
97 (1949), 842-843.
Differences in Massachusetts common law from
that of England.

802 _____. and SAMUEL E. EWING, III. "Spread of
Massachusetts law in the seventeenth century."
UPaLRev, 106 (1957-1958), 413-418.

803 HASSAM, FREDERICK F. Liberty tree, Liberty
hall. 1775. Lafayette and loyalty! Boston,
1891. Pp. 16.
Lafayette's visit of 1824.

804 HASSE, ADELAIDE ROSALIA. Index of economic
material in documents of the states of the
United States: Massachusetts, 1789-1904. Washington: Carnegie Institution of Washington, 1908.
Pp. 310.

805 HASTINGS, LEWIS MOREY. "An historical account
of some bridges over the Charles River."
CaHSP, 7 (1911-1912), 51-63.

806 HATCH, ALDEN. The Lodges of Massachusetts.
N.Y.: Hawthorn Books, 1973. Pp. viii, 360.
Lodge family.

807 [HAVEN, SAMUEL FOSTER]. A brief passage at
arms in relation to a small point of history.
Worcester: C. Hamilton, 1877. Pp. 29.
Whether Endecott and his company embarked in
a single ship.

808 HAWES, JOEL. 'One soweth and another reap-
eth' or, New England's indebtedness to the
Pilgrim Fathers, a discourse delivered in the First
Church in Hartford, Sabbath morning, May 8th, 1859.
Hartford: Hutchinson & Bullard, 1859. Pp. 23.

809 HAWKES, NATHAN MORTIMER. "Milestone memorials
along the Newburyport Turnpike." Lynn HSR,
No. 17 (1913), 123-151.

810 NO ENTRY

811 HAWTHORNE, NATHANIEL. Famous old people: being the second epoch of grandfather's chair.
Boston: E. P. Peabody, 1841. Pp. vii, 158.

812 _____. Grandfather's chair; true stories from
New England history and biography, (1841).
N.Y.: Univ. Publishing, 1901. Pp. viii, 183.

813 _____. Liberty tree: with the last words of
grandfather's chair. Boston: Tappan and
Dennet, 1842. Pp. viii, 156.
American Revolution.

814 HAXTUN, ANNIE ARNOUX. Signers of the Mayflower Compact. N.Y.: Reprinted from the
Mail and Express, 1896-1899. 3 pts. in 1 v.

815 HAYNES, GEORGE HENRY. "The causes of Know-
nothing success in Massachusetts." AHR, 3
(1897-1898), 67-82.
Election of 1854.

816 _____. "The conciliatory proposition in the
Massachusetts Convention of 1788." AASP, New
Ser., 29 (1919), 294-311.

817 _____. "How Massachusetts adopted the initia-
tive and referendum." PolSciQ, 34 (1919),
454-475.
1912-1917.

818 _____. "A Know-Nothing legislature." American Historical Association. Annual Report,
(1896), 177-187.
General Court of 1855.

819 _____. Representation and suffrage in Massachusetts, 1620-1691. Baltimore: Johns Hopkins Pr., 1894. Pp. 90.

873 ____. Oration delivered before the New England Society, in the City of New York...at their semi-centennial anniversary, December 22, 1855. n.p., [1856?]. Pp. 46.

874 HOLTON, EDITH AUSTIN. Yankees were like this. N.Y.: Harper & Bros., 1944. Pp. 268. Limited to Massachusetts; social life and customs.

875 HOMANS, ABIGAIL ADAMS. Education by uncles. Boston: Houghton Mifflin, 1966. Pp. 148. Adams family during nineteenth and twentieth centuries.

876 HORGAN, THOMAS PATRICK. Old Ironsides; an illustrated history of USS Constitution. Dublin, N.H.: Yankee, 1972. Pp. 122.

877 ____. Old Ironsides; the story of USS Constitution. Boston: Burdette, 1963. Pp. 98.

877A HORROCKS, J. W. "The Mayflower." Mariner's Mirror, 8 (1922), 2-9, 81-88, 140-147, 237-245, 354-362.

878 HORSFORD, CORNELIA. "Vinland and its ruins; some evidence that Northmen were in Massachusetts in pre-Columbian days." Popular Science, 56 (December, 1899), 160-176.

879 HOSMER, JEROME CARTER. "The narrative of Gen. Gage's spies, with biographical and other notes." BSPub, 9 (1912), 63-98.

880 HOWARD, ALAN B. "Art and history in Bradford's 'Of Plymouth Plantation.'" WMQ, 3 Ser., 28 (1971), 237-266.

881 HOWE, DANIEL WAIT. The Puritan republic of the Massachusetts Bay in New England. Indianapolis: Bowen-Merrill, 1899. Pp. xxxviii, 422.

882 HOWE, DONALD W. Quabbin, the lost valley. Roger Nye Lincoln, ed. Ware: Quabbin Book House, 1951. Pp. xviii, 631.

883 HOWE, FLORENCE THOMPSON. Asher Benjamin, country builders' assistant. Antiques, 40 (1941), 364-366. Houses designed by Benjamin.

884 HOWE, HENRY FORBUSH. Massachusetts: there she is--behold her. N.Y.: Harper, 1960. Pp. 290.

885 ____. Salt rivers of the Massachusetts shore. N.Y.: Rinehart, 1951. Pp. xiv, 370.

886 HOWE, MARK ANTONY DE WOLFE. Biographer's bait: a reminder of Edmund Quincy. MHSP, 68 (1944-1947), 377-391. Politics.

887 ____. The Humane Society of the Commonwealth of Massachusetts, an historical review, 1785-1916. Cambridge: Riverside Pr., 1918. Pp. xiv, 397.

888 HOWE, MARK DE WOLFE. "Creative period in the law of Massachusetts." MHSP, 69 (1947-1950), 232-251.

889 ____. and LOUIS F. EATON. "The Supreme Judicial power in the colony of Massachusetts Bay." NEQ, 20 (1947), 291-316.

890 HOWE, PAUL STURTEVANT. The religious and legal constitution of the Pilgrim state, the facts of early Pilgrim history. Cape May, N.J.: A. R. Hand, 1923. Pp. 129.

891 HOWE, WILLIAM HOWE, 5th viscount. General Sir William Howe's orderly book, at Charlestown, Boston and Halifax, June 17, 1775 to 1776, 26 May; to which is added the official abridgment of General Howe's correspondence with the English government during the siege of Boston, and some military returns, and now first printed from the original manuscripts; with an historical introduction by Edward Everett Hale. Benjamin Franklin Stevens, ed. London: B. F. Stevens, 1890. Pp. xix, 357. Subject and name index.

892 HOWIE, WENDELL DEARBORN. The reign of James the First; a historical record of the administration of James M. Curley as governor of Massachusetts. Cambridge: Warren Publications, 1936. Pp. 108.

893 ____. "Three hundred years of the liquor problem in Massachusetts." MassLQ, 18 (1933), 79-284.

894 HOWLAND, FREDERICK H. "Nativity and occupation of members of the Massachusetts Legislature." American Statistical Association. Publications, 4 (1894-1895), 15-19. 1847-1891.

895 HUBBARD, WILLIAM. A general history of New England from the discovery to MDCLXXX. (1815) 2d. ed. William Thaddeus Harris, ed. Boston: Charles C. Little and James Brown, 1848. Pp. vi, v, xvii, 768. Limited to Massachusetts.

896 HUESTIS, RUTH TERHUNE. The Pilgrims and the world they lived in. Book One. Group portrait. Pigeon Cove: Cove House Ventures, 1973. Pp. 75. MBNEH.

897 HUFFINGTON, PAUL and J. NELSON CLIFFORD. "Evolution of shipbuilding in southeastern Massachusetts." Economic Geography, 15 (1939), 362-378.

898 HULL, JOHN. "Diaries of John Hull, mint-master and treasurer of the colony of Massachusetts Bay." American Antiquarian Society. Transactions and Collections, 3 (1857), 109-316. Coinage.

899 HULTMAN, EUGENE CO. "The Charles River Basin." BSProc, (1940), 39-48.

900 HUMANE SOCIETY OF THE COMMONWEALTH OF MASSACHUSETTS. History of the Humane Society of the Commonwealth of Massachusetts: with a selected list of premiums awarded by the trustees, from its commencement to the present time, and a list of the members and officers. (1845) Boston: T. R. Marvin & Son, 1877. Pp. 116. Reprint of first edition with additions.

901 HUMPHREY, HEMAN. Character and sufferings of
       the Pilgrims, a sermon, December 22, 1820.
Pittsfield, 1821. Pp. 40.

902 HUMPHRY, JAMES, III. "For governor of Massa-
       chusetts: Long vs. Butler." Colby Library
Quarterly, 5 (1959-1961), 267-276.
       Election of 1879.

903 HUNNEWELL, JAMES FROTHINGHAM. "Early houses
       near Massachusetts Bay." MHSP, 2 Ser., 14
(1900-1901), 286-296.

904 HUNT, TIMOTHY DWIGHT. Address delivered be-
       fore the New England Society of San Francisco,
at the American Theatre, on the twenty-second day
of December, A.D. 1852. San Francisco: Cooke, Kenny, 1853. Pp. 20.
       Pilgrim Fathers.

905 HUNTER, JOSEPH. Collections concerning the
       church or congregation of Protestant Separa-
tists formed at Scrooby in North Nottinghamshire,
in the time of King James I: the founders of New-
Plymouth, the parent-colony of New-England. London: J. R. Smith, 1854. Pp. xiv, 205.

906 ____. Collections concerning the early his-
       tory of the founders of New Plymouth, the
first colonists of New England. London: John Russell Smith, 1849. Pp. 70.

907 HUNTINGTON, FREDERIC DAN. Massachusetts a
       field for church missions, a sermon preached
in Boston before the 'Diocesan Board of Missions,'
May 20, 1863. Boston: Dutton, 1863. Pp. 42.
       Episcopal Church.

908 HUNTINGTON, GALE. "The steamboat 'Helen Au-
       gusta.'" DCI, 7 (1965-1966), 298-304.
       Sailed between Martha's Vineyard and New Bed-
ford.

909 HUNTOON, DANIEL THOMAS VOSE. The province
       laws, their value, and the progress of the
new edition. Boston: Cupples, Upham, 1885.
Pp. 24.

910 HURD, CHARLES EDWIN. Genealogy and history
       of representative citizens of the Common-
wealth of Massachusetts. Boston: New England Historical Publishing Co., 1902. Pp. 835.

911 HURTUBIS, FRANCIS, JR. "First inauguration
       of John Hancock, governor of the Commonwealth
of Massachusetts." BSPub, 2 Ser., 1 (1916), 37-77.
       1780.

912 HUTCHINSON, THOMAS. The diary and letters of
       His Excellency Thomas Hutchinson.... Peter
Orlando Hutchinson, ed. London: S. Low, Marston,
Searle & Rivington, 1883-1886. 2v.

913 ____. The history of the colony and prov-
       ince of Massachusetts-Bay. (1764-1828) Law-
rence Shaw Mayo, ed. Cambridge: Harvard Univ.
Pr., 1936. 3v.
       Continued by George R. Minot in his 'Continu-
       ation of the history....' Further additions

by Catherine Barton Mayo appear in the Proceedings of the American Antiquarian Society
for April, 1949.

914 ____. The Hutchinson papers. (1769) Wil-
       liam H. Whitmore and William S. Appleton,
eds. Albany: Printed for the [Prince] Society by
J. Munsell, 1865. 2v.
       Supplementary papers in MHSC, 2 Ser., 10
       (1823), 181-188 and 3 Ser., 1 (1825), 1-152.
       First edition has title: 'A collection of
       original papers relative to the history of
       the colony of Massachusetts-Bay.

915 HUTHMACHER, J. JOSEPH. Massachusetts people
       and politics, 1919-1933. Cambridge: Har-
vard Univ. Pr., 1959. Pp. 328.

916 "IN western Massachusetts." Harper's Maga-
       zine, 61 (1880), 873-887.

917 "INFLUENCE of Berkshire and Essex counties in
       the formation of the Massachusetts Constitu-
tion." MassLQ, 1 (1916), 286-287.

918 INGLIS, ALEXANDER JAMES. The rise of the
       high school in Massachusetts. N.Y.: Colum-
bia Univ. 1911. Pp. 166.

919 INLAND Massachusetts illustrated: a concise
       résumé of the natural features and past his-
tory of the counties of Hampden, Hampshire, Franklin, and Berkshire, their towns, villages and cities, together with a condensed summary of their industrial advantages and development, and a comprehensive series of sketches descriptive of representative business houses, to which is prefixed a
short chapter on the Commonwealth at large.
Springfield: Elstner, 1890. Pp. 272.

920 INLAND Massachusetts illustrated: a concise
       résumé of the natural features and past his-
tory of Worcester, Bristol and Norfolk, and adjacent counties, their towns, villages, and cities,
together with a condensed summary of their industrial advantages and development, and a comprehensive series of sketches descriptive of representative business houses, to which is prefixed a short
chapter on the Commonwealth at large. Worcester:
Elstner, 1891. Pp. 292.

921 INSURANCE LIBRARY ASSOCIATION OF BOSTON. Re-
       ports of 1888-1900, with an account of the
early insurance offices in Massachusetts, from 1724
to 1801. Boston: F. Wood, 1901. Pp. 96.

922 ISHIHARA, HYŌEI. [Puritan Fathers. Tokyo:
       Yamamoto Shoten], 1963. Pp. 252.
       In Japanese.

923 IVERSON, MARION DAY. "Color in Pilgrim and
       Puritan dress." Antiques, 61 (1952), 240-
241.

924 JACKSON, GEORGE LEROY. The development of
       school support in colonial Massachusetts.
N.Y.: Columbia Univ., 1909. Pp. 95.

925 JACKSON, ROBERT TRACY. "History of the Oliver, Vassall and Royall Houses in Dorchester, Cambridge, and Medford." Genealogical Magazine, 2 (1907), 3-17.

926 JACOBS, WARREN. "America's oldest train." Cape Cod Magazine, 8 (September-October 1924), 21-22.
Fall River Line Steamboat Express, 1847.

927 _____. "The Morning Cape Express." Cape Cod Magazine, 8 (June, 1925), 29-21.
Boston to Provincetown, 1848.

928 _____. "100th anniversary of the opening of the first steam railroad in Massachusetts, from Boston to Newton, 1834-1934." RLHSB, No. 34 (1934), 67-68.

929 JAMESON, JOHN FRANKLIN. The arrival of the Pilgrims...a lecture delivered at Brown University, Providence, R. I., November 21, 1920. [Providence: Brown] University, 1920. Pp. 40.

930 JEFFERSON, HENRY. "Lincoln in Massachusetts." MagHist, 9 (1909), 109-110.
1848.

931 JENKS, WILLIAM. "The Massachusetts Colony Records." NEHGR, 8 (1854), 369-372.

932 JENNEY, CHARLES FRANCIS. "Paul's Bridge." DedHR, 1 (1890), 129-133.
Between Boston and Milton.

933 JENNINGS, JOHN EDWARD. Tattered ensign. N.Y.: Crowell, 1966. Pp. viii, 290.
The frigate 'Constitution.'

934 JESSETT, THOMAS E. "Planting the Prayer Book in Puritan Massachusetts." HMPEC, 21 (1952), 297-406.

935 JEWETT, JOHN FIGGIS. "Changing maternal mortality in Massachusetts." NEJMed, 256 (1957), 395-400.
1855-1955.

936 JILLSON, WILLARD ROUSE. The Mayflower Compact; bright torch of liberty and freedom. Frankfort, Ky: Roberts Print., 1966. Pp. 21.

937 JOHANNSEN, ROBERT W. "Stephen A. Douglas' New England campaign, 1860." NEQ, 35 (1962), 162-186.
Limited to Massachusetts.

938 "JOHN Brown in Massachusetts." Atlantic, 29 (1872), 420-433.

939 JOHNSON, ARTHUR L. "From 'Eastern State' to 'Evangeline'. a history of the Boston-Yarmouth, Nova Scotia steamship services." AmNep, 34 (1974), 174-187.

940 JOHNSON, E. A. J. "Some evidence of mercantilism in the Massachusetts-Bay." NEQ, 1 (1928), 371-395.

941 JOHNSON, EDWARD. Johnson's Wonder-working Providence, 1628-1651. J. Franklin Jameson, ed. N.Y.: C. Scribner's Sons, 1910. Pp. viii, 285.
Limited to Massachusetts; first edition of 1654 has title: 'A history of New England...'

942 JOHNSON, ROGER. "The dynamics of Massachusetts' industrial economy." Industry, 17 (August, 1952), 12-16.
Graphic presentation of decline and recovery in industrial employment, 1914-1952.

943 JONES, CHARLES. "The broom corn industry in the counties of Franklin and Hampshire, and in the town of Deerfield in particular." PVMA, 4 (1899-1904), 105-111.

944 JONES, EDWARD ALFRED. The loyalists of Massachusetts, their memorials, petitions and claims. London: Saint Catherine Pr., 1930. Pp. xxiv, 341.

945 JONES, KATHLEEN. "Horace Mann and early libraries of Massachusetts." Massachusetts Library Association. Bulletin, 27 (March, 1937), 19-21.

946 JONES, MATT BUSHNELL. "The early Massachusetts-Bay Colony seals." AASP, New Ser., 44 (1934), 13-44.
1628-1691.

947 _____. "An early silver mining promotion in Massachusetts Bay." MHSP, 65 (1932-1936), 372-386.

948 JONES, ROBERT E. "A potpourri of Pilgrim punishments." MayflowerQ, 35 (1969), 41-43.
Plymouth Colony.

949 JUDD, SYLVESTER. "The fur trade on Connecticut River in the seventeenth century." NEGHR, 11 (1857), 217-219.
Limited to Massachusetts.

950 KALISCH, PHILIP A. "Tracadie and Penikese Leprosaria: a comparative analysis of societal response in New Brunswick, 1844-1880, and Massachusetts, 1904-1921." BHistMed, 47 (1973), 480-512.
Leprosy.

951 KAPLAN, SIDNEY. "'Honestus' and the annihilation of the lawyers." South Atlantic Quarterly, 48 (1949), 401-420.
Shays' Rebellion.

952 _____. "Pay pension and power: economic grievances of the Massachusetts officers of the Revolution." BPLQ, 3 (1951), 15-34, 127-142.

953 _____. "Rank and status among Massachusetts Continental officers." AHR, 56 (1950-1951), 318-326.

954 _____. "Veteran officers and politics in Massachusetts, 1783-1787." WMQ, 3 Ser., 9 (1952), 29-57.

955   KATZ, MICHAEL B. The irony of early school
      reform; educational innovation in mid-nine-
teenth-century Massachusetts. Cambridge: Harvard
Univ. Pr., 1968. Pp. xii, 325.

956   KAWASHIMA, YASU. "Jurisdiction of the co-
      lonial courts over the Indians in Massachu-
setts, 1689-1763." NEQ, 42 (1963), 532-550.

957   _____. "Legal assigns of the Indian reserva-
      tion in colonial Massachusetts." AmJLegal
Hist, 13 (1969), 42-56.

958   KEAY, FRED E. "The Puritan and dress re-
      form." NEM, New Ser., 23 (1900-1901), 568-
573.

959   KEIR, ROBERT MALCOLM. "Some responses to en-
      vironment in Massachusetts." Geographical
Society of Philadelphia. Bulletin, 15 (1917), 121-
138, 167-185.
      Effect of geography on development of indus-
try.

960   KELBY, WILLIAM. "Notes on coins: the Massa-
      chusetts Shilling." HistMag, 2 Ser., 5
(1869), 115-116.

961   KELLOGG, AUGUSTA W. "The Charles River Val-
      ley." NEM, New Ser., 26 (1902), 645-666.

962   KELSO, ROBERT WILSON. The history of public
      poor relief in Massachusetts, 1620-1920.
Boston: Houghton Mifflin, 1922. Pp. 200.

963   KENNEALLY, JAMES J. "Catholicism and woman
      suffrage in Massachusetts." CathHistRev, 53
(1967-1968), 43-57.

964   _____. "Woman suffrage and the Massachusetts
      'Referendum' of 1895." The Historian, 30
(1967-1968), 617-633.

965   KENNEDY, CHARLES J. "Commuter services in
      the Boston area, 1835-1860." BusHr, 36
(1962), 153-170.
      Railroads.

966   _____. "The early business history of four
      Massachusetts railroads." BBHS, 25 (1951),
52-72, 84-98, 188-203, 207-229.
      Boston and Lowell, Boston and Worcester,
Eastern and Western.

967   KENNEDY, WILLIAM H. J. "Catholics in Massa-
      chusetts before 1750." CathHistRev, 17
(1931-1932), 10-28.

968   KENNEY, ROBERT J. and K. HEINZ MUEHLMANN.
      Manufacturing employment in the states' [sic]
standard metropolitan statistical areas 1960-1967.
Boston: Massachusetts Department of Commerce and
Development, 1970. Pp. 99.

969   _____ and _____. Personal income in Massa-
      chusetts, 1958-1966. [Boston]: Department
of Commerce and Development, 1970. 78 leaves.

970   KENT, THOMAS G. "The territory and bounda-
      ries of Massachusetts." Worcester HSProc,
(1891-1893), 402-412.

971   KEYSSAR, ALEXANDER. "Widowhood in eighteenth-
      century Massachusetts: a problem in the his-
tory of the family." Perspectives in American History, 8 (1974), 83-119.

972   KIMBALL, EDWIN FISKE. "On the shores of Buz-
      zards Bay." NEM, New Ser., 7 (1892-1893), 3-
25.

973   KIMBALL, JAMES M. "Story of the old Woburn
      Branch Railroad." RLHSB, No. 3 (1922), 1-13.

974   KING, HENRY MELVILLE. A summer visit of
      three Rhode Islanders to the Massachusetts Bay
in 1651. An account of the visit of Dr. John
Clarke, Obadiah Holmes and John Crandall, members of
the Baptist Church in Newport, R.I., to William Witter of Swampscott, Mass., in July 1651: its inno-
cent purpose and its painful consequences. (1880)
[Enlarged ed.] Providence: Preston and Rounds,
1896. Pp. vi, 115.
      First edition has title: Early Baptists de-
fended.

975   KING, JOSEPH EDWARD. "Judicial flotsam in
      Massachusetts-Bay, 1760-1765." NEQ, 27
(1954), 366-381.
      Vice-Admiralty courts.

976   KING, RUFUS. The life and correspondence of
      Rufus King; comprising his letters, private
and official, his public documents, and his speeches. Charles R. King, ed. N.Y.: G. P. Putnam's
Sons, 1894-1900. 6v.

977   KINGSBURY, SUSAN MYRA. Labor laws and their
      enforcement, with special reference to Massa-
chusetts. N.Y.: Longmans, Green, 1911. Pp. xxii,
419.
      Includes lengthy history of factory legisla-
tion in the state, 1825-1874.

978   KINNICUTT, LINCOLN NEWTON. "Plymouth's debt
      to the Indians." Harvard Theological Review,
13 (1920), 345-361.
      Plymouth Colony.

979   KIRKLAND, EDWARD CHASE. "The 'railroad
      scheme' of Massachusetts." JEconHist, 5
(1945), 145-171.
      Nineteenth century.

980   KITTREDGE, HENRY GRATTAN and A. C. GOULD.
      History of the American card-clothing indus-
try. Worcester: T. K. Earle, 1886. Pp. 96.

981   KLIMM, LESTER EARL. The relation between cer-
      tain population changes and the physical en-
vironment in Hampden, Hampshire, and Franklin counties, Massachusetts, 1790-1925. Philadelphia, 1933.
Pp. xiv, 128.

982   KLINGAMAN, DAVID C. "The coastwise trade of
      colonial Massachusetts." EIHC, 108 (1972),
217-234.

983   KNAPP, SAMUEL LORENZO. Biographical sketches
      of eminent lawyers, statesmen, and men of
letters.... Boston: Richardson and Lord, 1821.
Pp. iv, 360.

984   KNOLLENBERG, BERNHARD. "Did Samuel Adams provoke the Boston Tea Party and the clash at Lexington?" AASP, 70 (1960), 493-503.

985   KOEHLER, LYLE. "The case of the American Jezebels: Anne Hutchinson and female agitation during the years of Antinomian turmoil, 1636-1640." WMQ, 3 Ser., 31 (1974), 55-78.

986   KRUSELL, CYNTHIA HAGAR. "The land where first they trod." MayflowerQ, 36 (1970), 117-119. Paths and settlements of the Pilgrims.

987   KUCZYNSKI, ROBERT RENÉ. "The registration laws in the colonies of Massachusetts Bay and New Plymouth." American Statistical Association. Publications, 7 (1900-1901), 65-73. 1639-1692; vital statistics.

988   KUTLER, STANLEY I. Privilege and creative destruction; the Charles River Bridge case. Philadelphia: Lippincott, 1971. Pp. 191.

989   LAING, JEAN. "The pattern of population trends in Massachusetts." Economic Geography, 31 (1955), 265-271. 1870-1950.

990   LALLY, ALBERT V. The story of the Pilgrim fathers (1920) Boston: Vincent, 1930. Pp. 55.

991   "THE LAND Bank." Essex Antiq., 9 (1905), 135-137. 1740.

992   LANE, FRANCIS EMMET. American charities and the child of the immigrant; a study of typical child caring institutions in New York and Massachusetts between the years 1845 and 1880.... Washington: Catholic Univ. of America, 1932. Pp. xii, 172.

993   LANE, ROGER. "Crime and criminal statistics in nineteenth-century Massachusetts." JSoc Hist, 2 (1968-1969), 156-163.

994   LANGDON, GEORGE D. JR. "Bibliographic essay [on published and manuscript sources for the study of Plymouth Colony in the seventeenth century]." OPOCS, No. 1 (July, 1969), 41-50.

995   _____. "The franchise and political democracy in Plymouth Colony." WMQ, 3 Ser., 20 (1963), 513-526.

996   _____. Pilgrim colony; a history of New Plymouth, 1620-1691. New Haven: Yale Univ. Pr., 1966. Pp. xi, 257.

997   LAPHAM, SAMUEL. "Massachusetts maritime microcosm." AmNep, 19 (1959), 7-43. Eight generations of the Lapham family, shipbuilders.

998   LAZERSON, MARVIN. Origins of the urban school; public education in Massachusetts, 1870-1915. Cambridge: Harvard Univ. Pr., 1971. Pp. xix, 278.

999   _____. "Urban reform and the schools: kindergartens in Massachusetts, 1870-1915." HistEdQ, 11 (1971), 115-142.

1000   LEACH, DOUGLAS EDWARD. "The military system of Plymouth Colony." NEQ, 24 (1951), 342-364.

1001   LEADING manufacturers and merchants of central and western Massachusetts: historical and descriptive review of the industrial enterprises of Worcester, Hampden, Hampshire, Berkshire and Franklin counties. N.Y.: International Publishing, 1886. Pp. xi, 349.

1002   LEADING manufacturers and merchants of eastern Massachusetts: historical and descriptive review of the industrial enterprises of Bristol, Plymouth, Norfolk and Middlesex counties. N.Y.: International Publishing, 1887. Pp. x, 318.

1003   "A LEAF of Massachusetts history: Puritans, Indians and dogs." HistMag, 2 Ser., 2 (1867), 335; 3 (1868), 65-66. Christianizing of Indians and use of dogs for security purposes.

1004   [LEAVITT, PERCY METCALF]. Souvenir portfolio of Universalist churches in Massachusetts. Boston: Massasoit Pr., 1906. Pp. 112.

1005   LEAVITT, ROBERT KEITH. The chip on grandma's shoulder. Philadelphia: Lippincott, 1954. Pp. 255. Social life and customs.

1006   LEAVITT, STURGIS E. "Beaver business and the Pilgrims" MayflowerQ, 37 (1971), 81-82.

1007   LEAVITT, THOMAS W. "Textile manufacturers and the expansion of technical education in Massachusetts, 1869-1904." EIHC, 108 (1972), 244-251.

1008   LEE, E. ROSALIND. The Pilgrim Fathers, their trials and adventures. London: Sunday School Association, 1920. Pp. 83.

1009   "LEGAL qualifications of voters in Massachusetts." Essex Antiq, 12 (1908), 145-151.

1010   [LELAND, JOHN]. The Yankee spy, calculated for the religious meridian of Massachusetts, but will answer for New-Hampshire, Connecticut and Vermont, without any material alterations. By Jack Nips, pseud.... Boston: John Asplund, [1794]. Pp. 20. Criticism of religious discrimination in the Constitution and laws of Massachusetts.

1011   [LEONARD, DANIEL]. Massachusettensis: or, a series of letters, containing a faithful state of many important and striking facts which laid the foundation of the present troubles in the province of the Massachusetts-Bay; interspersed with animadversions and reflections, originally addressed to the people of that province, and worthy the consideration of the true patriots of this country. By a person of honor upon the spot. (1775) 4th ed. London: Reprinted for J. Mathews, 1776. Pp. viii, 118.

1012 LEVIN, MURRAY BURTON. The compleat politician; political strategy in Massachusetts. Indianapolis: Bobbs-Merrill, 1962. Pp. 334.
Twentieth century.

1013 LEVY, LEONARD WILLIAMS, comp. Blasphemy in Massachusetts: freedom of conscience and the Abner Kneeland case, a documentary record. N.Y.: Da Capo Pr., 1973. Pp. xxi, 592.

1014 _____. "Chief Justice Shaw and the church property controversy in Massachusetts." BULRev, 30 (1950), 219-235."
Ownership of property of Congregational churches in cases of schism, 1820-1830.

1015 _____. The law of the Commonwealth and Chief Justice Shaw. Cambridge: Harvard Univ. Pr., 1957. Pp. viii, 383.

1016 _____. "Satan's last apostle in Massachusetts." AmQ, 5 (1953), 16-30.
Blasphemy trial of Abner Kneeland.

1017 LEWIS, THEODORE B. "Land speculation and the Dudley Council of 1686." WMQ, 3 Ser., 31 (1974), 255-272.

1018 _____. "A Revolutionary tradition, 1689-1774: there was a revolution here as well as in England." NEQ, 46 (1973), 424-438.
Massachusetts in the 1770s compared with England in the 1680s.

1019 _____. and LINDA M. WEBB. "Voting for the Massachusetts Council of Assistants, 1674-1686." WMQ, 3 Ser., 30 (1973), 625-634.

1020 LINCOLN, RUFUS. The papers of Captain Rufus Lincoln, of Wareham, Mass. James Minor Lincoln, ed. Cambridge: Riverside Pr., 1904. Pp. 272.
Massachusetts 7th Infantry Regiment in the Revolution.

1021 LINEHAN, JOHN C. "Irish pioneers in Boston and vicinity." AIrHSJ, 6 (1906), 75-84.
Seventeenth and eighteenth centuries.

1022 LINES, PATRICIA M. and JOHN MCCLAUGHRY. Early American community development corporations: the trading companies. Cambridge: Center for Community Economic Development, 1970. Pp. 34, 3. M.
Plymouth Company and Massachusetts Bay Company.

1023 LINFORD, ALLEN A. Old age assistance in Massachusetts. Chicago: Univ. of Chicago Pr., 1949. Pp. viii, 418.

1024 LINSCOTT, ELISABETH SHOEMAKER. "New England's sea serpent." NEG, 6 (Fall, 1964), 10-18.
Sea serpents off the Massachusetts coast, 1817-1886.

1025 _____. "The river gods, their story in western Massachusetts." NEG, 8 (Winter, 1967), 20-25.
Flat bottom boats.

1026 LITT, EDGAR. The political cultures of Massachusetts. Cambridge: M.I.T. Pr., 1965. Pp. xiv, 224.

1027 LITTLE, NINA FLETCHER. "Country furniture: a symposium." Antiques, 93 (1968), 347-350.

1028 LITTLEFIELD, GEORGE EMERY. The early Massachusetts press, 1638-1711. Boston: Club of Odd Volumes, 1907. 2v.

1029 LOCKE, MARY STOUGHTON. "Indian missions in the Massachusetts and Plymouth colonies." DedHR, 3 (1892), 1-13, 60-69.

1030 LOCKWOOD, JOHN HOYT, et al. Western Massachusetts; a history, 1636-1925. N.Y.: Lewis Historical Publishing, 1926. 4v.
Vols. 3 and 4 are biographical.

1031 LODGE, HENRY CABOT. Life and letters of George Cabot. Boston: Little, Brown, 1877. Pp. xi, 615.
Politics.

1032 LONG, HENRY FOLLANSBEE. "The Newburyport and Boston Turnpike." EIHC, 42 (1906), 113-128.

1033 _____. "The salt marshes of the Massachusetts coast." EIHC, 47 (1911), 1-19.

1034 LONG, JOHN DAVIS. America of yesterday, as reflected in the journal of John Davis Long. Lawrence Shaw Mayo, ed. Boston: Atlantic Monthly Pr., 1923. Pp. x, 250.

1035 _____. Journal. Margaret Long, ed. Rindge, N.H.: R. R. Smith, 1956. Pp. ix, 363.

1036 LONGACRE, C. S. "The difference between the Pilgrim Fathers and the Puritans." Liberty, 25 (1930), 69-71, 86-87.

1037 LONGLEY, R. S. "Mob activities in revolutionary Massachusetts." NEQ, 6 (1933), 98-130.

1038 LORD, ARTHUR. "The Massachusetts Constitution and the constitutional conventions." MassLQ, 2 (1916-1917), 1-32.

1039 _____. "The Mayflower Compact." AASP, New Ser., 30 (1920), 278-294.

1040 _____. "The representative town meeting in Massachusetts." MassLQ, 4 (1918-1919), 49-102.

1041 LORD, ROBERT HOWARD, JOHN E. SEXTON and EDWARD T. HARRINGTON. History of the Archdiocese of Boston in the various stages of its development, 1604 to 1943. N.Y.: Sheed & Ward, 1944. 3v.

1042 LORD, VIVIAN SUTHERLAND. History of Massachusetts Daughters of the American Revolution, 1932-1959. Littleton, N.H.: Courier Printing, [1959?]. Pp. 247. [MFa].

1043   LORING, AUGUSTUS PEABODY. "A short account of the Massachusetts Constitutional Convention, 1917-1919." Pp. 99.
    Issued as supplement to 'New England Quarterly,' volume 6, 1933.

1044   LORING, GEORGE BAILEY. "The medical profession in Massachusetts during the Revolutionary War." Boston Medical and Surgical Journal, 92 (1875), 704-715.

1045   LOVELL, ARTHUR T. "The return of the British to Boston in 1903." NEM, New Ser., 29 (1903-1904), 137-156.
    A history of the Ancient and Honorable Artillery Company of Massachusetts.

1046   LOVETT, ROBERT W. "The Harvard Branch Railroad, 1849-1855. CaHSP, 38 (1959-1960), 23-50.
    Boston and Cambridge.

1047   LOWE, RICHARD G. "Massachusetts and the Acadians." WMQ, 3 Ser., 25 (1968), 212-229. 1755-1766.

1048   LOWENSTAM, BENJAMIN G. "Bay money." SWJ, 47 (1930), 516-525.
    Coins.

1049   LUCAS, PAUL R. "Colony or Commonwealth: Massachusetts Bay, 1661-1666." WMQ, 3 Ser., 24 (1967), 88-107.

1050   LUCAS, REX A. "A specification of the Weber thesis: Plymouth Colony." History and Theory; 10 (1971), 318-346.
    Capitalism inhibited by Calvinism.

1051   LUMMUS, HENRY TILTON. "The established church of Massachusetts." LynnHSR, (1901), 34-52.
    Congregational parish system.

1052   ____. "Statistics and successions in the Supreme Judicial Court and the Superior Court of Massachusetts to January 1, 1930. MassLQ, 15 (1930), Supplement No. 2, 1-68.
    Brief biographies of judges with references to other biographical sketches of them.

1053   LUMPKIN, KATHERINE DU PRE. Shutdowns in the Connecticut Valley: a study of worker displacement in the small industrial community. SCSH, 19 (1933-1934), 133-270.
    Limited to Massachusetts.

1054   LUTHIN, REINHARD H. "Abraham Lincoln and the Massachusetts Whigs in 1848. NEQ, 14 (1941), 619-632.

1055   LYMAN, GEORGE HINCKLEY, b. 1850. The story of the Massachusetts Committee on Public Safety, February 10, 1917-November 21, 1918. Boston: Wright & Potter, 1919. Pp. xi, 600.
    Civilian defense.

1056   MCAVOY, MARY C. "Catholic origins in Massachusetts." Catholic World, 132 (1930), 174-182.

1057   MCBRATNEY, WILLIAM H. "The one witness rule in Massachusetts." AmJLegalHist, 2 (1958), 155-160.
    Seventeenth century.

1058   MCBRIDE, MARION A. "Massachusetts Charitable Mechanics Association, founded 1795." Bostonian, 2 (1895), 25-32.

1059   MCCLELLAN, JAMES. "Comments on Kent Newmyer's paper 'Justice Joseph Story, the Charles River Bridge Case, and the Crisis of Republicanism.'" AmJLegalHist, 17 (1973), 271-273.

1060   MCCOY, JOHN J. History of the Catholic Church in the Diocese of Springfield. Boston: Hurd & Everts, 1900. Pp. 283. MB.

1061   ____. "The Irish element in the Second Massachusetts Volunteers in the recent war (with Spain)." AIrHSJ, 2 (1899), 85-88.

1062   MACCULLOCH, SUSAN L. "A tripartite political system among Christian Indians of early Massachusetts." Kroeber Anthropological Society. Papers, 34 (1966), 63-73.

1063   MACDONALD, WILLIAM. "The Massachusetts temper." CSMP, 27 (1927-1930), 328-341.
    Intellectual life.

1064   MACEACHEREN, ELAINE. "Emancipation of slavery in Massachusetts: a re-examination, 1770-1790." JNegroHist, 55 (1970), 289-306.

1065   MACFARLANE, RONALD OLIVER. "The Massachusetts Bay truck-houses in diplomacy with the Indians." NEQ, 11 (1938), 48-65.
    Fur industries.

1066   MCGRAW, ROBERT F. "Minutemen of '61: the pre-Civil War Massachusetts militia." Civil War History, 15 (1969), 101-115.

1067   MCILWAIN, CHARLES HOWARD. "The transfer of the charter to New England, and its significance in American constitutional history." MHSP, 63 (1929-1930), 53-65.

1068   MCINTYRE, RUTH A. Debts, hopeful and desperate: financing the Plymouth Colony. [Plymouth]: Plimoth Plantation, 1963. Pp. 86.

1069   MCKAY, ERNEST A. "Henry Wilson and the coalition of 1851." NEQ, 36 (1963), 338-357.
    Politics.

1070   MCKAY, RICHARD CORNELIUS. Some famous sailing ships and their builder, Donald McKay, a study of the American sailing packet and clipper eras, with biographical sketches of America's foremost designer and master-builder of ships, and a comprehensive history of his many famous ships. N.Y.: G. P. Putnam's Sons, 1928. Pp. xxvii, 395.

1071   MCKEAN, JOSEPH. "Deductions from select bills of mortality [in Massachusetts, 1772-1799]." American Academy of Arts and Sciences. Memoirs, 2 (1804), 66-70.

1072   MCKEE, CHRISTOPHER, ed. "'Constitution' in the quasi-war with France: the letters of John Roche, Jr., 1798-1801." AmNep, 27 (1967), 135-149.

1073   MCKEE, LINDA. "'Constitution' versus 'Guerriere.'" U. S. Naval Institute. Proceedings, 88 (August, 1962), 72-79.
       War of 1812.

1074   MACKENNAL, ALEXANDER. Homes and haunts of the Pilgrim Fathers. (1899) A new edition of Dr. Alexander Mackennal's work, rev. and partly rewritten by H. Elvet Lewis.... Philadelphia: G. W. Jacobs, 1920. Pp. xii, 143.

1075   MCKIRDY, CHARLES ROBERT. "A bar divided: the lawyers of Massachusetts and the American Revolution." AmJLegalHist, 16 (1972), 205-214.

1076   MACLEAR, JAMES FULTON. "The heart of New England rent: the mystical element in early Puritan history." MVHR, 42 (1955-1956), 621-652.

1077   MCNIFF, PHILIP JAMES. "A century of college libraries in Massachusetts." Massachusetts Library Association. Bulletin, 41 (1951), 24-26.

1078   MACPHERSON, DAVID H. "The Massachusetts Universalist Convention." Universalist Historical Society. Journal, 6 (1966), 5-24.
       Decline of Universalism, 1900-1950.

1079   MACRAE, DUNCAN, JR. "The role of the state legislator in Massachusetts." AmSocRev, 19 (1954), 185-194.

1080   _____. "Roll call and leadership." Public Opinion Quarterly, 20 (1957), 543-558.
       Massachusetts House of Representatives, 1947-1952.

1081   MCSPADDEN, JOSEPH WALKER. Massachusetts; a romantic story for young people. N.Y.: J. H. Sears, 1926. Pp. 128.

1082   MACY, JOHN. "A glance at the real Puritans." Harper's Magazine, 154 (1927), 742-750.

1083   MADDOX, ROBERT J. "The Adamses in America." AHI, 6 (July, 1971), 12-21.

1084   MAGOUN, F. ALEXANDER. The frigate Constitution and other historic ships. Salem: Marine Research Society, 1928. Pp. xvii, 154.

1085   "THE MAIL stage in Massachusetts." BBHS, 4 (January, 1930), 11-15.

1086   MALLAM, WILLIAM D. "Butlerism in Massachusetts." NEQ, 33 (1960), 186-206.
       Post Civil War politics. Benjamin Franklin Butler.

1087   MANN, JOEL. A discourse delivered in Bristol, [R.I.] December 22, 1820, on the anniversary of the landing of our ancestors at Plymouth. Warren [R.I.]: S. Randall, 1821. Pp. 19.
       Pilgrim Fathers.

1088   MANN, MOSES WHITCHER. "A pioneer railroad and how it was built." MedHR, 12 (1909), 49-67.
       Boston and Lowell Railroad.

1089   _____. "Why Mystic?" MedHR, 21 (1918), 49-56.
       The naming of the Mystic River.

1090   MANSFIELD, BLANCHE MCMANUS. The voyage of the Mayflower. N.Y.: E. R. Herrick, 1897. Pp. 72.

1091   MANSFIELD, EDWARD C. Work of the Massachusetts Volunteer Aid Association during the war with Spain, 1898. Boston: Alfred Mudge & Son, [1899?]. Pp. 185. M.

1092   MARBLE, ALBERT P. Geography of Massachusetts. Cincinnati: Van Antwerp, Bragg, 1878. Pp. 16.

1093   MARBLE, ANNIE RUSSELL. The women who came in the Mayflower. Boston: Pilgrim Pr., 1920. Pp. vi, 110.

1094   MARDEN, GEORGE AUGUSTUS, ed. Government of the Commonwealth of Massachusetts. A souvenir. Historical, descriptive, and biographical sketches. Boston: J. R. Osgood, 1880. 2v.
       Biographies of government officials.

1095   MARSDEN, REGINALD G. "Captain Christopher Jones and the Mayflower." English Historical Review, 19 (1904), 669-680.

1096   MARTEN, CATHERINE. "The Wampanoags in the seventeenth century: an ethnohistorical study." OPOCS, No. 2 (December, 1970), 3-40.
       Plymouth Colony.

1097   MARTIN, AUSTIN A. "Gleanings from early Massachusetts laws." Green Bag, 2 (1890), 295-298.

1098   MARTIN, GEORGE HENRY. Brief historical sketch of the Massachusetts public school system. Boston: Nathan Sawyer & Son, 1893. Pp. 8.

1099   _____. "The district school and the academy in Massachusetts." NEM, New Ser., 9 (1893-1894), 450-462.

1100   _____. "The early school legislation of Massachusetts." NEM, New Ser., 8 (1893), 526-538.

1101   The evolution of the Massachusetts public school system; a historical sketch. N.Y.: D. Appleton, 1894. Pp. xx, 284.

1102   _____. "Massachusetts schools before the Revolution." NEM, New Ser., 9 (1893-1894), 356-368.

1103   MARTIN, MARGARET ELIZABETH. Merchants and trade of the Connecticut River Valley, 1780-1820. Northampton: Department of History of Smith College, 1939. Pp. vii, 284.
       Limited to Massachusetts.

1104 MARTYN, CARLOS. The Pilgrim Fathers of New England: a history. N.Y.: American Tract Society, [1867]. Pp. 432.

1105 MASON, ALBERT. "A short history of the Supreme Judicial Court of Massachusetts." MassLQ, 2 (1916-1917), 82-100.

1106 MASON, ALPHEUS THOMAS. The Brandeis way; a case study in the workings of democracy. Princeton: Princeton Univ. Pr., 1938. Pp. vii, 336.
    Insurance and banking.

1107 MASON, EDWARD SAGENDORPH. The street railway in Massachusetts; the rise and decline of an industry. Cambridge: Harvard Univ. Pr., 1932. Pp. xvii, 222.

1108 MASSACHUSETTS (COLONY). Records of the Company of the Massachusetts Bay in New England, from 1628 to 1641, as contained in the first volume of the archives of the Commonwealth of Massachusetts. Samuel F. Haven, ed. Cambridge: Bolles and Houghton, 1850. Pp. cxxxviii, 107.

1109 _____. Records of the governor and company of the Massachusetts Bay in New England. Nathaniel B. Shurtleff, ed. Boston: W. White, 1853-1854. 5v. in 6.
    1628-1686.

1110 MASSACHUSETTS (COLONY) COURT OF ASSISTANTS. Records of the Court of Assistants of the colony of the Massachusetts Bay, 1630-1692.... John Noble and John F. Cronin, eds. Boston: County of Suffolk, 1901-1928. 3v.

1111 MASSACHUSETTS (COLONY) GENERAL COURT. HOUSE OF REPRESENTATIVES. Journals of the House of Representatives of Massachusetts.... [Boston]: Massachusetts Historical Society, 1919-.
    Covers 1715-1767 as of 1974.

1112 _____. Journals of the House of Representatives of His Majesty's province of the Massachusetts-Bay 1715. Worthington Chauncey Ford, ed. Boston, 1902. Pp. xviii, 104.

1113 MASSACHUSETTS (COLONY) LAWS, STATUTES, ETC. The acts and resolves, public and private, of the province of the Massachusetts Bay, to which are prefixed the charters of the province, with historical and explanatory notes, and an appendix. Boston: Wright & Potter, 1869-1922. 21v.
    Name and subject indexes; covers 1691-1780.

1114 MASSACHUSETTS (COLONY) PROVINCIAL CONGRESS. The journals of each Provincial Congress of Massachusetts in 1774 and 1775, and of the Committee of Safety, with an appendix, containing the proceedings of the county conventions--narratives of the events of the nineteenth of April, 1775-- papers relating to Ticonderoga and Crown Point, and other documents, illustrative of the early history of the American Revolution. Boston: Dutton and Wentworth, 1838. Pp. lix, 778.
    Edited and indexed.

1115 MASSACHUSETTS (COLONY) SUPERIOR COURT OF JUDICATURE. Reports of cases argued and adjudged in the Superior Court of Judicature of the province of Massachusetts Bay, between 1761 and 1772. By Josiah Quincy, Jr. Samuel M. Quincy, ed. Boston: Little, Brown, 1865. Pp. vii, 606.
    Appendix relates to the Writs of Assistance.

1116 MASSACHUSETTS. ADJUTANT-GENERAL'S OFFICE. Massachusetts soldiers, sailors, and marines in the Civil War. Boston: Wright & Potter, 1937. Pp. 634.

1117 _____. Records of the Massachusetts Volunteer Militia called out by the governor of Massachusetts to suppress a threatened invasion during the War of 1812-1814, John Baker, comp. Boston: Wright & Potter, 1913. Pp. xv, 448.

1118 MASSACHUSETTS. ANCIENT AND HONORABLE ARTILLERY COMPANY. Historical sketch of the Ancient and Honorable Artillery Company of Massachusetts, chartered 1638, and catalogue of museum of the company. Boston: Poole Printing, 1914. Pp. 98.

1119 MASSACHUSETTS. BOARD OF RAILROAD COMMISSIONERS. An index-digest of the reported decisions, precedents and general principles enunciated by the Board of Railroad Commissioners from 1870 to 1911, inclusive. Boston: Wright & Potter, 1912. Pp. xxv, 115.

1120 [_____]. Index of the special railroad laws of Massachusetts. Boston: Wright & Potter, 1874. Pp. xix, 493.
    1826-1873.

1121 MASSACHUSETTS. BOARD OF STATE CHARITIES. The public charities of Massachusetts during the century ending January 1, 1876. F. B. Sanborn, ed. Boston: Wright & Potter, 1876. Pp. 108.

1122 MASSACHUSETTS. BUREAU OF STATISTICS OF LABOR. Comparative wages and prices, 1860-1897. Horace G. Wadlin, ed. Boston: Wright & Potter, 1898. Pp. vi, 41.

1123 _____. History of wages and prices in Massachusetts: 1752-1883. Including comparative wages and prices in Massachusetts and Great Britain: 1860-1883. Carroll D. Wright, ed. Boston: Wright & Potter, 1885. Pp. 313, 57.

1124 _____. Strikes in Massachusetts, 1830-1880. Boston: State Printers, 1889. Pp. iv, 73. M.

1125 MASSACHUSETTS. CIVIL DEFENSE AGENCY. Massachusetts civil defense, 1953-1956. [Natick, 1956]. Pp. 35.

1126 _____. Plan and history of civil defense in Massachusetts, 1950-1953. [Boston], 1953. v.p. M.

1127 MASSACHUSETTS. CIVIL WAR CENTENNIAL COMMISSION. Massachusetts regiments in the Civil War, 1861-1865, their town, city or county origins and engagements in which they took part. [Boston], 1961. Unpaged. M.

1128   MASSACHUSETTS. COMMISSION ON LUNACY, 1854.
        Insanity and idiocy in Massachusetts: report
of the Commission on Lunacy, 1855. By Edward Jarvis. Cambridge: Harvard Univ. Pr., 1971. v.p.
        Includes critical introduction by Gerald N.
Grob.

1129   MASSACHUSETTS. COMMISSION ON MASSACHUSETTS'
        PART IN THE WORLD WAR. Report of the Com-
mission on Massachusetts' Part in the World War.
Boston: Wright & Potter, 1929-1931. 2v.
        Volume 2 was published first, contains
biographies.

1130   MASSACHUSETTS. COMMISSION TO INVESTIGATE
        AND STUDY TRANSPORTATION SERVICE IN SOUTH-
EASTERN MASSACHUSETTS. The Old Colony Railroad; an historically true narrative of one of the
pioneer railroad systems in America. Charles W.
Dow, ed. [Boston?], 1949. 52 leaves.

1131   MASSACHUSETTS. CONSTITUTION. The adjusted
        Constitution of Massachusetts; annulled and
fulfilled parts dropped; amendments embodied with
the original articles. J. Nelson Trask, ed. Boston: The Editor, 1884. Pp. xiv, 142.

1132   MASSACHUSETTS. CONVENTION, 1788. Debates
        and proceedings in the Convention of the
Commonwealth of Massachusetts, held in the year
1788, and which finally ratified the Constitution
of the United States. Bradford K. Peirce and
Charles Hale, eds. Boston: W. White, 1856.
Pp. vii, 442.
        Detailed index.

1133   MASSACHUSETTS. DEPARTMENT OF COMMERCE.
        Movements of retail trade in Massachusetts
cities and towns, 1939-1948. Melvin L. Morse,
comp. Boston: State Planning Board, 1951. Pp. 6.
M.

1134   _____. Movements of retail trade in Massa-
        chusetts 1948-1954. Boston, 1956. Unpaged.

1135   _____. Population movements between Massa-
        chusetts cities and towns, 1945-1955. Bos-
ton, 1956. 10 leaves. M.

1136   MASSACHUSETTS. DEPARTMENT OF COMMERCE. DI-
        VISION OF RESEARCH. Population movements in
Massachusetts, 1950-1960. Boston, 1961. 10 leaves.

1137   MASSACHUSETTS. DEPARTMENT OF COMMERCE AND
        DEVELOPMENT. BUREAU OF AREA PLANNING. Sta-
tistical abstract of Massachusetts' economy for selected years 1929-1968. Boston, 1970. Pp. vi, 94
leaves.

1138   MASSACHUSETTS. DEPARTMENT OF CORRECTION.
        An analysis of convictions of murder in the
first degree in Massachusetts from January 1, 1900
to December 31, 1962. William F. Bugden, ed. Boston, [1963?]. Pp. 4.

1139   MASSACHUSETTS. DEPARTMENT OF EDUCATION.
        1837-1930. n.p., [1930?]. unpaged. M.
        Brief survery of the Department of Education.

1140   _____. The Massachusetts Bay Colony and the
        General Court. The observance of the tercen-
tenary of the Massachusetts Bay Colony and of the
General Court and one hundred fiftieth anniversary
of the adoption of the constitution of the Commonwealth of Massachusetts. Washington: Govt. Print.
Off., 1930. Pp. iii, 35.

1141   _____. Material suggested for use in the
        schools in observance of the tercentenary of
Massachusetts Bay Colony and of the General Court
and one hundred fiftieth anniversary of the adoption
of the constitution of the Commonwealth. Boston,
1930. Pp. xiv, 222.

1142   MASSACHUSETTS. DEPARTMENT OF EDUCATION. DI-
        VISION OF ELEMENTARY AND SECONDARY EDUCATION
AND NORMAL SCHOOLS. The development of edu-
cation in Massachusetts, 1630-1930. Boston: State
Printers, 1930. Pp. 14. M.

1143   MASSACHUSETTS. DEPARTMENT OF LABOR AND IN-
        DUSTRIES. Statistics of manufactures in
Massachusetts, 1920-1938. [Boston? 1940?].
Pp. 132.

1144   _____. Trends in type and cost of new house-
        keeping dwelling construction in municipali-
ties in Massachusetts, 1926-1948, inclusive. Boston, 1949. Pp. 3. M.

1145   _____. Wages and hours of labor in the metal
        trades in Massachusetts, 1914-1919....
Boston: Wright & Potter, 1920. Pp. 72.

1146   MASSACHUSETTS. DEPARTMENT OF PUBLIC HEALTH.
        75th anniversary of the Massachusetts Depart-
ment of Public Health, 1869-1944. Boston, 1948.
Pp. 72. M.

1147   MASSACHUSETTS. DEPARTMENT OF PUBLIC WELFARE.
        DIVISION OF CHILD GUARDIANSHIP. Statistical
review of the quarter century 1925-1950.... Boston,
1951. Pp. 26. M.

1148   MASSACHUSETTS. DIVISION OF EMPLOYMENT SECU-
        RITY. Employment and unemployment 1950-1966.
[Boston], 1967. v.p. M.

1149   _____. Industrial pattern of Massachusetts,
        manufacturing industries, 1959-1965. Boston,
[1967?]. Pp. iii, 40. M.

1150   _____. Thirtieth anniversary of unemployment
        security in Massachusetts. [Boston: State
Printers, 1965]. Unpaged. M.

1151   MASSACHUSETTS. EXECUTIVE OFFICE OF ADMINIS-
        TRATION AND FINANCE. Massachusetts firsts.
[Boston], 1965. Pp. 33. M.

1152   MASSACHUSETTS. 1ST CORPS OF CADETS. The one
        hundred and fiftieth anniversary of the foun-
dation of the First Corps Cadets, Massachusetts Volunteer Militia, October 19, 1891. Boston: Nathan
Sawyer & Son, 1892. Pp. 84.

1153   MASSACHUSETTS. FUSILIER VETERAN ASSOCIATION.
        A historical sketch: Fusilier Veteran Asso-
ciation, 1787-1914. Cambridge: Murray and Emery,
1914. Pp. 21.

1154 MASSACHUSETTS. GENERAL COURT. Political
      complexion of the House of Representatives
and Senate, 1869-1968. n.p., [1968?]. Unpaged. M.

1155 ____. Public officers of the Commonwealth
      of Massachusetts. Boston: Buck Printing,
1945-. M.
      Biographies.

1156 ____. Reports of controverted elections in
      the Senate and House of Representatives of
the Commonwealth of Massachusetts from 1853 to 1885
inclusive. Edward P. Loring and Charles T. Russell,
Jr., eds. Boston: Wright & Potter, 1886.
Pp. xxxvi, 550.

1157 MASSACHUSETTS. GENERAL COURT, 1930. The
      General Court of Massachusetts, 1630-1930;
tercentenary exercises, commemorating its establishment three hundred years ago, and to note the
progress of the Commonwealth under nine generations
of lawmakers held at the State House, Boston, Massachusetts, at a special session in the chamber of
the House of Representatives, Monday, October twenty, nineteen thirty, eleven o'clock. (1930) [En-
larged ed.]. Boston: Wright & Potter, 1931.
Pp. 123.

1158 NO ENTRY

1159 MASSACHUSETTS. GENERAL COURT. HOUSE OF
      REPRESENTATIVES. Reports of controverted
elections in the House of Representatives, of the
Commonwealth of Massachusetts, from 1780 to 1852:
the cases from 1780 to 1834, inclusive, compiled
from the Journals, files, and printed documents of
the House, in pursuance of an order thereof, and
under the direction of a committee appointed for
the purpose...and the cases from 1835 to 1852, inclusive, in pursuance of a resolve of the General
Court, passed on the 18th of May, 1852. Luther S.
Cushing, Charles W. Storey, and Lewis Josselyn,
eds. Boston: Wright & Potter, 1853. Pp. xx, 757.

1160 MASSACHUSETTS. GENERAL COURT. JOINT SPE-
      CIAL RECESS COMMITTEE ON CONTESTED ELECTION
      CASES. Reports of contested election cases
in the Senate and House of Representatives of the
Commonwealth of Massachusetts for the years 1903-
1922, together with the opinions of the Supreme
Judicial Court relating to such elections. Paul D.
Howard, ed. Boston: White & Potter, 1923.
Pp. 240.

1161 MASSACHUSETTS. GOVERNOR, 1800-1807 (CALEB
      STRONG). Patriotism and piety. The speech-
es of His Excellency Caleb Strong, esq., to the
Senate and House of Representatives of the Commonwealth of Massachusetts; with their answers; and
other official publick papers of His Excellency,
from 1800 to 1807. Newburyport, Edmund M. Blunt,
1808. Pp. xii, 202.

1162 MASSACHUSETTS. LAWS, STATUTES, ETC. An in-
      dex to the public statutes of the Common-
wealth of Massachusetts and to the public acts of
1882 to 1887, both inclusive. By William V. Kellen.
Boston: Wright & Potter, 1888. Pp. iv, 559.

1163 ____. Metropolitan parks legislation, 1892-
      1918. Boston: Wright & Potter, 1918.
Pp. 162. MB.

1164 MASSACHUSETTS. NATIONAL GUARD. Historical
      and pictorial review...National Guard of...
Massachusetts. Baton Rouge, La., 1939.
Pp. xxxviii, 473. MB.

1165 MASSACHUSETTS. SECRETARY OF THE COMMON-
      WEALTH. Historical data relating to coun-
ties, cities and towns in Massachusetts. Prepared
by Kevin H. White. [Boston], 1966. Pp. 92.

1166 ____. List of persons whose names have been
      changed in Massachusetts. 1780-1892. Bos-
ton: Wright & Potter, 1893. Pp. 522.

1167 ____. Massachusetts soldiers and sailors
      of the Revolutionary War. Boston: Wright &
Potter, 1896-1908. 17v.
      Biographies.

1168 ____. Report of the lists of incorporations
      and their capitals granted by the legislature
of Massachusetts from the adoption of the Constitution in 1780 to 1836. [Boston?], 1836. Pp. 92.
MBNEH.

1169 ____. Schedule exhibiting the condition of
      the banks in Massachusetts for every year
from 1803 to 1837, inclusive. [Boston, 1838].
Pp. 30.

1170 ____. Tabular view of representation in the
      Commonwealth of Massachusetts, from 1780 to
1853. Ephraim M. Wright, ed. Boston: William
White, 1854. Pp. 162. M.

1171 MASSACHUSETTS. SPECIAL COMMISSION ON PRI-
      MARIES AND ELECTION LAWS. Reports of con-
tested election cases in the Senate and House of
Representatives of the Commonwealth of Massachusetts
for the years 1923-1942, together with the opinions
of the Supreme Judicial Court relating to such elections. Paul D. Howard, ed. Boston: Wright & Potter, 1942. Pp. xii, 295.

1172 MASSACHUSETTS. SPECIAL COMMISSION ON THE
      CELEBRATION OF THE TERCENTENARY OF THE FOUND-
      ING OF THE MASSACHUSETTS BAY COLONY. Histor-
ical markers erected by Massachusetts Bay Colony
Tercentenary Commission; text of inscriptions as revised by Samuel Eliot Morison.... Boston: Commonwealth of Massachusetts, 1930. Pp. 39.

1173 ____. Pathways of the Puritans. Mrs. N. S.
      Bell, comp. Framingham: Old America Co.,
1930. Pp. xx, 212.

1174 MASSACHUSETTS. SPECIAL COMMISSION ON THE
      CELEBRATION OF THE TERCENTENARY OF THE
      FOUNDING OF THE MASSACHUSETTS BAY COLONY.
      MARINE COMMITTEE. Massachusetts on the sea,
1630-1930, published by the Commonwealth of Massachusetts, in commemoration of the enterprise of the
seamen of the Massachusetts Bay Colony, and in recognition of the maritime accomplishments of their
descendants. (1930) 2d ed. [Boston], 1931.
Pp. 32.

1175 MASSACHUSETTS. STATE BOARD OF AGRICULTURE.
      Agriculture of Massachusetts, synoptical and
analytical index, 1837-1892. Frederick H. Fowler,
ed. Boston: Wright & Potter, 1893. Pp. 301.

1176 MASSACHUSETTS. STATE BOARD OF HEALTH. In-
      fantile paralysis in Massachusetts, 1907-
1912. Boston, 1914. Pp. 151. MB.

1177 _____. State Board of Health of Massachu-
      setts, a brief history of its organization
and its work, 1869-1912. Boston: Wright & Potter,
1912. Pp. 70.

1178 MASSACHUSETTS. STATE LIBRARY. Index of
      special reports authorized by the General
Court, 1900-1965. Boston: Wright and Potter, 1966.
Pp. 46.

1179 MASSACHUSETTS. STATE PLANNING BOARD. Devel-
      opment of retail trade in Massachusetts cit-
ies and towns, 1929-1939, based on United States
census of retail trade, Massachusetts. Melvin L.
Morse, ed. [Boston], 1941. 27 leaves.

1180 _____. In and out migration, cities and
      towns of Massachusetts, 1940-1945. Boston,
1948. Unpaged. M.

1181 MASSACHUSETTS. SUPERIOR COURT. Centennial
      of the Superior Court of the Commonwealth of
Massachusetts, 1859-1959. [Boston? 1959?].
Unpaged. MBNEH.

1182 MASSACHUSETTS. SUPREME JUDICIAL COURT.
      Catalogue of the records and files of the
Office of the Clerk, Supreme Judicial Court for the
county of Suffolk. (1890) Revised 1896. Boston:
Addison C. Getchell, 1897. Pp. 181. M.
      Relates to entire state; gives dates and
      places where court was held 1692-1797.

1183 _____. The two hundred fiftieth birthday of
      the Supreme Judicial Court of the Common-
wealth of Massachusetts, 1692-1942. n.p., 1942.
Pp. 28. M.

1184 MASSACHUSETTS AUDUBON SOCIETY. The Massa-
      chusetts Audubon Society, a brief history.
Lincoln, 1970. Pp. 3. M.

1185 MASSACHUSETTS BAR ASSOCIATION. Legal history
      of Massachusetts from 1630 to 1953: a story
told largely in pictures for the diamond jubilee of
the American Bar Association (1878-1953). Boston,
1953. Pp. 132.
      The August, 1953 issue of the 'Massachusetts
      Law Quarterly.'

1186 _____. Our Massachusetts Constitution; its
      history and purpose. [Boston? 1956]. Un-
paged.

1187 _____. Our Massachusetts heritage. [Bos-
      ton?], 1954. Unpaged.

1188 _____. The Supreme Judicial Court of Massa-
      chusetts, 1692-1942. Boston, [1942?]. v.p.

1189 MASSACHUSETTS BAY TERCENTENARY, INC. COMMIT-
      TEE ON RACIAL GROUPS. Historical review,
contributions to civilization; of the Armenians,
French, Germans, Greeks, Italians, Letts, Lithuani-
ans, Poles, Russians, Swedes, Syrians, Ukrainians.
[Boston? 1930?]. Unpaged.
      Collection of articles.

1190 MASSACHUSETTS BIBLE SOCIETY. The first hun-
      dred years of the Massachusetts Bible Soci-
ety, its founders and its friends, the workers and
the work, 1809-1909. Boston: Thomas Todd, [1909?].
Pp. 58. MB.

1191 MASSACHUSETTS BOARD OF CERTIFICATION IN PSY-
      CHOLOGY. Biographical directory of certified
psychologists in Massachusetts. Boston, 1964.
Pp. 56. MB.

1192 MASSACHUSETTS CHARITABLE MECHANIC ASSOCIA-
      TION. Annals of the Massachusetts Charitable
Mechanic Association. Joseph T. Buckingham, comp.
Boston: Crocker and Brewster, 1853. Pp. viii, 432.
      1795-1853.

1193 _____. Annals of the Massachusetts Charit-
      able Mechanic Association, 1795-1892. Bos-
ton: Rockwell and Churchill, 1892. Pp. vi, 1044.
      When the Annals of the association were
      printed in 1892 (621 p.) a portion only of
      the copies were bound. Early in 1900 the
      bound edition was nearly exhausted, and it
      was voted to continue the history of the as-
      sociation to the close of 1900, and to bind
      the same with the remaining unbound copies
      of the Annals. The additional material was
      issued therefore as 'Appendix, 1892-1900.
      Boston, Lincoln & Perry, Printers, 1903.'
      Pp. [623]-1044.

1194 _____. Annals of the Massachusetts Charit-
      able Mechanic Association, supplement, 1852
to 1860. n.p., [1860]. Pp. 427-623.

1195 MASSACHUSETTS COUNCIL OF CHURCHES. Churches
      in Massachusetts. Boston, 1956. Pp. 34.

1196 MASSACHUSETTS COUNCIL ON SOCIAL WELFARE.
      1953-1963, a continuing story. n.p.,
[1964?]. Pp. 34. M.
      History of the council.

1197 MASSACHUSETTS DENTAL SOCIETY. The story of
      dentistry in Massachusetts, presented by the
Massachusetts Dental Society on the occasion of its
centennial, 1864-1964. n.p., 1964. Pp. 63.

1198 "[MASSACHUSETTS] Division of Library Exten-
      sion celebrates 75th anniversary, 1890-1965."
Bay State Librarian, 55 (October, 1965), entire
issue.

1199 MASSACHUSETTS FEDERATION OF TAXPAYERS ASSOCI-
      ATIONS. A taxpayer's library; books and pam-
phlets helpful in studying government in Massachusetts. (1948) Rev. ed. Boston, 1961. Pp. iv, 19.

1200   MASSACHUSETTS GEODETIC SURVEY. Massachusetts
         localities: a finding list of Massachusetts
cities and towns; and of villages, certain lesser
localities, railroad stations, and post offices
whose location is not localized within the appropriate cities and towns by their names; and other generally related material. [Boston], 1938. Pp. 78.

1201   MASSACHUSETTS HISTORICAL SOCIETY. Lectures
         delivered in a course before the Lowell In-
stitute, in Boston, by members of the Massachusetts
Historical Society, on subjects relating to the
early history of Massachusetts. Boston, 1869.
Pp. viii, 498.

1202   _____. A pride of Quincys. Boston, 1969.
         Unpaged.
         Quincy family.

1203   _____. Warren-Adams letters, being chiefly
         a correspondence among John Adams, Samuel
Adams, and James Warren...1743-1814. [Boston]:
The Massachusetts Historical Society, 1917-1925.
2v.

1204   "MASSACHUSETTS immigrants." Massachusetts
         Labor Bulletin, No. 39 (1906), 1-15.
Statistical comparison of 1895 and 1905.

1205   MASSACHUSETTS INSTITUTE OF TECHNOLOGY. DIVI-
         SION OF MUNICIPAL AND INDUSTRIAL RESEARCH.
Municipal costs in Massachusetts from 1921 to
1929.... Cambridge, 1932. Pp. 16. MB.

1206   MASSACHUSETTS railroads, 1842 to 1855. Bos-
         ton: J. H. Eastburn's Pr., 1856. Pp. 23.

1207   MASSACHUSETTS SABBATH SCHOOL SOCIETY. A
         brief history of the Massachusetts Sabbath
School Society and the rise and progress of Sabbath
schools in the Orthodox Congregational denomination
in Massachusetts. Boston: Sabbath School Society,
1850. Pp. 36. M.

1208   MASSACHUSETTS SOCIETY FOR PROMOTING AGRICUL-
         TURE. Centennial year (1792-1892). Salem:
Salem Observer Office, 1892. Pp. 146. MBU.

1209   _____. An outline of the history of the
         Massachusetts Society for Promoting Agricul-
ture. Boston: Meador, 1942. Pp. 63.

1210   MASSACHUSETTS Society for Promoting Agricul-
         ture, 1792-1961. n.p., [1961?]. Pp. 9.
MSaE.

1211   MASSACHUSETTS SOCIETY FOR THE PREVENTION OF
         CRUELTY TO CHILDREN. 90th anniversary, Chil-
dren's Protective Service, 1878-1968. n.p.,
[1968?]. Unpaged. M.

1212   MASSACHUSETTS STATE FEDERATION OF WOMEN'S
         CLUBS. HISTORY COMMITTEE. Progress and
achievement: a history of the Massachusetts State
Federation of Women's Clubs, 1893-1962. (1932) 2d
ed. [Boston], 1962. Pp. 288.

1213   MASSEY, ROBERT K. "The Democratic laggard:
         Massachusetts in 1932." NEQ, 44 (1971),
553-574.

1214   MATHER, COTTON. Diary of Cotton Mather,
         1681-1724. Boston: The [Massachusetts His-
torical] Society, 1911-1912. 2v.

1215   MATHER, INCREASE. Diary by Increase Mather,
         March, 1675-December, 1676, together with
extracts from another diary by him, 1674-1687.
Samuel A. Green, ed. Cambridge: J. Wilson and Son,
1900. Pp. 54.

1216   MATHEWS, BASIL JOSEPH. The Argonauts of
         faith; the adventures of the 'Mayflower' Pil-
grims. N.Y.: George H. Doran, 1920. Pp. xi, 185.
Also issued the same year with the title
'The quest of liberty.'

1217   MATHEWS, NATHAN. "Early files of the county
         courts of Massachusetts." MHSP, 57 (1923-
1924), 20-28.

1218   MATTHEWS, ALBERT. "Acceptance of the explan-
         atory charter, 1725-1726." CSMP, 14 (1911-
1913), 389-400.

1219   _____. "Documents relating to the last meet-
         ings of the Massachusetts Royal Council,
1774-1776." CSMP, 32 (1933-1937), 460-504.

1220   _____. "The name 'New England' as applied to
         Massachusetts." CSMP, 25 (1922-1924), 382-
390.

1221   _____. "Notes on the Massachusetts Royal
         Commissions, 1681-1775." CSMP, 17 (1913-
1914), 2-111.

1222   _____. "The solemn league and covenant,
         1774." CSMP, 18 (1915-1916), 103-122.

1223   _____. "The term Pilgrim Fathers and early
         celebrations of Forefathers' Days." CSMP,
17 (1913-1914), 293-391.

1224   MAUDUIT, ISRAEL. A short view of the history
         of the New England colonies, with respect to
their charters and constitution. (1769) 4th ed.
London: Printed for J. Wilkie, 1776. v.p.
         First edition has title: 'A short view of
         the history of the colony of Massachusetts
         Bay.'

1225   MAUDUIT, JASPER. Jasper Mauduit, agent in
         London for the Province of the Massachusetts-
Bay, 1762-1765. [Boston]: Massachusetts Historical
Society, 1918. Pp. xxxvii, 194.

1226   MARVIN, ABIJAH PERKINS. "The Puritans of
         Massachusetts Bay. Who were they? What
caused them to leave England? Why did they come
here? What did they do here? Worcester HSProc,
(1887), 101-121.

1227   MAYFLOWER and the Pilgrims, the dramatic
         story.... Boston: Benson Publishing, 1957.
Pp. 32. MBNEH.

1228   MAYFLOWER descendants and their marriages for
         two generations after the landing; including
a short history of the church of the Pilgrim founders of New England. John Tannehill Landis, ed.
[Baltimore]: Southern Book, 1956. Pp. 37.

1229   MAYO, LAWRENCE SHAW.   "Thomas Hutchinson and his 'History of Massachusetts-Bay.'" AASP, New Ser., 41 (1931), 321-339.

1230   _____.   The Winthrop family in America. Boston: Massachusetts Historical Society, 1948. Pp. x, 507.

1231   MEAD, EDWIN DOAK.   The Massachusetts tercentenary. Boston: Thomas Todd, 1930. Pp. 16.

1232   _____.   "The meaning of Massachusetts." NEQ, 3 (1930), 25-54.
Massachusetts' contributions to America since 1630.

1233   _____.   "Why did the Pilgrim Fathers come to New England?" New Englander, 41 (1882), 711-741.

1234   MEADER, JOHN R.   "Shays' Rebellion." Americana, 5 (1910), 661-670.

1235   MELDER, KEITH E.   "Forerunners of freedom: the Grimké sisters in Massachusetts, 1837-1838." EIHC, 103 (1967), 223-249.
Antislavery.

1236   MEN of Massachusetts; a collection of portraits of representative men in business and professional life in the Commonwealth of Massachusetts. Boston: Rockwell and Churchill, 1903. Pp. xxiv, 386.
Includes index by occupation.

1237   MEN of progress; one thousand biographical sketches and portraits of leaders in business and professional life in the Commonwealth of Massachusetts, Richard Herndon, comp., Edwin M. Bacon, ed. Boston: New England Magazine, 1896. Pp. 1027.

1238   MERRILL, FRED W.   Right of petition, 1654. Hampton, N.H.: Charles Francis Adams, 1900. Pp. 12. MH.
Fifteen persons upheld their right to petition the General Court against disfranchisement of Robert Pike.

1239   MERRILL, GEORGE S.   "The Grand Army of the Republic in Massachusetts." NEM 4 (1886), 113-121.

1240   MERRILL, LOUIS TAYLOR.   "The Puritan policeman." AmSocRev, 10 (1945), 766-776.
Seventeenth-century punishment.

1241   MERRILL, WILLIAM PIERSON.   Our better portion...The thirteenth annual sermon of the New England Society in the City of New York, preached at the Brick Presbyterian Church on Sunday, December 15, 1912. [New York? 1912]. Pp. 17.
Puritans.

1242   MERRIMAN, TITUS MOONEY.   'Welcome Englishmen'; or, Pilgrims, Puritans and Roger Williams vindicated and his sentence of banishment ought to be revoked. (1892) 2d ed. Boston: Arena Publishing, 1896. Pp. xii, 320.
First edition has title: 'Pilgrims, Puritans and Roger Williams....'

1243   MERRITT, ARTHUR C.   "Paper making, ancient and modern." WNE, 3 (1913) 309-322.
Relates to Massachusetts.

1244   MESSERLI, JONATHAN C.   "The early education of Horace Mann: home, meeting house and village." The Historian, 29 (1966-1967), 263-390.

1245   _____.   "Localism and state control in Horace Mann's reform of the common schools." AmQ, 17 (1965), 104-118.

1246   MEYER, JACOB CONRAD.   Church and State in Massachusetts from 1740 to 1833, a chapter in the history of the development of individual freedom. Cleveland: Western Reserve Univ. Pr., 1930. Pp. viii, 276.

1247   MIDDLEKAUFF, ROBERT.   The Mathers: three generations of Puritan intellectuals, 1596-1728. N.Y.: Oxford Univ. Pr., 1971. Pp. xii, 440.

1248   MIDWINTER, EDWARD.   "The Society for the Propagation of the Gospel and the Church in the American colonies, III: Massachusetts." HMPEC, 4 (1935), 100-115.
Episcopal Church.

1249   MILLER, JOHN C.   "Religion, finance, and democracy in Massachusetts." NEQ, 6 (1933), 29-58.
Eighteenth century.

1250   MILLER, PERRY.   Orthodoxy in Massachusetts, 1630-1650. (1933) Boston: Beacon Pr., 1959. Pp. 319.
Contains a new preface by the author.

1251   MINOT, GEORGE RICHARDS.   Continuation of the history of the Province of Massachusetts Bay, from the year 1748 [to 1765]. Boston: Manning & Loring. Feb., 1798-June, 1803. 2v.

1252   _____.   The history of the insurrections in Massachusetts, in the year seventeen hundred and eighty six, and the rebellion consequent thereon. (1788) 2d ed. Boston: James W. Burditt, 1810. Pp. iv, 192.
Shays' Rebellion.

1253   "'MISHAWUM' and 'Mystic.'" Winchester Record, 2 (1886), 460-463.
Geographical names.

1254   MITCHELL, BETTY L.   "Massachusetts reacts to John Brown's Raid." Civil War History, 19 (1973), 65-79.

1255   MITCHELL, STEWART, ed.   "The founding of Massachusetts: a selection from the sources of the history of the settlement, 1628-1631. MHSP, 62 (1928-1929), 225-425.
Indexed.

1256   MONAHAN, THOMAS P.   "One hundred years of marriage in Massachusetts." AmJSoc, 56 (1950-1951), 534-545.

1257 MONK, LILLIAN HOAG. "Glimpses of the Pilgrims." Cape Cod Magazine, 8 (December, 1924), 10-11, 14.

1258 _____. Old Pilgrim days. Los Angeles: H. A. Miller, 1920. Pp. 188.

1259 _____. "Two Pilgrim leaders." Cape Cod Magazine, 7 (August, 1923), 15, 19-23. William Brewster and John Robinson.

1260 MOODY, ROBERT EARLE. "Massachusetts trade with Carolina, 1686-1709." North Carolina Historical Review, 20 (1943), 43-53.

1261 _____. "A re-examination of the antecedents of the Massachusetts Bay Company's charter of 1629." MHSP, 69 (1947-1950), 56-80.

1262 MOORE, ALICE E. "Increase and Cotton Mather." Bostonian, 2 (1895), 146-153.

1263 MOORE, GEORGE HENRY. "Appendix to 'Notes on the history of witchcraft in Massachusetts.'" AASP, New Ser., 2 (1882-1883), 182-192.

1264 _____. Final notes on witchcraft in Massachusetts: a summary vindication of the laws and liberties concerning attainders with corruption of blood, escheats, forfeitures for crime, and pardon of offenders, in reply to 'Reasons', etc. of Hon. Abner C. Goodell, Jr.... N.Y., 1885. Pp. 120.

1265 _____. The first folio of the Cambridge press, memoranda concerning the Massachusetts laws of 1648. N.Y., 1889. Pp. 16.

1266 _____. "History of witchcraft in Massachusetts and the act of 1711." MHSP, 2 Ser., (1884-1885), 77-118.

1267 _____. "The Massachusetts laws of 1648, and Joseph Hills." HistMag, 2 Ser., 3 (1868), 85-91.

1268 _____. "Notes on the bibliography of witchcraft in Massachusetts." AASP, New Ser., 5 (1887-1888), 245-273.

1269 _____. Notes on the history of slavery in Massachusetts. N.Y.: D. Appleton, 1866. Pp. iv, 256.

1270 _____. "Notes on the history of witchcraft in Massachusetts, with illustrative documents." AASP, New Ser., 2 (1882-1883), 162-181.

1271 _____. "Slave marriages in Massachusetts." HistMag, 2 Ser., 5 (1869), 135-137.

1272 _____. "'Woman's rights' in Massachusetts." HistMag, 2 Ser., 2 (1867), 21-22. Suffrage.

1273 MOORE, JACOB BAILEY. Memoirs of American governors. Vol. I. N.Y.: Gates & Stedman, 1846. Pp. iv, 439. Limited to Massachusetts. No more published; reissued in 1951 as: 'Lives of the governors of New Plymouth and Massachusetts Bay....'

1274 MOORE, MARTIN. "Brief historical notices of the Rev. John Eliot, and of the Indians who received the gospel by his labors." American Quarterly Register, 15 (1842-1843), 319-327.

1275 MORELAND, DONALD W. "John Augustus and his successors." National Probation Association. Yearbook, (1941), 1-22. Probation movement in the nineteenth century.

1276 MORGAN, EDMUND SEARS, ed. The founding of Massachusetts: historians and the sources. Indianapolis: Bobbs-Merrill, 1964. Pp. xii, 479.

1277 _____. "Thomas Hutchinson and the Stamp Act." NEQ, 21 (1948), 459-492.

1278 MORISON, SAMUEL ELIOT. Builders of the Bay Colony. (1930) Rev. and enl. Cambridge: Houghton Mifflin, 1964. Pp. vi, 405. Also published in 1930 with title: 'Massachusettensis de conditoribus.'

1279 _____. "The custom-house records in Massachusetts, as a source of history." MHSP, 54 (1920-1921), 324-331.

1280 _____. "Forcing the Dardanelles in 1810; with some account of the early Levant trade of Massachusetts." NEQ, 1 (1928), 208-225.

1281 _____. "The formation of the Massachusetts Constitution: address at the 175th anniversary of the Constituion of Massachusetts." MassLQ, 40 (December, 1955), 1-17.

1282 NO ENTRY

1283 _____. Historical background for the Massachusetts Bay tercentenary in 1930. Boston: Massachusetts Bay Tercentenary, Inc., 1928. Pp. 12.

1284 _____. A history of the Constitution of Massachusetts. Boston: Wright & Potter, 1917. Pp. 72.

1285 _____. The life and letters of Harrison Gray Otis, Federalist, 1765-1848. Boston: Houghton Mifflin, 1913. 2v.

1286 _____. The maritime history of Massachusetts, 1783-1860. (1921) Boston: Houghton Mifflin, 1941. Pp. xi, 420.

1287 _____. "The 'Mayflower's' destination and the Pilgrim Fathers' patents." CSMP, 38 (1947-1951), 387-413.

1288 _____. "The Pilgrim Fathers, their significance in history." CSMP, 38 (1947-1951), 364-379. A revision of the 1937 book with the same title.

1289 _____. "Plymouth Colony and Virginia." Virginia Magazine of History and Biography, 62 (1954), 147-165.

1290 _____. The story of the 'Old Colony' of New Plymouth, 1620-1692. N.Y.: Knopf, 1956. Pp. 296.

1291 _____. "The struggle over the adoption of the Constitution of Massachusetts, 1780." MHSP, 50 (1916-1917), 353-412.

1292 _____. "Those misunderstood Puritans." Forum, 85 (1931), 142-147.

1293 _____. "Three oathless centuries in Massachusetts." MassLQ, 21 (April, 1936), 61-68. Teachers' oath laws.

1294 _____. "The vote of Massachusetts on summoning a constitutional convention, 1776-1916." MHSP, 50 (1916-1917), 241-249.

1295 MORRIS, RICHARD B. "Massachusetts and the common law: the declaration of 1646." AHR, 31 (1925-1926), 443-453.

1296 _____. and JONATHAN GROSSMAN. "The regulation of wages in early Massachusetts." NEQ, 11 (1938), 470-500. Seventeenth century.

1297 MORRIS, RICHARD B. "Then and there the child independence was born." AmHeritage, 13 (February, 1962), 36-39, 82-84. Writs of Assistance.

1298 MORSE, ANSON ELY. The Federalist Party in Massachusetts to the year 1800. Princeton: [Princeton] Univ. Library, 1909. Pp. 231.

1299 MORSE, JOHN LOVETT. "The history of pediatrics in Massachusetts." NEJMed, 205 (1931), 169-180.

1300 MORSE, JOHN TORREY, JR. Memoir of Colonel Henry Lee; with selections from his writings and speeches. Boston: Little, Brown, 1905. Pp. viii, 441.

1301 MORSE, MELVIN L. Development of retail trade in cities and towns of Massachusetts, 1929-1939. [Boston]: Massachusetts State Planning Board, 1941. 27 leaves. M.

1302 _____. In and out migration, Massachusetts cities and towns, 1940-1950. Boston: State Planning Board, 1951. Unpaged. M.

1303 _____. "100 years of rubber in Massachusetts." Industry, 4 (September, 1939), 7-10.

1304 [MORTON, EDWARD THOMAS]. United States and possessions, Massachusetts, Volume No. Six, state's history series, 1620, 315 years progress, 1935. Boston: Producers Sales Service, 1935. Pp. 74. M.

1305 MORTON, NATHANIEL. New England's memorial. (1669) 6th ed. Also Governor Bradford's History of Plymouth Colony; portions of Prince's Chronology; Governor Bradford's dialogue; Governor Winslow's visits to Massasoit.... Sewall Harding, ed. Boston: Congregational Board of Publication, 1855. Pp. xxii, 515.

1306 MORTON, THOMAS. The new English Canaan of Thomas Morton. (1637) Charles Francis Adams, Jr., ed. Boston: Prince Society, 1883. Pp. vi, 381.

1307 MOURT'S RELATION. Mourt's relation or journal of the plantation at Plymouth. (1622) Henry Martyn Dexter, ed. Boston: J. K. Wiggin, 1865. Pp. xlvii, 176.

1308 MUEHLMANN, K. HEINZ and ROBERT J. KENNEY, JR. Economic changes in Massachusetts. [Boston]: Massachusetts Department of Commerce and Development, 1970. Pp. xi, 184. M. Since the 1950s.

1309 MUNROE, JAMES PHINNEY. The New England conscience. Boston: R. G. Badger, 1915. Pp. 219. Collection of essays.

1310 MURDOCH, RICHARD K. "Cod or mackerel: bounty payment disputes, 1829-1832." EIHC, 105 (1969), 306-337.

1311 MURDOCK, KENNETH BALLARD. "Clio in the wilderness: history and biography in Puritan New England." Church History, 24 (1955), 221-238. Historiography.

1312 _____. "Notes on Increase and Cotton Mather." UHSP, 1, Pt. 1, (1925), 22-44.

1313 MUSSEY, H. K. "Massachusetts 300 years ago." Nation, 131 (1930), 199-200.

1314 MYERS, DENYS PETER. Massachusetts and the first ten amendments to the Constitution. Washington: Govt. Print. Off., 1936. Pp. 41.

1315 MYERS, GUSTAVUS. Ye olden blue laws. N.Y.: Century Co., 1921. Pp. vi, 274.

1316 NASON, ELIAS. A gazetteer of the State of Massachusetts. (1874) Boston: B. B. Russell, 1890. Pp. 724.

1317 NASON, GEORGE WARREN. History and complete roster of the Massachuments regiments minute men of '61 who responded to the first call of President Abraham Lincoln, April 15, 1861, to defend the flag and Constitution of the United States...and biographical sketches of minute men of Massachusetts. Boston: Smith & McCance, 1910. Pp. 413.

1318 NATHANS, SYDNEY. "Daniel Webster, Massachusetts man." NEQ, 39 (1966), 161-181. 1836-1843; political career.

1319 NELSEN, ANNE KUSENER. "King Philip's War and the Hubbard-Mather rivalry." WMQ, 3 Ser., 27 (1970), 615-629.

1320 NELSON, JAMES. The Mine Workers' District 50; the story of the gas, coke and chemical unions of Massachusetts and their growth into a national union. N.Y.: Exposition Pr., 1955. Pp. 158.

1321   NELSON, LOVEDAY A. Our Pilgrim forefathers.
        Chicago: A. Flanagan, 1904. Pp. 31.

1322   NELSON, W. RIPLEY. "Bay State Historical
        League, a brief historical sketch." HistNan,
2 (July, 1954), 11-12.

1323   NELSON, WILLIAM E. "The legal restraint of
        powers in pre-Revolutionary America: Massa-
chusetts as a case study, 1760-1775." AmJLegalHist,
18 (1974), 1-32.

1324   _____. "The reform of common law pleading
        in Massachusetts, 1760-1830: adjudication
as a prelude to legislation." UPaLRev, 122 (1973-
1974), 97-136.

1325   "'NEW Bedford' revisited." Steamboat Bill,
        31 (1974), 6-8.
        Steamship.

1326   NEW ENGLAND GUARDS. Proceedings at the fif-
        tieth anniversary of the New England Guards,
October 15, 1862.... Boston: T. R. Marvin & Son,
1863. Pp. 92.

1327   NEW ENGLAND HISTORIC GENEALOGICAL SOCIETY.
        Proceedings on the twenty-fifth day of Octo-
ber, 1880, commemorative of the organization of the
government of Massachusetts under the Constitution
of the twenty-fifth day of October, 1780, together
with the proceedings at the State House and at the
City Hall on the same day. Boston, 1880. Pp. 67.

1328   "A NEW England secretary in curly maple."
        Antiques, 42 (1942), 304.
        Early 1700s.

1329   NEW PLYMOUTH COLONY. A declaration of the
        warrantable grounds and proceedings of the
first associates of the government of New-Plymouth;
in their laying the first foundations of this government, and in their making laws, and disposing of
the lands within the same. Together with the general fundamentals of their laws. Enacted, ordained,
and constituted, by the authority of the associates
of the colony of New-Plymouth. Boston: Greenleaf's
Printing-Office, 1773. Pp. 24.

1330   _____. Records of the Colony of New Ply-
        mouth, in New England. Nathaniel B. Shurt-
leff and David Pulsifer, eds. Boston: W. White,
1855-1861. 12v.
        Name and subject indexes.

1331   NEW PLYMOUTH COLONY. LAWS, STATUTES, ETC.
        The compact with the charter and laws of the
colony of New Plymouth: together with the charter
of the Council at Plymouth, and an appendix containing the Articles of Confederation of the United
Colonies of New England, and other valuable documents. William Brigham, ed. Boston: Dutton and
Wentworth, 1836. Pp. x, 357.

1332   NEWCOMB, WELLINGTON. "Anne Hutchinson versus
        Massachusetts." AmHer, 24 (1973-1974), 12-
15, 78-81.

1333   NEWCOMER, LEE NATHANIEL. The embattled
        farmers; a Massachusetts countryside in the

American Revolution. N.Y.: King's Crown Pr., 1953.
Pp. 274.

1334   _____. "Yankee rebels of inland Massachu-
        setts." WMQ, 3 Ser., 9 (1952), 156-165.
        Revolutionary western Massachusetts.

1335   NEWHALL, JAMES ROBINSON. Ye Great and Gen-
        eral Courte in collonie times. By Obadiah
Oldpath. Lynn: Nichols Pr., 1897. Pp. viii, 504.

1336   NEWMYER, KENT. "Justice Joseph Story, the
        Charles River Bridge case and the crisis of
Republicanism." AmJLegalHist, 17 (1973), 232-245.

1337   NEWTON, MASS. Eliot anniversary, 1646-1896.
        City of Newton, memorial exercises, Novem-
ber 11, 1896. Newton, 1896. Pp. 4, 102.
        Celebration of beginning of John Eliot's work
        in Christianizing the Indians.

1338   NICHOLAS, WILLIAM H. "Literary landmarks of
        Massachusetts." National Geographic Maga-
zine, 97 (1950), 279-310.

1339   NICHOLS, ARTHUR H. "The bells of Paul and
        Joseph W. Revere." EIHC, 47 (1911), 293-
316; 48 (1912), 1-16.

1340   _____. "The early bells of Paul Revere."
        NEHGR, 58 (1904), 151-157.

1341   NICHOLS, CHARLES L. "Notes on the almanacs
        of Massachusetts." AASP, New Ser., 22
(1912), 15-134.
        Includes bibliography, 1639-1850.

1342   NICHOLSON, LOWELL S. "Two hundred and fif-
        tieth anniversary of the Supreme Judicial
Court." Bar Bulletin, 13 (1942), 319-321.

1343   NICKERSON, WARREN SEARS. Land ho!--1620; a
        seaman's story of the Mayflower; her con-
struction, her navigation and her first landfall.
Boston: Houghton Mifflin, 1931. Pp. xix, 155.

1344   NOBLE, FREDERICK ALPHONSO. The Pilgrims.
        Boston: Pilgrim Pr., 1907. Pp. xvi, 483.

1345   NOBLE, JOHN. "A few notes on admiralty ju-
        risdiction in the colony and in the province
of the Massachusetts Bay." CSMP, 8 (1902-1904),
150-185.

1346   _____. "A few notes on the Shays' Rebel-
        lion." AASP, New Ser., 15 (1902-1903), 200-
232.

1347   _____. "A few notes touching strangers'
        courts in the colony." CSMP, 6 (1899-1900),
282-286.
        Seventeenth century.

1348   _____. "A glance at suicide as dealt with
        in the colony and in the province of Massa-
chusetts Bay." MHSP, 2 Ser., 16 (1902), 521-532.

1349   _____. "Legislation in regard to highway
        robbery in Massachusetts." MHSP, 2 Ser., 19
(1905), 178-190.
        Seventeenth and eighteenth centuries.

1350 _____. "Notes on the libel suit of Knowles v. Douglass in the Superior Court of Judicature, 1748 and 1749." CSMP, 3 (1895-1897), 213-240.

1351 _____. "Notes on the trial and punishment of crimes in the Court of Assistants in the time of the colony and in the Superiour Court of Judicature in the first years of the province." CSMP, 3 (1895-1897), 51-66.
Seventeenth century.

1352 _____. "The records and files of the Superior Court of Judicature and of the Supreme Judicial Court--their history and places of deposit." CSMP, 5 (1897-1898), 5-26.

1353 _____. "Some Massachusetts Tories." CSMP, 5 (1897-1894), 257-297.
1770s.

1354 NOE, SYDNEY PHILIP. "The coinage of Massachusetts Bay Colony." AASP, 60 (1950), 11-20.

1355 _____. The New England and Willow Tree coinages of Massachusetts. N.Y.: American Numismatic Society, 1943. Pp. 55.

1356 _____. The Oak Tree coinage of Massachusetts. N.Y.: American Numismatic Society, 1947. Pp. viii, 23.

1357 _____. The Pine Tree coinage of Massachusetts. N.Y.: American Numismatic Society, 1952. Pp. ix, 48.

1358 NORDHOFF, CHARLES. "Cape Cod, Nantucket and the Vineyard." Harper's Magazine, 51 (1875), 52-66.

1359 "NORFOLK and Bristol Street Railway Company." Transportation Bulletin, No. 66 (August, 1961-July, 1962).

1360 NORTHEND, MARY HARROD. "Some country and hunt clubs of Massachusetts." North Shore Reminder, 9 (August 27, 1910), 5-9.

1361 _____. We visit old inns. Boston: Small, Maynard, 1925. Pp. xii, 176.

1362 NORTHEND, WILLIAM DUMMER. "Address before the Essex Bar Association." EIHC, 22 (1885), 161-176, 257-278; 23 (1886), 17-30.
Law.

1363 _____. The Bay Colony; a civil, religious and social history of the Massachusetts Colony and its settlements from the landing at Cape Ann in 1624 to the death of Governor Winthrop in 1650. Boston: Estes and Lauriat, 1896. Pp. viii, 349.

1364 NORTON, THOMAS LOWELL. Trade-union policies in the Massachusetts shoe industry, 1919-1929. N.Y.: Columbia Univ. Pr., 1932. Pp. 377.

1365 NORTON, WILLIAM B. "Paper currency in Massachusetts during the Revolution." NEQ, 7 (1934), 43-69.

1366 NOURSE, HENRY STEDMAN. "The public libraries of Massachusetts." NEM, New Ser., 5 (1891-1892), 139-159.

1367 NOYES, ETHEL JANE RUSSELL CHESEBROUGH. The women of the Mayflower and women of Plymouth Colony. Plymouth: Memorial Pr., 1921. Pp. 197.

1368 NUTTING, WALLACE. Massachusetts beautiful. Framingham: Old America Co., 1923. Pp. 301.

1369 OAKES, EUGENE ERNEST. Studies in Massachusetts town finance. Cambridge: Harvard Univ. Pr., 1937. Pp. 237.

1370 OBER, FREDERICK C. "Historical interest: 150 years of thrift." Boston, 58 (December, 1966), 43-46.
Banks and banking.

1371 OBERHOLZER, EMIL. Delinquent saints; disciplinary action in the early Congregational churches of Massachusetts. N.Y.: Columbia Univ. Pr., 1956, 1955. Pp. x, 379.

1372 O'BRIEN, MICHAEL JOSEPH. "An authoritative account of the earliest Irish settlers of New England." AIrHSJ, 18 (1919), 110-144.

1373 _____. "The Kelly's, Burkes and Sheas of the Massachusetts line." AIrHSJ, 21 (1922), 107-110.

1374 _____. "Some stray historical nuggets from the early records of Massachusetts towns." AIrHSJ, 15 (1916), 172-190.
Irish.

1375 _____. "Some traces of Irish settlers in the colony of Massachusetts Bay." AIrHSJ, 18 (1919), 145-162.

1376 O'BRIEN, WILLIAM. "Did the Jennison case outlaw slavery in Massachusetts?" WMQ, 3 Ser., 17 (1960), 219-241.

1377 O'CONNOR, JOHNSON. "The Lowell Railroad bottle." Antique, 3 (1923), 72-74.
Trains pictured on bottles.

1378 O'CONNOR, THOMAS H. Massachusetts in the Civil War. Vol. I: the call to arms, 1860-1861. Boston: Massachusetts Civil War Centennial Commission, 1960. Pp. 46. M.

1379 _____. Massachusetts in the Civil War. Vol. V: the last trumpet, 1864-1865. Boston: Massachusetts Civil War Centennial Commission, 1965. Pp. 48. M.

1380 O'DWYER, GEORGE F. "Historical gleanings from Massachusetts records." AIrHSJ, 18 (1919), 216-223.
Irish.

1381 OEDEL, HOWARD TREDENNICK. Massachusetts in the Civil War. Vol. IV: a year of dedication, 1863-1864. Boston: Massachusetts Civil War Centennial Commission, 1964. Pp. 47. M.

1382   O'HARA, DWIGHT. "Progress in industrial
         health in Massachusetts." Industry, 8 (Au-
gust, 1943), 56, 58, 76-78.

1383   OLD COLONY RAILROAD. The Old Colony; or,
         Pilgrim land, past and present. [Boston]:
Fall River Line and Old Colony Railroad, 1886.
Pp. 84.

1384   "OLD Ironsides." SWJ, 41 (1927), 763-774.

1385   "THE OLD town meeting." MagHist, 13 (1911),
         303-305.

1386   OLIVER, FREDERICK, L. "The bridges of the
         Charles." BSProc, (1952), 33-47.

1387   OLIVER, PETER, 1713-1791. Origin & progress
         of the American rebellion; a Tory view. Doug-
lass Adair and John A. Schutz, eds. San Marino,
Calif: Huntington Library, 1961. Pp. xxi, 173.

1388   OLIVER, PETER, 1822-1855. The Puritan com-
         monwealth. An historical review of the Puri-
tan government in Massachusetts in its civil and ecclesiastical relations from its rise to the abroga-
tion of the first charter, together with some general reflections on the English colonial policy, and
on the character of Puritanism. Boston: Little,
Brown, 1856. Pp. xii, 502.

1389   OSGOOD, FLETCHER. "The gypsy moth in Massa-
         chusetts." NEM, New Ser., 21 (1899-1900),
677-694.
         1868-1899.

1390   OTIS, EDWARD O. JR. "The jewelry industry."
         Industry, 4 (February, 1939), 7-10, 48.

1391   OVERHOLSER, WINIFRED. "Psychiatry in the
         Massachusetts courts." Social Forces, 7
(1929), 77-87.

1392   PABST, MARGARET RICHARDS. Agricultural
         trends in the Connecticut Valley region of
Massachusetts, 1800-1900. Northampton, 1941.
Pp. xiv, 138.

1393   PAGE, WALTER GILMAN. "The Massachusetts So-
         ciety of Sons of the Revolution." NEM, New
Ser., 20 (1899), 3-15.

1394   ____. "The Society of Sons of the Revolu-
         tion in the Commonwealth of Massachusetts."
Sons of the Revolution, Massachusetts Society. Register, (1899), 129-142.
         Historical sketch.

1395   PAINE, DAVID. "Prominent country clubs."
         NEM, New Ser., 32 (1905), 322-336.

1396   PAINE, ROBERT TREAT, JR. "Massachusetts'
         historic attitude in regard to representative
government: the teachings of the Fathers." Arena,
38 (1907), 14-18.

1397   PAPER making as conducted in western Massa-
         chusetts, with a brief history of the busi-
ness from the earliest ages to the present time,
with interesting data regarding the manufacture of

paper in detail. Springfield: C. W. Bryan, 1874.
Pp. 71.

1398   "PAPER making in western New England." WNE,
         1 (1910-1911), 1-10.
         Limited to Massachusetts.

1399   PARK, CHARLES EDWARDS. "The first four
         churches of Massachusetts Bay." UHSP, 2,
Pt. 1, (1931), 1-19.

1400   ____. "Friendship as a factor in the set-
         tlement of Massachusetts." AASP, New Ser.,
28 (1918), 51-62.

1401   ____. "Puritans and Quakers." NEQ, 27
         (1954), 53-74.
         Seventeenth century, Massachusetts Bay Col-
ony.

1402   PARKER, FRANCIS JEWETT. A study of municipal
         government in Massachusetts. Boston: C. W.
Calkins, 1881. Pp. 24.

1403   PARKER, HENRY L. "The Anglican Church in the
         colonies." Worcester HSProc, (1887), 182-
207.
         Limited to Massachusetts.

1404   PARKER, JOEL. The first charter and the ear-
         ly religious legislation of Massachusetts, a
lecture in a course on the early history of Massa-
chusetts, by members of the Massachusetts Historical
Society, at the Lowell Institute, Boston, delivered
Feb. 9, 1869. Boston: J. Wilson and Son, 1869.
Pp. 85.

1405   PARKHURST, WELLINGTON EVARTS. "Indian paths
         and trails." Clinton HSHP, 1 (1912), 1-8.

1406   PARSONS, HERBERT COLLINS. "The source of the
         free school." PVMA, 3 (1890-1898), 158-171.

1407   THE PATH of the Pilgrim church, from its ori-
         gin in England to its establishment in New
England, an historical sketch. Boston: Massachusetts Sabbath School Society, 1862. Pp. 267.

1408   PATTERSON, RAYMOND SEARS and MARY CARR BAKER.
         75th anniversary of the Massachusetts Depart-
ment of Public Health, 1869-1944. Boston, 1947.
Pp. 71

1409   PATTERSON, STEPHEN E. Political parties in
         revolutionary Massachusetts. Madison: Univ.
of Wisconsin Pr., 1973. Pp. ix, 299.

1410   PAULLIN, CHARLES OSCAR. "The administration
         of the Massachusetts and Virgina navies in
the American Revolution" United States Naval Institute. Proceedings, 32 (1906), 131-164.

1411   ____. "Massachusetts navy of the American
         Revolution." NEM, New Ser., 35 (1906-1907),
571-578.

1412   PEABODY, OLIVER WILLIAM BOURN. A discourse,
         delivered in the church of the First Congre-
gational Society in Burlington, Sunday, December 21,
1845, the anniversary of the Sabbath, which preceded

(PEABODY, OLIVER WILLIAM BOURN.)
the landing of the Pilgrim Fathers at Plymouth.
Burlington, [Vt.]: Univ. Pr., 1846. Pp. 22.

1413 PEABODY, SUSAN WADE. Historical study of
legislation regarding public health in the
states of New York and Massachusetts. Chicago:
Univ. of Chicago, 1909. Pp. iv, 158.

1414 PEAIRS, C. A. "Corporate powers in Massachusetts, 1804-1947." BULRev, 28 (1948), 301-
334.

1415 PEARSON, GEORGE E. "Origin of the Massachusetts General Court." NEM, 54 (1915-1916),
33-38.

1416 PEIRCE, JOSEPHINE H. "New Englanders always
liked stoves." CEAIA, 2 (1937-1944), 157-
158.
Limited to Massachusetts.

1417 PELLETIER, MABEL C. "Massachusetts Daughters
of the Revolution and their recent celebration." Bostonian, 2 (1895), 109-119.

1418 [PEMBERTON, THOMAS]. "Account of fires in
Boston and other towns in Massachusetts,
1701-1800." MHSC, 2 Ser., 1 (1814), 81-103.

1419 PENNINGTON, EDGAR LEGARE. "Anglican beginnings in Massachusetts." HMPEC, 10 (1941),
242-289.

1420 PENNYPACKER, SAMUEL WHITAKER. Pennsylvania
and Massachusetts: a historical parallel.
Philadelphia: William J. Campbell, 1901. Pp. 27.
M.

1421 PENROSE, CHARLES. New England in the year
of grace 1766--and Sir Francis Bernard, his
outlook on trade and navigation. Princeton:
Princeton Univ. Pr., 1940. Pp. 28.

1422 PERLEY, SIDNEY. "Old-time lotteries." Essex
Antiq, 1 (1897), 77-79.

1423 _____. "Our Indians of the colonial period."
Lynn HSR, 23, Pt. 1, (1921-1923), 32-38.

1424 PERRY, THOMAS W. "New Plymouth and old England: a suggestion." WMQ, 3 Ser., 18
(1961), 251-265.
Plymouth Colony.

1425 PERRY, WILLIAM STEVENS. Historical sketch of
the Church Missionary Association of the
Eastern District of Massachusetts. Boston: Dutton,
1859. Pp. 39. MB.

1426 _____. Men and measures of the Massachusetts
Convention of 1784-1785, a discourse delivered in Christ Church, Cambridge, Mass. before the
Eastern Convocation of the Diocese of Massachusetts
on the occasion of the celebration of the centenary
of the founding of the diocese. Boston: Geo. F.
Crook, 1885. Pp. 24. MBNEH.

1427 _____. ed. Papers relating to the history of
the [Episcopal] Church in Massachusetts, A.D.
1676-1785. Boston: Priv. Print., 1873. Pp. 720.
MBNEH.

1428 PETERSON, HAROLD LESLIE. Arms and armor of
the Pilgrims, 1620-1692. Plymouth: Plimoth
Plantation and the Pilgrim Society, 1957. Pp. 28.

1429 _____. "the military equipment of the Plymouth and Bay Colonies, 1620-1690." NEQ, 20
(1947), 197-208.

1430 PETTIGROVE, FREDERICK G. An account of the
prisons of Massachusetts. Boston: Wright &
Potter, 1904. Pp. 47.

1431 PEW, WILLIAM ANDREWS. "The Bible Commonwealth of Massachusetts." EIHC, 66 (1930),
225-236.
1630-1684.

1432 PHELPS, ROSWELL F. "Number of wage-earners
in manufacturing establishments in Massachusetts, 1914-1921." American Statistical Association. Journal, 17 (1920), 495-496.

1433 PHILLIPS, MARY SCHUYLER. Colonial Massachusetts. Cincinnati: Ebbert & Richardson,
1916. Pp. 44.

1434 PIDGIN, CHARLES FELTON. History of the Bureau of Statistics of Labor of Massachusetts, and of labor legislation in that state from
1833 to 1876. Boston: Wright & Potter, 1876.
Pp. 101.

1435 PIERPONT, JOHN. The Pilgrims of Plymouth: a
poem delivered before the New-England Society
in the City of New York, at their semi-centennial
anniversary, December 22, 1855. Boston: Crosby,
Nichols, 1856. Pp. 30.

1436 THE PILGRIM fathers, or the lives of some of
the first settlers of New England. Portland,
[Me.]: Shirley, Hyde, 1830. Pp. vi, 123.

1437 PILGRIM SOCIETY, PLYMOUTH, MASS. An account
of the Pilgrim celebration at Plymouth, August 1, 1853, containing a list of the decorations
in the town, and correct copies of the speeches
made at the dinner-table. Boston: Crosby, Nichols,
1853. Pp. 182.
Plymouth Colony.

1438 _____. The proceedings at the celebration by
the Pilgrim Society, at Plymouth, August 1st,
1889, of the completion of the national monument to
the Pilgrims. William T. Davis, comp. Plymouth:
Avery & Doten, 1889. Pp. 176.

1439 _____. The proceedings at the celebration by
the Pilgrim Society at Plymouth, December 21,
1870, of the two hundred and fiftieth anniversary of
the landing of the Pilgrims. Cambridge: J. Wilson
and Son, 1871. Pp. 208.

1440 _____. The proceedings at the celebration by the Pilgrim Society at Plymouth, December 21, 1895, of the 275th anniversary of the landing of the Pilgrims. Plymouth: Avery & Doten, 1896. Pp. 76.

1441 PLOOIJ, DANIËL. The Pilgrim Fathers from a Dutch point of view. N.Y.: New York Univ. Pr., 1932. Pp. xi, 154.

1442 PLUMSTEAD, A. W., comp. The wall and the gardens; selected Massachusetts election sermons, 1670-1775. Minneapolis: Univ. of Minnesota Pr., 1968. Pp. viii, 390.

1443 POLE, J. R. "Suffrage and representation in Massachusetts: a statistical note." WMQ, 3 Ser., 14 (1957), 560-592.
1780-1860.

1444 POND, SHEPARD. "Medals of Massachusetts Bay tercentenary." Numismatist, 44 (1931), 377-400.

1445 PONTIUS, DALE. State supervision of local government, its development in Massachusetts. Washington: American Council on Public Affairs, 1942. Pp. xi, 165.

1446 POOL, DAVID DE SOLA. "Hebrew learning among the Puritans of New England prior to 1700." AJHSP, 20 (1911), 31-83.
Limited to Massachusetts.

1447 POOLE, WILLIAM FREDERIC, ed. "The witchcraft delusion of 1692. By Gov. Thomas Hutchinson." NEHGR, 24 (1870), 381-414.

1448 POOR, ALFRED EASTON. Colonial architecture of Cape Cod, Nantucket and Martha's Vineyard. N.Y.: W. Helburn, 1932. Pp. 6.

1449 POPE, CHARLES HENRY. The pioneers of Massachusetts, a descriptive list, drawn from records of the colonies, towns and churches and other contemporaneous documents. Boston, 1900. Pp. 549.
Biography.

1450 _____, ed. The Plymouth scrap book; the oldest original documents extant in Plymouth archives, printed verbatim, some reproduced...with a review of Bradford's History of Plimouth Plantation. Boston: C. E. Goodspeed, 1918. Pp. ix, 149.

1451 _____. Supplement to the pioneers of Massachusetts. [Boston, 1901]. Pp. xv.
Additions and corrections.

1452 POPE, FRANKLIN LEONARD. The western boundary of Massachusetts: a study of Indian and colonial history. Pittsfield: Priv. Print., 1886. Pp. 61.

1453 PORTER, KENNETH WIGGINS, ed. The Jacksons and the Lees; two generations of Massachusetts merchants, 1765-1844. Cambridge: Harvard Univ. Pr., 1937. 2v.

1454 PORY, JOHN. John Pory's lost description of Plymouth Colony in the earliest days of the Pilgrim Fathers, together with contemporary accounts of English colonization elsewhere in New England and in the Bermudas. Champlin Burrage, ed. Boston: Houghton Mifflin, 1918. Pp. xxiv, 65.

1455 POST, TRUMAN MARCELLUS. The Pilgrim Fathers. A discourse in commemoration of the Pilgrim Fathers, delivered in the Third Presbyterian Church, St. Louis, December 24, 1848. St. Louis: Union Job Office, 1849. Pp. iv, 47.

1456 POTTER, EDGAR. "Who made the first straw bonnet in Massachusetts?" OTNE, 11 (1920-1921), 72-78.

1457 POWELL, WALTER A. The Pilgrims and their religious, intellectual and civic life. Wilmington, Del.: Mercantile Printing, 1923. Pp. 266.

1458 "THE POWER industry." Industry, 1 (June, 1936), 7-10, 32.

1459 POWERS, EDWIN. Crime and punishment in early Massachusetts, 1620-1692: a documentary history. Boston: Beacon Pr., 1966. Pp. xiii, 647.

1460 POWERS, WILLIAM F. The one hundred year vigil: the story of the Massachusetts State Police. [Boston?], 1965. Pp. 62.

1461 POWICKE, FREDERICK JAMES, ed. "Some unpublished correspondence of the Rev. Richard Baxter and the Rev. John Eliot, 'the apostle to the American Indians,' 1656-1682." John Rylands Library Bulletin, 15 (1931), 138-176, 442-466.

1462 PRATT, HARVERY HUNTER. Three highways of the colonies...read before the Scituate Historical Society...February 22, 1918. n.p. [1918?]. Pp. 22. MBNEH.
Route from Plymouth to Boston.

1463 PRATT, PHINEHAS. A declaration of the affairs of the English people that first inhabited New England. Richard Frothingham, Jr., ed. Boston: T. R. Marvin & Son, 1858. Pp. 20.

1464 PREBLE, GEORGE HENRY. "Early shipbuilding in Massachusetts." NEHGR, 23 (1869), 38-41; 25 (1871), 15-21, 124-130, 362-369; 26 (1872), 21-29, 271-284.

1465 PRENDERGAST, FRANK M. "One hundred years ago in Massachusetts." Industry, 22 (October, 1956), 32.
Industry.

1466 _____. "Twenty-five years of editorial leadership." Industry, 24 (August, 1959), 19-20, 41.
Anniversary of "Industry," magazine.

1467 PRESSEY, EDWARD PEARSON. "The rise of the tide of life to New England hilltops." NEM, New Ser., 22 (1900), 695-711.
Social life and customs.

1468 PRINCE, L. BRADFORD. "The Mayflower spirit."
JAmHist, 15 (1921), 61-70.
Pilgrim Fathers.

1469 PUBLIC officials of Massachusetts.... Boston: Boston Review, 1906-1943/44. 27v.
Title varies.

1470 "THE PURITANS and Separatists." HistMag, 2 Ser., 2 (1867), 278-279.

1471 QUA, STANLEY E. "Some highlights in a half century of Massachusetts statutory history."
MassLQ, 42 (1957), 38-42.
1904-1957.

1472 QUIMBY, GEORGE F. "Development of factory classes in Massachusetts up to date." National Education Association. Addresses and Proceedings, (1922), 951-957.
Immigrant education.

1473 QUINCY, JOSIAH, 1802-1882. Figures of the past from the leaves of old journals, illustrated from old prints and photographs. (1883)
Mark Antony DeWolfe Howe, ed. Boston: Little, Brown, 1926. Pp. xvi, 347.

1474 NO ENTRY

1475 QUINT, ALONZO H. "Historical sketch of the General Association of Massachusetts."
CongQ, 1 (1859), 38-53; 11 (1869), 240.
Ministerial association.

1476 _____. "The normal schools of Massachusetts." CongQ, 3 (1861), 33-51.

1477 _____. "Some account of ministerial associations (Congregational) in Massachusetts."
CongQ, 5 (1863), 293-304; 7 (1865), 195-196; 8 (1866), 381.

1478 RAIKES, GEORGE ALFRED. The history of the Honourable Artillery Company. London: R. Bentley & Son, 1878. 2v.
Includes a history of the Ancient and Honorable Artillery Company of Massachusetts.

1479 RAND, JOHN CLARK, ed. One of a thousand, a series of biographical sketches of one thousand representative men resident in the Commonwealth of Massachusetts, A.D. 1888-'89. Boston: First National Publishing, 1890. Pp. 707.

1480 RANDOLPH, EDWARD. Edward Randolph: including his letters and official papers from the New England, middle, and southern colonies in America, with other documents relating chiefly to the vacating of the royal charter of the colony of Massachusetts Bay, 1676-1703. Robert Noxon Toppan and Alfred T. S. Goodrick, eds. Boston: Prince Society, 1898-1909. 7v.

1481 RANTOUL, ROBERT, 1805-1852. Memoirs, speeches and writings of Robert Rantoul, Jr. Luther Hamilton, ed. Boston: J. P. Jewett, 1854.
Pp. xii, 864.

1482 RANTOUL, ROBERT SAMUEL. "The cod in Massachusetts history." EIHC, 8 (1866), 129-138.

1483 _____. "Negro slavery in Massachusetts, portions of a paper and before the Beverly Lyceum, April, 1833." EIHC, 24 (1887), 81-108.

1484 RAPHAELSON, ARNOLD H. Massachusetts unemployment compensation, 1948-1961: a study in countercyclical finance. Boston: Federal Reserve Bank, 1966. Pp. iv, 160.

1485 RAPPARD, WILLIAM EMMANUEL. Les corporations d'affaires au Massachusetts; étude d'histoire économique et de législation comparée.... Paris: V. Giard & E. Brière, 1908. Pp. 278.

1486 RASAY, C. E. S. "The Ancient and Honorable Artillery Company." MagAmHist, 21 (1889), 456-486.

1487 RAWLYK, GEORGE A. Nova Scotia's Massachusetts: a study of Massachusetts-Nova Scotia relations 1630 to 1784. Montreal: McGill-Queen's Univ. Pr., 1973. Pp. xviii, 298.

1488 READ, CHARLES F. "Milestones in and near Boston." MagHist, 10 (1909), 151-156, 194-206.
Thoroughfares.

1489 REED, CHARLES A. "The province of Massachusetts Bay in the seventeenth century." Old Colony HSC, No. 2 (1880), 5-36.

1490 REID, WILLIAM JAMES. Massachusetts: a students' guide to localized history. N.Y.: Columbia Univ., 1965. Pp. x, 29.

1491 _____. and HERBERT G. REGAN. Massachusetts, history & government of the Bay State. N.Y.: Oxford Book Co., 1956. Pp. 300.

1492 RIEDER, KATHRYN. "Music that came in the Mayflower." Etude, 63 (1945), 383-412.

1493 "REMINISCENCES connected with the War of 1812." NEHGR, 19 (1865), 338-342.

1494 REPRESENTATIVE men and old families of southeastern Massachusetts, containing historical sketches of prominent and representative citizens and genealogical records of many of the old families.... Chicago: J. H. Beers, 1912. 3v.
Barnstable, Bristol and Plymouth counties.

1495 REPRESENTATIVE men of Massachusetts, 1890-1900. The leaders in official, business, and professional life of the Commonwealth. Everett: Massachusetts Publishing, 1898. Pp. 491.
Biography.

1496 REVERE, PAUL. Paul Revere's own account of his midnight ride, April 18-19, 1775, with a short account of his life, by S. E. Morison. Boston: Old South Association, [1922?]. Pp. 12.

1497 ____. Paul Revere's own story: an account of his ride as told in a letter to a friend, together with a brief sketch of his versatile career. Harriet E. O'Brien, comp. [Boston]: P. Walton, 1929. Pp. xiv, 47.

1498 "REVISED list of Massachusetts industries established 100 years or more." Industry, 22 (March, 1957), 31, 50-51.
 Arranged chronologically.

1499 REZNECK, SAMUEL. "Letters from a Massachusetts Federalist to a New York Democrat, 1823-1839." New York History, 48 (1967), 255-274.
 Francis Baylies to John E. Wool.

1500 RICH, E. N. "The Humane Society of the Commonwealth of Massachusetts." Nautical Research Guild. Secretary's Letter, 3 (1950), 20-22.
 1786-1916.

1501 RIGGS, SIDNEY N. "Christian Indians of colonial Massachusetts." DCI, 4 (August, 1962), 3-9.

1502 RILEY, STEPHEN THOMAS. "Dr. William Whiting and Shays' Rebellion." AASP, 66 (1956), 119-166.

1503 RIMBERT, SYLVIE. "L'immigration Franco-Canadienne au Massachusetts." Revue Canadienne de Geographie, 8 (1954), 75-85.

1504 ROBBINS, MAURICE, et al. "A brief review of the progress of the Massachusetts Archaeological Society." MASB, 10 (1948-1949), 50-59.
 1939-1948.

1505 ROBBINS, MAURICE. "Indians of the Old Colony: their relation with and their contributions to the settlement of the area." MASB, 17 (1955-1956), 59-74.

1506 ROBBINS, WILLIAM G. "The Massachusetts Bay Company: an analysis of motives." The Historian, 32 (1969-1971), 83-98.

1507 ROBERTS, OLIVER AYER. History of the military company of Massachusetts, now called the Ancient and Honorable Artillery Company of Massachusetts, 1637-1888. Boston: A. Mudge & Son, 1895-1901. 4v.

1508 ROBINSON, HARRIET JANE HANSON. Massachusetts in the woman suffrage movement. A general, political, legal and legislative history from 1774, to 1881. (1881) 2d ed. Boston: Roberts Bros., 1883. Pp. xi, 279.

1509 ROE, ALFRED SEELYE. "The governors of Massachusetts." NEM, 25 (1901-1902), 523-548, 651-672.
 Hancock to Crane, (1780-1902).

1510 ____. "Three April days." Worcester HS Proc., (1881), 25-43.
 April 19, 1689: Boston uprising against Governor Andros; April 19, 1775: Lexington and Concord; April 19, 1861: Massachusetts men killed in battle at Baltimore.

1511 ROGERS, ALBERT R. The historic voyage of the Arbella, 1630. Boston: Arbella Co., 1930. Pp. 31. M.

1512 ROGERS, E. H. "Pilgrim and profit sharing." Country Time and Tide, 1 (1902), 61-67.

1513 ROGERS, HENRY MUNROE, comp. Military Order of the Loyal Legion of the United States, annals of the Commandery of the State of Massachusetts from its institution, March 4, 1868, to May 1, 1918, and the proceedings at the fiftieth anniversary, March 6, 1918. Boston: Atlantic Printing Co., 1918. Pp. vii, 132.

1514 RONDA, JAMES P. "Red and white at the bench: Indians and the law in Plymouth Colony, 1620-1691." EIHC, 110 (1974), 200-215.

1515 ROOSEVELT, THEODORE. Address of President Roosevelt on the occasion of the laying of the corner stone of the Pilgrim Memorial Monument, Provincetown, Massachusetts, August 20, 1907. Washington: Govt. Print. Off., 1907. Pp. 64.

1516 ROOT, W. T. "The Massachusetts Book of Laws of 1648." Iowa Law Review, 15 (1929-1930), 179-185.

1517 ROSE-TROUP, FRANCES JAMES. "John Pierce and the Pilgrim Fathers." EIHC, 66 (1930), 237-256, 360-376.

1518 ____. John White, the patriarch of Dorchester (Dorset) and the founder of Massachusetts, 1575-1648, with an account of the early settlements in Massachusetts, 1620-1630. N.Y.: G. P. Putnam's Sons, 1930. Pp. xii, 483.

1519 ____. The Massachusetts Bay Company and its predecessors. N.Y.: Grafton Pr., 1930. Pp. xi, 176.

1520 ROSENBAUM, BETTY B. "Sociological basis of the laws relating to women sex offenders in Massachusetts, 1620-1860." Journal of Criminal Law, 28 (1938), 815-846.

1521 ROSENKRANTZ, BARBARA GUTMANN. Public health and the State; changing views in Massachusetts, 1842-1936. Cambridge: Harvard Univ. Pr., 1972. Pp. 259.

1522 ROSENMEIER, JESPER. "New England's perfection: the image of Adam and the image of Christ in the Antinomian crisis, 1634 to 1638." WMQ, 3 Ser., 27 (1970), 435-459.
 John Cotton's debates with Massachusetts Bay Colony elders.

1523 ROTH, ANNA ELIZABETH. A review of the first fifty years of the Massachusetts State Nurses' Association, 1903-1953. Boston: The Association, 1953. Pp. 34. M.

1524 ____. Thirty-five years of the Massachusetts State Nurses' Association.... Boston: Massachusetts State Nurses' Association, 1938. Pp. 62.
 1903-1938.

1525 [ROTHERY, AGNES EDWARDS]. The old Coast road from Boston to Plymouth, by Agnes Edwards, pseud. Boston: Houghton Mifflin, 1920. Pp. xxix, 203.
Norfolk and Plymouth counties.

1526 ROWLAND, WILLIAM FREDERIC. A sermon, delivered at Exeter [N.H.] December 22d, 1820, being the second centennial anniversary of the landing of the Pilgrims of New-England. Exeter [N.H.]: J. J. Williams, 1821. Pp. 19.

1527 ROWSE, A. L. "Pilgrims and Puritans." Am Heritage, 10 (October, 1959), 49-53, 78-83.

1528 ROY, THOMAS SHERRAD. Stalwart builders: a history of the Grand Lodge of Masons in Massachusetts 1733-1970. Boston: Masonic Education and Charity Trust of the Grand Lodge of Massachusetts, 1971. Pp. xiii, 411.

1529 ROZMAN, DAVID and RUTH EVELYN SHERBURNE. Historical trend in Massachusetts industries, 1837-1933. Amherst: Massachusetts State College, 1938. Pp. 31.

1530 _____ and _____. Population in Massachusetts...1900-1950. Amherst: Univ. of Massachusetts, [1951?]. Pp. 46. M.

1531 RUCHAMES, LOUIS. "Jim Crow railroads in Massachusetts." AmQ, 8 (1956), 61-75.

1532 _____. "Race and education in Massachusetts." NegroHistB, 13 (1949-1950), 53-59, 71.

1533 _____. "Race, marriage and abolition in Massachusetts." JNegroHist, 40 (1955), 250-273.

1534 RUGG, ARTHUR PRENTICE. "A famous colonial litigation." AASP, New Ser., 30 (1920), 217-250.
Richard Sherman v. Robert Keayne, 1642.

1535 RUSSELL, CHARLES THEODORE. Agricultural progress in Massachusetts for the last half century. Boston: Moody, 1850. Pp. 22. MB.

1536 RUSSELL, FOSTER WILLIAM. Mount Auburn biographies; a biographical listing of distinguished persons interred in Mount Auburn Cemetery, Cambridge, Massachusetts, 1831-1952. [Cambridge?], 1953. Pp. 216.
Primarily persons prominent in Massachusetts.

1537 RUTMAN, DARRETT BRUCE. "Governor Winthrop's garden crop: the significance of agriculture in the early commerce of Massachusetts Bay." WMQ, 3 Ser., 20 (1963), 396-415.

1538 _____. "My beloved and good husband." Am Heritage, 13 (August, 1962), 24-27, 94-96.
John and Margaret Winthrop.

1539 RYERSON, ADOLPHUS EGERTON. The loyalists of America and their times: from 1620 to 1816. Toronto: W. Briggs, 1880. 2v.

1540 SABLE, MARTIN HOWARD. A bio-bibliography of the Kennedy family. Metuchen, N.J.: Scarecrow Pr., 1969. Pp. 330.

1541 SADD, VICTOR and ROBERT TODD WILLIAMS. Causes of commercial bankruptcies. Washington: Govt. Print. Off., 1932. Pp. iv, 52.
Statistical analysis of 570 concerns in the jurisdiction of the bankruptcy courts of Middlesex, Norfolk, and Suffolk counties, 1930-1931.

1542 SALSBURY, STEPHEN. The state, the investor, and the railroad; the Boston & Albany, 1825-1867. Cambridge: Harvard Univ. Pr., 1967. Pp. xx, 404.

1543 SALTONSTALL, LEVERETT, b. 1892. "Some experiences in public life over the years in Massachusetts and Washington." MHSP, 74 (1961), 84-93.
1919-1961.

1544 SANDROF, IVAN. Massachusetts towns: an 1840 view. Barre: Barre Publishers, 1963. Pp. 116.

1545 _____. More Massachusetts towns. Barre: Barre Publishers, 1965. Pp. 102.

1546 SANFORD, EDWIN G. The Pilgrim Fathers and Plymouth Colony: a bibliographical survey of books and articles published during the past fifty years. Boston: Boston Public Library, 1970. Pp. 29.

1547 SANFORD, ENOCH. Sketch of the Pilgrims who founded the Church of Christ in New England. Boston: Perkins and Marvin, 1831. Pp. 71.

1548 SANGER, CHESTER F. "The divorce legislation of Massachusetts." BSM 3 (1885), 27-32.

1549 SAUNDERS, WILLIAM A., ed. "Correspondence relative to 'The history of Massachusetts Bay,' between its author Gov. Thomas Hutchinson, and Rev. Ezra Stiles." NEHGR, 26 (1872), 159-164, 230-233.

1550 SAVAGE, JAMES. Constitution of Massachusetts, address delivered before the Massachusetts Lyceum, January 26, 1832. Boston, 1832. Pp. 12.

1551 SAVINGS BANK LIFE INSURANCE COUNCIL, BOSTON. From acorn to mighty oak, Savings Bank Life Insurance, 1907-1947. Boston, 1947. Pp. 8. MB.

1552 SAWYER, ALFRED P. "Early mining operations near Lowell." Lowell HSC, 1 (1907-1913), 316-342.

1553 SAWYER, CHARLES WINTHROP. "American percussion pepperboxes." Antiques, 10 (1926), 285-289.
Firearms.

1554 SAWYER, JOSEPH DILLAWAY. History of the Pilgrims and Puritans, their ancestry and descendants: basis of Americanization. William Elliot Griffis, ed. N.Y.: Century History Co., 1922. 3v.

1555 SCHMECKEBIER, L. F. "How Maine became a state." Maine Historical Society. Collections, 2 Ser., 9 (1898), 146-171.

1556 SCHOLZ, ROBERT F. "Clerical consociation in Massachusetts Bay: reassessing the New England way and its origins. WMQ, 29 (1972), 391-414.

1557 SCHOULER, JAMES. "The Massachusetts Convention of 1853. MHSP, 2 Ser., 18 (1903-1904), 30-48.
Constitutional convention.

1558 _____. "The Whig Party in Massachusetts." MHSP, 50 (1916-1917), 39-53.

1559 SCHOULER, WILLIAM. A history of Massachusetts in the Civil War. Boston: E. P. Dutton, 1868-1871. 2v.
Contributions of cities and counties.

1560 SCHUTZ, JOHN A. "Imperialism in Massachusetts during the governorship of William Shirley, 1741-1756." Huntington Library Quarterly, 23 (1960), 217-236."

1561 _____. "Succession politics in Massachusetts, 1730-1741." WMQ, 3 Ser., 15 (1958), 508-520.

1562 SCHUYLER, LIVINGSTON ROWE. "The press in Massachusetts." MagHist, 1 (1905), 362-377.
Colonial period.

1563 SCOTT, BENJAMIN. The Pilgrim Fathers neither Puritans nor persecutors: a lecture delivered at the Friends' Institute, London, on the 18th January, 1866. (1866) 2d ed. London: A. W. Bennett, 1869. Pp. 39.

1564 SEGAL, ROBERT M. "Administrative procedure in Massachusetts: rule making and judicial review. BULRev, 33 (1953), 1-29.
1837-1952.

1565 SEIDMAN, AARON B. "Church and State in the early years of the Massachusetts Bay Colony." NEQ, 18 (1945), 211-233.

1566 SENTER, ORAMEL S. "The Cape region and Martha's Vineyard." Potter's AmMo, 9 (1877), 81-95.

1567 75TH ANNIVERSARY Massachusetts Department of Public Works, 1893-1968. Rod and Transit, 8 (June, 1968), entire issue.

1568 SEWALL, RICHARD H. John P. Hale and the Liberty Party, 1847-1848. NEQ, 37 (1964), 200-223.

1569 SEWALL, SAMUEL, 1652-1730. Diary of Samuel Sewall. 1674-1729. Boston: The [Massachusetts Historical] Society, 1878-1882. 3v.

1570 _____. The diary of Samuel Sewall, 1674-1729. Milton Halsey Thomas, ed. N.Y.: Farrar, Straus and Giroux, 1973. 2v.

1571 _____. Letter-book of Samuel Sewall. Boston: Massachusetts Historical Society, 1886-1888. 2v.
1685-1729.

1572 _____. The selling of Joseph; a memorial. Sidney Kaplan, ed. Amherst: Univ. of Massachusetts Pr., 1969. Pp. 66.
Slavery.

1573 SEXTON, JOHN EDWARD. "Massachusetts' religious policy with the Indians under Governor Bernard: 1760-1769." CathHistRev, 24 (1938), 310-328.

1574 SEYBOLT, ROBERT FRANCIS, ed. "Hunting Indians in Massachusetts: a scouting journal of 1758." NEQ, 3 (1930), 527-531.

1575 _____. "Note on the regulation of the practice of medicine in eighteenth-century Massachusetts." NEJMed, 202 (1930), 1067-1068.

1576 SHANKLE, GEORGE EARLIE. Massachusetts, state name, flag, seal, song, bird, flower, and other symbols; a study based on historical documents giving the origin and significance of the state name, nicknames, motto, seal, flag, flower, bird, song, and descriptive comments on the capitol building and on some of the outstanding state histories. N.Y.: H. W. Wilson, 1933. Pp. 16.

1577 SHAPIRO, SAMUEL. "The conservative dilemma: the Massachusetts Constitutional Convention of 1853." NEQ, 33 (1960), 207-224.

1578 SHATTUCK, HENRY LEE. "Martin Lomasney in the Constitutional Convention of 1917-1919." MHSP, 71 (1953-1957), 299-310.

1579 _____. "Some experiences of my political life." MHSP, 73 (1961), 81-91.
1920s and 1930s.

1580 SHAW, HUBERT KINNEY. Families of the Pilgrims. Boston: Massachusetts Society of Mayflower Descendants, 1956. Pp. 178.

1581 SHELDON, GEORGE. "Flintlock or matchlock?" Worcester HSProc, (1897-1899), 408-420.
King Philip's War.

1582 _____. "The flintlock used in Philip's War." Worcester HSProc, 17 (1900-1901), 67-92.

1583 _____. "Old time traffic and travel on the Connecticut [River]." PVMA, 3 (1890-1898, 117-129.
Limited to Massachusetts.

1584 SHERMAN, RICHARD B. "Charles Sumner Bird and the Progressive Party in Massachusetts." NEQ, 33 (1960), 325-340.

1585 _____. "The status revolution and Massachusetts progressive leadership." PolSciQ, 78 (1963), 59-65.
1912.

1586 SHINN, GEORGE WOLFE. Indebtedness of Massachusetts to its six bishops: Bass, Parker, Griswold, Eastburn, Paddock, and Brooks, 1797-1893. A discourse delivered before the Convention of the Diocese of Massachusetts...April 25, 1894. Boston: Damrell and Upham, 1894. Pp. 43. MBNEH.

1587 SHIPTON, CLIFFORD KENYON. "James Otis and the Writs of Assistance." BSProc, (1961), 17-25.

1588 SHIRLEY, WILLIAM. Correspondence of William Shirley, governor of Massachusetts and military commander in America, 1731-1760. Charles Henry Lincoln, ed. N.Y.: Macmillan, 1912. 2v.

1589 SHOEMAKER, ELISABETH. River gods, their story in Pioneer Valley, Massachusetts. Boston: Berkeley Pr., 1941. Pp. 16.
Hampden, Hampshire and Franklin counties.

1590 SHRINER, CHARLES A. Shays's Rebellion. Americana, 20 (1926), 235-252.

1591 SHY, JOHN W. "A new look at the colonial militia." WMQ, 3 Ser., 20 (1963), 175-185. Massachusetts and Virginia.

1592 SIEBENS, CAROLINE R. A historical sketch of the libraries of Cape Cod and Martha's Vineyard and Nantucket. Hyannis: Patriot Pr., 1952. Pp. 29. [MBaC].

1593 SIEBERT, WILBUR HENRY. "The underground railroad in Massachusetts." AASP, New Ser., 45 (1935), 25-100.

1594 _____. "The underground railroad in Massachusetts." NEQ, 9 (1936), 447-467.
Differs from above article.

1595 SILVER, ROLLO GABRIEL. "Government printing in Massachusetts-Bay, 1700-1750." AASP, 68 (1958), 135-162.

1596 _____. "Government printing in Massachusetts, 1751-1801." Studies in Bibliography, 16 (1963) 161-200.

1597 SIMMONS, JAMES RAYMOND. The historic trees of Massachusetts. Boston: Marshall Jones, 1919. Pp. xxi, 139.

1598 SIMMONS, RICHARD C. "Early Massachusetts: a Puritan Commonwealth." History Today, 18 (1968), 259-267.

1599 _____. "Godliness, property, and the franchise in Puritan Massachusetts: an interpretation." JAH, 55 (1968-1969), 495-511.

1600 _____. "The Massachusetts Revolution of 1689: three early American political broadsides." JAS, 2 (1968), 1-12.

1601 _____., ed. Richard Sadler's account of the Massachusetts churches. NEQ, 42 (1969), 411-425.
Seventeenth century.

1602 SIMPSON, LEWIS P. "'The intercommunity of the learned': Boston and Cambridge in 1800." NEQ, 23 (1950), 491-503.
Intellectual life.

1603 SKEDD, DORIS E. Bibliography of Massachusetts housing conditions. [Boston: Massachusetts Housing Association], 1931. 17 leaves. MB.
Lists publications issued from 1846-1931.

1604 SKELTON, EDWARD OLIVER. The story of New England, illustrated, being a narrative of the principal events from the arrival of the Pilgrims in 1620 and of the Puritans in 1624 to the present time. Boston: E. O. Skelton, 1910. Pp. 140.

1605 SLAFTER, EDMUND FARWELL, ed. John Checkley; or, the evolution of religious tolerance in Massachusetts Bay, including Mr. Checkley's controversial writings; his letters and other papers, with historical illustrations and a memoir. Boston: The Prince Society, 1897. 2v.

1606 SLEEPER, FRANK BRAMAN. "Fifty years of probation work in Massachusetts." MassMag, 1 (1908), 226-234.

1607 SLICER, THOMAS ROBERTS. The seventh annual sermon on Forefathers' Day...the seventh annual sermon preached before the New England Society in the City of New York in All Souls Church, Fourth Avenue, corner Twentieth Street, on Forefathers' Day, Sunday, December 16th, 1906. [New York]: Printed by order of the Society, [1906?]. Pp. 19.
Puritans.

1608 SLY, JOHN FAIRFIELD. Town government in Massachusetts (1620-1930). Cambridge: Harvard Univ. Pr., 1930. Pp. viii, 244.

1609 SMALL, ROBERT ORANGE. One goal: the history of training war production workers in and through the vocational schools of the Commonwealth of Massachusetts, 1940-1945. Boston: Massachusetts Vocational Association, 1950. Pp. xv, 371.
Technical education.

1610 SMITH, A. BRADFORD. "The Concord Turnpike." LexHSP, 3 (1900-1904), 110-116.

1611 SMITH, BRADFORD. Our debt to the Pilgrims. Plymouth: Choir Alley Pr., 1957. Pp. 20.

1612 SMITH, JONATHAN. "The depression of 1785 and Daniel Shays' Rebellion." WMQ, 3 Ser., 5 (1948), 77-94.

1613 _____. "How Massachusetts raised her troops in the Revolution." MHSP, 55 (1921-1922), 345-370.

1614 _____. Some features of Shays' Rebellion... address before the Clinton Historical Society, September 14, 1903. Clinton: W. J. Coulter, 1905. Pp. 12. M.

1615   [SMITH, MATTHEW HALE]. The Old Colony Rail-
        road: its connections, popular resorts, and
fashionable watering-places. By Burleigh, pseud.
Boston: Rand, Avery, 1875. Pp. 31.

1616   SMITH, PHILIP CHADWICK FOSTER. "Crystal
        blocks of Yankee coldness: the development
of the Massachusetts ice trade from Frederick Tudor
to Wenham Lake, 1806-1886. EIHC, 97 (1961), 197-
232.

1617   SMITH, SHERMAN MERRITT. The relation of the
        State to religious education in Massachu-
setts. Syracuse: Syracuse Univ. Book Store, 1926.
Pp. viii, 350.

1618   SNELL, THOMAS. "History of the General Asso-
        ciation of Massachusetts." American Quar-
terly Register, 11 (1838-1839), 160-173.
        Ministerial association.

1619   SNIDER, JOSEPH LYONS. Credit unions in Mas-
        sachusetts. Cambridge: Harvard Univ. Pr.
1939. Pp. 142.

1620   SNOW, ELLIOT and HARPER ALLEN GOSNELL. On
        the docks of 'Old Ironsides.' N.Y.: Mac-
millan, 1932. Pp. xx, 304.

1621   SOCIETY OF COLONIAL WARS. MASSACHUSETTS.
        The first half century of the Society of
Colonial Wars in the Commonwealth of Massachusetts,
1893-1943. Harold C. Durrell and Alexander B.
Ewing, eds. Boston: Arthur John Clark Sowdon Publication Fund, 1944. Pp. 229.

1622   SOCIETY OF THE CINCINNATI. MASSACHUSETTS.
        Memorials of the Massachusetts Society of
the Cincinnati. Bradford Adams Whittemore, ed.
Boston, 1964. Pp. xliv, 852.

1623   SOLEY, JOHN CODMAN. The fight between the
        'Constitution' and the 'Java.' [Boston]:
Military Historical Society of Massachusetts, 1901.
Pp. 20. MB.
        War of 1812.

1624   SOLOMON, BARBARA MILLER. Ancestors and im-
        migrants, a changing New England tradition.
Cambridge: Harvard Univ. Pr., 1956. Pp. ix, 276.
        Immigration Restriction League.

1625   "SOME Masonic buildings of Massachusetts,
        modern and historic." NOHR, 5 (July 21,
1906), 3-7.

1626   "SOME Massachusetts historical writers."
        MassMag, 1 (1908), 38-42, 112-116, 184-185,
274-277; 2 (1909), 51-53.
        Biographies of historians of Massachusetts.

1627   SOSIN, JACK M. "The Massachusetts Acts of
        1774: coercive or preventive?" Huntington
Library Quarterly, 26 (1963), 235-252.

1628   SOUTHWICK, HENRY LAWRENCE. The policy of
        the early colonists of Massachusetts toward
Quakers and others whom they regarded as intruders.
Boston: Old South Meeting House, 1885. Pp. viii,
21.

1629   SOUTHWICK, WALTER H. Early history of the
        Puritans, Quakers and Indians, with a biog-
raphy of the Quaker martyr Lawrence Southwick, emi-
grant founder of the Southwick family in America....
[Lynn, 1931]. Pp. 20.

1630   SOUTHWORTH, FRANKLIN. Some early vicissi-
        tudes of the Pilgrim Fathers. Meadville
Theological School. Quarterly Bulletin, 15 (January, 1926), 3-11.

1631   SPECK, FRANK GOULDSMITH. "A note on the
        Hassanamisco band of Nipmuc. MASB, 4 (1942-
1943), 49-56.
        Indians.

1632   _____. "Reflections upon the past and pre-
        sent of the Massachusetts Indians." MASB,
4 (1942-1943), 33-38.

1633   _____. Territorial subdivisions and bounda-
        ries of the Wampanoag, Massachusett and Nau-
set Indians. N.Y.: Museum of the American Indian,
1928. Pp. 152.

1634   _____. and RALPH WARREN DEXTER. "Utiliza-
        tion of marine life by Wampanoag Indians of
Massachusetts." Washington Academy of Sciences.
Journal, 38 (1948), 257-265.

1635   SPECTOR, ROBERT M. "The Quock Walker cases
        (1781-1783): the abolition of slavery and
Negro citizenship in early Massachusetts." JNegro
Hist, 53 (1968), 12-32.

1636   SPELVIN, GEORGE. "Massachusetts pioneered
        the banana industry." Industry, 12 (August,
1947), 13-16.

1637   SPENCER, A. W. "Prominent men in the shoe
        and leather trade." Bostonian, 1 (1894-
1895) 65-80, 173-188, 283-295, 408-421, 552-558,
657-661.
        Biographies.

1638   SPENCER, HENRY RUSSELL. Constitutional con-
        flict in provincial Massachusetts: a study
of some phases of the opposition between the Massachusetts governor and General Court in the early
eighteenth century. Columbus, Ohio: F. J. Heer,
1905. Pp. 135.

1639   SPINNEY, FRANK O. "Decoding the past."
        NEG, 1 (Fall, 1959), 26-30.
        Historic houses.

1640   SPOFFORD, AINSWORTH RAND. Massachusetts in
        the American Revolution.... Washington:
Printed for the [District of Columbia] Society [of
the Sons of the American Revolution], 1895. Pp. 37.

1641   SPOFFORD, JEREMIAH. A historical and statis-
        tical gazetteer of Massachusetts, with
sketches of the principal events from its settlement; a catalogue of prominent characters, and historical and statistical notices of the several cities and towns, alphabetically arranged.... (1828)
Haverhill: E. G. Frothingham, 1860. Pp. iv, 372.
        First edition has title: A gazetteer of
        Massachusetts.

1642 SPRAGUE, STUART SEELY. "The whaling ports: a study of ninety years of rivalry, 1784-1875." AmNep, 33 (1973), 120-130.

1643 SPRING, GARDINER. A tribute to New-England: a sermon, delivered before the New-England Society of the City and State of New York, on the 22d of December, 1820, being the second centennial celebration of the landing of the Pilgrims at Plymouth. N.Y.: L. & F. Lockwood, 1821. Pp. 44.
Pilgrim Fathers.

1644 SPRINGFIELD, MASS. CITY LIBRARY ASSOCIATION. The Pilgrim tercentenary, the Puritans, and the New England spirit. Springfield, 1921. unpaged.
A bibliography.

1645 SPRUNGER, KEITH L. "William Ames and the settlement of Massachusetts Bay." NEQ, 39 (1966), 66-79.
His influence on the Puritans even though he never came to America.

1646 STANWOOD, EDWARD. "The Massachusetts election in 1806." MHSP, 2 Ser., 20 (1906-1907), 12-21.

1647 _____. "The separation of Maine from Massachusetts." MHSP, 3 Ser., 1 (1907-1908), 125-164.

1648 STAPLES, CARLTON ALBERT. "The existence and the extinction of slavery in Massachusetts." LexHSP, 4 (1905-1910), 48-60.

1649 STAPLES, HAMILTON B. "The Province laws." AASP, New Ser., 3 (1883-1885), 158-177.

1650 STARBUCK, ALEXANDER. "Historical events leading up to the battles of Lexington and Concord." LexHSP, 4 (1905-1910), 127-157.

1651 STARK, JAMES HENRY. The loyalists of Massachusetts and the other side of the American Revolution. Boston, 1910. Pp. vii, 509.

1652 STARKEY, MARION LENA. A little rebellion. N.Y.: Knopf, 1955. Pp. 258.
Shays' Rebellion.

1653 STATE STREET TRUST CO., BOSTON. 300th anniversary of the Massachusetts Bay coinage known as Pine Tree, 1652-1952. Boston, [1952]. Pp. 23.

1654 "Statistics of the Massachusetts Congregational churches." CongQ, 8 (1866), 311.
1630-1865.

1655 STERN, T. NOEL. "Cost and adequacy of old age assistance in Massachusetts." BULRev, 32 (1952), 1-45.
1942-1951.

1656 STEWART, GEORGE RIPPEY. "Men's names in Plymouth and Massachusetts in the seventeenth century." Univ. of California Publications in English, 7 (1948), 109-137.

1657 STIFLER, SUSAN MARTHA REED. Church and State in Massachusetts, 1691-1740. Urbana, Ill., 1914. Pp. 208.

1658 STODDARD, FRANCIS RUSSELL. The truth about the Pilgrims. N.Y.: Society of Mayflower Descendants in the State of New York, 1952. Pp. 206.

1659 STONE, ORRA LAVILLE. History of Massachusetts industries; their inception, growth, and success. Boston: S. J. Clarke, 1930. 4v.
Vols. 3 and 4 are biographical.

1660 STONE, SARA A. "Some old trees." Historic Leaves, 5 (1906-1907), 1-9.

1661 STORER, MALCOLM. Numismatics of Massachusetts. [Boston]: Massachusetts Historical Society, 1923. Pp. xi, 318.

1662 _____. "Pine Tree shillings and other colonial money." OTNE, 20 (1929-1930), 65-86.

1663 STOUT, NEIL R. "The spies who went out in the cold." Am Heritage, 23 (1972), 52-55. 100-103.
William Brown and Henry DeBirniere on mission for General Gage, February, 1775.

1664 STUART, HENRY LONGAN. The inventive genius of Massachusetts men and its influence in the development of the trade and industry of America. [Boston?], 1915. Pp. 24.

1665 STURGES, WALTER KNIGHT. "Arthur Little and the colonial revival." SocArchHistJ, 32 (1973), 147-163.
Domestic architecture, 1870s-1890s.

1666 STURGIS, RUSSELL. "The young men's Christian associations of Massachusetts." BSM 1 (1884) 302-306.

1667 SULLIVAN, JAMES. The history of land titles in Massachusetts. Boston: I. Thomas and E. T. Andrews, 1801. Pp. x, 392.

1668 _____. One hundred years of progress; a graphic, historical, and pictorial account of the Catholic Church of New England: Archdiocese of Boston. Boston: Illustrated Publishing, 1895. Pp. 842. MB.

1669 SULLIVAN, JOHN P. "Twenty-fifth year of unemployment insurance system in Massachusetts." Industry, 25 (August, 1960), 19-20, 29.

1670 SULLIVAN, MARY XAVERIA, SISTER. The history of Catholic secondary education in the Archdiocese of Boston. Washington: Catholic Univ. of America Pr., 1946. Pp. xiii, 183.

1671 SULLIVAN, WILLIAM. A discourse delivered before the Pilgrim Society, at Plymouth, on the twenty second day of December, 1829. Boston: Carter and Hendee, 1830. Pp. 60.
Pilgrim Fathers.

1672 SULLIVAN, WILLIAM B. "The Bay Colony, the first to conceive the idea of independence." DanHC, 18 (1930), 40-46.

1673 SUNDERMAN, LLOYD FREDERICK. "Early music education in Massachusetts." Education, 72 (1951), 45-67.
   1720-1838.

1674 SURVEY OF FEDERAL ARCHIVES. The eleven original customs districts established in the Commonwealth of Massachusetts, in geographical order, from the New Hampshire to the Rhode Island borders, together with the names of collectors who served in them between 1789 and 1913. Boston: National Archives Project, 1941. 15 leaves.

1675 _____. Inventory of Federal archives in the states, Ser. III, the Department of the Treasury, No. 20, Massachusetts, Pt. II, the Bureau of Customs. Boston: National Archives Project, 1938. 443 leaves. MBNEH.

1676 SUZZALLO, HENRY. The rise of local school supervision in Massachusetts (the school committee, 1635-1827).... [N.Y.]: Printed for the author, 1905. Pp. vii, 155.

1677 SWAN, ROBERT T. "[Massachusetts town records in print.]" AHR, 1 (1896), 581-584, 771-772.

1678 SWAN, WILLIAM UPHAM. "Early visual telegraphs in Massachusetts." BSProc., (1933), 31-47.

1679 SWEET, MARY C. "Massachusetts and Maryland in the Revolution." MagHist, 20 (1915), 222-241.

1680 SWIFT, WILLIAM HENRY. Massachusetts railroads 1842 to 1855. Boston: J. H. Eastburn's Pr., 1856. Pp. 23. MB.

1681 SYRETT, DAVID. "Town meeting politics in Massachusetts, 1776-1786." WMQ, 3 Ser., 21 (1964), 352-366.

1682 TAFT, HERBERT C. "Early days of railroading." Lowell HSC, 1 (1907-1913), 388-417.

1683 "A TALE of two organs." HistNan, 10 (April, 1963), 5-14.

1684 TANIS, NORMAN EARL. "Education in John Eliot's Indian utopias, 1646-1675." HistEdQ, 10 (1970), 308-323.

1685 TAPLEY, HARRIET SILVESTER. "The 'Province Galley' of Massachusetts Bay, 1694-1716." EIHC, 58 (1922), 73-88, 153-175.

1686 TAPPAN, GEORGE ARTHUR, ed. Our State House, illustrated, historical, and biographical.... Boston: Tappan Publishing, 1900. Pp. 130.

1687 TARBOX, INCREASE NILES. "The Pilgrims and Puritans: Plymouth and the Massachusetts Bay." Old Colony HSC, [No. 1] (1878), 23-58.

1688 _____. "Plymouth and the Bay." CongQ, 17 (1875), 238-252.

1689 TATRO, KENNETH W. "People's banks: the constructive legacy of Josiah Quincy." Boston, 58 (December, 1966), 55-59.
   Savings and loan associations.

1690 TAYLOR, ROBERT JOSEPH, ed. Massachusetts, Colony to Commonwealth: documents on the formation of its Constitution, 1775-1780. Chapel Hill: Univ. of North Carolina Pr., 1961. Pp. xi, 166.

1691 _____. Western Massachusetts in the Revolution. Providence: Brown Univ. Pr., 1954. Pp. viii, 227.

1692 TEAFORD, JON. "The transformation of Massachusetts education, 1670-1780." HistEdQ, 10 (1970), 287-307.

1693 TELLER, WALTER MAGNES. Cape Cod and the offshore islands. Englewood Cliffs, N.J.: Prentice-Hall, 1970. Pp. x, 256.

1693A TENNEY, MARY ALICE, comp. The Pilgrims: A selected list of works in the Public Library of the City of Boston. Boston: The Trustees [of the Boston Public Library], 1920. Pp. 51. MB.

1694 TERCENTENARY CONFERENCE OF CITY AND TOWN COMMITTEES, INC. Celebrating a 300th anniversary; a report of the Massachusetts Bay tercentenary of 1930, commemorating the 300th anniversary of the founding by the Puritans of the Bay Colony in New England. Story of the organization, arrangement and conduct of the state-wide, localized celebration in 250 towns and cities of the Commonwealth from January 1 to December 31, 1930; together with complete schedule of the principal events to the number 2000 sponsored by the state, municipal and other agencies; and a list of the organizations and local committees concerned. Everett Bird Mero, comp. Boston, 1931. Pp. 131.

1695 THACHER, JENNIE WILLIAMS. "A trip to Boston seventy five years ago." PVMA, 7 (1921-1929), 154-159.
   From Deerfield.

1696 THAYER, JAMES BRADLEY. "A chapter of legal history in Massachusetts." HarvLRev, 9 (1895-1896), 1-12.
   Competency of witnesses.

1697 THOMAS, EDWARD LAW. "The New Bedford, Martha's Vineyard and Nantucket Steamboat Company." DCI, 10 (1968-1969), 151-159.

1698 THOMPSON, ABIJAH. "The Ancient and Honorable Artillery Company." Winchester Record, 1 (1-85), 161-165.

1699 THOMPSON, ELROY SHERMAN. History of Plymouth, Norfolk and Barnstable Counties, Massachusetts. N.Y.: Lewis Historical Publishing Co., 1928. 3v.
   Vol. 3 contains biographical material.

1700 THOMPSON, FRANCIS MCGEE. "Massachusetts Colony and Peter and John Schuyler." PVMA, 4 (1899-1904), 313-329.
   1689-1723.

1701 THOMPSON, LAWRENCE. "Some collectors in colonial Massachusetts." Colophon, 2 (Autumn,
1936), 82-100.
Book collectors.

1702 THOMPSON, MACK. "Massachusetts and New York
Stamp Acts." WMQ, 26 (1969), 253-258.
1755-1756.

1703 THOMTE, THEODORE. Battles of the frigate
Constitution. Chicago: Rand McNally, 1966.
Pp. 128.

1704 THORNDIKE, SAMUEL LOTHROP. "The psalmodies
of Plymouth and Massachusetts Bay." CSMP, 1
(1892-1894), 228-238.

1705 THORNTON, JOHN WINGATE. Index of persons
and places mentioned in Hutchinson's 'Massachusetts.' Charles Lowell Woodward, ed. New York,
1879. Pp. 15.

1706 THORPE, JAMES A. "Colonial suffrage in
Massachusetts: an essay review." EIHC, 106
(1970), 169-181.

1707 THWING, LEROY L. "Lighting in early colonial Massachusetts." NEQ, 11 (1938), 166-170.

1708 TILLINGHAST, CALEB BENJAMIN. The free public libraries of Massachusetts. Boston,
1891. Pp. 290.

1709 TODD, CHARLES BURR. In olde Massachusetts;
sketches of old times and places during the
early days of the Commonwealth. N.Y.: Grafton
Pr., 1907. Pp. viii, 253.

1710 TOLLES, FREDERICK B. "A Quaker's curse:
Humphrey Norton to John Endecott, 1658."
Huntington Library Quarterly, 14 (1950-1951), 415-
421.

1711 TOMLINSON, ABRAHAM and BENSON J. LOSSING,
comps. The military journals of two private
soldiers, 1758-1775...to which is added, a supplement, containing official papers on the skirmishes
at Lexington and Concord. Poughkeepsie, 1855.
Pp. 128.
Lemuel Lyon and Samuel Haws: includes siege
of Boston and battles of Lexington and Concord.

1712 TONER, JOSEPH M. "History of inoculation in
Massachusetts." Massachusetts Medical Society. Publications, 2 (1867-1868), 153-172.

1713 TOOMEY, DANIEL P. and THOMAS C. QUINN. Massachusetts of today; a memorial of the
state, historical and biographical. Boston: Columbia Publishing, 1892. Pp. 619.

1714 TOON, PETER. The Pilgrims' faith: historical research. Callington [England]: Gospel
Communication, 1970. Pp. 79.

1715 TORRINGTON, JOHN ALDEN. "Our oldest military company." Munsey's Magazine, 17 (1897),
33-38.
Ancient and Honorable Artillery Company.

1716 TOURTELLOT, ARTHUR BERNON. The Charles.
N.Y.: Farrar & Rinehart, 1941. Pp. x, 356.
Charles River.

1717 TOWNER, LAWRENCE WILLIAM. "'A fondness for
freedom': servant protest in Puritan society." WMQ, 3 Ser., 19 (1962), 201-219.
1629-1750; limited to Massachusetts.

1718 ____. "The Sewall-Saffin dialogue on slavery." WMQ, 3 Ser., 21 (1964), 40-52.
Samuel Sewall and John Saffin.

1719 TOWNSEND, CHARLES WENDELL. Sand dunes and
salt marshes. Boston: D. Estes, 1913.
Pp. 311.

1720 TOWNSEND, THOMAS S. "Massachusetts in the
Civil War." NEM, New Ser., (1895) 3-20.

1721 TRACY, JAMES J. "The origin of the Massachusetts militia." MagHist, 1 (1905), 1-9.

1722 TUCKER, CARLTON E. "Brockton Street Railway
Co." Transportation Bulletin, No. 63 (May-
July, 1960), entire issue.

1723 TURNER, FREDERICK JACKSON. "The first offi-
cial frontier of the Massachusetts Bay."
CSMP, 17 (1913-1914), 250-270.
Boundaries.

1724 TURNER, LYNN W. "The last war cruise of
Old Ironsides." AmHeritage, 6 (April, 1955),
56-61.

1725 TUTTLE, JULIUS HERBERT. Massachusetts and
her royal charter granted March 4, 1628-29.
Boston: Massachusetts Society of the Order of the
Founders and Patriots of America, 1924. Pp. 25.

1726 TWOMBLEY, ROBERT C. and RICHARD H. MOORE.
"Black Puritan: the Negro in seventeenth-
century Massachusetts." WMQ, 3 Ser., 24 (1967),
224-242.

1727 TYLER, LYON G. "Aristocracy in Massachusetts and Virginia." WMQ, 26 (1917-1918),
277-281.

1728 TYMESON, MILDRED MCCLARY. But one lamp.
[Boston?], 1964. Pp. 63.
Dentistry in Massachusetts, 1864-1964.

1729 TYNG, DUDLEY. Massachusetts Episcopalians,
1607-1957. Pascoag, R.I.: Delmo Pr., 1957.
Pp. 142. MWA.

1730 UHLENBERG, PETER R. "A study of cohort life
cycles: cohorts of native born Massachusetts women, 1830-1920." Population Studies, 23
(1969), 407-420.

1731 UNITED SPANISH WAR VETERANS. DEPARTMENT OF
MASSACHUSETTS. NATIONAL AUXILIARY. History
of the Department of Massachusetts, National Auxiliary...as presented in reports 1907-1929. Boston,
1929. Pp. 199. MB.
Ladies' auxiliary.

1732 U. S. BOSTON NATIONAL HISTORIC SITES COMMIS-
      SION. Final report of the Boston National
Historic Sites Commission. Washington: Govt.
Print. Off., 1961. Pp. xviii, 261.
      Relates to greater Boston area; includes
      partial list of 'lost' historic sites.

1733 U. S. BUREAU OF CONSTRUCTION AND REPAIR.
      United States Frigate 'Constitution.' A
brief account of her history, together with data for
model builders. Washington: Govt. Print. Off.,
1932. Pp. 15.

1734 U. S. PRESIDENT, 1921-1923 (HARDING). The
      achievement of the centuries, address of the
President delivered August 1, 1921, at the tercentenary celebration of the landing of the Pilgrims
at Plymouth.... Washington: Govt. Print. Off.,
1921. Pp. 8.

1735 UPDEGRAFF, HARLAN. The origin of the moving
      school in Massachusetts.... N.Y.: Columbia
Univ., 1908. Pp. 186.

1736 UPHAM, CHARLES WENTWORTH. An oration deliv-
      ered before the New England Society in the
City of New York, December 22, 1846. 2d ed. Boston: J. Munroe, 1847. Pp. 64.

1737 USEEM, JOHN. "Changing economy and rural
      security in Massachusetts." AgricHist, 16
(1942), 29-40.

1738 USHER, ROLAND GREENE. The Pilgrims and
      their history. N.Y.: Macmillan, 1918.
Pp. x, 310.

1739 VAN ANTWERP, LEE D. "The Mayflower, her
      passengers and their descendants." NEHGR,
124 (1970), 110-113.

1740 VANČURA, ZDENĚK. Otcové poutníci a počátky
      americké literatury. The Pilgrim Fathers
and the beginnings of American literature. Praha:
Universita Karlova, 1965. Pp. 90.
      In Czech, with summary in English.

1741 VAN DE WOESTYNE, ROYAL STEWART. State con-
      trol of local finance in Massachusetts.
Cambridge: Harvard Univ. Pr., 1935. Pp. xii, 184.

1742 VARNEY, GEORGE JONES. "The Scotch-Irish and
      the Bay State border." NEM, New Ser., 16
(1897), 347-352.

1743 VAUGHAN, ALDEN T. "The 'horrid and unnatural
      rebellion' of Daniel Shays." Am Heritage,
17 (June, 1966), 50-53, 77-81.

1744 VAUGHN, CONSTANT E. "Pilgrim foods." May-
      flowerQ, 35 (1969), 5-7.

1745 VERA, JOSEPH S. "Evidence of habit and cus-
      tom in Massachusetts civil cases." BULRev,
33 (1953), 205-217.
      1810-1940.

1746 VIETS, HENRY ROUSE. A brief history of medi-
      cine in Massachusetts. Boston: Houghton
Mifflin, 1930. Pp. x, 194.

1747 ____. "Some features of the history of
      medicine in Massachusetts during the colonial
period, 1620-1770." Isis, 23 (1935), 389-405.

1748 VINAL, WILLIAM GOULD. The rise and fall of
      ye district school in Plimouth Plantation
(1800-1900). Norwell: Vinehall, 1958. Pp. 144.

1749 VINOVSKIS, MARIS A. "Mortality rates and
      trends in Massachusetts before 1860." JEcon
Hist, 32 (1972), 184-213.

1750 ____. Trends in Massachusetts education,
      1826-1860." HistEdQ, 12 (1972), 501-529.
Statistical study.

1751 VIRGIN, HARRY. "Constitutional Convention of
      1819." Maine Historical Society. Collec-
tions, 3 Ser., 2 (1906), 416-464.

1752 VOSE, GEORGE L. "Notes on early transporta-
      tion in Massachusetts." Association of En-
gineering Societies. Journal, 4 (1884-1885), 53-
72.

1753 "VOYAGE of the Mayflower." CCAPL, 5 (July,
      1921), 17-18.

1754 VUILLEUMIER, MARION. "Their fate was in his
      hands." MayflowerQ, 37 (1971), 46-50.
Relations between the Pilgrims and Massasoit
(Wampanoags), 1620-1661.

1755 WADLIN, HORACE GREELEY. "The growth of cit-
      ies in Massachusetts." American Statistical
Association. Publications, New Ser., 2 (1890-1891),
159-173.
      Statistical tables.

1756 ____. Strikes and lockouts, 1881-1886.
      Boston: Wright & Potter, 1889. Pp. v, 117.

1757 WALETT, FRANCIS GUSTAF. "Governor Bernard's
      undoing: an earlier Hutchinson letters af-
fair." NEQ, 38 (1965), 217-226.
      1760s.

1758 ____. "The Massachusetts Council, 1766-
      1774: the transformation of a conservative
institution." WMQ, 3 Ser., 6 (1949), 605-627.

1759 ____. Massachusetts newspapers and the Rev-
      olutionary crisis, 1763-1776. Boston: Mas-
sachusetts Bicentennial Commission, 1974. Pp. 44.
M.

1760 WALKER, ALICE MOREHOUSE. Early days in the
      Connecticut Valley. Amherst, 1901. Pp. 51.
Limited to Massachusetts.

1761 WALKER, C. S. "The Smith charities." NEM,
      New Ser., 21 (1899-1900), 718-727.
Nineteenth century.

1762 WALKER, MACK. "The mercenaries." NEQ, 39
      (1966), 390-398.
Recruitment in 1864 of German immigrants by
Massachusetts agents to serve in the Union
army.

1763 WALL, ROBERT EMMET, JR. "The decline of the
        Massachusetts franchise, 1647-1666." JAH,
59 (1972-1973), 303-310.

1764 _____. "The Massachusetts Bay Colony fran-
        chise in 1647." WMQ, 27 (1970), 136-144.

1765 _____. Massachusetts Bay: the crucial dec-
        ade, 1640-1650. New Haven: Yale Univ. Pr.,
1972. Pp. x, 292.

1766 WALL, WILLIAM EDMUND. The oldest paint
        shops in Massachusetts: a paper read at the
nineteenth annual convention of the Society of Master House Painters and Decorators of Massachusetts,
held in the American House, Boston, January 13,
1910. Somerville, 1910. Pp. 74.

1767 WALLINGFORD, HOWARD and GEORGE MARSH. "New
        England's paper industry born on the Nepon-
set River." Industry, 16 (July, 1951), 13-15.

1768 WALSH, JAMES P. "Solomon Stoddard's open
        communion: a reexamination." NEQ, 43
(1970), 97-114.

1769 WALSH, LOUIS S. Archdiocese of Boston,
        growth of parochial schools in chronological
order 1820-1900. Newton Highlands: St. John's Industrial Training School, 1901. Pp. 16. MB.

1770 WALTERS, RONALD G. "New England society and
        'The Laws and Liberties of Massachusetts,
1648.'" EIHC, 106 (1970), 145-168.

1771 WARD, ANDREW HENSHAW. "Notes on anti-Revo-
        lutionary currency and politics." NEHGR,
14 (1860), 261-264.
        Land Bank, 1740.

1772 WARD, HARRY M. Statism in Plymouth Colony.
        Port Washington, N.Y.: Kennikat Pr., 1973.
Pp. 193.
        Civil rights.

1773 WARD, MAY ALDEN. Old Colony days. Boston:
        Roberts Bros., 1896. Pp. 280.
        Social life and customs.

1774 WARE, EDITH ELLEN. Political opinion in
        Massachusetts during Civil War and Recon-
struction. N.Y.: Columbia Univ. Pr., 1916.
Pp. 219.

1775 WARE, HORACE EVERETT. "The charter and the
        men." Society of Colonial Wars. Massachu-
setts. [Yearbook], (1906), 57-86.
        Massachusetts Bay Colony.

1776 _____. The transfer to Massachusetts of its
        charter government, 1630. Cambridge: John
Wilson and Son, 1912. Pp. 23.

1777 _____. "Was the government of the Massachu-
        setts Bay Colony a theocracy?" CSMP, 10
(1904-1906), 151-180.

1778 WÄRENSTAM, ERIC. Mayflower och pilgrimerna.
        Stockholm: Förlaget Filadelfia, 1957.
Pp. 232.

1779 WARNER, FRANCES LESTER. Pilgrim trails: a
        Plymouth-to-Provincetown sketchbook. Boston:
Atlantic Monthly Pr., 1921. Pp. 47.

1780 WARREN, CHARLES. "Elbridge Gerry, James War-
        ren, Mercy Warren and the ratification of the
Federal Constitution in Massachusetts." MHSP, 64
(1930-1932), 143-164.
        1787.

1781 _____. Jacobin and junto: or, early Ameri-
        can politics as viewed in the diary of Dr.
Nathaniel Ames, 1758-1822. Cambridge: Harvard
Univ. Pr., 1931. Pp. 324.

1782 WARREN, JAMES. A study in dissent: the
        Warren-Gerry correspondence, 1776-1792.
Clinton Harvey Gardiner, ed. Carbondale: Southern
Illinois Univ. Pr., 1968. Pp. xxxi, 269.

1783 WARREN, JOSEPH PARKER. "The Confederation
        and the Shays' Rebellion." AHR, 11 (1905-
1906), 42-67.

1784 WARREN, WINSLOW. "The colonial customs ser-
        vice in Massachusetts in its relation to the
American Revolution." MHSP, 46 (1912-1913), 440-
474.

1785 _____. "The Pilgrim spirit." CSMP, 24
        (1920-1922), 10-23.

1786 _____. "The Pilgrims in Holland and Ameri-
        ca." CSMP, 18 (1915-1916), 130-152.

1787 WASHBURN, EMORY. "Did the vacating of the
        colony charter annul the laws made under
it?" MHSP, (1873-1875), 451-459.

1788 _____. "Extinction of slavery in Massachu-
        setts." MHSP, (1855-1858), 188-203.

1789 _____. "The origin and sources of the Bill
        of Rights declared in the Constitution of
Massachusetts." MHSP, (1864-1865), 294-313.

1790 _____. Sketches of the judicial history of
        Massachusetts from 1630 to the Revolution in
1775. Boston: C. C. Little and J. Brown, 1840.
Pp. 407.

1791 _____. Slavery as it once prevailed in
        Massachusetts, a lecture for the Massachu-
setts Historical Society, Jan. 22, 1869. Boston:
John Wilson & Son, 1869. Pp. 35. MB.

1792 _____. "Transfer of the colony charter of
        1628 from England to Massachusetts."
MHSP, (1858-1860), 154-167.

1793 WASHBURN, ROBERT COLLYER. Prayer for profit:
        being the colorful story of our Pilgrim Fa-
thers. N.Y.: Sears Publishing, 1930. Pp. 305.

1794 WASHBURN, ROBERT MORRIS. Footprints on the
        sands of time. Boston, 1924. Pp. 111.
        Political affairs, 1900-1924.

1795 _____. Nine intimates of the past. Boston, 1942. Unpaged.
Francis P. Magoun, Maria K. M. Sherrill, Chester W. Lasell, William H. Coolidge, Charlotte G. W. Calkins, Ellen G. Loring, Elwood Worcester, Slater Washburn and Charles F. Choate, Jr.

1796 "WASHINGTON'S visit to New England in 1789." NEM, New Ser., 1 (1889-1890), 345-350.

1797 WATERS, JOHN J. The Otis family, in Provincial and Revolutionary Massachusetts. Chapel Hill: Univ. of North Carolina Pr., 1968. Pp. xi, 221.

1798 _____. and JOHN A. SCHUTZ. "Patterns of Massachusetts colonial politics: the Writs of Assistance and the rivalry between the Otis and Hutchinson families." WMQ, 3 Ser., 24 (1967), 543-567.

1799 WATERS, THOMAS FRANKLIN. "The early homes of the Puritans." EIHC, 33 (1898), 45-79.

1800 WATKINS, LURA WOODSIDE. "American silvered glass." Antiques, 42 (1942), 183-186.

1801 _____. "An antecedent of three mold glass." Antiques, 36 (1939), 68-70.

1802 _____. "Shaded glass of the Massachusetts glasshouses." Antiques, 28 (1935), 19-21.

1803 WATKINS, WALTER KENDALL. Massachusetts in the intended expedition to Canada in 1746. Boston, 1900. Pp. 55. MBNEH.

1804 _____. Massachusetts in the Lake George expedition. Boston, 1906. Pp. 54. MBNEH. 1755.

1805 WEBSTER, DANIEL. A discourse, delivered at Plymouth, December 22, 1820, in commemoration of the first settlement of New-England. (1821) 4th ed. Boston: Wells and Lilly, 1826. Pp. 60.

1806 WEEDEN, WILLIAM BABCOCK. War government, Federal and State, in Massachusetts, New York, Pennsylvania and Indiana, 1861-1865. Boston: Houghton Mifflin, 1906. Pp. xxv, 389.

1807 WEEKS, LOUIS, III. "Cotton Mather and Quakers." QH, 59 (1970), 24-33.

1808 WEEKS, LYMAN HORACE. "Early Massachusetts newspapers." American Historical Magazine, 3 (1908), 111-140.

1809 WEIR, FREDERICK LEWIS. "Early records of the seventeenth-century churches in Massachusetts which became Unitarian." UHSP, 7, Pt. 2 (1941), 11-22.

1810 _____. A short history of the Worcester Conference and Worcester Association...delivered...at Hudson, April 13, 1947. Leominster:

Enterprise Job Printing Department, [1947?]. Unpaged. MBNEH.
Ministerial association.

1811 WELCH, RICHARD E. JR. "Opponents and colleagues: George Frisbie Hoar and Henry Cabot Lodge, 1898-1904." NEQ, 39 (1966), 182-209.

1812 _____. "The Parsons-Sedgwick feud and the reform of the Massachusetts judiciary." EIHC, 92 (1956), 171-187.
Theophilus Parsons and Theodore Sedgwick, 1803-1811.

1813 WELLMAN, JOSHUA WYMAN. The church polity of the Pilgrims. Boston: Congregational Board of Publication. [1857]. Pp. 144.

1814 "WERE the Pilgrims Puritans?" HistMag, 2 Ser., 2 (1867), 277.

1815 WERTENBAKER, THOMAS JEFFERSON. The Puritan oligarchy: the founding of American civilization. N.Y.: C. Scribner's Sons, 1947. Pp. xiv, 359.
Church and State.

1816 WESTON, DAVID. A historical discourse preached at the fiftieth anniversary of the Worcester Baptist Association...September 22, 1869. Worcester: Tyler & Seagrave, 1869. Pp. 28. MWA.

1817 WESTON, HORACE C. "The less remembered years." PSN, No. 14 (May, 1964), entire issue.
Plymouth Colony.

1818 WHELAN, ELIZABETH MURPHY. "Estimates of the ultimate family: status of children born out of wedlock in Massachusetts, 1961-1968." Journal of Marriage and the Family, 34 (1972), 635-646.

1819 WHELPLEY, PHILIP MELANCTHON. A discourse delivered before the New-England Society of the City and State of New-York, Dec. 22, 1822, in commemoration of the Plymouth Colony. N.Y.: J. Seymour, 1823. Pp. 49, iv.

1820 WHIPPLE, GEORGE CHANDLER. State sanitation; a review of the work of the Massachusetts State Board of Health. Cambridge: Harvard Univ. Pr., 1917. 2v.
Vol. 1 is historical.

1821 WHITE, DANIEL APPLETON. An address, delivered at Ipswich, before the Essex County Lyceum, at their first annual meeting, May 5, 1830. Salem: Foote & Brown, 1830. Pp. 60.
Appendix contains a history of the lyceum movement in Massachusetts.

1822 WHITE, FRANCES J. Through the old-time haunts of the Norwottuck and Pocumtuck Indians. Springfield: F. A. Bassette, 1903. Pp. 42. Limited to Franklin and Hampshire counties.

1823 WHITE, LAURA A. "Was Charles Sumner shamming, 1856-1859?" NEQ, 33 (1960), 291-324. Republican politics.

1824 WHITE, LEONARD D. "The origin of utility commissions in Massachusetts." Journal of Political Economy, 29 (1921), 177-197.

1825 WHITEFIELD, EDWIN. Homes of our forefathers in Massachusetts. (1879) New ed. Dedham, 1892. 39 leaves.

1826 WHITEHILL, WALTER MUIR. "Who rules here? Random reflections on the national origins of those set in authority over us." NEQ, 43, (1970), 434-449.
Famous sons of Massachusetts and their origins.

1827 WHITING, MARGARET C. "The freedom suit." PVMA, 7 (1921-1929), 569-574.
Marriage customs.

1828 WHITMAN, BENJAMIN. An index to the laws of Massachusetts from the adoption of the Constitution [1780] to the year 1796. Worcester: Thomas, Son & Thomas, 1797. Pp. 152. MB.

1829 WHITMAN, ZACHARIAH GARDNER. Historical sketch of the Massachusetts Ancient and Honorable Artillery Company from its formation in 1637...to the present time. (1820) 2d. ed. Boston: John H. Eastburn, 1842. Pp. iv, 463. M.

1830 WHITMORE, WILLIAM HENRY. A bibliographical sketch of the laws of the Massachusetts colony from 1630 to 1686. In which are included the Body of Liberties of 1641, and the records of the Court of Assistants, 1641-1644, arranged to accompany the reprints of the laws of 1660 and 1672. Boston: Rockwell and Churchill, 1890. Pp. xliii, 150.

1831 _____. The Massachusetts civil list for the colonial and provincial periods, 1630-1774, being a list of the names and dates of appointment of all the civil officers constituted by authority of the charters, or the local government. Albany: J. Munsell, 1870. Pp. 172.

1832 _____. "Origin of the names of the towns in Massachusetts." MHSP (1871-1873), 393-419.

1833 WHITTELSEY, SARAH SCOVILL. Massachusetts labor legislation: an historical and critical study.... Philadelphia: American Academy of Political and Social Science, 1900. Pp. 157.

1834 WHITTEMORE, HENRY. The signers of the Mayflower Compact, and their descendants. N.Y.: Mayflower Publishing, 1899. Pp. 48.

1835 WHITTEN, ROBERT HARVEY. Public administration in Massachusetts; the relation of central to local activity.... N.Y.: Columbia Univ., 1898. Pp. x, 167.

1836 WHO'S who in Massachusetts; a volume containing a biographical history of every important living person in the Commonwealth. (1940) Vol. II, 1942-1943. Boston: Larkin, Roosevelt & Larkin, 1942. Pp. 742.
First edition is called 'volume one.'

1837 WILBUR, HERVEY. The Pilgrims, a sermon preached in Wendell, Dec. 22, 1820, it being the second centennial anniversary of the landing of our ancestors at Plymouth. Wendell: J. Metcalf, 1821. Pp. 20. M.

1838 WILDER, HARRIS HAWTHORNE. "Notes on the Indians of southern Massachusetts." American Anthropologist, New Ser., 25 (1923), 197-218.

1839 WILDER, JANET. "1939 - history in review - 1964. [Massachusetts Archaeological Society]." MASB, 25 (1963-1964) 46-49.

1840 WILDER, MARSHALL PINCKNEY. History and progress of the Massachusetts State Board of Agriculture for the first quarter of a century.... Boston: Rand, Avery, 1878. Pp. 21.

1841 WILKINSON, THOMAS OBERSON. Changes in younger population of Massachusetts, 1950-1960. Amherst: Cooperative Extension Service, Univ. of Massachusetts, 1963. Pp. 12.

1842 _____, SYLVIA DUGRE and JOYCE PARENT. Massachusetts population growth and redistribution, 1950-1960. Amherst: Cooperative Extension Service, Univ. of Massachusetts, 1963. Pp. 24.

1843 WILLARD, ASHTON R. "Charles Bulfinch, the architect." NEM, New Ser., 3 (1890-1891), 273-299.

1844 WILLARD, JOSEPH. "Naturalization in the American colonies, with more particular reference to Massachusetts." MHSP, (1858-1860), 337-364.

1845 WILLARD, JOSEPH AUGUSTUS. Half a century with judges and lawyers. Boston: Houghton Mifflin, 1895. Pp. iv, 371.
Social life and customs.

1846 WILLARD, SAMUEL. History of the rise, progress and consummation of the rupture, which now divides the Congregational clergy and churches of Massachusetts, in a discourse delivered in the First Church in Deerfield, Mass., September 22, 1857.... Greenfield: H. D. Mirick, 1858. Pp. 42.
Unitarianism.

1847 WILLIAMS, ROY FOSTER. "A.I.M.'s [Associated Industries of Massachusetts] golden anniversary." Industry, 30 (January, 1965), 10-12, 36-39, (March, 1965), 14-15, 33-37, (April, 1965), 28-29, 41-45, (July, 1965), 17-18, 39-43.
Manufacturers' association.

1848 _____. Seven romances of Bay State industry. N.Y.: Newcomen Society in North America, 1951. Pp. 56. MB.

1849 WILLIAMSON, JEFFREY G. "Consumer behavior in the nineteenth century: Carroll D. Wright's Massachusetts workers in 1875." EEH, 2 Ser., 4 (1966-1967), 98-135.

1850 WILLISON, GEORGE FINDLAY, ed. The Pilgrim
     reader; the story of the Pilgrims as told by
themselves & their contemporaries, friendly & un-
friendly. Garden City, N.Y.: Doubleday, 1953.
Pp. xvii, 585.

1851 _____. Saints and strangers, being the
     lives of the Pilgrim Fathers & their famil-
ies, with their friends & foes; & an account of
their posthumous wanderings in limbo, their final
resurrection & rise to glory, & the strange pilgrimages of Plymouth Rock. N.Y.: Reynal & Hitchcock, 1945. Pp. ix, 513.

1852 WILLS, LOIS BAILEY. "The old meeting
     house." NEG, 6 (Winter, 1965), 34-43.
General religious history.

1853 WILLSON, LAWRENCE. "Another view of the
     Pilgrims." NEQ, 34 (1961), 160-177.
As seen by Thoreau.

1854 WINSLOW, CHARLES EDWARD AMORY. "There were
     giants in those days." American Journal of
Public Health, 43 (June, 1953, Pt. 2), 15-19.
Public health, 1890-1910.

1855 WINSLOW, DOUGLAS KENELM. Mayflower heri-
     tage; a family record of the growth of
Anglo-American partnership. N.Y.: Funk & Wagnalls,
1957. Pp. 200.
Winslow family.

1856 WINSOR, JUSTIN. Massachusetts. Boston:
     Little, Brown, 1882. Pp. 29.

1857 WINTHROP, ROBERT CHARLES. An address, de-
     livered before the New England Society, in
the City of New York, December 23, 1839. Boston:
Perkins & Marvin, 1840. Pp. 60.
Pilgrim Fathers.

1858 _____. Introductory lecture to the course
     on the early history of Massachusetts, by
members of the Massachusetts Historical Society,
at the Lowell Institute, Boston, delivered Jan. 5,
1869. Boston: J. Wilson and Son, 1869. Pp. 27.
Caption title: Massachusetts and its early
history.

1859 WOLFORD, THORP LANIER. "Democratic-Republi-
     can reaction in Massachusetts to the embargo
of 1807." NEQ, 15 (1942), 35-61.

1860 WOOD, F. J. "Paper money and Shays' Rebel-
     lion." SWJ, 26 (1920), 333-345, 422-434.

1861 WOOD, GORDON S. "The Massachusetts mug-
     wumps." NEQ, 33 (1960), 435-451.
1880s.

1862 WOOD, HERBERT GEORGE. Venturers for the
     kingdom; a study in the history of the Pil-
grim Fathers. London: Hodder and Stoughton, 1920.
Pp. xiv, 254.

1863 WOOD, WILLIAM. Wood's New England's pros-
     pect. (1634) Charles Deane, ed. Boston:
The [Prince] Society, 1865. Pp. xxxi, 131.
Limited to Massachusetts.

1864 WOODBRIDGE, JOHN. The jubilee of New Eng-
     land, a sermon, preached in Hadley, December
22, 1820, in commemoration of the landing of our
fathers at Plymouth; being two centuries from that
event. Northampton: T. W. Shepard, 1821. Pp. 28.

1865 WOODBRIDGE, WILLIAM. An address delivered
     before the New England Society of Michigan,
December 22, 1847. Detroit: Harsha & Willcox,
1849. Pp. 24.
Pilgrim Fathers.

1866 WOODRUFF, EDWIN H. "Chancery in Massachu-
     setts." Law Quarterly Review, 5 (1889),
370-386.
     1628-1877.

1867 WOODS, AMY. "Shipwrecks along the New Eng-
     land coast." CCAPL, 6 (September, 1922),
11-15.

1868 WOODSON, CARTER G. "The relations of Negroes
     and Indians in Massachusetts." JNegroHist,
5 (1920), 45-57.

1869 WOODWARD, WILLIAM. History of the Massachu-
     setts savings banks. N.Y.: Homans, 1889.
Pp. 39. MB.

1870 WORCESTER BAPTIST ASSOCIATION, WORCESTER,
     MASS. Minutes of the Worcester Baptist Asso-
ciation at its fiftieth anniversary held with the
First Baptist Church in Worcester...with the semi-
centennial discourse. Worcester: Tyler & Seagrave, 1869. Pp. 46. MB.
     Churches are in several counties; not limit-
ed to Worcester and vicinity.

1871 WORTHINGTON, CHARLES. "The industrial trend
     of New England." SWJ, 37 (1925), 163-176.
Limited to Massachusetts, 1899-1924.

1872 WORTHLEY, HAROLD FIELD. "An historical es-
     say: the Massachusetts Convention of Con-
gregational Ministers." UHSP, 12, Pt. 1 (1958),
47-103.

1873 _____. An inventory of the records of the
     particular (Congregational) churches of
Massachusetts gathered 1620-1805. Cambridge: Harvard Univ. Pr., 1970. Pp. xiv, 716.

1874 WRIGHT, CARROLL DAVIDSON. Comparative wages
     and prices 1860-1883: Massachusetts and
Great Britain. Boston: Wright & Potter, 1885.
Pp. 57. MB.

1875 WRIGHT, CHARLES BAKER. Gleanings from Fore-
     fathers', a memorial souvenir. Middlebury,
Vt.: Middlebury Historical Society, 1926.
Pp. xvi, 96.
Pilgrim Fathers.

1876 WRIGHT, CONRAD. The beginnings of Unitari-
     anism in America. Boston: Starr King Pr.,
1955. Pp. 305.

1877 WRIGHT, HARRY ANDREW. The story of western
     Massachusetts. N.Y.: Lewis Historical Pub-
lishing, 1949. 4v.
Includes biography.

1878 _____. "Those human Puritans." AASP, 50 (1940), 80-90.

1879 WRITERS' PROGRAM. MASSACHUSETTS. The origin of Massachusetts place names of the state, counties, cities, and towns. N.Y.: Harian Publications, 1941. Pp. vi, 55.

1880 WROTH, L. KINVIN. "The Massachusetts Vice Admiralty Court and the Federal Admiralty Jurisdiction." AmJLegalHist, 6 (1962), 250-268, 347-367.
Eighteenth century.

1881 WURZBACH, CARL. "On the Massachusetts silver colonial coinage." Numismatic Review, 1 (June, 1943), 11-12.

1882 WYMAN, THEODORE C. "'Naushon' and 'New Bedford' at war." Steamboat Bill, 30 (1973), 200-203.
Steamships, World War II.

1883 YOUNG, ALEXANDER. Chronicles of the first planters of the colony of Massachusetts Bay, from 1623 to 1636. Boston: C. C. Little and J. Brown, 1846. Pp. viii, 571.

1884 _____. Chronicles of the Pilgrim Fathers of the colony of Plymouth, from 1602 to 1625. (1841) 2d. ed. Boston: C. C. Little and J. Brown, 1844. Pp. xvi, 502.

1885 YOUNG, BENJAMIN LORING. "Martin Lomasney as I knew him." MHSP, 75 (1963), 52-65.
Politics, early 20th century.

1886 YOUNT, HUBERT WILLIAM and RUTH EVELYN SHERBURNE. The cost of government in Massachusetts, 1910-1926. Amherst, [Agricultural Experiment Station], 1929. Pp. [168]-234.

1887 ZANGER, JULES. "Crime and punishment in early Massachusetts." WMQ, 3 Ser., 22 (1965), 471-477.

1888 ZEMSKY, ROBERT M. Merchants, farmers, and river gods; an essay on eighteenth-century American politics. Boston: Gambit, 1971. Pp. xiii, 361.

1889 _____. "Power, influence and status: leadership patterns in the Massachusetts Assembly, 1740-1755." WMQ, 3 Ser., 26 (1969), 502-520.

1890 ZILVERSMIT, ARTHUR. "Quok Walker, Mumbet and the abolition of slavery in Massachusetts." WMQ, 3 Ser., 25 (1968), 614-624.

1891 ZIMMERMAN, JOSEPH FRANCIS. "The executive veto in Massachusetts, 1947-1960." Social Science, 37 (1962), 162-168.

1892 _____. The Massachusetts town meeting; a tenacious institution. Albany: Graduate School of Public Affairs, State Univ. of New York, 1967. Pp. vii, 137.

1893 _____. "Rationale of veto use in Massachusetts." Social Science, 39 (1964), 204-207.
1939-1963.

1894 ZORN, ROMAN J. "The New England Anti-Slavery Society: pioneer abolition organization." JNegroHist, 42 (1957), 157-176.
Became Massachusetts Anti-Slavery Society in 1835.

1895 ZORNOW, WILLIAM FRANK. "Massachusetts tariff policies, 1775-1789." EIHC, 90 (1954), 194-215.

1896 ZUCKERMAN, MICHAEL. "The social context of democracy in Massachusetts." WMQ, 3 Ser., 25 (1968), 523-544.
Seventeenth and eighteenth centuries.

BARNSTABLE COUNTY

1897   ABOUT Cape Cod.... Boston: Thomas Todd,
        1936. Pp. 128.

1898   ACKERMAN, JOHN H. "The Cape Cod Canal."
        AHI, 1 (November, 1966), 32-39.

1899   ALEXANDER, LEWIS M. "The impact of tourism
        on the economy of Cape Cod, Massachusetts."
Economic Geography, 29 (1953), 320-326.
        1920-1950.

1900   ALLEN, EVERETT S. This quiet place; a Cape
        Cod chronicle. Boston: Little, Brown, 1971.
Pp. 280.
        Social life and customs.

1901   ALLEN, MERCY PAINE. "On Queen Anne Road."
        CCAPL, 5 (September, 1921), 11.

1902   ASHLEY, BURTON M. "Old Cape Cod fence
        posts." OTNE, 14 (1923-1924), 21-28.

1903   ASHLEY, ROBERT PAUL. "A canal, after 300
        years." The Cape, 2 (June, 1968), 23-28.
        Cape Cod Canal.

1904   ____. "The Cape Cod cottage." The Cape,
        2 (January, 1968), 9-12, 18-19.

1905   ____. "Cape Cod's other canal." The Cape,
        1 (June, 1967), 9-12.
        As conceived by Myles Standish in 1627.

1906   BANGS, MARY ROGERS. Old Cape Cod; the land:
        the men, the sea. (1920) New ed., rev. and
enl. Boston: Houghton Mifflin, 1931. Pp. 309.

1907   "THE BEAUTY of a Cape Cod house." Cape Cod
        Magazine, 8 (April, 1926), 7-8.

1908   BELL, ARTHUR WELLINGTON. Cape Cod color; be-
        ing a pot-pourri of promiscuous paragraphs
concerning fish, flesh, and fowl, with a few stray
observations upon flowers, fruits, and institutions
on the Cape. Boston: Houghton Mifflin, 1931.
Pp. x, 170.

1909   BELL, JOHN. "We are going to have a rail-
        road!" CCC, 25 (1972), 44-45, 85-86.
        Cape Cod Railroad.

1910   BERCHEN, WILLIAM and MONICA DICKENS. Cape
        Cod. N.Y.: Viking Pr., 1972. Pp. 94.
        Social life and customs.

1911   [BERGER, JOSEF]. Cape Cod pilot; Federal
        Writers' Project, Works Progress Administra-
tion for the State of Massachusetts, by Jeremiah
Digges, pseud. Provincetown: Modern Pilgrim Pr.,
1937. Pp. 403.

1912   BESTON, HENRY. The outermost house: a year
        of life on the great beach of Cape Cod.
N.Y.: Doubleday, Doran, 1928. Pp. xv, 222.

1913   BOICOURT, JANE. "Antiques on Cape Cod."
        Antiques, 61 (1952), 530-533.

1914   BRADFORD, GERSHOM. "Old days are typified
        by old houses." Cape Cod Magazine, 7 (De-
cember, 1923), 8-9.

1915   BRAY, MARY M. "Cape Cod myths and tradi-
        tions." Cape Cod Magazine, 1 (September,
1915), 27-28.

1916   BROWNSON, LYDIA BURGESS. "Cape Cod colonial
        furniture." CCAPL, 5 (June, 1921), 7-9,
(September, 1921), 7-10; 6 (April, 1922), 5-6.

1917   BUMSTED, JOHN M. "A caution to erring Chris-
        tians: ecclesiastical disorder on Cape Cod,
1717 to 1738." WMQ, 3 Ser., 28 (1971), 413-438.

1918   BURBANK, GEORGE EVERETT. "A history of the
        Cape Cod Canal." Cape Cod Magazine, 1
(March, 1916), 9-15.

1919   BURNETT, WANDA. "Cape Cod people and
        places." National Geographic Magazine, 89
(1946), 737-774.

1920   CAHOON, ROBERT H. "The old salt works."
        CCAPL, 6 (May, 1922), 13-14.

1921   ____. "Shipwrecks on the Cape." Cape Cod
        Magazine, 2 (September, 1916), 10-14.

1922   CAPE COD. CHAMBER OF COMMERCE. Ships logs
        and captains' diaries of old Cape Cod. Bos-
ton: Berkeley Pr., 1937. Pp. 36.

1923   "THE CAPE Cod cottage." Architectural Forum,
        90 (February, 1949), 88-94, (March, 1949),
100-106.

1924   "CAPE Cod in the Revolutionary War." Cape
        Cod Magazine, 2 (April, 1917), 12-14.

1925   CAPE COD sea reminiscences. Yarmouthport:
        C. W. Swift, 1913. Pp. 8.

1926   CHAMBERLAIN, NATHAN HENRY. "Sandwich and
        Yarmouth." NEM, New Ser., 1 (1889-1890),
301-315.

1927   CHASE, ALEXANDER B. Old shipmasters....
        Yarmouthport: Swift, 1924. Unpaged.
MBNEH.

1928   "CHRONOLOGY of events in Cape Cod history."
        Cape Cod Magazine, 1 (June, 1915), 29-31,
(July, 1915), 36-38, (September, 1915), 38, (October,
1915), 37-38, (November, 1915), 35-37, (December,
1915), 32-34, (January, 1916), 38-39, (February,
1916), 39, (March, 1916), 37.
        1006-1829.

1929   CLARK, ADMONT G. "Lighting the lower Cape."
        CCC, 23 (1970), 62-63.
        Lighthouses.

1930   CLARK, FRANCIS E. "A Cape Cod northeaster."
        AmNep, 24 (1964), 138-143.
        Storm of March 9-12, 1855.

1931   CONGREGATIONAL CHURCHES IN MASSACHUSETTS.
        BARNSTABLE ASSOCIATION. CONFERENCE. The
Barnstable Conference of Evangelical Congregational
Churches, comprising the constitution of the conference, with a concise history of the churches....
(1846) Yarmouthport: Register Pr., 1866. Pp. 50.

1932 CONNALLY, ERNEST ALLEN. "The Cape Cod house: an introductory study." SocArchHistJ, 19 (1960), 47-56.

1933 CORBETT, SCOTT. Cape Cod's way, an informal history. N.Y: Crowell, 1955. Pp. 310.

1934 _____. The Sea Fox; the adventures of Cape Cod's most colorful rumrunner. N.Y.: Crowell, 1956. Pp. 244.

1935 _____. We chose Cape Cod. N.Y.: Crowell, 1953. Pp. 307.

1936 CRANE, FERGUS. "Cape Cod Canal." Eclectic Magazine, 146 (1906), 277-282.

1937 CROCKER, ARTHUR B. "Old shipmasters of Cape Cod." Cape Cod Magazine, 1 (May, 1915), 18-20.
Biography.

1938 CROSBY, KATHARINE. Blue-water men and other Cape Codders. N.Y.: Macmillan, 1946. Pp. 288.
Descriptions of towns.

1939 _____. The Cape type of house. Yarmouthport: C. W. Swift, 1927. Pp. 6.

1940 _____. "When the first auto drove down the Cape." Cape Cod Magazine, 10 (November, 1926), 5-6, 14-16.
1901, Barnstable to Provincetown.

1941 CROWELL, JOSHUA FREEMAN. Cape Cod byways. Yarmouthport: C. W. Swift, 1935. Pp. 62
MBNEH.

1942 CUSACK, BETTY BUGBEE. Collector's luck; a thousand years at Lewis Bay, Cape Cod. Stoneham: G. R. Barnstead, 1967. Pp. xxiv, 238.

1943 DALTON, JOHN WILFRED. The life savers of Cape Cod. Boston: Barta Pr., 1902. Pp. 152.
United States Life Saving Service.

1944 DARLING, EDWARD and WILLIAM ANTHONY MILLER, JR. Three old timers: Sandwich, Barnstable, Yarmouth, 1639-1939. South Yarmouth: Wayside Studio, 1939. Pp. 47.
Historic houses.

1945 DAY, LOIS. "Cranberries--as old as the Cape itself." CCC, 4 (1949), 36-38.

1946 DE COSTA, BENJAMIN FRANKLIN. Cabo de Baxos; or, the place of Cape Cod in the old cartology.... N.Y.: T. Whitaker, 1881. Pp. 13.

1947 _____. "The first slaves brought into Massachusetts." HistMag, 2 Ser., 2 (1867), 373.

1948 DEYO, SIMEON L., ed. History of Barnstable County, Massachusetts: 1620-1637-1686-1890. N.Y.: H. W. Blake, 1890. Pp. xii, 1010.
Includes biography.

1949 DILLINGHAM, JOHN HOAG. The Society of Friends in Barnstable County, Massachusetts.... N.Y.: H. W. Blake, 1891. Pp. 39.

1950 DOANE, DORIS. A book of Cape Cod houses. Old Greenwich, Conn: Chatham Pr., 1970. Pp. 91.
Domestic architecture.

1951 DRIVER, GEORGE HIBBERT. Cape-scapes. Boston: Chapple, 1930. Pp. 62.
Informal sketches.

1952 EATON, WALTER PRICHARD. Cape Cod, a plain tale of the lure of the Old Colony country for many men of many minds--or, the joys of a vacation between Buzzards Bay and Provincetown. [N.Y.]: Imprinted for the New York, New Haven and Hartford Railroad Company, 1923. Unpaged.

1953 FAWSETT, MARISE. "Salt haying on old Cape Cod." NEG, 10 (Summer, 1968), 25-30.

1954 FISHER, HOPE. Cape Cod thru the centuries. Falmouth: Kendall Printing, n.d. Pp. 23. [MBaC].

1955 "FOLLOWING Thoreau on Cape Cod." MagHist, 21 (1915), 98-104.

1956 FREEMAN, FREDERICK. The history of Cape Cod: the annals of Barnstable County, including the district of Mashpee. Boston: Geo. C. Rand & Avery, 1858-1862. 2v.

1957 FRITZE, HATTIE BLOSSOM. Horse and buggy days on old Cape Cod. Barnstable: Great Marshes Pr., 1966. Pp. x, 197.
Social life and customs.

1958 FULLER, G. W. Historical discourses commemorative of the 50th anniversary of the Barnstable Baptist Association...1881. Boston: G. J. Stiles, 1881. Pp. 24. M.

1959 GIAMBARBA, PAUL. The picture story of Cape Cod, from Iyanough to John F. Kennedy. Centerville: Scrimshaw Pr., 1965. Pp. 63.

1960 HALL, LEMUEL C. "Cape Cod piratical lore." Cape Cod Magazine, 1 (August, 1915), 22-24.

1961 _____. "Cape Cod poets and poetry." CCAPL, 4 (March, 1921), 13-14.

1962 _____. "The cranberry industry." Cape Cod Magazine, 1 (October, 1915), 5-8.

1963 _____. "Legendary discovery of Cape Cod." CCAPL, 4 (June, 1920), 7-8.

1964 _____. "Literary history of Cape Cod." Cape Cod Magazine, 7 (March, 1924), 6-8.

1965 _____. "The portal of the Cape." CCAPL, 6 (June, 1922), 5-7.
Cape Cod Canal.

1966   HALL, WILLIAM. A statement of some of the principle facts, which took place in the Revolutionary War, in and about the county of Barnstable, on Cape Cod. Boston, 1831. Pp. 8.

1967   HATCH, MELLEN C. M. The log of Provincetown and Truro on Cape Cod. Provincetown, 1939 [i.e. 1951]. Pp. 86.

1968   HAWLEY, GIDEON. "Biographical and topographical anecdotes respecting Sandwich and Mashpee." MHSC, 3 (1794), 188-193.

1969   HAY, JOHN. The great beach. Garden City, N.Y.: Doubleday, 1963. Pp. 131.
       Natural history.

1970   _____. Nature's year; the seasons of Cape Cod. Garden City, N.Y.: Doubleday, 1961. Pp. 199.

1971   HEATON, CLAUDE E. "The Indians had a name for it." CCC, 20 (1967), 34-35, 78-79.
       Cape Cod place names.

1972   "HISTORIC Cape Cod Canal." Waterways Magazine, (February, 1931), 7-8, 18-19.

1973   "HISTORIC inns of Cape Cod." The Cape Cod Magazine, (1961), 27.

1974   HOWES, THOMAS PRINCE. Ancient houses. Yarmouthport: C. W. Swift, 1911. Unpaged.
       Dennis and Yarmouth.

1975   HYANNIS, Harwich, Harwichport, East and West Harwich, Cotuit, Osterville, Dennis, Dennisport, East and West Dennis, Yarmouthport, South Yarmouth and Chatham. N.Y.: American Suburbs Co., 1908. Pp. 16.

1976   "INCIDENTS of the Revolution." CCAPL, 4 (June, 1920), 11-13.

1977   "THE INDIANS had a name for it." CCC, 7 (1952), 53-56.
       Cape Cod place names.

1978   JACOBS, WARREN. "The railroad on the Cape." Cape Cod Magazine, 2 (November, 1916), 5-8.

1979   JENSEN, ALBERT C. "Cape Cod forests." American Forests, 65 (August, 1959), 28-29, 47-49.

1980   JOHNSON, JOHN SPERRY. Stories of Cape Cod, by Jack Johnson...A "discovery book," romantic facts of all the Cape Cod towns. Plymouth: Memorial Pr., 1944. Pp. 87.

1981   KELLOGG, MARY. "A Cape Cod house known as the Noah's ark on Meetinghouse Lane." House Beautiful, 59 (1926), 609-613.
       Specific house not identified.

1982   KEYES, LANGLEY CARLETON. Cape Cod passage; a history of the Cape in verse. New Bedford: Reynolds DeWalt, 1969. Pp. 247.

1983   KITTREDGE, HENRY CROCKER. "Cape Cod--Boston packets." CCB, 48 (March, 1937), 5-6, 20, (April, 1937), 25-27, (May, 1937), 23-25, (June 1, 1937), 24-26, (June 15, 1937), 21-23, (July 1, 1937), 26-28.

1984   _____. Cape Cod: its people and their history. (1930) 2d. ed. with a post-epilogue, 1930-1968 by John Hay. Boston: Houghton Mifflin, 1968. Pp. xii, 344.

1985   _____. "The merchant marine of Cape Cod." Harvard Graduates' Magazine, 34 (1926), 331-347.

1986   _____. Mooncussers of Cape Cod. Boston: Houghton Mifflin, 1937. Pp. vi, 226.
       Shipwrecks.

1987   _____. Shipmasters of Cape Cod. Boston: Houghton Mifflin, 1935. Pp. 319.

1988   KOEHLER, MARGARET. "Viking fever!" CCC, 25 (1972), 78-82, 84.
       Norsemen on the Cape?

1989   LAWSON, EVELYN. Theater on Cape Cod. Yarmouth Port: Parnassus Imprints, 1969. Pp. vii, 71.

1990   "THE LEGEND of cranberries." CCB, 48 (December, 1937), 39-40; 49 (January, 1938), 18-19, (February, 1938), 29-31.
       Growth of the industry on Cape Cod.

1991   LEIGHTON, CLARE VERONICA HOPE. Where land meets sea; the tide line of Cape Cod. N.Y.: Rinehart, 1954. Pp. 202.

1992   LEONARD, MARY HALL. "Early history of the Canal route." Cape Cod Magazine, 2 (March, 1917), 18-19.
       Cape Cod Canal.

1993   LINCOLN, JOSEPH CROSBY. Cape Cod yesterdays. Boston: Little, Brown, 1935. Pp. xv, 286.
       Social life and customs.

1994   [LIVERMORE, CHARLES W. and LEANDER CROSBY]. Ye antient wrecke--1626, loss of the Sparrow-Hawk in 1626, remarkable preservation and recent discovery of the wreck. Boston: A. Mudge & Son, 1865. Pp. 44.

1995   MCCUE, JAMES WESTAWAY. Romantic Cape Cod. Harwich: Goss Print, 1941. Unpaged.

1996   MASSACHUSETTS. DEPARTMENT OF LABOR AND INDUSTRIES. Population and resources of Cape Cod: a special report in recognition of the three hundredth anniversary of the settlement of New England. Boston: Wright & Potter, 1922. Pp. 121.
       Statistics and bibliography.

1997   MILLER, J. W. "The Cape Cod Canal." National Geographic Magazine, 26 (1914), 185-190.

1998   MITCHELL, EDWIN VALENTINE. It's an old Cape Cod custom. N.Y.: Vanguard Pr., 1949. Pp. 242.

1999   MITCHELL, F.   "Cape Cod." Century, 4 (1883),
        643-658.

2000   PAINE, GUSTAVUS SWIFT.   "Ungodly carriages
        on Cape Cod." NEQ, 25 (1952), 181-198.
        Calvinist-Unitarian controversy between Na-
        thaniel Stone and Samuel Osborn, 1718-1738.

2001   PAINE, JOSIAH. Eastham and Orleans histori-
        cal papers. Yarmouthport: C. W. Swift,
        1914. Pp. 29.

2002   PALFREY, JOHN GORHAM. A discourse pro-
        nounced at Barnstable on the third of Sep-
        tember, 1839, at the celebration of the second cen-
        tennial anniversary of the settlement of Cape Cod.
        Boston: Ferdinand Andrews, 1840. Pp. 50.

2003   PERRY, EZRA G. A trip around Cape Cod; our
        summer land and memories of my childhood.
        Boston: C. S. Binner, [1895?]. Pp. 188.

2004   POHL, FREDERICK JULIUS. The Vikings on Cape
        Cod; evidence from archaeological discovery.
        Pictou, Nova Scotia: Pictou Advocate Pr., 1957.
        Pp. 63.

2005   PRATT, AMBROSE E.   "The Barnstable County
        Fair." Cape Cod Magazine, 1 (September
        1915), 5-7, 38.

2006   PRATT, ENOCH. "Complete list of the Congre-
        gational ministers in the county of Barn-
        stable, Ms. from the settlement of the country to
        1842." American Quarterly Register, 15 (1842-1843),
        58-72.
              Gives information relating to birth, educa-
              tion, settlement, resignation and death.

2007   _____. A comprehensive history, ecclesiasti-
        cal and civil, of Eastham, Wellfleet and Or-
        leans, county of Barnstable, Mass., from 1644 to
        1844. Yarmouth: W. S. Fisher, 1844. Pp. viii,
        180.

2008   QUINN, WILLIAM P. Shipwrecks around Cape
        Cod: a collection of photographs, and data
        covering the period from the late 1800's to 1973
        on Cape Cod. Farmington, Me.: Knowlton & McLeary,
        1973. Pp. 239.

2009   RALEIGH, CHARLES S. "The wreck: a remark-
        able description of a marine disaster, il-
        lustrated in painting." Cape Cod Magazine, 1 (Sep-
        tember, 1915), 9-13.

2010   REID, WILLIAM JAMES. The building of the
        Cape Cod Canal, 1627-1914. [N.Y.?], 1961.
        Pp. xv, 131.

2011   _____. "The military value of the Cape Cod
        Canal." U. S. Naval Institute. Proceedings,
        91 (1965), 82-91.

2012   RICH, WILLIAM T. "Early Indian history."
        Cape Cod Magazine, 3 (September 1917), 25-
        27.

2013   ROGERS, FRED B. "'Pox Acres' on old Cape
        Cod." NEJMed, 278 (1968), 21-23.
        Title refers to isolated burial plots for
        smallpox victims.

2014   [ROTHERY, AGNES EDWARDS]. Cape Cod, new &
        old, by Agnes Edwards, pseud. Boston:
        Houghton Mifflin, 1918. Pp. xvi, 239.

2015   RYDER, MARION DAYTON CROWELL. Cape Cod re-
        membrances. Taunton: W. S. Sullwold, 1972.
        Pp. 128.

2016   SAGENDORPH, ROBB. "Authentic Cape Cod
        houses." CCC, 18 (1965), 40-43, 98.

2017   SANDWICH, MASS. Sandwich and Bourne, colony
        and town records. C. W. Swift, ed. Yar-
        mouthport: C. W. Swift, 1910. Unpaged.

2017   _____. Two hundred and fiftieth anniversary
        celebration of Sandwich and Bourne, at Sand-
        wich, Massachusetts, September 3, 1889. Ambrose E.
        Pratt, comp. Falmouth: Local Publishing and Print-
        ing Co., 1890. Pp. 131.

2019   [SCAIFE, ROGER LIVINGSTON]. Cape Coddities,
        by Dennis and Marion Chatham, pseud. Boston:
        Houghton Mifflin, 1920. Pp. 164.
        Essays.

2020   SETZER, DOROTHEA. "Cape Cod taverns." CCC,
        10 (1956), 29-33.

2021   SHAY, EDITH FOLEY and FRANK SHAY, eds. Sand
        in their shoes; a Cape Cod reader. Boston:
        Houghton Mifflin, 1951. Pp. xvi, 364.

2022   SHERMAN, BRADFORD. Souvenir; a letter from
        Cape Cod.... Orleans, 1913. Pp. 39.
        Historical sketch in the form of a letter.

2023   SHOEMAKER, ELISABETH, ed. Cape Cod legends.
        Boston: Berkeley Pr., 1935. Pp. 43.

2024   SMALL, ISAAC MORTON. Just a little about the
        lower Cape, from Provincetown to Brewster and
        the journey of the Mayflower Pilgrims. Truro, 1926.
        Pp. 71. [MHarB].

2025   _____. Shipwrecks on Cape Cod, the story of
        a few. North Truro, 1912. Pp. 48. MWA.

2026   SMITH EDWARD LEODORE. The ancient Nawsett of
        Plymouth Colony, now Eastham, Wellfleet and
        Orleans. n.p., 1914. Unpaged. MWA.

2027   SMITH, WILLIAM CHRISTOPHER. "Cape Cod wind-
        mills." Cape Cod Magazine, 6 (December,
        1922), 11.

2028   SNOW, EDWARD ROWE. A Pilgrim returns to Cape
        Cod. Boston: Yankee Publishing, 1946.
        Pp. 413.

2029   SPRAGUE, FRANCIS WILLIAM. Barnstable and
        Yarmouth sea captains and ship owners. Bos-
        ton: T. R. Marvin & Son, 1913. Pp. 52.

2030 SWIFT, CHARLES FRANCIS. Cape Cod, the right arm of Massachusetts, an historical narrative.... Yarmouth: Register Publishing, 1897. Pp. 391.

2031 _____. History of old Yarmouth, comprising the present towns of Yarmouth and Dennis, from the settlement to the division in 1794 with the history of both towns to these times. Yarmouth Port, 1884. Pp. 281.

2032 TABER, GLADYS BAGG. My own Cape Cod. Philadelphia: Lippincott, 1971. Pp. 251.

2033 TARBELL, ARTHUR WILSON. I retire to Cape Cod. N.Y.: S. Daye, 1944. Pp. xiv, 143.

2034 THOREAU, HENRY DAVID. Cape Cod. Dudley C. Lunt, ed. N.Y.: Norton, 1951. Pp. 300.

2035 _____. Guide to Cape Cod, based on Cape Cod. Alexander B. Adams, ed. N.Y.: Devin-Adair, 1962. Pp. x, 148.

2036 _____. Thoreau's Cape Cod. Thea Wheelwright, ed. Barre: Barre Publishers, 1971. Pp. xxviii, 102.

2037 TOWNE, SUMNER A., JR. "The legend of the Cape Cod half house." CCC, 22 (1969), 92-94.

2038 TREAT, LUCY E. "Along the Pamet trail." CCAPL, 4 (August, 1920), 14-15. Pamet and Nauset Indians.

2039 _____. "Early wrecks on Cape Cod." CCAPL, 5 (September, 1921), 12-14. Shipwrecks.

2040 _____. "Later wrecks on Cape Cod." CCAPL, 5 (November, 1921), 13-14. Shipwrecks.

2041 TRIPP, THOMAS A. Cape Cod and Buzzards Bay: reminders memories, contacts. N.Y.: Newcomen Society of England, American Branch, 1948. Pp. 32.

2042 VAN CLEEF, EUGENE. "The Finns on Cape Cod." NEQ, 6 (1933), 597-601.

2043 VUILLEUMIER, MARION. Churches on Cape Cod. Taunton: William S. Sullwold, 1974. Pp. 128.

2044 _____. Earning a living on olde Cape Cod. Craigville: Craigville Pr., 1968. Pp. 80. Industry.

2045 _____. Indians on olde Cape Cod. Taunton: W. S. Sullwold Pub., 1970. Pp. 96.

2046 _____. Sketches of old Cape Cod. Taunton: W. S. Sullwold, 1972. Pp. 96. Primarily historic houses.

2047 WADLIN, HORACE GREELEY. Social and industrial changes in the county of Barnstable. Boston, 1897. Pp. vii, 104. MB.

2048 WATERHOUSE, DOROTHY. "Old wallpapers of Cape Cod." CCC, 9 (1954), 50-56.

2049 WING, DANIEL. Old Cape Cod windmills. Yarmouthport: Swift, 1925. Pp. 15. MB.

2050 WISBEY, HERBERT A., JR. "Thoreau's last visit to Cape Cod." The South Shore and Cape Cod Magazine, (Season 1959), [7-8].

2051 YARMOUTH, MASS. The celebration of the two hundred and fiftieth anniversary of the founding of old Yarmouth, Mass., including the present towns of Yarmouth and Dennis. September 1 and 3, 1889. Yarmouth, 1889. Pp. 147.

BERKSHIRE COUNTY

2052 ALLEN, THOMAS. An historical sketch of the county of Berkshire, and town of Pittsfield. Boston: Belcher and Armstrong, 1808. Pp. 14.

2053 "ANOTHER distinction for Berkshire County, first wood pulp in America made in Curtisville, and first wood pulp paper at Lee." Berkshire Hills, 3 (1902-1903), 44-45. Stockbridge and Lee.

2054 ASHE, SYDNEY WHITMORE. Pioneer paper makers of Berkshire: reprint of a radio talk given by Sydney Whitmore Ashe over station WGY, Schnectady, 26 September 1928. Dalton, 1928. 9 leaves.

2055 BERKSHIRE ASSOCIATION OF CONGREGATIONAL MINISTERS. Proceedings at the centennial commemmoration of the organization of the Berkshire Association of Congregational Ministers, held at Stockbridge, Mass., October 28, 1863. Boston: J. E. Farwell, 1864. Pp. 56. Historical address by Albert Hopkins.

2056 "BERKSHIRE brass bands." Berkshire Hills, 1 (March 1, 1901), [1-5], (April 1, 1901), [1-7].

2057 BERKSHIRE COUNTY BIBLE SOCIETY. Proceedings of the Berkshire County Bible Society, at its fiftieth anniversary held at Lenox, January 9, 1867. Boston: T. R. Marvin & Son, 1867. Pp. 31. M.

2058 THE BERKSHIRE jubilee, celebrated at Pittsfield, Mass., August 22 and 23, 1844. Albany: W. C. Little, 1845. Pp. 244.

2059 BERKSHIRE LIFE INSURANCE COMPANY, PITTSFIELD, MASS. Drives and walks, Pittsfield and vicinity. Pittsfield, n.d. Pp. 74.

2060 "BERKSHIRE 150 years ago, the conflict of the pioneers with the red men." Berkshire Hills, 3 (1902-1903), 123-126.

2061 "BERKSHIRE organizations: the cradle of illustrated newspapers, local news and personal mention." Berkshire Hills, 4 (1903-1904), 184-185.

2062 "BERKSHIRE telegraphic sketch." Berkshire
Hills, 3 (1902-1903), 45-48.
Telegraphy in northern and central areas of
the county.

2063 "BERKSHIRE traditions: literary inspiration
in New England hills." MagHist, 6 (1907),
330-336.
Intellectual life.

2064 "BERKSHIRE'S old orchards." Berkshire Hills,
3 (1902-1903), 84.
Apple orchards, 1815-1860.

2065 "BERKSHIRE'S old 'underground railroads,'
recollections of men conductors and engineers." Berkshire Hills, 1 (January 1, 1901), [7].
Slavery.

2066 "BERKSHIRE'S two governors." Berkshire
Hills, 1 (August 1, 1901), [5-6].
George Nixon Briggs and Winthrop Murray
Crane.

2067 BIOGRAPHICAL review...containing life
sketches of leading citizens of Berkshire
County, Massachusetts.... Boston: Biographical Review Publishing Co., 1899. Pp. 596.

2068 BIRD, FRANICS WILLIAM. The last agony of
the great bore. 2d ed. Boston: E. P. Dutton, 1868. Pp. 96.
Hoosac Tunnel.

2069 _____. The road to ruin; or, the decline
and fall of the Hoosac Tunnel. Boston:
Wright & Potter, 1862. Pp. 44.

2070 BIRDSALL, RICHARD DAVENPORT. Berkshire Coun-
ty: a cultural history. New Haven: Yale
Univ. Pr., 1959. Pp. 401.
Intellectual life.

2071 _____. "Berkshire's golden age." AmQ, 8
(1956), 328-355.
Intellectual life, 1840s and 1850s.

2072 _____. "Country gentlemen of the Berkshires." NEG, 3 (Summer, 1961), 16-25.
Biography.

2073 _____. "The first century of Berkshire County." BPLQ, 9 (1957), 20-39.

2074 BOUTON, EUGENE. Berkshire County. Pittsfield: Pittsfield Public Schools, 1904.
Pp. 112. MPB.

2075 BROWN, RAYMOND H. "The Housatonic Indians:
the aboriginal inhabitants of southern Berkshire County." MASB, 19 (1957-1958), 44-50.

2076 BRYAN, CLARK W. The book of Berkshire, describing and illustrating its hills and .c.
homes. Great Barrington, 1886. Pp. 292.

2077 [_____]. A new book of Berkshire, which
gives the history of the past, and forecasts
the bright and glowing future of Berkshire's hills
and homes.... Springfield, 1890. Pp. 324.

2078 "'CHESHIRE Harbor' and 'New State:' queer
names given to Berkshire localities by the
pioneers." Berkshire Hills, 3 (1902-1903), 88.

2079 CHILD, HAMILTON, comp. Gazetteer of Berkshire county, Mass., 1725-1885. Syracuse:
Journal Office, 1885. 2 v. in 1.

2080 COOKE, ROLLIN HILLYER, ed. Historic homes
and institutions and genealogical and personal memoirs of Berkshire County, Massachusetts.
N.Y.: Lewis Publishing, 1906. 2v.
Biography.

2081 CUMMINGS, OSMOND RICHARD. "A history of the
Berkshire Street Railway." Transportation
Bulletin, No. 79 (January-December, 1972), entire
issue.

2082 CUTLER, JAMES TUCKER. "The literary associations of Berkshire." NEM, New Ser., 9
(1893-1894), 3-22.

2083 "EARLY Superior Court history: origin in
Berkshire County." Berkshire Hills, New
Ser., 2 (1905-1906), 134.

2084 EATON, WALTER PRICHARD. "The Berkshires:
old style." American Mercury, 22 (1931),
323-329.
1840-1860.

2085 _____. In Berkshire fields. N.Y.: Harper &
Bros., 1920. Pp. xiii, 312.
Natural history.

2086 EGGLESTON, NATHANIEL HILLYER. "Centennial
anniversary of the Berkshire Association."
CongQ, 6 (1864), 142-147.
Ministerial associations.

2087 _____. "The story of Hoosac Tunnel." Atlantic, 49 (1882), 289-304.

2088 "FAMOUS Berkshire hotels and their proprietors." Berkshire Magazine, 1 (January,
1907), 7-11.

2089 FEDERAL WRITERS' PROJECT. MASSACHUSETTS.
The Berkshire hills. N.Y.: Funk & Wagnalls,
1939. Pp. xiv, 368.

2090 FERRY, J. C. Berkshire hills: a description
of the thirty-two towns of Massachusetts'
most western county. Pittsfield: Sun Printing,
1886. Pp. 24. M.

2091 [FIELD, DAVID DUDLEY and CHESTER DEWEY], eds.
A history of the county of Berkshire, Massachusetts; in two parts. The first being a general
view of the county; the second, an account of the
several towns. By gentlemen in the county, clergymen and laymen. Pittsfield: S. W. Bush, 1829.
Pp. iv, 468.

2092 "THE FOUR Pontoosuck settlement forts."
Berkshire Hills, 4 (1903-1904), 234-235.
Fort Anson, Fort Goodrich, Fort Fairfield,
and Fort Ashley.

2093 [FRASER, JOHN H.]. Berkshire county.... Chicago: Parish, 1893. 20 leaves. Author attribution by Princeton University Library.

2094 GARDNER, FRANK A. "Colonel John Patterson's Regiment." MassMag, 8 (1915), 27-42, 75-83. Revolutionary; biography.

2095 GLADDEN, WASHINGTON. "Hoosac Tunnel." Scribner's Monthly, 1 (1870-1871), 143-159.

2096 "GOLD hunting in Berkshire." Berkshire Hills, 2 (June 1, 1902), [1-4].
1785-1902.

2097 GRINNELL, FRANK WASHBURN. "The influence of Thomas Allen and the Berkshire Constitutionalists on the constitutional history of the United States." ABAJ, 22 (1936), 168-174, 210-211.

2098 HARRISON, CONSTANCE CARY. "American rural festivals." Century Magazine, 50 (1895), 323-33.
Lenox and Stockbridge.

2099 HARRISON, JOSEPH LE ROY. The great bore; a souvenir of the Hoosac Tunnel. A history of the tunnel, with sketches of North Adams, its vicinity and drives; Williamstown and Mount Greylock. North Adams: Advance Job Print Works, 1891. Pp. 74.

2100 HIBBARD, FREEBORN. "Methodism in Berkshire, seventy years ago." Berkshire Hills, 1 (January 1, 1901), [5].

2101 "HISTORICAL Berkshire homes." Berkshire Hills, 1 (June 1, 1901), [12].

2102 HISTORY of Berkshire County, Massachusetts, with biographical sketches of its prominent men.... Thomas Cushing and Joseph E. A. Smith, eds. N.Y.: J. B. Beers, 1885. 2 v. in 1.

2103 HISTORY of the Hoosac tunnel.... Boston: E. S. Martin, 1880. Unpaged.

2104 HOOPER, JOSEPH. "The Protestant Episcopal Church in Berkshire." BHSSC, 1, Pt. 3 (1890), 185-212.

2105 "HOOSAC Tunnel centennial, 1873-1973." B & M Bulletin, 3 (September, 1973), entire issue.

2106 "HOOSAC Tunnel happenings." Berkshire Hills, New Ser. 1 (1904-1905), 21-24, 41-46, 61, 70; 2 (1905-1906), 109-117, 129-134, 149-153.
1819-1905.

2107 HORWITT, PINK and BERTHA SKOLE. Jews in Berkshire County. Williamstown: DOR, 1972. Pp. viii, 74.

2108 HOUSATONIC RAILROAD COMPANY. Ye olde Berkshire hills. N.Y.: American Bank Note Co., 1891. Pp. 105.

2109 HYDE, ALEXANDER. "Social life and customs of the early citizens of Berkshire. " BHSSC, 3 (1889-1913), 29-49.

2110 JARVIE, JEAN. Stories from our hills. North Adams: Excelsior Printing, 1926. Pp. 143.

2111 KEITH, H. F. "The early roads and settlements of Berkshire west of Stockbridge and Shefffield." BHSSC, 1, Pt. 1 (1886), 118-135.

2112 KELLOGG, ENSIGN HOMER. Address delivered before the Association of the Manufacturers of Berkshire County, at their first meeting in Pittsfield, Feb. 22, 1855, with an account of the introduction of woolen manufacture into the county, by Thaddeus Clapp, 3d, and a report of other proceedings of the day. Pittsfield: Chickering & Marsh, 1855. Pp. 34.

2113 KIRKLAND, EDWARD CHASE. "The Hoosac Tunnel route: the great bore." NEQ, 20 (1947), 88-113.

2114 LAWRENCE, ARTHUR. "Origin of the name Berkshire." BHSSC 2, Pt. 2 (1895), 79-80.

2115 MCCARRY, CHARLES. "Home to the enduring Berkshires." National Geographic, 138 (1970), 196-221.

2116 MARTIN, EDWARD S. History of the Hoosac Tunnel. North Adams: E. D. Angell, 1877. Pp. 21.

2117 "MASONIC history, American origin in Massachusetts: five blue lodges in Berkshire in the seventeenth century." Berkshire Hills, 1 (February 1, 1901), [1-3].

2118 MULLANY, KATHERINE FRANCES. Catholic Pittsfield and Berkshire. Pittsfield: Sun Printing, 1897-1924. 2v.
Vol. 2 has imprint: Pittsfield: Eagle Printing and Binding.

2119 NEWDICK, EDWIN W. "A new chapter in Hoosac Tunnel history." WNE, 1 (1910-1911), 29-36.

2120 "NORTHERN Berkshire masonry." Berkshire Hills, 4 (1903-1904), 273-278.
1794-1904; Freemasons.

2121 "THE OLD church edifices of Berkshire County." Berkshire Hills, 2 (March 1, 1902), [3-4].

2122 "THE OLD 'general trainings,' a sketch of the old military days and some of its characters." Berkshire Hills, 2 (January 1, 1902), [6-7].

2123 "THE OLD Liberty Party of Berkshire." Berkshire Hills, 2 (August 1, 1902), [11].
Anti-slavery.

2124 "THE OLD Masonic lodges of Berkshire." Berkshire Hills, 2 (February 1, 1902), [1-5].

2125 "OLD stage lines in northern Berkshire." Berkshire Hills, 1 (July 1, 1901), [3-4].

2126 PALMER, CHARLES JAMES. Berkshire County:
its past history and achievements. n.p.,
[1902?]. Pp. 24.
Includes origins of place names.

2127 _____. History of Lenox and Richmond.
Pittsfield: Sun Printing, 1904. Pp. 48

2128 PARKER, S. P. "History of Episcopal Church
in Berkshire County." BHSSC, 2, Pt. 2
(1895), 83-92.

2129 PARSONS, HERBERT COLLINS. "Hoosac Tunnel."
PVMA, 4 (1899-1904), 176-191.

2130 PEATTIE, RODERICK, ed. The Berkshires: the
purple hills. N.Y.: Vanguard Pr., 1948.
Pp. 414.
Anthology.

2131 PEIRSON, JOSEPH EDWARD. Historical scenes
in the Berkshire Hills, from Connecticut to
Vermont and over the Mohawk Trail. W. S. Weld,
comp. Pittsfield: Berkshire Life Insurance Co.,
1919. Unpaged.

2132 PETERSON, BERNARD. "Industrial jewels of
the Berkshires." Industry, 12 (October,
1946), 17-20, 42, 44, 46, 48, 50, 52, 54, 56, 58.
Adams and North Adams; industry.

2133 PHILLIPS, W. H. "Early recollections of
Berkshire County." Berkshire Hills, New
Ser., 2 (1905-1906), 103-104.
Nineteenth century.

2134 "PIONEER colored folks of Berkshire, mostly
fugitives from slavery." Berkshire Hills, 3
(1902-1903), 101-104.
Biography.

2135 "PIONEER picture takers in Pittsfield and
North Adams." Berkshire Hills, New Ser., 2
(1905-1906), 105-106.
1850s and 1860s.

2136 "POLITICAL campaign of 1856: lively recol-
lections of gatherings and flag raisings in
Great Barrington and Alford." Berkshire Hills, New
Ser., 1 (1904-1905), 35-36.

2137 PRESSEY, EDWARD PEARSON. "Hoosac Tunnel's
troubled story." NEM, New Ser., 26 (1902),
117-128.

2138 RAMSDELL, ROGER WEARNE. An architectural
monograph; wooden architecture in the Berkshires. St. Paul: White Pine Bureau, 1924.
Pp. 16.

2139 "RECOLLECTIONS of the log cabin campaign of
1840." Berkshire Hills, 3 (1902-1903), 120.
Harrison-Tyler election.

2140 "REMINISCENCES of the Hoosac Tunnel: demolition of rocky fastnesses with nitro-glycer-
ine." Berkshire Hills, 4 (1903-1904), 172-174.

2141 "REMINISCENT stories from southern Berkshire." Berkshire Hills, New Ser., 2
(1905-1906), 154-156.
Social life and customs.

2142 "A REVOLUTIONARY event: routes of the Burgoyne prisoners through Berkshire." Berkshire Hills, 1 (January 1, 1901), [6].

2143 RICHMOND, CLINTON Q. "Adams and North Adams." NEM, New Ser., 21 (1899-1900), 161-
181.

2144 "ROUGH times in Berkshire: sketch of Rev.
Billy Hibbard and his account of Shays' Re-
bellion--the cause of the uprising, its history and
the final battle at Sheffield." Berkshire Hills, 3
(1902-1903), 23-24.

2145 ROWE, HENRY G. and CHARLES T. FAIRFIELD, eds.
North Adams and vicinity illustrated, an illustrated book of North Adams, Adams and Williamstown, Massachusetts, their industries, past and present.... North Adams: Transcript Publishing, 1898.
Pp. 140.

2146 SEDGWICK, HENRY DWIGHT. "Reminiscences of
literary Berkshire." Century Magazine, 50
(1895), 552-568.

2147 _____. "The Sedgwicks of Berkshire."
BHSSC, 3 (1899-1913), 91-105.

2148 SLEEPER, ELIZABETH ALVENA HARDING. Among the
Berkshire Hills: an unconventional trio.
n.p., 1894. Pp. 40.

2149 SMITH, A. M. "Medicine in Berkshire."
BHSSC, 1, Pt. 3 (1890), 115-181.

2150 [SMITH, JOSEPH EDWARD ADAMS]. Taghconic; the
romance & beauty of the hills. (1852) By
Godfrey Greylock, pseud. Boston: Lee & Shepard,
1879. Pp. 381.

2151 [SNELL, RALPH MEEKER]. "Paper making in
Gt. Barrington and Stockbridge." Superior
Facts, 3 (February, 1930) 1-4.
Author attribution by Berkshire Athenaeum.

2152 "SOME Berkshire Tories in the Revolution,
their stubborn allegiance to King George."
Berkshire Hills, 3 (1902-1903), 37-38.
Biography.

2153 "SOME old-time taverns." Berkshire Hills, 1
(June 1, 1901), [1-5]; 2 (September 1, 1901),
[9-11], (December 1, 1901), [1-5].

2154 "SPELLING matches: revival of this popular
old time exercise and amusement in Pittsfield
in 1875--North Adams wins the county championship
and still holds the belt." Berkshire Hills, New
Ser., 1 (1904-1905), 78-79.

2155 SUTTON, HORACE. "The Berkshire story."
Town and Country, 103 (August, 1949), 20-29,
74, 77.
Social life and customs.

2156   TAFT, HENRY W. "Judicial history of Berk-
        shire." BHSSC, 1, Pt. 1 (1886), 89-115.

2157   TAGUE, WILLIAM H., ROBERT B. KIMBALL and
        RICHARD V. HAPPEL. Berkshire, two hundred
years in pictures, 1761-1961. Pittsfield: Berkshire Eagle, 1961. Pp. 113.

2158   TAGUE, WILLIAM H. "The rise and evaporation
        of the Mount Greylock tramway." Berkshire
Review, 3 (Summer, 1967), 4-15.

2159   "TELEGRAPHY in central and southern Berk-
        shire." Berkshire Hills, 3 (1902-1903), 65-
67.

2160   "TROUTING in Berkshire." Berkshire Hills, 3
        (1902-1903), 96.

2161   "THE TWO Berkshire hospitals: the House of
        Mercy at Pittsfield and the Free Hospital at
North Adams." Berkshire Hills, 4 (1903-1904), 145-
148.

2162   "TWO notable Berkshire pastors." Berkshire
        Hills, 4 (1903-1904), 217-218.
        Edward H. Purcell of Pittsfield and Charles
        Lynch of North Adams.

2163   "TWO notable hermits, their retreats in the
        Berkshire solitudes." Berkshire Hills, 4
(1903-1904), 202-203.
        George L. Tichnor of Tyringham and Freder-
        ick Pyncheon of Great Barrington.

2164   WAKEFIELD, ROWAN ALBERT and BARBARA FRANCES
        WAKEFIELD. Sheffield [and] Mt. Washington
in the Berkshires, Massachusetts. Sheffield:
1948. Pp. 31.

2165   WARNER, CHARLES FORBES. Picturesque Berk-
        shire...complete in two parts, with 1200 il-
lustrations. Northampton: Picturesque Publishing,
1893. 2v.

2166   WATSON, ELKANAH. History of the rise, prog-
        ress, and existing state of the Berkshire
Agricultural Society in Massachusetts.... Albany:
E. & E. Hosford, 1819. Pp. 80. MPB.

2167   WESTON, BYRON. "History of paper making in
        Berkshire County." BHSSC, 2, Pt. 2 (1895),
3-23.

2168   WILCOX, D. M. "An episode of Shays's Rebel-
        lion." MagHist, 22 (1916), 100-107.

2169   "THE WOODLANDS of Berkshire, immense drain
        upon the native forests in earlier and later
days and for what purposes." Berkshire Hills, New
Ser., 1 (1904-1905), 32-33.

2170   ZILVERSMIT, ARTHUR. "Mumbet: folklore and
        fact." Berkshire History, 1 (Spring, 1971),
3-14.
        Elizabeth Freeman.

BRISTOL COUNTY

2171   BRAYTON, ISRAEL. "History of the Slade
        lands." Fall River HSP, (1921-1926), 155-
162.

2172   BURGESS, J. H. City of New Bedford, 1914;
        descriptive and pictorial; commemorative of
the 250th anniversary of when Dartmouth became a
town, 1664, New Bedford being a part thereof. Also
a description of the city's beautiful suburb, Fairhaven. [New Bedford, 1914]. Pp. 62.

2173   CRAPO, HENRY HOWLAND. "The villages of Dart-
        mouth in the British raid of 1778." ODHS,
No. 23 (January, 1909), 10-16.
        Dartmouth and New Bedford.

2174   DEVOLL, MRS. DANIEL T. "Past industries of
        upper Acushnet River." ODHS, No. 7 (Septem-
ber, 1904), 5-8.

2175   ELLIS, LEONARD BOLLES. History of New Bed-
        ford and its vicinity, 1602-1892. Syracuse,
N.Y.: D. Mason, 1892. Pp. 731, 175.

2176   GARDNER, FRANK A. "Colonel Timothy Walker's
        regiment." MassMag, 3 (1910), 25-39.
        Revolutionary; biography.

2177   "A HOME for Spouter Inn." Old Dartmouth HSB,
        (Winter, 1954-1955), 1-4.
        Fairhaven and New Bedford hotels and taverns.

2178   HURD, DUANE HAMILTON, ed. History of Bristol
        County, Massachusetts, with biographical
sketches of many of its pioneers and prominent men.
Philadelphia: J. W. Lewis, 1883. Pp. xii, 922.

2179   HUTT, FRANK WALCOTT, ed. A history of Bris-
        tol County, Massachusetts. N.Y.: Lewis
Historical Publishing, 1924. 3v.

2180   LONGLEY, JONATHAN. "Complete list of the
        Congregational ministers in the county of
Bristol, Ms. [to the present time]." American Quarterly Register, 12 (1839-1840), 135-149.
        Gives information relating to birth, educa-
        tion, settlement, resignation and death.

2181   NEW BEDFORD, MASS. CITY COUNCIL. Centennial
        celebration. Proceedings in connection with
the celebration at New Bedford, September 14th,
1864, of the two hundredth anniversary of the incorporation of the town of Dartmouth. New Bedford:
E. Anthony & Sons, 1865. Pp. 129.

2182   NEWMAN, SYLVANUS CHACE. Rehoboth in the
        past. An historical oration delivered on
the Fourth of July, 1860...also an account of the
proceedings in Seekonk, (the ancient Rehoboth,) at
the celebration of the day, completing two hundred
and sixteen years of its history.... Pawtucket,
[R.I.]: Robert Sherman, 1860. Pp. 112.

2183   OUR county and its people; a descriptive and
        biographical record of Bristol County, Massa-
chusetts. [Boston]: Boston History Co., 1899.
Pp. xii, 799, 418.

2184 PEIRCE, EBENEZER WEAVER. Brief sketches of
      Freetown, Fall River, and Fairhaven. Boston:
D. Dudley, 1872. Pp. 25.

2185 RANDALL, GEORGE. "Rehoboth and Attleboro."
      NEM, New Ser., 11 (1894-1895), 225-243.

2186 RICKETSON, DANIEL. The history of New Bed-
      ford, Bristol County, Massachusetts: includ-
ing a history of the old township of Dartmouth and
the present townships of Westport, Dartmouth, and
Fairhaven, from their settlement to the present
time. New Bedford, 1858. Pp. xii, 412.

DUKES COUNTY

2187 ALLEN, JOSEPH CHASE. Tales and trails of
      Martha's Vineyard. Boston: Little, Brown,
1938. Pp. 234.

2188 _____. Vineyard fishing boats: their ori-
      gin and development. [New Bedford, 194-].
Pp. 21.

2189 _____. The wheelhouse loafer: selections
      from Joseph Chase Allen's weekly longshore
log, 'With the fishermen,' from the Vineyard Gazette, 1940-1960 [i.e. 1965]. Colbert Smith, ed.
Boston: Little, Brown, 1966. Pp. xiii, 304.

2190 BANKS, CHARLES EDWARD. "Capowack. Is it the
      correct Indian name of Martha's Vineyard?"
NEHGR, 52 (1898), 176-180.

2191 _____, The history of Martha's Vineyard,
      Dukes County, Massachusetts.... Boston:
G. H. Dean, 1911-1925. 3v.
      Vol. 3 published by Dukes County Historical
      Society.

2192 _____. "Martin's or Martha's? What is the
      proper nomenclature of the Vineyard?"
NEHGR, 48 (1894), 201-104.

2193 BLACKWELL, WALTER. Tracing the route of
      Martha's Vineyard Railroad, 1874-1896. Mi-
ami: Engelhard Printing Co., 1971. Pp. 18.

2194 BROWN, CHARLES H. Let your light shine.
      [New Bedford, 1923]. Pp. 13.
      Early Martha's Vineyard.

2195 BUTLER, WILLIAM. "Martha's Vineyard in
      1792--a diary." DCI, 8 (1966-1967), 23-33.
      Edited by Gale Huntington.

2196 COOPER, THOMAS. "Fabulous traditions and
      customs of the Indians of Martha's Vineyard."
MHSC, 1 (1792), 139-140.

2197 [DEVENS, SAMUEL ADAMS]. Sketches of Mar-
      tha's Vineyard, and other reminiscences of
travel at home, etc. By an inexperienced clergyman. Boston: J. Munroe, 1838. Pp. viii, 207.

2198 DUKES COUNTY, MASS. Dukes County To-Day-
      1915-Historical, Biographical, Statistical.
Edgartown: Vineyard Gazette, 1915. Unpaged. M.

2199 DUKES COUNTY HISTORICAL SOCIETY, EDGARTOWN,
      MASS. Martha's Vineyard, a short history by
various hands, together with a guide to points of
interest. Eleanor R. Mayhew, ed. Edgartown, 1956.
Pp. 160.

2200 EATON, WALTER PRICHARD. Marthas Vineyard, a
      pleasant island in a summer sea, a land of
old towns, new cottages, high cliffs, white sails,
green fairway, salt water, wild fowl, and the steady
pull of an ocean breeze. N.Y.: Kalkhoff Co., 1923.
Unpaged.

2201 EISENTAEDT, ALFRED and HENRY BEETLE HOUGH.
      Martha's Vineyard. N.Y.: Viking Pr., 1970.
Pp. 70.

2202 ELDRIDGE, GEORGE WASHINGTON. "Martha's Vine-
      yard, gem of the North Atlantic." NEM, New
Ser., 40 (1909), 163-179.

2203 _____. Martha's Vineyard: its history and
      advantages as a health and summer resort.
Providence, R.I.: E. L. Freeman & Son, 1889.
Pp. 60.

2204 ELVIN, JOSEPH B. "The passing of an era on
      the Vineyard." DCI, 5 (1963-1964), 84-119.
      Trap fishing.

2205 GANNETT, ALLEN. "A complete list of Congre-
      gational ministers of Dukes County, Mass.,
from the first settlement to the present time: with
accompanying notes, and some account of the mission-
aries to the Indians on Martha's Vineyard." American Quarterly Register, 15 (1842-1843), 492-498.
      Gives information relating to birth, educa-
      tion, settlement, resignation and death.

2206 GARDNER, RUSSELL HERBERT. "My Sanchekan-
      tackett." DCI, 12 (1970-1971), 47-67.
      Algonquin Indian village.

2207 GIFFORD, DORIS COTTLE. "Jonathan Mayhew and
      the missionary Mayhews." DCI, 8 (1966-1967),
50-56.

2208 GOELL, BLANCHE ISABEL. Tramping on Martha's
      Vineyard, a talk originally given before the
Appalachian Mountain Club of Boston and repeated before the Dukes County Historical Society at Edgartown, Massachusetts, October the twenty-ninth,
1925. [Edgartown, 1925]. Pp. 15.

2209 GOOKIN, WARNER FOOTE. Capawack, alias Mar-
      tha's Vineyard. Edgartown: Dukes County
Historical Society, 1947. Pp. 58.

2210 HALLOCK, WILLIAM ALLEN. The venerable May-
      hews, and the aboriginal Indians of Martha's
Vineyard, condensed from Rev. Experience Mayhew's
history printed in London in 1727, and brought down
to the present century. N.Y. American Tract Society, 1874. Pp. 190.

2211 HARE, LLOYD C. M. "An island girlhood one
      hundred years ago." DCI, 5 (August, 1963),
3-33.
      Charlotte Eliza Smith.

2212 HAWTHORNE, NATHANIEL. "Martha's Vineyard." American Magazine of Useful and Entertaining Knowledge, 2 (1836), 341-344.
Includes history from 1641 to end of the Revolution.

2213 HINE, CHARLES GILBERT. The history of Cedar Neck. n.p.: Priv. Print., 1907. Pp. viii, 104.

2214 _____. The story of Martha's Vineyard, from the lips of its inhabitants, newspaper files and those who have visited its shores, including stray notes on local history and industries. N.Y.: Hine Bros., 1908. Pp. v, 224.

2215 HOUGH, DORRIS S. "Some Vineyard authors." DCI, 3 (May, 1962), 14-24.

2216 HOUGH, GEORGE A. Disaster on Devil's Bridge. Mystic, Conn.: Marine Historical Association, 1963. Pp. 146.
Wreck of the 'City of Columbus' off Gay Head.

2217 HOUGH, HENRY BEETLE. "Martha's Vineyard and the theatre." DCI, 8 (1966-1967), 3-9.

2218 _____. Martha's Vineyard, summer resort, 1835-1935. Rutland, Vt.: Tuttle, 1936. Pp. 276.

2219 _____. Singing in the morning, and other essays about Martha's Vineyard. N.Y.: Simon and Schuster, 1951. Pp. xii, 242.

2220 _____. "Transition--approach to a period." DCI, 1 (May, 1960), [3-7].
History based on business directories.

2221 _____. Vineyard Gazette reader. N.Y.: Harcourt, Brace & World, 1967. Pp. 276.

2222 _____. "Vineyard jottings." DCI, 7 (1965-1966), 288-297.
Fragments of island history.

2223 _____. "Years of innocence on Martha's Vineyard." DCI, 2 (February, 1961), [3-12].
Social life and customs.

2224 HUGGINS, LEON M. The two Rogerses: George A., Vineyard whaleman, and Henry H., Standard Oil millionaire. North Tisbury: G. A. Hough, 1909. unpaged.

2225 HUNTINGTON, GALE. "Vinland and the Vineyard." DCI, 15 (1973-1974), 35-48.

2226 JOSEPHS, PETER COLT. "The remarkable brick barns of Martha's Vineyard." DCI, 15 (1973-1974), 99-118.

2227 LEACH, ROBERT J. "Quaker intruders on Martha's Vineyard." DCI, 4 (1962-1963), 55-63.

2228 LORD, ANNIE DAGGETT. "The language of Martha's Vineyard." DCI, 6 (1964-1965), 143-149.
Social life and customs.

2229 "MARTHA'S Vineyard." Saturday Review, 66 (1888), 520-521.

2230 MARTHA'S Vineyard and its attractions.... N.Y.: G. W. Richardson, [1914?]. Pp. 40.

2231 MAYHEW, EXPERIENCE. A discourse showing that God dealeth with men as reasonable creatures, preached at Boston, N.E., Nov. 23, 1718 with a brief account of the State of the Indians on Martha's Vineyard and the small islands adjacent in Dukes County from the year 1694 to 1720. Boston: B. Green for Samuel Gerrish, 1720. Pp. 34, 12. MB.

2232 _____. Indian converts: or, some account of the lives and dying speeches of a considerable number of the Christianized Indians of Martha's Vineyard, in New-England...to which is added, some account of those English ministers who have successively presided over the Indian work in that and the adjacent islands. By [Thomas] Prince. London: Printed for S. Gerrish, bookseller in Boston..., 1727. Pp. xxiv, 310.

2233 MAYHEW, MATTHEW. A brief narrative of the success which the Gospel hath had, among the Indians, of Martha's-Vineyard (and the places adjacent) in New-England. With some remarkable curiosities, concerning the numbers, the customes, and the present circumstances of the Indians on that island. Further explaining [sic] and confirming the account given of those matters, by Mr. Cotton Mather in the life of the renowned Mr. John Eliot, whereto is added, an account concerning the present state of Christianity among the Indians, in other parts of New-England: expressed in the letters of several worthy persons, best acquainted therewithall. Boston: Bartholomew Green, 1694. Pp. 55.

2234 MÉRAS, PHYLLIS. First spring; a Martha's Vineyard journal. Riverside, Conn.: Chatham Pr., 1972. Pp. 143.

2235 MOWRY, WILLIAM AUGUSTUS. "Martha's Vineyard." NEM, New Ser., 16 (1897), 543-560.

2236 _____. The Martha's Vineyard Summer Institute; a brief sketch of its establishment, its progress, its scope, and its present condition. Boston: R. H. Blodgett [1905]. Pp. 44.
For teachers.

2237 NORTON, HENRY FRANKLIN. Martha's Vineyard, historical, legendary, scenic, the story of its towns: Edgartown, Oak Bluffs, Tisbury (Vineyard Haven), West Tisbury, Chilmark, Gay Head. Hartford: H. F. Norton, R. E. Pyne, 1923. Pp. 94.

2238 "THE NOVEMBER gale of 1898." DCI, 12 (1970-1971), 99-105.

2239 OGDEN, J. G. "Forest history of Martha's Vineyard." American Midland Naturalist, 66 (1962), 417-430.

2240 PILLSBURY, A. "The Martha's Vineyard summer institute." NEM, 6 (1887-1888), 3-15.
For teachers.

2241   POOLE, DOROTHY COTTLE. "The lobster industry
       of Martha's Vineyard." DCI, 15 (1973-1974),
59-90.

2242   RIGGS, SIDNEY N. "The Episcopal churches of
       Martha's Vineyard." DCI, 2 (November,
1960), [3-4].

2243   _____. "Vineyard meeting houses." DCI, 2
       (August, 1960), [3-19].

2244   SCOVILLE, DOROTHY RADCLIFFE. Indian legends
       of Martha's Vineyard. Gay Head, 1970.
Pp. 28.

2245   _____. Shipwrecks on Martha's Vineyard.
       Gay Head, 1972. Pp. 64.

2246   SHALER, N. S. "Martha's Vineyard." Atlan-
       tic, 34 (1874), 732-740.

2247   SHEPARD, MARSHALL. "Captain Gosnold and the
       New World." DCI, 13 (1971-1972), 69-90.
       Edited by Harold C. Wilson.

2248   SIMON, ANNE W. No island is an island; the
       ordeal of Martha's Vineyard. Garden City,
N.Y.: Doubleday, 1973. Pp. xiii, 250.
       Threat of progress against forces of preser-
       vation.

2249   SMITH, COLBERT. "Grey's Raid: what hap-
       pened when the British stole the Vineyard's
livestock." CCC, 20 (1967), 10-14.
       Charles Grey, 1778.

2250   "SOME Vineyard newspapers of the past."
       DCI, 11 (1969-1970), 23-40.

2251   STROTHER, D. H. "A summer in New England:
       Martha's Vineyard." Harper's Magazine, 21
(1860), 442-461.

2252   TELLER, WALTER MAGNES. An island summer.
       N.Y.: Knopf, 1951. Pp. 221

2253   THAXTER, JOSEPH. "The hazards of seafaring-
       Martha's Vineyard 1780-1827." DCI, 10 (1968-
1969), 167-171.

2254   TRAVERS, MILTON A. The Wampanoag Indian tri-
       bute tribes of Martha's Vineyard; the story
of the Capowacks of Nope, the Takemmy-Wampanoags,
the Nunpaug-Wampanoags, the Aquinnah-Wampanoags of
Catachukutcho (Gay Head tribe), the Chappaquiddick-
Wampanoags. [New Bedford?], 1960. Pp. 78

2255   VINCENT, HEBRON. "The early settlement of
       Martha's Vineyard." DCI, 4 (November,
1962), 19-28.

2256   "A VISIT to Martha's Vineyard." Atlantic, 4
       (1859), 281-294.

2257   WHITING, EMMA MAYHEW. Vineyard Indian rel-
       ics. Edgartown, 1924. Pp. 8. MB.

2258   _____. and HENRY BEETLE HOUGH. Whaling
       wives. Boston: Houghton Mifflin, 1953.
Pp. xx, 293.

2259   WILSON, HAROLD C. "A faire island for Mar-
       tha." DCI, 10 (1968-1969), 201-207.
       Discovery and naming of Martha's Vineyard and
       surrounding islands by Bartholomew Gosnold,
       1599.

ESSEX COUNTY

2260   ADAMS, HERBERT BAXTER. Village communities
       of Cape Anne and Salem. Baltimore: Johns
Hopkins Univ., 1883. Pp. 81

2261   ALBION, ROBERT GREENHALGH. "From sails to
       spindles: Essex County in transition."
EIHC, 95 (1959), 115-136.
       Commerce and industry.

2262   ALONG the old roads of Cape Ann. Gloucester:
       F. S. & A. H. McKenzie, 1923. Pp. 106.

2263   AMBLER, EDWARD VASSAR. Know Cape Ann, the
       garden spot of the Atlantic. [Beverly?]:
North Shore Pr., 1931. Pp. 88.

2264   "AROUND Cape Ann, Annisquam to Marblehead."
       Century, 23 (1881), 49-57.

2265   ARRINGTON, BENJAMIN F., ed. Municipal his-
       tory of Essex County in Massachusetts....
N.Y.: Lewis Historical Publishing, 1922. 4v.
       Vols. 3 and 4 are biographical.

2266   ATHERTON, HORACE H., JR. Speech of Horace
       Atherton, Jr. upon the 100th anniversary of
the organization of the Essex Agricultural Society.
n.p., 1918. Pp. 12. MSaE.

2267   BABSON, JOHN JAMES. History of the town of
       Gloucester, Cape Ann, including the town of
Rockport. Gloucester: P. Smith, 1972. Pp. lxv,
610.
       Reprint of 1860 edition with new introduction
       and historical review by Joseph E. Garland.

2268   _____. Notes and additions to the history
       of Gloucester. Part first: early settlers.
Gloucester: M. V. B. Perley, 1876. Pp. 94.

2269   _____. Notes and additions to the history
       of Gloucester. Second series, with an appen-
dix containing indexes to parts I and II. Salem:
Salem Pr., 1891. Pp. 187.

2270   BABSON, THOMAS E. "Evolution of Cape Ann
       roads and transportation, 1623-1955." EIHC,
91 (1955), 302-328.

2271   BAILEY, SARAH LORING. Historical sketches of
       Andover, (comprising the present towns of
North Andover and Andover), Massachusetts. Boston:
Houghton Mifflin, 1880. Pp. xxiv, 626.

2272   BALCOMB, FRANK WIPPICH. "One hundred twenty-
       five years of Royal Arch Masonry in Salem and
vicinity." EIHC, 76 (1940), 299-313.

2273 BELKNAP, HENRY WYCKOFF. Artists and crafts-
men of Essex County, Massachusetts. Salem:
Essex Institute, 1927. Pp. viii, 127.
Biography.

2274 ____. Trades and tradesmen of Essex County,
Massachusetts, chiefly of the seventeenth
century. Salem: Essex Institute, 1929. Pp. 96.
Biography.

2275 BENJAMIN, S. G. W. "Gloucester and Cape
Ann." Harper's Magazine, 51 (1875), 465-474.

2276 BENSON, HENRY PERKINS. "Half century of mo-
toring in Essex County." EIHC, 85 (1949),
201-214.

2277 BIOGRAPHICAL review...containing life sketches of leading citizens of Essex County, Massachusetts.... Boston: Biographical Review Publishing, 1898. Pp. 618

2278 BRAGDON, JOSEPH H. Seaboard towns; or, traveller's guide book from Boston to Portland:
containing a description of the cities, towns and
villages, scenery and objects of interest along the
route of the Eastern railroad and its branches, and
the Portland, Saco and Portsmouth railroad, including historical sketches, legends &c.... Newburyport: Moulton & Clark, 1857. Pp. 204.

2279 BREBNER, WINSTON P. "The legendary North
Shore." Holiday, 28 (1960), 62-69, 110.
Social life and customs.

2280 BROWN, CHARLES RAYMOND. The Northern Con-
federacy according to the plans of the 'Essex Junto,' 1796-1814.... Princeton: Princeton
Univ. Pr., 1915. Pp. 123.

2281 BUCK, JOHN H. "The early church plate of
Newburyport, Newbury, West Newbury and Rowley." EIHC, 44 (1908), 293-304.

2282 "THE BUILDING of Essex Bridge." EIHC, 30
(1893), 53-105.
Between Beverly and Salem.

2283 BURNHAM, J. FORREST. "The story of Essex
North District Medical Society in Lawrence,
Methuen, Andover and North Andover from 1841 to
1930. NEJMed, 204 (1931), 665-667.

2284 BUSH-BROWN, ALBERT and CAROLINE SHILLABER.
"When the eye failed, and architecutre fell
to building or literature." EIHC, 95 (1959), 165-
175.
Nineteenth century.

2285 CAREY, GEORGE G. "Folklore from the printed
sources of Essex County, Massachusetts."
Southern Folklore Quarterly, 32 (1968), 17-43.
Witchcraft.

2286 CARPENTER, CHARLES CARROLL and THOMAS FRANK-
LIN WATERS. An historical sketch of the Essex South Association of Congregational ministers
and the Salem Association, reunited in Dec., 1885,

under the name of Essex South and Salem Association.... Salem: Salem Observer Book and Job Print,
1893. Pp. 33.
1716-1885.

2287 CARROLL, THOMAS. History of the leather industry in Salem and Danvers, Mass.. U.S.A.
n.p., [after June, 1902]. Pp. 20. MSaE.
A supplement issued by 'Hide and Leather.'

2288 CARTER, JAMES GORDON. A geography of Essex
County; for young children; embracing 1. a
short topographical and historical sketch of every
town: 2. a general view of the county, and the
employments of the people: 3. a glossary, explaining the geographical and other difficult terms.
Boston: Carter & Hendee, 1830. Pp. viii, 118.
Not juvenile literature.

2289 CHAPMAN, MARTHA A. Sunday school historical
address. [Marblehead, 188-?]. Pp. 10.
Methodist Sunday schools in the county.

2290 CHINN, GEORGE. The wheelman's hand-book of
Essex County, Massachusetts: containing
sketches of the cities and towns of the county...
also, sketch of the League of Essex County Wheelmen,
and a chapter on wheel literature. (1884) 3d ed.
Beverly: Citizen Steam Pr., 1886. Pp. 59.

2291 CITY IMPROVEMENT SOCIETY OF NEWBURYPORT,
MASS. Places of historical interest within
the limits of 'Ould Newbury.' Newburyport, Printed
for the City Improvement Society, 1897. Pp. 10.
Newbury and Newburyport.

2292 CLARK, WILLIAM HORACE. "Highlights of three
centuries of old Newbury, Massachusetts."
Americana, 31 (1937), 389-424.
Newbury and Newburyport.

2293 COFFIN, EDWARD M. Merrimac River shipping:
paper read before the Historical Society of
Old Newbury, May 27, 1926. Newburyport: Historical
Society of Old Newbury, 1926. Pp. 24.

2294 COFFIN, JOSHUA. A sketch of the history of
Newbury, Newburyport, and West Newbury, from
1635 to 1845. Boston: S. G. Drake, 1845.
Pp. viii, 416.

2295 COPELAND, MELVIN THOMAS and ELLIOTT C. ROG-
ERS. The saga of Cape Ann. Freeport, Me.:
Bond Wheelwright, 1960. Pp. 254.

2296 CROSBY, NATHAN. "Reminiscences of distinguished men of Essex County." EIHC, 17
(1880), 151-179.

2297 CUMMINGS, OSMOND RICHARD and GERALD F. CUN-
NINGHAM. "The Haverhill, Georgetown & Dan-
vers Street Railway; Georgetown, Rowley & Ipswich
Street Railway System, 1900-1906." Transportation
Bulletin, No. 67 (August, 1962-February, 1963), en-
tire issue.

2298 CURRIER, JOHN JAMES. Historical sketch of
ship building on the Merrimac River. Newburyport: William H. Huse, 1877. Pp. 80.
Limited to Massachusetts.

2299 DANVERS, MASS. Proceedings at the reception
and dinner in honor of George Peabody, esq.,
of London, by the citizens of the old town of Danvers, October 9, 1856; to which is appended an historical sketch of the Peabody Institute, with the
exercises at the laying of the corner-stone and at
the dedication.... Boston: H. W. Dutton & Son,
Printers, 1856. Pp. vi, 195.
Relates to Danvers and Peabody.

2300 DAVISSON, WILLIAM I. and DENNIS T. DUGAN.
"Commerce in seventeenth-century Essex County, Massachusetts." EIHC, 107 (1971), 113-142.

2301 DAVISSON, WILLIAM I. "Essex County price
trends: money and markets in 17-century Massachusetts." EIHC, 103 (1967), 144-185.

2302 _____. "Essex County wealth trends: wealth
and economic growth in 17th century Massachusetts." EIHC, 103 (1967), 291-342.

2303 _____. and DENNIS T. DUGAN. "Land precedents
in Essex County, Massachusetts." EIHC, 106
(1970), 252-276.
Seventeenth century.

2304 DEAN, JOHN WARD. "The Gerrymander." NEHGR,
46 (1892), 374-383.

2305 DECATUR, STEPHEN. "The Moulton silversmiths." Antiques, 39 (1941), 14-17.
Moulton family of Newbury and Newburyport.

2306 DEXTER, RALPH W. "The relationship of natural features to the place names of Cape Ann,
Massachusetts." EIHC, 88 (1952), 141-149.

2307 _____. "Utilization of natural resources in
the plaster of old houses in the vicinity of
Cape Ann, Massachusetts." EIHC, 106 (1970), 108-
111.

2308 DOW, GEORGE FRANCIS. "Essex County in the
Massachusetts Bay Colony as described by
early travelers." TopHC, 25 (1920), 1-72; 26
(1921), 1-112.
1605-1797.

2309 _____. "The French Acadians in Essex County and their life in exile." EIHC, 45
(1909), 293-307.
Eighteenth century.

2310 _____. "The River Agwam, an Essex County
waterway." TopHC, 28 (1923), 1-16.

2311 _____, comp. Two centuries of travel in Essex County, Massachusetts, a collection of
narratives and observations made by travelers,
1605-1799. Topsfield: Topsfield Historical Society, 1921. Pp. xvi, 189.

2312 DUREN, MARTHA WILLIAMSON FORSYTH. "Three
generations of Silsbees and their vessels."
EIHC, 61 (1925), 1-24, 113-128, 241-258.
"Continued," but no more appeared.

2313 "EARLY planted crops." Essex Antiq., 11
(1907), 97-100.

2314 "EARTHQUAKES in Essex County." Essex Antiq.,
6 (1902), 166-170.

2315 EMERY, SARAH ANNA SMITH. Reminiscences of a
nonagenarian. Newburyport: W. H. Huse,
1879. Pp. 336.
Newbury and Newburyport.

2316 ENDICOTT, CHARLES MOSES. "History of the Salem and Danvers Aqueduct." EIHC, 2 (1860),
105-115.

2317 ESSEX BAR ASSOCIATION, SALEM, MASS. Memorials of the Essex Bar Association, and brief
biographical notices of some of the distinguished
members of the Essex bar prior to the formation of
the Association. William D. Northend and Edward B.
George, eds. Salem: Newcomb and Gauss, 1900.
Pp. 253.
Spine says "volume one," but no more published.

2318 ESSEX--county history and directory.... Boston: C. A. & J. F. Wood, 1870. v.p.

2319 "ESSEX County loyalists." EIHC, 43 (1907),
289-316.

2320 ESSEX INSTITUTE, SALEM, MASS. Ship registers
of the district of Salem and Beverly, Massachusetts, 1789-1900. A. Frank Hitchings and Stephen
Willard Phillips, eds. Salem: The Essex Institute,
1906. Pp. 206.

2321 "ESSEX-Merrimack Bridge." ECHGR, 2 (1895),
49-51.
Bridge in two sections from Newburyport to
Salisbury with Deer Island between the spans.

2322 ESSEX NORTH ASSOCIATION. Contributions to
the ecclesiastical history of Essex County,
Mass. Boston: Congregational Board of Publication,
1865. Pp. xi, 396.

2323 FALES, DEAN A., JR. Essex County furniture--
documented treasures from local collections,
1660-1860." EIHC, 101 (1965), 165-244.

2324 _____. "Two Essex County clocks." Antiques,
84 (1963), 80-81.
Made by Henry Harmson and Edmund Currier.

2325 FELT, JOSEPH BARLOW. "Historical notices of
Ipswich and Hamilton." EIHC, 4 (1862), 225-
229.

2326 _____. History of Ipswich, Essex, and Hamilton. Cambridge: C. Folsom, 1834. Pp. xv,
304.

2327 _____. "A list of Congregational and Presbyterian ministers who have been settled in
the county of Essex, Mass. from its first settlement to the year 1834." American Quarterly Register, 7 (1834-1835), 246-261.
Gives information regarding birth, education,
settlement, resignation and death.

2328 FIORE, JORDAN DOMENIC. "The Temple-Bernard
affair, a royal custom house scandal in Essex County." EIHC, 90 (1954), 58-83.
Francis Bernard and John Temple, 1760s.

2329 FISCHER, DAVID H. "The myth of the Essex Junto." WMQ, 3 Ser., 21 (1964), 191-235. Federalism.

2330 FORBES, ALLAN. "Early Myopia festivities." EIHC, 78 (1942), 307-328. 1882-1916, Myopia Hunt Club.

2331 "A FORGOTTEN horror." EIHC, 35 (1899), 304. Smallpox epidemics and their treatment in Essex County.

2332 FOWLER, ALBERT E. "The British are coming!" NEG, 11 (Spring, 1970), 43-47. April, 1775.

2333 FUESS, CLAUDE MOORE. "Essex County metamorphosis." EIHC, 92 (1956), 4-17. Survey of the county's development.

2334 _____. "Essex County politics a century ago." EIHC, 95 (1959), 104-114.

2335 _____., ed. and SCOTT HURTT PARADISE, comp. The story of Essex County. N.Y.: American Historical Society, 1935. 4v. Vols. 3 and 4 are biographical.

2336 FULLER, SAMUEL. Education in the two Andovers: address at the dedication of the Punchard Free School, Tuesday, September 2nd, 1856. Andover: W. F. Draper, 1856. Pp. 42. Andover and North Andover.

2337 GAGE, THOMAS. The history of Rowley, anciently including Bradford, Boxford, and Georgetown, from the year 1639 to the present time, with an address, delivered September 5, 1839, at the celebration of the second centennial anniversary of its settlement. By Rev. James Bradford. Boston: Ferdinand Andrews, 1840. Pp. xx, 483.

2338 [GANNON, FREDERIC AUGUSTUS]. Leather in Salem and Peabody. n.p., n.d. 3v. MSaE. Author attribution by the Essex Institute.

2339 _____. "Salem and the North Shore, leather tercentenary, 1639-1939." Shoe and Leather Reporter, (July 22, 1939), 19-44.

2340 GARDNER, FRANK A. "Colonel James Frye's Regiment." MassMag, 3 (1910), 187-198, 246-256. Revolutionary; biography.

2341 _____. "Colonel John Mansfield's Regiment." MassMag, 6 (1913), 147-158; 7 (1914), 32-45. Revolutionary; biography.

2342 _____. "Colonel Moses Little's Regiment." MassMag, 9 (1916), 18-44. Revolutionary; biography.

2343 GARRETT, EDMUND HENRY. Romance & reality of the Puritan coast; with many little picturings authentic or fanciful. Boston: Little, Brown, 1897. Pp. 221.

2344 GETCHELL, EMILY A. "Newbury and Newburyport in the Lexington fight." Putnam's HM, New Ser., 3 (1895), 7-15.

2345 GOODELL, ABNER CHENEY, JR. "A biographical notice of the officers of probate for Essex County from the commencement of the colony to the present time." EIHC, 2 (1860), 157-166, 213-226; 3 (1861), 1-11, 147-154; 4 (1862), 97-111, 267-271.

2346 GRANT, PHILIP A., JR. "The elections of 1834 in Essex County, Massachusetts." EIHC, 106 (1970), 126-141.

2347 GRANT, ROBERT. The North Shore of Massachusetts. N.Y.: C. Scribner's Sons, 1896. Pp. 63.

2348 HAWKES, NATHAN MORTIMER. "Semi-historical rambles among the eighteenth-century places along Saugus River." EIHC, 25 (1888), 241-273.

2349 HAYES, BARTLETT H. "Arts and crafts in Essex County." Americana, 29 (1930), 460-513.

2350 HILL, BENJAMIN D. and WINFIELD SCOTT NEVINS. The North Shore of Massachusetts Bay: a guide and history of Marblehead, Salem Neck and Juniper Point, Beverly, and Cape Ann. Salem: Salem Pr., 1879. Unpaged.

2351 HISTORICAL RECORDS SURVEY. MASSACHUSETTS. Inventory of the county archives of Massachusetts, Essex County. Boston: Historical Records Survey, 1937. 370 leaves. Essex County was the only volume issued.

2352 HITCHINGS, A. FRANK. "Ship registers of the district of Salem and Beverly, 1789-1900." EIHC, 39 (1903), 185-208; 40 (1904), 49-72, 177-200, 217-240, 321-336; 41 (1905), 141-164, 309-332, 357-380; 43 (1906), 89-110.

2353 [HOMER, JAMES LLOYD]. Nahant, and other places on the North-Shore; being a continuation of notes on the sea-shore, by the Shade of Alden. Boston: W. Chadwick, 1848. Pp. vii, 48.

2354 HOUSE, ALBERT VIRGIL. "The lean-to house and the life it sheltered." DanHC, 11 (1923), 113-133. Relates to several houses.

2355 HUBER, MARY MEANS. "Essex County trade cards." EIHC, 98 (1962), 154-160. Merchants.

2356 HURD, DUANE HAMILTON, ed. History of Essex County, Massachusetts, with biographical sketches of many of its pioneers and prominent men. Philadelphia: J. W. Lewis, 1888. 2v.

2357 "INDIANS of Essex County, Massachusetts." ECHGR, 2 (1895), 74-75, 93-94. Biographies.

2358 IPSWICH, MASS. Outline of tercentenary program at Ipswich, Massachusetts including information in regard to Essex, Hamilton and Topsfield which were at one time part of Ipswich...in connection with the three hundredth anniversary of the founding of the Massachusetts Bay Colony. [Ipswich]: Chronicle Publishing, 1930. unpaged. MBNEH.

2359   JACKSON, RUSSELL LEIGH. "Old Essex as a fac-
        tor in the settlement of the great North-
west." Americana, 9 (1914), 982-994.

2360   _____. "The Pearsons and their mills."
        EIHC, 61 (1925), 345-352; 62 (1926), 65-80;
74 (1938), 49-62.
        "Continued," but no more appeared.

2361   _____. The physicians of Essex County. Sa-
        lem: Essex Institute, 1948. Pp. v, 152.

2362   _____. "The seafaring Browns." EIHC, 80
        (1944), 55-68.

2363   JENKINS, LAWRENCE WATERS. "The Essex
        Guards." EIHC, 47 (1921), 249-272; 58
(1922), 25-40.
        Militia.

2364   JONAS, MANFRED. "The wills of the early set-
        tlers of Essex County, Massachusetts."
EIHC, 96 (1960), 228-235.

2365   KENNEDY, CHARLES J. "Railroads in Essex
        County a century ago." EIHC, 95 (1959), 137-
148.

2366   KENNY, HERBERT A. Cape Ann: Cape America.
        Philadelphia: Lippincott, 1971. Pp. viii,
294.

2367   KEYES, HOMER EATON. "Dennis or a lesser
        light?" Antiques, 34 (1938), 296-300.
        Thomas Dennis' oak chairs, seventeenth cen-
tury.

2368   [KNAPP, SAMUEL LORENZO]. Extracts from the
        journal of Marshal Soult, pseud., addressed
to a friend: how obtained, and by whom translated
is not a subject of enquiry.... Newburyport: W. B.
Allen, 1817. Pp. 143.
        Social life and customs.

2369   KNAPP, WILLIAM P. "Stone age implements of
        Essex County." DanHC, 5 (1917), 24-31.

2370   KONIG, DAVID THOMAS. "Community custom and
        common law: social change and development
of land law in seventeenth-century Massachusetts."
AmJLegalHist, 18 (1974), 137-177.
        Limited to Essex County.

2371   _____. "A new look at the Essex 'French':
        ethnic frictions and community tensions in
seventeenth-century Essex County, Massachusetts.
EIHC, 110 (1974), 167-180.
        Huguenots.

2372   LAMSON, DARIUS FRANCIS. "Emigration from
        New England to New Brunswick, 1763-1764."
MagAmHist, 25 (1891), 118-119.
        Limited to Essex County.

2373   LAWTON, R. J. Industrial and mercantile
        Peabody and Danvers. n.p., 1909. Pp. 40.

2374   _____. Industrial and mercantile Salem and
        Marblehead illustrated. n.p., 1909. Pp. 69.
MSaE.

2375   LEWIS, ALONZO and JAMES ROBINSON NEWHALL.
        History of Lynn, Essex County, Massachusetts,
including Lynnfield, Saugus, Swampscott, and Nahant.
Lynn: G. C. Herbert, 1890-1897.
        Vol. 1 is a revision and continuation of
        Lewis' History of Lynn, first published in
        1829. Vol. 2 has imprint: Lynn: I. A.
        Newhall and H. M. Newhall. This edition
        covers 1629-1893.

2376   LONG, HENRY FOLLANSBEE. "The Newburyport
        and Danvers Railroads." EIHC, 46 (1910), 17-
55.

2377   LORING, KATHARINE PEABODY. "The earliest
        summer residents of the North Shore and their
houses." EIHC, 68 (1932), 193-208.
        Social life and customs.

2378   LOW, DAVID W. Address delivered before the
        Essex Agricultural Society, in Massachu-
setts, at their 58th annual exhibition.... Salem:
Observer Steam Printing Rooms, 1880. Pp. 23.
        Agriculture and fishing.

2379   LOWELL, WILLIAM D. "The ancient ferry ways
        of the Merrimack." Putnam's HM, New Ser., 3
(1895), 35-42, 71-77.

2380   LYDON, JAMES G. "North Shore trade in the
        early eighteenth century." AmNep, 28 (1968),
261-274.

2381   MCDANIEL, B. F. "Geology and mineralogy in
        Essex County, Mass." EIB, 16 (1884), 133-
140.
        Historical survey of scientific activities.

2382   MCDONALD, EDITH WILLOUGHBY. "The romance of
        the Old Bay Road." SWJ, 46 (1930), 341-369.

2383   MACSWIGGAN, AMELIA ELIZABETH. "Pioneer pot-
        teries of Danvers and Peabody, Massachu-
setts." Antiques Journal, 12 (February, 1957), 36-
37.

2384   MANNY, FRANK A. Essex County homes in three
        centuries. Manchester, 1929. Pp. 8. MB.

2385   MARBLEHEAD HISTORICAL SOCIETY. The North
        Shore Review; "old colonial days" number....
[Marblehead], Published in the interest of the Marblehead Historical Society, 1915. Unpaged.

2386   MASSACHUSETTS (COLONY). COUNTY COURT (ESSEX
        CO.) Records and files of the quarterly
courts of Essex County, Massachusetts.... George
Francis Dow, ed. Salem: Essex Institute, 1911-
1921. 8v.
        1636-1683; courts held at Salem 1636-1641
        and at Salem and Ipswich 1641-1692.

2387   MASSACHUSETTS (COLONY). PROBATE COURT (ES-
        SEX CO.) The probate records of Essex Coun-
ty, Massachusetts, 1635-1681. George Francis Dow,
ed. Salem: The Essex Institute, 1916-1921. 3v.

2388   MERRILL, JOSEPH. History of Amesbury, in-
        cluding the first seventeen years of Salis-
bury, to the separation in 1654; and Merrimac, from

(MERRILL, JOSEPH)
its incorporation in 1876. Haverhill: F. P. Stiles, 1880. Pp. xxiii, 451.

2389 MOODY, ROBERT EARLE, comp. The Saltonstall papers, 1607-1815. Volume I, 1607-1789. Selected and edited and with biographies of ten members of the Saltonstall family in six generations. Boston: Massachusetts Historical Society, 1972. Pp. xx, 574.

2390 MULLIKEN, SARAH ELIZABETH. "Plum Island." EIHC, 87 (1951), 99-113.

2391 "NATURAL and political history of the Gerrymander." AmHistRecord, 1 (1872), 504-507.

2392 NELSON, TRUMAN. "The matrix of place." EIHC, 95 (1959), 176-185.
        Hawthorne in Salem and Whittier in Danvers.

2393 NEVINS, WINFIELD SCOTT. "Summer days on the North Shore." NEM, New Ser., 5 (1891-1892), 17-37.
        Social life and customs.

2394 _____. "Witchcraft in Massachusetts." Americana, 16 (1922), 52-61.

2395 NEWHALL, JAMES ROBINSON. The Essex memorial, for 1836: embracing a register of the county. Salem: H. Whipple, 1836. Pp. vii, 281.

2396 NORTON, SUSAN L. "Marital migration in Essex County, Massachusetts, in the colonial and early federal periods." Journal of Marriage and the Family, 35 (1973), 406-418.

2397 O'BRIEN, MICHAEL JOSEPH. "The pioneer Irish of Essex County, Massachusetts." AIrHSJ, 26 (1927), 137-149.

2398 PARK, HELEN. "Seventeenth-century furniture of Essex County and its makers." Antiques, 78 (1960), 350-355.

2399 PERLEY, SIDNEY. "Early gravestones in Essex County." Essex Antiq, 3 (1899), 177-181.

2400 _____. "Essex County in the abolition of slavery." ECHGR, 1 (1894), 1-4, 25-27, 37-39, 52-54, 146-148; 2 (1895), 23-25.
        "Continued," but periodical ceased publication.

2401 _____. History of liquor in Essex County, Mass., for 260 years. n.p., [1890?]. Broadside, 15 x 10 1/2 inches. MSaE.

2401A _____. The Indian land titles of Essex County, Massachusetts. Salem: Essex Book and Print Club, 1912. Pp. 144.

2402 _____. "The manufacture of nails in Essex County." Essex Antiq, 2 (1898), 69-74.

2403 _____. "Parts of Salem and Marblehead in 1700." Essex Antiq, 13 (1909), 132-138.

2404 _____. "Persecution of the Quakers in Essex County." Essex Antiq, 1 (1897), 135-140.

2405 _____. The poets of Essex County, Massachusetts. Salem, 1889. Pp. 214.
        Biographies.

2406 PHILLIPS, JAMES DUNCAN. "Transportation in Essex County." EIHC, 85 (1949), 245-258.

2407 PICKARD, SAMUEL THOMAS. Whittier-land; a handbook of North Essex, containing many anecdotes of and poems by John Greenleaf Whittier never before collected. Boston: Houghton Mifflin, 1904. Pp. xi, 160.

2408 PIERCE, CALVIN P. Ryal Side from early days of Salem colony. Cambridge: Riverside Pr. for the Beverly Historical Society, 1931. Pp. xiv, 174.
        Salem, Beverly and Danvers.

2409 PLEASURE drives around Cape Ann. Gloucester: Procter Bros., 1896. Pp. 95.

2410 POOLMAN, KENNETH. Guns off Cape Ann; the story of the Shannon and the Chesapeake. Chicago: Rand McNally, 1962. Pp. 175.
        War of 1812.

2411 PRIME, DANIEL NOYES. The autobiography of an octogenarian, containing the genealogy of his ancestors, sketches of their history, and of various events that have occurred during his protracted life.... Newburyport: W. H. Huse, 1873. Pp. x, 293.
        Georgetown, Rowley and Ipswich.

2412 PROPER, DAVID RALPH. "Swami Vivekananda in Essex County." EIHC, 103 (1967), 40-52.
        1893-1894; Indian monk who pioneered Vedanta.

2413 PUTNAM, EBEN. "Militia officers, Essex Co., Mass. 1761-1771." EIHC, 29 (1892), 177-183.

2414 RANTOUL, ROBERT SAMUEL. "Essex County and the Indians, a lecture read before the Beverly Lyceum, Nov. 20, 1832." EIHC, 19 (1882), 126-142.

2415 _____. "The Essex Junto--the long embargo--and the great Topsfield caucus of 1808." EIHC, 19 (1882), 226-240.
        Federalism.

2416 _____. "Washington in Essex County." EIHC, 58 (1922), 1-19.
        1789.

2417 REED, JACOB W. "Old houses in Essex County, Mass." NEHGR, 22 (1868), 388-389.

2418 ROBINSON, FRANCIS JOSEPH GEORGE. Tragabigzanda; or, Cape Ann, an informer; the romance, legend, and history of Cape Ann, past and present. Boston: Progressive Print, 1935. Pp. 32.
        Tragabigzanda was name given to the area by Captain John Smith.

2419 ROBINSON, FRANK T. "Quaint Essex." NEM, New Ser., 11 (1894-1895), 100-114.

2420 _____. "The quaint North Shore." NEM, New Ser., 10 (1894), 654-668.

2421 ROBINSON, JOHN. "The pre-historic relics of Essex County." Essex Antiq., 13 (1909), 98-101.

2422 _____. "The progress of botany in Essex County during the last half century, especially as influenced by the Essex County Natural History Society and the Essex Institute, 1834-1884." EIB, 16 (1884), 122-132.

2423 _____. "Sketches of some of the early botanists." EIB, 12 (1880), 87-94.

2424 ROSE-TROUP, FRANCES. Roger Conant and the early settlements on the North Shore of Massachusetts. n.p., Roger Conant Family Association, Inc., 1926. Pp. 18.

2425 [ROTHERY, AGNES EDWARDS]. The romantic shore, by Agnes Edwards, pseud. Salem: Salem Pr., 1915. Pp. vii, 202.

2426 ROWELL, WILBUR E. "The Merrimack River." EIHC, 82 (1946), 12-25.

2427 SALEM, Beverly, Danvers and Peabody: their representative business men and points of interest. N.Y.: Mercantile Illustrating Co., 1893. Pp. 164.

2428 SAVILLE, MARSHALL HOWARD. "Champlain and his landings at Cape Ann, 1605, 1606." AASP, New Ser., 43 (1933), 447-469.

2429 SHAPIRO, SAMUEL. "Aristocracy, mud, and vituperation: the Butler-Dana campaign in Essex County in 1868." NEQ, 31 (1958), 340-360.
Benjamin F. Butler and Richard Henry Dana, Jr.

2430 SMITH, SYLVANUS. Fisheries of Cape Ann... [Gloucester]: Gloucester Times, 1915. Pp. vi, 131. MSaE.

2431 SOLOMON, BARBARA MILLER. "The growth of the population in Essex County 1850-1960." EIHC, 95 (1959), 82-103.

2432 "SOME Essex County Indians." Essex Antiq., 5 (1901), 39-40.
Biographies.

2433 SOUVENIR of the Grand Army of the Republic of Salem and vicinity, containing sketches, rosters and portraits: posts of Salem, Danvers, Beverly, Marblehead and Peabody. Salem: C. E. Trow, 1893. Pp. 41.

2434 NO ENTRY

2435 SPALDING, SAMUEL JONES. "The history of the Essex North Association, with sketches of its members." CongQ, 6 (1864), 161-175.
Ministerial association.

2436 STARK, JAMES HENRY and C. A. WOOD. Pictorial history of Essex County. Boston: Photo-Electrotype, [1880?]. Pp. 16. MSaE.

2437 STONE, EBEN F. "Address before the Essex Bar, Feb. 2, 1889." EIHC, 26 (1889), 1-50. Sketches of Rufus Choate, Caleb Cushing and Robert Rantoul, Jr.

2438 TEWKSBURY, ROBERT HASKELL. The Merrimack Valley: an address delivered May 13th, 1896, before the Methuen Historical Society. [Methuen, 1896]. Pp. 25.

2439 THORNTON, JOHN WINGATE. The landing at Cape Anne; or, the charter of the first permanent colony on the territory of the Massachusetts Company, now discovered and first published from the original manuscript, with an inquiry into its authority and a history of the colony, 1624-1628, Roger Conant, governor. Boston: Gould and Lincoln, 1854. Pp. xii, 84.

2440 [TRACY, CYRUS MASON]. Standard history of Essex County, Massachusetts, embracing a history of the county from its first settlement to the present time, with a history and description of its towns and cities. H. Wheatland, ed. Boston: C. F. Jewett, 1878. Pp. 424.
Copy at New England Historic Genealogical Society contains a typescript index of persons by Lois C. Perkins.

2441 UPTON, J. WARREN and HENRY KEMBLE OLIVER. Addresses of J. Warren Upton...and Hon. H. K. Oliver...delivered at the 50th anniversary of Essex County Teachers' Association, at Salem, April 4, 1879.... [Salem?, 1879]. Pp. 20.

2442 WADE, HERBERT T. "The Essex Regiment in Shays' Rebellion--1787." EIHC, 90 (1954), 317-349.

2443 WALETT, FRANCIS GUSTAF. "The election of 1888: Essex County men wave the bloody shirt." EIHC, 86 (1950), 150-154.

2444 WALLACE, MARY. Summer magic. Garden City, N.Y.: Doubleday, 1967. Pp. 95.
Reminiscences.

2445 WALLACE, WILLIAM HUSTON. "Merrimack Valley manufacturing, past and present." Economic Geography, 37 (1961), 283-308.

2446 WARE, BENJAMIN P. "Historical sketch of the Essex Agricultural Society." Essex Agricultural Society. Transactions, (1883) 142-146.

2447 WASSON, GEORGE S. "The vanished pinky." OTNE, 20 (1929-1930), 187-195.
Schooners.

2448 WATERS, THOMAS FRANKLIN. "Church troubles in ye olden times." MassMag, 8 (1915), 59-74.

2449 _____. History of the Essex Agricultural Society of Essex County, Massachusetts 1818-1918. Salem: Newcomb and Gauss, 1918. Pp. 56. M.

2450 _____. Plum Island, Ipswich, Mass. Salem: Printed for the [Ipswich Historical] Society, 1918. Pp. 64.
Island is not entirely in Ipswich.

2451 WATKINS, LURA WOODSIDE. "The Bayleys: Essex County potters." Antiques, 34 (1938), 253-255; 35 (1939), 22-27.

2452 _____. "Bridges over the Merrimac: Rocks Bridge." Covered Bridge Topics, 19 (January, 1962), 1-2.
Between Haverhill and West Newbury.

2453 WEBBER, CHARLES HENRY and WINFIELD SCOTT NEVINS. Old Naumkeag: an historical sketch of the city of Salem, and the towns of Marblehead, Peabody, Beverly, Danvers, Wenham, Manchester, Topsfield, and Middleton. Salem: A. A. Smith, 1877. Pp. x, 312.

2454 WHITAKER, NICHOLAS TILLINGHAST. Methodism on Cape Ann: an historical address delivered by Rev. N. T. Whitaker, pastor of the Elm St. Church, Gloucester, at the celebration of the semi-centennial anniversary, March 3, 1875. Gloucester: John D. Woodbury, 1875. Pp. 31. M.

2455 WHITEHILL, WALTER MUIR. "The topography of Essex County in 1859." EIHC, 95 (1959), 69-81.

2456 WHO'S who along the North Shore of Massachusetts Bay. Salem: Salem Pr., 1907-1910. 2v.

2457 WOODBURY, LOUIS AUGUSTUS. An historical sketch of Bradford, Mass., in the Revolution. (Including East Bradford, now Groveland). Groveland: Ambrose, 1895. Pp. viii, 112.

FRANKLIN COUNTY

2458 ANDREWS, ERASTUS. A historical discourse, delivered at the Baptist meeting-house at N. Leveret, [sic] on August 18th, 1847, in commemoration of the eightieth anniversary of the Baptist Church of Leverett and Montague. Amherst: J. S. & C. Adams, 1847. Pp. 24.

2459 BARNARD, DARWIN. Rambling reminiscences of life in Franklin Co. n.p., 1909. Pp. 10. M.

2460 BIOGRAPHICAL review: this volume contains biographical sketches of the leading citizens of Franklin County, Massachusetts. Boston: Biographical Review Publishing, 1895. Pp. 668.

2461 BORRUP, ROGER. "The Shelburne Falls and Colrain Street Railway Company." Transportation Bulletin, No. 75 (July 1967-December 1968), 1-32.

2462 CUMMINGS, OSMOND RICHARD. "Greenfield and Montague transportation area." Transportation Bulletin, No. 60 (October-December, 1959), entire issue.

2463 DAVENPORT, ELMER, F. Puzzle of Catamount Hill, being a report on pioneer life in Franklin County, Massachusetts, during the century after the War of Independence, 1780-1880. n.p., 1969. Unpaged. MBNEH.

2464 FULLER, MARY WILLIAMS. "Three early artists of Franklin County." PVMA, 7 (1921-1929), 178-186.
Chester Harding, Henry K. Brown and George Fuller.

2465 GRISWOLD, WHITING. Address delivered at the opening of court in the new [Franklin County] court house in Greenfield, Mass., March 18, 1873. Greenfield: E. D. Merriam, 1873. Pp. 51.
Contains biographies of prominent lawyers who practiced in the first Franklin County court house.

2466 PACKARD, THEOPHILUS. A history of the churches and ministers, and of Franklin Association, in Franklin County, Mass., and an appendix respecting the County. Boston: S. K. Whipple, 1854. Pp. vii, 456.

2467 SHELDON, GEORGE. "Forty years of frontier life in the Pocumtuck Valley." NEM, 4 (1886), 236-249.

2468 THOMPSON, FRANCIS NIMS. "The Probate Court and its judges." PVMA, 7 (1921-1929), 631-653.

2469 WARNER, CHARLES FORBES, ed. Picturesque Franklin. 1891. Northampton: Wade, Warner, 1891. Pp. 123.

2470 WATERS, THOMAS FRANKLIN. "Idylls of Franklin County." MassMag, 1 (1908), 123-131.

HAMPDEN COUNTY

2471 BIOGRAPHICAL review: this volume contains biographical sketches of the leading citizens of Hampden County, Massachusetts.... Boston: Biographical Review Publishing, 1895. Pp. 1138.

2472 BOYDEN, ARTHUR H., comp. Postal history information, Hampden County, Massachusetts 1789-1890. Casselberry, Fla., 1968. Unpaged. MS.

2473 CALKINS, MARSHALL. "The early physicians of Hampden County." CVHSP, 2 (1882-1903), 157-174.

2474 COPELAND, ALFRED MINOTT, ed. 'Our county and its people'; a history of Hampden County, Massachusetts.... Boston: Century Memorial Publishing, 1902. 3v.

2475 DUGRE, SYLVIA and THOMAS O. WILKINSON. Demographic correlates of metropolitan growth: Springfield, Chicopee, Holyoke, Massachusetts, 1950-1960. Amherst: Cooperative Extension Service, Univ. of Mass., 1963. Pp. 28.

2476   GREENOUGH, J. C.   "Historical relations of
         Springfield and Westfield." CVHSP, 2 (1882-
1903), 252-263.

2477   FLANAGAN, ANDREW J.   "The early dentists of
         Hampden County." CVHSP, 2 (1882-1903), 214-
242.

2478   HOWLETT, CARL C. Hampden. n.p., 1962.
         Pp. 7. MBNEH.

2479   JOHNSON, CLIFTON. Hampden County, 1636-
         1936. N.Y.: American Historical Society,
1936. 3v.
         Vol. 3 is biographical.

2480   "REMARKS and observations made by Justin Han-
         cock." Grafton Magazine of History and Biog-
raphy, 1 (March, 1909), 24-34.
         Granville and Springfield.

2481   SEIG, LOUIS. "Population change in the
         Springfield-Chicopee-Holyoke commuter re-
gion." Rocky Mountain Social Science Journal, 7
(1970), 77-87.
         1790-1960.

2482   SKETCHES of the churches and pastors in Hamp-
         den County, Mass.; and also, an address de-
livered to the pastors, by Rev. T. M. Colley, D. D.
at Mettineague, September 13, 1853. By a committee
of pastors. Westfield: S. W. Edson, 1854.
Pp. viii, 144.

2483   [WARNER, CHARLES FORBES], ed. Picturesque
         Hampden. Northampton: Picturesque Publish-
ing, 1891. 2v.

2484   WRIGHT, HARRY ANDREW. Early Springfield and
         Longmeadow, Massachusetts; with special ref-
erence to Benjamin Cooley, pioneer.... Rutland,
Vt., 1940. Pp. 59.

2485   _____, ed. Indian deeds of Hampden County,
         being copies of all land transfers from the
Indians recorded in the county of Hampden: Massachusetts, and some deeds from other sources, together with notes and translations of Indian place
names. Springfield, 1905. Pp. 194.

HAMPSHIRE COUNTY

2486   BIOGRAPHICAL review: this volume contains
         biographical sketches of the leading citi-
zens of Hampshire County, Massachusetts.... Boston: Biographical Review Publishing, 1896.
Pp. 580.

2487   CLARKE, OLIVE CLEAVELAND. Things that I re-
         member at ninety-five. n.p., 1881. Pp. 14.
         Reminiscences.

2488   A FULL and graphic account of the terrible
         Mill River disaster, caused by the breaking
of a reservoir in Hampshire County, Mass. May 16,
1874, with full details of the loss of life and
property at Williamsburg, Skinnerville, Haydenville
and Leeds. Springfield: Weaver Shipman, 1874.
Pp. 48.

2489   GARDNER, FRANK A.   "Colonel Timothy Daniel-
         son's Regiment." MassMag, 2 (1909), 69-83.
         Revolutionary; biography.

2490   GAY, WILLIAM BURTON, comp. Gazetteer of
         Hampshire County, Mass., 1654-1887. Syra-
cuse: W. B. Gay, [1886?]. 2 v. in 1.

2491   HAMPSHIRE COUNTY, MASS. TERCENTENARY EDITO-
         RIAL COMMITTEE. The Hampshire history, cel-
ebrating 300 years of Hampshire County, Massachusetts. Lawrence E. Wikander, Helen Terry and Mark
Kiley, comps. Northampton: Hampshire County Commissioners, 1964. Pp. xiv, 364.

2492   HAMPSHIRE COUNTY BUSINESS AND PROFESSIONAL
         WOMEN'S CLUB. Twentieth anniversary...1926-
1946. Northampton, 1946. Pp. 30. MNF.

2493   HANNAY, AGNES. A chronicle of industry on
         the Mill River. Northampton: Department of
History of Smith College, 1936. Pp. 142.
         Northampton and Williamsburg.

2494   JOHNSON, CLIFTON. Historic Hampshire in the
         Connecticut Valley; happenings in a charming
old New England county from the time of the dinosaur
down to about 1900. Springfield: Milton Bradley,
1932. Pp. 406.

2495   JUDD, SYLVESTER. History of Hadley, includ-
         ing the early history of Hatfield, South
Hadley, Amherst and Granby, Massachusetts; also fam-
ily genealogies by Lucius M. Boltwood. (1863)
[New ed.] Springfield: H. R. Huntting, 1905.
Pp. xliii, 504, 205.
         Introduction includes sketches of William
         Goffe and Edward Whalley by George Sheldon.

2496   LAW, F. H.   "Historical landmarks near Am-
         herst." Bachelor of Arts, 2 (1896), 333-
343.

2497   LEFAVOUR, HENRY.   "The proposed college in
         Hampshire County in 1762." MHSP, 66 (1936-
1941), 53-79.
         Queen's College; never established.

2498   LYMAN, PAYSON WILLISTON. Military service of
         the towns of Amherst, Belchertown and Granby,
in the Revolutionary War. Amherst, 1889. Pp. 22.

2499   MANWELL, JOHN P. A history of the Hampshire
         Association of Congregational Churches and
Ministers. Amherst: Newell Pr., [1941?]. Pp. 43.
MNF.

2500   MASSACHUSETTS (COLONY) COURTS (HAMPSHIRE
         COUNTY). Colonial justice in western Massa-
chusetts, 1639-1702; the Pynchon court record, an
original judges' diary of the administration of justice in the Springfield courts in the Massachusetts
Bay Colony. Joseph Henry Smith, ed. Cambridge:
Harvard Univ. Pr., 1961. Pp. ix, 426.

2501   NIEDERFRANK, EVLON JOY. The Massachusetts
         hill towns in wartime.... Upper Darby, Pa.:
U. S. Department of Agriculture, Bureau of Agricultural Economics, 1945. Pp. 26. MAJ.
         Chesterfield, Cummington, Goshen, Plainfield
         and Worthington.

2502 "STODDARDEANISM." New Englander, 4 (1846), 350-355.
Half-way Covenant.

2503 [WARNER, CHARLES FORBES], ed. Picturesque Hampshire; a supplement to the quarter-centennial [edition of the Hampshire County] Journal. Northampton: Wade, Warner, 1890. Pp. 112.

2504 WESTCOTT, GEORGE W. Hampshire County: agricultural census figures by towns for 1925 and 1935, county totals from 1880 to 1935. [Amherst]: Massachusetts State College, 1936. 56 leaves. MAJ.

2505 WESTERN HAMPSHIRE BOARD OF TRADE. The western Hampshire highlands. Springfield: F. A. Bassette, 1912. Pp. xx, 60. M.
Chesterfield, Cummington, Plainfield and Worthington.

MIDDLESEX COUNTY

2506 ADAMS, CHARLES FRANCIS, 1807-1886. "A paper on the Middlesex Canal." Towpath Topics, 11 (September, 1973), [3-7].

2507 AYER, JOHN F. "The old Medford Turnpike." Historic Leaves, 1 (July, 1902), 7-20.

2508 [BACON, GEORGE FOX]. Leading business men of Marlboro, Hudson, So. Framingham, Natick, and vicinity; embracing also Saxonville and Cochituate. Boston: Mercantile Publishing, 1890. Pp. 86.

2509 [BAYLES, JAMES]. Lowell, Chelmsford, Graniteville, Forge Village, Dracut, Collinsville, of to-day, their commerce, trade, and industries, descriptive and historical. Rev. and enl. ed. [Lowell]: Lowell Daily Citizen, 1893. Pp. 122.

2510 BIOGRAPHICAL review...containing life sketches of leading citizens of Middlesex County, Massachusetts.... Boston: Biographical Review Publishing, 1898. Pp. 838.

2511 BROOKS, CHARLES. The tornado of 1851, in Medford, West Cambridge and Waltham, Middlesex County, Mass. Boston: J. M. Usher, 1852. Pp. 72.

2512 BROWN, ABRAM ENGLISH. Flag of the minute men, April 19, 1775, its origin and history. [Bedford]: Bedford Historical Society, 1894. 10 leaves.

2513 BROWN, EPHRAIM. "Concord, Lexington, April 19, 1775, the crisis, the dates, the bridge, the men." ORHAL, 6 (1896-1904), 19-32.

2514 BUTLER, CALEB. History of the town of Groton, including Pepperell and Shirley, from the first grant of Groton Plantation in 1655, with appendices, containing family registers, town and state officers, population, and other statistics. Boston: T. R. Marvin, 1848. Pp. xx, 499.

2515 CADBURY, HENRY JOEL. "Quakers and their abettors, Middlesex County, Massachusetts, 1663." FHABull, 27 (Spring, 1938), 9-16.

2516 CARTER, JAMES GORDON and N. H. BROOKS. A geography of Middlesex County for young children, embracing 1. A short topographical and historical sketch of every town. 2. A general view of the county and the employments of the people. 3. A glossary explaining the geographical and other difficult terms. Cambridge: Hilliard and Brown, 1830. Pp. 106.
Not juvenile literature.

2517 CASAS, WILLIAM B. DE LAS. "The Middlesex Fells." NEM, New Ser., 18 (1898), 701-721.

2518 CLARK, JONAS. The fate of blood-thirsty oppressors, and God's tender care of his distressed people, a sermon, preached at Lexington, April 19, 1776, to commemorate the murder, bloodshed, and commencement of hostilities, between Great Britain and America, in that town, by a brigade of troops of George III, under the command of Lieutenant-Colonel Smith, on the nineteenth of April, 1775.... Boston: Powars & Willis, 1776. Pp. 31, 8.
Lexington and Concord.

2519 _____. Historic guide book, story of Arlington, Lexington, Concord; the Battle of Lexington portrayed by Jonas Clark. Cambridge: T. A. Scott, 1904. Unpaged. M.

2520 CONKLIN, EDWIN P. Middlesex County and its people; a history. N.Y.: Lewis Historical Publishing, 1927. 4v.

2521 COOKE, GEORGE. "Our aborigines." Winchester Record, 1 (1885), 264-275.

2522 _____. "Waterfield." Winchester Record, 2 (1886), 1-9.
Division of land from Charlestown which is now Winchester and Woburn.

2523 COWLEY, CHARLES. "The last of the Sachems of the Merrimac River Indians." ORHAL, 6 (1896-1904), 376-427.
Passaconaway and Wannalancet.

2524 CRITTENDEN, H. T. "The Billerica & Bedford Railroad." RLHSB, No. 57 (1942), 7-14.

2525 CULLEN, JOSEPH P. "Battles, leaders, and issues of the Revolution: at Concord and Lexington." AHI, 2 (June, 1967), 4-11, 52-56.

2526 CULLEN, MAURICE R., JR. Battle road; birthplace of the American Revolution. Old Greenwich, Conn.: Chatham Pr., 1970. Pp. 47.

2527 CUMMINGS, OSMOND RICHARD. "Concord, Maynard, and Hudson Street Railway." Transportation Bulletin, No. 74 (January-June, 1967), entire issue.

2528 CUTTER, WILLIAM RICHARD, ed. Historic homes and places and genealogical and personal memoirs relating to the families of Middlesex County, Massachusetts. N.Y.: Lewis Historical Publishing, 1908. 4v.

2529 ____. "School history." Winchester Record, 2 (1886), 64-69.
Winchester and Woburn.

2530 DAME, LORIN L. "The Middlesex Canal." BSM, 2 (1884-1885), 96-106.

2531 ____. "The Middlesex Canal." MedHR, 1 (1898), 33-51.
Varies slightly from above entry.

2532 DE BERNIERE, HENRY. General Gage's instructions, of 22d February 1775.... Boston: J. Gill, 1779. Pp. 20.
Battles of Concord and Lexington.

2533 DICKSON, BRENTON H. "The Middlesex Canal." CaHSP, 40 (1964-1966), 43-58.

2534 ____. "The Middlesex Canal." NEG, 7 (Spring, 1966), 12-21.
Differs slightly from above article.

2535 DRAKE, SAMUEL ADAMS. Historic mansions and highways around Boston, being a new and rev. ed. of "Old landmarks and historic fields of Middlesex." (1874) Boston: Little, Brown, 1899. Pp. xvi, 440.
First edition has title: Historic fields and mansions of Middlesex; it was subsequently published in 1876 and 1895 with the title: Old landmarks and historic fields of Middlesex.

2536 ____, ed. History of Middlesex County, Massachusetts, containing carefully prepared histories of every city and town in the county, by well-known writers; and a general history of the county, from the earliest to the present time. Boston: Estes and Lauriat, 1880. 2v.

2537 EATON, CHESTER WILLIAMS, WARREN E. EATON and WILL EVERETT EATON, eds. Proceedings of the 250th anniversary of the ancient town of Redding once including the territory now comprising the towns of Reading, Wakefield, and North Reading, with historical chapters. Reading: Loring & Twombly, 1896. Pp. 398.

2538 EATON, LILLEY. Genealogical history of the town of Reading, Mass., including the present towns of Wakefield, Reading, and North Reading, with chronological and historical sketches, from 1639 to 1874. Boston: A. Mudge & Son, 1874. Pp. xxviii, 815.
New England Historic Genealogical Society has a photocopy of a typescript index of names appearing in this work.

2539 ECHOES from Mystic side: Malden, Melrose, Everett. Boston: Educational Publishing, 1890. Pp. 94. MBNEH.

2540 [EDDY, CALEB]. Historical sketch of the Middlesex Canal, with remarks for the consideration of the proprietors, by the agent of the corporation. Boston: Samuel N. Dickinson, 1843. Pp. 53.

2541 ERSKINE, EDITH C. "The Concord River in history and literature." LowellHSC, 1 (1907-1913) 164-168.

2542 EUSTIS, H. L. "The tornado of August 22, 1851 in Waltham, West Cambridge and Medford." American Academy of Arts and Sciences. Memoirs, New Ser., 5 (1855), 169-178.

2543 EVERETT, EDWARD. An oration delivered at Concord, April the nineteenth, 1825. Boston: Cummings, Hilliard, 1825. Pp. 59.
Concord and Lexington.

2544 FARRINGTON, CHARLES C. Paul Revere and his famous ride. Bedford: Bedford Print Shop, 1923. Pp. 89.

2545 FORBES, HARRIETTE MERRIFIELD. "Some seventeenth-century houses of Middlesex County, Massachusetts." OTNE, 29 (1938-1939), 90-105.

2546 FREESE, JOHN W. Historic houses and spots in Cambridge, Massachusetts and near-by towns. Boston: Ginn, 1897. Pp. viii, 144.

2547 FRENCH, ALLEN. The day of Concord and Lexington, the nineteenth of April, 1775. Boston: Little, Brown, 1925. Pp. xiii, 295.

2548 ____. General Gage's informers: new material upon Lexington & Concord; Benjamin Thompson as loyalist & the treachery of Benjamin Church, Jr. Ann Arbor: Univ. of Michigan Pr., 1932. Pp. xv, 207.

2549 FRENCH, J. B. "Early recollections of an old resident." ORHAL, 1 (1874-1879), 252-264.
Steamships, coaches and railroads.

2550 GALVIN, JOHN R. The minute men: a compact history of the defenders of the American colonies, 1645-1775. N.Y.: Hawthorn Books, 1967. Pp. 286.

2551 GARDNER, FRANK A. "Colonel Ebenezer Bridge's Regiment." MassMag, 2 (1909), 203-227.
Revolutionary, biography.

2552 ____. "Colonel William Prescott's Regiment." MassMag, 1 (1908), 149-167, 235-259.
Revolutionary, biography.

2553 GARVIN, AGNES H. "The part borne by the parent towns of Lowell in the war of the Revolution." Lowell HSC, 2 (1921-1926), 299-304.
Chelmsford, Tewksbury and Dracut.

2554 GETTEMY, CHARLES FERRIS. "The true story of Paul Revere's ride." NEM, New Ser., 26 (1902), 131-151.

2555 GIDDINGS, HOWARD ALDEN. "The ride of Paul Revere." MagAmHist, 29 (1893), 360-366.

2556 GILMAN, ALFRED. "History of Central Bridge." ORHAL, 2 (1880-1883), 295-318.
Between Lowell and Dracut.

2557 GOERTZ, ARTHÉMISE. "The nineteenth of
April." JAmHist, 35 (1931), 93-102.
Concord and Lexington.

2558 GOULD, LEVI SWANTON. Ancient Middlesex with
brief biographical sketches of the men who
have served the country officially since its settlement. [Somerville]: Somerville Journal Print,
1905. Pp. 336.

2558A GREEN, JOHN O. "Lowell and Harvard College."
ORHAL, 1 (1874-1879), 229-234.
Lowell, Mass.

2559 HALE, RICHARD WALDEN, 1871-1943 and BENJAMIN
HUMPHREY DORR. Unicorn Country Club: a
brief history of the title to its lands in Stoneham
and Woburn, Middlesex County, Massachusetts. Boston: Court Square Pr., 1927. Pp. 31 [i.e. 34].

2560 HAMLIN, CYRUS. "Colonel Francis Faulkner
and the battle of Lexington." LexHSP, 1
(1886-1889), 110-116.

2561 HARRIS, NATHANIEL. Records of the court of
Nathaniel Harris, one of His Majesty's justices of the peace within and for the county of
Middlesex, holden at Watertown from 1734 to 1761...
together with a paper by F. E. Crawford read before
the Historical Society of Watertown, November 14,
1893. Watertown: Historical Society of Watertown,
1938. Pp. 135.

2562 "AN HISTORIC American road." Chamber's Journal, 5 Ser., 7 (1890), 721-724.
Battles of Lexington and Concord.

2563 HISTORY of the fight at Lexington, April 19,
1775, from the best authorities.... Boston:
Rand, Avery, 1875. Pp. 24.
Relates to battles of Lexington and Concord.

2564 HOLDEN, HARLEY P. "The Middlesex Canal."
Towpath Topics, 4 (January, 1966), entire
issue.

2565 HOLMES, JOHN ALBERT. "The ancient fish weir
on Menotomy River." CaHSP, 5 (1910), 32-43.

2566 _____. "The ancient name 'Menotomy' and the
river of that name." MedHR, 14 (1911), 57-
64.

2567 HOPKINS, ARTHUR T. "The old Middlesex Canal." NEM, New Ser., 17 (1897-1898), 519-
532.

2568 HOWELLS, WILLIAM DEAN. Three villages. Bos-
ton: J. R. Osgood, 1884. Pp. 198.
Lexington and Shirley, Massachusetts and
Gnadenhütten, Ohio.

2569 HUDSON, ALFRED SERENO. The annals of Sudbury, Wayland, and Maynard, Middlesex County, Massachusetts. Ayer, 1891. v.p.

2570 HURD, DUANE HAMILTON, ed. History of Middlesex County, Massachusetts, with biographical
sketches of many of its pioneers and prominent
men.... Philadelphia: J. W. Lewis, 1890. 3v.

2571 THE INDUSTRIAL advantages of Lowell, Mass.
and environs: South Lowell, North Chelms-
ford, South and East Chelmsford, Chelmsford Center,
Dracut, Billerica, North Billerica, Ayer's City,
Collinsville and Willow Dale. W. H. Goodfellow,
Sr., comp. Lowell: W. H. Goodfellow, 1895.
Pp. 168.

2572 INGRAHAM, ALEC. "An exacting study of the
complexities, obstacles, successes and fail-
ures encountered in the building and operation of
the Middlesex Canal." Towpath Topics, 7 (April,
1969), [2-8], (September, 1969), [1-4].

2573 JACOBS, SARAH SPRAGUE. Nonantum and Natick.
Boston: Massachusetts Sabbath School Society, 1853. Pp. 336.
Nonantum is in Newton; an 1858 printing has
title: the white oak and its neighbors.

2574 JEFFRIES, WALTER LLOYD. "Town rates of Newton and Billerica, Mass." NEHGR, 31 (1877),
302-307.
Taxation, 1688; includes tables.

2575 KENDALL, FRANCIS H. "Turnpike roads of Middlesex County." NEM, New Ser., 28 (1903),
711-717.

2576 KIMBALL, HERBERT W. "Lexington and Concord."
MagHist, 1 (1905), 239-244.
Battles.

2577 LACOCK, JOHN KENNEDY. Lexington and Concord:
an illustrated book of 70 views from original
photographs. Boston: Jordan & More, 1925.
Unpaged.
Includes a text.

2578 LAWRENCE, LEWIS M. The Middlesex Canal....
Boston, 1942. 148 leaves.

2579 LAWRENCE, ROSEWELL B. "Middlesex Fells."
Appalachia, 4 (1884-1886), 199-214.
Park.

2580 LAWSON, FRED, JR. "The Middlesex Canal."
Towpath Topics, 5 (August, 1967), [2-6].

2581 LAWTON, FREDERICK. "Historical sketch of the
Middlesex Mechanics Association." ORHAL, 6
(1896-1904), 279-322.

2582 "LEXINGTON and Concord." Potter's AmMo, 4
(1875), 250-256.
Battles.

2583 "LEXINGTON and Concord, 1775-1904." NOHR, 3
(July 2, 1904), 3-7.

2584 LITTLE, DAVID B. America's first centennial
celebration, the nineteenth of April 1875 at
Lexington and Concord, Massachusetts. (1961) 2d.
ed. Boston: Houghton Mifflin, 1974. Pp. 64.

2585 MANN, MOSES WHITCHER. "An eighteenth-century
enterprise." MedHR, 7 (1904), 1-19.
Middlesex Canal.

2586 ____. "The Middlesex Canal, an eighteenth-century enterprise." BSPub, 6 (1910), 69-87.

2587 MASSACHUSETTS. PROBATE COURT (MIDDLESEX COUNTY). Index to the probate records of the county of Middlesex, Massachusetts; first and second series.... Samuel H. Folsom and William E. Rogers, eds. Cambridge, 1912-1914. 3 v. in 2.
Second series was published first.

2588 "MEDFORD'S metes and bounds." MedHR, 18 (1915), 90-97.

2589 MELLOON, GLADYS L. "The Merrimack River in history and literature." Lowell HSC, 2 (1921-1926), 10-16.

2590 MIDDLESEX County manual. Lowell: Penhallow Printing, 1878. Pp. 144.
Includes historical sketch of the county by Charles Cowley.

2591 MIDDLESEX EAST DISTRICT MEDICAL SOCIETY. Semicentennial anniversary held at Woburn, Mass., October 23rd, 1900. Boston: Idea Pr., 1900. Pp. 48. MB.
Includes historical sketch of the society by Samuel Warren Abbott.

2592 MOREY, CHARLES FREDERIC. "Middlesex Canal." Canal News, 1 (January, 1964), 1-5.

2593 MORSE, ABNER. A genealogical register of the inhabitants and history of the towns of Sherborn and Holliston. Boston: Damrell & Moore, 1856. Pp. 340 [i.e. 347].

2594 MOTT, FRANK LUTHER. "The newspaper coverage of Lexington and Concord." NEQ, 17 (1944), 489-505.

2595 MURDOCK, HAROLD. The nineteenth of April, 1775, exhibiting a fair and impartial account of the engagement fought on that day, chiefly in the towns of Concord, Lexington, and Menotomy, between a detachment of His Britannick Majesty's regular troops and the militia of the province of Massachusetts Bay; with candid remarks upon certain relations of that sanguinary event set forth by other hands. Boston: Houghton Mifflin, 1923. Pp. x, 134.

2596 NAYLOR, ANNIE LOUISE. "The Concord River in history and literature." Lowell HSC, 1 (1907-1913), 169-174.

2597 OLD COLONY TRUST COMPANY, BOSTON. The Lexington-Concord battle road, April 19, 1775. 2d. ed. Boston, 1961. Pp. 74.

2598 PARKHURST, WELLINGTON EVARTS. Historical facts relating to the Cutler Mills school district of Ashland, nos. 6 and 5, formerly no. 13 of Framingham, including references to the Parks Corner (no. 3) district of Framingham, of which no. 13 was formerly a part. Clinton: W. J. Coulter, 1897. Pp. 35.

2599 PATTERSON, DAVID N. A necrology of the physicians of Lowell and vicinity, 1826-1898. Lowell: Courier-Citizen, 1899. Pp. 121. M. Biographies.

2600 ____. "Reminiscences of the early physicians of Lowell and vicinity." ORHAL, 2 (1880-1883), 329-448.

2601 QUARTER-MILLENIAL celebration of the incorporation of the towns of Sudbury and Wayland, September fourth [1889]. Lowell: Marden & Rowell, 1891. Pp. 42. MBNEH.

2602 QUIMBY, IAN M.G. "The Doolittle engravings of the battle of Lexington and Concord." Winterthur Portfolio, 5 (1968), 83-108.
Amos Doolittle.

2603 RANTOUL, ROBERT SAMUEL. "The cruise of the 'Quero': how we carried the news to the King." EIHC, 36 (1900), 1-30.
Battles of Lexington & Concord.

2604 REVERE, PAUL. Paul Revere's three accounts of his famous ride. Edmund S. Morgan, ed. Boston: Massachusetts Historical Society, 1961. Unpaged.

2605 RICHARDSON, LAURENCE EATON. Concord River. Barre: Barre Publishers, 1964. Pp. 73.

2606 RICHARDSON, WILLIAM A. "Judges of probate, county of Middlesex, Mass." NEHGR, 29 (1875), 61-66.
Biographies.

2607 ROBERTS, CHRISTOPHER. The Middlesex Canal, 1793-1860. Cambridge: Harvard Univ. Pr., 1938. Pp. xii, 252.

2608 RUSSELL, JAMES S. "How Pawtucket Bridge was built and owned." ORHAL, 4 (1888-1891), 1-16.
Between Lowell and Dracut.

2609 SANBORN, FRANK B. "Concord and Lexington." Education, 23 (1903), 490-501.

2610 [SANDERSON, GEORGE AUGUSTUS], comp. Petitions, remonstrances, and acts relating to Littleton and Boxborough, 1782 to 1869. Boston: G. E. Crosby, 1890. Pp. 16.

2611 SARGENT, AARON. "The Winter Hill Road in 1842." Historic Leaves, 1 (October, 1902), 19-22.

2612 SEELEY, O. GILBERT. Views and descriptive history of Lexington and Concord. Lexington, 1901. Pp. 50. M.

2613 SEWALL, SAMUEL, 1785-1868. "A brief survey of the Congregational churches and ministers in the county of Middlesex, and in Chelsea in the county of Suffolk, Ms., from the first settlement of the country to the present day." American Quarterly Register, 11 (1838-1839), 45-55, 174-197, 248-279, 376-402; 12 (1839-1840), 234-250; 13 (1840-1841),

(SEWALL, SAMUEL.)
37-57; 14 (1842), 251-264, 393-411.
    Gives information relating to birth, educa-
    tion, settlement, resignation and death.

2614   SHATTUCK, LEMUEL. A history of the town of
        Concord; Middlesex County, Massachusetts,
from its earliest settlement to 1832; and of the
adjoining towns, Bedford, Acton, Lincoln, and Carlisle; containing various notices of county and
state history not before published. Boston: Russell, Odiorne, 1835. Pp. viii, 392.

2615   SYMMES, LUTHER RICHARDSON. "Squa Sachem."
        Winchester Record, 1 (1885), 19-22.
    Indian queen who owned land in Winchester
    and surrounding towns.

2616   TAYLOR, WILLIAM R. and CHRISTOPHER LASCH.
        "Two 'kindred spirits': sorority and family
in New England, 1839-1846." NEQ, 36 (1963), 23-41.
    Luella J. B. Case of Lowell and Sarah Edgar-
    ton of Shirley.

2617   "TEMPERANCE societies." Winchester Record,
        2 (1886), 111-115.
    Winchester and Woburn.

2618   TEMPLE, JOSIAH HOWARD. Historical sketch of
        the Middlesex South Conference of Churches.
South Framingham: J. C. Clark, 1880. Pp. 23. MB.
    Congregational.

2619   TOURTELLOT, ARTHUR BERNON. A bibliography
        of the battles of Concord and Lexington.
N.Y., 1959. Pp. 45.

2620   _____. William Diamond's drum; the beginning
        of the war of the American Revolution. Gar-
den City, N.Y.: Doubleday, 1959. Pp. 311.

2621   U. S. BOSTON NATIONAL HISTORIC SITES COM-
        MISSION. The Lexington-Concord battle road,
April 19, 1775. (1960) 2d. ed. Boston: Old Colony Trust Co., 1961. Pp. 74. M.

2622   VARNEY, GEORGE JONES. The story of Patriot's
        Day, Lexington and Concord, April 19, 1775;
with poems brought out on the first observation of
the anniversary holiday, and the forms in which it
was celebrated. Boston: Lee and Shepard, 1895.
Pp. x, 170.

2623   WAKEFIELD, MASS. Wakefield souvenir of the
        celebration of the 250th anniversary of an-
cient Reading, at Wakefield...May 28th, Reading...
May 29th, 1894. Containing the official program
of the exercises in both towns.... Wakefield:
C. W. Eaton and W. E. Eaton, [1894]. Unpaged.

2624   WALKER, BENJAMIN. "The Middlesex Canal."
        ORHAL, 3 (1884-1887), 273-308.

2625   WALKER, LAWRENCE BREED. "The Billerica &
        Bedford Railroad of Massachusetts." RLHSB,
No. 44 (1937), 24-27.

2626   WEDGE, RUTH P. "The Merrimack River in his-
        tory and literature." Lowell HSC, 2 (1921-
1926), 17-23.

2627   WELLINGTON, GEORGE Y. "Origin of the Lexing-
        ton and West Cambridge Branch Railroad."
LexHSP, 3 (1900-1904), 58-61.

2628   WHEELER, RICHARD. "Voices of Lexington and
        Concord." Am Heritage, 22 (April, 1971), 9-
13, 98-103.

2629   WOOD, MAL. "The old Middlesex Canal." Tow-
        path Topics, 9 (January, 1971), [6-8],
(April, 1971), [2-8].

2630   WRIGHT, ELLEN M. "Elizur Wright and the Mid-
        dlesex Fells." MedHR, 4 (1901), 77-82.
    Park.

2631   WRIGHT, GENEVA ALDRICH. "The shot heard
        round the world, April 19, 1775." Daughters
of the American Revolution Magazine, 10 (1971), 393-
394, 464, 472.

2632   YEATON, HERBERT PIERCE. "Historical sketch
        of the old Middlesex Canal." Towpath Topics,
4 (September, 1966), [2-7]; 5 (March, 1967), [2-8].

NANTUCKET COUNTY

2633   SEE NANTUCKET.

NORFOLK COUNTY

2634   ADAMS, CHARLES FRANCIS, 1835-1915. History
        of Braintree, Massachusetts (1639-1708) the
north precinct of Braintree (1708-1792) and the
town of Quincy (1792-1889). Cambridge: Riverside
Pr., 1891. Pp. 365.

2635   ALDEN, EBENEZER. "Early history of the medi-
        cal profession in Norfolk County." Boston
Medical and Surgical Journal, 49 (1853), 149-156,
173-179, 199-205, 215-200, 237-245.

2636   BIOGRAPHICAL review...containing life
        sketches of leading citizens of Norfolk
County, Massachusetts.... Boston: Biographical
Review Publishing, 1898. Pp. 710.

2637   BIRD, FRANCIS WILLIAM. Facts in relation to
        the history and management of the Walpole and
Norfolk County Railroads. Boston: Damrell &
Moore, 1847. Pp. 24.

2638   CAMERON, JAMES REESE, comp. Index to Three
        hundred years of Quincy, 1625-1925 [by]
Daniel Munro Wilson. Quincy: Quincy Historical
Society, 1973. Pp. 24. MBNEH.

2639   _____. New beginnings: Quincy and Norfolk
        County, Massachusetts. Quincy: Quincy His-
torical Society, 1966. Pp. 27.
    Subdivision of old town of Braintree into
    Quincy, Braintree, and Randolph, and
    formation of the county, 1792-1793.

2640   CAPPERS, ELMER O. Place names in Norfolk
        County, Massachusetts. [Brookline]: Norfolk
County Trust Co., [1972?]. Pp. 40. MBNEH.

2641   CHENEY, WILLIAM FRANKLIN. "The English Church in Dedham and Stoughton." DedHR, 5 (1894), 45-52.

2642   CHICK, MRS. CHARLES G. "Ancient landmarks of Norfolk County." HPHR, 8 (1912), 49-50.

2643   CLARK, GEORGE KUHN. History of Needham, Massachusetts, 1711-1911; including West Needham, now the town of Wellesley, to its separation from Needham in 1881, with some references to its affairs to 1911. Cambridge: Univ. Pr., 1912. Pp. 746.

2644   COOK, LOUIS ATWOOD. History of Norfolk County, Massachusetts, 1622-1918. S. J. Clarke, 1918. 2v.
       Vol. 2 is biographical.

2645   CUMMINGS, OSMOND RICHARD. Blue Hill Street Railway. Chicago: Electric Railway Historical Society, 1957. Pp. 27. MB.

2646   DUNBAR, ELIJAH. A sermon, preached at the ordination of the Rev. William Richey, to the pastoral care of the church and society in Canton, July 1, 1807...also, an appendix, giving an historical account of the rise and formation of the several churches in the towns of Canton, Sharon and Stoughton.... Dedham: H. Mann, 1809. Pp. 29.

2647   EDWARDS, WILLIAM CHURCHILL and FREDERICK AMES COATES. Commemorative booklet of the third centennial anniversary exercises of the incorporation of the ancient town of Braintree with an appendix and the history of Quincy, 'the north precinct of the ancient town of Braintree.' Quincy: Golden Print, 1940. Unpaged.

2648   EVERETT, WILLIAM. "Connection of the Adams family with Quincy and Braintree." MHSP, 2 Ser., 10 (1895-1896), 371-374.

2649   FORBES, ALLAN. Sport in Norfolk County. Boston: Houghton Mifflin, 1938. Pp. xv, 274.

2650   GALLISON, JEFFERSON CUSHING. Franklin and Wrentham. Franklin: Sentinel Pr., 1904. Pp. 28.
       Slightly revised version of article in NEM, New Ser., 2 (1899-1900), 321-341.

2651   HISTORY and directory of Randolph and Holbrook for 1891, containing resident, street and business directory, ... Boston: Brown, 1891. Pp. 176.

2652   HURD, DUANE HAMILTON, ed. History of Norfolk County, Massachusetts, with biographical sketches of many of its pioneers and prominent men. Philadelphia: J. W. Lewis, 1884. Pp. xii, 1001.

2653   MASSACHUSETTS. PROBATE COURT (NORFOLK COUNTY). Probate index, Norfolk County, Massachusetts...1793-1900. Dedham: Transcript Pr., 1910. 2v.

2654   NOLEN, JOHN. New towns for old; achievements in civic improvement in some American small towns and neighborhoods. Boston: Marshall Jones, 1927. Pp. xxix, 177.
       Cohasset and Walpole.

2655   NOYES, THOMAS. "Complete list of the Congregational ministers in the county of Norfolk, Mass., from the settlement of the county to the present time." American Quarterly Register, 8 (1835-1836), 42-58.
       Gives information regarding birth, education, settlement, resignation and death.

2656   PATTEE, WILLIAM SAMUEL. A history of old Braintree and Quincy, with a sketch of Randolph and Holbrook. Quincy: Green & Prescott, 1878. Pp. xiv, 660.

2657   WARNER, SAMUEL. History and directory of Wrentham and Norfolk, Mass. for 1890...history of the towns, from the first settlement to the present time. Boston: Brown Bros., 1890. Pp. 141.

2658   WILSON, DANIEL MUNRO. Three hundred years of Quincy, 1625-1925, historical retrospect of Mount Wollaston, Braintree, and Quincy. Boston: Wright & Potter, 1926. Pp. xiv, 455.
       For index to this work see: Cameron, James Reese.

PLYMOUTH COUNTY

2659   BIOGRAPHICAL review...containing life sketches of leading citizens of Plymouth County, Massachusetts.... Boston: Biographical Review Publishing, 1897. Pp. 638.

2660   BLISS, WILLIAM ROOT. Colonial times on Buzzard's Bay. (1888) New ed. Boston: Houghton Mifflin, 1900. Pp. 252.
       Wareham, Rochester, Marion and Mattapoisett.

2660A BRIDGEWATER, MASS. Proceedings of the 250th anniversary of old Bridgewater at West Bridgewater, Massachusetts, June 13, 1906. Bridgewater: A. H. Willis, 1907. Pp. 149.
       Bridgewater, Brockton, West Bridgewater, and East Bridgewater.

2661   BRIGGS, LLOYD VERNON. History and records of St. Andrew's Protestant Episcopal Church, of Scituate, Mass., 1725-1811, of Hanover, Mass., 1811-1903, and other items of historical interest, being volume II of the church and cemetery records of Hanover, Mass. Boston: W. Spooner, 1904. Pp. ix, 188.

2662   _____. History of shipbuilding on North River, Plymouth County, Massachusetts; with genealogies of the shipbuilders, and accounts of the industries upon its tributaries. 1640 to 1872. Boston: Coburn Bros., 1889. Pp. xv, 420.
       Author's notes and correspondence relating to this work are in the New England Historic Genealogical Society.

2663   CUMMINGS, OSMOND RICHARD. "Brockton and Plymouth Street Railway." Transportation Bulletin, No. 59 (July-September, 1959), entire issue.

2664   FORD, LEWIS. The variety book containing life sketches and reminiscences. Boston: G. E. Crosby, 1892. Pp. 243.

2665 GARDNER, FRANK A. "Colonel Theophilus Cotton's Regiment." MassMag, 3 (1910), 99-116.
Revolutionary; biography.

2666 _____. "General John Thomas's and Colonel John Bailey's Regiments." MassMag, 7 (1914), 158-182.
Revolutionary; biography.

2667 HISTORY and directory of Rockland and Hanover for 1892.... Boston: Brown Bros., 1892. Pp. 187. MBNEH.

2668 HISTORY of Plympton, (Carver and a part of Halifax inclusive.) MHSC, 2 Ser., 4 (1816), 283-285.

2669 HORTON, HOWARD LEAVITT. Ship building on the North river. [Boston?, 195-]. Unpaged.

2670 HURD, DUANE HAMILTON, ed. History of Plymouth County, Massachusetts, with biographical sketches of many of its pioneers and prominent men. Philadelphia: J. W. Lewis, 1884. Pp. viii, 1199.

2671 KINNICUTT, LINCOLN NEWTON. Indian names of places in Plymouth, Middleborough, Lakeville and Carver, Plymouth County, Massachusetts, with interpretations of some of them. Worcester: Commonwealth Pr., 1909. Pp. 64.

2672 LEONARD, MARY HALL. "Old Rochester and her daughter towns." NEM, New Ser., 20 (1899), 613-635.
Includes Marion and Mattapoisett.

2673 LORD, ARTHUR. "Some objections made to the State Constitution, 1780." MHSP, 50 (1916-1917), 54-60.
Middleborough and Plymouth.

2674 MATTAPOISETT, MASS. Mattapoisett and old Rochester, Massachusetts; being a history of these towns and also in part of Marion and a portion of Wareham. (1907) 3d. ed. Mattapoisett: Mattapoisett Improvement Association, 1950. Pp. xii, 426. MBNEH.

2675 MERRITT, JOSEPH FOSTER. Old time anecdotes of the North River and South Shore. Rockland: Rockland Standard Publishing, 1928. Pp. 110. MBNEH.

2676 NOYES, THOMAS. "Complete list of the Congregational ministers, in the county of Plymouth, Mass. from the settlement of the country to the present time." American Quarterly Register, 8 (1835-1836), 144-159.

2677 PACKARD, WINTHROP. Old Plymouth trails. Boston: Small, Maynard, 1920. Pp. 351.

2678 PEIRCE, EBENEZER WEAVER. Historic sketches of Hanson, Lakeville, Mattapoisett, Middleboro', Pembroke, Plympton, Rochester, Wareham, and West Bridgewater. Boston, 1873. Pp. 75.

2679 PLYMOUTH COUNTY, MASS. Plymouth County celebration of centennial of the Superior Court of the Commonwealth of Massachusetts. Monday, May 18, 1959. Plymouth: Leyden Pr., 1960. Pp. 24. M.

2680 THE PLYMOUTH County directory, and historical register of the Old Colony, containing an historical sketch of the county, and of each town in the county; a roll of honor, with the names of all soldiers of the army and navy, from this county, who lost their lives in service; an alphabetical list of voters; a complete index to the mercantile, manufacturing, and professional interests of the county.... Middleboro: Stillman B. Pratt, 1867. v.p.

2681 ROBBINS, MAURICE. "Historical approach to Titicut." MASB, 11 (1949-1950), 48-73.
Historical archaeology.

2682 ROCHESTER, MASS. Rochester's official bicentennial record. Tuesday, July 22, 1879, containing the historical address of Rev. N. W. Everett; the responses by Lieut. Gov. Long, Hon. W. W. Crapo, M.C., Judge Thos. Russell, and others; also, a full account of the proceedings of the day. New Bedford: Mercury Publishing, 1879. Pp. 125.
Marion, Mattapoisett, Rochester and Wareham.

2683 RYDER, ALICE AUSTIN. Lands of Sippican, on Buzzards Bay. New Bedford: Reynolds, 1934.
Marion, Mattapoisett and Rochester.

2684 SHERMAN, ANDREW M. "Historic New England towns revisited or back on my native heath." Americana, 8 (1913), 29-56, 127-152, 227-254, 321-342.
Limited to Plymouth County.

2685 SWAN, MABEL MUNSON. "Two early Massachusetts houses." Antiques, 52 (1947), 106-109.
Winslow House, Marshfield and the Squire William Sever House, Kingston.

2686 YESTERDAYS of Abington, Rockland, and Whitman, a historical picture book. Abington: New England Art Publishers, 1962. Pp. 98. MBNEH.

SUFFOLK COUNTY

2687 ALPER, BENEDICT S. "Juvenile justice: a study of juvenile appeals to the Suffolk Superior Court, Boston, 1930-1935." Journal of Criminal Law, 29 (1938), 202-215.

2688 ATKINS, RICHARD ANNESLEY. "The first hundred years." National Municipal Review, 30 (1941), 90-95.
Courts and taxation.

2689 BRADFORD, ALDEN. "Juridical statistics for the County of Suffolk viz. judges of [the] Superior Court of Judicature and of [the] Supreme Judicial Court of Massachusetts; and barristers, counsellors, and attornies, with brief notices of those who have deceased or retired from public life." American Quarterly Register, 13 (1840-1841), 417-432.
Includes table relating to birth, education, date of admission to bar, person(s) with whom he read law, and death.

2690 BROWN, RICHARD D. "The confiscation and dis-
position of loyalists' estates in Suffolk
County, Massachusetts." WMQ, 3 Ser., 21 (1964),
534-550.

2691 DEXTER, GEORGE, ed. "Record book of the Suffolk Bar." MHSP, 19 (1881-1882), 141-179.
1770-1805.

2692 HASSAM, JOHN TYLER. "Early recorders and
registers of deeds for the county of Suffolk,
Massachusetts, 1639-1735." MHSP, 2 Ser., 12 (1895-
1896), 203-250.
Biographies.

2693 _____. "Registers of deeds for the county of
Suffolk." MHSP, 2 Ser., 14 (1900-1901), 34-
104.
Biographies.

2694 _____. "Registers of probate for the county
of Suffolk, Massachusetts, 1639-1799."
MHSP, 2 Ser., 16 (1902), 23-125.
Biographies.

2695 LANGWORTHY, ISAAC PENDLETON. A brief historical sketch of the Suffolk North Conference
of Congregational Churches. Boston: Alfred Mudge
& Son, 1887. Pp. 12.
1861-1886.

2696 MASSACHUSETTS (COLONY) COUNTY COURT (SUFFOLK
COUNTY). Records of the Suffolk County
Court, 1671-1680.... Samuel Eliot Morison, ed.
Boston: The [Colonial] Society [of Massachusetts],
1933. 2v.

2697 MASSACHUSETTS. PROBATE COURT (SUFFOLK COUN-
TY). Index to the probate records of the
county of Suffolk, Massachusetts from the year 1636
to and including the year 1893. Elijah George, ed.
Boston: Rockwell and Churchill, 1895. 3v.

2698 NOBLE, JOHN. "The early court files of the
county of Suffolk." CSMP, 3 (1895-1897),
317-326.

2699 PROFESSIONAL and industrial history of Suffolk County, Massachusetts.... Boston:
Boston History Co., 1894. 3v.

2700 SUFFOLK COUNTY, MASS. Suffolk deeds. Boston, 1880-1906. 14v.
1629-1697.

2701 SULLIVAN, WILLIAM. An address to the members of the bar of Suffolk [County], Mass. at
their stated meeting on the first Tuesday of March,
1824. Boston: I. R. Butts, 1825. Pp. 63.
Legal history.

2702 TARBOX, INCREASE NILES. The religious and
ecclesiastical contrast within the bounds of
the Suffolk West Conference between the years 1776
and 1876. An address read before the Suffolk West
Conference at its meeting in Auburndale, Oct. 11,
1876. Boston: The Conference, 1876. Pp. 23. M.
Congregationalism.

2703 WEBSTER, MARY PHILLIPS and CHARLES R. MORRIS.
The story of the Suffolk Resolves. I. Suffolk County and the propaganda war for American independence. II. Neponset Valley industry prepares
to supply the Continental army. Milton: Milton
Historical Commission, 1973. Pp. iii, 60. M.

WORCESTER COUNTY

2704 ADAMS, CHARLES JOSEPH, ed. Quabaug, 1660-
1910: an account of the two hundred and fiftieth anniversary celebration held at West Brookfield, Mass., September 21, 1910. Worcester: Davis
Pr., 1915. Pp. 127.
Brookfield, New Braintree, North Brookfield,
West Brookfield.

2705 ADAMS, HENRY B. "Old militia companies."
FitchHSP, 4 (1900-1906), 136-145.
Ashburnham and Fitchburg.

2706 ALDRICH, PELEG EMORY. History of Worcester
County, Massachusetts...from its first settlement to the present time, with a history and
description of its cities and towns. Boston: Jewett, 1879. 2v.

2707 ALLEN, GEORGE. Reminiscences of the Rev.
George Allen, of Worcester, with a biograph-
ical sketch and notes by Franklin P. Rice.
Worcester: Putnam and Davis, 1883. Pp. 127.
Biographical.

2708 ALLEN, JOSEPH. An address delivered in Leominster, June 21, 1854, on the 20th anniversary of the Worcester Sunday School Society.
Worcester: Howland, [1854]. Pp. 18.

2709 AMMIDOWN, HOLMES. Historical collections:
containing I. The Reformation in France;
the rise, progress and destruction of the Huguenot
Church. II. The histories of seven towns, six of
which are in the south part of Worcester County,
Mass., namely: Oxford, Dudley, Webster, Sturbridge,
Charlton, Southbridge, and the town of Woodstock,
now in Connecticut, but originally granted and settled by people from the province of Massachusetts,
and regarded as belonging to her for about sixty
years. (1874) 2d. ed. New York, 1877. 2v.

2710 ANDERSON, GLENN F. "The social effects of
the Wachusett Reservoir on Boylston and West
Boylston." HJWM, 3 (Spring, 1974), 51-58.

2711 BENEDICT, WILLIAM ADDISON and HIRAM AVERILL
TRACY, comps. History of the town of Sutton,
Massachusetts...including Grafton, Millbury...and
parts of Northbridge, Upton and Auburn. Worcester:
Sanford and Co., 1878-1952. 2v.
Vol. 2 published by the town; John C. Dudley
was chairman of the Historical Committee for
this volume.

2712 BIOGRAPHICAL review...containing life
sketches of leading citizens of Worcester
County, Massachusetts.... Boston: Biographical Review Publishing, 1899. Pp. 1229.

2713 BLACK, JOHN and GEORGE WILLIAM WESTCOTT. Rural planning of one county: Worcester County, Massachusetts. Cambridge: Harvard Univ. Pr., 1959. Pp. xv, 419.
Historical study of land use.

2714 BLAKE, FRANCIS EVERETT. Worcester County, Massachusetts, warnings, 1737-1788. Worcester: F. P. Rice, 1899. Pp. 101.
Newcomers were "warned out."

2715 BRAGG, LESLIE RAYMOND. The doctors of Dudley and Webster, Massachusetts. n.p., n.d., [1952?]. Pp. xi, 185.

2716 CARTER, JAMES GORDON and WILLIAM H. BROOKS. A geography of Worcester county; for young children. Embracing 1. A short topographical and historical sketch of every town. 2. A general view of the county, and the employments of the people. 3. A glossary, explaining the geographical and other difficult terms. Lancaster: Carter, Andrews, 1830. Pp. vii, 61.
Not juvenile literature.

2717 "A CATALOGUE of the several Congregational ministers in the county of Worcester." WMHJ, 2 (1826), 371-375.
1658-1826.

2718 CHAMBERLAIN, DANIEL HENRY. "Old Brookfield and West Brookfield." NEM, New Ser., 21 (1899-1900), 481-504.

2719 _____. "Wheeler's surprise, 1675; where?" Worcester HSProc, (1897-1899), 508-533.
Brookfield or Hardwick; King Philip's War.

2720 CHAMBERLAIN, HENRY H. "Worcester County cattle-shows." Worcester HSProc, (1897-1899), 199-208.

2721 COOMBS, ZELOTES WOOD. "Early blast furnace operations in Worcester County." Worcester HSPub, New Ser., 2 (1936-1943), 138-152.

2722 _____. "Worcester County: its history, with discussion of attempts to divide it." Worcester HSPub, New Ser., 1 (1928-1935), 169-184.

2723 COREY, CHARLES V. "Worcester South Agricultural Society." QHSL, 3, No. 2, 17-24.

2724 CRANE, ELLERY BICKNELL, ed. Historic homes and institutions and genealogical and personal memoirs of Worcester County, Massachusetts, with a history of Worcester Society of Antiquity. Lewis Publishing, 1907. 4v.

2725 _____. History of Worcester County, Massachusetts. Lewis Historical Publishing, 1924. 3v.
Includes biographies.

2726 CRANE, JOHN CALVIN. "Asa Waters, 2d, and the Sutton and Millbury Armory." Worcester HSProc, (1886), 76-82.

2727 _____. Peter Whitney, and his 'History of Worcester County.' Worcester: F. P. Rice, 1889. Pp. 25.

2728 [CUMMINGS, C. H.]. Leading business men of Worcester and vicinity; embracing Millbury, Grafton, Westboro, Upton, Uxbridge, Leicester, Whitinsville. Illustrated. Boston: Mercantile Publishing, 1889. Pp. 304.
Biography.

2729 DAVIS, ANDREW MCFARLAND. "The land bank mortgages in Worcester County." AASP, New Ser., 16 (1903-1904), 85-90.

2730 DAVIS, GEORGE. A historical sketch of Sturbridge and Southbridge. West Brookfield: O. S. Cooke, 1856. Pp. v, 233.

2731 DENNY, C. C. "An ancient road, and reminiscences of some Worcester families who dwelt on it." Worcester HSProc, (1891-1893), 368-383.
Great Post Road, Worcester to Brookfield.

2732 DENNY, DANIEL E. "The Worcester County Mechanics Association." Worcester Magazine, 12 (1909), 60-69.

2733 DRAPER, JAMES. History of Spencer, Massachusetts, from its earliest settlement to the year 1860: including a brief sketch of Leicester, to the year 1753. (1841) 2d ed. Worcester: H. J. Howland, [1860]. Pp. viii, 276.

2734 DRESSER, MRS. GEORGE K. "The Indians of this locality." QHSL, 1, No. 9, 107-120.

2735 EPLER, PERCY HAROLD. Master minds at the Commonwealth's heart. Worcester: F. S. Blanchard, 1909. Pp. 317.
Biographies.

2736 FOOT, JOSEPH IVES. An historical discourse, delivered at West Brookfield, Mass., Nov. 27, 1828, on the day of the annual thanksgiving, with Capt. Thomas Wheeler's narrative, now annexed, and additional notices of occurrences in the town, since the first publication of the discourse...(1829). West Brookfield: Merriam & Cooke, 1843. Pp. 96.
Brookfield and West Brookfield.

2737 GARDNER, FRANK A. "Colonel Ebenezer Learned's Regiment." MassMag, 5 (1912), 73-101.
Revolutionary; biography.

2738 GARFIELD, JAMES FREEMAN DANA. "Lunenburg and Leominster in the Revolution." FitchHSP, 1 (1892-1894), 123-134.

2739 HARDING, WILLIAM B. "Origin of the names of the towns in Worcester County." Worcester HSProc, (1883), 97-117.

2740 "HISTORY of the county of Worcester." WMHJ, 1 (1825-1826), 33-36, 86-91, 103-116, 129-133, 161-164, 193-197; 2 (1826), 205-212, 377.

2741 HISTORY of Worcester County, Massachusetts, embracing a comprehensive history of the county from its first settlement to the present time, with a history and description of its cities and towns.... Boston: C. F. Jewett, 1879. 2v.

2742   HOAR, GEORGE FRISBIE and ALFRED SEELYE ROE.
       "Worcester County inventors." NEM, New Ser.,
31 (1904-1905), 350-363, 469-492.

2743   HOWLAND, JOSEPH A.   "[Worcester County (South
       Division) Anti-slavery Society]." Worcester
HSProc, (1886) 82-87.
       1838-1865.

2744   HUNTLEY, SULLIVAN W.   "Ashburnham Reservoir
       flood." FitchHSP, 4 (1900-1906), 253-265.

2745   HURD, DUANE HAMILTON, ed. History of
       Worcester County, Massachusetts, with bio-
graphical sketches of many of its pioneers and prominent men. Philadelphia: J. W. Lewis, 1889. 2v.

2746   KENT, DANIEL. "The locations of the first,
       second and third jails in Worcester County."
Worcester HSPub, New Ser., 2 (1936-1943), 64-71.

2747   KINGSLEY, ELBRIDGE and FREDERICK KNAB. Pic-
       turesque Worcester.... Springfield: W. F.
Adams, 1895. 2v.
       Pt. 3 never published; Pt. 1 relates to
       Worcester proper and Pt. 2 relates to towns
       in northern section of the county.

2748   KINNICUTT, LINCOLN NEWTON. Indian names of
       places in Worcester County, Massachusetts,
with interpretations of some of them. Worcester:
Commonwealth Pr., 1905. Pp. 59.

2749   LEADING business men of Spencer, Brookfield
       and vicinity; embracing Spencer, North
Brookfield, Brookfield, East Brookfield, West
Brookfield, Warren and West Warren. Boston: Mer-
cantile Publishing, 1889. Pp. 66.

2750   LINCOLN, CHARLES H. "The reciprocal influ-
       ence of the city and county of Worcester in
their development." Worcester HSPub, New Ser., 1
(1928-1935), 401-417.

2751   MARBLE, ANNA T. "Notable women of Worcester
       and Worcester Co." Worcester HSPub, New
Ser., 2 (1936-1943), 269-281.

2752   MASSACHUSETTS (COLONY) COURT OF GENERAL
       SESSIONS OF THE PEACE. WORCESTER COUNTY.
Records of the Court of General Sessions of the
Peace for the county of Worcester, Massachusetts,
from 1731 to 1737. Franklin P. Rice, ed. Worcester: Worcester Society of Antiquity, 1882. Pp. 197.

2753   MASSACHUSETTS. PROBATE COURT (WORCESTER
       COUNTY). Index to the probate records of
the county of Worcester, Massachusetts.... George
Herbert Harlow, John W. Mawbey, Harry H. Atwood,
comps. Worcester: O. B. Wood, 1898-1920. 5v.
       1731-1920.

2754   MORGAN, PHILIP M. "The Boston, Barre and
       Gardner Railroad." Worcester HSPub, New
Ser., 3 (1964), 59-68.

2755   NATIVES OF MAINE. WORCESTER COUNTY, MASSA-
       CHUSETTS. Constitution of the natives of
Maine of Worcester County, Mass. with list of mem-
bers...with a brief history of the association.
Worcester: Charles Hamilton, 1886. Pp. 56. M.

2756   NELSON, JOHN. Worcester County; a narrative
       history. N.Y.: American Historical Society,
1934. 3v.

2757   NOURSE, HENRY STEDMAN. "Some notes upon the
       genesis of the power loom in Worcester Coun-
ty." AASP, New Ser., 16 (1903-1904), 22-46.

2758   NOYES, THOMAS. "Complete list of Congrega-
       tional ministers, in the county of Worcester,
Mass., from its settlement to the present time."
American Quarterly Register, 10 (1837-1838), 47-65,
126-145.
       Gives information regarding place of birth,
       education, settlement, resignation and death.

2759   PAIGE, LUCIUS ROBINSON. "Wheeler's defeat:
       1675: where?" AASP, New Ser., 5 (1887-
1888), 96-106.
       King Philip's War.

2760   ____. "Wickaboag? or Winnimisset? which
       was the place of Capt. Wheeler's defeat in
1675?" NEHGR, 38 (1884), 395-400.
       King Philip's War.

2761   RICE, FRANKLIN PIERCE. "The Worcester dis-
       trict in Congress, from 1789 to 1857."
Worcester HSProc, (1889), 77-95.
       Biographies of representatives.

2762   SEARS, CLARA ENDICOTT. The great powwow; the
       story of the Nashaway Valley in King Philip's
War. Boston: Houghton Mifflin, 1934. Pp. x, 288.

2763   SHELDON, GEORGE. "Wheeler's surprise - the
       cul-de-sac." Worcester HSProc, 17 (1900-
1901), 445-465.
       King Philip's War.

2764   SMITH, JONATHAN. "Toryism in Worcester
       County during the war for independence."
MHSP, 48 (1914-1915), 15-35.

2765   STAPLES, SAMUEL ELIAS. "The Worcester Coun-
       ty Musical Association." Worcester HSProc,
(1884), 19-42.

2766   STEARNS, EZRA SCOLLARY. "Notown, its grants
       and families." FitchHSP, 5 (1907-1913), 95-
117.
       Fitchburg and Westminster.

2767   STEVENS, EBEN S. "Quinebaug and its indus-
       tries." QHSL, 2, No. 22, 217-224.

2768   THOMPSON, GRACE AGNES. "Lancaster and Clin-
       ton." NEM, New Ser., 32 (1905), 353-377.

2769   TORREY, RUFUS CAMPBELL. History of the town
       of Fitchburg, Massachusetts; comprising also
a history of Lunenburg, from its first settlement to
the year 1764.... (1836) Fitchburg: Fitchburg
Centennial Committee, 1865. Pp. iv, 128.

2770   TYMESON, MILDRED MCCLARY. The Lancastrian
       towns. Barre: Barre Publisher, 1967.
Pp. 94.

2771 WHITAKER, GEORGE MASON. "The Mason family in connection with the early history of Sturbridge and Southbridge." QHSL, 1, No. 17, 205-214.

2772 WHITE, MARTHA E. D. "Westborough and Northborough." NEM, New Ser., 26 (1902), 721-738.

2773 WHITNEY, PETER. The history of the county of Worcester, in the Commonwealth of Massachusetts: with a particular account of every town from its first settlement to the present time; including its ecclesiastical state, together with a geographical description of the same, to which is prefixed, a map of the county, at large, from actual survey. Worcester: Isaiah Thomas, 1793. Pp. vi, 339.

2774 WILLIS, HENRY AUGUSTUS. "The division of Worcester County." FitchHSP, 3 (1897-1899), 70-83.

2775 WILSON, LEWIS G. "Milford and Hopedale." NEM, New Ser., 27 (1902-1903), 487-508.

2776 WORCESTER COUNTY, MASS. BAR. Addresses before the members of the bar, of Worcester County, Massachusetts: by Joseph Willard, October 2, 1829; Emory Washburn, February 7, 1856; Dwight Foster, October 3, 1878. Worcester: C. Hamilton, 1879. Pp. ix, 250.
   Series of biographical sketches of lawyers.

2777 WORCESTER BANK & TRUST COMPANY, WORCESTER, MASS. Forty immortals of Worcester & its county: A brief account of those natives or residents who have accomplished something for their community or for the nation. [Worcester], 1920. Pp. 72.

2778 "WORCESTER County Indian names." Worcester Magazine, 9 (1906), 102-105.

2779 WORCESTER COUNTY MECHANICS ASSOCIATION. Historical sketch...with the charter and by-laws, a list of members and a catalogue of the library. Worcester: Howland, 1854. Pp. 78. MB.

2780 WORCESTER SOUTH CONFERENCE OF CONGREGATIONAL CHURCHES. Worcester South chronicles: a brief history of the Congregational churches of the Worcester South Conference, of Massachusetts. 1670-1876. Worcester: L. P. Goddard, 1877. Pp. 66.

ABINGTON

2781 ABINGTON, MASS. Celebration of the one hundred and fiftieth anniversary of the incorporation of Abington, Massachusetts, June 10, 1862.... Boston: Wright & Potter, 1862. Pp. 114.

2782 ____. Official program of the commemorative exercises of the two hundredth anniversary of the incorporation of the town of Abington, Massachusetts, June 10, 1712, participated in by the town of Abington, Rockland and Whitman, comprising the original town of Abington, to be held June 9 to 15 inclusive, 1912.... Rockland: A. I. Randall, 1912. Pp. 72.

2783 ABINGTON, MASS. HIGH SCHOOL. Catalogue of the Abington High School, 1849-1912. Boston: Fort Hill Pr., [1912?]. Pp. 138. MBNEH.

2784 COUGHLAN, WILLIAM J. "Abington." NEM, 47 (1912), 113-128.

2785 GOODNOW, EARLE T. "Manufacture of tacks, brads, and sprigs." CEAIA, 1 (March, 1934), 1, 6.

2786 HISTORICAL SOCIETY OF OLD ABINGTON. Old Abington's 250th anniversary, 1712-1962; early history, Abington, 1962. 27 leaves.

2787 "HISTORY and description of Abington, Mass., Aug. 1816." MHSC, 2 Ser., 7 (1818), 114-124.

2788 HOBART, AARON. An historical sketch of Abington, Plymouth County, Massachusetts. Boston: S. N. Dickinson, 1839. Pp. 176.

2789 HOBART, BENJAMIN. History of the town of Abington, Plymouth County, Massachusetts, from its first settlement. Boston: T. H. Carter and Son, 1866. Pp. xix, 453.

2790 MESERVE, CHARLES FRANCIS. Abington's part in the building of a great commonwealth and a powerful nation. n.p., 1930. Pp. 20.

2791 O'BRIEN, ROBERT LINCOLN. Abington, Mass., commemorative address...200th anniversary... June 13, 1912. Boston, 1918. Pp. 26. MB.

2792 SNOW, CHARLES A. A historical discourse given on the 50th anniversary of the Baptist Church, South Abington, Mass., November 6, 1872. South Abington, 1873. Pp. 32. MB.

ACTON

2793 ACTON, MASS. Acton directory embracing also a brief history of the town.... South Acton: W. N. Sharp, 1883-1884. Pp. 52. MBNEH.

2794 ACTON, MASS. EVANGELICAL CHURCH. The confession of faith and covenant of the Evangelical Church in Acton, Mass., with regulations and catalogue of members. Detroit: Tribune Book and Job Printing, 1868. Pp. 52. MH.
   Includes historical sketch.

2795   ACTON-BOXBOROUGH REGIONAL SCHOOL DISTRICT,
        WEST ACTON, MASS. A decade of progress,
1955-1965. West Acton, [1966?]. Pp. 58. M.

2796   ACTON HISTORICAL SOCIETY, ACTON, MASS. A
        brief history of Acton. Acton, 1974.
Pp. 56. MBNEH.

2797   ADAMS, JOSIAH. An address delivered at Ac-
        ton, July 21, 1835, being the first centen-
nial anniversary of the organization of that
town.... Boston: J. T. Buckingham, 1835. Pp. 48.
        Also relates to battle of Concord.

2798   EASTERBROOK, GORHAM. Sermon delivered...fif-
        tieth anniversary of the West Acton Baptist
Church, July 12, 1896. Ayer: Huntley S. Turner,
[1896?]. Pp. 22.

2799   NOYES, FREDERICK BROOKS. "The tale of
        Brooks Tavern." NEM, New Ser., 27 (1902-
1903), 331-343.

2800   _____. Tell tale tomb or the Acton aspect of
        the Concord fight. Leicester, [not after
1939]. Pp. 15. MBNEH.

2801   PHALEN, HAROLD ROMAINE. History of the town
        of Acton. Cambridge, 1954. Pp. iii, 471.

2802   SOUVENIR of the celebration of the 120th an-
        niversary of the Concord fight. Acton:
April 19, 1895. Acton: F. P. Wood, 1895. Pp. 24.

ACUSHNET

2803   ACUSHNET centennial, Acushnet, Massachu-
        setts, land of the Cushenas, 1860-1960.
Acushnet: American Pr., 1960. Pp. 52.

2804   HOWLAND, FRANKLYN. A history of the town of
        Acushnet, Bristol County, state of Massachu-
setts. New Bedford, 1907. Pp. 398.

2805   SWIFT, CLEMENT N. "Old Acushnet." ODHS,
        No. 7 (September, 1904), 8-16.

ADAMS

2806   ADAMS, MASS. First records of the town of
        Adams, Massachusetts. Franklin P. Rice, ed.
Worcester: Massachusetts Record Society, 1892.
Pp. 11.

2807   GREYLOCK NATIONAL BANK, ADAMS, MASS. His-
        toric Adams; the past and the present of the
town and a bank. Boston: Walton Advertising &
Printing, 1941. Pp. 27.

2808   "THE JENKS family of Adams; inventors of the
        fire engine, the hand scythe and the iron
kettle." Berkshire Hills, 4 (1903-1904), 225-227.

2809   "L. L. Brown Paper Company." Industry, 7
        (January, 1942), 21-24, 46.

2810   NILES, GRACE GREYLOCK. "Greylock Park Res-
        ervation." NEM, New Ser., 45 (1911), 382-
395.

2811   "OLD Fort Massachusetts." Berkshire Hills, 3
        (1902-1903), 85-87; 4 (1903-1904), 289.

2812   PLUNKETT, W. C. AND SONS, ADAMS, MASS. One
        hundred years of business--W. C. Plunket &
Sons, 1814-1914. Adams: Andover Pr., 1914.
Unpaged. MPB.
        Cotton.

2813   "A RARE bit of history: attempt to divide
        the town of Adams in 1826." Berkshire Hills,
New Ser., 1 (1904-1905), 14.

2814   SLADE, D. D. "The site of old Fort Massachu-
        setts." MagAmHist, 20 (1888), 281-285.

2815   "SOUTH Adams reminiscences." Berkshire
        Hills, New Ser., 2 (1905-1906), 162-163.

2816   "A VENERABLE structure standing for 115
        years." Berkshire Hills, 1 (May 1, 1901),
[1-3].
        Friends meeting house, built 1786.

AGAWAM

2817   BIRCHARD, WILLIAM METCALF. A discourse de-
        livered at the centennial anniversary of the
First Congregational Church, in Agawam, (Feeding
Hills Parish), November 11, 1862. Springfield:
S. Bowles, 1863. Pp. 22.

2818   "WOOLEN makers for a century." WNE, 1 (1910-
        1911), 293-294.
        The Agawam Co.

ALFORD

2819   WARNER, HENRY C. "Old graveyards in Alford."
        Berkshire Hills, 1 (Dec. 1, 1900), [6].

2820   _____. "The old meeting house at Alford."
        Berkshire Hills, 3 (1902-1903), 128-129.
        Union meeting house.

AMESBURY

2821   AMESBURY, MASS. CONGREGATIONAL CHURCH. Re-
        port of the semi-centennial celebration of
the Congregational Church and Society, Amesbury,
Mass., December 4, 5, & 6, 1881, historical discourse, addresses and communications. Amesbury:
J. B. Rodgers, 1882. Pp. 47.
        Discourse by P. S. Boyd.

2822   "BAILEY was making electrics 70 years ago."
        Industry, 36 (April, 1971), 22.
        S. R. Bailey & Co., electric automobiles.

2823 BLANEY, WILLIAM C. "Pewter communion service of the Rocky Hill Meeting House." OTNE, 58 (1967-1968), 82-84.

2824 EVANS, JOHN Q. The plains of 200 years ago...a paper read at a meeting of the Town Improvement Society held at Batt's Hill, Salisbury, Mass., June 17, 1897. Amesbury: Morse, 1897. Pp. 8.

2825 FREEMASONS. AMESBURY, MASS. WARREN LODGE. Warren Lodge A.F. & A.M. centenary celebration, an account of its centenary celebration held at Amesbury, Massachusetts, June 17 and 18, 1923, including the historical address delivered by Right Worshipful Charles I. Pettingell.... Amesbury, 1925. Pp. 176.

2826 HILL, EVE. "The house of the month [Averill House]." The Shoreliner, 2 (January, 1952), 35-41.

2827 _____. "The Macy-Colby House." The Shoreliner, 2 (November, 1951), 10-13.

2828 LITTLE, NINA FLETCHER. "The treasurer's book of the Rocky Hill Church." OTNE, 57 (1966-1967), 46-48.

2829 LONGYEAR, MARY HAWLEY BEECHER. The history of a house (built by Squire Bagley, in Amesbury, Massachusetts) its founder, family and guests. (1925) 3d ed. rev. Brookline: Longyear Foundation, 1959. Pp. 70. MSaE.

2830 PETTENGELL, CHARLES IRELAND. "The west parish of Salisbury, Massachusetts, and the Rocky Hill Church." EIHC, 82 (1946), 97-121. 1634-1884.

2831 REDFORD, SARA LOCKE. History of Amesbury, Massachusetts, beginning with the arrival of the Winthrop Fleet 1630 at Salem and Boston through 1967. Amesbury: Whittier Pr., 1968. Pp. 239.

2832 RICE, MARGARET S. Sun on the river; the story of the Bailey family business, 1856-1956. Concord, N.H.: Rumford Pr., 1955. Pp. 146. The Bailey Co. formerly manufactured sleighs, carriages and electric vehicles; today it produces weather stripping and glass run channels for the automobile industry.

2833 SMITH, EMILY BINNEY. A chronological record of the principal events that have occured in Amesbury, Massachusetts, from the organization of the township of Merrimac in 1638 to 1900. Amesbury: J. E. Brierly, 1901. Pp. 38.

2834 SPARHAWK, FRANCES C. "Amesbury: the home of Whittier." BSM, 3 (1885), 418-428.

2835 WHITTIER HOME ASSOCIATION, AMESBURY, MASS. Amesbury home of Whittier. Amesbury: Whittier Pr., [1918?]. Pp. 30. MSaE.

2836 WOODWELL, ROLAND H. Amesbury Public Library, 1856-1956. Ambesbury, 1956. Pp. 35.

AMHERST

2837 ALLEN, MARY ADÈLE. Around a village green: sketches of life in Amherst. Northampton: Kraushar Pr., 1939. Pp. 94.

2838 _____. "The Boltwood House, memories of Amherst friends and neighbors." Amherst Graduates' Quarterly, 26 (August, 1937), 297-307. Social life and customs.

2839 ALPHA DELTA PHI. AMHERST CHAPTER. Amherst Alpha Delta Phi. 1837-1887. N.Y.: Fleming, Brewster & Alley, 1887. Pp. 176. Amherst College.

2840 AMHERST, MASS. Records of the town of Amherst from 1735 to 1788. J. F. Jameson, ed. Amherst: J. E. Williams, 1884. Pp. iv, 100.

2841 AMHERST, MASS. FIRST CHURCH OF CHRIST. An historical review, one hundred and fiftieth anniversary of the First Church of Christ in Amherst, Massachusetts. November 7, 1889. Amherst: Amherst Record, 1890. Pp. 121. MAJ.

2842 AMHERST, MASS. NORTH CONGREGATIONAL CHURCH. A brief history of the North Congregational Church, Amherst, Massachusetts, 1826-1926. Amherst: Carpenter & Morehouse, 1927. Pp. 42. MAJ.

2843 _____. Diamond jubilee of the North Congregational Church, Amherst, Mass. Nov. 15th, 1901. Fitchburg: Sentinel Printing, 1902. Pp. 73.

2844 AMHERST, MASS. SECOND CONGREGATIONAL CHURCH. Manual of the Second Congregational Church, Amherst, Mass. containing historic documents, list of pastors, by-laws of the incorporated church and a list of members received and dismissed from the date of organization, 1782. Amherst: Carpenter & Morehouse, 1924. Pp. 70.

2845 AMHERST COLLEGE. Causes of growth & decline of Amherst College from 1825-1846. n.p., n.d. Pp. 12.

2846 _____. Exercises at the semi-centennial of Amherst College, July 12, 1871. Springfield: Samuel Bowles, 1871. Pp. 149

2847 _____. A plea for a miserable world. I. An address, delivered at the laying of the corner stone of the building erecting for the charity institution in Amherst, Massachusetts, August 9, 1820, by Noah Webster, esq. II. A sermon, delivered on the same occasion, by Rev. Daniel A. Clark. III. A brief account of the origin of the institution. Boston: Ezra Lincoln, 1820. Pp. 48. Relates to the charity institution.

2848 "[AMHERST College centennial]." Amherst Graduates' Quarterly, 10 (August, 1921), entire issue.

2849 AMHERST, Massachusetts, this booklet is published by the town of Amherst; the Chamber of Commerce; Amherst College [and] the University of Massachusetts, as part of the town's observance of

(AMHERST, Massachusetts, this booklet...) its bicentennial anniversary, 1959. [Amherst?, 1959?]. Unpaged.

2850   ANDERSON, CHARLES R. "From a window in Amherst: Emily Dickinson looks at the American scene." NEQ, 31 (1958), 147-171.
Refers to Amherst people and events.

2851   ATKINS, WILLIAM H. Leave the light burning: South Amherst, Massachusetts. Marjorie Atkins Elliott, ed. McFarland, Wis.: Community Publications, 1973. Pp. xii, 148.

2852   BOWKER, WILLIAM HENRY. The old guard; the famous "Faculty of four"; the mission and future of the college; its debt to Amherst College, Harvard College and other institutions.... Boston: Wright and Potter, 1908. Pp. 19.
University of Massachusetts.

2853   BROWN, W. R. "Amherst." WNE, 2 (1912), 263-270.

2854   _____. Amherst, Massachusetts...a home of culture and agriculture. Amherst: Charles E. Ewell, n.d. Pp. 32.

2855   CANFIELD, FAYETTE CURTIS. "Farewell to College Hall." Amherst Graduates' Quarterly, 26 (August, 1937), 291-296.
Theater at Amherst College.

2856   _____. The seed and the sowers; a series of chapel talks on the history of Amherst College and a play about its founding. Amherst: Amherst College, 1955. Pp. 140.

2857   CARPENTER, EDWARD WILTON and CHARLES FREDERICK MOREHOUSE. The history of the town of Amherst, Massachusetts.... Amherst, 1896. Pp. xxiii, 640, 263.

2858   CARR, WILLIAM OTIS. The Amherst diary of William Otis Carr, 1853-1857. Frank O. Spinney, ed. Guilford, Conn.: Shore Line Times Publishing, 1940. Pp. x, 30. MNF.
Amherst College.

2859   CARY, HAROLD WHITING. The University of Massachusetts: a history of one hundred years. Amherst: Univ. of Massachusetts, 1962. Pp. 247.

2860   CASWELL, LILLEY BREWER. Brief history of the Massachusetts Agricultural College, semi-centennial, 1917. Springfield: F. A. Bassette, 1917. Pp. 72. MAJ.

2861   CAUSES of the growth and decline of Amherst College. n.p., 1847. Pp. 12. MH.

2862   "THE CRADLE of Amherst College." Amherst Graduates' Quarterly, 19 (May, 1930), 151-156.
Amherst Academy.

2863   CUTTING, GEORGE RUGG. Student life at Amherst College: its organizations, their membership and history.... Amherst: Hatch & Williams, 1871. Pp. 204.

2864   DAKIN, WINTHROP S. Historical sketch of Amherst Savings Bank, 1864-1964. n.p., [1964?]. Pp. 11. MAJ.

2865   DAUGHTERS OF THE AMERICAN REVOLUTION. MASSACHUSETTS. MARY MATOON CHAPTER, AMHERST. Amherst, Massachusetts, the chronology of events in the development of the town of Amherst, Massachusetts, 1727 to 1941. n.p., [1941?]. Pp. 16. MAJ.

2866   DICKINSON, MARQUIS FAYETTE. The beginnings of college history: an address delivered at the Massachusetts Agricultural College, Amherst, Mass., Oct. 2, 1907. Boston: Wright and Potter, 1908. Pp. 17.

2867   _____. Historical address delivered at the centennial celebration, in Amherst, Mass., July 4, 1876. Amherst: McCloud & Williams, 1878. Pp. viii, 44.
1876 also marked the centennial of Amherst.

2868   FISHER, GEORGE ELISHA. Centennial anniversary, historical discourse...at the Second Congregational Church, Amherst, Mass., Nov. 12, 1882. Amherst: J. E. Williams, 1882. Pp. 40.

2869   _____. Historical sketch, articles of faith, covenant and rules, of the North Church, Amherst, Mass. Amherst: J. S. & C. Adams, 1854. Pp. 35.
Author attribution by the American Congregational Association.

2870   FREEMASONS. AMHERST, MASS. PACIFIC LODGE. Historical sketch of Pacific Lodge, together with the by-laws, and a complete list of members. Amherst: H. M. McCloud, 1876. Pp. 28, 3

2871   FUESS, CLAUDE MOORE. Amherst, the story of a New England college. Boston: Little, Brown, 1935. Pp. xiii, 372.

2872   GOODELL, HENRY H. "The Massachusetts Agricultural College." NEM, New Ser., 3 (1890-1891), 224-231.

2873   GREEN, CHARLES ROBERT. "The Jones Library in Amherst." Amherst Graduates' Quarterly, 18 (February, 1929), 87-93.

2874   HAMMOND, WILLIAM GARDINER. Remembrance of Amherst, an undergraduate's diary, 1846-1848. George F. Whicher, ed. N.Y.: Columbia Univ. Pr., 1946. Pp. viii, 307.

2875   HAWLEY, JOHN AMON and FRANK PRENTICE RAND. Two hundred years in view and review, 1739-1939: a record of the observance of its two hundredth anniversary by the First Congregational Church in Amherst, Massachusetts, November 4-5, 1939. Amherst: Carpenter & Morehouse, 1939. unpaged.

2876   HEWLETT, HORACE W., ed. In other words; Amherst in prose and verse. Amherst: Amherst College Pr., 1964. Pp. x, 208.
Amherst College.

2877   "HISTORY of Amherst College." The Sprite, No. 6 (March, 1832), 161-170.

2878 HITCHCOCK, EDWARD, 1793-1864. Reminiscences of Amherst College, historical, scientific, biographical and autobiographical: also, of other and wider life experiences. Northampton: Bridgman & Childs, 1863. Pp. vii, 412.

2879 [HITCHCOCK, EDWARD], 1828-1911. A report of twenty years experience in the Department of Physical Education and Hygiene in Amherst College to the Board of Trustees, June 27, 1881.... Amherst: C. A. Bangs, 1881. Pp. 18. MNF.
        Author attribution by the Forbes Library, Northampton.

2880 HITCHCOCK, FREDERICK HILLS. The handbook of Amherst, Massachusetts. (1891) Rev. ed. Amherst, 1894. Pp. v, 188.

2881 HUMPHREY, HEMAN. "Revivals of religion in Amherst College." American Quarterly Register, 11 (1838-1839), 317-328.

2882 _____. Sketches of the early history of Amherst College. Northampton: Kingsbury Box & Printing, 1905. Pp. 32.

2883 JOHNSON, GEORGE H. Historical manual of the North Congregational Church and Society, Amherst, Mass.... Amherst: J. E. Williams Book & Job Printer, 1889. Pp. 64.

2884 KING, STANLEY. 'The Consecrated Eminence'; the story of the campus and buildings of Amherst College. Amherst: Amherst College, 1951 [i.e. 1952]. Pp. xi, 368.

2885 _____. A history of the endowment of Amherst College. Amherst: Amherst College, 1950. Pp. vii, 259.

2886 LE DUC, THOMAS HAROLD ANDRÉ. Piety and intellect at Amherst College, 1865-1912. N.Y.: Columbia Univ. Pr., 1946. Pp. ix, 165.

2887 LONG, J. C. "General Amherst and the College." Amherst Graduates' Quarterly, 23 (February, 1934), 89-95.
        Jeffery Amherst.

2888 MCKEON, NEWTON FELCH and KATHERINE CONOVER COWLES, eds. Amherst, Massachusetts imprints, 1825-1876. Amherst: Amherst College Library, 1946. Pp. 191.
        Includes a history of printing in the town.

2889 MARSH, DWIGHT WHITNEY. Historical address delivered at the semicentennial celebration of the North Congregational Church, Amherst, Mass., November 15th, 1876.... Fitchburg: Sentinel Printing, 1877. Pp. 23.

2890 MASSACHUSETTS. STATE COLLEGE, AMHERST. The Massachusetts Agricultural College, Bibliography of the College, Pt. 1, The Institution. Amherst, 1917. Pp. 69.
        Pt. 2, 'The Men,' was never published.

2891 PEASE, ARTHUR STANLEY. "Francis Howard Fobes [and his Snail's Pace Press]." HarvLibBul, 13 (1959), 125-134.

2892 PHI BETA KAPPA. MASSACHUSETTS BETA, AMHERST COLLEGE. Massachusetts Beta of Phi Beta Kappa, Amherst College; the second catalogue of the chapter. Amherst, 1934. Pp. iv. 58.
        Includes history of the chapter.

2893 RAND, FRANK PRENTICE. The Jones Library in Amherst, 1919-1969. Amherst: Jones Library, 1969. Pp. 115.

2894 _____. The village of Amherst, a landmark of light. Amherst: Amherst Historical Society, 1958. Pp. 337.

2895 _____. Yesterdays at Massachusetts State College, 1863-1933. Amherst: The Associate Alumni, Massachusetts State College, 1933. Pp. vi, 245.

2896 RILEY, HERBERT ELIHU, ed. An Amherst book: a collection of stories, poems, songs, sketches and historical articles of alumni and undergraduates of Amherst College. N.Y.: Republic Pr., 1896. Pp. x, 189.

2897 SARGENT, DAVID W., JR. "The railroad mania in Amherst: a critical study of the Amherst & Belchertown Railroad." RLHSB, No. 47 (1938), 11-45.
        1853-1864.

2898 SEE, ANNA PHILLIPS. Amherst past and present.... n.p., 1930. Pp. 52. MAJ.

2899 SHOOP, MAX PARDOE. Sabrina, the class goddess of Amherst College; a history. (1910) [2d ed.]. Springfield: Loring-Axtell, 1910. v.p. Bronze statue.

2900 SOME useful information concerning the places of interest in Amherst. Amherst: M. McCloud, 1875. Pp. 31.

2901 STEARNS, ALFRED ERNEST. An Amherst boyhood. Amherst: The College, 1946. Pp. x, 212. Amherst College.

2902 [SWEETSER, CHARLES HUMPHREYS]. Annals of Amherst College: the soil, the seed, the sowers, the presidents and the professors.... Northampton: Trumbull & Gere, 1860. Pp. 70.
        Author attribution by Newton McKeon and Katharine Cowley in their 'Amherst, Massachusetts imprints, 1825 to 1876.'

2903 TANNOUS, DAVID. "A short history of Walker Hall, Amherst College." Amherst Alumni News, (Spring, 1963), 7-13.
        Demolished in 1963.

2904 THAYER, CHARLES HIRAM. History of the Stockbridge House at Massachusetts State College, n.p., 1936. Pp. 20. MAJ.

2905 TUCKERMAN, FREDERICK. Amherst Academy; a New England school of the past, 1814-1861. Amherst, 1929. Pp. xii, 272.

2906 TYLER, WILLIAM SEYMOUR. History of Amherst
       College during its first half century, 1821-
1871. Springfield: C. W. Bryan, 1873. Pp. xii,
671.

2907 _____. A history of Amherst College during
       the administrations of its first five presi-
dents, from 1821 to 1891. N.Y.: Hitchcock, 1895.
Pp. xxxiii, 312.

2908 WALKER, ALICE MOREHOUSE. Historic homes of
       Amherst. Amherst: Carpenter & Morehouse,
1905. Pp. 100.

2909 _____. The story of a New England country
       church. Amherst, 1901. Pp. 29. MB.
North Congregational Church.

2910 _____. Through Turkey Pass to Amherst and
       beyond. Amherst, 1903. Pp. 52.

2911 _____. Ye Amherst girl of ye olden tyme.
       Amherst, 1901. Pp. 31

2912 WATTS, R. J. "The Massachusetts Agricultur-
       al College: historical sketch." The Sig-
net, New Ser., 1, No. 4 (1909), 3-14.

2913 WHICHER, GEORGE FRISBIE. Mornings at 8:50;
       brief evocations of the past for a college
audience. Northampton: Hampshire Bookshop, 1950.
Pp. viii, 159.
       Amherst College.

ANDOVER

2914 ABBOT, ABIEL, 1765-1859. History of Ando-
       ver, from its settlement to 1829. Andover:
Flagg and Gould, 1829. Pp. 204.

2915 ABBOT ACADEMY, ANDOVER, MASS. Abbot Acad-
       emy at Andover, Massachusetts. Andover:
Andover Pr., 1907. Pp. 40.
       History and general information.

2916 _____. Addresses delivered during the cele-
       bration of the one hundredth anniversary of
the founding of Abbot Academy. Andover, 1929.
Pp. 87.

2917 ANDOVER, MASS. Andover, Massachusetts: pro-
       ceedings at the celebration of the two hun-
dred and fiftieth anniversary of the incorporation
of the town, May 20, 1896. Andover: Andover Pr.,
1897. Pp. 173.

2918 _____. Historic Andover, 325th anniversary,
       1646-1971. [Andover?], 1971. Unpaged. M.

2919 ANDOVER, MASS. CHRIST CHURCH. History of
       the parish of the Christ Church, from its
origin to the present time, June, 1854. Andover:
John S. Flagg, 1854. Pp. 11. M.

2920 _____. Semi-centennial celebration, All-
       Saints Day, 1885. Andover, 1886. Unpaged.

2921 ANDOVER, MASS. FIRST CHURCH. Exercises at
       the celebration of the two hundred and fif-
tieth anniversary of the organization of the First
Church in Andover, Wednesday, October second, eighteen hundred and ninety-five, 1645-1895. n.p., n.d.
Pp. 27.

2922 ANDOVER, MASS. FREE CHRISTIAN CHURCH. Fif-
       tieth anniversary, May, 1896. n.p., n.d.
Pp. 29.
       Includes history of the church.

2923 ANDOVER, MASS. MEMORIAL HALL. Historical
       sketch of the Memorial Hall, Andover, Mass.
Lawrence: G. S. Merrill & Crocker, 1873. Pp. 19.
       A soldiers' memorial and library.

2924 ANDOVER, MASS. SOUTH CHURCH. Historical
       manual of the South Church in Andover, Mass.,
August, 1859. [George Mooar], comp. Andover:
W. F. Draper, 1859. Pp. 200.

2925 _____. The South Church, Congregational,
       Andover, Massachusetts, two hundred fiftieth
anniversary, October 15-22, 1961. n.p., [1961?].
Pp. 20. MSaE.

2926 _____. Supplementary manual of the South
       Church, Andover, Mass. August, 1882. An-
dover: W. F. Draper, 1882. Pp. 35.
       Supplements 'Historical manual' of 1859.

2927 ANDOVER, MASS. 325TH ANNIVERSARY COMMITTEE.
       Andover, 1946-1961. Andover, 1971. Pp. 59.
M.

2928 ANDOVER, MASS. WEST PARISH CHURCH. Histori-
       cal manual of the West Church and Parish in
Andover, Massachusetts...December fifth, 1826-1926.
Andover: Andover Pr., 1926. Pp. 59. MSaE.

2929 _____. Historical sketches of the West Par-
       ish Church, Andover, Massachusetts, 1906.
[Andover?], 1906. Pp. 81.

2930 _____. Supplement to the historical manual
       of the West Church and Parish in Andover,
Massachusetts, 1926-1951. n.p., [1951?]. Pp. 32.
MSaE.

2931 ANDOVER THEOLOGICAL SEMINARY. The Andover
       case; with an introductory historical state-
ment, a careful summary of the arguments of the re-
spondent professors and the full text of the arguments of the complainants and their counsel, together with the decision of the board of visitors.
Boston: Stanley and Usher, 1887. Pp. 194.

2932 _____. A memorial of the semi-centennial
       celebration of the founding of the Theologi-
cal Seminary at Andover. Andover: Warren F. Draper, 1859. Pp. viii, 242.

2933 ANDOVER TOWNSMAN, ANDOVER, MASS. Town of
       Andover, Mass; 250th anniversary souvenir,
including the official programme of the anniversary
celebration. Andover: Andover Pr., 1897. Pp. 46.

2934 BACON, LEONARD. A commemorative discourse, on the completion of fifty years from the founding of the Theological Seminary at Andover. Andover: W. F. Draper, 1858. Pp. 46.

2935 BALDWIN, SIMEON E. "Visitorial statutes of Andover Seminary." American Historical Association. Annual Report, (1891), 225-241.

2936 BULLEN, ADELAIDE K. and RIPLEY P. BULLEN. "Black Lucy's garden." MASB, 6 (1945-1946), 17-28.
　　Lucy Foster; historical archaeology.

2937 CARPENTER, CHARLES CARROLL. Andover Ministerial Association; one hundred and fiftieth anniversary, First Congregational Church, Lowell, October 7, 1913. Boston: Everett Pr., 1913. Pp. 23.
　　Includes historical sketch.

2938 CARPENTER, JANE BRODIE. Abbot and Miss Bailey and Abbot in the early days. Andover: Abbot Academy, 1959. Pp. 326.
　　Abbot Academy and Bertha Bailey.

2939 CARTER, FRANKLIN. The service of the Andover Theological Seminary in the cause of education; an address delivered at the one hundredth anniversary of the founding of the seminary, June 9, 1908. Williamstown, 1918. Pp. 22.

2940 "A CENTURY of service in review." Industry, 21 (June, 1956), 9-11, 44.
　　Tyer Rubber Co.

2941 DOUGLAS-LITHGOW, ROBERT ALEXANDER. "A group of early colonial houses at Andover, Mass." MassMag, 5 (1912), 4-9.

2942 DOWNS, ANNIE SAWYER. "Abbot Academy." NEM, 4 (1886), 136-152.

2943 ____. "Historic Andover." NEM, New Ser., 14 (1896), 483-507.

2944 ____. Poem: historic Andover, 1646-1896. Andover: Andover Pr., 1896. Pp. 56.

2945 FUESS, CLAUDE MOORE, ed. Andover, Massachusetts, in the World War. [Andover]: Andover Pr., 1921. Pp. 224.

2946 ____. Andover: symbol of New England; the evolution of a town. [Andover]: Andover Historical Society, 1959. Pp. 480.

2947 ____. In my time; a medley of Andover reminiscences. Andover: Phillips Academy, 1959. Pp. vi, 127.
　　Reminiscences of the academy.

2948 ____. Independent schoolmaster. Boston: Little, Brown, 1952. Pp. 371.
　　Phillips Academy.

2949 ____. An old New England school; a history of Phillips Academy, Andover. Boston: Houghton Mifflin, 1917. Pp. xi, 547.

2950 ____. "Witches at Andover." MHSP, 70 (1950-1953), 8-20.

2951 GOLDSMITH, BESSIE P. The townswoman's Andover. Andover: Andover Historical Society, 1964. Pp. 104. MSaE.

2952 GREVEN, PHILIP J., JR. "Family structure in seventeenth-century Andover, Massachusetts." WMQ, 3 Ser., 23 (1966), 234-256.

2953 ____. Four generations: population, land, and family in colonial Andover, Massachusetts. Ithaca: Cornell Univ. Pr., 1970. Pp. xvi, 329

2954 ____. "Old patterns in the New World: the distribution of land in seventeenth-century Andover." EIHC, 101 (1965), 133-148.

2955 ____. "Youth, maturity, and religious conversion: a note on the ages of converts in Andover, Massachusetts, 1711-1749." EIHC, 108 (1972), 119-134.

2956 HISTORIC houses in Andover, Massachusetts. n.p., 1946. Unpaged. MSaE.

2957 HOOKER, EDWARD W. "Sacred music in the Theological Seminary, Andover, Massachusetts." CongQ, 6 (1864), 268-275.

2958 JACKSON, SUSAN E. Reminiscences of Andover. Andover: Andover Pr., 1914. Pp. 38.

2959 KELSEY, KATHERINE ROXANNA. Abbot Academy sketches, 1892-1912. Boston: Houghton Mifflin, 1929. Pp. viii, 234.

2960 KEMPER, JOHN MASON. Phillips Academy at Andover: a national public school. N.Y.: Newcomen Society in North America, 1957. Pp. 28.

2961 KIMBALL, JAMES M. "A tragic railroad accident of 1853." Railroad Enthusiast, 8 (January-February, 1941), 32.

2962 KITTREDGE, HENRY AUSTIN. "Andover, past and present, with some recollections of my time." NEM, New Ser., 39 (1908-1909), 579-593.
　　Phillips Academy.

2963 LE BOUTILLIER, ADDISON B. An architectural monograph on early wooden architecture in Andover, Mass. St. Paul: White Pine Bureau, 1917. Pp. 16.

2964 MCKEEN, PHILENA and PHEBE F. MCKEEN. Annals of fifty years: a history of Abbot Academy, Andover, Mass., 1829-1879. Andover: W. F. Draper, 1880. Pp. xx, 259.

2965 MCKEEN, PHILENA. Sequel to the annals of 50 years: a history of the Abbot Academy, Andover, Mass. 1879-1892. Andover: W. F. Draper, 1897. MH.

2966 MAKEPEACE, FRANK BARROWS. "'An illustrious town'--Andover." NEM, 4 (1886), 301-318.

2967   MATTHEWS, ALBERT. "Washington youths at An-
        dover Academy, 1795-1797." CSMP, 14 (1911-
1913), 58-63.
        Augustine and Bushrod Washington.

2968   MORSS, GEORGE HENRY. History of the Mission
        Hill Sabbath School in Abbott Village. Ando-
ver: The Society of Inquiry, Phillips Academy,
1856. Pp. 38. MB.

2969   "THE OLD meeting-house of the South Parish,
        Andover, Ms." CongQ, 5 (1863), 170-172.

2970   PARADISE, SCOTT HURTT. A history of print-
        ing in Andover, Massachusetts, 1798-1931.
[Andover]: The Andover Pr., 1931. Unpaged.

2971   PARK, WILLIAM EDWARDS. Earlier annals of
        Phillips Academy. [Gloversville, N.Y.?
1882?]. Pp. 51. MH.

2972   PHILLIPS ACADEMY. ANDOVER, MASS. An Ando-
        ver primer: Phillips Academy and its histo-
ry, 1778-1928. Andover, 1928. Unpaged. MB.

2973   PHILLIPS ACADEMY, ANDOVER, MASS. PHILO-
        MATHEAN SOCIETY. Memorial, semi-centennial
of the Philomathean Society, Phillips Academy, Andover, Mass. Andover, [1875]. Pp. vii, 142.

2974   "PHILLIPS Academy, Andover." New Englander,
        44 (1885), 571-586.

2975   POORE, ALFRED. "A genealogical-historical
        visitation of Andover, Mass. in the year
1863." EIHC, 48 (1912), 276-292; 49 (1913), 50-64,
161-171, 239-252, 305-320; 50 (1914), 41-56, 253-
264; 51 (1915), 306-312; 52 (1916), 84-96, 281-288;
53 (1917), 54-64, 187-192; 54 (1918), 138-144, 246-
250; 55 (1919), 75-77.
        Biography.

2976   RAYMOND, SAMUEL, comp. The record of Ando-
        ver during the Rebellion. Andover: W. F.
Draper, 1875. Pp. viii, 232.
        Biography.

2977   ROBBINS, SARAH STUART. Old Andover days;
        memories of a Puritan childhood. Boston:
Pilgrim Pr., 1908. Pp. xi, 188.
        Social life and customs.

2978   ROBINSON, SUSAN E. Reminiscences of Andover.
        Andover: Andover Pr., 1914. Pp. 38. MSaE.

2979   SHAWSHEEN Village, the model community and
        home of the officers and staff of the Ameri-
can Woolen Co. Andover: American Woolen Co.,
1924. Unpaged. MBNEH.

2980   SMITH, MARY BYERS. "The founding of the
        Free Christian Church of Andover." EIHC, 82
(1946), 291-305.

2981   _____. "The founding of the Memorial Hall
        Library, Andover." EIHC, 79 (1943), 246-255.

2982   "THE SOUTH Church, Andover, Ms." CongQ, 5
        (1863), 20-22.

2983   STREET, OWEN. Discourse delivered on the
        twenty-fifth anniversary of the Andover Con-
ference, April 29, 1884, at the West Church, Andover. Lowell: Morning Mail Print, 1884. Pp. 22.
M.
        Ministerial association.

2984   TAYLOR, JOHN PHELPS. Historical discourse
        preached in the Seminary Chapel, Andover, on
May 17, 1896, being the Sunday prior to the 250th
anniversary of the incorporation of the town. Andover: Andover Pr., [1896?]. Pp. 16. MBNEH.
        General sketch of education in the town.

2985   THOMPSON, J. EARL, JR. "Abolitionism and
        theological education at Andover." NEQ, 42
(1974), 238-261.

2986   WILLIAMS, DANIEL DAY. The Andover liberals;
        a study in American theology. N.Y.: King's
Crown Pr., 1941. Pp. viii, 203.

2987   WOODS, LEONARD. History of the Andover The-
        ological Seminary. Boston: J. R. Osgood,
1885. Pp. 638.

ARLINGTON

2988   ARLINGTON, MASS. Arlington, Massachusetts:
        a short history with map. Arlington, 1930.
Unpaged.

2989   _____. The one hundredth anniversary of the
        incorporation of the town of Arlington, Mas-
sachusetts, Saturday, June first, 1907. Arlington:
Everett Pr., 1907. Pp. 65.

2990   ARLINGTON. Boston: Edison Electric Illumi-
        nating Co., 1909. Pp. 20. M.

2991   ARLINGTON, MASS. BAPTIST CHURCH. History of
        the Baptist Church in West Cambridge; togeth-
er with the articles of faith, church covenant regulations, and list of members. Boston: J. M. Hewes,
1855. Pp. 30. MB.

2992   ARLINGTON, MASS. FIRST CONGREGATIONAL
        CHURCH. The one hundred and fiftieth anni-
versary of the organization of the First Congregational Parish in Arlington, Massachusetts; an account of the commemorative services, the historic
sermon, and address of the pastor. Boston, 1889.
Pp. 31.

2993   ARLINGTON calendar. [Arlington?, 1901?].
        Unpaged.
        Events 1733-1900 appear next to appropriate
        day; appendix gives chronological lists of
        clergymen and postmasters.

2994   ARLINGTON COOPERATIVE BANK, ARLINGTON, MASS.
        Helping Arlington home owners for fifty years
1889-1939.... Arlington, 1939. Unpaged. M.

2995   ARLINGTON FIVE CENTS SAVINGS BANK, ARLINGTON,
        MASS. Souvenir statement commemorating the
70th anniversary of the Arlington Five Cents Savings

(ARLINGTON FIVE CENTS SAVINGS BANK, ARLING-
TON, MASS.)
Bank and the 300th anniversary of the founding of
Massachusetts Bay Colony. Boston: A. W. Ellis,
1930. Pp. 12.

2996 [BARTLETT, EDWARD H. H.]. How Arlington won
the flag on the town house. [Arlington?]:
Stedman Pr., [1905?]. Pp. 8.

2997 BROWN, ABRAM ENGLISH. "Menotomy parsonage."
NEM, New Ser., 26 (1902), 80-92.
Historic house and its dwellers.

2998 CALLAHAN, D. W. Centennial anniversary of
the town of Arlington. n.p., [1907?]. Unpaged. M.

2999 CUTTER, BENJAMIN and WILLIAM RICHARD CUTTER.
History of the town of Arlington, Massachusetts, formerly the second precinct in Cambridge or
district of Menotomy, afterward the town of West
Cambridge, 1635-1879. Boston: D. Clapp & Son,
1880. Pp. iv, 368.

3000 GILL, FREDERIC. The story of the First Con-
gregational Parish 'The Unitarian Church,'
Arlington, Massachusetts. Arlington?, 1930?.
Pp. 23.

3001 NEEDHAM, ROBERT FRANCIS. The Arlington Universalists and their church, a brief history
of the First Universalist Society of Arlington,
Massachusetts, from its informal beginnings to the
year 1941. Arlington, 1941. Unpaged.

3002 NYLANDER, ROBERT HARRINGTON. "Jason Russell
and his house in Menotomy." OTNE, 55 (1964-
1965), 29-42.

3003 PARKER, CHARLES SYMMES. Town of Arlington,
past and present; a narrative of larger
events and important changes in the village precinct
and town from 1637 to 1907. Arlington: C. S. Parker & Son, 1907. Pp. 331.

3004 PRENDERGAST, FRANK M. "A world of figur-
ines." Industry, 12 (September, 1947), 13-
15.
Sebastion studio.

3005 RUSSELL, JASON ALMUS. "An incident on the
battle road: cold-blooded murder of an old
and crippled American by the British troops during
their retreat from the Battle of Lexington, April
19, 1775." JAmHist, 24 (1930), 114-117.

3006 SMITH, SAMUEL ABBOT. West Cambridge on the
nineteenth of April, 1775, an address delivered in behalf of the Ladies' Soldiers' Aid Society of West Cambridge. Boston: A. Mudge & Son,
1864. Pp. 66.

ASHBURNHAM

3007 ASHBURNHAM, MASS. FIRST CONGREGATIONAL
CHURCH. Manual...containing a history of its
formation.... Fitchburg: Sentinel Printing, 1878.
Pp. 32. M.

3008 CUSHING, STEPHEN. Semi-centennial discourse
delivered in the Methodist Episcopal Church,
in Ashburnham, Mass.,...July 9, 1882.... Boston:
Deland & Barta, 1883. Pp. 27.

3009 HOLDEN, RAYMOND PECKHAM and BARBARA B. HOLD-
EN. Ashburnham, Massachusetts, 1885-1965.
Gardner: Hatton Printing, 1970. Pp. 222.

3010 STEARNS, EZRA SCOLLAY. History of Ashburnham, Massachusetts, from the grant of Dorchester Canada to the present time, 1734-1886....
Ashburnham: Published by the town, 1887. Pp. 1022.

ASHBY

3011 ASHBY, MASS. BICENTENNIAL JOURNAL COMMITTEE.
Official journal, Ashby, Massachusetts bicentennial, 1767-1967. Ashby, 1967. Pp. 120. M.

3012 BARBER, LAURENCE LUTHER. "The clockmakers of
Ashby, Massachusetts." Antiques, 23 (1932),
178-180.

3013 WILDER, DOROTHY T. A history of the Ashby
Band, Ashby, Massachusetts 1887-1967. Fitchburg: Fitchburg Sentinel, [1968?]. Unpaged. M.

3014 _____. A history of the First Parish Church,
Unitarian-Universalist, of Ashby, Massachusetts, 1767-1967. East Pepperell: Townell Printing, 1968. Pp. 38.

ASHFIELD

3015 ASHFIELD, MASS. BICENTENNIAL COMMITTEE.
Ashfield bicentennial, 1765-1965. n.p.,
1965. Pp. 48.

3016 HALL, CHARLES A. "Early Huntstown and Chil-
eab Smith. PVMA 5 (1905-1911) 198-214.

3017 HALL, GRANVILLE STANLEY. "Boy life in a
Massachusetts county town thirty years ago."
AASP, New Ser., 7 (1890-1891), 107-128.

3018 HOWES, BARNABAS. Historical sketches of the
times and men in Ashfield, Mass., during the
Revolutionary War.... North Adams: Mrs. W. B.
Walden, 1884. Pp. 22.

3019 _____. History of the town of Ashfield,
Mass., Vol. I. West Cummington: W. G. At-
kins, 1887. Pp. 24.
No more published.

3020 HOWES, FREDERICK G. Historical address given
at the dedication of the new Sanderson Academy and Field Memorial Hall Building, Ashfield,
Mass., July 24, 1889. Greenfield: E. A. Hall,
1889. Pp. 24. MB.
History of the academy.

3021 _____. History of the town of Ashfield,
Franklin County, Massachusetts from its settlement...; also a historical sketch of the town

(HOWES, FREDERICK G.)
written by Rev. Thomas Shepard in 1834. [Ashfield]:
Published by the town, [1910?]-1965. 2v.
1742-1960; Vol. 2 was written by citizens of
the town.

3022   HUNTINGTON, GEORGE PUTNAM. Historical ad-
        dress read in St. John's Church, Ashfield,
Mass...October 2, 1887...59th anniversary of the
consecration of the church. n.p., 1887. Pp. 8.
MDeeP.

3023   MCLAUGHLIN, WILLIAM G., ed. "Ebenezer
        Smith's ballad of the Ashfield Baptists,
1772." NEQ, 47 (1974), 97-108.

3024   RICHARDS, GEORGE. Ministerial duties and
        immunities, a sermon preached...in Ashfield
Dec. 3, 1851. Boston: T. R. Marvin, 1851. Pp. 31.
MB.
        Includes historical sketch by Theophilus
Packard, Jr.

3025   WATKINS, LURA WOODSIDE. "The stoneware of
        South Ashfield, Massachusetts." Antiques,
26 (1934), 94-97.

ASHLAND

3026   ASHLAND. Boston: Edison Electric Illuminat-
        ing Co., 1909. Pp. 8. MBNEH.

3027   HISTORICAL RECORDS SURVEY. MASSACHUSETTS.
        History of the town of Ashland. Framingham:
Lakeview Pr., 1942. Pp. 141.

3028   HOMER, MARTHA A. Evolution of the Indian
        trails of 300 years ago to the Ashland
streets and avenues of to-day. Ashland, 1908. Unpaged. M.

3029   METCALF, FRANK JOHNSON. History of the high
        school, Ashland, Mass., 1856-1890, with a
biographical record of its members. South Framingham: Lakeview Pr., 1890. Pp. 117. MB.

3030   "THE WARREN Telechron Company." Industry, 2
        (March, 1937) 9-11.
        Electric clocks.

ATHOL

3031   ATHOL, MASS. BOARD OF TRADE. Athol, Massa-
        chusetts: a little book about a big town.
Athol, 1919. Pp. 48.
        Includes brief historical sketch.

3032   ATHOL CO-OPERATIVE BANK. 50 glorious years,
        Athol Co-operative Bank, 1889-1939. Athol,
1939. Unpaged. M.

3033   BLAKE, HENRY AUGUSTUS. Historical addresses,
        with short accounts of the celebrations of
the 50th anniversary of the organization of the
Evangelical Congregational Church of Athol, Mass....
delivered Oct. 14 and Nov. 21, 1880. Athol: Athol
Transcript Co., 1880. Pp. 38.

3034   CASWELL, LILLEY BREWER. Athol, Massachu-
        setts, past and present. Athol, 1899.
Pp. vii, 448.
        Includes biographical sketches.

3035   _____. History of the Methodist Episcopal
        Church, Athol, Massachusetts, with sketch of
the 50th anniversary exercise, historical address,
etc. Athol: Athol Transcript Co., 1902. Pp. 26.

3036   CLARKE, SAMUEL FULTON. A centennial dis-
        course delivered September 9, 1850, before
the First Church and Society in Athol, at the celebration of the one hundredth anniversary of the
organization of said church. Boston: W. Crosby &
H. P. Nichols, 1851. Pp. 95.

3037   FARNUM, WALTER E. "Industry's map of Massa-
        chusetts: Athol." Industry, 3 (December,
1937), 35-36.

3038   "L. S. Starrett Co." Industry, 2 (February,
        1937), 9-11.
        Tools.

3039   LORD, WILLIAM GARDINER, comp. History of
        Athol, Massachusetts. Athol, 1953. Pp. 745.

3040   _____. and MARY B. LORD. History of the
        First Baptist Church of Athol, Massachusetts.
Athol: F. W. Gourlay, [1913?]. Pp. 92.

3041   NORTON, JOHN FOOTE. The home of the ancient
        dead restored: an address delivered at
Athol, Mass., July 4, 1859...at the re-consecration
of the ancient cemetery of Athol, and the erection
of a monument thereon. (1859) 2d ed. Athol: Rufus Putnam, 1859. Pp. 24.

3042   [_____]. The record of Athol, Massachusetts,
        in suppressing the great rebellion. Boston:
G. C. Rand & Avery, 1866. Pp. 264.
        Includes biography.

3043   SPRAGUE, HENRY HARRISON. A story of a New
        England town: address...given at Athol, Old
Home Week, July 26, 1903. Boston: Little, Brown,
1904. Pp. 48.

ATTLEBORO

3044   ATTLEBORO, MASS. CIVILIAN DEFENSE COMMITTEE.
        A brief history of Attleboro's civilian de-
fense. n.p., [1945]. Unpaged. M.

3045   ATTLEBORO, MASS. FIRST CONGREGATIONAL
        CHURCH. Baptizms [sic], marriages, deaths,
admitted to communion, Old Town Church, Attleboro;
first church, 1740-1856. Copied by Elizabeth J.
Wilmarth, comp. [Attleboro]: Marion Pearce Carter,
1928. 22 leaves.

3046   ATTLEBORO, MASS. SECOND CONGREGATIONAL
        CHURCH. Membership and vital records of the
Second Congregational Church of Attleboro, Massachu-
setts. Marion Williams Pierce Carter and Charles
Shepard, II, eds. Washington, 1924. 48 leaves.

3047 BARROWS, CHARLES M. "Attleboro, Mass."
NEM, 4 (1886), 27-36.

3048 COBB, BERTHA VINTON. Two hundredth anniversary observance, Second Congregational
Church, May 20-21-22-23, 1948, program and histories, souvenir booklet. Attleboro, [1948?].
Pp. 30. MBNEH.

3049 CRANE, JONATHAN. A historical sketch of the
Second Congregational Church in Attleborough:
delivered at its centennial meeting, December 7,
1848. Boston: Damrell & Moore, 1849. Pp. 44.

3050 DAGGETT, JOHN. A sketch of the history of
Attleborough, from its settlement to the
division. Amelia Daggett Sheffield, ed. Boston:
S. Usher, 1894. Pp. 788.
Includes biography.

3051 "FIFTY years of pioneering service to the
jewelry industry." Industry, 16 (November,
1950), 32g-32h, 65-66.
Sweet Mfg. Co., chains.

3052 HUNT, SAMUEL. A plea for the old parish:
a discourse preached in West Attleborough,
October 13th, 1872. Central Falls, [R.I.]: E. L.
Freeman, 1872. Pp. 23.
Congregational church.

3053 "JEWELRY was the road to success for 40-year
old L. G. Balfour Co." Industry, 18 (July,
1953), 21-22, 48-49.

3054 MCLOUGHLIN, WILLIAM G. "The Balkcom Case
(1782) and the pietistic theory of separation
of Church and State." WMQ, 3 Ser., 24 (1967), 267-
283.
Elijah Balkcom.

3055 "THE MASON Box Company, a 75-year old boxing
champion." Industry, 31 (June, 1966), 31.

3056 SULLIVAN, BARBARA. "The jewelry hub of
America." Industry, 33 (May, 1968), 15, 73.

3057 WELD, HABIJAH. "Note on Attleborough."
MHSC, 2 Ser., 1 (1814), 184-185.
1694-1727.

3058 WHITEHILL, JOHN. Early history of the First
Church of Christ in Attleboro.... Providence: J. C. Hall, 1894. Pp. 18. MB.

AUBURN

3059 FEDERAL WRITERS' PROJECT. MASSACHUSETTS.
A historical sketch of Auburn, Massachusetts, from the earliest period to the present day
with brief accounts of early settlers and prominent
citizens. Worcester: Chas. D. Cady, 1937. Pp. 63.

AVON

3060 SEE HISTORIES OF NORFOLK COUNTY.

AYER

3061 BATCHELDER, ROGER. The book of Fort Devens.
N.Y.: Grosset & Dunlap, 1941. Pp. 72.

3062 ____. Camp Devens, described and photographed.... Boston: Small, Maynard, 1918.
Pp. 94.

3063 BURNS, GEORGE J. Historical address delivered before St. Paul Lodge, F. and A.M. at
its centennial anniversary at Ayer, Mass., January
26, 1897.... Ayer, 1897. Pp. 21.

3064 CLARK, LYMAN. Historical discourse relative
to the South Groton Christian Union, 1855-
1864, and the First Unitarian Parish of Ayer, Mass.,
1864-1885. Ayer: J. H. Turner, [1886]. Pp. 20.

3065 COWLEY, CHARLES. Reminiscences of James C.
Ayer and the town of Ayer. 3d ed. Lowell:
Penhallow Printing, [1880]. Pp. 156.
Second edition is [1879?].

3066 FOSDICK, DAVID. A village ministry in Massachusetts: a farewell sermon preached July 1,
1860, in the meeting-house recently belonging to the
"South-Groton Christian Union." Boston: Crosby,
Nichols, Lee, 1861. Pp. 30.

3067 HUDSON, ALFRED SERENO. History and by-laws
of the First Congregational Church, Ayer,
Mass. Ayer: W. M. Sargent, 1887. Pp. 135.

3068 MENDING AND SERVICE BOARD, CAMP DEVENS. History of the mending and service board of Camp
Devens during the World War 1917-1919. n.p.,
[1922?]. Pp. 23. M.

3069 ROBINSON, WILLIAM JOSEPH. Forging the sword;
the story of Camp Devens, New England's army
cantonment. Concord, N.H.: Rumford Pr., 1920.
Pp. xi, 172.

BARNSTABLE

3070 ALLEN, GEORGE E. "A short story of a Cape
church." Cape Cod Magazine, 2 (July, 1916),
17-19.
West Barnstable Congregational Church.

3071 AREY, BERTHA M. Historical sketch of the
First Baptist Church in Hyannis, Massachusetts. Hyannis: F. B. & F. P. Goss, 1939. Unpaged. [MBaC].

3072 BACON, GASPAR G. The founding of the town of
Barnstable, Commonwealth of Massachusetts,
1639-1939, tercentenary address, August 25, 1939.
n.p., 1939. Pp. 17. M.

3073 BARNSTABLE, MASS. Barnstable town records.
C. W. Swift, ed. Yarmouthport: C. W.
Swift, 1910. Pp. 60.
1649 to 1779.

3074 _____. The Cape Cod centennial celebration at Barnstable, Sept. 3, 1839, of the incorporation of that town, Sept. 3, 1639, giving a full detail of the preliminary proceedings of the committees, and the speeches and toasts at the dinner. Barnstable: S. B. Phinney, 1840. Pp. 92.

3075 _____. Records of the proprietors of the common lands in the town of Barnstable, Massachusetts, 1703-1795. James F. McLaughlin, ed. Boston, 1935. Pp. 288.

3076 BARNSTABLE, MASS. BARNSTABLE TERCENTENARY COMMITTEE. Barnstable, a little guide to some of her historic scenes. Hyannis: F. B. & F. P. Goss, 1939. Pp. 31. MBNEH.

3077 _____. Report of proceedings of the tercentenary anniversary of the town of Barnstable, Massachusetts. Donald G. Trayser, ed. Hyannis, 1940. Pp. xv, 215.

3078 BARNSTABLE, MASS. WEST PARISH CHURCH. Records of the West Parish of Barnstable, Massachusetts, 1668-1807. Boston: Massachusetts Historical Society, 1924. 160 leaves.

3079 "BARNSTABLE Gorhams." MagHist, 22 (1916), 195-197.
Gorham family.

3080 BOWLES, FRANCIS TIFFANY. "The loyalty of Barnstable in the Revolution." CSMP, 25 (1922-1924), 265-348.

3081 BUSH-BROWN, ALBERT. Books, bass, Barnstable: an address delivered at the centennial celebration of the Sturgis Library, Barnstable, Massachusetts, August 26, 1967. Barnstable: Great Marshes Pr., 1967. Pp. 28.

3082 CENTERVILLE OLD HOME WEEK ASSOCIATION, CENTERVILLE, MASS. Old home week celebration, August 19-22, 1904, historical notes, Centerville, Massachusetts.... Boston: Sparrell Print, 1905. Pp. 148.
Historical notes by Julia E. Phinney.

3083 CHILDS, LILA B. "Cotuit." Cape Cod Magazine, 4 (July, 1918), 6-7.
Locality.

3084 CLARK, ADMONT G. "A college is born." CCC, 17 (1964), 66-70.
Cape Cod Community College, founded 1961.

3085 CLOSSON, ELIZABETH K. "House forsaken." CCC, 15 (1962), 36-37.
Robinson Hinckley House.

3086 CROCKER, AURIN B. "Hyannis--old and new." CCAPL, 6 (May, 1972), 14-15.

3087 CROCKER, HENRY E. "Old times and old families in the West Parish of Barnstable." Cape Cod Magazine, 6 (January 1923), 11, 13-14, (February-March, 1923), 7-9; 7 (April, 1923), 7-9, (May, 1923), 7-9, (June, 1923), 7-9, (July, 1923), 7-8.

3088 CROCKER, LIZZIE S. HINCKLEY. Sketch of Third Barnstable Baptist Church and meeting house, with membership enrollment. n.p., 1927. Pp. 28.

3089 CROSBY, KATHARINE. "Cape Cod's famous 'Crosby cats.'" Cape Cod Magazine, 8 (July 1, 1926), 5-6, 33.
Sailboats.

3090 DAMORE, LEO. The Cape Cod years of John Fitzgerald Kennedy. Englewood Cliffs, N.J.: Prentice-Hall, 1967. Pp. vii, 262.

3091 GOEHRING, WALTER R. Being an account of the church body in London in 1616...and particularly of West Parish Meetinghouse built in 1717 in West Barnstable, Mass. West Barnstable: West Parish Memorial Foundation, 1959. Pp. 36. MWA.

3092 GOODELL, EDWIN B., JR. "The meeting-house at West Barnstable, Mass." OTNE, 21 (1930-1931), 37-42.

3093 HALLETT, CLARA. An historical building, story of the old Masonic Temple in Hyannis. Hyannis: F. B. & F. P. Goss, 1938. Pp. 9. [MHy].

3094 HARRIS, CHARLES E. Hyannis sea captains. Yarmouthport: Register Pr., 1939. Pp. 162. MBNEH.

3095 HERRICK, PAUL FAIRBANKS and LARRY G. NEWMAN. Old Hyannis Port. New Bedford: Reynolds-Dewalt, 1968. Pp. 84. MWA.

3096 HINCKLEY, DESIRE E., comp. The Congregational Church in the East Precinct, Barnstable, Mass., 1646-1899. Barnstable: F. B. & F. P. Goss, 1899. Pp. 24.

3097 JENKINS, ELIZABETH C. "Turn back the years!" CCC, 9 (1954), 8-12.
West Parish Meeting House.

3098 KINGSLEY, KAY. "Barnstable rooftrees." Cape Cod Magazine, 9 (April, 1927), 5-6, 12.
Domestic architecture.

3099 KITTREDGE, HENRY CROCKER. Barnstable, 1639-1939; a brief historical sketch. Hyannis: F. B. & F. P. Goss, 1939. Pp. 39.

3100 "LARGEST Cape banking institution." Cape Cod Magazine, 9 (November-December, 1925), 7-8.
Hyannis Trust Co.

3101 MCCULLOCH, ROBERT and ALICE BEALE. "The Barnstable liberty pole." CCC, 16 (1963), 42-44.

3102 _____. and _____. "Silversmiths of Barnstable, Massachusetts." Antiques, 84 (1963), 72-74.

3103 MASSACHUSETTS. STATE TEACHERS COLLEGE, HYANNIS. Hyannis Normal School, anniversary booklet, 1897-1922. Boston: Wright and Potter, 1922. Pp. 77. M.

3104   NATIONAL ARCHIVES PROJECT. Alphabetical list
        of ship registers, district of Barnstable,
Massachusetts, 1814-1913. Boston, 1938. Pp. x,
163 leaves. [i.e. 164].
        Includes historical statistics.

3105   "THE OLD sail loft at Hyannis." Cape Cod
        Magazine, 8 (May, 1925), 19.

3106   "THE OLDEST public library." Cape Cod Maga-
        zine, 6 (December, 1922), 10-11.

3107   THE OLDEST public library building in the
        United States. Yarmouthport: C. W. Swift,
1923. Unpaged. MB.

3108   PAGET, ANN. "They built a business from a
        bayberry." Cape Cod Magazine, 9 (September,
1927), 18, 20.
        Colonial Candle Co.

3109   PARK, J. EDGAR. "An ancient church." CCC,
        7 (1952), 20-21.
        West Barnstable Church.

3110   PHINNEY, M. R. "Origin of the Cape cat
        boat." Cape Cod Magazine, 1 (September,
1915), 17-18.

3111   SAMUEL, ELIZABETH I. "The West Barnstable
        Congregational Church." OTNE, 21 (1930-
1931), 31-36.

3112   SPRAGUE, FRANCIS WILLIAM. Notes on old
        houses in Barnstable. [Barnstable?], 1917.
Pp. 2. MB.

3113   SPRAGUE, MARY AUGUSTA. Barnstable: a bit
        of nostalgia. Barnstable, 1964. Pp. 66.

3114   _____. A Cape Cod village from 'horse and
        buggy' to the 'space age.' Hyannis: Patriot
Pr., 1963. Pp. 101. MWA.

3115   THYGESEN, H. E. Articles of faith and cove-
        nant of the Congregational Church of West
Barnstable, Mass., with a brief historical sketch...
Sandwich: H. L. Chipman, 1917. Pp. 56. MBNEH.

3116   TRAYSER, DONALD GRANT, ed. Barnstable;
        three centuries of a Cape Cod town. Hyannis:
F. B. & F. P. Goss, 1939. Pp. xiv, 500.

3117   VUILLEUMIER, MARION. Craigville on Old Cape
        Cod. Taunton: W. S. Sullwold, 1972.
Pp. 48.

3118   _____. Craigville then and now. Boston:
        Charles A. Draper, 1964. Unpaged. [MBaC].

3119   WATKINS, WALTER KENDALL. "One Cape Cod
        homestead." MagHist, 22 (1916), 192-195.
        Gorham family.

3120   "WEQUAQUET Lake." Cape Cod Magazine, 1
        (January, 1916), 17-18.

3121   WHITEHILL, WALTER MUIR, ed. "The letters of
        the Reverend Thomas Walley of Barnstable to
the Reverend John Cotton of Plymouth." AASP, New
Ser., 58 (1948), 247-262.

3122   WILLIAMS, J. HAROLD. The woman who saved a
        meetinghouse. West Barnstable: The West
Parish Memorial Foundation, 1971. Pp. 48. [MBaC].

BARRE

3123   BARRE, MASS. A memorial of the one hundredth
        anniversary of the incorporation of the town
of Barre, June 17, 1874, containing the historical
discourse by Rev. James W. Thompson...the poem by
Charles Brimblecom...the speeches and other exercises of the occasion. Cambridge: J. Wilson and
Son, 1875. Pp. 281.

3124   DAY, JOHN ALPHONSO. Brief sketches of the
        Methodist Episcopal Church in Barre, 1844-
1887. Fitchburg: Sentinel Printing, 1887.
Pp. 42.

3125   GAYLORD, JOSEPH FITCH and CHARLES M. CROOKS.
        Two sketches of the history of the Evangeli-
cal Congregational Church, Barre, Mass. n.p.,
[1927?]. Pp. 34.

3126   SULLIVAN, JAMES E. American town: Barre,
        Massachusetts 1774-1974. [Barre]: Barre
Historical Society, 1974. Pp. 56. MBNEH.

3127   THOMPSON, JAMES WILLIAM. A discourse pro-
        nounced at Barre, June 17, 1874 on the one
hundredth anniversary of the incorporation of that
town. Cambridge: J. Wilson and Son, 1875.
Pp. 149. M.

3128   WOODS, JOSEPH EDWIN. A brief history of the
        Barre cattle shows. Worcester: Skelley
Print, 1914. Pp. 25.

BECKET

3129   ARCHER, CATHALINE ALFORD. Becket sons in a
        Massachusetts settlement of New Connecticut.
Northford, Conn.: L. W. Gibbons, 1953. Pp. 58.

3130   _____. Becket's first years: 1752-1802.
        n.p., [1952?]. Pp. 32.

3131   _____. The founding of the First Church of
        Becket. New Haven: Lincoln Printshop,
[1933]. Pp. 6.

3132   GREEN, SAMUEL ABBOTT. "Origin of the name of
        the town of Becket." MHSP, 2 Ser., 5 (1889-
1890), 166-167.

3133   MOULTHROP, ESTHER TURNER, comp., et al. A
        bicentennial history of Becket, Berkshire
County, Massachusetts, incorporated June 21, 1765.
Pittsfield, 1965. Pp. 215.

BEDFORD

3134   BEDFORD, MASS. Bedford in the World War: an
        account of the part played by the citizens of

(BEDFORD, MASS.)
the town of Bedford, military and civilian, in the
Great War with Germany, 1917-1919. n.p., [1926?].
Pp. 108.
    Biographies of servicemen.

3135   BEDFORD, MASS. CHURCH OF CHRIST. The con-
        fession of faith, and covenant of the Church
of Christ.... Boston: Crocker & Brewster, 1843.
Pp. 20.
    Includes history.

3136   BEDFORD. Boston: Edison Electric Illuminat-
        ing Co., 1909. Pp. 12. M.

3137   BROWN, ABRAM ENGLISH. Glimpses of old New
        England life, legends of old Bedford. Bos-
ton: R. H. Blodgett, 1892. Pp. 198.

3138   _____. "Governor Winthrop's farm, a chapter
        of old Bedford history." NEM, New Ser., 6
(1892), 325-336.

3139   _____. An historical address commemorative
        of the organization of the first Sabbath
school in Bedford, Mass. Boston: Geo. H. Ellis,
1888. Pp. 42.
    Seventieth anniversary.

3140   _____. History of the town of Bedford, Mid-
        dlesex County, Massachusetts, from its ear-
liest settlement to the year of Our Lord 1891...
with a genealogical register of old families. Bedford, 1891. Pp. 110, 48.

3141   _____. "The journal of the minister of Bed-
        ford." NEM, New Ser., 19 (1898), 434-442.
Samuel Stearns; an account based on the
journal.

3142   BROWN, LOUISE K. Wilderness town; the story
        of Bedford, Massachusetts. [Bedford?, 1968].
Pp. 218.

3143   GLEASON, JOHN F. A sermon preached in the
        Trinitarian Congregational Church, Bedford,
Mass., Sunday, September 18, 1870. Boston: David
Clapp & Son, 1870. Pp. 20. MBNEH.
    Relates to the church.

3144   HAYDEN, WILLIAM R. The past, present, and
        future of Bedford, Mass., reports of the re-
marks of W. R. Hayden at the railroad meeting, Bedford, Nov. 21, 1868. Concord: Tolman, 1868.
Pp. 4. MB.

3145   MANSUR, INA G. A cursory look at the rise
        of the First Parish Church in Bedford. [Bed-
ford], 1964. Pp. 9.

3146   _____. The story of the First Parish in Bed-
        ford Unitarian Universalist, compiled for
the 150th anniversary of the second meetinghouse,
1817-1967. [Bedford, 1967]. Unpaged.

3147   "SAMUEL Stearns and the Unitarian controversy
        in Bedford." CongQ, 10 (1868), 245-275.
1831-1839.

3148   STEARNS, JONATHAN FRENCH. Bedford sesqui-
        centennial celebration, Aug. 27, 1879. His-
torical discourse. Boston: A. Mudge & Son, 1879.
Pp. 84.

BELCHERTOWN

3149   BELCHERTOWN, MASS. Proceedings of the old
        Home Week celebration in Belchertown, Mass.,
July 26-29, 1902. Amherst: Carpenter & Morehouse,
1902. Pp. 59. MAJ.
    Includes historical sermon by Payson W. Ly-
man.

3150   BELCHERTOWN, MASS. BICENTENNIAL COMMITTEE.
        Belchertown, Massachusetts, founded 1731,
incorporated 1761. Springfield: Walter Whittum,
[1961?]. Pp. 64. MAJ.

3151   BELCHERTOWN, MASS. CONGREGATIONAL CHURCH.
        Centennial celebration of the dedication of
Belchertown Congregational Church, September 12th.
[1892] Palmer: C. B. Fiske, 1892. Pp. 62. M.

3152   _____. Manual of the Congregational Church,
        Belchertown, Mass., containing an historical
sketch of the church, its principles, articles of
faith, covenant, rules and catalogue. Springfield:
C. W. Bryan, 1874. Pp. 32.

3153   DOOLITTLE, MARK. Historical sketch of the
        Congregational Church in Belchertown, Mass.,
from its organization, 114 years, with notices of
the pastors and officers, and list of communicants
chronologically arranged, tracing genealogies, in-
termarriages and family relatives, also, embracing
numerous facts and incidents relating to the first
settlers and early history of the place. Northampton: Hopkins, Bridgman, 1852. Pp. xii, 282.

3154   _____. "Historical sketches of Belchertown,
        Mass." NEHGR, 2 (1848), 177-180.

3155   ENFIELD, MASS. The hundredth anniversary
        celebration, Enfield, Massachusetts, July the
2nd, 3rd, and 4th, Nineteen Sixteen. n.p., [1916?].
Unpaged. MAJ.

3156   ENFIELD, MASS. CONGREGATIONAL CHURCH. By-
        laws, creed and covenant, historical sketch,
and form of service for reception of members of the
Congregational Church, Enfield, Mass., adopted December 15, 1926. Belchertown: L. H. Blackmer,
1927. Pp. 28.
    History by Amanda Woods Ewing and John S.
Curtis.

3157   _____. The one hundred and fiftieth anniver-
        sary service of the Congregational Church,
Enfield, Massachusetts. Belchertown: Lewis H.
Blackmer, [1936?]. Pp. 22. MAJ.
    Historical sermon by Randolph Seaman Merrill.

3158   LYMAN, PAYSON WILLISTON. 150th anniversary
        of the incorporation of the town of Belcher-
town, July 2, 3 and 4, 1911; a sketch of the celebration and the historical address. Belchertown:
Lewis H. Blackmer, 1912. Pp. 23.

3159   RICHARDS, FREDERICK B. Historical sermon
       preached in [the] Congregational Church, En-
field, Mass., July 2, 1916, centennial of the town.
n.p., [1916?]. Pp. 20. MAJ.

3160   SHAW, WILLIAM E. History of Belchertown in
       the 18th century. William A. Doubleday, ed.
Amherst: Newell Pr., 1968. Pp. xvi, 116.

3161   UNDERWOOD, FRANCIS HENRY. Quabbin; the story
       of a small town with outlooks upon Puritan
life. Boston: Lee and Shepard, 1893. Pp. viii,
375.

BELLINGHAM

3162   BELLINGHAM. Boston: Edison Electric Illu-
       minating Co., 1909. Pp. 8. MBNEH.

3163   FISHER, ABIAL. Century sermons. Two dis-
       courses, delivered at Bellingham, (Mass.) in
the year 1822, the first giving the civil and ecclesiastical history of the town, from its incorporation, Nov. 27, 1719, to Nov. 27, 1819; and the second, the memoirs of the three ministers who died in
the town, during that period. Worcester: W. Manning, 1822.
       Elnathan Wight, Noah Alden, and Valentine
Whitman Rathbun.

3164   PARTRIDGE, GEORGE FAIRBANKS. History of the
       town of Bellingham, Massachusetts, 1719-
1919. [Bellingham]: The Town, 1919. Pp. 221.

BELMONT

3165   BALDWIN, FRANCES B., comp. From Pequossette
       Plantation to the town of Belmont, Massachu-
setts, 1630-1953. Belmont: Belmont Citizen, 1954.
Pp. 72.

3166   BELMONT, MASS. Fiftieth anniversary of the
       incorporation of the Town of Belmont, Massa-
chusetts, Thursday, June seventeenth, 1909. Boston:
Everett Pr., [1909?]. Pp. 23.

3167   "[BELMONT Municipal Light Department]."
       Belmont HSN, 6 (September, 1971), 1-5.

3168   "BELMONT town seal." Belmont HSN, 8 (June,
       1974), 1-2.

3169   BENTON, JAY ROGERS. "The founders of the
       plantation," an historic address deliv-
ered..., July 5th, 1930. Newton: Garden City Pr.,
1931. Pp. 359-381.
       From an unidentified work.

3170   _____. A thumb-nail sketch of the settle-
       ment of Pequusset Plantation of the Massa-
chusetts Bay Colony, today--the town of Belmont.
[Boston?, 1930?]. Pp. 11.

3171   "BENTON Library." Belmont HSN, 7 (June,
       1973), 1-4.

3172   "BRIGHTON Street School." Belmont HSN, 8
       (September, 1973), 1-6.

3173   "[BUSINESS in the Beaver Brook area of Bel-
       mont.]" Belmont HSN, 6 (December, 1971),
1-4.

3174   CHENERY, WINTHROP LOUIS, comp. Some statis-
       tics of the town of Belmont, Mass., for the
first thirty years of its corporate existence.
Boston: J. A. Cummings Printing, 1890. Pp. 25.

3175   "DANIEL Butler School, 1898." Belmont HSN,
       8 (March, 1974), 1-3.

3176   DUNCAN, ROGER F. The story of Belmont Hill
       School, 1923-1973. [Belmont?], 1973. Pp.
ix, 243.

3177   "EARLY fire alarm." Belmont HSN, 8 (Decem-
       ber, 1973), 5-6.
       Town fire alarm system.

3178   "EVOLUTION of the Belmont High School, 1868-
       1968." Belmont HSN, 3 (Winter, 1969), 2-3.

3179   "FANEUIL Hall market district." Belmont HSN,
       (June, 1971), 1-6.
       Belmont agriculture.

3180   FOOTE, HENRY WILDER, b. 1875. Remember the
       days of old. A discourse delivered at the
75th anniversary of the church in Belmont, Massachusetts on February 8, 1931. [Belmont, 1931].
Pp. 13.

3181   "HIGHLAND stock farm." Belmont HSN, 6
       (March, 1972), 1-5.
       Cattle breeding.

3182   JAYNES, MRS. HERBERT. "Old Waverly." Bel-
       mont HSN, 3 (October, 1968), 4-6.
       Section of the town.

3183   "ORIGINAL Daniel Butler School (now Waverly
       Fire Station)." Belmont HSN, 8 (December,
1973), 1-5.

3184   ROBBINS, SAMUEL DOWSE. Who's who in Belmont;
       biographical and autobiographical sketches of
residents of Belmont, Massachusetts. Belmont, 1972.
Pp. xiv, 432.

3185   "ROCK Meadow." Belmont HSN, 3 (Spring,
       (1969), 5-6.
       Land on which McLean Hospital is located.

3186   "TOWN farm--stable and tramp house, Concord
       Avenue 1877-1934." Belmont HSN, 7 (Septem-
ber, 1972), 1-5.
       Belmont's hobo problem.

BERKLEY

3187   ARNZEN, NIELS. "Report of Committe on Dight-
       on Rock." Old Colony HSC, No. 5 (1893), 94-
97.

3188   BERKLEY, MASS. CONGREGATIONAL CHURCH. The
        observance of the one hundred and fiftieth
anniversary of the organization of the Congregational Church in Berkley, Mass., November 2, 1887, containing the historical sermon by Rev. S. Hopkins
Emery, of Taunton, Mass., an abstract of addresses
and other proceedings.... Taunton: C. H. Buffington, 1888. Pp. 52.

3189   BRECHER, RUTH and EDWARD BRECHER. "The
        enigma of Dighton Rock." Am Heritage, 9
(June, 1958), 62-64, 91-92.

3190   DA SILVA, MANUEL LUCIANO. "Meaning of
        Dighton Rock." Medical Opinion and Review,
2 (1966), 82-86.

3191   _____. Portuguese pilgrims and Dighton Rock;
        the first chapter in American history.
Bristol, R.I.: Nelson D. Martins, 1971. Pp. 100.

3192   DAVIS, JOHN, 1761-1847. "An attempt to ex-
        plain the inscription on the Dighton Rock."
American Academy of Arts and Sciences. Memoirs, 3
(1809), 197-205.

3193   DELABARRE, EDMUND BURKE. Dighton Rock; a
        study of the written rocks of New England.
N.Y.: W. Neale, 1928. Pp. xv, 369.

3194   _____. "Dighton Rock: the earliest and most
        puzzling of New England antiquities." OTNE,
14 (1923-1924), 51-72.

3195   _____. "Early interest in Dighton Rock."
        CSMP, 18 (1915-1916), 235-299.

3196   _____. "Middle period of Dighton Rock his-
        tory." CSMP, 19 (1916-1917), 46-149.

3197   _____. "Recent history of Dighton Rock."
        CSMP, 20 (1917-1919), 286-462.

3198   "THE DIGHTON Rock." American Architect and
        Building News, 27 (1890), 93.

3199   "DIGHTON Rock." Old Dartmouth HSB, (Summer,
1955), 1-3.

3200   FRAGOSO, JOSEPH DAMASO. A historic report of
        twenty eight years of patriotic and dramatic
efforts to save Dighton Rock. New Bedford: Miguel
Corte-Real Society, 1954. Pp. 36. M.

3201   _____. In hono of Portugal, the Portugese
        Navy and the Dighton Rock. New Bedford,
1958. Pp. 16. M.

3202   GRAVIER, GABRIEL. Notice sur le roc de
        Dighton et le séjour des Scandinaves en
Amérique au commencement du onzième siècle. Nancy:
G. Crépin-Leblond, 1875. Pp. 27.

3203   HALL, JOHN W. D. "Dighton Writing Rock."
        Old Colony HSC, No. 4 (1889), 97-99.

3204   KENDAL, E. A. "Account of the writing rock
        in Taunton River." American Academy of Arts
and Sciences. Memoirs, 3 (1809), 165-191.

3205   LOPES, FRANCISCO FERNANDES. "The brothers
        Corte-Real." Studia, 16 (1965), 153-165.
Dighton Rock.

3206   MACLEAN, J. P. "Norse remains in America."
        American Antiquarian, 14 (1892), 189-196.
Dighton Rock.

3207   MARQUES, GILBERTO S. Pedra de Dighton; o
        professor Delabarre desvenda o mistério das
inscrições da Pedra de Dighton, fazendo a impor-
tantissima descoberta que foi o navegador português
Miguel Côrte Real, o primeiro europeu que habitou o
continente norte americano. New Bedford: Union
Printing, 1930. Pp. 45.
        Dighton Rock.

3208   RAU, CHARLES. "Observations on the Dighton
        Rock inscription." MagAmHist, 2 (1878), 82-
85.

3209   SANFORD, ENOCH. History of the town of Berk-
        ley, Mass., including sketches of the lives
of the two first ministers, Rev. Samuel Tobey, and
Rev. Thomas Andros, whose united ministry continued
ninety-one years. N.Y.: K. Tompkins, 1872.
Pp. 60.

3210   WINTHROP, JAMES. "Account of an inscribed
        rock at Dighton, in the Commonwealth of Mas-
sachusetts, accompanied with a copy of the inscription." American Academy of Arts and Sciences.
Memoirs, 2 (1804), 126-129.

3211   WORSAAE, J. J. A. "The Dighton Rock inscrip-
        tion; an opinion of a Danish archaeologist."
MagAmHist, 3 (1879), 236-238.

3212   YOUNG, GEORGE F. W. Miguel Corte-Real and
        the Dighton Writing-Rock. Taunton: Old
Colony Historical Society, 1970. Pp. 146.

BERLIN

3213   BERLIN, MASS. Memorial record of the sol-
        diers of Berlin, in the great rebellion,
with the exercises at the dedication of the tablets
of the deceased, Memorial Hall, and the Town House,
Wednesday, March 2d, 1870, Berlin, Mass. Clinton:
W. J. Coulter, 1870. P. 46.
        Includes biography.

3214   BERLIN, MASS. SESQUICENTENNIAL CELEBRATION
        COMMITTEE. Berlin Sesquicentennial, June 8,
9, 10, 1962. Berlin, 1962. Pp. 15. M.

3215   CARTER, AMORY. History of the parish and
        town of Berlin. Worcester, Mass., 1878.
Pp. 40.

3216   HOUGHTON, WILLIAM ADDISON. History of the
        town of Berlin, Worcester County, Mass.,
from 1784 to 1895. Worcester: F. S. Blanchard,
1895. Pp. viii, 584.

3217   KRACKHARDT, FREDERICK A. History of the town
        of Berlin, Worcester County, Mass., from
1784-1959. Berlin: Colonial Pr., [1959?].
Pp. xiv, 338. M.

BERNARDSTON

3218 BERNARDSTON, MASS. Bernardston, Massachu-
setts, sesqui-centennial; March 6, 1762-
August 7, 1912. Greenfield: E. A. Hall, [1912?].
Unpaged.

3219 KELLOGG, LUCY JANE CUTLER. History of the
town of Bernardston, Franklin County, Massachusetts. Greenfield: E. A. Hall, 1902-1962. 2v.
1736-1960; Vol. 2 written by townspeople and
published by the Cushman Library trustees.

3220 ____. "Settlement of Bernardston." PVMA,
3 (1890-1898), 94-115.

3221 POWERS INSTITUTE, BERNARDSTON, MASS. General
catalogue and history of Powers Institute,
its teachers and pupils, Bernardston, Mass., 1857-
1896. Holyoke: Powers Institute Alumni Association, 1896. Pp. 107. MB.

BEVERLY

BEATTIE, DONALD W. and J. RICHARD COLLINS. Washington's New England fleet: Beverly's role in
its origins, 1775-1777. Salem: Newcomb & Gauss,
1969. Pp. ix, 69.

3223 BEVERLY, MASS. 1630-1930. Beverly tercentenary, June 15-16-17. Beverly: Beverly
Trade School, [1930?]. Unpaged.

3224 BEVERLY, MASS. CHAMBER OF COMMERCE. Historic Beverly; being an account of the
growth of the city of Beverly from the earliest
times to the present, with short sketches of the
men and women who contributed so much to the up-
building of the community in the early days. Katharine Peabody Loring and Alice Gertrude Lapham,
comps. [Beverly]: Beverly Chamber of Commerce,
1937. Pp. 38.

3225 BEVERLY, MASS. DANE STREET CONGREGATIONAL
CHURCH. History and manual of the Dane
Street Congregational Church and Society of Beverly,
Mass. 1802-1897. Prepared by the pastor and the
clerk. Boston: F. Wood, 1897. Pp. 63.
The pastor and the clerk were Francis Van
Horn and Louis H. Baker, respectively.

3226 BEVERLY, MASS. FIRST BAPTIST CHURCH. An
outline of the history of the First Baptist
Church in Beverly. n.p., [1857?]. Pp. 4. MSaE.

3227 BEVERLY, MASS. FIRST PARISH CHURCH. The
First Parish Church, Unitarian, Beverly,
Massachusetts, a volume of historical interest published in honor of the two hundred and seventy-fifth
anniversary of the founding of the church on Sept.
20, 1667. Beverly: Times Publishing, 1942.
Pp. 120.

3228 ____. The register of baptisms of the First
Church in Beverly, 1667-1710. August A. Gal-
loupe, ed. Boston: Research Publication Co., 1903.
Pp. 50.

3229 ____. 300th anniversary of the First Parish
Church Unitarian, Beverly, Massachusetts, a
history. Beverly, 1967. Pp. 20. M.

3230 BEVERLY, MASS. SECOND CONGREGATIONAL CHURCH.
Two hundred and twenty-fifth anniversary,
1713-1938. n.p., 1938. Unpaged. MBNEH.

3231 BEVERLY, MASS. WASHINGTON STREET CHURCH.
Historical sketch, articles of faith and
covenant, and principles and rules of the Washington
Street Church, Beverly, Mass., with a list of offi-
cers and members to May, 1881. Beverly: Beverly
Citizen Print, 1881. Pp. 16. MB.

3232 BEVERLY FEMALE CHARITABLE SOCIETY, BEVERLY,
MASS. Celebration of the one hundredth anni-
versary of the Beverly Female Charitable Society,
December fourteenth, nineteen hundred and ten.
Beverly: [1910?]. Pp. 30.

3233 BEVERLY SAVINGS BANK, BEVERLY, MASS. 100th
anniversary, 1867-1967. Beverly: Wilks-
craft, [1967?]. Pp. 23. MSaE.

3234 BILLIAS, GEORGE ATHAN. "Beverly's seacoast
defenses during the Revolutionary War."
EIHC, 94 (1958), 119-131.

3235 BRADSTREET, ALVAH JUDSON. History of Im-
manuel Church, Ryal Side, Beverly. n.p.,
1948. Pp. 30. MSaE.

3236 BULKELEY, B. R. "Old Beverly." NEM, New
Ser., 40 (1909), 649-657.

3237 CARLMAN, BEVERLY C. "Samuel McIntire's Beverly schoolhouse." EIHC, 107 (1971), 194-
197.

3238 DOW, MARY LARCOM. Old days at Beverly Farms.
Beverly: North Shore Printing, 1921. Pp.
81.

3239 FROST, CHESTER E. and LAURANCE S. HOVEY.
Beverly tercentenary, 1668-1968; some important events in the history of Beverly, Mass. [Bev-
erly?]: Published in cooperation with Beverly Tercentenary Celebration Committee, 1968. Pp. 44.

3240 FROST, CHESTER E. B's diverse. n.p., 1969.
Unpaged.
Beverly and Bermuda.

3241 GOODELL, ABNER CHENEY, JR. "Beverly and the
settlement at Bass River." CSMP, 1 (1892-
1894), 77-84.

3242 HARMOND, RICHARD. "The time they tried to
divide Beverly." EIHC, 104 (1968), 19-33.
1880s.

3243 HOWE, OCTAVIUS T. "Beverly privateers in the
American Revolution." CSMP, 24 (1920-1922),
318-435.

3244 HUIGINN, EUGENE JOSEPH VINCENT. Freemasonry
in Beverly, 1779-1924, Amity Lodge, 1779-
1789, Liberty Lodge, 1824-1924. Beverly: North
Shore Printing, 1924. Pp. 74. MSaE.

3245 KILHAM, HENRIETTA B. "The Cabot-Lee-Kilham House, Beverly, Mass. and those who lived in it." OTNE, 15 (1924-1925), 147-155.

3246 KILHAM, WALTER HARRINGTON. "The Cabot-Lee-Kilham House, Beverly, Mass." OTNE, 15 (1924-1925), 156-163.

3246A KING, CHARLES A. "Beverly--settlement, town, and city." National Magazine, 17 (1902-1903), 413-417.

3247 KNOWLTON, KENNETH F. "Twenty-five years of water filtration progress." New England Water Works Association. Journal, 74 (1960), 289-311.

Salem and Beverly water supply board.

3248 LAPHAM, ALICE GERTRUDE. The old planters of Beverly in Massachusetts and the thousand acre grant of 1635. Cambridge: Riverside Pr. for the Beverly Historical Society and the Conant Family Association, 1930. Pp. vi, 133.

3249 LASH, DAVID C. and EMMA S. LASH. Index of names for History of Beverly by Edwin M. Stone. [Beverly]: Beverly Historical Society, 1958. Pp. 16. MBNEH.

3250 LOVETT, ROBERT W. "The Beverly Cotton Manufactory: or some light on an early cotton mill." BBHS, 26 (1952), 218-237.

3251 _____. "From social library to public library, a century of library development in Beverly, Massachusetts." EIHC, 88 (1952), 219-253. 1802-1896.

3252 _____. "A house and its inhabitants: the story of 27 Conant Street, Beverly including some remarks on No. 29." EIHC, 104 (1968), 42-52.

3253 _____. "A nineteenth-century Beverly partnership; the Pickett Coal Company, 1827-1910." EIHC, 96 (1960), 85-104, 207-227.

3254 _____. "A parish divided and reunited, the precinct of Salem and Beverly 1813-1903." EIHC, 99 (1963), 203-236. Second Congregational Church.

3255 _____. "A parish is formed, the precinct of Salem and Beverly, 1713-1753." EIHC, 98 (1962), 129-153. Second Congregational Church.

3256 _____. "A parish weathers war and dissension, the precinct of Salem and Beverly 1753-1813." EIHC, 99 (1963), 88-116. Second Congregational Church.

3257 _____. "Squire Rantoul and his drug store, 1796-1824." BBHS, 25 (1951), 99-114.

3258 MACSWIGGAN, AMELIA ELIZABETH. "A pioneer cotton mill of New England." Antiques Journal, 11 (February, 1956), 22-23, 36. Beverly Cotton Manufactory.

3259 MORGAN, WILLIAM C. Beverly, garden city by the sea: an historical sketch of the North Shore city, with a history of the churches, the various institutions, and societies, the schools, fire department, birds, and flowers. Beverly: Amos L. Odell, 1897. Pp. 207. M.

3260 PERLEY, SIDNEY. "Beverly in 1700." EIHC, 55 (1919), 81-102, 209-229, 273-303; 26 (1920), 33-49, 98-110, 209-222.

3261 RANTOUL, ROBERT, 1778-1858. "Memoranda of Beverly." MHSC, 3 Ser., 7 (1838), 250-255.

3262 RANTOUL, ROBERT SAMUEL. "The first cotton mill in America." EIHC, 33 (1898), 1-43. Beverly Cotton Manufactory.

3263 _____. "Three hundred years of Beverly." EIHC, 55 (1919), 103-110.

3264 STONE, EDWIN MARTIN. History of Beverly, civil and ecclesiastical, from its settlement in 1630 to 1842. Boston: J. Munroe, 1843. For an index of names appearing in this work see: Lash, David C.

3265 _____. A lecture comprising the history of the second parish in Beverly, and the origin and progress of the Church of Christ, worshipping in that place, delivered in the Meeting House of said parish, Sabbath evening, July 6, 1834. Mendon: G. W. Stacy, 1835. Pp. 35. MH.

3266 THAYER, CHRISTOPHER TOPPAN. An address delivered in the First parish, Beverly, October 2, 1867, on the two-hundredth anniversary of its formation.... Boston: Nichols and Noyes, 1868. Pp. 79.

3267 WEBBER, JOHN WHITING. "A Massachusetts pewterer." Antiques, 5 (1924), 26-28. Israel Trask.

3268 WOLKINS, GEORGE GREGERSON. Beverly men in the War of Independence: remarks before the Beverly Historical Society...April 9, 1930. Beverly: Beverly Historical Society, 1932. Pp. 39. MB.

3269 WOODBERRY, CHARLES. Independence Park, Beverly, Massachusetts. Historical events associated with the ground. [Beverly?, 1907?]. Pp. 32. M.

Revolutionary events.

BILLERICA

3270 BILLERICA, MASS. Celebration of the two hundredth anniversary of the incorporation of Billerica, Massachusetts, May 29th, 1855; including the proceedings of the committee, address, poem, and other exercises of the occasion. Lowell: S. J. Varney, 1855. Pp. 152.

3271 _____. Report of the official celebration held July 4th, 1919 by the town of Billerica in honor of her sons and daughters who served in the World War. n.p., [1919?]. Pp. 26. M.

3272 CUMINGS, HENRY. An half-century discourse, addressed to the people of Billerica, Feb. 21, 1813. Cambridge: Hilliard and Metcalf, 1813. Pp. 31.
First Congregational Church.

3273 "THE DITSON-Harnden House." Billerica, 3 (April, 1915), 3-4.

3274 EAMES, MARY R. "What Billerica women have done." Billerica, 1 (August, 1912), 3-5; (September, 1912), 4-6.

3275 FARMER, JOHN. An historical memoir of Billerica, in Massachusetts, containing notices of the principal events in the civil and ecclesiastical affairs of the town, from its first settlement to 1816.... Amherst, N.H.: R. Boylston, 1816. Pp. 36.

3276 _____. "Sketches of the early history of Billerica." BBNL, 1 (1826), 229-233.

3277 "FAULKNER Mills." Billerica, 1 (March, 1913), 10.
Wool.

3278 "THE FIRST Parish Church." Billerica, 2 (November, 1913), 4-5.

3279 HAZEN, HENRY ALLEN. History of Billerica, Massachusetts.... Boston: A. Williams, 1883. v.p.

3280 "HISTORIC Billerica: Bennett Hall." Billerica, 1 (December, 1912), 7.
Historic house.

3281 "HISTORICAL sketch of St. Anne's Mission, North Billerica." Billerica, 1 (February, 1913), 6-7.
Episcopal Church.

3282 "HISTORICAL sketch of Winning Rebekah Lodge, No. 108." Billerica, 1 (February, 1913), 5.
Odd Fellows.

3283 "HISTORY of the Howe School." Billerica, 3 (July, 1914), 4-6; (August, 1914), 5-7; (October, 1914), 6.

3284 HOWARD, LOUISE C. "The Manning Manse." Lowell HSC, 1 (1907-1913), 175-179.

3285 "THE JONES place." Billerica, 3 (September, 1914), 4-5.
Historic house.

3286 MANNING, WARREN H. "Billerica tree history notes." Billerica, 2 (January, 1914), 4-7.

3287 MANNING, WILLIAM H. "The Manning Homestead." MassMag, 1 (1908), 43.

3288 NASON, ELIAS. Billerica: a centennial oration, July 4, 1876.... Lowell: Marden and Rowell, 1876. Pp. 25.

3289 "NORTH Billerica recollections." Billerica, 3 (December, 1914), 8-11; (January, 1915), 5-6; (February, 1915), 6; (March, 1915), 7; (April, 1915), 5-6; (May, 1915), 3-5.

3290 SAGE, MARTHA HILL. Old families of the First Parish.... Boston: J. B. Holden, 1898. Pp. 19.

3291 "THE SEARLES House." Billerica, 3 (November, 1914), 4-5.

3292 "SOCIETIES and clubs in Billerica, arranged chronologically by date of organization." Billerica, 2 (July, 1913), 5-8.

3293 SPALDING, ALICE F. "Town improvement in Billerica." NEM, New Ser., 31 (1904-1905), 379-386.

3294 STEARNS, A. WARREN. "Cambridge grants and families in Billerica, 1641-1655." CaHSP, 9 (1914), 71-78.

3295 _____. "Population of Billerica." Billerica, 2 (November, 1913), 5-7.
1659-1910.

3296 _____. Slavery in Billerica. Billerica: Billerica Publishing, 1957. Unpaged. MBNEH.

3297 _____. "The story of the Cook House." Billerica, 2 (May, 1914), 6-7.

3298 "TALBOT Dyewood and Chemical Works." Billerica, 1 (March, 1913), 11-12.

3299 "TALBOT Mills." Billerica, 1 (March, 1913) 10-11.
Wool.

BLACKSTONE

3300 WALKER, GEORGE FREDERICK. Historical, a sermon preached in the Congregational Church, Blackstone, October 1, 1876. South Framingham: J. Clark, 1877. Pp. 16. M.

BLANDFORD

3301 BLANDFORD, MASS. Blandford's bicentennial official souvenir, published in connection with the 200th anniversary of the founding of the town of Blandford, Massachusetts.... Edgar Holmes Plummer, ed. [Blandford, 1935]. Unpaged.

3302 "BLANDFORD Free Library." Blandford Mo, 2 (March, 1903), 1-3.

3303 GIBBS, WILLIAM H. Address delivered before the Literary Association, Blandford, Mass., Sept. 21, 1850, upon the history of that town. Springfield: G. W. Wilson, 1850. Pp. 76.

3304 KEEP, JOHN. A discourse delivered at Blandford, Mass., Tuesday, March 20th, 1821, giving some account of the early settlement of the town and the history of the church. Ware: Charles W. Eddy, 1886. Pp. 23.

3305 LLOYD, JULIA. "Schools of olden times." Blandford Mo., 1 (December, 1902), 21-22.

3306 "NORTH Blandford industry fifty years ago." Blandford Mo., 1 (February, 1902), 12-13.

3307 "THE OLD hotel." Blandford, Mo., 1 (August, 1902), 7-8.

3308 "SEATING arrangements in the Blandford Church 105 years ago." Blandford Mo., 1 (March, 1902), 7-8, (June, 1902), 7-8.

3309 WOOD, SUMNER GILBERT. "A New England town in the French and Indian War." MagHist, 10 (1909), 29-36, 36a-36e, 157-162, 256-260; 11 (1910), 13-21.

3310 _____. "The old Blandford Church." Blandford Mo., 2 (August, 1903), 6-13.

3311 _____, comp. Soldiers and sailors of the Revolution from Blandford, Massachusetts. West Medway, 1933. Pp. 52.

3312 _____. The taverns & turnpikes of Blandford, 1733-1833. [Blandford], 1908. Pp. 329.

3313 _____. Ulster Scots and Blandford scouts. West Medway, 1928. Pp. 436.

BOLTON

3314 BOLTON, MASS. History of Bolton, 1738-1938. Bolton, 1938. Pp. viii, 274. MB.

3315 BOLTON, MASS. FIRST CONGREGATIONAL CHURCH. A historical sketch of the First Congregational Church in Bolton. Clinton: Ballard & Messinger, 1851. Pp. 28.

3316 EDES, RICHARD SULLIVAN. Address delivered in the First Parish Church in Bolton July 4th, 1876, at the centennial celebration of the anniversary of American independence; and also in observance of the 138th aniversary of the incorporation of the town. Clinton: W. J. Coulter, 1877. Pp. iv, 57.

3317 PARDEE, JOSEPH NELSON. "Thomas Goss vs. inhabitants of Bolton, 1770-1782." UHSP 2, Pt. 1, (1931), 20-30.
    Congregationalism.

BOSTON

3318 ABBATT, WILLIAM. "Boston seventy years ago." MagHist, 8 (1908), 15-21.
    1838.

3319 ABBOT, FRANCIS ELLINGWOOD. "The Boston Tea Party." Sons of the Revolution. Massachusetts Society. Register, (1899), 65-78.

3320 ABBOTT, SAMUEL, JR. History and by-laws of the Boston Veteran Firemen's Association, from 1833 to 1898.... Boston: O. P. Adams, 1898. Pp. 80.

3321 ABERTHAW CONSTRUCTION COMPANY, BOSTON. Aberthaw Construction Company; a quarter century of fulfilment. Boston, 1919. Pp. 92.

3322 ABORN, PELEG, ed. A descriptive and historical sketch of Boston Harbor and surroundings... Boston: W. M. Tenney, 1885. Pp. 86.

3323 AN ACCOUNT of the conflagration of the Ursuline Convent. At the request of several gentlemen, the author was induced to publish the following statement of facts, in relation to the Ursuline Convent, which was destroyed by fire, on the night of August 11th, 1834. By a friend of religious toleration.... Boston, 1834. Pp. 35.

3324 ACKLAND, THOMAS. "The Kelts of colonial Boston." AIrHSJ, 7 (1907), 80-95.
    Irish.

3325 ACTION FOR BOSTON COMMUNITY DEVELOPMENT. The Chinese in Boston, 1970. Boston, 1970. iv, 88, A-4 leaves. M.
    Includes history.

3326 _____. The discarded suburbs: Roxbury and North Dorchester, 1800-1950. Sam B. Warner, comp. [Boston], 1961. 16 leaves.

3327 ADAMS, CHARLES FRANCIS, 1835-1915. "The Battle of Bunker Hill." AHR, 1 (1895-1896), 401-413.

3328 _____. "The Battle of Bunker Hill from a strategic point of view." AASP, New Ser., 10 (1895), 387-398.

3329 ADAMS, EMMA SELLEW. "A remembrance of the Boston draft riot." MagHist, 10 (1909), 37-40.
    1863, Civil War.

3330 ADAMS, RANDOLPH GREENFIELD. "New light on the Boston Massacre." AASP, New Ser., 47 (1937), 259-354.

3331 ADAMS, WILLIAM T. "The schools of sixty years ago." Bostonian, 3 (1895-1896), 166-169.

3332 ADDISON, ALBERT CHRISTOPHER. The romantic story of the Puritan Fathers and their founding of new Boston and the Massachusetts Bay Colony; together with some account of the conditions which led to their departure from old Boston and the neighbouring towns in England. Boston: L. C. Page, 1912. Pp. xiv, 243.

3333 ALDEN, EBENEZER. Historical sketch of the origin and progress of the Massachusetts Medical Society. Boston: W. S. Damrell, 1838. Pp. 48.

3334 ALDEN, JOHN. "The New Hampshire Exchange Club and its Boston home." Granite Mo., 35 (1903), 291-315.

3335 ALDEN, JOHN ELIOT. "A season in Federal Street: J. B. Williamson and the Boston Theatre, 1796-1797." AASP, 65 (1955), 9-74.

3336 ALGER, WILLIAM ROUNSEVILLE. Historical sketch of the Bulfinch St. Society. Boston: John Wilson and Son, 1861. Pp. 16.
A Universalist church.

3337 ALLEN, ELEANOR W. "Boston's Women's Educational and Industrial Union." NEG, 6 (Spring, 1965), 30-39.
Historical sketch.

3338 ALLEN, FREDERICK BAYLIES. Historical address...at the service commemorating the seventy-fifth anniversary of the incorporation of the Episcopal City Mission, St. Paul's Cathedral, May 2, 1919. Boston, [1919?]. Pp. 26.

3339 _____. "The very beginnings of Boston." BSPub, 2 Ser., 3 (1919), 69-85.

3340 ALLEN, WILLIAM. An historical discourse, delivered in Dorchester, January 2, 1848, on occasion of the fortieth anniversary of the gathering of the Second Church, under the pastoral care of the late Rev. John Codman.... Boston: Marvin, 1848. Pp. 30.

3341 ALLIS, FREDERICK SCOULLER, JR. "Boston and the Alien and Sedition Laws." BSProc, (1951), 25-51.

3342 _____. and H. A. CROSBY FORBES. Boston & the China Trade. Boston: Massachusetts Historical Society, 1970. Pp. 30. M.

3343 "ALLYN and Bacon: 100 year-old paradox." Publishers' Weekly, 194 (July 1, 1968), 22-26.

3344 AMADON, ELIZABETH REED. Faneuil Hall, Dock Square and Merchants Row, Boston, Mass., 1742: historical report. Boston: Architectural Heritage, 1969. Pp. 20. MB.

3345 _____. No. 46 Joy Street, Smith Schoolhouse, Boston, Mass., 1834. Boston: Architectural Heritage, 1970. Pp. 23. MB.

3346 _____. Old State House: State and Washington Streets, Boston, Mass., 1713: historical report. Boston: Architectural Heritage, 1969. Pp. 24. MB.

3347 _____. Park Street Church, Zero Park Street, Boston, Mass., 1809. Boston: Architectural Heritage, 1969. v.p. MB.

3348 _____. Parker House, 60 School Street, Boston, Mass., 1854: historical report. Boston: Architectural Heritage, 1969. Pp. 39. MB.
Hotel.

3349 AMERICAN CONGREGATIONAL ASSOCIATION, BOSTON. Celebration of the fiftieth anniversary of the American Congregational Association in Tremont Temple, Boston, Monday, May twenty-fifth, MCMIII.... Boston: American Congregational Association, 1903. Pp. 61.

3350 _____. Historical sketch of its organization, with addresses at the dedication of the new building. Boston, 1899. Pp. 40.

3351 _____. Proceedings at the dedication of the Congregational House, Boston, February 12th, 1873, together with a brief history of the American Congregational Association, by the corresponding secretary [Isaac Pendleton Langworthy]. Boston: American Congregational Association, 1873. Pp. 99.

3352 "THE [AMERICAN Meteorological] Society's new home, 45 Beacon Street, Boston, home of Harrison Gray Otis, 1806-1848." American Meteorological Society. Bulletin, 41 (1960), 507-517.

3353 AMERICAN PUBLISHING AND ENGRAVING CO., N.Y. Boston and Bostonians.... N.Y.: American Publishing and Engraving, [1894]. Pp. 225.
Industries.

3354 AMERICAN TRACT SOCIETY, BOSTON. A brief history of the American Tract Society, instituted at Boston, 1814, and its relations to the American Tract Society at New York, instituted 1825. Boston: T. R. Marvin, 1857. Pp. 48.

3355 AMERICAN TRUST COMPANY. BUNKER HILL BRANCH, CHARLESTOWN, MASS. A century of banking in historic Charlestown. 1825-1925. Boston: Priv. Print, 1925. Pp. 30.

3356 AMERICAN WOOLEN COMPANY. A sketch of the mills of the American Woolen Company. Boston, 1901. Pp. 144.

3357 AMES, ELLIS. "The Garrison mob." MHSP, 18 (1880-1881), 341-343.
William Lloyd Garrison, 1835.

3358 AMORY, CLEVELAND. The proper Bostonians. N.Y.: E. P. Dutton, 1947. Pp. 381.
Social life and customs.

3359 ANCIENT ARABIC ORDER OF THE NOBLES OF THE MYSTIC SHRINE FOR NORTH AMERICA. BOSTON. ALEPPO TEMPLE. History of Aleppo Temple, Ancient Arabic Order Nobles of the Mystic Shrine, preceded by history of the Ancient Arabic Order and history of the Imperial Council Nobles of the Mystic Shrine for North America. Boston: Hall Pub., 1915. 2v.

3360 "ANCIENT paper-hangings in Dorchester, Mass." NEHGR, 19 (1865), 170.

3361 ANDERSON, EDWARD A. PCC cars of Boston, 1937-1967. Cambridge: Boston Street Railway Association, 1968. Pp. 51.
Title refers to: President's Conference Committee of the American Transit Association.

3362 ANDERSON, GREGG. "The Merrymount Press: an appraisal of its books." PM: An Intimate Journal for Production Managers, 4 (October-November, 1938), 17-48.

3363 ANDERSON, THOMAS F. "Boston as a world port." NEM, New Ser., 38 (1908), 393-409.

3364 _____. "Historic Boston." NEM, New Ser., 38 (1908), 559-576.

3365 ANDREWS, AGNES. "The light of March 17, 1776." NEM, 52 (1914-1915), 208-210.
Dorchester Heights.

3366 ANDREWS, CHARLES MCLEAN. "Boston merchants and the non-importation movement." CSMP, 19 (1916-1917), 159-259.
Eighteenth century.

3367 ANGOFF, CHARLES. "Memories of Boston." Menorah Journal, 49 (1962), 136-147.
Jewish life; early twentieth century.

3368 ANTHOLOGY SOCIETY, BOSTON. Journal of the proceedings of the Society which conducts the Monthly Anthology & Boston Review, October 3, 1805, to July 2, 1811. M. A. DeWolfe Howe, ed. [Boston]: Boston Athenaeum, 1910. Pp. 344.

3369 APOLLONIO, THORNTON D. Boston public schools, past and present, with some reflections on their characters and characteristics. Boston: Wright & Potter, 1923. Pp. 166.

3370 APPLETON, WILLIAM. Selections from the diaries of William Appleton, 1786-1862. Susan Mason Loring, ed. Boston: Merrymount Pr., 1922. Pp. 250.
Insight into business world.

3371 APPLETON, WILLIAM SUMNER. "The Province House, 1922." OTNE, 62 (1971-1972), 87-91.

3372 THE APPLETON Temporary Home. A record of work. (1874) Rev. and enl. ed. Boston, 1876. Pp. 320.
Treatment of alcoholics.

3373 ARCHER, GLEASON LEONARD. Building a school; a fearless portrayal of men and events in the Old Bay State, 1906-1919. Boston, 1919. Pp. 316.
Suffolk University Law School.

3374 _____. The impossible task; a story of present day Boston, and how through faith, courage and sacrifice came victory at last. Boston: Suffolk Law School Pr., 1926. Pp. 255.
Suffolk University Law School.

3375 ARMSTRONG, IRENE. "Boston banks." SWJ, 46 (1930), 768-773.

3376 _____. "A school of pottery." Our Boston, 3 (September, 1928), 17-20.
Paul Revere pottery.

3377 ARMSTRONG, JOSEPH. The mother church, a history of the building of the original edifice of the First Church of Christ, Scientist, in Boston, Massachusetts (1897) 17th ed. Boston: Christian Science Publishing Society, 1911. Pp. ix, 107.

3378 ARNOLD, HAROLD GREENE. First Parish West Roxbury. Historical Notes. n.p., n.d. Broadside 9 1/2 x 5 5/8 inches. MBNEH.

3379 ARNOLD, HOWARD PAYSON. The evolution of the Boston medal. Boston, 1901. Pp. 31.

3380 ARRINGTON, JOSEPH EARL. "Lewes and Bartholomew's mechanical panorama of the Battle of Bunker Hill." OTNE, 52 (1961-1962), 50-58, 81-89. Minard Lewis and Truman C. Bartholomew.

3381 "ARTEMUS Ward in Boston, 1864." MagHist, 19 (1914), 191-192.

3382 ASPINWALL, WILLIAM. A volume relating to the early history of Boston, containing the Aspinwall notarial records from 1644 to 1651. William H. Whitmore and Walter K. Watkins, eds. Boston: Municpal Printing Office, 1903. Pp. x, 455.

3383 "THE 'ATLANTIC'S' pleasant days in Tremont Street." Atlantic Monthly, 100 (1907), 716-720.
'Atlantic Monthly.'

3384 AUGUSTUS, JOHN. A report of the labors of John Augustus, for the last ten years, in aid of the unfortunate: containing a description of his method of operations; striking incidents, and observations upon the improvement of some of our city institutions, with a view to the benefit of the prisoner and of society. Boston: Wright & Hasty, 1852. Pp. 104.

3385 AULT, WARREN ORTMAN. Boston University: the College of Liberal Arts, 1873-1973. Boston: Boston Univ., 1973. Pp. xii, 283.

3386 AUSTIN, ARTHUR WILLIAMS. Address at dedication of the town-house at Jamaica Plain, West Roxbury. Boston: A. Mudge & Son, 1868. Pp. 39.

3387 AUSTIN, GEORGE LOWELL. "Lee and Shepard." BSM, 2 (1884-1885), 309-316.
Publishers.

3388 AUSTIN, WILLIAM. An oration, pronounced at Charlestown, at the request of the Artillery Company, on the seventeenth of June; being the anniversary of the Battle of Bunker Hill, and of that Company.... Charlestown: Samuel Etheridge, 1801. Pp. 29.

3389 AUTHENTIC and comprehensive guide and history of Boston.... Boston: Shepard, Norwell, [1878]. Pp. 96.

3390 AYARS, CHRISTINE MERRICK. Contributions to the art of music in America by the music industries of Boston, 1740-1936. N.Y.: H. W. Wilson, 1937. Pp. xv, 326.

3391 AYER, JAMES BOURNE. "Boston at the time of the Battle of Bunker Hill." Bunker Hill Monument Association. Proceedings, (1905), 35-43.

3392 AYER, MARY FARWELL. Boston Common in colonial and provincial days. Boston: D. B. Updike, 1903. Pp. 5, 47.

3393 ____, comp. Check-list of Boston newspapers, 1704-1780...with bibliographical notes by Albert Matthews. Boston: The [Colonial] Society [of Massachusetts], 1907. Pp. xvii, 527.

3394 ____. Early days on Boston Common. Boston: Merrymount Pr., 1910. Pp. vii, 78.

3395 ____. "The South Meeting-House, Boston." NEHGR, 59 (1905), 265-267.
1669-1729.

3396 AYLMER, KEVIN J. "The fire last time. Boston, 60 (January, 1968), 51-57.
1872.

3397 AYRES, IDA. "The story of Shirley Place." NEM, New Ser., 15 (1896-1897), 743-755.
Home of Governor William Shirley.

3398 BABCOCK, MARY KENT DAVEY. Christ Church, Salem Street, Boston, the Old North Church of Paul Revere fame; historical sketches, colonial period, 1723-1775. Boston: Thomas Todd, 1947. Pp. xiii, 271.

3399 ____. "Dr. Cutler entertains the clergy." HMPEC, 13 (1944), 83-93.
Timothy Cutler and the convention of Episcopal clergy of New England, 1738.

3400 ____. "Early organists of Christ Church, Boston, 1736-1824." HMPEC, 14 (1945), 337-351.

3401 ____. "Old Christ Church Boston." HMPEC, 8 (1939), 166-169.

3402 ____. "The organs and organ builders of Christ Church, Boston: 1736-1945." HMPEC, 14 (1945), 241-261.

3403 ____. "The weather-vane on Christ Church." OTNE, 32 (1941-1942), 63-65.

3404 BABST, HENRY J. "A brief history of the Massachusetts Memorial Hospitals." NEJMed, 253 (1955), 859-865.
1855-1955.

3405 BACON, EDWIN MUNROE. Bacon's dictionary of Boston; with an historical introduction.... Boston: Houghton Mifflin, 1886. Pp. xiv, 469.

3406 ____. The book of Boston: fifty years' recollections of the New England metropolis. Boston: Book of Boston Co., 1916. Pp. 534.

3407 ____. and ARTHUR P. GAY. The East Boston ferries and the free ferries issue, a significant chapter of municipal history. Boston: W. B. Clarke, 1909. Pp. 32.

3408 BACON, EDWIN MUNROE. King's Dictionary of Boston; with an historical introduction by George Edward Ellis. Cambridge: Moses King, 1893. Pp. xvi, 616.

3409 ____. Rambles around old Boston. Boston: Little, Brown, 1914. Pp. viii, 205.

3410 [____]. Washington street, old and new; a history in narrative form of the changes which this ancient street has undergone since the settlement of Boston. Boston: C. B. Webster, 1913. Unpaged.

3411 BACON, FRED P. and EDWARD O. SKELTON. Commemorative record of the Handel and Haydn Society of Boston, 1815-1903. Boston: Handel & Haydn Society. [1903?]. Pp. 84.

3412 BAKER, DANIEL WELD. "The grasshopper in Boston." NEHGR, 49 (1895), 24-28.
Weather vanes on Faneuil Hall and on summer house in Peter Faneuil's garden.

3413 ____. Historical sketch of the Dorchester First Parish. Mary Baker Ordway, ed. Albany: F. H. Evory, 1916. Pp. 77.

3414 BAKER, PETER CARPENTER. The Battle of Bunker Hill, an oration delivered before Bunker Hill Chapter, O. U. A., at the celebration of the anniversary of the Battle of Bunker Hill, June 17, 1853, at the Broadway Tabernacle. N.Y.: Baker, Godwin, 1853. Pp. 25.

3415 BAKER, RAY STANNARD. New ideals in healing. N.Y.: F. A. Stokes, 1909. Pp. viii, 105.
Emmanuel Movement (mental healing) in Boston and Social Service Department of Massachusetts General Hospital.

3416 BAKER, WILLIAM A. A history of the Boston Marine Society, 1742-1967. Boston: Boston Marine Society, 1968. Pp. x, 369.

3417 "BAKER'S plays marks centenary year." Publishers' Weekly, 148 (September 8, 1945), 966-969.
Walter H. Baker Co., publisher.

3418 BALCH, MARION C. History of the Jamaica Plain Neighborhood House Association. [Jamaica Plain], 1953. Pp. 37.

3419 BALDWIN, THOMAS. A brief sketch of the revival of religion in Boston, in 1803-5. Boston: Lincoln and Edmands, 1826. Pp. 8.

3420 ____. A discourse delivered in the Second Baptist Meeting-house in Boston, on the first Lord's day in January, 1824, with an appendix, containing historical sketches of the church and society, from their commencement to the present time. Boston: Lincoln & Edmands, [1824]. Pp. 32.

3421 BALDWIN, WILLIAM HENRY. Our farewell to the old meeting-house, address at Brighton, Mass. March 31, 1895 [Boston, 1895]. Pp. 24.

3422 BALFOUR, DAVID M. "Beacon Hill before the houses." BSM, 1 (1884), 389-394.

3423   _____. "The taverns of Boston in ye olden
time." BSM, 2 (1884-1885), 106-119.

3424   BALFOUR, MARY DEVENS. First Parish memen-
tos.... n.p., [1886?]. Unpaged.
250th anniversary.

3425   BALL, WILLIAM T. W. "The old Federal Street
Theatre." BSPub, 8 (1911), 43-91.

3426   BALLARD, JOSEPH. Account of the poor fund
and other charities held in trust by the Old
South Society, city of Boston; with copies of original papers relative to the charities and to the
late trial before the Supreme Court of Massachusetts in 1867. Boston: G. C. Rand & Avery, 1868.
Pp. vi, 234.

3427   BALLOU, ELLEN B. The building of the house;
Houghton Mifflin's formative years. Boston:
Houghton Mifflin, 1970. Pp. xv, 695.

3428   "'BANK Houses' of the Massachusetts Bank
1784-1903." About the First, (April, 1934),
4-5.

3429   BANKETTE COMPANY, INC., BOSTON. The tercentenary art book of Boston. Boston, 1930.
Pp. 54.

3430   "BANKING parallels and contrasts, 1784,
1934." About the First, (July, 1934), 4-5,
10-11.
Massachusetts Bank and First National Bank.

3431   BANKS, LOUIS ALBERT. White slaves; or, the
oppression of the worthy poor. Boston: Lee
and Shepard, 1892. Pp. 327.
Laboring classes.

3432   BANKS, N. HOUSTON. "Abby Folsom and Judge
Story." MagAmHist, 10 (1883), 427-429.
Abolition, 1833.

3433   BAPTIST EDUCATION SOCIETY OF THE YOUNG MEN
OF BOSTON. A sketch of the history of the
Baptist Auxiliary Education Society of the Young
Men of Boston, with the constitution and list of
members. Boston: Putnam & Damrell, 1833. Pp. 22.

3434   BARBER, SAMUEL. Boston Common; a diary of
notable events, incidents, and neighboring
occurences. (1914) 2d ed. Boston: Christopher
Publishing House, 1916. Pp. 288, xlvii.

3435   BARBER, WILLIAM. "Dr. Jackson's discovery
of ether." National Magazine, 5 (1896-
1897), 46-58.

3436   BARBEY, JACOB A. The early history of the
New England Mutual Life Insurance Company.
Boston, 1923. Pp. 39.

3437   BARKER, JOHN, fl. 1775. The British in Boston, being the diary of Lieutenant John Barker of the King's own regiment from November 15,
1774 to May 31, 1776, with notes by Elizabeth Ellery Dana. Cambridge: Harvard Univ. Pr., 1924.
Pp. x, 73.

3438   BARR, LOCKWOOD. "The forerunner of the Willard banjo." Antiques, 75 (1959), 282-285.
Clocks.

3439   "THE BARRELL farm or garden near Milk, Summer and Franklin Streets." OTNE, 37 (1946-
1947), 69-71.
Seventeenth and eighteenth centuries.

3440   BARRETT, JOHN T. "The inoculation controversy in Puritan New England." BHistMed, 12
(1942), 169-190.
1720s in Boston.

3441   BARRON, CLARENCE WALKER and JOSEPH G. MARTIN.
The Boston Stock Exchange, with brief sketches of prominent brokers, bankers, banks and moneyed
institutions of Boston. Boston: Hunt & Bell, 1893.
Unpaged.

3442   BARROWS, CHARLES M. "Old Dorchester." BSM,
3 (1885), 39-47.

3443   BARROWS, JOHN STUART. "The beginning and
launching of the United States Frigate Constitution." BsProc, (1925), 23-37.

3444   _____. "The National Lancers." NEM, New
Ser., 34 (1906), 401-416.
Boston troop of cavalry.

3445   BARRY, ELIZABETH G. House: 1682 Washington
Street, corner Worcester Square. [Boston,
1963?]. 6 leaves.

3446   BARTLETT, HARRIETT MOULTON. 50 years of
social work in the medical setting: past
significance, future outlook. N.Y.: National Association of Social Workers, 1957. Pp. 46.
Massachusetts General Hospital Social Service
Department.

3447   BARTLETT, JOSIAH. "A historical sketch of
Charlestown, in the county of Middlesex, and
Commonwealth of Massachusetts." MHSC, 2 Ser., 2
(1814), 163-184.

3448   BATES, WILLIAM CARVER. "Boston writing masters before the Revolution." NEM, New Ser.,
19 (1898-1899), 403-418.

3449   _____. "A Boston writing-school before the
Revolution." MagAmHist, 21 (1889), 499-503.

3450   "THE BATTLE of Breed's and Bunker Hills."
Potter's AmMo, 4 (June, 1875), 410-412.

3451   "THE BATTLE of Bunker Hill, June 17, 1775."
About the First, (June, 1938), 4-7.

3452   BAUER, ANN. "The Charlestown State Prison."
HJWM, 2 (Fall, 1973), 22-29.

3453   BAXTER, SYLVESTER. "Architectural features
of Boston parks." American Architect and
Building News, 61 (1898), 19-20, 51-52, 83-84.

3454   _____. "Boston at the century's end." Harper's Magazine, 99 (1899), 823-846.

3455 ____. "Boston's Fenway as an educational center." Outlook, 86 (1907), 894-907.

3456 BAXTER, WILLIAM THREIPLAND. The house of Hancock; business in Boston, 1724-1775. Cambridge: Harvard Univ. Pr., 1945. Pp. xxvii, 821.

3457 [BAXTON, CHARLES]. Boston and the Back Bay. Boston: Reed & Lincoln, 1884. Pp. 93.

3458 BEALES, ROSS W., JR. "The Half-Way Covenant and religious scrupulosity: the First Church of Dorchester, Massachusetts, as a test." WMQ, 31 (1974), 465-480.

3459 BEALL, OTHO T., JR. "Cotton Mather's early 'Curiosa Americana' and the Boston Philosophical Society of 1683." WMQ, 3 Ser., 18 (1961), 360-372.

3460 BEALS, VICTOR. "Nearly sixty years ago at the old Hollis." NEG, 11 (Spring, 1970), 48-53.
        Theater.

3461 BEARDSLEY, DAVID. "Boston and the first printers and publishers." American Printer, 75 (August 20, 1922), 35-37.

3462 BEARSE, AUSTIN. Reminiscences of fugitive-slave law days in Boston. Boston: W. Richardson, 1880. Pp. 41.

3463 BEEBE, LUCIUS MORRIS. Boston and the Boston legend. N.Y.: D. Appleton-Century, 1935. Pp. xv, 372.

3464 BELL, CHARLES HENRY. New Hampshire at Bunker Hill, an address delivered before the Bunker Hill Monument Association, in Boston, June 17, 1891. Cambridge: J. Wilson and Son, 1891. Pp. 26.

3465 BENEVOLENT FRATERNITY OF CHURCHES, BOSTON. Seventy-fifth anniversary of the founding of the Ministry-at-Large in the city of Boston by Rev. Joseph Tuckerman. Boston: Ellis, 1901. Pp. 29.
        Organization of Unitarian churches.

3466 BENSON, ALBERT EMERSON. History of the Massachusetts Horticultural Society. Norwood: Printed for the Massachusetts Horticultural Society, 1929. Pp. ix, 553.

3467 BENT, SAMUEL ARTHUR. "Colonnade row." BSPub, 11 (1914), 9-57.
        Residential block on Tremont St. built in 1811.

3468 BENTON, JOSIAH HENRY. The story of the old Boston Town House, 1658-1711. Boston: Merrymount Pr., 1908. Pp. xi, 212.
        Includes punishments inflicted by orders of the colony courts 1630-1691.

3469 BENZAQUIN, PAUL. Fire in Boston's Cocoanut Grove; holocaust. (1959) New ed. Boston: Branden Pr., 1967. Pp. 248.
        First edition has title: Holocaust!

3470 BERKELEY SCHOOL, BOSTON. A decade's work. 1884-1894. Boston: Clapp & Son, 1895. Pp. 59. MB.

3471 "BERKELEY St. Congregational Church, Boston, Ms." CongQ, 6 (1864), 33-38.

3472 BERRY, LAWRENCE FREDERICK. "Greenwood Memorial Church" (Methodist Episcopal) Dorchester, Massachusetts; its ancestry and growth with the neighborhood. Roxbury: Warren Pr., 1936. Pp. 120.

3473 BEST, WILLIAM J. A history of the Pacific National Bank of Boston, Mass. Washington: Judd & Detweiler, 1884. Pp. 52.

3474 BETHESDA SOCIETY, BOSTON. A brief account of the origin and progress of the Boston Female Society for Missionary Purposes.... Boston: Lincoln & Edmands, [1818]. Pp. 24.

3475 BETTS, JOHN R. "The Negro and the New England conscience in the days of John Boyle O'Reilly." JNegroHist, 51 (1966), 246-261.
        1870s and 1880s.

3476 "BIBLIOGRAPHY of Boston." Boston Public Library Bulletin, 2 Ser., 3 (1898), 42-47; 4 (1899), 295-313.

3477 BIGELOW, ALBERT FRANCIS. Twenty-five years of legal aid in Boston, 1900-1925. Boston: Boston Legal Aid Society, [1926]. Pp. 33.

3478 BILLINGTON, RAY ALLEN. "The burning of the Charlestown Convent." NEQ, 10 (1937), 4-24.

3479 "BILLS of mortality in Dorchester." MHSC, 1 (1792), 116.
        1749-1792.

3480 "BILLS of mortality of Boston." MHSC, 2 Ser., 7 (1818), 134-135; 8 (1819), 40-41; 3 Ser., 1 (1825), 278-286; 4 (1834), 323-330; 5 (1836), 288-290; 6 (1837), 285; 7 (1838), 284.
        1815-1837.

3481 "BIOGRAPHY of the 'Boston Courier.'" Hist Mag, 10 (1866), 45-47.
        Newspaper.

3482 BLAGDEN, GEORGE WASHINGTON. Memorial discourses delivered in the Old South Church, Boston, on the two hundredth anniversary of its organization, May 23, 1869.... Cambridge: Welch, Bigelow, 1870. Pp. 45.

3483 BLAKE, FRANCIS EVERETT. "The British raid on Dorchester Neck, February, 1776." NEHGR, 53 (1899), 177-185.

3484 ____, comp. History of the South Baptist Church of Boston, with notes relating to the Fourth Street Baptist Church. Boston, 1899. Pp. 51.

3485 BLAKE, JAMES, EBENEZER CLAPP, JR., JAMES M. ROBBINS, and EDWARD HOLDEN, eds. Annals of the town of Dorchester, 1750. Boston: D. Clapp, Jr., 1846. Pp. vi, 95.

3486 BLAKE, JOHN BALLARD. "The inoculation controversy in Boston: 1721-1722." NEQ, 25
(1952), 489-506.

3487 _____. "Lemuel Shattuck and the Boston water supply." BHistMed, 29 (1955), 554-562.
1844-1845.

3488 _____. "The medical profession and public
health in colonial Boston." BHistMed, 26
(1952), 218-230.

3489 _____. Public health in the town of Boston,
1630-1822. Cambridge: Harvard Univ. Pr.,
1959. Pp. x, 278.

3490 _____. "Smallpox inoculation in colonial
Boston." JHistMed, 8 (1953), 284-300.

3491 _____. "'Yellow Jack' in Boston." NEG, 6
(Fall, 1964), 19-26.
Yellow fever, 1796-1802 and 1819.

3492 BLAKE, MAURICE CARY. "Boston hand stamps:
the first known use, February 27, 1769."
Stamps, 45 (1944), 416-418, 425-427.

3493 _____, ed. "A mast-fleet letter of 1709."
MHSP, 78 (1966), 133-142.
Efforts to protect trees marked to become
masts.

3494 _____. and WILBUR W. DAVIS. Postal markings
of Boston, Massachusetts, to 1890. Portland, Me.: Severn-Wylie-Jewett Co., 1949.
Pp. xvii, 367.

3495 BLAKE, MORISON. "The shipping days of Boston." SWJ, 43 (1928), 771-787.

3496 BLASBERG, ROBERT W. "Grueby art pottery."
Antiques, 100 (1971), 246-249.
Grueby Faïence and Tile Company, 1897-1910.

3497 BLELOCK, GEORGE H. Boston past and present,
being an outline of the history of the city
as exhibited in the lives of its prominent citizens.
Cambridge: Riverside Pr., 1874. Pp. xiv, 543.
Biography.

3498 BLENKIN, G. B. "Boston, England, and John
Cotton in 1621." NEHGR, 28 (1874), 125-139.
Boston during reign of James I.

3499 BLODGETT, GEOFFREY T. "The mind of the Boston mugwump." MVHR, 48 (1961-1962), 614-
634.
1880s.

3500 BLODGETT, STEPHEN H. "Early Boston history
revealed in the story of smallpox inoculation." Our Boston, 3 (October, 1928), 7-12, (November, 1928), 18-22; 4 (January, 1929), 14-18,
(February, 1929), 13-21, (May-June, 1929), 9-16.
Not completed, as periodical ceased publication.

3501 BLOOD, W. H., JR. "Bunker Hill Monument."
SWJ, 42 (1928), 783-791.

3502 BLOOD in the streets: the Boston Massacre,
5 March 1770. Boston: Revolutionary War
Bicentennial Commission, 1970. Unpaged.
Contains an essay by John Eliot Alden.

3503 BODFISH, J. P. "The old Franklin Street
Church." BSProc, (1898), 44-59.
Roman Catholic.

3504 BODGE, GEORGE MADISON. "The Dutch pirates in
Boston 1694-1695." BSPub, 7 (1910), 33-60.

3505 BOIES, JEREMIAH SMITH. "Historical reminiscences, 1715-1775." NEHGR, 6 (1852), 255-
258.

3506 BOLLES, JAMES AARON. The anniversary sermon
and report preached in the Church of the Advent, Boston, Mass., the first Sunday in Advent,
A. D., 1860, being the sixteenth anniversary of the
foundation of the parish. Boston: Henry W. Dutton
and Son, 1860. Pp. 40.

3507 _____. The Church of the Advent, a saluta-
tory sermon preached in the Church of the
Advent, Boston, Mass. on the first Sunday in Advent,
1859, being the fifteenth anniversary of the foundation of the parish. Boston: Henry W. Dutton and
Son, 1859. Pp. 40.

3508 BOLLES, JOHN A. "Escape from Fort Warren."
Civil War Times Illustrated, 5 (1966), 44-
48.

Unsuccessful attempt by Charles W. Read.

3509 BOLSTER, EDITH R. "Dorchester before annexation." Our Boston, 1 (April, 1926), 7-12.

3510 BOLTON, CHARLES KNOWLES. "The Boston Athenaeum." SWJ, 42 (1928), 475-487.

3511 _____. "Circulating libraries in Boston,
1765-1865." CSMP, 11 (1906-1907), 196-207.

3512 _____. "A half-forgotten tragedy of 1755."
OTNE, 11 (1920-1921), 12-14.
Punishment of Negro servants for poisoning
their master.

3513 _____. "Social libraries in Boston." CSMP,
12 (1908-1909), 332-338.

3514 BOND, HENRY F. "Old Summer Street, Boston."
NEM, New Ser., 19 (1898-1899), 333-356.

3515 BOOTH, JOHN NICHOLLS. The story of the Second Church in Boston, the original Old North;
including the Old North Church mystery. Boston,
1959. Pp. 92.

3516 BORTMAN, MARK. "Paul Revere and Son and
their Jewish correspondents." AJHSP, 43
(1953-1954), 199-229.

3517 BOSTON. Boston and its story, 1630-1915.
Edward M. Hartwell, Edward W. McGlenen and
Edward O. Skelton, eds. Boston: Printing Depart-
ment, 1916. Pp. 200.

3518 _____. A catalogue of the city councils of Boston, 1822-1908, Roxbury, 1846-1867, Charlestown, 1847-1873 and of the selectmen of Boston, 1634-1822, also of various other town and municipal officers. (1891) Printed by order of the City council.... [Boston]: City of Boston Printing Department, 1909. Pp. 402.

3519 _____. Celebration of the centennial anniversary of the Battle of Bunker Hill, with an appendix containing a survey of the literature of the battle, its antecedents and results. Boston: Printed by order of the City Council, 1875. Pp. viii, 174.
　　　Appendix prepared by Justin Winsor.

3520 _____. Celebration of the two hundred and fiftieth anniversary of the settlement of Boston, September 17, 1880. Boston: Printed by order of the City Council, 1880. Pp. 172.

3521 _____. March 17th, 1876. Celebration of the centennial anniversary of the evacuation of Boston by the British army, March 17th, 1776; reception of the Washington medal; oration delivered in Music Hall, and a chronicle of the Siege of Boston. George L. Ellis, ed. Boston: Printed by order of the City Council, 1876.

3522 _____. A memorial of the American patriots who fell at the Battle of Bunker Hill, June 17, 1775. With an account of the dedication of the memorial tablets on Winthrop Square, Charlestown, June 17, 1889, and an appendix containing illustrative papers. (1889) 4th ed. Boston: Printed by order of the City Council, 1896. Pp. 274.
　　　Appendix prepared by William H. Whitmore.

3523 _____. Monument to Joseph Warren, its origin, history and dedication, 1898-1904. Boston: Municipal Printing Office, 1905. Pp. 110.

3524 _____. Re-dedication of the Old State House, Boston, July 11, 1882. (1882) 6th ed. Boston: Printed by order of the City Council, 1893. Pp. 236.
　　　Detailed history of the building.

3525 _____. 1776-1926, a patriotic celebration commemorating the 150th anniversary of the evacuation of Boston by the British troops, conducted by the City of Boston, Honorable Malcolm E. Nichols, Mayor, Wednesday evening, March 17, 1926, Mechanics Hall, Boston, Massachusetts. [Boston, 1926]. Unpaged.

3526 _____. A short narrative of the horrid massacre in Boston, perpetrated in the evening of the fifth day of March, 1770, by soldiers of the 29th regiment, which with the 14th regiment were then quartered there; with some observations on the state of things prior to that catastrophe. (1770) N.Y.: J. Doggett, Jr., 1849. Pp. 122.
　　　Notes and illustrations by John Doggett, Jr.

3527 BOSTON. ARLINGTON STREET CHURCH. The century and quest; commemorating the centennial celebration of the Arlington Street Church, Unitarian-Universalist, Boston, Mass., 1861-1961. Boston, 1961. Unpaged.

3528 _____. A memorial of the Federal-street meeting-house. A discourse preached on Sunday morning, March 13, 1859, by Rev. Ezra S. Gannett; and addresses delivered in the afternoon of that day, by Rev. S. B. Cruft, Rev. A. Smith, Rev. F. W. Holland, Rev. R. P. Rogers [and] Rev. R. C. Waterston.... Boston: Crosby, Nichols, Lee, 1860. Pp. 89.

3529 BOSTON. BALDWIN PLACE BAPTIST CHURCH. A concise history of the Baldwin Place Baptist Church, together with the articles of faith and practice, also an alphabetical and chronological calendar of the present members. Boston: Wm. H. Hutchinson, 1854. Pp. 96.

3530 BOSTON. BERKELEY STREET CONGREGATIONAL CHURCH. Semi-centennial of the Berkeley Street Congregational Church, commemorated September 30, 1877. Boston: Noyes, Snow, 1877. Pp. 54.

3531 BOSTON. BOARD OF HEALTH. Comparative view of twenty-five of the principal causes of death during the years 1872 to 1887, inclusive. Boston: Rockwell and Churchill, 1888. Unpaged.

3532 BOSTON. BOWDOIN SQUARE BAPTIST CHURCH. Bowdoin Square Church book: comprising a brief history of the formation and organizations of the church; its articles of faith, covenant, etc. R. W. Cushman, ed. Boston: S. N. Dickinson, 1843. Pp. 126.

3533 BOSTON. BOWDOIN STREET CHURCH. The articles of faith and covenant of the Bowdoin Street Church, Boston, with a list of the members. Boston: T. R. Marvin, 1856. Pp. 71.
　　　Includes a brief history.

3534 BOSTON. BRATTLE SQUARE CHURCH. The Manifesto Church, records of the church in Brattle Square, Boston, with lists of communicants, baptisms, marriages, and funerals, 1699-1872. Boston: Benevolent Fraternity of Churches, 1902. Pp. xvi, 448.
　　　Indexed.

3535 BOSTON. BUNKER HILL DAY CELEBRATION COMMITTEE. Celebration of the sesquicentennial anniversary of the Battle of Bunker Hill, June 17, 1925. Boston: Printing Department, 1925. Pp. 42.

3536 BOSTON. CEMETERY DEPT. Historical sketch and matters appertaining to the Copp's Hill burial-ground. Boston: Municipal Printing Office, 1901. Pp. 26.

3537 _____. Historical sketch and matters appertaining to the Granary burial-ground. Boston: Municipal Printing Office, 1902. Pp. 37.

3538 _____. Historical sketch and matters appertaining to the King's Chapel burying ground.... Boston: Municipal Printing Office, 1903. Pp. 52.

3539 BOSTON. CHAMBER OF COMMERCE. BUREAU OF COMMERCIAL AND INDUSTRIAL AFFAIRS. The Boston fire, November 9, 1872.... Boston: Boston Chamber of Commerce, Bureau of Commercial and Industrial Affairs, 1922. Pp. 32.

3540 BOSTON. CHAMBER OF COMMERCE. CIVIC DEPT.
Metropolitan Boston; a collection of three
publications on the history and present characteristics of the region. Boston, 1947. v.p.

3541 BOSTON. CHILDREN'S HOSPITAL. The Children's
Hospital, 1869-1951, eighty-two years of
service to the community and to the nation: The
Children's Medical Center, 1946-1951. [Boston,
1951?]. Pp. 65.

3542 _____. The Children's Hospital, 1869-1939;
School of Nursing, 1889-1939. [Boston,
1939]. Pp. 50.

3543 _____. Medical and surgical report of the
Children's Hospital, 1869-1894. T. M.
Rotch and Herbert L. Burrell, eds. Boston: Board
of Managers, 1895. Pp. xv, 367.

3544 BOSTON. CHILDREN'S MUSEUM. For 25 years:
Boston's Children's Museum. Jamaica Plain:
Pinkham Pr., 1940. Pp. 16.

3545 BOSTON. CHRIST CHURCH. Christ Church, Salem Street, Boston, 1723, a guide. Boston,
1941. Unpaged.
Not a guide book.

3546 _____. Pictorial history of Christ Church,
Boston, the Old North Church of Paul Revere
fame. Everett: Acme Printing, [1960?]. Unpaged.
M.

3547 BOSTON. CHURCH OF THE ADVENT. The Church
of the Advent. Boston, 1938. Pp. 26.

3548 _____. The Parish of the Advent in the city
of Boston, a history of one hundred years,
1844-1944. Boston, 1944. Pp. vii, 212.

3549 _____. Sketch of the history of the parish,
1844-1894. Boston: George H. Ellis, 1894.
Pp. 87. MB.

3550 BOSTON. CHURCH OF THE DISCIPLES. A record
of the celebration of the seventy-fifth anniversary of the Church of the Disciples, Boston,
April 2-27, 1916. Boston: Geo. H. Ellis, 1916.
Pp. 26.

3551 BOSTON. CITY COUNCIL. Brighton day: celebration of the one hundredth anniversary of
the incorporation of the town of Brighton, held on
August 3, 1907. Boston: Municipal Printing Office,
1908. Pp. 63.

3552 _____. Celebration of the one hundred and
twenty-fifth anniversary of the evacuation
of Boston by the British army, March 17, 1901....
Boston: Municipal Printing Office, 1901. Pp. 162.

3553 _____. Leverett street jail. [Boston,
1841]. Pp. 11.

3554 BOSTON. CITY COUNCIL. JOINT COMMITTEE ON
INTERMENTS. A sketch of the origin and his-
tory of the Granary burial-ground. Boston, 1879.
Pp. 21.

3555 BOSTON. CITY HOSPITAL. A history of the
Boston City Hospital from its foundation un-
til 1904. David W. Cheever, et al., eds. Boston:
Municipal Printing Office, 1906. Pp. vi, 422.

3556 _____. Semicentennial observance of the
opening of the Boston City Hospital, 1864-
1914. Boston: Printing Department, 1914. Pp. 14.
M.

3557 BOSTON. CITY HOSPITAL. DEPT. OF SOCIAL
WORK. Ten years of social work at the Boston
City Hospital. Boston, 1925. Pp. 38.

3558 BOSTON. CITY PLANNING BOARD. From Trimoun-
taine to Boston. 1630. 1930. A brief history of the city of Boston, together with a statement of its commercial and industrial opportunities;
its points of special interest; a list of its historical tablets and other statistical data. Elisabeth M. Herlihy, comp. Boston: Printing Department, 1930. Pp. 76.

3559 BOSTON. CIVIC SERVICE HOUSE. Helps for new
Americans: the record of Civic Service
House, a social settlement founded in 1901. Boston,
1915. Pp. 47. M.

3560 BOSTON. CLARENDON STREET BAPTIST CHURCH. A
brief history of the Clarendon St. Baptist
Church (formerly Federal Street, afterwards Rowe
Street Church), Boston; with the declaration of
faith, church covenant, list of members, etc. Boston: Gould & Lincoln, 1872. Pp. 126.

3561 _____. A brief history of the Rowe Street
Baptist Church, Boston; with the declaration
of faith, church covenant, and list of members.
Boston: Gould and Lincoln, 1858. Pp. 90.

3562 BOSTON. COMMISSION ON MARKING HISTORICAL
SITES. Report of the Commission on Marking
Historical Sites of the City of Boston, 1924-1937.
Boston, [1937?]. Pp. 151.

3563 BOSTON. COMMITTEE ON COMPILATION OF THE TER-
CENTENARY CELEBRATION. Tercentenary of the
founding of Boston, an account of the celebration
marking the three hundredth anniversary of the settlement of the site of the city of Boston, Massachusetts. Boston: Printing Department, 1930.
Pp. xii, 392.

3564 BOSTON. COMMITTEE ON PUBLIC BUILDINGS. The
City Hall, Boston, corner stone laid, Monday,
September 17, 1865. Boston: City Council, 1866.
Pp. vii, 130.

3565 BOSTON. COMMUNITY CHURCH. The Community
Church of Boston: history and principles.
[Boston, 1939]. Pp. 24.

3566 BOSTON. EMMANUEL CHURCH. Emmanuel Church
in the city of Boston, 1860-1960, the first
one hundred years. [Boston]: The Vestry, 1960.
Pp. 70. MBNEH.

3567   BOSTON. ENGLISH HIGH SCHOOL. Catalogue of the scholars and teachers of the English High School, Boston, Mass., from 1821 to 1890, together with pictures of the head masters and schoolhouses, and an historical sketch of the school. Boston: English High School Association, 1890. Pp. xxviii, 109.

3568   _____. Semi-centennial anniversary of the English High School, May 2, 1871. Boston: English High School Association, 1871. Pp. 112.

3569   BOSTON. ENGLISH HIGH SCHOOL ASSOCIATION. CENTENARY COMMITTEE. One hundred years of the English High School of Boston. [Boston], 1924. Pp. v, 87.

3570   BOSTON. FINANCE COMMISSION. A chronology of the Boston public schools. George A. O. Ernst, ed. Boston: Printing Department, 1912. Pp. 39.

3571   BOSTON. FIRST BAPTIST CHURCH. Bi-centenary commemoration, Sunday, March 21, 1880, of the reopening of the First Baptist meeting-house in Boston, after its doors had been 'nailed up' by order of the Governor and Council of the Colony of Massachusetts, March, 8th, 1680. Historical discourse, by the pastor, Cephas B. Crane, D.D., with other exercises. Boston: Tolman & White, 1880. Pp. 27.

3572   _____. A brief history of the First Baptist Church in Boston.... Boston: S. N. Dickinson, 1843. Pp. 36.

3573   _____. The commemorative services of the First Baptist Church of Boston, Massachusetts, on the occasion of the two hundred and fiftieth anniversary of its foundation, Saturday, Sunday and Monday, June 5, 6, and 7, 1915. Edwin P. Wells, ed. [Boston], 1915. Pp. xiii, 233.

3574   _____. Historical sketch of the First Baptist Church, Boston.... Boston: C. A. Heyer & Son, 1886. Pp. 64. MB.

3575   _____. Manual, with historical sketch, of the First Baptist Church, Boston.... Boston: Franklin Pr., 1880. Pp. 45.

3576   BOSTON. FIRST CHURCH. The commemoration by the First Church in Boston of the completion of two hundred and fifty years since its foundation, on Thursday, November 18, 1880. Boston: Hall & Whiting, 1881. Pp. xx, 218.

3577   _____. The records of the First Church in Boston, 1630-1868. Richard D. Pierce, ed. Boston: Colonial Society of Massachusetts, 1961. 3v.

3578   _____. Sermons and addresses commemorating the 275th anniversary of the founding of the First Church in Boston, Sunday, November 5, and Sunday, November 12, 1905. Boston, 1906. Pp. 56.

3579   BOSTON. FIRST CHURCH, JAMAICA PLAIN. 150th anniversary of the First Congregational Society, Jamaica Plain, Mass., commemoration service, 1769-1919. December 31, 1919. [Jamaica Plain, 1919]. Unpaged.

3580   BOSTON. FIRST FREE CONGREGATIONAL CHURCH. Brief history of the First Free Congregational Church.... Boston: Dow and Jackson, 1840. Pp. 48.

3581   BOSTON. FIRST METHODIST EPISCOPAL CHURCH. First Church Herald; historic illustrated edition, published in commemoration of the 100th anniversary of the erection of the Temple Street Church, December 6-13, 1936. [Boston, 1936]. Unpaged.

3582   BOSTON. FIRST NATIONAL BANK. The Battle of Bunker Hill. Boston: First National Bank of Boston, 1939. Pp. 28.

3583   _____. 1784-1934, the First National Bank of Boston; a brief history of its 150 years of continual existence with emphasis on the early days of its first forebear, the Massachusetts Bank--organized in 1784. Boston: Priv. Print, 1934. Pp. 67.

3584   BOSTON. FLOATING HOSPITAL. Historical sketch of the origin and development of the Boston Floating Hospital. Boston, [1903?]. Pp. 35. M.

3585   BOSTON. FRANKLIN STREET CHURCH. Origin and formation of the Franklin Street Church.... Boston: Light and Stearns, 1836. Pp. 23. M.

3586   BOSTON. GIRLS' HIGH SCHOOL. A brief sketch of the history of the Girls' High School of Boston, 1902-1927, together with an account of the celebration of the seventy-fifth anniversary of the school. [Boston, 1927]. Pp. 66.

3587   BOSTON. HAWES SCHOOL. OLD HAWES SCHOOL BOYS' ASSOCIATION. The Hawes School memorial, containing an account of five re-unions of the Old Hawes School Boys' Association, one re-union of the Hawes School Girls' Association, and a series of biographical sketches of the old masters.... Boston: D. Clapp & Son, 1889. Pp. 277.

3588   BOSTON. HISTORIC CONSERVATION COMMITTEE. Beacon Hill: The North Slope. [Boston], 1963. Pp. 34. M.

3589   _____. Marlborough Street/Back Bay, a proposal to establish the Marlborough Street Historic District. [Boston], 1966. 23 leaves. M. Architectural history of individual houses.

3590   BOSTON. HOLY TRINITY CHURCH. Geschichte der deutschen katholischen hl. Dreifaltigkeits-Gemeinde in Boston, Mass.; Jubiläums-Andenken an die 50 jährige Gedächtnisfeier des ersten Gottesdienstes in der alten hl. Dreifaltigkeits-Kirche. [Boston]: F. X. Nopper, 1894. Pp. 99.

3591   _____. Golden jubilee celebration of the consecration of the Holy Trinity German Catholic Church, 1877-1927. Boston, [1927]. Pp. 56.

3592   _____. Holy Trinity Parish, Boston, Mass.; a historical review. Boston: E. L. Grimes, 1927. Pp. 69.

3593   BOSTON. HOME FOR AGED WOMEN. A brief his-
        tory of the Home for Aged Women; one hun-
dredth anniversary, 1849--April 30--1949. n.p.,
[1949]]. Pp. 10.

3594   BOSTON. HOUSE OF THE GOOD SAMARITAN. 'To
        wider spheres of usefulness'; the hundredth
anniversary of the House of the Good Samaritan.
Boston, 1961. Pp. 26. M.
        M.

3595   BOSTON. INDUSTRIAL SCHOOL FOR CRIPPLED AND
        DEFORMED CHILDREN. Boston Common in the
seventeenth century. Boston, 1903. Unpaged.

3596   _____. 75 years of service, 1894-1969.
        Boston, 1969. Unpaged. M.

3597   BOSTON. KING'S CHAPEL. A brief sketch of
        the history of King's Chapel. n.p.,
[1898?]. Unpaged. M.

3598   _____. The commemoration by King's Chapel,
        Boston, of the completion of two hundred
years since its foundation, on Wednesday, December
15, 1886.... Boston: Little, Brown, 1887.
Pp. vi, 200.
        Historical sermons by Henry Wilder Foote.

3599   BOSTON. LEYDEN CHURCH. Manual for the use
        of the members of the Church of Christ in
Leyden Chapel, Boston, Mass. Joseph H. Towne, ed.
Boston, 1846. Pp. vi, 192. M.
        Includes brief history.

3600   BOSTON. MAVERICK CONGREGATIONAL CHURCH.
        Condensed history and manual of the Maverick
Congregational Church, East Boston, Mass., from its
organization May 31st, 1836 to June 30, 1894. Boston, 1894. Pp. 227. MBNEH.

3601   BOSTON. MAYOR, 1910-1914 (JOHN F. FITZGER-
        ALD). The advance of Boston, a pictorial
review of municipal progress by this city during
four years 1910-1913, Honorable John F. Fitzgerald,
Mayor. Boston, [1913]. Pp. ix, 113.

3602   BOSTON. MECHANIC APPRENTICES' LIBRARY ASSO-
        CIATION. Semicentennial festival, February
22, 1870, address by Charles W. Slack, with appendix, giving a report of the festival by W. B. Smart.
Boston: Wright & Potter, 1870. Pp. 51. MB.

3603   BOSTON. MERCANTILE LIBRARY ASSOCIATION.
        Mercantile Library Association: its charter,
constitution, by-laws, a sketch of its history, etc.
Boston, 1882. Pp. 28.

3604   _____. The Mercantile Library Association:
        its charter, constitution, by-laws...with an
account of its seventy-fifth anniversary. Boston
1895. Pp. 38.

3605   BOSTON. MOUNT VERNON CONGREGATIONAL CHURCH.
        The confession of faith and covenant of the
Mount Vernon Congregational Church, in Boston,
Mass., organized June 1, 1842. Boston: J. H. Barn-
ard, 1872. Pp. 96.
        Includes brief historical sketch.

3606   BOSTON. MUNICIPAL GOVERNMENT. City of Bos-
        ton, a sketch of the origin and history of
the Granary burial-ground.... Boston, 1879.
Pp. 21. MB.

3607   BOSTON. MUSEUM OF FINE ARTS. Back Bay Bos-
        ton: the city as a work of art, with essays
by Lewis Mumford and Walter Muir Whitehall. [Bos-
ton, 1969]. Pp. 149.

3608   _____. Museum of Fine Arts, Boston, 1870-
        1920. [Boston, 1921]. Pp. 38.

3609   BOSTON. MUSEUM OF SCIENCE. 10 years at
        Science Park, 1951-1961. Boston, 1961. Un-
paged. M.

3610   BOSTON. OLD SOUTH CHURCH. An historical
        catalogue of the Old South Church (Third
Church) Boston. Hamilton A. Hill and George F.
Bigelow, eds. Boston: Printed for Private Distri-
bution, 1883. Pp. x, 370.
        1669-1882.

3611   _____. History of the Old South Church of
        Boston. Boston: Published for the Benefit
of the Old South Fund, 1929. Pp. 71. M.

3612   _____. Old South Chapel prayer meeting, its
        origin and history.... Boston: J. E. Til-
ton, 1859. Pp. 199. M.
        A non-denominational meeting held in the
        Old South Chapel, 1850-1859.

3613   _____. Old South Church (Third Church) Bos-
        ton, memorial addresses, Sunday evening,
October 26, 1884. Boston: Cupples, Upham, 1885.
Pp. 131.
        Sketches of ministers from 1670 to 1882.

3614   _____. Our heritage, Old South Church, 1669-
        1919. Norwood: Plimpton Pr., 1919. Pp. 94.

3615   _____. The two hundred and fiftieth anni-
        versary of the founding of the Old South
Church (Third Church, 1669) in Boston. Norwood:
Plimpton Pr., 1919. Pp. ix, 138.
        Historical discourse is by George A. Gordon.

3616   BOSTON. PARK STREET CHURCH. The articles of
        faith and covenant, of Park Street Church,
Boston, with a list of members. Boston: T. R. Marvin, 1850. Pp. 43. M.
        Includes brief history.

3617   _____. Commemorative exercises at the one
        hundredth anniversary of the organization of
Park Street Church, February 26-March 3, 1909.
A. Z. Conrad, ed. Boston: Park Street Centennial
Committee, 1909. Pp. 293.

3618   _____. The semi-centennial celebration of
        the Park Street Church and Society; held on
the Lord's Day, February 27, 1859, with the festival on the day following. Boston: H. Hoyt, 1861.
Pp. 166.
        Includes historical sketch.

3619 ____. Seventy-fifth anniversary of Park Street Congregational Church, John L. Withrow...sermon and address, Sunday, March 2, 1884.... Boston: Brown, [1884?]. Pp. 46.

3620 BOSTON. PAUPER BOYS' SCHOOL. DEER ISLAND. History and description.... Boston: Rockwell and Churchill, 1876. Pp. 13. MB.

3621 BOSTON. PHILLIPS CONGREGATIONAL CHURCH. Seventy-fifth anniversary...December 12th, 1898, South Boston, Mass. Boston, 1898. Pp. 20. MB.

3622 BOSTON. PITTS STREET CHAPEL. History of the Ministry at Large in connection with the Pitts Street Chapel. Boston: John Wilson, 1850. Pp. 12. MBNEH.

3623 BOSTON. PUBLIC LIBRARY. Proceedings at the dedication of the building for the public library of the city of Boston, January 1, 1858. Boston: City Council, 1858. Pp. 194.
    Includes a history of the library.

3624 BOSTON. PUBLIC LIBRARY. CENTENNIAL COMMISSION. Building a great future upon a glorious past. Boston, 1953. Pp. 36.

3625 BOSTON. PUBLIC LIBRARY. CITY POINT BRANCH. A short history of South Boston. [Boston, 1930]. Unpaged.

3626 BOSTON. REGISTRY DEPT. Bills of mortality, 1810-1849, city of Boston. With an essay on the vital statistics of Boston, from 1840 to 1841 by Lemuel Shattuck. Boston: Registry Department, 1893. Pp. xiii, 87.

3627 ____. Records relating to the early history of Boston.... William H. Whitmore, et al., eds. Boston: Rockwell and Churchill, 1876-1909. 39v.
    Imprint varies.

3628 BOSTON. ST. AUGUSTINE'S CEMETERY. A short history of St. Augustine's Cemetery, So. Boston, Mass. n.p., n.d. Pp. 16.

3629 BOSTON. ST. MARY'S CHURCH. 1847-1922, diamond jubilee of the Society of Jesus, St. Mary's Church, North End, Boston, Massachusetts. November 19-23. Boston, 1922. Unpaged.
    Contains a sketch of the church.

3630 ____. Golden jubilee of the Society of Jesus in Boston, Mass., 1847-1897, St. Mary's Parish, Oct. 3, 4, 5 and 6, 1897. Boston: Jubilee Committee, 1898. Pp. 112.

3631 BOSTON. ST. MATTHEW'S CHURCH. Centennial book of the 'Parish of St. Matthew's in Boston,' incorporated June 20, 1816. Boston, 1916. Unpaged.

3632 BOSTON. SALEM AND MARINER'S CHURCH. Memorial volume of Salem Church, Boston, Mass. [Boston?]: Published by the Committee, 1874. Pp. 52.

3633 BOSTON. SCHOOL COMMITTEE. Boston Latin and high schools, 1635-1935, organization and administration; tercentenary report, 1935....

Boston: Printing Department, 1935. Pp. 138.
    Includes a chronology.

3634 ____. Dorchester celebration, 250th anniversary of the establishment of the first public school in Dorchester, June 22, 1889. Boston: Rockwell and Churchill, 1890. Pp. 77.

3635 BOSTON. SCHOOL OF EXPRESSION. Twenty years of ideals and experiences. Boston, [1900]. Unpaged.

3636 BOSTON. SECOND CHURCH. The historical and other records belonging to the Second Church in Boston. [Boston, 1888]. Pp. 12.
    Signed: Francis H. Brown.

3637 ____. The Second Church in Boston; commemorative services held on the completion of two hundred and fifty years since its foundation, 1649-1899. Boston, 1900. Pp. xv, 206.

3638 BOSTON. SECOND SOCIETY OF UNIVERSALISTS. An account of the celebration of the seventy-fifth anniversary of the Second Society of Universalists, Boston, December 18, 1892.... Boston: Universalist Publishing House, 1893. Pp. 129.
    Historical discourse by A. A. Miner.

3639 BOSTON. SESQUICENTENNIAL HISTORICAL COMMITTEE. A patriotic celebration commemorating the 150th anniversary of the evacuation of Boston by the British troops. n.p., [1926?]. Unpaged. M.
    Includes history of the evacuation by Pierce Edward Buckley.

3640 BOSTON. SHAW MONUMENT COMITTEE. The monument to Robert Gould Shaw, its inception, completion and unveiling, 1865-1897. Boston: Houghton Mifflin, 1897. Pp. 97. M.

3641 BOSTON. SHAWMUT CONGREGATIONAL CHURCH. The articles of faith and covenant of the Shawmut Congregational Church, Boston. Boston: Rand, Avery & Frye, 1871. Pp. 58.
    Includes brief history.

3642 BOSTON. SOUTH BAPTIST CHRUCH. History, with the articles of faith, covenant and list of members, 1865. Boston: Mudge, 1865. Pp. 48.

3643 BOSTON. SOUTH CONGREGATIONAL CHURCH. Memorials of the history for half a century... collected for its jubilee celebration, February 3, 1878. Boston: Rand, Avery, 1878. Pp. 119.
    Includes two sermons by Edward Everett Hale.

3644 BOSTON. SOUTH END HOUSE. South End House, a university settlement; 1892-1899. [Boston, 1899]. Pp. 9.

3645 ____. South End House at the end of its twenty-first year, 1891-1912. [Boston], 1913. Pp. 60.
    Settlement house.

3646 BOSTON. SPRINGFIELD STREET PRESBYTERIAN CHURCH. The history of the Springfield Street Presbyterian Church, Boston, Mass. Boston: Brown, 1883. Pp. 16.

3647   BOSTON. STATISTICS DEPT. The growth of Boston in population, area, etc. Dr. Edward M. Hartwell, ed. Boston: Printing Department, 1911. Pp. 8.

3648   BOSTON. SUFFOLK SCHOOL FOR BOYS. A brief history of Rainsford Island. Boston, 1915. Pp. 8.
    Hospital and reform school.

3469   BOSTON. TERCENTENARY COMMITTEE. SUBCOMMITEE ON MEMORIAL HISTORY. Fifty years of Boston: a memorial volume issued in commemoration of the tercentenary of 1930. Elisabeth M. Herlihy, ed. Boston, 1932. Pp. xx, 799.
    Planned as a fifth volume to Justin Winsor's Memorial History of Boston.

3650   BOSTON. TRANSIT COMMISSION. The ferry, the Charles-River bridge and the Charlestown bridge, historical statement.... George G. Crocker, ed. Boston: Rockwell and Churchill, 1899. Pp. 12.

3651   BOSTON. TREMONT STREET METHODIST EPISCOPAL CHURCH. Quarter centennial of the dedication of Tremont Street Methodist Episcopal Church...Jan. 2, 1887. Boston: W. S. Best, 1887. Pp. 24. M.

3652   BOSTON. TRINITY CHURCH. Consecration services of Trinity Church, Boston, February 9, 1877, with the consecration sermon, by Rev. A. H. Vinton, D. D., an historical sermon, by Rev. Phillips Brooks, and a description of the church edifice by H. H. Richardson, architect. Boston: Printed by order of the Vestry, 1877. Pp. 76.

3653   _____. Trinity Church in the city of Boston, Massachusetts, 1733-1933. Boston: Printed for the Wardens & Vestry of Trinity Church, 1933. Pp. x, 219.

3654   BOSTON. TRUSTEES OF THE FRANKLIN FUND. A sketch of the origin, object and character of the Franklin Fund, for the benefit of young married mechanics of Boston. Boston, 1866. Pp. 38.
    A loan fund to assist tradesmen in establishing businesses. Preface signed S. F. M. [Samuel Foster McCleary].

3655   BOSTON. TWELFTH BAPTIST CHURCH. One hundred and five years by faith, a history of the Twelfth Baptist Church...Boston, Massachusetts. [Boston, 1946]. Pp. 141.
    1840-1945.

3656   BOSTON. TWENTY-EIGHTH CONGREGATIONAL CHURCH. PARKER-FRATERNITY. The Parker-Fraternity: its constitution and by-laws, officers...with a sketch of its origin and operations. Boston, 1864. Pp. 46.

3657   BOSTON. UNION CONGREGATIONAL CHURCH. A brief view of the church. [Boston, 1834]. Pp. 12.

3658   _____. Confession of faith, and covenant, also a brief history of the Union Church, Essex Street. Boston: Peirce and Williams, 1830. Pp. 36.

3659   _____. Confession of faith and covenant, also a brief history of Union Church, Essex Street, Boston. Boston: Wright and Hasty, 1852. Pp. 66.

3660   _____. An ecclesiastical memoir of Essex Street Religious Society, Boston, in a series of letters addressed to some gentlemen of this city. Boston: Ezra Lincoln, 1823. Pp. 128.

3661   _____. The one hundredth anniversary of the founding of Union Church, Boston, 1822; with a history of Berkeley Temple, 1827. [Boston, 1922]. Pp. 53.

3662   _____. Seventy-fifth anniversary, 1822-1897, Sunday evening, October 24, 1897, Union Church.... Boston: F. Wood, 1897. Pp. 32.
    Historical address by Jonathan A. Lane.

3663   BOSTON. UNION TEMPLE BAPTIST SABBATH SCHOOL. Twelfth anniversary...Tremont Temple...May 21, 1876.... Boston, 1876. Pp. 12.

3664   BOSTON. WEST CHURCH. The West Church, Boston: commemorative services on the fiftieth anniversary of its present ministry, and the one hundred and fiftieth of its foundation, on Tuesday, March 1, 1887.... Boston: Damrell and Upham, 1887. Pp. 124.
    Preface signed C. A. B. [Cyrus Augustus Bartol].

3665   _____. The West Church and its ministers, fiftieth anniversary of the ordination of Charles Lowell, D. D. Boston: Crosby, Nichols, and Co., 1856. Pp. 242.

3666   "[BOSTON]." Town and Country, 116 (April, 1962), entire issue.
    General popular articles.

3667   BOSTON and its vicinity, past and present. Boston, 1851. Pp. 358.

3668   BOSTON AND MASSACHUSETTS GENERAL HOSPITAL. TRAINING SCHOOL FOR NURSES. ALUMNAE ASSOCIATION. History...with extracts from the minutes, from Feb. 14, 1895, to May, 1906. Boston: David Clapp & Son, 1907. Pp. 31. MB.

3669   "BOSTON and the fugitive slave law." BBHS, 4 (May, 1930), 1-7.

3670   "BOSTON as the paradise of the Negro." Colored American Magazine, 7 (1904), 309-317.

3671   BOSTON ATHENAEUM. The Athenaeum centenary: the influence and history of the Boston Athenaeum from 1807 to 1907, with a record of its officers and benefactors and a complete list of proprietors.... [Boston], 1907. Pp. xiii, 236.

3672   "BOSTON Athenaeum." Public Library Monthly, 1 (October, 1903), 35-39.

3673   BOSTON CLEARING HOUSE ASSOCIATION. 100th anniversary, 1856-1956. [Boston, 1956]. Pp. 32.

3674 BOSTON CLUB. Brief history, officers and members for 1903, and prospectus and plans for the new club house. [Boston, 1903]. Unpaged.

3675 "BOSTON Common." SWJ, 43 (1928), 350-362.

3676 THE BOSTON Common; or, rural walks in cities: By a friend of improvement.... Boston: G. W. Light, 1838. Pp. 64.

3677 "BOSTON Custom-house." BBHS, 8 (1934), 42-44.
1843.

3678 BOSTON DEAF MUTE CHRISTIAN ASSOCIATION. History of the origin and progress of the Boston Deaf Mute Christian Association, with the constitution, list of officers.... Boston: Davis & Farmer, 1865. Pp. 20.

3679 _____. [The origin, objects, wants and recommendations, with a list of donors]. Boston: Gribben & Kiley, 1868. Pp. 22.

3680 BOSTON DISPENSARY. Highlights of the story of New England's oldest medical charity. [Boston, 1946?]. Pp. 23.

3681 _____. An historical report of the Boston Dispensary for one hundred and one years. 1796-1897. Robert W. Greenleaf, ed. Brookline: Riverdale Pr., 1898. Pp. 64.

3682 BOSTON EDISON COMPANY. Souvenir, twenty-fifth anniversary of the Edison Electric Illuminating Company of Boston, February 20, 1886-February 20, 1911. Boston: Barta Pr., 1911. Pp. 43.

3683 _____. A war-time record: an illustrated account of the war-time activities of the Edison Electric Illuminating Company of Boston during the great World War, 1914-1918. Boston: Priv. Print., 1922. Pp. 108.

3684 BOSTON ELEVATED RAILWAY COMPANY. Fifty years of unified transportation in metropolitan Boston. Boston, 1938. Pp. 112.

3685 BOSTON EVENING TRANSCRIPT. A golden anniversary: The Transcript's fiftieth birthday, a long look backward. [Boston]: Priv. Print., 1880. Pp. 51.

3686 BOSTON EYE BANK. Ten years of progress, 1946-1956. n.p., [1956?]. Unpaged. M.

3687 "BOSTON; fifty years of progress in the New England field." Southern Lumberman, (December 15, 1931), 143, 146.

3688 "[BOSTON fire of 1872]." Weekly Underwriter, 147 (September 19, 1942), entire issue.

3689 BOSTON FIVE CENTS SAVINGS BANK. A century, a city and a five cent piece; pictures and memories of old Boston, published for the pleasure of our friends. Boston, 1955. Unpaged.
1854-1954.

3690 _____. Fiftieth anniversary of incorporation, May 2, 1904: historical address, responses of invited guests. Boston: G. H. Ellis, 1904. Pp. 59.

3691 BOSTON GLOBE. The Boston Globe was twice born, first in 1872 and again in 1958. [Boston?, 1958]. Unpaged. M.

3692 _____. Boston, the gateway to New England.... [Boston], 1922. Pp. 48.

3693 _____. The great Boston fire, 1872: a disaster with a villain: old-style politics. Boston, 1972. Pp. 55. MB.

3694 _____. The old corner 1712-1964. Boston, 1964. Unpaged.
Bookstore.

3695 BOSTON HERALD. Historical, descriptive, statistical review of Boston with a representation of her leading business and professional firms, in the English, German, French and Spanish languages. [Boston], 1896. Pp. 181.

3696 "THE BOSTON Herald." BSM, 2 (1884-1885), 22-35.

3697 BOSTON history in the Boston poets. Boston: Old South Meeting House, 1907. Unpaged.

3698 "BOSTON in 1774." American Historical Magazine, 1 (1836), 110-113.

3699 BOSTON in the Revolution illustrated: a souvenir for patriotic Americans. Boston: Rand Avery, 1888. Pp. 15.

3700 BOSTON INSURANCE COMPANY. Marine and fire insurance in Boston: an illustrated epitome of its origin and growth together with the story of the Boston Insurance Company. Boston: Walton Advertising and Printing, 1914. Pp. 42.

3701 "THE BOSTON Latin School." BSM, 3 (1885), 74-75.

3702 BOSTON LATIN SCHOOL ASSOCIATION. Catalogue of the Boston Public Latin School, established in 1635, with an historical sketch, prepared by Henry F. Jenks.... Boston: Boston Latin School Association, 1886. v.p.

3703 _____. The oldest school in America, an oration by Phillips Brooks, D. D., and a poem by Robert Grant, at the celebration of the two hundred and fiftieth anniversary of the foundation of the Boston Latin School, April 23, 1885. Boston: Houghton Mifflin, 1885. Pp. 106.

3704 _____. Proceedings and addresses of the Boston Latin School tercentenary, 1635-1935. Lee J. Dunn, ed. Boston, 1937. Pp. 221.

3705 _____. Two hundred and seventy-fifth anniversary of the Boston Latin school, 1635-1910. [Boston], 1910. Pp. 44.

3706 BOSTON LEGAL AID SOCIETY. Twenty five years of legal aid in Boston, 1900-1925. Boston, 1926. Pp. 33. M.

3707 BOSTON LIFE UNDERWRITERS ASSOCIATION. Annals of the Boston Life Underwriters Association, 1890. C. M. Barrows, comp. Boston: Priv. Print., 1890. Pp. 209. M.

3708 BOSTON LOTOS CLUB. 'Lotos leaves,' or a night in October, being a complete and official transcript of the proceedings at the first anniversary banquet, Young's Hotel, Saturday evening, October 2, 1880. J. Austin Fynes, ed. Boston, 1880. Pp. 36.
Includes a history of the club.

3709 BOSTON LYING-IN HOSPITAL. Its past, present, future. [Boston, 189-?]. Pp. 7.

3710 BOSTON MALACOLOGICAL CLUB. Golden jubilee, 1910-1960. [Boston], 1960. Unpaged.

3711 BOSTON MARINE SOCIETY. A brief history of the Boston Marine Society, its character and usefulness, from June 1, 1742, to November 1, 1891. Boston: Wright & Potter, 1891. Pp. 13.

3712 _____. Charter and by-laws of the Boston Marine Society. Began June 1, 1742, incorporated February 2, 1754, together with a brief history of the Society, its condition November 12, 1907, list of members, and other statistical information. Boston, 1908. Pp. 123.

3713 _____. Gleanings from the records of the Boston Marine Society, through its first century, 1742 to 1842. Nath'l Spooner, comp. Boston, 1879. Pp. 191.

3714 "THE BOSTON Massacre." All the Year Round, New Ser., 7 (1872), 349-354.

3715 "THE BOSTON Massacre." AmHist Record, 1 (1872), 123-124.

3716 BOSTON MEDICAL LIBRARY. Celebration of the fiftieth anniversary of the Boston Medical Library, January 19, 1926. Norwood: Plimpton Pr., 1926. Pp. 30.

3717 THE BOSTON mob of 'Gentleman of Property and Standing,' proceedings of the anti-slavery meeting...on the twentieth anniversary of the mob of October 21, 1835. Phonographic report by J. M. W. Yerrinton. Boston: R. F. Wallcutt, 1855. Pp. 76. M.

3718 BOSTON MUNICIPAL RESEARCH BUREAU. Boston city charter, 1909-1946; a report prepared for the Special Charter Commission of 1946. [Boston], 1946. Pp. 22.

3719 _____. Boston's city finances of 1924-1934 and the financial outlook for 1935. Boston, 1935. Pp. iii, 47.

3720 _____. A decade of city finances, 1929-1938. Boston, 1939. Pp. 16.

3721 BOSTON MUSEUM. History of the Boston Museum. Boston, 1892. Pp. 35.
A theater.

3722 "BOSTON newspapers." BBNL, 1 (1826), 66-67, 82, 102-104, 166, 174-175, 195-196, 303-304; 2 (1826), 109-114, 133-136, 260-263, 268-272.

3723 BOSTON past and present; being an outline of the history of the city as exhibited in the lives of its prominent citizens.... Cambridge: Riverside Pr., 1874. Pp. xiv, 543.

3724 BOSTON PIER, OR THE LONG WHARF CORPORATION. Centennial of the Boston Pier, or the Long Wharf Corporation, 1873. Cambridge: J. Wilson and Son, 1873. Pp. 38.

3725 BOSTON PRESS CLUB. The Boston Press Club: a sketch of its career from its organization in 1886 to 1911, its aims and achievements. Alfred T. Waite, ed. Boston, 1911. Unpaged.
Includes detailed history.

3726 BOSTON prints and printmakers, 1670-1775; a conference held by the Colonial Society of Massachusetts, 1 and 2 April 1971. Boston: Colonial Society of Massachusetts, 1973. Pp. xxv, 294.

3727 BOSTON REDEVELOPMENT AUTHORITY. PLANNING DEPARTMENT. Survey of new housing in Boston, 1960-1972. [Boston?], 1972. Unpaged. M.

3728 "BOSTON Regiment in colonial days." Colonial Wars, 1 (1913), 30-40.

3729 "BOSTON riot of 1765." BBHS, 7 (June, 1933), 12-13.

3730 "[BOSTON Seamen's Friend Society, one hundredth anniversary, 1827-1927]." Sea Breeze, 40 (January, 1928), entire issue.
Charity.

3731 BOSTON, 1630-1880. Boston: Rand, Avery, 1880. Pp. 8.

3732 BOSTON SOCIETY FOR THE CARE OF GIRLS. An account of the rise, progress, and present state of the Boston Female Asylum.... (1803) Boston: Russell and Cutler, 1810. Pp. 40.

3733 _____. One hundred years of work with girls in Boston. Boston, 1919. Pp. 24.

3734 _____. Reminiscences of the Boston Female Asylum. Boston: Eastburn's Pr., 1844. Pp. 88.
Sabin attributes authorship to Abby L. Wales.

3735 BOSTON SOCIETY OF NATURAL HISTORY. The Boston Society of Natural History, 1830-1930. Percy R. Creed, ed. Boston, 1930. Pp. xii, 117.

3736 BOSTON SOCIETY OF THE NEW JERUSALEM. A brief sketch of the history of the Boston Society of the New Jerusalem. Boston, 1852. Pp. 24.

3737 _____. Semi-centennial celebration of the Society, formed August 15, 1818. Boston, 1869. Pp. 86.

3738 _____. A sketch of the history of the Boston Society of the New Jerusalem.... Boston: W. Carter and Brother, 1863. Pp. 66.

3739 _____. A sketch of the history of the Boston Society of the New Jerusalem, with a list of its members. Boston: J. C. Regan, 1873. Pp. 116.

3740 "THE BOSTON Stock Exchange: an uncommon market." Boston, 57 (September, 1965), 31-49.

3741 THE BOSTON Stock Exchange, its inception, early history, and the important contribution it has made to developing New England as a financial and investment centre. Boston: Priv. Print., 1930. Pp. 32.

3742 BOSTON SYMPHONY ORCHESTRA. The past and present of the Boston Symphony Orchestra, together with an account of its conductors and activities. [Boston, 1951?]. Pp. 10.

3743 "BOSTON, the building of a heritage, the rebuilding of a city, the shaping of a region, Boston tomorrow." Architectural Forum, 12 (June 4, 1964), entire issue.
Includes brief architectural history of the city.

3744 BOSTON UNIVERSITY. First quarter centennial of Boston University, program and addresses. Brookline: Riverdale Pr., 1898. Pp. xiii, 84.

3745 BOSTON UNIVERSITY. COLLEGE OF LIBERAL ARTS. Seventy-fifth anniversary. Boston, 1948. Pp. 48. MBU.

3746 BOSTON UNIVERSITY. SCHOOL OF THEOLOGY. Historical sketch. Boston, 1896. Pp. 32.

3747 BOSTON, yesterday and today. Boston: Court Square Pr., 1939. Pp. 31.
Collection of essays.

3748 BOSTONIANS as seen by Boston newspaper cartoonists. Boston, 1906. Unpaged.
Includes biographical information.

3749 "BOSTON'S first city charter." Boston Public Library Bulletin, 4 Ser., 4 (1922), 7-12.

3750 BOUDINOT, ELIAS. Elias Boudinot's journey to Boston in 1809. Milton Halsey Thomas, ed. Princeton, N.J.: Princeton Univ. Library, 1955. Pp. xii, 97. MB.

3751 BOUVÉ, THOMAS TRACY. Historical sketch of the Boston Society of Natural History; with a notice of the Linnaean Society which preceded it. Boston: Boston Society of Natural History, 1880. Pp. vii, 250.

3752 BOWDITCH, ERNEST. "The great Boston fire of 1872...and how the valuables of the Massachusetts Bank were saved." About the First, (September, 1935), 8-11.

3753 [BOWDITCH, NATHANIEL INGERSOLL. 'Gleaner' articles]. Boston: Rockwell and Churchill, 1887. Pp. x, 232.
Real property.

3754 _____. A history of the Massachusetts General Hospital. (1851) 2d ed., with a continuation to 1872. Boston: Printed by the Trustees from the Bowditch Fund, 1872. Pp. xvii, 734.
Continuation and editing by George E. Ellis.

3755 BOWEN, ABEL. Bowen's picture of Boston, or the citizens and stranger's guide to the metropolis of Massachusetts, and its environs, to which is affixed the annals of Boston.... (1829) 3d ed. Boston: Otis, Broaders, 1838. Pp. 304.

3756 BOWEN, HELEN. "The fishing lady and Boston Common." Antiques, 4 (1923), 70-73.
Needlepoint tapestries.

3757 BOWER, ROBERT T. "Note on 'Did Labor Support Jackson?: the Boston story.'" PolSciQ, 65 (1950), 441-444.
Commentary on an article by Edward Pessen, entry 5220.

3758 BOYD, JAMES. Address before the Charitable Irish Society in Boston at their centennial anniversary, March 17, 1837. Boston: Dow, 1837. Pp. 40. MB.

3759 BOYDEN, ALBERT. Ropes-Gray, 1865-1940. Boston: Lincoln & Smith Pr., 1942. Pp. 215.
Law firm.

3760 BOYER, PAUL S. "Boston book censorship in the twenties." AmQ, 15 (1963), 3-24.
1920s.

3761 BOYLE, ISAAC. An historical memoir of the Boston Episcopal Charitable Society. Boston, 1840. Pp. 31.

3762 BOYLSTON, ZABDIEL. Historical account of the small-pox inoculated in New England, upon all sorts of persons, whites, blacks, and of all ages and constitutions. With some account of the nature of the infection in the natural and inoculated way, and their different effects on human bodies. With some short directions to the unexperienced in this method of practice. (1726) 2d ed., cor. Boston: Reprinted for S. Gerrish and T. Hancock, 1730. Pp. vi, vi, 53.
Limited to Boston.

3763 "THE BOYLSTON market building, Boston, Mass." OTNE, 37 (1946-1947), 1-6.
Demolished, 1888.

3764 [BRADFORD, ALDEN]. A particular account of the battle of Bunker, or Breed's Hill, on the 17th of June, 1775. By a Citizen of Boston. (1825) 2d ed. Boston: Cummings, Hilliard, 1825. Pp. 27.

3765 BRADFORD, GAMALIEL, 1831-1911. The government of the city of Boston, address of Gamaliel Bradford, at the Lyceum Hall, Dorchester, March 14, 1884 [Boston?, 1884?]. Pp. 12.

3766 BRADISH, FRANK E. "The old corner book store." BSPub, 2 Ser., 2 (1917), 71-100.

3767 BRADLEE, CALEB DAVIS. Farewell; a sermon preached on Sunday, April 21st, 1872, a slight sketch of the Church of the Redeemer, and of its happy and holy work, for eight blessed years.... Boston: J. Wilson, 1872. Pp. 12.

3768 _____. Thirtieth anniversary of the foundation of the Harrison Square Church, Dorchester District, Boston, Mass., Oct. 13, 1878, a sermon. Boston: Fred W. Barry, 1878. MB.

3769 BRADLEE, FRANCIS BOARDMAN CROWNINSHIELD. The Boston and Lowell Railroad, the Nashua and Lowell Railroad. Salem: Essex Institute, 1918. Pp. 64.

3770 _____. "The ship 'Great Republic' and Donald McKay, her builder." EIHC, 63 (1927), 193-216, 309-322.

3771 _____. "The steamboat 'Massachusetts' and the beginnings of steam navigation in Boston Bay." EIHC, 50 (1914), 193-213. Nineteenth century.

3772 [BRADLEE, NATHANIEL J.] History of the introduction of pure water into the city of Boston, with a description of its Cochituate water works.... Comp. by a member of the Water Board. Boston: A. Mudge & Son, 1868. Pp. xxi, 299.

3773 BRAYLEY, ARTHUR WELLINGTON. "The churches of Boston fifty years ago." Bostonian, 2 (1895), 346-378.

3774 _____. A complete history of the Boston Fire Department, including the fire-alarm service and the protective department, from 1630 to 1888.... Boston: J. P. Dale, 1889. Pp. xx, 729.

3775 [_____], comp. A history of the Boston Yacht Club, embracing an interesting record of the events of this, the pioneer yacht club of New England, from its organization to the present time, together with features of value and interest to all yachtsmen.... Boston: L. P. Hager, [1891?]. Pp. 174.

3776 _____. Schools and schoolboys of old Boston; an historical chronicle of the public schools of Boston from 1636 to 1844, to which is added a series of biographical sketches, with portraits of some of the old schoolboys of Boston.... Boston: L. P. Hager, 1894. Pp. 439.

3777 _____. "Woods' Boston Museum; what razing of an old landmark disclosed." Bostonian, 2 (1895), 125-130.

3778 BRAYLEY, GEORGE. "Early instrumental music in Boston." Bostonian, 1 (1894-1895), 189-196.

3779 BRAZER, ESTHER STEVENS. "Early Boston Japanners." Antiques, 43 (1943), 208-211. Eighteenth century.

3780 BRECK, SAMUEL. Recollections of Samuel Breck, with passages from his note-books, (1771-1862). H. E. Scudder, ed. London: S. Low, Marston, Searle, & Rivington, 1877. Pp. 318. Social life and customs.

3781 BREWER & LORD, BOSTON. 100 years of being ready when--or the life and times of Brewer & Lord Insurance. Boston, 1859. Unpaged. MB.

3782 BRIDENBAUGH, CARL. "The high cost of living in Boston, 1728." NEQ, 5 (1932), 800-811.

3783 A BRIEF history of Boston's esplanade concerts. n.p., [1948]. Unpaged. M.

3784 "A BRIEF history of the Manufactory House 1753-1806." About the First, (March, 1934), 3, 7. Home of the Massachusetts Bank, 1784-1792.

3785 A BRIEF sketch of the history of King's chapel. [Boston, 1898]. Unpaged.

3786 "A BRIEF sketch of the Hyde Park Historical Society." HPHR, 1 (1891-1892), 2.

3787 BRIGGS, LLOYD VERNON. History of the Psychopathic Hospital, Boston, Massachusetts. Boston: Wright & Potter, 1922. Pp. xxiii, 222

3788 BRIGHAM, CLARENCE SAUNDERS. "Boston Massacre, 1770." Antiques, 68 (1955), 40-43. Engravings by Paul Revere, Henry Pelham, and Jonathan Mulliken.

3789 BRIGHTMAN, ANNA. "Window curtains in colonial Boston and Salem." Antiques, 86 (1964), 184-187.

3790 _____. "Woolen window curtains - luxury in colonial Boston and Salem." Antiques, 86 (1964), 722-727.

3791 BRIGHTON, MASS. EVANGELICAL CONGREGATIONAL CHURCH. One hundredth anniversary, 1827-1927, Brighton Evangelical Congregational Church. Brighton, 1927. Pp. 12.

3792 BRIGHTON, MASS. FIRST PARISH. Historical addresses by Anna H. Sanderson and George B. Livermore. Boston: Walker, Young, 1894. Pp. 66. History of the church and the ladies' association.

3793 BRIGHTON, MASS. OUR LADY OF PRESENTATION PARISH. Your glory and your pride: a brief history of the parish of Our Lady of the Presentation, Brighton, Mass., issued on the occasion of the golden jubilee of the setting of the cornerstone of the present church. Boston, 1963. Pp. 44. MB.

3794 BRIGHTON, MASS. ST. GABRIEL'S MONASTERY (PASSIONIST). Silver jubilee 1936, of Saint Gabriel Laymen's Retreat League, in grateful tribute to its father and founder, William, Cardinal O'Connell, Archbishop of Boston. Sunday, December 13, 1936. Brighton, [1936?]. Pp. 32.

3795 "THE BRIGHTON market." About the First, (March, 1940), 6-8.

3796 BRISSOT DE WARVILLE, JACQUES PIERRE. Boston in 1788. Boston: Directors of the Old South Work, 1902. Pp. 20.

3797 "A BRITISH officer in Boston in 1775." Atlantic, 39 (1877), 389-401, 544, 554.

3798 BRITT, ALBERT. "The cradle of liberty 1742-1942." BSProc, (1943), 33-50.
Faneuil Hall.

3799 BROCHES, SAMUEL. "A chapter in the history of the Jews of Boston." Yivo Bleter, 9 (1954), 205-211.

3800 BROCK, GEORGE E. Brighton Evangelical Congregational Church, 1827-1927. J. M. Ayer, ed. Brighton: Item Pr., [1927?]. Pp. 36.

3801 "BROOK Farm community." Country Time and Tide, 4 (1903), 176-180; 5 (1903-1904), 1-8.

3802 BROOKS, JOHN GRAHAM. Memorial sermons in recognition of the two hundred and fiftieth anniversary of the founding of the First Religious Society in Roxbury, March 26, 1882, April 2, 1882. Boston: Geo. H. Ellis, 1882. Pp. 60.

3803 BROOKS, PHILLIPS. "The Boston Latin School." NEM, New Ser., 8 (1893), 681-704.

3804 _____. "Trinity Church, Boston." NEM, New Ser., 8 (1893), 139-158.

3805 BROOKS, VAN WYCK. "Boston in the nineties, a second glimpse of New England's Indian summer." Harper's Magazine, 181 (1940), 321-328.

3806 _____. "Dr. Holmes' Boston: New England after the flowering." Harper's Magazine, 181 (1940), 138-146.
Saturday Club.

3807 BROWN, ABBIE FARWELL. The lights of Beacon Hill; a Christmas message. Boston: Houghton Mifflin, 1922. Pp. 15.

3808 _____. The New England Poetry Club; an outline of history 1915-1923. [Boston?], 1923. Pp. 21.

3809 BROWN, ABRAM ENGLISH. "Beacon Hill." NEM, New Ser., 28 (1903), 631-650.

3810 _____. "Faneuil Hall." NEM, New Ser., 21 (1899-1900), 519-540.

3811 _____. Faneuil Hall and Faneuil Hall Market; or, Peter Faneuil and his gift. Boston: Lee and Shepard, 1900. Pp. x, 218, 671.

3812 BROWN, FRANK CHOUTEAU. "The Clough-Langdon House, 21 Unity Street, Boston." OTNE, 37 (1946-1947), 79-84.

3813 _____. "The first Boston theatre, on Federal Street." OTNE, 36 (1945-1946), 1-7.

3814 _____. "The first residential 'row houses' in Boston." OTNE, 37 (1946-1947), 60-69.

3815 _____. "John Smibert, artist, and the first Faneuil Hall." OTNE, 36 (1945-1946), 61-63.

3816 _____. 'Zero' Park Street, Boston, Massachusetts, the home of General Electric refrigerators. [Boston, 1929]. Pp. 28.
An architectural study.

3817 BROWN, HERBERT R. "Elements of sensibility in 'The Massachusetts Magazine.'" American Literature, 1 (1929), 286-296.
Published in Boston, 1789-1796.

3818 BROWN, IRA V. "The Millerites and the Boston press." NEQ, 16 (1943), 592-614.
1843-1844.

3819 BROWN, JOHN PERKINS and ELEANOR RANSOM. The Thomas Creese house, Boston, Massachusetts, being the description of a typical townhouse of the early eighteenth century and containing a history of the site thereof from the time of Anne Hutchinson to the present day. Boston, 1940. Pp. 43.
Also known as the 'Old Corner Book Store.'

3820 BROWN, MARY LOUISE. "John Welch, carver." Antiques, 9 (1926), 28-30.
Relates to codfish in visitors gallery, House of Representatives, State House.

3821 [BROWN, REBECCA WARREN]. Stories about General Warren, in relation to the fifth of March massacre, and the Battle of Bunker Hill. By a Lady of Boston. Boston: J. Loring, 1835. Pp. 112.

3822 BROWN, RICHARD D. "Massachusetts towns reply to the Boston Committee of Correspondence, 1773." WMQ, 3 Ser., 25 (1968), 22-39.

3823 _____. Revolutionary politics in Massachusetts; the Boston Committee of Correspondence and the towns, 1772-1774. Cambridge: Harvard Univ. Pr., 1970. Pp. xiv, 282.

3824 BRUCE, JAMES L. "Filling in of the Back Bay and the Charles River development." BSProc, (1940), 25-38.

3825 _____. "The Rogers Building and Huntington Hall." BSProc, (1941), 29-36.
First building of Massachusetts Institute of Technology, demolished in 1939.

3826 _____. "The towers of the new Old South." BSProc, (1938), 41-46.
Old South Church.

3827 BRUCE, ROBERT ERNEST. A chronicle of achievement; thirty years of the Professor Augustus Howe Buck Educational Fund. Boston: Boston Univ. Pr., 1948. Pp. xii, 459.
A Boston University endowment.

3828 BRUSH, JOHN WOOLMAN. Legacy of faith, a short history of the First Baptist Church of Boston. Groveland: Boyd-James Pr., 1965. Pp. 68. M.

3829 BRYANT AND STRATTON COMMERCIAL SCHOOL, BOS-
TON. 75 years of achievement of Bryant and
Stratton Commercial School, with historic notes of
Boston, 1865-1940. Boston, 1940. Pp. 24. M.

3830 BUCKMASTER, HENRIETTA. "One hundred years
ago." NEG, 5 (Summer, 1963), 17-25.
Anti-slavery movements.

3831 BUCKNAM, WILTON FRANCIS, comp. and ed. A
history of Boston Division Number Sixty-one
Brotherhood of Locomotive Engineers. Boston: A. T.
Bliss, 1906. Pp. 201.

3832 BUDINGTON, WILLIAM IVES. The history of the
First Church, Charlestown, in nine lectures,
with notes. Boston: Charles Tappan, 1845.
Pp. 258.

3833 _____. Our Puritan Fathers, our glory: a
sermon preached in commemoration of the
220th anniversary of the founding of the First
Church in Charlestown, Mass., Sunday, November 14,
1852. Charlestown: McKim & Cutter, 1852. Pp. 32.

3834 BUGBEE, JAMES MCKELLAR. The city government
of Boston. Baltimore: N. Murray, 1887.
Pp. 60.

3835 _____. Sketch of the city of Boston. n.p.,
n.d. Pp. 13. M.

3836 BUGBEE, JOHN S. Address before the Everett
Literary Association on the occasion of its
seventh anniversary, June 26, 1862. Boston: Nil-
son, 1862. Pp. 12. MB.

3837 BUHLER, KATHRYN C. "John Edwards, goldsmith,
and his progeny." Antiques, 59 (1951), 288-
292.

3838 "[BUNKER Hill centennial]." Frank Leslie's
Illustrated Newspaper, 40 (1875), issues of
June 26 and July 3.

3839 BUNKER HILL centennial June 17, 1875. [An
illustrated paper containing an account of
the Battle of Bunker Hill.] Boston, 1875. Pp. 8.

3840 BUNKER HILL TIMES, CHARLESTOWN, MASS. "Souvenir of the 50th anniversary of the dedication of Bunker Hill Monument, 1843-1893. Charlestown: Tafft-Gardner-Shepard, [1893?]. Pp. 86.

3841 "BUNKER'S Hill." HistMag, 2 Ser., 3 (1868),
321-442.

3842 BUNTING, BAINBRIDGE. Houses of Boston's Back
Bay; an architectural history, 1840-1917.
Cambridge: Harvard Univ. Pr., 1967. Pp. xvii, 494.

3843 _____. "The plan of the Back Bay area in
Boston." SocArchHistJ, 13 (May, 1954), 19-
25.

3844 BUNTING, WILLIAM HENRY. Portrait of a port:
Boston, 1852-1914. Cambridge: Belknap Pr.,
1917. Pp. xviii, 519.

3845 BURDETT, EVERETT WATSON. History of the Old
South Meeting-house in Boston. Boston:
B. B. Russell, 1877. Pp. 106.

3846 BURNES, JACOB MADEIRA. West End House; the
story of a boys' club. Boston: Stratford
Co., 1934. Pp. 222.

3847 BURRAGE, WALTER LINCOLN. A history of the
Massachusetts Medical Society, with brief
biographies of the founders and chief officers,
1781-1922. Norwood: Plimpton Pr., 1923. Pp. xii,
503.

3848 BURRAGE, WILLIAM CLARENCE. "The visit of
the West Point cadets to Boston, 1821."
BSPub, 6 (1910), 53-66.

3849 BURRILL, ELLEN MUDGE. "The State House as an
historical museum." Lynn HSR, No. 14 (1910),
154-177.

3850 BURROUGHS, HARRY ERNEST. Boys in men's
shoes, a world of working children. N.Y.:
Macmillan, 1944. Pp. xx, 370.
Burroughs Newsboys Foundation; charity.

3851 BURROUGHS, HENRY. A historical account of
Christ Church, Boston, an address, delivered
on the one hundred and fiftieth anniversary of the
opening of the church, December 29th, 1873. Boston:
A. Williams, 1874. Pp. 44.

3852 BURTON, KATHERINE KURZ. Paradise planters,
the story of Brook Farm. N.Y.: Longmans,
Green, 1939. Pp. x, 336.

3853 [BUSCH, JOHN J.] An historic tour; a pil-
grimmage to the birthplace of American liberty, and the homes of our foremost authors. Boston:
Hudson Printing, 1913. Pp. 38.
Boston, Lexington and Concord.

3854 BUSHEE, FREDERICK ALEXANDER. Ethnic factors
in the population of Boston. N.Y.: Macmillan, 1903. Pp. vi, 171.

3855 _____. "The growth of the population of Boston." American Statistical Association.
Publications, 6 (1898-1899), 239-274.

3856 _____. "Italian immigrants in Boston."
Arena, 17 (1896-1897), 722-734.

3857 BUSHNELL, ROBERT T. "Banned in Boston."
North American Review, 229 (1930), 518-525.

3858 "BUSINESS and the coffee house." BBHS, 2
(May, 1928), 11-13.
Exchange Coffee House.

3859 BUTLER, GERALD W. "The key to Boston Harbor." Periodical, 5 (Summer, 1973), 27-37.
Fort Warren.

3860 BUTTERFIELD, LYMAN HENRY. "Bostonians and
their neighbors as pack rats." American
Archivist, 24 (1961), 141-159.
Historical societies.

3861 BYNNER, EDWIN LASSETTER. "The old Bunch of Grapes Tavern." Atlantic, 64 (1889), 721-735.

3862 BYRNE, JOHN F. The glories of Mary in Boston; a memorial history of the Church of Our Lady of Perpetual Help (Mission Church) Roxbury, Mass., 1871-1921. Boston: Mission Church Pr., 1921. Pp. 584.

3863 BYRNE, JOHN JOSEPH, ed. A history of the Boston City Hospital, 1905-1964. Boston, 1964. Pp. 406.

3864 CABOT, NANCY GRAVES. "The fishing lady and Boston Common." Antiques, 40 (1941), 28-31. Needlepoint tapestries.

3865 CABOT, STEPHEN. Report of the 'Draft riot' in Boston, July 14th, 1863. [Boston, 1902]. Unpaged.

3866 CADBURY, HENRY JOEL. "Quaker relief during the Siege of Boston." CSMP, 34 (1937-1942), 39-179.

3867 CALDWELL, OTIS WILLIAM and STUART A. CORTIS. Then & now in education, 1845:1923; a message of encouragement from the past to the present. N.Y.: World Book, 1924. Pp. ix, 400. Limited to Boston; development of its school system since 1845.

3868 CAMERON, E. H. "Of Yankee granite." Technology Review, 54 (1952), 359-364, 388, 419-422, 438, 440, 442, 444, 446. Bunker Hill Monument.

3869 CAMERON, RICHARD MORGAN. Boston University School of Theology, 1839-1968. Boston: Boston Univ. School of Theology, 1968. Pp. v, 170. MBU.

3870 CAMPBELL, CLEMENTINE. "Fort Warren: the key to Boston Harbor." Bostonian, 2 (1895), 259-269.

3871 CAMPBELL, WILLIAM ROGERS. Historical discourse delivered at the celebration of the fiftieth anniversary of the Highland Congregational Sunday School...January 25, 1903.... [Boston], 1903. Pp. 16.

3872 CANAVAN, MICHAEL JOSEPH. "The old Boston Public Library, 1656-1747." CSMP, 12 (1908-1909), 116-132.

3873 _____. "Where were the Quakers hanged?" BSProc, (1911), 37-49.

3874 CANDAGE, RUFUS G. F. "Boston Light and the Brewsters." NEM, New Ser., 13 (1895-1896), 131-147. Brewster Islands.

3875 _____. "Boston ships, past and present." BSProc, (1901), 26-41.

3876 CANHAM, ERWIN D. Commitment to freedom; the story of the Christian Science Monitor. Boston: Houghton Mifflin, 1958. Pp. 454.

3877 CANNON, IDA MAUD. On the social frontier of medicine; pioneering in medical social service. Cambridge: Harvard Univ. Pr., 1952. Pp. 273 Social Service Department, Massachusetts General Hospital.

3878 CAPEN, SAMUEL BILLINGS. Address...at the twenty-fifth anniversary of the West Roxbury Co-Operative Bank held in Boston...March twenty-second, nineteen hundred and six. [Boston, 1906]. Pp. 7.

3879 CAPLAN, NIEL, ed. "Some unpublished letters of Benjamin Colman, 1717-1725." MHSP, 77 (1965), 101-142.

3880 CAREW, PETER. "Boston saints." Blackwood's Magazine 268 (1950), 460-471. Seventeenth-century politics.

3881 CARNEY HOSPITAL. BOSTON. Carney Hospital, Boston, one hundredth anniversary. Boston, [1963?]. Unpaged. M.

3882 _____. Diamond jubilee, 1863-1938. Boston, 1938. Pp. 74. MB.

3883 CARPENTER, EDMUND JANES. "The Province House." NEM, New Ser., 21 (1899-1900), 428-437.

3884 _____. "The story of the Boston Public Library." NEM, New Ser., 12 (1895), 737-756.

3885 CARRINGTON, HENRY B. "Bunker Hill." BSM, 1 (1884), 290-302.

3886 _____. "The Siege of Boston developed." BSM, 1 (1884), 36-44.

3887 CARRUTH, FRANCES WESTON. "Boston in fiction." The Bookman, 14 (1901-1902), 236-254, 364-385, 507-521, 590-604.

3888 CARTER, RUTH N. "The Puritan post: a history of the post office in Boston." BSProc, (1957), 27-38.

3889 CARTER, WILLIAM. A genuine detail of the several engagements, positions, and movements of the royal and American armies; with an accurate account of the blockade of Boston, and a plan of the works on Bunker's Hill, at the time it was abandoned by His Majesty's forces, on the seventeenth of March, 1776. [London, 1784?]. Pp. 50.

3890 CARTER'S INK COMPANY. Little known Boston; a collection of landmarks from drawings by Francis Hight.... Boston, 1927. Pp. 45.

3891 CARTY, JOHN E. "Public Works Department-- Bridge and Ferry Division." Our Boston, 3 (September, 1928), 7-10.

3892 CARVEN, CHRISTOPHER J. "Public Works Department--Water Division." Our Boston, 4 (March, 1929), 9-12.

3893　CARVER, ROBIN.　History of Boston.　Boston: Lilly, Wait, Colman, and Holden, 1834. Pp. viii, 160.

3894　_____.　Stories about Boston, and its neighborhood.　Boston:　Lilly, Wait and L. C. Bowles, 1833.　Pp. 184.

3895　CASALE, OTTAVIO M.　"Battle of Boston:　a revaluation of Poe's lyceum appearance."　American Literature, 45 (1973), 423-428. 1845.

3896　CASE, HAROLD CLAUDE.　Harvest from the seed; Boston University in mid-century.　N.Y.: Newcomen Society in North America, 1957.　Pp. 24.

3897　CASH, PHILIP.　Medical men at the Siege of Boston, April, 1775-April, 1776; problems of the Massachusetts and Continental armies.　Philadelphia:　American Philosophical Society, 1973. Pp. xi, 185.

3898　"CENTENNIAL celebration, June 17, 1875, [of the Battle of Bunker Hill]."　Bunker Hill Monument Association.　Proceedings, (1875), 11-216.

3899　"CENTENNIAL tea-party in Boston."　Leisure Hour, 23 (1874), 789-791. Signed: G. G. R.

3900　"A CENTURY of the Massachusetts State Library."　LJ, 51 (1926), 229-230.

3901　CESTRE, C.　"La premiére formule de l'éthique commerciale aux Etas-Unis."　Revue Anglo-Américaine, 6 (1928-1929), 193-207. Charge against Robert Keayne for profiteering, 1639, and John Cotton's sermon.

3902　CHADWICK, JAMES READ.　The medical libraries of Boston; a report read at the first annual meeting of the Boston Medical Library Association, held on Oct. 3, 1876.　Cambridge: Riverside Pr., 1876.　Pp. 11.

3903　CHAFEE, ZECHARIAH.　The censorship in Boston.　Boston:　Civil Liberties Committee of Massachusetts, 1929.　Pp. 22.

3904　CHAFFEE, JOHN R.　The history of the First Methodist Episcopal Church, Dorchester, Massachusetts.　Boston:　Pilgrim Pr., 1917.　Pp. 247.

3905　[CHAMBERLAIN, A. C. ALLEN].　By broomstick train, little journeys about Boston's suburbs on the electric cars.　Boston:　Boston Transcript, 1895.　Pp. 45.

3906　CHAMBERLAIN, ALLEN.　"Beacon Hill Christmas candles."　OTNE, 26 (1935-1936), 69-73.

3907　_____.　Beacon Hill, its ancient pastures and and early mansions.　Boston:　Houghton Mifflin, 1925.　Pp. xiv, 309.

3908　CHAMBERLAIN, MELLEN.　"The old Province House."　MHSP, 2 Ser., 2 (1885-1886), 122-131.

3909　_____.　"Samuel Maverick's palisade house of 1630."　MHSP, 2 Ser., 1 (1884-1885), 366-373.

3910　CHAMBERLIN, JOSEPH EDGAR.　The Boston Transcript, a history of its first hundred years.　Boston:　Houghton Mifflin, 1930.　Pp. xii, 241.

3911　CHANDLER, FRANCIS WARD, ed.　Municipal architecture in Boston, from designs by Edmund M. Wheelwright, city architect, 1891 to 1895.　Boston: Bates & Guild, 1898.　2v.

3912　CHANDLER, JOSEPH EVERETT.　"Notes on the Paul Revere House."　Walpole Society Notebook, (1944), 15-20.

3913　CHANDLER & co.'s full account of the great fire in Boston! and the ruins.　Boston, 1872. Pp. 62.

3914　CHANEY, GEORGE LEONARD.　Hollis Street Church, 1862-1877.　A historical discourse.　Boston:　Geo. H. Ellis, 1879.　Pp. 23.

3915　_____.　Hollis Street Church from Mather Byles to Thomas Starr King, 1732-1861, two discourses given in Hollis Street Meeting-house, Dec. 31, 1876, and Jan. 7, 1877.　Boston:　G. H. Ellis, 1877.　Pp. 70.

3916　CHAPMAN, GRACE OLIVE.　Stanton Avenue Methodist Episcopal Church, Dorchester (Boston) Massachusetts, 1886-1936.　[Boston], 1937.　Pp. 117.

3917　CHAPPLE, JOE MITCHELL.　"The house that Baker built."　National Magazine, 24 (June, 1906), [10 unnumbered pages at end of issue]. Walter Baker Co.; chocolate.

3918　"CHAPTERS from 'Horn Book' history."　Horn Book, 38 (1962), 192-193, 298-299, 401-403, 509-511, 624-625; 39 (1963), 92-93, 207-210, 327-330, 412-415. Periodical.

3919　CHARITABLE IRISH SOCIETY, BOSTON.　Address delivered before the Charitable Irish Society in Boston at the celebration of the centennial anniversary, March 17, 1827.　Boston:　James B. Dow, 1837.　Pp. 40.　M. Address is by James Boyd.

3920　CHARLESTOWN, MASS.　Charlestown land records.　Boston:　Rockwell and Churchill, 1878. Pp. vii, 273. 1638-1802.

3921　CHARLESTOWN, MASS. FIRST BAPTIST CHURCH.　History, covenant, and catalogue of the First Baptist Church, Charlestown, Mass.　Boston: Mudge, 1873.　Pp. 24.

3922　_____.　A short history of the First Baptist Church in Charlestown.　Boston:　Howe, 1852. Pp. 88.

3923　CHARLESTOWN, MASS. FIRST CHURCH.　The commemoration of the two hundred and fiftieth anniversary of the First Church, Charlestown, Mass., November 12, 1882.　Cambridge:　J. Wilson and Son, 1882.　Pp. 60.

3924 _____. Manual of the First Church in Charlestown, Boston, Mass., with a brief history.... Cambridge: Harvard Printing, 1896. Pp. xxiv, 16. M.

3925 _____. Manual...with a brief history of its organization...and list of membership, commencing 1856. Boston: Jones & Co., 1876. Pp. 23.

3926 _____. Records of the First Church in Charlestown, Massachusetts, 1632-1789. Boston: D. Clapp and Son, 1880. Pp. 168, xxvii.

3927 _____. Semi-centennial celebration of the First Sabbath-school Society in Massachusetts, and the First Parish Sabbath School, Charlestown, held on the Lord's Day, October 14, 1866. Boston: Arthur W. Locke, 1867. Pp. 97.

3928 CHARLESTOWN, MASS. FIRST UNIVERSALIST CHURCH. Articles of faith, covenant, and form of church government...with a historical sketch. Boston: Spooner, 1867. Pp. 11.
Historical sketch by William H. Finney.

3929 _____. A memorial of its centennial year. Excercises held in the church April 23, 24, and 25, 1911. Boston: Everett Pr., 1911. Pp. 31.

3930 CHARLESTOWN, MASS. FIRST UNIVERSALIST SOCIETY. A memorial of its one hundred and twenty-fifth anniversary...May 17 and 18, 1936. n.p., [1936?]. Pp. 12. M.

3931 CHARLESTOWN, MASS. HARVARD CHURCH. History of the Harvard Church in Charlestown, 1815-1879; with services at the ordination of Mr. Pitt Dillingham, October 4, 1876, the proceedings of the council and the pastor's first sermon.... Boston: The Society, 1879. Pp. 294.
History by Henry Herbert Edes.

3932 CHARLESTOWN, MASS. HIGH SCHOOL. Charlestown High School: historical sketches of the school. Boston: Rand, Avery, 1881. Pp. 106. MB.

3933 CHARLESTOWN, MASS. HIGH STREET BAPTIST CHURCH. History of the High Street Baptist Church in Charlestown, Ms., with the names of members. Boston: Howe, 1853. Pp. 36.

3934 CHARLESTOWN, MASS. ST. JOHN'S CHURCH. The challenge of one hundred years, St. John's Church in old Charlestown, 1840-1940. n.p., [1940?]. Unpaged. MBNEH.

3935 CHARLESTOWN, MASS. WINTHROP CHURCH. Semi-centennial manual, Winthrop Church (Charlestown), Boston, Mass., with historical sketch and list of members from Jan. 9, 1833, to Jan. 9, 1883. Boston: Alfred Mudge & Son, 1883. Pp. 77, 32.

3936 CHARLESTOWN CITY GUARD. A souvenir history of the Charlestown City Guard, Company H, 5th Regiment, Infantry, MVM. Boston: Hanover Printing, 1897. Pp. 46. M.
Established 1850.

3937 THE CHARLESTOWN convent; its destruction by a mob, on the night of August 11, 1834, with a history of the excitement before the burning.... Boston: P. Donahoe, 1870. Pp. 98.

3938 CHARLESTOWN SAVING BANK, CHARLESTOWN, MASS. A banking tradition that started in Charlestown. Charlestown, 1960. Pp. 35.

3939 CHARLESTOWN, something of its history. The early days of the settlement during the Revolution and since. Boston: Bunker Hill Times, 1875. Pp. 12.

3940 CHARVAT, WILLIAM. "James T. Fields and the beginning of book promotion." Huntington Library Quarterly, 8 (1944-1945), 75-94.

3941 CHASE, FRANK W. "White slave traffic in Boston." NEM, New Ser., 41 (1909-1910), 531-539.
Prostitution.

3942 CHASE, GEORGE B. "Daniel Webster's libel suit." MHSP, 19 (1881-1882), 281-284. 1828, against Theodore Lyman, Jr., editor of the 'Jackson Republican.'

3943 CHECKLEY, SAMUEL. "Diary of the Rev. Samuel Checkley, 1735." CSMP, 12 (1908-1909), 270-306.
Ed. by Henry Winchester Cunningham.

3944 [CHERRINGTON, WILLIAM PETER], comp. The A B C of American independence, a concise history of the Old South Church.... Boston: Hooper, Lewis, 1901. Pp. 17.

3945 CHESTER, ARTHUR HERBERT. Trinity Church in the city of Boston: an historical and descriptive account (illustrated) with a guide to its windows and paintings. (1888) Rev. and enl. by Charles Edward Chester, comp. Boston: Wallace & Spooner, 1910. Pp. 101. M.

3946 CHEVALIER, S. A. "The history of the Catalogue Department." More Books, 2 (1927), 215-219.
Boston Public Library.

3947 CHIANG, YEE. The silent traveller in Boston. N.Y.: W. W. Norton, 1959. Pp. xii, 275.

3948 CHICK, CHARLES G. "Hyde Park High School." HPHR, 3 (1903), 9-12.

3949 _____. "James Otis and Samuel Adams." BSProc, (1909), 40-50.

3950 _____. "A sketch of the [Hyde Park] Historical Society." HPHR, 3 (1903), 43-46.

3951 CHICKERING & SONS, BOSTON. Achievement: an ascending scale, being a short history of the House of Chickering and Sons. Boston, 1920. Unpaged.

3952 _____. The commemoration of the founding of the House of Chickering & Sons upon the eightieth anniversary of the event, 1823-1903. Boston: Priv. Print., 1904. Pp. 93.

3953 _____. 1823-1923, Jonas Chickering centennial celebration to honor the memory and achievement of one of Boston's most distinguished citizens and one of the world's greatest inventors. Cheltenham, N.Y., 1923. Unpaged. MB.
Piano manufacturers; centennial of the firm.

3954 _____. The Jonas Chickering centennial celebration; a tribute to the life and work of Jonas Chickering, one of the world's greatest inventors, in celebration of the hundredth anniversary of the founding by him of the House of Chickering & Sons in 1823. N.Y.: Chickering & Sons, 1924. Pp. 55.
Piano manufacturers.

3955 CHIDSEY, DONALD BARR. The Siege of Boston; an on-the-scene account of the beginning of the American Revolution. N.Y.: Crown, 1966. Pp. 186.

3956 CHRISTIAN, HENRY ASBURY, comp. Kappa Pi Eta Dinner Club, 1871-1946. Boston: Priv. Print., 1946. Pp. 19.
Harvard Medical School Alumni.

3957 CHRISTMAS, EARL. The house of goodwill; a story of Morgan Memorial. Boston: Morgan Memorial Pr., 1924. Pp. 161.

3958 CHURCH, BENJAMIN. An oration delivered March fifth, 1773, at the request of the inhabitants of the town of Boston; to commemorate the bloody tragedy of the fifth of March, 1770. (1773) 4th ed. Boston: J. Greenleaf, 1773. Pp. 20.

3959 "CHURCHES in Boston." American Quarterly Register, 7 (1834-1835), 53-57.

3960 CLAPP, DAVID, comp. The ancient proprietors of Jones's Hill, Dorchester, including brief sketches of the Jones, Stoughton, Tailer, Wiswall, Moseley, Capen and Holden families, the location and boundaries of their estates, &c. Boston: Printed for Private Distribution, 1883. Pp. vi, 68.

3961 CLAPP, EBENEZER. A brief history of the Dorchester Conversation Club. Boston: George H. Ellis, 1878. Pp. 12.

3962 CLAPP, EDWIN JONES. The port of Boston: a study and a solution of the traffic and operating problems of Boston, and its place in the competition of the north Atlantic seaports. New Haven: Yale Univ. Pr., 1916. Pp. xii, 402.

3963 CLAPP, JOHN BOUVÉ. A century of service, 1815-1915. Boston: S. Peirce, 1915. Pp. 77.
S. S. Peirce and Company, grocers.

3964 CLAPP, OTIS. The Washingtonian Home and its sixteen years' work, an address delivered at the dedication of its new building...Sunday, December 21, 1873. South Framingham: J. C. Clark, 1874. Pp. 16.
Treatment of alcoholics.

3965 CLAPP, WILLIAM WARLAND. A record of the Boston stage. Boston: J. Munroe, 1853. Pp. xiii, 479.
A typewritten index to plays mentioned is in the Boston Public Library.

3966 CLARK, E. S., JR. "The first lighthouse in the United States." United States Naval Institue. Proceedings, 63 (1937), 507-510.
Boston Light.

3967 CLARK, JOSEPH BOURNE. An historical discourse commemorative of the twenty-fifth anniversary of the gathering of the Central Congregational Church, Jamaica Plain; delivered Feb. 10, 1878. Boston: Gunn, Bliss, 1878. Pp. 34.

3968 CLARK, SYDNEY AYLMER. The first hundred years of the New England Mutual Life Insurance Company, 1835-1935. Boston: New England Mutual Life Insurance Company, 1935. Pp. 135.

3969 CLARK, THOMAS MARCH. The memorial: a discourse delivered in King's Chapel on Easter Tuesday, 1874, the 150th anniversary of the Boston Episcopal Charitable Society. Boston: Williams, 1874. Pp. 28.

3970 CLARK, WILLIAM HORACE. The first fifty years of the Massachusetts Forest and Park Association (Massachusetts Forestry Association), 1898-1932, 1898-1948. Boston: Massachusetts Forest and Park Association, 1948. Pp. 31.

3971 CLARKE, BRADLEY H. Rapid transit Boston. Cambridge: Boston Street Railway Association, 1971. Pp. 35.

3972 _____. Transit Boston, 1850-1970. Cambridge: Boston Street Railway Association, 1970. Pp. 30.

3973 _____. The trackless trolleys of Boston. Cambridge: Boston Street Railway Association, 1970. Pp. 63, xi.

3974 CLARKE, CATHERINE GODDARD. The Loyolas and the Cabots: the story of the Boston heresy case. Boston: Ravengate Pr., 1950. Pp. xi, 301.

3975 CLARKE, HERMANN F. "Jeremiah Dummer, silversmith (1645-1718)." Antiques, 28 (1935), 142-145.

3976 CLARKE, JOHN. An impartial and authentic narrative of the battle fought on the 17th of June, 1775, between His Brittanic Majesty's troops and the American Provincial Army, on Bunker's Hill, near Charles Town, in New-England, with a true and faithful account of the officers who were killed and wounded in that memorable battle. To which are added some particular remarks and anecdotes which have not yet transpired. The while being collected and written on the spot. (1775) 2d ed., with extracts from three letters lately received from America; and all the promotions in the Army and Marines, since the said battle. London: J. Millan, 1775. Pp. 36.

3977 CLARKE, LOIS W. "The story of Dorchester Heights." NEM, New Ser., 18 (1898), 221-231.

3978 CLARKE, STEPHEN J. "Education and catastrophe." Boston, 58 (August, 1966), 22-25. Schools since 1925.

3979 CLEMENT, EDWARD H. "19th-century Boston journalism." NEM, New Ser., 35 (1906-1907), 277-288, 415-421, 523-528, 707-713; 36 (1907), 41-49, 170-176, 321-330, 462-467, 558-564, 729-735; 37 (1907-1908), 92-98.

3980 "CLOCKS by Lemuel Curtis." Antiques, 41 (1942), 53-54.

3981 "CLOCKS from the Roxbury Community." Antiques, 17 (1930), 232-233.

3982 CLOVER CLUB OF BOSTON. Golden jubilee year book, 1883-1933. Boston, 1933. Pp. 54.

3983 ____. Year book--60th anniversary, 1886-1943. Boston, 1943. Pp. 55.

3984 CLUB OF ODD VOLUMES, BOSTON. Historical sketch of the Club of Odd Volumes. Boston, 1950. Pp. 24.

3985 COADY, JAMES D. "Charlestown--old and new." Our Boston, 1 (October, 1926), 7-14.

3986 COBB, B. F. "Evolution of the lumber delivery wagon in Boston." Lumber World Review, (January 10, 1912), 30-31.

3987 COBB, SAMUEL CROCKER. An historical address delivered on the occasion of the centennial celebration at Boston, Massachusetts, July 4, 1883. Boston: Printed by order of the Society, 1883. Pp. 50.
    Society of the Cincinnati.

3988 COBB, WILLIAM H. "The Congregational House, Boston." NEM, New Ser., 21 (1899-1900), 219-230.
    Headquarters and library of American Congregational Association.

3989 COBURN, FREDERICK WILLIAM. "The Johnstons of Boston." Art in America, 21 (1933), 27-36. Eighteenth-century artists.

3990 CODMAN, JOHN, 1782-1847. Review of the past, a sermon, delivered in Dorchester, December 7, 1845, being the 37th anniversary of the author's ordination. Boston: T. R. Marvin, 1846. Pp. 27.
    History of the Second Church.

3991 CODMAN, JOHN, II. "A story of old Charlestown." NEM, New Ser., 3 (1891), 796-807. Execution of two Negroes in 1755; also Battle of Bunker Hill.

3992 CODMAN, JOHN THOMAS. "The Brook Farm Association." Coming Age, 2 (1899), 33-38.

3993 ____. Brook Farm: historic and personal memoirs. Boston: Arena Publishing, 1894. Pp. viii, 335.

3994 CODMAN, OGDEN. Index of obituaries in Boston newspapers, 1704-1800. Boston: G. K. Hall, 1968. 3v.

3995 COFFIN, CHARLES, comp. History of the Battle of Breed's Hill, by Major-Generals William Heath, Henry Lee, James Wilkinson and Henry Dearborn. Saco, [Me.]: W. J. Condon, 1831. Pp. 38.

3996 COFFIN, CHARLES CARLETON. "Faneuil Hall." BSPub, 3 (1906), 41-71.

3997 ____. Oration delivered before the New England Historic Genealogical Society, April 19, 1895, to commemorate its fiftieth anniversary.... Boston: The Society, 1895. Pp. 42.

3998 [____.] The story of the great fire, Boston, November 9-10, 1872, by 'Carleton,' pseud., an eye-witness. Boston: Shepard and Gill, 1872. Pp. 32.

3999 COGGESHALL, SAMUEL WILDE. Introduction of Methodism into Boston: a discourse delivered at the formation of the New England Methodist Historical Society at the Bromfield St. Church, Boston, Monday, Feb. 28, 1859. Boston: Rand and Avery, 1859. Pp. 53.

4000 COHEN, AMY. Fire/police station: Engine and Hose House No. 33, Police Station No. 16, 941-953 Boylston St., 1885-1886: historic report. Boston: Architectural Heritage, 1969. Pp. 7. MB.

4001 COLBETH, HAROLD L. "The Boston Marine Society." BSProc, (1945), 29-53.

4002 COLE, EDWARD H. A school and a man: a short history of Chauncy Hall School and a memoir of Franklin Thomas Kurt.... Newtonville: Oakwood Pr., 1951. Pp. 18. MB.

4003 COLE, WILLIAM ISAAC. "Boston's Insane Hospital." NEM, New Ser., 19 (1898-1899), 753-768.

4004 ____. "Boston's penal institutions." NEM, New Ser., 17 (1897-1898), 613-629.

4005 ____. "Early churches at the North End, Boston." NEM, New Ser., 26 (1902), 241-256.

4006 COLEMAN, EARLE. Edward Everett Hale: preacher as publisher. PBSA, 46 (1952), 139-150.
    J. Stilman Smith & Co.

4007 COTESWORTHY, DANIEL CLEMENT. John Tileston's school, Boston, 1778-1789: 1761-1766; also his diary from 1761 to 1766. Boston: Antiquarian Book Store, 1887. Pp. 80.

4008 "A COLLECTION of banjo clocks." Antiques, 26 (1934), 10-11.

4009 COLLIER, ELEANOR RUST. The Boston University College of Basic Studies, 1949-1962. Boston: Boston University, 1963. 27 leaves. MBU.

4010 _____. The Boston University College of Business Administration, 1913-1958. [Boston?, 1959?]. 33 leaves. MBU.

4011 _____. The Boston University School of Law, 1872-1960. [Boston?, 1960]. 72 leaves.

4012 _____. The Boston University School of Public Relations and Communications, 1947-1960. Boston: Boston University, 1960. 73 leaves. MBU.

4013 _____. The Boston University School of Religious Education and Social Service, 1918-1940. Boston, 1959. 40 leaves. MBU.

4014 _____. A history of Boston University, Sargent College. Boston, 1958. 35 leaves. MBU.

4015 _____. Origins of Boston University School of Theology in Newbury, Vermont and Concord, New Hampshire, prior to moving to Boston to become the Boston Theological Seminary. Boston, 1958. 35 leaves. MBU.

4016 "COLONEL Sprague's administration, Boston Girls' High School, 1876-1885." Journal of Education, 74 (1911), 685-686.
Homer Baxter Sprague.

4017 COLUMBIAN NATIONAL LIFE INSURANCE CO., BOSTON. Our first fifty: the story of Columbian National. Boston, 1952. Pp. 40. MH-BA.

4018 COMBINED JEWISH APPEAL, BOSTON, MASS. Fiftieth anniversary year book, 1895-1945, commemorating half a century of organized Jewish philanthropies in Boston. Boston, [1945]. Pp. 309. [MWalAJHi].

4019 COMMAGER, HENRY STEELE. "Tempest in a Boston tea cup." NEQ, 6 (1933), 651-675.
Transcendentalism.

4020 THE COMMERCIAL BULLETIN, BOSTON. The Commercial Bulletin, Boston: Saturday, June 11, 1892, commercial, industrial and financial development of Boston. Boston, 1892. Unpaged.

4021 COMMINS, MABEL P. "Fort Winthrop: its past and present history." Bostonian, 2 (1895), 491-501.

4022 COMSTOCK, HELEN. "Paintings and antiques, the home of Mr. and Mrs. Allan Forbes." Antiques, 66 (1954), 40-43.

4023 CONANT, RICHARD KEITH. Fifty years of growth, an account of the early development of the School of Social Work of Boston University. Boston: Boston Univ. School of Social Work, 1968. Pp. 37. MB.

4024 CONFAR, LEONARD. Charlestown, a limited study of church and community. [Boston?]: Department of Research and Strategy, Massachusetts Council of Churches, 1950. 33 leaves.
Protestant churches; historical and statistical study.

4025 "THE CONGREGATIONAL Library Association: its origin and objects." CongQ, 1 (1859), 70-73.

4026 CONGREGATIONAL PUBLISHING SOCIETY. A brief historical sketch of the Congregational Sunday-School and Publishing Society with its organization and present condition, January, 1894. Boston, 1894. Pp. 16.

4027 CONNECTICUT RIVER LUMBER CO. Boston: its commerce, finance and literature...1892. N.Y.: A. F. Parsons Publishing, 1892. Pp. x, 285.

4028 CONNELLY, JOHN. A century-old concern, business of Jones, McDuffee & Stratton, founded by Otis Norcross, the elder, in 1810, unbroken record of growth and progress, the largest wholesale and retail crockery, china and glassware establishment in the country.... Boston: G. H. Ellis, 1910. Pp. 52.

4029 CONNELLY, PATRICK JOSEPH. Islands of Boston Harbor, 1630-1932, 'green isles of romance.' Dorchester: Chapple Publishing, 1932. Pp. 47.

4030 CONRAD, ARCTURUS ZODIAC, ed. Boston's awakening, a complete account of the great Boston revival under the leadership of J. Wilbur Chapman and Charles M. Alexander, January 26th to February 21st, 1909. Boston: King's Business Publishing, 1909. Pp. 290.

4031 CONTE, GAETANO. Dieci anni in America, impressioni e ricordi.... Palermo: G. Spinnato, 1903. Pp. 223.
Major emphasis on Boston.

4032 "CONTRIBUTIONS to trade history, No. XXX: D. Lothrop & Co." American Bookseller, New Ser., 19 (1886), 281-283.
Publisher.

4033 CONWAY, FRANK. "The Boston Bust Company, the story of a scramble for a name." National Magazine, 26 (1907), 98-102.
Corset manufacturer.

4034 CONWAY, KATHERINE ELEANOR. The Good Shepherd in Boston, silver jubilee memorial. Boston: Flynn & Mahony, 1892. Pp. 18.
Reformatory.

4035 CONWELL, RUSSELL HERMAN. History of the great fire in Boston, November 9 and 10, 1872. Boston: B. B. Russell, 1873. Pp. 312.

4036 COOK, ARTHUR MALCOLM. Boston goes to Massachusetts. Boston, [England]: Church House, 1945. Pp. 44.
Boston, England.

4037 COOKE, GEORGE WILLIS. "Brook Farm." NEM, New Ser., 17 (1897-1898), 391-407.

4038 _____. "The Free Religious Association." NEM, New Ser., 28 (1903), 484-499.
Protest against conservative Unitarianism.

4039 _____. "The Saturday Club." NEM, New Ser., 19 (1898-1899), 24-34.

4040 COOLIDGE, JAMES I. T. Discourse preached on the third Sunday after Trinity, 1866, being the fiftieth anniversary of the celebration of the Holy Communion in St. Matthew's Church, South Boston. Boston: David Clapp & Son, 1913. Pp. 14. MBNEH.

4041 COPELAND, MELVIN THOMAS. And mark an era: the story of the Harvard Business School. Boston: Little, Brown, 1958. Pp. 368.

4042 COPELAND, ROBERT MORRIS. The most beautiful city in America. Boston: Lee & Shepard, 1872. Pp. 46.

4043 CORBETT, ALEXANDER. "The first Boston town house, 1658-1711." BSProc, (1930), 24-47.

4044 CORBETT, ALEXANDER, JR. "The Boston Theatre." Bostonian, 1 (1894-1895), 3-18.

4045 CORDINGLEY, W. W. "Shirley Place, Roxbury, Massachusetts, and its builder, Governor William Shirley." OTNE, 12 (1921-1922), 51-63.

4046 CORTHELL, JAMES ROLAND. "The story of Camp Meigs." NEM, New Ser., 32 (1905), 385-395.

4047 COVELL, WILLIAM KING. "The old Boston Music Hall organ." OTNE, 18 (1927-1928), 183-189.

4048 COX, ALBERT SCOTT. "Ye ancient burial grounds of Boston." NEM, New Ser., 7 (1892-1893), 607-625.

4049 COX, HARRIET CARYL. "Paul Revere House." MassMag, 1 (1908), 133-136.

4050 COYLE, PHILIP E. "Early Boston fires." BSProc, (1955), 40-59.

4051 [CRAFTS, WILLIAM AUGUSTUS]. Forest Hills cemetery: its establishment, progress, scenery, monuments, etc.... Roxbury: J. Backup, 1855. Pp. iv, 237.

4052 "CRAFT'S Journal of the Siege of Boston with notes by Samuel P. Fowler." EIHC, 3 (1861), 51-57, 133-140, 167-174, 219-228. Benjamin Craft.

4053 CRAM, RALPH ADAMS. "Christ Church bells." NEM, New Ser., 11 (1894-1895), 640-647.

4054 CRANDALL, RUTH. "Wholesale commodity prices in Boston during the eighteenth century." RevEconStat, 16 (1934), 117-128, 178-183.

4055 CRAWFORD, MARY CAROLINE. "The Boston Athenaeum." National Magazine, 20, (1904), 272-277.

4056 _____. Old Boston days & ways from the dawn of the Revolution until the town became a city. Boston: Little, Brown, 1909. Pp. xv, 463. Continuation of the author's 'St. Botolph's town.'

4057 _____. One hundred years of Boston hospitality as mirrored in the lusty life of a century old firm: the Anniversary Epicure, 1831-1931. Boston: S. S. Pierce, [1931?]. Pp. 22. MBNEH. S. S. Pierce, grocers.

4058 _____. Romantic days in old Boston; the story of the city and its people during the nineteenth century. Boston: Little, Brown, 1910. Pp. xix, 411. Social life and customs.

4059 _____. St. Botolph's town; an account of old Boston in colonial days. Boston: L. C. Page, 1908. Pp. xii, 365. Published in 1922 with title: 'Old Boston in colonial days.'

4060 "THE CRESCENT that waned." Antiques, 30 (1936), 27. Franklin Crescent (1796-1855).

4061 CROCKER, GEORGE GLOVER. From the stage coach to the railroad train and the street car: an outline review written with special reference to public conveyances in and around Boston in the nineteenth century. Boston: W. B. Clarke, 1900. Pp. 32.

4062 _____. "The passenger traffic of Boston and the subway." NEM, New Ser., 19 (1898-1899), 523-541.

4063 CROCKER AND BREWSTER, BOSTON. Fiftieth anniversary of the co-partnership of Crocker & Brewster, November, 1868. Boston: G. C. Rand and Avery, 1869. Pp. 32.

4064 CROSBY, DONALD F. "Boston's Catholics and the Spanish Civil War: 1936-1939." NEQ, 44 (1971), 82-100.

4065 CROSBY, IRVING BALLARD. Boston through the ages; the geological story of greater Boston. Boston: Marshall Jones, 1928. Pp. xvii, 166.

4066 CROSS, HELEN REEDER. "Boston Common--the uncommon village green." NEG, 10 (Spring, 1969), 31-41.

4067 _____. "Bunker Hill Monument and the petticoats." NEG, 3 (Spring, 1962), 30-36. Support for construction of Bunker Hill Monument by Sarah Josepha Hale.

4068 CROSS, JACK L. "Influence of the politicians in the Massachusetts Historical Society." NEQ, 29 (1956), 503-509.

4069 CROSWELL, ANDREW. A narrative of the founding and settling the new-gathered Congregational Church in Boston; with the opposition of the South Church to the minister, his defence of himself before the council, and expostulatory letter to that church afterwards, to which is added, by way of appendix, the defence of that doctrine of justifying faith, which hath been so much condemned in England, written by Messrs. Boston, Erskines, &c. when the same was cried down in Scotland, Anno Dom. 1721. Boston: Rogers and Fowle, 1749. Pp. 37.

4070 CROWE, CHARLES R. "Christian Socialism and
      the First Church of Humanity." Church Histo-
ry, 35 (1966), 93-106.
      1847-1854.

4071 _____. "This unnatural union of Phalanste-
      ries and Transcendentalists." Journal of
the History of Ideas, 20 (1959), 495-502.
      Brook Farm.

4072 _____. "Transcendentalist support of Brook
      Farm: a paradox." Historian, 21 (1958-
1959), 281-295.

4073 CROWLEY, JAMES A. "Yes! We have historic
      background." B and M Employees' Magazine,
14 (March, 1946), 4-6.
      Battle of Bunker Hill.

4074 CUDAHY, BRIAN J. Change at Park Street Un-
      der: the story of Boston's subways. Brat-
tleboro, Vt.: S. Greene Pr., 1972. Pp. 63.

4075 CULLEN, JAMES BERNARD, ed. The story of the
      Irish in Boston, together with biographical
sketches of representative men and noted women.
(1889) Boston: H. A. Plimpton, 1893. v.p.

4076 CULLIS, CHARLES. History of the Consump-
      tives' Home, no. 11 Willard St. Boston,
1869. v.p.

4077 CUMMINGS, ABBOTT LOWELL. "The beginnings of
      India Wharf." BSProc, (1962), 17-24.

4078 _____. "Charles Bulfinch and Boston's van-
      ishing West End." OTNE, 52 (1961-1962), 31-
49.

4079 _____. "The first Harrison Gray Otis House
      in Boston: a study in pictorial evidence."
OTNE, 60 (1969-1970), 105-108.
      Cambridge Street.

4080 _____. "The Foster-Hutchinson House."
      OTNE, 54 (1963-1964), 59-76.

4081 _____. "The old feather store in Boston."
      OTNE, 48 (1957-1958), 85-104.
      Demolished 1860.

4082 CURRAN, JEAN ALONZO. Founders of the Harvard
      School of Public Health, with biographical
notes, 1909-1946. [N.Y.]: Josiah Macy, Jr., Foundation, 1970. Pp. xviii, 294.

4083 CURTIS, BENJAMIN R. "The Boston University
      Law School." NEM, 4 (1886), 218-225.

4084 CURTIS, EDITH ROELKER. "A season in utopia."
      Am Heritage, 10 (April, 1959), 58-63, 98-100.
      Brook Farm.

4085 _____. A season in utopia: the story of
      Brook Farm. N.Y.: Nelson, 1961. Pp. 346.

4086 CURTIS, GEORGE TICKNOR. The rights of con-
      science and of property; or the true issue of
the convent question. Boston: C. C. Little and
J. Brown, 1842. Pp. 39.
      Ursuline convent.

4087 "THE CURTIS House, Jamaica Plain." Potter's
      AmMo, 6 (1876), 162-165.

4088 CUSHING, THOMAS. Historical sketch of
      Chauncy-Hall School, with catalogue of teach-
ers and pupils, and appendix, 1828-1894. Boston:
D. Clapp & Son, 1895. Pp. 216.

4089 _____. "Reminiscences of schools and teach-
      ers in Dorchester and Boston." American
Journal of Education, 34 (1884), 177-192.

4090 DALL, CAROLINE WELLS HEALEY. Otis, the story
      of an old house. [Washington, 1892].
Pp. 22.
      Otis family and house at 34 Chambers Street,
      Boston.

4091 DALLAS, CHARLES DONALD. The spirit of Paul
      Revere--a glorious heritage for American
industry. Princeton: Princeton Univ. Pr., 1944.
Pp. 52.

4092 DAMON, S. FOSTER. "The Genesis of Boston."
      Atlantic, 156 (1935), 487-491.
      Social life.

4093 DAMRELL, CHARLES STANHOPE. A half century
      of Boston's building: the construction of
buildings, the enactment of building laws and ordinances, sanitary laws, the ancient and modern building, building statistics, Boston's valuation, a
chapter of Boston's big fire, fire losses, public
lands account, prominent architects, contractors
and builders, building materials and their source of
supply, inspection of buildings, the building and
plumbing associations. Boston: L. P. Hager, 1895.
Pp. 524.

4094 DAMRELL, JOHN STANHOPE. Address delivered
      before the Boston Veteran Firemen, February
2, 1886. Boston: Bass & Stephens, 1886. Pp. 31.
      Boston fire of 1872.

4095 DANA, HERMAN. The early days of the Beth
      Israel Hospital, 1911-1920. [Boston?]:
Priv. Print., 1950. Pp. 25.

4096 _____. The story of the Myer Dana Memorial
      Chapel, dedicated May 30, 1950. [Boston?]:
Priv. Print., 1954. Pp. 36.
      Cemetery of Congregation Adath Jeshurun.

4097 DANIELS, ABRAHAM GETZEL. Memories of Ohabei
      Shalom, 1843-1918...in commemoration of the
75th anniversary of Temple Ohabei Shalom, in the
City of Boston, Massachusetts, Feb. 26, 1918-5678.
[Boston, 1918]. unpaged.

4098 DANIELS, JOHN. In freedom's birthplace; a
      study of the Boston Negroes. Boston: Hough-
ton Mifflin, 1914. Pp. xiii, 496.

4099 DARLING, ARTHUR BURR. "Prior to Little Rock
      in American education: the 'Roberts' case of
1849-1850." MHSP, 72 (1957-1960), 126-142.
      Sarah Roberts.

4100   DAUGHTERS OF THE REVOLUTION. MASSACHUSETTS.
         MARY WARREN CHAPTER, ROXBURY. Glimpses of
early Roxbury. Boston: Merrymount Pr., 1905.
Pp. 30.

4101   [DAVENPORT, DANIEL]. The sexton's monitor,
         and Dorchester cemetery memorial. (1826)
3d ed. Boston: A. Mudge, 1845. Pp. 86 [i.e. 36].
Some historical and statistical material.

4102   DAVIDSON, CARLA. "Boston painters, Boston
         ladies." Am Heritage, 23 (1972), 4-17.

4103   DAVIES, PHILIP. History of the North Street
         Union Mission to the Poor. Boston: Ripley,
1870. Pp. 15.

4104   DAVIS, ANDREW MCFARLAND. "Boston 'Banks'--
         1681-1740 - those who were interested in
them." NEHGR, 57 (1903), 274-281.

4105   _____. "The Fund at Boston in New England."
         AASP, New Ser., 15 (1902-1903), 368-384.
         1680s.

4106   _____. "The prospectus of Blackwell's Bank,
         1687." MHSP, 2 Ser., 18 (1903-1904), 63-81.

4107   DAVIS, ELMER. "Boston." Harper's Magazine,
         156 (1928), 140-153.

4108   DAVIS, LANCE EDWIN and PETER LESTER PAYNE.
         "From benevolence to business: the story of
two savings banks." BusHR, 32 (1958), 386-406.
         Provident Institution for Savings in the
         Town of Boston and Savings Bank of Baltimore,
         1818-1861.

4109   DAVIS, MRS. M. G. "New England Conservatory
         of Music." Granite Mo, 7 (1884), 372-379.

4110   DAVIS, PERLEY BACON. Historical sermon,
         preached April 10, 1892, on the 25th anni-
versary of his pastorate over the First Congregational Church, Hyde Park, Mass. Hyde Park, 1892.
Pp. 25.

4111   DAVIS, WALTER, E. Story of Eliot Church.
         Boston: Eliot Congregational Church of Rox-
bury, [1959?]. Pp. vi, 89. MB.

4112   DAVIS, WILBUR W. "The history of Boston as
         disclosed in the digging of the Commonwealth
Avenue underpass and other traffic tunnels." BS
Proc., (1938), 29-40.

4113   DAVISON, PETER. "After 50 years, people
         still ask: what is the Atlantic Monthly
Press?" Publishers' Weekly, 192 (October 16, 1967),
32-34.

4114   _____. "Literary lions and battling Brah-
         mins." Boston, 62 (June, 1970), 84-94.
Houghton Mifflin Co. and other Boston publishing houses since 1832.

4115   DAVOLL, RALPH. "Boston Art Club." NEM, New
         Ser., 43 (1910-1911), 427-436.

4116   DAY, ALAN and KATHERINE DAY. "Another look
         at the Boston 'Caucus.'" JAS, 5 (1971),
19-42.
         North End Caucus, an 18th-century political
         club.

4117   DEAN, H. L. "'The New-England Courant'
         against the ministers." NEG, 5 (Winter,
1964), 3-13.
         1721-1726.

4118   DE ANGELIS, RONALD and MARK DE ANGELIS.
         "Work horses of Boston Harbor." Steamboat
Bill, 28 (1971), 135-136.
         Boston Tow Boat Co.

4119   DEARBORN, HENRY. An account of the Battle of
         Bunker's Hill.... Boston: Munroe & Francis,
1818. Pp. 8, 12.

4120   DEARBORN, HENRY ALEXANDER SCAMMEL. An ad-
         dress delivered on the viii of October,
MDCCCXXX, the second centennial anniversary, of the
settlement of Roxbury. Roxbury: C. P. Emmons,
1830. Pp. 40.

4121   DEARBORN, NATHANIEL. Boston notions; being
         an authentic and concise account of 'that
village,' from 1630 to 1847. Boston: W. D. Ticknor, 1848. Pp. xx, 426.

4122   _____. Dearborn's reminiscences of Boston,
         and guide through the city and environs.
Boston, [1851]. Pp. xii, 180.

4123   DE COSTA, BENJAMIN FRANKLIN. The story of
         Mt. Benedict. [Somerville]: Citizen Pr.,
1893. Pp. 14.
         Convent.

4124   DEEM, WARREN H. The problem of Boston's
         Metropolitan Transit Authority. [Cambridge]:
Graduate School of Public Administration, Harvard
Univ., 1953. 70 leaves.
         Includes history.

4125   DENEHEY, JOHN WILLIAM, comp. A historical,
         biographical and commercial history--Boston
Fruit and Produce Exchange. Boston: Boston Fruit
and Produce Exchange, [1895]. Pp. 100. M.

4126   DE NORMANDIE, JAMES. The ancient landmark: a
sermon...May 4, 1902. Boston: South End Industrial
School, 1902. Pp. 18.
         First Church.

4127   _____. "The First Church in Roxbury, and
         Revolutionary times." Bunker Hill Monument
Association. Proceedings, (1903), 23-32.

4128   _____. An historical sketch of the First
         Church in Roxbury, 1896. [Roxbury, 1896].
Pp. 18.

4129   _____. "The Manifesto Church." MHSP, 47
         (1913-1914), 223-231.

4130   _____. "The Roxbury Latin School." NEM, New
         Ser., 12 (1895), 388-406.

4131 DERBY, ELIAS HASKET. Boston: a commercial metropolis in 1850: her growth, population, wealth and prospects. Boston: Redding, 1850. Pp. 16.

4132 _____. "City of Boston." Hunt's Merchants' Magazine and Commercial Review, 23 (1850), 482-497.

4133 DESAUTELS, RAYMOND E. "Domestic policies." Boston, 59 (January, 1967), 43, 45, 46. Insurance.

4134 DEVENS, CHARLES, JR. "An oration on the one-hundredth anniversary of the Battle of Bunker Hill, June 17, 1775." NEHGR, 29 (1875), 395-416.

4135 DEVENS BENEVOLENT SOCIETY OF THE CITY OF CHARLESTOWN. The Female Benevolent Society, organized under...the name of the Devens Benevolent Society, December 26, 1856, historical sketch, 1818-1894. Charlestown: Allbe & Pratt, 1895. Unpaged.

4136 [DE VOE, EDWIN]. Celebration of the 17th of June, 1871, by the City of Charlestown, with complete programme of the celebration. Charlestown, 1871. Unpaged.
        Author attribution by Boston Public Library; contains an illustrated history of the Battle of Bunker Hill.

4137 DEXTER, FRANKLIN BOWDITCH. "A report of the trial of Mrs. Anne Hutchinson before the Church in Boston, March, 1638." MHSP, 2 Ser., 4 (1887-1889), 159-191.

4138 DIAMOND, SIGMUND. "Bunker Hill, Tory propaganda, and Adam Smith." NEQ, 25 (1952), 363-374.

4139 DICKERSON, OLIVER MORTON, comp. Boston under military rule (1768-1769) as revealed in a journal of the times. Boston: Chapman & Grimes, 1936. Pp. xiii, 137.

4140 _____. "The commissioners of customs and the 'Boston Massacre.'" NEQ, 27 (1954), 307-325.

4141 _____. "Opinion of Attorney General Jonathan Sewall of Massachusetts in the case of the 'Lydia.'" WMQ, 3 Ser., 4 (1947), 499-504. 1768.

4142 DICKSON, HARRY ELLIS. Gentlemen, more dolce, please: an irreverent memoir of thirty years in the Boston Symphony Orchestra. Boston: Beacon Pr., 1969. Pp. xi, 162.

4143 DICKSON, MARGUERITE STOCKMAN. "Parks and parkways in Boston." Our Boston, 1 (July, 1926), 7-18.

4144 DILLAWAY, CHARLES KNAPP. A history of the Grammar School, or 'The Free Schoole of 1645 in Roxburie,' with biographical sketches of the ministers of the First Church, and other trustees. Roxbury: J. Backup, 1860. Pp. viii, 202.

4145 [DIX, JOHN]. Local loiterings, and visits in the vicinity of Boston. By a Looker-on. Boston: Redding, 1845. Pp. 147.

4146 DOGGETT, LAURENCE LOCKE. History of the Boston Young Men's Christian Association. Boston: The Young Men's Christian Association, 1901. Pp. vii, 130.

4147 DOGGETT, SAMUEL BRADLEE. "The model of the Bradlee-Doggett House, Hollis Street, Boston." OTNE, 19 (1928-1929), 174-180. Demolished 1898.

4148 DOHERTY, RICHARD M. Political and economic problems of the Boston metropolitan area: an annotated bibliography. [Boston], 1958. Pp. 76.

4149 DONAHOE, PATRICK. History of the first Catholic church in Boston, or, a chapter of what is being prepared for the press. The introduction and progress of the Church throughout the New England states. By a clergyman. n.p., [not after 1882]. Pp. 32. M.
        Signed by the author at end.

4150 DONALD, ELIJAH WINCHESTER. Twenty years of parish life, Trinity Church in the City of Boston.... Boston: W. Spooner, 1897. Pp. 20. M.

4151 DOOLEY, WILLIAM GERMAIN. "Early Boston seen in prints." Antiques, 44 (1943), 278-280. 1722-1872.

4152 DORCHESTER, MASS. Dorchester celebration, 250th anniversary of the establishment of the first public school in Dorchester, June 22, 1889. Boston: Rockwell and Churchill, 1890. Pp. 77.

4153 _____. Dorchester town records. (1880) 3d ed. Boston: Rockwell and Churchill, 1896. Pp. v, 329.

4154 [DORCHESTER, MASS. CHRIST CHURCH]. The Dorchester book.... Boston: G. H. Ellis, 1899. Pp. viii, 58.

4155 DORCHESTER, MASS. FIRST BAPTIST CHURCH. Declaration of faith and covenant...together with a brief history of the Church, and a list of the members, January 1, 1843. Boston: Howe, 1843. Pp. 24.

4156 DORCHESTER, MASS. FIRST CHURCH. Dedication of the sixth meeting-house, Thursday, May 6, 1897.... Boston: Geo. H. Ellis, n.d. Pp. 57.

4157 _____. Proceedings of the two hundred and fiftieth anniversary of the gathering in England, departure for America, and final settlement in New England, of the First Church and Parish of Dorchester, Mass., coincident with the settlement of the town, observed March 28 and June 17, 1880. Boston: G. H. Ellis, 1880. Pp. 176.

4158 _____. Records of the First Church at Dorchester, in New England, 1636-1734. S. J. Barrows and William B. Trask, eds. Boston: G. H. Ellis, 1891. Pp. xxvi, 270.

4159 DORCHESTER, MASS. FIRST PARISH. First Parish in Dorchester, historical sketch, list of members.... Boston: George H. Ellis, 1898. Pp. 45. MBNEH.

4160 DORCHESTER, MASS. INDUSTRIAL SCHOOL FOR GIRLS. Paper read at the fiftieth anniversary of the Dorchester Industrial School, June 7, 1904. [Boston, 1904]. Pp. 10.

4161 DORCHESTER, MASS. PILGRIM CHURCH. History, articles of faith and covenant of Pilgrim Church (Trinitarian Congregational) in Dorchester District of Boston. Boston: Beacon Pr., 1888. Pp. 62. MBNEH.

4162 DORCHESTER, MASS. ST. MARY'S CHURCH. Fiftieth anniversary of the foundation of St. Mary's Parish, Dorchester, 1847-1897. [Boston], 1898. Pp. 152.
Historical sermon by Lindall W. Saltonstall.

4163 DORCHESTER, MASS. SAINT MARK'S CHURCH. Golden jubilee, 1905-1955, Sunday, Nov. 20 to Thursday Nov. 24, 1955. [Boston?, 1955]. Pp. 31.

4164 DORCHESTER, MASS. SECOND CHURCH. Sermon and addresses commemorative of the seventy-fifth anniversary of the Second Church, Dorchester, December 31, 1882, and January 1, 1883. Boston: Wood, 1883. Pp. 64.

4165 DORCHESTER, MASS. TERCENTENARY COMMITTEE. Dorchester, 1630--old and new--1930, in the old Bay Colony; historic and pictorial record commemorating the three hundredth anniversary of the founding of Dorchester, Massachusetts, in the old Bay Colony, where government by town meeting was first organized and where the first free school supported by public taxation was established. Richard Peterson Bonney, ed. Dorchester: Chapple Publishing, 1930. Pp. 78.

4166 DORCHESTER ANTIQUARIAN AND HISTORICAL SOCIETY, DORCHESTER, MASS. History of the town of Dorchester, Massachusetts. Ebenezer Clapp, et al., eds. Boston, 1859. Pp. xii, 672.

4167 "DORCHESTER Antiquarian and Historical Society: a sketch." HistMag, 1 (1857), 131-132.

4168 DORCHESTER ARGUS-CITIZEN. A chronicle of Dorchester history in honor of the 333rd anniversary of the founding of Dorchester. [Hyde Park?, 1963]. Pp. 64.

4169 [DORCHESTER HISTORICAL SOCIETY, DORCHESTER, MASS.] Dorchester day; celebration of the two hundred and seventy-seventh anniversary of the settlement of Dorchester, June 8th, 1907, including also a brief description of the origin of Dorchester day and the three preceding celebrations. James H. Stark, ed. Boston: Municipal Printing Office, 1907. Pp. 117.

4170 ____. Dorchester day; celebration of the two hundred and seventy-ninth anniversary of the settlement of Dorchester, June 5, 1909, under the auspices of the Dorchester historical society; including also the celebration of Dorchester day, June 6, 1908...and the flagstaff dedication at Upham's corner, Patriots' day, April 19, 1909. James H. Stark, ed. Boston: Printing Department, 1909. Pp. 116.

4171 DORCHESTER in the old Bay Colony; historic and pictorial record commemorating the anniversary of the founding of Dorchester, Mass., in the old Bay Colony, where government by town meeting was first organized and where the first free school supported by public taxation was established. [Dorchester]: Tribune Publishing, [1972]. Pp. 64.

4172 DORCHESTER TEMPLE BAPTIST CHURCH, DORCHESTER, MASS. Dorchester Temple Baptist Church, seventy-fifth anniversary, November 8, 1961. n.p., [1961?]. Pp. 23. MBNEH.

4173 "DORCHESTER, the birthplace of public schools." National Magazine, 58 (1930), 383-389.

4174 DORION, EUSTACHE CHARLES EDOUARD. The redemption of the South End, a study in city evangelization. N.Y.: Abingdon Pr., 1915. Pp. 124.
Morgan Memorial; a social settlement.

4175 DORR, FRANK IRVING. Hayseed and sawdust. Boston: Wormsted, Smith, 1934. Pp. 228.
Raymond's; a department store.

4176 DOUGLAS-LITHGOW, ROBERT ALEXANDER. "Andrew Oliver House, Dorchester." MassMag, 3 (1910), 57-61.

4177 ____. "The Province House, Boston." Mass Mag, 3 (1910), 199-203.
Official residence of the former royal governors; built by Peter Sergeant, 1679.

4178 DOUGLASS, EMMONS E. The Boston Protective Department. [Medford], 1964. 27 leaves.
1849-1959, insurance.

4179 [DOWNER, CHARLES]. A visit to the 'Old North Church.' Boston, Mass. [Boston], 1893. Pp. 20.

4180 DOWNES, WILLIAM HOWE. "Boston as an art centre." NEM, New Ser., 30 (1904), 155-166.

4181 ____. "Boston painters and paintings." Atlantic, 62 (1888), 89-98, 258-266, 382-394, 500-510, 646-656, 777-786.

4182 DOWNS, JOSEPH. "John Cogswell, cabinetmaker." Antiques, 61 (1952), 322-324.

4183 DOWST, HENRY PAYSON. Random notes of Boston. Boston: H. B. Humphrey, 1913. Pp. 91.

4184 DRAKE, FRANCIS SAMUEL. "The Boston Tea Party." Old and New, 9 (1874), 97-107.

4185 ____. The town of Roxbury: its memorable persons and places, its history and antiquities, with numerous illustrations of its old landmarks and noted personages. Roxbury, 1878. Pp. vi, 475.

4186 DRAKE, SAMUEL ADAMS. Around the Hub, a boys' book about Boston. Boston: Roberts Bros., 1881. Pp. 267.
Not juvenile literature.

4187 _____. Bunker Hill: the story told in letters from the battle field by British officers engaged. Boston: Nichols & Hall, 1875. Pp. 76.

4188 _____. "Edward Everett's birthplace, Dorchester." Appleton's Journal, 9 (1873), 719-721.

4189 _____. "North Square, Boston." Appleton's Journal, 9 (1873), 461-462.

4190 _____. Old Boston taverns and tavern clubs. (1886) New illustrated ed., with an account of 'Cole's Inn,' 'The Bakers' Arms,' and 'Golden Ball,' by Walter K. Watkins; also a list of taverns, giving the names of the various owners of the property, from Miss Thwing's work on 'The inhabitants and estates of the town of Boston, 1630-1800,' in the possession of the Massachusetts Historical Society. Boston: W. A. Butterfield, 1917. Pp. 124.

4191 _____. Old landmarks and historic personages of Boston. (1873) Rev. ed. Boston: Little, Brown, 1900. Pp. xviii, 484.

4192 DRAKE, SAMUEL GARDNER. An address delivered at the annual meeting of the New England Historical and Genealogical Society, held...January 20th, 1858. Boston: H. W. Dutton and Son, 1858. Pp. 20.
History of the society.

4193 _____. The history and antiquities of Boston...from its settlement in 1630, to the year 1770, also, an introductory history of the discovery and settlement of New England. Boston: L. Stevens, 1856. Pp. x, 840.

4194 _____. "Printers, publishers, and booksellers, in Boston, before the year 1800." HistMag, 2 Ser., 7 (1870), 216-220.

4195 DRUMMEY, JOHN. "Cultured capers at the Sign of the Bear." Boston, 55 (April, 1963), 84-87, 98.
Tavern Club.

4196 DUANE, CHARLES WILLIAMS. A historical sermon delivered on the one hundred and seventy-fifth anniversary of Christ Church, Boston, also historical notes on its name, the North Church.... Boston: Carrie, [1901]. Pp. 57.

4197 DUFFY, JOHN. "A sidelight on colonial newspapers." The Historian, 18 (1955-1956), 230-239.
Limited to Boston.

4198 DUNIGAN, DAVID RONAN. A history of Boston College. Milwaukee: Bruce Publishing, 1947. Pp. xviii, 362.

4199 DUNSTAN, JOHN LESLIE. A light to the city; 150 years of the City Missionary Society of

Boston, 1816-1966. Boston: Beacon Pr., 1966. Pp. xiii, 294.

4200 DURYEE, KITTIE S. More peaks than valleys--the story of the first campaign, 1897-1900. Boston: Massachusetts Civic League, [1974?]. M. Pp. 31.
History of the Massachusetts Civic League.

4201 DUTTON, E. P., & COMPANY. Seventy-five years; or, the joys and sorrows of publishing and selling books at Duttons, from 1852 to 1927.... N.Y., 1927. Pp. 91.

4202 DWIGHT, JOHN S. "The Handel and Haydn Society." NEM, New Ser., 1 (1889-1890), 382-393.

4203 DWIGHT, TIMOTHY. Boston at the beginning of the 19th century. Boston: Old South Work, 1903. Pp. 24.

4204 DYER, JULIA KNOWLTON. "The islands of Boston Harbor." BSPub, 2 (1905), 107-131.

4205 DYER, WALTER A. "The Boston rocker." Antiques, 13 (1928), 389-392.

4206 EAGER, GEORGE HENRY. Historical sketch of the Second Church in Boston. Boston: Robinson Printing, 1894. Pp. 43.

4207 EARLE, ALICE MORSE. "A Boston schoolgirl in 1771." Atlantic, 72 (1893), 218-224.
Anna Green Winslow.

4208 EARLIEST meeting houses in West Roxbury. West Roxbury: West Roxbury Historical Society, n.d. Unpaged. MBNEH.

4209 "EARLY Boston--visual telegraphs and how they aided shipping." About the First, (May, 1938), 4-8.

4210 EAST BOSTON SAVINGS BANK. Into a second century, 1848-1948. East Boston, [1948]. Pp. 10.

4211 EASTMAN, RALPH MASON. "Boston and aviation." BSProc, (1946), 27-48.

4212 _____. Pilots and pilot boats of Boston Harbor, presenting stories and illustrations of the skilled, resourceful men of stout hearts who, with their trim, weatherly boats of sturdy construction, have played such an important role in the maritime life of Boston. Boston: Priv. Print., 1956. Pp. 91.

4213 EATON, ASA. Historical account of Christ Church, Boston: a discourse, delivered in said church, Dec. 28, 1823, by the rector. Boston: J. W. Ingraham, 1824. Pp. 39.

4214 EATON, LEONARD KIMBALL. "Charles Bulfinch and the Massachusetts General Hospital." Isis, 41 (1950), 8-11.

4215 _____. "Medicine in Philadelphia and Boston, 1805-1830." PMHB, 75 (1951), 66-75.

4216 EATON, MARION GOODWIN. "Where Boston began." SWJ, 43 (1928), 651-661.
Charlestown.

4217 EATON, QUAINTANCE. The Boston Opera Company. N.Y.: Appleton-Century, 1965. Pp. xiv, 338.

4218 EDDY, DANIEL CLARKE. The memorial sermon preached in the Baldwin-Place Meeting House on the last Sabbath of its occupancy by the Second Baptist Church. Boston: Graves & Young, 1865. Pp. 62.
Contains history of various Baptist churches in Boston.

4219 EDES, HENRY HERBERT. "Hall's Coffee House, Boston." CSMP, 14 (1911-1913), 400-408.

4220 _____. "The places of worship of the Sandemanians in Boston." CSMP, 6 (1899-1900), 109-123.
Eighteenth century religious society.

4221 EDWARDS, RICHARD H. Tales of the Observer. Boston: Jordan Marsh, 1950. Pp. 116.
Jordan Marsh Co., a department store.

4222 EGAN, JOSEPH BURKE. Citizenship in Boston. Philadelphia: John C. Winston, 1925. Pp. xxii, 423.
Includes historical portions.

4223 EHRENFRIED, ALBERT. A chronicle of Boston Jewry, from the colonial settlement to 1900. [Boston?, 1963]. Pp. viii, 771.

4224 EKLUND, EMMET E. "Swedish Lutheran congregations of the Boston area, 1867-1930." Swedish Pioneer Historical Quarterly, 16 (1965), 56-75.

4225 ELDRIDGE, D. "Camp Meigs, Readville, Mass." HPHR, 6 (1908), 10-28.

4226 ELDRIDGE, ELISHA DONNE. Last century recollections, collection of facts of early life in the boot and shoe trade of Boston. Boston: Boot and Shoe Recorder, 1904. Pp. 16.

4227 ELDRIDGE, GEORGE WASHINGTON. The Marston restaurants; a brief history. Boston: Oxford-Print, 1912. Pp. 23.

4228 ELIOT, CHRISTOPHER RHODES. "The Boston Public Garden; Horace Gray, Sr.; Charles Francis Barnard." BSProc, (1939), 27-45.

4229 _____. "The origin and early history of the Boston Association of Ministers." UHSP, 7, Pt. 1 (1940), 21-38.

4230 [ELIOT, EPHRAIM]. Historical notices of the New North Religious Society in Boston, with anecdotes of Rev. Andrew and John Eliot. Boston: Phelps and Farnham, 1822. Pp. 51.
Author attribution by Harvard University Library.

4231 ELIOT, SAMUEL ATKINS, 1862-1950. "A cradle of liberty, being the story of the West Church in Boston, 1737-1937." UHSP, 5, Pt. 2 (1937), 1-13.

4232 _____. "From scalping knife to can opener: a sketch of the origins & work of an old Massachusetts society." MHSP, 66 (1936-1941), 107-125.
Society for Propagating the Gospel among the Indians and others in North America.

4233 [ELIOT, WILLIAM HARVARD]. A description of Tremont House, with architectural illustrations.... Boston: Gray and Bowen, 1830. Pp. 36, xxxi.

4234 ELIOT SCHOOL, JAMAICA PLAIN, MASS. The Eliot School, 1676-1905. Boston: South End Industrial School, 1905. Pp. 35.

4235 ELL, CARL STEPHENS. Northeastern at Boston: adventures in education to develop latent talents! N.Y.: Newcomen Society in North America, 1956. Pp. 24.

4236 ELLIS, ARTHUR BLAKE. "The abode of John Hull and Samuel Sewall." MHSP, 2 Ser., 1 (1884-1885), 312.

4237 _____. History of the First Church in Boston, 1630-1880. Boston: Hall & Whiting, 1881. Pp. lxxxviii, 356.

4238 ELLIS, CHARLES MAYO. The history of Roxbury town. Boston: Samuel G. Drake, 1847. Pp. 146.

4239 ELLIS, GEORGE EDWARD. A commemorative discourse delivered in the New South Church, Church Green, Boston on Sunday, December 25, 1864, on the fiftieth anniversary of its dedication. Boston: H. W. Dutton and Son, 1865. Pp. 42.

4240 _____. "General Burgoyne in Boston." MHSP, (1875-1876), 233-248.
1775.

4241 _____. History of the Battle of Bunker's [Breed's] Hill, on June 17, 1775, from authentic sources in print and manuscript. Boston: Lee & Shepard, 1895. Pp. 152.

4242 _____. An oration delivered at Charlestown, Massachusetts, on the 17th of June, 1841, in commemoration of the Battle of Bunker Hill. Boston: W. Crosby, 1841. Pp. 72.

4243 _____. "Sick and wounded at Bunker Hill." Boston Medical and Surgical Journal, 92 (1875), 731-732.

4244 _____. Sketch of the cities of Boston and Cambridge.... Boston: Little, Brown, 1875. Pp. 28.

4245 [_____]. Sketches of Bunker Hill battle and monument, with illustrative documents. Charlestown: C. P. Emmons, 1843. Pp. 172.

4246 ELLIS, RUFUS. The last sermon preached in First Church, Chauncy Street, May 10, 1868; being the Lord's day previous to the removal of the congregation to the chapel of their fifth house of worship, on the corner of Berkeley and Marlborough Streets. Boston: J. Wilson and Son, 1868. Pp. 32.

4247   ELLIS, WARREN B. "Freemasonry in Boston." NEM, New Ser., 13 (1895-1896), 3-20.

4248   ELLSWORTH, EDWARD W. "Sea birds of Muscovy in Massachusetts." NEQ, 33 (1960), 3-18. Visit of Russian vessels to Boston in 1864.

4249   ELSON, LOUIS CHARLES. "The Boston Symphony Orchestra." NEM, New Ser., 1 (1889-1890), 235-241.

4250   EMERSON, EDWARD WALDO. The early years of the Saturday Club, 1855-1870. Boston: Houghton Mifflin, 1918. Pp. xii, 515. Predecessor of the 'Later years of the Saturday Club, 1870-1920' by Mark Antony DeWolfe Howe and 'The Saturday Club: a century completed, 1920-1956' by Edward W. Forbes.

4251   EMERSON, HAVEN. The Baker Memorial, a study of the first ten years of a unit for people of moderate means at the Massachusetts General Hospital. N.Y.: The Commonwealth Fund, 1941. Pp. ix, 75.

4252   EMERSON, RALPH WALDO. "Boston." Atlantic, 69 (1892), 26-35.

4253   EMERSON, WILLIAM. An historical sketch of the First Church in Boston, from its formation to the present period, to which are added two sermons, one on leaving the old, and the other on entering the new house of worship. Boston: Munroe & Francis, 1812. Pp. 256.

4254   EMERSON HOSPITAL, BOSTON. Medical, surgical and obstetrical report of the Emerson Hospital, Forest Hills, Boston, 1907 to 1911 inclusive. Cambridge: University Pr., 1912. Pp. 93.

4255   _____. Medical, surgical and obstetrical report of the Emerson Hospital from January 1, 1912 to January 1, 1923, also statistical resumé of results since the opening of the hospital twenty years ago. Cambridge: Univ. Pr., [1923?]. Pp. 72. M.

4256   EMERY, HORACE T. "Headquarters of the visiting state delegations of the Christian Endeavor convention." Bostonian, 2 (1895), 323-345. Histories of Boston area churches.

4257   EMERY, SUSAN LAVINIA. A Catholic stronghold and its making: a history of St. Peter's Parish, Dorchester, Massachusetts, and of its first rector, the Rev. Peter Ronan. Boston: Geo. H. Ellis, 1910. Pp. 95.

4258   EMMONS, WILLIAM. An address commemorative of the Battle of Bunker Hill, June 17, 1775. Boston: J. Q. Adams, 1834. Pp. 16.

4259   _____. An address in commemoration of the Boston Massacre of March 5, 1770...on the evening of March 5, 1825. 2d. ed. corrected. [Boston, 1825]. Pp. 14.

4260   _____. An oration on Bunker Hill battle, delivered on the battle ground, in Charlestown, 18th of June, 1827.... Boston, 1827. Pp. 16.

4261   ENGELHARDT, GEORGE WASHINGTON. Boston, Massachusetts. [Boston], 1897. Pp. 306. Economic conditions.

4262   ENGLIZIAN, H. CROSBY, Brimstone Corner; Park Street Church, Boston. Chicago: Moody Pr., 1968. Pp. 286.

4263   ERLANGER, STEVEN J. The colonial worker in Boston, 1775. Boston: U. S. Department of Labor, Bureau of Labor Statistics, New England Regional Office, 1975. Pp. 24. MBNEH.

4264   ERNST, CARL WILHELM. "The American town in the Revolution." Society of Colonial Wars. Massachusetts. [Yearbook], (1906), 87-97.

4265   _____. "Boston and transportation." BSProc, (1898), 18-31.

4266   _____. Constitutional history of Boston, Massachusetts. [Boston, 1894]. Pp. 173.

4267   _____. "Words coined in Boston." BSProc, (1897), 19-27; (1900), 39-47.

4268   ERNST, ELLEN LUNT FROTHINGHAM. The First Congregational Society of Jamaica Plain (the Third Parish Church in Roxbury) 1769-1909. n.p., Priv. Print., 1909. Pp. 79.

4269   _____. "Jamaica Plain before annexation." Our Boston, 1 (September, 1926), 17-21.

4270   ERNST, GEORGE ALEXANDER OTIS. "The movement for school reform in Boston." Educational Review, 28 (1904), 433-443. 1897-1904.

4271   "EVACUATION of Boston." Potter's AmMo, 6 (1876), 166-172.

4272   EVANGELICAL BAPTIST BENEVOLENT AND MISSIONARY SOCITY, BOSTON. Constitution, with a history of the Tremont Temple enterprise. Boston: Hewes, 1876. Pp. 16. MB.

4273   EVANS, GEORGE HILL. The burning of the Mount Benedict Ursuline Community House. Somerville: Somerville Public Library, 1934. Pp. 31.

4274   EVERETT, ALEXANDER HILL. An address delivered at Charlestown, Mass., on the 17th of June, 1836, at the request of the young men, without distinction of party, in commemoration of the Battle of Bunker Hill. Boston: Beals & Greene, 1836. Pp. 71.

4275   EVERETT, EDWARD. An address delivered on the 28th of June, 1830, the anniversary of the arrival of Governor Winthrop at Charlestown. Charlestown: W. W. Wheildon, 1830. Pp. 51.

4276   _____. Dorchester in 1630, 1776, and 1855, an oration delivered on the Fourth of July, 1855...also an account of the proceedings in Dorchester at the celebration of the day. Boston: D. Clapp, 1855. Pp. viii, 158.

4277   ____. An oration delivered at Charlestown, on the seventy-fifth anniversary of the Battle of Bunker Hill, June 17, 1850. Boston: Redding, 1850. Pp. 77.

4278   EWING, WILLIAM. The Sunday-school century, containing a history of the Congregational Sunday-school and Publishing Society. Boston: Pilgrim Pr., 1918. Pp. xvi, 141.

4279   "F. du Sud," pseud. "Masonic lodges of Boston." Bostonian, 2 (1895), 540-559.

4280   FAGAN, JAMES OCTAVIUS. The New England squeak and other stories, being the strange adventure of heroic yet primitive people. Boston: Geo. H. Ellis, 1931. Pp. 88.
        Historical anecdotes.

4281   ____. The Old South; or, the romance of early New England history. Boston: Geo. H. Ellis, 1923. Pp. 141.
        Old South Church.

4282   FALES, DEAN A., JR. "Joseph Barrell's Pleasant Hill." CSMP, 43 (1956-1963), 373-390.
        House, demolished 1896.

4283   ____. "Two Boston cabinetmakers of the 1820s." Antiques, 103 (1973), 1002-1003.
        Moses Mellen and George and Jacob Smith.

4284   FALES, MARTHA GANDY. "Obadiah Rich, Boston silversmith." Antiques, 94 (1968), 565-569.

4285   FAMILY WELFARE SOCIETY OF BOSTON. Then and now a friend in need; Associated Charities of Boston, 1879-1921; the Family Welfare Society of Boston, 1921-1929. n.p., [1929?]. Pp. 31.

4286   ____. Yesterday and tomorrow, the sixtieth anniversary, 1879-1939. Boston, 1939. Pp. 14. M.

4287   FARLOW, JOHN WOODFORD. The history of the Boston Medical Library. Norwood: Plimpton Pr., 1918. Pp. 240.

4288   ____. "Yellow fever in Boston, 1798." MHSP, 59 (1925-1926), 157-158.

4289   FARMER, LAURENCE. "When Cotton Mather fought the smallpox." Am Heritage, 8 (August, 1957), 40-43, 109.

4290   FAXON, NATHANIEL WALES. The Massachusetts General Hospital, 1935-1955. Cambridge: Harvard Univ. Pr., 1959. Pp. 490.

4291   FAY, FREDERIC HAROLD. The population and finances of Boston: a study of municipal growth. Boston: Municipal Printing Office, 1901. Pp. 33.

4292   FEDER, SID. The great Brink's holdup. Completed by Joseph F. Dinneen. Garden City, N.Y.: Doubleday, 1961. Pp. 263.

4293   FEDERATED JEWISH CHARITIES OF BOSTON. Purim Ball...to celebrate the fiftieth anniversary of the founding of the United Hebrew Benevolent Association, March 5, 1914. Boston, 1914. Pp. 55. M.

4294   FELLMAN, MICHAEL. "Theodore Parker and the abolitionist role in the 1850s." JAH, 61 (1974), 666-684.

4295   FERDINAND, THEORDORE N. "The criminal patterns of Boston since 1849." AmJSoc, 73 (1967-1968), 84-99.

4296   "FIFTIETH anniversary of the Boston City Hospital, June 20, 1914." Boston Medical and Surgical Journal, 171 (July 16, 1914), 89-98.

4297   "FIFTY years of textbook publishing: D. C. Heath & Co. celebrates its golden anniversary." Publishers' Weekly, 127 (April 13, 1935), 1508-1511.

4298   FILLEBROWN, CHARLES BOWDOIN. The A B C of taxation, with Boston object lessons, private property in land, and other essays and addresses. (1909) 4th ed. rev. Garden City, [N.Y.]: Doubleday, Page, 1916. Pp. 236.

4299   FINCH, J. "On the forts around Boston which were erected during the War of Independence." American Journal of Science, 8 (1824), 338-348.

4300   FIREY, WALTER IRVING. Land use in central Boston.... Cambridge: Harvard Univ. Pr., 1947. Pp. xv, 367.

4301   ____. "Sentiments and symbolism as ecological variables." AmSocRev, 10 (1945), 140-148.
        Spatial patterns as related to historic landmarks, Beacon Hill and the North End.

4302   "FIRST blood of the Revolution, destruction of tea." American Pioneer, 1 (1842), 412-413.

4303   "THE FIRST Harrison Gray Otis House, Boston, and its architect." OTNE, 36 (1945-1946), 85-86.
        Cambridge St.; attributed to Charles Bulfinch.

4304   "THE FIRST organized football club in the United States." OTNE, 15 (1924-1925), 7-13.
        Oneida Football Club, 1862.

4305   FISHER, CHARLES EBEN. "The Hinkley Locomotive Works." RLHSB, No. 25, (1931), 6-11.

4306   FISHER, J. B. "Who was Crispus Attucks?" AmHist Record, 1 (1872), 531-533.

4307   FISHER, WILLIAM ARMS. Notes on music in old Boston. Boston: Oliver Ditson, 1918. v. p.

4308   ____. One hundred and fifty years of music publishing in the United States: an historical sketch with special reference to the pioneer publisher, Oliver Ditson Company, Inc., 1783-1933. Boston: Oliver Ditson, 1933. Pp. xvi, 146.

4309 FISKE, JOHN, 1842-1901. "Crispus Attucks, King George, and the Tea Party." Sons of the Revolution, Massachusetts Society. Register, (1899), 104-126.

4310 FITCH, ROBERT G. "The great Boston fire of 1872." NEM, New Ser., 21 (1899-1900), 358-377.

4311 FITZ, REGINALD H. "Zabdiel Boylston, inoculator, and the epidemic of smallpox in Boston in 1721." Johns Hopkins Hospital Bulletin, 22 (1911), 315-327.

4312 FITZGERALD, DAVID. Carney Hospital, Boston: one hundredth anniversary, 1863-1963. [Boston, 1963?]. Unpaged.

4313 FITZGERALD, DESMOND. History of the Boston Water Works, from 1868 to 1876, being a supplement to a 'History of the introduction of pure water into the city of Boston with a description of its Cochituate waterworks, etc. 1868.' Boston: Rockwell & Churchill, 1876. Pp. vi, 290.
    'History of the introduction...' is by Nathaniel J. Bradlee.

4314 FLAGG, MILDRED BUCHANAN. Boston authors now and then: more members of the Boston Authors Club, 1900-1966. Cambridge: Dresser, Chapman & Grimes, 1966. Pp. 269.
    Sequel to 'Notable Boston authors.'

4315 _____. Notable Boston authors: members of the Boston Authors Club, 1900-1966. Cambridge: Dresser, Chapman & Grimes, 1965. Pp. 268.

4316 FLEMING, THOMAS J. Now we are enemies: the story of Bunker Hill. N.Y.: St. Martin's Pr., 1960. Pp. 366.

4317 _____. "Verdicts of history I: the Boston Massacre." Am Heritage, 18 (December, 1966), 6-10, 102-111.

4318 FLETCHER, WILLIAM I. "Some recollections of the Boston Athenaeum, 1861-1866." LJ, 38 (1914), 579-583.

4319 FLEXNER, JAMES THOMAS. "Providence rides a storm." Am Heritage, 19 (December, 1967), 13-17, 98-99.
    Battle of Dorchester Heights.

4320 FLOWER, B. O. "A graveyard with a history." Arena, 19 (1898), 618-631.
    Copp's Hill.

4321 FLOYD, ALICE P. The history of the Parish of All Saints (Ashmont) Dorchester, Boston, Massachusetts. Boston: Sheldon Pr., 1945. Pp. 89.

4322 FLOYD, MARGARET HENDERSON. "A terra-cotta cornerstone for Copley Square: Museum of Fine Arts, Boston, 1870-1876, by Sturgis and Brigham." SocArchHistJ, 32 (1973), 83-103.
    John H. Sturgis and Charles Brigham.

4323 FOLEY, SUZANNE. "Christ Church, Boston." OTNE, 51 (1960-1961), 67-85.

4324 FOOTE, HENRY WILDER, 1838-1889, HENRY H. EDES and JOHN C. PERKINS. Annals of King's Chapel from the Puritan age of New England to the present day. Boston: Little, Brown, 1882-1940. 3v.

4325 FOOTE, HENRY WILDER, 1838-1889. The centenary of the King's Chapel liturgy, discourse by Rev. Henry Wilder Foote and address by Rev. James Freeman Clarke...given in King's Chapel, Sunday, April 12, 1885.... Boston: Geo. H. Ellis, 1885. Pp. 34.

4326 _____. James Freeman and King's Chapel, 1782-1787: a chapter in the early history of the Unitarian movement in New England. Boston: L. C. Bowles, 1873. Pp. 29.

4327 _____. King's Chapel and the evacuation of Boston, a discourse by Henry Wilder Foote, given in King's Chapel, Sunday, March 12, 1876.... Boston: G. H. Ellis, 1876. Pp. 23.

4328 FOOTE, HENRY WILDER, b. 1875. "The Church of England in the first Boston Town House." BSPub, 8 (1911), 9-39.

4329 _____. "The historical background of the present King's Chapel." UHSP, 8, Pt. 2 (1950), 34-46.

4330 _____. "Musical life in Boston in the eighteenth century." AASP, New Ser., 49 (1939), 293-313.

4331 FOOTLIGHT CLUB, JAMAICA PLAIN, MASS.... Fiftieth anniversary and 161st performance. Eliot Hall, Jamaica Plain, December 8-11, 1926. Pp. 22.
    Contains an historical sketch of the club.

4332 FORBES, ALLAN and PAUL F. CADMAN. Boston and some noted émigrés; a collection of facts and incidents, with appropriate illustrations, relating to some well-known citizens of France who found homes in Boston and New England, with which are included accounts of several visits made by one of the authors to La Rochelle and to the homes of the ancestors of Paul Revere. [Boston]: State Street Trust Co., 1938. Pp. 98.
    Reprinted in Cottonport, Louisiana in 1971 with title: 'Boston French.'

4333 FORBES, ALLAN. 40 years in Boston banking--not forgetting ship models! N.Y.: Newcomen Society of England, American Branch, 1948. Pp. 28.

4334 _____. and RALPH MASON EASTMAN. Other statues of Boston as a sequel to our brochure of 1946 entitled 'Some statues of Boston.' Boston: State Street Trust Co., 1947. Pp. 93.

4335 _____. and _____. Some statues of Boston: reproductions of some of the statues for which Boston is famous, with information concerning the personalities and events so memorialized. Boston: State Street Trust Company, 1946. Pp. 75.

4336 FORBES, EDWARD WALDO and JOHN H. FINLEY, JR. The Saturday Club: a century completed, 1920-1956. Boston: Houghton Mifflin, 1958. Pp. xix, 410.
Successor to 'The early years of the Saturday Club' by Edward Waldo Emerson and the 'Later years of the Saturday Club' by Mark Antony DeWolfe Howe.

4337 FORBES, FRANK H. "The old wharves of Boston." BSProc, (1952), 25-32.

4338 FORBES, HARRIETTE MERRIFIELD. "The Lamsons of Charlestown, stone cutters." OTNE, 17 (1926-1927), 125-139.

4339 FORBES, JOHN D. "Boston smuggling, 1807-1815." AmNep, 10, (1950), 144-154.

4340 _____. "European wars and Boston trade." NEQ, 11 (1938), 709-730.

4341 _____. "Shepley, Bulfinch, Richardson and Abbott, Architects: an introduction." SocArchHistJ, 17 (Fall, 1958), 19-31.

4342 "THE FORBES Lithograph Manufacturing Company." Industry, 3 (March, 1938), 7-10, 54-55.

4343 "FORBES Lithograph marks 100th milestone." Industry, 27 (May, 1962), 15, 44-46.

4344 FORD, WORTHINGTON CHAUNCEY. The Boston book market, 1679-1700. Boston: Club of Old Volumes, 1917. Pp. xi, 197.

4345 _____, ed. Boston in 1775: Letters from General Washington, Captain John Chester, Lieutenant Samuel B. Webb, and Joseph Barrell.... Brooklyn: Historical Printing Club, 1892. Pp. 38.

4346 _____. "Franklin's 'New England Courant.'" MHSP, 57 (1923-1924), 336-353.

4347 "FORT Independence in Boston Harbor." Hist Mag, 5 (1861), 310-313.
Castle Island, 1633-1798; signed B.F.D. [Benjamin Franklin De Costa].

4348 FORTY-FOUR CLUB. BOSTON. Annals of the Forty Four Club, seventy years, 1844-1914. Boston: The Barta Pr., [1947?]. Pp. 69.
Preface signed W.E.H. [William Edwards Huntington].

4349 "FORTY years of the 'Atlantic Monthly.'" Atlantic, 80 (1897), 571-576.

4350 FOULDS, MARGARET HADLEY. "The Massachusetts Bank, 1784-1865." JEBH, 2 (1929-1930), 256-270.

4351 FOWLE, JOHN ALLEN. Paper on the old Dorchester burying ground, read before the [Dorchester Historical] Society, November 22nd, 1901. (1901) 2d. ed. Dorchester: Published by the Society at 'ye old Blake House,' 1907. Pp. 22.

4352 FOWLER, MOSES FIELD. Review of the management of the Metropolitan Railroad Co. from 1860 to 1865. Boston: For sale at Howard's News Agency, 1865. Pp. 78.

4353 FOX, STEPHEN R. The guardian of Boston: William Monroe Trotter. N.Y.: Atheneum, 1970. Pp. ix, 307.

4354 FOX, THOMAS A. "A brief history of the Beacon Hill State-House." American Architect and Building News, 48 (1895), 127-129; 49 (1895), 55-56.

4355 FRAGMENT SOCIETY, BOSTON, MASS. Souvenir yearbook, one hundred and fiftieth anniversary of the Fragment Society. Jamaica Plain: Fandel Pr., 1962. Pp. 61. M.
Includes history, 1812-1962.

4356 _____. Souvenir year book, one hundredth anniversary of the Fragment Society (Sewing Circle), instituted Oct., 1812, incorporated Dec. 1816-1916. Boston: Bliss, 1916. Pp. 47.

4357 FRANKLIN TYPOGRAPHICAL SOCIETY, BOSTON. A few facts relating to the Franklin Typographical Society, its aims and purposes together with some things it has done in the past seventy-five years.... Cambridge: Univ. Pr., 1900. Pp. 27.

4358 _____. Proceedings of the Franklin Typographical Society, at the observance of the semi-centennial of its institution, January 17, 1874, with a brief historical sketch. Boston, 1875. Pp. 60.

4359 _____. A sketch of the history of the Franklin Typographical Society, and of its library, read before the Society at its April meeting, by the librarian. Boston: H. W. Dutton & Son, 1860. Pp. 16.
The librarian was Henry Squire.

4360 FRASER, ESTHER STEVENS. "Did Paul Revere make lace-edge trays?" Antiques, 31 (1937), 76-77.

4361 FREEDOM and the Old South Meeting-house. Boston: Old South Work, 1910. Pp. 30.

4362 FREEMAN, DONALD. Boston architecture. Cambridge: MIT Pr., 1971. Pp. 122.

4363 FREEMAN, JAMES and SAMUEL CARY. Funeral sermons preached at Kingschapel, Boston. Boston: Printed by Sewell Phelps, no. 5, Court street, 1820. Pp. 68.
Sketches of Susan A. Bulfinch, Samuel Cary, and Joseph Coolidge.

4364 FREEMASONS. BOSTON. ADELPHI LODGE. Fiftieth anniversary, 1865-1915: history of the lodge by Worshipful Brother Edward F. Estes, October the sixth, nineteen hundred and fifteen. [Boston, 1915]. Pp. 51.

4365 FREEMASONS. BOSTON. COLUMBIAN LODGE. Centenary of Columbian Lodge A. F. and A. M., Boston, Mass., 1795--June--1895. Boston, 1895. Pp. 254.

4366 FREEMASONS. BOSTON. JOSEPH WARREN LODGE. Joseph Warren Lodge F. & A. M., 100th anniversary celebration, Friday, September 21, 1956, reception to Grandmaster, Friday, September 28, 1956. n.p., [1956?]. Unpaged. MBNEH.

4367 FREEMASONS. BOSTON. JOSEPH WEBB LODGE. Jubilee year, Joseph Webb Lodge, A. F. and A. M., Boston, Massachusetts: the fiftieth anniversary program, March 7, 8, 10 and 13, 1926. Boston: Insurance Pr., [1926?]. Pp. 14.

4368 FREEMASONS. BOSTON. KNIGHTS TEMPLARS. BOSTON COMMANDERY. A sketch of Boston Commandery of Knights Templars, 1769-1895. [Boston]: Triennial Committee, 1895. Pp. 48.

4369 FREEMASONS. BOSTON. KNIGHTS TEMPLARS. PILGRIM COMMANDERY, NO. 9. Semi-centennial, Pilgrim Commandery, No. 9, K. T. 1855-1905. [Boston, 1905]. Pp. 75.

4370 FREEMASONS. BOSTON. LODGE OF SAINT ANDREW. Commemoration of the one hundred and fiftieth anniversary of the Lodge of Saint Andrew, Boston, New England, November 30, 1906. Boston, 1907. Pp. 306.

4371 _____. Commemoration of the one hundred twenty fifth anniversary of the Lodge of Saint Andrew, 1881, Nov. 30. Boston, 1887. Pp. 122.

4372 _____. The Lodge of Saint Andrew, and the Massachusetts Grand Lodge: conditi et dicati, anno lucis 5756-5769. Boston, 1870. Pp. 292. 1756-1769.

4373 _____. Lodge of St. Andrew bi-centennial memorial, 1756-1956. Boston, 1958. Pp. 197.

4374 FREEMASONS. BOSTON. MASSACHUSETTS LODGE. By-laws of the Massachusetts Lodge, Boston, chartered 1770, together with a historical sketch of the lodge, a list of members, and biographical sketches. Boston, 1871. Pp. 132.

4375 _____. Celebration of the one hundred-twenty-fifth anniversary of the Massachusetts Lodge, 1770--May 17--1895, with historical notes, by-laws, and a list of members. Boston, 1896. Pp. 143.

4376 _____. Centennial festival of Massachusetts Lodge, with the exercises of commemoration, including the historical address by Worshipful Brother Charles W. Slack, the proceedings at the banquet, and other incidents, May 12, 1870. Boston, 1870. Pp. 73.

4377 _____. History, charter and by-laws with the original and admitted members, past masters, honorary and active members, &c. Boston, 1863. Pp. 36.

4378 FREEMASONS. BOSTON. MT. LEBANON LODGE. Centennial of Mt. Lebanon Lodge, A. F. and A. M., Boston, Mass., 1801--June 10--1901. [Boston], 1901. Pp. 97.

4379 FREEMASONS. BOSTON. ROYAL ARCH MASONS. ST. ANDREW'S CHAPTER. Celebration of the one hundred and twenty-fifth anniversary, 1769-1894. Boston, 1894. Pp. 145. Historical address by W. B. Ellis.

4380 _____. Centennial celebration of St. Andrew's Royal Arch Chapter, held at Masonic Temple, on Wednesday, September 29, 1869. Boston, 1870. Pp. 78.

4381 _____. Exercises commemorating the one hundred fiftieth anniversary of the organization of St. Andrew's Royal Arch Chapter, Boston, Massachusetts, October the first, nineteen nineteen, 1769, 1919. [Boston], 1920. Pp. 169.

4382 FREEMASONS. BOSTON. ST. JOHN'S LODGE. History of St. John's Lodge of Boston in the Commonwealth of Massachusetts as shown in the records of the First Lodge, the Second Lodge, the Third Lodge, the Rising Sun Lodge, the Master's Lodge, St. John's Lodge, Most Worshipful Grand Lodge. Boston: Priv. Print., 1917. Pp. 263.

4383 _____. One hundred and seventy-fifth anniversary of the institution of St. John's Lodge A. F. & A. M. October 4, 5 and 6, 1908. Boston, [1908]. Pp. 20.

4384 FREEMASONS. BOSTON, MASS. WINSLOW LEWIS LODGE. By-laws of Winslow Lewis Lodge, with an historical sketch and list of members. Boston: Rand, Avery, 1874. Pp. 94.

4385 _____. Proceedings of fiftieth anniversary of Winslow Lewis Lodge, Hotel Brunswick, Boston, December 8, 1905, together with an address by the Hon. Charles Levi Woodbury, delivered at the twenty-fifth anniversary, December 10, 1881. Boston: Rockwell and Churchill, 1906. Pp. 60.

4386 FREEMASONS. DORCHESTER, MASS. UNION LODGE. An historical sketch of Union Lodge, Dorchester, from 1796 to 1876. James H. Upham, William Sayward and William T. Adams, eds. Boston: Rockwell and Churchill, 1877. Pp. 147.

4387 FREEMASONS. ROXBURY, MASS. LAFAYETTE LODGE. By-laws, organizations, list of members, and historical sketch. Boston: Richter, 1896. Pp. 39.

4388 FREEMASONS. ROXBURY, MASS. WASHINGTON LODGE. Historical sketch and centennial anniversary of Washington Lodge A. F. and A. M., Roxbury, Mass., 1796-1896.... Roxbury, 1896. Pp. 245.

4389 _____. History and by-laws of Washington Lodge, Roxbury, Mass., February 1st, A. L. 5866. John W. Dadmun and John F. Newton, comps. Boston: G. C. Rand & Avery, 1866. Pp. 74.

4390 FREEMASONS. SOUTH BOSTON. ST. PAUL'S LODGE. Fiftieth anniversary of Saint Paul's Lodge, A. F. & A. M., South Boston, Massachusetts, Tuesday evening, March 30, 1897. Boston, 1899. Pp. 31.

4391 FRENCH, ALLEN. "The Hallowell-Graves fisti-
cuffs, 1775." MHSP, 63 (1929-1930), 23-48.
'Encounter in the street' between Benjamin
Hallowell, Commissioner of Customs & Samuel
Graves, Admiral of the British Fleet, Aug.
11, 1775.

4392 ____. The Siege of Boston. N.Y.: Macmillan, 1911. Pp. xi, 450.

4393 FRENCH, CHARLES ELWELL, ed. Six years of
drama at the Castle Square Theatre, with
portraits of the members of the company and complete
programs of all plays produced, May 3, 1897--May 3,
1903. Boston, 1903. Pp. 406.

4394 FRENCH, EDWARD VINTON, comp. 1860--fifty
years--1910, Arkwright Mutual Fire Insurance
Company, one of the associated factory mutual fire
insurance companies, often called the 'New England
mutuals' or the 'factory mutuals.'... Boston:
Priv. Print., 1912. Pp. 123.

4395 FRENCH, MRS. GEORGE A. Dorchester Historical Society and its three houses. Boston:
Thomas Todd, 1960. Pp. 15. MBNEH.

4396 FRENCH, H. W. "A famous old church, Christ
Church, Boston." Potter's AmMo, 17 (1881),
481-494.

4397 FRENCH, HANNAH DUSTIN. "The amazing career
of Andrew Barclay, Scottish bookbinder of
Boston." Studies in Bibliography, 14 (1961), 145-
162.

4398 ____. "Bound in Boston by Henry B. Legg."
Studies in Bibliography, 17 (1964), 135-139.

4399 ____. John Roulstone's Harvard bindings."
HarvLibBul, 18 (1970), 171-182.
Early nineteenth century.

4400 FRENCH, RUTH HAWTHORNE. History and notables
of Pinckney Street.... [Boston?], 1952.
Pp. 33.

4401 FRESE, JOSEPH R. "James Otis and Writs of
Assistance." NEQ, 30 (1957), 496-508.
1760s.

4402 FRIEDMAN, DANIEL J. White militancy in Boston: a reconsideration of Marx and Weber.
Lexington: Lexington Books, 1973. Pp. xxiii, 162.

4403 FRIEDMANN, KAREN J. "Victualling colonial
Boston." AgricHist, 47 (1973), 189-205.

4404 FRIEDMAN, LEE MAX. "The Battle of Bunker
Hill and the Jews' burying ground." OTNE,
39 (1948-1949), 49-51.

4405 ____. "A Beacon Hill synagogue." OTNE, 33
(1942-1943), 1-5.
Congregation Anshe Libawitz.

4406 ____. "Boston in American Jewish history."
AJHSP, 42 (1952-1953), 333-340.

4407 ____. Three centuries of American Jewish
history in Massachusetts." BSProc, (1955),
25-39.

4408 FRIENDS, SOCIETY OF. BOSTON. YEARLY MEET-
ING. An historical account of the various
meeting-houses of the Society of Friends in Boston,
being the report of a committee of the representative meeting. Boston: Getchell, 1874. Pp. 37.

4409 "FROM sperm oil to solvenized gasoline."
Industry, 2 (July, 1937), 33-34.
125th anniversary of Jenney Manufacturing Co.

4410 FROST, JOHN EDWARD. Boston, America's home
port: a sketch book. Boston: Hawthorne
Pr., 1955. Pp. 92.

4411 ____. Channels of grace; a souvenir of the
Catholic Archdiocese of Boston. Warren Car-
berg, ed. Boston: Hawthorne Pr., 1954. Unpaged.

4412 FROTHINGHAM, FRANK E. The Boston fire, November 9th and 10th, 1872, its history, together with the losses in detail of both real and
personal estate, also, a complete list of insurance
losses, and an appendix containing the city loan,
insurance, and building acts. Boston: Lee & Shepard, 1873. Pp. 115.

4413 FROTHINGHAM, NATHANIEL LANGDON. The shade of
the past, for the celebration of the close of
the second century since the establishment of the
Thursday Lecture. Boston: Lee & Shepard, 1873.
Pp. 115.

4414 ____. Two hundred years ago, a sermon
preached to the First Church, on the close of
their second century, 29 August, 1830. Boston,
1830. Pp. 20.

4415 FROTHINGHAM, OCTAVIUS BROOKS. Boston Unitarianism, 1820-1850; study of the life and work
of Nathaniel Langdon Frothingham. N.Y.: G. P. Putnam's Sons, 1890. Pp. 272.

4416 FROTHINGHAM, PAUL REVERE. The fulfilment of
fifty years; an anniversary sermon preached
in the Arlington Street Church, Sunday, December 10,
1911. Boston: Geo. H. Ellis, 1912. Pp. 17.

4417 FROTHINGHAM, RICHARD. The alarm on the night
of April 18, 1775. (1876) [2d. ed.].
[Boston, 1877?]. Pp. 12.
Paul Revere's signal lanterns.

4418 ____. The battle-field of Bunker Hill:
with a relation of the action by William
Prescott, and illustrative documents; a paper com-
municated to the Massachusetts Historical Society,
June 10, 1875, with additions. Boston, 1876.
Pp. 46.

4419 ____. The centennial: Battle of Bunker
Hill.... Boston: Little, Brown, 1875.
Pp. 136.
Later printings have title: 'Battle of
Bunker Hill.'

4420 _____. The command in the Battle of Bunker
Hill, with a reply to 'Remarks on Frothing-
ham's history of the battle, by S. Swett.' Boston:
C. C. Little and J. Brown, 1850. Pp. 56.

4421 _____. The history of Charlestown, Massachusetts. Charlestown: C. P. Emmons, 1845-
1849. Pp. 368.

4422 _____. History of the Siege of Boston, and
of the battles of Lexington, Concord, and
Bunker Hill, also an account of the Bunker Hill
monument, with illustrative documents. (1849) 6th
ed. Boston: Little, Brown, 1896. Pp. ix, 422.

4423 _____. Oration delivered before the city
government and citizens of Boston, in Music
Hall, July 4, 1874. Boston: Rockwell & Churchill,
1874. Pp. 55.
Appendix: The action of Boston, Charlestown,
Dorchester, and Roxbury on the question of
independence.

4424 _____. "The Sam Adams Regiments in the
town of Boston." Atlantic, 9 (1862), 701-
720; 10 (1862), 179-203; 12 (1863), 595-616.

4425 FROTHINGHAM, THOMAS GODDARD. "The Siege of
Boston." MHSP, 59 (1925-1926), 292-301.

4426 FUCHS, LAWRENCE H. "Presidential politics
in Boston: the Irish response to Stevenson."
NEQ, 30 (1957), 435-447.
Election of 1956.

4427 FULLER, ARTHUR BUCKMINSTER. An historical
discourse, delivered in the New North Church,
October 1, 1854. Boston: Crosby, Nichols, 1854.
Pp. 33.
Relates to the church.

4428 FULTON, JUSTIN DEWEY. The work of God in
Tremont Temple, a historical discourse;
sketches of Tremont Temple and its pastor by Rev.
Gilbert Haven, and Prof. Norman Fox.... Boston:
Union Temple Baptist Church, 1871. Pp. 28.

4429 "FUNERAL processions in Boston from 1770 to
1800." BSPub, 4 (1907), 125-149.

4430 NO ENTRY

4431 GAFFEY, JAMES P. "The changing of the guard:
the rise of Cardinal O'Connell of Boston."
CathHistRev, 59 (1973), 225-244.

4432 GALLAGHER, CHARLES T. Proceedings at the
centenary of the founding of a Republican
Institution in the Town of Boston, 1819-1919. Boston, 1919. Pp. 14. M.
Political club

4433 GAMET, VERA. "The pianos of Jonas Chickering." OTNE, 31 (1940-1941), 1-9.

4434 GANS, HERBERT J. The urban villagers; group
and class in the life of Italian-Americans.
N.Y.: Free Press of Glencoe, 1962. Pp. xvi, 367.
West End.

4435 GARDINER, ABRAHAM SYLVESTER. Bunker Hill; a
centennial oration, delivered [in] Reading,
Mass., in commemoration of the Battle of Bunker Hill
fought June 17, 1775. Stoneham: Sentinel Pr.,
1875. Pp. 16.

4436 GARDNER, INEZ J. "Boston and the Woman's
Club." NEM, New Ser., 34 (1906), 597-605.

4437 GARDNER, JAMES B. "New England Guards."
BSPub, 4 (1907), 9-53.

4438 GARLAND, JOSEPH E. Every man our neighbor;
a brief history of the Massachusetts General
Hospital, 1811-1961. Boston: Little, Brown, 1961.
Pp. 56.

4439 _____. An experiment in medicine; the first
twenty years of the Pratt Clinic and the New
England Center Hospital of Boston. Cambridge: Riverside Pr., 1960. Pp. 107.

4440 _____. "The New England Journal of Medicine,
1812-1968." JHistMed, 24 (1969), 125-139.

4441 GARRETT, WENDELL D. "Figures and figureheads: the maritime collection at the State
Street Bank and Trust Company, Boston." Antiques,
90 (1966), 816-823.

4442 GARRISON, WILLIAM FLOYD. "Boston anti-slavery days." BSPub, 2 (1905), 81-104.

4443 GASSETT, HELEN MARIA. Categorical account of
the Female Medical College, to the people of
the New England states. Boston, 1855. Pp. 138.
New England Female Medical College.

4444 GATES, BURTON NOBLE. "Boston earthenware:
Frederick Mear, potter." Antiques, 5 (1924),
310-311.
Boston Earthenware Manufacturing Co.

4445 GEDDES, JAMES. Sketch of the Department of
Romance Languages, Boston University, 1876-
1900. [Boston], 1902. Pp. 16.

4446 GENDROT, ALMIRA TORREY BLAKE FENNO. Artists
I have known. Boston: Warren Pr., [1923].
Pp. 46.
Nineteenth-century Boston arts and artists.

4447 GENERAL FOODS CORPORATION. A calendar of
Walter Baker & Company, Inc., and its times
1765-1940.... Bruce Millar, ed. [N.Y., 1940].
65 leaves.
Chocolate manufacture.

4448 "THE GENESIS of the Roxbury Historical Society." Roxbury HSY, (1917), 9-13.

4449 GERLACH, DON R. "A note on the Quartering
Act of 1774." NEQ, 39 (1966), 80-88.

4450   GERRIER, EDITH. "The Suffolk Bank." Bostonian, 2 (1895), 603-611.

4451   GERRY, SAMUEL L. "The old masters of Boston." NEM, New Ser., 3 (1890-1891), 683-695.

4452   GETCHELL, EVERETT LAMONT. Field lessons in
the geography and history of the Boston Basin: a handbook for teachers. Boston: Little,
Brown, 1910. Pp. xiii, 186.

4453   GARLAND, ADELAIDE HARRIET. Ten years later,
1894-1904; an address given before the All
Around Dickens Club, April 6, 1904. Boston: Southgate Pr., 1904.
        History of the club.

4454   GIFFEN, JANE C. "Susanna Rowson and her
academy." Antiques, 98 (1970), 436-440.

4455   GILLESPIE, CHARLES BANCROFT, comp. Illustrated history of South Boston, issued in
conjunction with and under auspices of the South
Boston Citizens' Association; comprising an historic
record and pictorial description of the district,
past and present. South Boston: Inquirer Publishing, 1900. Pp. 258.

4456   GILLETT, E. H., ed. "The speech of Mr. John
Checkley, upon his tryal, at Boston, in New-
England, 1724." HistMag, 2 Ser., 3 (1868), 209-
223.

4457   GILMAN, ARTHUR. "The Hancock House and its
founder." Atlantic, 11 (1863), 692-707.

4458   _____. The story of Boston. N.Y.: G. P.
Putnam's Sons, 1889. Pp. viii, 507.

4459   GILMAN, CAROLINE HOWARD. Recollections of
the private centennial celebration of the
overthrow of the tea, at Griffin's Wharf, in Boston
Harbor, December 16, 1773, in honor of Samuel Howard, one of the actors, at Cambridge, Mass., December, 1873. Cambridge: J. Wilson and Son, 1874.
Pp. 51.

4460   GILMER, ALBERT H. "Boston and emancipation."
MagHist, 16 (1913), 141-147.

4461   GILMORE, PATRICK SARSFIELD. History of the
National Peace Jubilee and Great Musical
Festival, held in the city of Boston, June, 1869,
to commemorate the restoration of peace throughout
the land. Boston: Lee and Shepard, 1871. Pp. x,
758.

4462   GLADDEN, SANFORD CHARLES. An index to the
vital records of Boston, 1630-1699. Boulder,
Colo.: Empire Reproduction and Print, 1969. Pp.
ii, 188.

4463   _____. An index to the vital records of Dorchester, Massachusetts through 1825. [Boul-
der?, Colo.], 1970. Pp. iii, 148.

4464   GLUECK, SHELDON and ELEANOR T. GLUECK. Juvenile delinquents grown up. N.Y.: Commonwealth Fund, 1940. Pp. viii, 330.
        Sequel to 'One Thousand Juvenile Delin-
        quents.'

4465   _____. and _____. One thousand juvenile
delinquents; their treatment by court and
clinic. Cambridge: Harvard Univ. Pr., 1934.
Pp. xxix, 341.

4466   GODFREY, CARLOS E. "When Boston was New Jersey's capital." New Jersey Historical Society, Proceedings, 51 (1933), 1-23.
        Under Edmund Andros, 1688.

4467   GOHDES, CLARENCE. "A Brook Farm labor record." American Literature, 1 (1929), 297-
303.

4468   GOLDENBERG, JOSEPH. "A forgotten dry dock
in colonial Charlestown." AmNep, 30 (1970),
56-62.

4469   GOLDSTEIN, FANNY. "West End Branch Library:
yesterday and today." Bay State Librarian,
47 (Winter, 1957), 1-2.
        Boston Public Library.

4470   GOOD GOVERNMENT ASSOCIATION, BOSTON. Its
purpose, its methods, its history. Boston,
1920. Unpaged. M.

4471   GOODELL, ABNER CHENEY, JR. The Boston Massacre. [Boston, 1887]. Pp. 11.

4472   _____. "Charges against Samuel Adams."
MHSP, 20 (1882-1883), 213-226.
Failure to give surety as tax collector,
1760s.

4473   _____. "The murder of Captain Codman."
MHSP, 20 (1882-1883), 122-157.
Poisoning of master by slaves; trial account,
1755.

4474   GOODMAN, PAUL. "Ethics and enterprise: the
values of the Boston elite: 1800-1860."
AmQ, 18 (1966), 437-451.

4475   GOODSPEED, CHARLES ELIOT. Yankee bookseller:
being the reminiscences of Charles E. Goodspeed.... Boston: Houghton Mifflin, 1937.
Pp. xiii, 325.

4476   GOODWIN, DANIEL, JR. Provincial pictures by
brush and pen: an address delivered before
the Bostonian Society, in the council chamber of the
old State-House, Boston, May 11, 1886.... Chicago:
Fergus Printing, 1886.
        Sketches of members of the Pitts and Bowdoin
        families.

4477   GOODWIN, M. C. "The castle - a sketch of
Fort Independence." Bostonian, 2 (1895),
644-654.

4478   GOODY, MARVIN E. and ROBERT P. WALSH, eds.
Boston Society of Architects: the first hundred years, 1867-1967. [Boston]: Boston Society
of Architects, 1967. Pp. 150.

4479   GORDON, ADONIRAM JUDSON. The fiftieth year:
a sermon, preached on the semi-centennial
anniversary of the Clarendon-Street Baptist Church
in Boston, October 21st, 1877. Boston, 1878.
Pp. 35.

4480   GORDON, GEORGE ANGIER. "The ancient line
        fields of Charlestown." NEHGR, 48 (1894),
57-59.

4481   GORE, HENRY WATSON, comp. The Independent
        Corps of Cadets of Boston, Mass., at Fort
Warren, Boston Harbor, in 1862. Boston: Rockwell
and Churchill, 1888. Pp. 447.

4482   GOSS, ELBRIDGE HENRY. "First newspaper in
        Boston." AmHist Record, 1 (1872), 460-461.

4483   GOSSE, ELIZABETH MERRITT. "Old Roxbury
        town." MagHist, 20 (1915), 260-264.

4484   GOULD, AUGUSTUS A. "Notice of the origin,
        progress, and present condition of the Bos-
ton Society of Natural History." American Quarterly Register, 14 (1842), 236-241.

4485   [GOULD, ELIZABETH PORTER]. An offering in
        behalf of the deaf. [Boston]: Boston Par-
ents Education Association, 1903. Pp. 28.
        History of the Horace Mann School.

4486   GOULD, GEORGE L. Historical sketch of the
        paint, oil, varnish and allied trades of
Boston since 1800, A.D. [Boston?, 1914?]. Pp. 148.

4487   GRAND ARMY OF THE REPUBLIC. DEPARTMENT OF
        MASSACHUSETTS. R. A. PEIRCE POST NO. 190,
        NEW BEDFORD. The Bunker Hill drum, captured
June 17, 1775, historical sketch. New Bedford:
Standard Print, 1904. Pp. 10.

4488   GRANT, ALINE. "Nearly a hundred years ago
        in Boston." NEG, 14 (Winter, 1973), 35-42.
Social life and customs.

4489   GRAS, NORMAN SCOTT BRIEN. "The building of
        the Business School, 1919-1942." Harvard
Business School. Alumni Bulletin, 18 (1942), 219-
235.

4490   _____. The Massachusetts First National
        Bank of Boston, 1784-1934. Cambridge: Har-
vard Univ. Pr., 1937. Pp. xxiv, 768.

4491   [GRAY, THOMAS]. Obituary notice of Rev.
        John Bradford, with a brief historical
sketch of the Congregational churches in Roxbury by
Rev. John Pierce. Boston: Christian Register,
[1825]. Pp. 12.
        Author attribution by the Massachusetts His-
        torical Society.

4492   _____. A sermon, delivered to the church
        and congregation, on Jamaica Plain, Roxbury,
the afternoon of the Lord's day, immediately suc-
ceeding the twelfth anniversary of his ordination,
March 31, 1805. Boston: Russell and Cutler, 1805.
Pp. 22.
        An historical sketch of the Third Parish of
        Roxbury.

4493   "THE GREAT elm and its scion." NEHGR, 64
        (1910), 141-144.
        The Liberty Tree.

4494   THE GREAT organ in the Boston Music Hall, be-
        ing a brief history of the enterprise from
its commencement, with a description of the instrument; together with the inaugural ode, and some account of the opening ceremonies on the evening of
November 2, 1863; to which is appended a short account of the principal organs in England and on the
continent of Europe. Boston: Ticknor and Fields,
1866. Pp. 102.

4495   GREEN, MARTIN BURGESS. The problem of Bos-
        ton; some readings in cultural history.
N.Y.: W. W. Norton, 1966. Pp. 234.
        Intellectual life.

4496   GREEN, SAMUEL ABBOTT. "The Boston Magazine."
        MHSP, 2 Ser., 18 (1903-1904), 326-330.
        1783-1785.

4497   _____. "The Boston Massacre, March 5, 1770."
        AASP, New Ser., 14 (1900-1901), 40-53.

4498   _____. "Colonel William Prescott; and Groton
        Soldiers at the Battle of Bunker Hill."
MHSP, 43 (1909-1910), 92-99.

4499   _____. "Description of Peter Fanueil, and
        notes on the earliest teaching of medicine
in Massachusetts." MHSP, 2 Ser., 1 (1884-1885), 42-
47.

4500   _____. "Formation and growth of the Soci-
        ety's Library." MHSP, 2 Ser., 8 (1892-1894),
312-344.
        Massachusetts Historical Society.

4501   _____. "Minutes of the tea meetings."
        MHSP, 20 (1882-1883), 11-17.
        Boston Tea Party.

4502   GREENE, CHARLOTTE. While on the hill, a
        stroll down Chestnut Street. Boston: Four
Seas Co., 1930. Pp. 31.

4503   GREENE, JEREMIAH EVARTS. Debt of Massachu-
        setts to Dorchester: town meeting and free
school, address...in Pilgrim Church, Dorchester,
January 27, 1894. Worcester: Hamilton, 1894.
Pp. 9.

4504   _____. "The Roxbury Latin School--an out-
        line of its history." AASP, New Ser., 4
(1885-1887), 348-366; 5 (1887-1888), 146-147.

4505   GREENE, JOHN GARDNER. "The Charles Street
        Meeting-house, Boston." OTNE, 30 (1939-
1940), 87-93.

4506   _____. "The Emmanuel Movement." NEQ, 7
        (1934), 494-532.
        Religious therapeutics.

4507   GREENLEAF, EDWARD H. "The Museum of Fine
        Arts, Boston." Art Review, 3 (July-August,
1888), 1-8.

4508   GREENOUGH, CHARLES PELHAM. "The experiences
        of an Irish immigrant, 1681." MHSP, 49
(1915-1916), 99-106.
        Henry Sharlot.

4509 GREENWOOD, FRANCIS WILLIAM PITT. A history of King's Chapel, in Boston, the first Episcopal church in New England; comprising notices of the introduction of Episcopacy into the northern colonies. Boston: Carter, Hendee, 1833. Pp. xii, 215.

4510 GREGORY, AMELIO FRANCIS. Historic Fort Independence and Castle Island. Cambridge: L. F. Weston, 1908. Pp. viii.

4511 GRIFFIN, SARA SWAN. "The Battle of Bunker Hill and those who participated therein from the towns from which Lowell was formed." Lowell HSC, 1 (1907-1913), 418-436.

4512 GRIMKE, ARCHIBALD H. "Anti-slavery Boston." NEM, New Ser., 3 (1890-1891), 441-459.

4513 GRINNELL, FRANK WASHBURN. "A brief history of the Social Law Library." MassLQ, 10 (1925), 48-53.

4514 GRISWOLD, WESLEY S. The night the Revolution began: the Boston Tea Party, 1773. Brattleboro, Vt.: S. Greene Pr., 1972. Pp. xv, 160.

4515 "THE GROWTH of a great publishing house: D. C. Heath & Company." Journal of Education, 71 (1910), 652-653.

4516 "THE GROWTH of a great publishing house: D. C. Heath & Company." School Journal, 58 (1899), 749-752.

4517 GUILD, COURTENAY. "Address of Vice President Guild: The Bostonian Society." BSProc, (1932), 21-26.
Historical sketch.

4518 _____. "Men and market of 1826." BSProc, (1927), 24-36.

4519 GUILD, CURTIS. "Bits of old Boston and word pictures of the past." BSPub, 2 Ser., 1 (1916), 9-35.

4520 GUINDON, FREDERICK A. Boston and her story. Boston: D. C. Heath, 1921. Pp. iv, 145.

4521 GULLIVER, FREDERIC PUTNAM. "The geographical development of Boston." Journal of Geography, 2 (1903), 323-329.

4522 HACKER, FRANCIS H. "The British lion roars, but--." NEG, 11 (Winter, 1970), 3-9.
Non-payment of tax by John Hancock on a cargo of wine.

4523 HAGELIN, WLADIMIR and RALPH A. BROWN. "Connecticut farmers at Bunker Hill: the diary of Colonel Experience Storrs." NEQ, 28 (1955), 72-93.

4524 HAGEMANN, HENRY FREDERICK. History does point the way! Rockland Atlas National Bank of Boston, 1833-1958. N.Y.: Newcomen Society in North America, 1958. Pp. 28.

4525 [HAGER, LOUIS P.]. Development of the West End Street Railway of Boston, its transition from primitive horse cars to the grandest and most comprehensive electric railway system in the world, with a complete account of the individuals, firms and corporations that have contributed to the magnificent equipment of the road.... Boston: Hager & Handy, 1893. Pp. 188.

4526 _____. History of the West End Street Railway, in which is included sketches of the early street railways of Boston--consolidation of the various lines--foreign street railways--the Berlin viaduct--anecdotes, etc., together with speeches by President Henry M. Whitney, and others.... Boston, [1892]. Pp. 296.

4527 HALE, EDWARD EVERETT. "Boston Tea Party." Old and New, 9 (1874), 145-150.

4528 _____. "Churches and ministers of Boston." National Magazine, 6 (1897), 533-540.

4529 _____. The contribution of Boston to American independence: oration delivered before the mayor and citizens of Boston at the one hundred and twenty-first celebration of the Declaration of Independence, Monday, July 5, 1897. Boston, 1897. Pp. 40.

4530 _____. "Hills, coves and streets of old Boston." National Magazine, 6 (1897), 434-440.

4531 _____. Historic Boston and its neighborhood.... N.Y.: D. Appleton, 1898. Pp. xv, 186.

4532 _____. Memories of a hundred years. (1902) New ed., rev. N.Y.: Macmillan, 1904. 2v.

4533 _____. "A New England boyhood." Atlantic, 70 (1892), 148-160, 338-346, 495-505, 608-617, 765-776.
Reminiscences.

4534 _____. One hundred years ago: how the war began, a series of sketches from original authorities. Boston: Lockwood, Brooks, 1875. Pp. 40.
Revolution.

4535 _____. "School Street in 1830." BSProc, (1923), 35-37.

4536 [HALE, JAMES W.]. Old Boston Town, early in this century; by an 1801-er. N.Y.: G. F. Nesbitt, [1883?]. Pp. 56.
Signed: Oxygenairian.

4537 HALE, MABEL F. "Boz bewitched Boston." NEG. 10 (Fall, 1968), 22-30.
Charles Dickens' visit in 1842.

4538 _____. "Longfellow hears a nightingale." NEG, 6 (Winter, 1965), 15-24.
A Jenny Lind concert, 1850.

4539   HALE, RICHARD WALDEN, b. 1909. "The first
       independent school in America." CSMP, 35
(1942-1946), 225-297.
       Roxbury Latin School.

4540   _____. "The Shirley-Eustis House." Historic
       Preservation, 20 (1968), 22-25.

4541   _____. Tercentenary history of the Roxbury
       Latin School, 1645-1945. Cambridge: River-
side Pr., 1946. Pp. iv, 170.

4542   HALL, CHARLES WINSLOW. "Jabez Hamlen at
       Bunker Hill." National Magazine, 14 (1901),
271-284.
       Eyewitness account.

4543   HALL, NATHANIEL. A sermon preached in the
       meeting-house of the First Church, Dorches-
ter, on Sunday, June 19, 1870, being the two hundred
and fortieth anniversary of the first assembling of
the church for divine service after its landing in
America. Boston: E. Clapp, 1870. Pp. 27.

4544   HALPERT, STEPHEN and RICHARD JOHNS, comps.
       A return to Pagany; the history, correspond-
ence, and selections from a little magazine, 1929-
1932. Boston: Beacon Pr., 1969. Pp. xviii, 519.

4545   HALSEY, RICHARD TOWNLEY HAINES. The Boston
       Port Bill as pictured by a contemporary Lon-
don cartoonist. N.Y.: Grolier Club, 1904.
Pp. xxix, 333.
       Author attributes cartoons to Philip Dawe.

4546   _____. "English sympathy with Boston during
       the American Revolution." OTNE, 46 (1955-
1956), 85-95.

4547   _____. The influence of the Hancock House
       in the colonies. [N.Y.?, 1924?]. Unpaged.

4548   HAM, WILLIAM T. "Associations of employers
       in the construction industry of Boston."
JEBH, 3 (1930-1931), 55-80.

4549   HAMMOND, JOHN W. "Long Wharf and the old
       salt house." Bostonian, 3 (1895-1896), 181-
185.

4550   HANCOCK, JOHN, 1737-1793. An oration deliv-
       ered March 5, 1774, at the request of the
inhabitants of the town of Boston: to commemorate
the bloody tragedy of the fifth of March 1770.
(1774) 2d. ed. Boston: Edes and Gill, 1774.
Pp. 20.

4551   HANDEL AND HAYDN SOCIETY, BOSTON. History
       of the Handel and Haydn Society of Boston,
Massachusetts.... Boston: A. Mudge & Son, 1883-
1934. 2v. in 3.
       1815-1933.

4552   HANDLIN, OSCAR. Boston's immigrants; a
       study in acculturation. (1941) Rev. and
enl. ed. Cambridge: Harvard Univ. Pr., 1959.
Pp. 382.
       1790-1880.

4553   _____. "A Russian anarchist visits Boston."
       NEQ, 15 (1942), 104-109.
       Michael Bakounin in 1861.

4554   HANDY, DANIEL NASH. The first sixty years,
       the story of the Insurance Library Associa-
tion of Boston, incorporated December 28, 1887; an
historical sketch. Boston, 1947. Pp. 168.

4555   "THE HANOVER Church, Boston." CongQ, 7
       (1865), 29-31.
       Destroyed by fire in 1830.

4556   HANSEN, DAVID. "The First Corps of Cadets of
       Boston." BSProc, (1944), 27-57.

4557   HANSEN, HARRY. The Boston Massacre; an epi-
       sode of dissent and violence. N.Y.: Has-
tings House, 1970. Pp. 191.

4558   HAPGOOD, RICHARD LOCKE. History of the Har-
       vard Dental School. Boston: Harvard Univ.
Dental School, 1930. Pp. xix, 343.

4559   HARASZTI, ZOLTAN. "Brook Farm letters."
       More Books, 12 (1937), 49-68, 93-114.

4560   _____. "A hundred years ago." BPLQ, 4
       (1952), 115-124.
       Centennial of Boston Public Library.

4561   _____. "A hundred years ago." More Books,
       23 (1948), 83-89.
       Boston Public Library.

4562   _____. "Mr. Updike and the Merrymount
       Press." More Books, 10 (1935), 157-173.
       Daniel Berkeley Updike.

4563   HARDAWAY, PAUL A. "Samuel Finley Breese
       Morse and the electric telegraph in Boston."
BSProc, (1947), 31-55.

4564   HARRIMAN, FRANK G. "The Old North Church,
       Boston." Granite Mo, 7 (1884), 46-49.

4565   HARRINGTON, THOMAS FRANCIS. The Harvard
       Medical School; a history, narrative and
documentary, 1782-1905. James Gregory Mumford, ed.
N.Y.: Lewis Publishing, 1905. 3v.

4566   HARRIS, CHARLES E. "Figureheads of the 'Con-
       stitution.'" Antiques, 30 (1936), 10-13.

4567   HARRIS, HENRY. "Church affairs in Boston,
       1720-1730." HistMag, 3 Ser., 1 (1873), 196-
204.
       Ed. by William Stevens Perry.

4568   HARRIS, LOUISE. None but the best; or, the
       story of three pioneers: The Youth's Compan-
ion, Daniel Sharp Ford [and] C. A. Stephens. Providence: C. A. Stephens Collection, Brown Univ.,
1966. Pp. 185.
       'The Youth's Companion' was a periodical pub-
lished in Boston 1827-1929.

4569 HARRIS, MICHAEL H. and GERARD SPIEGLER. "Everett, Ticknor and the common man; the fear of societal instability as the motivation for the founding of the Boston Public Library." Libri, 24 (1974), 249-275.
Edward Everett and George Ticknor.

4570 HARRIS, NEIL. "The Gilded Age revisited: Boston and the museum movement." AmQ, 14 (1962), 545-566.

4571 HARRIS, THADDEUS MASON. "Chronological and topographical account of Dorchester." MHSC, 9 (1804), 147-199.

4572 _____. "Dorchester (Mass.) town records." NEHGR, 21 (1867), 163-168, 269-277, 329-338; 22 (1868), 48-55.
Edited by William Blake Trask.

4573 _____. Memorials of the First Church in Dorchester, from its settlement in New England, to the end of the second century, in two discourses, delivered July 4, 1830.... Boston: Daily Advertiser, 1830. Pp. 67.

4574 HARRISON, LEONARD VANCE. Police administration in Boston. Cambridge: Harvard Univ. Pr., 1934. Pp. viii, 203.

4575 HARRISSON, DAVID, JR. A voice from the Washingtonian Home; being a history of the foundation, rise, and progress of the Washingtonian Home, an institution established at No. 36 Charles Street, Boston, for the reformation of the inebriate; also, a review of some of the evils of intemperance in England, together with a sketch of the temperance reform in America. Boston: Redding, 1860. Pp. xii, 324.

4576 HART, ALBERT BUSHNELL. "Address of Professor Hart: Washington as a Bostonian." BSProc, (1932), 27-41.

4577 HARTE, WALTER BLACKBURN. "The Back Bay: Boston's throne of wealth." Arena, 10 (1894), 1-22.

4577A HARVARD MUSICAL ASSOCIATION, BOSTON. The Harvard Musical Association, 1837-1912. Boston: G. H. Ellis, 1912. Pp. 88.

4578 HARVARD UNIVERSITY. DENTAL SCHOOL. A report of the twentieth anniversary of the Harvard Dental School, March 11, 1889. Boston: A. Mudge & Son, 1890. Pp. 68.

4579 _____. The 75th anniversary of the founding of the dental school of Harvard University; a record of the celebration held at the Harvard Club of Boston, April 16, 1943. 1868-1943. Cambridge, 1944. Pp. 52.

4580 HARVARD UNIVERSITY. MEDICAL SCHOOL. The Harvard Medical School 1783-1933, the celebration of the one hundred and fiftieth anniversary of the opening of the school, October 6th & 7th 1933. Boston, 1933. Unpaged.

4581 _____. The Harvard Medical School, 1782-1906. Harold C. Ernst, ed. [Boston?, 1906]. Pp. xi, 212.

4582 _____. The new century and the new building of the Harvard Medical School, 1783-1883; addresses and exercises at the one hundredth anniversary of the foundation of the medical school of Harvard University, October 17, 1883. Cambridge: J. Wilson and Son, 1884. Pp. 55.
Address by Oliver Wendell Holmes.

4583 HASKELL, CALEB. Caleb Haskell's diary: May 5, 1775-May 30, 1776, a revolutionary soldier's record before Boston and with Arnold's Quebec expedition. Lothrop Withington, ed. Newburyport: W. H. Huse, 1881. Pp. 23.

4584 HASSAM, JOHN TYLER. "The Castle Tavern in Boston." NEHGR, 33 (1879), 400-403.

4585 _____. "The King's Arms Tavern in Boston." NEHGR, 34 (1880), 41-48.

4586 _____. No. 47 Court Street, Boston. Boston: David Clapp & Son, 1903. Pp. 7.

4587 HASTINGS, DANA M. "Boston's little-known packet lines." AmNep, 15 (1955), 133-141.
Early nineteenth century.

4588 HATLEN, THEODORE W. "'Margaret Fleming' and the Boston independent theatre." Educational Theatre Journal, 8 (1956), 17-21.
Play by James A. Herne and its performance in 1891.

4589 HAWES, ALICE M. Glimpses of the old Mount Vernon Church: an informal talk given to the Mount Vernon Young People's Society, Herrick House, December 30, 1923. Boston: Thomas Todd, 1924. Pp. 19. M.

4590 HAWES, FRANK MORTIMER. "Charlestown schools after 1812." Historic Leaves, 4 (1905-1906), 63-74.

4591 _____. "Charlestown schools after 1825." Historic Leaves, 5 (1906-1907), 16-26, 46-52, 67-83, 92-100.

4592 _____. "Charlestown schools after 1793." Historic Leaves, 4 (1905-1906), 38-46.

4593 _____. The Charlestown schools from 1819-20." Historic Leaves, 4 (1905-1906), 90-101.

4594 _____. "Charlestown schools in the 18th century." Historic Leaves, 2 (1903-1904), 58-65; 3 (1904-1905), 11-20.

4595 _____. "Charlestown schools in the 17th century." Historic Leaves, 2 (1903-1904), 15-21, 32-42.

4596 _____. "Charlestown schools within the peninsula." Historic Leaves, 3 (1904-1905), 43-48, 64-68.

4597 _____. "Charlestown schools without the peninsula." Historic Leaves, 4 (1905-1906), 14-22.

4598 _____. "The schools of Charlestown beyond the neck--Revolutionary period." OTNE, 3 (1904-1905), 87-93.

4599 HAWES, JOSIAH JOHNSON. The legacy of Josiah Johnson Hawes; 19th century photographs of Boston. Rachel Johnston Homer, ed. Barre: Barre Publisher, 1972. Pp. 131.
1840-1870.

4600 HAWKES, BENJAMIN. "Letters relating to the destruction of the Ursuline Convent, Charlestown." United States Catholic Historical Magazine, 3 (1890), 274-277.

4601 [HAWKES, JAMES]. A retrospect of the Boston Tea-Party, with a memoir of George R. T. Hewes, a survivor of the little band of patriots who drowned the tea in Boston Harbour in 1773. By a Citizen of New-York. N.Y.: S. S. Bliss, 1834. Pp. 209.

4602 HAYDEN, WILLIAM R. "The discovery of ether." Bostonian, 3 (1895-1896), 315-328.
William Thomas Green Morton, at Massachusetts General Hospital.

4603 HAYES, JOHN S. Souvenir of Coeur de Lion Commandery, Knights Templars, Charlestown, Mass. Somerville: Somerville Journal, 1896. Pp. 53. MB.

4604 HAYNES, GIDEON. Pictures from prison life: an historical sketch of the Massachusetts State Prison, with narratives and incidents, and suggestions on discipline. Boston: Lee and Shepard, 1869. Pp. 290.

4605 HAYWARD, ARTHUR H. "Boston's second tea party." OTNE, 30 (1939-1940), 10-14.
An 1874 'guessing contest.'

4606 _____. "When Boston Harbor froze." OTNE, 39 (1948-1949), 76-79.
1844.

4607 HEALY, WILLIAM and AUGUSTA F. BONNER. Delinquents and criminals, their making and unmaking; studies in two American cities. N.Y.: Macmillan, 1926. Pp. viii, 317.
Boston and Chicago.

4608 HEARD, JOHN R. Boston theatres and halls, with historical notes past and present; chronology of principal dramatic and musical events. Boston: W. B. Jones, 1907. Unpaged.

4609 HEARD, JOHN THEODORE. A historical account of Columbian Lodge of Free and Accepted Masons of Boston, Mass. Boston: A. Mudge and Son, 1856. Pp. xi, 592.

4610 HEATH, D. C. AND COMPANY. Forty years of service, published in commemoration of the fortieth anniversary of D. C. Heath and Company.... Boston, 1925. Pp. 61.

4611 HEATH, EDWIN G. "From 'Round Marsh' to Public Garden." Bostonian, 2 (1895), 629-636.
Park.

4612 HELMS, EDGAR JAMES. Pioneering in modern city missions. Boston: Morgan Memorial, 1927. Pp. 136.
Morgan Memorial.

4613 HENDERSON, A. F. Boston national banks and trust companies, 1898-1909; showing in detail all changes which have taken place and a comparative table of growth of all institutions during the past ten years. Boston: Lovell & Henderson, 1909. Unpaged.

4614 HENDRICK, IVES, ed. The birth of an institute: twenty-fifth anniversary, the Boston Psychoanalytic Institute, November 30, 1958. Freeport, Me.: B. Wheelwright, 1961. Pp. xiv, 164.

4615 HENRETTA, JAMES A. "Economic development and social structure in colonial Boston." WMQ, 3 Ser., 22 (1965), 75-92.

4616 HENSHAW, WILLIAM. The orderly book of Colonel William Henshaw, of the American army, April 20-Sept. 26, 1775, including a memoir by Emory Washburn, and notes by Charles C. Smith. Harriet E. Henshaw, ed. Boston: A. Williams, 1881. Pp. xiv, 167.
Orderly books for September 1, 1775 through October 3, 1776 appear in the 'Proceedings' of the American Antiquarian Society for April, 1947.

4617 HEPBURN, ANDREW. Boston: the story of a great American city and its contribution to our national heritage. N.Y.: Scholastic Book Services, 1966. Pp. 158.

4618 HERLIHY, ELISABETH M. "The physical development of Boston." Our Boston, 1 (March, 1926), 7-15.

4619 HERNDON, RICHARD, comp. Boston of to-day; a glance at its history and characteristics, with biographical sketches and portraits of many of its professional and business men. Edwin Munroe Bacon, ed. Boston: Post Publishing, 1892. Pp. vi, 461.

4620 HERSEY, HORATIO BROOKS. "The old West End, Boston." OTNE, 20 (1929-1930), 162-177.

4621 HEWLETT, RICHARD G. "Josiah Quincy: reform mayor of Boston." NEQ, 24 (1951), 179-196.

4622 HEYWOOD, HERBERT. "China in New England." NEM, New Ser., 28 (1903), 473-483.
Boston's Chinese community.

4623 HICHBORN, BENJAMIN. An oration, delivered March 5th, 1777, at the request of the inhabitants of the town of Boston; to commemorate the bloody tragedy of the fifth of March, 1770. Boston: Edes and Gill, 1777. Pp. 18.

4624 HIGHAM, ROBIN D. S. "The port of Boston and the embargo of 1807-1809." AmNep, 16 (1956), 189-210.

4625 HILDRETH, RICHARD. My connection with the Atlas newspaper; including a sketch of the history of the Amory Hall party of 1838, and an account of the senatorial and representative elections in the city of Boston for the year 1839, so far as the question of sustaining the license law of 1838 was involved therein. Boston: Whipple and Damrell, 1839. Pp. 24.

4626 HILL, AMELIA L. "The news of the evacuation of Boston and the Declaration of Independence." NEM, New Ser., 14 (1896), 317-322.

4627 HILL, EDWIN BURLINGAME. "Musical Boston in the gay 90's." Etude, 67 (1949), 9, 53, 55, 71, 118-119, 148, 186, 224, 264-265, 290, 298.

4628 HILL, HAMILTON ANDREWS. "Boston and Liverpool packet lines, sail and steam." NEM, New Ser., 9 (1893-1894), 545-563.

4629 _____. Boston's trade and commerce for forty years, 1844-1884. Boston: T. R. Marvin & Son, 1884. Pp. 20.

4630 _____. "Governor Winthrop's homestead." NEM, New Ser., 13 (1895-1896), 727-736.

4631 _____. History of the Old South Church (Third Church) Boston, 1669-1884. Boston: Houghton Mifflin, 1890. 2v.
Vol. 2 contains an extensive bibliography by A. P. C. Griffin.

4632 _____. "Old Milk Street, Boston." NEM, New Ser., 12 (1895), 97-106.

4633 _____. 1669-1882, an historical catalogue of the Old South Church (Third Church) Boston. Boston, 1883. Pp. x, 370.

4634 _____. The trade and commerce of Boston, 1630 to 1890. Boston: Damrell & Upham, 1895. Pp. 163.

4635 HILL, WILLIAM CARROLL. A century of genealogical progress, being a history of the New England Historic Genealogical Society, 1845-1945. Boston: New England Historic Genealogical Society, 1945. Pp. 99.

4636 _____. History of the Cecilia Society, Boston, Mass. 1874-1917. [Boston, 1917].
Pp. 24.
A choral society.

4637 "HILLS and vallies [sic] of Boston Common, 1772, and first celebration of American independence in the town, 1777." AmHist Record, 2 (1873), 167-169.
Signed: "Robinson."

4638 HILTON, WILLIAM B. "A checklist of Boston plane makers." CEAIA, 27 (1974), 23-27.

4639 HIRSHBERG, ALBERT. The Red Sox, the bean and the cod. Boston: Waverly House, 1947. Pp. viii, 220.

4640 "HISTORIC processions in Boston from 1789 to 1824." BSPub, 5 (1908), 65-119.

4641 HISTORICAL review of the Boston Bijou Theatre, with the original casts of all the operas that have been produced at the Bijou, and with photographs illustrative of the various scenes in them. Boston: Edward O. Shelton, 1884. Unpaged.

4642 A HISTORICAL sketch of Boston, containing a brief account of its settlement, rise and progress, with a glance at its present and prospective prosperity. Boston: E. L. Mitchell, 1861. Pp. 96.

4643 "HISTORICAL sketch of the first public Mass in Boston." American Catholic Historical Researches, 6 (1889), 19-20.
1789.

4644 "HISTORY of the Boston Type Foundry." Printers' Bulletin, (June, 1867).

4645 HISTORY of the great conflagration; or, Boston and its destruction, embracing a brief history of its early settlement and progress to date: together with a full and graphic account of its destruction by fire, on the 9th and 10th of November, 1872.... Philadelphia: W. Flint, 1872. Pp. iii, 142.

4646 "HISTORY of the New England Water Works Association, 1877-1974." New England Water Works Association. Journal, 88 (1974), 119-167.

4647 THE HISTORY of the Westminster Case. Boston, 1902. Unpaged. M.
Height of public buildings.

4648 HITCHCOCK, HENRY RUSSELL. Boston architecture, 1637-1954; including other communities within easy driving distance. N.Y.: Reinhold Publishing, 1954. Pp. 64.

4649 _____. "The Boston State House." Architectural Record, 65 (1929), 98.

4650 HITCHINGS, SINCLAIR H. "Joseph Belknap's printing in Boston." PAGA, 6 (1958), 95-107; 7 (1958), 23-26.

4651 _____. and CATHERINE H. FARLOW. A new guide to the Massachusetts State House. [Boston, 1964]. Pp. 108.

4652 HITCHINS, MRS. JOHN B. "Notes on Summer Street and Church Green." About the First, (May, 1939), 4-5.

4653 HODGKINSON, HAROLD DANIEL. "Miracle in Boston." MHSP, 84 (1972), 71-81.
Major public building projects, 1952-1972.

4653A HOFF, HEBBEL E. and JOHN F. FULTON. "The centenary of the first American Physiological Society founded at Boston by William A. Alcott and Sylvester Graham." BHistMed, 5 (1937), 687-734.

4654 HOLBROOK, STEWART H. "Boston's temple of burlesque." American Mercury, 58 (1944), 411-416.
Old Howard Theater.

4655 _____. "Murder at Harvard." American Scholar, 14 (1945), 425-434.
John W. Webster's murder of George Parkman.

4656 HOLDEN, WHEATON A. "The Peabody touch: Peabody and Stearns of Boston, 1870-1917." Soc ArchHistJ, 32 (1973), 114-131.
Robert S. Peabody and John G. Stearns.

4657 HOLLIS, HELEN RICE. "Jonas Chickering: 'the father of American pianoforte-making.'" Antiques, 104 (1973), 227-230.

4658 HOLMES, CHARLES NEVERS. "The beacon on Beacon Hill." MagHist, 20 (1915), 41-42.

4659 HOLMES, OLIVER WENDELL. Dr. Holmes's Boston. Caroline Ticknor, ed. Boston: Houghton Mifflin, 1915. Pp. xiv, 213.
Nineteenth-century intellectual life.

4660 HOLMES, PAULINE. One hundred years of Mount Vernon Church, 1842-1942. Boston: Mount Vernon Church, 1942. Pp. xv, 221.

4661 _____. A tercentenary history of the Boston Public Latin School, 1635-1935. Cambridge: Harvard Univ., 1935. Pp. xxiv, 541.

4662 HOLMES, THOMAS JAMES. "The bookbindings of John Ratcliff and Edmund Ranger, seventeenth-century Boston bookbinders." AASP, New Ser., 38 (1928), 31-50.

4663 HOLT, ANNA C. "The library of the Harvard Medical School, 1847 and 1947." HarvLibBul, 2 (1948), 32-43.

4664 HOLZMAN, THOMAS. Municipal employee unions in Boston: 1900-1970. Lynn: Massachusetts Public Finance Project, 1974. Pp. 55. M.

4665 [HOMANS, ISAAC SMITH]. History of Boston, from 1630 to 1856.... Boston: F. C. Moore, 1856. Pp. 246.

4666 [_____]. Sketches of Boston, past and present, and of some few places in its vicinity.... Boston: Phillips, Sampson, 1851. Pp. viii, 246, 112.

4667 HOME AND SCHOOL VISITORS ASSOCIATION, BOSTON. Past and present, what of the future? n.p., 1941. Pp. 16. M.
Social service agency.

4668 HOME SAVINGS BANK, BOSTON. 60 years on Tremont Street. n.p., [1929?]. Unpaged. M.

4669 HORR, GEORGE EDWIN J. Sermon on the seventy-fifth anniversary of the First Baptist Sunday School, Charlestown, Mass...April 15, 1888. Boston: McDonald, Gill, [1888?]. Pp. 17. M.

4670 HORSFORD, EBEN NORTON. "The Indian names of Boston, and their meaning." NEHGR, 40 (1886), 94-103.

4671 HORTON, HOWARD LEAVITT. New England aspects: Boston, Hingham and the South Shore.... [Boston?], 1949. Unpaged.

4672 _____. New England sampler: Boston, Hingham and the South Shore. Boston, 1950. v.p. MB.

4673 HOSPITAL COUNCIL OF BOSTON. Five years, 1935-1939. Boston, [1940]. Pp. 16. M.

4674 _____. Five years, 1940-1944. Boston, [1945?]. Pp. 15. M.

4675 HOUGHTON GORNEY FLOWER SHOP. Park Street in ye olde tymes, being a few interesting facts about Centry Street and the vicinity close by. Boston, 1929. Unpaged.

4676 [HOUGHTON MIFFLIN COMPANY]. Fifty years of publishing: a history of the Educational Department of Houghton Mifflin Company. Boston, 1930. Pp. 31.

4677 _____. A half-century of children's books. Boston: Houghton, 1930. Pp. 32.
Juvenile department, 1880-1930.

4678 _____. Of the making of books and of the part played therein by the publishing house of Houghton Mifflin Company. [Boston, 191-?]. Pp. 16.

4679 _____. Park Street, new and old, 1828-1923. Boston, 1923. Pp. 15.
Houghton Mifflin, publishers.

4680 HOUSING ASSOCIATION OF METROPOLITAN BOSTON. A statistical review of ten years of building activity in Boston (residential construction and demolition), 1930-1940. Boston, 1940. 13 leaves.

4681 [HOVEY, WILLIAM ALFRED], comp. A golden anniversary, the Transcript's fiftieth birthday, a long look backward. Boston, 1880. Pp. 51.
Boston Evening Transcript.

4682 HOWARD, MARION. "Three Boston judges." Granite Mo, 14 (1892), 147-151.
Caleb Blodgett, William Josiah Forsaith and Joseph Henry Hardy.

4683 _____. "Two Boston artists." Granite Mo, 14 (1892), 53-55.
Daniel J. Strain and Scott Leighton.

4784 HOWARD BENEVOLENT SOCIETY IN THE CITY OF BOSTON. Historical sketch...with the 42d annual report, amended act of incorporation and by-laws. Boston, 1852. Pp. 20.
Charity.

4685 HOWARD SUNDAY SCHOOL, BOSTON. The Howard Sunday School during seventy-five years, and the work of Rev. S. H. Winkley. Boston: Alfred Mudge & Son, 1902. Pp. 41.

4686   HOWE, DANIEL WALKER. The Unitarian con-
        science: Harvard moral philosophy, 1805-
1861. Cambridge: Harvard Univ. Pr., 1970.
Pp. viii, 398.

4687   HOWE, HELEN HUNTINGTON. The gentle Ameri-
        cans, 1864-1960; biography of a breed. N.Y.:
Harper & Row, 1965. Pp. xix, 458.
        Intellectual life.

4688   HOWE, JULIA WARD. "A chronicle of Boston
        clubs." NEM, New Ser., 34 (1906), 610-615.

4689   _____. "Social Boston, past and present."
        Harper's Bazaar, 43 (1909), 105-110.

4690   HOWE, MARK ANTONY DE WOLFE, ed. The articu-
        late sisters: passages from journals and
letters of the daughters of President Josiah Quincy
of Harvard University. Cambridge: Harvard Univ.
Pr., 1946. Pp. 249.
        Social life and customs.

4691   _____. The Atlantic Monthly and its makers.
        Boston: Atlantic Monthly Pr., 1919.
Pp. 106.

4692   _____. Boston Common: scenes from four cen-
        turies. Cambridge: Riverside Pr., 1910.
Pp. x, 87.

4693   _____. Boston landmarks. N.Y.: Hastings
        House, 1946. Pp. 133.

4694   _____. "'The Boston religion.'" Atlantic,
        91 (1903), 729-738.
        Unitarian controversy.

4695   _____. and JOHN N. BURK. The Boston Sym-
        phony Orchestra, 1881-1931. (1914) Semi-
centennial ed., rev. and extended. Boston: Houghton Mifflin, 1931. Pp. vii, 273.

4696   HOWE, MARK ANTONY DE WOLFE. Boston, the
        place and the people. N.Y.: Macmillan,
1903. Pp. xv, 397.

4697   _____. "Episodes of Boston commerce." At-
        lantic, 91 (1903), 175-184.

4698   [_____]. I'm from Boston: scenes from the
        living past, illustrated by picture and sto-
ry. Boston: Atlantic Monthly Pr., 1920. Unpaged.
        Historic houses.

4699   _____, ed. Later years of the Saturday Club,
        1870-1920. Boston: Houghton Mifflin, 1927.
Pp. xvii, 427.
        Successor to 'The early years of the Satur-
        day Club, 1855-1870' by Edward Waldo Emerson
        and predecessor of 'The Saturday Club:
        a century completed, 1920-1956' by Edward W.
        Forbes.

4700   _____. Memories of a hostess; a chronicle
        of eminent friendships drawn chiefly from
the diaries of Mrs. James T. Fields. Boston: Atlantic Monthly Pr., 1922. Pp. 312.
        Includes Oliver Wendell Holmes, Charles
        Dickens, Sarah Orne Jewett and Annie Adams
        Fields.

4701   _____. A partial (and not impartial) semi-
        centennial history of the Tavern Club, 1884-
1934. [Boston]: Tavern Club, 1934. Pp. x, 273.

4702   HOWELLS, WILLIAM DEAN. "Recollections of an
        Atlantic editorship." Atlantic, 100 (1907),
594-606.
        Atlantic Monthly.

4703   HOYT, ALBERT H. "Brief history of the Reg-
        ister." NEHGR, 30 (1876), 184-188.
        'New England Historical and Genealogical
        Register,' 1846-1876.

4704   HUBBARD, JAMES MASCARENE. "Boston in 1710:
        preparing for a small war." BSPub, 3 (1906),
9-37.
        Arrival of small English fleet, at first
        thought to be French.

4705   _____. "Boston's last town meetings and
        first city election." BSPub, 6 (1910), 91-
117.
        1822.

4706   HUDSON, CHARLES. Doubts concerning the Bat-
        tle of Bunker Hill, addressed to the Chris-
tian public. Boston: J. Munroe, 1857. Pp. 41.

4707   HUGGINS, NATHAN IRVIN. Protestants against
        poverty: Boston's charities, 1870-1900.
Westport, Conn.: Greenwood, 1971. Pp. xiv, 225.

4708   HULTMAN, EUGENE C. "A brief history of the
        Boston Fire Department." Our Boston, 2
(February, 1927) 14-16.

4709   _____. "History of Boston's water supply,
        1652-1940." BSProc, (1948), 41-51.

4710   HUMPHREY, GRACE. Father takes us to Boston.
        Philadelphia: Penn Publishing, 1928.
Pp. 239.

4711   HUMPHREY, MARTHA BURNHAM. An eye for music.
        Boston: Algonquin Pr., 1949. Pp. 108.
        Boston Symphony Orchestra.

4712   HUNNEWELL, JAMES FROTHINGHAM. "An American
        shrine: the First Church." NEHGR, 24
(1870), 273-285.
        First Church, Charlestown.

4713   _____. Bibliography of Charlestown, Massa-
        chusetts, and Bunker Hill.... Boston:
J. R. Osgood, 1880. Pp. vii, 100.
        Additions appear in Hunnewell's 'A century of
        town life.' Boston, 1888, pp. 261-300.

4714   _____. A century of town life: a history of
        Charlestown, Massachusetts, 1775-1887, with
surveys, records and twenty-eight pages of plans and
views. Boston: Little, Brown, 1888. Pp. xiv, 316.

4715   _____. "The condition of Naval affairs in
        Boston in 1812." MHSP, 2 Ser., 16 (1902),
181-186.

4716   _____. "A very old corner of Boston."
        BSPub, 2 (1905), 7-27.
        Head of State Street.

4717 HUNTER, ALEXANDER. "Confederate prisoners in Boston." NEM, New Ser., 23 (1900-1901), 683-697.

4718 HUNTER, EDWARD W. "China's role in the Boston Tea Party." China Weekly Review, 57 (June 6, 1931), 37.

4719 HURLEY, JOHN F. "Hyde Park." Our Boston, 2 (June, 1927), 14-17.

4720 HURST, CHARLES W. French and German immigrants into Boston, 1751. Milford, Conn., 1968. Pp. 15. MBNEH.

4721 HURWICH, LOUIS. "Jewish education in Boston." Jewish Education, 26 (1956), 22-34. 1843-1954.

4722 HUSE, CHARLES PHILLIPS. The financial history of Boston from May 1, 1822, to January 31, 1909. Cambridge: Harvard Univ. Pr., 1916. Pp. ix, 395.

4723 HYDE PARK, MASS. Memorial sketch of Hyde Park, Mass., for the first twenty years of its corporate existence, also its industries, statistics, and organizations, together with the anniversary addresses, delivered by Rev. Perley B. Davis, and Rev. Richard J. Barry. Jos. King Knight, Edmund Davis, Henry B. Humphrey, comps. Boston: L. Barta, 1888. Pp. 96.
1868-1888.

4724 HYDE PARK, MASS. FIRST BAPTIST CHURCH. Directory of the First Baptist Church, Hyde Park, Mass. with historical sketch. Hyde Park: Fairmount Pr., 1909. Unpaged. MBNEH.

4725 _____. Historical sketch and directory of the First Baptist Church, Hyde Park, Mass. Hyde Park: Hyde Park Gazette, 1905. Pp. 44. MBNEH.
Historical sketch by Jennie M. Stone.

4726 _____. Manual of the First Baptist Church, Hyde Park, containing historical sketch.... Boston: W. Richardson, 1878. Pp. 33.

4727 "HYDE Park and Fairmount Society for Mutual Improvement." HPHR, 2 (1892-1893), 13-14. Civic improvement society.

4728 HYDE PARK CENTENNIAL COMMITTEE. The first hundred years, 1868-1968. [Hyde Park, 1968]. Pp. 64.

4729 ILLUSTRATED Boston, the metropolis of New England. 1889. N.Y.: American Publishing and Engraving, [1889]. Pp. xiii, 305.

4730 IN and about historic Boston. Portland, Me.: L. H. Nelson, 1908. Unpaged.

4731 "IN BUSINESS one hundred years." American Lumberman, (March 18, 1911), 67. Davenport, Peters, Co., lumber.

4732 "INCIDENTS in the Siege of Boston, in 1775." AmHist Record, 1 (1872), 546-550.

4733 "INDIANS at Boston." Palimpsest, 9 (1928), 338-346. Arrived from Iowa in 1837.

4734 INGRAHAM, FERN. "A visit to the Harrison Gray Otis House." OTNE, 29 (1938-1939), 21-31.
Cambridge Street.

4735 INSTITUTION FOR SAVINGS IN ROXBURY, ROXBURY, MASS. A century of savings bank service; the story of the First Savings Bank in Roxbury, published in the 100th anniversary of the incorporation of the Institution for Savings in Roxbury and its Vicinity. Boston: Livermore & Knight, 1925. Pp. 22.

4736 INSURANCE LIBRARY ASSOCIATION OF BOSTON. A catalogue of the library of the Insurance Library Association of Boston; to which is added a sketch of the history and work of the association, together with other information. Henry E. Hess, comp. Boston: F. Wood, 1899. Pp. xiv, 267.

4737 "AN INTERESTING Boston handicraft." SWJ, 43 (1928), 499-506. Paul Revere Pottery, established 1908.

4738 INTERNATIONAL TYPOGRAPHICAL UNION OF NORTH AMERICA. UNION NO. 13, BOSTON. Illustrated historical souvenir, fiftieth aniversary, 1848-1898, Boston Typographical Union, No. 13, December 14, 1898. Boston: Rockwell & Churchill, 1898. Pp. 160.

4739 _____. Leaves of history from the archives of Boston Typographical Union no. XIII, from the foundation of the Boston Typographical Society to the diamond jubilee of its successor. Boston: Wright & Potter, 1923. Pp. xiv, 125.

4740 JACKSON, FRANK H. Monograph of the Boston Opera House, MDCCCCIX. Boston: W. A. Butterfield, 1909. Unpaged.

4741 JACKSON, MARY C. Statement of the history and operation of the loan fund [of the Associated Charities of Boston]. [Boston, 1898]. Pp. 15.

4742 JACKSON, RUSSELL LEIGH. "Benjamin Leigh and the Boston Massacre." OTNE, 34 (1943-1944), 31-33.

4743 JACKSON & CURTIS, BOSTON. Fifty years of finance. Boston, 1929. Pp. 59. Investment bankers.

4744 JACOBITE CLUB, BOSTON. The Jacobite Club. [Boston], 1909. Pp. 26. The club consisted of members of the Harvard class of 1857; historical sketch signed: J. M. [Joseph May].

4745 JACOBS, DONALD M. "The nineteenth-century struggle of segregated education in Boston schools." JNegroEd, 39 (1970), 76-85.

4746 _____. "William Lloyd Garrison's 'Liberator' and Boston's Blacks, 1830-1865." NEQ, 44 (1971), 259-277.

4747 JACOBS, WARREN. "Boston: old depots."
RLHSB, No. 4 (1923), 3-13.

4748 JAHER, FREDERIC COPLE. "Businessman and
gentleman: Nathan and Thomas Gold Appleton—
an exploration in intergenerational history."
EEH, 2 Ser., 4 (1966-1967), 17-39.

4749 _____. "Nineteenth-century elites in Boston
and New York." JSocHist, 6 (1972-1973),
32-77.

4750 JAMAICA PLAIN, MASS. BAPTIST CHURCH. A
brief history of the Jamaica Plain Baptist
Church of West Roxbury.... Boston: Rand, Avery &
Frye, 1871. Pp. 59.

4751 JAMAICA PLAIN, MASS. ST. ANDREW'S METHODIST
CHURCH. Fiftieth anniversary, November 2-9,
1941.... n.p., [1941?]. Unpaged. MBNEH.

4752 JANEWAY, JAMES. A seasonable and earnest address to the citizens of London, soon after
the dreadful fire which consumed the famous metropolis, in the year 1666...to which is added, Dr.
Smollett's account of the said conflagration, and
the imputed causes thereof, taken from his History
of England, together with a particular relation of
the great fire of Boston, in New-England; which
broke out at the Brazen-Head, in Cornhill, about two
o'clock in the morning, on March 20, 1760. Boston:
Fowle and Draper, 1760. Pp. 55.

4753 JARMAN, RUFUS. "Big boom in Boston." Am
Heritage, 20 (October, 1969), 46-49, 81-82.
An 1869 musical extravaganza known as the
National Peace Jubilee.

4754 JEFFRIES, B. JOY. "The experiences of a
loyalist physician in Boston in 1775." Mag
Hist, 5 (1907), 357-364.
John Jeffries.

4755 JENKES, FRANCIS H. "Boston musical compos-
ers." NEM, New Ser., 1 (1889-1890), 475-483.

4756 JENKS, HENRY F. "Old School Street." NEM,
New Ser., 13 (1895-1896), 259-272.

4757 JENKS, WILLIAM. "An account of the Massachusetts Historical Society." MHSC, 3 Ser.,
7 (1838), 5-26.

4758 JENNEY, CHARLES FRANCIS. "Historical field
day." HPHR, 4 (1904), 101-111.
Historic houses in Hyde Park.

4759 JENNINGS, JOHN EDWARD. Boston, cradle of
liberty, 1630-1776. Garden City, N.Y.:
Doubleday, 1947. Pp. x, 335.

4760 "JOHN Brown and his friends." Atlantic, 30
(1872), 50-61.
Visit to Boston, March, 1858.

4761 JOHN Hancock Mutual Life Insurance Company,
Boston. The first seventy-five years.
[Boston, 1937]. Pp. 67.

4762 "JOHN P. Squire Company." Industry, 7
(March, 1942), 19-22.
Pork products.

4763 "JOHN Singleton Copley's houses on Beacon
Hill, Boston." OTNE, 25 (1934-1935), 85-95.

4764 JOHNSON, ARTHUR MENZIES and BARRY E. SUPPLE.
Boston capitalists and western railroads: a
study in the nineteenth-century railroad investment
process. Cambridge: Harvard Univ. Pr., 1967.
Pp. x, 392.

4765 JOHNSON, FRED L. "A review of the proceedings of the Society since 1892." HPHR 3
(1903), 36-42; 4 (1904), 92-100; 5 (1905), 58-67;
6 (1908), 57-64; 7 (1909), 55-63; 8 (1912), 59-63.
Hyde Park Historical Society.

4766 JOHNSON, FREDERICK. "The ancient fishweir
in the Back Bay." BSProc, (1943), 27-32.

4767 JOHNSON, HAROLD EARLE. Hallelujah, amen!
The story of the Handel and Haydn Society of
Boston. Boston: B. Humphries, 1965. Pp. 256.

4768 _____. Musical interludes in Boston, 1795-
1830. N.Y.: Columbia Univ. Pr., 1943.
Pp. xv, 366.

4769 _____. "The musical Von Hagens." NEQ, 16
(1943), 110-117.
Family of musicians who also published music,
1796-1833.

4770 _____. Symphony Hall, Boston; with a list of
works performed by the Boston Symphony Orchestra, compiled by members of the staff of Symphony Hall. Boston: Little, Brown, 1950. Pp. vii, 431.

4771 JOHNSON, HARRIET E. "The early history of
Arlington Street Church." UHSP, 5, Pt. 2,
(1937), 15-33.

4772 JOHNSON, JAMES C. "East Boston long ago."
Bostonian, 2 (1895), 409-411.

4773 _____. "The introduction of the study of
music into the public schools of Boston and
of America." Bostonian, 1 (1894-1895), 622-632.

4774 _____. "The new land, the site of the old
Mill Pond in 1827." Bostonian, 2 (1895),
72-76.

4775 JOHNSON, THOMAS LYNN. The early years of the
Saturday Club. Cleveland: The Rowfant Club,
1921. Pp. 69.

4776 JONES, FRANK N. "The old State House." Bostonian, 2 (1895), 77-82.

4777 JONES, H. L. "The part played by Boston publishers of 1860-1900 in the field of children's books." Horn Book, 45 (1969), 20-28, 153-159,
329-336.

4778 JONES, JOHN E. "State House of Massachusetts." National Magazine, 28 (April, 1908),
[12 unnumbered pages at end of issue].

4779 JONES, JOSHUA H., JR. "Boston Harbor and its islands." Our Boston, 1 (July, 1926), 18-25.

4780 _____. "Boston's market problem awaits the attention of women." Our Boston, 1 (January, 1926), 13-18.

4781 JORDAN MARSH & CO., BOSTON. The story of a store: a brief record by word and picture showing the development, extent and convenient arrangement of New England's largest retail store. Boston, [1912?]. Pp. 32.

4782 ["JORDAN Marsh Co. diamond jubilee."]. Fellow Worker, 9, No. 1, (1926), entire issue.

4783 JUDGE, JOSEPH. "Those proper and other Bostonians." National Geographic Magazine, 146 (1974), 352-380.
Social life and customs.

4784 JUDGE BAKER GUIDANCE CENTER, BOSTON. The story of twenty-five years, 1917-1942, Judge Baker Guidance Center, a service for childhood and youth, formerly the Judge Baker Foundation, established by Frederick Pickering Cabot. Boston, 1942. Pp. 29.
Reform school.

4785 JULIEN, MATTHEW CANTINE. The Huguenots of old Boston. [New York?, 1895?]. Pp. 21.

4786 KAESE, HAROLD. The Boston Braves. N.Y.: G. P. Putnam's Sons, 1948. Pp. ix, 269.

4787 KAPLAN, SIDNEY. "The reduction of teachers' salaries in post-Revolutionary Boston." NEQ, 21 (1948), 373-379.

4788 KARNAGHAN, ANNE WEBB. "Early days of the Museum and present functions." Our Boston, 3 (April, 1928), 7-11.
Museum of Fine Arts.

4789 _____. "Fifty years of the Museum School." Our Boston, 3 (February, 1928), 12-15.
Museum of Fine Arts.

4790 KATZ, MICHAEL B. "The emergence of bureaucracy in urban education: the Boston case, 1850-1884." HistEdQ, 8 (1968), 155-188, 319-357.

4791 KEITH, ELMER D. and WILLIAM L. WARREN. "Peter Banner, architect, moves from New Haven to Boston." OTNE, 57 (1966-1967), 57-76.

4792 KELLOGG, AUGUSTA W. "The Boston Athenaeum." NEM, New Ser., 29 (1903-1904), 167-185.

4793 KELLY, RALPH. Boston in the 1830's--and the 'William Penn.' N.Y.: Newcomen Society of England, American Branch, 1947. Pp. 40.
Boston and Worcester Railroad.

4794 KENNEDY, ALBERT JOSEPH. "The South End." Our Boston, 2 (December, 1926), 13-19.

4795 _____. and ROBERT A. WOODS. The zone of emergence; observations of the lower middle and upper working class communities of Boston, 1905-1914. (1962) Abridged and edited, with a preface by Sam Bass Warner, Jr. 2d ed. Cambridge: M.I.T. Pr., 1969. Pp. vi, 219.

4796 KENNEY, WILLIAM F. Centenary of the See of Boston: a newspaper man's compilation of the leading events of the one hundredth anniversary of the Diocese of Boston, Oct., Nov., 1908. Boston: J. K. Waters, 1909. Pp. 264.

4797 KENT, LOUISE ANDREWS and ELIZABETH KENT TARSHIS. In good old colony times; a historical picture book. Boston: Houghton Mifflin, 1941. Pp. xii, 99.
Social life and customs.

4798 KERBER, LINDA K. "Science in the early republic: the Society for the Study of Natural Philosophy." WMQ, 3 Ser., 29 (1972), 263-280.

4799 KETCHUM, RICHARD M. The battle for Bunker Hill. Garden City, N.Y.: Doubleday, 1962. Pp. 232.

4800 KEYES, FREDERICK ANTHONY, ed. The Guild of Saint Apollonia, a brief historical sketch. Boston: Pilot Publishing, 1924. Pp. 120.
Roman Catholic dentists.

4801 KEYES, HOMER EATON. "The Boston State House in blue Staffordshire." Antiques, 1 (1922), 115-120.

4802 _____. "A note on the Seymour manner." Antiques, 32 (1937), 179-180.
John and Thomas Seymour, cabinetmakers.

4803 KIDDER, FREDERIC. History of the Boston Massacre, March 5, 1770; consisting of the narrative of the town, the trial of the soldiers: and a historical introduction, containing unpublished documents of John Adams, and explanatory notes. Albany: J. Munsell, 1870. Pp. 291

4804 KILEY, JOHN C. "Changes in realty values in the nineteenth and twentieth centuries." BBHS, 15 (1941), 33-41.

4805 KILGOUR, RAYMOND LINCOLN. Estes and Lauriat: a history, 1872-1898: with a brief account of Dana Estes and Company, 1898-1914. Ann Arbor, Univ. of Michigan Pr., 1957. Pp. 238.
Publisher and bookseller.

4806 _____. Messrs. Roberts Brothers, publishers. Ann Arbor: Univ. of Michigan Pr., 1952. Pp. xv, 307.

4807 KILHAM, WALTER HARRINGTON. Boston after Bulfinch: an account of its architecture 1800-1900. Cambridge: Harvard Univ. Pr., 1946. Pp. xv, 114.

4808 KIMBALL, FISKE. "The first remodeling of the Province House, 1728." OTNE, 62 (1971-1972), 93-94.

4809 KIMBALL, GEORGE A. "The Boston Elevated Railway." NEM, New Ser., 24 (1901), 455-468.

4810   KIMBALL, HERBERT W., ed. "A British officer in Boston in 1775." MagHist, 18 (1914), 1-15.
An unsigned diary which Kimball attributes to Lt. Thorne or Lt. Hamilton of the King's Own 4th Regiment.

4811   KIMBALL, JAMES. "The one hundredth anniversary of the destruction of tea in Boston Harbor." EIHC, 12 (1874), 197-239.

4812   KING, DEXTER S., ed. History of the North Russell Street M. E. Church and Sabbath School; with a brief account of St. John's Church at the Odeon. Boston: Geo. C. Rand & Avery, 1861. Pp. 99.

4813   KING, HENRY MELVILLE. Historical discourse delivered on the fiftieth anniversary of the organization of the Dudley-Street Baptist Church, Boston (formerly Roxbury), Mass., March 9, 1871. Boston: Rand, Avery, & Frye, 1871. Pp. 67.

4814   KING, MARY FIFIELD. First Parish Church in Dorchester: tercentenary celebration, 1630-1930, the story of the Church. [Dorchester, 1930]. Pp. 8.

4815   KING, MOSES. The Back-Bay district and the Vendome. [Boston], 1880. Pp. 31.
Vendome Hotel.

4816   _____, ed. King's hand-book of Boston.... (1878) 7th ed. Cambridge, 1885. Pp. 387.

4817   KING, WILLIAM FULLER, JR. "The sailmakers and ship chandlers of 79 Commercial Street, Boston." AmNep, 15 (1955), 220-231.
George Matthews Co.

4818   "KING'S Chapel, Boston." AmHist Record, 2 (1873), 155-157.
Signed: 'Robinson.'

4819   [KIRBY, GEORGIANA BRUCE]. "Before I went to Brook Farm." Old and New, 3 (1871), 175-185.
Author attribution by the editor.

4820   _____. "My first visit to Brook Farm." Overland Monthly, 5 (1870), 9-19.

4821   [_____]. "Reminiscences of Brook Farm." Old and New, 3 (1871), 425-438; 4 (1871-1872), 347-358; 5 (1872), 517-530.
Author attribution by the editor.

4822   KIRKER, HAROLD. "The Boston Exchange Coffee House." OTNE, 52 (1961-1962), 11-13.

4823   _____. and JAMES KIRKER. Bulfinch's Boston, 1787-1817. N.Y.: Oxford Univ. Pr., 1964. Pp. ix, 305.

4824   KIRKER, HAROLD "Bulfinch's design for the Massachusetts State House." OTNE, 55 (1964-1965), 43-46.

4825   KIRKER, JAMES. "Bulfinch's houses for Mrs. Swan." Antiques, 86 (1964), 442-444.
Mrs. James Swan.

4826   KIRKLAND, EDWARD CHASE. "Boston during the Civil War." MHSP, 71 (1953-1957), 194-203.

4827   KITTREDGE, HENRY CROCKER. "The Boston Packets." AmNep, 24 (1964), 127-137.

4828   [KNAPP, SAMUEL LORENZO]. Extracts from a journal of travels in North America, consisting of an account of Boston and its vicinity. By Ali Bey, pseud. Boston: Thomas Badger, 1818. Pp. 124.
Social life and customs.

4829   KNIGHT, JOSEPH KING. "Fifty years of the First Congregational Church of Hyde Park, Massachusetts." HPHR, 9 (1913), 5-63.

4830   KNIGHTS, PETER R. The plain people of Boston, 1830-1860: a study in city growth. N.Y.: Oxford Univ. Pr., 1971. Pp. xx, 204.

4831   KNOLLENBERG, BERNHARD. "Bunker Hill reviewed: a study in the conflict of historical evidence." MHSP, 72 (1957-1960), 84-100.

4832   KOBRE, SIDNEY. "The first American newspaper: a product of environment." Journalism Quarterly, 17 (1940), 335-345.
'Publick Occurrences.'

4833   KOREN, JOHN. Boston, 1822 to 1922: The story of its government and principal activities during one hundred years. [Boston]: City of Boston Printing Department, 1922. Pp. 255.

4834   KRAUS, JOE WALKER. "Messrs. Copeland and Day--publishers to the 1890's." Publishers' Weekly, 141 (March 21, 1942), 1168-1171.

4835   KULIKOFF, ALLAN. "The progress of inequality in Revolutionary Boston." WMQ, 3 Ser., 28 (1971), 375-412.

4836   KURTZ, HENRY I. "The Battle of Bunker Hill." AHI, 2 (November, 1967), 4-11, 47-53.

4837   KYLE, GEORGE ALEXANDER. The eighteen fifties: being a brief account of School Street, the Province House and the Boston Five Cents Savings Bank. Boston: Boston Five Cents Savings Bank, 1926. Pp. 106.

4838   KYPER, FRANK. "Boston's anonymous railroad reaches end of the track." RLHSB, No. 123 (1970), 58-61.
Union Freight Railroad.

4839   _____. "The diminutive high iron of Massachusetts Bay: the Fore River Railroad Corporation, the Union Freight Railroad Company." RLHSB, 120 (1969), 7-30.

4840   LABAREE, BENJAMIN WOODS. The Boston Tea Party. N.Y.: Oxford Univ. Pr., 1964. Pp. viii, 347.

4841   _____. "The Boston Tea Party and the American Revolution." CaHSP, 39 (1961-1963), 144-164.

4842 _____. Catalyst for revolution: the Boston Tea Party, 1773. Boston: Massachusetts Bicentennial Commission, 1973. Pp. 23.

4843 LA DAME, MARY. The Filene store; a study of employes' relation to management in a retail store. N.Y.: Russell Sage Foundation, 1930. Pp. 541.

4844 LADIES' EXCELSIOR CHARITABLE ASSOCIATION, BOSTON. From the slavery of 1776 to the freedom of 1876, an account of the labors of the Ladies' Charitable Association of Boston, in recognition of, and homage to the Declaration of Independence. Boston: Wright & Potter, 1876. Pp. 18.
A charity administered by Black women.

4845 NO ENTRY

4846 LAFORCE, J. CLAYBURN. "Gresham's law and the Suffolk System: a misapplied epigram." BusHR, 40 (1966), 149-166.
Banking.

4847 LAING, DIANA WHITEHILL. "The Cushing-Endicott House: 163 Marlborough Street." BSProc, (1960), 15-52.

4848 LAKE, WILFRED S. "The end of the Suffolk System." JEconHist, 7 (1947), 183-207.
Banking.

4849 [LANDIS, STELLA MCGEHEE]. The Mayflower Club, 1893-1931. Cambridge: Riverside Pr., 1933. Pp. 59.
Women's club.

4850 LANE, ROGER. "James Jeffrey Roche and the Boston 'Pilot.'" NEQ, 33 (1960), 341-363.
Roman Catholic diocesan newspaper, 1890-1905.

4851 _____. Policing the city: Boston, 1822-1885. Cambridge: Harvard Univ. Pr., 1967. Pp. x, 299.

4852 LANGTRY, ALBERT PERKINS, ed. Metropolitan Boston; a modern history.... N.Y.: Lewis Historical Publishing, 1929. 5v.

4853 LANKEVICH, GEORGE J. Boston: a chronological and documentary history, 1602-1970. Dobbs Ferry, N.Y.: Oceana Publications, 1974. Pp. vii, 152.

4854 LAPOMARDA, VINCENT A. "Maurice Joseph Tobin: the decline of bossism in Boston." NEQ, 43 (1970), 355-381.
Twentieth century.

4855 LATHROP, JOHN. God our protector and refuge in danger and trouble, a discourse, delivered at the public lecture in Boston, on Thursday, March 16, 1797...with an appendix, containing an account of several daring attempts to set fire to the town and rob the inhabitants.... Boston: Manning & Loring, 1797. Pp. 30.

4856 LAUGHLIN, HENRY ALEXANDER. An informal sketch of the history of Houghton Mifflin Company. Cambridge: Riverside Pr.,, 1957. Pp. 14.

4857 LAURIE, THOMAS. An historical discourse preached to the South Evangelical Church, West Roxbury, June 10, 1860. Boston: O. S. Thayer, 1861. Pp. 24.
Relates to the church.

4858 _____. Semi-centennial discourse, delivered at West Roxbury, (Boston), Mass. on the fiftieth anniversary of the South Evangelical Church, June 7, 1885. Boston: Beacon Pr., 1885. Pp. 15.

4859 LAWLER, THOMAS BONAVENTURE. Seventy years of textbook publishing: a history of Ginn and Company, 1867-1937.... Boston: Ginn, 1938. Pp. xiii, 304.

4860 LAWRANCE, WILLIAM IRVIN. A history of the Third Religious Society in Dorchester, 1812-1888. Boston: The Society, 1888. Pp. 48.

4861 LAWRENCE, AMOS. Extracts from the diary and correspondence of the late Amos Lawrence; with a brief account of some incidents of his life. William R. Lawrence, ed. Boston: Gould and Lincoln, 1855. Pp. xiv, 369.

4862 LAWRENCE, ROBERT MEANS. Old Park Street and its vicinity. Boston: Houghton Mifflin, 1922. Pp. ix, 172.

4863 _____. The site of Saint Paul's Cathedral, Boston, and its neighborhood. Boston: R. G. Badger, 1916. Pp. 299.

4864 LAWRENCE, SARAH B. "The great Peace Jubilee." NEM, New Ser., 32 (1905), 161-172.
An 1869 music festival.

4865 LAWRENCE, WILLIAM. An historical address by the Rt. Rev. William Lawrence...at the two hundredth anniversary of the Boston Episcopal Charitable Society, held in the Cathedral Church of St. Paul, Boston, Easter Tuesday, April 22, 1924.... Boston, 1924. Pp. 28.

4866 _____. The 75th anniversary of the consecration of St. Paul's Church, Boston, May 26th, 1895. A sermon.... Boston, 1895. Pp. 40.

4867 LAWRENCE, WILLIAM RICHARDS. A history of the Boston Dispensary. Boston: Wilson, 1859. Pp. xiii, 244.

4868 LAWSON, MURRAY G. "The Boston merchant fleet of 1753." AmNep, 9 (1949), 207-215.

4869 _____. "The routes of Boston's trade, 1752-1765." CSMP, 38 (1947-1951), 81-120.

4870 LEADING business men of Back Bay, South End, Boston Highlands, Jamaica Plain and Dorchester.... Boston: Mercantile Publishing, 1888. Pp. 224.
Biography.

4871 LEAHY, WILLIAM AUGUSTINE. The Catholic churches of Boston and its vicinity and St. John's Seminary, Brighton, Mass., a folio of photogravures with notes and historical information. Boston: McClellan, Hearn, 1892. 43 leaves.

4872 LEASE, BENJAMIN. "Robert Carter, James Russell Lowell and John Neal: a document." Jahrbuch für Amerikastudien, 13 (1968), 246-252.
'The Pioneer,' a Boston monthly periodical.

4873 LEBOWICH, JOSEPH. "The Jews in Boston till 1875." AJHSP, 12 (1904), 101-112.

4874 LECHFORD, THOMAS. Note-book kept by Thomas Lechford, esq., lawyer, in Boston, Massachusetts Bay, from June 27, 1638, to July 29, 1641. Edward Everett Hale, Jr., ed. Cambridge: J. Wilson and Son, 1885. Pp. xxviii, 460.

4875 LEE, G. W. "Hale House Farm, an experiment with boys." NEM, New Ser., 28 (1903), 241-252.
Social settlement.

4876 LEE, HENRY, 1817-1898. "The Clark and Hutchinson Houses." MHSP, 18 (1880-1881), 344-351.

4877 _____. A Massachusetts savings bank; being an account of the Provident Institution for Savings, together with a discussion of some problems of savings-bank management and legislation.... [Boston?]: Committee on Charities and Correction to Massachusetts Board of Managers, World's Fair, 1893. Pp. 44.

4878 LEE, HENRY, b. 1925. "Boston's greatest hotel." OTNE, 55 (1964-1965), 97-106.
Tremont House, demolished in 1895.

4879 _____. "Lafayette's son comes to Boston." BSProc, (1964), 12-22.
George Washington Lafayette.

4880 _____. The Shattucks of Boston. Boston: Massachusetts Historical Society, 1971. Pp. 32. M.

4881 LEE, JOSEPH. "Boston's playground system." NEM, New Ser., 27 (1902-1903), 521-536.

4882 LEE, WILLIAM H. Index to the City Council minutes from July 1, 1868 - January 3, 1880. Boston: Rockwell & Churchill, 1885. Pp. 391.

4883 LEICHENTRITT, HUGO. "Music in Boston in the nineties." More Books, 21 (1946), 367-380; 22 (1947), 11-19.

4884 LEONARD, AMOS M. "History of the Lawrence and Mather Schools, South Boston." BSProc, (1922), 24-45.

4885 LEVIN, MURRAY BURTON. The alienated voter: politics in Boston. N.Y.: Holt, Rinehart and Winston, 1960. Pp. 84.

4886 LEVY, LEONARD WILLIAMS. "The 'Abolition Riot:' Boston's first slave rescue." NEQ, 25 (1952), 85-92.
1836.

4887 _____. and HARLAN B. PHILLIPS. "The Roberts Case: source of the 'separate but equal' doctrine." AHR, 56 (1950-1951), 510-518.
Segregated schools, 1849.

4888 LEWIS, EDWIN J., JR. "The Unitarian churches of Boston in 1860." UHSP, 1, Pt. 2, (1928), 1-27.

4889 LIDSTONE, JAMES TORRINGTON SPENCER. The Bostoniad: giving a full description of the principal establishments, together with the most honorable and substantial business men, in the Athens of America. Boston: Hollis & Gunn, 1853. Pp. 62.
In verse.

4890 LIEB, FREDERICK GEORGE. The Boston Red Sox. N.Y.: G. P. Putnam's Sons, 1947. Pp. xiii, 257.

4891 LIFE in town, or the Boston spy, being a series of sketches illustrative of whims and women in the 'Athens of America.' By an Athenian.... Boston: Redding, 1844. Pp. 24.
Social life and customs.

4892 LINDEMANN, FRIEDRICH. Geschichte der Ev. Luth. Zions-Gemeinde, zu Boston, Massachusetts. West Roxbury, 1889. Pp. 19. MB.

4893 LINDSAY, J. D. "The Boston Massacre." National Magazine, 17 (1893), 239-250.

4894 LINSCOTT, ELISABETH SHOEMAKER. "Early years of our first historical society." NEG, 9 (Winter, 1968), 18-24.
Massachusetts Historical Society.

4895 LINSCOTT, ROBERT NEWTON, ed. State of mind: a Boston reader. N.Y.: Farrar, Straus, 1948. Pp. xiv, 428.
Social life and customs.

4896 LITTLE, NINA FLETCHER. "Early buildings of the asylum at Charlestown, 1795-1846." OTNE, 59 (1968-1969), 29-52.
McLean Hospital.

4897 _____. Early years of the McLean Hospital, recorded in the journal of George William Folsom, apothecary at the asylum in Charlestown. Boston: Francis A. Countway Library of Medicine, 1972. Pp. viii, 176.

4898 _____. "The good samaritan, symbol of the Boston Dispensary." Antiques, 70 (1956), 360-362.
Seal of the dispensary.

4899 LITTLE, BROWN AND COMPANY. One hundred and twenty-five years of publishing, 1837-1962. Boston, 1962. Pp. 84.

4900 _____. One hundred years of publishing, 1837-1937. Boston, 1937. Pp. 83.

4901 "LITTLE, Brown & Company centenary." Saturday Review of Literature, 15 (March 27, 1937), 1A-23A.
Publisher.

4902 "LITTLE, Brown & Company, 1837-1937." Publishers' Weekly, 131 (March 13, 1937), 1233-1237.

4903 "LITTLE, Brown's 125 years of publishing." Publishers' Weekly, 181 (March 19, 1962), 22-27.

4904 LITTLEFIELD, GEORGE EMERY. Early Boston booksellers 1642-1711. Boston: Club of Odd Volumes, 1900. Pp. 256.

4905 LOCKWOOD, ALICE G. B. "Furnishing and embellishments of Boston houses, 1694-1770." OTNE, 30 (1939-1940), 15-24.

4906 LODGE, HENRY CABOT. Boston. N.Y.: Longmans, Green, 1891. Pp. xi, 242.

4907 LOGUE, EDWARD J. "Boston, 1960-1967--seven years of plenty." MHSP, 84 (1972), 82-96.

4908 LOOMIS, C. GRANT. "Davy Crockett visits Boston." NEQ, 20 (1947), 396-400.
1834.

4909 LORD, DONALD C. "The removal of the Massachusetts General Court from Boston, 1769-1772." JAH, 55 (1968-1969), 735-755.
Reassembled in Cambridge.

4910 LORD, MYRA BELLE HORNE. History of the New England Woman's Press Association, 1885-1931. Newton: Graphic Pr., 1932. Pp. 393.

4911 LORIMER, GEORGE CLAUDE. Tremont Temple sketch book, containing a brief history of Tremont Temple Church.... Boston: St. Botolph Pr., 1896. Unpaged.

4912 LORING, JAMES SPEAR. The hundred Boston orators appointed by the municipal authorities and other public bodies, from 1770 to 1852; comprising historical gleanings, illustrating the principles and progress of our republican institutions. (1852) 4th ed. Boston: J. P. Jewett, 1855. Pp. viii, 727.
Biography.

4913 LORING, JOHN GREELEY. An address delivered before the First Christian Church in Boston, on Sabbath afternoon, June 30th, 1844, it being the fortieth anniversary of the organization of said church. Boston: Published by a committee of the Church, 1844. Pp. 26.

4914 LORING, LOUIS P. "Early railroads in Boston." Bostonian, 1 (1894-1895), 299-309.

4915 LOSSING, BENSON J. "The Boston Tea Party." Harper's Magazine, 4 (1851), 1-11.

4916 _____. "The Curtis House, Jamaica Plain." Potter's AmMo, 6 (1876), 161-165.

4917 _____. "Faneuil Hall." Potter's AmMo, 7 (1876), 321-327.

4918 _____. "The Province House, Boston." Potter's AmMo, 5 (1875), 881-887.

4919 LOTHROP, SAMUEL KIRKLAND. A history of the church in Brattle Street, Boston. Boston: W. Crosby and H. P. Nichols, 1851. Pp. vi, 217.
Brattle Square Church.

4920 _____. Memorial of the church in Brattle Square, a discourse preached in the church in Brattle Square, on the last Sunday of its use for public worship, July 30, 1871.... Boston: J. Wilson and Son, 1871. Pp. 56.

4921 LOVELL, JAMES. An oration delivered April 2d, 1771, at the request of the inhabitants of the town of Boston; to commemorate the bloody tragedy of the fifth of March, 1770. Boston: Edes and Gill, 1771. Pp. 9.

4922 LOVETT, A. S. More than half a century on State Street. Boston: Boston Board of Fire Underwriters, 1923. Pp. 43.
Fire insurance business, no particular firm.

4923 LOVETT, JAMES D'WOLF. Old Boston boys and the games they played. Boston: Riverside Pr., 1906. Pp. vi, 241.

4924 LOWELL, DANIEL OZRO SMITH. The story of the origin of the Palmer Memorial Hospital of Boston, Mass. Boston, 1926. Pp. 16.

4925 LUNT, PAUL. Paul Lunt's diary, May-December, 1775. Samuel A. Green, ed. Boston: J. Wilson and Son, 1872. Pp. 19.

4926 LURIE, REUBEN LEVI. The challenge of the forums; the story of Ford Hall and the open forum movement.... Boston: R. G. Badger, 1930. Pp. 218.
Adult education.

4927 LYMAN, GEORGE HINCKLEY, 1819-1890. Historical sketch of the Obstetrical Society of Boston in the War of the Rebellion. Boston: Clapp, 1887. Pp. 62.
Biographies.

4928 LYMAN, THEODORE, 1833-1897, ed. Papers relating to the Garrison mob. Cambridge: Welch, Bigelow, 1870. Pp. 73.
A vindication of the conduct of Mayor Theodore Lyman (1792-1849) at the time of the mobbing of William Lloyd Garrison in 1835.

4929 LYNDON, BARRY. "The House of Ticknor, with a glimpse of the Old Corner Bookstore." BSM, 3 (1885), 266-269.

4930 LYONS, DONALD H. The Cathedral Church of St. Paul, Boston, an historical sketch. [Boston, 195-]. Pp. 15.

4931   LYONS, LOUIS MARTIN. Newspaper story; one
       hundred years of the Boston Globe. Cam-
bridge: Harvard Univ. Pr., 1971. Pp. xv, 482.

4932   LYONS, RICHARD L. "The Boston Police Strike
       of 1919." NEQ, 20 (1947), 147-168.

4933   MABEE, CARLETON. "A Negro boycott to inte-
       grate Boston Schools." NEQ, 41 (1968), 341-
361.
       1840s.

4934   MCBRIDE, MARION A. "Some old Dorchester
       houses." NEM, New Ser., 2 (1890), 314-321.

4935   MCCLAIN, MINOR H. History and master plan,
       Georges Island and Fort Warren, Boston Har-
bor. [Boston]: Metropolitan District Commission,
1960. Pp. 60. M.

4936   MCCLEAN, ROBERT A. "Century old tradition
       of hospitality, Boston's good old Charles
Street Jail." Boston, 56 (September, 1964), 52-57,
74-76.

4937   MCCLEARY, OREN C. Charlestown: A bibli-
       ography.... Boston: Boston Public Library,
1973. 18 leaves. MB.

4938   MCCLEARY, SAMUEL F. "Boston writing schools
       in 1755." MHSP, 2 Ser., 4 (1887-1889), 193-
194.

4939   _____. "The origin, purpose and results of
       the Franklin Fund." MHSP, 2 Ser., 12 (1897-
1899), 17-29.
       Medals for outstanding Boston students.

4940   MCCLELLAND, NANCY. "The Washington memorial
       paper." Antiques, 6 (1924), 138-139.
       Wallpaper.

4941   MCCORD, DAVID THOMPSON WATSON. About Bos-
       ton; sight, sound, flavor & inflection.
Garden City, N.Y.: Doubleday, 1948. Pp. 192.

4942   _____. The fabrick of man: fifty years of
       the Peter Bent Brigham. Boston: Fiftieth
Anniversary Celebration Committee, 1963. Pp. 128.
       Hospital.

4943   [MCCUSKER, HONOR]. "The British in Boston:
       General Gage's orderly book, December 1774--
June 1775." More Books, 22 (1947), 163-174, 209-
224, 257-262.
       Author attribution by the editor.

4944   _____. "Connecticut troops in the Siege of
       Boston." More Books, 11 (1936), 377-380.

4945   _____. "Fifty years of music in Boston."
       More Books, 12 (1937), 341-359, 397-408,
451-462.
       1840-1890.

4946   MACDONALD, EDWARD. Old Copp's Hill and bur-
       ial ground, with historical sketches. (1879)
20th ed. Boston: Industrial School Pr., 1902.
Pp. 57.

4947   MACDONALD, WENDELL D. "Profiles of worker
       family living in Boston, 1875-1950." Monthly
Labor Review, 80 (1957), 271-280.

4948   MACELANEY, HUGH J., ed. Roxbury past and
       present, written by the Dudley School boys.
Boston, 1918. Pp. iii, 98. MB.

4949   MCGLENEN, EDWARD WEBSTER. "Christ Church and
       the signal lights." Society of Colonial
Wars. Massachusetts. [Yearbook], (1906), 99-134.

4950   MCGLINCHEE, CLAIRE. The first decade of the
       Boston Museum. Boston: B. Humphries, 1940.
Pp. 370.
       A theater.

4951   MCINTIRE, ALICE. "The Albanians in Boston."
       Our Boston, 1 (January, 1926), 19-22.

4952   MCKAY, GEORGE E. "Faneuil Hall Market."
       BSProc, (1910), 34-47.

4953   MACKENZIE, FREDERICK. A British fusilier in
       revolutionary Boston; being the diary of
Lieutenant Frederick Mackenzie, adjutant of the Roy-
al Welch Fusiliers, January 5-April 30, 1775, with
a letter describing his voyage to America. Allen
French, ed. Cambridge: Harvard Univ. Pr., 1926.
Pp. x, 83.

4954   MCKENZIE, W. S. "Tremont Temple." NEM, 6
       (1887-1888), 377-381.
       Baptist church.

4955   MACKEY, PHILIP ENGLISH. "An all-star debate
       on capital punishment, Boston, 1854." EIHC,
110 (1974), 181-199.

4956   MACKINTOSH, CHARLES G. Some recollections of
       the pastors and people of the Second Church
of old Roxbury, afterwards First Church, West Roxbury, of Brook Farm and the ancient road and landmarks from Elliot [sic] Square, Roxbury Hill, to
Memorial Square, Dedham. Salem: Newcomb & Gauss,
1901. Pp. 72. MB.

4957   MCLOUGHLIN, WILLIAM G. and MARTHA WHITING
       DAVIDSON, eds. "The Baptist debate of April
14-15, 1668." MHSP, 76 (1964), 91-133.

4958   MCNAMARA, KATHERINE and CAROLINE SHILLABER.
       The Boston metropolitan district, its physi-
cal growth and governmental development: a bibliography. Cambridge: Harvard Graduate School of
Public Administration and Harvard Graduate School of
Design, 1946. Pp. 197.

4959   MACULLAR PARKER COMPANY. In 1849: interest-
       ing facts about Boston seventy-five years
ago, also a brief review of the establishment and
growth of Macullar Parker, Co. Boston, 1924. Unpaged. MB.

4960   _____. Some old sites on an old thoroughfare
       and an account of some early residents there-
on. Boston, 1918. Pp. 30.
       Washington Street.

4961 _____. Washington Street old and new; a history in narrative form of the changes which this ancient street has undergone since the settlement of Boston. Boston, 1913. Unpaged. MB.

4962 MCVEY, T. H. Historic Brighton, events and places. n.p., [1967?]. Pp. 12. M.

4963 MCVICKAR, HARRY WHITNEY and JOSEPHINE POLLARD. The Boston Tea Party, December 1773. N.Y.: Dodd, Mead, 1882. Pp. 32.

4964 MAGINNES, DAVID R. "The case of the Court house rioters in the rendition of the fugitive slave Anthony Burns, 1854." JNegroHist, 56 (1971), 31-42.

4965 MAHONEY, WILLIAM H. "Benevolent hospitals in metropolitan Boston." American Statistical Association. Publications, 13 (1912-1913), 419-448.
Historical and statistical.

4966 MAKRIS, JOHN N., ed. Boston murders. N.Y.: Duell, Sloan and Pearce, 1948. Pp. 223.

4967 MALLAM, WILLIAM D. "The fight for the old granite block." NEW, 36 (1963), 42-62.
Politics at the Boston custom house, 1874.

4968 MALONE, MICHAEL T. "The ecclesiastical trials in Massachusetts of Oliver Sherman Prescott." Church History, 41 (1972), 94-107.
Prescott tried at Trinity Church for his views on private auricular confession, 1850-1852.

4969 MAMMEN, EDWARD WILLIAM. The old stock company school of acting; a study of the Boston Museum. Boston: Trustees of the Public Library, 1945. Pp. 89.
A shorter version appeared in 'More Books' during 1944.

4970 MANN, ALBERT WILLIAM, ed. Walks & talks about historic Boston.... Boston: Mann Publishing, 1917. Pp. 586.

4971 MANN, ARTHUR, ed. Growth and achievement: Temple Israel, 1854-1954. Cambridge: Riverside Pr., 1954. Pp. 131.
Congregation Adath Israel.

4972 MANN, DOROTHEA LAWRANCE. A century of book selling: the story of the Old Corner Book Store on the occasion of its one hundredth birthday. Boston: The Old Corner Book Store, 1928. Pp. 31.

4973 MARK, KENNETH LAMARTINE. Delayed by fire, being the early history of Simmons College.... Concord, N.H.: Rumford Pr., 1945. Pp. vii, 163.

4974 MARNELL, WILLIAM H. and DOUGLASS SHAND TUCCI. Saint Peter's Church, 1872-1972. Boston: Fandel Pr., 1972. Pp. 51. MB.

4975 MARSDEN, K. GERALD. "Philanthropy and the Boston playground movement, 1885-1907." Social Service Review, 35 (1961), 48-58.

4976 MARSH, DANIEL LASH. "All noisy on the medical front, the romantic story of the Boston University School of Medicine." Centerscope, (March/April, 1973), 7-31.
Centennial; published posthumously.

4977 _____. Three 'solid men of Boston,' Founders Day address at Boston University, March 13, 1933. Boston, 1933. Pp. 21. MB.
Alden Speare, Edward H. Dunn, and Roswell R. Robinson.

4978 _____. Traditions of Boston University. Boston: Boston Univ. Pr., [1945?]. Pp. 51. MBU.

4979 MARSHALL, ERNEST C. "The early history of the Massachusetts College of Pharmacy." Massachusetts College of Pharmacy. Quarterly Bulletin, No. 3 (1911), 5-20.

4980 MARSON, PHILIP. Breeder of democracy. Cambridge: Schenkman Publishing, 1963. Pp. viii, 199.
Boston Latin School.

4981 MARSTON, EVERETT C. Origin and development of Northeastern University, 1898-1960. Boston: Northeastern Univ., 1961. Pp. 234.

4982 MARTIN, GEORGE HENRY. "Boston schools one hundred years ago." NEM, New Ser., 26 (1902), 628-642.

4983 MARTIN, JOSEPH GREGORY. A century of finance, Martin's history of the Boston stock and money markets, one hundred years, from January, 1798, to January, 1898, comprising the annual fluctuations of all public stocks and investment securities...also a review of the Boston money market, 1831 to 1898.... Boston, 1898. Pp. viii, 232.

4984 MARTIN, LAWRENCE. "Women fought at Bunker Hill." NEQ, 8 (1935), 467-479.

4985 MASON, JONATHAN. An oration delivered March 6, 1780, at the request of the inhabitants of the town of Boston to commemorate the bloody tragedy of the fifth of March, 1770. Boston: John Gill, 1780. MWA.
Boston Massacre.

4986 MASSACHUSETTS. BOARD OF MANAGERS, WORLD'S FAIR, CHICAGO. Origin...Workingmen's Loan Association. Boston, 1893. Pp. 18. MB.

4987 MASSACHUSETTS. BUREAU OF STATISTICS. Changes in conducting retail trade in Boston since 1874. Boston: State Printers, 1900. Pp. v, 69. M.

4988 _____. The Massachusetts Bureau of Statistics, 1869-1915: a sketch of its history, organization and functions, together with a list of its publications and illustrative charts. Charles F. Gettemy, ed.... Boston: Wright & Potter, 1915. Pp. 115.

4989 MASSACHUSETTS. FINANCE COMMISSION OF THE CITY OF BOSTON. A chronology of the Boston public schools. Boston: City of Boston Printing Department, 1912. Pp. 39. M.

4990 MASSACHUSETTS. GENERAL COURT. Centennial of the Bulfinch State House, exercises before the Massachusetts legislature, January 11, 1898. Boston: Wright & Potter, 1898. Pp. 74.

4991 MASSACHUSETTS. GENERAL COURT. HOUSE OF REPRESENTATIVES. COMMITTEE ON HISTORY OF THE EMBLEM OF THE CODFISH. A history of the emblem of the codfish in the hall of the House of Representatives.... Boston: Wright and Potter, 1895. Pp. 62.

4992 MASSACHUSETTS. METROPOLITAN DISTRICT COMMISSION. Description of the Metropolitan Water Works, 1846-1932. Boston, 1932. Pp. 15. MB.
  Essays by William E. Foss and Frank E. Winsor.

4993 MASSACHUSETTS. METROPOLITAN PARK COMMISSION. A history and description of the Boston metropolitan parks. Boston: State Printers, 1900. Pp. 36. M.

4994 MASSACHUSETTS. REVOLUTIONARY WAR BICENTENNIAL COMMISSION. The Battle of Bunker Hill. Boston: Revolutionary War Bicentennial Commission and Massachusetts Historical Society, 1968. Unpaged. M.

4995 MASSACHUSETTS. STATE LIBRARY. The Massachusetts State House. Boston, 1953. Pp. 155.

4996 MASSACHUSETTS CHARITABLE FIRE SOCIETY. An old Boston institution: a brief history of the Massachusetts Charitable Fire Society, organized 1792--incorporated 1794. By its secretary, Henry H. Sprague. Boston: Little, Brown, 1893. Pp. x, 188.

4997 MASSACHUSETTS CONGREGATIONAL CHARITABLE SOCIETY. Act of incorporation, regulations, and members of the Massachusetts Congregational Charitable Society, with a brief sketch of its origin, progress, and purpose. Boston: John Eliot, 1815. Pp. 20. MB.

4998 MASSACHUSETTS DEAF MUTE CHRISTIAN UNION. Massachusetts Deaf Mute Christian Union. Boston: Gribben & Kiley, 1869. Pp. 14. MB.
  Sunday school.

4999 MASSACHUSETTS EYE AND EAR INFIRMARY. The story of the Massachusetts Eye and Ear Infirmary. [Boston, 1970?]. Pp. 28.

5000 MASSACHUSETTS FISH AND GAME ASSOCIATION. Massachusetts Fish and Game Association, a brief history. Cambridge, 1935. Pp. 32. MB.

5001 MASSACHUSETTS GENERAL HOSPITAL. The Massachusetts General Hospital, 1810-1900: a brief statement of the origin, growth, and scope of the Massachusetts General Hospital and its most important contributions to medical and surgical science. Boston: A. Mudge and Son, 1900. Pp. 8. M.

5002 _____. Memorial & historical volume, together with the proceedings of the centennial of the opening of the hospital. Boston, 1921. Pp. 303.

5003 MASSACHUSETTS HISTORICAL SOCIETY. The Battle of Bunker Hill. Boston, 1968. Unpaged.

5004 _____. Boston and the China trade. Boston, 1970. Unpaged.

5005 _____. Here we have lived: the houses of the Massachusetts Historical Society. Boston, 1967. Unpaged.

5006 _____. The Massachusetts Historical Society, 1791-1959. By Stephen T. Riley. Boston, 1959. Pp. 62.

5007 _____. Pro bono publico: the Shattucks of Boston. Boston, 1971. Unpaged.

5008 _____. Proceedings of a special meeting of the Massachusetts Historical Society, December 16, 1873; being the one hundredth anniversary of the destruction of the tea in Boston Harbor. Boston: J. Wilson and Son, 1874. Pp. 70.

5009 _____. A short account of the Massachusetts Historical Society, originally prepared by Charles Card Smith, together with the act of incorporation, additional acts and by-laws and a list of officers and members, January 1791-June 1918. Boston, 1918. Pp. 99.

5010 MASSACHUSETTS HORTICULTURAL SOCIETY. History of the Massachusetts Horticultural Society, 1829-1878. Robert Manning, ed. Boston, 1880. Pp. viii, 545.

5011 MASSACHUSETTS MEDICO-LEGAL SOCIETY. The Massachusetts Medico-Legal Society: a biographical directory, 1877-1937, also a transcript of the laws governing medical examiners, by Timothy Leary, and a list of papers read before the Society and later published. Boston, 1937. Pp. 190.

5012 MASSACHUSETTS NATIONAL BANK. [Circular containing a history of the bank, 1784-1892]. Boston, 1892. Pp. 12. MB.

5013 MASSACHUSETTS SCHOOL SUFFRAGE ASSOCIATION. Brief history of the Massachusetts School Suffrage Association. Boston, 1893. Pp. 16.
  Allowance of women as candidates for election to the Boston School Committee.

5014 MASSACHUSETTS STATE FEDERATION OF WOMEN'S CLUBS. HISTORY COMMITTEE. Progress and achievement: a history of the Massachusetts State Federation of Women's Clubs, 1893-1931. Mrs. Walter A. Hall, Mrs. Joseph S. Leach and Mrs. Frederick G. Smith, eds. [Boston], 1932. Pp. xii, 249.

5015 MASSACHUSETTS STATE PRISON, CHARLESTOWN, MASS. Description and historical sketch of the Massachusetts State Prison.... Charlestown: S. Etheridge, Jr., 1816. Pp. 38. MB.

5016   MASSACHUSETTS TEMPERANCE ALLIANCE. History
       of the Massachusetts Temperance Alliance.
Boston, [1875?]. Pp. 4. MB.

5017   MASSACHUSETTS TOTAL ABSTINENCE SOCIETY.
       Historical address, M.T.A. Society, Feb. 22,
1901. [Boston?, 1901?]. Pp. xii. MB.
       Celebration of 30th anniversary.

5018   MATERA, JAMES J. "100 years of public water
       supply for Boston." New England Waterworks
Association. Journal, 63 (1949), 150-164.
       1652-1948.

5019   MATHER, COTTON. "An account of the great
       fire in Boston, in the year 1711." MHSC,
[5] (1798), 52-53.

5020   [_____]. The Bostonian Ebenezer: some his-
       torical remarks, on the state of Boston, the
chief town of New-England, and of the English America, with some, agreeable methods, for preserving
and promoting, the good state of that, as well as
any other town, in the like circumstances, humbly
offer'd. By a Native of Boston.... Boston: B.
Green & J. Allen, 1698. Pp. 82 (i.e. 84).

5021   MATHER, SAMUEL. "Account of the settlement
       of Boston." MHSC, 1 (1792), 256.

5022   MATHIESON, MOIRA B. Records of Boston archi-
       tecture in the architectural records of the
Smithsonian Institution. n.p., 1969. Pp. 224.
MBSpnea.

5023   MATTHEWS, ALBERT. "A Dorchester religious
       society of young men." NEHGR, 60 (1906),
30-40.
       Eighteenth century.

5024   _____. "Early Sunday schools in Boston."
       CSMP, 21 (1919), 259-285.

5025   MATTOX, WILLIAM COURTNEY. Walworth Manufac-
       turing Company: its history and traditions.
n.p., [1921?]. Pp. 50. MH-BA.
       Valves.

5026   MAYNADIER, GUSTAVUS HOWARD. Sixty years of
       the Union Boat Club... [and] a list of mem-
bers and the more important races of the club from
1851 to 1911. Boston, 1913. Pp. vi, 333.

5027   MEANS, JAMES HOWARD, 1823-1894. Dorchester,
       past and present: a sermon preached in the
Second Church, Dorchester, December 26, 1869. Boston: Moses H. Sargent, 1870. Pp. 24.

5028   _____. An historical discourse on occasion
       of the fiftieth anniversary of the gathering
of the Second Church, Dorchester, delivered January
3, 1858. Boston: T. R. Marvin & Son, 1858.
Pp. 32.

5029   _____. An historical discourse on occasion
       of the seventieth anniversary of the gather-
ing of the Second Church, Dorchester, delivered
January 6, 1878. Boston: Frank Wood, 1878.
Pp. 28.

5030   MEANS, JAMES HOWARD, b. 1885. Ward 4; the
       Mallinckrodt Research Ward of the Massachu-
setts General Hospital. Cambridge: Harvard Univ.
Pr., 1958. Pp. 187.

5031   MEANY, THOMAS, et al. The Boston Red Sox.
       N.Y.: Barnes, 1956. Pp. 237.

5032   MELCHER, ELIZABETH G. "The genesis and his-
       tory of King's Chapel and of Christ Church."
Bostonian, 1 (1894-1895), 596-610.

5033   MELCHER, FREDERIC GERSHOM. "A Boston book-
       store at the turn of the century." AASP, 66
(1956), 37-50.
       Estes and Lauriat.

5034   MEMORIAL, Bunker Hill, 1775, June 17th, 1875.
       Boston: J. R. Osgood, 1875. Pp. 16.
       Sketches by Oliver Wendell Holmes, James M.
Bugbee and Nathaniel L. Frothingham.

5035   MEMORIAL of Jesse Lee and the old elm:
       eighty-fifth anniversary of Jesse Lee's ser-
mon under the old elm, Boston Common, held Sunday
evening, July 11, 1875, with a historical sketch of
the great tree. Boston: J.P. Magee, 1875. Pp. 55.
       Sermon and sketch by John W. Hamilton.

5036   MEMORIAL volume of the one hundredth anniver-
       sary celebration of the dedication of the
Church of the Holy Cross, Boston. [Boston]: New
England Catholic Historical Society, 1904. Pp. 137.

5037   MEN of Boston and New England. [Boston]:
       Boston American, 1913. Pp. 186.
       Brief biographical sketches below each por-
trait.

5038   MERINO, JAMES A. "Cooperative schemes for
       greater Boston: 1890-1920." NEQ, 45 (1972),
196-226.

5039   MERK, LOIS BANNISTER. "Boston's historic
       public school crisis." NEQ, 31 (1958), 172-
199.
       Allowance of women as candidates for election
to the Boston School Committee.

5040   MERRIAM, JOHN MCKINSTRY. "Historic burial-
       places of Boston and vicinity." AASP, New
Ser., 7 (1890-1891), 381-417.

5041   MERRITT, EDWARD PERCIVAL. "The Club of Odd
       Volumes." PBSA, 9 (1915), 21-44.

5042   _____. "The French Protestant Church in Bos-
       ton." CSMP, 26 (1924-1926), 323-348.
       1696-1748.

5043   _____. "The King's gift to Christ Church,
       Boston, 1733." CSMP, 19 (1916-1917), 299-
331.
       Bible, Prayer Books, communion plate and
altar furnishings.

5044   _____. "Note on the 'Courier Politique de
       l'Univers,' Boston, 1792-1793." CSMP, 24
(1920-1922), 296-299.
       Newspaper.

5045 _____. The parochial library of the eighteenth century in Christ Church, Boston. Boston: Merrymount Pr., 1917. Pp. 86.

5046 _____. "Sketches of the three earliest Roman
Catholic priests in Boston." CSMP, 25 (1922-
1924), 173-229.
Claude Florent Bouchard de la Poterie, Louis
de Rousselet and John Thayer.

5047 MERWICK, DONNA. Boston priests, 1848-1910;
a study of social and intellectual change.
Cambridge: Harvard Univ. Pr., 1973. Pp. xiii, 276.

5048 METCALF, PRISCILLA. "Boston before Bulfinch:
Harrison's King's Chapel." SocArchHistJ, 13
(March, 1954), 11-14.
Peter Harrison.

5049 MIKAL, ALAN. Exploring Boston Harbor. North
Quincy: Christopher Publishing House, 1973.
Pp. 128.
History and legends.

5050 MILES, JAMES B. Discourse preached in the
First Church, Charlestown, on Sunday, Janu-
ary 2, 1859. Boston: W & E Howe, 1859. Pp. 20.
Relates to the church.

5051 MILES, PLINY. The advantages of ocean steam
navigation, foreign and coastwise, to the
commerce of Boston and the manufactures of New England. Boston: Moore, 1857. Pp. 96. MB.

5052 MILLAR, DONALD. "Notes on the Hancock House,
Boston." OTNE, 17 (1926-1927), 121-124.
Demolished, 1863.

5053 MILLER, JOHN C. "The Massachusetts Convention, 1768." NEQ, 7 (1934), 445-474.

5054 MINER, HENRY B. "The Hyde Park Public Library." HPHR, 3 (1903), 5-8.

5055 MITCHELL, ANN MARIA. "Massachusetts Diocе-
san Library and the parish historian."
HMPEC, 7 (1938), 277-286.
Diocese of Massachusetts.

5056 MODEL, F. PETER. "The Quincy quandary."
Boston, 59 (November, 1967), 38-41.
Quincy markets.

5057 MONTGOMERY, DAVID. "The working classes of
the pre-industrial American city, 1780-1830."
LabHist, 9 (1968), 3-22.
Boston is one of the four cities investi-
gated.

5058 THE MONTHLY ANTHOLOGY, AND BOSTON REVIEW.
The Federalist literary mind: selections
from the Monthly Anthology, and Boston Review, 1803-
1811, including documents relating to the Boston
Athenaeum. Lewis P. Simpson, ed. [Baton Rouge]:
Louisiana State Univ. Pr., 1962. Pp. 246.

5059 MONTRESOR, JOHN. "Notes on Castle William."
New-York Historical Society. Collections,
14 (1881), 399-410.
Fort.

5060 MOODY, ROBERT EARLE. Boston men and the
winning of American independence: the story
of America shown in the lives of some of the most
illustrious men of Boston in New England, and illustrated by portraits now in the American history room
of Boston University. Boston, 1948. Pp. iv, 23.
Biography.

5061 MOORE, GEORGE HENRY. "Discovery of America
by Columbus: Boston and New York celebrations one hundred years ago." MagAmHist, 22 (1889),
317-323.
1792.

5062 _____. "The New England Synod of 1637."
HistMag, 2 Ser., 3 (1868), 26-29.

5063 _____. Prytaneum Bostoniense: notes on the
history of the Old State House, formerly
known as the Town House in Boston--the Court House
in Boston--the Province Court House--the State
House--and the City Hall. Boston: Cupples, Upham,
1885-1886. 2v.

5064 _____. Prytaneum Bostoniense. Examination of
Mr. William H. Whitmore's Old State House Memorial and reply to his appendix N.... 2d ed., with
additions. Boston: Cupples, Upham, 1887. Pp. 39.

5065 MOORE, MARTIN. Boston revival, 1842: a
brief history of the Evangelical churches of
Boston, together with a more particular account of
the revival of 1842. Boston: J. Putnam, 1842.
Pp. viii, 148. MB.

5066 MOORE, THOMAS EDWARD, JR. "The early years
of the Harvard Medical School: its founding
and curriculum, 1782-1810." BHistMed, 27 (1953),
530-561.

5067 MORGAN, EDMUND SEARS. "A Boston heiress and
her husbands, a true story." CSMP, 34 (1937-
1942), 499-513.
Anna Keayne, Edward Lane and Nicholas Paige;
seventeenth century.

5068 MORISON, SAMUEL ELIOT. "Boston traders in
the Hawaiian Islands 1789-1823." MHSP, 54
(1920-1921), 9-47.

5069 _____. "The commerce of Boston on the eve of
the Revolution." AASP, New Ser., 32 (1922),
24-51.

5070 _____. One boy's Boston, 1887-1901. Boston:
Houghton Mifflin, 1962. Pp. 81.
Social life and customs.

5071 MORRIS, AGNES. "South Boston." Our Boston,
1 (May, 1926), 11-13.

5072 MORRISON, ALLAN. "Black patriots were heroes
at first major battle of Revolution." Ebony,
19 (February, 1964), 44-46, 48-50, 52-53.
Bunker Hill.

5073 MORRISON, C. L. "The Boston Tea Party."
Granite Mo, 7 (1884), 115-116.

5074   MORSE, JOHN TORREY, JR. "Recollections of
        Boston and Harvard before the Civil War."
MHSP, 65 (1932-1936), 150-163.

5075   MORSE, MARY HARROWER. "Two women of Boston."
        NEG, 13 (Winter, 1972), 27-35.
        Mary Dyer and Anne Hutchinson.

5076   MORSMAN, OLIVER. A history of Breed's (com-
        monly called) Bunker's Hill battle, fought
between the provincial troops and the British, June
17, 1775. Sacket's Harbor, [N.Y.]: T. W. Haskell,
1830. Pp. iv, 17.

5077   MOSES, FRANKLIN J. "Mob or martyrs? Cris-
        pus Attucks and the Boston Massacre." Bos-
tonian, 1 (1894-1895), 641-650.

5078   MOTT, FRANK LUTHER. "The 'Christian Disci-
        ple' and the 'Christian Examiner.'" NEQ, 1
(1928), 197-207.
        Nineteenth-century periodicals.

5079   MOULTON, ROBERT SELDEN. The Cocoanut Grove
        nightclub fire, Boston, Massachusetts, Nov.
28, 1942. Boston: National Fire Protection Association, 1962. Pp. 16. M.

5080   MOWRY, WILLIAM AUGUSTUS. "The first Ameri-
        can public school." Education, 21 (1900-
1901), 535-548.

5081   ____. "The Young Men's Christian Associa-
        tion." HPHR, 3 (1903), 13-21.

5082   MUDGE, ENOCH REDINGTON. Address at the open-
        ing of the Huntington House, being a history
of the Emmanuel Church Mission, now the Chapel of
the Good Shepherd. n.p., [1865?]. Pp. 9. MB.

5083   MUGRIDGE, DONALD H. "In Roxbury camp: an
        American orderly book of 1775." Quarterly
Journal of Current Acquisitions, 19 (1962), 63-76.
        Periodical was published by the Library of
Congress.

5084   MUMFORD, LEWIS. "The making of a precedent,
        1840-1890." Boston, 61 (October, 1969),
42-46, 62, 66.
        Back Bay architecture.

5085   MUNROE, JAMES PHINNEY. "The destruction of
        the convent at Charlestown, Massachusetts,
1834." NEM, New Ser., 23 (1900-1901), 637-649.

5086   MUNSTERBERG, MARGARET. "Early views of
        Beacon Hill." BPLQ, 8 (1956), 171-180.

5087   ____. "The Weston sisters and the Boston
        controversy." BPLQ, 10 (1958), 38-50.
        Antislavery.

5088   ____. "The Weston sisters and the 'Boston
        Mob.'" BPLQ, 9 (1957), 183-194.
        Antislavery.

5089   MURDOCK, HAROLD. Bunker Hill: notes and
        queries on a famous battle.... Boston:
Houghton Mifflin, 1927. Pp. x, 149.

5090   ____. Earl Percy dines abroad: a Boswelli-
        an episode. Boston: Houghton Mifflin, 1924.
Pp. x, 46.
        Battle of Bunker Hill.

5091   ____. "The great Boston fire, and some
        contributing causes." BSProc, (1913), 49-61.

5092   ____. "Notes on Bunker Hill." CSMP, 26
        (1924-1926), 95-100, 107-158.

5093   MURDOCK, KENNETH BALLARD. "The teaching of
        Latin and Greek at the Boston Latin School in
1712." CSMP, 27 (1927-1930), 21-29.

5094   MURPHEY, RHOADS. "Boston's Chinatown."
        Economic Geography, 28 (1952), 244-255.
        Since the 1830s.

5095   MURPHY, JOHN ALLEN. Walworth, 1842-1942, (a
        history of one hundred years of valve manu-
facturing). [New York]: Walworth Co., 1945.
Pp. 72. MH-BA.

5096   MURRAY, EDWARD G., JOSEPH S. SHUBOW and ANSON
        PHELPS STOKES. "Religion in Boston: a gen-
eration of change." Boston, 59 (June, 1967), 32-34,
61-67.

5097   MUSSEY, HENRY RAYMOND. "The Christian Sci-
        ence censor." Nation, 130 (1930), 147-149,
175-178, 241-243, 291-293.

5098   MYERS, GRACE WHITING. History of the Massa-
        chusetts General Hospital, June, 1872 to De-
cember, 1900. Boston: Griffith-Stillings Pr.,
[1929?]. Pp. 224. MB.

5099   NADOLNY, JOE. "A century and a quarter of
        service to industry." Industry, 24 (Septem-
ber, 1959), 16e.
        Howe & French, Inc., industrial chemists.

5100   NASH, RAY. Printing as an art. Cambridge:
        Harvard Univ. Pr., 1955. Pp. xi, 141.
        A history of the Society of Printers, 1905-
1955.

5101   ____. "The Society of Printers and the
        [Boston] Public Library." More Books, 20
(1945), 221-226.

5102   NASON, JERRY. The story of the Boston mara-
        thon, from 1897. Boston: Boston Globe,
1966. Pp. 51.

5103   NATIONAL REVERE BANK. History of the Revere
        Bank of Boston, incorporated March, 1859; for
private circulation. Cambridge: Riverside Pr.,
1886. Pp. 32.

5104   NATIONAL UNION BANK OF BOSTON. A condensed
        record of the National Union Bank...from
1792 to 1904. Boston: J. A. Lowell, 1904. Unpaged. M.

5105   NAUWKERIGE Beschrijving van den Grooten Brand
        te Boston, 9, 10, en 11 November, 1872. Door
een Ooggetuige. Amsterdam: Scheltema & Holkema,
1872. Pp. 32. MB.
        Fire of 1872; by an eyewitness.

5106 NAVAL LIBRARY AND INSTITUTE, NAVY YARD, BOSTON. Statutes of the Naval Library and Institute, Navy Yard, Charlestown, Mass., adopted December 31, 1866, with an account of its origin and purpose, and a list of the officers and members past and present. Boston: J. E. Farwell, 1867. Pp. 36.

5107 NEALE, ROLLIN HEBER. An address delivered on the two hundredth anniversary of the organization of the First Baptist Church, Boston, June 7, 1865. Boston: Gould and Lincoln, 1865. Pp. 80.

5108 NELSON, HOWARD JOSEPH. "Walled cities of the United States." Association of American Geographers. Annals, 51 (1961), 1-22.
Boston is one of the cities studied.

5109 NESMITH, GEORGE W. "The British act of Parliament, known as the Boston Port Bill of 1774, and the liberality of New Hampshire, and other places, for the relief of the sufferers in Boston." Granite Mo, 2 (1879), 126-128.

5110 ____. "New Hampshire men at Bunker Hill." Granite Mo, 2 (1879), 266-272.

5111 NETTELS, CURTIS. "The economic relations of Boston, Philadelphia and New York, 1680-1715." JEBH, 3 (1930-1931), 185-215.

5112 NEUSNER, JACOB. "The impact of immigration and philanthropy upon the Boston Jewish community (1880-1914)." AJHSP, 46 (1956-1957), 71-85.

5113 NEW ENGLAND CATHOLIC HISTORICAL SOCIETY. Memorial volume of the 100th anniversary, Church of the Holy Cross, Boston. Boston, 1904. Pp. 137. MB.

5114 NEW ENGLAND ELECTRIC RAILWAY HISTORICAL SOCIETY. Surface cars of Boston, 1903-1963. Forty Fort, Pa.: H. E. Cox, 1963. Pp. 70.

5115 NEW ENGLAND HISTORIC GENEALOGICAL SOCIETY. Meeting of the New England Historic Genealogical Society, October 22, 1909, to commemorate its sixty-fifth anniversary. Boston, 1910. Pp. 21. M.

5116 NEW ENGLAND HOSPITAL FOR WOMEN AND CHILDREN. History and description. Boston, 1899. Pp. viii, 57. MB.
1859-1899.

5117 ____. History and description of the New England Hospital for Women and Children, Codman Avenue, Boston Highlands. Boston: W. L. Deland, 1876. Pp. 31. MB.

5118 NEW ENGLAND MANUFACTUERS' AND MECHANICS' INSTITUTE. Souvenir-album of the New England manufacturers' & Mechanics' Institute (past and future). Boston: Rand, Avery, 1884. Pp. 32.

5119 NEW ENGLAND MUTUAL LIFE INSURANCE CO. Back Bay since 2500 B.C. (1961) Rev. ed. Boston, 1965. Pp. 21. M.

5120 ____. Brief historical sketch. Boston, 1875. Pp. 7. MB.

5121 ____. First hundred years of the NEMLIC, 1835-1935, as recounted by Sydney A. Clark. Boston, 1935. Pp. 135. MB.

5122 "A NEW England sugar box of 1702." Antiques, 32 (1937), 309.
Edward Winslow, designer.

5123 NEW HAMPSHIRE INFANTRY. 2d REGT., 1775-1783. Orderly book kept by Jeremiah Fogg; Adjutant Colonel Enoch Poor's Second New Hampshire Regiment on Winter Hill, during the Siege of Boston, October 28, 1775, to January 12, 1776.... Albert A. Folsom, ed. Exeter, N.H.: Reprinted from the Exeter Newsletter, 1903. Pp. 85.

5124 NEWELL, LYMAN CHURCHILL. "Chemistry in old Boston." Bostonia, 4 (May, 1930), 3-15.
Early Boston industries.

5125 NICHOLLS, JOHN SAUNDERS CLYMO. The rise and growth of the East Boston courts: an historical and statistical account, with a forecast of the social and economical conditions in the district in the year 1980. East Boston, 1933. Pp. 173.

5126 NICHOLS, ARTHUR H. "Christ Church bells, Boston, Mass." NEHGR, 28 (1904), 63-71.

5127 NICKERSON HOME FOR CHILDREN. Historical report of the Nickerson Home for Children, 14 Tyler St., Boston, 1835-1910. Boston, [1910?]. Pp. 13. M.

5128 "NINETY years on." Living Age, 346 (1934), 198-224.
'Living Age,' periodical.

5129 NOBLE, JOHN. "The case of Maria in the Court of Assistants, 1681." CSMP, 6 (1899-1900), 323-335.
Execution of a Negro woman.

5130 NORCROSS, FREDERIC WALTER. "Ye ancient inns of Boston town." NEM, New Ser., 25 (1901-1902), 315-325.

5131 NORFOLK House and its historic surroundings. Providence: Livermore and Knight, 1901. Pp. 16. MB.
Hotel.

5132 NORMAN-WILCOX, GREGOR. "Staffordshire views of the Boston State House." Antiques, 20, (1931), 363-366.

5133 NORRIS, CURTIS B. "Boston's underground streams." NEG, 11 (Summer, 1970), 57-63.

5134 "NORTHEASTERN College: a history." National Magazine, 49 (1920-1921), 207-208.

5135 NORTHEND, MARY HARROD. "Quaint old Boston." Century, 100 (1920), 369-375.

5136 NORTON, JOHN. Historical sketch of Copp's Hill burying ground, with inscriptions and quaint epitaphs. (1910) 17th ed. [Boston], 1921. Pp. 32.

5137 NORTON, PAUL F. "Boston building ordinances, 1631-1714." SocArchHistJ, 20 (1961), 90-92.

5138 "NOTES from the history of Boston, Mass." About the First, (August, 1938), 4-7.

5139 "NOTES on the Boston Tea Party." NEM, New Ser., 8 (1893), 541-544.

5139A NUTTER, CHARLES READ. 125 years of the Harvard Musical Association. n.p., 1968. Pp. 17. MB.

5140 NYLANDER, JANE. "Vose and Coats, cabinet-makers." OTNE, 64 (1974), 87-91. 1789-1825.

5141 O'BRIEN, MICHAEL JOSEPH, ed. The Irish at Bunker Hill: evidence of Irish participation in the battle of 17 June 1775. Catherine Sullivan, ed. N.Y.: Devin-Adair, 1968. Pp. xi, 231. Also published in 1968 by Irish Univ. Pr.

5142 OBST, STELLA D. The story of Adath Israel: issued on the occasion of the tenth anniversary of the dedication of the present house of worship of the congregation. Boston: Daniels Printing, 1917. Pp. 33. [MWalAJHi].

5143 OBSTETRICAL SOCIETY OF BOSTON. Historical and biographical sketches by [Benjamin E.] Cotting and [William W.] Wellington. Boston: D. Clapp & Son, 1881. Pp. 73.

5144 ODD FELLOWS, INDEPENDENT ORDER OF. BOSTON. LIBRARY. Catalogue of books contained in the Odd Fellows' library, with a short history of the library, regulations, etc., etc. Fred W. Calkins, comp. Boston, 1875. Pp. x, 71.

5145 ODD FELLOWS, INDEPENDENT ORDER OF. BOSTON. MASSACHUSETTS LODGE, NO. 1. Statistics of Massachusetts Lodge, No. 1, I. O. of O. F., from its organization, March 26th, 1820, to May 1st, 1845, together with a directory of its members; also, a brief history of Odd Fellowship in the State of Massachusetts from the year 1819, to 1839. Simon B. Freeman, comp. Boston: A. Mudge, 1845. Pp. 46.

5146 ODD FELLOWS, INDEPENDENT ORDER OF. BOSTON. NORFOLK LODGE, NO. 48. Norfolk Lodge No. 48, I.O.O.F., instituted October 17, 1844, Norfolk Hall, Washington Street, Dorchester, fiftieth anniversary celebration and dedication of new hall. [Boston?, 1894?]. Pp. 31. MB. Includes history of the lodge.

5147 ODD FELLOWS, INDEPENDENT ORDER OF. CHARLESTOWN, MASS. HOWARD LODGE, NO. 22. Constitution, by-laws and rules of order of Howard Lodge, No. 22...together with extracts from the history of the lodge and a sketch of the life of John Howard. Boston: Alfred Mudge and Son, 1875. Pp. 136. M.

5148 ODIORNE, JAMES C. A complete list of the ministers of Boston of all denominations, from 1630 to 1642, arranged in the order of their settlement. NEHGR, 1 (1847), 134-136, 240-243, 318-321.

5149 O'KEEFE, JOSEPH JAMES. The men who robbed Brink's: the inside story of one of the most famous holdups in the history of crime, as told by Specs O'Keefe to Bob Considine, in co-operation with the FBI. N.Y.: Random House, 1961. Pp. 279.

5150 "OLD and new churches of Boston." NOHR, 5 (July 7, 1906), 2-5.

5151 OLD COLONY TRUST COMPANY. Building the Back Bay. Boston, 1926. Unpaged. MB.

5152 OLD Colony Trust Company, 1890-1915. Boston, 1915. Unpaged. MB.

5153 "THE OLD Corner Book-Store, the famous literary land-mark of Boston, and the men who met there." NEM, New Ser., 29 (1903-1904), 303-316.

5154 OLD Dorchester, recovery of some materials for its history, general and particular." NEHGR, 5 (1851), 389-402, 465-468. Biographies of inhabitants in 1641.

5155 THE OLD SCHOOL-BOYS OF BOSTON. The Old School Boys of Boston, organized 1880. Boston, 1903. Pp. 283. Biography.

5156 "OLD South Meeting House." SWJ, 46 (1930), 506-514.

5157 THE OLD Town-House of Boston (1883).... [2d. ed.]. Boston, 1887. Pp. 11.

5158 OLIVER, JEAN N. "The Copley Society of Boston." NEM, New Ser., 31 (1904-1905), 605-617. Formerly the Boston Art Students' Association.

5159 OLIVER, PETER, 1901-1959. "The Boston Theatre, 1800." CSMP, 34 (1937-1942), 554-570.

5160 O'MALLEY, CHARLES J. "American Irish Progress in Boston." AIrHSJ, 24 (1925), 183-190.

5161 O'MALLEY, THOMAS FRANCIS. New England's first convent school. [Somerville?]: Priv. Print., 1901. Pp. 9. MB. Ursuline Convent.

5162 "ONE hundred years of usefulness: the Massachusetts Historical Society." MagAmHist, 25 (1891), 250-253.

5163 ORATIONS, delivered at the request of the inhabitants of the town of Boston, to commemorate the evening of the fifth of March, 1770; when a number of citizens were killed by a party of British troops, quartered among them, in a time of peace. (1785) 2d. ed. Boston: Wm. T. Clap, 1807. Pp. 198. Annually, 1771-1783.

5164 ORCUTT, WILLIAM DANA. Good old Dorchester: a narrative history of the town. 1630-1893. (1893) 2d. ed. Cambridge: Univ. Pr., 1904. Pp. xv, 496.

5165 ORDWAY, WARREN. Carols and candles on Christmas eve. Boston: Lincoln & Smith, 1930. Unpaged.
Social life and customs.

5166 "ORIGIN of the New England Historic-Genealogical Society." NEHGR, 9 (1855), 2-12.

5167 "THE ORIGINAL Liberty Hall, Boston, Mass." MNEH, 1 (1891), 8-13.
Site surrounding the Liberty Tree, rallying point for Sons of Liberty.

5168 ORVIS, MARIANNE DWIGHT. Letters from Brook Farm, 1844-1847. Amy L. Reed, ed. Poughkeepsie, N.Y: Vassar College, 1928. Pp. xv, 191.

5169 OSGOOD, SAMUEL. "Echoes of Bunker Hill." Harper's Magazine, 51 (1875), 230-238.

5170 OTIS, HERBERT F. The story of India Wharf from an address...delivered on the centennial of the erection of India Wharf.... Boston: Merrymount Pr., 1916. Pp. 19. MB.

5171 "OUR bordering streets, Milk, Devonshire and Federal." About the First, (November, 1935), 4-7.

5172 OUR defenders: historical sketch and souvenir, Charlestown Artillery, Company D, Ninth Regiment Infantry, M.V.M. Boston: John A. Lowell, [1895?]. Pp. 65. MB.
Established in 1786.

5173 'OUR first men': a calendar of wealth, fashion and gentility; containing a list of those persons taxed in the city of Boston, credibly reported to be worth one hundred thousand dollars, with biographical notices of the principal persons... (1846) Rev. ed. Boston: Published by all the booksellers, 1846. Pp. 48.
Biography.

5174 OWEN, BARBARA. The organs and music of King's Chapel, 1713-1964. Boston: King's Chapel, 1966. Pp. 44.

5175 PACKARD, ALPHEUS S. History of the Bunker Hill Monument. Portland, Me.: Brown Thurston, 1853. Pp. 33. MBNEH.

5176 PALFREY, JOHN FORMAN. A sermon preached in the church in Brattle Square, in two parts, July 18, 1824.... Boston: Phelps & Farnham, 1825. Pp. 81.
Relates to the church.

5177 PALMER, GLENN. "From stables to studios." NEM, 54 (1915-1916), 106-110.
West End.

5178 PALMER, JULIUS A. "Hanover Church, Boston." CongQ, 14 (1872), 259-281.
Bowdoin St. Church as of 1831.

5179 PALTSITS, VICTOR HUGO. "New light on 'Publick Occurrences' America's first newspaper." AASP, 59 (1959), 75-88.

5180 "PAPER dealers of old Boston: Carter Rice & Co." Hurlbut's Papermaker Gentleman, 2 (Fall, 1934), 5-13.

5181 PARK, CHARLES EDWARDS. "Two ruling elders of the First Church in Boston: Thomas Leverett and Thomas Oliver." CSMP, 13 (1910-1911), 82-95.

5182 PARK, CHARLES FRANCIS. A history of the Lowell Institute School, 1903-1928. Cambridge: Harvard Univ. Pr., 1931. Pp. 192.

5183 PARKER, AMORY. Twenty crucial years: the story of Incorporated Investors, a pioneer investment company, 1925-1945. Boston: Parker Corporation, [1946?]. Pp. 126.

5184 PARKER, BARBARA N. "An early view of Boston." Antiques, 45 (1944), 192-193.
'View of Boston from Pemberton Hill,' painted in 1829 by Robert Salmon.

5185 PARKER, BOWDOIN S. What one Grand Army post has accomplished: history of the Edward W. Kinsley Post, No. 113...Boston, Mass. Norwood: Norwood Pr., 1913. Pp. xii, 420. MB.

5186 PARKER, FRANCIS JEWETT. "Could Putnam command at Bunker Hill?" NEHGR, 31 (1877), 403-413.
Israel Putnam.

5187 PARKER, KATHARINE HELEN. "The first epoch of art in Boston, progress of the Massachusetts Normal Art School." Bostonian, 1 (1894-1895), 662-670.

5188 PARKER, RICHARD GREEN. Sketch of the history of the Grammar School in the Easterly Part of Roxbury. Roxbury: Thomas S. Watts, 1826. Pp. 32. MB.

5189 PARKER, WILDER, AND COMPANY. Looking back one hundred years, from the beginning in 1820 to the present in the history of Parker, Wilder, & Co. of Boston. Boston, 1920. Pp. 24. M.
Dry goods.

5190 PARSONS, FRANCIS. The British attack at Bunker Hill, a paper read at a meeting of the Colonel Jeremiah Wadsworth Branch, Connecticut Society of the Sons of the American Revolution, Hartford Club, April 9, 1920. Hartford: Published by the Branch through the favor of Captain Clarence Horace Wickham, 1921. Pp. 35.

5191 PARSONS, HENRY S. "'The Boston Gazette' and the Boston Massacre." Antiques, 27 (1935), 96-98.

5192 _____. "Captain Quelch, pirate, and the colonial press." Antiques, 31 (1937), 190-193.

5193 PARSONS, SUSAN and WENDELL D. GARRETT. "The second Harrison Gray Otis House in Boston." Antiques, 92 (1967), 536-541.
Mount Vernon Street.

5194 PARTRIDGE, ALBERT L. "Simon Willard's regulator clocks." OTNE, 46 (1955-1956), 29-35.

5195   PATTEE, CHARLES H. "Recollections of old play-bills." Arena, 4 (1891), 604-614.

5196   PATTEN FANNY GORDON. History of the Winthrop School. Boston: Winthrop School Association, [1908?]. Pp. 101. MB.

5197   "PAUL Revere's lantern." Antiques, 18 (1930), 503.

5198   PAYNE, EDWARD F. Dickens days in Boston: a record of daily events.... Boston: Houghton Mifflin, 1927. Pp. xv, 274.
        Intellectual life, 1842 and 1867.

5199   _____. 68 of those 300 years: 1862-1930. Boston: Forbes Lithograph Manufacturing Co., 1930. Pp. 26. MB.
        History of the Forbes Lithograph Manufacturing Co.

5200   PAYSON, GILBERT R. "Long Wharf and the old water front." BSProc, (1928), 23-40.

5201   PAYSON, MRS. J. WENTWORTH. Reunion souvenir: a monograph of the first three decades, 1856-1886, bygones of Fairmount and Hyde Park revive the pleasant past, an address...at the first reunion of early settlers, Grand Army Hall, May 15, 1886. n.p., [1886?]. Unpaged. MBNEH.

5202   PEABODY, ANDREW PRESTON. "Boston mobs before the Revolution." Atlantic, 62 (1888), 321-333.

5203   PEABODY, HENRY GREENWOOD. Colonial and revolutionary landmarks of Boston: an illustrated lecture. Pasadena, Calif., 1913. Pp. 21.
        Historic houses.

5204   [PEABODY, MARY J.] Old Boston for young eyes.... [Cambridge]: J. Wilson and Son, 1880. Pp. 27.
        Not juvenile literature.

5205   [PEARSON, E. W.] City of Boston, its steam interests and leading engineers. Boston: Historical Publishing, 1886. Pp. xii, 272. MB.
        Author attribution by Boston Public Library; biography.

5206   PEASE, WILLIAM H. and JANE H. PEASE. "Boston Garrisonians and the problem of Frederick Douglass." CanJHist, 2 (September, 1967), 29-48.
        Antislavery.

5207   PEIRCE, HEMAN WINTHROP. Early days of the Copley Society, formerly the Boston Art Students' Association, 1879-1891. Boston: Rockwell and Churchill, 1903. Pp. 26.

5208   _____. The history of the School of the Museum of Fine Arts, Boston, 1877-1927. Boston: T. O. Metcalf, 1930. Pp. 129.

5209   [PEMBERTON, THOMAS]. "Account of fires in Boston, and other towns in Massachusetts in addition to those published in the description of Boston in the 3d volume of the Collections of the Massachusetts Historical Society." MHSC, 2 Ser., 1 (1814), 81-103.
        1701-1800; author attribution by the editor.

5210   [_____]. A topographical and historical description of Boston, 1794 by the author of the Historical Journal of the American War." MHSC, 3 (1794), 241-294.
        Author attribution by the editor; includes chronological list of Boston fires, 1653-1794.

5211   PENITENT FEMALES' REFUGE SOCIETY. Brief history of the rise and progress of the Penitent Females' Refuge, instituted Jan. 12, 1825. Boston: William D. Ticknor, 1849. Pp. 16. MB.
        Home for prostitutes; later called Bethesda Society.

5212   PENNINGTON, EDGAR LEGARE. "The Reverend Samuel Myles and his Boston ministry." HMPEC, 11 (1942), 154-178.
        King's Chapel.

5213   PEPPEARD, BERTHA A. "Before the days of Governor Square." Our Boston, 4 (December, 1928), 14-21.

5214   PERKINS, AUGUSTUS THORNDIKE. "Sketch of some of the losses to the departments of literature and the fine arts, occasioned by the great fire in Boston of 1872." NEHGR, 27 (1873), 369-375.

5215   PERKINS, JOHN CARROLL. "Some distinguished laymen in King's Chapel." UHSP, 5, Pt. 1 (1936), 1-17.

5216   PERRY, BLISS. "The Arlington Street incarnation." Atlantic, 150 (1932), 515-518.
        75th anniversary of the 'Atlantic Monthly.'

5217   _____. Park-Street papers. Boston: Houghton Mifflin, 1908. Pp. vii, 276.
        Houghton Mifflin, publisher.

5218   PERRY, EDWIN A. The Boston Herald and its history, how, when and where it was founded, its early struggles and hard-won successes.... Boston, 1878. Pp. 93.

5219   PESSEN, EDWARD. "Did fortunes rise and fall mercurially in antebellum America? The tale of two cities: Boston and New York." JSocHist, 4 (1970-1971), 339-358.

5220   _____. "Did labor support Jackson? The Boston story." PolSciQ, 64 (1949), 262-274.
        1828-1836; see also a commentary on this article by Robert T. Bower. entry 3757.

5221   PETER BENT BRIGHAM HOSPITAL. At the heart of a great medical centre, a record of the past and a promise for the future, 1913-1938. Cambridge: Abbey Pr., 1938. Pp. 46. M.

5222   PETERS, THOMAS MCCLURE. A picture of town government in Massachusetts Bay Colony at the middle of the seventeenth century, as illustrated by the town of Boston.... N.Y.: McWilliams Printing, [1890]. Pp. 73.

5223 PETERSON, BERNARD. "Boston firm spans life of the elevator industry." Industry, 16 (September, 1951), 16-18, 66.
George T. McLauthlin Co.

5224 _____. "The story of Underwood deviled ham." Industry, 12 (March, 1947), 23-25, 61-62.
William Underwood Company--canned food.

5225 PHILLIPS, ASA E. Historic tour of Boston, prepared for the meeting of the General Court of the Order of the Founders and Patriots of America. Boston: Hutcheson, 1971. Pp. 35. MBNEH.

5226 PHILLIPS, JAMES DUNCAN. "Recollections of Houghton Mifflin Company fifty years ago." Publishers' Weekly, 152 (November 1, 1947), 2165-2167.

5227 PHILPOTT, J. A. "The First National Bank of Boston marks its 150th anniversary." About the First, (May, 1934), 3-5, 12-18.

5228 PICKENS, BUFORD. "Wyatt's Pantheon, the State House in Boston and a new view of Bulfinch." SocArchHistJ, 29 (1970), 124-131.

5229 PICTORIAL history of Boston, 250th anniversary, 1630, 1880. Boston: Photo-electrotype Co., [1880]. Pp. 16.

5230 PIERCE, EDWARD LILLIE. The diary of John Rowe, a Boston merchant, 1764-1779.... Cambridge: J. Wilson and Son, 1895. Pp. 108.
Social life and customs.

5231 PIERCE, JOHN. A discourse delivered at Dorchester, on 17 June, 1830, to commemorate the completion of the second century from its settlement by our Pilgrim Fathers. Boston: W. L. Lewis, 1830. Pp. 36.

5232 PIERCE, S. S. CO., BOSTON. Annals of a corner grocery, 80th birthday of S. S. Pierce Co., 1831-1911. [Boston?, 1911?]. Unpaged.

5233 PIKE, JAMES, ed. History of the churches of Boston, giving a full account in denominational divisions, of all the church, organizations of the city, from their formation to the present time, with dates and complete statistics.... Boston: Ecclesia Publishing, 1883. Pp. 122.
This volume called 'Division 1, Baptist and Presbyterian.' No more published.

5234 PINANSKI, ABRAHAM EDWARD. The street railway system of metropolitan Boston. N.Y.: McGraw, 1908. Pp. 58.

5235 "A PIONEER in the rubber industry." Industry, 22 (July, 1957), 21-23, 60.
Davidson Rubber Co., centennial.

5236 "PIONEERS in water purification equipment." Industry, 16 (April, 1951), 17-18, 36.
Barnstead Still & Sterilizer Co.

5237 PITKIN, R. B. "A look at Boston, Massachusetts." American Legion Magazine, 82 (June, 1967), 24-29, 51-52.
Changes since 1940.

5238 PIZER, DONALD. "The radical drama in Boston, 1889-1891." NEQ, 31 (1958), 361-374.

5239 PLACE, CHARLES A. "The New South Church. Boston, Mass." OTNE, 11 (1920-1921), 51-53.

5240 PLECK, ELIZABETH H. "The two-parent household: Black family structure in late nineteenth-century Boston." JSocHist, 6 (1972-1973), 3-31.

5241 PLUTO CLUB, BOSTON. Journal of the Pluto Club, & selections from the Hades Gazette. Boston: Priv. Print., 1878. Pp. 102. MB.
Social club.

5242 POIRIER, PASCAL. "Des Acadiens déportés à Boston en 1755." Royal Society of Canada. Proceedings and Transactions, 3 Ser., 2, Section 1 (1908), 125-180.

5243 POND, SHEPARD. "History of the Boston Numismatic Society." Numismatist, 48 (1935) 426-434.

5244 PORTER, ALEXANDER S. "Changes of values in real estate in Boston the past one hundred years." BSPub, 1 (1886-1888), 57-74.

5245 PORTER, EDWARD GRIFFIN. Rambles in old Boston, New England. Boston: Cupples, Upham, 1887. Pp. xviii, 439.
Historic buildings.

5246 POSSE GYMNASIUM, BOSTON. Posse Gymnasium: history, location, aim. Boston: Everett Pr., 1897. Pp. 14. MB.

5247 POTTER, JOSEPH S. The past, present and future of Boston, speech...on the subject of uniting certain cities and towns with the city of Boston, delivered in the Massachusetts Senate, Thursday, April 24, 1873.... Boston: Wright & Potter, 1873. Pp. 84.

5248 POTTER, WILLIAM JAMES. Free Religious Association: its twenty five years. Boston: Free Religious Association of America, 1892. Pp. 31. MB.

5249 PRATT, ROBERT IRVING. "The 'traitors' who changed the world." Boston, 55 (July, 1963), 36-44.
Revolutionary Boston.

5250 PRAY, LEWIS GLOVER. Historical sketch of the Twelfth Congregational Society in Boston. Boston: John Wilson, 1863. Pp. 123. MBNEH.

5251 PRELUDE to revolt: steps to the Boston Massacre; readings from the Annals of America. Chicago: Encyclopaedia Brittanica Educational Corp., 1969. Pp. 32.

5252 PRENDERGAST, FRANK M. "Dedicated to high ethical standards." Industry, 22 (March, 1957), 17-19, 46.
Otis Clapp & Son, pharmaceuticals.

5253 PRESCOTT, WILLIAM. "Judge Prescott's account of the Battle of Bunker Hill." MHSP (1875-1876), 68-79.

5254 PRESSEY, PARK. "Early Boston churches." OTNE, 41 (1950-1951), 56-60.

5255 PRINCE, JOHN TUCKER. "Boston in 1813, reminiscences of an old school boy." BSPub, 3 (1906), 75-101.

5256 ____. "Boston's lanes and alleys." BSPub, 7 (1910), 9-29.

5257 PRINCE, THOMAS. Account of the revival of religion in Boston, in the years 1740-1-2-3. Boston: S. T. Armstrong, 1823. Pp. 55. MB.

5258 PRINDLE, FRANCES WESTON CARRUTH. Fictional rambles in & about Boston. N.Y.: McClure, Phillips, 1902. Pp. xxiii, 380.
Not fiction.

5259 PROVIDENT INSTITUTION FOR SAVINGS, BOSTON. One hundred years of savings bank service, a brief account of the origin, growth and present condition of the Provident Institution for Savings in the Town of Boston. Boston, 1916. Pp. 35.

5260 "THE PUBLISHER of the first regular American newspaper." HistMag, 8 (1864), 30-31.
John Campbell and 'The News-Letter.'

5261 PULSIFER, DAVID. An account of the Battle of Bunker Hill...with General Burgoyne's account of the battle. Boston: A. Williams, 1875. Pp. 75.

5262 PURCELL, HUGH DEVEREUX. "Don't give up the ship!" United States Naval Institute. Proceedings, 91 (1965), 82-94.
Capture of U.S. frigate 'Chesapeake' off Boston in the War of 1812.

5263 PUTNAM, ELIZABETH C. The Massachusetts Auxiliary Visitors. n.p., [1900?]. Pp. 18. MB.
Charity.

5264 QUARLES, BENJAMIN. "Crispus Attucks." AHI, 5 (November, 1970), 38-42.
Boston Massacre.

5265 QUEN, JACQUES M. "Early nineteenth-century observations on the insane in the Boston Almshouse." JHistMed, 23 (1968), 80-85.

5266 QUINCY, JOSIAH, 1772-1864. An address to the citizens of Boston, on the XVIIth of September, MDCCCXXX, the close of the second century from the first settlement of the city. Boston: J. H. Eastburn, 1830. Pp. 68.

5267 ____. The history of the Boston Athenaeum, with biographical notices of its deceased founders. Cambridge: Metcalf, 1851. Pp. xii, 263.

5268 ____. A municipal history of the town and city of Boston, during two centuries, from September 17, 1630, to September 17, 1830. Boston: C. C. Little and J. Brown, 1852. Pp. xi, 444.

5269 QUINCY, JOSIAH, 1859-1919. An address commemorative of the organization of city government in Boston, May 1, 1822, delivered at the request of the City Council on September 17, 1897. Boston: Municipal Printing Office, 1897. Pp. 72.

5270 QUINLAN, RICHARD J. "Growth and devolopment of Catholic education in the Archdiocese of Boston." CathHistRev, 22 (1936-1937), 27-41.

5271 NO ENTRY

5272 RADWAY, G. FRANK. Brahmins & bullyboys: G. Frank Radway's Boston Album. Stephen Halpert and Brenda Halpert, eds. Boston: Houghton Mifflin, 1973. Pp. xii, 143.

5273 RAILEY, JULIA HOUSTON. Retail and romance. Boston: Walker Lithograph & Publishing, 1926. Pp. 32.
Jordan Marsh Co.; department store, 1851-1926.

5274 RANDALL, RICHARD H., JR. "Boston chairs." OTNE, 54 (1963-1964), 12-20.

5275 ____. "William Randall, Boston japanner." Antiques, 105 (1974), 1127-1131.
Worked in Boston, 1715-1749.

5276 ____. "Works of Boston cabinetmakers; 1795-1825." Antiques, 81 (1962), 186-189, 412-415.

5277 RANDOLPH, WARREN. Mercies remembered: an anniversary and historical discourse preached at the Harvard Street Baptist Church in Boston, on Lord's Day, April 23d, 1865. Boston: The Church, 1865. Pp. 23. MB.

5278 RANSOM, WILL. "Private presses and the books they have given us, XIV: Daniel Berkeley Updike, the Merrymount Press, Boston." Publishers' Weekly, 113 (April 14, 1928), 1615-1619.

5279 RAUBENHEIMER, HERBERT C. Pharmacy and pharmacists in colonial Boston, Massachusetts. [Boston, 1966]. v.p.

5280 READ, CHARLES F. "The Brimmer School." BSProc, (1919), 31-46.

5281 ____. "The old State House, and its predecessor the first Town House." BSProc, (1908), 32-50.

5282 ____. "Washington's visits to Boston." BSProc, (1912), 56-68.
1756, 1776, 1789.

5283 REARDON, WILLIAM R. "The tradition behind Bostonian censorship." Educational Theatre Journal, 7 (1955), 97-101.
   Censorship of the theatre prior to 1806.

5284 "RED devil born on Boston wharf." Industry, 37 (August, 1972), 14-15.
   William Underwood Co.; canned food.

5285 REED, EDWARD F. "Reminiscences of Boston in the early days of the Civil War." BSProc, (1907), 28-42.

5286 REED, GEORGE B., (FIRM) BOSTON. After forty years, 1866-1906. [Boston?, 1906?]. Pp. 7. MBNEH.
   Law publishers.

5287 REGAN, MARY JANE. Echoes from the past: reminiscences of the Boston Athenaeum. [Boston]: Boston Athenaeum, 1927. Pp. 90.

5288 REICHMANN, FELIX. "Prelude to the Boston Massacre." American-German Review, 10 (June, 1944), 22-23.
   February, 1770; episode of Ebenezer Richardson and the death of Christopher Snider.

5289 REID, JOHN PHILLIP. "A lawyer acquitted: John Adams and the Boston Massacre trial." AmJLegalHist, 18 (1974), 189-207.

5290 "REMARKABLE superstitions." NEHGR, 2 (1848), 54-56.
   Spiritualism, seventeenth century.

5291 "REMINISCENCES of old Boston." BSProc, (1896), 23-42.

5292 REPORT of a French Protestant refugee, in Boston, 1687. Brooklyn, 1868. Pp. v, 42.

5293 "REPRESENTATIVES of the town of Boston in the General Court before the American Revolution." MHSC, 2 Ser., 10 (1823), 23-29.
   1634-1774.

5294 REYNOLDS, GRINDALL. Discourse preached on the occasion of leaving the old meeting house, Jamaica Plain, West Roxbury, March 20, 1853. Boston: Joseph G. Torrey, 1853. Pp. 28. MBNEH.

5295 ____. "Siege and evacuation of Boston." Unitarian Review and Religious Magazine, 5 (1876), 242-266.

5296 RHOADES, ELIZABETH and BROCK JOBE. "Recent discoveries in Boston japanned furniture." Antiques, 105 (1974), 1082-1091.

5297 RHODES, LEONARD H. Brief history of Tremont Temple. n.p., 1917. Pp. 29. MBNEH.

5298 RICE & HUTCHINGS, INC. A retrospect, 1866-1916; Rice & Hutchins, Inc. Cambridge: Univ. Pr., 1916. Pp. 54.
   Shoes.

5299 RICH, FRANK B. "The Butler School: the oldest school-house in Hyde Park." HPHR, 1 (1891-1892), 9-12.

5300 RICH, ROBERT. "'A wilderness of Whigs': the wealthy men of Boston." JSocHist, 4 (1970-1971), 263-276.
   Nineteenth century.

5301 RICHARDSON, GEORGE L. "History of Stony Brook." HPHR, 3 (1903), 47-54.

5302 ____. "Lyman Hall." HPHR, 2 (1892-1893), 64-69.
   Multi-purpose historic building.

5303 RICHARDSON, HENRY HOBSON. "Description of Trinity Church." NEM, New Ser., 8 (1893), 158-165.

5304 RIDEING. WILLIAM H. "The gateway of Boston." Harper's Magazine, 69 (1884), 352-361.

5305 ____. "Some Boston artists and their studios." American Magazine, 7 (1887-1888), 331-343, 466-478.

5306 RIDLEY, FLORIDA RUFFIN. "The Negro in Boston." Our Boston, 2 (January, 1927), 15-20.

5307 RILEY, STEPHEN THOMAS. "A monument to Colonel Robert Gould Shaw." MHSP, 75 (1963), 27-38.

5308 ROBB, RUSSELL. "Stone & Webster organization: early history of the firm." SWJ, 1 (1907), 4-6.

5309 ROBBINS, CHANDLER, 1810-1882. A history of the Second Church, or Old North, in Boston, to which is added a history of the New Brick Church.... Boston: J. Wilson & Son, 1852. Pp. viii, 320.

5310 ROBERTS, JOSEPHINE E. "Elizabeth Peabody and the Temple School." NEQ, 15 (1942), 497-508.
   Amos Bronson Alcott's school in the Masonic Temple, 1835.

5311 ____. "Horace Mann and the Peabody sisters." NEQ, 18 (1945), 164-180.
   1830s.

5312 ROBERTSON, JANET L. and ANDREW RICHARDS, comps. Puritan heritage; a brief history of Second Church in Dorchester. Boston, 1955. Unpaged.

5313 ROBIN, ABBÉ. "Boston eighty years ago." HistMag, 6 (1862), 242-245.

5314 ROBINSON, DWIGHT P. Massachusetts Investors Trust, pioneer in open end investment trusts. N.Y.: Newcomen Society in North America, 1954. Pp. 28.

5315 ROBINSON, LILLIAN V. Children's house: a history of the Hawthorne Club. Boston: Marshall Jones, 1937. Pp. 116.
   Social settlement.

5316 RODWIN, LLOYD. Housing and economic progress: a study of the housing experiences of
Boston's middle-income families. Cambridge: Harvard Univ. Pr. & Technology Pr., 1961. Pp. 228.

5317 _____. "Income and housing cost trends of
Boston's middle-income groups, 1846-1947."
Land Economics, 25 (1950), 368-382.

5318 _____. "The paradox of Boston's middle income housing progress." Appraisal Journal,
19 (1951), 42-55.
1913-1947.

5319 _____. "Rent control and housing: a case
study." Land Economics, 27 (1951), 314-323.
1920-1930.

5320 _____. "Studies in middle income housing."
Social Forces, 30 (1952), 292-299.
Building and loan associations and the suc-
cess of 'three deckers,' 1880-1948.

5321 ROE, ALFRED SEELYE. "The Massachusetts State
House." NEM, New Ser., 19 (1898-1899), 659-
677.

5322 _____. The Massachusetts State House: a
sketch of its history and a guide to its
points of interest. Worcester: F. S. Blanchard,
1899. Pp. 32. M.

5323 _____. The old Representatives' Hall, 1798-
1895: an address delivered before the Massachusetts House of Representatives, January 2,
1895. Boston: Wright and Potter, 1895. Pp. 72.

5324 ROLLINS, CARL PURINGTON. "D. B. Updike:
the Merrymount Press." Publishers' Weekly,
137 (March 2, 1940), 1005-1007.

5325 ROLLINS, JAMES W. "History of the Boston
dry dock...." Boston Society of Civil Engineers. Journal, 4 (1917), 261-288.

5326 ROMAINE, LAWRENCE B. "American hardware--
1795." CEAIA, 9 (1956), 21-22.
Ledger and store of Samuel Richards.

5327 _____. "Bag, bucket, bedkey and screw
driver." OTNE, 47 (1956-1957), 72-77.
Alert Eagle Fire Society.

5328 _____. "Weather vanes." CEAIA, 1 (January,
1937), page 21-8.
J. Harris & Son.

5329 "THE ROMANCE of chocolate." Industry, 12
(February, 1947), 29-32.
Walter Baker Co.

5330 ROMIG, EDGAR DUTCHER. The story of Trinity
Church in the city of Boston. [Boston]:
The Wardens and Vestry, 1952. Pp. 66.

5331 ROSEN, BENJAMIN. The trend of Jewish population in Boston: a study to determine the
location of a Jewish communal building. [Boston,
1921]. Pp. 28.

5332 ROSLINDALE, MASS. SACRED HEART CHURCH. Tent
to the temple: Sacred Heart Church, Roslindale, Mass., diamond jubilee, 1893-1968. Roslindale, 1968. Pp. 72. MB.

5333 ROSS, MARJORIE DRAKE. The book of Boston:
the colonial period, 1630 to 1775. N.Y.:
Hastings House, 1960. Pp. 127.

5334 _____. The book of Boston: the Federal period, 1775 to 1837. N.Y.: Hastings House,
1961. Pp. 176.

5335 _____. The book of Boston: the Victorian
period, 1837 to 1901. N.Y.: Hastings House,
1964. Pp. 166.

5336 ROSSITER, MARGARET W. "Benjamin Silliman
and the Lowell Institute: the popularization
of science in nineteenth-century America." NEQ, 44
(1971), 602-626.

5337 ROSSITER, WILLIAM SIDNEY, ed. Days and ways
in old Boston. Boston: R. H. Stearns, 1915.
Pp. 144.

5338 ROSTENBERG, LEONA. "Number thirteen West
Street." Book Collector's Packet, 4 (Septem-
ber, 1945), 7-9.
Elizabeth Peabody's Bookstore, 1839-1845.

5339 ROTUNDO, BARBARA. "The literary lights were
always bright at 148 Charles Street." Am
Heritage, 22 (February, 1971), 10-15.
Home of James T. Fields in nineteenth century.

5340 ROWE, GEORGE HOWARD MALCOLM. Historical description of the buildings and grounds of
the Boston City Hospital, together with chronological tables, statistics of appropriations, cost,
maintenance, etc. Boston, 1906. Pp. 102. MB.

5341 ROWE, HENRIETTA GOULD. "Old Dorchester Burying Ground." Putnam's HM, New Ser., 3
(1895), 81-86.

5342 ROWE, JOHN. Letters and diary of John Rowe,
Boston merchant, 1759-1762, 1764-1779, with
extracts from a paper written for the Massachusettts
Historical Society, by Edward Lillie Pierce. Anne
Rowe Cunningham, ed. Boston: W. B. Clarke, 1903.
Pp. 453.

5343 ROWELL, BENJAMIN WINSLOW and ALBERT L. RICH-
ARDSON, comps. Massachusetts Consistory of
Sublime Princes of the Royal Secret, thirty-second
degree of the Ancient and Accepted Scottish Rite for
the northern jurisdiction of the United States, Boston, Massachusetts. Instituted at Lowell, July 10,
1860. Chartered May 15, 1861. Formed a union with
De Witt Clinton and Boston Consistories and removed
to Boston, February 15, 1871. Boston: Griffith-
Stillings Pr., 1908. Pp. xv, 142.

5344 ROXBURY, MASS. Roxbury centennial, an account of the celebration in Roxbury, November
22, 1876, with the oration of Gen. Horace Binney
Sargent, speeches at the dinner and other matters.
Boston: Rockwell and Churchill, 1877. Pp. 104.

5345 ROXBURY, MASS. ALL SOULS UNITARIAN CHURCH. BRANCH ALLIANCE. The Roxbury Magazine, published by the Branch Alliance of the All Souls Unitarian Church, Roxbury, Mass. Boston: G. H. Ellis, 1899. Pp. 48.

5346 ROXBURY, MASS. DUDLEY STREET BAPTIST CHURCH. History of the Dudley Street Baptist Church, Roxbury. Boston: Gould & Lincoln, 1855. Pp. 54. MB.

5347 ROXBURY, MASS. ELIOT CONGREGATIONAL CHURCH. First hundred years. n.p., [1934?]. Pp. 8. MBNEH.

5348 ROXBURY, MASS. FIRST CHURCH. Historical sketch.... n.p., 1896. Pp. 18. MBNEH.

5349 ROXBURY, MASS. FIRST RELIGIOUS SOCIETY. Tercentenary celebration of the First Church in Roxbury...1630-1930. Roxbury, 1930. Pp. 23. MB.

5350 ROXBURY, MASS. HIGHLAND CONGREGATIONAL CHURCH. Directory...historical sketch.... Boston: Beacon Pr., 1886. Pp. 31. MB.

5351 _____. Manual of the Highland Congregational Church, comprising its history, articles of faith.... Boston: Rockwell and Churchill, 1870. Pp. 17. M.

5352 ROXBURY, MASS. TRINITY LUTHERAN CHURCH. History of Trinity Lutheran Church, Parker and Gore Streets, Roxbury, Massachusetts, 1871-1946. South Boston: Lawton Pr., 1946. Unpaged. MB.

5353 ROXBURY, MASS. UNIVERSALIST CHURCH. Semi-centennial memorial of the Universalist Church, Roxbury, Mass. Boston: Universalist Publishing House, 1871. Pp. 108. MBNEH.

5354 ROXBURY CHARITABLE SOCIETY. Celebration of the one hundredth anniversary of the Roxbury Charitable Society, November 22, 1894...with historical notes and a list of members. [Boston?, 1895?]. Pp. 84.

5355 ROXBURY HOME FOR AGED WOMEN. Roxbury Home for Aged Women 1856-1916. Boston: Geo. H. Ellis, 1916. Pp. 12. M.

5356 "ROXBURY'S historical landmarks." Roxbury HSY, (1917), 14-17.

5357 ROZ, FIRMIN. "Boston." France-Amérique, 21 (1930), 311-314. In French.

5358 RUBIN, JULIUS. Canal or railroad? Imitation and innovation in the response to the Erie Canal in Philadelphia, Baltimore, and Boston. Philadelphia: American Philosophical Society, 1961. Pp. 106.

5359 RUDWICK, ELLIOTT M. "Race leadership struggle: background on the Boston Riot of 1903." JNegroEd, 3 (1962), 16-24.

5360 RUGGLES, THEODORE SLEEPER. "Governor William Shirley and his Roxbury mansion." Roxbury HSY, (1919), 14-25.

5361 RUSS, W. A. "Boston's historic tree: the old elm on the Common." Potter's AmMo, 19 (1882), 291-293.

5362 _____. "The old cradle of Liberty--Faneuil Hall." The Manhattan, 2 (1883), 456-465.

5363 RUSSELL, BANJAMIN. "Boston, the town of the bean and the cod is a cosmopolitan city; all racial strains join in perpetuating its traditions." Holiday, 2 (August, 1947), 26-41, 86-87.

5364 RUSSELL, FRANCIS. "Coming of the Jews." Antioch Review, 15 (1955-1956), 19-38. Dorchester and Mattapan in the 1920s.

5365 _____. "Coolidge and the Boston Police Strike." Antioch Review, 16 (1956-1957), 403-415. 1919.

5366 _____. Forty years on: the old Roxbury Latin School of Kearsarge Avenue.... West Roxbury, 1970. Pp. 104. MB.

5367 _____. The great interlude: neglected events and persons from the First World War to the depression. N.Y.: McGraw-Hill, 1964. Pp. 212.

5368 _____. "Living and dying in Boston." National Review, 25 (1973), 1292-1296. Dorchester.

5369 _____. "Lost elegance." Am Heritage, 8 (June, 1957), 36-39, 107. Shirley Place, historic house.

5370 _____. "Seventy-five years of the Bostonian Society." BSProc, (1956), 27-41.

5371 _____. "The strike that made a President." Am Heritage, 14 (October, 1963), 44-47, 90-94. Calvin Coolidge and the Boston Police Strike, 1919.

5372 RUSSELL, THOMAS H. "Central Church, Boston." CongQ, 12 (1870), 519-523.

5373 "THE RUSSIAN festival in Boston." AmHist Record, 2 (1873), 272-274. Festival in honor of Russian achievements over their French invaders, 1813.

5374 RUTMAN, DARRETT BRUCE. Winthrop's Boston: portrait of a Puritan town, 1630-1649. Chapel Hill: Univ. of North Carolina Pr., 1965. Pp. x, 324.

5375 RUTTER, OWEN. A brief history of the firm of Messrs. Davison, Newman & Co., now incorporated with the West Indian Produce Association, Ltd. London: Davison, Newman, 1938. Pp. 39. MB. Shipper of the tea thrown into Boston Harbor.

5376 RYAN, GEORGE E. Botolph of Boston. North
Quincy: Christopher Publishing House, 1971.
Pp. 268.

5377 ____. "No kingdom for a horse." Boston,
58 (March, 1966), 20-21.
Social life and customs.

5378 RYAN, KATE. Old Boston Museum days. Boston:
Little, Brown, 1915. Pp. xii, 264.
A theater.

5379 SAINT BOTOLPH CLUB, BOSTON. XIIth night
revel of the St. Botolph Club to celebrate
its XXth anniversary, Friday, January the fifth,
1900. Boston: Mudge, 1900. Pp. 12. MB.

5380 ST. ELIZABETH'S HOSPITAL, BOSTON. One hundred years of service, 1869-1969. Boston,
1969. Unpaged. MB.

5381 SAINT MONICA'S HOME FOR SICK COLORED WOMEN
AND CHILDREN. St. Monica's Home 1888-1967,
under the direction of the Sisters of St. Margaret.
n.p., [1968?]. Pp. 11. M.

5382 SALEM AND MARINER'S CHURCH. Memorial volume. Boston: The Committee, 1874. Pp. 52.
MB.

5383 SAMS, HENRY W., ed. Autobiography of Brook
Farm. Englewood Cliffs, N.J.: Prentice-
Hall, 1958. Pp. 271.

5384 SAMSON, JOSEPHINE. Celebrities of Louisburg
Square. Greenfield, Mass.: Record Pr.,
1924. Pp. 24. MB.
Social life and customs.

5385 SANBORN, ALVAN FRANCIS. Moody's lodging
house, and other tenement sketches. Boston:
Copeland and Day, 1895. Pp. 175.

5386 SARGENT, AARON. "Recollections of Boston
merchants in the eighteen-forties." BSProc,
(1904), 25-37.

5387 SARGENT, GEORGE HENRY. "American book clubs:
The Bibliophile Society." Literary Collect-
or, 7 (1903-1904), 161-167.

5388 ____. Lauriat's, 1872-1922; being a sketch
of early Boston booksellers, with some account of Charles E. Lauriat Company and its founder,
Charles E. Lauriat. Boston: Priv. Print, 1922.
Pp. 58.

5389 ____. "Paul Revere's 'Boston Massacre.'"
Antiques, 11 (1927), 214-216.
An engraving.

5390 [SARGENT, JOHN TURNER]. The crisis of Uni-
tarianism in Boston, as connected with the
Twenty-Eighth Congregational Society, with some ac-
count of the origin and decline of that organiza-
tion. By Bronze Beethoven, pseud. Boston: Walker,
Wise, 1859. Pp. 26. MWA.
Author attribution by American Antiquarian
Society.

5391 ____. The ministry at Suffolk Street Chapel: its origin, progress and experience.
Boston: B. H. Greene, 1845. Pp. 40. M.

5392 [SARGENT, LUCIUS MANLIUS]. Notices of the
histories of Boston. By Sigma, pseud. Boston: A. Williams, 1857. Pp. 7.

5393 SARGENT, MARY ELIZABETH FISKE, ed. Sketches
and reminiscences of the Radical Club of
Chestnut Street, Boston. Boston: J. R. Osgood,
1880. Pp. xii, 418.

5394 SATURDAY EVENING GIRLS. The story of the
Saturday Evening Girls...especially written
for the reunion, Thursday, evening, Dec. 12, 1929
at the West End House, Boston.... Boston, 1929.
Pp. 16. MB.
Club.

5395 SAUL, NORMAN E. "The beginnings of American-
Russian Trade, 1763-1766." WMQ, 3 Ser., 26
(1969), 596-600.

5396 SAVAGE, EDWARD HARTWELL, comp. Boston
events: a brief mention and the date of more
than 5,000 events that transpired in Boston from
1630 to 1880, covering a period of 250 years, together with other occurrences of interest, arranged
in alphabetical order. Boston: Tolman & White,
1884. Pp. 218.

5397 ____. Police records and recollections; or,
Boston by daylight and gaslight for two hundred and forty years. Boston: J. P. Dale, 1873.
v.p.

5398 SAWYER, JOSEPH DILLAWAY. The last leaf on
the tree: reminiscence of the Old North
Church. Boston, 1930. Pp. 40. MBNEH.

5399 [SAWYER, SAMUEL ELWELL]. History of the
West Roxbury Park: how obtained, disregard
of private rights, absolute injustice, arbitrary
laws, right of eminent domain, 1873 to 1887....
Gloucester: Cape Ann Breeze Print, 1887. Pp. 103.
Now Franklin Park; dedication signed S. E. S.

5400 SAWYER, TIMOTHY THOMPSON. Old Charlestown:
historical, biographical, reminiscent. Boston: J. H. West, 1902. Pp. 527.

5401 SAXTON, F. WILLARD. "A few reminiscences of
Brook Farm." PVMA, 6 (1912-1920), 371-386.

5402 SAYLES, ADELAIDE K. BURTON. The story of the
Children's Museum of Boston from its beginnings to November 18, 1936. Boston: G. H. Ellis,
1937. Pp. xii, 87.

5403 SCALES, JOHN. "Men of old Nottingham [N.H.]
at the battle of Bunker Hill." Granite Mo,
2 (1879), 204-207.

5404 SCANLAN, MICHAEL JAMES. Brief history of the
Archdiocese of Boston. Boston: Nicholas M.
Williams, 1908. Pp. 60. MB.

5405 A SCHEDULE of the ancient colored inhabitants, of Charlestown, Mass., on record prior
to 1800.... [Charlestown?, 1870?]. Unpaged.

5406   SCHINDLER, SOLOMON. Israelites in Boston: a tale describing the development of Judaism in Boston. Boston: Berwick & Smith, 1889. Unpaged. MB.

5407   SCHLESINGER, ARTHUR MEIER. "Propaganda and the Boston newspaper press, 1767-1770." CSMP, 32 (1933-1937), 396-416.

5408   SCHOFIELD, MIKE. "The Old North Church isn't." Metro, 1 (April, 1971), 28-34.

5409   SCHOFIELD, WILLIAM GREENOUGH. Freedom by the Bay: the Freedom Trail. Chicago: Rand McNally, 1974. Pp. 160.

5410   SCHOULER, JAMES. "Abraham Lincoln at Tremont Temple in 1848." MHSP, 42 (1908-1909), 70-83.

5411   SCHOULER, WILLARD C. "Cattle industry of Boston." NEM, New Ser., 41 (1909-1910), 328-337.

5412   SCHULBERG, HERBERT C. and FRANK BAKER. "The history and development of Boston State Hospital: 1839-1963." Massachusetts Journal of Mental Health, 2 (Fall, 1971), 20-30.

5413   SCHULTZ, STANLEY KENTON. The culture factory: Boston public schools, 1789-1860. N.Y.: Oxford Univ. Pr., 1973. Pp. xvi, 394.

5414   SCHUYLER, MONTGOMERY. "Boston, ancient and modern." Pall Mall Magazine, 28 (1902), 325-337.

5415   SCHWAB, EMIL. 'The John Hancock': an historical sketch. Boston: John Hancock Mutual Life Insurance, 1912. Pp. 109. MB. Semicentennial.

5416   SCHWARTZ, HAROLD. "Fugitive slave days in Boston." NEQ, 27 (1954), 191-212.

5417   SCOTS' CHARITABLE SOCIETY, BOSTON. The celebration of the 182d anniversary...November 30, 1839. Boston, 1840. Pp. 29. MB.

5418   SCUDDER, HORACE ELISHA. "The Battle of Bunker Hill." Atlantic, 36 (1875), 79-91.

5419   _____. Boston town. Boston: Houghton Mifflin, 1881. Pp. viii, 243.

5420   _____. "The Siege of Boston." Atlantic, 37 (1876), 466-481.

5421   SCUDDER, WINTHROP SALTONSTALL, ed. "A history of the Gardiner Greene Estate on Cotton Hill, now Pemberton Square, Boston." BSPub, 12 (1915), 39-62.

5422   SEABURG, CARL. Boston observed. Boston: Beacon Pr., 1971. Pp. 328.

5423   SEARS, JOHN VAN DER ZEE. My friends at Brook Farm. N.Y.: D. FitzGerald, 1912. Pp. 172.

5424   SEARS, MARIAN V. "The National Shawmut Bank consolidation of 1898." BusHR, 39 (1965), 368-390.

5425   SEAVER, FRED. Founders and incorporators of the Third Parish in Jamaica Plain. Jamaica Plain, 1917. Pp. 11. MBNEH.

5426   SEAVER, WILLIAM J. An octogenarian's rambling recollections of Boston, 1840-1851. Brookline: Brookline Print, 1917. Unpaged. M.

5427   SEDGWICK, ORA GANNETT. "A girl of sixteen at Brook Farm." Atlantic, 85 (1900), 394-404.

5428   SELLECK, GEORGE A. "Boston Friends and the pastoral ministry, 1870-1926." QH, 61 (1972), 67-81.

5429   SEXTON, JOHN EDWARD and ARTHUR JOSEPH RILEY. History of Saint John's Seminary, Brighton. Boston: Roman Catholic Archbishop of Boston, 1945. Pp. 320.

5430   SEYBOLT, ROBERT FRANCIS. "Lithotomies performed by Dr. Gardiner of Boston, 1739 and 1741." NEJMed, 202 (1930), 109. Silvester Gardiner.

5431   _____. "The ministers at the town meetings in colonial Boston." CSMP, 32, (1933-1937), 300-304.

5432   _____. The private schools of colonial Boston. Cambridge: Harvard Univ. Pr., 1935. Pp. 106.

5433   _____. "The private schools of seventeenth-century Boston." NEQ, 8 (1935), 418-424.

5434   _____. The public schoolmasters of colonial Boston. Cambridge: Harvard Univ. Pr., 1939. Pp. 31.

5435   _____. The public schools of colonial Boston, 1635-1775. Cambridge: Harvard Univ. Pr., 1935. Pp. viii, 101.

5436   _____. "Schoolmasters of colonial Boston." CSMP, 27 (1927-1930), 130-157; 32 (1933-1937), 184-185. 1635-1776.

5437   _____. The town officials of colonial Boston, 1634-1775. Cambridge: Harvard Univ. Pr., 1939. Pp. xiii, 416.

5438   SHACKLETON, ROBERT. The book of Boston. Philadelphia: Penn Publishing, 1916. Pp. 332.

5439   SHAKIR, W. E. "The Syrians." Our Boston, 1 (April, 1926), 12-16.

5440   SHARF, FREDERIC ALAN. "Daniel Webster in bronze." OTNE, 56 (1965-1966), 77-80. Statue in front of State House.

5441 SHATTUCK, LEMUEL. "On the vital statistics of Boston." American Journal of the Medical Sciences, New Ser., 1 (1841), 369-373.

5442 SHAW, CHARLES. A topographical and historical description of Boston, from the first settlement of the town to the present period; with some account of its environs. Boston: Oliver Spear, 1817. Pp. 311.

5443 SHAW, CHARLES G. "A metropolitan antique." Antiques, 50 (1946), 385.
Louisburg Square.

5444 SHAW, HELEN. "Brighton." Our Boston, 1 (November, 1926), 15-21.

5445 SHAW, JOSEPH THOMPSON. The wool trade of the United States: history of a great industry; its rise and progress in Boston, now the second market of the world.... Washington: Govt. Print. Off., 1909. Pp. 73.

5446 SHAW, SAMUEL SAVAGE. The Boston Library Society: historical sketch. Boston: G. H. Ellis, 1895. Pp. 23.

5447 SHEA, J. G. "The Boston of Winthrop." American Catholic Quarterly Review, 12 (1887), 193-209.
Roman Catholics.

5448 SHEPARD, CHARLES A. B. "Contributions to trade history, No. XIX: [Boston book trade]." American Bookseller, New Ser., 17 (1885), 507-508.

5449 SHEPARD, HARVEY N. "Century of Boston: historical address at municipal centennial observance, Fanueil Hall, April 19, 1922." City Record, 14 (1922), 383-387.

5450 _____. "The Eliot School." BSProc, (1914), 39-57.

5451 SHEPPARD, JOHN HANNIBAL. "A brief history of the New England Historic-Genealogical Society." NEHGR, 16 (1862), 203-212.

5452 _____. "The new Masonic Temple." NEHGR, 26 (1872), 144-146.

5453 "THE SHEPPARD library." Massachusetts College of Pharmacy. Bulletin, 11 (1922), entire issue.
Library of the college.

5454 SHERMAN, CLARENCE E. "D. B. Updike and the Merrymount Press." Rhode Island History, 8 (1949), 21-25.

5455 SHERMAN, CONSTANCE D. "Boston from the State House belvedere a century ago." NEQ, 32 (1959), 521-530.
Excerpt from journal of Jacques Gerard Milbert in early nineteenth century.

5456 _____. "Through an eighteenth-century looking glass." NEQ, 27 (1954), 515-521.
Boston in 1789 as seen by Jean Joseph Marie Toscan.

5457 SHERWIN, OSCAR. "Sons of Otis and Hancock." NEQ, 19 (1946), 212-223.
1854 seizure of Anthony Burns, fugitive slave.

5458 "SHINING examples of craftsmanship." Antiques, 36 (1939), 240-241.
Silverware made in Boston.

5459 SHULTZ, JOHN R. Beacon Hill and the carol singers. Boston: Wood, Clarke Pr., 1923. Pp. 20.

5460 SHURCLIFF, ARTHUR ASAHEL. "The Boston park system." Journal of Geography, 2 (1903), 302-314.

5461 _____. "Development of the easterly portion of Boston Common in relation to the State House approaches." SWJ, 21 (1917), 415-423.

5462 _____. History and description of Boston metropolitan parks. Boston: Metropolitan Park Commissioners, 1900. Pp. 36. MB.

5463 SHURTLEFF, NATHANIEL BRADSTREET. "The Green Dragon Tavern, Boston." HistMag, 3 Ser., 1 (1872), 28-31.

5464 _____. A history of the old building... erected 1712, on the corner of School and Washington Streets, Boston. Boston: Damrell and Upham, 1898. Pp. 16.
Old Corner Bookstore.

5465 _____. "Negro election day." MHSP, (1873-1875), 45-46.
Day before Ascension Day, 1693-1832.

5466 _____. A topographical and historical description of Boston. (1871) 3d. ed. Boston, 1891. Pp. lvi, 720.

5467 SIEBERT, WILBUR HENRY. "The Vigilance Committee of Boston." BSProc, (1953), 23-45.
The underground railroad.

5468 SIGLER, RUTH. Charlestown: footsteps thru history. Marblehead, 1972. Pp. 37. MB.

5469 SILVER, ROLLO GABRIEL. "Abstracts from the wills and estates of Boston printers, 1800-1825." Studies in Bibliography, 7 (1955), 212-218.

5470 _____. "Belcher & Armstrong set up shop: 1805." Studies in Bibliography, 4 (1951-1952), 201-204.
Printers.

5471 _____. "Benjamin Edes, trumpeter of sedition." PBSA, 47 (1953), 248-268.
Eighteenth-century printer.

5472 _____. "The Boston book trade, 1800-1825." NYPLB, 52 (1948), 487-500, 557-573, 635-650.

5473 _____. "The Boston lads were undaunted." LJ, 74 (1949), 995-997.
Mechanic Apprentices' Library, 1819-1892.

5474 _____. "Buckets, bags, and bed key: some remarks concerning the Conservative Fire Society." American Notes and Queries, 8 (1948-1950), 3-10.
Printing.

5475 _____. "Publishing in Boston, 1726-1757: the accounts of Daniel Henchman." AASP, 66 (1956), 17-36.

5476 "SILVER Burdett completes 50 years." Publishers' Weekly, 127 (May 18, 1935), 1895-1898.
Publisher.

5477 SIMMONS, RICHARD C. "The founding of the Third Church in Boston." WMQ, 3 Ser., 26 (1969), 241-252.

5478 SIMONDS, THOMAS C. History of South Boston: formerly Dorchester Neck, now ward XII of the city of Boston. Boston: D. Clapp, 1857. Pp. 331.

5479 SIMPSON, LEWIS P. "A literary adventure of the early republic: the Anthology Society and the 'Monthly Anthology.'" NEQ, 27 (1954), 168-190.
Early nineteenth century.

5480 "SIX superior clocks." Antiques, 28 (1935), 64-65.
Made by Simon Willard.

5481 SKELTON, EDWARD OLIVER. Historical review of the Boston Bijou Theatre, with the original casts of all the operas that have been produced at the Bijou, and with photographs illustrative of the various scenes in them. Boston: Forbes Lithograph Manufacturing, 1884. Unpaged.

5482 A SKETCH of the Battle of Bunker Hill, also a sketch of the Boston Tea Party. n.p., [1843?]. Pp. 24. M.

5483 SKETCHES of Boston, 1848-1929. Boston: L. P. Hollander, 1929. Pp. 74. MBNEH.

5484 "SKETCHES of early life in Boston." Appleton's Journal, 1 (1869), 44-45, 85-87, 181-183, 211-213, 246-249.

5485 SKETCHES of some historic churches of greater Boston. Boston: Beacon Pr., 1918. Pp. 307.
Preface signed: Katharine Gibbs Allen.

5486 "SKETCHES of the publishers: Charles B. Richardson." Round Table, 3 (1866), 266-267.

5487 "SKETCHES of the publishers: Gould & Lincoln." Round Table, 3 (1866), 329-330.

5488 "SKETCHES of the publishers: Ticknor & Fields." Round Table, 3 (January 20, 1866), 42-43, (January 27, 1866), 58-59, (February 3, 1866), 74-75.

5489 "SKETCHES of the publishers: Walker, Fuller & Co., Boston [American Unitarian Association]." Round Table, 3 (March 31, 1866), 202-203.

5490 SLAFTER, EDMUND FARWELL. Discourse delivered before the New-England Historic, Genealogical Society, Boston, March 18, 1870, on the occasion of the twenty-fifth anniversary of its incorporation. Boston: New-England Historic, Genealogical Society, 1870. Pp. 59.

5491 SMART, GEORGE K. "A New England experimentation in idealism." Travel, 84 (November, 1939), 14-16.
Brook Farm.

5492 SMITH, ARTHUR WARREN. Baptist situation of Boston proper: a survey of historical and present conditions. Boston: Griffith-Stillings Pr., 1912. Pp. 80.

5493 SMITH, CHARLES C. "Historical sketch of the [Massachusetts Historical] Society." MHSP, 19 (1881-1882), 390-392.

5494 _____, ed. "A journal kept by Jabez Fitch, Jr., at the Siege of Boston." MHSP, 2 Ser., 9 (1894-1895), 40-92.

5495 SMITH, FITZ-HENRY, JR. "Centennial of Dickens' first visit to Boston: the testimonial to Captain Hewitt of the Britannia." BSProc, (1942), 24-29.

5496 _____. "Cotton Mather's account of the great tide of February, 1723." BSProc, (1942), 47-50.

5497 _____. "The French at Boston during the Revolution." BSPub, 10 (1913), 9-75.

5498 _____. "Some old-fashioned winters in Boston." MHSP, 65 (1932-1936), 269-305.

5499 _____. "Storms and shipwrecks in Boston Bay and the record of the life savers of Hull." BSPub, 2 Ser., 2 (1917), 9-66.
Massachusetts Humane Society.

5500 _____. "The story of Boston light, with some account of the beacons in Boston Harbor." BSPub, 7 (1910), 63-126.

5501 SMITH, HARRIETTE KNIGHT. The history of the Lowell Institute. Boston: Lamson, Wolfe, 1898. Pp. x, 125.
Adult education.

5502 _____. "The Lowell Institute." NEM, New Ser., 11 (1894-1895), 713-730.
Adult education.

5503 SMITH, HENRY NASH. "The 'backwoods' bull in the 'Boston' china shop." Am Heritage, 12 (August, 1961) 33, 108-111.
Mark Twain at Whittier's 70th birthday dinner, 1877.

5504 SMITH, ISAAC T. "A historic meeting-house." MagAmHist, 17 (1887), 474-482.
First Baptist Church, Salem Street.

5505 SMITH, J. C. V. "Ancient and modern Boston." New Boston, 2 (1911), 167-171.

5506   SMITH, JEROME VAN CROWNINSHIELD. An oration, delivered before the inhabitants of South Boston, on Saturday, July 4, 1835, the fifty-ninth anniversary of American independence. Boston: Russell, Odiorne, 1835. Pp. 56.
         Relates to South Boston.

5507   SMITH, ROBERT CHENEY. The shrine of Bowdoin Street, 1883-1958, the story of the Mission Church of Saint John the Evangelist in the city of Boston, Massachusetts, as told at the time of its 75th anniversary.... [Boston?, 1958?]. Pp. 76. M.

5508   SNEDEKER, LENDON. One hundred years at Children's [Hospital]. Boston, 1969. Pp. 100. M.

5509   SNOW, CALEB HOPKINS. A geography of Boston, county of Suffolk and the adjacent towns, with historical notes. Boston: Carter and Hendee, 1830. Pp. iv, 162.
         Contains historical descriptions by wards.

5510   _____. A history of Boston, the metropolis of Massachusetts, from its origin to the present period; with some account of the environs. (1824) 2d. ed. Boston: A. Bowen, 1828. Pp. iv, 427.

5511   SNOW, EDWARD ROWE. The Boston Young Men's Christian Union, one hundred years of service, 1851-1951. [Boston, 1952?]. Pp. 40.

5512   _____. Castle Island, its 300 years of history and romance. Andover: Andover Pr., 1935. Pp. 45.
         In Boston Harbor.

5513   _____. Historic Fort Warren. Boston: Yankee Publishing, 1941. Pp. 87.
         Civil War prison.

5514   _____. The islands of Boston Harbor, 1630-1971. N.Y.: Dodd, Mead, 1971. Pp. xiv, 274.

5515   _____. The islands of Boston Harbor, their history and romance, 1626-1935. Andover: Andover Pr., 1935. Pp. 367.

5516   _____. The romance of Boston Bay. Boston: Yankee Publishing, 1944. Pp. 319.

5517   _____. Sailing down Boston Bay. Boston: Yankee Publishing, 1941. Pp. 57.

5518   _____. The story of Minot's Light. Boston: Yankee Publishing, 1940. Pp. 139.

5519   _____. Two forts named Independence. n.p., 1967. Unpaged.
         In Boston Harbor and at Hull.

5520   SNOW, SAMUEL T. Fifty years with the Revere Copper Co., a paper read at the stockholders' meeting held on Monday 24 March, 1890, by its Treasurer. (1890) 2d. ed. Boston: Revere Copper Co., 1891. Pp. 49. MBNEH.

5521   SNYDER, ELLEN. A preliminary study of Boston rents and sales prices, 1960-1969. Boston: Boston Redevelopment Authority, 1970. Unpaged. M.

5522   SOCIETY TO ENCOURAGE STUDIES AT HOME. Society to Encourage Studies at Home, founded in 1873 by Anna Eliot Ticknor.... Cambridge: Riverside Pr., 1897. Pp. 218.

5523   [SOHIER, ELIZABETH PUTNAM]. History of the Old South Church of Boston.... Boston: R. Hildreth, 1876. Pp. 73.

5524   SOLOMON, BARBARA MILLER. Pioneers in service: the history of the Associated Jewish Philanthropies of Boston. Boston, 1956. Pp. 197.

5525   "SOME early experiments in banking." About the First, (September, 1936), 10-11.

5526   "SOME notes on an early school in the North End of Boston." OTNE, 38 (1947-1948), 32-34.

5527   SOMERSET CLUB, BOSTON. A brief history of the Somerset Club of Boston, with a list of past and present members, 1852-1913. Cambridge: Riverside Pr., 1913. Pp. 68.

5528   SONS OF THE AMERICAN REVOLUTION. MASSACHU-SETTS SOCIETY. Boston in the Revolution; a souvenir of the Seventeenth Congress, National Society of the Sons of the American Revolution.... Edwin S. Crandon, Edward W. McGlenen and Walter Kendall Watkins, comps. Boston, 1906. Pp. 48.

5529   SOUTH BOSTON. PHILLIPS CHURCH. Manual of the Phillips Church, Boston. Boston: Alfred Mudge and Son, 1882. Pp. 89. M.
         Includes historical sketch.

5530   SOUTH BOSTON SAVINGS BANK. The 100th anniversary of the South Boston Savings Bank, 1863-1963. n.p., [1963]. Pp. 27. M.

5531   SOUTH END HISTORICAL SOCIETY. A picture of the South End; or, the citizens and strangers guide to the metropolis of Massachusetts and its southerly environs, with curious addenda. Boston: Hutcheson, 1968.
         Historic houses.

5532   SOUTHACK, JOHN. The life of John Southack: written by himself. Containing an account of the sinking of the brigantine Hannah, for which the author suffered in 1803; and an account of all the other vessels insured at different places, which were to have been sunk. To which is added, a history of the state prison in Charlestown, with observations on this excellent institution.... [Charlestown?], 1809. Pp. 119.

5533   SOUTHGATE, HORATIO. A sermon preached on the occasion of the second anniversary of the Holy Guild of the Church of the Advent, Boston, Mass. on the evening of the first Sunday in Advent, 1854. Boston: J. Howe, 1855. Pp. 21. M.

5534   SOUVENIR of the 50th anniversary of the dedication of Bunker Hill Monument, 1843-1893. Charlestown: Bunker Hill Times, 1893. Pp. 86.
         A history of the city and biographical sketches.

5535   SPAIN, MAY R. The Society of Arts & Crafts, 1897-1924. Boston: Society of Arts & Crafts, 1924. Pp. 34.

5536 SPANG, JOSEPH PETER, JR. Look sharp! Feel sharp! Be sharp! Gillette Safety Razor Company: fifty years, 1901-1951. N.Y.: Newcomen Society in North America, 1951. Pp. 26.

5537 SPAULDING, HENRY GEORGE. Sixty years of the Unitarian Sunday School Society. Boston, 1887. Pp. 22. MB.

5538 SPEARE, EDWARD RAY. Interesting happenings in Boston University's history, 1839 to 1951. Boston: Boston Univ. Pr., 1957. Pp. 204.

5539 SPECTOR, BENJAMIN. A history of Tufts College Medical School, prepared for its semicentennial, 1893-1943. Boston: Tufts College Medical Alumni Association, 1943. Pp. 414 (i.e. 416).

5540 SPENCER, CHARLES ELDRIDGE. The First Bank of Boston, 1784-1949. N.Y.: Newcomen Society in North America, 1949. Pp. 32.

5541 SPRACKLING, HELEN. "Another American candle cup." Antiques, 73 (1958), 341.
Seventeenth-century silver made by Jeremiah Drummer.

5542 SPRAGUE, HENRY HARRISON. City government in Boston: its rise and development. Boston, 1890. Pp. 54. MB.

5543 _____. The founding of Charlestown by the Spragues, a glimpse of the beginning of the Massachusetts Bay settlement. Boston: W. B. Clarke, 1910. Pp. 39.

5544 SPRAGUE, HOWARD B. "Some aspects of medicine in Boston in the eighteenth century." OTNE, 13 (1922-1923), 14-19.

5545 SPRAGUE, JULIA A., comp. History of the New England Women's Club from 1868 to 1893. Boston: Lee and Shepard, 1894. Pp. 99.

5546 SPRAGUE, PHILO WOODRUFF. A sermon preached at the fiftieth anniversary of St. John's Church, Charlestown, 1840-1890. n.p., [1890?]. Unpaged. M.

5547 SPRING, JAMES WHEELOCK. Boston and the Parker House; a chronicle of those who have lived on that historic spot where the new Parker House now stands in Boston. Boston: J. R. Whipple, 1927. Pp. xiii, 230.

5548 STAINTON, JOHN. Urban renewal and planning in Boston. [Boston?]: Citizens' Housing and Planning Association, 1972. 76 leaves. M. 1960s.

5549 STANDARD, PAUL. "D. B. Updike: the Merrymount Press." Penrose Annual, 38 (1936), 17-22.

5550 STANLEY, RAYMOND W. The four Thompsons of Boston Harbor, 1621-1965. Boston, 1966. Pp. 78.
Thompson's Island; David Thompson, who owned it; John Thompson, his son; and Thompson Academy.

5551 _____. and ROSEMARY E. PHELAN, eds. Mr. Bulfinch's Boston. Boston: Old Colony Trust Co., 1963. Pp. 74.
Architecture.

5552 STAPLES, SAMUEL ELIAS. The Thursday lecture. Worcester: Clark Jillson, 1883. Pp. 7. MBNEH.
Adult education.

5553 STARK, JAMES HENRY. Antique views of ye towne of Boston. Boston: Photo-electrotype Engraving, 1882. Pp. 378.
Extensive text: not primarily pictorial.

5554 _____. History of the old Blake House, and a brief sketch of the Dorchester Historical Society. [Dorchester?], 1907. Pp. 13.

5555 _____. Illustrated history of Boston Harbor, compiled from the most authentic sources, giving a complete and reliable history of every island and headland in the harbor, from the earliest date to the present time.... Boston: Photo-electrotype Co., 1879. Pp. 167.

5556 STATE HOUSE WOMEN'S CLUB, BOSTON, MASS. [Constitution, by-laws and list of members], 1934-1935. n.p., [1934?]. M.
Includes a brief history of the club.

5557 STATE STREET TRUST COMPANY. Boston, England, and Boston, New England, 1630-1930; reproductions of rare prints with a commentary of historic notes.... Boston, 1930. Pp. vii, 45.

5558 _____. Boston, one hundred years a city: a collection of views made from rare prints and old photographs showing the changes which have occurred in Boston during the one hundred years of its existence as a city, 1822-1922. Boston, 1922. Pp. xii, 49.

5559 _____. Boston's growth: a bird's-eye view of Boston's increase in territory and population from its beginning to the present. Boston, 1910. Pp. 45.

5560 _____. Copley Square, a brief description of its history.... Boston: Walton Advertising, 1941. Pp. 34. M.

5561 _____. Forty of Boston's historic houses: a brief illustrated description of the residences of historic characters of Boston who have lived in or near the business section. Boston, 1912. Unpaged.

5562 _____. Forty of Boston's immortals: showing illustrations and giving a brief sketch of forty men of the past whose work would entitle them to a niche in a Boston hall of fame. Boston, 1910. Unpaged.

5563 _____. Mayors of Boston: an illustrated epitome of who the mayors have been and what they have done. Boston, 1914. Pp. 48.

5564 _____. Old shipping days in Boston. Boston, 1918. Pp. 49.

5565 ____. Other merchants and sea captains of old Boston: being more information about the merchants and sea captains of old Boston who played such an important part in building up the commerce of New England, together with some quaint and curious stories of the sea. Boston, 1919. Pp. vii, 70.

5566 ____. Some events of Boston and its neighbors. Boston, 1917. Pp. v, 62.

5567 ____. Some interesting Boston events. Boston, 1916. Pp. 78.

5568 ____. Some merchants and sea captains of old Boston: being a collection of sketches of notable men and mercantile houses prominent during the early half of the nineteenth century in the commerce and shipping of Boston. Boston, 1918. Pp. vii, 53.

5569 ____. Some ships of the clipper ship era, their builders, owners, and captains: a glance at an interesting phase of the American Merchant Marine so far as it relates to Boston. Boston, 1913. Pp. 45.

5570 ____. State Street: a brief account of a Boston way. Boston, 1906. Pp. 42.

5571 ____. State Street events: a brief account of divers notable persons & sundry stirring events having to do with the history of this ancient street. Boston, 1916. Pp. 51.

5572 STEARNS, FRANK PRESTON. "John Brown and his eastern friends." NEM, New Ser., 42 (1910), 589-599.
John Brown in Boston, early January, 1857; Kansas Aid Committee.

5573 STEBBINS, OLIVER B. "A famous Boston amateur dramatic club." Bostonian, 2 (1895), 131-140.
Aurora Club.

5574 ____. "The oldest theatre now in Boston." Bostonian, 1 (1894-1895), 113-130.
Boston Museum, established 1841.

5575 STEBBINS, THEODORE E., JR. "Richardson and Trinity Church: the evolution of a building." SocArchHistJ, 27 (1968), 281-298.
Henry H. Richardson.

5576 STEELE, DANIEL J. "The clocks of Simon Willard," Antiques, 1 (1922), 69-73.

5577 STERN, MADELEINE B. "Elliott, Thomes and Talbot and their blue backs." Publishers' Weekly, 149 (June 15, 1946), 3146-3151.

5578 ____. "James P. Walker and Horace B. Fuller: transcendental publishers." BPLQ, 6 (1954), 123-140.

5579 ____. "James Redpath and his books for the times." Publishers' Weekly, 148 (December 15, 1945), 2649-2653.

5580 ____. "Rise and fall of A. K. Loring." Publishers' Weekly, 149 (March 16, 1946), 1654-1658.

5581 ____. "Roberts Brothers, Boston." More Books, 20 (1945), 419-423.
Publishers.

5582 STETSON, AMOS W. Eighty years: an historical sketch of the State Bank, 1811-1865; the State National Bank, 1865-1891. [Boston, 1893]. Pp. ix, 94.

5583 STEVENS, BENJAMIN FRANKLIN. Boston Massacre. n.p., n.d. Pp. 18. MBNEH.

5584 ____. Reminiscences of the past half century: April 9, 1847, to April 9, 1897. Boston: N. Sawyer & Son, 1897. Pp. 44.
New England Mutual Life Insurance Co.

5585 ____. "Some old inns and taverns of Boston." Bostonian, 2 (1895), 17-24.

5586 ____. Some thoughts on old Boston: an address delivered before the Commercial Club of Boston, December 18, 1897. Boston: Rockwell & Churchill, 1898. Pp. 17. MB.

5587 ____. "The Tremont House: the exit of an old landmark." Bostonian, 1 (1894-1895), 329-344.
Hotel.

5588 STEVENS, CHARLES W. "The Boston Public Garden." NEM, New Ser., 24 (1901), 343-354.

5589 STEVENS, SOLON WARD. "The true significance of Bunker Hill Monument." MagHist, 1 (1905), 388-392.

5590 STEWART, JANE A. "Boston's experience with municipal baths." AmJSoc, 7 (1900-1901), 416-422.

5591 STIMSON, F. J. "Boston, the ebb tide." Scribner's Magazine, 83 (1928), 310-317.

5592 STODDARD, RICHARD. "Isaiah Rogers' Tremont Theatre, Boston." Antiques, 105 (1974), 1314-1319.

5593 ____. "A reconstruction of Charles Bulfinch's first Federal Street Theatre, Boston." Winterthur Portfolio, 6 (1970), 185-208.

5594 STONE, EDWIN A. A century of Boston banking. Boston: Rockwell & Churchill, 1894. Pp. 111.

5595 STONE, ELMA A. "The old Trescott House." HPHR, 3 (1903), 73-76.

5596 ____. Sketch of the First Baptist Sunday School...Hyde Park...1876-1883. n.p., [1883?]. Pp. 16. MBNEH.

5597   STONE, JAMES EDWARD. Register of the
        Charlestown men in the service during the
Civil War, 1861-1865. Boston: Old Charlestown
School Boys Association, 1919. v.p.

5598   STONE, JENNIE M. "The First Baptist Church
        of Hyde Park." HPHR, 7 (1909), 5-11.

5599   STONE, P. M. "The Boston waterfront at the
        turn of the century." Steamboat Bill, 14
(1957), 64-67, 91-94.
        Steamboats.

5600   _____. John Craig Players with Mary Young
        and their outline history of the famous
Castle Square Theatre, Boston, Massachusetts.
n.p., 1960. Pp. 32.

5601   STONE, WILLIAM L. "Early history of print-
        ing and [the] newspaper press in Boston and
New York." Continental Monthly, 4 (1863), 256-268.

5602   _____. "The early newspaper press of Boston
        and New-York." AmHist Record, 1 (1872), 387-
392.

5603   STONE & WEBSTER, INC. Stone & Webster...a
        brief account of the history of this organi-
zation and of the services developed during 44
years. N.Y., 1932. Pp. 26.
        Engineers.

5604   STONEMAN, VERNON C. John and Thomas Seymour,
        cabinetmakers in Boston, 1794-1816. Boston:
Special Publications, 1959. Pp. 393.

5605   STORER, MALCOLM. "Boston 'shinplasters' of
        the Civil War." OTNE, 13 (1922-1923), 23-27.
        Currency.

5606   _____. "The Franklin Boston school medals."
        MHSP, 55 (1921-1922), 189-198.
        Given to Boston children on merit under the
        will of Benjamin Franklin.

5607   STORY, DOUGLAS. "The city of a great tradi-
        tion." Munsey's Magazine, 28 (1902-1903),
1-9.

5608   "THE STORY of Allyn and Bacon, Inc." Book
        Production Magazine, 80 (July, 1964), 30-33.
        Publisher.

5609   "THE STORY of Little, Brown and Company."
        Book Production Magazine, 77 (June, 1963),
50-54.
        Publishers.

5610   "STORY of Tileston and Hollingsworth Co.;
        'oldest U. S. mill' is one of the most pro-
gressive." Pacific Pulp Paper Industry, 18 (July,
1944), 7-9.

5611   STOVER, AUGUSTUS W. A retrospect on the fif-
        tieth anniversary of the incorporation of
the Charlestown Five Cent Savings Bank, being a paper read before the Board of Trustees at their
quarterly meeting, April 13, 1904. Boston, 1904.
Pp. 42. MB.

5612   STOW, BARON. A discourse delivered at the
        one hundredth anniversary of the Baldwin
Place Baptist Church, July 27, 1843. Boston:
Gould, Kendall, and Lincoln, 1843. Pp. 107. MBNEH.

5613   STRICKLAND, CHARLES RUTAN. "Rebuilding the
        Old North Church steeple." Antiques, 68
(1955), 54-56.

5614   STROMBERG, ROLAND N. "Boston in the 1820s
        and 1830s." History Today, 11 (1961), 591-
598.

5615   STURGIS, RUSSELL. "The Boston Young Men's
        Christian Association." BSM, 1 (1884), 249-
258.

5616   SUFFOLK LAW SCHOOL. Historical souvenir: a
        history of the school and sketches of the
members of the faculty with photographs. Boston,
1912. Pp. 24. M.

5617   SUFFOLK SAVINGS BANK FOR SEAMEN AND OTHERS.
        One hundred years of the Suffolk Savings Bank
for Seamen and Others: a history of the origin and
growth of the bank with sketches of its officers together with a description of the waterfront of Boston as it was in 1833.... Boston: Walton Advertising & Printing, 1933. Pp. 82.

5618   SULLIVAN, JACK. "Watching prelates." Prose,
        No. 5 (Fall, 1972), 143-158.
        Roman Catholic clergy.

5619   SULLIVAN, JOSEPH MATTHEW. "The Quincy
        School." NEM, 51 (1914), 7-9.

5620   _____. "South Cove memories." NEM, 54
        (1915-1916), 5-7.

5621   SULLIVAN, JOSEPH T. "Boston Common: home
        of the first freedom." Boston, 55 (Septem-
ber, 1963), 54-58.

5622   SULLIVAN, JULIA E. The Boston Teacher's
        Club: 1898-1948. Boston: Blanchard,
[1948]. Pp. 32. M.

5623   SULLIVAN, ROBERT. The disappearance of Dr.
        Parkman. Boston: Little, Brown, 1971.
Pp. xiv, 241.
        Murder of George Parkman, Harvard professor,
        1850.

5624   _____. "The murder trial of Dr. Webster,
        Boston 1850." CaHSP, 41 (1967-1969), 55-88.
        For murder of George Parkman.

5625   SULLIVAN, THOMAS RUSSELL. Boston, new and
        old. Boston: Houghton Mifflin, 1912.
Pp. viii, 108.

5626   SUMNER, WILLIAM HYSLOP. A history of East
        Boston: with biographical sketches of its
early proprietors, and an appendix. Boston: J. E.
Tilton, 1858. Pp. viii, 801.

5627   _____. "Reminiscences relating to General
        Warren and Bunker Hill." NEHGR, 12 (1858),
113-122, 225-230.

5628   _____. "Some recollections of Washington's
        visit to Boston." NEHGR, 14 (1860), 161-166.
        1789.

5629   SURVEY OF FEDERAL ARCHIVES. Ship registers
        and enrollments of Boston and Charlestown.
Boston: National Archives Project, 1942. Pp. xvi,
248 leaves.
        1789-1795.

5630   SUTHERLAND, ROBERT T., JR. "The blockade of
        Boston." United States Naval Institute.
Proceedings, 63 (1937), 195-198.
        War of 1812.

5631   SUTTON, STEPHANNE BARRY. The Arnold Arbore-
        tum: the first century. [Jamaica Plain]:
Arnold Arboretum of Harvard Univ., 1971. Pp. 72.

5632   SWALLOW, SUSAN S. "The North End." SWJ, 42
        (1928), 651-661.

5633   SWAN, MABEL MUNSON. The Athenaeum gallery,
        1827-1873: the Boston athenaeum as an early
patron of art.... [Boston]: Boston Athenaeum,
1940. Pp. xiv, 312.

5634   _____. "Boston's carvers and joiners." An-
        tiques, 53 (1948), 198-201, 281-283.
        Eighteenth century.

5635   _____. "Furnituremakers of Charlestown."
        Antiques, 46 (1944), 203-206.

5636   _____. "The furniture of his excellency,
        John Hancock." Antiques, 31 (1937), 119-121.

5637   _____. "Furniture of the Boston Tories."
        Antiques, 41 (1942), 186-189.

5638   _____. "General Stephen Bedlam--cabinet and
        looking glass maker." Antiques, 65 (1954),
380-383.

5639   _____. "John Seymour and Son, cabinet-
        makers." Antiques, 32 (1937), 176-179.

5640   _____. "The Johnstons and the Reas--japan-
        ners." Antiques, 43 (1943), 211-213.
        Eighteenth century.

5641   _____. "The man who made brass works for
        Willard clocks." Antiques, 17 (1930), 524-
526.
        William Hunneman.

5642   _____. "The man who made Simon Willard's
        clock cases, John Doggett of Roxbury." An-
tiques, 15 (1929), 196-200.

5643   SWAN, SARAH H. "The story of an old house
        and the people who lived in it." NEM, New
Ser., 17 (1897-1898), 170-184.
        Washington and Winter Streets, demolished in
        1846.

5644   SWASEY, ROBERT. "The toy theater of Boston."
        NEM, 50 (1913-1914), 351-352.

5645   SWEETSER, FRANK LOEL. Patterns of change in
        the social ecology of Metropolitan Boston,
1950-1960. [Boston]: Massachusetts Department of
Mental Health, 1962. Pp. 158.
        Population.

5646   _____. The social ecology of metropolitan
        Boston: 1950. [Boston]: Massachusetts De-
partment of Mental Health, 1961. Pp. iv, 231
leaves.
        Population.

5647   _____. The social ecology of metropolitan
        Boston: 1960. [Boston]: Massachusetts De-
partment of Mental Health, 1962. Pp. 239.
        Population.

5648   SWETT, SAMUEL. History of Bunker Hill bat-
        tle, with a plan. (1818) 2d. ed. Boston:
Munroe and Francis, 1826. Pp. 58.
        First edition has title: Historical and
        topographical sketch of Bunker Hill battle.

5649   _____. "Horatio Greenough, the designer of
        Bunker Hill Monument." NEHGR, 18 (1864),
61-65.
        Building the monument.

5650   _____. Notes to his sketch of Bunker-hill
        battle. Boston: Munroe and Franics, 1825.
Pp. 30.

5651   _____. Who was the commander at Bunker Hill?
        Boston: J. Wilson, 1850. Pp. 39.

5652   SWIFT, LINDSAY. Brook Farm: its members,
        scholars, and visitors. N.Y.: Macmillan,
1900. Pp. x, 303.

5653   SYFORD, ETHEL. "Fifty years of the New Eng-
        land Conservatory of Music." NEM, New Ser.,
55 (1916), 139-145.

5654   "T Wharf, past and present." BSProc, (1948),
        27-40.

5655   TAGGART, JOSEPH HERMAN. The Federal Reserve
        Bank of Boston. Boston: Bankers Publishing,
1938. Pp. xii, 283.

5656   TALBOT, EMILY. "Old West Church." NEM, New
        Ser., 2 (1890), 174-184.

5657   TALMADGE, JOHN E. "Georgia tests the Fugi-
        tive Slave Law." Georgia Historical Quar-
terly, 49 (1965), 57-64.
        Boston abolitionists thwart return of escaped
        slaves.

5658   TANSELLE, GEORGE THOMAS. "Author and pub-
        lisher in 1800: letters of Royall Tyler and
Joseph Nancrede." HarvLibBul, 15 (1967), 129-139.

5659   TAPPAN, GEORGE ARTHUR. A 20th century sou-
        venir: the officers and the men, the stations
without and within of the Boston Police. Boston:
Twentieth Century Biography, 1901. Pp. 234. M.

5660 TARBELL, ARTHUR WILSON. "The Brook Farm experiment." National Magazine, 7 (1897-1898), 197-203.

5661 TARBOX, INCREASE NILES. "A reminiscence of the Stackpole House." New Englander, 32 (1873), 706-717.

5662 TATHAM, DAVID. "The Pendleton-Moore Shop." OTNE, 62 (1971-1972), 29-46.
Lithographic artists, 1825-1840.

5663 TAYLOR, ALICE. Boston. Garden City, N.Y.: N. Doubleday, 1957. Pp. 63.

5664 TAYLOR, DAVID HENRY. The Baptist denomination in Boston. Boston, 1885. Pp. 16. MB.

5665 TAYLOR, GEORGE ROGERS. "The beginnings of mass transportation in urban America." Smithsonian JHist, 1 (Summer, 1966), 35-50, (Fall, 1966), 31-54.
Boston, New York and Philadelphia.

5666 TEA leaves: being a collection of letters and documents relating to the shipment of tea to the American colonies in the year 1773, by the East India Tea Company. Francis S. Drake, ed. Boston: A. O. Crane, 1884. Pp. clxxxiv, 375.

5667 "A TEA party a hundred years ago." AmHist Record, 2 (1873), 529-531.
Boston Tea Party.

5668 NO ENTRY

5669 THACHER, PETER. A sermon preached to the church and society in Brattle-Street, Boston, Dec. 29, 1799, and occasioned by the completion of a century from its first establishment. Boston: Young & Minns, 1800. Pp. 18.
Brattle Square church.

5670 THACHER, PETER OXENBRIDGE. An address, pronounced on the first Tuesday of March, 1831 before the members of the bar of the county of Suffolk, Massachusetts. Boston: Hilliard, Gray, Little and Wilkins, 1831. Pp. 40.
Biographies of Boston lawyers.

5671 THARP, LOUISE HALL. The Appletons of Beacon Hill. Boston: Little, Brown, 1973. Pp. xvi, 368.

5672 ____. "They danced with the prince." NEG, 9 (Summer, 1967), 3-10.
Dancing classes of Lorenzo Papanti, 1829-1872.

5673 [THATCHER, BENJAMIN BUSSEY]. Traits of the Tea Party: being a memoir of George R. T. Hewes, one of the last of its survivors; with a history of that transaction; reminiscences of the massacre, and the siege, and other stories of old times. By a Bostonian. N.Y.: Harper & Bros., 1835. Pp. viii, 265.

5674 THAYER, WILLIAM ROSCOE. "An Italian nobleman's glimpse of Boston in 1837." MHSP, 43 (1909-1910), 88-92.
Count Francesco Arese.

5675 THERNSTROM, STEPHAN. "The case of Boston." MHSP, 79 (1967), 109-122.
Social mobility in late nineteenth and early twentieth centuries.

5676 ____. The other Bostonians: poverty and progress in the American metropolis, 1880-1970. Cambridge: Harvard Univ. Pr., 1973. Pp. xvi, 345.

5677 ____. Poverty, planning, and politics in the new Boston: the origins of ABCD. N.Y.: Basic Books, 1969. Pp. xiii, 199.
Action for Boston Community Development, urban renewal agency.

5678 THOMAS, J. WESLEY. "The Conversational Club." NEQ, 16 (1943), 296-298.
1847-1848, a literary society.

5679 THOMPSON, AUGUSTUS CHARLES. Eliot memorial: sketches historical and biographical of the Eliot Church and Society, Boston. Boston: Pilgrim Pr., 1900. Pp. viii, 503.

5680 ____. Feeding the lambs, quarter century memorial, Eliot Sabbath School, Roxbury. Boston: Damrell & Moore, 1859. Pp. 200. MB.

5681 THOMPSON, GRACE AGNES. "The Boston Floating Hospital, where science and philanthropy meet." NEM, 52 (1914-1915), 261-262, 286-291.

5682 ____. "The story of a great New England enterprise." NEM, 53 (1915), 12-24.
United Fruit Co.

5683 THOMPSON, JOHN ALEXANDER. History of the Boston Highlands Society of the New Jerusalem. Boston: The Society, 1887. Pp. 109. MB.

5684 THOMPSON, JOSEPH. A short history of Charlestown, for the past 44 years, and other subjects. Charlestown: De Costa & Homans, 1848. Pp. 71.

5685 THOMPSON'S ISLAND, BOSTON HARBOR. FARM AND TRADES SCHOOL. One hundredth anniversary of the organization of the...school at the Old South Church...Boston...March 21st, 1914. Boston, 1914. Pp. 29. MB.

5686 THOMSON, HELEN. Murder at Harvard. Boston: Houghton Mifflin, 1971. Pp. xii, 318.
George Parkman, Harvard professor murdered in Boston in 1850.

5687 THORNDIKE, SAMUEL LOTHROP. Past members of the Union Club of Boston and a brief sketch of the history of the club, July 1893. Boston, 1893. Pp. 58. MBNEH.

5688 THURSTON, PHILANDER. Historical discourse commemorating the fiftieth anniversary of the Village Church, Dorchester, delivered March 9, 1879. Boston: Beacon Pr., 1879. Pp. 39. M.

5689　THWING, ANNIE HAVEN.　The crooked & narrow
　　　　streets of the town of Boston 1630-1822.
Boston: Marshall Jones, 1920.　Pp. xi, 282.

5690　THWING, LEROY.　"The Bulfinch State House."
　　　　OTNE, 42 (1951-1952), 63-67.

5691　THWING, LEROY L.　"Boston street lighting in
　　　　the eighteenth century."　OTNE, 28 (1937-
1938), 72-78.

5692　_____.　"The four carving Skillins."　An-
　　　　tiques, 33 (1938), 326-328.

5693　THWING, WALTER ELIOT.　History of the First
　　　　Church in Roxbury, Massachusetts, 1630-1904.
Boston: W. A. Butterfield, 1908.　Pp. xxi, 428.

5694　TICKNOR, HOWARD MALCOM.　"The passing of the
　　　　Boston Museum."　NEM, New Ser., 28 (1903),
379-396.
　　　　Theater.

5695　TICKNOR (FIRM) BOSTON.　The cost books of
　　　　Ticknor and Fields, and their predecessors,
1832-1858.　Warren S. Tryon & William Charvat, eds.
N.Y.: Bibliographical Society of America, 1949.
Pp. L, 508.
　　　　Publisher.

5696　TIFFANY, NINA MOORE.　From colony to common-
　　　　wealth: stories of the Revolutionary days
in Boston.　Boston: Ginn, 1891.　Pp. viii, 180.

5697　TILLY, ALICE E.　"Slick slickers."　Indus-
　　　　try, 12 (June, 1947), 29-30, 45.
　　　　A. J. Tower Co., raincoats.

5698　TILTON, ELEANOR M.　"Lightning-rods and the
　　　　earthquake of 1755."　NEQ, 13 (1940), 85-97.

5699　TITUS, ANSON.　"Boston when Ben Franklin was
　　　　a boy."　BSProc, (1906), 55-72.

5700　_____.　"Boston when Ben Franklin was a
　　　　boy."　Worcester HSProc, 20 (1904), 250-252.

5701　TITUS, LILLIE B.　"How the ladies of Boston
　　　　finished Bunker Hill Monument."　MassMag, 1
(1908), 63-72.

5702　_____.　"How the ladies of Boston helped to
　　　　finish the Bunker Hill Monument."　Bostonian, 2 (1895), 238-242.
　　　　Differs from above article.

5703　TOMLINSON, ELLEN BROOKS.　"East Boston."
　　　　Our Boston, 2 (February, 1927), 17-22.

5704　TOMPKINS, EUGENE and QUINCY KILBY.　The his-
　　　　tory of the Boston Theatre, 1854-1901.　Boston: Houghton Mifflin, 1908.　Pp. xv, 550.

5705　TONER, JAMES VINCENT.　The Boston Edison
　　　　story, 1886-1951, 65 years of service.　N.Y.:
Newcomen Society in North America, 1951.　Pp. 32.

5706　TOOMEY, JOHN J. and EDWARD P. B. RANKIN.
　　　　History of South Boston (its past and present) and prospects for the future, with sketches of
prominent men.　Boston, 1901.　v.p.

5707　TOWER, ELLEN M.　"The North End Union."　Bos-
　　　　tonian, 2 (1895), 393-398.
　　　　Charity.

5708　TOWNER, LAWRENCE WILLIAM.　"The indentures of
　　　　Boston's poor apprentices: 1734-1805."
CSMP, 43 (1956-1963), 417-468.

5709　TRASK, WILLIAM BLAKE.　"Early matters relat-
　　　　ing to the town and First Church of Dorchester."　NEHGR, 40 (1886), 253-261.

5710　TREMONT STREET MEDICAL SCHOOL.　Tremont
　　　　Street Medical School, March, 1857; catalogue
of the past and present students...with an account
of its origin and plan of instruction.　Boston:
David Clapp, 1857.　Pp. 32.　MBNEH.

5711　TREUDLEY, MARY BOSWORTH.　"Formal organiza-
　　　　tion and the Americanization process with
special reference to the Greeks of Boston."　AmSoc
Rev, 14 (1949), 44-53.

5712　TRUAX, RHODA.　The doctors Warren of Boston:
　　　　first family of surgery.　Boston: Houghton
Mifflin, 1968.　Pp. xiii, 369.

5713　[TRUE, CHARLES KITTREDGE].　Shawmut: or, the
　　　　settlement of Boston by the Puritan Pilgrims....　Boston: Waite, Pierce, 1845.　Pp. 136.
　　　　Also published with the title: Tri-mountain,
　　　　or the early history of Boston.

5714　TRUMBULL, JAMES HAMMOND.　"Conference of the
　　　　elders of Massachusetts with the Rev. Robert
Lenthal of Weymouth, held at Dorchester, Feb. 10,
1639."　CongQ, 19 (1877), 232-248.
　　　　Congregationalism.

5715　TRYON, WARREN STENSON.　"Book distribution in
　　　　mid-nineteenth century America, illustrated
by the publishing records of Ticknor and Fields,
Boston."　PBSA, 41 (1947), 210-230.

5716　_____.　Parnassus Corner.　Boston: Houghton
　　　　Mifflin, 1963.　Pp. xiv, 445.
　　　　Ticknor and Fields, publishers.

5717　_____.　"The publications of Ticknor and
　　　　Fields in the South, 1840-1865."　Journal of
Southern History, 14 (1948), 305-330.

5718　_____.　"Ticknor and Fields' publications in
　　　　the Old Northwest, 1840-1860."　MVHR, 34
(1947-1948), 589-610.

5719　TUCCI, DOUGLASS SHAND.　Church building in
　　　　Boston 1720-1970, with an introduction to the
work of Ralph Adams Cram and the Boston Gothicists.
[Boston]: Dorchester Savings Bank, 1974.　Pp. 134.
M.

5720　_____.　Gothic churches of Dorchester.　Bos-
　　　　ton: Tribune Publishing Co., 1972.　Pp. 63.
MB.

5721 ____. Gothic churches of Dorchester, a companion volume; All Saints Church: an introduction to the architecture of Ralph Adams Cram. Boston: Dorchester Savings Bank, 1973. Pp. 214. M.

5722 ____. The second settlement 1875-1925, a study in the development of Victorian Dorchester. [Boston]: St. Margaret's Hospital, 1974. v.p. M.
History of St. Margaret's Hospital and architecture of Jones Hill area.

5723 TUCKER, EPHRAIM. "The burning of the Ursuline Convent." Worcester HSProc, (1889), 40-61.

5724 TUCKER, THOMAS WAIT. Bannisters Lane 1708-1899: being sundry remarks, some historical, and all new and interesting on Bannisters Lane, now named Winter Street, and the district immediately thereabout. Boston, 1899. Pp. 46. MB.

5725 TUDOR, JOHN. Deacon Tudor's diary; or, 'Memorandoms from 1709, &c., by John Tudor, to 1775 & 1778, 1780 and to '93.' A record of more or less important events in Boston, from 1732 to 1793, by an eye-witness. William Tudor, ed. Boston: W. Spooner, 1896. v.p.

5726 TUDOR, WILLIAM, 1750-1819. An oration, delivered March 5th, 1779, at the request of the inhabitants of the town of Boston; to commemorate the bloody tragedy of the fifth of March, 1770. Boston: Edes & Gill, 1779. Pp. 23 [i. e. 21].

5727 TUDOR, WILLIAM, 1779-1830. Discourse delivered before the Humane Society at their anniversary, May, 1817. Boston: John Eliot, 1817. Pp. 64. MBNEH.
Historical appendix.

5728 TUOHEY, GEORGE V., comp. A history of the Boston Base Ball Club being a public testimonial to the players of the 1897 team.... Boston: M. F. Quinn, 1897. Pp. 236. MB.

5729 TURNER, JOSEPH W. History of the Island Rangers, a juvenile Zouave company. East Boston, 1864. Pp. 63. MB.

5730 TUTTLE, JULIUS HERBERT. "The Boston petitions of 1664." MHSP, 52 (1918-1919), 312-316.
For preservation of charter privileges.

5731 ____. "The Society in retrospect." MHSP, 61 (1927-1928), 91-103.
Massachusetts Historical Society.

5732 "TWENTY fifth anniversary of the Gillette Safety Razor Co., 1901-1926." Gillette Blade, 9 (September, 1926), entire issue.

5733 TYLER, LESLIE. "Old Hinckley Locomotive Works demolished." Railroad Enthusiast, 8 (January-February, 1941), 10-11.

5734 UNION CLUB OF BOSTON. 100th anniversary celebration: Union Club of Boston, Inc. Frederick Milton Kimball, ed. Boston, 1964. Pp. 53.

5735 ____. A report of the celebration of the fiftieth anniversary of the founding of the Union Club of Boston, 1863-1913. Cambridge: Riverside Pr., [1913?]. Pp. 99.

5736 "THE UNITARIAN spring at Brook Farm." UHSP, 7, Pt. 2 (1941), 1-10.

5737 UNITARIAN TEMPERANCE SOCIETY. The Unitarian Temperance Society: a brief record of its history, work and purpose. Boston, [190-?]. Pp. 17. MB.

5738 U. S. BUREAU OF LIGHT-HOUSES. Two-hundredth anniversary of Boston light, September 25, 1916. Washington: Govt. Print. Off., 1916. Pp. 13.

5739 U. S. CENSUS OFFICE. 11th CENSUS, 1890. Vital statistics of Boston and Philadelphia covering a period of six years ending May 31, 1890. Washington: Govt. Print. Off., 1895. Pp. vii, 269.

5740 U. S. INFORMATION AGENCY. Boston: city of tradition. Washington: U. S. Information Service, [1961?]. Pp. 35.

5741 "AN UNWRITTEN chapter in the history of the Siege of Boston." PMHB, 1 (1877), 168-174.

5742 UPHAM, LULU. "The Public Garden pond." Bostonian, 2 (1895), 379-382.

5743 UPHAM, WILLIAM PHINEAS. "Incidents during the occupancy of Boston by the British troops in 1775-6." EIB, 8 (1876), 21-23.

5744 [UPSON, STEPHEN H. R.]. St. George's Syrian Orthodox Church in Boston: a brief history. Boston, 1950. Unpaged. MB.
Author attribution by Boston Public Library.

5745 UPTON, L. F. S. "Proceedings of ye body respecting the tea." WMQ, 3 Ser., 22 (1965), 287-300.
Boston Tea Party.

5746 VAN METER, MARY. "Bay Village or the Church-Street district: a survey of its history and some of its buildings and inhabitants." BSProc, (1969), 33 unnumbered pages between p. [20] and p. [23].

5747 VAN NESS, JAMES S., ed. "The diary of Rev. Joseph Perry written during the Siege of Boston, February 16 to March 28, 1776." BSProc, (1963), 19-56.

5748 VAN NESS, THOMAS. "A nest of liberty." Outlook, 75 (1903), 549-560.
Second Church.

5749 VAN TASSEL, DAVID D. "Gentlemen of property
      and standing: Compromise sentiment in Bos-
ton in 1850." NEQ, 23 (1950), 307-319.
      Compromise of 1850.

5750 VAN DE WETERING, JOHN E. "The 'Christian
      History' of the Great Awakening." Journal
of Presbyterian History, 44 (1966), 122-129.
      A weekly periodical, 1743-1745.

5751 VARNEY, GEORGE JONES. "The Massachusetts
      capitol." NEM, 5 (1886-1887), 66-69.

5752 _____. "The stars and stripes, a Boston
      idea." NEM, New Ser., 26 (1902), 539-548.

5753 VIETS, HENRY ROUSE. "The earliest printed
      references in newspapers and journals to the
first public demonstration of ether anesthesia in
1846." JHistMed, 4 (1949), 149-169.
      At Massachusetts General Hospital.

5754 _____. "The resident house staff at the
      opening of the Boston City Hospital in
1864." JHistMed, 14 (1959), 179-190.

5755 _____. "The War of 1812 and the Marine Hos-
      pital for the port of Boston." BHistMed, 10
(1941), 53-56.

5756 VILLARD, FANNY GARRISON. "How Boston re-
      ceived the Emancipation Proclamation." Re-
view of Reviews, 47 (1913), 177-178.

5757 VILLAUME, WILLIAM J. Protestantism in East
      Boston, Massachusetts, 1920-1946: an un-
churched minority in an overchurched community.
[Boston?]: Massachusetts Council of Churches, 1947.
Pp. 134, 47. MB.

5758 VISITING NURSES ASSOCIATION OF BOSTON. The
      hospital without walls, 1896-1936. Boston,
[1936?]. Pp. 23. M.
      Charity.

5759 VOGEL, SUSAN MAYCOCK. "Hartwell and Rich-
      ardson: an introduction to their work."
SocArchHistJ, 32 (1973), 132-146.
      Henry W. Hartwell and William C. Richardson.

5760 VOIGT, DAVID QUENTIN. "The Boston Red
      Stockings: the birth of major league base-
ball." NEQ, 43 (1970), 531-549.

5761 VON KLENZE, CAMILLO. "German literature in
      the 'Boston Transcript,' 1830-1880." Philo-
logical Quarterly, 11 (1932), 1-25.

5762 VOSE, JOHNSON T. "The first monument on
      Bunker Hill." Bostonian, 2 (1895), 227-237.

5763 VOSE, PETER E. "The great Boston fire of
      1760." NEHGR, 34 (1880), 288-293.

5764 "W. F. Schrafft & Son Corporation." Indus-
      try, 6 (February, 1941), 7-10, 38.
      Candy.

5765 WADLIN, HORACE GREELEY. The Public Library
      of the City of Boston: a history. Boston:
The Trustees [of the Boston Public Library], 1911.
Pp. xx, 236.

5766 [WADSWORTH, LUE STUART]. Souvenir of Hancock
      Tavern, Corn Court, Boston. Boston, 1900.
Unpaged. MB.
      Author attribution by Boston Public Library.

5767 WAITE, EMMA FORBES. "The Tontine Crescent
      and its architect [Charles Bulfinch]." OTNE,
43 (1952-1953), 74-77.
      A residential block.

5768 WAITE, FREDERICK CLAYTON. History of the New
      England Female Medical College, 1848-1874.
Boston: Boston Univ. School of Medicine, 1950.
Pp. 132.
      Merged with Boston University in 1874.

5769 WAKEFIELD, M. B. "Disaster at the 'tin
      bridge.'" RLHSB, No. 95 (1956), 85-87.
      Train derailment.

5770 WAKSTEIN, ALLEN M. "Boston's search for a
      metropolitan solution." American Institute
of Planners. Journal, 38 (1972), 285-296.
      Since the nineteenth century.

5771 WALL, CALEB ARNOLD. The historic Boston Tea
      Party of December 16, 1733, its men and ob-
jects: incidents leading to, accompanying, and following the throwing overboard of the tea, including
a short account of the Boston massacre of March 5,
1770.... Worcester: F. S. Blanchard, 1896.
Pp. 87.

5772 WALSH, ROBERT A. "The Massachusetts College
      of Pharmacy, 1823-1973." Massachusetts Col-
lege of Pharmacy. Bulletin, 62 (Fall, 1973), 5-59.

5773 "WALTER Baker & Company." Industry, 2 (No-
      vember, 1936), 9-11.
      Chocolate.

5774 WALTON, PERRY. Devonshire Street: a collec-
      tion of facts and incidents together with re-
productions of illustrations pertaining to an old
Boston street. Boston: Second National Bank, 1912.
Pp. 47.

5775 WARD, DAVID. "Comparative historical geogra-
      phy of street-car suburbs in Boston, Massa-
chusetts and Leeds, England, 1850-1920." Association of American Geographers. Annals, 54 (1964),
477-489.

5776 _____. "The emergence of central immigrant
      ghettoes in American cities: 1840-1920."
Association of American Geographers. Annals, 58
(1968), 343-359.
      Emphasis on Boston.

5777 _____. "The Industrial Revolution and the
      emergence of Boston's central business dis-
trict." Economic Geography, 42 (1966), 152-171.
      1835-1890.

5778 WARD, JULIUS H. "The Benedict Club." NEM,
      New Ser., 14 (1896), 461-471.

5779 WARDEN, GERARD B. Boston, 1689-1776.
      Boston: Little, Brown, 1970. Pp. 404.

5780 _____. "The Caucus and democracy in colonial Boston." NEQ, 43 (1970), 19-45.

5781 WARE, HENRY. Two discourses containing the history of the Old North and New Brick Churches, united as the Second Church in Boston, delivered May 20, 1821, at the completion of a century from the dedication of the present meetinghouse in Middle Street. Boston: J. W. Burditt, 1821. Pp. 61.

5782 WARNER, CALEB H. National Bank of Commerce of Boston. Cambridge: Univ. Pr., 1892. Pp. 47. MBNEH.
1850-1892.

5783 WARNER, FRANCES LESTER. Merry Christmas from Boston. Boston: Atlantic Monthly Pr., 1921. Unpaged.
Social life and customs.

5784 WARNER, RICHARD F. "Boston sees the joke." Outlook, 154 (1930), 210-211, 233.
Literary censorship.

5785 WARNER, SAM BASS. Crime and criminal statistics in Boston. Cambridge: Harvard Univ. Pr., 1934. Pp. x, 150.

5786 _____. and HENRY B. CABOT. Judges and law reform. Cambridge: Harvard Univ. Pr., 1936. Pp. viii, 246.

5787 WARNER, SAM BASS., JR. Streetcar suburbs, the process of growth in Boston, 1870-1900. Cambridge: Harvard Univ. Pr., 1962. Pp. xxi, 208.

5788 WARREN, CHARLES. "Samuel Adams and the Sans Souci Club in 1785." MHSP, 60 (1926-1927), 318-344.

5789 WARREN, CHARLES V. "Half a century of housing experiment." Our Boston, 2 (May, 1927), 12-15.

5790 WARREN, GEORGE WASHINGTON. The history of the Bunker Hill Monument Association during the first century of the United States of America. Boston: J. R. Osgood, 1877. Pp. xix, 426.

5791 WARREN, JOHN COLLINS. The great tree on Boston Common. Boston: J. Wilson & Son, 1855. Pp. 20.

5792 WARREN, WILLIAM FAIRFIELD. The historical heritage of Boston University: quartercentennial address, June 1, 1898. Boston, 1898. Pp. 23.

5793 _____. Origin and progress of Boston University. Boston: University Offices, 1893. Pp. 64. MBU.

5794 WARREN, WILLIAM MARSHALL. Beacon Hill and Boston University. n.p., 1933. Pp. 21. MBU.

5795 _____. Notes on the founders and associate founders of Boston University. [Boston?]: Boston Univ., College of Liberal Arts, for the first 'founders' day, March 13, 1931, 1931. Pp. 18.

5796 _____. Roundabout of the four homes of Boston University College of Liberal Arts.... Boston, [1948?]. Pp. 23. MBU.

5797 WARREN, WINSLOW. "Boston customs record." MHSP, 43 (1909-1910), 423-428.
Loss of customs records at the time of the evacuation of Boston in 1776.

5798 WASHBURN, FREDERIC AUGUSTUS. The Massachusetts General Hospital: its development, 1900-1935. Boston: Houghton Mifflin, 1939. Pp. xiii, 643.

5799 "WASHINGTON'S journey to Boston 150 years ago." About the First, (October, 1939), 4-6.

5800 WATERMAN, F. A. "Concise facts regarding historic Boston." National Magazine, 12 (1900), 277-282.

5801 WATERMAN, HENRY. "A famous American street." Americana, 5 (1910), 343-348.
Summer Street.

5802 WATERMAN, THOMAS TILESTON. "Certain brick houses in Boston from 1700 to 1776." OTNE, 23 (1932-1933), 22-27.

5803 _____. "The Province House demolition." OTNE, 62 (1971-1972), 107-113.

5804 WATERSTON, ROBERT CASSIE. "Boston schools." MHSP, (1871-1873), 387-391.
Seventeenth century.

5805 _____. "The old elm on Boston Common." MHSP, (1875-1876), 300-316.

5806 WATKINS, LURA WOODSIDE. "The Boston Crown Glass Company." Antiques, 37 (1940), 288-291.
1787-1829.

5807 _____. "George Richardson, pewterer." Antiques, 31 (1937), 194-196.

5808 _____. "Glassmaking in South Boston." Antiques, 48 (1945), 140-143, 216-218.

5809 _____. "New light on Boston stoneware and Frederick Carpenter." Antiques, 101 (1972), 1052-1057.

5810 WATKINS, WALTER KENDALL. "The Blue Anchor Tavern, Boston." OTNE, 20 (1929-1930), 154-161.

5811 _____. "Boston in the last days of the town." BSProc, (1923), 23-34.

5812 _____. "The Boston of Franklin's time." OTNE, 37 (1946-1947), 84-89.

5813 _____. "Boston one hundred years ago." BSProc, (1905), 25-40.

5814 _____. "Boylston Hotel, School Street." BSPub, 2 Ser., 1 (1916), 107-115.

5815 _____. "The defense of Boston in the War of 1812." BSProc, (1899), 35-57.

5816 _____. "The early use and manufacture of paper hangings in Boston." OTNE, 12 (1921-1922), 109-117.
Wallpaper.

5817 _____. Franklin's Head: a story of Court Street, Boston. Boston, 1909. Pp. 50. MBNEH.

5818 _____. "The great street to Roxbury Gate, 1630-1830." BSPub, 2 Ser., 3 (1919), 89-126.
Washington Street.

5819 _____. "The Hancock House and its builder." OTNE, 17 (1926-1927), 3-19.
Demolished in 1863.

5820 _____. "The Melvill House in Green Street." BSProc, (1917), 26-37.

5821 _____. "The New England Museum and the home of art in Boston." BSPub, 2 Ser., 2 (1917), 103-130.

5822 _____. "Notes on the Savage House." OTNE, 17 (1926-1927), 110-115.

5823 _____. "The Province House and its occupants." OTNE, 62 (1971-1972), 95-105.

5824 _____. "The Robert Gibbs House, Boston." OTNE, 22 (1931-1932), 193-196.

5825 _____. "Robert Orchard, or the art and mystery of feltmakers, of Boston in New England." BSPub, 4 (1907), 79-102.
Seventeenth century.

5826 _____. "The site of Faneuil Hall." BSPub, 7 (1910), 131-138.
Seventeenth and eighteenth centuries.

5827 _____. "Subscription list for building the first Town House." BSPub, 3 (1906), 105-149.
Collected biographies.

5828 _____. "Tarring and feathering in Boston in 1770." OTNE, 20 (1929-1930), 30-43.

5829 _____. Ye Crown Coffee House: a story of old Boston. Boston: Henderson & Ross, 1916. Pp. 55.

5830 WATSON, JOHN LEE. "Paul Revere's signal: the true story of the 'signal lanterns' in Christ Church, Boston." MHSP, (1876-1877), 164-177.

5831 WEBSTER, PHILIP J. "The Handel and Haydn Society." Boston, 55 (November, 1963), 34-39, 69, 73.

5832 [WEBSTER, REDFORD]. Selections from the chronicle of Boston and from the book of retrospections and anticipations; compiled in the last month of the last year of the town and the first month of the first year of the city, being the year of Lord MDCCCXXII. Boston, 1822. Pp. 132. MB.
Author attribution by Boston Public Library; satirical.

5833 WEDGWOOD, HAZEL. "The nursing service of the Boston Health Department." Our Boston, 2 (June, 1927), 17-21.

5834 WEDNESDAY EVENING CLUB. Centennial celebration of the Wednesday Evening Club: instituted June 21, 1777. Boston: J. Wilson, 1878. Pp. 145. MB.

5835 WEEKS, EDWARD. The Lowells and their Institute. Boston: Little, Brown, 1966. Pp. xli, 202.
Adult education.

5836 _____. Men, money and responsibility: a history of Lee, Higginson Corporation, 1848-1962. Boston, 1962. Pp. 29.
An investment trust.

5837 _____. "A state of mind surrounded by water." Boston, 57 (June, 1965), 25-28.
Reminiscences.

5838 WEINBERG, HELENE BARBARA. "John La Farge and the decoration of Trinity Church, Boston." SocArchHistJ, 33 (1974), 323-353.

5839 WEINHARDT, CARL J., JR. "The domestic architecture of Beacon Hill 1800-1850." BSProc, (1958), 11-32.

5840 WEIS, CARRIE M. W. History of the Village Congregational Church, Dorchester, Mass. Dorchester: Underhill, 1929. Pp. 32. MB.

5841 WEISER, FRANCIS XAVIER. Holy Trinity Parish, Boston, Mass., 1844-1944. Boston: Holy Trinity Rectory, 1944. Pp. 52.

5842 WELD, ANNA H. "The old Sumner Homestead." HPHR, 2 (1892-1893), 23-30.
Sumner family.

5843 WELD, JOHN G. "Sidelights of the old Boston militia companies." BSProc, (1949), 25-43.

5844 WELLINGTON, LEAH L. NICHOLS. History of the Bowdoin School, 1821-1907. Manchester, N.H.: Ruemely Pr., 1912. Pp. 178. MB.

5845 WELLS, AMOS RUSSEL. The Christian Endeavor Building, its history and surroundings. Boston: United Society of Christian Endeavor, 1919. Pp. 38. MBNEH.

5846 WELLS, KATE GANNETT. "The Boston club woman." Arena, 6 (1892), 369-371.

5847 _____. "In and about the old Bumstead Place." NEM, New Ser., 9 (1894), 649-658.

5848 WELLS MEMORIAL INSTITUTE. A summary of its history and present activities, 1880-1900. Boston, 1900. Pp. 31. MB.
A workingman's association.

5849 WENHAM, EDWARD. "The silversmiths of early Boston." Antiquarian, 17 (July, 1931), 31-34, 60.

5850 WEST ROXBURY, MASS. FIRST PARISH. West Roxbury Magazine, published by a committee for the First Parish, West Roxbury, West Roxbury, Mass.... Hudson: E. F. Worcester Pr., 1900. Pp. 56.

5851 WEST ROXBURY, MASS. SOUTH EVANGELICAL CHURCH. Seventy-fifth anniversary, 1835-1910. West Roxbury, 1910. Pp. 30. MB.

5852 WESTON, GEORGE F., JR. Boston ways: high, by, and folk. (1957) 3d. ed. Boston: Beacon Pr., 1974. Pp. xiv, 306.

5853 _____. "A portfolio of historical Boston." Food Marketing in New England, 13 (May, 1953), 11-22.

5854. THE WHARF RAT. T Wharf: notes and sketches collected during a quarter century of living on Boston's waterfront, presented by the Wharf Rat, a magazine of limited circulation and doubtful value published now and then since 1928. William Hauk, comp. Boston, Alden-Hauk, 1952. Pp. 185.

5855 WHEELER, ALEXANDER STRONG. Address on Boston, fifty years since, delivered before the Commercial Club of Boston, Nov. 21, 1896. Boston: Rockwell & Churchill, 1896. Pp. 25. MB.

5856 _____. Reminiscences of an old lawyer: an address by our fellow-member, Mr. A. S. Wheeler, delivered before the Commercial Club of Boston, December 18, 1897. Boston: Rockwell and Churchill, 1898. Pp. 20.
      Recollections of Boston lawyers.

5857 WHEELER, WARREN GAGE. "Fifty years on Boylston Street." MHSP, 78 (1966), 38-49.
      Massachusetts Historical Society, 1913-1963.

5858 WHEILDON, WILLIAM WILLDER. "Beacon Hill, the Beacon and the monuments." Bunker Hill Monument Association. Proceedings, (1889), 51-60.

5859 _____. Curiosities of history: Boston September seventeenth, 1630-1880. (1880) 2d. ed. Boston: Lee and Shepard, 1880. Pp. x, 141.

5860 _____. History of Paul Revere's signal lanterns, April 18, 1775, in the steeple of the North Church: with an account of the tablet on Christ Church and the monuments at Highland Park and Dorchester Heights. Concord, 1878. Pp. 63.

5861 _____. Semi-centennial celebration of the opening of the Faneuil Hall Market, August 26, 1876, with a history of the market. Boston: L. F. Lawrence and Co., 1877. Unpaged. MB.

5862 _____. Sentry, or Beacon Hill; the beacon and the monument of 1635 and 1790. Concord, 1877. Pp. vii, 116.

5863 _____. Siege and evacuation of Boston and Charlestown, with a brief account of pre-Revolutionary public buildings. Boston: Lee & Shepard, 1876. Pp. 64.

5864 "WHEN was Readville so named?" HPHR, 2 (1892-1893), 30.
      Section of Hyde Park.

5865 WHIPPLE, J. RAYNER. "'John Brown's Body Lies A Mouldering in the Grave': the popular Civil War song which originated at Fort Warren, Boston Harbor." OTNE, 32 (1941-1942), 97-100.

5866 WHITCHER, WILLIAM F. "The relation of New Hampshire men to the Siege of Boston." Mag Hist, 6 (1907), 63-85.

5867 WHITCOMB, HARRIET MANNING. Annals and reminiscences of Jamaica Plain. Cambridge: Riverside Pr., 1897. Pp. 64.

5868 WHITCOMB, WEAD AND CO. Then and now, some comparisons showing Boston's growth in fifteen years. Boston, 1905. Pp. 34. M.
      Industry, 1890-1905.

5869 WHITE, ARTHUR O. "The Black leadership class and education in antebellum Boston." JNegro Ed, 42 (1973), 504-515.

5870 _____. "Integrated schools in antebellum Boston: the implications of Black victory." Urban Education, 6 (1971), 131-145.

5871 WHITE, CHARLES H. "Boston town." Harper's Magazine, 113 (1906), 666-674.

5872 WHITE, GERALD TAYLOR. A history of the Massachusetts Hospital Life Insurance Company. Cambridge: Harvard Univ. Pr., 1955. Pp. 229.

5873 WHITE, OLIVE B. Centennial history of the Girls' High School of Boston. Boston, 1952. Pp. 80. MB.

5874 WHITE, Z. L. "The first owner of Boston." American Magazine, 7 (1888), 707-716.
      William Blaxton.

5875 WHITEFIELD, EDWIN. Homes of our forefathers in Boston, Old England and Boston, New England. Boston, 1889. Pp. 138.
      Historic houses.

5876 WHITEHILL, WALTER MUIR. "The apotheosis of the codfish." NEG, 5 (Summer, 1963), 10-16.
      Codfish in the House of Representatives chamber.

5877 _____. Boston: a topographical history. (1959) 2d. ed., enl. Cambridge: Harvard Univ. Pr., 1968. Pp. xl, 299.

5878 _____. Boston and the Civil War. Boston: Boston Athenaeum, 1963. Pp. 17.

5879 _____. Boston Athenaeum anthology, 1807-1972; selected from its annual reports. Boston: Boston Athenaeum, 1973. Pp. 48. M.

5880   _____, ed. Boston furniture of the eighteenth century: a conference held by the
Colonial Society of Massachusetts 11 and 12 May,
1972. Boston: Colonial Society of Massachusetts,
1974. Pp. xvi, 316.

5881   _____. Boston in the age of John Fitzgerald
Kennedy. Norman: Univ. of Oklahoma Pr.,
1966. Pp. xv, 208.
        Intellectual and social life.

5882   _____. Boston Public Library: a centennial
history. Cambridge: Harvard Univ. Pr.,
1956. Pp. 274.

5883   _____. Boston statues. Barre: Barre Publishers, 1970. Pp. 120.

5884   _____. "The centenary of the Dowse Library."
MHSP, 71 (1953-1957), 167-178.
        Massachusetts Historical Society.

5885   _____. The Club of Odd Volumes, Boston,
1887-1973, an address given at the Philo-
biblon Club [Philadelphia] on 19 April 1973.
[North Hills, Pa.]: Bird & Bull Pr., 1973. Pp. 13.
M.

5886   _____. Destroyed Boston buildings. Boston:
Massachusetts Historical Society, 1965.
Pp. 31.

5887   _____. "The early history of the American
Academy of Arts and Sciences." American
Academy of Arts and Sciences. Bulletin, 24 (1970-
1971), 3-23.

5888   _____. "The King's Chapel Library." CSMP,
38 (1947-1951), 274-289.

5889   _____. "The making of an architectural mas-
terpiece--the Boston Public Library."
American Art Journal, 2 (1970), 13-35.
        1854-1912.

5890   _____. "The metamorphoses of Scollay and
Bowdoin Squares." BSProc, (1972-1973),
[49-81].

5891   _____. Museum of Fine Arts, Boston: a centennial history. Cambridge: Belknap Pr.,
1970. 2v.

5892   _____. "The neighborhood of the Tavern
Club, 1630-1971." BSProc, (1970-1971),
[49-90].

5893   _____. "Perez Morton's daughter revisits
Boston in 1825." MHSP, 82 (1970), 21-47.

5894   _____. "Portrait busts in the library of
the Boston Athenaeum." Antiques, 105
(1973), 1141-1156.

5895   _____. The Provident Institution for Savings in the Town of Boston, 1816-1966: a
historical sketch. Boston, 1966. Pp. 122. MB.

5896   _____, et al. A seidel for Jake Wirth.
Lunenburg, Vt.: Stinehour Pr., 1964.
Pp. 45. MBNEH.
        Jacob Wirth Co., restaurant.

5897   _____. "Two destroyed Boston houses of the
eighteenth century." BSProc, (1959), 11-28.
        Bulfinch House and Vassall-Hubbard-Geyer-
Gardner House.

5898   _____. "The vicissitudes of Bacchante in
Boston." NEQ, 27 (1954), 435-454.
        Controversy over statue given to Boston Pub-
lic Library for its courtyard by Charles F.
McKim and its subsequent withdrawal, 1895-
1897.

5899   WHITESIDE, WILLIAM B. The Boston Y.M.C.A.
and community need: a century's evolution,
1851-1951. N.Y.: Association Pr., 1951. Pp. 239.

5900   WHITING, CHARLES F. "Historical associations of Charlestown and Cambridge." CaHSP,
33 (1949-1950), 134-155.
        History, not historical societies.

5901   WHITING, LILIAN. Boston days, the city of
beautiful ideals; Concord, and its famous
authors; the golden age of genius; dawn of the twentieth century; first decade of twentieth century.
(1902) Boston: Little, Brown, 1911. Pp. xii,
543.
        Social and intellectual life.

5902   _____. "The Old Corner Bookstore." Literary
Era, 8 (1901), 540-545.

5903   WHITING, MARGARET ABBOTT. "Another centenary." SWJ, 44 (1929), 327-339.
        Massachusetts Horticultural Society.

5904   WHITMAN, MRS. BERNARD. "Early Dorchester."
NEM, New Ser., 4 (1891), 327-334.

5905   WHITMAN, WILLIAM & COMPANY, INC. A brief
outline of the business of William Whitman &
Co.... Cambridge: Univ. Pr., 1910. Pp. 95.
        Textiles.

5906   WHITMAN, ZACHARIAH GARDNER. An address delivered before Massachusetts Lodge, at the
installation of officers, December 26, 5822, to
which is annexed an appendix containing a short
history of the lodge and a list of all who have been
masters or wardens of Massachusetts Lodge. Boston:
Bowen, 1823. Pp. 27.

5907   WHITMORE, WILLIAM HENRY. An historical summary of fires in Boston. Boston, 1872.
Pp. 12.

5908   _____. The Old State-House defended from un-
founded attacks upon its integrity, being a
reply to Dr. G. H. Moore's second paper, read before
the Bostonian Society, Feb. 9, 1886. Boston, 1886.
Pp. 8.

5909   WHITNEY, DAVID RICE. The Suffolk Bank. Cambridge: Riverside Pr., 1878. Pp. 73.

5910 WHITNEY, JAMES LYMAN. "Incidents in the history of the Boston Public Library." LJ, 27 (July, 1902), 16-24.

5911 [WHITNEY, LOUISA GODDARD]. The burning of the convent: a narrative of the destruction, by a mob, of the Ursuline School on Mount Benedict, Charlestown, as remembered by one of the pupils. Boston: J. R. Osgood, 1877. Pp. vi, 198.
    Preface signed: L. W.

5912 WHO'S who in Boston, D. Pittler, comp. Boston, [1931]. 36 leaves.

5913 WHYTE, WILLIAM FOOTE. "Race conflicts in the North End of Boston." NEQ, 12 (1939), 623-642.
    Irish and Italian.

5914 ____. Street corner society: the social structure of an Italian slum. (1943) Enl. ed. Chicago: Univ. of Chicago Pr., 1955. Pp. xxii, 366.
    North End.

5915 WIEDER, ARNOLD A. The early Jewish community of Boston's North End: a sociologically oriented study of an Eastern European Jewish immigrant community in an American big-city neighborhood between 1870 and 1900. Waltham: Brandeis Univ., 1962. Pp. 100.

5916 WIGGINS, JAMES HENRY. "A vanished architectural group." Bostonian, 2 (1895), 165-171.
    Several Boston churches.

5917 WIGGLESWORTH, EDWARD. "Sketch of the Boston Athenaeum." American Quarterly Register, 2 (1839-1840), 149-153.

5918 WIGHTMAN, JOSEPH MILNER. Annals of the Boston Primary School Committee, from its first establishment in 1818, to its dissolution in 1855. Boston: G. C. Rand & Avery, 1860. Pp. 8, 305.

5919 WILDER, CATHERINE KERLIN. "Artemas Ward and the Siege of Boston." CaHSP, 37 (1957-1958), 45-63.

5920 WILLARD, ASHTON R. "Recent church architecture in Boston." NEM, New Ser., 1 (1889-1890), 641-662.

5921 WILLARD, JOHN WARE. A history of Simon Willard, inventor and clockmaker...his sons, his apprentices.... Boston: E. O. Cockayne, 1911. Pp. 133. MBSpnea.

5922 WILLIAMS, ALEXANDER W. A social history of the greater Boston clubs. [Barre]: Barre Publishers, 1970. Pp. viii, 176.

5923 WILLIAMS, GEORGE WASHINGTON. History of the Twelfth Baptist Church, Boston, Mass., from 1840 to 1874.... Boston: J. H. Earle, 1874. Pp. 79. MB.

5924 WILLIAMS, THOMAS FRANKLIN. "Cabot, Peabody, and the care of the patient." BHistMed, 24 (1950), 462-481.
    Biographical studies of Richard C. Cabot and Francis W. Peabody, physicians.

5925 WILLIAMSON, MARGARET. The Mother Church extension. Boston: Christian Science Publishing Society, 1939. v.p.

5926 WILLOUGHBY, CHARLES CLARK. "An ancient Indian fish-weir." American Anthropologist, 29 (1927), 105-108.

5927 WILSON, HERBERT A. "History of the Boston Police Department." Our Boston, 1 (August, 1926), 17-20.

5928 WILSON, JOHN B. "The antecedents of Brook Farm." NEQ, 15 (1942), 320-331.

5929 ____. "Grimm's law and the Brahmins." NEQ, 38 (1965), 234-239.
    Intellectual life.

5930 [WILSON, THOMAS L. V.]. The aristocracy of Boston; who they are and what they were: being a history of the business and business men of Boston, for the last forty years. By One who knows them. Boston, 1848. Pp. 32.

5931 WINCHELL, JAMES MANNING. Jubilee sermons: two discourses exhibiting an historical sketch of the First Baptist Church in Boston 1665 to 1818. (1819) 2d. ed. Boston: J. Loring, 1820. Pp. 48. MB.

5932 WINCHESTER HOME FOR AGED WOMEN, CHARLESTOWN, MASS. Semicentennial, 1865-1915. Charlestown, 1915. Pp. 28. MB.

5933 [WINES, ENOCH COBB]. A trip to Boston, in a series of letters to the editor of the United States Gazette. By the author of 'Two years and a half in the navy.' Boston: C. C. Little and J. Brown, 1838. Pp. xii, 224.

5934 WINKLEY, HOBART W. "Annals of Louisburg Square." BSProc, (1926), 22-37.

5935 WINSHIP, GEORGE PARKER, ed. Boston in 1682 and 1699; a trip to New-England, by Edward Ward, and a letter from New England, by J. W. Providence: Club for Colonial Reprints, 1905. Pp. xxviii, 95.

5936 ____. Daniel Berkeley Updike and the Merrymount Press of Boston, Mass., 1860-1894-1941. Rochester, N.Y.: Leo Hart, 1947. Pp. x, 141. MB.

5937 ____. "Two or three Boston papers." PBSA, 14 (1920), 57-81.
    Eighteenth-century French newspapers.

5938 ____. "Updike and Merrymount Press." Direct Advertising, 28 (July, 1942), 4-11.
    Daniel Berkeley Updike.

5939 WINSHIP, JOHN PERKINS CUSHING. Historical Brighton: an illustrated history of Brighton and its citizens. Boston, G. A. Warren, 1899-1902. 2v.
Biography.

5940 WINSLOW, ANNA GREEN. Diary of Anna Green Winslow, a Boston school girl of 1771. Alice Morse Earle, ed. Boston: Houghton Mifflin, 1894. Pp. xx, 121.

5941 WINSLOW, CHARLES EDWARD AMORY. History of the Prince School in the city of Boston, 1872-1902. Boston, 1902. Pp. 36. MB.

5942 WINSLOW, EDWARD. "The early charitable organizations of Boston." NEHGR, 44 (1890), 100-103.

5943 WINSLOW, ERVING. "The Boston Athenaeum." Bostonian, 3 (1895-1896), 227-236.

5944 _____. "A loyalist in the Siege of Boston." NEHGR, 56 (1902), 48-54.
Isaac Winslow.

5945 WINSLOW, FREDERIC I. Chronological table of Boston Water Works. Boston: City Printing Department, 1912. Pp. 16. M.

5946 WINSLOW, HELEN M. "Industrial features in the Boston public schools." NEM, New Ser., 9 (1893-1894), 369-377.

5947 WINSLOW, OLA ELIZABETH. A destroying angel: the conquest of smallpox in colonial Boston. Boston: Houghton Mifflin, 1974. Pp. x, 137.

5948 WINSOR, FRANK E. "Some changes since Boston was settled three hundred years ago." Boston Society of Civil Engineers. Journal, 17 (1930), 311-323.
Sanitation and water supply.

5949 WINSOR, JUSTIN, ed. The memorial history of Boston, including Suffolk County, Massachusetts, 1630-1880. Boston: J. R. Osgood, 1880-1881. 4v.

5950 WINTHROP, ROBERT CHARLES. "Early portrait-painters in Boston." MHSP, 20 (1882-1883), 113-121.

5951 _____, et al. "Tea-Party anniversary." MHSP, (1873-1875), 151-216.

5952 "WINTHROP Church, Charlestown, Mass." CongQ, 9 (1867), 36-38.

5953 WISNER, BENJAMIN BLYDENBURG. The history of the Old South Church in Boston, in four sermons, delivered May 9, & 16, 1830, being the first and second Sabbaths after the completion of a century from the first occupancy of the present meeting house. Boston: Crocker & Brewster, 1830. Pp. 122.

5954 WITHINGTON, ROBERT. "A French comment on the Battle of Bunker Hill." NEQ, 22 (1949), 235-240.
Marquis de Chastellux, 1782.

5955 WOLBACH, WILLIAM W. Boston Safe Deposit and Trust Company; the story of New England's largest independent trust organization. N.Y.: Newcomen Society in North America, 1962. Pp. 28.

5956 WOLFE, ALBERT BENEDICT. The lodging house problem in Boston. Boston: Houghton Mifflin, 1906. Pp. 200.

5957 WOLKINS, GEORGE GREGERSON. "The Boston customs district in 1768." MHSP, 58 (1924-1925), 418-445.

5958 _____. "Daniel Malcolm and Writs of Assistance." MHSP, 58 (1924-1925), 5-84.

5959 _____. "Historic Boston." Education, 23 (1903), 583-605.

5960 _____. "The Prince Society." MHSP, 66 (1936-1941), 222-254.
Historical Society.

5961 _____. "The seizure of John Hancock's sloop 'Liberty.'" MHSP, 55 (1921-1922), 239-284. 1768.

5962 _____. "Village enterprise." OTNE, 41 (1950-1951), 83-88.
Joseph H. Billings Co., wool combers.

5963 WOMAN'S SEAMAN'S FRIEND SOCIETY, BOSTON. Woman's Seaman's Friend Society, its foundation and growth. n.p., 1955. Unpaged. M.

5964 WOMEN'S EDUCATIONAL AND INDUSTRIAL UNION, BOSTON. The Union--its history and aims. Boston, 1915. Pp. 22. MB.

5965 WOMEN'S TRADE UNION LEAGUE OF MASSACHUSETTS. The history of trade unionism among women in Boston. Boston, 1915. Pp. 33.

5966 WOOD, JAMES PLAYSTED. Boston. N.Y.: Seabury Pr., 1967. Pp. 143.

5967 WOOD, NATHAN EUSEBIUS. The history of the First Baptist Church of Boston (1665-1899). Philadelphia: American Baptist Publication Society, 1899. Pp. x, 378.

5968 WOODRUFF, JOHN. "America's oldest living theatre--the Howard Athenaeum." Theatre Annual, 8 (1950), 71-81.
1845-1950.

5969 WOODS, AMY. "The Boston Floating Hospital." NEM, New Ser., 31 (1904-1905), 187-201.

5970 _____. "An historical snow storm." NEM, New Ser., 29 (1903-1904), 754-761.
1898.

5971 WOODS, LUCY RICE. History of the Girls' High School of Boston, 1852-1902. Cambridge: Riverside Pr., 1904. Pp. 89. MB.

5972 WOODS, ROBERT ARCHEY, ed. Americans in process; a settlement study by residents and associates of the South End House, North and West Ends, Boston. Boston: Houghton Mifflin, 1902. Pp. ix, 380.

5973 _____. The city of wilderness; a settlement study by residents and associates of the South End House, South End, Boston. Boston: Houghton Mifflin, 1898. Pp. vii, 319.

5974 _____. The neighborhoods in nation-building: the running comment of thirty years at the South End House. Boston: Houghton Mifflin, 1923. Pp. viii, 348.

5975 WOODS (S. A.) MACHINE COMPANY, BOSTON. The fifth freedom, freedom to work. Boston, 1942. Pp. 28.
Labor controversy.

5976 WOOLMER-WILLIAMS, CHARLES. Incidents in the history of the Honourable Artillery Company. An abridged version of Major Raikes' history of the company from 1537 to 1887, including also a history of the American branch of the regiment, known as the Ancient and Honourable Company of Boston. London: R. Bentley, 1888. Pp. xvi, 203. MB.

5977 WORKINGMEN'S CO-OPERATIVE BANK, BOSTON. From Cheapside to Cornhill. Issued to commemorate the 50th anniversary of the Bank. Boston, 1930. Pp. 16. MB.

5978 WORRELL, DOROTHY. "Disposal of Boston's refuse." Our Boston, 1 (December, 1925), 13-20.

5979 _____. The Women's Municipal League of Boston, a history of thirty-five years of civic endeavor. Boston: Women's Municipal League Committees, 1943. Pp. xvi, 224.

5980 WORTHEN, SAMUEL COPP. "Bunker Hill." Granite Mo, 58 (1926), 182-186.

5981 WORTHY, WILLIAM. The story of the two first colored nurses to train in Boston City Hospital, Boston, Mass. [Boston?, 1942]. Pp. 15.

5982 WRENN, GEORGE L., III. "The Boston City Hall, Bryant and Gilman, architects, 1862-1865." SocArchHistJ, 21 (1962), 188-192.

5983 WRIGHT, CARROLL DAVIDSON. The social, commercial, and manufacturing statistics of the city of Boston...from the United States census returns for 1880, and from original sources, with an account of the railroad and shipping facilities of the city. Boston: Rockwell and Churchill, 1882. Pp. viii, 259.
Includes statistics of imports and exports, 1870-1881.

5984 WRIGHT, JOHN. Growth of St. Matthew's Parish, a discourse delivered on Sunday evening, June 26, 1877 in St. Matthew's Church, So. Boston. Boston: Damrell & Upham, 1887. Pp. 13. MBNEH.

5985 WRIGHT, LIVINGSTON. "Drove Boston's first horse-car." SWJ, 47 (1930), 239-241.

5986 WRIGHT, NATHALIA. "The monument that Jonathan built." AmQ, 5 (1953), 166-174.
Bunker Hill Monument.

5987 WRIGHT AND POTTER PRINTING COMPANY, BOSTON. The plant and its resources with a short history of its development during the last century. Boston, 1924. Pp. 36. MH.

5988 WRITERS' PROGRAM. MASSACHUSETTS. Boston looks seaward, the story of the port, 1630-1940. Boston: B. Humphries, 1941. Pp. 14, 316.

5989 WROTH, LAWRENCE COUNSELMAN. "The work of the Merrymount Press." New England Printer, 12 (December, 1935), 5-7.

5990 WYMAN, THOMAS BELLOWS. The genealogies and estates of Charlestown, in the county of Middlesex and Commonwealth of Massachusetts, 1629-1818. Henry H. Edes, ed. Boston: D. Clapp and Son, 1879. 2v.

5991 YEHIA, MARY ELLEN. "Chairs for the masses, a brief history of the L. White Chair Company, Boston, Massachusetts." OTNE, 58 (1972-1973), 33-44.
1864-1869.

5992 YODELIS, M. A. "Boston's first major newspaper war: a 'great awakening' of freedom." Journalism Quarterly, 51 (1974), 207-212.
Thomas Fleet.

5993 YORKE, DANE. Able men of Boston; the remarkable story of the first 100 years of the Boston Manufacturers Mutual Fire Insurance Company, its men, its times, and its growth in insurance protection, in fire prevention know-how, in ever vital service and security to North American industry, 1850-1950. Boston: Boston Manufacturers Mutual Fire Insurance Co., 1950. Pp. 253.

5994 YOUNG, ADA M. "Five secretaries and the Cogswells." Antiques, 88 (1965), 478-485.
Collected biographies of cabinet-makers.

5995 YOUNG, EDWARD JAMES. Minister's club, 1870-1899: an historical sketch read at the Hotel Brunswick in Boston. Cambridge: Univ. Pr., 1900. Pp. 56. MB.

5996 ZAITZEVSKY, CYNTHIA. "A new Richardson building." SocArchHistJ, 32 (1973), 164-166.
Hayden Building, Washington and LaGrange Streets.

5997 _____. "The Olmsted firm and the structures of the Boston park system." SocArchHistJ, 32 (1973), 167-174.

5998 ZIRNGIEBEL, FRANCES. "Teachers' school of science." Appleton's Popular Science Monthly, 55 (1899), 451-464, 640-652.

5999   ZOBEL, HILLER BELLIN. The Boston Massacre.
        N.Y.: W. W. Norton, 1970. Pp. xi, 372.

6000   _____. "Newer light on the Boston Massa-
        cre." AASP, 78 (1968), 119-128.

BOURNE

6001   ALEXANDER, FRED. Pocasset Heights (Mass.)
        and vicinity. A short description with some
historical data. n.p., 1957. Pp. 20. [MBo].

6002   BOURNE HISTORICAL SOCIETY. Aptucxet - the
        zero milestone in America's commercial prog-
ress. Bourne: Bourne Historical Society, 1928.
4 leaves.

6003   BROWNSON, LYDIA BURGESS. "The old house on
        the hill." Cape Cod Magazine, 3 (May, 1917),
18-21.
        Burgess House.

6004   _____. "The town of Bourne." CCAPL, 5 (No-
        vember, 1921), 7-8.

6005   CHRISTIE, TREVOR L. "Cleveland on the
        Cape." Saturday Review, 54 (March 8, 1971),
56-58.
        Grover Cleveland.

6006   DELABARRE, EDMUND BURKE. "The Indian petro-
        glyph at the Aptucxet Trading Post in
Bourne, Massachusetts." OTNE 26 (1935-1936), 110-
112.

6007   ELDRIDGE, GENEVA and SYDNEY A. CLARK. The
        story of Christian growth in Sagamore, Massa-
chusetts, Swift Memorial Methodist Church. Hyannis:
Patriot Office, 1941. Pp. 22. [MHy].

6008   A HISTORY of the Pocasset tragedy! With the
        three sermons preached in New Bedford by the
Rev. William J. Potter, Rev. C. S. Nutter, and Rev.
W. C. Stiles. New Bedford: Charles W. Knight,
1879. Pp. 43 MB.
        Murder of his daughter by Charles F. Free-
        man of Pocasset.

6009   KEENE, BETSEY D. History of Bourne from
        1622 to 1937. Yarmouthport: C. W. Swift,
1937. Pp. vi, 221, xiv.

6010   LEAVENS, JOHN M. "Those special thirteen
        years at Gray Gables." CCC, 26 (1973), 52-
56, 58-60.
        President Cleveland and his home at Monu-
        ment Beach.

6011   LOMBARD, GEORGE F. "Aptucxet, a trading
        place of the Pilgrims." BBHS, 8 (1934),
108-111.

6012   LOMBARD, PERCIVAL HALL. "The Aptucxet Trad-
        ing Post." OTNE, 23 (1932-1933), 159-174.

6013   _____. "The first trading post of the Plym-
        outh Colony." OTNE, 18 (1927-1928), 70-86.

6014   _____. "The old trading post." CCAPL, 5
        (July, 1921), 7-9.

6015   SHERMAN, MRS. ROBERT M. "Aptucxet Trading
        Post." MayflowerQ, 33 (1967), 63-64.

BOXBOROUGH

6016   BOXBOROUGH, MASS. Historical address, poem,
        reminiscences, and speeches, delivered at
the centennial celebration of the town of Boxborough, Feb. 24, 1883. Lowell: Marden and Rowell,
1883. Pp. 61.
        Address by Nathan Thompson.

6017   HAGER, LUCIE CAROLINE GILSON. Boxborough: a
        New England town and its people.... Phila-
delphia: J. W. Lewis, 1891. Pp. 218.

BOXFORD

6018   MANNY, FRANK A. and ANNETTE S. MANNY. Jour-
        ney's End, Boxford, 1672-1817-1942. Box-
ford, 1942. Unpaged. MSaE.
        Historic house.

6019   MASSACHUSETTS. BUREAU OF TRANSPORTATION.
        PLANNING AND DEVELOPMENT. Historic sites
study: report. Boston, 1967. Pp. 40.

6020   PARKHURST, JOHN W. Memoirs of happenings in
        and out of the Old Match Factory, Boxford,
Massachusetts, also the many families connected
therewith. n.p., 1938. Unpaged. MSaE.
        Biography.

6021   PARKHURST, WINNIFRID CHADWICK. History of
        the First Congregational Church, Boxford,
Massachusetts, 1702-1952. Topsfield: Perkins Pr.,
1952. Pp. v, 114.
        Contains a bibliography.

6022   _____. 125th anniversary, Ladies' Benevolent
        Society, First Church Congregational, Box-
ford, Massachusetts. Boxford, 1971. Unpaged.
MSaE.

6023   PEARL, EDWARD EVERETT. "History of the [West
        Boxford Public] Library from January 14,
1881." Ingalls Memorial Public Library Bulletin,
(September, 1931) [4-5].

6024   _____. Landmarks and watermarks of old Box-
        ford. [Manchester?, 1929?]. Pp. 7. MBNEH.

6025   PERLEY, SIDNEY. "The Ames murder." Essex
        Antiq, 2 (1898), 1-7.
        Ruth Perley Ames, 1769.

6026   _____. The dwellings of Boxford, Essex Coun-
        ty, Mass. Salem: Essex Institute, 1893.
Pp. 275.

6027 ____. The history of Boxford, Essex County, Massachusetts, from the earliest settlement known to the present time: a period of about two hundred and thirty years. Boxford, 1880. Pp. vii, 418.

6028 ____. "Mining and quarrying, and smelting of ores, in Boxford." EIHC, 25 (1888), 295-311.

6029 PHILLIPS, JAMES DUNCAN. "Boxford as a typical Puritan community." EIHC, 82 (1946), 334-342.

BOYLSTON

6030 AINSWORTH, ISRAEL. A brief history of the First Congregational Church, Boylston, Mass., being a sermon preached by the pastor, Sunday evening, August 15, 1886, as a precursor to the centennial of the town, observed on the following Wednesday.... Worcester: Sanford & Davis, 1887. Pp. 15.

6031 BOYLSTON, MASS. Centennial celebration of the incorporation of the town of Boylston, Massachusetts, August 18, 1886. Worcester: Sanford & Davis, 1887. Pp. 140.

6032 DAVENPORT, MATTHEW. A brief historical sketch of the town of Boylston; in the county of Worcester; from its first settlement to the present time. Lancaster: Carter, Andrews, 1831. Pp. 28.

6033 SANFORD, WILLIAM HOWE. The years of many generations considered: two sermons, preached in Boylston, Massachusetts, October 17 and 24, 1852, giving a history of the Congregational Church and ministry in said town, and also embracing many facts relating to the first settlers of the place.... Worcester: C. B. Webb, 1853. Pp. 71.

BRAINTREE

6034 ADAMS, CHARLES FRANCIS, 1807-1886. An address on the occasion of opening the new town hall, in Braintree, July 29, 1858. Boston: W. White, 1858. Pp. 86.

6035 ADAMS, CHARLES FRANCIS, 1835-1915. "Some phases of sexual morality and church discipline in colonial New England." MHSP, 2 Ser., 6 (1890-1891), 477-516.
Based on Braintree records.

6036 BATES, FRANK AMASA. Thomas Farm. [South Braintree?, 1904]. Pp. 17.

6037 BATES, SAMUEL AUSTIN. The ancient iron works at Braintree, Mass., (the first in America). South Braintree: Frank A. Bates, 1898. Pp. 29.

6038 ____. Bowditch Mill privilege. [South Braintree?, 1904]. Pp. 7.

6039 ____. The early schools of Braintree. South Braintree: Frank A. Bates, 1899. Pp. 35.

6040 BRAINTREE, MASS. Centennial celebration at Braintree, Mass., July 4, 1876. Boston: A. Mudge, 1877. Pp. 95.

6041 ____. Records of the town of Braintree, 1640 to 1793. Samuel A. Bates, ed. Randolph: D. H. Huxford, 1886. Pp. 939.

6042 BRAINTREE, MASS. FIRST CONGREGATIONAL CHURCH. A church manual: with brief historical notices of the First Congregational Church in Braintree and its pastors, from the date of its organization, till the close of 1859.... Boston: Hayden & Randall, 1860. Pp. 41.

6043 ____. Historical notices of the First Congregational Church in Braintree, from its organization in 1707, to the beginning of 1830. Boston: Marvin, 1830. Pp. 24.

6044 BRAINTREE, MASS. ST. THOMAS MORE CHURCH. Commemorating the 25th anniversary of St. Thomas More Church, Braintree, Massachusetts. [Braintree?], 1963. Unpaged.

6045 BRAINTREE, MASS. TERCENTENARY COMMITTEE. A brief history of the town of Braintree in Massachusetts, prepared for the observance of the tercentenary celebration of its founding, 1640-1940. Marion Sophia Arnold, ed. Boston: Thomas Todd, 1940. Pp. 64.

6046 BRIEF history of the town of Braintree in Massachusetts, U.S.A.; prepared for the citizens of Braintree, Essex, England, in honor of their 750th celebration. Braintree: Observer Pr., 1949. Pp. 95. MBNEH.

6047 "THE CODDINGTON School lands, Braintree, Massachusetts." MNEH, 1 (1891), 228-238.

6048 METAYER, ELIZABETH. Braintree, our town. Braintree: the Philergians of Braintree, 1970. Pp. 100. M.

6049 "PHENOMENAL industrial growth of South Braintree." Industry, 18 (July, 1953), 17-20, 53. Armstrong Cork Company.

6050 SHUSTER, RUTH W. Gathered in 1707: a history of the First Congregational Church, Braintree, Massachusetts, 1707-1957. [Braintree?], 1957. Pp. 138.

6051 SNYDER, JAMES W., ed. "Papers relating to the building of the ship 'Massachusetts' at Braintree, 1787, from the papers of William Hacket of Salisbury." EIHC, 74 (1938), 239-250.

6052 SPRAGUE, WALDO CHAMBERLAIN. Braintree Iron Works, erected in 1644 and 1645 by John Winthrop, Jr. An account of the furnace at West Quincy and the forge at Braintree, Massachusetts where the first iron was produced in the country for commercial purposes. Quincy, 1955. Pp. 20. MB.

6053 [STEVENS, ANNA AUGUSTA]. Reunion of the
    alumni of Hollis Institute or Academy.
n.p., [1904?]. Pp. 74. MBNEH.
    Author attribution by the New England His-
    toric Genealogical Society.

6054 THAYER, GEORGE AUGUSTINE. The Braintree
    soldiers' memorial: a record of the serv-
ices in the War of the Rebellion of the men of
Braintree, Massachusetts...with appendices containing a list of Braintree volunteers in the Union
army and navy from 1861 to 1865, the proceedings at
the dedication of the monument, June 17, 1874, and
a notice of the Braintree branch of the Sanitary
Commission. Boston: Alfred Mudge & Son, 1877.
Pp. 52.

6055 VINTON, JOHN ADAMS. The Braintree Iron
    Works. South Boston, 1857. Pp. 11. MBNEH.

6056 _____. The Vinton memorial, comprising a
    genealogy of the descendants of John Vinton
of Lynn, 1648: also, genealogical sketches of
several allied families...with an appendix containing a history of the Braintree Iron Works, and other historical matter. Boston: S. K. Whipple,
1858. Pp. xv, 534.

BREWSTER

6057 CAHOON, ROBERT H. "The old Dillingham
    House." CCAPL, 5 (February, 1922), 23-24.

6058 "CAPE Cod's distinguished school of the arts
    founded by Martha Atwood Baker." Musician,
45 (1940), 88.

6059 DOANE, DONALD. "Old Dillingham House in
    Brewster." CCC, 5 (1950), 31.

6060 DUGAN, CARO A. "A new-old industry." Cape
    Cod Magazine, 8 (July, 1924), 8.
    Spinning and weaving.

6061 FOSTER, MRS. J. E. "The old Dillingham
    House." Cape Cod Magazine, 2 (October,
1916), 27.

6062 LINCOLN, JOSEPH CROSBY. Our village. N.Y.:
    D. Appleton, 1909. Pp. 182.
    Social life and customs.

6063 READ, GEORGIA C. "Incredible Tawasantha."
    CCC, 20 (1967), 42-43, 80-81.
    Mansion of Albert Crosby.

6064 SEARS, JOSEPH HENRY. Brewster ship masters.
    Yarmouthport: C. W. Swift, 1906. Pp. ix,
80.

6065 WALTERS, RUTH. "First Parish Church of
    Brewster." CCC, 10 (1956), 59-60.

BRIDGEWATER

6066 BOYDEN, ALBERT GARDNER. History and alumni
    record of the State Normal School, Bridge-
water, Mass., to July, 1876. Boston: Noyes and
Snow, 1876. Pp. vii, 182.

6067 BOYDEN, ARTHUR CLARKE. The history of
    Bridgewater Normal School. Bridgewater:
Bridgewater Normal Alumni Association, 1933.
Pp. xi, 156.

6068 BRIDGEWATER, MASS. Celebration of the two-
    hundredth anniversary of the incorporation
of Bridgewater, Massachusetts, at West Bridgewater,
June 3, 1856; including the address by Hon. Emory
Washburn, of Worcester; poem by James Reed...and
other exercises of the occasion. Boston: J. Wilson and Son, 1856. Pp. viii, 167.

6069 BRIDGEWATER ACADEMY, BRIDGEWATER, MASS. His-
    torical notice of the Academy, from its
foundation in 1799, to the year 1858. Boston: Dutton, 1859. Pp. 35.

6070 THE BRIDGEWATER book.... Boston: George H.
    Ellis, 1899. Pp. 40.

6071 BRIDGEWATER NORMAL ASSOCIATION. Brief sketch
    of the pioneers in establishing the first
state normal school in America [and] a brief sketch
of the first principals of the state normal schools,
1839-'40. n.p., 1907. Unpaged. M.

6072 BRYANT, SETH. Shoe and leather trade of the
    last hundred years. Boston, 1891. Pp. 136.

6073 "A DESCRIPTION of Bridgewater, 1818." MHSC,
    2 Ser., 7 (1818), 137-176.
    Includes ecclesiastical history.

6074 DUNN, GERALD C. "Indians in Bridgewater."
    MASB, 3 (1941-1942), 31-33.

6075 A FEW facts and documents relating to the
    origin and progress of the Anti-Church Party
near Trinity Church in Bridgewater, Mass. Boston:
C. Stimpson, 1850. Pp. 27. MBNEH.

6076 HODGES, RICHARD MANNING. A semi-centennial
    discourse before the First Congregational
Society in Bridgewater, delivered on Lord's day,
17th September, 1871, with historical notes. Cambridge: J. Wilson and Son, 1871. Pp. 59.

6077 HOOPER, ARTHUR. A history of Bridgewater in
    the Rebellion. Boston: F. W. Barry, 1880.
Pp. 85.

6078 HUNTINGTON, DANIEL. A discourse delivered
    in the North Meeting-House in Bridgewater,
on Friday, Dec. 22, 1820, being the second centurial anniversary of the landing of the Pilgrims at
Plymouth. Boston: Lincoln, 1821. Pp. 24.
    Contains a history of the town.

6079 JACKSON, GEORGE ANSON. Old Bridgewater, Mass., a classic town whose early learned ministers were moulders of New England character: an address delivered...before the Old Bridgewater Historical Society, June 25, 1904. [Bridgewater]: Edward Alden, 1905. Unpaged.

6080 MASSACHUSETTS. STATE TEACHERS COLLEGE, BRIDGEWATER. Semicentennial exercises, August 28, 1890.... Boston: State Printers, 1892. Pp. 63. M.
Historical sketch by Albert Gardner Boyden.

6081 _____. Seventy-fifth anniversary of the State Normal School, Bridgewater, Massachusetts, June 19, 1915. Bridgewater: A. H. Willis, 1915. Pp. 87.

6082 MITCHELL, NAHUM. History of the early settlement of Bridgewater, in Plymouth County, Massachusetts, including an extensive family register. Boston: Kidder & Wright, 1840. Pp. 400.

BRIMFIELD

6083 BRIMFIELD, MASS. Historical celebration of the town of Brimfield, Hampden County, Mass., Wednesday, October 11, 1876, with the historical address of Rev. Charles M. Hyde, D. D., and other addresses, letters, documents, etc., relating to the early history of the town. Springfield: C. W. Bryan, 1879. Pp. vi, 487.

6084 CHASE, FLORENCE ELIZABETH. Echoes of memory. Brimfield, 1907. Pp. 16. MS.
Recollections of the town.

6085 [MORSE, JASON]. Annals of the church in Brimfield. By the pastor of the church.... Springfield: Samuel Bowles, 1856. Pp. 83.

6086 TARBELL, MARY ANNA. Stage days in Brimfield, a century of mail and coach. Springfield: F. A. Bassette, 1909. Pp. 32.

6087 _____. A village library. Boston, 1905. Pp. 19. MB.

6088 VAILL, JOSEPH. An historical sermon delivered at Brimfield, January 7, 1821, on the occasion of a new year. Springfield: A. G. Tannatt, 1829. Pp. 27. MB.
Relates to the town.

BROCKTON

6089 ANDEM, JAMES. The rise and progress of the First Baptist Church, North Bridgewater, Ms., being the first annual sermon, preached on Sunday, January 26, 1851.... Boston: Hewes, 1851. Pp. 16.

6090 BROCKTON, MASS. FIRST EVANGELICAL LUTHERAN CHURCH. Centennial brochure of the First Evangelical Lutheran Church, 1867-1967, Brockton, Mass. Brockton: Centennial Booklet Committee, 1967. Unpaged. M.

6091 BROCKTON HIGH SCHOOL. Dedication ceremonies for the new Brockton High School, September 1970-June 1971. Brockton, 1970. Unpaged.
Includes history of Brockton public schools, 1821-1970.

6092 BROCKTON WORLD WAR VICTORY ASSOCIATION. Brockton's honor roll of her sons who made the supreme sacrifice in the World War. [Brockton]: Brockton World War Victory Association, 1919. Pp. 108.
Biographies.

6093 BURRILL, ERNEST A. The story of Brockton's fight against influenza, September-October, nineteen eighteen. Brockton: Nichols & Eldridge, [1918?]. Pp. 25.

6094 CALDWELL, WARREN H. Brockton...photographs...representing the leading manufacturing industries, public buildings...with historical sketch and general description. Brockton: W. H. Caldwell, 1898. Pp. 165. M.

6095 CAMPELLO CO-OPERATIVE BANK. Campello Co-Operative Bank, Campello Station, Brockton, Mass.... Brockton, 1927. Unpaged. M.
1877-1927.

6096 CARY, MOSES. A genealogy of the families who have settled in the North Parish of Bridgewater, to which is added an historical sketch of North-Bridgewater. Boston: Bannister and Marvin, 1824. Pp. 48.

6097 "THE ELECTRIC and power business of Brockton, Massachusetts: the Edison Electric Illuminating Company--some distinctions in its history--a new plant installed--peculiarities of the growth of the business." SWJ, 2 (1908), 914-918.

6098 FORBUSH, W. A. "The street lighting system of the city of Brockton." SWJ, 26 (1920), 182-187.

6099 HAYWARD, ELIZABETH, comp. A genealogist's index of Bradford Kingman's 'History of Brockton....' West Hartford, Conn.: Chedwato Service, 1957. Pp. 15.
Names of persons.

6100 HOLMES, GEORGE CLARENCE, ed. Fire service of Brockton: a souvenir containing an account of the service from leather bucket times to the present fire department. Brockton: Brockton Firemen's Relief Association, 1888. Pp. 83. MB.

6101 KINGMAN, BRADFORD. "Congregational Church, Campello, Mass." CongQ, 7 (1865), 182-184.

6102 _____. "First Congregational Church in North Bridgewater, Mass." CongQ, 6 (1864), 294-299.

6103 _____. History of Brockton, Plymouth County, Massachusetts, 1656-1894. Syracuse, N.Y.: D. Mason, 1895. Pp. 814, 122.
See entry under Elizabeth Hayward for index.

6104 _____. History of North Bridgewater, Plymouth County, Massachusetts, from its first settlement to the present time, with family registers. Boston, 1866. Pp. xii, 696.

6105 _____. "The Porter Evangelical Church in North Bridgewater, Mass." CongQ, 6 (1864), 362-365.

6106 LANDERS, WARREN PRINCE, ed. Brockton and its centennial, chief events as town and city 1821-1921: the organization and story of its one hundredth anniversary, June 12-18, 1921. Brockton: City of Brockton, 1921. Pp. 200.

6107 LAWSON, EVALD B. "Christina Nilsson's visit to Brockton, Mass., in November, 1870." Augustana Historical Society. Publications, 3 (1933), 81-96.

6108 LOWE, HAMILTON. "Brockton, city of enterprise." NEM, New Ser., 45 (1911-1912), 67-80.

6109 MEADE, MARGARET. Yankeeville, U.S.A.: a village dialogue commemorating the 150th anniversary of the northern zone of Bridgewater, which rises from the wilderness in the year of our Lord 1821 and becomes the town of North Bridgewater, later to be Brockton, shire city of Plymouth County in the ancient and venerable state of Massachusetts. [Brockton, 1971]. Pp. 43. M.

6110 PIERCE, ALBERT F. History of the Brockton Relief Fund in aid of sufferers from the R. B. Grover & Co. factory fire, Brockton, Mass., March 20, 1905. Boston: Fort Hill Pr., 1907. Pp. 117.

6111 PRENDERGAST, FRANK M. "Craftsmanship in leather." Industry, 15 (June, 1950), 17-19, 42-43.
Field and Flint Co., shoes.

6112 THAYER, BETHIA HAYWARD. Brockton women.... N.Y.: Albertype Co., 1892. Unpaged.

6113 THOMPSON, ELROY SHERMAN. "Brockton, Massachusetts: enterprise and accomplishments of the great shoe city." NEM, New Ser., 34 (1906), 233-252.

BROOKFIELD

6114 BARTLETT, FRANCES. A story of old Brookfield, read at the annual meeting of the Quaboag Historical Society, at West Brookfield, Mass., October 7th, 1902.... Columbia, S.C.: R. L. Bryan, 1902. Pp. 13.

6115 BROOKFIELD, MASS. FIRST PARISH CHURCH. Anniversary exercises commemorating the 187th anniversary of the church, and the 150th of the precinct, held in the First Parish Church, October 16 and 17, 1904.... Spencer: W. J. Heffernan-Leader Print, 1905. Pp. 42.
Includes history by William L. Walsh.

6116 BROOKFIELD, MASS. 300th ANNIVERSARY CELEBRATION COMMITTEE. 300th anniversary celebration of the settlement of Quaboag Plantation 1660-1960. n.p., [1960?]. Pp. 96. MWA.

6117 BULLOCK, CHANDLER. "The Bathsheba Spooner murder case." Worcester HSPub, New Ser., 2 (1936-1943), 205-221.
1778.

6118 CHAMBERLAIN, LEANDER TROWBRIDGE. An address on the early history of old Brookfield, Mass., delivered at West Brookfield, Mass.... Brooklyn: Larkin, [1895?]. Pp. 36.

6119 COES, ELIZABETH CARLTON. Colonial Quaboag: published on the occasion of the 300th anniversary of the Quaboag Plantation settlement. Brookfield: Podunk Pedlar Pr., 1960. Pp. 35.

6120 DUNHAM, SAMUEL. An historical discourse delivered at West Brookfield, Mass., on occasion of the one hundred and fiftieth anniversary of the First Church in Brookfield, Oct. 16, 1867. Springfield: Samuel Bowles, 1867. Pp. 123.

6121 FISKE, NATHAN. "Historical account of the settlement of Brookfield." MHSC, 1 (1792), 257-271.

6122 _____. Remarkable providences to be gratefully recollected, religiously improved, and carefully transmitted to posterity. A sermon preached at Brookfield on the last day of the year 1775, together with some marginal notes &c. giving an account of the first settling of the town in the year 1660; its desolation by the Indians in Philip's War, in 1675; its distresses in Queen Anne's War; and its increase and improvements to the present time. Boston: Thomas and John Fleet, 1776. Pp. 31.

6123 FLETCHER, WILLIAM G. The Oliver Crosby House 1797. Brookfield: Harlan W. Angier, 1960. Pp. 22. MWA.

6124 FOOT, JOSEPH IVES. An historical discourse, delivered at Brookfield, Mass., Nov. 27, 1828, the day of the annual thanksgiving. Brookfield: E. and G. Merriam, 1829. Pp. 64.

6125 HODGES, JOSEPH, JR. Historical sketch of the Baptist Church in Brookfield. Brookfield, 1850. Pp. 8. MB.

6126 HORTON, FRANCIS. Memorials of Brookfield: a poem, delivered at West Brookfield, Mass., October 16, 1867, the one hundred and fiftieth anniversary of the Congregational Church. Springfield: S. Bowles, 1868. Pp. 20.

6127 REYNOLDS, GRINDALL. "King Philip's War; with special reference to the attack on Brookfield in August, 1675." AASP, New Ser., 5 (1887-1888), 77-95.

6128 ROY, LOUIS E. Quaboag Plantation alias Brookefeild; a seventeenth-century Massachusetts town. West Brookfield, 1965. Pp. 308.

6129 STONE, MICAH. Reminiscences of a half-century pastorate: a discourse delivered... [at] the Evangelical church in Brookfield, March 11, 1851.... West Brookfield: O. S. Cooke, 1851. Pp. 72.

6130 WAITE, HENRY E. "Early history of Brookfield, Mass." NEHGR, 35 (1881), 333-341.

6131 WALKER, AMASA. The nature and uses of money and mixed currency, with a history of the Wickaboag Bank. Boston: Crosby, Nichols, 1857. Pp. 83.

6132 WHITING, LYMAN. A bi-centennial oration made in West Brookfield, July 4, 1860, at the celebration of the two hundredth anniversary of the settlement of the town of Brookfield. West Brookfield: Thomas Morey, 1869. Pp. 92.

BROOKLINE

6133 ANDERSON, THOMAS F. "Wealthiest town in the world, and best governed." NEM, New Ser., 39 (1908-1909), 265-277.

6134 BAKER, EDWARD W. "Brookline Volunteer Fire Department." Brookline HSP, (1904), 18-41. 1784-1871.

6135 ____. "The Devotion School Fund." Brookline HSP, (1908), 13-25. Edward Devotion School Fund, 1762.

6136 ____. "The old burying ground." Brookline HSP, (1906), 19-36.

6137 BIGELOW, ROBERT PAYNE. A sketch of the history of St. Paul's Church in Brookline. Brookline, 1949. Pp. 21. 1849-1949.

6138 BOLTON, CHARLES KNOWLES. Brookline; the history of a favored town. Brookline: C. A. W. Spencer, 1897. Pp. 213.

6139 ____. "Some works relating to Brookline, Massachusetts, from its settlement to the year 1900." Brookline HPSP, No. 19-20 (1900), 89-179. Bibliography.

6140 BRIGGS, KATHERINE ROBINSON. "Brookline in the Civil War." Brookline HPSP, No. 10 (1896), 143-158.

6141 BROOKLINE, MASS. Muddy River and Brookline records. 1634-1838. [Boston]: J. E. Farwell, 1875. Pp. 703.

6142 ____. Proceedings at the dedication of the Town Hall, Brookline, February 22, 1873. Cambridge: J. Wilson & Son, 1873. Pp. 64.

6143 BROOKLINE, MASS. BAPTIST CHURCH. Addresses at the seventy-fifth anniversary of the founding of the Church, June...1903. Brookline: Spencer, 1903. Pp. 56.

6144 ____. Brief historical sketch of the Baptist Church in Brookline, Mass...constituted June 5, 1828. Brookline: Chronicle Pr., 1894. Pp. 63. MBNEH.

6145 ____. Celebration of the semi-centennial anniversary of the Baptist Church of Brookline; with an historical discourse by the pastor, the Rev. Henry C. Mabie, Sunday and Monday, June 2 and 3, 1878. Brookline: Chronicle Book and Job Print, 1878. Pp. 34.

6146 BROOKLINE, MASS. CHRIST'S CHURCH, LONGWOOD. Brief sketch of Christ's Church, Longwood. n.p., [1868]. Pp. 18.

6147 BROOKLINE, MASS. FIRST BAPTIST CHURCH. Historical sketch of the First Baptist Church, Brookline, Mass. with the declaration of faith, the church covenant, and a list of the officers and members, Brookline, 1877. Pp. 59. MB.

6148 BROOKLINE, MASS. FIRST UNITARIAN CHURCH. The First Parish in Brookline, 1717-1967. 250th anniversary celebration, October 27-29, 1967. n.p., [1967?]. Pp. 24. M.

6149 BROOKLINE, MASS. METHODIST EPISCOPAL CHURCH. History and year book, Brookline Methodist Episcopal Church. Pittsburgh, Pa., 1927. MBNEH.

6150 BROOKLINE. Boston: Edison Electric Illuminating Co., 1909. Pp. 28. M.

6151 BROOKLINE EDUCATION SOCIETY. Brookline Education Society: a chronicle of its work between the years 1895-1908. Brookline: Riverdale Pr., 1908. Pp. 112.

6152 BROOKLINE EDUCATION SOCIETY. HISTORY COMMITTEE, BROOKLINE, MASS. A guide to the local history of Brookline, Mass. Brookline: Riverdale Pr., 1897. Pp. 24. Chiefly the work of Annie B. Tomlinson.

6153 BROOKLINE Magazine. Brookline: Spencer, 1897. Pp. 70. MB. Collection of historical, descriptive, and other articles relating to Brookline; not a periodical.

6154 BROOKLINE UNION. A review of the work carried on by the various organizations having their headquarters in the Union Building, December, 1890. Brookline, 1890. Pp. 24.

6155 CANDAGE, RUFUS G. F. "[Houses and buildings in Brookline]." Brookline HSP, (1903), 7-15; (1904), 9-17; (1905), 10-21; (1906), 8-17.

6156 ____. "President's annual address." Brookline HSP, (1902), 5-14.
Brief description and history of Brookline.

6157 CHASE, ELLEN and CHARLES F. WHITE. "The Woodward-Goldsmith House, Clyde Street, Brookline." Brookline HSP, (1908), 27-37.

6158 THE CHRONICLE, BROOKLINE, MASS. Brookline, the Chronicle souvenir of the bicentennial. Brookline: C. A. W. Spencer, 1905. Pp. 64.

6159 THE COUNTRY CLUB, BROOKLINE, MASS. History of curling at the Country Club. Brookline, 1968. Pp. 72. MBNEH.

6160 CUMMINGS, EMMA GERTRUDE. Brookline's trees: a history of the Committee for Planting Trees of Brookline, Massachusetts and a record of some of its trees. [Brookline]: Brookline Historical Society and the Committee for Planting Trees, 1938. Pp. 97.

6161 CURTIS, JOHN GOULD. History of the town of Brookline, Massachusetts. Boston: Houghton Mifflin, 1933. Pp. xxiii, 349.

6162 CURTISS, FREDERIC HAINES and JOHN HEARD. The Country Club, 1882-1932. Brookline: Priv. Print, 1932. Pp. x, 213.

6163 DUNCKLEE, CHARLES B. One hundredth anniversary of Harvard Church; an account of the activities of the church and the congregation at Brookline, Massachusetts from 1844 to 1944. Brookline, 1944. Pp. 35.

6164 [DENEHY, JOHN WILLIAM]. A history of Brookline, Massachusetts, from the first settlement of Muddy River until the present time; 1630-1906; commemorating the two hundredth anniversary of the town, based on the early records and other authorities and arranged by leading subjects, containing portraits and sketches of the town's prominent men past and present; also illustrations of public buildings and residences. Brookline: Brookline Pr., 1906. Pp. 255.

6165 DOLIBER, MRS. THOMAS. "Two old Brookline homesteads." Brookline HSP, (1905), 29-60.
Homes of John Heath and Ebenezer Craft.

6166 DRISCOLL, MICHAEL. "Some extracts from Muddy River Records of the town." Brookline HSP, (1912), 15-37.
Special reference to the Middle and Heath Schools.

6167 FLETCHER, HERBERT HERVEY. A history of the Church of Our Saviour, Protestant Episcopal, in Longwood, Massachusetts, from its founding in 1868 to 1936. Brookline: Parish Council of the Church, 1936. Pp. xvi, 173.

6168 FLOWER, B. O. "Brookline: a model town under the referendum." Arena, 19 (1898), 505-519.

6169 ____. "Democracy and municipal government, or, how the richest town in the world is ruled by the referendum." Arena, 32 (1904), 377-391.

6170 FORBES, ETHEL H. "The history of the Brookline Fire Department." Brookline HSP, (1915), 35-43.

6171 FRANCIS, CARLETON SHURTLEFF. "Colonial Brookline." Brookline HSP, (1929), 10-27.
1633-1784.

6172 ____. "Walks and talks about Brookline." Brookline HSP, (1930), 9-24.

6173 FRANCIS, ELAINE T. "Two patriots of Brookline, Massachusetts." MagHist, 12 (1910), 97-104.
Aspinwall and Gardner families.

6174 GODDARD, JULIA. "The Goddard House, Warren Street, Brookline, built about 1730: its owners and occupants." Brookline HSP, (1903), 16-34.

6175 ____. The history of 'Green Hill.' Boston: Hooper, Lewis, & Co., 1911. Unpaged. MB.
Historic house.

6176 GODDARD SAMUEL ASPINWALL. Recollections of Brookline, being an account of the houses, the families, and the roads, in Brookline, in the years 1800 to 1810. Birmingham, England: E. C. Osborne, 1873. Pp. 16.

6177 GRIGGS, SUSAN VINING. "The Devotion family of Brookline." Brookline HPSP, No. 14 (1898), 35-46.

6178 HOWE, REGINALD HEBER. Anniversary sermon preached in the Church of Our Saviour, Longwood, Sunday, February the second MCMII, being the twenty-fifth anniversary of his rectorate. Boston: The Guild, 1902. Pp. 12.

6179 JONES, THEODORE FRANCIS. Land ownership in Brookline from the first settlement, illustrated by six maps, 1636, 1667, 1693, 1746, 1786, 1822, continued by four maps 1844, 1855, 1888, 1916, by Brookline surveyors, with genealogical additions, by Charles F. White. Brookline: Riverdale Pr., 1923. Pp. 44.

6180 KELLOGG, CHARLES W., JR. "The Brookline town meeting." Brookline HPSP, No. 13 (1897), 21-34.

6181 KENT, LOUISE ANDREWS. The Brookline trunk. Boston: Houghton Mifflin, 1955. Pp. 306.

6182 LITTLE, NINA FLETCHER. Some old Brookline houses built in this Massachusetts town before 1825 and still standing in 1948: a compilation of existing data, to which has been added architectural and biographical notes, constructional details, photographs and floor plans. [Brookline]: Brookline Historical Society, 1949. Pp. 160.

6183 [LYON, WILLIAM HENRY]. The First Parish in Brookline: an historical sketch. Brookline: Riverdale Pr., 1898. Pp. 48.
Author attribution by New England Historic Genealogical Society.

6184 ____. The history of the First Parish in Brookline, as a mirror on the history of the town, a sermon preached in the First Parish Meeting House, November 12, 1905.... [Brookline]: The Parish, [1905]. Pp. 26.

6185 MARVIN, JOHN R. Relations of Brookline to
Norfolk County. n.p., n.d. Unpaged.
MBNEH.
Historical statistics.

6186 MATTHEWS, GRACE ELISABETH. "The history of
the lyceum movement in Brookline." Brookline HPSP, No. 9 (1896), 137-142.

6187 MAY, MARGARET ELIZABETH. "Brookline in the
Revolution." Brookline HPSP, No. 3 (1895),
15-34.

6188 PIERCE, JOHN. An address at the opening of
the Town Hall, in Brookline, on Tuesday, 14
October, 1845. Boston: White & Potter, 1846.
Pp. 52.
Appendix contains biographical and histori-
cal sketches.

6189 _____. A discourse at Brookline, 24 November 1805, the day which completed a century
from the incorporation of the town. Cambridge:
William Hilliard, 1806. Pp. 32. MB.

6190 _____. A discourse delivered 9 November,
1817, the Lord's Day after the completion of
a century from the gathering of the Church in
Brookline. Boston: John Eliot, 1818. Pp. 32.
MB.
First Church.

6191 _____. "Historical sketch of Brookline."
MHSC, 2 Ser., 2 (1814), 140-161; 3 (1815),
284-285.
Second part is a note by J. Savage.

6192 _____. Reminiscences of forty years, delivered, 19 March, 1837, the Lord's Day after the completion of forty years from his settlement in the ministry, in Brookline. Boston: M.
Pratt, 1837. Pp. 35.

6193 SCALISE, VICTOR F., JR. Merging for mission.
Valley Forge: Judson Pr., 1972. Pp. 127.
United Parish Church; union of Baptist,
Congregational and Methodist churches.

6194 SHARP, MARION L. "Three glimpses of Brookline, in 1700, 1800 and 1900." Brookline
HPSP, No. 11 (1897), 1-15.

6195 STEARNS, CHARLES HENRY. Reminiscences of
Harvard Street [and] Old Harvard Street by
Edward Wild Baker. Brookline: Brookline Historical
Society, 1935. Pp. 24. MB.

6196 _____. "The Sewall House." Brookline HSP,
(1903), 35-45.

6197 _____. "A short history of Pierce Hall with
some personal recollections." Brookline
HSP, (1907), 16-23.
Adjoined the First Parish.

6198 THOMAS, REUEN. 1844-1894, Harvard Church
(Brookline) historical address delivered on
May 13, 1894. Brookline: The [Harvard Congrega-
tional] Society, [1894?]. Pp. 26. MBNEH.

6199 TOOGOOD, ANNA COXE. John Fitzgerald Kennedy
National Historic Site, Massachusetts. Washington: U. S. Office of History and Historic Architecture, Eastern Service Center, 1971. Pp. vii, 74.

6200 TSOUMAS, GEORGE J. "The founding years of
Holy Cross Greek Orthodox Theological School,
1937-1942." Greek Orthodox Theological Review, 12
(1967), 241-282.

6201 WATERMAN, JOHN. "Beaconfield Terraces."
NEM, New Ser., 5 (1892), 625-636.
Houses.

6202 WILLIAMS, HAROLD PARKER. "Brookline in the
anti-slavery movement." Brookline HPSP,
No. 18 (1899), 75-87.

6203 WINTHROP, ROBERT CHARLES. Address at the
dedication of the new Town Hall of Brookline,
on the 22d of February, 1873. Cambridge: J. Wilson
and Son, 1873. Pp. 42.
Relates to the town.

6204 WOODS, HARRIET F. Historical sketches of
Brookline, Mass. Boston: R. S. Davis,
1874. Pp. vii, 430.
Index in 'Brookline Library Bulletin' for
April, 1895.

BUCKLAND

6205 BUCKLAND, MASS. Buckland centennial, September 10, 1879, addresses, poems, songs....
Northampton: Metcalf, [1879?]. Pp. 40.

6206 KENDRICK, FANNIE SMITH SHAW. The history of
Buckland, 1779-1935, with genealogies by
Lucy Cutler Kellogg. Buckland, 1937. Pp. ix, 799.

6207 ROBINSON, OLIVE CRITTENDEN. "Ezra Wood, pro-
file cutter." Antiques, 42 (1942), 69-70.
Silhouettes.

6208 _____. "A forgotten clockmaker, reminiscences of 'Clock Hollow,' Buckland, Massachusetts." Antiques, 34 (1938), 140-141.
William Sherman.

BURLINGTON

6209 CURTIS, MARTHA E. SEWALL. Ye old meeting
house: addresses and verses relating to the
meeting house, Burlington, Middlesex County, Massachusetts, built 1732, and other historical addresses. Boston: Anchor Linotype Print, 1909. Pp. 62.

CAMBRIDGE

6210 ABBOTT, Edward. The bell's own story as told
at the public reception of the Paul Revere
Bell in [St. James Church], April 19th, 1901. Cambridge: Powell, 1901. Pp. 24.

6211 _____. St. James's Parish, Cambridge: forty years of parish history 1864-1904.... Cambridge: Caustic-Claflin, 1909. Pp. 139.

6212 "ACCOUNT-BOOKS of treasurers of Harvard College from 1669 to 1752." MHSP, (1862-1863), 337-356.

6213 ADAMS, CHARLES FRANCIS, 1835-1915. "Examinations for Harvard." MHSP, 2 Ser., 14 (1900-1901), 198-205.
1751 and 1821.

6214 ALLEN, HELEN B. "The old library, 1764-January 24-1939." Harvard Alumni Bulletin, 41 (1939), 543-547.

6215 ALLYN, ALICE C. "A history of Berkeley Street, Cambridge, Massachusetts." CaHSP, 21 (1930-1931), 58-71.

6216 ALMY, CHARLES. "The history of the Third District Court of Eastern Middlesex." CaHSP, 17 (1923-1924), 16-27.

6217 AMES, JAMES BARR. "The founding of the Mount Auburn Hospital." CaHSP, 39 (1961-1963), 39-49.

6218 AMES, MRS. JAMES BARR. "A history of the Cambridge Branch of the Massachusetts Indian Association from 1886 to 1923." CaHSP, 17 (1923-1924), 84-91.
Charity.

6219 AMES, OAKES I. "Mount Auburn's sixscore years." CaHSP, 34 (1951-1952), 77-95.
Cemetery.

6220 AMORY, THOMAS COFFIN. "Old Cambridge and new." NEHGR, 25 (1871), 221-244.

6221 APPLETON, NATHAN, 1843-1906. "Harvard College during the War of Rebellion." NEM, New Ser., 4 (1891), 3-23.

6222 ARMSTRONG, STEVEN. "Christ Church, Cambridge." Harvard Magazine, 77 (January, 1975), 37-41.
Architecture.

6223 ATWATER, EDWARD C., ed. "Morrill Wyman and the aspiration of acute pleural effusions, 1850: a letter from New England." BHistMed, 46 (1972), 235-256.

6224 ATWOOD, WILLIAM T. "Massachusetts Institute of Technology." NEM, New Ser., 42 (1910), 396-405.

6225 BACON, GEORGE FOX. Cambridge and vicinity: its representative business men and its points of interest.... Newark, N.J.: Mercantile Publishing, 1892. Pp. 150.
Limited to Cambridge; biography.

6226 BAIL, HAMILTON VAUGHN. "Harvard fiction." AASP, 68 (1957-1958), 211-347.

6227 _____. "Harvard's Commemoration Day, July 21, 1865." NEQ, 15 (1942), 256-279.

6228 _____. "Views of Harvard to 1860: an iconographic study." HarvLibBul, 1 (1947), 11-28, 185-211, 339-376; 2 (1948), 44-82, 179-221, 309-343; 3 (1949), 44-95, 436-438.

6229 BAILEY, HOLLIS RUSSELL. "The beginning of the First Church in Cambridge." CaHSP, 10 (1915), 86-113.

6230 _____. "The beginning of the First Parish in Cambridge." CaHSP, 17 (1923-1924), 92-97.

6231 BAILEY, JULIA BAYNARD PECKARD. "The distaff side of the ministerial succession in the First Parish Church in Cambridge." CaHSP, 22 (1932-1933), 80-96.

6232 BAILEY, SOLON IRVING. The history and work of Harvard Observatory, 1839 to 1927: an outline of the origin, development, and researches of the Astronomical Observatory of Harvard College together with brief biographies of its leading members. N.Y.: McGraw-Hill, 1931. Pp. xiii, 301.

6233 BAKER, CHRISTINA HOPKINSON. The story of Fay House. Cambridge: Harvard Univ. Pr., 1929. Pp. vi, 135.
Radcliffe College.

6234 BAKER, DANIEL WELD. History of the Harvard College Observatory during the period 1840-1890. Cambridge, 1890. Pp. 32.

6235 BALLOU, ELLEN B. "Horace Elisha Scudder and the 'Riverside Magazine.'" HarvLibBul, 14 (1960), 426-452.

6236 BALLOU, HOSEA STARR. "The Harvard Yard before Dunster." NEHGR, 80 (1926), 131-138.
Seventeenth century.

6237 BARNEY, J. DELLINGER and SAMUEL ELIOT MORISON. "The Yard in 1811-1812 and the old college pump." Harvard Alumni Bulletin, 38 (1936), 534-538.

6238 BATCHELDER, CHARLES FOSTER. An account of the Nuttall Ornithological Club, 1873 to 1919. Cambridge, 1937. Pp. 109.

6239 BATCHELDER, SAMUEL. "Title and history of the Henry Vassall Estate, Cambridge." NEHGR, 45 (1891), 191-197.

6240 BATCHELDER, SAMUEL F. "Washington in Christ Church, Cambridge." OTNE, 54 (1963-1964), 40-47.

6241 BATCHELDER, SAMUEL FRANCIS, 1870-1927. Bits of Cambridge history. Cambridge: Harvard Univ. Pr., 1930. Pp. 349.

6242 _____. Bits of Harvard history. Cambridge: Harvard Univ. Pr., 1924. Pp. xiv, 328.

6243 _____. "Burgoyne and his officers in Cambridge, 1777-1778." CaHSP, 13 (1918), 17-80.

6244 _____. Christ Church, Cambridge: some account of its history and present condition. Cambridge: [Graves and Henry], 1893. Pp. 88.

6245 _____. "Old times at the Law School." Atlantic, 90 (1902), 642-655.
Harvard Law School.

6246 _____. "The Washington Elm tradition." CaHSP, 18 (1925), 46-75.
Historical events under the elm.

6247 _____. The Washington Elm tradition, 'Under this tree Washington first took command of the American army.' Is it true? The evidence collected and considered. [Cambridge], 1925. Pp. 36.

6248 BEALE, JOSEPH H. "The history of local government in Cambridge." CaHSP, 22 (1932-1933), 17-28.

6249 BEALLE, MORRIS ALLISON. The history of football at Harvard, 1874-1948. Washington: Columbia Publishing, 1948. Pp. 541.

6250 BEMIS, SAMUEL FLAGG. "Harvard, 1913-1916." NEG, 11 (Winter, 1970), 10-19.

6251 BENTINCK-SMITH, WILLIAM. "Archibald Cary Coolidge and the Harvard Library." HarvLib Bul, 21 (1973), 229-253, 402-442; 22 (1974), 76-110, 185-225, 317-353, 429-454.

6252 BENTLEY, BYRON R. "Colonial Harvard: its progressive and liberal spirit." Harvard Graduates' Magazine, 38 (1929-1930), 416-424.

6253 BEVIS, ALMA DARST MURRAY. Diets and riots; an interpretation of the history of Harvard University. Boston: Marshall Jones, 1936. Pp. xiii, 127.

6254 BEYER, CLARA E. MORTENSON. History of labor legislation for women in three states. Washington: Govt. Print. Off., 1932. Pp. vi, 137.
Massachusetts, New York and California.

6255 BIDDLE, FRANCIS B. "Fifty years ago." Harvard Lampoon, 145 (December, 1956), 24-25, 39, 42-45.
Harvard University.

6256 BIGELOW, JACOB. A history of the cemetery of Mount Auburn. Boston: J. Munroe, 1860. Pp. xii, 263.

6257 BILLINGTON, RAY ALLEN. "Frederick Jackson Turner comes to Harvard." MHSP, 74 (1962), 51-83.
1910.

6258 BOLSTER, CHARLES S. "Cambridge court houses." CaHSP, 39 (1961-1963), 55-70.

6259 BOLSTER, ELIZABETH W. "Behind the scenes at 47 workshop." CaHSP, 40 (1964-1966), 110-122.
English 47, playwriting course at Harvard, 1904-1924.

6260 BOLTON, CHARLES KNOWLES. "The Harvard University Library." NEM, New Ser., 9 (1893-1894), 433-449.

6261 BOND, ELIZABETH L. "The observatory of Harvard College and its early founders." CaHSP, 25 (1938-1939), 75-85.

6262 BOND, WILLIAM CRANCH. History and description of the astronomical observatory of Harvard College. Cambridge: Metcalf, 1856. Pp. cxci.

6263 BOWDITCH, CHARLES PICKERING. An account of the trust administered by the trustees of the Charity of Edward Hopkins. Cambridge: Univ. Pr., 1889. Pp. 88.
A trust at Harvard University.

6264 BOWDOIN, JAMES. "Harvard University seventy-six years ago." HistMag, 1 (1857), 34-36.

6265 BOWEN, MARIA. "Reminiscences of Follen Street." CaHSP, 20 (1927-1929), 91-101.

6266 _____. and MARY D. DEXTER and ROSALBA P. S. PROELL. "Reminiscences of Sparks Street." CaHSP, 22 (1932-1933), 46-57.

6267 BOYD, LYLE G. "Mrs. Henry Draper and the Harvard College Observatory." HarvLibBul, 17 (1969), 70-97.

6268 BRADBURY, WILLIAM FROTHINGHAM and ELBRIDGE SMITH. The Cambridge High School: history and catalogue. Cambridge: Moses King, 1882. Pp. 94.

6269 BRADFORD, ALDEN. "Historical sketch of Harvard University." American Quarterly Register, 9 (1836-1837), 329-366.

6270 BREW, JOHN OTIS. Early days of the Peabody Museum at Harvard University. Cambridge: Published by the Museum, 1966. Pp. 18.
Archaeology and ethnology.

6271 _____. People and projects of the Peabody Museum, 1866-1966. Cambridge: Peabody Museum of Harvard Univ., 1966. Pp. iv, 59.

6272 BRIGGS, WALTER B. "Sundry observations upon four decades of Harvard College Library." CaHSP, 27 (1941), 29-41.

6273 BROWN, B. KATHERINE. "Puritan democracy: a case study." MVHR, 50 (1963-1964), 377-396.

6274 BROWN, EDWARD HOAGLAND. "Harvard and the Ohio Mounds." NEQ, 22 (1949), 205-228.

6275 BROWN, JOHN PERKINS. "Christ Church, Cambridge." CaHSP, 23 (1934-1935), 17-23.

6276 BROWN, ROLLO WALTER. Harvard Yard in the golden age. N.Y.: Current Books, 1948. Pp. 208.
Biographies of twelve nineteenth-century professors.

6277 BROWNING, JOHN S. One decade (1873-1882): a brief history of the Webster Graduates' Association, its constitution, by-laws, and membership...also an outline history of the Webster Grammar School, and a list of its teachers, with their terms of service.... Cambridge, 1883. Pp. 60.

6278 BRUNDIN, ROBERT E. "Justin Winsor of Harvard and the liberalizing of the college library." JLibHist, 10 (1975), 57-70.

6279 BUCK, PAUL. "Harvard attitudes toward Radcliffe in the early years." MHSP, 74 (1962), 33-50.

6280 BUCKINGHAM SCHOOL. The Buckingham School, 1889-1949. Cambridge, [1949?]. Unpaged.

6281 BUDKA, METCHIE J. E., ed. "A visit to Harvard College: 1798, from the diary of Julian Ursyn Niemcewicz." NEQ, 34 (1961), 510-514.

6282 BULFINCH, ELLEN SUSAN. Cambridge Branch of the Massachusetts Indian Association: historical sketch prepared for the twenty-fifth anniversary. Cambridge: Caustic-Claflin, [1911]. Pp. 23.

6283 _____. "The Tudor House at Fresh Pond." CaHSP, 3 (1908), 100-109.

6284 BUNDY, MCGEORGE. "Were those the days?" Daedalus, 99 (1970), 531-567.
Harvard University, 1949-1960.

6285 BURCHARD, JOHN ELY. Q.E.D.: M.I.T. in World War II. N.Y.: J. Wiley, 1948. Pp. xvi, 354.

6286 BUSH, GEORGE GARY. Harvard, the first American University. Boston: Cupples, Upham, 1886. Pp. vi, 160.

6287 BUTLER, J. D. "Statistics of the triennial catalog of Harvard University for 1839." American Quarterly Register, 12 (1839-1840), 393.
A table showing number of graduates and number who became ministers from classes of 1642-1839.

6288 BYNUM, DAVID E. "Child's legacy enlarged: oral literary studies at Harvard since 1856." HarvLibBul, 22 (1974), 237-267.
Francis James Child.

6289 CADBURY, HENRY JOEL. "Early Quakers at Cambridge." CaHSP, 24 (1936-1937), 67-82.

6290 _____. "Harvard College Library and the libraries of the Mathers." AASP, 50 (1940), 20-48.

6291 CALKINS, RAYMOND. The three hundred twenty-fifth anniversary of the First Church in Cambridge, 1636-1961. Cambridge: Archives Committee, First Church Congregational, 1965. Pp. 12.

6292 CAMBRIDGE, MASS. Cambridge fifty years a city, 1846-1896: an account of the celebration of the fiftieth anniversary of the incorporation of the city of Cambridge, Massachusetts, June 2-3, 1896. Walter Gee Davis, ed. Cambridge: Riverside Pr., 1897. Pp. 191.

6293 _____. Cambridge in the 'centennial.': Proceedings, July 3, 1875, in celebration of the centennial anniversary of Washington's taking command of the Continental Army, on Cambridge Common. Cambridge, 1875. Pp. 125.

6294 _____. Cambridge seventy-five years a city, 1846-1921: a brief account of the interesting events in connection with the celebration of the seventy-fifth anniversary of the city of Cambridge, Massachusetts, October 9-11-12, 1921. Cambridge: City Council Committee, 1922. Pp. 128.

6295 _____. Exercises in celebrating the two hundred and fiftieth anniversary of the settlement of Cambridge, held December 28, 1880. Cambridge: C. W. Sever, 1881. Pp. iv, 163.

6296 _____. The first three centuries. n.p., [1947?]. Pp. 96. M.

6297 _____. Memorial to the men of Cambridge who fell in the first battle of the Revolutionary War, services of dedication, Nov. 3, 1870. Cambridge: J. Wilson and Son, 1870. Pp. 40.
Address by Alexander McKenzie.

6298 _____. The records of the town of Cambridge (formerly Newtowne) Massachusetts, 1630-1703; the records of the town meetings, and of the selectmen, comprising all of the first volume of records, and being volume II. of the printed records of the town. Cambridge, 1901. Pp. vi, 397.
Has a detailed subject index.

6299 CAMBRIDGE, MASS. CITY COUNCIL. Historic spots in Cambridge, Massachusetts. n.p., 1925. Pp. 12. MH.

6300 CAMBRIDGE, MASS. EPWORTH METHODIST EPISCOPAL CHURCH. Fortieth anniversary manual of the Epworth Methodist Episcopal Church, Cambridge, Mass. Cambridge, 1907. Pp. 31. MBNEH.

6301 CAMBRIDGE, MASS. FIRST BAPTIST CHURCH. A brief history of the First Baptist Church, in Cambridge; with the declaration of faith, the church covenant, and a list of members. (1860) Cambridge: John Ford & Son, 1884. Pp. 119. M.

6302 CAMBRIDGE, MASS. FIRST CHURCH. History of the First Church in Cambridge, in connection with the Shepard Congregational Society; with its confession of faith, practical rules, ecclesiastical principles, standing rules, form of admission, and the names of members. Cambridge, 1872. v.p.

6303 _____. Records of the Church of Christ at Cambridge in New England, 1632-1830, comprising the ministerial records of baptisms, marriages, deaths, admission to covenant and communion, dismissals and church proceedings. Stephen Paschall Sharples, ed. Boston: Eben Putnam, 1906. Pp. viii, 579.
Has a detailed subject index.

6304 _____. Some passages in the history of the First Church, in connexion with the Shepard Congregational Society in Cambridge.... Cambridge: Thurston and Torry, 1842. Pp. 95.

6305 CAMBRIDGE, MASS. FIRST EVANGELICAL CONGREGATIONAL CHURCH IN CAMBRIDGEPORT. Manual of the First Evangelical Congregational Church in Cambridgeport, containing the history of the church, its rules, articles of faith, convenant and catalogue of members. Boston: T. R. Marvin, 1857. Pp. 26.

6306 CAMBRIDGE, MASS. FIRST PARISH (UNITARIAN). An account of the controversy in the First Parish in Cambridge, 1827-1829. Boston: Marvin, 1829. Pp. 58. MB.

6307 _____. The Paine Fund of the First Parish in Cambridge. Cambridge: Univ. Pr., 1912. Pp. 70.

6308 _____. Report on the connection at various times existing between the First Parish in Cambridge and Harvard College. Cambridge: Metcalf 1851. Pp. 52. MH.

6309 _____. Services at the celebration of the two hundred and fiftieth anniversary of the organization of the First Church in Cambridge, February 7-14, 1886. Cambridge: J. Wilson and Son, 1886. Pp. 174.

6310 CAMBRIDGE, MASS. HISTORICAL COMMISSION. Report one: East Cambridge. Cambridge, 1965. Pp. 101.
Architecture.

6311 _____. Report three: Cambridgeport. Cambridge, 1971. Pp. 159.
Architecture.

6312 _____. Report two: mid Cambridge. Antoinette F. Downing, Elisabeth McDougall, and Eleanor Pearson, comps. Cambridge, 1967. Pp. 118. MH.
Architecture.

6313 CAMBRIDGE, MASS. NO-LICENSE COMMITTEE. Ten no-license years in Cambridge. Cambridge, 1898. Pp. xi, 209.

6314 _____. Twenty-five years of no license: addresses delivered on the occasion of the celebration of the twenty-fifth consecutive year of no license in Cambridge Board of Trade Hall, Wednesday evening, May 15, 1912. Cambridge, [1912]. Pp. 35.

6315 CAMBRIDGE, MASS. NORTH AVENUE BAPTIST CHURCH. SABBATH SCHOOL. Memorial of the twenty-fifth anniversary of the North Avenue Sabbath School, Cambridge...Sept. 24, 1871. [Boston], 1872. Pp. 49.

6316 CAMBRIDGE, MASS. NORTH AVENUE CONGREGATIONAL CHURCH. Manual...historical sketch. Chelsea: Geo. B. Lawton, 1877. Pp. 52. MBNEH.

6317 _____. Manual...containing a historical sketch, a form of admission to the church... a catalogue of members to June 1899 and a parish directory. Boston: S. Usher, 1899. Pp. 70. M.

6318 CAMBRIDGE, MASS. NORTH CHURCH (CONGREGATIONAL). One hundredth anniversary, October 20-27, 1957.... n.p., [1957]. Pp. 11.
Historical notes by John F. Davis.

6319 CAMBRIDGE, MASS. OLD CAMBRIDGE BAPTIST CHURCH. History of the Old Cambridge Baptist Church with the declaration of faith, the church covenant, general regulations, and a list of the officers and members. Boston, 1860. Pp. 54.

6320 _____. Old Cambridge Baptist Church. [Cambridge, 1957?]. Unpaged.

6321 CAMBRIDGE, MASS. PROPRIETORS. The register book of the lands and houses in the 'New Towne' and the town of Cambridge, with the records of the proprietors of the common lands, being the records generally called 'the proprietors' records. Cambridge: J. Wilson & Son, 1896. Pp. vii, 409. 1634-1829.

6322 CAMBRIDGE, MASS. PUBLIC LIBRARY. The Cambridge Public Library: its history, rules and regulations, list of officers, past and present, etc. Charles Walker and Almira L. Hayward, comps. Cambridge: J. Wilson and Son, 1891. Pp. 73.

6323 _____. 1858-1908, history of the Cambridge Public Library, with the addresses at the celebration of its fiftieth anniversary, lists of its officers, etc. Cambridge, 1908. Pp. 96.

6323A _____. Selected list of books, pamphlets, etc., relating to Cambridge. Cambridge, 1905. Pp. 31.

6324 CAMBRIDGE, MASS. ST. BARTHOLOMEW'S CHURCH. Story of St. Bartholomew's Church, Columbia St., Cambridgeport. Cambridge, 1896. Pp. 12. MH.

6325 CAMBRIDGE, MASS. ST. JAMES'S PARISH. St. James's Parish, centennial year, highlighting one hundred years of parish life, 1864-1964. Cambridge, 1964. Pp. 62. MBNEH.

6326 CAMBRIDGE, MASS. ST. PAUL AFRICAN METHODIST EPISCOPAL CHURCH. One hundredth anniversary, 1873-1973. n.p., 1973. Pp. 84. M.

6327 CAMBRIDGE, MASS. ST. PAUL PARISH. St. Paul Parish, ninetieth anniversary, 1875-1965, reunion Mass and dinner. Cambridge: Franklin Print, [1965?]. Pp. 40. M.
Includes a brief history of the parish.

6328   CAMBRIDGE, MASS. VACATION SCHOOL COMMITTEE.
        The story of the Cambridge Vacation School
and its adoption by the city. Cambridge, 1900.
Pp. 10. MB.

6329   CAMBRIDGE CHRONICLE. Semi-centennial souve-
        nir of Cambridge, '46-'96. Cambridge,
[1896]. Pp. 138.

6330   _____. Seventy-fifth anniversary, Cambridge,
        Mass., Oct. 8, 1921. [Cambridge, 1921?].
Pp. 60.
        Anniversary of both the city and the news-
paper.

6331   CAMBRIDGE CLUB. Cambridge Club, 1879-1939,
        historical sketch.... Cambridge: Cosmos
Pr., 1939. Pp. 47. MH.

6332   CAMBRIDGE EDITORIAL RESEARCH, INC. The Cam-
        bridge book, 1966. Cambridge: Cambridge
Civic Association, 1966. Pp. 122.

6333   CAMBRIDGE FIREMEN'S RELIEF ASSOCIATION.
        History of the fire service, a souvenir.
Cambridge, 1888. Pp. 77. MB.

6334   CAMBRIDGE HUMANE SOCIETY. An account of the
        Cambridge Humane Society. Cambridge, 1819.
Pp. 7. MB.

6335   CAMBRIDGE SKATING CLUB. Cambridge Skating
        Club, 1898-1948. [Cambridge, 1948?].
Pp. 69.

6336   CAMBRIDGE TRIBUNE. Cambridge, a souvenir...
        1630-1890. Cambridge, 1890. Pp. 32. M.

6337   _____. Cambridge semi-centennial, 1846-
        1896. Boston, 1896. Pp. 64.
        Includes biography.

6338   _____. Cambridge, the Harvard Bridge, a
        souvenir, 1630, 1890, the university city....
Cambridge: F. S. Hill, 1890. Pp. 32.

6339   CAMBRIDGE UNION TEMPERANCE SOCIETY. Report,
        embracing a history of the society and a
statement of the condition of the cause in East
Cambridge, Jan. 8, 1843. [Cambridge, 1843].
Pp. 12.

6340   CARPENTER, HAZEN C. "Emerson, Eliot, and
        the elective system." NEQ, 24 (1951), 13-
34.
        Influence of Emerson on Eliot of Harvard,
        1869-1909.

6341   CARROLL, MARK. "The Belknap Press of Har-
        vard University Press." HarvLibBul, 18
(1970), 248-253.

6342   CHADWICK, JOHN WHITE. "The Harvard Divinity
        School." NEM, New Ser., 11 (1894-1895),
740-755.

6343   CHAMBERLAIN, JOSHUA LAWRENCE, WILLIAM R.
        THAYER and CHARLES E. L. WINGATE, eds. Har-
vard University: its history, influence, equipment
and characteristics, with biographical sketches and

portraits of founders, benefactors, officers and
alumni. Boston: R. Herndon, 1900. **v.p.**

6344   CHASE, PHILIP PUTNAM. "Some Cambridge re-
        formers of the eighties or Cambridge contri-
butions to Cleveland democracy in Massachusetts."
CaHSP, 20 (1927-1929), 24-52.

6345   CLAPP, CLIFFORD BLAKE. "Christo et Eccle-
        siae." CSMP, 25 (1922-1924), 59-83.
        Motto of Harvard College.

6346   COLE, ARTHUR H. "College expenses of 1806-
        1810." Harvard Alumni Bulletin, 38 (1936),
539-543.

6347   COMPTON, KARL TAYLOR. Massachusetts Insti-
        tute of Technology, 'Tomb of the dead lan-
guages.' N.Y.: Newcomen Society of England,
American Branch, 1948. Pp. 32.

6348   COOKE, GEORGE WILLIS. "The 'Dial': an his-
        torical and biographical introduction with a
list of the contributors." Journal of Speculative
Philosophy, 19 (1885), 225-265, 322-323.
        Periodical.

6349   COOLIDGE, ROSAMOND. "The history of Coolidge
        Hill." CaHSP, 32 (1946-1948), 96-103.

6350   CRANDALL, RUTH. The Research Center in En-
        trepreneurial History at Harvard University,
1948-1958: a historical sketch. Cambridge: [Har-
vard Univ.], 1960. Pp. iv, 67 leaves.

6351   CROTHERS, MRS. SAMUEL MCCHORD. "Reminiscen-
        ces of Cambridge." CaHSP, 31 (1945), 7-21.

6352   CUMMINGS, THOMAS HARRISON. An address on the
        first American flag: Washington's flag.
Cambridge: Cambridge Tribune Pr., [1921?]. Pp. 22.
MH.

6353   _____. An address on the first flag of Amer-
        ican independence. n.p., [1925?]. Pp. 8.
MH.

6354   _____. An address on the first flag of the
        Revolution. n.p., [1924?]. Pp. 8. MH.

6355   _____. An address on the Revolutionary flag,
        Washington's flag. n.p., [1923?]. Pp. 12.
MH.

6356   CURRIER, MARGARET. "Cataloguing at Harvard
        in the sixties." Harvard University Library
Notes, 4 (1942), 67-73.

6357   CURTIS, CHARLES PELHAM. "Learning and liquor
        at Harvard College 1792-1846." MHSP, 70
(1950-1953), 56-64.
        Phi Beta Kappa and the Porcellian Club.

6358   _____. "Liquor and Learning in Harvard Col-
        lege, 1792-1846." NEQ, 25 (1952), 344-353.
        Porcellian Club and Phi Beta Kappa; differs
        from previous article.

6359   CUTTER, WATSON GRANT. Family traditions con-
        cerning the Washington Elm. [Cambridge?,
1907]. Pp. 10.

6360 DANA, HENRY WADSWORTH LONGFELLOW. "The Dana-Palmer House." CaHSP, 33 (1949-1950), 7-36.

6361 _____. The Dana saga: three centuries of the Dana family in Cambridge. Cambridge: Cambridge Historical Society, 1941. Pp. 61.

6362 _____. Longfellow House. Cambridge, [19--]. Pp. 16. MH.

6363 _____. "The Longfellow House, Cambridge, Massachusetts." OTNE, 38 (1947-1948), 81-96.

6364 _____. "The Stephen Sewall House, Cambridge, Massachusetts." OTNE, 37 (1946-1947), 95-99. Demolished in 1946.

6365 DANA, RICHARD HENRY, b. 1851. Century and a half...150th anniversary of Christ Church... October 16, 1911. n.p., [1911?]. Unpaged. M.

6366 DANA, MRS. RICHARD HENRY. "The Female Humane Society." CaHSP, 9 (1914), 62-70. Charity.

6367 DAUGHTERS OF THE AMERICAN REVOLUTION, MASSACHUSETTS. HANNAH WINTHROP CHAPTER, CAMBRIDGE. The Cambridge houses. Cambridge, 1906. Unpaged.

6368 _____. An historic guide to Cambridge. Cambridge, 1907. Pp. 207.

6369 DAVIS, ANDREW MCFARLAND. An analysis of the early records of Harvard College, 1636-1750. Cambridge: Library of Harvard Univ., 1895. Pp. 21.

6370 _____. "The Cambridge Press." AASP, New Ser., 5 (1887-1888), 295-302. Stephen Daye.

6371 _____. "The early College buildings at Cambridge." AASP, New Ser., 6 (1889-1890), 323-349.

6372 _____. "The exhibitions of Harvard College prior to 1800." NEHGR, 46 (1892), 233-244. Beneficiary trusts for students.

6363 _____. "The first scholarship at Harvard College." AASP, New Ser., 5 (1887-1888), 129-139.

6374 _____. "Harvard commencement programme of 1723." CSMP, 3 (1895-1897), 400-404.

6375 _____. "The Indian College at Cambridge." MagAmHist, 24 (1890), 33-39.

6376 _____. "Investments of Harvard College, 1776-1790: an episode in the finances of the Revolution." QJEcon, 20 (1906), 399-418.

6377 _____. "The Lady Mowlson Scholarship at Cambridge." AASP, New Ser., 8 (1892-1893), 274-280. Harvard College.

6378 _____. "A search for a lost building." Atlantic, 66 (1890), 211-219. Harvard's first building.

6379 _____. "The site of the first College building at Cambridge." AASP, New Ser., 5 (1887-1888), 469-484.

6380 DAVIS, JOHN F. "The life story of Cambridge water." CaHSP, 41 (1967-1969), 7-15.

6381 DAY, GARDINER MUMFORD. The biography of a church; a brief history of Christ Church, Cambridge, Massachusetts. Cambridge: Riverside Pr., 1951. Pp. 186.

6382 _____. The friendship of Harvard and Christ Church and two other historical addresses. Cambridge, 1961. Pp. 20.

6383 "A DAY in old Cambridge." NOHR, 3 (August 27, 1904), 2-6.

6384 DEANE, CHARLES. "Washington's head-quarters in Cambridge." MHSP, (1871-1873), 257-263.

6385 DEARBORN, NATHANIEL. A concise history of, and guide through Mount Auburn, with a catalogue of lots laid out in that cemetery; a map of the grounds, and terms of subscription, regulations concerning visitors, interments, &c., &c. Boston, 1843. Pp. 74.

6386 DERRY, CECIL THAYER. Brief history of the Old Cambridge Baptist Church, 1844-1944. Cambridge, [1944?]. Pp. 49. MH.

6387 _____. "Pages from the history of the Cambridge High and Latin School." CaHSP, 35 (1953-1954), 91-109.

6388 DE VOTO, BERNARD. "Literary censorship in Cambridge." Harvard Graduates' Magazine, 39 (September, 1930), 30-42.

6389 DEXTER, GEORGE. "Tutor Sever's argument." MHSP, (1878), 50-67. Nicholas Sever advocated the right of instructors in Harvard College to a place in the Corporation, 1723.

6390 DONALLAN, JOHN WHITING. History of the Second Baptist Church, Cambridge, Mass. Lawrence: George S. Merrill, 1866. Pp. 120.

6391 DONOVAN, FRANCES COOPER-MARSHAL. "The Y.W.C.A. in Cambridge." CaHSP, 36 (1955-1956), 41-51.

6392 DOW, GEORGE FRANCIS, ed. The Holyoke diaries, 1709-1856; Rev. Edward Holyoke, Marblehead and Cambridge, 1709-1768, Edward Augustus Holyoke, M.D., Cambridge, 1742-1747, John Holyoke, Cambridge, 1748, Mrs. Mary (Vial) Holyoke, Salem, 1760-1800, Margaret Holyoke, Salem, 1801-1823, Mrs. Susanna (Holyoke) Ward, Salem, 1793-1856. Salem: The Essex Institute, 1911. Pp. xviii, 215.

6393 DRUMMEY, JACK. "Angier joins Interchemical in silver anniversary year." Industry, 22 (December, 1956), 25-27, 32b-32c.
Angier Products, adhesives.

6394 DUNDEE, R. ROBERT. "Football at Harvard College." Bostonian, 3 (1895-1896), 115-136.

6395 ECONOMY CLUB, CAMBRIDGE, MASS. Twenty fifth anniversary of the Economy Club, Cambridge, Massachusetts, June 21, 1897. Cambridge: Louis F. Weston, [1897?]. Unpaged. MH.

6396 ELIOT, CHARLES WILLIAM. Harvard memories. Cambridge: Harvard Univ. Pr., 1923. Pp. vii, 142.

6397 _____. "Personal recollections of Dr. Morrill Wyman, Professor Dunbar, Professor Sophocles, and Professor Shaler." CaHSP, 12 (1917), 25-45.
Harvard.

6398 ELIOT, FRANCES H. "The romance of street names in Cambridge." CaHSP, 32 (1946-1948), 25-29.

6399 ELIOT, SAMUEL ATKINS, 1798-1862. A sketch of the history of Harvard College, and of its present state. Boston: C. C. Little and J. Brown, 1848. Pp. xiii, 190.

6400 ELIOT, SAMUEL ATKINS, 1862-1850. A history of Cambridge, Massachusetts (1630-1913), together with biographies of Cambridge people. Cambridge: Cambridge Tribune, 1913. Pp. 308.

6401 _____. "A significant Cambridge anniversary." CaHSP, 32 (1946-1948), 104-114.
Tercentenary of Cambridge Synod of 1648.

6402 _____. "Some Cambridge pundits and pedagogues." CaHSP, 26 (1940), 13-35.
Biography.

6403 _____. "Some musical memories of Cambridge." CaHSP, 32 (1946-1948), 79-95.

6404 ELKINS, KIMBALL C. "Foreshadowings of Lamont: student proposals in the nineteenth century." Harvard LibBul, 8 (1954), 41-53.
Harvard College Library.

6405 _____ "Honorary degrees at Harvard." Harv LibBul, 12 (1958), 326-353.

6406 EMERTON, EPHRAIM. "Recollections of sixty years in Cambridge." CaHSP, 20 (1927-1929), 53-59.

6407 EVARTS, PRESCOTT. "On a certain deplorable tendency among the most respectable members of the community to abstain from church-going --as observed in the year 1796." CaHSP, 16 (1922), 97-109.
Congregationalism.

6408 FARLOW, MRS. WILLIAM G. "Quincy Street in the fifties." CaHSP, 18 (1925), 27-45.

6409 FARRINGTON, CHARLES C. Historic Cambridge Common. Bedford: Bedford Print Shop, 1918. Pp. 32.

6410 FICKETT, RALPH SEWARD. The history of the Marshall Club, Harvard Law School. [Cambridge, 1910]. Pp. 49.

6411 "FIRESIDE travels: Cambridge thirty years ago." Putnam's Monthly Magazine, 3 (1854), 379-386, 473-482.

6412 FLAGG, WILSON. Mount Auburn: its scenes, its beauties, and its lessons. Boston: J. Munroe, 1861. Pp. xii, 371.
Cemetery.

6413 FOOTE, HENRY WILDER, b. 1875, ed. The Cambridge Platform of 1648: tercentenary commemoration at Cambridge, Massachusetts, October 27, 1948. Boston: Beacon Pr., 1949. Pp. 119.

6414 _____. "The Harvard Divinity School as I have known it." CaHSP, 36 (1955-1956), 53-74.

6415 FORBES, EDWARD WALDO. "The Agassiz School." CaHSP, 35 (1953-1954), 35-55.

6416 _____. "The beginnings of the Art Department and of the Fogg Museum of Art at Harvard." CaHSP, 27 (1941), 11-27.

6417 FORBES, ELLIOT. "The musical scene at Harvard." CaHSP, 41 (1967-1969), 89-104.

6418 FORBES, HARRIETTE MERRIFIELD. "Early Cambridge diaries." CaHSP, 11 (1916), 57-83.
Includes a listing of diaries.

6419 FOSS, ALDEN S. "Boston Woven Hose and Rubber Company: eighty four years in Cambridge." CaHSP, 40 (1964-1966), 23-42.

6420 FOSTER, FRANCIS APTHORP. "The burning of Harvard Hall, 1764, and its consequences." CSMP, 14 (1911-1913), 2-43.

6421 FOSTER, MARGERY SOMERS. "The cost of a Harvard education in the Puritan period." CaHSP, 38 (1959-1960), 7-22.

6422 _____. 'Out of smalle beginnings...' an economic history Harvard College in the Puritan period (1636 to 1712). Cambridge: Harvard Univ. Pr., 1962. Pp. 243.

6423 FOWLER, FRANCES. "Kirkland Place." CaHSP, 23 (1934-1935), 76-94.

6424 FOXCROFT, FRANK. "Mount Auburn." NEM, New Ser., 14 (1896), 419-438.
Cemetery.

6425 _____. "No-license in Cambridge." CaHSP, 13 (1918), 9-16.
Temperance.

6426 FRASER, ESTHER STEVENS. "Excavating old time wall papers." Antiques, 3 (1923), 216-221.
John Hicks House, (1762).

6427 ____. "The John Hicks House, Cambridge, Mass." OTNE, 22 (1931-1932), 99-113.

6428 FREEMASONS. CAMBRIDGE, MASS. AMICABLE LODGE. Amicable Lodge A. F. & A. M., one hundred and twenty-fifth anniversary June 10 and 11, 1930, 1805-1930. Cambridge: Masonic Temple, [1930?]. Pp. ix, 132.

6429 ____. Exercises at the celebration of the 75th anniversary of Amicable Lodge, F. & A. M., June 10, 1880. [Boston, 1880]. Pp. 37.

6430 ____. Exercises at the centennial anniversary of the institution of Amicable Lodge, A. F. & A. M., Cambridge, Mass. June 6, 1905. Boston: Parkhill, 1906. Pp. 128.

6431 FRENCH, STANLEY. "The cemetery as cultural institution: the establishment of Mount Auburn and the 'rural cemetery' movement." AmQ, 26 (1974), 37-59.

6432 FROST, JOHN EDWARD. Harvard and Cambridge: a sketch book. N.Y.: Coward-McCann, 1940. Pp. vi, 89.

6433 GARDINER, JOHN HAYS. Harvard. N.Y.: Oxford Univ. Pr., 1914. Pp. vii, 333.

6434 GARRETT, WENDELL D. Apthorp House, 1760-1960. Cambridge: Adams House, Harvard Univ., 1960. Pp. 100.
Residence of master of Adams House.

6435 ____. "The topographical development of Cambridge, 1793-1896." CaHSP, 39 (1961-1963), 108-124.

6436 GEROULD, FLORENCE RUSSELL. "Historical sketch of the First Church in Cambridge (Unitarian)." CaHSP, 31 (1945), 61-65.

6437 GILMAN, ARTHUR, ed. The Cambridge of eighteen hundred and ninety-six, a picture of the city and its industries fifty years after its incorporation. Cambridge: Riverside Pr., 1896. Pp. xx, 424.

6438 ____, ed. Theatrum majorum, the Cambridge of 1776: wherein is set forth an account of the town, and of the events it witnessed: with which is incorporated the diary of Dorothy Dudley, now first publish'd; together with an historicall sketch; severall appropriate poems; numerous anecdotes.... (1876) 2d. ed. Boston: Lockwood, Brooks, 1876. Pp. v, 123.

6439 GILMAN, ROGER. "Victorian houses of old Cambridge." CaHSP, 26 (1940), 38-48.

6440 ____. "Windmill Lane to Ash Street." CaHSP, 31 (1945), 22-36.

6441 GOODHUE, ALBERT, JR. "The reading of Harvard students, 1770-1781, as shown by the records of the Speaking Club." EIHC, 73 (1937), 107-129.

6442 GOTLIEB, HOWARD B. "The friendship and the House: Phillips Brooks and Edwin Hale Abbot." HMPEC, 32 (1963), 37-48.
Phillips Brook House, Harvard University.

6443 GOZZALDI, MARY ISABELLA JAMES DE. "The Bates-Dana House." CaHSP, 20 (1927-1929), 60-62.

6444 ____. "Elmwood and its owners." CaHSP, 15 (1920-1921), 41-45.
Historic house.

6445 ____. "A few old Cambridge houses." CaHSP, 6 (1911), 17-26.

6446 ____. "Gerry's Landing and its neighborhood." CaHSP, 13 (1918), 81-88.
Section of the city.

6447 ____. History of Cambridge, Massachusetts, 1630-1877, with a genealogical register, by Lucius R. Paige, supplement and index, comprising a biographical and genealogical record of the early settlers and their descendants; with references to their wills and the administration of their estates in the Middlesex County registry of probate. Cambridge: Cambridge Historical Society, 1930. Pp. iv, 860.
This volume is supplement and index only to basic volume by Paige, entry 6627.

6448 ____. "The Hooper-Lee-Nichols House." CaHSP, 16 (1922), 18-20.

6449 ____. "Merchants of old Cambridge in the early days." CaHSP, 8 (1913), 30-40.

6450 ____. "The Ruggles-Fayerweather House." CaHSP, 17 (1923-1924), 54-59.

6451 ____. "The seal of the [Cambridge Historical] Society." CaHSP, 3 (1908), 5-19.

6452 ____. and ELIZABETH ELLERY DANA and DAVID T. POTTINGER. "The Vassall House." CaHSP, 21 (1930-1931), 78-118.

6453 GRAS, NORMAN SCOTT BRIEN. Harvard Co-operative Society past and present, 1882-1942. Cambridge: Harvard Univ. Pr., 1942. Pp. xi, 191.

6454 GRAUSTEIN, JEANNETTE E. "Natural history at Harvard College, 1788-1842." CaHSP, 38 (1959-1960), 69-86.

6455 GRAY, ROLAND. The trustees of the Charity of Edward Hopkins; supplemental account, 1889-1943. [Cambridge?]: Priv. print., 1948. Pp. 20.

6456 ____. "The William Gray House in Cambridge." CaHSP, 14 (1919), 104-106.

6457 GREEN, SAMUEL ABBOTT. "Early commencements at Harvard College." MHSP, 2 Ser., 10 (1895-1896), 194-206, 360; 2 Ser., 12 (1897-1899), 73.

6458 _____. "Old laws of Harvard College."
MHSP, 2 Ser., 11 (1896-1897), 200-209.

6459 _____. Remarks on the early history of
printing in New England. [Boston, 1897].
Pp. 16.

6460 GREEN, SAMUEL SWETT. "The Craigie House,
Cambridge." AASP, New Ser., 13 (1899-1900),
312-352.

6461 GREENE, JEROME DAVIS. The tercentenary of
Harvard College, a chronicle of the tercen-
tenary year, 1935-1936. Cambridge: Harvard Univ.
Pr., 1936. Pp. xiv, 492.

6462 GRIEDER, ELMER M. "The Littauer Center Library: a few notes on its origins." Harvard University Library Notes, 4 (1942), 97-104.

6463 GRISCOM, LUDLOW. "Early history of Cambridge ornithology." CaHSP, 35 (1953-1954),
11-16.

6464 HALE, EDWARD EVERETT. "My college days."
Atlantic, 71 (1893), 355-363, 458-467.
Harvard reminiscences.

6465 HALL, EDWARD HENRY. "The Cambridge Humane
Society." CaHSP, 6 (1911), 27-32.

6466 HALL, EDWIN HERBERT. "Historical sketch of
charitable societies in Cambridge." CaHSP,
18 (1925), 11-26.

6467 HALL, RICHARD W. "Recollections of the Cambridge Social Dramatic Club." CaHSP, 38
(1959-1960), 51-67.
Nineteenth century.

6468 HANSON, CHARLES LANE. "Four years at Harvard College, 1888-1892." CaHSP, 34 (1951-
1952), 37-57.

6469 HARASZTI, ZOLTÁN. The enigma of the Bay
Psalm Book. Chicago: Univ. of Chicago Pr.,
1956. Pp. xiii, 143.

6470 HARRER, JOHN A. "The Reverend José Glover
and the beginnings of the Cambridge Press."
CaHSP, 38 (1959-1960), 87-110.

6471 HARRIS, SEYMOUR EDWIN. Economics of Harvard.
N.Y.: McGraw-Hill, 1970. Pp. lxvii, 519.
Historical.

6472 HART, ALBERT BUSHNELL. "Harvard College and
the First Church." MHSP, 2 Ser., 5 (1889-
1890), 396-416.

6473 HARVARD ADVOCATE. Catalogue of the editors
of the Harvard Advocate, 1866-1886, to
which is prefixed a short history of the paper.
Cambridge: Harvard Univ., 1886. Pp. 36, 24.

6474 HARVARD College and its benefactors. Boston:
C. C. Little and J. Brown, 1846. Pp. 37.

6475 "HARVARD College statistics." American Quarterly Register, 8 (1835-1836), 162-163.
Average age of graduates in classes from
1744-1773.

6476 THE HARVARD CRIMSON. The Harvard Crimson,
1873-1906. [Cambridge]: Harvard Crimson,
1906. Pp. 121.
Newspaper.

6477 _____. The Harvard Crimson, fiftieth anni-
versary, 1873-1923. Cambridge: Harvard
Univ. Pr., 1923. Pp. xi, 257.
Newspaper.

6478 NO ENTRY

6479 HARVARD TRUST COMPANY, CAMBRIDGE, MASS.
America's unknown city, Cambridge, Massachusetts, 1630-1936: the Harvard Trust Company pre-
sents a part of the history of Cambridge heretofore
little emphasized.... [Cambridge?, 1936]. Pp. 27.

6480 _____. Seventy-five years old, being a history of the Harvard Trust Company, embracing
an account of the changing conditions through
seventy-five years and the manner in which the bank
has met them and thereby continuously provided adequate banking service to the entire community....
Cambridge, 1935. Unpaged.

6481 HARVARD UNIVERSITY. Education, bricks and
mortar: Harvard buildings and their contribution to the advancement of learning. Cambridge,
1949. Pp. 99.

6482 _____. Harvard College records...corporation
records, 1636-[1767].... Boston: The [Co-
lonial] Society [of Massachusetts], 1925-1935. 3v.

6483 _____. A record of the commemoration, November fifth to eighth, 1886, on the two hundred
and fiftieth anniversary of the founding of Harvard
College. Cambridge: J. Wilson and Son, 1887.
Pp. 379.

6484 _____. The tercentenary of Harvard College:
a chronicle of the tercentenary year, 1935-
1936. Cambridge: Harvard Univ. Pr., 1937.
Pp. xiv, 492.

6485 HARVARD UNIVERSITY. HARVARD LAW SCHOOL ASSO-
CIATION. The centennial history of the Har-
vard Law School, 1817-1917. [Boston]: Harvard Law
School Association, 1918. Pp. x, 412.

6486 _____. The Harvard Law School, 1817-1917....
[Boston]: Harvard Law School Association,
1917. Pp. 164.

6487 HARVARD UNIVERSITY. HASTY PUDDING CLUB. An
illustrated history of the Hasty Pudding Club
theatricals. (1897) 3d. ed. Cambridge, 1933.
Unpaged.

6488 HARVARD UNIVERSITY. LIBRARY. Gore Hall, the library of Harvard College, 1838-1913. Cambridge: Harvard Univ. Pr., 1917. Unpaged. Demolished in 1913.

6489 _____. Harvard University Library, 1638-1968. Text by Rene Kuhn Bryant. [Cambridge, 1969]. Pp. 53.

6490 HARVARD UNIVERSITY. MUSEUM OF COMPARATIVE ZOOLOGY. An account of the organization and progress of the Museum of Comparative Zoölogy at Harvard College, in Cambridge, Mass. Cambridge: Welch, Bigelow, 1873. Pp. 31.

6491 HARVARD UNIVERSITY. PHILLIPS BROOKS HOUSE. Phillips Brooks House, account of its origin, dedication and purpose. Boston, 1900. Pp. 71. MB.

6492 HASTINGS, LEWIS MOREY. "The streets of Cambridge, some account of their origin and history." CaHSP, 14 (1919), 31-78.

6493 HATCH, MARY R. P. "Harvard University: some account of its makers, its library and other buildings, and its club life." NEM, New Ser., 33 (1905-1906), 307-322.

6494 HAWKINS, HUGH. Between Harvard and America: the educational leadership of Charles W. Eliot. N.Y.: Oxford Univ. Pr., 1972. Pp. xi, 404.

6495 HAYES-CAVANAUGH, DORIS. "Early glass making in East Cambridge." CaHSP, 19 (1926), 32-45.

6496 _____. "Early glassmaking in East Cambridge, Mass." OTNE, 19 (1928-1929), 113-122. Differs from above article.

6497 HERRICK, ROBERT FREDERICK, comp. Red Top: reminiscences of Harvard rowing. Cambridge: Harvard Univ. Pr., 1948. Pp. vi, 255.

6498 HIGGINSON, THOMAS WENTWORTH. Old Cambridge. N.Y.: Macmillan, 1899. Pp. v, 203.

6499 HILL, BENJAMIN THOMAS. "Life at Harvard a century ago." AASP, New Ser., 20 (1909-1910), 197-248. 1813-1817.

6500 HISTORICAL facts: an outline of the salient events in the history of Cambridge, Mass., for the boys and the girls of our beloved city, by a graduate of the Cambridge High School. Boston: Newetowne Publishing, 1914. Pp. 16.

6501 THE HISTORY and traditions of Harvard College. Cambridge: Harvard Crimson, 1936. Pp. 76.

6502 HODGES, GEORGE. "The Kappa Delta of Cambridge, 1804-1819." MHSP, 50 (1916-1917), 123-132. Harvard fraternity.

6503 HOLMES, ABIEL. "History of Cambridge." MHSC, 7 (1800), 6-66.

6504 _____. A sermon, preached at Cambridge, January 4, 1801, the first Lord's Day in the nineteenth century. Cambridge: W. Hilliard, 1801. Pp. 27. Relates to the First Church.

6505 HOPPIN, NICHOLAS. One soweth and another reapeth: a commemorative sermon on the one hundredth anniversary of Christ Church, Cambridge, Mass., Tuesday, October 15, 1861. Cambridge: Miles and Dillingham, 1861. Pp. 36.

6506 _____. A sermon on the re-opening of Christ Church, Cambridge, Mass., preached on the twenty-fourth Sunday after Trinity, November 22, 1857; with a historical notice of the church. Boston: Ide and Dutton, 1858. Pp. 79.

6507 HOSMER, SAMUEL DANA. "Reminiscences of Cambridge and Harvard College." Worcester HSProc, (1888), 15-24.

6508 HOWE, ARCHIBALD MURRAY. "The state arsenal and the identification of the cannon on the Cambridge Common." CaHSP, 6 (1911), 5-15.

6509 HOWE, LOIS LILLEY, et al. "The Cambridge Plant Club." CaHSP, 35 (1953-1954), 17-33.

6510 _____. "Harvard Square in the 'seventies and 'eighties." CaHSP, 30 (1944), 11-27.

6511 _____. "The history of Garden Street." CaHSP, 33 (1949-1950), 37-57.

6512 _____. "Memories of nineteenth-century Cambridge." CaHSP, 34 (1951-1952), 59-76.

6513 HOWE, WILLARD. "An excommunication in Harvard Square." CaHSP, 29 (1943), 68-81. Three cases of discipline in First Parish Church, 1805-1819.

6514 HOWELLS, WILLIAM DEAN. "Some literary memories of Cambridge." Harper's Magazine, 101 (1900), 823-839.

6515 HOYT, JAMES S. The First Evangelical Congregational Church, Cambridgeport, Mass. Cambridge: Univ. Pr., 1878. Pp. 287.

6516 HUDSON, WINTHROP S. "The Morison myth concerning the founding of Harvard College." Church History, 8 (1939), 148-159. Samuel Eliot Morison.

6517 "INDUSTRY'S map of Massachusetts: city of Cambridge." Industry, 2 (February, 1937), 21-22, 48-49.

6518 "THE JOHN E. Cain Company, half a century of progress." Industry, 29 (June, 1964), 11-12, 39-41. Food.

6519 JONES, BESSIE JUDITH ZABAN. "Diary of two Bonds, 1846-1849, first directors of the Harvard College Observatory." HarvLibBul, 15 (1967), 368-386; 16 (1968), 49-71, 178-207.

6520 _____ and LYLE GIFFORD BOYD. The Harvard College Observatory: the first four directorships, 1839-1919. Cambridge: Harvard Univ. Pr., 1971. Pp. xi, 493.

6521 JONES, PAULINE. Cambridge Social Dramatic Club, 1890-1940; a collection of facts and incidents relating to the founding and history of the club. [Cambridge, 1940]. Pp. 18.

6522 KAHN, ELY JACQUES. Harvard: through change and through storm. N.Y.: W. W. Norton, 1969. Pp. 388.

6523 KIMBER, SIDNEY ARTHUR. Cambridge Press title-pages, 1640-1665; a pictorial representation of the work done in the first printing office in British North America. Takoma Park, Md.: W. L. Kimber, 1954. Pp. 123.

6524 _____. The story of an old press (the Stephen Daye press). (1937) 2d. ed. Cambridge: Univ. Pr., 1939. Pp. 47.

6525 KIMBER, SIDNEY ARTHUR. Three hundred years of printing in New England; being an account of the first printer in the British colonies in North America & his successors, with historical notes. Cambridge: Univ. Pr., 1938. Pp. 14.

6526 KING, MOSES. The Harvard anniversary handbook, 1636-1886; a serviceable guide, programme, and souvenir of the celebration of the two hundred and fiftieth anniversary of the founding of Harvard College at Cambridge, November 5, 6, 7, and 8, 1866. Boston: R. Avery, 1886. Pp. 95.

6527 KRAMER, SIDNEY. A history of Stone & Kimball and Herbert S. Stone & Co., with a bibliography of their publications, 1893-1905. Chicago: N. W. Forgue, 1940. Pp. xxii, 379.

6528 KYDRYŃSKI, JULIUSZ. Do widzenia, Claudio. Kraków: Wydawn. Literackie, 1966. Pp. 306. Intellectual life.

6529 LANCASTER, SOUTHWORTH. "Fire in Cambridge." CaHSP, 36 (1955-1956), 75-92.

6530 LANE, WILLIAM COOLIDGE. "The building of Holworthy Hall." CaHSP, 7 (1911-1912), 63-69.
Harvard University dormitory.

6531 _____. "The building of Massachusetts Hall, 1717-1720." CSMP, 24 (1920-1922), 81-110. Harvard University.

6532 _____. "Harvard College and Franklin." CSMP, 10 (1904-1906), 229-239.

6533 _____. "New Hampshire's part in restoring the library and apparatus of Harvard College after the fire of 1764." CSMP, 25 (1922-1924), 24-33.

6534 _____. "The rebellion of 1766 in Harvard College." CSMP, 10 (1904-1906), 32-59. Quality of food in the commons.

6535 _____. "A religious society at Harvard College, 1719." CSMP, 24 (1920-1922), 309-312.

6536 LARRABEE, HAROLD A. "Electives before Eliot." Harvard Alumni Bulletin, 42 (1940), 893-897.

6537 LAWRENCE, WILLIAM. Seventy-three years of the Episcopal Theological school, Cambridge, 1867-1940, a narrative. n.p., 1940. Pp. 35.

6538 LEAVITT, GEORGE ROSWELL. A brief history of Pilgrim Church, Cambridgeport, Mass. Cambridge, 1885. Pp. iv, 67.

6539 LEE, RUTH WEBB. "Peachblow glass." Antiques, 24 (1933), 48-50.

6540 LEVIN, ABRAHAM NATELSON and HENRY BERNHEIM GOODFRIEND. Harvard debating 1892 to 1913 (Harvard, Yale and Princeton). Cambridge: Caustic-Claflin, 1914. Pp. 77. MH.

6541 LILLIE, RUPERT BALLOU. Cambridge in 1775. [Wenham?, 1949]. Pp. 42.

6542 _____. "The gardens and homes of the loyalists." CaHSP, 26 (1940), 49-62.

6543 LIONS, ZELDA and GORDON W. ALLPORT. "Seventy-five years of continuing education: the Prospect Union Association." CaHSP, 40 (1964-1966), 139-158.
Founded in 1891.

6544 "A LIST of graduates of Harvard University, of anti-Revolutionary or loyalist principles, in the classes prior to the Revolution." American Quarterly Register, 13 (1840-1841), 403-416; 14 (1842), 167-172.
Includes biographical sketches.

6545 LITCHFIELD, I. W. "The Technology semi-centennial." SWJ, 19 (1916), 15-25.
Massachusetts Institute of Technology.

6546 [LIVERMORE, GEORGE]. A brief account of the Dana Hill Public School, Cambridge, 1849. Cambridge, 1849. Pp. 19.
Includes brief history; author attribution by Harvard University Library.

6547 LORD, ELIOT. "Harvard's youngest three." NEM, New Ser., 7 (1892-1893), 639-648.
Youngest at graduation, Cotton Mather, Paul Dudley and Andrew Preston Peabody.

6548 LOVETT, ROBERT W. "Harvard Union Library, 1901 to 1948." HarvLibBul, 2 (1948), 230-237.

6549 _____. "Hasty Pudding Club Library, 1808-1948." HarvLibBul, 2 (1948), 393-401.

6550 _____. "The Pennoyer Scholarship at Harvard." HarvLibBul, 4 (1950), 213-238.

6551 ____. "The undergraduate and the Harvard Library, 1877-1937." HarvLibBul, 1 (1947), 221-237.
For 1765-1877 and 1937-1947 see entry 6581.

6551A LOWELL, JAMES RUSSELL. Cambridge thirty years ago, 1854; a memoir addressed to the Edelmann Storg in Rome. Boston: Houghton Mifflin, 1910. Pp. 67.

6552 LYTTLE, CHARLES. "A sketch of the theological development of Harvard University, 1636-1805." Church History, 5 (1936), 301-329.

6553 MCCAUGHEY, ROBERT A. "The transformation of American academic life: Harvard University 1821-1892." Perspectives in American History, 8 (1974), 229-332.

6554 MCCORD, DAVID THOMPSON WATSON. An acre for education: being notes on the history of Radcliffe College. (1938) Rev. [ed.]. Cambridge, 1958. Pp. 97.
Author's name does not appear in the first edition.

6555 ____. Notes on the Harvard tercentenary.... Cambridge: Harvard Univ. Pr., 1936. Pp. 99.

6556 MCKENZIE, ALEXANDER. "'Address.'" CaHSP, 1 (1905-1906), 35-40.
First Church.

6557 ____. "The First Church in Cambridge." CongQ, 15 (1873), 384-394.

6558 ____. Lectures on the history of the First Church in Cambridge. Boston: Congregational Publishing Society, 1873. Pp. iv, 289. MB.

6559 ____. "Some Cambridge men I have known." CaHSP, 3 (1908), 19-36.

6560 ____. "Washington in Cambridge." Atlantic, 36 (1875), 92-98.
1775.

6561 MCMURTRIE, DOUGLAS C. "Die ersten Drücke im Englisch-sprachigen Nord-Amerika." Gutenberg-Jahrbuch, (1926), 136-143.
Stephen Daye's press.

6562 MACNAIR, WILLIAM M. "One hundred years of church life: a brief history of the Prospect Congregational Church in Cambridge, Massachusetts." CaHSP, 20 (1927-1929), 63-83.

6563 MACOMBER, GEORGE A. "Rambling notes on the Cambridge Trust Company; or tales of a wayside bank." CaHSP, 41 (1967-1969), 40-54.

6564 MAGUIRE, MARY HUME. "The curtain raiser to the founding of Radcliffe College." CaHSP, 36 (1955-1956), 23-39.

6565 MANDERS, ERIC I. "Notes on the troop units in the Cambridge army, 1775-1776." Military Collector and Historian, 23 (1971), 69-74.

6566 MANSION HOUSE ICE CREAM CO., EAST CAMBRIDGE, MASS. Lechmere Point souvenir, being a little narrative of events from the beginning of Governor William Phipps' farm in East Cambridge through the establishment of the old Mansion House and the present successful development of the famous Mansion House ice cream. East Cambridge, 1915. Pp. 47. MBNEH.

6567 MARSHALL, HELEN E. "The story of the 'Dial', 1840-1844." New Mexico Quarterly, 1 (1931), 147-165.
Literary magazine.

6568 MASON, DANIEL GREGORY. "At Harvard in the nineties." NEQ, 9 (1936), 43-70.

6569 MASSACHUSETTS INSTITUTE OF TECHNOLOGY. The Massachusetts Institute of Technology, a brief account of its foundation, character, and equipment. Boston, 1904. Pp. 42.

6570 MATHER, COTTON. The history of Harvard College. Boston: Directors of the Old South Work, 1907. Pp. 32.

6571 MATTHEWS, ALBERT. "Comenius and Harvard College." CSMP, 21 (1919), 146-190.

6572 ____. "Draught of a royal charter for Harvard College, 1723." CSMP, 25 (1922-1924), 390-400.

6573 ____. "Harvard College charter of 1672." CSMP, 21 (1919), 363-402.

6574 ____. "Harvard commencement days, 1642-1916." CSMP, 18 (1915-1916), 309-384.

6575 ____. "Teaching of French at Harvard College before 1750." CSMP, 17 (1913-1914), 216-232.

6576 ____. "Tentative lists of temporary students at Harvard College, 1639-1800." CSMP, 17 (1913-1914), 271-285.

6577 MAY, RALPH. "The Cambridge Boat Club." CaHSP, 39 (1961-1963), 125-143.

6578 MEANY, EILEEN G. "The Avon Home." CaHSP, 38 (1959-1960), 121-129.
Orphanage.

6579 MERRILL, ESTELLE MINERVA HATCH, ed. Cambridge sketches by Cambridge authors. [Cambridge]: Cambridge Young Women's Christian Association, 1896. Pp. xiii, 264.

6580 METCALF, KEYES DEWITT. "Spatial growth in the Harvard Library, 1638-1947." HarvLibBul, 2 (1948), 98-115.

6581 ____. "The undergraduate and the Harvard Library, 1765-1877; 1937-1947." HarvLibBul, 1 (1947), 29-51, 288-305.
For 1877 to 1937 see entry 6551.

6582 MEYER, ISIDORE S. "Hebrew at Harvard (1636-1760)." AJHSP, 35 (1939), 145-170.

6583 MITCHELL, STEWART. "Henry Adams and some of his students." MHSP, 66 (1936-1941), 294-312.
Harvard, 1870s.

6584 MOE, ALFRED KEANE. A history of Harvard. Cambridge: Harvard Univ., 1896. Pp. 121.
A burlesque.

6585 MOORE, MRS. JAMES LOWELL. "The Fayerweather House." CaHSP, 25 (1938-1939), 86-96.

6586 MOORE, KATHRYN MCDANIEL. "The dilemma of corporal punishment at Harvard College." HistEdQ, 14 (1974), 335-346.
1636-1724.

6587 MORGAN, MORRIS HICKY. "The first Harvard Doctors of Medicine." CSMP, 12 (1908-1909), 312-321.

6588 MORISON, SAMUEL ELIOT. "Academic seniority in colonial Harvard." Harvard Alumni Bulletin, 35 (1933), 576-578.

6589 _____. "A conjectural restoration of the 'old college' at Harvard." OTNE, 23 (1932-1933), 131-158.

6590 _____, ed. The development of Harvard University since the inauguration of President Eliot, 1869-1929. Cambridge: Harvard Univ. Pr., 1930. Pp. xc, 660.

6591 _____. The founding of Harvard College. Cambridge: Harvard Univ. Pr., 1935. Pp. xxvi, 472.

6592 _____. "The great rebellion in Harvard College, and the resignation of President Kirkland." CSMP, 27 (1927-1930), 54-112.
1828.

6593 _____. "Harvard and academic oaths." Harvard Alumni Bulletin, 37 (1935), 682-686.

6594 _____. Harvard College in the seventeenth century. Cambridge: Harvard Univ. Pr., 1936. 2v.

6595 _____. "Harvard degree diplomas." Harvard Alumni Bulletin, 35 (1933), 804-813.

6596 _____. "Harvard in the Colonial Wars, 1675-1748." Harvard Graduates' Magazine, 26 (1918), 554-574.

6597 _____. "The Harvard presidency." NEQ, 31 (1958), 435-446.
Biographical.

6598 _____. "The Harvard School of Astronomy in the seventeenth century." NEQ, 7 (1934), 3-24.

6599 _____. "Harvard seals and arms." Harvard Graduates' Magazine, 42 (1933-1934), 1-15.

6600 _____. "Harvard's past." Harvard Alumni Bulletin, 38 (1935), 265-274.

6601 _____. "Mistress Glover's household furnishings at Cambridge, Massachusetts, 1638-1641." OTNE, 25 (1934-1935), 29-32.

6602 _____. "Precedence at Harvard College in the seventeenth century." AASP, New Ser., 42 (1932), 371-431.
1642-1772, order of names of graduates.

6603 _____. Three centuries of Harvard, 1636-1936. Cambridge: Harvard Univ. Pr., 1936. Pp. viii, 512.

6604 _____. "Virginians and Marylanders at Harvard College in the seventeenth century." WMQ, 2 Ser., 13 (1933), 1-9.

6605 MULLER, JAMES ARTHUR. The Episcopal Theological School, 1867-1943. Cambridge: Episcopal Theological School, 1943. Pp. x, 246.

6606 MUNROE, JAMES PHINNEY. "The Massachusetts Institute of Technology." NEM, New Ser., 27 (1902-1903), 131-158.

6607 [MURRAY, ALBERT N]. The story of Kendall Square, a bit of history concerning the new location of Murray and Emery Company. Cambridge: Murray and Emery, 1916. Pp. 16.

6608 MUSSEY, BARROWS. "Stephen Daye 300 years later." Publishers' Weekly, 134 (December 24, 1938), 2148-2150.
Printer.

6609 NEWELL, WILLIAM. A discourse on the Cambridge church-gathering in 1636; delivered in the First Church, on Sunday, February 22, 1846. Boston: James Munroe, 1846. Pp. 65.

6610 _____. Two discourses delivered before the First Parish in Cambridge; one, upon leaving the old meeting house, and the other, at the dedication of the new. Cambridge: J. Munroe, 1834. Pp. 56.

6611 NICHOLAS, ARTHUR H. "Bells of Harvard College." NEHGR, 65 (1911), 275-284.

6612 "NINETY years of progress." Industry, 33 (September, 1968), 25, 56-57.
Peter Gray Corporation, umbrellas.

6613 NOBLE, JOHN. "Harvard College lotteries." CSMP, 27 (1927-1930), 162-186.

6614 _____. "An old Harvard commencement programme, 1730." CSMP, 6 (1899-1900), 265-278.

6615 _____. "A trial, in 1685, for frequenting the College contrary to law." CSMP, 3 (1895-1897), 448-470.
Harvard.

6616 NORRIS, ALBERT P. "Cambridge land holdings fraud from the proprietors' records of 1635." CaHSP, 22, (1932-1933), 58-79.

6617　NORTON, ARTHUR O.　"Harvard text-books and reference books of the seventeenth century." CSMP, 28 (1930-1933), 361-438.

6618　NORTON, CHARLES ELIOT.　"Reminiscences of old Cambridge." CaHSP, 1 (1905-1906), 11-23.

6619　NOYES, PENELOPE BARKER.　"From Lover's Lane to Sparks Street." CaHSP, 41 (1967-1969), 156-170.
　　　　Neighborhood reminiscences.

6620　NO ENTRY

6621　THE OATH of a free-man..., with a historical study by Lawrence C. Wroth and a note on the Stephen Daye Press by Melbert B. Cary, Jr.　N.Y.: Pr. of the Wooly Whale, 1939. Unpaged.
　　　　Relates to first work printed in British North America; no copies extant.

6622　OLD CAMBRIDGE SHAKESPEARE ASSOCIATION.　The Old Cambridge Shakespeare Association, 1860-1940. Cambridge: Cosmos Pr., 1940. Pp. 75.

6623　O'MALLEY, THOMAS FRANCIS.　"Gallows Hill, the ancient place of execution." CaHSP, 17 (1923-1924), 46-53.

6624　____.　"Old North Cambridge." CaHSP, 20 (1927-1929), 125-135.

6625　ORCUTT, WILLIAM DANA.　"Clubs and club life at Harvard." NEM, New Ser., 6 (1892), 81-98.

6626　OSWALD, JOHN CLYDE.　"Matthew, not Stephen, Day was America's first printer." American Printer, 91 (October, 1930), 63-66.

6627　PAIGE, LUCIUS ROBINSON.　History of Cambridge, Massachusetts, 1630-1877, with a genealogical register. Boston: H. O. Houghton, 1877. Pp. xvi, 731.
　　　　For supplement and index, see entry 6447.

6628　____.　"Stewards at Harvard." MHSP, (1860-1862), 154-160.
　　　　Seventeenth and eighteenth centuries.

6629　PAINTER, NELL.　"Jim Crow at Harvard: 1923." NEQ, 44 (1971), 627-634.
　　　　Exclusion of blacks from freshman dormitories.

6630　PALFREY, SARAH HAMMOND.　"Reminiscences of old Cambridge." National Magazine, 11 (1899-1900), 438-441.

6631　PALMER, FOSTER M.　"Horse car, trolley, and subway." CaHSP, 39 (1961-1963), 78-107.

6632　PALMER, MARY TOWLE.　"Extracts from 'The story of the bee.'" CaHSP, 17 (1923-1924), 63-83.
　　　　Sewing circle.

6633　PARK, CHARLES FRANCIS.　A history of the Lowell Institute School, 1903-1928. Cambridge: Harvard Univ. Pr., 1931. Pp. 192.
　　　　Training in the industrial arts.

6634　PARKER, JOEL.　The Law School of Harvard College. N.Y.: Hurd and Houghton, 1871. Pp. 56.

6635　PARTRIDGE, ALBERT L.　"An early gift of land to Harvard College." OTNE, 40 (1949-1950), 139-145.

6636　PAYSON, WILLIAM L.　"Notes on some Tory Row land titles." CaHSP, 37 (1957-1958), 7-27.
　　　　Eighteenth century.

6637　PEABODY, FRANCIS GREENWOOD.　"The centenary of the Cambridge Book Club." CaHSP, 28 (1942), 109-119.

6638　PEABODY, W. RODMAN.　"The Browne and Nichols School." CaHSP, 22 (1932-1933), 105-112.

6639　PEASE, ARTHUR STANLEY.　"The classics at Harvard in the nineties." HarvLibBul, 11 (1957), 258-267.

6640　PEIRCE, BENJAMIN.　A history of Harvard University, from its foundation, in the year 1636, to the period of the American Revolution. Cambridge: Brown, Shattuck, 1838. Pp. xix, 316, 159.

6641　PEIRCE, BRADFORD K.　"Riverside Press and its founder." Golden Rule Magazine, 4 (1879), 169-179.
　　　　Henry O. Houghton.

6642　PERRIN, PORTER G.　"Possible sources of technologia at early Harvard." NEQ, 7 (1934), 718-724.

6643　PHELPS, REGINALD G.　"150 years of Phi Beta Kappa at Harvard." American Scholar, 1 (1932), 58-64.

6644　PHILLIPS, JAMES DUNCAN.　"The Riverside Press." CaHSP, 19 (1926), 15-31.

6645　PICKERING, EDWARD CHARLES.　Statement of work done at the Harvard College Observatory during the years 1877-1882. Cambridge: J. Wilson and Son, 1882. Pp. 23.

6646　PIER, ARTHUR STANWOOD.　The story of Harvard. Boston: Little, Brown, 1913. Pp. 255.

6647　PIERCE, JOHN.　"Some notes on the Harvard commencements, 1803-1848." MHSP, 2 Ser., 5 (1889-1890), 167-263.
　　　　Edited by Charles C. Smith.

6648　PIPER, ELIZABETH B.　"Memories of the Berkeley Street School." CaHSP, 32 (1946-1948), 30-48.

6649 PORTER, KENNETH WIGGINS. "The Oxford-Cap War at Harvard." NEQ, 14 (1941), 77-83. Student riot, 1842.

6650 PORTER, LUCY KINGSLEY. "The owners of Elmwood." CaHSP, 33 (1949-1950), 58-93. Historic house.

6651 POTTER, ALFRED CLAGHORN. "The Harvard College Library, 1723-1735." CSMP, 25 (1922-1924), 1-13.

6652 _____. and CHARLES KNOWLES BOLTON. The librarians of Harvard College 1667-1877. Cambridge: Library of Harvard Univ., 1897. Pp. 47.

6653 POTTER, ALFRED CLAGHORN. The library of Harvard University: descriptive and historical notes. (1903) 4th ed. Cambridge: Harvard Univ. Pr., 1934. Pp. 186.

6654 POTTINGER, DAVID T. "I, too, in Arcadia." CaHSP, 35 (1953-1954), 111-124. Harvard University.

6655 _____. "Old Cambridge." CaHSP, 22 (1932-1933), 97-104.

6656 _____. "Thirty-eight Quincy Street." CaHSP, 23 (1934-1935), 24-48. Historic house.

6657 POTTS, DAVID B. "The Prospect Union: a conservative quest for social justice." NEQ, 35 (1962), 347-366. Adult education.

6658 POUND, ROSCOE. "The Harvard Law Library." HarvLibBul, 5 (1951), 290-303.

6659 PRENDERGAST, FRANK M. "Sixteen businesses in one." Industry, 19 (March, 1954), 13-16. Carter's Ink Co.

6660 PRESCOTT, SAMUEL CATE. When M.I.T. was 'Boston Tech,' 1861-1916. Cambridge: Technology Pr., 1954. Pp. xviii, 350.

6661 PROSPECT UNION, CAMBRIDGE, MASS. The Prospect Union, 1891-99. Cambridge, 1899. Pp. 68.

6662 QUINCY, JOSIAH, 1772-1864. The history of Harvard University. Cambridge: J. Owen, 1840. 2v.

6663 RADCLIFFE COLLEGE. Radcliffe College, 1879-1929. Cambridge, 1929. Pp. 25. MB.

6664 RAND, CHRISTOPHER. Cambridge, U. S. A.: hub of a new world. N.Y.: Oxford Univ. Pr., 1964. Pp. 195 Has been translated into Russian.

6665 RAND, EDWARD KENNARD. "Liberal education in seventeenth-century Harvard." NEQ, 6 (1933), 525-551.

6666 "RECORDS of the Cambridge Association of Ministers." MHSP, 17 (1879-1880), 262-281. Edited.

6667 REED, CHRISTOPHER. "The march up Tory Row." Harvard Magazine, 77 (September, 1974), 28-37. Insurgency on September 2, 1774.

6668 REED, HELEN LEAH. "Radcliffe College." NEM, New Ser., 11 (1894-1895), 609-624.

6669 RICHARDSON, C. F. "Cambridge on the Charles." Harper's Magazine, 52 (1876), 191-208.

6670 RICHARDSON, WILLIAM A. "The government of Harvard College, past and present." NEHGR, 51 (1897), 26-33.

6671 _____. "Harvard University college presidents and the election of Messrs. Quincy and Eliot." NEHGR, 49 (1895), 59-64.

6672 RICHMOND, HAROLD B. "Cambridge, a pioneer home of electronics." CaHSP, 34 (1951-1952), 111-124.

6673 ROBERTS, C. HOWARD. "100 years at the Riverside Press." Publishers' Weekly, 162 (August 2, 1952), 558-562, 564, 566.

6674 ROBINSON, GEORGE FREDERICK. "How the First Parish in Cambridge got a new meetinghouse." CaHSP, 24 (1936-1937), 49-66.

6675 RODEN, ROBERT F. The Cambridge Press, 1638-1692: a history of the first printing press established in English America, together with a bibliographical list of the issues of the press. N.Y.: Dodd, Mead, 1905. Pp. 193.

6676 ROGERS, MILLARD F., JR. "New England Glass Company marks." Antiques, 89 (1966), 724-729.

6677 _____. "The New England Glass Company: some discoveries." Antiques, 86 (1964), 77-81.

6678 ROGOVIN, GERALD A. "Modern distillery started with oar and drum." Industry, 36 (January, 1971), 21-22. Federal Distillers, Inc.

6679 ROLFE, WILLIAM JAMES and CLARENCE W. AYER, comps. 1858-1908: history of the Cambridge Public Library with the addresses at the celebration of its fiftieth anniversary, lists of its officers, etc. Cambridge, 1908. Pp. 96.

6680 ROSENMEIER, JESPER. "Veritas: the sealing of a promise." HarvLibBul, 16 (1968), 26-37. Origin of Harvard University seal of 1643.

6681 ROTUNDO, BARBARA. "Mount Auburn Cemetery: a proper Boston institution." HarvLibBul, 22 (1974), 268-279.

6682 RYDER, WILLIAM H. "Andover in Cambridge." NEM, New Ser., 41 (1909-1910), 673-679. Andover Theological Seminary.

6683 SAUNDERSON, HENRY HALLAM. "Cambridge, the focal point of Puritan life." CaHSP, 32 (1946-1948), 49-78.

6684 SAUNDERSON, LAURA DUDLEY. "The evolution of Cambridge Heights." CaHSP, 38 (1959-1960), 111-120.

6685 ____. "Forty years in the Fogg Museum." CaHSP, 35 (1953-1954), 57-78.

6686 SCHLESINGER, ELIZABETH BANCROFT. "Two early Harvard wives: Eliza Farrar and Eliza Follen." NEQ, 38 (1965), 147-167.

6687 SCUDDER, WINTHROP SALTONSTALL. The Longfellow Memorial Association, 1882-1922, an historical sketch. Cambridge: [Longfellow Memorial] Association, 1922. Pp. 21.
       Dissolved in 1922.

6688 "THE SEAL and bookmark of Harvard College." AmHist Record, 3 (1874), 464-466.
       Engraved by Nathaniel Hurd.

6689 SEDGWICK, ELLERY. "Second growth in New England: there were real grants in those days." Saturday Review of Literature, 26 (May 22, 1943), 10-12.
       Harvard University in the 1890s.

6690 SESSIONS, RUTH H. "A Harvard man's budget in 1790." Harvard Graduates' Magazine, 42 (1933-1934), 121-147.

6691 SEWARD, JOSIAH LAFAYETTE. "Early Harvard." BSM, 1 (1884), 149-154.

6692 SEYBOLT, ROBERT FRANCIS. "Student expenses at Harvard, 1772-1776." CSMP, 28 (1930-1933), 301-305.

6693 ____. "Student libraries at Harvard, 1763-1764." CSMP, 28 (1930-1933), 449-460.

6694 SHARPLES, STEPHEN PASCHALL. "The Lawrence Scientific School." CaHSP, 4 (1909), 79-86.
       Harvard University.

6695 SHERMAN, CHARLES WINSLOW. "Fort Washington." Technology Review, 61 (January, 1959), 150-152.

6696 SHILLABER, CAROLINE. Massachusetts Institute of Technology School of Architecture and Planning, 1861-1961: a hundred year chronicle. Cambridge: Massachusetts Institute of Technology, 1963. Pp. 134.

6697 SIBLEY, JOHN LANGDON. "Catalogues of Harvard University." MHSP, (1864-1865), 9-75.
       1674-1865.

6698 SIBLEY'S Harvard graduates: biographical sketches of those who attended Harvard College.... John Langdon Sibley and Clifford K. Shipton, eds. Boston: Massachusetts Historical Society, 1873-19--.
       Sibley edited the first three volumes, and Shipton edited volumes four through sixteen.

6699 SIMPSON, ALAN. "A candle in the corner: how Harvard College got the Hopkins Legacy." CSMP, 43 (1956-1963), 304-324.

6700 SIMPSON, LEWIS P. "'The Literary Miscellany' and 'The General Repository': two Cambridge periodicals of the early republic." Library Chronicle of the University of Texas, 3 (1947-1950), 177-190.

6701 [SIMPSON, SOPHIA SHUTTLEWORTH]. Two hundred years ago; or, a brief history of Cambridgeport and East Cambridge, with notices of some of the early settlers, a Christmas and birthday gift for young persons. Boston: Otis Clapp, 1859. Pp. vi, 111.
       Critical and explanatory notes to this work, by Thomas F. O'Malley, appear in CaHSP, 16 (1922), 69-96.

6702 "SKETCHES of the publishers: Riverside Press [and Hurd & Houghton]. Round Table, 3 (1866), 281-283.

6703 SMALL, BESSIE EVELYN. A history of St. Peter's Episcopal Church, Cambridge, Massachusetts, 1842-1942. Boston: Libbie Printing, 1942. Pp. 40.

6704 THE SOCIETY for the Collegiate Instruction of Women, commonly called 'the Harvard Annex.' The story of its beginning and growth, its organization and present supporters.... Cambridge: W. H. Wheeler, 1891. Pp. 50.
       Radcliffe College.

6705 SPALDING, ELIOT B. "The founder and three editors of the Cambridge Chronicle." CaHSP, 36 (1955-1956), 107-121.

6706 SPALDING, WALTER RAYMOND. Music at Harvard: a historical review of men and events. N.Y.: Coward-McCann, 1935. Pp. xiv, 310.

6707 STARKEY, LAWRENCE G. "Benefactors of the Cambridge Press: a reconsideration." Studies in Bibliography, 3 (1950-1951), 267-270.

6708 ____. "The printing by the Cambridge Press of 'A platform of church discipline, 1649.'" Studies in Bibliography, 2 (1949-1950), 79-93.

6709 STEARNS, FRANK PRESTON. Cambridge sketches. Philadelphia: J. B. Lippincott, 1905. Pp. 374.
       Biography.

6710 STEELE, CHAUNCEY DEPEW, JR. "A history of inns and hotels in Cambridge." CaHSP, 37 (1957-1958), 29-44.

6711 STERN, MADELEINE B. "Hilliard, Gray & Company: booksellers to the University." Publishers' Weekly, 15 (October 19, 1946), 2380-2388.

6712 STEVENS, EDMUND H. "Cambridge physicians I have known." CaHSP, 20 (1927-1929), 103-109.

6713 STEVENS, THOMAS W. "[Bruce Rogers and his Riverside Press books]." Inland Printer, 30 (1902-1903), 900-904.

6714 STEVENSON, EARL PLACE. 'Scatter acorns that oaks may grow,' Arthur D. Little, Inc., 1886-1953. N.Y.: Newcomen Society in North America, 1953. Pp. 32.

6715 STIGER, EDWIN T. "Old 'Tory Row.'" NEM, 50 (1913-1914), 479-480, 485-488, 493-494. Brattle Street.

6716 STIMPSON, MARY STOYELL. "Harvard Lampoon: its founders and contributors." NEM, New Ser., 35 (1906-1907), 579-590.

6717 STOREY, MOORFIELD. Harvard in the sixties: address...before the Harvard Memorial Society at Sanders Theater, Cambridge, April 3, 1896. Boston: Mills, Knight, 1896. Pp. 24. MB.

6718 STORY, JOSEPH. An address delivered on the dedication of the cemetery at Mount Auburn, September 24, 1831, to which is added an appendix, containing a historical notice and description of the place, with a list of the present subscribers. Boston: J. T. & E. Buckingham, 1831. Pp. 32.

6719 THE STORY of Harvard, a short history. Cambridge: University Information Center, 1964. Pp. 33.

6720 THE STORY of Harvard University Press, told by a friend, being an informal history on the occasion of the fiftieth anniversary of its founding. Cambridge, [1963?]. Unpaged.

6721 SUTHERLAND, ARTHUR EUGENE. "The Harvard Law School's four oldest houses." CaHSP, 41 (1967-1969), 117-131.

6722 _____. "A house and three centuries." CaHSP, 37 (1957-1958), 65-74. Nichols-Lee House.

6723 _____. The law at Harvard; a history of ideas and men, 1817-1967. Cambridge: Harvard Univ. Pr., 1967. Pp. xv, 408.

6724 SWAN, BRADFORD FULLER. "Some thoughts on the Bay Psalm Book of 1640, with a census of copies." Yale University Library Gazette, 22 (1947-1948), 49-76.

6725 SWIFT, LINDSAY. "A course in history at Harvard College in the seventies." MHSP, 52 (1918-1919), 69-77. Henry Adams' course in American history, 1876-1877.

6726 TAYLOR, CHARLES L. "The story of the Episcopal Theological School." CaHSP, 36 (1955-1956), 7-21.

6727 THAYER, WILLIAM ROSCOE. "George Washington in Cambridge." MHSP, 52 (1918-1919), 146-148. 1775.

6728 _____. "John Harvard and the early college." NEM, New Ser., 25 (1901-1902), 131-146. Harvard College.

6729 "THREE hundred years of printing." Industry, 3 (May, 1938), 29-31, 48. The University Press.

6730 "THE THREE original churches of Cambridge." HistMag, 2 Ser., 4 (1868), 140-142. Signed: F.A.W.

6731 TILLINGHAST, WILLIAM HOPKINS, comp. A bundle of statistics relating to the graduates of Harvard University, gathered for the two hundred and fiftieth anniversary, November 5-8, 1886. [Cambirdge?, 1886]. Unpaged.

6732 TODD, EDGELEY WOODMAN. "Philosophical ideas at Harvard College, 1817-1837." NEQ, 16 (1943), 63-90.

6733 TOLL, CHARLES HANSEN. Cambridge land owned in 1635 by certain early settlers. Amherst: Priv. Print., 1963. 44 leaves.

6734 TREAT, PRISCILLA GOUGH. "College redbooks and the changing social mores." CaHSP, 41 (1967-1969), 141-155. Radcliffe freshman handbooks.

6735 TURNER, HOWARD M. "The Cambridge water supply." New England Waterworks Association. Journal, 66 (1952), 142-166. 1856-1951.

6736 "THE UNITED-Carr Fastener Corporation." Industry, 4 (June, 1939), 7-9.

6737 THE UNIVERSITY PRESS, CAMBRIDGE, MASS. Stephen Daye and his successors: the establishment of a printing plant in what was formerly British North America and the development of the art of printing at the University Press, of Cambridge, Massachusetts, 1639-1921. Cambridge, 1921. Pp. 49.

6738 UNTERMEYER, LOUIS. A century of candymaking, 1847-1947; the story of the origin and growth of New England Confectionery Company which parallels that of the candy industry in America. n.p., [1947]. Pp. 84.

6739 VAILLE, FREDERICK OZNI and HENRY ALDEN CLARK, comps. The Harvard Book: a series of historical, biographical and descriptive sketches. Cambridge: Welch, Bigelow, 1875. 2v.

6740 WAGNER, CHARLES ABRAHAM. Harvard: four centuries and freedoms. N.Y.: Dutton, 1950. Pp. 326.

6741 WALCOTT, HENRY P. "Some Cambridge physicians." CaHSP, 16 (1922), 110-131.

6742 WALDO, FRANK. "Cambridge: historic, literary, scientific." Education, 23 (1903), 559-568.

6743 WALL, ROBERT EMMET, JR. "A new look at Cambridge." JAH, 52 (1965-1966), 599-605. Suffrage.

6744 WALTON, CLARENCE ELDON. An historical prospect of Harvard College, 1636-1936. Boston: Society for the Preservation of New England Antiquities, 1936. Pp. 48.

6745 _____. The three-hundredth anniversary of the Harvard College Library. Cambridge: Harvard College Library, 1939. Pp. iv, 46.

6746 WARREN, CHARLES. History of the Harvard Law School and of early legal conditions in America. N.Y.: Lewis Publishing, 1908. 3v.

6747 "WARREN Brothers Company." Industry, 1 (August, 1936), 7-9.
      Pavements, asphalt, macadam, etc.

6748 "THE WASHINGTON Elm, Cambridge." OTNE, 14 (1923-1924), 143-146.

6749 WATKINS, LURA WOODSIDE. Cambridge glass, 1818 to 1888: the story of the New England Glass Company. Boston: Marshall Jones, 1930. Pp. xxi, 199.

6750 _____. "Early glass pressing at Cambridge and Sandwich." Antiques, 28 (1935), 151-152, 242-243.

6751 WAY, W. IRVING. "The Riverside Press and Mr. Bruce Rogers." Inland Printer, 26 (1900-1901), 264-267.

6752 WELLS, JAMES ALVORD. Short history of the Old Cambridge Photographic Club. Boston, 1905. Pp. 43. MH.

6753 WEST, EMORY J. "Harvard and the Black man, 1635-1850: the first stages of struggle." Harvard Bulletin, 74 (November 22, 1971), 21-26.

6754 WHEELOCK, LOVEJOY AND CO., INC. 100 years of continuous service to industry, 1846-1946. n.p., [1946?]. Pp. 45. MB.
      Iron and steel.

6755 WHEELWRIGHT, JOHN BROOKS. "The Valentine-Fuller House." OTNE, 28 (1937-1938), 68-71.

6756 WHEELWRIGHT, JOHN TYLER. Lines read at the centennial celebration of the Hasty Pudding Club of Harvard College, 1795-1895. Boston: Little, Brown, 1896. Pp. 20. MB.

6757 WHITE, NORMAN HILL, JR. "Printing in Cambridge since 1800." CaHSP, 15 (1920-1921), 16-23.

6758 WHITEHILL, WALTER MUIR. "Edward Everett sinks the Harvard navy." Harvard Lampoon, 145 ([December], 1956), 30-31, 54-56.
      Custom of assigning high naval rank to seniors of the lowest academic standing.

6759 WHITING, CHARLES F. "Francis Avenue and the Norton Estate: the development of a community." CaHSP, 41 (1967-1969), 16-39.

6760 WHITMAN, EDMUND ALLEN. The Cambridge idea in temperance reform and Massachusetts laws dealing with drunkenness. Boston: Geo. H. Ellis, 1893. Pp. 35. MH.

6761 WILDER, CATHARINE KERLIN. "Eighty-five aromatic years in Harvard Square." CaHSP, 41 (1967-1969), 105-116.
      Leavitt & Peirce, tobacconists.

6762 WILLIAMS, EDWIN EVERITT. "The Metcalf administration, 1937-1955." HarvLibBul, 17 113-130.
      Keyes D. Metcalf as librarian of Harvard.

6763 WILLIAMS, GEORGE HUNTSTON, ed. The Harvard Divinity School: its place in Harvard University and in American culture. Boston: Beacon Pr., 1954. Pp. xvi, 366.

6764 WINSHIP, GEORGE PARKER. The Cambridge Press, 1638-1692, a reëxamination of the evidence concerning the Bay Psalm Book and the Eliot Indian Bible, as well as other contemporary books and people. Philadelphia: Univ. of Pennsylvania Pr., 1945. Pp. ix, 385.

6765 _____. "A document concerning the first Anglo-American press." The Library, 4 Ser., 20 (1939-1940), 51-70.
      Stephen Daye Press.

6766 _____. "Facts and fancies about the Cambridge Press." Colophon, New Ser., 3 (1938), 531-557.

6767 _____. "The first press in English America." Gutenberg Jahrbuch, (1939), 291-294.

6768 WINTERICH, JOHN T. "Harvard's press marks half century of publishing." Publishers' Weekly, 183 (April 22, 1963), 14-21.

6769 WINTHROP, ROBERT CHARLES. "Reminiscences of a night passed in the library of Harvard College." MHSP, 2 Ser., 3 (1886-1887), 216-218. 1834.

6770 WOOD, JOHN W. "Cambridgeport: a brief history." CaHSP, 35 (1953-1954), 79-89.

6771 _____. "Some aspects of the East Cambridge story." CaHSP, 36 (1955-1956), 93-105.

6772 WOODWORTH, JAY BACKUS. "The origin and nature of the old gravestones of the Cambridge Burial Yard." CaHSP, 17 (1923-1924), 28-41.

6773 WRIGHT, GEORGE GRIER. "Early Cambridge newspapers." CaHSP, 20 (1927-1929), 84-90.

6774 _____. "The schools of Cambridge, 1800-1870." CaHSP, 13 (1918), 89-112.

6775 YOUNG, WILLIAM J. "The history and restoration of the wallpaper in the Emerson House in Cambridge." CaHSP, 39 (1961-1963), 50-54.

CANTON

6776   AMES, ELLIS, comp. History of the Redman
        Farm, so called, and of the title thereto,
situate in Canton, Norfolk County, Massachusetts.
Boston: W. Bense, 1870. Pp. 32.

6777   BROWN, THERON. The Canton Baptist Memorial,
        being a historical discourse delivered be-
fore the Baptist Church in Canton, Mass. at the
celebration of their fiftieth anniversary, Wednesday, June 22, 1864. Boston: G. C. Rand & Avery,
1865. Pp. vi, 89, 29.

6778   BURKE, GERALD F. 150 years of yesterdays.
        Canton, 1947. Pp. 32. MBNEH.

6779   CANTON, MASS. 175TH ANNIVERSARY COMMITTEE.
        175th anniversary, Canton, a recollection.
n.p., [1972]. Pp. 18. M.

6780   CANTON. Boston: Edison Electric Illuminat-
        ing Co., 1909. Pp. 16. M.

6781   CANTON HIGH SCHOOL ASSOCIATION. Alumni Reg-
        ister 1869-1896. Prepared by a committee.
Boston: Washington Pr., 1897. Pp. 66. M.
        Includes biographical sketches of teachers.

6782   CHEIMETS, SHEILA. Canton industry–now and
        then. Canton: Canton 175th anniversary
committee, [1972]. Unpaged. M.

6783   ENDICOTT, CHARLES. Centennial celebration
        at Canton, Mass.: historical address. Bos-
ton: W. Bense, 1876. Pp. 47.
        Historical sketch of the town.

6784   GALVIN, E. D. "The Canton Viaduct." Rail-
        road History, No. 129 (1973), 71-85.

6785   HARLOW, SAMUEL ALLEN. One hundred years in
        the life of a church: historical sermon,
June 10, 1928, in commemoration of the organization
of the Evangelical Congregational Church. n.p.,
[1928]. Pp. 22.

6786   HUNTOON, DANIEL THOMAS VOSE. "The Doty Tav-
        ern." Potter's AmMo, 7 (1876), 24-26.

6787   _____. History of the town of Canton, Nor-
        folk County, Massachusetts. Cambridge: J.
Wilson and Son, 1893. Pp. xiv, 666.

6788   _____. "The old English Church in Canton,
        Mass." NEHGR, 29 (1875), 73-81.

6789   _____. "The powder-mill in Canton." NEHGR,
        31 (1877), 272-276.

6790   STIMPSON, MARY STOYELL. "Canton among the
        Blue Hills." NEM, New Ser., 34 (1906), 111-
128.

6791   TEDESCO, PAUL H. Economic change and the
        community: Canton, Massachusetts, 1797-
1965. Braintree: D. H. Mark, 1970. Pp. iv, 34.

CARLISLE

6792   BULL, SIDNEY AUGUSTUS. History of the town
        of Carlisle, Massachusetts, 1754-1920; with
biographical sketches of prominent persons. Cambridge: Murray Printing, 1920. Pp. xi, 365.

6793   LAPHAM, DONALD A. Carlisle, composite com-
        munity: historical facts concerning the
settlers in present Carlisle, Massachusetts, in the
colonial period. n.p., [1970?]. Pp. ix, 86.
MBNEH.

6794   TWISS, JAMES J. A discourse upon the history
        of the establishment of the First Parish in
Carlisle, Massachusetts, delivered...February 23,
1879. Lowell: Stone, Bacheller & Livingston, 1879.
Pp. 21.

6795   WILKINS, MRS. BENSON PERLEY. "The century-
        old houses of Carlisle, Massachusetts."
OTNE, 23 (1932-1933), 45-55.

CARVER

6796   GRIFFITH, HENRY S. History of the town of
        Carver, Massachusetts: historical review,
1637-1910. New Bedford: E. Anthony & Sons, 1913.
Pp. xiii, 366.

6797   MOORE, BETSY THANKFUL. The well sweep.
        Silver Lake: J. W. McCue, 1950. Pp. 95.
Benjamin Hammond House.

6798   MURDOCK, W. B. Cast iron and cranberries.
        n.p., [1937?]. 2 leaves. MBNEH.
South Carver.

CHARLEMONT

6799   BIRD, IVY MANNING. "My memories of Zoar."
        Rowe HSB, 9 (Winter, 1972), 19-20.

6800   CHARLEMONT, MASS. One hundred fiftieth anni-
        versary, Charlemont, Massachusetts, official
programme and historical sketch, 1765-1915. Springfield: Loring-Axtell, [1915?]. Unpaged. MDeeP.

6801   CHARLEMONT, MASS. 200TH ANNIVERSARY COMMIT-
        TEE. Charlemont 200th anniversary, 1765-
1965. n.p., [1965?]. Pp. 10. MDeeP.

6802   HAWKS, HELEN A. "Some reminiscences of
        Charlemont history." PVMA, 3 (1890-1898),
139-154.

6803   HEALY, ALLAN. Charlemont, Massachusetts,
        frontier village and hill town. Charlemont:
The Town, 1965. Pp. xi, 222.

6804   [_____]. Hall Tavern, the tale of an old
        inn. Evanston, Ill.: Pocumtuck Pr., 1939.
Pp. 11.
        Moved from Charlemont to Deerfield in 1947.

6805 JOHNSON, JONATHAN. An ancient township: historically sacred places still need to be marked in Charlemont, a paper read at the old oak tree gathering of August, 1893. n.p., [1893?]. Pp. 3.

6806 OLD FOLKS' ASSOCIATION OF CHARLEMONT, MASS. Sketch of the origin and growth of the Association. R. W. Field, Kate Upson Clark, and E. C. Hawks, comps. Greenfield, 1883. Pp. 65.

6807 "ROWE'S neighbors and the road that goes their way." Rowe HSB, 6 (Summer, 1969), entire issue.

6808 TAYLOR, ISADORE P. "Memories of Hall Tavern." PVMA, 7 (1921-1929), 526-532.

6809 TRUESDELL, LEON E. "The Truesdell sawmill in Zoar, 1886-1901." Rowe HSB, 7 (Summer, 1970), 9-15.

6810 WHITE, JOSEPH. Charlemont as a plantation: an historical discourse at the centennial anniversary of the death of Moses Rice, the first settler of the town, delivered at Charlemont, Mass., June 11, 1855. Boston: T. R. Marvin & Son, 1858. Pp. 48.

CHARLTON

6811 CHARLTON, MASS. Address at the dedication of the Dexter Memorial Town Hall, Charlton, Mass. by Hon. Charles J. McIntire, Tuesday, February the twenty-first, 1905; with exercises, and an appendix. n.p., [1906]. Pp. 84.

6812 COCHRAN, JOHN M. "Old Charlton taverns." QHSL, 3, No. 5, 53-63.

6813 DODGE, RUFUS B. Historical sketch, read, in part, at the third annual reunion of the present and past residents of Charlton, at Charlton, Sept. 4, 1899. Boston: Weymouth Publishing, 1899. Pp. 76.

6814 HAVEN, JOHN. Historical address, delivered in Charlton, July 4, 1876. Southbridge: Journal Print, 1876. Pp. 17.
    Brief sketch of town history.

6815 KING, WILLIAM H. "Charlton in the Civil War." QHSL, 1, No. 16, 201-204.

6816 LITTLE, NINA FLETCHER. "The General Salem Towne House at Old Sturbridge Village." Antiques, 75 (1959), 358-365.
    Built 1796, moved to Old Sturbridge Village in 1952.

6817 SPINNEY, FRANK O. "Chapman Lee, country cabinet maker." NEG, 1 (Winter, 1960), 34-38.

6818 _____. "A tale of two mirrors." NEG, 1 (Summer, 1959), 20-22.
    In home of Salem Towne, Jr.; house moved to Old Sturbridge Village in 1952.

6819 TITUS, ANSON. Charlton historical sketches. Southbridge: G. M. Whitaker, 1877. Pp. 28.

CHATHAM

6820 BALLOU, G. H. "Monomy." Harper's Magazine, 28 (1864), 305-311.
    Reminiscences.

6821 "BEACONS of Cape Cod, Chatham Light." CCB, 48 (Late July, 1937), 11.

6822 "BEACONS of Cape Cod, Monomoy Point." CCB, 48 (March, 1937), 21-22.

6823 BEARSE, CLARKSON P. The tragedy of Monomoy Beach, the graveyard of the Atlantic.... Harwich: Goss Print, 1943. Pp. 70.

6824 CHATHAM, MASS. The two hundredth anniversary of the incorporation of the town of Chatham, Massachusetts; a memorial or report of the celebration of August 1st and 2nd, 1912, and of the Sunday services August 4th, 1912. [Chatham]: The Town Celebration Committee, 1913. Pp. 119.

6825 CHATHAM HISTORICAL SOCIETY. Houses built in Chatham 1825 or before. West Harwich: Jack Viall, 1967. Pp. 32. MWA.

6826 _____. Interesting old Chatham houses. [West Harwich?, Jack Viall?], 1964. Pp. 32. MWA.

6827 _____. Some early Chatham homes. West Harwich: Jack Viall, 1965. Pp. 31. MWA.

6828 _____. Some more old Chatham houses. West Harwich: Jack Viall, 1963. Pp. 36. MWA.

6829 _____. Some old Chatham houses. West Harwich: Jack Viall, [1962]. Pp. 31. MWA.

6830 CROSBY, A. MORRIS. "Wreck of the tanker 'Pendleton.'" HistNan, 15 (July, 1967), 5-7.

6831 GUILD, ALICE WALKER. History of the First Methodist Church, Chatham, Massachusetts. [Hyannis]: Patriot Pr., 1949. Pp. 29. [MChaE].

6832 HAMILTON, THOMAS, JR. Some account of the small-pox, in the town of Chatham, in the year 1766. n.p., 1769. Pp. 7.

6833 HAWES, JAMES WILLIAM. Historical address delivered by James W. Hawes, August 1, 1912, on the occasion of the celebration of the 200th anniversary of the incorporation of Chatham, confined chiefly to the period before 1860. Yarmouthport: C. W. Swift, 1912. Pp. 38.

6834 HENDERSON, ELEANOR. Short history of transportation in Chatham. n.p., n.d. Unpaged. MWA.

6835 LINCOLN, JOSEPH CROSBY. "The saving of a landmark." Cape Cod Magazine, 8 (August 1, 1926), 5-6, 24.
    Atwood House.

6836 MITCHELL, HENRY. A chapter in the physical
history of the coast, being a report to
Prof. Benj. Pierce...concerning Chatham and the
peninsula at Monomoy. Boston: Wright and Potter,
1873. Pp. 17. MB.
Bound with the Boston Public Library copy is
the 'Report of Professor Mitchell; additional particulars concerning the changes in the
neighborhood of Chatham and Monomoy' which
is pages 69-80 of the 8th annual report of
the Massachusetts Board of Harbor Commissioners dated January 1874.

6837 [MITCHELL, HENRY]. Monomoy and its shoals.
Boston: Wright & Potter Printing, 1887.
Pp. 14.

6838 ROGERS, FRED B. "Dr. Samuel Lord and the
smallpox epidemic of 1765-66 at Chatham,
Massachusetts." NEJMed, 276 (1967), 322-324.

6839 SMITH, WILLIAM CHRISTOPHER. Congregational
Church in Chatham 1720-1920: historical address on the two hundredth anniversary of the organization of the church. [Chatham]: Chatham Monitor Print, 1920. Pp. 31.

6840 SMITH, WILLIAM CHRISTOPHER. A history of
Chatham, Massachusetts, formerly the con-
stablewick or village of Monomoit. Hyannis: F. B.
& F. P. Goss, 1909-1947. 4v.
Volume 4 has imprint: [Chatham]: Chatham
Historical Society.

6841 SOUTHWORTH, MURIEL C. "Yesterday at Monomoy." CCC, 20 (1967), 92-95.

6842 STEELE, GEORGE B. "The old grist mill."
Cape Cod Magazine, 1 (November, 1915), 25.

CHELMSFORD

6843 ALLEN, GEORGE H. Centennial address, delivered on the one hundredth anniversary of
the organization of the First Baptist Church, South
Chelmsford, Mass., with the poem written by Mrs.
M. B. C. Slade, with the original hymns, and an account of the centennial celebration. Lowell: Marden & Rowell, 1871. Pp. 33.

6844 ALLEN, WILKES. The history of Chelmsford,
from its origin in 1653, to the year 1820--
together with an historical sketch of the church,
and biographical notices of the four first pastors,
to which is added a memoir of the Pawtuckett tribe
of Indians. Haverhill: P. N. Green, 1820.
Pp. 192.

6845 CHELMSFORD, MASS. Chelmsford, Massachusetts:
proceedings at the celebration of the 250th
anniversary of the incorporation of the town, May
28, 29, 30, 31, 1905; report of the committee of
arrangements. Wilson Waters, ed. n.p., [1905].
Pp. 83.

6846 COWLEY, CHARLES. "John Eliot's work at Wamesit." ORHAL, 6 (1896-1904), 220-233.

6847 CUMINGS, IDA F. "Chelmsford." Lowell HSC,
2 (1921-1926), 131-136.

6848 [DALTON, CHARLES HENRY]. A wintersnight
tale. Boston: D. B. Updike, 1904. Pp. 21.
Reminiscences.

6849 DURHAM, MILDRED M. "Chelmsford." Lowell
HSC, 2 (1921-1926), 124-130.

6850 PARKHURST, ELEANOR. "Poor relief in a Massachusetts village in the eighteenth century."
Social Service Review, 11 (1937), 446-464.

6851 PERHAM, HENRY SPAULDING. "The early schools
of Chelmsford." ORHAL, 4 (1888-1891), 217-
235.

6852 _____. "The Wamesit Purchase." ORHAL, 6
(1896-1904), 125-147.

6853 STONE, ZINA EUGENE. "Before the power-loom,
the earliest cotton and woolen industries at
East Chelmsford and vicinity, and their promoters."
ORHAL, 6 (1896-1904), 46-74.

6854 WATERS, WILSON. History of Chelmsford, Massachusetts. Lowell: Courier-Citizen, 1917.
Pp. xiv, 893.
First chapter was written by Henry S. Perham before his death in 1906.

6855 _____. Sunday, July 15, 1860--Sunday, July
15, 1900, historical sketch of the founding
of All Saints' Church, Chelmsford, Mass.... Lowell: Courier-Citizen, [1900?]. Unpaged. MBNEH.

CHELSEA

6856 ADAMS, JOHN G. B. "The Massachusetts Soldiers' Home." NEM, New Ser., 2 (1890), 689-
697.

6857 CARY, THOMAS GREAVES. Gold from California,
and its effect on prices, a lecture, delivered at North Chelsea, Massachusetts, March 25th,
1856, with some reminiscences of the place. N.Y.:
George W. Wood, 1856. Pp. 20.

6858 CHAMBERLAIN, MELLEN, ed. A documentary his-
tory of Chelsea, including the Boston pre-
cincts of Winnisimmet, Rumney Marsh, and Pullen
Point, 1624-1824. Boston: Massachusetts Historical
Society, 1908. 2v.
Prepared for the press after the death of
the author by Jenny C. Watts and William R.
Cutter.

6859 CHELSEA, MASS. Roll of honor of the city of
Chelsea, a list of the soldiers and sailors
who served on the quota of Chelsea, in the great
Civil War for the preservation of the Union from
1861 to 1865, with a partial record of each man...
also an appendix including the names of Chelsea men
who served to the credit of other states, cities and
towns. Chelsea: H. Mason & Son, 1880. Pp. 213.
Biographies.

6860 CHELSEA, MASS. CENTRAL CONGREGATIONAL CHURCH. The manual of the Central Congregational Church in Chelsea, Mass.... Boston: Alfred Mudge & Son, 1878. Pp. 115.
Includes historical sketch.

6861 CHELSEA, MASS. FIRST CONGREGATIONAL CHURCH. Manual of the First Congregational Church, Chelsea, Mass., containing a historical sketch, a form of admission to the church...a form for the baptism of children, with the regulations and a catalogue of members to January 3, 1875. Boston: J. A. Butler, 1875. Pp. 73.

6862 CHELSEA, MASS. ST. LUKE'S CHURCH. The Parish Church of Chelsea, Massachusetts; St. Luke's, Washington Avenue, 1840-1930. Chelsea: Pike & Co., 1930. Pp. 72.

6863 CHELSEA, MASS. THIRD CONGREGATIONAL CHURCH. Historical sketch, articles of faith and covenant, and regulations of the Third Congregational Church, with a list of officers and members of church and sabbath school, to March 12, 1878. Boston: J. A. Butler, 1878. Pp. 23.

6864 CHELSEA. Boston: Edison Electric Illuminating Co., 1909. Pp. 28. M.

6865 FREEMASONS. CHELSEA, MASS. ROYAL ARCH MASONS. CHAPTER OF THE SHEKINAH. Fiftieth anniversary of the Royal Arch 'Chapter of the Shekinah,' Chelsea, Mass., January 31st, 1906; poem by comp. Rev. R. Perry Bush, historical address by R. E. Comp. Edwin S. Crandon. Chelsea: Charles H. Pike, 1906. Pp. 31. MB.

6866 ____. Twenty-fifth anniversary of the Royal Arch 'Chapter of the Shekinah,' Chelsea, Mass., December 30, 1880.... Boston: Rockwell and Churchill, 1881. Pp. 50.

6867 FREEMASONS. CHELSEA, MASS. STAR OF BETHLEHEM LODGE. 21st anniversary of Star of Bethlehem Lodge, address, by Charles H. Leonard; poem, by B. P. Shillaber. Boston, 1865. Pp. 42.

6868 GILLESPIE, CHARLES BANCROFT. The city of Chelsea, Massachusetts...her history, her achievements, her opportunities. Chelsea: Chelsea Gazette, 1898. Pp. 203.

6869 HAWES, LLOYD E. "Hugh Cornwall Robertson and the Chelsea period." Antiques, 89 (1966), 409-413.
Pottery, 1866-1895.

6870 LAMB, FRED WILLIAM. "Battle of Chelsea Creek." Granite Mo, 50 (1918), 120-121.
May 27, 1775.

6871 LANGWORTHY, ISAAC PENDLETON. A historical discourse, delivered at Chelsea, Mass., Sept. 20, 1866, at the twenty-fifth anniversary of the Winnisimmet Congregational Church. Chelsea: J. A. Butler, 1866. Pp. 47.

6872 MCCLINTOCK, WILLIAM E. "Chelsea." BSM, 1 (1884), 107-128.

6873 ____. "The new Chelsea." NEM, New Ser., 42 (1910), 15-25.

6874 PRATT, WALTER MERRIAM. The burning of Chelsea. Boston: Sampson Publishing, 1908. Pp. 149.

6875 ____. Seven generations: a story of Prattville and Chelsea. Norwood: Priv. Print., 1930. Pp. xiii, 419.

6876 SCANLAN, MICHAEL JAMES. An historical sketch of St. Rose, Chelsea, Massachusetts. Chelsea, 1927. Pp. 119.

6877 SMITH, THOMAS P. Spice mill on the marsh. Norfolk Downs: Pneumatic Scale Corp., 1925. Pp. 37. MB.
D & L Slade Company.

6878 TITSWORTH, ADONIRAM JUDSON. Fifteen years: an historical sermon covering the years 1866-1881, delivered at Chelsea, Mass., Sept. 18, 1881, at the fortieth anniversary of the First (Winnisimmet) Congregational Church. Boston: T. Todd, 1881. Pp. 31. M.

6879 WATKINS, LURA WOODSIDE. "Low's art tiles." Antiques, 45 (1944), 250-252.
John Gardner Low, nineteenth century.

CHESHIRE

6880 BARKER, J. M. "Early settlements in Cheshire." BHSSC, 1, Pt. 2, (1889), 63-108.

6881 CHESHIRE, MASS. METHODIST CHURCH. Centennial booklet, the Methodist Church, Cheshire, Massachusetts, July 9-16, 1944. n.p., [1944?]. Unpaged. MB.
Includes brief history by Muriel E. Andrews.

6882 CHESHIRE, MASS. SAINT MARY OF THE ASSUMPTION PARISH. Anniversaries...fiftieth church dedication, fifth parish foundation 1879 [and] 1931. n.p., [1931?]. Unpaged. MPB

6883 THE COLE House and its Masonic emblems. n.p., n.d. Unpaged. MPB.

6884 HARMON, BETSEY B. "New Providence, or Stafford's Hill." Berkshire Hills, 1 (Sept. 1, 1900), [9].

6885 "MASONIC blue lodges in Berkshire County, sketch history number one: Franklin Lodge of Stafford's Hill, or Cheshire." Berkshire Hills, 1 (Dec. 1, 1900), [1-3].

6886 MELLQUIST, ORVILLE KENNETH. The growth of a church: the drama of a century and a half at the Cheshire Baptist Church. Cheshire Baptist Church. Cheshire, 1940. 28 leaves. MPB.

6887 RAYNOR, ELLEN M. and EMMA L. PETITCLERC. History of the town of Cheshire, Berkshire County, Mass. Holyoke: Clark W. Bryan, 1885. Pp. 214.

6888 REYNOLDS, STEPHEN D. Brief history of Cheshire, Massachusetts, 1968. Cheshire: 175 Anniversary Committee, 1968. Pp. 48. M.

6889 "STAFFORD'S Hill." Berkshire Hills, 1 (Dec. 1, 1900), [9-11].

6890 "[STAFFORD'S Hill, Massachusetts]." Narraganset Historical Register, 7 (1889), 227-229.

CHESTER

6891 COPELAND, ALFRED MINOTT. A history of the town of Murrayfield, earlier known as Township No. 9, and comprising the present towns of Chester and Huntington, the northern part of Montgomery, and the southeast corner of Middlefield, 1760-1763. Springfield: C. W. Bryan, 1892. Pp. 175.

6892 _____. "History of Township Number Nine, formerly called Murrayfield, more lately Chester." CVHSP, 2 (1882-1903), 41-65.

CHESTERFIELD

6893 CHESTERFIELD, MASS. One hundred and fiftieth anniversary of the incorporation of Chesterfield, Mass., 1762-1912. Springfield: F. A. Bassette, 1912. Pp. 16. MNF.

6894 CHESTERFIELD, MASS. BICENTENNIAL CELEBRATION COMMITTEE. Two-hundredth anniversary of the incorporation of Chesterfield, Mass., 1762-1962. Northampton: Gazette Printing, [1962?]. Pp. 72.

6895 CHESTERFIELD, MASS. BICENTENNIAL GENEALOGY COMMITTEE. History and genealogy of the families of Chesterfield, Massachusetts, 1762-1962. [Chesterfield, 1963?]. Pp. 427.

CHICOPEE

6896 "A. G. Spalding & Bros." Industry, 4 (May, 1939), 7-10. Sporting goods.

6897 BELCHER, BILDAD B. Semi-centennial of the Chicopee Falls Congregational Sabbath School, 1830-1880, an address, delivered...December 12, 1880. Springfield: Springfield Printing, 1881. Pp. 51.

6898 BURNHAM, COLLINS G. "The city of Chicopee." NEM, New Ser., 18 (1898), 361-379.

6899 CHICOPEE, MASS. FIRST CONGREGATIONAL CHURCH. One hundred fiftieth anniversary, First Congregational Church, Chicopee, Massachusetts, September 28 and 29, 1902. Canaan Four Corners, N.Y.: Connecticut Valley Congregationalist, 1903. Pp. 61.

6900 CHICOPEE FALLS SAVINGS BANK. A half century of helping people to save and prosper, fiftieth anniversary of the Chicopee Falls Savings Bank, Chicopee Falls, Massachusetts, 1875-1925. Chicopee, 1925. Pp. 15. M.

6901 CLARK, ELI BENEDICT. A centennial discourse, delivered before the First Congregational Society in Chicopee, Sept. 26, 1852.... Springfield: George W. Wilson's Steam Power Presses, 1852. Pp. 23.

6902 DOYLE, JOHN E. "Chicopee's Irish (1830-1875)." HJWM, 3 (Spring, 1974), 13-23.

6903 "THE FISKE Rubber Corporation." Industry, 3 (February, 1938), 5-8. Tires.

6904 JOHNSON, L. L. Chicopee illustrated, 1896. Holyoke: Transcript Publishing, 1896. Pp. 135.

6905 PALMER, CLARISSA ELIZABETH SKEELE. Annals of Chicopee street: records and reminiscences of an old New England parish for a period of two hundred years. Springfield: Henry R. Johnson, 1899. 1899. Pp. 87. 1675-1875.

6906 SHLAKMAN, VERA. Economic history of a factory town: a study of Chicopee, Massachusetts. Northampton: Department of History of Smith College, 1935. Pp. 264.

6907 SZETELA, THADDEUS M. History of Chicopee. Chicopee: Szetela & Rich, 1948. Pp. vii, 291. MB.

CHILMARK

6908 DAVIS, ARTHUR W. "Recollections of many years." DCI, 4 (August, 1962), 11-13.

6909 DELABARRE, EDMUND BURKE and CHARLES W. BROWN. "The runic rock on No Man's Land, Massachusetts." NEQ, 8 (1935), 365-377.

6910 HOLAND, HJALMAR RUED. "The runic inscription on No Man's Land." NEQ, 17 (1944), 56-70.

6911 MARSTRAND, VILHELM. "The runic inscription on No Man's Land." NEQ, 22 (1949), 85-92.

6912 WOOD, ANNIE MOULTON. Noman's Land: isle of romance. New Bedford: Reynolds Printing, 1931. Pp. 166.

CLARKSBURG

6913 MARSDEN, ETHEL MAE. Clarksburg, Massachusetts, then and now, 1749-1962. [Adams]: Adams Specialty and Printing, 1963. Pp. 112.

CLINTON

6914 "THE BLAKE Manufacturing Corporation." In-
     dustry, 6 (August, 1941), 13-15.
Flashlights: a division of Ray-O-Vac.

6915 BOWERS, CHARLES M. "History of Clinton Bap-
     tist Church." Clinton HSHP, 1 (1912), 110-
122.

6916 _____. "Memories of former Clinton minis-
     ters." Clinton HSHP, 1 (1912), 79-88.
Collected biography.

6917 BOWERS, WALTER P. "Early history of Clinton
     Hospital." Clinton HSHP, 1 (1912), 89-93.

6918 BURDETT, GEORGE W. "Reminiscences of school
     days." Clinton HSHP, 1 (1912), 44-46.

6919 CLINTON, MASS. Clinton centennial volume,
     1850-1950: the story of Clinton, Massachu-
setts, incorporated March 14, 1850, and the Clinton
centennial celebration. Clinton, 1951. Pp. 223.

6920 _____. Semi-centennial celebration of the
     incorporation of the town of Clinton, Mar.
14, 1850; June 17-18-19, 1900. Andrew E. Ford, ed.
Clinton: W. J. Coulter, 1900. Pp. 176.

6921 CLINTON SAVINGS BANK. Clinton Savings Bank,
     1851-1951, a record of one hundred years.
Clinton, 1951. Pp. 27. M.

6922 FORD, ANDREW ELMER History of the origin
     of the town of Clinton, Massachusetts, 1653-
1865. Clinton: W. J. Coulter, 1896. Pp. viii,
696.

6923 MORSE, GEORGE M. "Clintonville in 1846."
     Clinton HSHP, 1 (1912), 62-78.

6924 PARKHURST, WELLINGTON EVARTS. "High Street
     in 1853." Clinton HSHP, 1 (1912), 47-56.
Historic houses.

6925 _____. "History of Chapel Hill School."
     Clinton HSHP, 1 (1912), 97-109.

6926 SMITH, JONATHAN. Masonic history: story of
     Trinity Lodge as told by Judge Jonathan
Smith at the fiftieth anniversary of the lodge,
held Monday, September 7th, 1908. [Clinton, 1908].
Pp. 10.

6927 STONE, CHRISTOPHER. "Old houses in Clinton."
     Clinton HSHP, 1 (1912), 39-43.

6928 THISSELL, JOSHUA. "Clinton in the Civil
     War." Clinton HSHP, 1 (1912), 21-31.

6929 _____. "First seven years in Clinton."
     Clinton HSHP, 1 (1912), 57-61.

6930 WALKER, NEIL. "Phases in the evolution of
     Clinton's greatest industry." Clinton HSHP,
1 (1912), 94-96.
Cotton mills.

COHASSET

6931 BEECHWOOD, MASS. EVANGELICAL UNION CHURCH.
     Historical sketch of Beechwood Church togeth-
er with the exercises of dedication, January 15,
1867. Boston: Alfred Mudge & Son, 1867. Pp. 20.

6932 BIGELOW, EDWIN VICTOR. A narrative history
     of the town of Cohasset, Massachusetts.
[Cohasset]: Committee on Town History, 1898-1956.
2v.
     Volume 2 is by Burtram J. Pratt.

6933 COHASSET, MASS. Addresses at the unveiling
     of a memorial, July 4, 1914, commemorating
the discovery of Cohasset in 1614 by Captain John
Smith. Cohasset, 1914. Pp. 19.

6934 _____. Centennial anniversary of the town
     of Cohasset, May 7, 1870, oration by Hon.
Thomas Russell, speeches by Gov. Claflin, Hiram
Revels, Loring Lothrop, Solomon Lincoln, George B.
Loring, and others. Boston: Wright & Potter, 1870.
Pp. 69.

6935 _____. Commemoration of the one hundred and
     fiftieth anniversary of the independent
government of the town of Cohasset, July fourth and
eighth to eleventh, 1921. Cohasset: Pageant Committee, 1922. Pp. 48.

6936 COHASSET SAVINGS BANK, COHASSET, MASS. 100th
     anniversary of the founding of the Cohasset
Savings Bank, incorporated February 28, 1845. Cohasset, 1945. Unpaged. M.

6937 COLLIER, EDMUND POMEROY. Cohasset's deep sea
     captains. Boston: Priv. Print., 1900.
Pp. 59.

6938 "THE CUBA Dam." Scituate HSB, 7 (June,
     1955), 1-2.
Built at mouth of Little Harbor circa 1758;
destroyed by a storm in 1851.

6939 DAVENPORT, GEORGE LYMAN and ELIZABETH O. DAV-
     ENPORT, comps. The genealogies of the fam-
ilies of Cohasset, Massachusetts...supplementary to
the narrative history of Cohasset, by Rev. E. Victor
Bigelow, published in 1898. [Cohasset]: Committee
on Town History, 1909. Pp. xii, 631.

6940 FLINT, JACOB. Two discourses, containing the
     history of the Church and Society in Cohas-
set, delivered December 16, 1821; being the first
Lord's day after the completion of a century from
the gathering of the church in that place, and the
ordination of the first pastor, with a geographical
sketch of Cohasset. Boston: Munroe and Francis,
1822. Pp. 28.
     Portions subsequently appeared in: MHSP,
3 Ser., 2 (1830), 84-109.

6941 HARNEY, MARTIN P. "The wreck of the brig
     'Saint John', a tragic episode of the Irish
famine immigration." Catholic World, 169 (1949),
360-364.
     October, 1849.

6942   HOWE, OLIVER H. "A brief history of Cohasset, Massachusetts." OTNE, 32 (1941-1942), 43-51.

6943   _____. Evolution of the Cohasset Historical Society, 1894-1944. Cohasset: Cohasset Historical Society, 1944. Unpaged. MBNEH.

6944   LAWRENCE, CHARLES A. "The building of Minot's Lodge Lighthouse." NEM, New Ser., 15 (1896-1897), 131-144.

6945   ROWLANDS, JOHN J. Spindrift from a house by the sea. N.Y.: Norton, 1960. Pp. 232.

COLRAIN

6946   COLRAIN, MASS. Colrain, Mass...a brief historical sketch of the town, the past and the present in perspective, a souvenir of the reunion of its former residents, August 26th, 1896. n.p., [1896?]. Unpaged.

6947   JOHNSON, KARLTON C. The Venerable House. Colrain: Colrain Congregational Church, 1950. Pp. 44.
       Colrain Congregational Church, 1750-1950.

6948   KEMP, ADELAIDE R. "The first recorded schoolhouse flag." OTNE, 26 (1935-1936), 136-137.

6949   MCCLELLAN, CHARLES H. The early settlers of Colrain, Mass.; or, some account of ye early settlement of 'Boston Township No. 2, alias Colrain,' 'adjoyning on ye north sid of Deerfield': an address delivered before H. S. Greenleaf Post No. 20, G. A. R., at Colrain, May 30, 1885. Greenfield: W. S. Carson, 1885. Pp. 86.

6950   PATRIE, LOIS MCCLELLAN. A history of Colrain, Massachusetts, with genealogies of early families. [Troy, N.Y.], 1974. Pp. vii, 337.

6951   SMITH, CARL G. "From homesteads to cellar holes on Catamount Hill, Colrain, Massachusetts." NEHGR, 96 (1942), 60-69.

6952   THOMPSON, FRANCIS MCGEE. The beginning of Colrain: address delivered at Colrain, Mass., Old Home Week, 1904. Greenfield, [1904?]. Pp. 16. MBNEH.

CONCORD

6953   ABBOTT, KATHARINE MIXER. "A summer visit to Concord." Critic, 43 (1903), 142-145.

6954   ACKERMAN, EDWARD. "Sequent occupance of a Boston suburban community." Economic Geography, 17 (1941), 61-74.

6955   AHL, HENRY CURTIS. A visit to Orchard House, Concord, Massachusetts. Concord, 1938. Pp. 15. M.

6956   ALLEN, GRANT. "Sunday at Concord." Fortnightly Review, New Ser., 43 (1888), 675-690.

6957   ANAGNOS, JULIA ROMANA HOWE. Philosophiae quaestor; or, days in Concord. Boston: D. Lothrop, 1885. Pp. 59.
       Concord School of Philosophy.

6958   BARRETT, AMOS. The Concord fight; an account by Amos Barrett; the personal experiences of the author who participated in the fight; written on the fiftieth anniversary. Allen French, ed. Boston: Thomas Todd, 1924. Pp. 14.

6959   BARTLETT, GEORGE BRADFORD. Concord: historic, literary and picturesque. (1880) 15th ed., rev. Boston: Lothrop Publishing, 1895. Pp. 200.
       First edition has title: The Concord guide book.

6960   _____. "Concord men and memories." BSM, 3 (1885), 224-232.

6961   BEERS, HENRY AUGUSTIN. "A Pilgrim in Concord." Yale Review, New Ser., 3 (1914), 673-688.
       Concord School of Philosophy.

6962   BLANDING, THOMAS. "Of New Bedford 'feeloosofers' and Concord real estate." Concord Saunterer, 8 (June, 1973), 2-8.
       Correspondence between Thoreau and Daniel Ricketson; the latter is 'house hunting' in Concord.

6963   BRADY, SARITA M. "Centennial Concord." Appleton's Journal, 13 (1875), 523-526.
       Battle.

6964   BREWSTER, WILLIAM. October farm, from the Concord journals and diaries of William Brewster. Smith Owen Dexter, comp. Cambridge: Harvard Univ. Pr., 1966. Pp. xv, 285.

6965   BRODERICK, JOHN CARUTHERS. "Thoreau, Alcott and the poll tax." Studies in Philology, 53 (1956), 612-626.

6966   BROWN, MARY HOSMER. Memories of Concord. Boston: Four Seas, 1926. Pp. 111.
       Biographies.

6967   CAMERON, KENNETH WALTER, comp. Concord harvest: publications of the Concord School of Philosophy and Literature with notes on its successors and other resources for research in Emerson, Thoreau, Alcott and the later transcendentalists. Hartford: Transcendental Books, 1970. 2v.

6968   _____, ed. Emerson, Thoreau, and Concord in early newspapers: biographical and historical lore for the scholar and general reader. Hartford: Transcendental Books, 1958. 355 leaves.

6969   CONCORD, MASS. Celebration of the two hundred and fiftieth anniversary of the incorporation of Concord, September 12, 1885, 1635-1885. John S. Keyes, G. M. Brooks and S. Hoar, eds. Concord, 1885. Pp. 95.

6970 _____. Concord, Massachusetts, births, marriages, and deaths, 1635-1850. Boston: T. Todd, 1895. Pp. vii, 496.
      Index of names and places.

6971 _____. Proceedings at the centennial celebration of Concord fight, April 19, 1875. Concord, 1876. Pp. 176.

6972 _____. The soldiers and sailors of Concord; report of the committee appointed by the town to procure a list of names of those who served in the Civil and Spanish-American Wars. Concord, 1908. Pp. 70.
      Biography.

6973 _____. Tercentenary, 1635-1935, Concord, Massachusetts, September 11, 12, 13, and 14, 1935. Boston: Thomas Todd, 1935. Pp. 35.

6974 CONCORD, MASS. BOARD OF TRADE. Concord, Massachusetts; some of its history and pictures of the points of interest. Concord, [1952?]. Unpaged.

6975 CONCORD, MASS. FIRST PARISH. Dedication of the restored meeting house of the First Parish in Concord, Thursday October 3rd, 1901. Concord, [1901]. Pp. 50.

6976 CONCORD, MASS. FREE PUBLIC LIBRARY. Concord Free Public Library, seventy-fifth anniversary, October 1, 1948. [Concord, 1948]. 16 leaves.

6977 CONCORD, MASS. LYCEUM. Semi-centennial, proceedings of the fiftieth anniversary of the organization of the Concord Lyceum.... Concord, 1879. Pp. 32.

6978 CONCORD ANTIQUARIAN SOCIETY, CONCORD, MASS. Celebration of the two hundred sixty-ninth birthday of Concord by the Antiquarian Society of that town, September the twelfth, 1904, report of the eighteenth anniversary of the Concord Antiquarian Society, with address by Mr. P. K. Walcott, together with a list of members of the society. Boston: Beacon Pr., 1904. Pp. 30.

6979 CONCORD, a few of the things to be seen there. Concord: Patriot Pr., 1902. Pp. 15.

6980 CONCORD SCHOOL OF PHILOSOPHY. Concord lectures on philosophy, comprising outlines of all the lectures at the Concord Summer School of Philosophy in 1882, with an historical sketch. Raymond L. Bridgman, comp. Cambridge: M. King, 1883. Pp. 168.

6981 COOKE, GEORGE WILLIS. "Concord history and life." NEM, New Ser., 18 (1898), 425-445.

6982 CURTIS, GEORGE WILLIAM. "An oration on the one-hundredth anniversary of 'Concord fight,' April 19, 1775." NEHGR, 29 (1875), 380-395.

6983 [EDES, PRISCILLA RICE]. Some reminiscences of old Concord. Gouverneur, N.Y.: C. A. Livingston, 1903. Unpaged.

6984 EMERSON, RALPH WALDO. A historical discourse, delivered before the citizens of Concord, 12th September, 1835, on the second centennial anniversary of the incorporation of the town. Concord: G. F. Bemis, 1835. Pp. 52.

6985 ERICKSON, RICHARD B. "Sounds of a New England village." NEG, 9 (Winter, 1968), 3-9.

6986 FALES, DEAN A., JR. "Hosmer family furniture." Antiques, 83 (1963), 548-549.

6987 FENN, MARY R. Tales of old Concord. Concord: Women's Parish Association, 1965. Pp. 40.

6988 FRENCH, ALLEN. "The British expedition to Concord, Massachusetts in 1775." Society for Army Historical Research. Journal, 15 (Spring, 1936), 17-31.

6989 _____. The drama of Concord: a pageant of three centuries, by Allen French; a part of the tercentenary celebration of the incorporation of Concord, Massachusetts, given in the Veterans Building under the direction of the Concord Players on the evenings of September 11, 12 and 14, 1935. Concord: Production Committee, 1935. Pp. xv, 101.

6990 _____. Old Concord. Boston: Little, Brown, 1915. Pp. xii, 186.

6991 _____. "Two Concord laymen: John and Samuel Hoar." UHSP, 5, Pt. 1 (1936), 19-37.

6992 GELLER, LAWRENCE D. Between Concord and Plymouth: the Transcendentalists and the Watsons, with the Hillside Collection of manuscripts. Concord: Thoreau Foundation, Inc., 1973. Pp. xviii, 237.

6993 "GENERAL Radio Company marks 50th year." Industry, 31 (December, 1965), 18-19, 45-46.

6994 GRINNELL, FRANK WASHBURN. "The resolution of the town of Concord on October 22, 1776, and its constitutional significance." MassLQ, 13 (August, 1928), 60-65.
      Massachusetts Constitution.

6995 GROUT, HENRY MARTYN. Trinitarian Congregationalism in Concord: an historical discourse, delivered at Concord, Mass., June 4, 1876, on occasion of the completion of the first half century of the Trinitarian Congregational Church.... Boston: T. Todd, 1876. Pp. 31.

6996 HOAR, EBENEZER ROCKWOOD. Address in the old Concord meeting house, April 19, 1894. Boston: Beacon Pr., 1894. Pp. 12.
      Battle of Concord.

6997 HOELTJE, HUBERT H. "Emerson, citizen of Concord." American Literature, 11 (1940), 367-378.

6998 HUDSON, ALFRED SERENO. The history of Concord, Massachusetts. Volume 1. Concord: Erudite Pr., 1904. Pp. 496.
      No more published.

6999 HUDSON, FREDERIC. "The Concord fight." Harper's Magazine, 50 (1874-1875), 777-804.

7000 HUDSON, H.R. "Concord books." Harper's Magazine, 51 (1875), 18-32.

7001 HURST, J. F. "Historic Concord." Chautauquan, 25 (1897), 266-273.

7002 JARVIS, EDWARD. Financial connection of the use of spirits and wine with the people of Concord, Massachusetts. Boston: T. Todd, 1883. Pp. 14.
Temperance.

7003 _____. "The supposed decay of families illustrated from Concord records." NEHGR, 38 (1884), 385-395.
Brief biographies and list of all settlers before 1700.

7004 KETTEL, RUSSELL H. Cummings E. Davis and his Concord furniture. Concord: Concord Antiquarian Society, n.d. Unpaged. M.

7005 _____. "Cummings E. Davis and the Concord Antiquarian Society." Antiques, 58 (1950), 108-109.

7006 KEYES, JOHN SHEPARD. Story of an old house: read before the Concord Antiquarian Society. [Concord]: Concord Antiquarian Society, [1902?]. Pp. 17.
Jones House.

7007 LEWIS, ALFRED HENRY. "Concord, the historic." Everybody's Magazine, 9 (1903), 773-780.

7008 LISTER, JEREMY. Concord fight, being so much of the narrative of Ensign Jeremy Lister of the 10th Regiment of Foot as pertains to his services on the 19th of April, 1775, and to his experiences in Boston during the early months of the siege. Cambridge: Harvard Univ. Pr., 1931. Pp. 55.

7009 LITTLE, DAVID B. "Cruising the Concord." NEG, 8 (Spring, 1962), 16-27.
Concord River.

7010 _____. "'Twas the nineteenth of April in (18)75--and the centennial was coming unstuck." Am Heritage, 23 (1972), 18-25, 102-103.

7011 [LOTHROP, HARRIET MULFORD STONE]. Old Concord, her highways and byways. (1888) Rev. and enl. ed., by Margaret Sidney, pseud. Boston: D. Lothrop, 1892. Pp. 178.

7012 LOTHROP, MARGARET MULFORD. The Wayside: home of authors. N.Y.: American Book Co., 1940. Pp. xii, 202.

7013 _____. "The Wayside, home of three authors." Elementary English Review, 10 (1933), 98-100, 111.
Margaret Sidney, Louisa May Alcott, and Nathaniel Hawthorne.

7014 _____. "Wayside--the home of three American authors." OTNE, 20 (1929-1930), 51-64.
Margaret Sidney, Louisa May Alcott and Nathaniel Hawthorne.

7015 LOW, ALVAH H. "The Concord Lyceum." OTNE, 50 (1959-1960), 29-42.

7016 MERRIAM, JOHN MCKINSTRY. "Concord." AASP, New Ser., 9 (1893-1894), 253-269.

7017 MERWIN, SAMUEL. Old Concord, seen through western spectacles. Boston: Houghton Mifflin, 1926. Pp. 32.

7018 MUNROE, ALFRED. Concord and the telegraph; read before the Concord Antiquarian Society, January 6, 1902. [Concord]: Concord Antiquarian Society, [1902]. Pp. 22.

7019 MURDOCK, HAROLD. "The British at Concord - April 19, 1775." MHSP, 56 (1922-1923), 70-94.

7020 NYREN, DOROTHY. "The Concord Academic Debating Society." Massachusetts Review, 4 (1962), 81-84.

7021 "A PIONEER in radio." Industry, 18 (December, 1952), 23-26.
General Radio Co.

7022 RANTOUL, ROBERT, JR. An oration delivered at Concord, on the celebration of the seventy-fifth anniversary of the events of April 19, 1775. Boston: Dutton & Wentworth, 1850. Pp. 135.

7023 REID, STUART J. "A summer day at Concord, Massachusetts." Manchester Quarterly, 1 (1882), 1-13.

7024 REYNOLDS, GRINDALL. A collection of historical and other papers. Alice Reynolds Keyes, ed. Concord: The Editor, 1895. Pp. xv, 499.

7025 _____. "Concord fight." Unitarian Review and Religious Magazine, 3 (1875), 383-398.

7026 _____. Concord fight, April 19, 1775. Boston: A. Williams, 1875. Pp. 23.

7027 _____. The story of a Concord farm and its owners. [Concord?, 1883?]. Pp. 29.
Farm known as Lee's Hill.

7028 RICHARDSON, LAURENCE EATON. Concord at the turn of the century: [paper] for the Morning Study Group, Concord Antiquarian Society, May 26, 1960. [Concord]: Concord Antiquarian Society, 1960. Pp. 21. M.

7029 _____. Concord chronicle, 1865-1899. Concord, 1967. Pp. 144.

7030 RIPLEY, EZRA. A history of the fight at Concord, on the 19th of April, 1775, with a particular account of the military operations and interesting events of that ever memorable day; showing that then and there the first regular and forcible

(RIPLEY, EZRA.)
resistance was made to the British soldiery, and
the first British blood was shed by armed Americans,
and the Revolutionary War thus commenced. (1827)
2d. ed. Concord: H. Atwill, 1832. Pp. iv, 40.

7031 ROBBINS, ROLAND WELLS. Discovery at Walden.
Stoneham: G. R. Barnstead & Son, 1947.
Pp. xvi, 60.

7032 _____. The story of the Minute Man....
Stoneham: G. R. Barnstead & Son, 1945.
Pp. 30.

7033 SANBORN, FRANK B. "Emerson and his friends
in Concord." NEM, New Ser., 3 (1890-1891),
411-431.

7034 _____. "New Hampshire men at the Concord
fight." MagHist, 7 (1908), 125-137.

7035 SAWITZKY, WILLIAM. "Ralph Earl's historical
painting, 'A view of the town of Concord.'"
Antiques, 28 (1935), 98-100.

7036 SCOTT, KENNETH and RUSSELL H. KETTELL. "Joseph Hosmer, cabinetmaker." Antiques, 73
(1958), 356-359.

7037 SCUDDER, TOWNSEND. Concord: American town.
Boston: Little, Brown, 1947. Pp. 421.

7038 SOCIAL CIRCLE IN CONCORD, CONCORD, MASS.
Centennial of the Social Circle in Concord,
March 21, 1882. Cambridge: Riverside Pr., 1882.
Pp. 176. MBNEH.

7039 _____. Memoirs of members of the Social
Circle in Concord. 2d. Ser., from 1795 to
1840.... Cambridge: Riverside Pr., 1888.
Pp. xiii, 386.

7040 _____. Memoirs of members of the Social
Circle in Concord. Third Ser., from 1840
to 1895.... Cambridge: Riverside Pr., 1907.
Pp. xiii, 260.

7041 _____. Memoirs of members of the Social Circle in Concord. Fourth Ser., from 1895 to
1909.... Cambridge: Riverside Pr., 1909.
Pp. xiii, 343.

7042 _____. Memoirs of members of the Social Circle in Concord. Fifth Ser., from 1900 to
1939.... Cambridge: Univ. Pr., 1940. Pp. 401.
MBNEH.

7043 STOWELL, ROBERT FREDERICK. A Thoreau gazetteer. Calais, Vt.: Poor Farm Pr., 1948.
5 leaves.

7044 SWAYNE, JOSEPHINE LATHAM, ed. The story of
Concord told by Concord writers. (1906)
2d. rev. ed. Boston: Meador Publishing, 1939.
Pp. 428.

7045 STEWART, RANDALL. "The Concord Group: a
study of relationships." Sewanee Review, 44
(1936), 434-446.
Emerson, Thoreau and Hawthorne.

7046 TEWKSBURY, GEORGE A. Manual of the Trini-
tarian Congregational Church of Concord.
Boston: Beacon Pr., 1895. Pp. 102. MBNEH.
Lengthy history.

7047 _____. Trinitarian Congregational Church of
Concord...supplementary to the manual of
eighteen hundred and ninety-four. Boston: Beacon
Pr., 1901. Pp. 67. MBNEH.

7048 THOREAU, HENRY DAVID. Men of Concord and
some others as portrayed in the journal of
Henry David Thoreau. Francis H. Allen, ed. Boston:
Houghton Mifflin, 1936. Pp. xi, 255.

7049 TICKNOR, CAROLINE, ed. Classic Concord, as
portrayed by Emerson, Hawthorne, Thoreau and
the Alcotts. Boston: Houghton Mifflin, 1926.
Pp. ix, 271.
Social life and customs.

7050 TOLMAN, ADAMS. Indian relics in Concord;
read before the Concord Antiquarian Society.
[Concord]: Concord Antiquarian Society, [1902?].
Pp. 26.

7051 TOLMAN, GEORGE. The Concord minute men; read
before the Concord Antiquarian Society,
March 4, 1901. [Concord: Concord Antiquarian] Society, [1902?]. Pp. 27.

7052 _____. Concord, some of the things to be
seen there. Concord: H. L. Whitcomb, 1903.
Pp. 32. M.

7053 _____. Early town records: a paper read before the Concord Antiquarian Society in April
April, 1896. Concord: Priv. Print., 1915. Pp. 20.

7054 _____. Events of April nineteenth; read before the Concord Antiquarian Society. [Con-
cord]: Concord Antiquarian Society, [1902?].
Pp. 36.

7055 _____. 'Graves and worms and epitaphs'; read
before the Concord Antiquarian Society.
[Concord]: Concord Antiquarian Society, [1902?].
Pp. 30.

7056 _____. "John Jack, the slave, and Daniel
Bliss, the Tory." Worcester HSProc, (1891-
1893), 246-265.

7057 _____. Preliminaries of Concord fight; read
before the Concord Antiquarian Society.
[Concord]: Concord Antiquarian Society, [1901?].
Pp. 28.

7058 _____. Wright's tavern; read before the Concord Antiquarian Society. [Concord]: Concord Antiquarian Society, [1901?]. Pp. 26.

7059 TOOGOOD, ANNA COXE. The Wayside; Minute Man
National Historical Park, Massachusetts.
Washington: Office of History and Historic Architecture, Eastern Service Center, 1970. Pp. viii,
165.

7060 TORRES-REYES, RICARDO. Captain Brown's
House: historic data; Minute Man National
Historical Park, Concord, Massachusetts. [Washing-
ton]: U. S. Division of History, Office of Archaeology and Historic Preservation, 1969. Pp. ii, 39
leaves.

7061 WAGNER, C. E. "Concord: her ancient glory
and abiding charm." Reformed Church Review,
4 Ser., 8 (1904), 22-41.

7062 WALCOTT, CHARLES HOSMER. Concord in the
colonial period: being a history of the
town of Concord, Massachusetts, from the earliest
settlement to the overthrow of the Andros government, 1635-1689. Boston: Estes and Lauriat, 1884.
Pp. xiv, 172.

7063 WALKER, EUGENE H. "Minerals of Concord."
Concord Saunterer, 9 (September, 1974), 1-6.
Social life and customs.

7064 WALTON, PERRY. Concord: a pilgrimage to
the historic and literary center of America;
illustrated by reproductions of photographs which
show the natural beauty of Concord and its historic
landmarks, together with a brief history of the
town and an account of the incidents and people that
have made it famous.... (1922) 3d. ed. Boston,
1930. Pp. 27.

7065 WARREN, AUSTIN. "The Concord School of
Philosophy." NEQ, 2 (1929), 198-232.

7066 WHEELER, RUTH ROBINSON. Concord: climate
for freedom. Concord: Concord Antiquarian
Society, 1967. Pp. xv, 253.

7067 _____. Our American mile. Concord: Concord Antiquarian Society, 1957. Pp. 40.
Domestic architecture.

7068 WHEILDON, WILLIAM WILDER. New chapter in
the history of the Concord fight; Groton
minute-men at the North Bridge, April 19, 1775....
Boston: Lee & Shepard, 1885. Pp. 32.

7069 WIREN, GEORGE R. "A reminder of Paul Revere's ride." SWJ, 36 (1925), 389-395.
Samuel Hartwell and his farm.

7070 WOOD, ALBERT EDWARD. How our great-grand-
fathers lived; read before the Concord Antiquarian Society. [Concord]: Concord Antiquarian
Society, [1902?]. Pp. 25.
Social life and customs.

7071 _____. The plantation at Musketequid; read
before the Concord Antiquarian Society.
[Concord]: Concord Antiquarian Society, [1902?].
Pp. 26.

CONWAY

7072 CONWAY, MASS. Celebration of the hundredth
anniversary of the incorporation of Conway,
Massachusetts, at Conway, June 19th, 1867; including a historical address by Rev. Charles B. Rice...

poem by Harvey Rice...oration by William Howland....
Northampton: Bridgman & Childs, 1867. Pp. 137
(i.e. 136).

7073 CONWAY, MASS. BICENTENNIAL COMMITTEE. Town
of Conway Bicentennial, 1967. [Conway?,
1967?]. Pp. 64. M.

7074 CUTLER, ELIJAH. Conway's second century: a
lecture delivered before the Y.M.C.A., Conway, Mass., March 8, 1868. Springfield: Samuel
Bowles, 1868. Pp. 20.

7075 LEE, DEANE, ed. Conway, 1767-1967. [Con-
way]: The Town, 1967. Pp. 260.

7076 MACLEISH, ARCHIBALD. An evening's journey
to Conway, Massachusetts; an outdoor play.
Northampton: Gehenna Pr., 1967. Pp. 20.

7077 MILLER, HORACE ELMER. Sketches of Conway.
Conway, 1890. Unpaged. MB.

7078 PEASE, CHARLES STANLEY, ed. History of Conway (Massachusetts) 1767-1917, by the people
of Conway. Springfield: Springfield Printing and
Binding, 1917. Pp. 345.

7079 SHAW, DONALD E. "Conway Electric Street
Railway." Transportation, 3 (April-June,
1949), 13-30.

CUMMINGTON

7080 DUNCAN, HARRY. "The Cummington Press." New
Colophon, 2 (1949), 221-236.

7081 FOSTER, HELEN H. and WILLIAM W. STREETER.
Only one Cummington: a book in two parts.
Cummington: Cummington Historical Commission, 1974.
Pp. 452.

7082 MILLER, HORACE ELMER. Sketches and directory
of the town of Cummington. West Cummington,
1881. Pp. 46.
Biography.

7083 NAHMER, HENRIETTA S. "Bryant's New England
home." NEM, New Ser., 6 (1892), 65-80.
William Cullen Bryant.

DALTON

7084 AMERICAN LEGION. MASSACHUSETTS. BENJAMIN F.
SULLIVAN POST, NO. 155. Dalton and the World
War, being the story of the service rendered their
country by the people of Dalton, Massachusetts, in
the World War of 1917-1918. n.p., [1922?].
Pp. 148. M.

7085 "THE BIRTHPLACE of paper making in Berkshire." Berkshire Hills, 3 (1902-1903), 121.
Zenas Crane, 1799.

7086 "A CENTURY of service." Industry, 28 (February, 1963), 20, 36.
Byron Weston Co., paper.

7087 "CRANE & Company." Industry, 4 (March, 1939), 7-10, 52.
Paper manufacturers.

7088 DALTON, MASS. The 150th anniversary of the town of Dalton, Massachusetts, 1784-1934. Pittsfield: Eagle Printing and Binding, [1934?]. Pp. 101.

7089 _____. 175th anniversary celebration, Sept. 19-20, 1959. n.p., [1959?]. Unpaged. MPB.
Includes history.

7090 DALTON, MASS. FIRST CONGREGATIONAL CHURCH. Historical sketch and manual of the First Congregational Church in Dalton, Mass., February 1785.' Pittsfield: Axtell & Pomeroy, 1881. Pp. 19. MPB.

7091 "DALTON memories: old times in the noted paper mill town." Berkshire Hills, 1 (July 1, 1901), [9].

7092 "THE OLD Berkshire mill." Berkshire Hills, New Ser., 1 (1904-1905), 11-13.
Paper.

7093 "OLD churches of the past: exterior and interior views of the Congregational Church in Dalton in 1811 and 1835. Berkshire Hills, New Ser., 2 (1905-1906), 96-99.

7094 SMITH, CORA HITT. A history of Dalton Methodism. n.p., 1927. Pp. 51. MPB.

DANVERS

7095 ABBOTT, RALPH F. "Early recollections of residences on the corner of Locust and Poplar Streets, and vicinity, as well as the people who occupied them." DanHC, 35 (1947), 41-50.

7096 AHERN, ELIZABETH A. "Sketch of the Roman Catholic parish in Danvers." DanHC, 8 (1920), 71-83.

7097 ALLEN, NELLIE BURNHAM. "District number five." DanHC, 26 (1938), 1-12.
Schools.

7098 _____. "The old farmhouse on the Newburyport Turnpike." DanHC, 37 (1949), 1-17.
Allen House.

7099 ALLEN, RUTH HOWARD. "The history of the Danvers Grange." DanHC, 42 (1964), 51-58.

7100 _____. "The hundredth anniversary of Holten High School." DanHC, 39 (1951), 56-65.

7101 _____. "Some Putnam houses on Locust Street." DanHC, 26 (1938), 50-64; 27 (1939), 29-39; 28 (1940), 46-52; 37 (1949), 53-62.
'Continued,' but no more appeared.

7102 _____. "Walnut Grove Cemetery." DanHC, 31 (1943), 6-14.

7103 ARDIFF, WILLIAM BIRRELL. King's Grant Motor Inn and Restaurant, Route 128, Danvers, Mass. A historical sketch. n.p., 1960. Pp. 8. MSaE.
Relates to land on which motel is located.

7104 BELL, GEORGE P. "Danvers about sixty-five years ago." DanHC, 31 (1943), 65-72.

7105 BRADSTREET, CLARA SOUTHWICK. "Olden days in West Peabody." DanHC, 36 (1948), 1-15.

7106 BRADSTREET, SARAH ELIZABETH. "'The underground railway' in Danvers." DanHC, 4 (1916), 129-130.

7107 BROWN, THURL D. "Danvers town halls." DanHC, 42 (1964), 99-115.

7108 _____. "Danvers town seal." DanHC, 43 (1967), 89-96.

7109 COOK, ELEANOR. "Lester Sanger Couch: his architectural heritage in Danvers." DanHC, 42 (1964), 79-83.

7110 COOK, MADELINE BROWN. "The history of Creese and Cook Company, Inc. of Danvers." DanHC, 34 (1946), 50-65.
Leather manufacturers.

7111 CROSSMAN, CARL L. "Eight fine old Danvers houses: their relations to architectural trends." DanHC, 42 (1964), 26-36.

7112 _____. The McIntire garden house on the Endicott estate. Middletown, Conn.: Wesleyan University Art Laboratory, 1962. Unpaged. MSaE.

7113 DAMON, FRANK C. "The Danvers Light Infantry, 1818-1851." DanHC, 14 (1926), 1-24; 15 (1927), 49-64.

7114 _____. "Danvers Riding Park." DanHC, 29 (1941), 40-53.

7115 _____. "Ezra Batchelder, clockmaker." DanHC, 22 (1934), 28-45; 23 (1935), 28-32.
'Continued,' but no more appeared.

7116 DANVERS, MASS. Account of the centennial celebration in Danvers, June 16, 1852, together with the proceedings of the town in relation to the donation of George Peabody.... Boston: Dutton and Wentworth, 1852. Pp. 208.

7117 _____. The celebration of the one hundred and fiftieth anniversary of the establishment of the town of Danvers, Massachusetts, as a separate municipality. June 15, 16, 17, 1902. Boston: S. Usher, 1907. Pp. 222.

7118 _____. Danvers (Mass. Bay) tercentenary. [Danvers]: Mirror Pr., [1930?]. Pp. 32. MSaE.
Includes historical sketch by Mabel Gilliland.

7119 _____. 200th anniversary, 1752-1952, Danvers, Massachusetts, official program. n.p., [1952?]. Pp. 32. MSaE.

7120 DANVERS, MASS. COMMITTEE TO REVISE THE SOLDIERS' RECORD. Report of the committee appointed to revise the soldiers' record. Danvers: The Town, 1895. Pp. vii, 165 (i.e. 169).
Four extra pages, 112*-115* are inserted between 112 and 113.

7121 DANVERS, MASS. FIRST CHURCH. Exercises in celebration of the two hundred and fiftieth anniversary of the First Church, Congregational, Danvers, Massachusetts, October 8th to 15th, 1922, with an address at the centennial of the Sunday school, November 17th, 1918. Salem: Newcomb & Gauss, 1922. Pp. 131.

7122 _____. Proceedings at the celebration of the two hundredth anniversary of the First Parish at Salem Village, now Danvers, October 8, 1872; with an historical address by Charles B. Rice.... Boston: Congregational Publishing Society, 1874. Pp. 272.

7123 DANVERS, MASS. FIRST UNIVERSALIST SOCIETY. Semicentennial, First Universalist Society of Danvers, October 19th, 1879. n.p., [1879?]. Pp. 19. MSaE.
History by Henry P. Forbes.

7124 DANVERS, MASS. MAPLE STREET CONGREGATIONAL CHURCH. The history, standing rules, confession of faith, covenant & members of the Maple Street Congregational Church, in Danvers, Mass.; compiled by order of the church, and extending to May, 1871. Salem: Observer, 1871. Pp. 44.

7125 "DANVERS centennial celebration." Littell's Living Age, 34 (1852), 85-87.

7126 DANVERS HISTORICAL SOCIETY, DANVERS, MASS. Old anti-slavery days: proceedings of the commemorative meeting, held by the Danvers Historical Society, at the Town Hall, Danvers, April 26, 1893, with introduction, letters and sketches. A. P. Putnam, ed. Danvers: Danvers Mirror Print, 1893. Pp. xxvii, 151.

7127 DANVERS SAVINGS BANK. Seventy-three years of the Danvers Savings Bank, 1850-1923. n.p., [1923?]. Pp. 22. MSaE.

7128 "ELECTION Day and other holidays." DanHC, 4 (1916), 126-129.

7129 EMERSON, GEORGE W. "Some annals of the birthplace of General Israel Putnam, Danvers, Mass." OTNE, 13 (1922-1923), 165-168.

7130 FOWLER, SAMUEL PAGE, 1800-1888. "Biographical sketch and diary of Rev. Joseph Green, of Salem Village." EIHC, 8 (1866), 91-96, 165-168, 215-224; 10 (1869-1870), 73-104; 36 (1900), 325-330.

7131 _____. "Biographical sketches of Rev. Joseph Green, Rev. Peter Clark, and Rev. Benjamin Wadsworth, ministers of Salem Village (now Danvers Centre). EIHC, 1 (1859), 56-66.

7132 FOWLER, SAMUEL PAGE, JR., b. 1838. "The 'King' Hooper House and its early occupants." DanHC, 1 (1913), 87-89.

7133 _____. "The New Mills Social Library." DanHC, 1 (1913), 95-96.

7134 _____. "Old-time schools in Danvers." DanHC, 12 (1924), 105-112.

7135 _____. "The old town of Danvers in 1765." DanHC, 8 (1920), 61-65.

7136 FRIEDMAN, LEE MAX. "Bernard & Friedman's Danvers tannery." DanHC, 38 (1950), 21-30.

7137 GAY, CLAIRE S. "History of the Danvers Visiting Nurse Association on the occasion of its fiftieth anniversary, (1908-1958)." DanHC, 41 (1961), 54-57.

7138 GOULD, ELIZABETH PORTER. "The home of Rebecca Nurse." Essex Antiq, 4 (1900), 135-137.

7139 HANSON, JOHN WESLEY. History of the town of Danvers, from its early settlement to the year 1848. Danvers, 1848. Pp. vii, 304.

7140 HARMOND, RICHARD. "Profits and practicality: the Danvers Arc Lighting Station and the municipal ownership movement in Massachusetts, 1888-1891." EIHC, 108 (1972), 75-85.
Street lighting.

7141 HARRINGTON, ARTHUR H. "Hathorne Hill in Danvers, with some account of Major William Hathorne." EIHC, 48 (1912), 97-112.

7142 HINES, EZRA DODGE. "Browne Hill (formerly called Long Hill and Leach's Hill) and some history connected with it." EIHC, 32 (1897), 201-238.

7143 _____. "George Jacobs and his home." DanHC, 1 (1913), 66-71.

7144 _____. Historic Danvers. Danvers: Frank E. Moynahan, 1894. unpaged.

7145 _____. "An historical trip through Danvers." DanHC, 4 (1916), 18-27; 6 (1918), 1-10. 'Continued,' but no more appeared.

7146 _____. "School District No. 2, New Mills." DanHC, 16 (1928), 20-36; 17 (1929), 33-54.

7147 _____. Some Danvers acres and associations connected therewith, 1897. Salem: Newcomb & Gauss, 1930. Pp. 22.

7148 HOLBROOK, CHARLES F. "First Baptist Church of Danvers." DanHC, 12 (1924), 1-17.

7149 HOUSE, ALBERT VIRGIL. "Forgotten paths in Danvers." DanHC, 13 (1925), 123-147.

7150 _____. "Historic cellar holes." DanHC, 15 (1927), 87-107.
Houses and their dwellers.

7151 _____. Historical address...at the 250th anniversary, First Church, Danvers, October 8, 1922. Danvers: Mirror Pr., [1922?]. Pp. 26. MSaE.

7152 HUTCHINSON, ALFRED. "A century in the history of Danvers Highlands, 1864-1964." DanHC, 42 (1964), 86-98.
Western section of the town.

7153 _____. "A thumb-nail sketch of Danvers' early history, 1632-1952." DanHC, 40 (1952-1953), 75-90.

7154 HYDE, WILLIAM L. "Reminiscences of Danvers in the forties and fifties." DanHC, 5 (1917), 1-20.

7155 INDEPENDENT AGRICULTURAL SCHOOL OF THE COUNTY OF ESSEX, DANVERS, MASS. Twenty fifth anniversary, 1913-1938. Salem: Newcomb and Gauss, [1938?]. Pp. 24. MSaE.

7156 KEIFE, CATHERINE AMANDA. "Drone Street in 1875." DanHC, 24 (1936), 101-110.

7157 _____. "Holten High School in the early eighties." DanHC, 25 (1937), 39-47.

7158 _____. "The Wadsworth School." DanHC, 23 (1935), 19-27.

7159 KENNEY, W. J. C. "Danvers fires and fire companies." DanHC, 5 (1917), 84-86.

7160 KING, DANIEL PUTNAM. An address commemorative of seven young men of Danvers, who were slain in the Battle of Lexington; delivered in the Old South Meeting House, in Danvers, on the sixtieth anniversary of the battle. Salem: W. & S. B. Ives, 1835. Pp. 32.

7161 LAMSON, WILLIAM. "Danversport fifty years ago." DanHC, 12 (1924), 113-117.

7162 LEAROYD, JESSIE PUTNAM. "Fifty years, 1889-1939." DanHC, 27 (1939), 1-13.
Danvers Historical Society.

7163 _____. "The Hunt Memorial Hospital." DanHC, 16 (1928), 122-130.

7164 MCELROY, PAUL SIMPSON. "On building a new church." DanHC, 39 (1951), 23-40.
Maple Street Congregational Church.

7165 MAPLE, MARY HINES and BESSIE PUTNAM ROPES. "History of First Universalist Church in Danvers." DanHC, 36 (1948), 30-49.

7166 MAPLE, MARY HINES. "Old time Danversport." DanHC, 35 (1947), 1-26.

7167 MASON, JOHN B. "Calvary Church." DanHC, 22 (1934), 99-102.

7168 MASSEY, DUDLEY ALDEN, ed. History of free-masonry in Danvers, Mass., from September, 1778, to July, 1896, containing a history of the United States Lodge, as taken from the archives of the Grand Lodge of Mass.: of Jordan, Amity and Mosaic Lodges and Holten Royal Arch Chapter, as taken from their respective records...and, as far as ascertainable, a genealogical, biographical, and a full masonic register of all the masons having connection with masonry in Danvers and Peabody. Peabody: C. H. Shepard, 1896. Pp. 734.

7169 MERRIAM, FRANK E. "Early Danvers railroads." DanHC, 33 (1945), 50-57.

7170 MOYNAHAN, FRANK E. "Danvers, Massachusetts." NEM, New Ser., 27 (1902-1903), 220-233.

7171 _____, ed. Danvers, Massachusetts: a résumé of her past history and progress, together with a condensed summary of her industrial advantages and development, biographies of prominent Danvers men and a series of comprehensive sketches of her representative manufacturing and commercial enterprises. Danvers: Danvers Mirror, 1899. Pp. 202.

7172 _____. Historic Danvers. Danver, 1894. Unpaged. MBNEH.

7173 MUDGE, FLORENCE A. "History of the Benevolent Society of the First Church." DanHC, 23 (1935), 33-40.

7174 NEWHALL, CHARLES. "The Danvers Post Office: its establishment and history." DanHC, 7 (1919), 1-21.

7175 _____. "Historical sketch of Ward Post 90, G. A. R." DanHC, 25 (1937), 83-86.

7176 NICHOLS, ANDREW. Danvers: a poem written for the centennial celebration, June 16, 1852. Boston: Dutton and Wentworth, 1852. Pp. 40. MSaE.

7177 _____. "The old Dyson Road." DanHC, 2 (1914), 101-104.

7178 _____. "The original lot of Col. Jeremiah Page." DanHC, 3 (1915), 101-109.

7179 "OLD shipmasters and seamen of Danvers." DanHC, 2 (1914), 88-99.

7180 [OSGOOD, GEORGE]. Historical sketch, of School District Number Thirteen, North Danvers: or, as it is known abroad, Danvers Plains: or, by its ancient name, Porter's Plains, to distinguish it from Shillaber's Plains, South Danvers. Salem: Gazette Office, 1855. Pp. 32.

7181 PAGE, ANNE L. "A Negro slave in Danvers, Mass." MassMag, 7 (1914), 137-138.
"Dill" owned by Jeremiah Page.

7182 "THE PAGE House." Spirit of '76, 1 (1894-1895), 29.

7183 PEABODY INSTITUTE, DANVERS, MASS. History of the Peabody Institute, Danvers, Mass., 1852-1911. Boston: Thomas Todd, [1911?]. Pp. 166. MSaE.
Library.

7184 PERLEY, SIDNEY. "Center of Salem Village in 1700." EIHC, 54 (1918), 225-245.

7185 _____. "Endicott lands, Salem, in 1700." EIHC, 51 (1915), 361-382.

7186 _____. "Hathorne: part of Salem Village in 1700." EIHC, 53 (1917), 332-344; 54 (1918), 115-137.

7187 _____. "The Nurse House." EIHC, 62 (1926), 1-3.

7188 _____. "A part of Salem Village in 1700." DanHC, 3 (1915), 65-84; 5 (1917), 33-47.
Real property.

7189 _____. "Part of Salem Village in 1700." EIHC, 52 (1916), 177-191.

7190 PHILBRICK, JULIA A. "The old schoolhouse in District No. 4." DanHC, 1 (1913), 23-29.

7191 _____. "Slaves in Danvers families." Dan HC, 4 (1916), 121-125.

7192 POOLE, FITCH. "The old Bell Tavern." Dan HC, 17 (1929), 9-12.

7193 PORTER, FREDERICK. "Reminiscences of Fox Hill School House." DanHC, 17 (1929), 7-8.

7194 PRATT, ANNETTE MUDGE. "Centre Street folks and the homes they lived in." DanHC, 32 (1944), 1-26.

7195 _____. "E. & A. Mudge & Co." DanHC, 34 (1946), 1-11.
Shoe manufacturers.

7196 PRIEST, GEORGE F. "Old houses of Salem Village." DanHC, 3 (1915), 1-12.

7197 _____. "Salem Village parsonage." DanHC, 16 (1928), 1-19.

7198 _____. "School District Number Five." DanHC, 12 (1924), 18-30.

7199 PRINCE, MOSES. "List of houses and cellar holes in District No. 5 about 1852." DanHC, 24 (1936), 21-27.
Houses and their dwellers; edited by Florence A. Mudge.

7200 PUTNAM, A. LEWIS. "Reminiscenses of Danvers." DanHC, 4 (1916), 89-96.

7201 PUTNAM, ALFRED PORTER. "Danvers people and their homes." DanHC, 1 (1913), 3-22; 3 (1915), 87-100; 5 (1917), 74-83; 7 (1919), 68-74; 9 (1921), 57-64; 11 (1923), 50-54; 17 (1929), 55-73; 19 (1931), 18-22; 23 (1935), 7-18; 24 (1936), 29-42; 25 (1937), 28-34; 26 (1938), 13-22; 27 (1939), 14-25; 30 (1942), 20-29; 31 (1943), 15-27; 34 (1946), 79-93.

7202 _____. "Fiftieth anniversary of the Universalist Church." DanHC, 36 (1948), 50-57.

7203 _____. "Schoolhouses in District No. Three." DanHC, 35 (1947), 67-69.

7204 PUTNAM, ALLEN. "History of parts of the Putnam family." DanHC, 37 (1949), 25-46.

7205 PUTNAM, ARTHUR ALWYN. The Putnam Guards of Danvers, Mass.: story of the company in the early war time of 1861. Danvers: Danvers Mirror Office, 1887. Pp. 22.

7206 _____. "Recollections of the church choirs of North Danvers." DanHC, 1 (1913), 52-60.

7207 [_____]. The Village Bank in Danvers: a glance at its history with other relevant matter, for the consideration of the stockholders and the community interested. By a Citizen. Boston: McIntire and Moulton, 1862. Pp. 36. MSaE.
Author attribution by the Essex Institute.

7208 PUTNAM, EBEN. "The king unwilling - how Danvers became a town." Putnam's HM, New Ser., 5 (1897), 141-160.

7209 PUTNAM, ELIZABETH G. and MARION EATON MULRY. "Memories of our neighborhood (Holten Street); a dialogue." DanHC, 38 (1950), 1-17.

7210 RICE, CHARLES B. Proceedings at the celebration of the two hundredth anniversary of the First Parish at Salem Village, now Danvers, October 8, 1872.... Boston: Congregational Publishing Society, 1874. Pp. 272. MBNEH.

7211 _____. "Recent First Parish history with review and general observations." DanHC, 2 (1914), 105-118.

7212 SHEHAN, THOMAS. "The old Twilight League." DanHC, 42 (1964), 9-22.
Baseball.

7213 "SOME business firms in Danvers in 1875." DanHC, 3 (1915), 63-64.

7214 "SOME Danvers schools and teachers." DanHC, 4 (1916), 30-32.

7215 SPOFFORD, MABEL. "Seventy-five years ago." DanHC, 41 (1961), 17-22.
Danvers Women's Association.

7216 STONE, THOMAS T. "Reminiscences." DanHC, 3 (1915), 37-41.

7217 SULLIVAN, WILLIAM B. "Celtic Danvers." Dan HC, 1 (1913), 74-86.
Irish.

7218 TAPLEY, CHARLES SUTHERLAND. "The Berry Tavern." DanHC, 42 (1964), 59-66.

7219 ____. Country estates of old Danvers. Danvers: Mirror Pr., [1960?]. Pp. 71. MSaE.
Historic houses.

7220 ____. "Danvers roads and other roads." DanHC, 12 (1924), 75-87.

7221 ____. "The first hundred years of the Danvers Savings Bank." DanHC, 38 (1950), 18-20.

7222 ____. "Fortieth anniversary of Danvers Visiting Nurse Association, 1948." DanHC, 37 (1949), 20-22.

7223 ____. From Muddy Boo to Blind Hole. Danvers: Priv. Print., 1940. Pp. 24.
Title refers to sections of the town.

7224 ____. "Glen Magna Farms." DanHC, 41 (1961), 7-16.
An estate.

7225 ____. "Historic address." DanHc, 40 (1952-1953), 36-39.
Relates to the town.

7226 ____. "The old Danvers State House." DanHC, 32 (1944), 33-38.
Putnam-Fellows-Masury House which was frequented by politicans.

7227 ____. "The one hundredth anniversary of the Maple Street Church." DanHC, 33 (1945), 16-21.

7228 ____. "75th anniversary, Mosaic Lodge, A. F. & A. M. observed October 24, 1946." DanHC, 35 (1947), 37-40.

7229 TAPLEY, HARRIET SILVESTER. "Capt. Samuel Page and his vessels." DanHC, 11 (1923), 92-111; 13 (1925), 56-63; 14 (1926), 25-30; 15 (1927), 37-45; 16 (1928), 37-50; 17 (1929), 20-32; 18 (1930), 97-103.
'Continued,' but no more appeared.

7230 ____. Chronicles of Danvers (old Salem Village) Massachusetts, 1632-1923. Danvers: Danvers Historical Society, 1923. Pp. xii, 283.

7231 ____. "Early physicians of Danvers." DanHC, 4 (1916), 73-88; 6 (1918), 50-83; 7 (1919), 56-58; 8 (1920), 66-67.

7232 ____. "Gilbert Tapley of Salem and some of his descendants." DanHC, 29 (1941), 75-92; 30 (1942), 32-48.

7233 ____. "'Neck of land' records." DanHC, 31 (1943), 1-5.
Land dispute.

7234 ____. "Old tavern days in Danvers." DanHC, 8 (1920), 1-32.

7235 ____. "Primitive shoemaking, first factory in the United States at Danvers." Boot and Shoe Recorder, (July 15, 1896).

7236 ____. "The schooner 'Sally' of Danvers." DanHC, 19 (1931), 23-32.

7237 UPHAM, CHARLES WENTWORTH. "Salem Village-- its parsonages and their occupants." Hist Mag, 2, Ser. 6 (1869), 353-355.

7238 VALENTINE, ELMER. The scholar's manual, containing questions and answers to the history and geography of Danvers. Danvers: G. R. Carlton, 1846. Pp. 54. MSaE.

7239 WILKINS, CARRIE F. B. "The history of the General Israel Putnam Chapter, D. A. R., 1895 to 1931." DanHC, 28 (1940), 18-36.

7240 WINSLOW, ANNIE M. "First Baptist Church." DanHC, 37 (1949), 47-52.

7241 ____. "Program of adult alien education in Danvers." DanHC, 42 (1964), 23-25. 1919-1943.

7242 ZOLLO, RICHARD P. "Danvers Square--an informal history." DanHC, 43 (1967), 1-79.

7243 ____. "Whittier's Oak Knoll." DanHC, 41 (1961), 58-66.
House.

DARTMOUTH

7244 ALLEN, WALTER SPOONER. "The family of George Allen, the immigrant, and its connection with the settlement of Dartmouth." ODHS, No. 18 (September, 1907), 12-22.

7245 ANDREWS, STEPHEN M. A sketch of Elder Daniel Hix, with the history of the First Christian Church in Dartmouth, Mass., for one hundred years. New Bedford: E. Anthony & Sons, 1880. Pp. vi, 204.

7246 BULLARD, JOHN MORGAN. Friends' Academy, 1810-1960: a history of the first one hundred fifty years. New Bedford, 1960. Pp. 120.

7247 CRAPO, HENRY HOWLAND. "Banks of old Dartmouth." ODHS, No. 46 (March, 1917), 23-51.

7248 ____. The Slocum House at Barney's Joy. [New Bedford, 1910]. Pp. 10.

7249 CRAPO, WILLIAM WALLACE. "Dartmouth traditions." ODHS, No. 2 (September, 1903), 4-5.

7250 DARTMOUTH, MASS. Proceedings in connection with the celebration at New Bedford, September 14, 1864 of the two hundredth anniversary of the incorporation of the town of Dartmouth. New Bedford: E. Anthony & Son, 1865. Pp. 129. MBNEH.

7251 GIDLEY, JOB S. "Historical glimpses of Dartmouth schools." ODHS, No. 10 (July, 1905), 11-16.

7252   HOWLAND, ELLIS L.   "The salt industry of
        Padanaram." ODHS, No. 2 (September, 1903),
11-16.
        Section of the town.

7253   LITTLEFIELD, L. A.   "Traditions of Padana-
        ram." ODHS, No. 2 (September, 1903), 8-10.
        Section of the town.

7254   LOOMIS, SALLY.   "The evolution of Paul
        Cuffe's Black Nationalism." Negro HistB, 37
(1974), 298-302.

7255   LOWRY, ANN GIDLEY.   Quakers and their meet-
        ing house at Apponegansett. [New Bedford?,
1947?]. unpaged. MB.

7256   RICKETSON, OLIVER G.   "Dartmouth dig: 1951;
        a survey of the Russell Garrison." BJCH,
(Summer, 1964), 4-15.

7257   RODMAN, THOMAS R.   "The King Philip War in
        Dartmouth." ODHS, No. 3 (December, 1903),
9-15.

7258   "SMITH Mills." New Bedford Free Public Li-
        brary. Monthly Bulletin, 2 (1897), 79-80.

7259   TABER, MARY KEMPTON.   "The Kempton family in
        old Dartmouth." ODHS, No. 21 (June, 1908),
5-10.

7260   TRIPP, THOMAS A.   Apponegansett meeting
        houses. [New Bedford?], 1931. unpaged. MB.

7261   WING, WILLIAM A.   "Five John's of old Dart-
        mouth." ODHS, No. 25 (June, 1909), 11-13.
        John Smith, John Russell, John Akin, John
        Shepherd and John Howland.

7262   WORTH, HENRY BARNARD.   "The homesteads at
        Apponeganset before 1710." ODHS, No. 25
(June, 1909), 6-9.
        Land.

7263   _____. "Smith Mills." ODHS, No. 20 (March,
        1908), 15-31.

7264   _____. "Ten ancient homes." ODHS, No. 3
        (December, 1903), 7-9.

DEDHAM

7265   AUSTIN, WALTER.   Tale of a Dedham tavern:
        history of the Norfolk Hotel, Dedham, Massa-
chusetts. Cambridge: Riverside Pr., 1912.
Pp. 195.

7266   "THE AVERY School." DedHR, 7 (1896), 41-43.

7267   BABCOCK, SAMUEL BRAZER.   A historical dis-
        course delivered at the closing of the old
Episcopal (St. Paul's) Church, Dedham, November 30,
1845. Dedham: H. Mann, 1846. Pp. 23.

7268   BATES, JOSHUA.   A discourse, delivered Febru-
        ary 15, 1818, being the Sabbath preceding
the dissolution of the pastoral relation between
the author and the First Church in Dedham. Dedham:
Abel D. Alleyne, 1818. Pp. 23.
        Historical sketch of the church.

7269   BEACH, SETH CURTIS.   A brief history of the
        last three pastorates of the First Parish in
Dedham, 1860-1888: a sermon preached November 11,
1888. Dedham: The Parish, 1888. Pp. 27.
        Benjamin H. Bailey, George M. Folsom, and the
        author.

7270   BOYD, HARRIET TRACY.   "The early days of the
        Dedham Branch Railroad." DedHR, 5 (1894),
97-101.

7271   _____. "Vine Rock Bridge in Dedham." DedHR,
        2 (1891), 83-88.

7272   "BRIEF sketch of the Dedham Historical Soci-
        ety." DedHR, 1 (1890), 3-4.

7273   BROWN, B. KATHERINE.   "Puritan democracy in
        Dedham, Massachusetts: another case study."
WMQ, 3 Ser., 24 (1967), 378-396.
        Suffrage.

7274   COBB, JONATHAN HOLMES.   "The stone court
        house, 1827." DedHR, 4 (1893), 5-14.

7275   COGSWELL, WILLIAM.   A sermon, containing a
        brief history of the South Church and Parish
in Dedham, delivered, June 23, 1816. Dedham: Abel
D. Alleyne, 1816. Pp. 23.

7276   COOK, EDWARD M., JR.   "Social behavior and
        changing values in Dedham, Massachusetts,
1700 to 1775." WMQ, 3 Ser., 27 (1970), 546-580.

7277   CRAWFORD, MARY CAROLINE.   The female ex-pris-
        oner: a real home for the reform and recla-
mation of castaways. [Boston?, 190-?]. Pp. 4.
        Dedham Asylum for Discharged Female Pris-
        oners.

7278   DEDHAM, MASS.   An alphabetical abstract of
        the record of births, in the town of Dedham,
Massachusetts, 1844-1890. Don Gleason Hill, comp.
Dedham: Dedham Transcript, 1894. Pp. xviii, 206.

7279   _____. An alphabetical abstract of the rec-
        ord of deaths, in the town of Dedham, Massa-
chusetts, 1844-1890. Don Gleason Hill, comp. Dedham: Dedham Transcript, 1895. Pp. ix, 217.

7280   _____. An alphabetical abstract of the rec-
        ord of marriages, in the town of Dedham, Mas-
sachusetts, 1844-1890, arranged under the names of
the grooms, with an index of the names of brides.
Don Gleason Hill, comp. Dedham: Dedham Transcript,
1896. Pp. iv, 165.

7281   _____. The early records of the town....
        Dedham: Dedham Transcript Pr., 1886-1968.
7v.

        Vols. 1-5 edited by Don G. Hill; vol. 6 ed-
        ited by Julius H. Tuttle; vol. 7, edited by
        Benjamin Fisher, has imprint: Norwood: Nor-
        wood Printing Co.; detailed indexes.

7282 _____. Proceedings at the celebration of the two hundred and fiftieth anniversary of the founding of the free school at Dedham, Massachusetts, January 11, 1895. Dedham, 1895. Pp. viii, 48.

7283 _____. Proceedings at the celebration of the two hundred and fiftieth anniversary of the incorporation of the town of Dedham, Massachusetts, September 21, 1886. Cambridge, John Wilson and Son, 1887. Pp. vii, 214.

7284 _____. Proceedings at the dedication of the Avery School building, Dedham, Mass. September 2, 1895. Dedham, 1896. Pp. ix, 51.

7285 _____. The record of the town meetings, and abstract of births, marriages, and deaths, in the town of Dedham, Massachusetts, 1887-1896. Don Gleason Hill, ed. Dedham: Transcript Steam Job Print, 1896. Unpaged.

7286 DEDHAM, MASS. FIRST CHURCH. Dedham pulpit: or, sermons by the pastors of the First Church in Dedham, in the XVIIth and XVIIIth centuries; with a centennial discourse by the present pastor. Boston: Perkins & Marvin, 1840. Pp. viii, 517.
> Includes statistical table of churches and ministers in the territory of ancient Dedham.

7287 _____. Covenant of the First Church in Dedham, with some facts of history and illustrations of doctrine. Dedham: H. H. McQuillen, 1878. Pp. iv, 123.

7288 DEDHAM, MASS. FIRST CONGREGATIONAL CHURCH. MEN'S CLUB. 'Old Dedham days and ways': an historical festival under the auspices of the Men's Club of the First Congregational Church and the personal direction of Miss Margaret McLaren Eager, of Boston, Memorial Hall, Dedham, Mass., November 29, 30 and December 1, at 8 p.m. Boston: Metcalf Pr., 1904. Pp. 24.

7289 DEDHAM, MASS. FIRST PARISH. Commemorative services at the two hundred and fiftieth anniversary of the gathering of the First Church in Dedham, Mass., observed November 18 and 19, 1888. Dedham: Joint Committee of the Two Churches, 1888. Pp. 114.
> Services held by the First Parish Church and the First Congregational Church, both having originated from the First Church.

7290 DEDHAM, MASS. HIGH SCHOOL. Historical catalogue of the Dedham High School, teachers and students, 1851-1889. Dedham: H. H. McQuillen, 1889. Pp. 213.

7291 DEDHAM, MASS. TERCENTENARY COMMITTEE. Official commemoration and chronicle issued in honor of the 300th anniversary of the historic town of Dedham, 1636-1936, containing an account of the exercises enacted in commemoration of the three hundredth anniversary of the historic town of Dedham, the shiretown of Norfolk County in Massachusetts. Dedham: Transcript Pr., 1936. Pp. 204.

7292 DEDHAM. Boston: Edison Electric Illuminating Co., 1909. Pp. 16. M.

7293 DEDHAM HISTORICAL SOCIETY. A list of revolutionary soldiers who served Dedham in the Revolution, 1775-1783; this list is based upon the Massachusetts soldiers and sailors of the Revolutionary War, published by the Commonwealth and supplemented by the town and parish records of Dedham. [Dedham]: Dedham Historical Society, 1917. Pp. 13.

7294 _____. Notes on historic Dedham. Dedham: Dedham Historical Society, [not after 1947]. unpaged. MBNEH.

7295 _____. A plan of Dedham Village, Mass., 1636-1876, with descriptions of the grants of lots to the original owners, transcribed from the town records; the plan showing approximately the situation of the original grants with relation to the present village. [Dedham]: Dedham Historical Society, 1883. Pp. 15.

7296 DEDHAM INSTITUTION FOR SAVINGS. Centenary, March 19, 1931. Dedham: Elson, 1931. 5 leaves.

7297 DEDHAM NATIONAL BANK. One hundred years of the Dedham National Bank, being a selection of the most interesting events in the history of the Dedham National Bank. Dedham, 1914. Pp. 31. MBNEH.

7298 DEDHAM TRANSCRIPT. Historic Dedham, issued by the Dedham Transcript Press incorporated to commemorate the fiftieth anniversary of the Dedham Transcript, 1870-1920. Dedham, 1920. Pp. 51. MBNEH.
> Relates to the town, not the newspaper.

7299 _____. Town of Dedham 325th anniversary, 1636-1961; Dedham Transcript 90th anniversary, 1870-1960. [Dedham, 1960]. Pp. 88.

7300 "DEDHAM Village in 1795." DedHR, 14 (1903), 39-48.

7301 DEXTER, SAMUEL. Our fathers God, the hope of posterity, some serious thoughts on the foundation, rise and growth of the settlements in New England; with a view to the edification of the present, and the instruction and admonition of future generations; a discourse delivered at Dedham, on the day of publick thanksgiving, Nov. 23. 1738, upon the conclusion of the first century, since a Church of Christ was gathered in that place. (1738) 2d. ed. Boston: Thomas Fleet, Jr., 1796. Pp. ii, 51.
> Relates to Dedham.

7302 "DIARY of Nathaniel Ames, 1758-1821," DedHR, 1 (1890), 9-16, 49-52, 111-114, 144-148; 2 (1891), 25-28, 59-60, 96-99, 148-150; 3 (1892), 20-24, 69-73, 129-133, 184-186; 4 (1893), 24-25, 65-68, 100-102, 170-172; 5 (1894), 32-33, 66, 134-135, 172-174; 6 (1895), 20-22, 68-70, 109-111, 133-134; 7 (1896), 33-34, 77-78, 115-117, 145-146; 8 (1897), 27-28, 54-56, 90-91, 137-138; 9 (1898), 24-26, 62-63, 96-98, 110-113; 10 (1899), 25-27, 63-65, 79-82, 120-121; 11 (1900), 17-19, 48-50, 102-104, 147-149;

("DIARY of Nathaniel Ames...")
12 (1901), 9-10, 33-34, 58-60, 107-108, 123-125; 13 (1902), 25-27, 49-53, 80-82, 112-114; 14 (1903), 35-36, 71-72, 99-100, 129-130.
1758-1807 only; periodical ceased publication with volume 14.

7303   DURFEE, CALVIN. A centennial discourse: delivered before the South Church and Society, in Dedham, Mass., June 26, 1836. Boston: D. K. Hitchcock, 1836. Pp. 44.
Church history.

7304   EASTMAN, MAX. "Is this the truth about Sacco and Vanzetti?" National Review, 11 (1961), 261-264.

7305   EDWARDS, JONATHAN, 1820-1894. Two sermons preached fifty years from the building of the 'new meeting-house,' for the First Church, Dedham, January, 1870.... Dedham: John Cox, Jr., 1870. Pp. 22.

7306   ERNST, CARL WILHELM. "Dedham as a postal centre." DedHR, 6 (1895), 86-89.

7307   ____. "Dedham mail coaches." DedHR, 7 (1896), 14-15.

7308   EVANS, ELIZABETH GLENDOWER GARDINER. Outstanding features of the Sacco-Vanzetti case, together with letters from the defendants. Boston: New England Civil Liberties Committee, 1924. Pp. 46.

7309   FELIX, DAVID. Protest: Sacco-Vanzetti and the intellectuals. Bloomington: Indiana Univ. Pr., 1965. Pp. 274.

7310   FERGUSON, RACHEL MARION. "Domestic utensils and furniture used in Dedham since 1635." DedHR, 2 (1891), 125-130.

7311   NO ENTRY

7312   FISHER, GEORGE F. "Recollections of the old Dedham Branch Railroad, via Readville." DedHR, 1 (1890), 141-143.

7313   FOLSOM, ALBERT A. "Camp of the French Army, Dedham 1782." DedHR, 12 (1901), 8-10.

7314   FOWLER, LAURA WENTWORTH. "The Fairbanks House, Dedham." MagHist, 12 (1910), 273-275.

7315   FRANKFURTER, FELIX. The case of Sacco and Vanzetti: a critical analysis for lawyers and laymen. Boston: Little, Brown, 1927. Pp. 118.

7316   FREEMASONS. DEDHAM, MASS. CONSTELLATION LODGE. Proceedings at the celebration of the twenty-fifth anniversary of Constellation Lodge, A. F. and A. M., Dedham, Massachusetts, March 16, 1897. Dedham, 1898. Pp. ix, 113.

7317   GAY, FREDERICK LEWIS. "Quaker persecutions in Dedham." DedHR, 4 (1893), 32-36.

7318   GROSSMAN, JAMES. "The Sacco-Vanzetti case reconsidered." Commentary, 33 (1962), 31-44.

7319   GUILD, CALVIN. "Connecticut Corner, Dedham, before 1810." DedHR, 5 (1894), 40-42.

7320   ____. The first Sabbath School in Dedham: historical sketch, delivered before the First Congregational Sabbath School at the 250th anniversary of the gathering of the First Church in Dedham, November 18, 1888. Dedham, 1888. Pp. 12.

7321   ____. "The stone mill, and the water privilege bought by Thomas Barrows in 1862." DedHR, 4 (1893), 51-54.

7322   GUILD, REUBEN ALDRICH. "A district school seventy years ago." NEM, New Ser., 18 (1898), 452-456.

7323   HAVEN, SAMUEL FOSTER. An historical address delivered before the citizens of the town of Dedham, on the twenty-first of September, 1836, being the second centennial anniversary of the incorporation of the town. Dedham: Herman Mann, 1837. Pp. 79.

7324   HAWES, LLOYD E. The Dedham Pottery and the earlier Robertson's Chelsea potteries. Dedham: Dedham Historical Society, 1968. Pp. 52. Chelsea 1859-1895, Dedham 1896-1943.

7325   HEWINS, ANNIE JOSEPHINE. "The brute enemies of the early settlers of Dedham." DedHR, 2 (1891), 16-22.
Indians and wild animals.

7326   HILL, DON GLEASON. "The Dedham Institution for Savings." DedHR, 3 (1892), 145-152.

7327   ____. "The landing place on Charles River, Dedham Village." DedHR, 13 (1902), 67-77.

7328   ____. "The record of a New England town from the passage of the Stamp Act to the Declaration of Independence." National Magazine, 16 (1892), 160-174.

7329   HISTORY and directory of Dedham, Mass., for 1889, containing a complete resident, street and business directory, town officers, schools, societies, churches, post offices...census of Massachusetts, and a history of the town from the first settlement to the present time. Boston: A. E. Foss, 1889.

7330   "THE HOUSE that sentiment built." Industry, 20 (August, 1955), 9-12.
Rust Craft, greeting cards.

7331   HUMPHREY, GEORGE WASHINGTON. "Bibliography of Dedham." DedHR, 1 (1890), 37, 70-71.

7332   ____. "The old chestnut trees, Dedham." DedHR, 1 (1890), 106-108.

7333   "INDIAN deeds of Dedham." DedHR, 9 (1898), 42-45.

7334 JENNEY, CHARLES FRANCIS. "Northerly part of ancient line between Dedham and Dorchester. DedHR, 1 (1890), 41-48, 94-100.

7335 JONES, ALVIN LINCOLN. "Old Fairbanks House." DedHR, 8 (1897), 1-4.

7336 JOUGHLIN, GEORGE LOUIS and EDMUND M. MORGAN. The legacy of Sacco and Vanzetti. N.Y.: Harcourt, Brace, 1948. Pp. xvii, 598.

7337 LAMSON, ALVAN. A history of the First Church and Parish in Dedham, in three discourses, delivered on occasion of the completion, November 18, 1838, of the second century since the gathering of said church. Dedham: Herman Mann, 1839. Pp. 104.

7338 LATHROP, JOSEPH HENRY. "Dedham in the Rebellion." DedHR, 1 (1890), 35-37, 61-64; 2 (1891), 30-33, 63-67, 101-106, 135-142; 3 (1892), 31-34, 88-91, 133-138, 193-197; 4 (1893), 36-41, 70-75, 107-118, 162-165; 5 (1894), 17-22, 76-83, 122-127, 165-170; 6 (1895), 34-40, 58-65, 101-108, 140-145; 7 (1896), 19-26, 65-70, 111-115.

7339 LOCKE, CALVIN STOUGHTON. "Incidents in the history of West Dedham." DedHR, 1 (1890), 17-24.

7340 _____. Other men have labored: a sermon preached December 7th, 1879. Dedham: H. H. McQuillen, 1880. Pp. 29. First Church.

7341 LOCKRIDGE, KENNETH A. and ALAN KREIDER. "The evolution of Massachusetts town government, 1640-1740." WMQ, 3 Ser., 23 (1966), 549-574. Dedham and Watertown.

7342 LOCKRIDGE, KENNETH A. "The history of a Puritan Church, 1637-1736." NEQ, 40 (1967), 399-424.

7343 _____. A New England town: the first hundred years, Dedham, Massachusetts, 1636-1736. N.Y.: Norton, 1970. Pp. xv, 208.

7344 _____. "The population of Dedham, Massachusetts, 1636-1736." EconHistRev, 2 Ser., 19 (1966), 318-344.

7345 LOSSING, BENSON J. "The Fairbanks House, Dedham." Potter's AmMo, 7 (1876), 241-247.

7346 MANN, HERMAN. Historical annals of Dedham, from its settlement in 1635, to 1847. Dedham, 1847. Pp. viii, 136.

7347 MUSMANNO, MICHAEL ANGELO. After twelve years. N.Y.: A. A. Knopf, 1939. Pp. 415. Sacco-Vanzetti.

7348 NORFOLK MUTUAL FIRE INSURANCE CO. One hundred years of insurance. Dedham, 1925. Pp. 32. MBNEH.

7349 O'CONNOR, TOM. Current developments in the Sacco-Vanzetti case. Springfield, 1960. 19 leaves.

7350 "THE OLD saw-mill and grist-mill on Mother Brook." DedHR, 6 (1895), 113-116.

7351 "THE OLD training ground." DedHR, (1898), 99-102.

7352 "THE OLD Whiting Mills on Mother Brook." DedHR, 13 (1902), 97-98.

7353 PACKARD, J. F. "Baptist beginnings at Mill Village." DedHR, 11 (1900), 107-111.

7354 _____. "The First Baptist Meeting-House in Mill Village." DedHR, 12 (1901), 4-8. 1843.

7355 PARKHURST, J. W. Historical sermon giving the concise history of the First Baptist Church in Dedham from its origin down to the present time, delivered August 2d, 1846. Boston: J. Putna, 1846. Pp. 20. M.

7356 PAUL, EDWARD CRANE. "The Paul Homestead in Dedham." DedHR, 10 (1899), 103-113.

7357 "THE POWDER House." DedHR, 4 (1893), 91-94.

7358 PRATT, GRACE JOY. Church of the Good Shepherd, Dedham, Massachusetts, seventy-fifth anniversary, Trinity Sunday, 1948. Dedham, 1948. Pp. 23. M.

7359 PUTNAM, EBEN. "The Fairbanks House in Dedham, Mass." Genealogical Quarterly Magazine, 5 (1904-1905), 147-149.

7360 RILEY, DORA. "Reminiscences of the old Draper House." DedHR, 7 (1896), 109-111.

7361 RUDD, EDWARD HUNTTING. Dedham's ancient landmarks and their national significance. Dedham: Dedham Transcript Printing and Publishing, 1908. Pp. 57.

7362 RUSSELL, FRANCIS. "Sacco-Vanzetti: was the trial fair?" Modern Age, 19 (1975), 30-41.

7363 _____. "Son of Sacco." National Review, 25 (1973), 887-890. Dante Sacco.

7364 _____. "A tragedy in Dedham." Am Heritage, 9 (October, 1958), 52-57, 109; 11 (December, 1959), 89-93. Sacco-Vanzetti.

7365 _____. "Tragedy in Dedham: a retrospect of the Sacco-Vanzetti trial." Antioch Review, 15 (1955-1956), 387-398.

7366 _____. Tragedy in Dedham: the story of the Sacco-Vanzetti case. N.Y.: McGraw-Hill, 1962. Pp. 478.

7367 SACCO, NICOLA. The letters of Sacco and Vanzetti. Marion Denman Frankfurter and Gardner Jackson, eds. N.Y.: Viking Pr., 1928 Pp. xi, 414.

7368 _____, defendant. The Sacco-Vanzetti case: transcript of the record of the trial of Nicola Sacco and Bartolomeo Vanzetti in the courts of Massachusetts and subsequent proceedings 1920-7. Prefatory essay by William O. Douglas. (1928-1929) 2d. ed. Mamaroneck, N.Y.: P. P. Appel, 1969. 5v.

7369 _____, defendant. Sacco y Vanzett, un grave error judical. José Augustín Martínez, ed. Habana: Cultural, 1930. Pp. 386.

7370 SHELDON, N. L. "The birthplace of the American free public school." NEM, New Ser., 27 (1902-1903), 509-517.

7371 SLAFTER, CARLOS. A record of education: the schools and teachers of Dedham, Massachusetts, 1644-1904. [Dedham]: Dedham Transcript Pr., 1905. Pp. 330.

7372 _____. "The 250th anniversary of the establishment of the free public school in Dedham, Massachusetts." DedHR, 6 (1895), 1-11.

7373 SMITH, FRANK. "Controversy over Dedham's grant to the Natick Indians." DedHR, 9 (1898), 37-41.

7374 _____. Dedham in picture and story. n.p., [1924?-1929?]. 6v. MBNEH.

7375 _____. A history of Dedham, Massachusetts. Dedham: Transcript Pr., 1936. Pp. 543.

7376 SMITH, JAMES MORTON. The Federalist 'Saints' versus 'The devil of sedition': the liberty pole cases of Dedham, Massachusetts, 1798-1799. NEQ, 28 (1955), 198-215.

7377 SMITH, MARTHA ABBY. "A study of the growth of town government in colonial days." DedHR, 3 (1892), 101-111.

7378 SWAN, MABEL MUNSON. "The Dedham pottery." Antiques, 10 (1926), 116-121.

7379 "THE STRIPED pig." HPHR, 2 (1892-1893), 44-53. Temperance, 1838.

7380 TITUS, LILLIE B. "The old Fairbanks House at Dedham, Mass." MassMag, 1 (1908), 25-26.

7381 TRANSCRIPT PRESS, INC., DEDHAM. The Dedham Transcript, celebrating a century of service, 1870-1970. [Dedham], 1970. Pp. 111.

7382 WALLED in this tomb: questions left unanswered by the Lowell Committee in the Sacco-Vanzetti case and their pertinence in understanding the conflicts sweeping the world at this hour, for especial consideration by the alumni of Harvard University during its tercentenary celebration. Boston: Excelsior Pr., 1936. Pp. 29. MB.

7383 WHITE, JOHN. A centennial discourse delivered before the Congregational Scoiety in the Third Parish of Dedham, January 17, 1836. Dedham: H. Mann, 1836. Pp. 34. MB.

7384 WIGHT, DANFORTH PHIPPS. "Dedham Village sixty years ago, in 1807." DedHR, 5 (1894), 145-149.

7385 WORTHINGTON, ARTHUR MORTON. History of Saint Paul's Episcopal Church in Dedham, with addenda covering the last fity years, by Thomas E. Jansen, Jr. [Dedham?, 1958]. Pp. 43. Originally appeared in the 'Dedham Transcript' in 1908.

7386 WORTHINGTON, ERASTUS. "The Dexter House during the Siege of Boston, 1775-6." DedHR, 5 (1894), 150-158.

7387 _____. "The first court house, 1793." DedHR, 4 (1893), 1-5.

7388 _____. "The frigate Constitution and the Avery Oak." DedHR, 9 (1898), 1-5.

7389 _____. Historical sketch of Mother Brook, Dedham, Mass...showing the diversion of a portion of the Charles River into the Neponset River and the manufacturing on the stream from 1639 to 1900. Dedham: C. G. Wheeler, 1900. Pp. 16. M.

7390 _____. The history of Dedham, from the beginning of its settlement, in September, 1635, to May, 1827. Boston: Dutton and Wentworth, 1827. Pp. 146.

7391 WORTHINGTON, JOHN WINTHROP. "The penal institutions of Dedham." DedHR, 1 (1890), 27-31.

7392 YE OLD Fayerbanke House, Dedham, Mass., built in 1636. Boston: E. L. Grimes, [1936?]. Pp. 31. MBNEH.

DEERFIELD

7393 ALLEN, MARY ELECTA. "Blue and White needlework of Deerfield." The House Beautiful, 3 (1898), 166-169. Embroidery by the Blue and White Society.

7394 _____. "Handicrafts in old Deerfield." Outlook, 69 (1901), 592-597.

7395 _____. "Old Deerfield." NEM, New Ser., 7 (1892-1893), 33-46.

7396 ANDREWS, SIBYL STETSON. Miracle of the snow: a true story of the events in Deerfield, Massachusetts, during the years 1704-1714. Turners Falls: Franklin County Pr., 1971. Pp. 115. MDeeP.

7397 ASHLEY, GERTRUDE PORTER. Memories of old Deerfield. Deerfield, 1934. Pp. 45.

7398 "ASHLEY House, Deerfield, Massachusetts." Interior Design and Decoration, 19 (July, 1949), 18-19.

7399 BAKER, CHARLOTTE ALICE. "Settlement of Deerfield." PVMA, 1 (1870-1879), 72-102.

7400 BOUVE, PAULINE CARRINGTON. "Deerfield renaissance." NEM, New Ser., 33 (1905-1906), 162-172.

7401 BOYDEN, ELIZABETH. "The 250th anniversary of the Massacre." Deerfield Alumni Journal, 10 (January, 1954), 5-11.

7402 THE CENTENNIAL of the PVMA [Pocumtuck Valley Memorial Association] and the dedication of the Heritage Foundation Library, Deerfield, Massachusetts, May 22nd, 1970. [Meriden, Conn.]: Meriden Gravure, 1970. Pp. 27. MBNEH.
Historical address by Wilmarth Sheldon Lewis.

7403 CHANDLER, AMARIAH. A brief review of a historical sermon, delivered at Deerfield, Mass., September 22, 1857, by Rev. Samuel Willard. Greenfield: Eastman, 1859. Pp. 27.
Unitarianism.

7404 CHASE, CORNELIUS THURSTON. Eaglebrook: the first fifty years, 1922-1972. [Deerfield]: Eaglebrook School, [1972?]. Pp. 223.

7405 CLARK, PERKINS K. Sacrifices for our country: a discourse delivered July 17, 1864, in the First Church, South Deerfield, Mass., at a funeral service for James T. Stebbins and Myron E. Stowell, who were killed in the armies of the Union, with an appendix, containing sketches of other deceased soldiers, from the same place.... Greenfield: Eastman, 1864. Pp. 44.
Biographies of soldiers.

7406 COLEMAN, EMMA LEWIS. "The Frary House, Deerfield, Massachusetts." OTNE, 23 (1932-1933), 89-98.

7407 _____. A historic and present day guide to old Deerfield. Boston, 1907. Pp. 116.

7408 COWAN, RORY and LEE PHILLIPS. A sign of change: the greening of Deerfield Academy. Bedford: Camera Stat Associates, 1971. Pp. 109. MDeeH.

7409 DAVIS, GEORGE T. "'The St. Regis Bell.'" MHSP, (1869-1870), 311-321.
Legend connected with Deerfield.

7410 "DEERFIELD." Antiques, 70 (1956), 223-267.

7411 DEERFIELD ACADEMY. Deerfield Academy.... Deerfield, 1929. Unpaged.

7412 "[DEERFIELD Academy, 150th anniversary]." Deerfield Alumni Journal, 5, No. 3 (1949), entire issue.

7413 "DEERFIELD doors." The House Beautiful, 6 (November, 1899), 243-250.

7414 "DEERFIELD revisited." Antiques, 75 (1959), 464-469.

7415 "DEERFIELD Village industries." Pallette and Bench, 2 (June, 1910), 240-241.

7416 DICKINSON, RODOLPHUS. A description of Deerfield, in Franklin County, intended as an exhibition of the plan of a contemplated gazetteer of Massachusetts proper. Deerfield: G. J. Newcomb, 1817. Pp. 8.

7417 _____. A geographical, statistical, and historical view of the town of Deerfield, in the county of Franklin, and state of Massachusetts; intended as an exhibition of the plan and execution of a contemplated gazetteer of Massachusetts proper. Deerfield: Graves & Wells, 1815. Pp. 29.

7418 "EARLY history of the town of Deerfield." Deerfield, 29 (Spring, 1972), 3-4.

7419 EVERETT, EDWARD. An address delivered at Bloody Brook, in South Deerfield, September 30, 1835, in commemoration of the fall of the 'Flower of Essex,' at that spot, in King Philip's War, September 18, (o.s.) 1675. Boston: Russell, Shattuck, & Williams, 1835. Pp. 44.

7420 FLYNT, HELEN G. and HENRY N. FLYNT. The Dwight-Barnard House, Deerfield, Massachusetts. Worcester: Commonwealth Pr., 1954. Pp. 28.
House was moved from Springfield in 1954.

7421 _____ and _____. An old custom, the liberty pole of Deerfield, 1774. [Greenwich?, Conn.]: Priv. Print., 1946. Unpaged.

7422 FLYNT, HENRY N. and HELEN G. FLYNT. Asa Stebbins House, 1799, Deerfield, Mass. n.p.: Priv. Print., 1958. Pp. 16. MDeeH.

7423 _____ and _____. Ashley House in Old Deerfield, Massachusetts. Deerfield: Priv. Print., [1949?]. Pp. 16. MDeeH.

7424 _____ and _____. Deerfield meeting house, Deerfield, Mass. Deerfield: Priv. Print., 1952. Pp. 8. MDeeH.
First church.

7425 _____ and _____. Hall Tavern, 1760, in old Deerfield, Mass. n.p.: Priv. Print., n.d. Pp. 15. MDeeH.

7426 _____ and _____. John Wilson Printing House, Deerfield, Mass. Deerfield: Priv. Print., 1951. Pp. 8. MDeeH.

7427 FLYNT, HENRY N. "Old Deerfield." Connecticut Antiquarian, 5 (1953), 19-25.

7428 _____. "Old Deerfield, a living community." Art in America, 43 (1955), 40-47, 73-74.

7429 FRIARY, GRACE T. "Silversmithing in Deerfield, Massachusetts." The Magazine Silver, 5 (1972), 15-16.

7430 FULLER, MARY WILLIAMS. The story of Deerfield. Brattleboro: Vermont Printing, 1930. Pp. 48.

7431 GOSS, ELBRIDGE HENRY. "King Philip's War-- the Battle of Bloody Brook." Potter's AmMo, 5 (1875), 735-743.

7432   GRISWOLD, F. K. "Home industries in old
       Deerfield." Independent, 73 (1912), 1047-
1051.

7433   HADDON, RAWSON W. An architectural mono-
       graph on old Deerfield, Massachusetts.
St. Paul: White Pine Bureau, 1920. Pp. 16.

7434   HAIGIS, JOHN W., JR. "The Deerfield Massa-
       cre, a new appraisal." Deerfield Alumni
Journal, 15 (October, 1958), 4-10.
       1704.

7435   HARRIS, MARGARET. "Origin and history of
       Deerfield Academy." PVMA, 5 (1905-1911),
495-500.

7436   HAWKS, SUSAN BELLE. "A Deerfield chest
       dated 1699." American Collector, 10 (Sep-
tember, 1941), 8-9.

7437   HERITAGE FOUNDATION, DEERFIELD, MASS. Old
       Deerfield Meeting House, 1838-1958. Deer-
field, 1958. Pp. 28. MDeeH.
       Orthodox Congregational Church and the
       Martha Goulding Pratt Memorial.

7438   "HISTORY of Memorial Hall." PVMA, 1 (1870-
       1879), 434-442.

7439   "HISTORY of the founding of Deerfield Acad-
       emy." PVMA, 1 (1870-1879), 397-405.

7440   HITCHCOCK, NATHANIEL. "Recollections of the
       old Indian House." PVMA, 1 (1870-1879),
277-280.

7441   HOWE, MARGERY BURNHAM. Early American em-
       broideries in Deerfield, Massachusetts.
Deerfield, Heritage Foundation, [1964?]. Pp. 32.
MDeeH.

7442   [HOYT, ELIHU]. A brief sketch of the first
       settlement of Deerfield, Mass., together
with a few of the events which took place there in
early times. By one of the descendants of the
first settlers of the town. Greenfield: James P.
Fogg, 1833. Pp. iv, 48.
       Preface signed: E. H.

7443   INDIAN HOUSE MEMORIAL, INC., DEERFIELD,
       MASS. Indian House memorial, Old Deerfield,
Massachusetts. Deerfield, 1945. Pp. 89.
       Signed: Marion Pendleton Drew and Kelsey
       Flower.

7444   JOHNSON, CLIFTON. An unredeemed captive:
       being the story of Eunice Williams, who, at
the age of seven years, was carried away from Deerfield by the Indians in the year 1704, and who
lived among the Indians in Canada as one of them
the rest of her life. Holyoke: Griffith, Axtell &
Cady, 1897. Pp. 54.

7445   LARNED, AUGUSTA. "A Massachusetts Arcadia."
       MagHist, 21 (1915), 151-155.

7446   LELAND, MARINE. A Canadian explorer in Deer-
       field, Jacques de Noyen, 1668-1745. Spring-
field: Connecticut Valley Historical Museum, 1955.
Pp. 9. MDeeH.

7447   LYNNDE, ELMER. "Deerfield--old and new."
       Potter's AmMo, 9 (1877), 199-200.

7448   MCCRACKEN, ELIZABETH. "The small town of
       Deerfield." Outlook, 86 (May 25, 1907), 161-
168.

7449   MCDOWELL, BART. "Deerfield keeps a truce
       with time." National Geographic Magazine,
135 (1969), 780-809.

7450   MARPLE, ELLIOT. "'The Beehive,' Deerfield,
       Mass." OTNE, 24 (1933-1934), 129-131.
       Former tavern.

7451   MERRITT, BRUCE G. "Loyalism and social con-
       flict in Revolutionary Deerfield, Massachu-
setts." JAH, 57 (1970-1971), 277-289.

7452   MILLER, AMELIA FULLER and JOSEPH P. SPANG,
       III. The Deerfield town records: how they
were found. Deerfield: Heritage Foundation, 1970.
Pp. 6. MDeeH.

7453   MILLER, AMELIA FULLER. Hannah Beaman lifts
       the latch: a story of the Allen House in
old Deerfield, Massachusetts. n.p.: Priv. Print,
1947. Pp. 15. MDeeH.

7454   ____. The Reverend Jonathan Ashley House,
       Deerfield, Massachusetts. [Deerfield]:
Heritage Foundation, 1962. Pp. xiv, 153.

7455   "OLD Deerfield: symbol of America." Inte-
       rior Design, 26 (December, 1955), 98-99, 122,
125-126.
       Old Manse, 1768.

7456   PARKMAN, FRANCIS. "The village of Deerfield,
       1704." MagAmHist, 28 (1892), 68-71.

7457   PARSONS, HERBERT COLLINS. "Fifty years of the
       Pocumtuck Valley Memorial Association."
PVMA, 6 (1912-1920), 554-565.
       Historical society.

7458   PATTERSON, GERARD A. "...the enemy came in
       like a flood upon us." AHI, 1 (November,
1966), 14-19.
       Massacre of 1704.

7459   PHELPS, FLORA L. "Pioneers in Massachu-
       setts." Américas, 22 (February, 1970), 21-
30.

7460   PINKHAM PRESS, BOSTON. Old Deerfield, con-
       taining an appreciation of early New England
as evidenced by the now standing seventeenth-century
houses of Deerfield, Massachusetts; illustrated with
reproductions of pencil sketches made from the
houses themselves. Boston: Pinkham Pr., 1927. 24
leaves.

7461   POCUMTUCK VALLEY MEMORIAL ASSOCIATION, DEER-
        FIELD, MASS. The first 100 years of the Po-
cumtuck Valley Memorial Association. Deerfield,
1972. Pp. 30. MDeeP.
        Historical society.

7462   PRATT, FRANK WRIGHT. Boyhood memories of
        old Deerfield. Portland, Me.: Southworth-
Anthoensen Pr., 1936. Pp. 308.

7463   PRATT, JANE. "From Merton Abbey to old
        Deerfield." Craftsman, 5 (1903), 183-191.
Arts and crafts.

7464   SHELDON, GEORGE. "Biographical sketches of
        the settlers at Pocumtuck before Philip's
War." PVMA, 1 (1870-1879), 69-72.

7465   ____. "The conference at Deerfield, Mass.,
        August 27-31, 1735, between Gov. Belcher
and several tribes of western Indians." NEHGR, 60
(1906), 256-261.

7466   ____. "Gossip about the Pocumtuck gun."
        PVMA, 1 (1880-1889), 28-35.

7467   ____. A history of Deerfield, Massachu-
        setts--a facsimile of the 1895-96 edition
published in recognition of the tercentenary of the
town of Deerfield in 1973, with a new foreword by
Amelia F. Miller and Donald R. Friary. Somersworth,
N.H.: New Hampshire Publishing Co. in collaboration
with the Pocumtuck Valley Memorial Association,
Deerfield, 1972. 2v. M.

7468   ____. "The little brown house on the Al-
        bany Road." NEM, New Ser., 19 (1898-1899),
36-54.
        Epaphras Hoyt House.

7469   ____. "Negro slavery in old Deerfield."
        NEM, New Ser., 8 (1893), 49-60.

7470   ____. "New tracks in an old trail." PVMA,
        3 (1899-1904), 11-28.
French and Indian attack of 1704 and capture
of John Williams.

7471   ____. "The old Deerfield cannon." PVMA,
        3 (1890-1898), 241-243.

7472   ____ and JENNIE MARIA ARMS SHELDON. The
        Rev. John Williams House. Deerfield, 1918.
Pp. 32.

7473   SHELDON, GEORGE. "'Tis sixty years since:
        the passing of the stall-fed ox and the farm
boy." PVMA, 3 (1890-1898), 472-490.
        Raising oxen for the Boston and New York
markets prior to advent of railroads.

7474   SHELDON, JENNIE MARIA ARMS. "The evolution-
        ary history of a New England homestead, or
the Colonel Joseph Stebbins Homestead in Deerfield,
Massachusetts." PVMA, 7 (1921-1929), 159-177.

7475   ____. "John Sheldon and the old Indian
        House Homestead." PVMA, 5 (1905-1911), 238-
254.

7476   ____. "The 'old Indian House' at Deerfield,
        Mass., and the effort made in 1847 to save it
from destruction." OTNE, 12 (1921-1922), 99-108.

7477   ____. Pitted stones. Deerfield, 1925.
        Pp. 65.

7478   SHELDON, JOHN. "The common field of Deer-
        field." PVMA, 5 (1905-1911), 238-254.

7479   ____. "Telling what happened to Deerfield
        February 29, 1704." PVMA, 7 (1921-1929),
204-209.
        French and Indian attack.

7480   SPANG, JOSEPH PETER, III. "Brick architec-
        ture in Deerfield, Massachusetts, 1797-
1825." Antiques, 106, (1974), 628-633.

7481   ____. "The Parker and Russell Silver Shop
        in old Deerfield: Clesson House." Antiques,
81 (1962), 638-641.

7482   ____. "Preservation project: Deerfield's
        Memorial Hall." Antiques, 94 (1968), 206-
209.

7483   ____. "The Wells-Thorn House in Deerfield,
        Massachusetts." Antiques, 89 (1966), 730-
733.

7484   SPOONER, LEWIS G. Directory and history of
        the Orthodox Congregational Church, Deer-
field, Massachusetts. n.p., [1915?]. Pp. 16.
MDeeP.

7485   STAGG, A. "Old Deerfield: enchantingly re-
        captures the spirit of the eighteenth cen-
tury." House and Garden, 134 (October, 1968), 34+.

7486   [STRONG, TITUS]. The Deerfield captive, an
        Indian story; being a narrative of facts for
the instruction of the young. (1832) 4th ed.
Greenfield: A. Phelps, 1842. Pp. 68. ICN.

7487   SWEDLUND, ALAN C. The genetic structure of
        an historical population; a study of marriage
and fertility in old Deerfield, Massachusetts.
Prescott, Ariz.: Center for Man and Environment,
Prescott College, 1971. Pp. v, 78.

7488   "THE STORY of Deerfield." Antiques, 60
        (1951), 108-112.

7489   TAYLOR, JOHN. A century sermon, preached at
        Deerfield, February 29, 1804, in commemora-
tion of the destruction of the town by the French
and Indians. Greenfield: John Denio, 1804.
Pp. 32. MB.

7490   THOMPSON, FRANCIS MCGEE. "Messengers of war
        and messengers of peace." PVMA, 4 (1899-
1904), 9-11.
        French and Indian attack of 1704.

7491   THOMPSON, FRANCIS NIMS. "Evolution and hu-
        man progress illumed by history." PVMA, 7
(1921-1929), 231-235.
        Nims family.

7492   WELLS, CAROLYN. "The welcoming doorways of Deerfield." Craftsman, 24 (1913), 413-420.

7493   WHITING, MARGARET C. "A Deerfield discovery." PVMA, 7 (1921-1929), 131-133. Wall paintings in Ware House.

7494   WILLIAMS, JOHN. The redeemed captive returning to Zion: or, a faithful history of remarkable occurrences in the captivity and deliverance of Mr. John Williams, minister of the gospel in Deerfield, who in the desolation which befel that plantation by an incursion of the French and Indians, was by them carried away, with his family and his neighborhood, into Canada, drawn up by himself. (1707) Stephen W. Williams, ed. Northampton: Hopkins, Bridgman, 1853. Pp. viii, 192.

7495   WILLIAMS, STEPHEN WEST. A biographical memoir of the Rev. John Williams, first miniter of Deerfield, Massachusetts, with a slight sketch of ancient Deerfield, and an account of the Indian wars in that place and vicinity, wtih an appendix, containing the journal of the Rev. Doctor Stephen Williams, of Longmeadow, during his captivity, and other papers relating to the early Indian wars in Deerfield. Greenfield: C. J. J. Ingersoll, 1837. Pp. vi, 127.

7496   "THE WILLIAMS House at Deerfield." Mass Mag, 2 (1909), 41.

7497   WINSHIP, ALBERT E. "Pocumtuck Valley in the world's arena." PVMA, 4 (1899-1904), 251-261.

7498   WRIGHT, ROXA. "Blue and White Deerfield embroidery." Woman's Day, (June, 1962), 53-60.
Blue and White Society, 1896-1925.

7499   YALE, CATHARINE B. Story of the old Willard House of Deerfield, Mass., written for and read at the eighteenth annual meeting of the Pocumtuck Valley Memorial Association, February 22, 1887. Boston: Houghton, Mifflin, 1887. Pp. 24.

DENNIS

7500   BRAGDON, WILLIAM B. The South Dennis Meeting House.... Yarmouthport: Swift, 1924. Pp. 22.

7501   "THE CAPE Playhouse." CCC, 2 (1947), 16-21.

7502   CLARK, ADMONT G. "They built clipper ships in their backyard." AmNep, 22 (1962), 233-251.
Shiverick Shipyard.

7503   CRAIG, POLLY. "Autobiography of a church." The Cape, 1 (June, 1967), 24-25.
Congregational Church of South Dennis.

7504   CROSBY, KATHARINE. "When the Cape built clipper ships." Cape Cod Magazine, 8 (August 16, 1926), 5-6, 20, 25.
Shiverick Shipyard.

7505   EVANS, SYLVANUS C. The Baker zone in West Dennis.... Yarmouthport, 1928. Unpaged. Area of the town occupied by the Baker family.

7506   HALL, LEMUEL C. "The town of Dennis." CCAPL, 4 (April, 1921), 15.

7507   HALL, THOMAS F. Shipbuilding at East Dennis.... Yarmouthport, 1925. Pp. 8.

7508   KINGSLEY, KAY. "The house a Howes built." Cape Cod Magazine, 9 (December, 1926), 9. Howes-Hall House.

7509   O'NEIL, NEVA. Master mariners of Dennis. [Dennis]: Dennis Historical Society, 1965. Pp. v, 48.

7510   PERRY, ERNESTINE. The white spire: history of the West Dennis Community Church and Village, 1835-1885. West Dennis: West Dennis Community Church, 1967. Pp. 44.

7511   STOCKDALE, SABRA. "The tower on Scargo Hill." The Cape, 1 (March, 1967), 12-14 Stone tower.

DIGHTON

7512   DIGHTON, MASS. 250th anniversary, town of Dighton, Mass., 1712-1962. Taunton: Davol Printing, 1962. Pp. 71. M.

7513   DIGHTON, MASS. UNITARIAN CHURCH. Yearbook and church directory of the Unitarian Church, Dighton, Mass. n.p., [1933?]. Unpaged. MBNEH.
Contains historical sketch.

7514   LANE, HELEN HOLMES. History of the town of Dighton, Massachusetts, the South Purchase, May 30, 1712. [Dighton]: The Town, 1962. Pp. 263.

7515   PARKIN, FRANK P. History of the Methodist Episcopal Church in North Dighton, Mass. [Dighton?]: The Official Board, 1888. Pp. 71. M.

7516   TOWN of Dighton bi-centennial, 1712-1912. Taunton: C. A. Hack & Son, 1912. Pp. 169.

7517   WALTON ADVERTISING AND PRINTING CO., BOSTON. From grey to beauty: an account of the industry carried on at North Dighton by the Mount Hope Finishing Company. Boston: Priv. Print., 1927. Pp. 81. MB.
Bleaching, dyeing and finishing of cloth.

DOUGLAS

7518   EAST DOUGLAS, MASS. CONGREGATIONAL CHURCH. The confession of faith and covenant...with a brief history, and a list of members, May, 1875. East Douglas: C. J. Batcheller, 1875. Pp. 33.

7519   EMERSON, WILLIAM ANDREW. History of the
       town of Douglas, (Massachusetts,) from the
earliest period to the close of 1878. Boston:
F. W. Bird, 1879. Pp. 359.

7520   KEBABIAN, JOHN S. "The Douglas Axe Manufac-
       turing Company, East Douglas, Mass." CEAIA,
25 (1972), 43-46.

DOVER

7521   DOVER. Boston: Edison Electric Illuminat-
       ing Co., 1909. Pp. 8. M.

7522   DOVER HISTORICAL AND NATURAL HISTORY SOCIETY,
       DOVER, MASS. Dedication of the Sawin Memo-
rial Building, Dover, Massachusetts, Tuesday, May
14th, 1907. [Dover], 1908. Pp. 40.

7523   _____. Old Home Day in the town of Dover,
       August 19th, 1903. Natick: Natick Bulle-
tin, 1903. Pp. 55.
       Historical address by Frank Smith.

7524   _____. Old Home Day: proceedings of the
       one hundred and twenty-fifth anniversary of
the incorporation of the town of Dover, Massachusetts, Wednesday, July 7th, 1909.... [Dover?],
1910. Pp. 73.
       Historical address by F. J. Stimson.

7525   _____. The proceedings of the dedication of
       the Soldiers' Monument, Dover, Massachusetts,
June 18, 1910; to which has been added the exercises
of dedication of the new grammar school house, November 12, 1910, the unveiling of headstones to the
memory of Revolutionary soldiers, May 10, 1911, the
dedication of the tablet erected in memory of the
Indians, January 13, 1912. [Dover], 1912. Pp. 83.

7526   JONES, ALICE JOHNSON. In Dover on the
       Charles: a contribution to New England folk-
lore. Newport, R.I.: Milne Printery, 1906.
Pp. 114.
       Social life and customs.

7527   SMITH, FRANK. Biographical sketch of the
       residents of that part of Dedham, which is
now Dover, who took part in King Philip's War, the
last French and Indian War, and the Revolution; --
together with the record of the services of those
who represented Dover in the War of 1812; the war
with Mexico; the Civil War; and the war with Spain.
Dover: The Town, 1909. Pp. 88, iv.

7528   _____. Biographical sketches of the resi-
       dents of Dover, Massachusetts, who during
the first century of the town's corporate existence,
1748-1848, graduated from college. [Dover?, 189-?].
Pp. 12.

7529   _____. The deeds of our fathers: a Memorial
       Day address delivered in the Town House,
Dover, Massachusetts, May 30, 1904. [Dover?]:
Memorial Day Committee, 1904. Pp. 19.

7530   _____. Dover farms; in which is traced the
       development of the territory from the first
settlement in 1640 to 1900. Dover: Historical and
Natural History Society, 1914. Pp. viii, 152.

7531   _____. Dover fifty years ago. [Dover?,
       1930]. Pp. 14.

7532   _____. "Dover, Mass., the Springfield or
       Fourth Parish of Dedham in the Revolutionary
War." DedHR, 2 (1891), 118-120; 3 (1892), 25-28.

7533   _____. The founders of the First Parish,
       Dover, Massachusetts, with descriptions of
all the houses now standing which were built before
the Revolution. [Dover?]: First Parish, 1908.
Pp. 24.

7534   _____. A geographical and historical cate-
       chism of Dover, Mass. n.p., 1891. Pp. 18.
MB.

7535   _____. Narrative history: a history of Do-
       ver, Massachusetts, as a precinct, parish,
district, and town. Dover: The Town, 1897.
Pp. xv, 354.

7536   _____. One hundredth anniversary of the
       First Parish Sunday School, Dover, Mass.;
address...November 10, 1918. Dover, 1918. Pp. 8.
MBNEH.

7537   _____. The Williams Tavern, Dover, Mass.:
       a paper read before the Dover Historical
Society, July 11, 1908. [Dover, 1908]. Pp. 7.

7538   TILDEN, WILLIAM SMITH. "The legend of Tub-
       wreck Brook." DedHR, 9 (1898), 80-85.

DRACUT

7539   COBURN, SILAS ROGER. "Description of grants
       of land, which in 1701 was included in the
territory called Dracut." Lowell HSC, 2 (1921-
1926), 137-151.

7540   _____. History of Dracut, Massachusetts,
       called by the Indians Augumtoocooke and be-
fore incorporation, the Wildernesse North of the
Merrimac, first permanent settlement in 1669 and incorporated as a town in 1701. Lowell: Courier-
Citizen, 1922. Pp. xii, 433.

7541   DRACUT, MASS. Report of 200th anniversary of
       the incorporation of [the] town of Dracut,
June 12, 1901. Lowell: Butterfield Printing,
[1901?]. Pp. 46.

7542   GORDON, GEORGE ANGIER. Early grants of land
       in the Wildernesse North of [the] Merri-
mack.... Lowell: Morning Mail, 1892. Pp. 44.
MBNEH.

DUDLEY

7543 BATES, JOSHUA. An anniversary discourse, delivered at Dudley, Massachusetts, March 20, 1853, with topographical and historical notices of the town. Boston: T. R. Marvin, 1853. Pp. 58.

7544 CONANT, HEZEKIAH, comp. A souvenir of the Conant Memorial Church, its inception, construction, and dedication.... Boston: Forbes Lithograph Manufacturing, 1893. Pp. viii, 130.

7545 CONANT, SAMUEL MORRIS. "The settlement of Dudley." QHSL, 1, No. 8, 99-106.

7546 CRAWFORD, PEARLE L. "Stevens Linen, its first century and a half." NEG, 9 (Winter, 1968), 33-40.

7547 DUDLEY, MASS. The book of Dudley, published as an official souvenir of the celebration of the 200th anniversary of the incorporation of the town. Webster: Times Publishing, 1932. Unpaged. M.

7548 DUDLEY, MASS. FIRST CONGREGATIONAL CHURCH. Historical notice of the Congregational Church in Dudley, with the articles of faith, covenant, &c. Worcester: Henry J. Howland, 1845. Pp. 16.

7549 EDDY, WILLIAM PENN. "Ancient perambulation of selectmen in Dudley." QHSL, 1, No. 23-24, 283-303.

7550 _____. "The old stone monument on the Durfee Farm in Dudley." QHSL, 1, No. 18-19, 215-240.

7551 _____. "Rattlesnake Hill Trail in Dudley and how it became a white man's highway." QHSL, 1, No. 20, 241-256.

7552 FRANCIS, JAMES HANMER. Copy of a discourse delivered on Fast-day, April 9, 1835, by Rev. James H. Francis, containing an historical sketch of the town of Dudley, Mass. n.p.: Printed for Samuel Morris Conant, 1892. 2 leaves.

7553 MORTON, ELIAS P. "Dudley in the Civil War." QHSL, 3, No. 1, 1-16.

DUNSTABLE

7554 GATES, CURTIS H., ed. Dunstable Village. Nashua, N.H.: Accurate Printing, 1973. Pp. 95. M.

7555 LORING, GEORGE BAILEY. Historical sketches of Dunstable, Mass., bi-centennial oration of Hon. George B. Loring, September 17, 1873. Lowell: G. M. Elliott, 1873. Pp. 19.

7556 NASON, ELIAS. A history of the town of Dunstable, Massachusetts, from its earliest settlement to the year of our Lord 1873. Boston: A. Mudge & Son, 1877. Pp. 316.

7557 [SPALDING, EDWARD H.], comp. Bi-centennial of old Dunstable, address by Hon. S. T. Worcester, October 27, 1873, also Colonel Bancroft's personal narrative of the Battle of Bunker Hill, and some notices of persons and families of the early times of Dunstable, including Welds, Tyngs, Lovewells, Farwells, Fletchers, Bancrofts, Joneses and Cutlers. By J. B. Hill. Nashua, N.H.: E. H. Spalding, 1878. Pp. 189.

7558 TURNER, BERTHA M. "The Thompson Farm." VIAA, 51 (1946), 1, 7.

DUXBURY

7559 ALDEN, CHARLES LAFORESTT. The story of the John Alden House, built 1653, Duxbury, Massachusetts. Duxbury, 1938. Pp. 26.

7560 ALDEN, EDWARD SMITH. Alden homestead, Duxbury, Mass., shrine of millions of descendants of John Alden and his wife, Priscilla Mullens. Holyoke: Alden Pr., 1932. Pp. 64.

7561 BRADFORD, ALDEN. "Notes on Duxbury." MHSC, 2 Ser., 10 (1823), 57-71. Seventeenth century.

7562 BRADFORD, GERSHOM. "The Ezra Westons, shipbuilders of Duxbury." AmNep, 14 (1954), 29-41.

7563 _____. Historic Duxbury in Plymouth County, Massachusetts. Boston, 1920. Pp. 44.

7564 BRADFORD, LAURENCE. Historic Duxbury in Plymouth County, Massachusetts. (1900) Gershom Bradford, II, ed. 3d. ed. Boston: N. Sawyer & Son, 1910. Pp. 160.

7565 DUXBURY, MASS. Copy of the old records of the town of Duxbury, Mass., from 1642 to 1770, made in the year 1892. Plymouth: Avery & Doten, 1893. Pp. 348. Indexed.

7566 _____. The two hundred and fiftieth anniversary of the settlement of Duxbury, June 17, 1887. Plymouth: Avery & Doten, 1887. Pp. 96. Oration by Justin Winsor.

7567 DUXBURY fifty years ago. Philadelphia, 1864. Pp. 30. Harvard University Library attributes authorship to Henry Winsor.

7568 "THE DUXBURY, Mass. home of John Alden." MayflowerQ, 34 (1968), 13.

7569 FISH, HENRY A. Duxbury, Massachusetts, ancient and modern: a sketch, with map and key. Binghamton, N.Y., 1924. Pp. 17.

7570 HATHAWAY, JERUSHA FAUNCE. Duxbury sketches. Dorchester: Underhill Pr., 1921. Pp. 34. MBNEH.

7571 HIGGINS, LUCY PORTER. "Old ship-building days at Duxbury." MNEH, 3 (1893), 215-226.

7572 _____. "When and where some of the first ships were built in New England." Americana, 13 (1919), 244-252.

7573 HUIGINN, EUGENE JOSEPH VINCENT. The graves of Myles Standish and other Pilgrims. (1892) Rev. and enl. Beverly, 1914. Pp. 218.

7574 LONG, ELLESLEY WALDO, ed. The story of Duxbury, 1637-1937. Duxbury: The Duxbury Tercentenary Committee, [1937]. Pp. xiv, 237.

7575 [MCKINNEY, WILLIAM LORD]. King Caesar: a story of colonial Duxbury in Massachusetts. Duxbury: Duxbury Rural and Historical Association, [not after 1967]. Unpaged. M.
    Author attribution by the editor; Ezra Weston and his home, the King Caesar mansion.

7576 PERRY, C. C. "White Pine in Duxbury, Massachusetts, 1808-1920." Journal of Forestry, 42 (December, 1944), 927.

7577 THE PILGRIM town of Duxbury. Plymouth: A. S. Burbank [1900]. Unpaged.

7578 "A TOPOGRAPHICAL description of Duxborough, in the county of Plymouth." MHSC, 2 (1793), 3-8.

7579 WENTWORTH, DOROTHY. Settlement and growth of Duxbury, 1628-1870. Duxbury: Duxbury Rural and Historical Society, 1973. Pp. xiv, 144. M.

7580 WINSOR, JUSTIN. History of the town of Duxbury, Massachusetts, with genealogical registers. Boston: Crosby & Nichols, 1849. Pp. viii, 360.

EAST BRIDGEWATER

7581 BRYANT, SETH. Old and new Joppa, and other historical sketches. Lynn: L. C. Parker, 1895. Pp. 24.
    Relates to the village of Elmwood, formerly called Joppa.

7582 HILL, LEONARD ERSKINE. Meteorological and chronological register; comprising a record of the weather, with especial reference to the position of the wind, and the moon on the occasion of sudden changes, untimely frosts, &c., from a personal diary of the author from 1806 to 1869, with an appendix. Plymouth: M. Bates, 1869. Pp. 396.

7583 RICH, PAUL JOHN. The history of East Bridgewater. East Bridgewater: Arthur Baggia Pr., [19--]. Pp. 28.

7584 WILSON, DAVID K. The East Bridgewater sesquicennial, 1823-1973. East Bridgewater: East Bridgewater Sesquicentennial, 1973. Pp. 96.

EAST BROOKFIELD

7585 EAST BROOKFIELD, MASS. Baby town of the Commonwealth 1920-1970, fiftieth anniversary souvenir program. n.p., [1970?]. Pp. 45. M.
    Includes brief history of the town by Mary D. Putnam.

7586 ROY, LOUIS E. History of East Brookfield, Massachusetts, 1686-1970. Worcester: Heffernan Pr., 1970. Pp. xii, 432.

EAST LONGMEADOW

7587 CHAMPLIN, WINSLOW S. The history of the town of East Longmeadow written to commemorate the town's fiftieth anniversary, 1894 to 1944. John Stacy Beebe, ed. East Longmeadow, 1948. Pp. 126. MBNEH.

7588 GOODLATTE, JEANNE P. History of the town of East Longmeadow. Springfield: New England Blue Print Paper Co., 1969. Pp. viii, 182. MDeeH.

7589 PRESTON, T. DAVIS. One hundredth anniversary of the First Congregational Church, East Longmeadow, Massachusetts. East Longmeadow, 1929. Pp. 20. MAJ.

EASTHAM

7590 "BEACONS of Cape Cod, Eastham 1897-1937." CCB, 48 (April, 1937), 7.

7591 "HISTORY of Eastham." MHSC, 8 (1802), 159-186.

7592 KOEHLER, MARGARET H. "The house that whales built." CCC, 19 (1966), 22-23, 68. Penniman House.

7593 LOWE, ALICE ALBERTA. Nauset on Cape Cod: a history of Eastham. Falmouth: Kendall Printing, 1968. Pp. 155.

7594 PAINE, JOSIAH. Founders' day edition, August 26, 1916, of the early settlers of Eastham, containing sketches of all early settlers of Eastham. Yarmouthport: C. W. Swift, 1916. 2v.

7595 RICHARDSON, WYMAN. The house on Nauset Marsh. N.Y.: Norton, 1955. Pp. 223. Natural history.

7596 SMITH, EDITH M. "Camp meeting days in Eastham." Cape Cod Magazine, 10 (October, 1926), 9, 16.
    Mid-nineteenth century.

7597 TRAYSER, DONALD GRANT. Eastham, Massachusetts, 1651-1951: Eastham's three centuries. Nauset on Cape Cod [by] Alice Alberta Lowe. Eastham: Eastham Tercentenary Committee, 1951. Pp. xii, 183.

7598 WARNER, JULIA. "Eastham celebrates, 1651-
1951." CCC, 6 (1951), 12-18.

EASTHAMPTON

7599 BOOK of the chronicles of the city of Samuel:
being a sketch of the history of Easthampton.
Easthampton: Union Printing, 1867. Pp. 27.
A satire in biblical style.

7600 EASTHAMPTON, MASS. Commemorating the 175th
anniversary and homecoming 1785-1960. n.p.,
[1960?]. Pp. 166. MNF.

7601 _____. Report of the centennial celebration
at Easthampton, Mass., Wednesday, June 17th,
1885. Easthampton: L. E. Torrey, 1885. Pp. 138.

7602 EASTHAMPTON, MASS. PAYSON CHURCH. Manual
of the Payson Church, Easthampton, Mass.,
including its history, and its present members.
Easthampton: H. M. Converse, 1880. Pp. 36. M.

7603 EASTHAMPTON, MASS. SESQUICENTENNIAL CELE-
BRATION COMMITTEE. 1785-1935, 150th anniversary of Easthampton, Massachusetts, June 17,
1935. n.p., [1935?]. Pp. 128. MNF.

7604 "EASTHAMPTON: a town of varied assets."
WNE, 1 (1910-1911), 247-263.

7605 EASTHAMPTON SAVINGS BANK. 80th anniversary...1870-1950. Easthampton, [1950?].
Pp. 39. MNF.

7606 KELLOGG, ENSIGN HOSMER. Address of Hon. E.
H. Kellogg of Pittsfield, Mass., together
with other exercises connected with the dedication
of the Town Hall, at Easthampton, Mass., June 29,
1869. Easthampton: Frank A. Bartlett, 1869.
Pp. 39.

7607 LYMAN, PAYSON WILLISTON. Historical address
delivered at the centennial celebration, in
Easthampton, Mass., July 4, 1876. Springfield:
C. W. Bryan, 1877. Pp. viii, 100.
Relates to the town.

7608 _____. The historical address delivered...
on the one hundredth anniversary of the
founding of the First Church, Easthampton, Mass.,
November 17, 1885.... Easthampton: Easthampton
News, 1887. Pp. 74.

7609 _____. History of Easthampton: its settlement and growth; its material, educational,
and religious interests, together with a genealogical record of its original families. Northampton:
Trumbull & Gere, 1866. Pp. iv, 192.

7610 SAWYER, JOSEPH HENRY. A history of the
Williston Seminary. Easthampton: The
Trustees, 1917. Pp. 336. MB.

7611 SMITH, L. S. "Easthampton, Mass." NEM,
New Ser., 31 (1904-1905), 314-329.

7612 "THIRD quarter-centennial [of Williston
Academy]." Williston Bulletin, 2 (July,
1917), entire issue.

7613 WILLISTON SEMINARY. Baccalaureate sermon,
oration and addresses delivered at the semi-
centennial celebration of Williston Seminary, Easthampton, Mass., June 14-17, 1891. Springfield:
Springfield Printing and Binding, [1891]. Pp. 95.

7614 _____. Historical discourse and oration delivered at the quarter century celebration
of Williston Seminary, Easthampton, Mass., July 2,
1867. Northampton: Trumbull & Gere, 1867. Pp. iv,
63. MAJ.

7615 "WILLISTON Seminary." New Englander, 44
(1885), 265-279.

7616 WRIGHT, LUTHER, 1796-1870. Historical sketch
of Easthampton, Mass., delivered before the
Young Men's Association, of Easthampton, Oct. 7,
1851. Northampton: Gazette Office, 1852. Pp. 32.

EASTON

7617 AMES, DAVID. The Ames family of Easton,
Massachusetts. [Easton]: Easton Historical
Society, [1972]. Pp. 14. M.

7618 ARCHITECTURE of Henry Hobson Richardson in
North Easton, Massachusetts. Easton: Oakes
Ames Memorial Hall Association and the Easton His-
torical Society, 1969. Pp. 28. M.

7619 BUMSTED, JOHN M. "Presbyterianism in 18th-
century Massachusetts: the formation of a
church at Easton." Journal of Presbyterian History,
46 (1968), 243-253.

7620 CHAFFIN, WILLIAM LADD. History of the town
of Easton, Massachusetts. Cambridge: J.
Wilson and Son, 1886. Pp. xviii, 838.

7621 _____. The religious history of Easton,
Massachusetts: a sermon. North Easton:
Unity Church, 1905. Pp. 25.

7622 OLIVER, DUNCAN B. Easton's pictorial past,
printed from the Easton Historical Society's
archives in honor of the town's 250th anniversary.
[Easton]: Easton Historical Society, [1975]. Unpaged. M.

7623 RICH, PAUL JOHN. History of the First Church
in Easton, based on materials compiled by
Mrs. Edwin H. White. n.p., [1972?]. Unpaged.
MBNEH.

EDGARTOWN

7624 HALL, JOHN GOODMAN. An historical discourse,
delivered in the Congregational meeting-
house, at Edgartown, Mass., November 6, 1878. Boston: Beacon Pr., 1878. Pp. 19.
Also known as the Mayhew Church; relates to
the church.

7625 HOUGH, HENRY BEETLE. Country editor. N.Y.: Doubleday, Doran, 1940. Pp. viii, 325.
Vineyard Gazette.

7626 _____. Once more the thunderer. N.Y.: Washburn, 1950. Pp. 316.
Vineyard Gazette.

7627 PEASE, JEREMIAH. "Excerpts from Jeremiah Pease's diary." DCI, 16 (1974-1975), 39-51.
1819 and 1820; edited by Gale Huntington.

7628 REID, GLADYS PEASE. "Tom's Neck Farm." DCI, 16 (August, 1974), 3-18.
Social life and customs on Chappaquidick Island.

7629 NO ENTRY

EGREMONT

7630 SOUTH EGREMONT, MASS. CONGREGATIONAL CHURCH. Manual of the Congregational Church, South Egremont, Mass., 1884. Great Barrington: Clark W. Bryan, 1884. Pp. 16. MPB.
Includes historical sketch.

7631 WARNER, HENRY C. "The ancient burial grounds of Egremont." Berkshire Hills, 1 (April 1, 1901), [10-11].

ERVING

7632 BROWN, LILLA L. W., et al. Erving, Massachusetts in retrospect, 1838-1938. Orange: Enterprise and Journal, [1938?]. Unpaged. MBNEH.

ESSEX

7633 CALDWELL, AUGUSTINE. "The Cogswell House, Essex, 1732." The Visitor, 2 (1892), 11-12.

7634 CHOATE, RUFUS, 1847-1935. Historical address delivered October twenty-second, nineteen hundred and five at the reopening of the Congregational Church in Essex, Massachusetts, after extensive repairs. Essex: Burnham's Job Print, [1905?]. Pp. 24. MWA.

7635 CROWELL, ROBERT. History of the town of Essex, from 1634 to 1868...with sketches of the soldiers in the War of the Rebellion, by Hon. David Choate. Essex: The Town, 1868. Pp. xx, 488.

7636 _____. History of the town of Essex from 1634 to 1700. Boston: C. C. P. Moody, 1853. Pp. 166, 3.

7637 DOW, GEORGE FRANCIS. "The Choate House at Essex, Massachusetts, and its recent restoration." OTNE, 12 (1921-1922), 6-13.

7638 ESSEX, MASS. FIRST CONGREGATIONAL CHURCH. Congregational Church and Parish, Essex, Mass., two hundred and fiftieth anniversary, 1683-1933. Ipswich: Chronicle Publishing, [1933?]. Pp. 60. MSaE.

7639 _____. Two centuries of church history: celebration of the two hundredth anniversary of the organization of the Congregational Church & Parish in Essex, Mass., August 19-22, 1883. Salem: J. H. Choate, 1884. Pp. 214.
Historical discourse by Edward P. Crowell.

7640 ESSEX, MASS. SESQUICENTENNIAL COMMITTEE. Essex in picture. Essex: Essex Historical Society and Essex United Methodist Church, 1969. Unpaged. M.
Pictorial history.

7641 HARRIS, LESLIE. 150 years a town: a running account of life in the town of Essex since incorporation in 1819. Manchester: Cricket Pr., 1969. Pp. 94.

7642 HILL, ROBERT W. "Our coastal pioneers." EIHC, 78 (1942), 24-40.
Ship building.

7643 LITTLE, NINA FLETCHER. "John Cogswell's Grant and some of the houses thereon, 1636-1839." EIHC, 76 (1940), 152-173.

7644 MORELAND, HELEN F. Colonial communion silver and pewter of the First Congregational Church, Essex, Massachusetts. Essex, 1961. Unpaged. MSaE.
Includes history of the church.

7645 "SHIPBUILDING and shoe business in Essex in 1845." EIHC, 81 (1945), 305-306.

7646 "SKETCH of proceedings in relation to building the first meeting, Second Parish, Ipswich, called Chebacco Parish, now Essex, Mass." NEHGR, 18 (1864), 72-74.

7647 STORY, DANA A. and JOHN M. CLAYTON. The building of a wooden ship: 'sawn frames and trunnel fastened.' Barre: Barre Publishers, 1971. Unpaged.

7648 STORY, DANA A. Frame-up!: the story of Essex, its shipyards and its people. Barre: Barre Publishers, 1964. Pp. viii, 128.

7649 WINCHESTER, ALICE. "Living with antiques: Cogswell's Grant, the Essex County home of Mr. and Mrs. Bertram K. Little." Antiques, 95 (1969), 242-251.

EVERETT

7650 "CARPENTER-Morton Company." Industry, 5 (March, 1940), 7-9, 63-65.
Paints and varnishes.

7651 "THE CHEMICAL industry." Industry, 1
    (March, 1936), 5-8.
    Merrimac Chemical Company.

7652 EVERETT centennial, 1870-1970. Everett:
    Daniels Printing, [1970?]. Unpaged.
MBNEH.

7653 EVERETT souvenir, 1870-1893. Dudley P. Bai-
    ley and Walter L. Colby, eds. [Everett]:
Everett Souvenir Co., [1893]. Pp. 136.

7654 KYLE, GEORGE ALEXANDER. The straight road:
    a short account of the Newburyport Turnpike
and early days in Everett Massachusetts. [Everett]:
Everett National Bank, 1927. Pp. 38.

FAIRHAVEN

7655 BROWN, FRANK CHOUTEAU. "The sunken garden
    at the Captain Thomas Bennett House, Fair-
haven, Mass." OTNE, 36 (1945-1946), 81-84.

7656 DEXTER, FRANKLIN BOWDITCH. Two lectures on
    the history of Fairhaven, Massachusetts.
Fairhaven: Waldron, 1919. Pp. 46.

7657 FAIRHAVEN IMPROVEMENT ASSOCIATION. Histori-
    cal sketch, 1882-1903; by-laws & officers.
Fairhaven: Star Office, 1903. Unpaged.

7658 [FAIRHAVEN OLD HOME WEEK ASSOCIATION]. A
    brief history of the town of Fairhaven,
Massachusetts, prepared in connection with the cel-
ebration of Old Home Week, July 26-31, 1903. James
L. Gillingham, et al, eds. New Bedford: Standard
Print, 1903. Pp. 100.

7659 FEDERAL WRITERS' PROJECT. MASSACHUSETTS.
    Fairhaven, Massachusetts. [Fairhaven?],
1939. Pp. 60.

7660 HARRIS, CHARLES AUGUSTUS. Old-time Fair-
    haven, erstwhile eastern New Bedford. New
Bedford: Reynolds Printing, 1947-1954. 3v.

7661 JUDD, LEWIS S., JR. Fairhaven: a descrip-
    tive and historical sketch.... Boston:
Franklin Engraving, 1896. Pp. 53.

7662 MILLICENT LIBRARY. Fiftieth anniversary of
    the Millicent Library, January, the thirty-
first, nineteen hundred forty-three. New Bedford:
Reynolds, 1943. Pp. 41.

7663 POPE, JOSHUA LORING. An account of the first
    naval battle of the Revolutionary War....
[New Bedford]: New Bedford Chapter, Sons of the
American Revolution, [1930?]. Pp. 6.
    May 14, 1775 on Buzzard's Bay, south of
    Fairhaven.

7664 TABER, THOMAS. "Oxford Village, Fairhaven."
    ODHS, No. 43 (March, 1915), 9-13.

7665 TRIPP, GEORGE HENRY. "The town of Fairhaven
    in four wars." ODHS, No. 6 (June, 1904),
9-15.

7666 TRIPP, JOB CARVER. "Fifty years on the Fair-
    haven School Board." ODHS, No. 6 (June,
1904), 5-8.

7667 ____. The old men of Fairhaven. [New Bed-
    ford, 1909?]. Pp. 10.

FALL RIVER

7668 BORDEN, PHILIP D. "A rambling history of
    the Fall River Irons Works." Fall River HSP,
(1921-1926), 81-107.

7669 ____. "Villages and other localities in
    early Fall River." Fall River HSP, (1921-
1926), 163-165.

7670 BRADLEY, FRANCIS JAMES. A brief history of
    the Diocese of Fall River, Mass. Michael V.
McCarthy, ed. N.Y., 1931. Pp. 63.

7671 BRAYTON, ALICE. Life on the stream. New-
    port, R.I.: Wilkinson Pr., [not after 1967].
2v. M.
    General history of the city.

7672 BRAYTON, JOHN SUMMERFIELD. Brown University
    alumni of Fall River, Mass. Paper read...
before the Association of the Sons of Brown University in Fall River and vicinity. Fall River,
[1888]. Pp. 23.
    Biographies.

7673 BRONSON, ASA. Address on the anniversary of
    the fire, delivered in Pearl Street Christ-
ian Chapel, July 2, 1844.... Fall River, 1844.
Pp. 15.
    Fire of 1843.

7674 CARR, ELIZABETH VALENTINE DURFEE, JULIA A. S.
    THURSTON, and MARY A. R. HOLMES, comp. His-
tory, annals and sketches of the Central Church of
Fall River, Massachusetts. A.D. 1842-A.D. 1905.
Henry H. Earl, ed. Fall River: The Church, 1905.
Pp. xii, 331.

7675 DERBY, ELIAS HASKET, comp. Statistics of the
    resources of the city of Fall River...ad-
dressed to Blake, Brothers & Co., of London...and
letter from Brooks, Ball & Storey...showing the authority and legality of an issue of $600,000 funding
loan bonds to Blake, Brothers & Co...by the city of
Fall River, Mass., 1874. [Fall River, 1874?].
Pp. 26.
    Economic conditions.

7676 DONAHUE, JOHN R., comp. Causes of the finan-
    cial breakdown of the local government of
Fall River, Mass., and means taken by Massachusetts
to re-establish the finances of that city. [Hart-
ford]: Tax Commissioners of Connecticut, 1933.
Pp. 40. M.

7677 DUBUQUE, HUGO ADELARD. Les Canadiens fran-
    çais de Fall River, Mass., notes histor-
iques.... Fall River: H. Boisseau, 1883. Pp. 21.

7678 ___. Fall River Indian Reservation. Fall River, 1907. Pp. iii, 100.

7679 ___. Le guide Canadien-Français (ou, almanach des adresses) de Fall River, et notes historiques sur les Canadiens de Fall River; contenant aussi un recensement complete de la population Canadienne, la biographie des membres du clergé, des hommes de profession, des présidents de sociétés; et une histoire des paroisses et des sociétés, des annonces et d'autres renseignements utiles. Fall River: E. U., E. F. Lamoureux, 1888. Pp. 263.

7680 DUPONT, RALPH P. "The 'Holder Borden.'" NEQ, 27 (1954), 355-365.
Whaling vessel built at Fall River.

7681 DURFEE, JOSEPH. Reminiscences of Col. Joseph Durfee relating to the early history of Fall River and of Revolutionary scenes. [Fall River?, 1834?]. Pp. 12.

7682 EARL, HENRY HILLIARD and FREDERICK M. PECK. Fall River and its industries: an historical and statistical record of village, town, and city, from the date of the original charter of the freemen's purchase in 1656 to the present time, with valuable statistical tables, family genealogies, etc., illustrated by views and portraits on steel. N.Y.: Atlantic Publishing and Engraving, 1877. Pp. 280.
Same as Earl's 'Centennial history of Fall River' (1877) except that genealogies are here substituted for pages 220-248 of that work.

7683 EARL, HENRY HILLIARD. "Old landmarks and reminiscences of Fall River, 1831-1924." Fall River HSP, (1921-1926), 74-80.

7684 "81 years of service." Bristol, 4 (July, 1971), 9,34.
Fall River Boys' Club.

7685 EMERY, WILLIAM MORRELL. "Fall River's first daily paper with a pen picture of the town in 1848." Fall River HSP, (1921-1926), 136-154.
The Spark.

7686 FALL RIVER, MASS. FIRST BAPTIST CHURCH. A brief history of the...Church, with...a list of the members. Fall River: Robertson, 1872. Pp. 73.

7687 FALL RIVER, MASS. FIRST CONGREGATIONAL CHURCH. LADIES' BENEVOLENT SOCIETY. History of the Ladies' Benevolent Society of the First Congregational Church, Fall River, Massachusetts. Fall River: J. H. Franklin, 1904. Pp. 168.

7688 FALL RIVER, MASS. TERCENTENARY COMMITTEE. Fall River in history, a brief presentation, in word and picture, of some of the historical objects and places in and about Fall River. Fall River: Munroe Pr., 1930. Pp. 27.

7689 FALL RIVER, MASS. TRUESDALE HOSPITAL. Twenty-five years of progress, 1905-6-1930-1. Fall River, [1931?]. Pp. 42.

7690 FALL RIVER, an historical sketch of her industry, progress, and improvement. Fall River: W. W. Armstrong, 1870. Pp. 144.

7691 FALL RIVER FIVE CENTS SAVINGS BANK. The big story of the big five: one hundred years of useful banking service, 1855-1955. Fall River, 1955. Pp. 25. M.

7692 FALL RIVER NATIONAL BANK. Birth and rebirth, the story of Fall River and the Fall River National Bank; 125th anniversary, 1825-1950. Fall River, 1950. Pp. 25. M.

7693 FALL RIVER SAVINGS BANK. The centenary of the Fall River Savings Bank; being the story of the growth of a famous institution, 1828-1928. Boston: Lincoln & Smith, 1928. Pp. 30.

7694 FENNER, HENRY MILNE. History of Fall River, Massachusetts, comp. for the cotton centennial, under the direction of the historical committee of the Merchants Association.... [Fall River]: Fall River Merchants Association, 1911. Pp. 106.

7695 ___. and BENJAMIN BUFFINTON. History of Fall River. N.Y.: F. T. Smiley, 1906. Pp. 264.

7696 FOWLER, ORIN. History of Fall River, with notices of Freetown and Tiverton, as published in 1841, together with a sketch of the life of Rev. Orin Fowler; an epitome of the Massachusetts and Rhode Island boundary question; an account of the great fire of 1843; and ecclesiastical, manufacturing, and other statistics. Fall River: Almy & Milne, 1862. Pp. 100.

7697 JENNINGS, ANDREW J. "The Fall River bar--past and present." Fall River HSP, (1921-1926), 9-18.

7698 LINCOLN, JONATHAN THAYER. The city of the dinner-pail. Boston: Houghton Mifflin, 1909. Pp. 186.

7699 LINTNER, SYLVIA CHACE. "Mill architecture in Fall River: 1865-1880." NEQ, 21 (1948), 185-203.

7700 LYMAN, PAYSON WILLISTON. "Fall River Massachusetts." NEM, New Ser., 24 (1901), 291-312.

7701 ___. The historical address delivered at the dissolution of the Fowler Congregational Church, Fall River, Mass., April 1, 1917; also the register of the church membership. Fall River: Munroe Pr., [1917?]. Pp. 32. M.

7702 LYNCH, THOMAS E. History of the fire department of Fall River, Mass. [Fall River]: Charles J. Leary, 1900. Pp. 176. M.

7703 NATIONAL FIRE PROTECTION ASSOCIATION. The Fall River conflagration, February 2-3, 1928.... Boston: National Fire Protection Association, 1928. Pp. 39.

7704 "THE OLDEST house in Fall River heated by gas." SWJ, 42 (1928), 494-496.

7705 PECKHAM, A. C. "The early physicians of Fall River." Fall River HSP, (1921-1926), 63-73.

7706 PHILLIPS, ARTHUR SHERMAN. The Phillips history of Fall River. Norman S. Easton, ed. Fall River: Dover Pr., 1944-1946. 3v. MBNEH.

7707 PHILLIPS, EDWARD L. Collective bargaining and craft unions; an historical and analytical study of a strike for collective bargaining rights by craft unions in the textile industry of Fall River, Massachusetts. Fall River: Loomfixers' Union, 1950. Pp. vii, 116.
Strike took place in 1943.

7708 PLOURDE, ANTONIN M. "Sainte-Anne de Fall River, 1869-1969, les Dominicains à Fall River." Le Rosaire, Nos. 843-844 (Juin-Août, 1969), entire issue.

7709 PORTER, EDWIN H. The Fall River tragedy: a history of the Borden murders, a plain statement of the material facts pertaining to the most famous crime of the century, including the story of the arrest and preliminary trial of Miss Lizzie A. Borden and a full report of the superior court trial, with a hitherto unpublished account of the renowned Trickey-McHenry affair. Fall River: G. R. H. Buffinton, 1893. Pp. 312.

7710 "SAINT Anne's centennial 1869-1969: this famous church and its role in Fall River history." Bristol, [2] (Summer, 1969), 17-20.

7711 SEGAL, MARTIN. "Interrelationship of workers under joint demand: the case of the Fall River textile workers." QJEcon, 70 (1956), 464-477.
1873-1955.

7712 SMITH, THOMAS RUSSELL. The cotton textile industry of Fall River, Massachusetts; a study of industrial localization. N.Y.: King's Crown Pr., 1944. Pp. x, 175.

7713 SULLIVAN, ROBERT. Goodbye, Lizzie Borden. Brattleboro, Vt.: S. Greene Pr., 1974. Pp. viii, 245.

7714 [WILLIAMS, CATHERINE R. ARNOLD]. Fall River, an authentic narrative, by the author of 'Tales, National, Revolutionary'.... Boston: Lilly, Wait, 1834. Pp. viii, 198.
Circumstances leading to trial of Rev. Ephraim K. Avery for the murder of Sarah M. Cornell in 1832.

7715 WRIGHT, CARROLL DAVIDSON. Fall River, Lowell, and Lawrence. Boston: Rand Avery, 1882. Pp. 226. MWA.
Labor.

FALMOUTH

7716 CARMICHAEL, CAMPBELL B. One hundred and fiftieth anniversary, 1808-1958, the John Wesley Methodist Church, Falmouth, Massachusetts. Falmouth: Kendall Printing, 1958. Unpaged. [MFa].

7717 DUNHAM, J. W. "The town of Falmouth." CCAPL, 5 (May, 1921), 7-9.

7718 ELPHICK, ROBERT. Falmouth past and present.... Falmouth: Kendall Printing, [1958?]. Pp. 100. MBNEH.

7719 FALMOUTH, MASS. The celebration of the two hundredth anniversary of the incorporation of the town of Falmouth, Massachusetts, June 15, 1886. Falmouth, 1887. Pp. vi, 153.

7720 FALMOUTH, MASS. BOARD OF TRADE AND INDUSTRY. Falmouth-by-the-sea: the Naples of America. Falmouth, 1896. Pp. 214.
Includes historic houses.

7721 FALMOUTH, MASS. FIRST CONGREGATIONAL CHURCH. Two hundredth anniversary, 1708-1908, First Congregational Church, Falmouth, Massachusetts, October 11, 12 and 13, 1908. n.p., [1908]. Pp. 85. MWA.

7722 "FALMOUTH inner harbor." CCAPL, 6 (June, 1922), 23-24.

7723 "FALMOUTH'S famous families." Cape Cod Magazine, 8 (June, 1926), 7, 20.

7724 FAUGHT, MILLARD CLARK. Falmouth, Massachusetts: problems of a resort community. N.Y.: Columbia Univ. Pr., 1945. Pp. 190.
Social and economic conditions.

7725 FURBUSH, WILLIAM F. "Where scientists study sea life." Cape Cod Magazine, 10 (January, 1928), 13-15.
Marine Biological Laboratory at Woods Hole.

7726 GIFFORD, ARNOLD B. "Saconesset homestead-- a colonial ship's bottom roof house." Historic Preservation, 19 (1967), 84-86.

7727 JENKINS, CHARLES W. Three lectures on the early history of...Falmouth, covering the time from its settlement to 1812, delivered in the year 1843.... Falmouth: L. F. Clarke, 1889. Pp. 113.
Original manuscript of this work is in the Massachusetts State Library.

7728 NIGHTINGALE, LLOYD T. From Falmouth's past; Vikings, Indians, minutemen, whalers, makers of Falmouth history in story and picture. Falmouth, 1936. Pp. 71. [MFa].

7729 ROGERS, FRED B. "Pioneer inoculators on Cape Cod." NEJMed, 270 (1964), 664-666.
Francis Wicks and Hugh George Donaldson, late eighteenth century.

7730 "THE SACONESSET Homestead." The Cape, 1 (May, 1967), 6-7.

7731 A SHORT history of Falmouth, Cape Cod, Massachusetts. [Falmouth]: Falmouth Enterprise, 1942. Pp. 16. [MFa].

7732 TEATICKET school, 25th anniversary, 1928-1953. Falmouth: Kendall Printing, 1953. unpaged. [MFa].

7733 WALTON, PERRY. Falmouth on Cape Cod, picturesque, romantic, hostoric.... Boston, 1925. Pp. 47.

7734 [WAYMAN, DOROTHY GODFREY]. "Around the elm-girt heart of Falmouth." Cape Cod Magazine, 9 (May, 1927), 5-6, 16.
Historic houses; signed Theodate Geoffrey, a pseudonym.

7735 [_____]. Suckanesset; wherein may be read a history of Falmouth, Massachusetts, by Theodate Geoffrey, pseud. Falmouth: Falmouth Publishing, 1930. Pp. 168.

7736 WOODS Hole and the ter-centenary of the landing of Gosnold, August 15th, 1907. n.p., [1907?]. Pp. 55. M.

7737 "WOODS Hole whalers." Cape Cod Magazine, 8 (February - March, 1925), 17-19.

FITCHBURG

7738 [BACON, GEORGE FOX]. Leading business men of Fitchburg and vicinity: embracing also Clinton, Ayer, Gardner, Leominster, Winchendon, Ashburnham, and Baldwinsville.... Boston: Mercantile Publishing, 1890. Pp. 159.

7739 BAILEY, E. FOSTER. "Reminiscences of the old Town Hall." FitchHSP, 4 (1900-1906), 65-79.

7740 _____. "Reminiscences relating to the Second Meeting-House in Fitchburg." FitchHSP, 4 (1900-1906), 52-64.

7741 BAILEY, EBENEZER. "Early history of the City Hall." FitchHSP, 4 (1900-1906), 266-275.

7742 _____. "An early workingmen's association of Fitchburg." FitchHSP, 4 (1900-1906), 242-252.

7743 _____. "The Fitchburg Philosophical Society." FitchHSP, 1 (1892-1894), 188-201.

7744 _____. "Fitchburg preparatory to the Revolution." FitchHSP, 4 (1900-1906), 125-135.

7745 _____. "Historical sketch of Fitchburg." BSM, 2 (1884-1885), 226-231.

7746 BAILEY, HARRISON. "Early real estate owners in Fitchburg." FitchHSP, 4 (1900-1906), 105-112.

7747 BOUTWELL & CO. Boutwell's ready reference book and pocket memoranda for Fitchburg. Leominster, 1888. Pp. 56.

7748 CURRIER, FREDERICK A. The old city and other divisions of Fitchburg, read at a meeting of the Fitchburg Historical Society, November 18, 1918. N.p., n.d. Pp. 8. MWA.

7749 _____. "The old stores of Fitchburg." FitchHSP, 3 (1897-1899), 159-223.

7750 _____. "The post-offices and post-masters of Fitchburg." FitchHSP, 1 (1892-1894), 87-112.

7751 _____. "Tavern days and the old taverns of Fitchburg." FitchHSP, 2 (1894-1897), 85-125.

7752 EDGERLY, JOSEPH G. "Fitchburg, Massachusetts." NEM, New Ser., 12 (1895), 321-337.

7753 EMERSON, ALFRED. A centenary discourse delivered in the meeting house of the Calvinistic Congregational Church, in Fitchburg, Mass., March 1, 1868. Fitchburg: Kellogg & Simonds, 1868. Pp. 21. M.

7754 EMERSON, WILLIAM ANDREW. Fireside legends: incidents, anecdotes, reminiscences, etc., connected with the early history of Fitchburg, Massachusetts, and vicinity. (1890) 2d. ed. [Fitchburg?], 1900. Pp. 336.

7755 _____. Fitchburg past and present. (1887) New illustrated ed. Fitchburg, 1903. Pp. 368.

7756 FAHLSTROM, CLIFFORD I. "Fitchburg Yarn at fifty years keeps city textile tradition." Industry, 22 (January, 1957), 32e-32g, 53-54.

7757 FISHER, CHARLES EBEN. Locomotives of the Boston & Maine Railroad: Fitchburg Railroad." RLHSB, No. 37 (1935), 41-56.

7758 FITCHBURG, MASS. The old records of the town of Fitchburgh, Massachusetts.... Walter A. Davis, comp. Fitchburg: Sentinel Printing, 1898-1913. 8v.

7759 FITCHBURG, MASS. FIRST BAPTIST CHURCH. Semi-centennial celebration...including an account of the services, the poem, the historical address and the memorial sermon, held June 8th, 1881. Fitchburg: Sentinel Printing, 1881. Pp. 61.

7760 FITCHBURG, MASS. ROLLSTONE CONGREGATIONAL CHURCH. Jubilee services of the Rollstone Congregational Church, May, 1890 in view of the final payment of the original debt upon the church edifice. Fitchburg: Sentinel Printing, 1890. Pp. 17. MBNEH.
1868-1890.

7761 FITCHBURG, MASS. ST. JOSEPH PARISH. Diamond jubilee program. [Fitchburg, 1965?]. Unpaged.

7762   FITCHBURG MUTUAL FIRE INSURANCE CO.   75th
          anniversary, 1847-1922. Fitchburg, [1922?].
Pp. 57.

7763   FITCHBURG SAVINGS BANK. One hundred years
          of the Fitchburg Savings Bank, 'The old
bank with the new ideas,' 1846-1946. [Fitchburg],
1946. Pp. 35.

7764   "FITCHBURG, 1719-1914: an epitome." Fitch-
          burg Public Library Bulletin, 10 (1914), 21,
28.
          Chronology of events.

7765   FOSDICK, CHARLES. "Some transplanted build-
          ings in Fitchburg." FitchHSP, 5 (1907-
1913), 213-224.

7766   FREEMASONS. FITCHBURG, MASS. AURORA LODGE.
          Centennial memorial of Aurora Lodge A. F.
and A. M., A.D. 1801-1901. Frederick A. Currier,
ed. Fitchburg, 1901. Pp. 166.

7767   FREEMASONS. FITCHBURG, MASS. KNIGHTS TEM-
          PLARS. JERUSALEM COMMANDERY, NO. 19. Fif-
tieth anniversary 1865-1915. Frederick A. Currier,
ed. [Fitchburg?], 1916. Pp. vii, 126.

7768   FREEMASONS. FITCHBURG, MASS. ROYAL ARCH
          MASONS. THOMAS CHAPTER. Centennial memori-
al of Thomas Royal Arch Chapter, Fitchburg, Massachusetts, 1821-1921. Frederick A. Currier, ed.
Fitchburg, 1923. Pp. 114.

7769   GARFIELD, JAMES FREEMAN DANA. "Falulah."
          Fitchburg HSP, 5 (1907-1913), 207-212.
          Tract of land.

7770   _____. "Fitchburg soldiers of the Revolu-
          tion." FitchHSP, 4 (1900-1906), 172-232.

7771   _____. "Fitchburg's response to the Lexing-
          ton alarm." FitchHSP, 1 (1892-1894), 113-
122.

7772   _____. "The meeting-house controversy."
          FitchHSP, 5 (1907-1913), 197-206.
          Eighteenth-century dispute regarding loca-
tion of a new meeting-house.

7773   _____. "On the early history of the fire
          service of Fitchburg." FitchHSP, 1 (1892-
1894), 50-57.

7774   _____. "Pioneer printers of Fitchburg."
          FitchHSP, 1 (1892-1894), 157-169.

7775   _____. Sketch of journalism in Fitchburg,
          Mass. Fitchburg, 1888. Pp. 43.

7776   _____. "A tour in Main Street." FitchHSP,
          5 (1907-1913), 250-260.

7777   GOODFELLOW, MAUD A. State Normal School,
          Fitchburg, Mass., the first twenty-five
years, 1895-1920, under the direction of J. G.
Thompson, principal; historical sketch and lists of
former faculty and students. Fitchburg: State
Normal School Practical Arts Pr., 1920. Pp. 104.

7778   GOODRICH, HENRY AUGUSTUS. "A connecting
          link in the military history of Fitchburg."
FitchHSP, 4 (1900-1906), 146-153.
          Fitchburg Fusiliers.

7779   _____. "The first half-century of high
          schools in Fitchburg, 1830-1880." FitchHSP,
2 (1894-1897), 193-240.

7780   _____. Fitchburg town and city: first of a
          series of talks under the auspices of Fitch-
burg Y.M.C.A. Fitchburg, 1897. Pp. 15.

7781   _____. "The verse writers of Fitchburg, past
          and present." FitchHSP, 3 (1897-1899), 104-
138.

7782   GREENMAN, WALTER F. "An interlude of church
          discipline in Fitchburg." FitchHSP, 2
(1894-1897), 258-280.
          1804-1813.

7783   HARDY, GEORGE H. History of the meeting
          house in Fitchburg commonly known as 'the
Lord's barn.' Fitchburg: Sentinel Printing, 1910.
Pp. 17.
          Nondenominational.

7784   HITCHCOCK, GEORGE A. "The first half-century
          of the Calvinistic Congregational Church."
FitchHSP, 4 (1900-1906), 35-51.

7785   _____. "From hamlet to city." FitchHSP, 5
          (1907-1913), 261-269.

7786   _____. A history of the Calvinistic Congre-
          gational Church and Society, Fitchburg, Mas-
sachusetts...with an introduction on the separation
of Church and State also a historical sketch of the
C. C. Sunday School, by Ebenezer Bailey. Fitchburg: The Society, 1902. Pp. iv, 145.

7787   HULING, RAY GREENE. The teachers and gradu-
          ates of the Fitchburg High School, 1849-
1883; preceeded by some mention of teachers in the
Fitchburg Academy, 1830-1848. Fitchburg: Sentinel
Printing, 1884. Pp. 66.

7788   "INDUSTRY'S map of Massachusetts: Fitch-
          burg." Industry, 2 (September, 1937), 23-24.

7789   KIRKPATRICK, DORIS. The city and the river.
          [Fitchburg]: Fitchburg Historical Society,
1971-.

7790   KOLEHMAINEN, JOHN ILMARI. Sow the golden
          seed. Fitchburg: Raivaaja Publishing, 1955.
Pp. 150.
          'Raivaaja,' a Finnish newspaper.

7791   MASON, ATHERTON P. "The Fitchburg Athenaeum
          (1852-1859)." FitchHSP, 1 (1892-1894), 202-
219.

7792   _____. "Fitchburg in 1885." BSM, 2 (1884-
          1885), 341-358.

7793   _____. "School affairs in Fitchburg fifty
          years ago." FitchHSP, 2 (1894-1897), 241-
249.

7794 _____. "A town meeting-house and town politics in the last century." NEM, 4 (1886), 127-135.

7795 MILLER, G. W. "Fitchburg, the Pittsburg of Massachusetts." National Magazine, 17 (1902-1903), 260-264.

7796 O'CONNOR, D. CHARLES. "Eastern city with western ideas." NEM, New Ser., 39 (1908-1909), 199-213.

7797 "THE 125-year story of Simonds Saw and Steel." Industry, 22 (August, 1957), 25-28, 59.

7798 "OSUUSTOIMINTA Fitchburgissa." Sürtokansan Kalenteri, (1946), 188-190.
Title: Cooperation in Fitchburg; in Finnish.

7799 "REMINISCENCES of early Fitchburg." Town Talk, 1 (November 15, 1890), 11.

7800 SIMONDS MANUFACTURING COMPANY. Seventy five years of business progress and industrial advance, 1832-1907. Cambridge: Univ. Pr., 1907. Pp. 54. MB.
Saw manufacturers.

7801 SNOW, CHARLES HENRY BOYLSTON. Address, at the centennial celebration, of the town of Fitchburg, June 30th, 1864. Fitchburg: Piper & Boutelle, 1876. Pp. 36, 55.

7802 SPAULDING, J. CALVIN. "Reminiscences of South Fitchburg." FitchHSP, 5 (1907-1913), 241-249.

7803 STEARNS, EZRA SCOLLAY. "An early hospital of Fitchburg." FitchHSP, 4 (1900-1906), 233-241.
Eighteenth century.

7804 _____. "Old clocks in Fitchburg." Fitch HSP, 5 (1907-1913), 118-156.

7805 STEBBINS, CALVIN. 1700-1900, the story of a church for two centuries: a sermon at the First Parish Church, Framingham, June tenth, nineteen hundred. South Framingham: Geo. L. Clapp, 1900. Pp. 30.

7806 [SYRJALA, SAVELE]. Fifty years of service 1914-1964, Workers' Credit Union, Fitchburg, Mass. [Fitchburg?, 1964?]. Pp. 32. MFi.

7807 _____. The story of a cooperative; a brief history of United Co-operative Society of Fitchburg. Fitchburg: United Co-operative Society, 1947. Pp. 64.

7808 TOLMAN, MARTHA D. "An historical sketch of the Third Trinitarian Congregational Church of Fitchburg." FitchHSP, 5 (1907-1913), 45-68.

7809 "TYOVAEN Pankki." Kalenteri Amerikan Suomalaiselle Tyoväelle, (1915), 164-173.
Workers' Credit Union; in Finnish.

7810 UNITED COOPERATIVE FARMERS, INC. Twenty-fifth anniversary of UCF, a record of cooperative achievement 1928-1953. Boston: Excelsior Pr., [1953?]. Pp. 36. MFi.

7811 WELLMAN, LOUISE H. "A dame school in Fitchburg sixty years ago." FitchHSP, 2 (1894-1897), 250-257.

7812 WHEELWRIGHT, WILLIAM BOND and SUMNER KEAN. The lengthened shadow of one man. Fitchburg: Crocker, Burbank, 1957. Pp. 181.
Crocker, Burbank & Co., paper.

7813 WILLIS, HENRY AUGUSTUS. "The birth of Fitchburg--its first settlers and their homes." FitchHSP, 2 (1894-1897), 29-84.

7814 _____. "The early days of railroads in Fitchburg." FitchHSP, 1 (1892-1894), 27-49.

7815 _____. Fitchburg in the War of the Rebellion. Fitchburg: S. Shepley, 1866. Pp. 282.

7816 WINCHESTER, ALICE. "A painted wall." Antiques, 49 (1946), 310-311.
Home of Mr. & Mrs. Charles Howard, mural paintings from the 1830s and 1840s.

FLORIDA

7817 SEE HISTORIES OF BERKSHIRE COUNTY.

FOXBOROUGH

7818 CARPENTER, ROBERT W. History and directory of Foxboro, Mass., for 1890, containing a complete resident, street and business directory, town officers, schools, societies, churches, post offices, etc...history of the town from the first settlement to the present time. Boston: A. E. Foss, 1890.

7819 "FIFTY years of leadership in instrument development." Industry, 23 (June, 1958), 43-45.
Foxboro Company.

7820 FOXBOROUGH, MASS. Foxborough's official centennial record, Saturday, June 29, 1878. Boston: Rockwell & Churchill, 1879. Pp. 248.
Historical address by E. P. Carpenter.

7821 KNIGHT, DOROTHY CLARE. "Crack Rock." SWJ, 47 (1930), 170-176.
Section of the town.

7822 LANE, CLIFFORD W. and MRS. CLIFFORD W. LANE. This was Foxborough! Foxborough: Rea-Craft Pr., 1966. Pp. viii, 277.

7823   SPENCER, WILLIAM HENRY. Historical dis-
       course delivered at the rededication of the
Baptist Meeting-House, in Foxborough, Mass., Janu-
ary 22, 1879. Foxboro: R. W. S. Blackwell, 1879.
Pp. 64. M.

7824   WEYGAND, JAMES LAMAR. "Red Barn Press."
       American Book Collector, 14 (January, 1964),
8.

FRAMINGHAM

7825   [BALLARD, WILLIAM]. A sketch of the history
       of Framingham, supposed to have been written
by Oudeise [transliterated from the Greek] while in
prison, aided in the obtaining of documents, by his
brothers Nemo and Aucun; authors of A residence in
the South; and, A tour through the West.... Boston, 1827. Pp. iv, 70.

7826   BARRY, WILLIAM. A history of Framingham,
       Massachusetts, including the Plantation,
from 1640 to the present time, with an appendix,
containing a notice of Sudbury and its first proprietors; also, a register of the inhabitants of
Framingham before 1800, with genealogical sketches.
Boston: J. Munroe, 1847. Pp. iv, 456.

7827   BURGESS, J. H., ed. Town of Framingham,
       Massachusetts, past and present, progress
and prosperity; souvenir, 1906. Framingham: Lakeview Pr., 1906. Pp. 32.

7828   DENNISON MANUFACTURING CO. Seventy-five
       years, 1844-1919. Framingham, [1920?].
Pp. 71.

7829   EDGELL GROVE CEMETERY. Edgell Grove Ceme-
       tery, 1848-1938. n.p., [1938?]. unpaged.
MBNEH.

7830   ESTY, CONSTANTINE C. Historical address...
       at the bi-centennial anniversary of the in-
corporation of the Town of Framingham. Mount
Wayte, 1900. Pp. 16.

7831   FENWICK, THOMAS. "Framingham of today."
       NEM, New Ser., 39 (1908-1909), 739-753.

7832   FISHER, CHARLES P. "Structural history of
       the Pike-Haven-Foster House, Framingham,
Massachusetts." OTNE, 45 (1954-1955), 29-36.

7833   FRAMINGHAM, MASS. Memorial of the bi-centen-
       nial celebration of the incorporation of the
town of Framingham, Massachusetts, June, 1900....
South Framingham: G. L. Clapp, [1900?]. Pp. xvi,
252.

7834   FRAMINGHAM, MASS. FIRST CHURCH. Services
       at the bi-centennial of the First Parish
in Framingham, October thirteenth, nineteen hundred and one. Boston: Wright and Potter, 1902.
Pp. 68.

7835   FRAMINGHAM, MASS. PLYMOUTH CHURCH. Manual
       of the Church of Christ, in Framingham,
Mass., organized October 8, 1701: including the
confession of faith, covenant, standing rules, list
of officers and members, and historical notes. Boston: Wright and Potter, 1870. Pp. 91

7836   ____. Revised manual, Plymouth Church in
       Framingham; present church by-laws, histori-
cal notes; membership list continued from the manual of 1701-1870 to September 1, 1930. John H.
Temple, comp. Framingham: Lakeview Pr., 1930.
Pp. 126.

7837   FRAMINGHAM. Boston: Edison Electric Illu-
       minating Co., 1909. Pp. 20. M.

7838   FRAMINGHAM COOPERATIVE BANK. Fiftieth anni-
       versary 1889-1939; the growth of an institu-
tion.... Framingham, 1931. Unpaged. M.

7839   FRAMINGHAM NATIONAL BANK. A century of ser-
       vice, 1833-1933. Framingham: Lakeview Pr.,
1933. Pp. 42.

7840   FRAMINGHAM TRUST COMPANY. Golden jubilee--
       Framingham Trust Company...a half century of
service to Greater Framingham. Framingham, 1959.
Unpaged. M.

7841   GRAGIN, ISABELLA SOPHRONIA. Framingham old
       & new. Framingham: Framingham Camera and
Sketch Club, 1904. Pp. 32. M.

7842   HAYES, E. P. "History of the Dennison Manu-
       facturing Company." JEBH, 1 (1928-1929),
467-502; 2 (1929-1930), 163-202.
       Paper products; continuation in volume 2 is
       by Charlotte Heath.

7843   HEATH, CHARLOTTE. Dennison beginnings:
       1840-1878. [Framingham?, 1927]. Pp. 116.

7844   HOWARD, R. H. Saxonville Methodism: a memo-
       rial and historical discourse delivered...
January 9, 1881, ensuing the dedication of the New
Methodist Church, Saxonville. [Framingham]: Angier
Potter, 1881. Pp. 21. M.

7845   HURD, THEODORE C. Address of Theodore C.
       Hurd at the bicentennial anniversary of the
incorporation of the town of Framingham, June 13,
1900. n.p., [1900?]. Pp. 19. MWA.

7846   MASSACHUSETTS STATE TEACHERS COLLEGE, FRA-
       MINGHAM. Semi-centennial celebration, state
normal school, Framingham, July 2, 1889, established
in 1839, at Lexington, report of Alumnae Association
of the first state normal school in the world. Boston: Beacon Pr., 1889. Pp. 75.

7847   MERRIAM, JOHN MCKINSTRY. "The First Parish
       of Framingham, 1701-1951." UHSP, 9, Pt. 2
(1952), 1-24.

7848 _____. Five Framingham heroes of the American Revolution: a paper read upon invitation of the Framingham Chapter of the Daughters of the American Revolution.... Framingham: Lakeview Pr., 1925. Pp. 22.
Micajah Gleason, Jonathan Maynard, John Nixon, Thomas Nixon and Peter Salem.

7849 _____. The Framingham of one hundred years ago: a paper read at the centennial of the coming of the State Teachers College to Framingham ...in the program prepared by Dr. Martin F. O'Connor, president, October 29th, 1953. [Framingham, 1954?]. Pp. 15.

7850 _____. Sketches of Framingham.... Boston: Bellman, 1950. Pp. 132.

7851 PEIRCE, CYRUS. The first state normal school in America: the journals of Cyrus Peirce and Mary Swift. Arthur O. Norton, ed. Cambridge: Harvard Univ. Pr., 1926. Pp. lvi, 299.

7852 SABINE, LORENZO. Framingham in the Revolution: an address read before the Middlesex South Agricultural Society, March 14, 1853 and published in 1933 by the Framingham Historical and Natural History Society. Framingham: Lakeview Pr., 1933. Pp. 37. MBNEH.

7853 SAFFORD, HENRY G. Twenty-fifth anniversary, historical address delivered Sunday evening, Mar. 16, 1879 in the Baptist Church, So. Framingham. So. Framingham: J. C. Clark, 1879. Pp. 32. M.
Relates to the city.

7854 SOUTH FRAMINGHAM-PARK STREET BAPTIST CHURCH. One century of service: South Framingham-Park Street Baptist Church, 1854-1954. n.p., [1954?]. Pp. 23. MBNEH.

7855 "STORY of a famous name in carpets." Industry, 23 (November, 1957), 32c-32e, 32h.
Roxbury Carpet Company.

7856 TEMPLE, JOSIAH HOWARD. History of Framingham, Massachusetts, early known as Danforth's Farms, 1640-1880; with a genealogical register. Framingham: The Town, 1887. Pp. vii, 794.

7857 _____. History of the first Sabbath school in Framingham, Mass., from 1816 to 1868; with a sketch of the rise of Sabbath schools. Boston: Wright & Potter, 1868. Pp. 158.

FRANKLIN

7858 BLAKE, MORTIMER. A history of the town of Franklin, Mass.: from its settlement to the completion of its first century, 2d March, 1878; with genealogical notices of its earliest families, sketches of its professional men, and a report of the centennial celebration. Franklin: The Committee of the Town, 1879. Pp. 289.

7859 CUSHMAN, HENRY IRVING. "The Dean Academy." NEM, 6 (1887-1888), 150-155.

7860 FOSS, A. E. & CO., NEEDHAM, MASS. History and directory of Franklin, Mass. for 1890.... Boston: F. I. Brown, 1890. Pp. 139. M.
History by Mrs. E. L. Morse.

7861 FRANKLIN, MASS. The one hundred and fiftieth anniversary of the incorporation of the town of Franklin, Massachusetts, 1778-1928, September 1, 2, and 3, 1928. Franklin: Sentinel Pr., 1928. Pp. 80.

7862 _____. The record of births, marriages and deaths in the town of Franklin, from 1778 to 1872. Orestes T. Doe, ed. Franklin: Franklin Sentinel, 1898. Pp. vii, 232.

7863 FRANKLIN, MASS. FIRST CONGREGATIONAL CHURCH. Manual of the First Congregational Church, Franklin, Mass. Boston: Rand, Avery & Frye, 1870. Pp. 42. M.
Includes history.

7864 _____. Our retrospect, 1738-1888; a memorial volume, containing the historical discourse, addresses, reminiscences, letters, etc., given at the sesqui-centennial celebration of the First Congregational Church, Franklin, Mass., Wednesday and Thursday, June 13, 14, 1888. Walpole: The Committee of Arrangements, 1888. Pp. 87.

7865 SMALLEY, ELAM. Centennial sermon, delivered before the Church and Congregation in Franklin, Mass., Feb. 25, 1838. Boston: Manning & Fisher, 1838. Pp. 56. MB.

FREETOWN

7866 BUMSTED, JOHN M. "Orthodoxy in Massachusetts: the ecclesiastical history of Freetown, 1683-1776." NEQ, 43 (1970), 274-284.

7867 HERBERT, MARY PHILLIPS, comp. Freetown, Mass., marriage records (Bristol County) 1686-1844. Glendale, Calif.: Margaret P. Creer, 1934. 63 leaves.

7868 A HISTORY of the town of Freetown, Massachusetts, with an account of the old home festival, July 30th, 1902. Fall River: J. H. Franklin, 1902. Pp. 287.

7869 PEIRCE, EBENEZER WEAVER. "The original owners and early settlers of Freetown and Assonet." Old Colony HSC, No. 3 (1885), 113-130.

GARDNER

7870 GARDNER, MASS. FIRST BAPTIST CHURCH. Memorial pamphlet of the First Baptist Church, Gardner, September 28, 1880; issued at the time of their fiftieth anniversary.... Gardner: A. G. Bushnell, 1880. Pp. 29.

7871 GEARAN, MARIE MARGARET. The early Irish settlers in the town of Gardner, Massachusetts. Fitchburg, 1932. Pp. 73.

7872   GLAZIER, LEWIS. History of Gardner, Massa-
        chusetts, from its earliest settlement to
1860. Worcester: C. Hamilton, 1860. Pp. vii,
163.

7873   GREENWOOD, RICHARD N. The five Heywood
        brothers, 1826-1951; a brief history of the
Heywood-Wakefield Company during 125 years. N.Y.:
Newcomen Society in North America, 1951. Pp. 32.
        Furniture manufacturers.

7874   HALLOCK, F. PAUL. "Industry's map of Massa-
        chusetts: Gardner." Industry, 3 (August,
1938), 19-22, 40.

7875   HERRICK, WILLIAM DODGE. History of the town
        of Gardner, Worcester County, Mass., from
the incorporation, June 27, 1785, to the present
time. Gardner: The Committee, 1878. Pp. xv, 535.

7876   HEYWOOD-WAKEFIELD COMPANY. A completed cen-
        tury, 1826-1926: the story of Heywood-
Wakefield company. Boston, 1926. Pp. 4, iii.
        Furniture.

7877   LEBLANC, CYRILLE and THOMAS F. FLYNN. Gard-
        ner in World War II. Gardner: Hatton Pr.,
1947. Pp. 557.

7878   MOORE, ESTHER GILMAN, et al. History of
        Gardner, Massachusetts, 1785-1967. Gardner:
Hatton Print., 1967. Pp. 334.

7879   PEHRSON, BENGT. "Heywood-Wakefield Company
        marks its 125th anniversary." Industry, 16
(August, 1951), 15-17.
        Furniture.

7880   "WINDSOR chairs through five generations."
        Industry, 22 (April, 1957), 17-19.
        Nichols & Stone Co.

GAY HEAD

7881   AWFUL tale of shipwreck, loss of steamer
        City of Columbus, which foundered on Devil's
Bridge Reef, off Gay Head, Jan. 18, 1884, by which
catastrophe one hundred and two persons lost their
lives, a full and graphic account, a story of suf-
fering, sorrow and heroic achievement. New Bedford:
Mercury Publishing, 1884. Pp. 23.

7882   BAYLIES, WILLIAM "Description of Gay Head."
        American Academy of Arts and Sciences. Mem-
oirs, 2, Pt. 1 (1793), 150-155.

7883   BURGESS, EDWARD SANDFORD. "The old South
        Road of Gay Head." DCI, 12 (1970-1971),
1-35.

7884   KIMBALL, CAROL W. "The loss of the U. S. S.
        Galena on Gay Head." DCI, 9 (1967-1968),
32-40.
        Shipwreck, 1891.

7885   POOLE, DOROTHY COTTLE. "Full circle." DCI,
        10 (1968-1969), 121-142.
        Whaling.

7886   SCAGLION, RICHARD. "The Moshop tale: a
        chronological analysis of a Wampanoag Indian
myth." DCI, 8 (August, 1974), 19-26.

7887   TRIPP, JOHN. "Native church at Gay Head."
        MNEH, 3 (1893), 250-253.

GEORGETOWN

7888   EWELL, WILLIAM STICKNEY. "The meal chest
        story." EIHC, 81 (1945), 274-281.
        Spiritualism and witchcraft.

7889   FIELD, JANE. A brief history of Georgetown,
        Massachusetts, 1838-1963. Georgetown:
Georgetown Historical Society, 1963. Pp. 38.

7890   FREEMASONS. GEORGETOWN, MASS. CHARLES C.
        DAME LODGE. One hundredth anniversary,
Charles C. Dame Lodge, A. F. & A. M., instituted
April 5, 1867, Georgetown, Massachusetts, a century
of Masonic brotherhood, 1867-1967. n.p., [1967?].
Pp. 50. MSaE.

7891   GEORGETOWN, MASS. PEABODY MEMORIAL CHURCH.
        The Peabody Memorial Church in Georgetown,
Mass.; its origin, the exercises connected with the
laying of the cornerstone, the dedication, and the
ordination of its pastor. Georgetown, 1869.
Pp. 77.

7892   HULL, FORREST P. Georgetown, story of one
        hundred years, 1838-1938. Georgetown: cen-
tennial celebration of the incorporation, 1938.
Pp. 87. MB.

7893   PERLEY, SIDNEY. "Centre of Georgetown in
        the year 1800." Essex Antiq, 2 (1898), 103-
108.

7894   SPOFFORD, ELLEN W. "Personal sketches of
        early inhabitants of Georgetown, Mass."
EHIC, 41 (1905), 165-179.

GILL

7895   "GILL'S centennial celebration." PVMA, 3
        (1890-1898), 175-213.
        Incorporated in 1793.

GLOUCESTER

7896   ADAMS, HERBERT BAXTER. "The Fisher Planta-
        tion at Cape Anne." EIHC, 19 (1882), 81-90.
        Seventeenth century.

7897   ALABISO, AL. "City of time and tide." In-
        dustry, 38 (August, 1973), 14,16.

7898   AYER, SILAS HIBBARD, comp. Souvenir of Bass
        Rocks, Gloucester, Mass. Boston: Bass Rocks
Improvement Association, 1905. Pp. 49.

7899 BABSON, HELEN CORLISS. The Finns in Lanes-
ville, Massachusetts. Los Angeles, Calif:
Southern California Sociological Society, Univ. of
Southern California, [1920]. Pp. 12.

7900 BABSON, JOHN JAMES. "Historical sketch of
Annisquam." EIB, 4 (1872), 128-130.

7901 BETTS, L. W. "Gloucester, the Fishing City."
Outlook, 68 (1901), 61-69.

7902 BISBEE, FREDERICK ADELBERT. 1770-1920, from
Good Luck to Gloucester, the book of the
pilgrimage; being the record of the celebration by
means of a great pageant of the one hundred and
fiftieth anniversary of the landing of John Murray,
his reception by Thomas Potter, and the preaching
of the first Universalist sermon at Good Luck, New
Jersey, and the establishing of the first Universalist Church at Gloucester, Massachusetts. Boston:
Murray Pr., 1920. Pp. 373.

7903 BOHDAN, CAROL. "Beauport, in Gloucester,
Massachusetts." Antiques, 103, (1973), 520-
532.
House.

7904 _____. "History in houses: Beauport, in
Gloucester, Massachusetts." Antiques, 103
(1973), 520-532.

7905 BROOKS, ALFRED MANSFIELD. "The First Parish
in Gloucester, 1642-1942." UHSP, 8, Pt. 1
(1947), 37-41.

7906 _____. "The Fitz Lane House in Gloucester."
EIHC, 78 (1942), 281-283.

7907 _____. "The Pearce-Parrot Garden in Gloucester." EIHC, 80 (1944), 283-285.

7908 _____. "A picture of Gloucester about 1800."
EIHC, 87 (1951), 333-338.

7909 BROWN, FRANK CHOUTEAU. "Interior details
and furnishings of the William Haskell
dwelling, built before 1650, at West Gloucester,
Massachusetts." Pencil Points, 20 (1939), 113-128.

7910 CHADBOURNE, ROBERT A. "Diversification means
success for Le Page's." Industry, 19 (May,
1954), 11-14.
Glue; 75th anniversary.

7911 CHAMBERLAIN, NARCISSA G. "History in
houses: the White-Ellery House at Gloucester, Massachusetts." Antiques, 78 (1960), 570-573.

7912 CHAMBERLAIN, SAMUEL and PAUL M. HOLLISTER.
Beauport at Gloucester, the most fascinating
house in America. N.Y.: Hastings House, 1951.
Pp. 84.

7913 COFFIN, E. W. "Historical notices of the
Third Parish at Annisquam." EIB, 4 (1872),
124-127.

7914 COFFIN, JAMES R. "Le Beau Port, sea-
browned fishing town of Gloucester." NEM,
New Ser., 42 (1910), 167-178.

7915 CONNOLLY, JAMES BRENDAN. The book of the
Gloucester fishermen. (1927) New ed., rev.
and enl. John Day, 1930. Pp. 303.
London edition of 1928 has title: Fishermen
of the banks.

7916 _____. The port of Gloucester. N.Y.: Doubleday, Doran, 1940. Pp. ix, 333.

7917 CONTI, FRANCES A. "...city of technology."
Industry, 38 (August, 1973), 18-20, 37.
Industrial history.

7918 COX, FRANK L. The Gloucester book. Gloucester: White, 1921. Pp. 80.

7919 COXE, R. C. "In Gloucester Harbor." Century, 44 (1892), 518-522.

7920 CUSHING, RICHARD JAMES. Our Lady of Good
Voyage, Gloucester, Massachusetts. [Glouces-
ter?, 1946?]. Pp. 57.
A church history.

7921 DEXTER, RALPH W. "The scientific period of
the Cape Ann Scientific and Literary Association, and its successors, 1873-1952." EIHC, 109
(1973), 165-174.

7922 EATON, G. F. Historical sketch of the Elm
Street Methodist Episcopal Church, Glouces-
ter, Mass., March, 1883. Gloucester: Woodbury &
Haskell, 1883. Pp. 66.

7923 EDDY, RICHARD. Universalism in Gloucester,
Mass.: an historical discourse on the one
hundredth anniversary of the first sermon of Rev.
John Murray in that town, delivered in the Indepen-
dent Christian Church, November 3, 1874....
Gloucester: Procter Bros., 1892. Pp. 245.

7924 ELDREDGE, DAVID S. "The Gloucester fishing
industry in World War II." AmNep, 27 (1967),
202-210.

7925 ELSON, LOUIS CHARLES. A Gloucester sketch-
book and souvenir. Gloucester: Procter
Bros., 1904. Pp. 22.

7926 ERICKSON, EVARTS. "When New England saw the
serpent." Am Heritage, 7 (April, 1956), 26-
27.

7927 ESSEX INSTITUTE, SALEM, MASS. Ship registers
of the district of Gloucester, Massachusetts,
1789-1875, compiled from the Gloucester customs
house records, now on deposit at the Essex Institute, with an introduction by Stephen Willard Phillips. Salem: Essex Institute, 1944. Pp. 196.

7928 FIFIELD, CHARLES WOODBURY. Along the
Gloucester waterfront. [Melrose?], 1955.
Pp. 69.

7929 THE FISHERIES of Gloucester from the first
catch by the English in 1623, to the centennial year, 1876, giving an account of the settlement
of the town; development of the fishing business;
various branches; statistics of catch; models of

(THE FISHERIES...) vessels; the granite interest; the advantages of Cape Ann as a place of summer resort, etc., etc. Gloucester: Procter Bros., 1876. Pp. 88.

7930 THE FISHERMEN'S own book, comprising the list of men and vessels lost from the port of Gloucester, Mass., from 1874 to April 1, 1882, and a table of losses from 1830, together with valuable statistics of the fisheries, also notable fares, narrow escapes, startling adventures, fishermen's off-hand sketches, ballads, descriptions of fishing trips and other interesting facts and incidents connected with this branch of maritime industry. Gloucester: Procter Bros., 1882. Pp. iv, 274.

7931 FOSTER, MRS. E. G. and ALICE W. FOSTER. The story of Kettle Cove. Magnolia, 1902. Pp. 39. M.

7932 FULLER, DANIEL. The diary of the Rev. Daniel Fuller with his account of his family & other matters, written at Gloucester, in Massachusetts, circa 1775. Daniel Fuller Appleton, ed. N.Y.: De Vinne Pr., 1894. Pp. 49.

7933 GANNETT, J. H. "History of the Baptist Church in East Gloucester." EIB, 3 (1871), 106-109.

7934 GARLAND, JOSEPH E. Eastern Point: a nautical, rustical, and social chronicle of Gloucester's outer shield and inner sanctum, 1606-1950. Peterborough, N.H.: Noone House, 1971. Pp. xiv, 424.

7935 _____. The Gloucester guide: a retrospective ramble. Gloucester: Gloucester 350th Anniversary Celebration Inc., 1973. Pp. xiv, 137. Historical.

7936 GLOUCESTER, MASS. Century celebration held at City Hall, Gloucester, Mass., Dec. 31, 1900, Jan. 1, 1901. Gloucester: Cape Ann Breeze, 1901. Pp. 73.

7937 _____. Memorial of the celebration of the two hundred and fiftieth anniversary of the incorporation of the town of Gloucester, Mass., August, 1892.... Boston: A. Mudge & Son, 1901. Pp. x, 369.

7938 _____. Tabular statement of the appropriations, receipts and expenditures of some of the departments...[of government].... n.p., [1883?]. Unpaged. M.
1864-1883.

7939 GLOUCESTER, MASS. BOARD OF TRADE. Gloucester, Mass. Gloucester, 1909. Unpaged.

7940 GLOUCESTER, MASS. EVANGELICAL CONGREGATIONAL CHURCH. Exercises at the fiftieth anniversary of the Evangelical Congregational Church. Gloucester, Mass., November 18, 1879. Gloucester: Cape Ann Bulletin Pr., 1880. Pp. 75.
Historical address by Frank G. Clark.

7941 GLOUCESTER, MASS. FIRST BAPTIST CHURCH. Semi-centennial of the First Baptist Church, Gloucester, Mass. [Gloucester]: Procter Bros., 1881. Pp. 42.

7942 GLOUCESTER, MASS. FIRST CHURCH. The First Church in Gloucester, an authentic historical statement, showing also the legal relations of parishes and churches. Gloucester: Procter Bros., 1880. Pp. 27.

7943 GLOUCESTER, MASS. HIGH SCHOOL. Fiftieth anniversary, Gloucester, Massachusetts High School, Cadets, R.O.T.C., May 30-31, 1935. Gloucester: Cape Ann Ticket and Label, [1935?]. Pp. 43. MSaE.

7944 GLOUCESTER, MASS. ORTHODOX CONGREGATIONAL CHURCH. Manual of the Orthodox Congregational Church in Lanesville, Mass. Gloucester: John S. E. Rogers, 1870. Pp. 36. M.

7945 GLOUCESTER, MASS. TRINITY CONGREGATIONAL CHURCH. Exercises in observance of the seventy-fifth anniversary of the Trinity Congregational Church, Gloucester, Mass., Sunday, November 13th, Wednesday, November 16th, 1904. Gloucester: Procter Bros., [1904?]. Pp. 47. MSaE.

7946 GLOUCESTER LYCEUM AND SAWYER FREE LIBRARY. Gloucester Lyceum and Sawyer Free Library, Inc., 1830-1930: the record of a century. Gloucester, 1930. Unpaged. M.

7947 _____. Outline of history and dedication of the Sawyer Free Library, of Gloucester, Mass., Tuesday, July 1, 1884, sermon, press notices, etc.... Gloucester: Cape Ann Bulletin Steam Book and Job Print, 1884. Pp. 96.

7948 GLOUCESTER 350TH ANNIVERSARY CELEBRATION, INC. Gloucester's 350th anniversary. Gloucester, 1973. Unpaged. M.

7949 "GLOUCESTER'S deserted village." Essex Antiq, 1 (1897), 43-44.
Dogtown.

7950 HART, LAWRENCE J. "The romance of Gloucester." Industry, 2 (July, 1937), 35-39.

7951 HARTT, HILDEGARDE TO. Magnolia, once Kettle Cove. n.p., 1962. Pp. 65. MSaE.

7952 HAWES, CHARLES BOARDMAN. Gloucester, by land and sea: the story of a New England seacoast town. Boston: Little, Brown, 1923. Pp. xiv, 226.

7953 HAYES, DAVID F. "The role of the Finnish immigrant in the history of Lanesville, Massachusetts, 1870-1957." EIHC, 95 (1959), 313-347.

7954 JEWETT, JAMES S. "A short historical sketch of Annisquam Parrish." EIHC, 21 (1884), 176-180.

7955 [KNOWLTON, HELEN MARY]. "The Hunt studio."
Magnolia Leaves, 2 (1882), 115-116.
William Morris Hunt, artist: author attri-
bution by the editor.

7956 LANE, C. A. History of the Annisquam Female
Benevolent Society, May 24, 1889. Glouces-
ter: Breeze Print, [1889?]. Unpaged. MBNEH.
Charity.

7957 LITTLE, NINA FLETCHER. "The old White-El-
lery House, Gloucester, Massachusetts."
OTNE, 37 (1946-1947), 53-59.
Signed: Mrs. Bertram K. Little.

7958 MCCLURE, W. RAYMOND. They that go down to
the sea in ships: more essays in remembrance. Rutlant, Vt.: Sharp Offset Print., 1968.
Pp. 87.

7959 MCFARLAND, RAYMOND. The masts of Gloucester: recollections of a fisherman. N.Y.:
W. W. Norton, 1937. Pp. x, 268.

7960 MANN, CHARLES EDWARD. In the heart of Cape
Ann; or, the story of Dogtown. (1896) [2d.
ed.]. Gloucester: Procter Bros., 1906. Pp. 77,
31.
Final 31 pages has a separate title: Beginnings of Dogtown.

7961 ONE of freedom's battles: where it was
fought and to whom the victory was due.
n.p., n.d. Pp. 24. MBNEH.
Universalism.

7962 PARSONS, PETER and PETER ANASTAS. When
Gloucester was Gloucester: toward an oral
history of the city. Gloucester: Gloucester 350th
Anniversary Celebration, Inc., 1973. Pp. x, 82.

7963 PETERSON, FREDERICK. "The fishermen of
Gloucester." Americana, 31 (1937), 461-491.

7964 POWERS, LEVI M. Sketch of the Independent
Christian Church and the Sargent Murray Gil-
man House, Gloucester, Massachusetts. Boston:
Murray Pr., 1920. Pp. 32. MB.

7965 PRENDERGAST, FRANK M. "Made in the Gloucester tradition." Industry, 11 (January,
1946), 14-16.
Cape Anne Manufacturing Company, clothing.

7966 PRINGLE, JAMES ROBERT, comp. The book of
the three hundredth anniversary observance
of the foundation of Massachusetts Bay Colony at
Cape Ann in 1623 and the fiftieth year of the incorporation of Gloucester as a city. Lynn: Nic-
hols-Ellis Pr., 1924. Pp. 280. M.

7967 ____. History of the town and city of
Gloucester, Cape Ann, Massachusetts.
Gloucester, 1892. Pp. 340.

7968 PROCTER, GEORGE H. "An American fishing
port." Lippincott's Magazine, 1 (1868),
497-505.

7969 ____. The fishermen's memorial and record
book, containing a list of vessels and their
crews, lost from the port of Gloucester from the
year 1830 to October 1, 1873...including those lost
in the gale of August 24, 1873: it also contains
valuable statistics of the fishing business, off-
hand sketches, big trips, tales of narrow escapes,
maritime poetry, and other matters of interest to
these toilers of the sea. Gloucester: Procter
Bros., 1873. Pp. iv, 172.

7970 RECCHIA, KITTY PARSONS. The story of Our
Lady of Good Voyage, founded in 1890, erected for the Portuguese fishermen of Gloucester, Mass.
in 1893. North Montpelier, Vt.: Driftwind Pr.,
1945. Unpaged. MSaE.

7971 THE SARGENT-Murray-Gilman-Hough House Association. n.p., [1964?]. M.

7972 "SHIP registers of the district of Gloucester, 1789-1875." EIHC, 77 (1941), 363-378;
78 (1942), 41-64, 177-192, 265-280, 387-402; 79
(1943), 65-80, 177-192, 293-308, 387-402; 80 (1944),
71-78, 180-191.

7973 SOMES, JOHN J. "Gloucester as an ideal summer resort." National Magazine, 18 (1903),
674-678.

7974 ____. The Gloucester Fire Department: its
history and work from 1793 to 1893, the old
machines, fire clubs, hand engines, steamers, etc.,
etc., and the part each performed in fighting fires,
with a record of fires from 1656 to 1893. [Glouces-
ter]: Procter Bros., 1892. Pp. viii, 275.

7975 ____. "Linzee's attack on Gloucester."
MagHist, 2 (1905), 85-89.
John Linzee; August 8, 1775.

7976 SPAULDING, H. C., comp. Magnolia souvenir.
Boston: F. Wood, 1886. Pp. 52.

7977 START, EDWIN A. "Round about Gloucester."
NEM, New Ser., 6 (1892), 687-703.

7978 STORY of an interesting and historic old
house in Gloucester, Mass., built by Winthrop
Sargent about 1768. Boston: Murray Pr., [not after
1919]. Pp. 15. MBNEH.
Sargent-Murray-Gilman-Hough House.

7979 "THE THIRD Parish, Annisquam, Gloucester."
ECHGR, 1 (1894), 129-130.

7980 THOMAS, GORDON W. Builders of Gloucester's
prosperity: life stories of famous fishing
vessels. [Gloucester], 1952. Pp. 92.

7981 ____. Fast and able: life stories of great
Gloucester fishing vessels. Paul B. Kenyon,
ed. Gloucester: Gloucester 350th Anniversary Celebration, Inc., 1973. Pp. xii, 212.

7982 TIBBETS, FREDERICK WASHINGTON. The story of
Gloucester, Massachusetts, permanently settled 1623; an address...given before the convention
of the Massachusetts State Firemen's Association at

(TIBBETS, FREDERICK WASHINGTON.)
City Hall, Gloucester, Thursday afternoon, September 21, 1916. [Gloucester]: Clark the Printer, 1917. Pp. 52.

7983 WILMERDING, JOHN. "Interpretations of place: views of Gloucester, Mass. by American artists." EIHC, 103 (1967), 53-65.

GOSHEN

7984 BARRUS, HIRAM. History of the town of Goshen, Hampshire County, Massachusetts, from its first settlement in 1761 to 1881. Boston, 1881. Pp. 262.

7985 GOSHEN, MASS. Centennial anniversary of the incorporation of the town of Goshen, Mass., June 22, 1881, including addresses, poems, letters, and other matters relating to the occasion. Reading: Chronicle Job Print, 1881. Pp. 64.
Historical address by Hiram Barrus.

7986 _____. Goshen, Massachusetts, 175th anniversary program 1781-1956, August 3-4, 1956. n.p., [1956?]. Unpaged. MAJ.

7987 WHITMAN, SAMUEL. An impartial history of the proceedings of the church and people of Goshen, (Mass.) in the dismission of their minister, and in the settling of another; containing facts and documents from some time in the year 1816, till towards the close of the year 1821.... Boston: Lincoln & Edmands, 1824. Pp. 84. MB.

GOSNOLD

7988 ANDERSON SCHOOL OF NATURAL HISTORY, PENIKESE ISLAND. The organization and progress of the Anderson School of Natural History at Penikese Island, report of the trustees for 1873. Cambridge: Welch, Bigelow, 1874. Pp. 30.
Administered by Harvard School of Comparative Zoology.

7989 BROWN, ALEXANDER CROSBY. "Enchanted voyage." AmNep, 7 (1947), 213-223.
Pasque Island.

7990 _____. "Reminiscences of the last voyage of the bark 'Wanderer.'" AmNep, 9 (1949), 17-30.
Wrecked in hurricane off Cuttyhunk, 26 August 1924.

7991 CORNISH, LOUIS CRAIG. "Agassiz's school on Penikese." Scientific Monthly, 57 (1943), 315-321.

7992 CRAPO, WILLIAM WALLACE. "Gosnold's voyage." MHSP, 2 Ser., 16 (1902), 247-249.

7993 EMERSON, AMELIA FORBES. Early history of Naushon Island. Boston: Thomas Todd, 1935. Pp. xi, 502.

7994 _____, comp. Naushon data. Concord, 1963. Pp. 235.

7995 HALL, ARTHUR CLEVELAND. "Cuttyhunk." NEM, New Ser., 17 (1897-1898), 36-51.

7996 HASKELL, LOUISE TAYLOR. The story of Cuttyhunk. New Bedford: Reynolds Print., 1953. Pp. 53.

7997 HOWLAND, ALICE FORBES. "The story of Pasque and the Pasque Island Club." DCI, 3 (February, 1962), entire issue.
Fishing club.

7998 _____. Three islands; Pasque, Nashawena, and Penikese. [Boston?], 1964. Pp. xvi, 127.

7999 [LATTIN, FRANK H.]. Penikese, a reminiscence by one of its pupils. Albion, N.Y., 1895. Pp. 95. MB.
Anderson School of Natural History; author attribution by Boston Public Library.

8000 "NAUSHON Island." About the First, (February, 1941), 4-5.

8001 SHEPARD, MARSHALL. Our enchanted island. Edgartown: Dukes County Historical Society, 1940. Pp. 16. M.
Cuttyhunk Island.

8002 "VISIT to the Elizabeth Islands." North American Review, 5 (1817), 313-324.

8003 WILSON, HAROLD C. "A field trip for Louis Agassiz." DCI, 15 (1973-1974), 23-34.
John Anderson School of Natural History.

8004 _____ and WILLIAM C. CARR. "Gosnold's Elizabeth isle: Cuttyhunk or Naushon." AmNep, 33 (1973), 131-145.
Location of Gosnold Fort.

8005 WILSON, HAROLD C. Those pearly isles; the enchanting story of the Elizabeth Islands. Falmouth: Kendall Printing, 1973. Pp. vii, 74.

GRAFTON

8006 BEALES, ROSS W., JR., ed. "Solomon Prentice's narrative of the Great Awakening." MHSP, 83 (1971), 130-147.
Written in 1744.

8007 BRIGHAM, CHARLES, JR. Book of questions and answers relating to the town of Grafton.... Worcester: M. Spooner, 1831. Pp. 20. MWA.

8008 BRIGHAM, WILLIAM. An address delivered before the inhabitants of Grafton, on the first centennial anniversary of that town, April 29, 1835. Boston: Light & Horton, 1835. Pp. 40.

8009 CUMMIN, HAZEL E. "A Willard clock of unusual interest." Antiques, 16 (1929), 46-47.
The only dated Simon Willard clock marked 'Grafton.'

8010 DEXTER, HENRY MARTYN, ed. "Result of a council at Grafton, Ms. in 1744." CongQ, 4 (1862), 247-252.

8011 FLAGG, CHARLES ALCOTT. "The old Merriam House." MassMag, 2 (1909), 98.

8012 GOULDING, FRANK PALMER. Address delivered at the celebration of the one hundred and fiftieth anniversary of the incorporation of the town of Grafton, Mass., April 29, 1885. Worcester: C. Hamilton, 1886. Pp. 42.

8013 GRAFTON, MASS. EVANGELICAL CONGREGATIONAL CHURCH. The confession of faith and covenant of the Evangelical Congregational Church in Grafton, Mass., with a brief history and list of its members, January 1, 1842. Worcester: Spooner, Howland, and Merriam, 1842. Pp. 60.

8014 GRAFTON, MASS. EVANGELICAL CONGREGATIONAL CHURCH, LADIES' SEWING CIRCLE. The fiftieth anniversary, being the proceedings at the semi-centennial of the Ladies' Sewing Circle, connected with the Evangelical Church, Grafton, Mass. March 5, 1879. Worcester: Lucius P. Goddard, 1879. Pp. 24. M.

8015 HARLOW, SAMUEL ALLEN. One hundred and seventy-five years in the life of a church, historical sermon...anniversary of the organization of the Church of Christ in Hassanimisco Plantation, now Grafton, Mass...Dec. 30, 1906.... Worcester: Davis Pr., [1906?]. Pp. 29.

8016 HOWE, ELIJAH FRANKLIN. Grafton: historical oration delivered at the centennial celebration held at Grafton, Mass., July 4th, 1876. Worcester: C. Hamilton, 1878. Pp. 46.

8017 PIERCE, FREDERICK CLIFTON. History of Grafton, Worcester County, Massachusetts, from its early settlement by the Indians in 1647 to the present time, 1879.... Worcester: C. Hamilton, 1879. Pp. xiv, 623.

8018 SAUNDERS, RICHARD. "The Willard Homestead in Grafton, Massachusetts." Antiques, 102 (1972), 84-89.

8019 WILLSON, EDMUND BURKE. Address delivered at the consecration of the Riverside Cemetery in Grafton; April 29, 1851, to which is added an account of the cemetery. Boston: John Wilson, 1851. Pp. 16. MBNEH.
Historical sketch by T. C. Biscoe.

8020 _____. A sermon preached in Grafton, Sunday, December 27, 1846 containing historical notes of the Congregational Church in said town. Worcester: National Aegis, 1847. Pp. 39. M.

GRANBY

8021 GRANBY, MASS. CHURCH OF CHRIST. Manual of the Church of Christ in Granby, Mass., including a historical sketch.... Springfield: Clark W. Bryan, 1875. Pp. 12. MNF.

8022 GRANBY bicentennial, 1768-1968, Granby, Massachusetts; incorporated June 11, 1768. Granby: The Town, 1968. Pp. 283.

8023 SNYDER, ESTHER GALLUP. Old houses: Granby, Massachusetts. Granby: Granby Woman's Club, 1954. Pp. 50. MBNEH.

GRANVILLE

8024 GRANVILLE, MASS. FIRST CHURCH OF CHRIST. The Granville jubilee, celebrated at Granville, Mass., August 27 and 28, 1845. Springfield: H. S. Taylor, 1845. Pp. 139.
Historical discourse by Timothy M. Cooley.

8025 GRANVILLE jubilee, the First Church of Christ, Granville, Massachusetts, August 28th, 1895. Pittsfield: Sun Printing, 1895. Pp. 15. M.
Centennial of the beginning of the pastorate of Timothy Mather Cooley.

8026 SHEPARDSON, FRANCIS WAYLAND. "The old Granville and the new." NEM, New Ser., 20 (1899), 97-117.
"The new" is Granville, Ohio.

8027 WILSON, ALBION BENJAMIN. History of Granville, Massachusetts. Hartford: Connecticut Printers, 1954. Pp. xiv, 381.

GREAT BARRINGTON

8028 CHAPMAN, GERARD. St. James' Parish, Great Barrington, Massachusetts, 1762-1962. [Great Barrington]: Protestant Episcopal Society of Great Barrington, 1962. Pp. xxiv, 92.

8029 CONN, HOWARD JAMES. The First Congregational Church of Great Barrington, 1743-1943, a history. [Great Barrington]: The Anniversary Year Committee, 1943. Pp. 121.

8030 DURFEE, CALVIN. Advantages of retrospection, a commemorative discourse, delivered before the Congregational Church and Society in Great Barrington, May 13, 1866, with an appendix. Boston: T. R. Marvin & Son, 1866. Pp. 48.

8031 DWIGHT, R. HENRY W. "Old Great Barrington." MagHist, 23 (1916), 173-184.

8032 "THE FIRST Methodist meeting house, Great Barrington." Berkshire Hills, 2 (March 1, 1902), [10-11].
1845.

8033 GREAT BARRINGTON, MASS. Great Barrington, bi-centennial 1761-1961. n.p., [1961?]. Pp. 399. M.

8034 _____. Great Barrington, Mass., town diary, 1676-1911, and souvenir program.... Great Barrington: Berkshire Courier Print, [1911?]. Unpaged.

8035 _____. Great Barrington, Massachusetts, town diary, 1676-1930 and program [of] tercentenary celebration and Old Home Week, July 20-26, 1930. Great Barrington: Berkshire Courier, [1930?]. Unpaged. MPB.

8036 MUNSON, L. E. "Old Indian fordway." BHSSC, 3 (1899-1913), 353-359.

8037 NATIONAL MAHAIWE BANK. The story of a country bank, 1847-1947. Great Barrington, [1947?]. Pp. 56. MPB.

8038 POPE, S. G. "The first shoe factory in Berkshire County." Berkshire Hills, 2 (August 1, 1902), [8-9].

8039 SAHLER, LOUIS HASBROUCK VON. "The earliest records of Saint James' Episcopal Church, Great Barrington, Massachusetts with brief notes of the town, church and first rector." Putnam's HM, New Ser., 7 (1899), 152-156, 199-201; Genealogical Quarterly Magazine, 1 (1900), 53-67, 126-139, 179-187, 227-232; 2 (1901), 16-28.

8040 TAYLOR, CHARLES JAMES, RALPH W. POPE and GEORGE E. MCCLEAN. History of Great Barrington (Berkshire) Massachusetts. [Great Barrington], 1928. Pp. xvii, 620.
1676-1922.

8041 TODD, JOHN. The pulpit tested: a sermon delivered at the centennial anniversary of the Congregational Church in Great Barrington, December 23, 1843. Pittsfield: E. P. Little, 1844. Pp. 123. MB.
Lengthy historical appendix by J. W. Turner.

8042 WARNER, H. E. "War recollections as connected with Great Barrington from 1861 to 1864." Berkshire Hills, 4 (1903-1904), 188-189.

8043 _____. "War recollections: the raising of troops in Great Barrington in 1861." Berkshire Hills, 4 (1903-1904), 177-178.

8044 WARNER, HENRY C. "Historic Boulder Monument: old Indian fordway on the Houstanic River at Great Barrington." Berkshire Hills, 4 (1903-1904), 287-288.

GREENFIELD

8045 ADAMS, ELIZABETH L. A history of the Mansion house corner, Greenfield, Massachusetts. N.Y.: American Historical Society, 1928. Pp. 32.

8046 ALDRICH, ETHELYN A. A directory of the book trade in Greenfield, Massachusetts, 1792-1899. Charlottesville: Bibliographical Society of the University of Virginia, 1954. Pp. 102.

8047 ALLEN, S. AND SONS, GREENFIELD, MASS. History of S. Allen & Sons, 1812-1912. [Greenfield]: Published at Allen's Corner, [1912?]. Pp. 15. [MGreen].
Hardware store.

8048 ALVORD, HENRY ELIJAH. Old Home observance; Thursday, July thirty one, nineteen hundred and two. Greenfield, Massachusetts; address of Major Henry E. Alvord, letter of Honorable John E. Russell.... [Greenfield, 1902]. Pp. 42.

8049 [BACON, GEORGE FOX]. Leading business men of Greenfield and vicinity; embracing also Turners Falls, Orange, and Athol.... Boston: Mercantile Publishing, 1889. Pp. 72.

8050 BUTEMONT, MALCOLM. A concise history of Republican Lodge. n.p., [1945?]. Pp. 16. MDeeP.
Freemasons.

8051 CORSS, CHARLES C. "Recollections of the old meetinghouse." PVMA, 3 (1890-1898), 255-259.

8052 DARLING, HERBERT E. and DORIS M. PAULIN. History of Greenfield Tap and Die, one hundredth anniversary, 1872-1972. n.p., 1972. Unpaged. MDeeP.

8053 ELKS, BENEVOLENT AND PROTECTIVE ORDER OF, GREENFIELD, MASS. Greenfield Lodge, fiftieth anniversary, 1913-1963. n.p., [1963?]. Pp. 36. [MGreen].

8054 FOSS, WESLEY B. "Industry's map of Massachusetts: Greenfield." Industry, 3 (June, 1938), 27-29.

8055 FRANKLIN COUNTY PUBLIC HOSPITAL, GREENFIELD, MASS. SCHOOL OF NURSING. 70 years of the Franklin County Public Hospital School of Nursing, 1895-1965. n.p., 1965. Pp. 22. [MGreen].

8056 FRANKLIN SAVINGS INSTITUTION, GREENFIELD, MASS. Franklin Savings Institution, commemorating its one hundredth anniversary, 1834-1934. Greenfield: Minott Printing and Binding, [1934?]. Pp. 15. M.

8057 GATES, WINFRED C. "Journal of a cabinet maker's apprentice." CEAIA, 15 (1962), 23-24, 35-36.
Edward Jenner Carpenter, 1844-1845.

8058 GREENFIELD, MASS. Official souvenir program, Greenfield (Massachusetts) sesqui-centennial, 1753 June 9 1903.... [Greenfield]: E. A. Hall, 1903. Unpaged.
Includes history.

8059 GREENFIELD, MASS. FIRST CONGREGATIONAL CHURCH. A history of the First Church (Congregational) Greenfield, Massachusetts, originally the "North Parish" of Deerfield. Greenfield: E. A. Hall, 1963. Pp. 110. MDeeP.

8060 _____. Manual of the First Congregational Church, Greenfield, Mass. with a catalogue of members, 1878. Greenfield: Franklin Printing Office, 1878. Pp. 19. M.
Includes brief history.

8061 GREENFIELD, MASS. FIRST NATIONAL BANK. 125 curious stories and little known facts, past and present about money and banking in Greenfield and its environs. Greenfield: Channing L. Bete, [1947?]. Unpaged. M.

8062 _____. One hundred years in Greenfield, 1822-1922, issued to commemorate a century of banking, the First National Bank. Greenfield, 1922. Pp. 47.

8063 GREENFIELD, MASS. HOLY TRINITY CHURCH. Holy Trinity Church, Greenfield, 1868-1968. n.p., [1968?]. Pp. 96. [MGreen].

8064 GREENFIELD SAVINGS BANK. Greenfield Savings Bank, a history. [Greenfield], 1974. Unpaged. MDeeH.

8065 GREENFIELD TAP AND DIE CORPORATION. [Historical booklet, 1872-1918]. Hartford, 1918. Pp. 23.

8066 "THE GREENFIELD Tap & Die Corporation." Industry, 6 (July, 1941), 11-14.

8067 HORTON, JAMES A. History of Edwin E. Day Post, No. 174, G. A. R., Department of Massachusetts, 1870 to 1926. Greenfield, 1926. Pp. 32.

8068 KELLOGG, LUCY JANE CUTLER. Alliance women of the past...given before the All Souls Branch Alliance, Greenfield, Massachusetts, November 3, 1937. [Greenfield]: Greenfield Commercial School, 1927. 17 leaves. MDeeH.

8069 _____. Hearth stone tales: a condensed history of Greenfield, Massachusetts. Hartford: Case, Lockwood & Brainard, 1936. Pp. viii, 125.

8070 _____. Historical Greenfield.... [Greenfield]: Greenfield Historical Society, 1926. Pp. 19. MDeeH.

8071 LEE, JOHN CARLL. "Grand old Greenfield." WNE, 2 (1912), 151-166.

8072 _____. "Greenfield's achievements in varied manufactures." WNE, 2 (1912), 174-188.

8073 [LEONARD, CLARA]. "Memories of Bluemeadow." NEM, New Ser., 13 (1896), 694-704; 14 (1896), 86-93, 220-226, 345-350. Signed: Charlotte Lyon, a pseudonym; events of 50 years before, names are fictitious.

8074 LODGE, HENRY CABOT. Address of Hon. Henry Cabot Lodge, delivered at Greenfield, June 9, 1903, on the 150th anniversary of the incorporation of the town. [Greenfield, 1904?]. Pp. 21.

8075 _____. A frontier town, and other essays. N.Y.: C. Scribner's Sons, 1906. Pp. 274.

8076 "THE MILLERS Falls Company." Industry, 6 (December, 1940), 13-16. Tools.

8077 MOODY, C. M. Greenfield 150 years ago. Greenfield, 1903. Unpaged. [MGreen].

8078 PARSONS, HERBERT COLLINS. "Greenfield." NEM, New Ser., 15 (1896-1897), 609-629.

8079 PEABODY, W. RODMAN. A history of the Greenfield Electric Light and Power Company, Greenfield, Massachusetts. Boston: Pinkham Pr., [1924?]. Pp. 77. MAJ.

8080 SHUMWAY, HARRY I. "The Potter House, Greenfield, Massachusetts." House Beautiful, 45 (February, 1919), 61-64.

8081 SMITH, MARY PRUDENCE WELLS. The Third Congregational (Unitarian) Society of Greenfield, Mass. an historical sketch. [Greenfield?]: Franklin County Branch of the National Alliance of Unitarian and Other Christian Women, 1897. Pp. 28. MDeep.

8082 THOMPSON, FRANCIS MCGEE. "An early bee hunter's adventures." MassMag, 8 (1915), 84-90. John Smead and John Gillett, 1696.

8083 _____. "Greenfield and its First Church." PVMA, 1 (1870-1879), 474-480.

8084 _____. History of Greenfield, shire town of Franklin County, Massachusetts. Greenfield: T. Morey & Son, 1904-54. 4v. 1682-1953; volume 3, by Lucy Cutler Kellogg, has title: History of Greenfield, 1900-1929. Volume 4, by Charles Sidney Severance, was published by the town and has title: History of Greenfield, 1930-1953.

8085 WHITEMAN, JOHN B. St. James Parish, Greenfield, Mass., 1812-1912. Greenfield: E. A. Hall, 1912. Pp. 125. [MGreen].

8086 WILLARD, DAVID. Willard's history of Greenfield.... Greenfield: Kneeland & Eastman, 1838. Pp. iv, 180.

8087 WINSLOW, CHARLES E., ed. A pictorial history of Greenfield, Massachusetts. [Greenfield]: Greenfield Historical Society, 1953. Unpaged. MDeeH.

8088 WYLIE, MAUDE GEORGE. "Across the thresholds of Greenfield's homes." WNE, 2 (1912), 167-171. Architecture.

GROTON

8089 AMORY, WILLIAM. Reminiscences of Groton, during the years 1823 and 1824. Groton, Mass., 1884. Pp. 13. MB.

8090 BOUTWELL, FRANCIS MARION. Old highways and landmarks of Groton, Massachusetts. Groton 1884. Pp. 20.

8091 _____. Old homesteads of Groton, Massachusetts. Groton, 1883. Pp. 11.

8092 _____. People and their homes in Groton, Massachusetts, in olden time. Groton, 1890. Pp. 18.

8093 [BUTLER, CALEB]. Collection of facts and documents relating to ecclesiastical affairs in Groton, Mass.... Boston: Stephen Foster, 1827. Pp. 44.

8094 CONANT, WALLACE B. "Groton, an ancient town and its famous schools." NEM, New Ser., 33 (1905-1906), 468-478.

8095 GREEN, SAMUEL ABBOTT. An account of the early land-grants of Groton, Massachusetts.... Groton, 1879. Pp. 58.

8096 _____. An account of the lawyers of Groton, Massachusetts, including natives who have practised elsewhere, and those also who have studied law in the town. Groton, 1892. Pp. 158.

8097 _____. An account of the physicians and dentists of Groton, Massachusetts, including those who, born there, have practised their profession elsewhere. Groton, 1890. Pp. 90.

8098 _____. The boundary lines of old Groton. Groton, 1885. Pp. 105.

8099 _____. A brief account of some of the early settlers of Groton, Massachusetts, being the appendix to 'Groton epitaphs.' Groton, 1878. Pp. 28.
    Biography.

8100 _____. "Chapters in the early history of Groton." NEHGR, 36 (1882), 21-28, 167-174.

8101 _____. Facts relating to the history of Groton, Massachusetts. Groton, 1912-1914. 2v.
    Volume one has title: The natural history and topography of Groton, Massachusetts.

8102 _____. The geography of Groton, Massachusetts, prepared for the use of the members of the Appalachian Club, on a proposed visit to that town, Saturday, September 18, 1886. Groton, 1886. Pp. 20.

8103 _____. Groton as a shire town.--Destructive tornado.--Two Groton conventions.--The soapstone quarry. Groton, 1884. Pp. 20.

8104 _____. "Groton during Shays's Rebellion." MHSP, 2 Ser., 1 (1884-1885), 298-312.

8105 _____. Groton during the Indian wars. Groton, 1883. Pp. 214.

8106 _____. Groton during the Revolution, with an appendix. Groton, 1900. Pp. 343.

8107 _____. Groton historical series: a collection of papers relating to the history of the town of Groton, Massachusetts. Groton, 1887-1899. 4v.

8108 _____. Groton in the witchcraft times. Groton, 1883. Pp. 29.

8109 _____. An historical address, bi-centennial and centennial, delivered at Groton, Massachusetts, July 4, 1876, by request of the citizens. (1876) 2d. ed. Groton, 1876. Pp. 89.

8110 _____. An historical address delivered at Groton, Massachusetts, February 20, 1880... at the dedication of three monuments erected by the town. Groton, 1880. Pp. 56.
    First meeting house, King Philip's War and William Prescott.

8111 _____. An historical address delivered at Groton, Massachusetts, July 12, 1905, by request of the citizens, on the celebration of the two hundred and fiftieth anniversary of the settlement of the town. Groton, 1905. Pp. 52.

8112 _____. "The old stores or the post-office of Groton." BSM, 1 (1884), 70-79.

8113 _____. "The old stores, the post office, the old taverns and stage coaches of Groton." Granite Mo, 9 (1886), 195-204, 230-239.

8114 _____. "The old taverns and stage-coaches of Groton." BSM, 1 (1884), 10-19.

8115 _____. "The old town of Groton." MagHist, 2 (1905), 185-198.

8116 _____. "Papers relating to Thomas Lawrence's Company, 1758." MHSP, 2 Ser., 6 (1890-1891), 21-33.
    Militia.

8117 _____. "The population of Groton at different times and the provincial census of 1765." MHSP, 2 Ser., 4 (1887-1889), 136-141.

8118 _____. Remarks on Nonacocicus, the Indian name of Major Willard's farm at Groton, Mass.... [Cambridge, 1893?]. Pp. 4.

8119 _____. "Result of a council held at Groton in 1712." MHSP, 2 Ser., 13 (1899-1900), 298-302.
    Congregational ministers.

8120 _____. "Slavery at Groton in provincial times." MHSP, 42 (1908-1909), 196-202.

8121 GROTON, MASS. Addresses delivered at Groton, Massachusetts, July 12, 1905, by request of the citizens, on the celebration of the two hundred and fiftieth anniversary of its settlement. Groton, 1905. Pp. 100.

8122 _____. The early records of Groton, Massachusetts, 1662-1707. Samuel A. Green, ed. Groton, 1880. Pp. 200.

8123 _____. The Groton bi-centennial celebration, October 31, 1855. Groton, 1886. Pp. 23.

8124 _____. Proceedings of the centennial cele-
bration at Groton, Mass., July 4th, 1876, in
commemoration of the destruction of the town,
March, 1676, and the Declaration of Independence,
July 4th, 1776, with an oration by Samuel Abbott
Green, M.D. Groton, 1876. Pp. xi, 89.

8125 _____. Tercentenary, 1655-1955. Virginia
A. May, ed. [Groton?], 1955. Pp. 94.

8126 _____. The town records of Groton, Massachusetts. 1662-1678. Samuel A. Green, ed.
Groton, 1879. Pp. 46.

8127 GROTON, MASS. UNION CONGREGATIONAL CHURCH.
Historical addresses delivered at the Union
Congregational Church, Groton, Massachusetts,
Wednesday, January first, 1902, seventy-fifth anni-
versary, 1827-1902. Ayer: Huntley Turner Pr.,
[1902?]. Pp. 31.
Addresses by Mary T. Shumway, Henry W. Whit-
ing and Darwin P. Keyes.

8128 LAWRENCE ACADEMY. Financial history of Lawrence Academy, at Groton, Massachusetts,
with a statement of its funds now available. Groton, 1895. Pp. 28.

8129 _____. The jubilee of Lawrence Academy, at
Groton, Mass., July 12, 1854. N.Y.: Standard Steam Psesses [sic], 1855. Pp. 76.

8130 _____. 'Massachusetts' most famous school
town.' Groton: Ayer: H. S. Turner, 1903.
Pp. 7.

8131 _____. Proceedings at the celebration of
the ninetieth anniversary of the founding of
Lawrence Academy, Groton, Massachusetts, June 21,
1883. Groton, 1883. Pp. 48.

8132 LAWRENCE ACADEMY. ALUNMI ASSOCIATION. A
general catalogue of the trustees, teachers,
and students of Lawrence Academy, Groton, Massachusetts, from the time of its incorporation. 1793-
1893, with an account of the celebrations of the
ninetieth and the one hundredth anniversaries.
Groton, 1893. Pp. 241.

8133 RICHARDSON, EDWARD ADAMS. The Community,
Groton, Massachusetts: the story of a
neighborhood, March, 1911, Ayer, Massachusetts.
Ayer: H. S. Turner, 1911. Pp. 15.
William Miller and the Second Coming.

8134 _____. Moors School at old District No. 2,
Groton, Massachusetts; the story of a dis-
trict school. Ayer: Huntley S. Turner, 1911.
Pp. 32.

8135 SHUMWAY, MARY T. The Groton Public Library:
a paper read before the Groton Historical
Society in 1898. Rev., 1905. Boston: Sparrell
Print, 1905. Pp. 15.

8136 WRIGHT, ELIZUR. Reminiscences of Groton
during the years 1826 and 1827. Groton:
Marsh, 1884. Pp. 14. MB.

GROVELAND

8137 BERRY, LOUIS F. The old church bell used in
the Groveland Congregational Meeting-House,
1795-1895, a centennial anniversary sermon delivered
Dec. 22, 1895. Haverhill: Chase Bros., 1896.
Pp. 18.

8138 GROVELAND, MASS. CONGREGATIONAL CHURCH OF
CHRIST. Historical address delivered at the
one hundred and seventy-fifth anniversary of the
Congregational Church of Christ of Groveland, Mass.,
together with a list of officers and members.
Haverhill: Torrey & Torrey, [1902?]. Pp. 41. MHi.
1727-1902.

8139 PARKER, SARAH DEWHIRST. Outline of Groveland
history. Groveland, 1950. Pp. 93. MB.

8140 POORE, ALFRED. "A genealogical-historical
visitation of Groveland, Mass., in the year
1863." EIHC, 55 (1919), 241-248.
'Continued' but no more appeared.

8141 _____. "Groveland localities and place-
names." EIHC, 46 (1910), 161-177.

8142 _____. "The houses and buildings of Groveland, Mass." EIHC, 46 (1910), 193-208, 289-
304; 47 (1911), 25-40, 133-148, 261-276.

8143 SPOFFORD, JEREMIAH. "Merrimack Academy."
EIB, 4 (1872), 108-114.
Founded in 1821.

8144 _____. Reminiscences of seventy years; including half a century in the practice of
medicine in this place, delivered in the First
Church in Groveland, June 22, 1867. Haverhill:
E. G. Frothingham, 1867. Pp. 40.

HADLEY

8145 ANDREW, MARJORIE, et al. War over old Had-
ley. Amherst: Massachusetts State College,
Department of Economics, 1946. 36 leaves. MAJ.
Economic conditions, 1941-1945.

8146 BAYNE, JULIA TAFT. "Old Hadley." NEM, New
Ser., 7 (1892-1893), 329-344.

8147 BONNEY, FRANKLIN and ELBRIDGE KINGSLEY.
"The original settlers of Hadley and the lots
of land granted them." Grafton Magazine of History,
2 (1909-1910), 3-37.

8148 CALLAHAN, ELLEN ELIZABETH. "Hadley: a study
of the political development of a typical New
England town from the official records, 1659-1930."
SCSH, 16 (1930-1931), 1-106.

8149 DWYER, MARGARET CLIFFORD. Hopkins Academy &
the Hopkins Fund, 1664-1964, a history. Hadley: Trustees of Hopkins Academy, 1964. Pp. xiii,
316.

8150 ELKINS, STANLEY and ERIC MCKITRICK. "Meaning for Turner's frontier: the Southwest frontier and New England." PolSciQ, 69 (1954), 565-602.
Frederick Jackson Turner; 'New England' refers to Hadley.

8151 FISHER, GEORGE ELISHA. Historical address by the pastor, with addresses and letters at the semi-centennial celebration of the Congregational Church, in South Hadley Falls, Mass., Aug. 9, 1874. Holyoke: Transcript Book and Job Printing House, 1874. Pp. 46.

8152 HADLEY, SAMUEL P. "Historical sketch of the police court of Hadley." Lowell HSC, 2 (1921-1926), 36-81.

8153 HADLEY, MASS. Celebration of the two hundredth anniversary of the settlement of Hadley, Massachusetts, at Hadley, June 8, 1859; including the address by Rev. Prof. F. D. Huntington... poem by Edward C. Porter...and the other exercises of the occasion. Northampton: Bridgman & Childs, 1859. Pp. 98.

8154 HADLEY, MASS. COMMITTEE FOR OPEN HOUSES. Old houses, 1659-1959, Hadley tercentenary celebration. Hadley, 1959. Pp. 22.

8155 HADLEY, MASS. FIRST CHURCH. Manual of the First Church in Hadley; history, confession of faith.... Northampton: Hopkins, Bridgman, 1855. Pp. 12. MNF.

8156 _____. The three hundredth anniversary of the First Congregational Church in Hadley, July 12-August 2, 1959. Hadley: Tercentenary Publications Committee, 1959. Pp. 101.

8157 HADLEY, MASS. SAINT JOHN'S PARISH. Saint John's Parish, Hadley, Massachusetts, 1915-1965. n.p., [1965?]. Unpaged. MAJ.

8158 HADLEY, MASS. SECOND CONGREGATIONAL CHURCH. Exercises at the semi-centennial of the dedication of the church edifice in North Hadley, November 20, 1884. Northampton: Gazette Printing, 1885. Pp. 36. MAJ.

8159 _____. 125th anniversary of the Second Congregational Church of Hadley, Massachusetts 1831-1956, October 28, 1956. Amherst: Hamilton I. Newell, [1956?]. Pp. 64. MAJ.

8160 _____. Services at the centennial celebration of the organization of the Congregational Church in North Hadley, observed Sunday, June 28, 1931. Northampton: Metcalf, 1931. Pp. 58.

8161 HADLEY, the regicides, Indian, and general history; a souvenir in honor of Major-General Joseph Hooker, and in anticipation of the memorial exercises at his birthplace, Tuesday, May 7, 1895. Northampton: Picturesque Publishing, [1895]. Unpaged.

8162 HOPKINS ACADEMY. History of the Hopkins Fund, Grammar School and Academy, in Hadley, Mass...1657-1890. Amherst: Amherst Record Pr., 1890. Pp. 198.

8163 HUNTINGTON, ARRIA SARGENT. Under a colonial roof-tree: fireside chronicles of early New England. Boston: Houghton Mifflin, 1891. Pp. 133. Social life and customs.

8164 HUNTINGTON, JAMES LINCOLN. Forty Acres: the story of the Bishop Huntington House. N.Y.: Hastings House, 1949. Pp. 68.
Porter-Phelps-Huntington House.

8165 _____. How and why the families Porter, Phelps and Huntington came to Hadley and built the house at Forty Acres. [Hadley: Porter-Phelps-Huntington Foundation, 1966?]. Unpaged. MDeeH.

8166 JOHNSON, CLIFTON. Historic Hadley: quarter millennial souvenir, 1659-1909. Hadley, 1909. Pp. 40.

8167 [_____], ed. Old Hadley: quarter millennial celebration, 1909, Sunday, Monday, Tuesday and Wednesday August 1-2-3 and 4: the story of the four days with the various addresses and numerous illustrations. Springfield: F. A. Bassette, [1909]. Pp. 94.

8168 LUTHER, CLAIR FRANKLIN. "The Hadley chest." Antiques, 14 (1928), 338-340.

8169 _____. The Hadley chest. Hartford: Case, Lockwood & Brainard, 1935. Pp. xxii, 144.

8170 _____. "A late Hadley chestmaker." Antiques, 16 (1929), 202-203.
Eliakim Smith.

8171 MARTULA, MRS. JOHN T., RICHARD MARTULA and SUSAN MARTULA, eds. Hadley tercentenary 1659-1959. n.p., [1959?]. Unpaged. MNF.

8172 NOSTRAND, RICHARD L. "The colonial New England town." Journal of Geography, 72 (October, 1973), 45-53.
Limited to Hadley.

8173 ORR, WILLIAM. "An educational experiment that worked." School and Society, 39 (1934), 675-679.
Hopkins Academy.

8174 POTTER, DOROTHY MAY, comp. Tercentenary chronology, Hadley, Massachusetts; 1659-1959. n.p., [1963]. Pp. 134.

8175 SHELDON, GEORGE. "The traditionary story of the attack upon Hadley and the appearance of Gen. Goffe, Sept. 1, 1675: has it any foundation in fact?" NEHGR, 28 (1874), 379-391.
King Philip's War.

8176 SMITH, HELEN EVERTSON. "An unpublished legend of the Regicides." NEM, New Ser., 31 (1904-1905), 55-59.
William Goffe and Edward Whalley.

8177 TRUMAN, NATHAN E. "Did General Goffe defend Hadley?" Americana, 15 (1921), 155-168.

8178 WALKER, ALICE MOREHOUSE. Historic Hadley: a story of the making of a famous Massachusetts town. N.Y.: Grafton Pr., 1906. Pp. xii, 130.

8179 WARREN, ISRAEL PERKINS. The three judges: story of the men who beheaded their king. N.Y.: Warren and Wyman, 1873. Pp. xii, 303. John Dixwell, William Goffe and Edward Whalley.

8180 WINCHESTER, ALICE. "The Prentis House at the Shelburne Museum." Antiques, 71 (1957), 440-442. Built 1733, moved to Shelburne, Vt. in 1955.

HALIFAX

8181 [DAVIS, SAMUEL]. "Notes on Halifax." MHSC, 2 Ser., 4 (1816), 279-283. Author attribution by Charles A. Flagg.

HAMILTON

8182 CUTLER, MANASSEH. A century discourse, delivered in Hamilton, in Thursday, October 27, 1814. Salem: Thomas C. Cushing, 1815. Pp. 26. Anniversary of the First Congregational Church.

8183 EARLY history of Hamilton, the Ordinance of 1787, life of Dr. Manasseh Cutler, the Ohio Company; recreation of the trek of the pioneers of the Ohio Company on December 3, 1787, Ipswich Hamlet, now Hamilton, Massachusetts. Salem: Newcomb & Gauss, 1937. Pp. 27. MB.

8184 FORBES, ALLAN. "Early Myopia at Hamilton." EIHC, 78 (1942), 201-225. Myopia Hunt Club.

8185 HAMILTON, MASSACHUSETTS. Celebration of the 150th anniversary of the incorporation of the town of Hamilton, Massachusetts, 1739-1943. n.p., Stanley Hall, [1943?]. Pp. 28. MSaE.

8186 _____. The celebration of the one hundredth anniversary of the incorporation of the town of Hamilton, Mass., June 21, 1893. Salem: Barry & Lufkin, 1895. Pp. 48.

8187 HAMILTON, MASS. 175TH ANNIVERSARY COMMITTEE. Town of Hamilton, Massachusetts, 175th anniversary, June 21, 1968. Salem: Newcomb & Gauss, [1968?]. Pp. 29. MSaE. History by Janice G. Pulsifer.

8188 PULSIFER, JANICE GOLDSMITH. "The Cutlers of Hamilton." EIHC, 107 (1971), 335-408. Cutler family.

8189 SPRAGUE, GEORGE H. A history of the First Congregational Church of Hamilton, the Third Church of Ipswich, the church of Manasseh Cutler, 1714-1764. [Salem?: Newcomb & Gauss?, 1964]. Pp. 24. MSaE.

8190 WOOD, GRACE A. Hamilton tercentenary, July 19 and 20, 1930. Salem: Newcomb & Gauss, 1930. Pp. 12. MBNEH.

HAMPDEN

8191 CHASE, EDWARD A. Historical address delivered...at the centennial celebration of the Congregational Church, Hampden, Mass., November 18, 1885. Hartford: Case, Lockwood & Brainard, 1898. Pp. 69.

8192 HOWLETT, CARL C. Early Hampden, its settlers and the homes they built. Hampden: Yola Guild of the Federated Community Church, 1958. Pp. 182. MBNEH.

8193 _____. Federated Community Church, Hampden, Massachusetts; historical sketch of the Protestant churches of Hampden. Hampden, 1954. Pp. 27. MS.

HANCOCK

8194 "MT. Zion on the Taconic Hills." Berkshire Hills, New Ser., 1 (1904-1905), 5-7. Shakers.

HANOVER

8195 BARRY, JOHN STETSON. A historical sketch of the town of Hanover, Mass., with family genealogies. Boston: S. G. Drake, 1853. Pp. v, 448.

8196 CUTLER, SAMUEL. The origin, progress, and present condition of St. Andrew's Church Hanover, Ms.; a sermon delivered in St. Andrew's Church, Hanover, on the twenty-second Sunday after Trinity, November 8, 1846. Boston: A. Forbes, 1848. Pp. 24.

8197 DWELLEY, JEDEDIAH and JOHN F. SIMMONS. History of the town of Hanover, Massachusetts, with family genealogies. [Hanover]: The Town, 1910. Pp. 291, 474.

8198 FORD, DAVID BARNES. History of Hanover Academy. Boston: H. M. Hight, 1899. Pp. 221.

8199 HANOVER, MASS. A copy of the records of births, marriages and deaths and of intentions of marriage of the town of Hanover, Mass., 1727-1857, as recorded by the several town clerks for the said town of Hanover.... Rockland: Rockland Standard, 1898. Pp. vi, 319.

8200   HANOVER, MASS. 200th anniversary incorpora-
        tion of town of Hanover, Massachusetts, 1727-
1927, Hanover, Mass., June 14, 1927. Boston:
McGrath-Sherrill, 1927. Pp. 32.

8201   HANOVER, MASS. FIRST CONGREGATIONAL CHURCH.
        History and records of the First Congrega-
tional Church, Hanover, Mass., 1727-1865, and inscriptions from the headstones and tombs in the
cemetery at Centre Hanover, Mass., 1727-1894, being
volume I of the church and cemetery records of Hanover, Mass. L. Vernon Briggs, ed. Boston: W.
Spooner, 1895. Pp. vi, 316.

8202   HANOVER, MASS. METHODIST EPISCOPAL CHURCH.
        Souvenir and directory.... n.p., [1898?].
Pp. 48. MBNEH.
        1845-1898.

HANSON

8203   HANSON, MASS. FIRST CONGREGATIONAL CHURCH.
        Two hundredth anniversary, 1748-1948....
n.p., 1948. Unpaged. MBNEH.

8204   HANSON, MASS. PICTORIAL HISTORY COMMITTEE.
        A pictorial history of the town of Hanson,
incorporated 1820. Hanson: Hanson Historical Society, 1962. Unpaged. MBNEH.

HARDWICK

8205   PAIGE, LUCIUS ROBINSON. An address at the
        centennial celebration in Hardwick, Mass.,
November 15, 1838. Cambridge: Metcalf, Torry,
and Ballou, 1838. Pp. iv, 76.

8206   _____. History of Hardwick, Massachusetts,
        with a genealogical register. Boston:
Houghton Mifflin, 1883. Pp. xii, 555.

8207   SMITH, HENRY W. History of the struggle and
        progress of religious liberty in Greenwich,
Massachusetts. n.p., 1886. Pp. 71. MWA.

HARVARD

8208   ATHERTON, PERCY ARAD. Remarks on the his-
        tory of the town of Harvard at a meeting of
the Bay State Historical League, July 22, 1931.
n.p.: Printed Privately, 1939. Unpaged.

8209   CHANDLER, SETH. An historical discourse de-
        livered before the First Congregational So-
ciety in Harvard, Massachusetts, October 22, 1882.
Boston: G. E. Littlefield, 1884. Pp. 28.
        Appendix by Samuel A. Green is a sketch of
the early history of the town.

8210   CLARK, ANNIE MARIA LAWRENCE. The Alcotts in
        Harvard. Lancaster: J. C. L. Clark, 1902.
Pp. 43.

8211   GREEN, SAMUEL ABBOTT. Old manuscripts relat-
        ing to Harvard, Massachusetts, communicated
to the Massachusetts Historical Society.... Boston,
1913. Pp. 24.

8212   HARVARD, MASS. Celebration of the one hun-
        dred seventy-fifth anniversary of the incor-
poration of the town of Harvard, July 4, 1907.
Ayer: Wm. M. Sargent, 1908. Pp. 31. MBNEH.

8213   HARVARD, MASS. PUBLIC LIBRARY. Proceedings
        at the dedication of Harvard Public Library
at the town hall, June 22, 1887, together with an
historical sketch of the town and its public institutions by Selah Howell, A. M., and other documents
relating to the library and its benefactors. Boston: G. H. Ellis, 1888. Pp. 46.

8214   NOURSE, HENRY STEDMAN. History of the town
        of Harvard, Massachusetts, 1732-1893. Har-
vard: W. Hapgood, 1894. Pp. ix, 605.

8215   O'BRIEN, HARRIET ELLEN. Lost Utopias; a
        brief description of three quests for happi-
ness: Alcott's Fruitlands, old Shaker House, and
American Indian Museum, rescued from oblivion, recorded and preserved by Clara Endicott Sears on
Prospect Hill in the old township of Harvard, Massachusetts. (1929) 3d. ed. Brookline, 1947.
Pp. 70.

8216   SAMSON, GEORGE WHITEFIELD. Baptist succes-
        sion, or Baptist principles in church his-
tory...a centennial discourse delivered, June 27th,
1876, before the Baptist Church in Harvard, Mass.
N.Y.: James Huggins, 1878. Pp. 93. MB.
        Contains incidents in the history of the
church.

8217   SAVAGE, FREDERICK SCHILLOW. Memoirs of old
        Harvard days, from 1863 to 1924, also the
men and women and their descendants who made old
Harvard what it is today. Still River, 1924.
Pp. 77.

8218   SEARS, CLARA ENDICOTT, comp. Bronson Al-
        cott's Fruitlands...with Transcendental wild
oats, by Louisa M. Alcott. Boston: Houghton Mifflin, 1915. Pp. xvii, 185.

8219   _____. Gleanings from old Shaker journals.
        Boston: Houghton Mifflin, 1916. Pp. xiii,
298.

8220   WEST, ARTHUR T. "Reminiscences of life in a
        Shaker village." NEQ, 11 (1938), 343-360.

HARWICH

8221   CROSBY, KATHARINE. "The second century of
        living in the venerable homes of Harwich
Port." Cape Cod Magazine, 8 (July 15, 1926), 7-8.

8222   DOANE, VIRGINIA S. The birth of a building:
        the Harwich Exchange, 1885-1964. West Har-
wich: Jack Viall, 1965. Pp. 24. [MBaC].

8223 "EARLY history of Harwich." CCAPL, 5 (January, 1922), 15, 18-19.

8224 ELDRIDGE, L. EUGENE. "Burgess Homestead, Bank St., Harwich." Cape Cod Magazine, 7 (November, 1923), 9-11.

8225 GOSS, ALTON P. "History of Harwich in miniature." Cape Cod Magazine, 2 (May, 1916), 5-9.

8226 HARWICH, MASS. 275 COMMITTEE. 275th anniversary, Harwich, Massachusetts, a sketch of the years 1694-1969 in text and pictures. Harwich: Jack Viall, 1969. Pp. 56. M.

8227 HARWICH HISTORICAL COMMISSION. Indian history of Harwich, Massachusetts. [Harwich]: Harwich Historical Society, 1972. Pp. 30. [MBaC].

8228 MACMAHON, WILLIAM. "The art of shoemaking in Harwich." Cape Cod Magazine, 9 (March, 1927), 9, 16-17.

8229 PAINE, JOSIAH. A history of Harwich, Barnstable County, Massachusetts, 1620-1800; including the early history of that part now Brewster; with some account of its Indian inhabitants. Rutland, Vt.: Tuttle, 1937. Pp. iv, 503.

HATFIELD

8230 BARTON, CHESTER M. and DANIEL W. WELLS, comps. 212th anniversary of the Indian attack on Hatfield, and field-day of the Pocumtuck Valley Memorial Association, at Hatfield, Massachusetts, Thursday, Sept. 19th, 1889. Northampton: Gazette Printing, 1890. Pp. 95.

8231 ENGLEHARDT, CYNTHIA, ed. This is our Hatfield. [Hatfield?], 1973. Pp. vii, 136. MNF.

8232 HATFIELD, MASS. FIRST CONGREGATIONAL CHURCH. 300th anniversary celebration, October 11th-18th, 1970, First Congregational Church, Hatfield, Massachusetts.... n.p., [1970?]. Unpaged. MAJ.

8233 HATFIELD, MASS. ST. JOSEPH'S PARISH. 75th anniversary, 1899-1974. n.p., [1974?]. Unpaged. MNF.

8234 HATFIELD, MASS. TERCENTENARY COMMITTEE. Historical Capawonk, June 21-28, 1970. [Amherst?]: Warner Bros., 1970. Unpaged. M.

8235 HATFIELD TERCENTENARY ORGANIZATION. HISTORY COMMITTEE. Hatfield, 1670-1970. Northampton: Gazette Printing, 1970. Pp. xi, 92.

8236 MILLER, MARGARET. "The little old schoolhouse in the middle of the road." PVMA, 7 (1921-1929), 115-126.

8237 _____. "A Whig parson and a Tory colonel at Hatfield." PVMA, 5 (1905-1911), 418-431. Joseph Lyman and Israel Williams.

8238 PAPERS concerning the attack on Hatfield and Deerfield by a party of Indians from Canada, September nineteenth, 1677. N.Y.: Bradford Club, 1859. Pp. viii, 82. Preface signed F. B. H., [Franklin Benjamin Hough].

8239 STEBBINS, GILES BADGER. "The home of Sophia and Oliver Smith." NEM, New Ser., 19 (1898-1899), 166-175.

8240 WELLS, DANIEL WHITE and REUBEN F. WELLS. A history of Hatfield, Massachusetts, in three parts: I. An account of the development of the social and industrial life of the town from its first settlement. II. The houses and homes of Hatfield, with personal reminiscences of the men and women who have lived there during the last one hundred years; brief historical accounts of the religious societies and of Smith Academy; statistical tables, etc. III. Genealogies of the families of the first settlers. Springfield: F. C. H. Gibbons, 1910. Pp. 536.

8241 WIGHT, CHARLES ALBERT. The Hatfield book. Springfield: F. A Bassette, 1908. Pp. 59.

8242 WRIGHT, HARRY ANDREW. "The technique of seventeenth-century Indian land purchasers." EIHC, 77 (1941), 185-197.

HAVERHILL

8243 ANTHONY, FRANCIS W. "History of the practice of medicine in Haverhill and vicinity since 1836--based on the recollections of fifty years and the records of one hundred years." NEJMed, 204 (1931), 661-665.

8244 BARNES, HENRY ELBERT. The glory of worship: a sermon preached at the re-dedication of the Centre Congregational Church, Haverhill, Mass., November 19, 1878 to which is appended a brief historical sketch. Haverhill: Daily Bulletin Steam Book and Job Print Office, 1878. Pp. 20.

8245 _____. Semi-centennial of Center Congregational Church and Society, Haverhill, Mass., with a historical discourse...to which is added a historical appendix, September 30, and October 1, 1883. Haverhill: C. C. Morse & Son, 1884. Pp. 36.

8246 [BARROWS, ELIZABETH A. CATE]. A memorial of Bradford Academy. Boston: Congregational S. S. and Publishing Society, 1870. Pp. 189. Now Bradford Junior College.

8247 BARTLETT, ALBERT LE ROY. Haverhill, an historical address...given at the exercises commemorative of the two hundred and seventy-fifth anniversary of the settlement of the city, on Sunday, October the tenth, nineteen hundred and fifteen. Haverhill: Record Printing, 1915. Pp. 63.

8248 _____. "Some annals of old Haverhill." NEM, New Ser., 2 (1890), 505-522.

8249 _____. Some memories of old Haverhill in Massachusetts. Haverhill, 1915. Pp. 105.

8250 BEDFORD, HENRY F. "The 'Haverhill Social Democrat,' spokesman for socialism." Lab Hist, 2 (1961), 82-89.
Newspaper.

8251 _____. "The socialist movement in Haverhill." EIHC, 99 (1963), 33-47.
1890-1900.

8252 BOSSART, BONNIE. "Haverhill founded on shoe industry." Industry, 35 (November, 1970), 18, 54.

8253 BRADFORD, MASS. FIRST CHURCH. Articles of faith and covenant adopted by the First Church of Christ in Bradford, Mass., with is standing rules and practical principles, a catalogue of its officers and members, from its first organization, in 1682, up to 1665, and an appendix, containing facts in its history. Haverhill: C. C. Morse & Son, 1886. Pp. 79.

8254 "THE BRADFORD Academy." EIB, 12 (1880), 130-132.

8255 CAMPBELL, DONALD. Haverhill and the American heritage. Merrimac: Martin Lithograph, n.d. Unpaged. MSaE.

8256 CARY, GEORGE E. "The First Church of Christ, Bradford, Massachusetts." EIHC, 86 (1950), 1-14.

8257 CHASE, GEORGE WINGATE. The history of Haverhill, Massachusetts, from its first settlement, in 1640, to the year 1860.... Haverhill, 1861. v.p.

8258 COGSWELL, WILLARD GOODRICH. "Highways and low ways in Haverhill from Grant to McKinley." MHSP, 71 (1953-1957), 272-286.

8259 COLE, JOHN F. "The brick trade in early Haverhill." OTNE, 58 (1967-1968), 49-50, 59.

8260 CORLISS, JOHN B. The first era in the history of Haverhill, Mass., comprising the period from the settlement of the plantation of Pentucket (1640) to the conclusion of permanent peace with the Indians (1715). Haverhill: C. C. Morse & Son, 1885. Pp. 40.

8261 CORNING, CHARLES ROBERT. An exploit in King William's War, 1697: Hannah Dustan.... Concord, N.H.: Printed by the Republican Press Association, 1890. Pp. 39.

8262 CRONAN, FRANCIS W. Red Sunday: the Saltonstalls, the Dustons, and the fighting Ayers, Merrimack Valley history. Haverhill, 1965. Pp. 260.

8263 CROWELL, JOHN. The colonial and revolutionary history of Haverhill, a centennial oration, delivered before the city government and the citizens of Haverhill, July 4, 1876.... Haverhill: Gazette Print, 1877. Pp. 38.

8264 DAVIS, HARRY R. "The First Baptist Church of Haverhill looking back one hundred and seventy-five years." EIHC, 82 (1946), 193-210.

8265 DODGE, JOSHUA. A sermon, delivered in Haverhill, December 22, 1820, being the second centesimal anniversary of the landing of New-England fathers, at Plymouth. Haverhill: Burrill & Hersey, 1821. Pp. 28.

8266 DOUGLASS, ALICE MAY. "Whittier's birthplace." MassMag, 1 (1908), 11-12.

8267 EVERTS, WILLIAM WALLACE, JR. Historical discourse delivered on the 125th anniversary of the First Baptist Church of Haverhill, Mass., May 9, 1890; and the historical sketch of the Sunday school, by J. H. Davis. Haverhill: Chase Bros., 1890. Pp. 79.

8268 GAGE, HOWARD H. "Haverhill, queen city of the Merrimack." National Magazine, 17 (1902-1903), 546-550.

8269 GAGEY, EDMOND M. "General Booth with his big bass drum enters into Haverhill, Massachusetts." NEQ, 45 (1972), 508-525.
Salvation Army.

8270 GILMORE, FRANK ALBERT. Historical sketch of First Parish, Haverhill, Mass...Oct. 31, 1895. Haverhill: C. C. Morse & Son, 1895. Pp. 28.

8271 GRAVES, HENRY CLINTON. Historical sketch of the Baptist Religious Society of Haverhill, Massachusetts, and of the church edifices built under its direction, with an account of the dedication services, November 22d, 1883. Haverhill: James A. Hale, 1886. Pp. 68.

8272 GRIFFITH, GEORGE BANCROFT. "Birthplace and home of Whittier." Potter's AmMo, 14 (1880), 258-261.

8273 HALL, ARTHUR HOWARD. Old Bradford schooldays. Norwood: Plimpton Pr., 1910. Pp. 181.

8274 HAVERHILL, MASS. 'Haverhill on the March,' official pictorial magazine and program of events, 325th anniversary celebration, June 19-27, 1965. Groveland: Boyd, James Pr., 1965. Pp. 116. M.

8275 _____. The story of a New England town; a record of the commemoration, July second and third, 1890, on the two hundred and fiftieth anniversary of the settlement of Haverhill, Massachusetts.... Jones Frankle, ed. Boston: J. G. Cupples, 1891. 2v.
Historical address by S. W. Duncan.

8276 _____. 250th anniversary of ye anciente towne of Haverhill...July 2 and 3, 1890. Worcester: F. S. Blanchard, 1890. Pp. 20. MSaE.

8277 HAVERHILL, MASS. BOARD OF TRADE. History of the city of Haverhill, Massachusetts, showing its industrial and commercial interests and opportunities; the commercial centre of a population of over 125,000, and the first shoe city in the world. [Haverhill], 1905. Pp. 118.

8278 ____. Haverhill, Massachusetts: an industrial and commercial center. Haverhill: Chase Bros., 1889. Pp. 260.

8279 HAVERHILL, MASS. CENTER CONGREGATIONAL CHURCH. Seventy-fifth anniversary exercises held October 11-12, 1908, containing a summary, the historical sermon, and other papers read on that occasion. Haverhill: Chase Pr., 1908. Pp. 36.
     Sermon by Calvin M. Clark.

8280 HAVERHILL, MASS. CHAMBER OF COMMERCE. The Haverhill book. Haverhill: Record Pr., 1919. Pp. 127.

8281 HAVERHILL, MASS. FIRST BAPTIST CHURCH. Centennial discourse delivered on the one hundredth anniversary of the organization of the Baptist Church, Haverhill, Mass., on the ninth of May, 1865, by Arthur Savage Train, with an account of the centennial celebration, and historical notes. Boston: Gould & Lincoln, 1865. Pp. iv, 96.

8282 ____. Historical sketch of the Baptist Religious Society of Haverhill, Massachusetts and the church edifices built under its direction, with an account of the dedication services, November 22d, 1883. Haverhill: J. A. Hale, 1886. Pp. 68. M.

8283 HAVERHILL, MASS. FIRST REFORMED BAPTIST CHURCH. A brief narrative of the origin of the 'First Reformed Baptist Church' in Haverhill, Mass. Haverhill: Iris Office, 1833. Pp. 30. MSaE.

8284 HAVERHILL, MASS. HIGH SCHOOL. ALUMNI ASSOCIATION. The Haverhill Academy and the Haverhill High School, 1827-1890, an historical sketch by Albert L. Bartlett.... Haverhill: Chase Bros., 1890. Pp. 227.

8285 HAVERHILL, MASS. NORTH CONGREGATIONAL CHURCH. Manual...containing its articles of faith...and history. Haverhill: Chase Bros., 1882. Pp. 64. M.
     Historical address by Raymond H. Seeley.

8286 HAVERHILL, MASS. PORTLAND STREET BAPTIST CHURCH. A brief history.... Haverhill: Nichols, 1890. Pp. 69.

8287 ____. Fiftieth anniversary, Portland Street Church, Haverhill, Mass. 1859-1909. [Haverhill]: A. E. Lord, [1909?]. Unpaged. MSaE.

8288 HAVERHILL, MASS. SOUTH CHRISTIAN CHURCH. One hundred years for Christ, the South Christian Church, Haverhill, Mass., one hundredth anniversary, April 6, 7, 8, 1906. n.p., [1906?]. Unpaged. MSaE.

8289 HAVERHILL, MASS. TERCENTENARY COMMITTEE. Official pictorial magazine of the Haverhill tercentenary celebration, 1640-1940. [Haverhill]: The Record Pr., [1940]. Pp. 80.
     Includes substantial text.

8290 HAVERHILL, MASS. WEST CONGREGATIONAL CHURCH. Exercises commemorative of the one hundred and fiftieth anniversary of the West Congregational Church, Haverhill, Mass., including historical addresses, poem, reminiscences, and letters from former pastors, October 22, 1885. Haverhill: C. C. Morse and Son, 1886. Pp. 59.
     Historical discourse by John N. Lowell.

8291 THE HAVERHILL aqueduct, its history, ownership, management, value and relationship to the city. Haverhill, 1884. Pp. 35.

8292 HAVERHILL, foundation facts concerning its settlement, growth, industries, and societies, etc., etc. Haverhill: Bridgman & Gay, 1879.

8293 HAVERHILL MONDAY EVENING CLUB. Proceedings at the twenty-fifth anniversary of the Haverhill Monday Evening Club, Monday evening, Nov. 19, 1885. Boston: Cupples, Upham, 1886. Pp. 53.

8294 HAVERHILL POST OFFICE EMPLOYEES' MUTUAL BENEFIT ASSOCIATION. Haverhill postal guide, including a history of the Haverhill Post Office from 1775 to 1910 with additional postal information. Haverhill: Chase Pr., 1910. Pp. 80. MSaE.

8295 HAVERHILL SAVINGS BANK. The first one hundred years of the Institution for Savings in Haverhill and its Vicinity, subsequently known as the Haverhill Savings Bank. Haverhill, [1928?]. Pp. 33. M.
     1828-1928.

8296 HAYNES, GEORGE HENRY. An historical, biographical, and commercial illustrated review of the city of Haverhill, its progress in manufacturing, the professions and in social and municipal life. Haverhill: Chase Pr., 1900. Pp. 50. MSaE.

8297 HILL, MABEL. "Bradford Academy: a jubilee sketch." NEM, New Ser., 28 (1903), 345-368.

8298 "AN HISTORICAL sketch of Haverhill, in the county of Essex, and Commonwealth of Massachusetts; with biographical notices." MHSC, 2 Ser., 4 (1816), 121-176.

8299 HORSCH, RAY LYNNWOOD. Under the X-ray. Haverhill: Record Publishing, 1939. Pp. 103.
     Biographies.

8300 KIMBALL, EMMA ADELINE. The Peaslees and others of Haverhill and vicinity. Haverhill: Chase Bros., 1899. Pp. 72.

8301 KINGSBURY, JOHN DENNISON. Memorial history of Bradford, Mass...including addresses delivered at the two hundredth anniversary of the First Church of Bradford, December 27, 1882. Haverhill: C. C. Morse and Son, 1883. Pp. xii, 192.

8302 MABIE, HAMILTON WRIGHT. "A New England
        school anniversary, [the centennial at Brad-
ford Academy]." Outlook, 74 (1903), 500-502.

8303 MERRILL, JOSEPH. "History of Bradford Acad-
        emy." American Quarterly Register, 13
(1840-1841), 70-74.

8304 MIRICK, BENJAMIN L. The history of Haver-
        hill, Massachusetts. Haverhill: A. W.
Thayer, 1832. Pp. 227.
        The Library of Congress indicates that the
        work was "probably written in large part by
        J. G. Whittier, who turned his manuscript
        over to Mirick."

8305 MOODY, ROBERT EARLE, ed. "Records of the
        Magistrates' Court at Haverhill, Massachu-
setts, kept by Nathaniel Saltonstall, 1682-1685."
MHSP, 79 (1967), 151-186.

8306 NELSON, HARRIET O. and BETSEY GREENLEAF KEN-
        DALL. Reminiscences of Bradford Academy,
two papers read at the annual meeting of the alumnae, October 10, 1891. Haverhill: Mitchell &
Hoyt, 1892. Pp. 27. MSaE.

8307 ODD FELLOWS, INDEPENDENT ORDER OF. HAVER-
        HILL, MASS. MUTUAL RELIEF LODGE, NO. 83.
Constitution, by-laws and rules of Mutual Relief
Lodge, Number 83, of the Independent Order of Odd
Fellows, to which is added a history of the
lodge...instituted September 4, 1845 at Haverhill,
Mass. Boston: Solon Thornton, 1871. Pp. 163.
MSaE.

8308 PERLEY, SIDNEY. "Part of Haverhill in
        1700." Essex Antiq, 3 (1899), 161-168.

8309 PERRY, GARDNER BRAMAN. A discourse, deliver-
        ed in the East Parish in Bradford, December
22, 1820; two hundred years after the first settlement in New-England, containing a history of the
town. Haverhill: Burrill and Hersey, 1821.
        Reprinted in 1872 with title: History of
        Bradford, Mass. from the earliest period
        to the close of 1820.

8310 PHILLIPS, JAMES DUNCAN. "Folks in Haverhill
        in 1783." EIHC, 82 (1946), 137-154.

8311 POND, JEAN SARAH. Bradford, a New England
        school (Bradford, a New England academy)
(1930) Sesquicentennial ed., rev. and supplemented
by Dale Mitchell. Bradford, 1954 [i.e. 1955].
Pp. 380.
        Now Bradford Junior College.

8312 ROGERS, Ida Clifford. "Haverhill--yesterday
        and to-day." NEM, New Ser., 32 (1905), 225-
257.

8313 SMITH, SADIE ADAMS. "Heroes of the Dustin
        family." JAmHist, 15 (1921), 213-216.
        Massacre of 1697.

8314 SNOW, JOSEPH CROCKER. History of the First
        Universalist Church, Kenoza Avenue, Haver-
hill, Mass. Haverhill, 1900. Unpaged. MBNEH.

8315 SOCIETY FOR THE PROMOTION OF TEMPERANCE IN
        HAVERHILL. An account of the origin and
doings of the Society for the Promotion of Temperance in Haverhill and Vicinity. Haverhill: A. W.
Thayer, 1830. Pp. 27. MB.

8316 SPENCER, WILLIAM HENRY. A sketch of the his-
        sory of the First Parish Church of Haverhill,
Mass.... Haverhill: C. C. Morse & Son, 1872.
Pp. 16. M.

8317 "THROAT distemper in Haverhill, 1735-7."
        Essex Antiq, 1 (1897), 10-13.

8318 [WATKINS, WALTER KENDALL]. 250th anniversary
        of ye anciente towne of Haverhill, 1640-1890.
Worcester: F. S. Blanchard, 1890. Pp. 20.

8319 WORTH, EDMUND. Semi-centennial...Baptist
        Church, East Haverhill.... Haverhill: Wood-
ward & Palmer, 1872. Pp. 40. MBNEH.

HAWLEY

8320 ATKINS, WILLIAM GILES. History of the town
        of Hawley, Franklin County, Massachusetts,
from its first settlement in 1771 to 1887, with family records and biographical sketches. West Cummington, 1887. Pp. 130.

8321 JOHNSON, LOUISE HALE. History of the town
        of Hawley, Franklin County, Massachusetts,
1771-1951, with genealogies. Mystic, Conn.: Charter Oak House, 1953. Pp. 380.

8322 ROBINSON, OLIVE CRITTENDEN. "A forgotten
        clockmaker: Simeon Crittenden, Junior."
Antiques, 46 (1944), 82-83.

HEATH

8323 GUILD, EDWARD P. "Heath: a historic hill
        town." MassMag, 1 (1908), 219-225.

8324 HEATH, MASS. Centennial anniversary of the
        town of Heath, Mass., August 19, 1885, ad-
dresses, speeches, letters, statistics, etc., etc.
Edward P. Guild, ed. Boston, 1885. Pp. vii, 148.

8325 _____. Sesquicentennial anniversary of the
        town of Heath, Mass., August 25-29, 1935,
addresses, speeches, letters, statistics. Howard
Chandler Robbins, ed. [Heath]: Heath Historical
Society, [1935]. Pp. 170.

8326 HEATH, MASS. FIRST CHURCH OF CHRIST. Arti-
        cles of faith and covenant of the First
Church of Christ in Heath, Mass. Boston: T. R.
Marvin & Son, 1873. Pp. 8. M.
        Includes 'Historical note.'

8327 MILLER, MOSES. A historical discourse, de-
        livered by...[the] former pastor of the
First Congregational Church in Heath, at the request
of said church, October 13, 1852, with some of the
accompanying exercises. Shelburne Falls: Geo. W.
Mirick, 1853. Pp. 80.
        Relates to the town.

8328 PERRY, ARTHUR LATHAM. "Fort Shirley."
      BSM, 3 (1885), 341-347.

HINGHAM

8329 "ALMSHOUSES in Hingham." The Hinghamite,
      No. 12 (December, 1941), [5].

8330 "BEGINNINGS of the Hingham Historical Soci-
      ety." The Hinghamite, No. 6 (June, 1941),
[1-2].

8331 BURR, FEARING and GEORGE LINCOLN. The town
      of Hingham in the late Civil War, with
sketches of its soldiers and sailors, also the address and other exercises at the dedication of the
soldiers' and sailors' monument. Boston: Rand,
Avery, 1876. Pp. 455.

8332 "CLAM, Oyster.and Plum Pudding Corporation."
      The Hinghamite, No. 8 (August, 1941), [1-2];
No. 9 (September, 1941), [1-3].
      A club, 1855-1883.

8333 COATSWORTH, ELIZABETH JANE. South Shore
      town. N.Y.: Macmillan, 1948. Pp. xii, 201.

8334 COLLIER, PRICE. "The old meeting-house in
      Hingham, Mass." NEM, New Ser., 8 (1893),
477-489.

8335 COOLIDGE, JOHN. "Hingham builds a meeting-
      house." NEQ, 34 (1961), 435-461.
      Old Ship Church.

8336 CORNISH, LOUIS CRAIG. The settlement of
      Hingham, Massachusetts. Boston: Rockwell &
Churchill, 1911. Pp. 23.

8337 CORSE, MURRAY P. "The Old Ship Meetinghouse
      in Hingham, Mass." OTNE, 21 (1930-1931),
19-30.

8338 CUSHING, DANIEL. Extracts from the minutes
      of Daniel Cushing, of Hingham, with a photo-
graph of his manuscript, entitled, a list of the
names of such persons as came out of the town of
Hingham, and towns adjacent, in the county of Norfolk, England, into New England, and settled in
Hingham, N.E., also, some account of John Cutler.
H. A. Whitney, ed. Boston: John Wilson & Son,
1865. Pp. 28.

8339 DAUGHTERS OF THE AMERICAN REVOLUTION. MAS-
      SACHUSETTS. OLD COLONY CHAPTER, HINGHAM.
Hingham: a story of its early settlement and life,
its ancient landmarks, its historic sites and buildings.... [Hingham], 1911. Pp. 123.

8340 GARVER, AUSTIN S. "The old meeting-house at
      Hingham." Potter's AmMo, 4 (1875), 20-21.
      Old Ship Church.

8341 GAY, EBENEZER. Old man's calendar, a dis-
      course on Joshua XIV:10 delivered in the
First Parish of Hingham...August 26, 1781. Hingham:
Re-printed by Jedidiah Farmer, 1846. Pp. 32. M.
      Appendix to this edition concerns the early
      ministers of the parish.

8342 GREGMORE, HOMER. "Historic Hingham." NEM,
      New Ser., 33 (1905-1906), 335-350.

8343 HERSEY, ALAN F. Historic Hingham. [Hingham,
      1948]. Pp. 34.

8344 HINGHAM, MASS. The celebration of the two
      hundred and fiftieth anniversary of the set-
tlement of the town of Hingham, Massachusetts, September 15, 1885. Hingham: Committee of Arrangements, 1885. Pp. vi, 134.

8345 _____. History of the town of Hingham, Mas-
      sachusetts.... Hingham, 1893. ev.

8346 HINGHAM, MASS. FIRST PARISH. The commemora-
      tive services of the First Parish in Hingham
on the two hundredth anniversary of the building of
its meeting-house, Monday, August 8, 1881. Hingham,
1882. Pp. vi, 169.

8347 _____. Old meeting house, Hingham, Massachu-
      setts. [Hingham?, 1930?]. Pp. 7.

8348 _____. The two hundred and twenty-fifth an-
      niversary of the opening of the old meeting
house in Hingham, Massachusetts, for public worship,
January 20, 1907, 1682-1907. Boston: Geo. H. Ellis, 1907. Pp. 44.

8349 HINGHAM, MASS. TERCENTENARY COMMITTEE.
      Hingham old and new. Hingham, 1935. Pp. 96,

8350 HINGHAM and Quincy bridges: their freedom
      and the manner in which it was obtained. By
One Who Knows, pseud. Boston: Wright & Potter,
1864. Pp. 20. MB.

8351 HINGHAM MAGAZINE. Boston: Geo. H. Ellis,
      1898. Pp. 52, xxvi.
      No more published.

8352 HINGHAM MUTUAL FIRE INSURANCE COMPANY. The
      first hundred years of the Hingham Mutual
Fire Insurance Company, incorporated 1826, Hingham,
Massachusetts. Providence: Livermore and
Knight, 1926. Pp. 32.

8353 HORTON, EDWARD AUGUSTUS. Discourse delivered
      to the First Parish in Hingham on the two
hundredth anniversary of the opening of its meeting-
house for public worship, Sunday, January 8, 1882.
Hingham: The Parish, 1882. Pp. 57.

8354 HORTON, HOWARD LEAVITT. Aspects of a New
      England town (Hingham, Mass.) from the horse
and buggy days to the event of World War I, with a
treatise on 'Life in the army, World War II.'
Philadelphia: Hans L. Raum, 1945. Pp. 35.

8355 _____. Hingham: maritime history, ship-
      building, mackerel fisheries: packets,
1790 to 1900. Buzzard's Bay, 1969. Unpaged.

8356 _____. Hingham: Melville Garden, Downer
      Landing; Boston & Hingham Steamboat Co.;
Nantasket Beach Railroad Co.; South Shore Railroad.
[Hingham], 1948. Pp. 6.

8357   _____. The South Shore sketch book:
          Glimpses of Hingham, and a short story, The
old hulk sails again.... [Boston], 1948. Pp. 16.

8358   INTIMATE recollections of the Village Press
          by three friends: In the beginning by Will
Ransom, Hingham interlude by Charles E. Park, Metropolitan memo by Mitchell Kennerley.... Marlborough, N.Y., 1938. Unpaged.

8359   LINCOLN, CALVIN. A discourse delivered to
          the First Parish in Hingham, September 8,
1969, on re-opening their meeting-house.... Hingham: The Parish, 1873. Pp. 79.

8360   LINCOLN, FRANCIS HENRY. "Hingham." BSM, 3
          (1885), 258-265.

8361   _____. The old meeting-house, Hingham, Mass.
          Hingham, 1902. Pp. 16.

8362   LINCOLN, SOLOMON. An address delivered be-
          fore the citizens of the town of Hingham,
on the 28th of September, 1835, being the two hundredth anniversary of the settlement of the town.
Hingham: J. Farmer, 1835. Pp. 63.

8363   _____. "The beginnings of Hingham." The
          Hinghamite, No. 11 (November, 1941), [1-2],
No. 12 (December, 1941), [1-2]; 2 (January, 1942),
[2-3], (February, 1942), [2-3], (March, 1942),
[2-4], (April, 1942), [2-4], (May, 1942), [2-4],
(June, 1942), [3-5], (July, 1942), 4, (August,
1942), [3-4], (September, 1942), [4], (October,
1942), [4], (November, 1942), [3-4].

8364   _____. History of the town of Hingham,
          Plymouth County, Massachusetts. Hingham:
C. Gill, Jr., and Farmer and Brown, 1827. Pp. iv,
183.

8365   NORTON, CHARLES ELIOT. Address at the cele-
          bration of the 200th anniversary of the
building of the old meeting house at Hingham, on
the eighth of August, 1881. Cambridge: Wilson,
1881. Pp. 36. MB.

8366   "OLD Thaxter Mansion." The Hinghamite,
          No. 10 (October, 1941), [1].
Demolished in 1864.

8367   OUR old burial grounds.... Hingham, 1842.
          Pp. 24.

8368   "OUT of the past." The Hinghamite, No. 4
          (April 1941), [1].
Foulsham-Cushing-Sprague House, demolished
in 1875.

8369   PITCHER, ALBERT R. Origin and growth of the
          fire department in Hingham, Massachusetts,
1635-1942. Weymouth: Smith Print, 1946. Pp. 69.
MB.

8370   "A RAINBOW whist in a rainbow roof cottage."
          The Hinghamite, No. 7 (July, 1941), [1].
Wilder House.

8371   SEARS, ORIN BREWSTER. The old salt works.
          Auburndale: Norumbega Pr., 1916. Pp. 11.
MBNEH.

8372   SMITH, DANIEL SCOTT. "Family limitation,
          sexual control and domestic feminism in Vic-
torian America." Feminist Studies, 1 (Winter-
Spring, 1973), 40-57.
          Includes statistics for Hingham.

8373   _____. "Parental power and marriage pat-
          terns: an analysis of historical trends in
Hingham, Massachusetts." Journal of Marriage and
the Family, 35 (1973), 419-428.

8374   _____. "Underregistration and bias in pro-
          bate records: an analysis of data from
eighteenth-century Hingham, Massachusetts." WMQ, 3
Ser., 32 (1975), 100-110.

8375   STARK, GLADYS TEELE DETWYLER. The Old Ship
          Meeting House of Hingham, Massachusetts.
Boston: Beacon Pr., 1951. Pp. 32.

8376   STUDLEY, MARIAN H. "An 'August first' in
          1844." NEQ, 16 (1943), 567-577.
          Anti-slavery picnic.

8377   WATERS, JOHN J. "Hingham, Massachusetts,
          1631-1661: an East Anglian oligarchy in the
New World." JSocHist, 1 (1967-1968), 351-370.

HINSDALE

8378   HINSDALE, MASS. CONGREGATIONAL CHURCH. Com-
          memoration of the centennial of the Congrega-
tional Church, Hinsdale, Mass., organized December
17th, 1795, August 28th, 1895. Pittsfield: Sun
Printing, 1896. Pp. 173.

HOLBROOK

8379   FRENCH, LINDA M. The Winthrop Congregational
          Church 1856-1956. Holbrook: Anniversary
Committee, [1956?]. Pp. 48.

8380   HOLBROOK, MASS. CENTENNIAL COMMITTEE. Hol-
          brook, 1872-1972, 100th anniversary. Canton:
Blue Hills Regional Technical High School, 1972.
Unpaged. M.

8380A   "SEVENTY years of leadership in lighting."
          Industry, 16 (October, 1950), 19-20, 65-67.
          Wheeler Reflector Co.

HOLDEN

8381   DAMON, SAMUEL CHENERY. The history of Hol-
          den, Massachusetts, 1667-1841. Worcester:
Wallace and Ripley, 1841. Pp. viii, 154.

8382   ESTES, DAVID FOSTER. The history of Holden,
          Massachusetts, 1684-1894. Worcester: C. F.
Lawrence, 1894. Pp. x, 446.

8383   HOLDEN, MASS. 225TH ANNIVERSARY COMMITTEE, INC. 225th anniversary, Holden, Massachusetts, 1741-1966. n.p., 1966. Unpaged. M.

8384   PROUTY, FLORENCE NEWELL. History of the town of Holden, Massachusetts, 1667-1941. Worcester: Stobbs Pr., 1941. Pp. 370.

HOLLAND

8385   LOVERING, MARTIN. History of the town of Holland, Massachusetts. Rutland, Vt.: Tuttle, 1915. Pp. 749.

HOLLISTON

8386   ADAMS, GEORGE MOULTON. A historical discourse delivered at the celebration of the one hundred and fiftieth anniversary of the formation of the Congregational Church, Holliston, Massachusetts, June 11, 1879. So. Framingham: J. C. Clark, 1879. Pp. 65.

8387   BENNETT, ALBERT ARNOLD. The first ten years of the Holliston First Baptist Church: an address delivered before the church, on the seventeenth anniversary of its organization, August 28th, 1877, to which is appended the church, covenant and a list of members. Framingham: J. C. Clark, 1878. Pp. 52.

8388   BRAGG, ERNEST ATHERTON. A history of the towns of Holliston, Medway, and Milford, including the counties of Worcester, Middlesex, and Norfolk, which join in this area, from 1667 to 1950. n.p., 1958. Pp. 27.

8389   _____. The origin and growth of the boot and shoe industry in Holliston, where it began in 1793, and in Milford, Massachusetts, where it continued in 1795 and remained into 1950. [Boston?], 1951. Pp. 100.

8390   DOWSE, EDMUND. Centennial address delivered in Holliston, July 4, 1876. So. Framingham: J. C. Clark, 1877. Pp. 32.
       Town history.

8391   FITCH, CHARLES. View of Holliston in its first century, a century sermon, delivered in Holliston, Mass., Dec. 4, 1826. Dedham: H. & W. H. Mann, 1827. Pp. 36.

8392   HOLLISTON, MASS. The two hundredth anniversary of the town of Holliston, Mass., August 30, 31 and September 1, 2, 1924, souvenir program. n.p., [1924]. Pp. 32.

8393   HOLLISTON, MASS. FIRST CONGREGATIONAL CHURCH. Manual of the First Congregational Church, in Holliston, Mass., containing its history, articles of faith, covenant, and standing rules, with a list of the members. Holliston: David Heard, Jr., 1849. Pp. 8.

8394   _____. Manual of the First Congregational Church in Holliston, Mass., containing its history, articles of faith, covenant and standing rules with a list of the members. Holliston: Parker & Plimpton, 1825. Pp. 12.

8395   _____. Record of the celebration of the two hundredth anniversary, 1728-1928. n.p., [1928?]. Pp. 27. MBNEH.

8396   HOLLISTON. Boston: Edison Electric Illuminating Co., 1909. Pp. 12. M.

8397   LOOMIS, SILAS LAURENCE. Record of Holliston Academy, 1836 to 1844, Holliston, Mass.... Washington, D.C.: Gibson Bros., 1876. Pp. 86.

8398   REES, DOROTHY DRINKWATER. Holliston, Massachusetts, 1724-1974, the story of a New England town. Holliston: Holliston's 250th Anniversary Committee, 1973. Pp. 100. M.

HOLYOKE

8399   BAGG, EDWARD PARSONS and AARON MOORE BAGG, JR. The first hundred years of the Second Congregational Church of Holyoke, 1849-1949. [Holyoke, 1949]. Pp. 68.

8400   BILODEAU, THERESE. "The French in Holyoke, (1850-1900)." HJWM, 3 (Spring, 1974), 1-12.

8401   FOOTE, H. L. Historical sketch of the first twenty-five years of the life of St. Paul's Church, Holyoke, Mass. Holyoke, 1889. Pp. 27.

8402   GABRIEL, RALPH HENRY. The founding of Holyoke, 1848. Princeton: Princeton Univ. Pr., 1936. Pp. 23.

8403   GINGER, RAY. "Labor in a Massachusetts cotton mill, 1853-60." BusHR, 28 (1954), 67-91. Lyman Mills; known as Hadley Falls Co. until 1854.

8404   GREATER HOLYOKE COUNCIL OF CHURCHES. CHRISTIAN LIFE AND WORK DEPARTMENT. Holyoke's Negro families: report to the Greater Holyoke Council of Churches of a survey, prepared by Bulkeley Smith, Jr. [Holyoke]: Greater Holyoke Council of Churches, 1962. 17 leaves.

8405   GREEN, CONSTANCE MCLAUGHLIN. Holyoke, Massachusetts: a case history of the industrial revolution in America. New Haven: Yale Univ. Pr., 1939. Pp. ix, 425.

8406   HADLEY FALLS COMPANY, HOLYOKE, MASS. A report of the history and present condition of the Hadley Falls Company at Holyoke, Massachusetts. Boston: John Wilson & Son, 1853. Pp. 22. Cotton mill.

8407   "HISTORICAL notes of Holyoke." Paper, 21 (September 12, 1917), 20-21. Paper manufacturer.

8408 HOLYOKE, MASS. PUBLIC LIBRARY. The story of
Holyoke, Massachusetts, in painting and in
prose: mural paintings by Sante Graziani attained
by the bequest of the late Joseph Allen Skinner to
the Holyoke Public Library; interpretive essays by
Arthur Ryan and others. Holyoke, 1954. Pp. 32.

8409 HOLYOKE, MASS. SECOND BAPTIST CHURCH. Quarter centennial of the Second Baptist Church
and Sunday school...June 21, 1874. Holyoke:
Transcript Book & Job Printing House, 1874.
Pp. 43.

8410 HOLYOKE WATER POWER COMPANY. Connecticut
River flood at Holyoke, Massachusetts, November 5-6, 1927. Holyoke, 1928. Unpaged.

8411 HUTNER, FRANCES CORNWALL. The Farr Alpaca
Company: a case study in business history.
Northampton: Department of History of Smith Col-
lege, 1951. Pp. v, 107.

8412 "INDUSTRY'S map of Massachusetts: Holyoke."
Industry, 2 (May, 1937), 35-36.

8413 JOHNSON, FANNY M. "A model industrial city."
BSM, 3 (1885), 328-339.

8414 JOHNSON, L. L. Holyoke past and present,
1745-1895. Holyoke: Transcript Publishing,
1895. Pp. 160.

8415 KENDALL, W. E., ed. Fire services of Holyoke, Mass. Holyoke, 1888. Pp. 79.

8416 KIRTLAND, EDWIN L. "The city of Holyoke."
NEM, New Ser., 17 (1897-1898), 715-737.

8417 "MEETING change and challenges for more than
100 years." Industry, 25 (September, 1960)
19-22.
National Blank Book Co.; record keeping supplies.

8418 NATIONAL BLANK BOOK CO., HOLYOKE, MASS. The
story of an American achievement. Holyoke,
1943. Pp. 89.

8419 OSGOOD, GILBERT C. Story of the Holyoke
churches. Holyoke: Transcript Publishing,
1890. Pp. 115.
Includes history of the Y.M.C.A.

8420 QUIGLEY, FRANK. "Holyoke, the paper metropolis." National Magazine, 19 (1903-1904),
386-391.

8421 UNDERWOOD, KENNETH WILSON. Protestant and
Catholic: religious and social interaction
in an industrial community. Boston: Beacon Pr.,
1957. Pp. xxi, 484.

8422 ZACK, CHARLES SUMNER. Holyoke in the Great
War...including the towns of South Hadley,
Willimansett, Belchertown, Fairview and Granby.
Holyoke: Transcript Publishing, 1919. Pp. 475.

HOPEDALE

8423 BALLOU, ADIN. History of the Hopedale Community, from its inception to its virtual
submergence in the Hopedale Parish. William S. Heywood, ed. Lowell: Thompson & Hill, 1897.
Pp. xvii, 415.

8424 CHASE, WILLIAM HENRY. Five generations of
loom builders: a story of loom building
from the days of the craftsmanship of the hand loom
weaver to the modern automatic loom of Draper Corporation, with a supplement on the origin and development of the arts of spinning and weaving. Hopedale: Draper Corporation, 1951. Pp. xi, 87.

8425 DRAPER, GEORGE OTIS. History of the Northrop
loom evolution; containing correspondence,
reports, records, digests and explanatory matter.
Milford: Cook, 1897-1899. 2v.

8426 "HIGH honors for Draper Corporation." Industry, 17 (June, 1952), 24, 26, 32, 34, 36,
38-43.
150th anniversary; looms.

8427 HOPEDALE reminiscences: papers read before
the Hopedale Ladies Sewing Society and Branch
Alliance, April 27, 1910. [Hopedale]: School Pr.,
[1910?]. Pp. 71. MWA.

8428 JOHNSON, G. SHERMAN. "Massachusetts garden
spot." NEM, New Ser., 40 (1909), 607-613.

8429 PERRY, LEWIS. "Adin Ballou's Hopedale Community and the theology of antislavery."
Church History, 39 (1970), 372-389.

8430 WEST, THOMAS HENRY. 'The loom builders':
the Drapers as pioneer contributors to the
American way of life. N.Y.: Newcomen Society in
North America, 1952. Pp. 36.
Draper Corporation.

8431 WILSON, LEWIS G. "Hopedale and its founder."
NEM, New Ser., 4 (1891), 197-212.
Adin Ballou.

HOPKINTON

8432 DEXTER, HENRY MARTYN, ed. "The result of an
ecclesiastical council publickly declared to
the Church of Christ in Hopkinton, Sept. 19th,
1735." CongQ, 5 (1863), 342-346.

8433 HOPKINTON, MASS. FIRST CONGREGATIONAL
CHURCH. Manual of the First Congregational
Church in Hopkinton, Mass., organized Sept. 2, 1724,
including the confession of faith, covenant, standing rules, list of officers and members, and historical sketch. Boston: A. Mudge, 1881. Pp. 53.

8434 HOPKINTON. Boston: Edison Electric Illuminating Co., 1909. Pp. 12. M.

8435 HOWE, NATHANAEL. A century sermon, delivered in Hopkinton, Mass., on Lord's day, December 24, 1815. (1816) 4th ed. With a memoir of the author and explanatory notes by Elias Nason. Boston: John P. Jewett, 1851. Pp. 56.
Centennial of the town.

8436 KAPLAN, SIDNEY. "Harvard College and the Shays Rebellion." BPLQ, 7 (1955), 110-111.
Real estate in Hopkinton owned by Harvard.

8437 NASON, ELIAS. "Public worship in the old church at Hopkinton, (Mass.), in the old colonial times." NEHGR, 20 (1866), 122-123.

8438 OLESON, O. N. Hopkinton and vicinity. [Milford]: Milford Journal, [1906?].
Pp. 36. MWA.

8439 SAFFORD, FRANCES, A. A brief history of Hopkinton. n.p., 1915. Pp. 44. M.

HUBBARDSTON

8440 HUBBARDSTON, MASS. An address, in commemoration of the one hundredth anniversary of the incorporation of the town of Hubbardston, Mass., delivered June 13th, 1867, by Rev. John M. Stowe, of Sullivan, N.H.; a poem, prepared by Dea. Ephraim Stowe; together with other proceedings and exercises connected with the occasion.... Worcester: C. Hamilton, 1867. Pp. 109.

8441 HUBBARDSTON, MASS. BICENTENNIAL COMMITTEE. Program and souvenir, 200th anniversary celebration, Hubbardston, Mass., 1769-1967. n.p., 1967. Pp. 20. M.

8442 STOWE, JOHN MURDOCK. An address, in commemoration of the one hundredth anniversary of the incorporation of the town of Hubbardston, Mass., delivered June 13th, 1867.... Worcester: Chas. Hamilton, 1867. Pp. 109. MBNEH.

8443 _____. History of the town of Hubbardston, Worcester County, Mass., from the time its territory was purchased of the Indians in 1686, to the present, with the genealogy of present and former resident families. Hubbardston: Publishing Committee, 1881. Pp. xix, 383.

HUDSON

8444 CHAPPLE, JOE MITCHELL. "Hudson, Massachusetts." National Magazine, 27 (October, 1907), [6 unnumbered pages at end of issue].

8445 HUDSON, CHARLES. Abstract of the history of Hudson, Mass. from its first settlement to the centennial anniversary of the declaration of our national independence, July 4, 1876, with the action of the town, and the proceedings at the celebration. [Boston], 1877. Pp. 78.

8446 HUDSON, MASS. EUREKA ENGINE COMPANY, NO. 1. A brief history of the company, from its organization to the present time...with sketches and portraits of leading members, etc. Hudson: Enterprise Pr., 1886. Unpaged.

8447 JOSLIN, JAMES THOMAS. Historical address delivered at the dedication of the remodelled church of the First Unitarian Society, Hudson, Massachusetts on December nineteenth, nineteen hundred one, with which are included the portraits of the ministers: et cetera. Hudson: Ed. Worcester, [1902?]. Pp. 56.

8448 MURRAY, CAROL. "Hudson firm celebrates centennial." Industry, 29 (March, 1964), 20, 48-50.
Thomas Taylor & Sons, fabrics.

8449 "PIONEERS in the art of broaching." Industry, 10 (May, 1945), 19-21.
Lapointe Machine Tool Co.

8450 ROMAINE, LAWRENCE B. "An ingenious fly trap." CEAIA, 2 (1937-1944), 41-42.
Made by Edson Manufacturing Co.

8451 WILLIAMS, ROY FOSTER. "Broaching pioneers' 50th anniversary." Industry, 17 (May, 1952), 22-24.
Lapointe Machine Tool Co.

8452 WORCESTER, EDWARD F. Hudson, past and present. Hudson: Enterprise Printing, 1899. unpaged.

HULL

8453 BERGAN, WILLIAM M. Old Nantasket. (1968) Rev. ed. North Quincy: Christopher Publishing, 1969. Pp. 154.

8454 [HOMER, JAMES LLOYD]. Notes on the seashore; or, random sketches, in relation to the ancient town of Hull, its settlement, its inhabitants, and its social and political institutions; to the fisheries, fishing parties, and boat sailing; to Boston Harbor and its islands.... By the 'Shade of Alden.' Boston: Redding, 1848. Pp. vii, 54.

8455 [LINCOLN, SOLOMON]. Sketch of Nantasket: (now called Hull,) in the county of Plymouth. Hingham: Gazette Pr., 1830. Pp. 16.
Signed: L.

8456 MATTHEWS, ALBERT. "The naming of Hull, Massachusetts." NEHGR, 59 (1905), 177-186.

8457 ROCKWOOD, CHARLES M. "At the gateway of Boston Harbor." NEM, New Ser., 42 (1910), 693-699.

8458 SMITH, MRS. JOHN E. "Point Allerton." MayflowerQ, 37 (1971), 5-7.

HUNTINGTON

8459   BISBEE, JOHN HATCH. History of the town of
        Huntington, in the county of Hampshire,
Mass., from its first settlement to the year 1876.
Springfield: C. W. Bryan, 1876. Pp. 40.

IPSWICH

8460   APPLETON Farms tercentenary, Ipswich, Massa-
        chusetts...July Third, nineteen hundred and
thirty-eight...1638-1938. n.p., n.d. Pp. 10.
MSaE.

8461   BARROW, THOMAS C. "The town records of Ips-
        wich." EIHC, 97 (1961), 294-302.

8462   BAXTER, SYLVESTER. The Hotel Cluny of a New
        England village, and An old Ipswich house,
with the history of the house, and proceedings at
the annual meeting Dec. 3, 1900. Salem: Salem
Pr., 1901. Pp. 53.
        Whipple House; 'An old Ipswich house' is
        by William H. Downes.

8463   BROWN, ABBIE FARWELL. "Old Ipswich town."
        NEM, New Ser., 28 (1903), 416-423.

8464   CALDWELL, LYDIA A. Our honored seminary,
        April 23, 1828, the seventy-fifth anniver-
sary of the coming of Miss Grant and Miss Lyon to
Ipswich, April 23, 1903. n.p., n.d. Pp. 7.
        Ipswich Seminary.

8465   "THE CAPT. Matthew Perkins House, Ipswich,
        Mass." OTNE, 15 (1924-1925), 125-127.
        Formerly the Norton-Cobbet House.

8466   CHOATE, WASHINGTON. The oration...and the
        poem by Rev. Edgar F. Davis, on the 200th
anniversary of the resistance to the Andros tax,
at Ipswich, July 4, 1887. Salem: Salem Observer
Book & Job Print, 1894. Pp. 30.

8467   "CHOATE Bridge, Ipswich." ECHGR, 1 (1894),
        5-6, 23-24.

8468   "THE CHOATE Bridge, Ipswich, Mass." OTNE,
        11 (1920-1921), 88-89.

8469   CLEAVELAND, JOHN. A short and plain narra-
        tive of the late work of God's spirit at
Chebacco in Ipswich, in the years 1763 and 1764:
together with some account of the conduct of the
Fourth Church of Christ in Ipswich, in admitting
members.... Boston: Z. Fowle, 1767. Pp. 81.

8470   COGSWELL, JOHN H. "The early Church." Old
        Ipswich, 1 (1899), 21-26.
        1648.

8471   COMSTOCK, HELEN. "An Ipswich account book
        1707-1762." Antiques, 66 (1954), 188-192.
        Furniture.

8472   COWLES, EUNICE CALDWELL. Autumnal memories,
        read at the First Church, Ipswich, Mass.,

October 30, 1898. [Ipswich]: Augustine Caldwell,
1898. Pp. 11.
        Sabbath schools.

8473   _____. Historical sketch: read at the six-
        tieth anniversary of the First Parish Sabbath
School. Ipswich, Mass., Sunday, June 30, 1878.
[Ipswich?, 1878]. Pp. 12.

8474   CROWELL, ROBERT. A sketch of the history of
        the Second Parish in Ipswich, a discourse
delivered in the said parish on Lord's Day, Jan. 1,
1815. Andover: Flagg and Gould, 1815. Pp. 32.

8475   "DANIEL Hovey's house." Antiquarian Papers,
        3 (April, 1882), [1].

8476   DENISON memorial: Ipswich, Mass., September
        20, 1882, two hundredth anniversary of the
death of Major-General Daniel Denison. Biographical
sketch by Prof. D. D. Slade; historical sketch by
Augustine Caldwell. Ipswich, 1882. Pp. 52.
        Historical sketch: 1633-1682.

8477   DOW, ARTHUR W. "Historic houses." Anti-
        quarian Papers, 1 (December, 1879), [1].

8478   EAGER, MARGARET MACLAREN. Ipswich historical
        pageant, to celebrate the 20th anniversary
of the Ipswich Historical Society. n.p., [19--?].
Unpaged.

8479   "AN EARLY court session, 1645." Putnam's
        HM, 2 (1893-1894), 173-176.

8480   FEWKES, JESSE. Fine thread, lace and hosiery
        in Ipswich, and Ipswich mills and factories,
proceedings at the annual meeting December 7, 1903.
Salem: Salem Pr., 1904. Pp. 48.
        Ipswich mills and factories is by Thomas F.
        Waters.

8481   "THE FIRST American stone-arched bridge."
        MagHist, 3 (1905), 119.
        Choate Bridge.

8482   FITZ, DANIEL. Old meeting house, the last
        day of assembling in the old meeting house
of the South Parish, Ipswich, Mass., Dec. 31, 1837.
n.p., 1899. Pp. 28. MBNEH.

8483   GOODHUE, CHARLES E. Ipswich, proud settle-
        ment in the province of the Massachusetts-
Bay. N.Y.: Newcomen Society in North America,
1953. Pp. 36.

8484   HAMMATT, ABRAHAM. "History of Mr. Hammatt's
        house." Antiquarian Papers, 1 (October,
1879), [1-2].

8485   _____. "Ipswich Grammar School." NEHGR, 6
        (1852), 64-71, 159-167.

8486   _____. "Physicians of Ipswich." NEHGR, 4
        (1850), 11-16.

8487   _____. "Two hundredth anniversary of the
        foundation of the Grammar School in Ipswich,
instituted January 11-21, 1650-51." Antiquarian

(HAMMATT, ABRAHAM.)
Papers, 1 (November, 1879), [1-3], (December, 1879),
[1-3], (December, 1879), [2-3], (January, 1880),
[2-3], (March, 1880), [3-4], (April, 1880), [2-3].
(July, 1880), [1-3], (September, 1880), [2-3].

8488   HEARD, GEORGE W. "Early meeting houses."
       Antiquarian Papers, 4 (June, 1884), [1-4].

8489   "HOUSE of William and Lydia (Lull) Caldwell,
       High St., Ipswich." Antiquarian Papers, 4
(July, 1884), [1].

8490   IPSWICH, MASS. The ancient records of the
       town of Ipswich...from 1634 to 1650. George
A. Schofield, ed. Ipswich: Chronicle Motor Pr.,
1899. Unpaged.

8491   _____. The celebration of the two hundred
       and fiftieth anniversary of the incorporation
of the town of Ipswich, Massachusetts, August 16,
1884. Boston: Little, Brown, 1884. Pp. vi, 149.
       Historical address by John C. Kimball.

8492   _____. Chronicle report of the 250th anni-
       versary exercises of Ipswich, August 16th,
1894. Ipswich: Ipswich Chronicle, 1884. Pp. 74.

8493   IPSWICH, MASS. FIRST CHURCH OF CHRIST.
       Anniversary Sunday, August 17, 1884, the two
hundred and fiftieth anniversary of the organization
of the First Church, Ipswich, Mass. Ipswich: Ipswich Antiquarian Papers, 1884. Pp. 28. MB.
       Sermons by Edwin Beaman Palmer and Increase
Niles Tarbox.

8494   _____. Concise history of the First Church
       of Christ, 1634-1879.... Ipswich: L. H.
Daniels, 1879. Pp. 36. MSaE.

8495   IPSWICH, MASS. SALT MARSH COMMITTEE. The
       Ipswich marshes. n.p., n.d. Unpaged.
MSaE.

8496   IPSWICH, MASS. SOUTH PARISH CHURCH. The
       old meeting house, 1747-1838. Ipswich:
Caldwell, 1899. Pp. 28. MB.

8497   IPSWICH, MASS. YE OLDE BURNHAM HOUSE. Ye
       olde Burnham house in Ipswich, Massachusetts,
kept by Martha Lucy Murray, built in 1640, quaintest
place in all New England.... n.p., [193-?]. 10
leaves.

8498   "THE IPSWICH Female Seminary." American
       Quarterly Register, 11 (1838-1839), 368-375.

8499   IPSWICH HISTORICAL SOCIETY, IPSWICH, MASS.
       Order of exercises at the dedication of the
ancient house now occupied by the society and the
proceedings at the annual meeting, Dec. 5, 1898,
including a history of the house by the president
[Thomas Franklin Waters]. Ipswich: Independent
Pr., 1899. Pp. 49.

8500   _____. Thomas Dudley and Simon and Ann
       Bradstreet; a study of house-lots to deter-
mine the location of their homes, and the exercises

at the dedication of tablets, July 31, 1902. Proceedings at the annual meeting Dec. 1, 1902. Salem:
Salem Pr., 1903. Pp. 54.

8501   IPSWICH, Massachusetts, resources, develop-
       ment and progress, a series of comprehensive
sketches. Biddeford, Me.: Historical Publishing,
1902. Pp. 25. MSaE.

8502   IPSWICH MILLS. The hosiery industry of Ips-
       wich, 1822-1922. Ipswich, 1922. Pp. 24.
M.

8503   "THE IPSWICH Paines." Antiquarian Papers, 1
       (1879), [3].

8504   "JOHN Knowlton's house, 1691-2." Antiquarian
       Papers, 3 (May, 1883), [1].

8505   JOHNSON, EDWARD. "Ipswich." Antiquarian
       Papers, 3 (February, 1882), [2-3].

8506   KIMBALL, DAVID TENNEY. The fruits of Con-
       gregationalism: a centennial discourse, de-
livered before the First Church and Religious Society in Ipswich, August 10, 1834. Boston: L. W.
Kimball, 1834. Pp. 32.

8507   _____. The last sermon preached in the an-
       cient meeting house of the First Parish in
Ipswich, February 22, 1846. Boston: Temperance
Standard Pr., 1846. Pp. 32.
       Historical review.

8508   _____. A sketch of the ecclesiastical his-
       tory of Ipswich, the substance of a dis-
course, in two parts, delivered in that town, December 1820. Haverhill: Gazette and Patriot Office, 1823. Pp. 44.

8509   LYON, IRVING P. "The oak furniture of Ips-
       wich, Massachusetts." Antiques, 32 (1937),
230-233, 298-301; 33 (1938), 73-75, 198-203, 322-
325; 34 (1938), 79-81.

8510   "MADAME Rogers' School." Antiquarian Papers,
       4 (February, 1884), [1].

8511   NORTON, SUSAN L. "Population growth in colo-
       nial America: a study of Ipswich, Massachu-
setts." Population Studies, 25 (1971), 433-452.
       1633-1790.

8512   O'DWYER, GEORGE F. "The Irish in Ipswich,
       1630-1700." Catholic World, 115 (1922),
805-814.

8513   PARK, HELEN. "Thomas Dennis, Ipswich joiner:
       a re-examination." Antiques, 78 (1960), 40-
44.

       Furniture; seventeenth century.

8514   PATCH, JOHN. "The Winthrop, Symonds and
       Patch place." Antiquarian Papers, 3 (Septem-
ber, 1883), [1-2], (December, 1883), [1-2].
       Historic house.

8515   PERKINS, LUCY A. Historical sketch of the
       Ladies' Aid Society...at the 70th anniversa-
ry of the Society, May 28, 1902. [Ipswich]: Chas.
G. Hull, 1903. Pp. 16. MSaE.

8516   PERLEY, MARTIN VAN BUREN. Millend, Ips-
       wich, 1635-1640. Portsmouth, N.H., 1901.
Pp. 16. MBNEH.
       Section of town in vicinity of the mill.

8517   PERLEY, SIDNEY. "Part of Ipswich in 1700."
       Essex Antiq, 6 (1902), 14-19.

8518   PERZEL, EDWARD S. "Landholding in Ipswich."
       EIHC, 104 (1968), 303-328.
       Seventeenth century.

8519   PICTORIAL Ipswich, with complete historical
       annotations. Portsmouth, N.H.: M. V. B.
Perley, 1900. 72 leaves.

8520   POTTER, I. J. Chronicle report of the 250th
       anniversary exercises of Ipswich, August 16,
1884, together with a few sketches about town....
Ipswich: Chronicle Pr., 1884. Pp. 74.

8521   "THE PROCTOR House." Antiquarian Papers, 1
       (October, 1879), [3].

8522   "REV. NATHANIEL Rogers' House, 1728." An-
       tiquarian papers, 2 (July, 1881), [3-4].

8523   "SHATSWELL House, High Street." Antiquarian
       Papers, 2 (March, 1881), [1-2].

8524   SHURCLIFF, SIDNEY NICHOLS. Upon the road
       Argilla: a record of the first quarter cen-
tury of a unique summer colony. Boston: Priv.
Print., 1958. Pp. 152. MSaE.

8525   SHURCLIFF, WILLIAM A. A casual history of
       the upper part of Argilla Road, Ipswich,
Mass., since 1897. n.p., [not after 1966]. 95
leaves. MSaE.

8526   "1667, a busy year." Antiquarian Papers, 3
       (March, 1882), [4].
       Houses built in that year.

8527   "SPARKE'S Tavern, 1671." Antiquarian Papers,
       4 (February, 1884), [3].

8528   THOMPSON, KATHERINE S. "Dr. Manning's mill."
       OTNE, 55 (1964-1965), 11-22.
       Woolen mill.

8529   WADE, HERBERT T. "Nathaniel Wade and his
       Ipswich minute men." EIHC, 89 (1953), 213-
252.

8530   "THE WALLEY-Dana House." Antiquarian Pa-
       pers, 2 (April, 1881), [1].

8531   WATERS, THOMAS FRANKLIN. Candlewood, an
       ancient neighborhood in Ipswich; with gene-
alogies of John Brown, William Fellows, Robert Kinsman.... Salem: Salem Pr., 1909. Pp. 161.

8532   _____. The development of our town govern-
       ment and common lands and commonage. Salem:
Salem Pr., 1900. Pp. 29.

8533   [_____]. The early homes of the Puritans,
       and some old Ipswich houses.... Salem:
Salem Pr., 1898. Pp. 106.

8534   _____. Glimpses of everyday life in old
       Ipswich. [Salem], 1925. Pp. 39.

8535   _____. An historical address delivered on
       the 140th anniversary of the organization of
the South Church, Ipswich, Sunday, July 31, 1887.
Ipswich, 1887. Pp. 31. MSaE.

8536   _____. A history of the old Argilla Road in
       Ipswich, Massachusetts. Salem: Salem Pr.,
1900. Pp. 43.

8537   _____. "Houses of the early settlers, size,
       value, duration." ECHGR, 1 (1894), 161-162;
2 (1895), 97-100.
       'To be continued,' but periodical ceased
publication.

8538   _____. Ipswich in the Massachusetts Bay
       Colony. Ipswich: Ipswich Historical Soci-
ety, 1905-1917. 2v.
       1633-1917.

8539   _____. Ipswich in the World War. [Salem],
       1920. Pp. 244.

8540   _____. Ipswich River, its bridges, wharves
       and industries. [Salem], 1923. Pp. 40.

8541   _____. Ipswich Village and the old Rowley
       Road. [Salem], 1914. Pp. 77.

8542   _____. Jeffrey's Neck and the way leading
       thereto with notes on Little Neck. Salem:
Salem Pr., 1912. Pp. vi, 94.

8543   _____. The John Whipple House in Ipswich,
       Mass., and the people who have owned and
lived in it. [Ipswich?], 1915. Pp. 55.

8544   _____. The meeting house green and a study
       of houses and lands in that vicinity....
Salem: Salem Pr., 1902. Pp. 52.

8545   _____. The old Bay Road from Saltonstall's
       Brook and Samuel Appleton's farm, and a ge-
nealogy of the Ipswich descendants of Samuel Appleton.... Salem: Salem Pr., 1907. Pp. 62.

8546   _____. "The so-called Saltonstall House in
       Ipswich." Putnam's HM, 2 (1893-1894), 3-4.

8547   _____. "Some old Ipswich houses." EIHC, 33
       (1898), 197-241.

8548   _____ and EUNICE W. FARLEY FELTEN [sic].
       Two Ipswich patriots. [Salem], 1927.
Pp. 41.

8549   WHIPPLE, SHERMAN LELAND and THOMAS FRANKLIN
        WATERS. Puritan homes. [Salem], 1929.
Pp. 99.

8550   WHITTIER, JOHN GREENLEAF. "The great Ipswich
        fright." Antiquarian Papers, 4 (March,
1884), [1-2].
        Rumor of British landing, April 21, 1775.

8551   WIGGLESWORTH, EDWARD. "Observations on the
        longevity of the inhabitants of Ipswich and
Hingham, and the proposals for ascertaining the
value of estates held for life and the reversion of
them." American Academy of Arts and Sciences, Memoirs, 1 (1875), 565-568.

8552   WILLCOMB, OLIVER CLIFTON. Genealogy of the
        Willcomb family of New England (1655-1902),
together with a condensed history of the town of
Ipswich, Mass.... Lynn, 1902. Pp. vii, 302.

8553   "THE WINTHROP and Burnham House, 1633."
        Antiquarian Papers, 3 (October, 1883), [1-2].

KINGSTON

8554   BAILEY, SARAH Y. The civic progress of
        Kingston [and] a history of her industries,
two hundred years, 1726-1926. Kingston: The Two
Hundredth Anniversary Committee, 1926. Pp. 53.
        'A history of her industries' is by Emily F.
        Drew.

8555   _____. The story of Jones River in pilgrim
        Plymouth, 1620-1726; which in the latter
year became Kingston, Massachusetts. Kingston:
Alliance of Unitarian Women, 1929. Pp. 48.

8556   CHASE, SALLY F. D. and EMILY F. DREW. A few
        highlights regarding the old [Major John
Bradford] House, the region where it stands and the
family which lived there from earliest days until
the American Revolution. n.p., [1946?]. Unpaged.
M.

8557   DREW, THOMAS BRADFORD. The ancient estate
        of Governor William Bradford. Boston:
T. P. Smith, 1897. Pp. 43.

8558   HOBART, ETHEL. "Kingston, Massachusetts."
        NEM, New Ser., 32 (1905), 505-511.

8559   JONES, HENRY M. Ships of Kingston, 'Good-
        bye, fare ye well.' Plymouth: Memorial
Pr., 1926. Pp. 130.
        c1714-1887.

8560   KINGSTON, MASS. Report of the proceedings
        and exercises at the one hundred and fif-
tieth anniversary of the incorporation of the town
of Kingston, Mass., June 27, 1876. Boston: E. B.
Stillings, 1876. Pp. 151.

8561   KINGSTON, MASS. BAPTIST CHURCH. 155th
        year celebration...March 27, 1960. n.p.,
1960. Pp. 25. M.

8562   SHERMAN, MRS. ROBERT M. "The Major John
        Bradford House--Kingston, Mass.--1674."
MayflowerQ, 35 (1969), 11-12.

LAKEVILLE

8563   ROMAINE, LAWRENCE B. "The Ward House, née
        Sproat, Lakeville, Mass., 1711-1963 or who
buried George III in a vase of flowers?" MiddAntiq,
5 (November, 1963), 6-7.

8564   SEAVER, JANE MONTGOMERY. "Personal recollec-
        tions of the Precinct Congregational Church
in Lakeville, Massachusetts, in 1850." OTNE, 30
(1939-1940), 101-105.

8565   VIGERS, GLADYS DE MARANVILLE. History of the
        town of Lakeville, Massachusetts, 1852-1952;
one hundredth anniversary of the town of Lakeville.
[Lakeville, 1952]. Pp. 247.

LANCASTER

8566   BROWN, JOHN PERKINS. "Notes on the Bulfinch
        Church at Lancaster, Mass." OTNE, 27 (1936-
1937), 148-151.
        First Church of Christ.

8567   CLARK, JOHN CALVIN LAWRENCE, comp. Notable
        historic spots in Lancaster, Massachusetts.
[Lancaster]: South Lancaster Printing, 1928. Unpaged.

8568   CUSHING, JOHN DANIEL. "Lancaster Circulating
        Library." NYPLB, 64 (1960), 432-436.

8569   "DESTRUCTION of Lancaster." WMHJ, 1 (1825-
        1826), 280-284.
        King Philip's War.

8570   EMERSON, WILLIAM ANDREW and JOHN CALVIN
        LAWRENCE CLARK. Lancaster on the Nashua,
picturesque and historical. Leominster: M. A. Tolman, 1904. Pp. 96.

8571   GOODWIN, ISAAC. An oration, delivered at
        Lancaster, February 21, 1826, in commemora-
tion of the one hundred and fiftieth anniversary of
the destruction of that town by the Indians.
Worcester: Rogers & Griffin, 1826. Pp. 15.
        King Philip's War.

8572   HARRINGTON, TIMOTHY. A century sermon,
        preached at the First-Parish, in Lancaster,
May 28th, 1753. (1753) Leominster: S. & J. Wilder, for Mr. Joshua Fletcher, of Lancaster, July,
1806. Pp. 25.
        Centennial of the town.

8573   LANCASTER, MASS. The birth, marriage, and
        death register, church records and epitaphs
of Lancaster, Massachusetts, 1643-1850. Henry S.
Nourse, ed. Lancaster, 1890. Pp. 508.

8574 _____. Commemoration of the two hundred and fiftieth anniversary of the incorporation of Lancaster, Massachusetts, Tuesday, June 30, 1903. Lancaster, 1904. Pp. 43.

8575 _____. The early records of Lancaster, Massachusetts, 1643-1725. Henry S. Nourse, ed. Lancaster, 1884. Pp. 364.

8576 "LANCASTER." BBNL, 1 (1826), 118-120.

8577 "LANCASTER, Mass." Ballou's Pictorial Drawing-Room Companion, 11 (1856), 360-361.

8578 MARVIN, ABIJAH PERKINS. History of the town of Lancaster, Massachusetts, from the first settlement to the present time, 1643-1879. Lancaster: The Town, 1879. Pp. 798.

8579 MORISON, SAMUEL ELIOT. "The Plantation of Nashaway--an industrial experiment." CSMP, 27 (1927-1930), 204-222.

8580 MORSE, GEORGE F. A short history of Lancaster, Mass. n.p., 1916. Pp. 12. M.

8581 NOURSE, HENRY STEDMAN. Lancastriana: I. A supplement to the early records and military annals of Lancaster, Massachusetts. Lancaster, 1900. Pp. 45.

8582 _____. Lancastriana: II. A bibliography compiled for the Public Library of Lancaster, Massachusetts. Lancaster, 1901. Pp. 46.

8583 _____. "The loyalists of Lancaster." BSM, 1 (1884), 377-386.

8584 _____. The military annals of Lancaster, Massachusetts, 1740-1865, including lists of soldiers serving in the colonial and Revolutionary wars, for the Lancastrian towns: Berlin, Bolton, Harvard, Leominster, and Sterling. Lancaster, 1889. Pp. 402.

8585 ROWLANDSON, MARY WHITE. The narrative of the captivity and restoration of Mrs. Mary Rowlandson, first printed in 1682 at Cambridge, Massachusetts, & London, England, whereunto are annexed a map of her removes & biographical & historical notes. Frederick L. Weis, ed. Boston: Houghton Mifflin, 1930. Pp. vi, 86.

8586 SAFFORD, MARION FULLER. Historical sketch of the First Church of Lancaster. Lancaster, 1916. Pp. 16. MBNEH.

8587 _____. The story of colonial Lancaster (Massachusetts). Rutland, Vt.: Tuttle, 1937. Pp. 190.

8588 SMITH, JONATHAN. History of old Trinity Lodge of Lancaster, Mass., chartered, January 30, 1778, became extinct (about) 1832. Clinton: W. J. Coulter, 1896. Pp. vi, 241.

8589 THAYER, NATHANIEL. A sermon delivered at Lancaster, Dec. 29, 1816, the last Lord's Day in which there was religious worship in the old meeting-house. Worcester: William Manning, 1817. Pp. 39. MBNEH.

8590 WEIS, FREDERICK LEWIS. Historical sketch of the Lancaster Town Library, 1790-1862-1950. Lancaster, 1950. Unpaged. MBNEH.

8591 WILLARD, JOSEPH. An address in commemoration of the two-hundredth anniversary of the incorporation of Lancaster, Massachusetts. Boston: J. Wilson & Son, 1853. Pp. vi, 230.

8592 _____. "History of Lancaster." WMHJ, 2 (1826), 257-344.

8593 _____. Topographical and historical sketches of the town of Lancaster, in the Commonwealth of Massachusetts; furnished for the Worcester Magazine and Historical Journal. Worcester: C. Griffin, 1826. Pp. 90.

LANESBOROUGH

8594 BENNETT, ANNA FULLER. History of the Berkshire Union Chapel. Pittsfield: J. C. Gerst Pr., 1934. Pp. 23. MPB.

8595 _____. A summary of historical facts relating to the Lanesboro Congregational Church. n.p., [1945?]. Unpaged. MPB.

8596 MARTIN, FRANCES S. Lanesborough, Massachusetts: the story of a wilderness settlement, 1765-1965. Lanesborough, 1965. Pp. 110.

8597 "OLD Home Week, celebration in Lanesboro, July, 1902." Berkshire Hills, 3 (1902-1903), 1-5, 13-19.

8598 PALMER, CHARLES JAMES. History of town of Lanesborough, Massachusetts, 1741-1905... Pt. 1. n.p., [1905?]. Pp. 168. No more published.

8599 _____. "150th anniversary of granting the charter of the town of Lanesborough." BHSSC, 2, Pt. 4 (1897), 281-303.

8600 _____. Sermon preached at St. Luke's Church, Lanesborough, Mass., August 28, 1892, on the 150th anniversary of the town. Pittsfield: Sun Printing, 1892. Pp. 15. M.

8601 _____. Sermon preached in St. Luke's Church, Lanesborough, Mass., October 16, 1892, on the 125th anniversary of the organization of the parish. Pittsfield: Geo. T. Denny, 1893. Pp. 18.

8602 "THE PLATTS and Meads: two old time notable families of Lanesboro--the managers of its once famous marble quarries, etc." Berkshire Hills, 4 (1903-1904), 152.

8603 "RARE bit of Berkshire history, the notable old time family of James Greene of Lanesboro." Berkshire Hills, 4 (1903-1904), 228-231.

8604 SHAW, S. BRENTON. A centennial sermon delivered in St. Luke's Church, Lanesborough, October 6, 1867. Pittsfield: Chickering & Axtell, 1867. Pp. 22. M.

8605 THOMSON, EDITH PARKER. "The home of Josh Billings." NEM, New Ser., 19 (1898-1899), 696-703.

LAWRENCE

8606 ARLINGTON MILLS, LAWRENCE, MASS. The Arlington Mills: a historical and descriptive sketch, with some account of the worsted dress-goods manufacture in the United States.... Boston: Rockwell and Churchill, 1891. Pp. 134.

8607 _____. Arlington Mills, 1865-1925. Norwood: Plimpton Pr., 1925. Pp. 112.

8608 _____. Arlington Mills, seventy-five years of progress 1865-1940. Norwood: Plimpton Pr., [1940]. Pp. 14.

8609 _____. Tops, a new American industry: a study in the development of the American worsted manufacture, the Arlington Mills.... Cambridge: Riverside Pr., 1898. Pp. x, 137.

8610 "THE ARLINGTON Mills." Industry, 5 (September, 1940), 7-11.
        Wool.

8611 AN AUTHENTIC history of the Lawrence calamity, embracing a description of the Pemberton Mill, a detailed account of the catastrophe, a chapter of thrilling incidents, list of contributions to the relief fund, names of the killed and wounded, abstracts of the sermons on the subject, report of the coroner's inquest, &c. Boston: J. J. Dyer, 1860. Pp. 96.
        Building collapsed and caught fire.

8612 BARROWS, JOHN HENRY. The history of the Eliot Congregational Church, Lawrence, Mass., an anniversary sermon, preached March 14, 1880.... Lawrence: Geo. S. Merrill & Crocker, 1880. Pp. 29.

8613 BAY STATE BANK, LAWRENCE, MASS. History. Boston: Samuel Ward, [1905]. Unpaged. MSaE.

8614 BOWDEN, ERNEST J. Unitarians in Lawrence. n.p., [1922?]. Pp. 12. MSaE.
        First Unitarian Society, 1847-1922.

8615 CAHN, WILLIAM. Mill town: a dramatic, pictorial narrative of the century-old fight to unionize an industrial town.... N.Y.: Cameron & Kahn, 1954. Pp. 286.

8616 CATHOLIC ORDER OF FORESTERS, LAWRENCE, MASS., COURT SAINT ANN, NO. 268. Golden jubilee, Sunday, June 9, 1946. n.p., [1946?]. Unpaged. MeU.

8617 "CENTRAL Congregational Church, Lawrence, Ms." CongQ, 3 (1861), 18-20.

8618 CHENEY, MABEL J. History of the Church of the Good Shepherd of the First Universalist Society of Lawrence, Massachusetts, 1847-1947. [Lawrence]: Eagle Tribune Job Print, [1947?]. Unpaged. MSaE.

8619 COLE, DONALD B. "The collapse of the Pemberton Mill." EIHC, 96 (1960), 47-55.
        1860.

8620 _____. Immigrant city: Lawrence, Massachusetts, 1845-1921. Chapel Hill: Univ. of North Carolina Pr., 1963. Pp. ix, 248.

8621 _____. "Lawrence, Massachusetts: model town to immigrant city 1845-1912." EIHC, 92 (1956), 349-375.

8622 DONIGAN, BERNARD E. "The city of Lawrence, Massachusetts." National Magazine, 17 (1902-1903), 264-274.

8623 DORGAN, MAURICE B. History of Lawrence, Massachusetts, with war records. [Lawrence], 1924. Pp. ix, 267.

8624 _____. Lawrence yesterday and today (1845-1918) a concise history of Lawrence, Massachusetts--her industries and institutions; municipal statistics and a variety of information concerning the city. Lawrence: Dick & Trumpold, 1918. Pp. 263.

8625 EAGLE AND TRIBUNE, LAWRENCE, MASS. 1853-1903, fifty years a city: a souvenir of the semi-centennial anniversary of Lawrence, Massachusetts. Lawrence: Hildreth & Rogers, 1903. Pp. 161. MWA.

8626 FECTEAU, EDOUARD. Les Franco-Américains de Lawrence et des environs. Lowell: Lowell Association des Anciens Elèves, 1941. Pp. 24. MeU.

8627 FREEMASONS. LAWRENCE, MASS. GRECIAN LODGE. Grecian Lodge, A. F. & A. M., Lawrence, Massachusetts, report of the proceedings of the seventy-fifth anniversary December fourteenth, nineteen hundred. n.p., [1900]. Pp. 41. MSaE.
        Historical sketch by Charles H. Littlefield.

8628 HAYES, JONATHAN FRANKLIN CHESLEY. History of the city of Lawrence. Lawrence: E. D. Green, 1868. Pp. 168.

8629 JURAS, PRANCIŠKUS. Šv. Pranciškaus Lietuviu Parapija; 30 Metu Sukakluvēms Paminēti, 1903-1933. Lawrence, [1933?]. Unpaged. MH.
        St. Frances Lithuanian Parish.

8630 KEOGH, J. P. Semicentennial history of Lawrence, Massachusetts.... Lawrence: Bailey and Rushforth, 1903. Pp. 179. MSaE.

8631 KNOWLES, MORRIS and C. G. HYDE. "The Lawrence city filter: a history of its installation and maintenance." American Society of Civil Engineers. Transactions, 46 (1901), 257-378.
        Water supply; detailed statistics, 1895-1900.

8632 LAWRENCE, MASS. BOARD OF TRADE. A brief history of the city of Lawrence, its textile industries, etc. Lawrence, 1902. Pp. 124.

8633   LAWRENCE, MASS. SOUTH CONGREGATIONAL CHURCH.
        Manual...organized May 13, 1868. Lawrence:
Lawrence Daily Eagle Steam Print, 1882. Pp. 20.
M.
        Includes brief history.

8634   LAWRENCE COOPERATIVE BANK. ...50 years of
        security and service for Lawrence fami-
lies.... Lawrence, 1938. Pp. 16. M.

8635   LAWRENCE MONDAY NIGHT CLUB. Twenty-fifth
        anniversary of the Lawrence Monday Night
Club, February eighth, 1897. Boston: Thomas Todd,
[1897?]. Pp. 30. MSaE.

8636   LAWRENCE SAVINGS BANK. Fiftieth anniversary,
        Lawrence Savings Bank, 1868-1918, Lawrence,
Massachusetts. Lawrence, 1918. Pp. 38. M.

8637   LAWRENCE up to date, 1845-1895. Lawrence:
        Rush & Donoghue, 1895. Pp. 172, A-87.
MBNEH.

8638   LOOKING backward in Lawrence: a story read
        at the second anniversary of the Y.P.S.C.E.
[Young People's Society of Christian Endeavor] of
the Lawrence Street Congregational Church, Lawrence
Mass., Sept. 25, 1889. [Lawrence]: Daily Eagle
Print, [1889?]. Pp. 24. MSaE.

8639   MCCARTHY, JOSEPH. "Great industries of New
        England, greatest mill in the world." NEM,
New Ser., 39 (1908-1909), 769-774.
        Wood Worsted Mill.

8640   MASSACHUSETTS. DEPARTMENT OF PUBLIC HEALTH.
        Proud heritage: a review of Lawrence Ex-
periment Station, past, present, future. [Boston,
1953]. Pp. 36.

8641   MERRILL, CHARLES G. The Lawrence gazetteer,
        containing a record of the important events
in Lawrence and vicinity from 1845 to 1894, also,
a history of the corporations, industrial establishments, churches, societies, clubs, and other
organizations; national, state and municipal statistics, and a variety of useful information. Lawrence, 1894. Pp. 165.

8642   MUTUAL RELIEF ASSOCIATION, LAWRENCE, MASS.
        Fire service of Lawrence...leather basket
times to the present fire department. Lawrence,
1888. Pp. 63. MB.

8643   O'MAHONEY, KATHARINE A. O'KEEFE. Sketch of
        Catholicity in Lawrence and vicinity. Law-
rence: Sentinel Steam Printing, 1882. Pp. iii,
290.

8644   PACIFIC MILLS, LAWRENCE, MASS. Memoirs of a
        corporation: the story of Mary and Mack and
Pacific Mills. Boston, 1950. 12v. M.
        Issued monthly during 1950 to commemorate
        centennial of the firm.

8645   "THE PACIFIC Mills." Industry, 2 (December,
        1936), 11-13.
        Wool.

8646   PETERSON, BERNARD. "A path around the world
        on paper." Industry, 17 (May, 1952), 7-12,
48.
        Champion-International Co.

8647   PRATT, WALTER MERRIAM. "The Lawrence revo-
        lution." NEM, 47 (1912), 7-16.
        Labor strife.

8648   THE REPORT of the Lawrence survey; studies
        in relation to Lawrence, Massachusetts, made
in 1911, under the advice of Francis H. McLean by
Robert E. Todd and Frank B. Sanborn at the procure-
ment of the White Fund. Lawrence, 1912. Pp. 263.
        Primarily concerned with housing.

8649   SAUNDERS, EDITH ST. LOE. The first hundred
        years of Grace Church. Andover: Andover
Pr., 1946. Pp. 96.

8650   SMITH, FREDERICK MORTON. The Essex Company
        on the Merrimack at Lawrence. N.Y.: New-
comen Society of England, American Branch, 1947.
Pp. 32.

8651   SUŽIEDĖLIS, SIMAS. The story of St. Francis
        Lithuanian Parish.... Lawrence, 1953.
Pp. 416. MB.
        In English and Lithuanian.

8652   TEWKSBURY, ROBERT HASKELL. Historical
        sketch, the fall of Pemberton Mill on the
tenth of January, 1860 at Lawrence, Massachusetts...
forty years after the occurence and verified by
testimony and records. n.p., 1900. Pp. 12.
MSaE.

8653   TYLER, ROBERT L. "The Lawrence Strike of
        1912: a view of textiles and labor fifty
years ago." CottHR, 2 (1961), 123-131.

8654   VORSE, MARY MARVIN HEATON. A footnote to
        folly: reminiscences of Mary Heaton Vorse.
N.Y.: Farrar & Rinehart, 1935. Pp. viii, 407.
        Strike of 1912.

8655   WADSWORTH, HORACE ANDREW, comp. History of
        Lawrence, Massachusetts, with portraits and
biographical sketches of ex-mayors up to 1880 and
other distinguished citizens.... Lawrence: H.
Reed, 1880. Pp. v, 179.
        First issued in 1878 with title: Quarter
        centennial history of Lawrence, Massachu-
        setts.

8656   WHITING, LYMAN. A sermon preached at the
        dedication of the meeting-house of the Law-
rence Street Congregational Society, Lawrence, Oct.
11, 1848, with historical notices of the church
and society. Lawrence: Hayes, 1849. Pp. 16. MB.

8657   WILLIAMS, ROY FOSTER. "Pacific Mills fin-
        ishes its first century." Industry, 15
(March, 1950), 24e-24g, 38, 40, 42.

8658   YOUNG, GEORGE H. "The city of Lawrence,
        Massachusetts." NEM, New Ser., 17 (1897-
1898), 581-597.

LEE

8659 ASHE, SYDNEY WHITMORE. Early paper makers
of Lee: a radio talk...over station WGY,
Schenectady, April 20, 1929. Lee: Smith Paper,
[1929?]. Unpaged. MPB.

8660 "EARLY papermaking in East Lee, Mass." Superior Facts, 2 (February, 1929), 1-4, 6, 9.

8661 GALE, AMORY. History of the town of Lee,
Mass.: a lecture delivered before the Young
Men's Association of Lee, Mar. 22d, 1854. Lee:
French & Royce, 1854. Pp. 48.

8662 HYDE, ALVAN. A sermon occasioned by the
death of Mrs. Abigail Bassett, consort of
Mr. Cornelius Bassett, Jun. who died, at Lee, Massachusetts, Dec. 8th, 1812, in the 54th year of her
age; with an appendix, containing a brief account
of three seasons of the revival of religion, in
Lee. Stockbridge, 1815. Pp. 20.
1792, 1800, 1806.

8663 HYDE, CHARLES MCEWEN and ALEXANDER HYDE,
comps. Lee: the centennial celebration,
and centennial history of the town of Lee, Mass.
Springfield: C. W. Bryan, 1878. Pp. iv, 352.

8664 LEE, MASS. Records of the town of Lee from
its incorporation to A. D. 1801; all the
extant records of the town clerks, town treasurers,
Hopland School District and Congregational Church
for that period; also inscriptions from the cemeteries, with an appendix containing a brief account
of the town's incorporation, state and county taxes,
and other matters relating to the early history of
the town. Dorvil Miller Wilcox, ed. Lee: The
Valley Gleaner, 1900. Pp. 374.

8665 _____. Vital records of Lee, Massachusetts,
1777-1801, from the records of the town,
Congregational Church and inscriptions in the early
burial grounds; all the family birth records continued beyond 1801 given as fully as recorded; containing also the baptisms and names of church members in the records of the Congregational Church
from its organization in 1780 to 1801. Dorvil Miller Wilcox, ed. Lee: The Valley Gleaner, 1899.
Pp. vii, 108.

8666 LEE, MASS. FIRST CONGREGATIONAL CHURCH.
Historical address delivered by Rev. Nahum
Gale...at the semi-centennial celebration of the
Congregational Sunday School, Lee, December 23,
1869, with the other exercises. Lee: J. A. Royce,
1870. Pp. 41.

8667 _____. One hundred and fiftieth anniversary
of the founding of the First Congregational
Church, Lee, Massachusetts. Pittsfield: Sun Printing, 1931. Pp. 61.

8668 "PAPER making in South Lee, Mass." Superior
Facts, 2 (January, 1929), 1-5, 9.

8669 "PAPERMAKING in Lee Village." Superior
Facts, 2 (March, 1929), 1-4, 8-11.

8670 SCULL, PENROSE. Papermaking in the Berkshires, the story of the Hurlbut Paper Company published in commemoration of the one hundred
and fiftieth anniversary of the founding of the
company in April, 1806. South Lee: Hurlbut Paper
Company, [1956?]. Pp. 39. MPB.

LEICESTER

8671 [BURNETT, MAUD KNOWLTON], ed. Handbook of
historical data concerning Leicester, Massachusetts.... Spencer: W. J. Heffernan, 1912.
Pp. 34.

8672 CHADWICK, JOHN WHITE. "The town of Leicester, Massachusetts." NEM, New Ser., 22
(1900), 349-368.

8673 CHENOWETH, CAROLINE VAN DUSEN. History of
the Second Congregational Church and Society
in Leicester, Massachusetts.... [Worcester], 1908.
Pp. vii, 199.

8674 COOLEY, BENJAMIN FRANKLIN. Rochdale jubilee,
1823-1873, historical sermon. Worcester:
Fiske, 1873. Pp. 19.

8675 COOLIDGE, AMOS HILL. The religious history
of the First Congregational Church in Leicester, a sermon...April 24, 1887. Worcester: C. Hamilton, 1887. Pp. 32.

8676 GREENVILLE BAPTIST CHURCH, LEICESTER, MASS.
The Greenville Baptist Church in Leicester,
Massachusetts: exercises on the 150th anniversary
of its formation, September 28, 1888, including a
historical discourse by the pastor [H. C. Estes] and
addresses commemorative of its first pastor, Rev.
Thomas Green, M.D. Worcester: C. F. Lawrence,
1889. Pp. 126.

8677 "HISTORY of Leicester." BBNL, 1 (1826), 294-
296.

8678 "HISTORY of Leicester Academy." American
Quarterly Register, 7 (1834-1835), 51-53.

8679 LADIES CHARITABLE SOCIETY, LEICESTER, MASS.
Celebration of the fiftieth anniversary of
the organization of the Ladies Charitable Society,
Leicester, Mass., Sept. 21, 1882. Worcester: C.
Hamilton, 1882. Pp. 28.

8680 LEICESTER, MASS. Celebration of the centennial anniversary of American independence,
at Leicester; July 4th, 1876. Worcester: C. Hamilton, 1876. Pp. 36.
Relates to the town.

8681 _____. Celebration of the one hundred and
fiftieth anniversary of the organization of
the town of Leicester, July 4, 1871. Cambridge:
J. Wilson & Son, 1871. Pp. 77.

8682 LEICESTER, MASS. SCHOOL COMMITTEE. Report
of the School Committee of the town of
Leicester for 1849-50 together with a historical

(LEICESTER, MASS. SCHOOL COMMITTEE.)
sketch of the district schools from the first settlement of the town. Worcester: Massachusetts
Spy, 1850. Pp. 34. M.

8683 LEICESTER ACADEMY. The centenary of Leicester Academy held September 4, 1884, including the historical address by Hon William W. Rice,
and the poem by Rev. Thomas Hill, D. D., with historical supplement. Worcester: C. Hamilton, 1884.
Pp. 113.

8684 _____. Festival at Leicester Academy, on
the seventy-first anniversary, August 7,
1855; with the address, by Rev. Alonzo Hill...and
the poem, by Isaac F. Shepard.... Worcester:
Fiske & Reynolds, 1885. Pp. 72.

8685 _____. Leicester Academy, 1784-1934, being
a record of the one hundred and fiftieth
anniversary exercises held at Smith Hall, Leicester, Massachusetts, September 4, 1934. Worcester:
Davis Pr., [1934?]. Pp. 99.

8686 MAY, SAMUEL. "Leicester Academy." Worcester HSProc, (1883), 77-87.

8687 [OLNEY, CATHERINE]. St. Thomas Episcopal
Church, Cherry Valley, Massachusetts.
[Leicester?, 1907?]. Pp. 20. MBNEH.
1873-1907; author attribution by the New
England Historic Genealogical Society.

8688 PEIRCE, JOSEPHINE H. "The American card-
clothing industry." CEAIA, 5 (1952), 40.
Began in Leicester.

8689 RUSSELL, JOHN EDWARDS. Oration delivered in
the Town Hall, Leicester, Mass., July 4th,
1876. Worcester: Charles Hamilton, 1876. Pp. 18.
Relates to the town.

8690 WASHBURN, EMORY. An address commemorative
of the part taken by the inhabitants of the
original town of Leicester, in the events of the
Revolution: delivered at Leicester, July 4, 1849.
Boston: C. C. P. Moody, 1849. Pp. 48.

8691 _____. Brief sketch of the history of
Leicester Academy, Pt. 1. Boston: Phillips,
Sampson, 1855. Pp. vii, 158.
No more published.

8692 _____. Historical sketches of the town of
Leicester, Massachusetts, during the first
century from its settlement. Boston: J. Wilson
and Son, 1860. Pp. 467.

8693 _____. "Topographical and historical
sketches of the town of Leicester." WMHJ,
2 (1826), 65-128.

8694 WRIGHT, LUTHER, 1796-1870. Education: an
address before the trustees and students of
Leicester Academy, convened to dedicate the new
edifice, Dec. 25, 1833, added, a concise history of
the institution. Worcester: S. H. Colton, 1834.
Pp. 35. MB.

8695 WROTH, L. KINVIN. "The Rev. Nathaniel Green
and the tax assessors: passive resistance in
eighteenth-century Massachusetts." NEG, 9 (Fall,
1967), 15-21.

LENOX

8696 BERKSHIRE MUSIC CENTER, STOCKBRIDGE, MASS.
A Tanglewood dream, the Berkshire Music Cen-
ter 25th anniversary album. Lenox: Koussevitzky
Music Foundation, 1965. Unpaged.

8697 COLTON, OLIVE A. Lenox. n.p., n.d. Pp. 48.
MPB.

8698 CURRY, ROBERT L. Lenox School: not to be
served but to serve. N.Y.: Newcomen Society
in North America, 1966. Pp. 24.

8699 HALL, WILLIAM. "Yokun: residence of the
Hon. Richard Goodman, Lenox, Berkshire County, Mass." Potter's AmMo, 13 (1879), 442-444.

8700 HIBBARD, GEORGE ABIAH. Lenox. N.Y.:
Charles Scribner's Sons, 1896. Pp. 54.

8701 _____. "Lenox." Scribner's Magazine, 16
(1894), 420-434.

8702 HOLLAND, JAMES R. Tanglewood. Barre:
Barre Publishers, 1973. Pp. 96.

8703 HOWE, MARK ANTONY DE WOLFE. The tale of
Tanglewood, scene of the Berkshire music festivals. N.Y.: Vanguard Pr., 1946. Pp. 101.

8704 LENOX, MASS. July 4, 1876! Centennial celebration at Lenox, Mass., historical address
by Julius Rockwell. Pittsfield: Chickering & Axtell, 1876. Pp. 41.

8705 LENOX, MASS. CONGREGATIONAL CHURCH. The
centennial anniversary of the dedication of
the old church on the hill, Lenox, Massachusetts,
June twelfth, nineteen hundred and six. Pittsfield:
Sun Printing 1908. Pp. 82.

8706 LENOX, MASS. LIBRARY ASSOCIATION. The second hundred years. n.p., [1963?]. Unpaged.
M.

8707 LENOX, MASS. TRINITY CHURCH. History of
Trinity Church, Lenox, Massachusetts, 1763-
1895. Cambridge: John Wilson & Son, 1895.
Pp. 54. MBNEH.

8708 LENOX ACADEMY. One hundredth anniversary of
the founding of Lenox Academy; an account of
the celebration and the day's doings; October first
nineteen hundred three. Pittsfield: Sun Printing,
1905. Pp. 76.

8709 LINCOLN, CHARLES M. "The summer colony at
Lenox." Munsey's Magazine, 17 (1897), 674-
680.

8710 LYNCH, FREDERICK. "The church on the Lenox hilltop and round about it." NEM, New Ser., 23 (1900-1901), 192-211.

8711 MACDONALD, HELEN and MARY MACDONALD. A history of the Lenox Library, written for its 100th anniversary. Lenox, 1956. Pp. 20. MB.

8712 MAHANNA, JOHN G. W. Music under the moon. A history of the Berkshire Symphonic Festival, Inc. Pittsfield: Eagle Printing, 1955. Pp. 123. M.

8713 MALLARY, RAYMOND DE WITT. Lenox and the Berkshire highlands. N.Y.: G. P. Putnam's Sons, 1902. Pp. xiii, 363.

8714 ____. "Lenox in literature." Critic, 41 (1902), 31-40.

8715 ____. "Picturesque Lenox." Independent, 55 (1903), 1328-1333.

8716 "THE OLD Lenox Academy." Berkshire Hills, 4 (1903-1904), 176.

8717 SHAKESPEARE CLUB, LENOX, MASS. Lenox, Massachusetts-bicentennial, 1767-1967, historical souvenir and official program. n.p., 1967. Pp. 42. M.

8718 WOOD, DAVID H. Lenox: Massachusetts shire town. Lenox: The Town, 1969. Pp. xiv, 219.

LEOMINSTER

8719 "CLUETT, Peabody & Company, Leominster." Industry, 3 (June, 1938), 5-7, 55. Arrow shirts.

8720 "E. I. du Pont de Nemours & Company, Doyle Works, Leominster." Industry, 4 (October, 1938), 7-10, 71. Plastics.

8721 EMERSON, WILLIAM ANDREW. Leominster, Massachusetts, historical and picturesque. Gardner: Lithotype Publishing, 1888. Pp. xv, 320.

8722 ____. Leominster traditions. Leominster, 1891. Pp. 99.

8723 "THE F. A. Whitney Carriage Company." Industry, 3 (July, 1938), 5-8. Baby carriages.

8724 FIELD, CALEB CLESSON. Statistics of comb-making in Leominster, 1852. Worcester: Franklin P. Rice, 1893. Pp. 14.

8725 HORTON, EDWARD AUGUSTUS. An historical address commemorating the semi-centennial anniversary, of the dedication of the 1st Congregational Meeting-House, in Leominster, delivered... Oct. 15, 1873. Leominster: Enterprise Office. Pp. 32.

8726 KEVILLE, JOHN J. "The history of plastics in Leominster." Industry, 33 (July, 1968), 15-16.

8727 LEOMINSTER, MASS. CENTRAL BAPTIST CHURCH. Manual...containing its covenant, articles of faith, by-laws and rules of order, together with an historical discourse...Dec. 23, 1874 by Rev. A. F. Mason, Pastor. Leominster: Enterprise Book & Job Office, 1875. Pp. 38. Semicentennial.

8728 LEOMINSTER, MASS. FIRST CONGREGATIONAL SOCIETY, UNITARIAN. First Congregational Society, Unitarian, two hundredth anniversary, September 19, 1943. n.p., [1943?]. Pp. 24. MWA.

8729 LEOMINSTER, MASS. ORTHODOX CONGREGATIONAL CHURCH. The statment of faith and covenant of the Orthodox Congregational Church, Leominister, with historical sketch, standing rules, lists of officers and living members, adopted 1877. Leominster: Enterprise Office, 1877. Pp. 31.

8730 LEOMINSTER, MASS. PUBLIC LIBRARY. A history of the Leominster Public Library.... Leominster, 1957. Pp. 28.

8731 LEOMINSTER, MASS. TWIN ANNIVERSARY GENERAL COMMITTEE. Souvenir brochure. [Leominster]: Laurier, 1965. Unpaged. M. Includes historical sketches.

8732 LEOMINSTER HISTORICAL SOCIETY. Leominster's contribution to the Massachusetts Bay Colony tercentenary and the 190th anniversary of the town. [Leominster, 1930?]. Unpaged. MBNEH.

8733 "LEOMINSTER, Mass." BBNL, 1 (1826), 38-40, 49-50.

8734 MILLER, G. W. "Leominster, city of shirts and baby carriages." National Magazine, 17 (1902-1903), 258-260.

8735 POPE, FRANK H. "Leominster's lesson to growing cities of Massachusetts." NEM, New Ser., 39 (1908-1909), 709-721.

8736 RICHARDSON, EDWARD ADAMS. Leominster, Massachusetts, July 4th and 5th, 1915, 175th anniversary souvenir. Leominster: Leominster Enterprise, 1915. Pp. 20. M.

8737 STEBBINS, RUFUS PHINEAS. A centennial discourse delivered to the First Congregational Church and Society in Leominster, September 24, 1843.... Boston: C. C. Little & J. Brown, 1843. Pp. 112.

8738 WALTON, PERRY, ed. Comb making in America, an account of the origin and development of the industry for which Leominster has become famous, to which are added pictures of many of the early comb makers and views of the old time comb shops, compiled...in commemoration of the one hundred and fiftieth anniversary of the founding of the comb industry in Leominster, Massachusetts. Boston, 1925. Pp. xiv, 158.

8739   WEISS, HARRY B. "Chapman Whitcomb, early
        American publisher and peddler of chap-
books." Book Collector's Packet, 3 (April, 1939),
1-3.
        Firm established in 1796.

8740   WHITNEY, F. A. CARRIAGE CO., LEOMINSTER,
        MASS. Chronicles of a baby carriage....
Leominster, 1923. Pp. 45. MH-BA.

8741   WILDER, DAVID. The history of Leominster,
        or the northern half of the Lancaster new or
additional grant, from June 26, 1701, the date of
the deed from George Tahanto, Indian sagamore, to
July 4, 1852. Fitchburg: Reveille Office, 1853.
Pp. 263.

LEVERETT

8742   BRAMLAGE, GEORGENE and WILLIAM BRAMLAGE.
        Leverett, the community. n.p., [1974?].
Pp. 44. M.

8743   EASTMAN, DAVID. "Brief history of the Con-
        gregational Church of Leverett." PVMA, 1
(1870-1879), 246-255.

8744   LEVERETT, MASS. BICENTENNIAL COMMITTEE. A
        history of Leverett, Massachusetts, 1774-
1974. Northampton: Gazette Printing, 1974.
Pp. 126. M.

8745   NEWTON, B. "History of the Baptist Church
        in North Leverett." PVMA, 1 (1870-1879),
255-271.

8746   WATSON, J. P. "Settlement of Leverett."
        PVMA, 1 (1870-1879), 229-246.

LEXINGTON

8747   ABERCROMBIE, JAMES. A British account of
        the Battle of Lexington; and the last meet-
ing in the Dowse Library at No. 30 Tremont St.,
Boston. n.p., [1897?]. Pp. 4.

8748   ADAMS, WILLIAM, 1807-1880. Sermon delivered
        ...in the town hall, Lexington, Sunday even-
ing, April 18, 1875, on the occasion of the centennial celebration of the Battle of Lexington. n.p.,
1875. Pp. 15.

8749   AYLMER, KEVIN J. "The banker and his bat-
        tle: Lexington, 1775." AHI, 8 (October,
1973), 10-17.
        Story of Harold Murdock's study of the
        Battle of Lexington.

8750   BACHELLER, CARRIE E. Munroe Tavern, the
        custodian's story. [Lexington: Lexington
Historical Society, 1925]. Pp. 32.

8751   BARRETT, ESTHER TIDD. "Growth of the Bap-
        tist Church." LexHSP, 4 (1905-1910), 164-
165.

8752   BLISS, EDWARD P. "The old taverns of Lexing-
        ton." LexHSP, 1 (1886-1889), 73-87.

8753   BROWN, FRANCIS H. "Recollections of the
        Third meetinghouse in Lexington, erected
1794." LexHSP, 3 (1900-1904), 82-94.

8754   BRYANT, ALBERT W. "The anti-Masonic move-
        ment, particularly in Lexington." LexHSP,
4 (1905-1910), 24-47.

8755   _____. "Lexington sixty years ago." LexHSP,
        2 (1890-1899), 19-64.

8756   _____. "The military organizations of Lex-
        ington." LexHSP, 2 (1890-1899), 85-98.

8757   _____. "The Munroe Tavern." LexHSP, 3
        (1900-1904), 142-154.

8758   CARY MEMORIAL LIBRARY, LEXINGTON, MASS. A
        century of service, 1868-1968. Lexington,
[1968?]. Unpaged.

8759   _____. Contemporary Lexington authors, cen-
        tennial year 1968-69. Lexington, [1969?].
29 leaves. MB.
        Centennial of the library.

8760   COBURN, FRANK WARREN. The battle of April
        19, 1775, in Lexington, Concord, Lincoln,
Arlington, Cambridge, Somerville and Charlestown,
Massachusetts. (1912) 2d. ed., rev. and with additions. Lexington: Lexington Historical Society,
1922. Pp. xxviii, 189.

8761   _____. The battle on Lexington Common, April
        19, 1775, consisting of an account of that
action, now first published and a reprint of my lecture entitled 'Fiction and truth about the battle
on Lexington common' published in 1918, also a complete roster of Captain John Parker's company; a
list of the seventy-seven men who were with him that
morning; and a list of the eight men who are known
to have returned the British fire. Lexington, 1921.
v.p.

8762   CUMINGS, HENRY. A sermon preached at Lexing-
        ton, on the 19th of April, 1781, being the
anniversary of the commencement of hostilities between Great-Britain and America, which took place
in that town, on the 19th of April, 1775. Boston:
Benjamin Edes & Sons, 1781. Pp. 39.

8763   DANA, RICHARD HENRY, 1815-1882. Oration at
        Lexington, April 19, 1875. Boston: Lock-
wood, Brooks, 1875. Pp. 19.

8764   DEANE, CHARLES, ed. "Letter of Paul Revere
        to Jeremy Belknap." MHSP, (1878), 370-376.
Battle of Lexington.

8765   EMMONS, WILLIAM. An address in commemoration
        of Lexington battle delivered April 19,
1826.... Boston, 1826. Pp. 16.

8766 [_____]. Emmons' oration on Lexington battle, delivered Apr. 19th, 1827. n.p.,
[182-?]. Pp. 7.
Author attribution by Harvard University
Library.

8767 EVERETT, EDWARD. An address, delivered at
Lexington, on the 19th (20th) April, 1835.
Charlestown: W. W. Wheildon, 1835. Pp. 66.

8768 FERNALD, HELEN CLARK. The Jonathan Harrington House. Lexington: Adams Pr., 1937.
Pp. ix, 61.

8769 _____. "Sketches of old Lexington." SWJ,
47 (1930), 329-349.

8770 GOODWIN, ALICE D. "Some memories of the
Baptist Church in Lexington." LexHSP, 4
(1905-1910), 158-163.

8771 GREELEY, WILLIAM ROGER. Notes on the history of the First Parish Church of Lexington,
1691-1941. [Lexington, 1941?]. Pp. 22.

8772 HARRINGTON, ELIZABETH W. "Clock making in
Lexington." LexHSP, 3 (1900-1904), 134-137.

8773 HOWELLS, WILLIAM DEAN. "Lexington." Long-
man's Magazine, 1 (1882-1883), 41-61.

8774 HUDSON, CHARLES. Abstract of the history of
Lexington, Mass., from its first settlement
to the centennial anniversary of the declaration of
our national independence, July 4, 1876. Boston:
T. R. Marvin & Son, 1876. Pp. 28.

8775 _____. Corrections and additions to the
History of Lexington. [Boston?, 1918].
Pp. 8.

8776 _____. History of the town of Lexington,
Middlesex County, Massachusetts, from its
first settlement to 1868...rev. and continued to
1912 by the Lexington Historical Society....
(1868) Boston: Houghton Mifflin, 1913. 2v.

8777 HUDSON, MARY E. "Early days of the Lexington High School." LexHSP, 3 (1900-1904),
117-133.

8778 _____. "Some memories of the Lexington centennial." LexHSP, 3 (1900-1904), 62-81.

8779 _____. "Work of Lexington women in the War
of the Rebellion." LexHSP, 2 (1890-1899),
197-214.

8780 LEXINGTON, MASS. 150th anniversary: Battle
of Lexington, April 19 and 20, 1925, 1775-
1925. Lexington, 1925. Pp. 24.

8781 _____. An oration delivered at Lexington on
the dedication of the Town and Memorial Hall,
April 19, 1871, being the 96th anniversary of the
Battle of Lexington, by Dr. George B. Loring, with
proceedings and a historical appendix. Boston:
T. R. Marvin & Son, 1871. Pp. 76.

8782 _____. Proceedings & addresses commemorative
of the two hundredth anniversary of the incorporation of the town of Lexington. Cambridge:
Riverside Pr., 1914. Pp. 36.

8783 _____. Proceedings at the centennial celebration of the Battle of Lexington, April
19, 1875. Lexington, 1875. Pp. 170.

8784 _____. Record of births, marriages, and
deaths to January 1, 1898.... Boston:
Wright & Potter, 1898. Pp. ix, 484.

8785 LEXINGTON, MASS. FIRST BAPTIST CHURCH.
Declaration of faith, with the church cove-
nant...constituted Dec. 11, 1833. Boston: J.
Howe, 1839. Pp. 25. M.
Includes brief history of the church.

8786 LEXINGTON. Boston: Edison Electric Illumi-
nation Co., 1909. Pp. 16. M.

8787 "LEXINGTON and the nineteenth of April, '75."
BBNL, 1 (1826), 265-269, 277-281, 289-294,
301-303.

8788 LEXINGTON SAVINGS BANK. A calender history
of Lexington, Massachusetts, 1620-1946,
issued by the Lexington Savings Bank in observance
of its seventy-fifth anniversary, 1871-1945. Lexington, 1946. Pp. 148.

8789 LOCKE, ALONZO E. "The early schools of Lexington." LexHSP, 4 (1905-1910), 5-13.

8790 MERRITT, ELIZABETH. "The Lexington alarm,
April 19, 1775: messages sent to the south-
ward after the battle." Maryland Historical Magazine, 41 (1946), 89-114.

8791 MUNROE, JAMES PHINNEY and E. S. CUMMINGS.
"Proceedings and addresses commemorative of
the two hundredth anniversary of the incorporation
of the town of Lexington." MagHist, 20 (1915),
199-221.

8792 MUNROE, JAMES PHINNEY. "Washington's dinner
at the Munroe Tavern." LexHSP, 1 (1886-1889),
xlix-lxii.

8793 MURDOCK, HAROLD. "Earl Percy's retreat to
Boston on the nineteenth of April, 1775."
CSMP, 24 (1920-1922), 257-292.
Hugh Percy.

8794 _____. "Historic doubts on the Battle of
Lexington." MHSP, 49 (1915-1916), 361-386.

8795 MUZZEY, ARTEMAS B. "Battle of Lexington."
Religious Magazine and Monthly Review, 45
(1871), 386-394.

8796 _____. "Battle of Lexington, with personal
recollections of men engaged in it." NEHGR,
31 (1877), 377-393.

8797 PAYSON, PHILLIPS. A memorial of Lexington battle, and of some signal interpositions of Providence in the American Revolution, a sermon preached at Lexington, on the nineteenth of April, 1782, the anniversary of the commencement of the war between Great-Britain and America, which opened in a most tragical scene, in that town, on the nineteenth of April, 1775. Boston: Benjamin Edes & Sons, 1782. Pp. 24.

8798 PHINNEY, ELIAS. History of the Battle at Lexington, on the morning of the 19th April, 1775. Boston: Phelps & Farnham, 1825. Pp. 40.

8799 PIPER, FRED SMITH. "Architectural yesterdays in Lexington: a fragmentary account of some of the older buildings and their builders." LexHSP, 4 (1905-1910), 114-126.

8800 _____. Lexington: the birthplace of American liberty; a handbook containing a brief summary of the events leading up to the outbreak of the American Revolution--Paul Revere's narrative of his famous ride--an account of the Battle of Lexington--a sketch of the town and the places of historic interest--inscriptions on all historic tablets--directory. (1902) 11th ed. Lexington: Lexington Historical Society, 1963. Pp. 60.

8801 PORTER, EDWARD GRIFFIN and H. M. STEPHENSON. Souvenir of Lexington, 1775-1875. Boston: J. R. Osgood, 1875. Pp. 16.
Battle.

8802 PULLEN, DORIS L. and DONALD B. COBB. The celebration of April the nineteenth from 1776 to 1960 in Lexington, Massachusetts, 'The birthplace of American liberty.' Lexington, 1960. Pp. 32.

8803 SAMPSON, WALTER. "Lexington in 1775 and in 1861." LexHSP, 1 (1886-1889), 117-128.

8804 SCHEIDE, JOHN HINSDALE. "The Lexington alarm." AASP, 50 (1940), 49-79.

8805 SCOTT, A. E. "Lexington Academy." LexHSP, 1 (1886-1889), 88-94.

8806 _____. "Origin of the name Lexington." LexHSP, 1 (1886-1889), 9-15.

8807 SCOTT, OTTO J. The creative ordeal; the story of Raytheon. N.Y.: Atheneum, 1974. Pp. 429.

8808 "THE second meeting-house in Lexington, erected by the town in 1714." LexHSP, 1 (1890), 129-130.

8809 SMITH, A. BRADFORD. "History of the Stone Building." LexHSP, 2 (1890-1899), 144-157.

8810 _____. "Kite End." LexHSP, 2 (1890-1899), 99-122.
Part of the 'south district' of Lexington.

8811 SMITH, GEORGE O. "The milk business and milk men of earlier days." LexHSP, 2 (1890-1899), 187-196.

8812 _____. "Reminiscences of the fur industry." LexHSP, 2 (1890-1899), 171-186.

8813 "SOME facts relating to the third meeting house in Lexington." LexHSP, 1 (1886-1889), 130-137.

8814 STAPLES, CARLTON ALBERT. "Early schools and school-masters." LexHSP, 2 (1890-1899), 158-170.

8815 _____. "The first English proprietors of the site of Lexington Village." LexHSP, 2 (1890-1899), 5-18.

8816 _____. "The parish of Cambridge Farms." LexHSP, 3 (1900-1904), 25-41.
Congregational church.

8817 _____. "A sketch of the history of Lexington Common." LexHSP, 1 (1886-1889), 17-37.

8818 _____. Two old time ministers of Lexington. n.p., n.d. Pp. 18. MBNEH.
Jonas Clark and John Hancock.

8819 _____. "Washington's visit to Lexington." LexHSP, 1 (1886-1889), xxxiii-xlix.

8820 STARBUCK, ALEXANDER. "The first normal school in America." NHAP, (1909), 41-57.
Lexington Normal School, 1839.

8821 TYLER, J. E. "An account of Lexington in the Rockingham Mss. at Sheffield." WMQ, 3 Ser., 10 (1953), 98-107.
Battle; Lord Rockingham's papers are in the City Library, Sheffield, England.

8822 VILES, REBECCA. "Lexington Normal School." LexHSP, 1 (1886-1889), 95-100.

8823 WAITT, ERNEST . "How the news of the Battle of Lexington reached England." NEM, New Ser., 40 (1909), 92-97.

8824 WESTCOTT, HENRY. Lexington centennial sermons, delivered in the First Congregational Church, Lexington, Mass., April 11th, 18th and 25th, 1875. Boston: F. Wood, 1875. Pp. 53.

8825 WHITMORE, WILLIAM HENRY. "The origin of the name of the town of Lexington." MHSP, (1871-1873), 269-276.

8826 WILLIAMS, AVERY. A discourse delivered at Lexington, March 31, 1813, the day which completed a century from the incorporation of the town. Boston: Samuel T. Armstrong, 1813. Pp. 34.

8827 WINSLOW, JOHN. Battle of Lexington as looked at in London in the trial of John Horne for libel on the British government. N.Y., 1897. Pp. 39. MB.

8828 WINTHROP, ROBERT CHARLES. "Battle of Lexington." MHSP, (1858-1860), 22-25.
How the news reached England.

8829   WORTHEN, EDWIN B. A brief history of the
       Lexington Historical Society in observance
of its seventy-fifth anniversary, 1886-1961. Lexington: Lexington Historical Society, 1962.
Pp. 35.

LEYDEN

8830   ARMS, WILLIAM TYLER and MASHA E. ARMS. His-
       tory of Leyden, Massachusetts, 1676-1959.
Orange: Enterprise and Journal, 1959. Pp. 220.

LINCOLN

8831   ADAMS, CHARLES FRANCIS, 1835-1915. A mile-
       stone planted, address of Charles Francis
Adams at Lincoln, Massachusetts, April 23, 1904 on
the one hundred and fiftieth anniversary of the incorporation of the town. [Lincoln, 1904]. Pp. 137.

8832   FITCH, MARION and JANE POOR. Hartwell Farm.
       n.p., [between 1934 and 1968]. Unpaged.
MSaE.
       Historic house.

8833   HERSEY, FRANK WILSON CHENEY. Heroes of the
       battle road: a narrative of events in Lin-
coln on the 18th and 19th of April, 1775, wherein
are set forth the capture of Paul Revere, escape of
Samuel Prescott, heroism of Mary Hartwell, and
other stirring incidents. Boston: P. Walton, 1930.
Pp. 39.

8834   LINCOLN, MASS. An account of the celebration
       by the town of Lincoln, Massachusetts, April
23rd, 1904, of the 150th anniversary of its incorporation, 1754-1904. Lincoln, 1905. Pp. v, 239.

8835   _____. Dedication of the new Town House in
       Lincoln, Massachusetts, May 26, 1892....
Boston: T. R. Marvin & Son, 1893. Pp. 90.

8836   LINCOLN, MASS. FIRST CONGREGATIONAL CHURCH.
       Proceedings in observance of the one hundred
and fiftieth anniversary...of the organization of
the First Church in Lincoln, Mass., August 21 and
September 4, 1898. Cambridge: Univ. Pr., 1899.
Pp. 102.

8837   PORTER, EDWARD GRIFFIN. A sermon commemora-
       tive of one hundred and fifty years of the
First Church in Lincoln, Massachusetts, delivered
September 4, 1898, containing biographical sketches
of the pastors and some of the citizens of the town.
Cambridge: Univ. Pr., 1899. Pp. 48.

8838   RICHARDSON, HENRY JACKSON. Historical manu-
       al of the Church of Christ, Lincoln, Mass.
Boston: Tolman & White, 1872. Pp. 107. MBNEH.

LITTLETON

8839   CONANT, ALBERT FRANCIS. "History of Little-
       ton schools." Littleton HSP, No. 1,
(1894-1895), 49-62.

8840   FAIRFIELD, OLIVER JAY. The town of Little-
       ton, Massachusetts, past and present. Lit-
tleton: Littleton Improvement Society, 1914.
Pp. 16. M.

8841   FOSTER, EDMUND. The works of God declared
       by one generation to another: a sermon,
preached at Littleton, Dec. 4, 1815, on the completion of a century from the incorporation of that
town. Concord: Joseph T. Peters, 1815. Pp. 28.

8842   HARWOOD, HERBERT JOSEPH. "An incident of
       King Philip's War connected with this place."
Littleton HSP, No. 1 (1894-1895), 39-46.

8843   _____. "The Indians of Nashoba." Littleton
       HSP, No. 1 (1894-1895), 96-106.

8844   HARWOOD, LUCY M. "Recollections of Littleton
       about the year 1838." Littleton HSP, No. 2
(1906), [3-5].

8845   KIMBALL, JOHN A. "Old roads in Littleton."
       Littleton HSP, No. 2 (1906), [1-2].

8846   LITTLETON, MASS. Records of Littleton, Mas-
       sachusetts, first installment, births and
deaths from the earliest records in the town books
begun in 1715.... J. A. Harwood, comp. Littleton,
1900. Pp. 542, 178.
       Index of places and persons.

8847   LITTLETON, MASS. LYCEUM. Semi-centennial,
       proceedings on the fiftieth anniversary of
the organization of the Littleton Lyceum, Tuesday,
Dec. 23, 1879, consisting of historical address by
Miss H. P. Hodge of Littleton.... Boston: Conant
& Newhall, 1881. Pp. 36.

8848   "LITTLETON, Mass." BBNL, 1 (1826), 97-100.

8849   PRIEST, FRANK BIGELOW. "The Garrison House
       at Nashoba." Littleton HSP, No. 1 (1894-
1895), 20-22.

8850   SANDERSON, GEORGE W. "Some reminiscences of
       seventy years." Littleton HSP, No. 3 (1908),
3-7.

LONGMEADOW

8851   BLISS, JULIA M. "Two centuries and a half
       in Longmeadow." NEM, New Ser., 18 (1898),
582-599.

8852   _____. Longmeadow's sesquicentennial offi-
       cial souvenir; published in connection with
the 150th anniversary of the founding of the town
of Longmeadow, Massachusetts.... Edgar Holmes
Plummer, ed. [Longmeadow]: Longmeadow 150th Anniversary Association, [1933]. Unpaged.

8853   _____. Proceedings at the centennial cele-
       bration of the incorporation of the town of
Longmeadow, October 17th, 1883, with numerous historical appendices and a town genealogy.... Richard
S. Storrs and John W. Harding, eds. [Longmeadow],
1884. Pp. 321, 97.

LOWELL

8854 ALLEN, NATHAN. "Health of Lowell." ORHAL, 3 (1884-1887), 145-158.

8855 ANDERSON, EVELYN C. "The mills of Lowell." Lowell HSC, 2 (1921-1926), 275-279.

8856 APPLETON, NATHAN, 1779-1861 and JOHN AMORY LOWELL. Correspondence between Nathan Appleton and John A. Lowell in relation to the early history of the city of Lowell. Boston: Eastburn's Pr., 1848. Pp. 19.

8857 APPLETON, NATHAN, 1779-1861. Introduction of the power loom, and origin of Lowell. Lowell: B. H. Penhallow, 1858. Pp. v, 36.

8858 BARROWS, CHARLES DANA. Sermon delivered at Kirk St. Congregational Church, Lowell, Mass., June 13, 1875, the thirtieth anniversary of the organization of the church. Lowell: Stone, Huse, 1875. Pp. 24.

8859 BAYLES, JAMES. "The American Venice: some account of the rivers, canals and bridges of Lowell." ORHAL, 4 (1888-1891), 182-191.

8860 [_____]. Lowell: past, present and prospective. Lowell: Citizen Newspaper, 1891. Pp. 74.

8861 BETTS, L. W. "Lowell, the city of spindles." Outlook, 69 (1901), 373-378.

8862 BOURBONNIÈRE, AVILA, ed. Les canadiens-français de Lowell, Mass.; recensement, valeur commerciale, valeur immobilière, condition religieuse, civile, et politique, noms et adresses, suivis de la constitution et des reglements de L'Union Franco-américaine. Lowell, 1896. Pp. 192.

8863 CADDELL, ALDRED M. "The Lowell High School, its history, and the history its boys and girls have made." Lowell HSC, 1 (1907-1913), 129-134.

8864 CARNEY, GEORGE J. "The semi-centennial history of the Lowell Institution for Savings." ORHAL, 1 (1874-1879), 386-393.

8865 CARY, THOMAS GREAVES. Profits on manufactures at Lowell, a letter from the treasurer of a corporation to John S. Pendleton, esq., Virginia. Boston: C. C. Little & J. Brown, 1845. Pp. 23.

8866 "A CENTURY of Lowell." Putnam's HM, 1 (1892-1893), 91-95.
Textiles.

8867 "A CENTURY of machine knife manufacturing." Industry, 13 (August, 1948), 25-26.
D. Lovejoy & Son.

8868 CHADBOURNE, ROBERT A. "America's oldest shirt maker." Industry, 18 (April, 1953), 13-16.
C. F. Hathaway Company.

8869 CHAMBRÉ, ALBERT ST. JOHN. Historical sermon, delivered in Saint Anne's Church, Lowell, Mass...March 15, 1885, in commemoration of the sixtieth anniversary of the consecration, March 16, 1825. Boston: The Vestry, 1885. Pp. 23.

8870 CHASE, C. C. "Brief biographical notices of the prominent citizens of the town of Lowell--1826 to 1836." ORHAL, 4 (1888-1891), 293-325.

8871 _____. "Lives of postmasters." ORHAL, 4 (1888-1891), 128-141.

8872 _____. "Reminiscences of the high school." ORHAL, 3 (1884-1887), 113-144.

8873 CLARK, EDWIN R. "Early locomotive building in Lowell, Mass." RLHSB, No. 7 (1924), 25-57.

8874 CLÉMENT, ANTOINE, ed. L'Alliance Française de Lowell. Manchester, N.H.: L'Avenir National, 1937. Pp. 301.

8875 _____. L'Alliance française de Lowell, 1937-1948. Manchester, N.H.: L'Avenir National, 1948. Pp. 294.

8876 COBURN, FREDERICK WILLIAM. History of Lowell and its people. N.Y.: Lewis Historical Publishing, 1920. 3v.

8877 CONKLIN, HAROLD P. "The Lowell High School and the history its boys and girls have made." Lowell HSC, 1 (1907-1913), 135-139.

8878 COOLIDGE, JOHN PHILLIPS. Mill and mansion: a study of architecture and society in Lowell, Massachusetts, 1839-1865. N.Y.: Columbia Univ. Pr., 1942. Pp. xi, 261.

8879 COWLEY, CHARLES. "Foreign colonies of Lowell." ORHAL, 2 (1880-1883), 163-179.

8880 _____. A history of Lowell. (1856) 2d. rev. ed. Boston: Lee & Shepard, 1868. Pp. 235.
First edition has title: A handbook of business in Lowell, with a history of the city; also issued in 1868 with title: Illustrated history of Lowell.

8881 _____. "Lowell in the navy during the war." ORHAL, 5 (1894), 294-308.
Biographies; Civil War.

8882 _____. Memories of the Indians and pioneers of the region of Lowell. Lowell: Stone & Huse, 1862. Pp. 24.
Pennacook Indians.

8883 _____. "Public monuments of Lowell." ORHAL, 6 (1896-1904), 98-112.

8884 CUYLER, THEODORE LEDYARD. "A day at Lowell." Godey's Magazine and Lady's Book, 33 (1846), 183-184.

8885   DAVID, PAUL A. "The 'Horndal Effect' in
        Lowell 1834-1856: a short run learning curve
for integrated cotton textile mills." EEH, 2 Ser.,
10 (1972-1973), 131-150.
        Growth of productivity.

8886   DORCHESTER, DANIEL. An historical sketch of
        the formation and progress of St. Paul's
Church; it being the first Methodist Episcopal
Church in Lowell, Mass. Boston: Geo. C. Rand &
Avery, 1866. Pp. 92.
        Includes statistics.

8887   EDSON, THEODORE. The commemoration of the
        40th anniversary of the consecration of St.
Anne's Church, Lowell, March 19, 1865, the ser-
mon...and the proceedings of the vestry. Lowell:
James, 1865. Pp. 27.

8888   _____. Historical discourse on the occasion
        of the fiftieth anniversary of the first in-
troduction of stated public worship into the village of East Chelmsford, now the City of Lowell...
given...March 8, 1874. Lowell: Marden & Rowell,
1874. Pp. 48.

8889   _____. A sermon, delivered in St. Anne's
        Church, Lowell, Sunday, March 18, 1855, in
commemoration of the thirtieth anniversary of the
consecration of said church. Lowell: B. C. Sar-
geant, 1855. Pp. 24.

8890   ENO, ARTHUR LOUIS. Les avocats franco-
        americains de Lowell, Massachusetts, 1886-
1936. Lowell: Eno Printing, 1936. Pp. 52.

8891   FAY, SAMUEL. "Carpet weaving and the Lowell
        Manufacturing Company." ORHAL, 1 (1874-
1879), 52-61.

8892   FELLOWS, J. K. "Insurance in Lowell."
        ORHAL, 2 (1880-1883), 133-151.

8893   FOSTER, EDNA H. "The old Bay State in a
        retrospect glance: the Commonwealth of Mas-
sachusetts reviews its social, economic and educational progress--how the city of Lowell contributed to advancement by its manufactures, banks
and the experimentation of one of the first high
schools in the United States." National Magazine,
58 (1930), 364-366.

8894   FREEMASONS. LOWELL, MASS. PILGRIM COM-
        MANDERY. NO. 9. KNIGHTS TEMPLARS. Semi-
centennial...1855-1905. n.p., [1905?]. Pp. 75.
MBNEH.

8895   GIBB, GEORGE SWEET. "Three early railroad
        equipment contracts." BBHS, 21 (1947), 10-
17.
        Locks and Canals Co. as a builder of loco-
motives.

8896   GILMAN, ALFRED. "History of Lowell grammar
        schools." ORHAL, 4 (1888-1891), 87-109.

8897   _____. "The newspaper press of Lowell."
        ORHAL, 2 (1880-1883), 233-267.

8898   _____. "Reminiscences of an ex-postmaster."
        ORHAL, 4 (1888-1891), 142-150.

8899   GRIFFIN, SARA SWAN. "Old homes and historic
        byways of Lowell." Lowell HSC, 1 (1907-
1913), 451-466.

8900   _____. Quaint bits of Lowell history: a
        few interesting stories of earlier days.
Lowell: Butterfield, 1913. Pp. 112.

8901   GROVER, WALTER, B. "The American Hide and
        Leather Company." Industry, 6 (January,
1941), 9-12, 67-69.

8902   HADLEY, SAMUEL P. "Boyhood reminiscences of
        Middlesex Village." Lowell HSC, 1 (1907-
1913), 180-205.

8903   _____. "Early legislation relating to Lowell
        and vicinity." Lowell HSC, 2 (1921-1926),
228-238.

8904   _____. and MABEL HILL. "Lowell: a character
        sketch of the city." NEM, New Ser., 19
(1898-1899), 625-646.

8905   HADLEY, SAMUEL P. "Personal reminiscences of
        Lowell, fifty years ago." ORHAL, 5 (1894),
277-293.

8906   _____. "Reminiscences of Lowell book-
        sellers." Lowell HSC, 2 (1921-1926), 285-
298.

8907   HEDRICK, GEORGE. "Reminiscences, and recol-
        lections of Lowell." ORHAL, 1 (1874-1879),
253-372.

8908   HILL, FRANK PIERCE, comp. and ed. Lowell
        illustrated: a chronological record of
events and historical sketches of the large manufacturing corporations. Lowell, 1884. 92 leaves.

8909   HORWITZ, RICHARD P. "Architecture and cul-
        ture: the meaning of the Lowell boarding
house." AmQ, 25 (1973), 64-82.

8910   HOVEY, CHARLES. "Discount banks of Lowell."
        ORHAL, 3 (1884-1887), 258-269.

8911   _____. "Early trade and traders of Lowell."
        ORHAL, 2 (1880-1883), 152-164.

8912   _____. "History of an old firm." ORHAL, 1
        (1874-1879), 235-242.
        Carleton Apothecary.

8913   _____. "History of St. Anne's Church, Low-
        ell." ORHAL, 3 (1884-1887), 309-323.

8914   _____. "Organized charities of Lowell."
        ORHAL, 3 (1884-1887), 13-19.

8915   _____. "The Wyman Farm and its owner."
        ORHAL, 2 (1880-1883), 83-91.

8916   ILLUSTRATED history of Lowell and vicinity,
        Massachusetts: done by divers hands....
Lowell: Courier-Citizen, 1897. Pp. 881.

8917 IN and about Lowell. Lowell: Nelson's Colonial Department Store, 1908. Unpaged.

8918 JOSEPHSON, HANNAH GEFFEN. The golden threads; New England's mill girls and magnates. N.Y.: Duell, Sloan and Pearce, 1949. Pp. ix, 325.

8919 KENNGOTT, GEORGE FREDERICK. The record of a city: a social survey of Lowell, Massachusetts. N.Y.: Macmillan, 1912. Pp. xiv, 257.

8920 KOPYCINSKI, JOSEPH V. "Early history of the Locks and Canals Corporation." Towpath Topics, 5 (November, 1967), [3-4].
       Water supply.

8921 LARCOM, LUCY. "American factory life--past, present, and future." Journal of Social Science, No. 16 (1882), 141-146.

8922 _____. "Among Lowell mill-girls: a reminiscence." Atlantic, 48 (1881), 593-612.

8923 LAWSON, T. B. "Lowell and Newburyport." ORHAL, 1 (1874-1879), 212-228.

8924 LINCOLN, VARNUM. "My schools and teachers in Lowell sixty years ago." ORHAL, 5 (1894), 125-146.

8925 LOWELL, MASS. Exercises at the seventy-fifth anniversary of the incorporation of the town of Lowell, Friday, the first day of March, nineteen hundred and one. Lowell: Courier-Citizen, 1901. Pp. 62. M.
       Addresses by Solon Ward Stevens and Francis Cabot Lowell.

8926 _____. Exercises of the fiftieth anniversary commemorative of the incorporation of the city of Lowell, Thursday, April 1, 1886. Lowell: S. W. Huse, 1886. Pp. 107.

8927 _____. Proceedings in the city of Lowell at the centennial observance of the incorporation of the town of Lowell, Massachusetts, March 1st, 1926. [Lowell], 1926. Pp. 88.

8928 _____. Proceedings in the city of Lowell at the semi-centennial celebration of the incorporation of the town of Lowell, March 1st, 1876. Lowell: Penhallow, 1876. Pp. 151, 11.

8929 LOWELL, MASS. BOARD OF TRADE. City of Lowell, Massachusetts, its manufacturing interests and business advantages, review of board of trade work, description of Textile School and its work. [Lowell], 1902. Pp. 136.

8930 LOWELL, MASS. ELIOT CHURCH. The semi-centennial volume of the Eliot Church, Lowell, Mass., containing a sermon from each pastor, papers and letters furnished for the jubilee celebration, confessions of faith, etc. John M. Greene, ed. Lowell: Huse, Goodwin, 1881. Pp. 351.

8931 LOWELL, MASS. FIRST BAPTIST CHURCH. Jubilee exercises...fiftieth anniversary... February 8, 1876. Lowell: Marden & Rowell, 1876. Pp. 69. M.
       Sermon by Daniel Clarke Eddy.

8932 LOWELL, MASS. FIRST CONGREGATIONAL CHURCH. Semi-centennial of the First Congregational Church, Lowell, Mass., Tuesday, June 6th, 1876. Lowell: Stone, Huse, 1876. Pp. 72.

8933 LOWELL, MASS. FIRST UNITARIAN SOCIETY. Exercises, 75th anniversary, First Unitarian Society...September 25-26, 1904. Lowell: Butterfield Pr., 1904. Pp. 54. MBNEH.

8934 _____. Semi-centennial anniversary of the South Congregational Society (Unitarian), in Lowell, Friday, Sept. 26, 1879. Lowell: Huse, Goodwin, 1880. Pp. 122.

8935 LOWELL, MASS. FIRST UNIVERSALIST CHURCH. Commemoration of the fortieth anniversary of the dedication of the First Universalist Church, Lowell, Mass., December 25th, 1868. Lowell: Knapp & Morey, 1869. Pp. 42.

8936 LOWELL, MASS. JOHN STREET CONGREGATIONAL CHURCH. Fortieth anniversary, Lowell, Mass., May 9th and 11th, 1879. Lowell: Huse, Goodwin, 1879. Pp. 54.

8937 _____. Observance of its semi-centennial anniversary, May 9 and 12, 1889. Lowell: S. W. Huse, 1889. Pp. 26. M.

8938 LOWELL, MASS. TRADES AND LABOR COUNCIL. Lowell, a city of spindles: being a series of illustrated historical articles pertaining to the social and industrial growth of Lowell, with a compilation of the laws relating to labor. Lowell: Lawler & Company, 1900. Pp. 456.

8939 "LOWELL." BSM, 1 (1884), 161-200.

8940 "LOWELL and its manufactures." Merchants' Magazine, 16 (1847), 356-362.

8941 LOWELL BAR ASSOCIATION. 125th anniversary of District Court of Lowell, Lowell, Massachusetts, 1833-1958. Lowell, 1958. Pp. 20.

8942 THE LOWELL book. Boston: George H. Ellis, 1899. Pp. 52.
       Collection of descriptive essays.

8943 LOWELL HOSPITAL. Report of the Lowell Hospital, from 1840 to 1849, made to the trustees, June 12th, 1849, by Gilman Kimball. Lowell, 1849. Pp. 16.

8944 LOWELL INSTITUTION FOR SAVINGS. At the 'Meeting of the waters,' a sketch of Lowell life from the discovery of the Merrimack to the present day, 1829-1929. Lowell, 1929. Pp. 32.

8945 _____. Four score and ten years of the Lowell Institution for Savings.... Lowell, 1919. Pp. 33. M.

8946 MACBRAYNE, LEWIS E. "Lowell, a city of industry." National Magazine, 17 (1902-1903), 113-118.

8947 MCCLINTOCK, JOHN N. "Lowell." Granite Mo, 9 (1886), 299-338.

8948 MACDONALD, ALLAN. "Lowell: a commercial utopia." NEQ, 10 (1937), 37-62.

8949 MASSACHUSETTS INSTITUTE OF TECHNOLOGY. DE-PARTMENT OF ENGLISH AND HISTORY. Lowell, an early American industrial community.... Lynwood S. Bryant and John B. Rae, comps. Cambridge: Technology Pr., 1950. Pp. 306.

8950 "THE MAYORS of Lowell." ORHAL, 1 (1871-1879), 137-187.

8951 MERRILL, GILBERT R. "History of the Lowell Technological Institute." TextHR, 3 (1962), 82-96.

8952 MERRILL, JOSHUA. "School District No. 5 and my connection with it." ORHAL, 1 (1874-1879), 25-41.

8953 MERRILL, LOUIS TAYLOR. "Mill town on the Merrimack." NEQ, 19 (1946), 19-31.

8954 MESERVE, HARRY CHAMBERLAIN. Lowell--an industrial dream come true. Boston: National Association of Cotton Manufacturers, 1923. Pp. 126.

8955 METCALF, H. H. "New Hampshire men in Lowell." Granite Mo, 5 (1882), 273-275, 303-308, 324-327.
Biographies.

8956 MILES, HENRY ADOLPHUS. A glance at our history, prospects and duties, a Thanksgiving discourse preached in the South Congregational Church, Lowell, November 30, 1843. Lowell: Stearns and Taylor, 1844. Pp. 16. MB.
Relates to the city.

8957 _____. Lowell, as it was, and as it is. (1845) 2d. ed. Lowell: N. L. Dayton, 1847. Pp. 234.

8958 MOUSSET, PAUL. "Un îlot de vieille France en Nouvelle-Angleterre." France Illustration, No. 384 (February 21, 1953), 249-252.

8959 O'DWYER, GEORGE F. Irish Catholic genesis of Lowell. Lowell: Sullivan Bros., 1920. Unpaged.

8960 _____. "Lowell's first schools." United States Catholic Historical Society Records and Studies, 21 (1932), 235-238.

8961 ORDWAY, H. M. "The drama in Lowell, with a short sketch of the life of Perez Fuller." OHRAL, 2 (1880-1883), 268-288.

8962 _____. "The first Burns celebration in Lowell." ORHAL, 3 (1884-1887), 42-46.
Scottish population.

8963 PARKER, MARGARET TERRELL. Lowell: a study of industrial development. N.Y.: Macmillan, 1940. Pp. xii, 238.

8964 PERHAM, HENRY S. "The early settlers of that part of Chelmsford now Lowell." ORHAL, 5 (1894), 57-82.

8965 _____. "The folks at the Neck (now Lowell) in ye olden time." ORHAL, 6 (1896-1904), 234-251.

8966 PEVEY, SUSAN RICHARDSON. "Reminiscences of Middlesex Village." Canal News, 1 (October, 1963), [2, 4].

8967 ROBINSON, HARRIET JANE HANSON. "The life of the early mill girls." Journal of Social Science, No. 16 (1882), 127-140.
1832-1848.

8968 _____. Loom and spindle: or life among the early mill girls, with a sketch of the 'Lowell Offering' and some of its contributors. N.Y.: T. Y. Crowell, 1898. Pp. vii, 216.

8969 _____. "The Lowell Offering." NEM, New Ser., 1 (1889-1890), 461-467.
Periodical.

8970 ROBINSON, JOHN P. "The Melvin suits." ORHAL, 2 (1880-1883), 201-205.
Proprietors of Locks and Canals on Merrimack River vs. Melvin family, 1832-1849.

8971 ROELKER, WILLIAM GREENE. The Abbotts of Lowell, Massachusetts, in the Civil War, read as a lecture before the Lowell Historical Society at its annual meeting, February 12th, 1941. Lowell: Lowell Historical Society, 1941. Pp. 12.

8972 ROSEN, GEORGE. "The medical aspects of the controversy over factory conditions in New England, 1840-1850." BHistMed, 15 (1944), 483-497.

8973 RUSSELL, JAMES S. "The Lowell Cemetery." ORHAL, 4 (1888-1891), 272-281.

8974 _____. "Reminiscences of the Lowell High School." ORHAL, 2 (1880-1883), 12-32.

8975 _____. "Residences on Nesmith Street." ORHAL, 4 (1888-1891), 352-358.

8976 _____. "St. Luke's Episcopal Church in Lowell." ORHAL, 5 (1894), 159-164.

8977 SANTERRE, RICHARD. Centenaire de la Fête Saint-Jean-Baptiste à Lowell Massachusetts. n.p., [1968?]. Pp. 36. MeU.

8978 _____. The Franco-Americans of Lowell, Massachusetts. Lowell: Franco-American Day Committee, 1972. Unpaged.

8979 _____. [Marist Brothers in Lowell.] n.p., [1967?]. Unpaged. MeU.

8980 SARGENT, GEORGE HENRY. "The beginning of the house organ." Antiques, 7 (1925), 260-262.
'The Lowell Offering,' 1840.

8981 SCORESBY, WILLIAM. American factories and their female operatives; with an appeal on behalf of the British factory population.... London: Longmans, Brown, Green & Longmans, 1845. Pp. viii, 122.
Primarily conditions in Lowell.

8982 "SKETCH of the town of Lowell." BBNL, 1 (1826), 157-160.

8983 STEVENS, SOLON WARD. "A local musical society of 1824." ORHAL, 4 (1888-1891), 24-33.
Beethoven Musical Society.

8984 STONE, ZINA EUGENE. "The families living in East Chelmsford (or 'Chelmsford Neck,' now Lowell) in 1802." ORHAL, 1 (1874-1879), 275-284.

8985 ____. "Gen. Jackson in Lowell." ORHAL, 1 (1874-1879), 105-135.
1833.

8986 ____. "Introduction of the telegraph, the telephone, and the daguerreotype into Lowell." ORHAL, 5 (1894), 165-188.

8987 ____. "Lowell's once-popular newspaper, 'Vox Populi'--1841-1896, its rise, progress and decline, with biographical sketches of those who were prominently connected with it during its more than fifty-four years of life." ORHAL, 6 (1896-1904), 172-206.

8988 ____. "Masonic events in the early days of Lowell." ORHAL, 5 (1894), 223-226.

8989 ____. "The Old Residents' Historical Association: its origin and its history for twenty-five years." ORHAL, 5 (1894), 337-365.

8990 THESSIAY, HELEN. "The streets of Lowell." Lowell HSC, 2 (1921-1926), 248-255.

8991 THOMAS, EDWARD W. "A retrospect of the early manufacturing in city of Lowell." Lowell HSC, 2 (1921-1926), 451-469.

8992 VARNUM, ATKINSON C. History of the Pawtucket Church and Society with reminiscences of pastors and founders, sketches of Congregational Churches in Lowell, and a brief outline of congregationalism. Lowell: Morning Mail, 1888. Pp. 195. MB.

8993 WALKER, BENJAMIN. "Early recollections of Lowell." ORHAL, 4 (1888-1891), 237-258.

8994 WALSH, LOUIS S. The early Irish Catholic schools of Lowell, Massachusetts, 1835-1852. Boston: T. A. Whalen, 1901. Pp. 20.

8995 WATERS, WILSON. Historical sketch of St. Anne's Church, Lowell, Massachusetts.... [Lowell]: Courier Citizen, 1925. Pp. 96. MBNEH.

8996 WATKINS, LURA WOODSIDE. "Bridges over the Merrimac at Lowell." Covered Bridge Topics, 29 (April, 1962), 1, 7-8, 11.

8997 WEBSTER, MARY A. "Reminiscences of Lowell High School." Lowell HSC, 2 (1921-1926), 108-123.

8998 WEBSTER, PRENTISS, ed. Story of the City Hall Commission...and Memorial Hall. Lowell: Citizen Newspaper, 1894. Pp. 233. MBNEH.
Includes the public library.

8999 WEISBERGER, BERNARD A. "The working ladies of Lowell." Am Heritage, 12 (February, 1961), 42-45, 83-90.

9000 WRIGHT, A. B. "Lowell in 1826." ORHAL, 3 (1884-1887), 402-434.

9001 WRIGHT, HELENA. "The uncommon mill girls of Lowell." History Today, 28 (1973), 10-19.

LUDLOW

9002 LUDLOW, MASS. FIRST CONGREGATIONAL CHURCH. Proceedings of the First Congregational Church in Ludlow, Mass. Ware: Charles Hamilton, 1851. Pp. 24. MS.
Early history of church.

9003 LUDLOW SAVINGS BANK. Seventy five years of savings banking, 1888-1963, Ludlow Savings Bank.... Ludlow, 1963. Unpaged. M.

9004 NOON, ALFRED, comp. The history of Ludlow, Massachusetts, with biographical sketches of leading citizens, reminiscences, genealogies, farm histories, and an account of the centennial celebration, June 17, 1874.... (1875) 2d. ed., rev. and enl. Springfield: Springfield Printing and Binding, 1912. Pp. xiv, 592.

LUNENBURG

9005 LUNENBURG, MASS. The early records of the town of Lunenberg, Massachusetts, including that part which is now Fitchburg; 1719-1764, a complete transcript of the town meetings and selectmen's records contained in the first two books of the general records of the town; also a copy of all the vital statistics of the town previous to the year 1764. Walter A. Davis, comp. Fitchburg, 1896. Pp. vi, 384.

9006 LUNENBURG, MASS. PROPRIETORS. The Proprietors' records of the town of Lunenburg, Massachusetts, including Fitchburg and a portion of Ashby, 1729-1833.... Walter A. Davis, comp. Fitchburg, 1897. Pp. x, 374.

9007 "TOPOGRAPHICAL and historical sketch of the town of Lunenburgh." MHSC, 2 Ser., 1 (1814), 181-184.

LYNN

9008 ADAMS, CHARLES. A discourse delivered at the First Methodist Church in Lynn, February 28, 1841, on occasion of the fiftieth anniversary of the establishment of the Methodist Church, in that town. Lynn: Perley & Stoneham, 1841. Pp. 36.

9009 ADAMS, IDA G. "New Hampshire Club in Lynn, Mass." Granite Mo, 38 (1906), 176-177.

9010 BARTON, WALTER. Historical address delivered on the occasion of the two hundred and fiftieth anniversary of the First Church of Christ, Lynn, Congregational Trinitarian, Thursday, June 8, 1882. Lynn: McCarty, 1882. Pp. 30.

9011 BETTS, L. W. "Lynn: a city by the sea." Outlook, 69 (1901), 207-211.

9012 BREED, WARREN MUDGE. "Banks and bankers of old Lynn." Lynn HSR, No. 20 (1916), 35-64.

9013 _____. "Some abandoned industries of Lynn." Lynn HSR, No. 14 (1910), 178-207.

9014 BUFFUM, CHARLES. "Reminiscences of a business life in Lynn." Lynn HSR, No. 12 (1908), 92-108.
    Shoes.

9015 BURRILL, ELLEN MUDGE. "The Burrill family of Lynn." Lynn HSR, No. 11, (1907), 64-109.

9016 _____. Essex Trust Company, Lynn, Massachusetts, 1814, 1914, an historical sketch of the bank, for its centennial year. Lynn, 1913. Pp. lxx.

9017 _____. "Lynn in our grandfathers' time." Lynn HSR, No. 21 (1917), 36-108.

9018 CARROLL, THOMAS. "A sketch of the leather and morocco business of Lynn, Massachusetts." Hide and Leather, (February 14, 1903), Supplement.

9019 CLARK, WILLIAM ROBINSON. A discourse on the formation and progress of the first Methodist Episcopal Church in Lynn, delivered on the Sabbath following the reopening of the church. Boston: Rand & Avery, 1859. Pp. 37.

9020 COOKE, PARSONS. A century of Puritanism, and a century of its opposites; with results contrasted to enforce Puritan principles, and to trace what is peculiar in the people of Lynn to what is peculiar in its history. Boston: S. K. Whipple, 1855. Pp. 444.

9021 COPELAND, AUGUSTA THOMAS. In commemoration of the 300th anniversary of the First Church of Christ in Lynn...June 5, 1932. Lynn, 1932. Pp. 43.

9022 CUMBLER, JOHN T. "Labor, capital, and community: the struggle for power." LabHist, 15 (1974), 395-415.
    Leather workers, 1890.

9023 DAY, A. F. "When streetcars were young." Railroad Magazine, 65 (November, 1954), 48-50, 52.

9024 DELNOW, MERRILL FILLMORE. "The Athenian Club." Lynn HSR, No. 11 (1907), 44-55. Debating society.

9025 _____. "The Lynn Young Men's Christian Association, its beginnings." Lynn HSR, No. 13 (1909), 117-130.

9026 DEXTER, RALPH W. "The Lynn Natural History Society (1842-1855)." EIHC, 98 (1962), 175-183.

9027 EARLY, ELEANOR. "Sing a song of Lydia Pinkham." NEG, 5 (Winter, 1964), 34-40. Patent medicine.

9028 EQUITABLE COOPERATIVE BANK, LYNN, MASS. 50th anniversary of the Equitable Cooperative Bank. Lynn, [1927?]. Pp. 16. M.

9029 "THE EVERETT Debating Society." Lynn HSR, No. 12 (1908), 85-91.

9030 FALER, PAUL. "Cultural aspects of the Industrial Revolution: Lynn, Massachusetts shoemakers and industrial morality." LabHist, 15 (1974), 367-394.

9031 FENNO, HENRY, ed. Our police: the official history of the police department of the city of Lynn from the first constable to the latest appointee. Lynn: The City, 1895. Pp. 229. MSaE.

9032 FREEMASONS. LYNN, MASS. MOUNT CARMEL LODGE. One hundred years, Mount Carmel Lodge, Ancient Free and Accepted Masons, of Lynn, Massachusetts, instituted June 10, A. D. 1805, A. L. 5805. [Lynn], 1905. Pp. xii, 152.

9032A GANNON, FREDERIC AUGUSTUS. The last forty years of footwear in Lynn. Lynn: Lynn Mailing Co., 1938. Unpaged. MSaE.

9033 _____. The ways of a worker of a century ago as shown by the diary of Joseph Lye, shoemaker. Salem: Newcomb & Gauss, 1918. Pp. 25.

9034 GENERAL ELECTRIC COMPANY, LYNN, MASS. Fifty years of watthour-meter manufacture. [Lynn], 1939. Unpaged. MSaE.

9035 "GENERAL Electric Company." Industry, 1 (April, 1936), 5-8.

9036 GOODELL, ABNER CHENEY, JR. Address of greeting from the Essex Institute to the Lynn Historical Society on the occasion of its tenth anniversary celebration, December 18, 1906. [Salem?, 1906?]. Pp. 7.

9037 GRANT, WILLIAM THOMAS. The story of W. T. Grant and the early days of the business he founded, as told to G. Lynn Sumner. [N.Y.?], 1954. Pp. 47.

9038   GRAVES, EDWIN J.   Historical address deliv-
       ered at the seventy-second anniversary of
St. Paul's Methodist Episcopal Sunday School, Lynn,
Mass., Sunday, January 30, 1887. Lynn: G. H. and
W. A. Nichols, 1888. Pp. 38. M.

9039   GREAT Lynn fire of November 26, 1889, graph-
       ic tale of the most disastrous conflagration
that ever visited the city of shoes. Prepared by
one of the sufferers. Salem: Hutchinson and Son,
[1889?]. Pp. 16. MSaE.

9040   HACKER, SALLIE H.   "The Society of Friends
       at Lynn, Mass." EIHC, 41 (1905), 333-353.

9041   HARTLEY, EDWARD NEAL.   Ironworks on the
       Saugus; the Lynn and Braintree ventures of
the Company of Undertakers of the Ironworks in New
England. Norman: Univ. of Oklahoma Pr., 1957.
Pp. 328.

9042   HAWKES, NATHAN MORTIMER.   "The Flagg-Gray
       House." Lynn HSR (1900), 9-10.

9043   _____.   Hearths and homes of old Lynn, with
       studies in local history. Lynn: T. P.
Nichols & Sons, 1907. Pp. xvi, 350.

9044   _____.   Historical address before the Bay
       State Lodge, No. 40, I.O.O.F. at its fifti-
eth anniversary, Lynn, Mass., March 6 A.D. 1894.
Lynn: Nichols Pr., 1894. Pp. 24. MBNEH.

9045   _____.   In Lynn Woods, with pen and camera.
       Lynn: T. B. Nichols, 1893. Pp. vi, 104.

9046   _____.   Increase Newhall's house; or, the
       Minute Men's Tavern, random gleanings con-
cerning a nook of old Lynn about which the tides of
human activity have ebbed and flowed before and
since 1775. [Lynn?, 1917?]. Pp. 15.

9047   _____.   "Lynnmere: gleanings from the rec-
       ords and pen sketches of a picturesque re-
gion of old Lynn, its mineral springs and hotel,
its prior and later tenants." Lynn HSR, No. 16
(1912), 96-120.

9048   _____.   "The meeting house." Lynn HSR,
       (1901), 9-11.
       Third Parish.

9049   _____.   "The meeting-house of the Second
       Church in Lynn." Lynn HSR, (1899), 9-11.

9050   _____.   "Why the old town house was built
       and some things which have been talked of
within its walls since." Salem Press Historical
and Genealogical Register, 2 (1891-1892), 177-189.

9051   HILL, JAMES L.   Decade of history in the
       North Church, Lynn. Lynn: Leech & Lewis,
[1879?]. Pp. 35. MB.

9052   "AN HISTORICAL sketch of the great shoe
       town." Shoe and Leather Reporter, 54 (Au-
gust 4, 1892), Supplement, lxv-lxxv.

9053   HOBBS, CLARENCE W.   Lynn and surroundings.
       Lynn: Lewis & Winship, 1886. Pp. 161.

9054   JOHNSON, BENJAMIN N.   "The first twenty-five
       years of the life of the [Lynn Historical]
Society." Lynn HSR, 23, Pt. 1 (1921-1923), 21-23.

9055   JOHNSON, DAVID NEWHALL.   Sketches of Lynn;
       or, the changes of fifty years. Lynn: Thos.
P. Nichols, 1880. Pp. vii, 490.

9056   LYNN, MASS.   Centennial memorial of Lynn, Es-
       sex County, Massachusetts, embracing an his-
torical sketch, 1629-1876, by James R. Newhall, and
notices of the mayors, with portraits. Lynn, 1876.
Pp. viii, 204.

9057   _____.   The city hall of Lynn: being a his-
       tory of events leading to its erection, and
an account of the ceremonies at the dedication of
the building, Nov. 30, 1867. Lynn: Thos. P. Nichols, 1869. Pp. xviii, 132.

9058   _____.   City of Lynn, Massachusetts semi-
       centennial of incorporation, events and ex-
ercises of the 50th anniversary celebration held
May 13th, 14th and 15th, 1900. Walter L. Ramsdell,
ed. Lynn: Whitten & Cass, 1900. Pp. xvi, 292.

9059   _____.   Proceedings in Lynn, Massachusetts,
       June 17, 1879, being the two hundred and
fiftieth anniversary of the settlement, embracing
the oration, by Cyrus M. Tracy, and the addresses,
correspondence, etc., with an introductory chapter
and a second part, by James R. Newhall. Lynn, 1880.
Pp. vi, 224.

9060   _____.   Records of ye towne meetings of Lyn.
       Lynn: Lynn Historical Society, 1949-. 7v.
7 volumes, covering 1691-1783, have appeared
as of 1974.

9061   LYNN, MASS.   BOSTON STREET METHODIST EPISCO-
       PAL CHURCH. An account of the commemoration
of the twenty-fifth anniversary of the Boston
Street Church, May 20, 1878. Lynn: Leech and Lewis, 1880. Pp. 40. M.

9062   _____.   An account of the fifty-first anni-
       versary of the Church, and of Methodist be-
ginnings in Lynn, a semi-centennial jubilee, held
in the Church June 19, 21, 24, 1904. William Henry
Meredith, ed. Lynn: Whitten and Cass, 1904.
Pp. 92.

9063   LYNN, MASS.   CENTRAL CONGREGATIONAL CHURCH.
       Confession of faith, covenant and membership
of the Central Congregational Church, Lynn, Mass.,
with a historical discourse.... Lynn: Thos. P.
Nichols, 1881. Pp. 32.

9064   LYNN, MASS.   CHAMBER OF COMMERCE. Lynn,
       Massachusetts. Lynn, 1916. Unpaged.

9065   LYNN, MASS.   FIRST CHURCH OF CHRIST. Cele-
       bration of the two hundred and fiftieth an-
niversary of the organization of the First Church of
Christ, in Lynn, (Congregational Trinitarian) at
Lynn, Massachusetts...June 8, 1882. Lynn: J. F.
McCarty & Bros., 1882. Pp. 135.
       Historical address by Walter Barton.

9066 ____. Celebration of the 275th anniversary of the First Church of Christ, organized June 8, 1632, Lynn, Massachusetts, Sunday, June ninth, nineteen hundred seven. Lynn: Thos. P. Nichols & Sons, 1907. Pp. 153.

9067 LYNN, MASS. FIRST CONGREGATIONAL CHURCH. Manual of the First Congregational Church in Lynn; containing the history of the church, its rules, declaration of faith, covenant, address and catalogue of members. Lynn: A. H. Carsley, 1874. Pp. 38. M.

9068 LYNN, MASS. FIRST METHODIST EPISCOPAL CHURCH. Centennial anniversary of the First Methodist Episcopal Church, Lynn, Mass., observed February 19-22, 1891. John D. Pickles, ed. Lynn: Geo. C. Herbert, 1891. Pp. 147.

9069 LYNN, MASS. FIRST UNIVERSALIST PARISH. Constitution and by-laws...with an historical abstract 1874. Boston: Rand and Avery, 1874. Pp. 23. MB.

9070 ____. The First Universalist Parish of Lynn, by-laws adopted April 23, 1907, and our church and the people who made it; an historical address by Ellen Mudge Burrill, delivered Sunday afternoon, March 22, 1908, for the seventy-fifth anniversary, with the program...a register of ministers, clerks, treasurers, superintendents of the Sunday school, and present officers in all branches of the parish. [Lynn], 1908. Pp. 39.

9071 LYNN, MASS. PUBLIC LIBRARY. Lynn one hundred years a city, prepared by the Lynn Public Library and the Lynn Historical Society. Lynn, 1950. Pp. x, 63.

9072 LYNN, MASS. SECOND CONGREGATIONAL SOCIETY. Address, poems and speeches delivered at the semi-centennial anniversary of the Second Congregational Society of Lynn, Wednesday, April 30, 1873, at Odd Fellows' Hall. Lynn: Thos. P. Nichols, 1873. Pp. 96.

9073 "[LYNN CENTENNIAL]." Boot and Shoe Recorder, 21 (August 10, 1892), entire issue.

9074 LYNN FIVE CENT SAVINGS BANK. Seventy-fifth anniversary...1855-1930. Lynn: Nichols Pr., 1930. Pp. 28.

9075 LYNN INSTITUTION FOR SAVINGS. A century of service...the record of one hundred years, incorporated June twentieth, 1826. Lynn, 1926. Unpaged. M.

9076 ____. Lynn Institution for Savings, 1825-1951. n.p., [1951?]. Pp. 27. MSaE.

9077 LYNN TEMPERANCE REFORM CLUB. Anniversary of th Lynn Temperance Reform Club, 1916. n.p., [1916?]. Unpaged. MSaE.
Includes brief historical sketch by Amos P. Wilson.

9078 LYNN TYPOGRAPHICAL UNION, NO. 120. Silver anniversary, 1912. Lynn: M'Carty & Son, [1912?]. Unpaged. MSaE.
History by Edward F. Giblin.

9079 LYNN YACHT CLUB. Thirty-fourth annual ball, Lynn Yacht Club, Casino Hall April 18th, 1912. Lynn: Frank S. Whitten, [1912?]. Pp. 24. MSaE.
Includes club history.

9080 MANGAN, JOHN J. "The newspapers of Lynn." Lynn HSR, No. 13 (1909), 131-168.

9081 MANN, CHARLES EDWARD. "The three Lynn captains." Lynn HSR, No. 14 (1910), 81-128. Robert Bridges, Thomas Marshall and Richard Walker.

9082 MARTIN, GEORGE HENRY. "The First Church of Christ in Lynn." Lynn HSR, (1905), 9-11.

9083 ____. "Glimpses of colonial life in Lynn in the Indian war days." Lynn HSR, No. 17 (1913), 98-122.

9084 ____. "The Lynn Academy." Lynn HSR, No. 12 (1908), 58-84.

9085 ____. "Lynn in the early Indian wars." Lynn HSR, No. 13 (1909), 61-86.

9086 ____. "The public services of Strawberry Brook." Lynn HSR, (1904), 58-78.

9087 ____. "The unfolding of religious faith in Lynn." Lynn HSR, No. 16 (1912), 47-72.

9088 MURPHY, JOSEPH W. "Lynn Woods." NOHR, 3 (August 13, 1904), 3-6.

9089 NATIONAL CITY BANK, LYNN, MASS. Semi-centennial of the National City Bank of Lynn, Massachusetts, October 1, 1904. Lynn: T. P. Nichols, 1904. Pp. 44. MB.

9090 NEWHALL, ASA T., GEORGE H. NEWHALL and ROBERT W. THOMPSON. "The great fire of Lynn, Nov. 26, 1889." Lynn HSR, 23, Pt. 1 (1921-1923), 10-13.

9091 NEWHALL, HOWARD MUDGE. "The First Methodist Meeting House built in 1812." Lynn HSR (1903), 9-11.

9092 ____. "Ten years of the Lynn Historical Society." Lynn HSR, (1906), 10-12.

9093 [NEWHALL, JAMES ROBINSON]. Lin: or, notable people and notable things in the early history of Lynn, the Third Plantation of Massachusetts Colony. (1862) By Obadiah Oldpath, pseud. New ed. Lynn: G. C. Herbert, 1890. Pp. viii, 500.
First edition has title: Lin: or jewels of the Third Plantation.

9094 NEWHALL, JOHN BREED. "Early Lewis, Broad and Nahant Streets." Lynn HSR (1906), 59-83.

9095 NEWHALL, WILBUR F. "The Exploring Circle." Lynn HSR, No. 11 (1907), 56-63. Scientific society.

9096 ODD FELLOWS, INDEPENDENT ORDER OF. LYNN, MASS. RICHARD W. DROWN LODGE NO. 106. Twenty-fifth anniversary, Saturday, August 11, 1906. n.p., [1906?]. Unpaged. MSaE. Includes brief history.

9097 OXFORD CLUB, LYNN, MASS. Oxford Club souvenir, description of the social, religious, and industrial characteristics of Lynn. John Myron Potter, ed. [Lynn?]: Potter & Potter, 1892. Pp. 148. MB.

9098 PARKER, JOHN R. "Lynn, city of shoes and electricity." National Magazine, 17 (1902-1903), 107-113.

9099 PERCIVAL, BENJAMIN. "Abolitionism in Lynn and Essex County." Lynn HSR, No. 12 (1908), 109-130.

9100 PERLEY, SIDNEY. "Historical sketch of the First Church in Lynn." Essex Antiq, 1 (1897), 151-157.

9101 PINKHAM, ARTHUR WELLINGTON and FRANK E. BRUCE. 1854-1929: men and money at the National City Bank of Lynn, Massachusetts, during the last seventy-five years. Lynn: Nichols Pr., 1929. Pp. 83. M.

9102 PIPER, HELEN J. and MABEL A. FRENCH. History stories of Lynn retold and illustrated by the pupils of grade IV, V, and VI of the Lynn public schools. Lynn: Lynn School Committee, 1931. Pp. 255. MSaE.

9103 PORTER, MARGARET E. "Old Woodend and its neighboring territory." Lynn HSR, No. 15 (1911), 106-138.

9104 PRATT, RICHARD. Commonplace book of Richard Pratt of Lynn, Mass. Nathan Mortimer Hawkes, ed. Lynn: Nichols Pr., 1900. Pp. 75. MBNEH. 1755-1798.

9105 A REVIEW of Lynn: or observations on the manners and customs of the place.... By a Passenger from Lynn. Boston, 1821. Pp. 48. MB.

9106 REVIEW of the attempt to manufacture iron at Lynn & Braintree in Massachusetts and the successful enterprise at Taunton in the Old Colony. Taunton: C. A. Hack & Son, [1901?]. Pp. 15. MBNEH.

9107 ROTARY CLUB, LYNN, MASS. The Rotary Club of Lynn, 50th anniversary banquet, Saturday, March 2, 1968, New Ocean House, Swampscott, Mass. n.p., [1968?]. Unpaged. MSaE. Includes club history.

9108 RUSSELL, EUGENE D. "Harvard College and Lynn in colonial times." Lynn HSR, No. 16 (1912), 73-95.

9109 SANDERSON, HOWARD KENDALL. Lynn in the Revolution. Boston: W. B. Clarke, 1909. 2v.

9110 "SHOE manufacturing in Lynn from its settlement to 1892." Boot and Shoe Recorder, 21 (August 10, 1892).

9111 START, EDWIN A. "The city of Lynn." NEM, New Ser., 4 (1891), 497-520.

9112 STONE, WILLIAM. "Lynn and its old shoemaker shops." Lynn HSR, No. 15 (1911), 79-100.

9113 TAPLEY, HENRY FULLER, et al. Memorials read before the Whiting Club, Lynn, Mass. n.p., n.d. Pp. 23. MBNEH. Augustus H. Amory, Philip A. Chase, Charles S. Fuller, Charles H. Newhall, and Howard M. Newhall.

9114 ____, ed. "An old New England town as seen by Joseph Lye." Lynn HSR, No. 19 (1915), 36-54.

9115 TOLLES, FREDERICK B. "The new-light Quakers of Lynn and New Bedford." NEQ, 32 (1959), 291-319. 1820s.

9116 WOODBURY, CHARLES JEPTHA HILL. "The bells of Lynn." Lynn HSR, No. 18 (1914), 109-166.

9117 ____. "The floating bridge at Lynn on the Salem and Boston Turnpike." EIHC, 34 (1898), 67-76.

9118 ____. "Historic priorities in Lynn." Lynn HSR, No. 17 (1913), 53-87.

9119 ____. "The old tunnel." Lynn HSR, No. 13 (1909), 92-98. Congregational meeting house.

LYNNFIELD

9120 "GEOGRAPHICAL names of old Lynnfield." Historical Lynnfield, 1 (March, 1955), 2.

9121 "THE HASKELL House." Historical Lynnfield, 13 (May, 1967), 1-2.

9122 HAYWOOD, CHARLES. "The railroad through Lynnfield Center." Historical Lynnfield, 1 (March, 1955), 1-2.

9123 MACGREGOR, GEORGE C. "The old Garrison House." Historical Lynnfield, 2 (March, 1956), 1-2.

9124 MACKENZIE, NEIL D. "The First Parish Meetinghouse, Lynnfield Center, Massachusetts." OTNE, 45 (1954-1955), 103-106.

9125 "METHODISTS in Lynnfield." Historical Lynnfield, 12 (November, 1965), 1-2.

9126 "MURDER in Lynnfield, 1897." Historical
Lynnfield, 2 (September, 1955), 1.
John Gallo murdered by Alfred C. Williams.

9127 "OLD school salient in town's history."
Historical Lynnfield, 8 (February, 1962),
1-2.

9128 PARSONS, MARY A. "The old meeting house in
Lynnfield Centre." Essex Antiq, 4 (1900),
119-120.

9129 PARSONS, EVEN. "A sketch of the First Religious Society in Lynnfield, read before the
Essex Unitarian Conference, Sept. 8, 1881." EIHC,
19 (1882), 1-17.

9130 "PLACE names in Lynnfield and why." Historical Lynnfield, 15 (January, 1969), 1-2,
(March, 1969), 1-2.

9131 ROSS, KATHERINE WELLMAN. History of the
Centre Congregational Church, 1720-1970.
Boston: Winthrop Printing, 1970. Pp. 64. MSaE.

9132 _____. "Indians in Lynnfield." Historical
Lynnfield, 5 (May, 1959), 1-2.

9133 _____. "Lynnfield Methodist Religious Society." Historical Lynnfield, 15 (November,
1969), 1-2.

9134 "A 1740 house." Historical Lynnfield, 10
(March, 1964), 2.
Daniel Mansfield House.

9135 TUCK, LOUIS B. "History of water in Lynnfield." Historical Lynnfield, 5 (January,
1959), 1-2.

9136 WELLMAN, THOMAS BARTHOLOMEW. "The first
library society." Historical Lynnfield, 12
(January, 1966), 2; (March, 1966), 2.

9137 _____. History of the town of Lynnfield,
Mass., 1635-1895. Boston: Blanchard &
Watts, 1895. Pp. xv, 268.

9138 WORTHEN, KEN. "Roundy's Store...Worthen's
Food Mart." Historical Lynnfield, 20
(March, 1973), 1-2.

MALDEN

9139 BAXTER, SYLVESTER. "Bell Rock, its monument and its tablets." MalHR, No. 1 (1910-
1911), 5-11.

9140 BOWMAN, J. RUSSELL, comp. Short history of
the First Parish in Malden, 1649-1949 and of
the First Parish in Malden, Universalist, 1828-
1949. Malden: First Parish in Malden, Universalist, 1949. Unpaged. MBNEH.

9141 BRUCE, CHARLES EMERSON. City of Malden
directory.... Boston: G. E. Crosby, [1882]-
1887. 2v.

First volume contains an 'Outline history
for 250 years' of over 300 pages.

9142 CHAMBERLAIN, GEORGE WALTER. "The early Baptists of Malden." MalHR, No. 5 (1917-1918),
13-38.

9143 _____. "The Old Hill Tavern and its occupants." MalHR, No. 4 (1915-1916), 14-29.

9144 CHILD, RUTH L. S. History of the schools of
Malden, 1649-1934. Malden, [1950?].
Pp. 236. M.

9145 COLSON, WILLIAM WYMAN, comp. Malden, Massachusetts: 1882-1917, thirty-fifth anniversary, city of Malden; 1892-1917, twenty-fifth anniversary, Malden Evening News. [Malden]: Malden
Evening News, [1917?]. Pp. 79. M.

9146 COREY, DELORAINE PENDRE. The history of Malden, Massachusetts, 1633-1785. Malden, 1899.
Pp. xvii, 870.

9147 _____. Malden, past and present, issued on
the occasion of the two hundred and fiftieth
anniversary of Malden, Mass., May, 1899. Malden:
Malden Mirror, 1899. Pp. 112. MBNEH.

9148 _____. "The Old Brick." MalHR, No. 6 (1919-
1920), 5-12.
First Parish Church.

9149 _____. "Two centuries and a half in Malden."
NEM, New Ser., 20 (1899), 357-378.
Established as a town in 1649.

9150 _____. "A walk up Salem Street." MalHR,
No. 5 (1917-1918), 5-12.

9151 GREEN, JAMES DIMAN. An oration delivered at
Malden, on the two hundredth anniversary of
the incorporation of the town, May 23, 1849. Boston: G. C. Rand, 1850. Pp. 53.

9152 HAVEN, GILBERT. "The original Methodist
Church of Malden Center." MalHR, No. 6
(1919-1920), 31-46.

9153 LAWRENCE, WILLIAM. Address at the union
service of the churches of Malden in connection with the 250th anniversary of the founding of
the city. Cambridge: Univ. Pr., 1899. Pp. 11.

9154 MALDEN, MASS. The bi-centennial book of Malden, containing the oration and poem delivered on the two hundredth anniversary of the incorporation of the town, May 23, 1849; with other proceedings on that day; and matters pertaining to the history of the place.... Boston: Geo. C. Rand, 1850.
Pp. 251.

9155 _____. Births, marriages and deaths in the
town of Malden, Massachusetts, 1649-1850.
Deloraine P. Corey, comp. Cambridge: Univ. Pr.,
1903. Pp. xiv, 393.

9156 ____. City of Malden, official souvenir program of the quarter millenial celebration...May 21, 22 & 23, 1899. Boston: Caslon Pr., [1899?]. Pp. 56. M.

9157 ____. Memorial of the celebration of the two hundred and fiftieth anniversary of the incorporation of the town of Malden, Massachusetts, May, 1899.... Cambridge: Univ. Pr., 1900. Pp. xii, 340.

9158 ____. Oration, poem, speeches, chronicles, &c., at the dedication of the Malden Town Hall on Thursday evening, October 29th, 1857. Malden: C. C. P. Moody, 1857. Pp. 52.

9159 ____. Proceedings of the two hundred seventy-fifth anniversary of Malden, Massachusetts, Malden Auditorium, May 25, 1924.... [Malden]: Malden Historical Society, 1925. Pp. 44.

9160 MALDEN, MASS. CENTRE METHODIST EPISCOPAL CHURCH. Centre Methodist Episcopal Church, Malden, Mass., celebration of the one hundredth anniversary of the organization of the church, May 1-8, 1921. Cambridge: Murray, [1921?]. Pp. 32. MBNEH.

9161 MALDEN, MASS. FIRST BAPTIST CHURCH. A brief history of the First Baptist Church, Malden: declaration of faith, the church covenant, and list of members. Boston: J. M. Hewes, 1859. Pp. 32. M.

9162 ____. Judson centennial services, a compilation of addresses...by J. Nelson Lewis. [Malden]: A. G. Brown, 1888. Pp. 75. M.
Includes history of church; centennial of the birth of Adoniram Judson.

9163 MALDEN, MASS. ST. PAUL'S CHURCH. The first hundred years of St. Paul's Church and Parish, Malden, Mass., 1867-1967. Malden, 1967. Pp. 56. M.

9164 MALDEN, MASS. SCHOOL COMMITTEE. City of Malden, public school souvenir, to commemorate the two hundred fiftieth anniversary of the municipality, 1649-1899. Malden, 1899. Pp. 242.

9165 "[THE MALDEN and Melrose Gas Light Company and the Malden Electric Company]." Tenney Service, 16 (1928), 261-376.

9166 MALDEN HISTORICAL SOCIETY. Malden's celebration of the Massachusetts Bay Colony Tercentenary. Malden, 1931. Pp. 122. MB.

9167 MALDEN SAVINGS BANK. Seventy-fifth anniversary of the Malden Savings Bank, 1860-1935. Malden, 1935. Pp. 17. MBNEH.

9168 "MALDEN'S presidential votes from Washington to Roosevelt." Malden Outlook, 1 (November 12, 1904), 1.

9169 MANN, CHARLES EDWARD. "The governor's lady." MalHR, No. 6 (1919-1920), 13-30.
Origin of the name "Coytmore Lea"; one of the city's parks.

9170 ____. "Methodist beginnings in Malden." MalHR, No. 4, (1915-1916), 30-64.

9171 MANN, MARY LAWRENCE. "Some notable women in the annals of Malden." MalHR, No. 2 (1911-1912), 54-62.

9172 "MILESTONES in megacycles." Industry, 15 (March, 1950), 17-19.
National Co., founded 1914; television sets.

9173 MUDGE, JAMES. "The Mudges of Malden." MalHR, No. 5, (1917-1918), 39-54.

9174 "THE NEWHALL family." Malden Outlook, 1 (January 14, 1905), 1; (January 21, 1905), 3.

9175 WATKINS, WALTER KENDALL. "Malden's old meetinghouses." MalHR, No. 2 (1911-1912), 33-53.

9176 ____. "The Revolutionary patriots of Malden and their descendants." Malden Outlook, 1 (December 31, 1904), 1-2; (January 28, 1905), 1-2; (February 4, 1905), 5.

9177 "A WELL known quartette." Malden Outlook, 1 (October 29, 1904), 1.
George W. Stiles, Alvin E. Bliss, and their wives.

9178 WELLMAN, JOSHUA WYMAN. A historical discourse delivered May 21, 1899 at the celebration of the 250th anniversary of the organization of the First Church of Christ in Malden, Mass. Cambridge: Univ. Pr., 1899. Pp. 29. M.

9179 WRIGHT, SAMUEL OSGOOD. An historical discourse delivered at Malden, Mass...December 1, 1831, containing a sketch of the history of that town...to the present time. Boston: Light & Harris, 1832. Pp. 36. MB.

MANCHESTER

9180 "DID Winthrop land at Manchester?" EIHC, 34 (1898), 209-218.

9181 FLOYD, FRANK L. 'Manchester-by-the-sea.' 2d. ed. [Manchester]: Floyd's News Store, 1945. Pp. 209.

9182 LAMSON, DARIUS FRANCIS. History of the town of Manchester, Essex County, Massachusetts, 1645-1895. [Manchester]: The Town, [1895]. Pp. xii, 425, xiv.

9183 ____. "A Sunday in olden times: Manchester, Massachusetts." MagAmHist, 24 (1890), 214-218.

9184 MANCHESTER, MASS. Manchester-by-the-Sea, 1645-1970. [Manchester]: The Town, 1970. Pp. 58. MSaE.

9185 ____. Souvenir program of Manchester's celebration of the 300th anniversary of the Massachusetts Bay Colony. n.p., [1930?]. Pp. 32. MSaE.

9186 MANCHESTER, MASS. ORTHODOX CONGREGATIONAL
    CHURCH. Brief history, articles of faith,
covenant and living members of the Orthodox Congregational Church in Manchester, Mass.... Boston:
Wright & Hasty, 1851. Pp. 31.

9187 _____. Two hundred fiftieth aniversary of
    the founding of the Orthodox Congregational
Church Manchester, Massachusetts. n.p., [1966?].
Unpaged. M.

9188 MANCHESTER YACHT CLUB. Soundings: Manches-
    ter Yacht Club, 1892-1964. n.p., [1964?].
Pp. 69. MSaE.

MANSFIELD

9189 COPELAND, JENNIE FREEMAN. Every day but
    Sunday: the romantic age of New England in-
dustry.... Brattleboro, Vt.: Stephen Daye Pr.,
1936. Pp. 294.
    Limited to Mansfield.

9190 _____. "The Fisher-Richardson House."
    OTNE, 21 (1930-1931), 168-178.

9191 HISTORY and directory of Mansfield, Mass.,
    for 1891.... Boston: F. I. Brown, 1891.
Pp. 122. MBNEH.

9192 MANSFIELD, MASS. Program: 150th anniver-
    sary [of the] incorporation of Mansfield as
a town, August 23-24-25-26, 1925. [Mansfield?,
1925?]. Unpaged. MB.
    Includes historical section by Jennie F.
Copeland.

9193 ROCKWOOD, CHARLES M. "Mansfield, an econom-
    ic study." NEM, New Ser., 39 (1908-1909),
493-499.

9194 STEARNS, ISAAC. Right and wrong, in Mans-
    field, Mass., or, an account of the pro-
slavery mob of October 10th, 1836: when an anti-
slavery lecturer [Charles C. Burleigh] was silenced
by the beat of drums, &c., with some reasoning in
favor of emancipation; appendix, containing a list
of officers and members of the Mansfield Anti-
slavery Society. Pawtucket, Mass.: Robert Sherman,
1837. Pp. 61.

MARBLEHEAD

9195 ALDRICH, WILLIAM TRUMAN. An architectural
    monograph on Marblehead, its contribution to
eighteenth- and early nineteenth-century American
architecture. Saint Paul: White Pine Bureau, 1918.
Pp. 16.

9196 BARNARD, THOMAS. A sermon preached at the
    ordination of the Rev. William Whitwell, to
the joint pastoral care of the First Church and congregation in Marblehead, with the Rev. John Barnard,
August 25, 1762, together with the charge given
Mr. Whitwell, by the Rev. John Barnard, preceded by

an introductory discourse in defence of the ecclesiastical establishment of these churches, and
followed by an historical account of the First
Church in Marblehead, and also the right hand of
fellowship given by the Rev. Mr. Simon Bradstreet
of Marblehead. Boston: J. Dpaper [sic], 1762.
Pp. 51.

9197 BARROW, THOMAS C. "Church politics in Mar-
    blehead, 1715." EIHC, 98 (1962), 121-127.
St. Michael's Church, First Congregational
Church and Second Congregational Church.

9198 BEACH, GEORGE K., CHARLES CONRAD WRIGHT and
    DANA MCLEAN GREELEY. Three sermons for the
250th anniversary celebration of the Unitarian
Church of Marblehead, 1716-1966. n.p., [1966].
Unpaged. MSaE.

9199 BILLIAS, GEORGE ATHAN. General John Glover
    and his Marblehead mariners. N.Y.: Holt,
1960. Pp. xii, 243.
    Revolutionary regiment.

9200 _____. "Pox and politics in Marblehead,
    1773-1774." EIHC, 92 (1956), 43-58.

9201 BOWDEN, WILLIAM HAMMOND. "The commerce of
    Marblehead, 1665-1775." EIHC, 68 (1932),
117-146.

9202 BOWEN, ASHLEY. The journals of Ashley Bowen
    (1728-1813) of Marblehead. Philip Chadwick
Foster Smith, ed. Boston: Colonial Society of
Massachusetts, 1973. 2v.

9203 BRADLEE, FRANCIS BOARDMAN CROWNINSHIELD.
    Marblehead's foreign commerce, 1789-1850,
compiled...from Marblehead custom house records.
Salem: Essex Institute, 1929. Pp. 182.

9204 CHADWELL, PAULINE SOROKA. "The Colonel Jere-
    miah Lee Mansion." Antiques, 48 (1945)
353-355.

9205 CHADWICK, JOHN WHITE. "Old Marblehead."
    NEM, New Ser., 12 (1895), 611-628.

9206 CHAMBERLAIN, NARCISSA G. "The neighbors of
    Jeremiah Lee and the boundaries of his prop-
erty." EIHC, 105 (1969), 128-136.

9207 DANA, SAMUEL. A discourse, on the history of
    the First Christian Church and Society in
Marblehead; delivered to his people January 7,
1816. Boston: Samuel T. Armstrong, 1816. Pp. 31.

9208 DOANE, HELEN PAINE. "Historic background of
    Clifton (Marblehead), Massachusetts." EIHC,
82 (1946), 229-248.

9209 DURNIN, RICHARD GERRY. "Marblehead Academy,
    1788-1865." EIHC, 100 (1964), 145-154.

9210 FEAREY, RUTH. Old Marblehead. Canandaigua,
    N.Y., 1932. Pp. 26.

9211 FELD, STUART PAUL. "St. Michael's Church,
    Marblehead, Massachusetts, 1714." OTNE, 52
(1961-1962), 91-113; 53 (1962-1963), 31-48.

9212   FOSTER, CHARLES HENRY WHEELWRIGHT. The East-
        ern Yacht Club ditty box, 1870-1900. Nor-
wood: Plimpton Pr., 1932. Pp. xix, 317.

9213   FROTHINGHAM, THOMAS GODDARD. "Service of
        Marblehead to the United States Navy."
United States Naval Institute. Proceedings, 52
(1926), 2413-2418.

9214   GARDNER, FRANK A. "Colonel John Glover's
        Marblehead Regiment." MassMag, 1 (1908),
14-20, 85-102.
        Revolutionary; biography.

9215   GOULD, BARTLETT. "The Burgess story."
        American Aviation Historical Society. Jour-
nal, 10 (1965), 79-87, 241-249; 11 (1966), 270-
278; 12 (1967), 273-280; 13 (1968), 37-42.
        Burgess Co., airplane builders, 1910-1918.

9216   GREGORY, JAMES J. H. "Indian relics of Mar-
        blehead." Essex Antiq, 4 (1900), 39-40.

9217   HALL, HELEN. "The Lee Mansion, Marble-
        head." Country Life, 151 (1972), 144-148.

9218   _____. "Marblehead, Massachusetts." Coun-
        try Life, 151 (1972), 18-22.

9219   HATHAWAY, STEPHEN PUTNAM. Historical sketch
        of Philanthropic Lodge., F. and A. M., of
Marblehead, Mass., delivered at the one hundred and
twenty-fifth anniversary of the lodge, March 25,
1885. Boston: Rand Avery, 1888. Pp. 23.

9220   _____. "The Second Congregational Church in
        Marblehead." EIHC, 22 (1885), 81-102.

9221   HORNBY, LESTER G. An artist's sketch-book
        of old Marblehead., with text by Sylvester
Baxter. Boston: A. w. Elson, 1906. 40 leaves.

9222   KIMBALL, F. R. Handbook of Marblehead Neck.
        Boston: Rand, Avery, 1882. Pp. 45.
        Includes history.

9223   KNIGHT, RUSSELL W. "Fire, smoak, & Elbridge
        Gerry." EIHC, 106 (1970), 32-45.
        Appearance of three British naval vessels
        off Marblehead, December 1, 1775.

9224   LACOCK, JOHN KENNEDY. Marblehead, the his-
        toric landmarks and points of interest and
how to see them. Medford: J. C. Miller, Jr.,
1929. Pp. 16.
        Historic houses.

9225   LEE, THOMAS A. "The Lee family of Marble-
        head." EIHC, 52 (1916), 329-344; 53 (1917),
153-168.

9226   LEEK, JOHN W. Historical sermon, preached
        by the Rev. John W. Leek, rector of St.
Michael's Church, Marblehead, Mass., at the occa-
sion of its 158th anniversary, on St. Michael's
Day, September 29th, 1872.... Peabody: Peabody
Pr., 1873. Pp. 25.

9227   LORD, PRISCILLA SAWYER and VIRGINIA C. GAM-
        AGE. Marblehead; the spirit of '76 lives
here. Philadelphia: Chilton, 1971. Pp. xii, 395.

9228   MARBLEHEAD, MASS. FIRST CHURCH OF CHRIST.
        Historical sketch, confession of Faith, cove-
nant, and membership of the First Church of Christ,
Marblehead, Mass. Marblehead: N. Willis Sanborn,
1876. Pp. 38. MBNEH.

9229   MARBLEHEAD, MASS. FIRST CONGREGATIONAL
        CHURCH. The bi-centennial...August 13,
1884. Marblehead: N. Allen Lindsey, 1884. Pp. x,
90. MB.

9230   _____. Manual and historical sketch of the
        First Congregational Church, Marblehead,
Mass., 1684 to 1901. Marblehead: N. A. Lindsey,
[1901?]. Pp. 107.

9231   MARBLEHEAD, MASS. ST. MICHAEL'S CHURCH. St.
        Michael's Church, Marblehead, Mass., order of
exercises commemorating its restoration, Wednesday
afternoon, April 18, 1888. Boston: Geo. F. Crook,
1888. Pp. 55. MWA.
        Includes historical sketch by Samuel Roads,
        Jr.

9232   _____. St. Michael's Church, Marblehead,
        Mass., 1714-1924. Marblehead: N. A. Lind-
sey, 1924. Pp. 44.
        Copy at New England Historic Genealogical So-
        ciety contains a manuscript index of persons.

9233   MARBLEHEAD, MASS. THIRD CONGREGATIONAL
        CHURCH. Historical notices of the Third Con-
gregational Church of Christ in Marblehead, A.D.
1858. Salem: Salem Gazette Pr., 1859. Pp. 18.
MSaE.

9234   MARBLEHEAD, MASS. 300TH ANNIVERSARY COMMIT-
        TEE. Town of Marblehead, 1649-1949....
Marblehead, 1949. Pp. 40. MSaE.

9235   "MARBLEHEAD." Harper's Magazine, 49 (1874),
        181-202.

9236   MARBLEHEAD centennial almanac. n.p., 1876.
        Unpaged. M.
        Includes chronological table of historical
        events in the town.

9237   MARBLEHEAD HISTORICAL SOCIETY. Marblehead
        historical society...[list of officers, his-
tory and by-laws]. Marblehead: N. A. Lindsey,
1905. Pp. 13.

9238   _____. Old Marblehead sea captains and the
        ships in which they sailed.... Benjamin J.
Lindsey, comp. [Marblehead], 1915. Pp. 137.

9239   _____. Ye old colonial days celebration:
        in connection with the exercises, August 29
and 30, 1913, commemorative of Marblehead's place in
colonial history, this souvenir book is issued by
the Marblehead Historical Society.... Marblehead,
1913. Unpaged.

9240 OPEN house day in olde Marblehead, July 10, 1954. n.p., [1954?]. Unpaged. MSaE. Historic houses.

9241 PEABODY, ROBERT EPHRAIM. "Peach's Point, Marblehead." EIHC, 102 (1966), 3-20.

9242 PERLEY, SIDNEY. "Fountain Inn, Marblehead." Essex Antiq, 2 (1898), 125-127.

9243 ____. "Marblehead in the year 1700." EIHC, 46 (1910), 1-16, 178-184, 221-246, 305-316; 47 (1911), 67-95, 149-166, 250-252, 341-349; 48 (1912), 79-84.

9244 ____. "Parts of Marblehead in 1700." Essex Antiq, 13 (1909), 175.

9245 ROADS, SAMUEL, JR. The history and traditions of Marblehead. (1880) 3d. ed. Marblehead: N. A. Lindsey, 1897. Pp. xxiv, 595.

9246 ____, comp. The Marblehead manual. Marblehead: Statesman Publishing, 1883. Pp. 96.

9247 ROBINSON, JOSEPH STANLEY. The story of Marblehead. Lynn, 1936. Pp. 91.

9248 SANBORN, NATHAN PERKINS. The Fountain Inn, Agnes Surriage and Sir Harry Frankland: a paper read before the Marblehead Historical Society, December 8, 1904. [Marblehead:] The [Marblehead Historical] Society, 1903. Pp. 43.

9249 ____. Gen. John Glover and his Marblehead Regiment in the Revolutionary War; a paper read before the Marblehead Historical Society, May 14, 1903. [Marblehead:] The [Marblehead Historical] Society, 1903. Pp. 56.

9250 SANBORN, TRACY LEWIS. Two centuries of Freemasonry: the history of Philanthropic Lodge. [Marblehead?, 1960]. Pp. 55.

9251 SEARLE, RICHARD WHITING. "History of Catta Island off Marblehead." EIHC, 83 (1947), 308-352.

9252 ____. "Marblehead Great Neck." EIHC, 73 (1937), 203-239.

9253 A SOUVENIR of Marblehead. J. F. Brown, ed. [Marblehead]: Observer Book and Job Print, [1895?]. Pp. 40.

9254 THOMPSON, WINFIELD M. "Marblehead." The Rudder, 19 (1908), 115-128.

9255 THORN, FANNY ROPES. "A day in quaint old Marblehead." NOHR, 3 (August 20, 1904), 2-6.

9256 THURSTON, WILLIAM A., ed. Centennial celebration of the Methodist Episcopal Church of Marblehead, Mass., Sunday, Monday and Tuesday, Nov. 1, 2 and 3, 1891. Salem: Salem Pr., 1892. Pp. 80. MSaE.

9257 "A TOPOGRAPHICAL and historical account of Marblehead." MHSC, 8 (1802), 54-78.

9258 TUTT, HANNAH. The Lee Mansion, what it was and what it is. Boston: C. B. Webster, 1911. Pp. 16.

9259 TUTT, RICHARD. "Washington's fleet and Marblehead's part in its creation." EIHC, 81 (1945), 291-304. 1770s.

9260 WIDGER, THURLOW STANLEY. Historic Marblehead, a guided tour and chronology of events to 1950. Wellesley, 1957. Pp. 52. MSaE.

9261 ____. Marblehead's fishing, foreign commerce, and shoe industry. [Framingham?, 1962?]. 37 leaves. MSaE.

MARION

9262 JOBB, LEANDER. Historical sketch of the Congregational Church in Marion, Mass.; a sermon, Dec. 29, 1861. New Bedford: Standard Steam Printing, 1862. Pp. 16.

MARLBOROUGH

9263 BALDWIN, FOY SPENCER, EMILY G. BALCH and WILLIAM L. RUTAN. The strike of the shoe workers in Marlboro, Mass., Nov. 14, 1898-May 5, 1899, a report, prepared for the Twentieth Century Club of Boston. Boston: Boston Co-operative Pr., 1899. Pp. 23.

9264 BIGELOW, ELLA A. FISHER. Historical reminiscences of the early times in Marlborough, Massachusetts, and prominent events from 1860 to 1910, including...an account of the celebration of the two hundred and fiftieth anniversary of the incorporation of the town. Marlborough: Times Publishing, 1910. Pp. xvii, 488.
      A typescript index of names by Wilhelmina M. Wilder is at the New England Historic Genealogical Society.

9265 BURHOE, J. T. History of the Baptist Church in Marlboro, from April 14th, 1868, to April 14th, 1878. Marlboro: Cook & Townsend, 1878. Pp. 16.

9266 FELTON, CYRUS. A record of more than four hundred and fifty events with the date of their occurrence, in Marlborough and vicinity.... n.p., [1879]. Pp. 21. MBNEH.

9267 ____. A record of upwards of six hundred events, with the dates of their occurrence, in Marlborough and neighboring towns.... Marlborough: Times Publishing, 1880. Pp. 43.
      Does not supersede previous entry.

9268 FIELD, LEVI ALPHEUS. An historical sketch of the First Congregational Church in Marlborough, Mass., with the exercises at the celebration of the fiftieth anniversary of Rev. Sylvester F. Bucklin's ordination, as pastor of said church. Worcester: Henry J. Howland, 1859. Pp. iv, 82.

9269   GREEN, SAMUEL ABBOTT. Note-book kept by the
        Rev. William Brinsmead, the first minister
of Marlborough, Mass.; remarks made before the
Massachusetts Historical Society, February 14,
1889. Cambridge: J. Wilson and Son, 1889. Pp. 7.

9270   HAYWARD, EDWARD FARWELL. History of the Sec-
        ond Parish Church (Unitarian) Marlborough,
Massachusetts. [Marlborough?], 1906. Pp. 48.

9271   HUDSON, CHARLES. History of the town of
        Marlborough, Middlesex County, Massachu-
setts, from its first settlement in 1657 to 1861;
with a brief sketch of the town of Northborough, a
genealogy of the families in Marlborough to 1800,
and an account of the celebration of the two hundredth anniversary of the incorporation of the
town. Boston: T. R. Marvin & Son, 1862. Pp. xvi,
544.

9272   "MARLBORO'S 250th anniversary." Worcester
        Magazine, 13 (1910), 191-193.

9273   MARLBOROUGH, MASS. PUBLIC SCHOOLS. History,
        Marlborough public schools, 1894. Marlboro:
Times Printing, 1894. Pp. 12. M.

9274   MARLBOROUGH, MASS. WEST CHURCH. The church
        record being a concise sketch of the origin
and history of the West Church in Marlborough. Boston: John Wilson, 1850. Pp. 22. M.

9275   PACKARD, ASA. "A description of Marlbor-
        ough." MHSC, [4] (1795), 46-47.

9276   PITMAN, JOSEPH ASBURY, comp. Notes on the
        history of Marlborough. Marlborough:
Times Publishing, 1905. Pp. 12 (i.e. 22).

9277   WINCHESTER, ALICE. "Living with antiques:
        Time Stone Farm in Marlboro, Massachusetts."
Antiques, 59 (1951), 460-464.

MARSHFIELD

9278   [ALDEN, EBENEZER]. ...Historical sketch of
        the First Church in Marshfield, October,
1854.... Boston: C. C. P. Moody, 1854. Pp. 33.

9279   BRADFORD, RUTH A. "Marshfield and its his-
        toric houses." NEM, New Ser., 24 (1901),
422-444.

9280   FORD, DAVID BARNES. The centennial history
        of the First Baptist Church, Marshfield,
Mass., 1788-1888. Boston: J. H. Earle, [1888?].
Pp. 39.

9281   LEONARD, GEORGE. Marshfield sixty years
        ago, a lecture delivered in Marshfield, A
April 23, 1872. Boston: J. Frank Farmer, 1872.
Pp. 25.

9282   MARSHFIELD, MASS. BOARD OF TRADE. Marsh-
        field's open door, 1640-1940, tercentenary
celebration, July 21-28 inclusive. n.p., [1940?].
Pp. 52. M.

9283   MARSHFIELD, 70°-40′ W:42°-5′N; the autobiog-
        raphy of a Pilgrim town; being an account of
three hundred years of a New England town; founded
by the Pilgrims; lived in and developed by the Roy-
alists; adopted by Daniel Webster; beloved by many
of the ancestors of those who today make it their
home, 1640-1940. Marshfield: Marshfield Tercentenary Committee, 1940. Pp. xix, 334.

9284   RICHARDS, LYSANDER SALMON. History of Marsh-
        field. Plymouth: Memorial Pr., 1901-1905.
2v.

        Copy at New England Historic Genealogical
        Society contains a typescript index of
        names.

9285   ROBINSON, THOMAS P. "The historic Winslow
        House at Marshfield, Massachusetts, and its
restoration." OTNE, 11 (1920-1921), 107-112.

9286   SHERMAN, MRS. ROBERT M. "The Winslow House
        at Marshfield, Mass." MayflowerQ, 33 (1967),
47-48.

9287   SHURTLEFF, NATHANIEL BRADSTREET. "A few
        facts in the early history of the town of
Marshfield." NEHGR, 7 (1853), 276-278.

9288   _____. Thunder & lightning; and deaths at
        Marshfield in 1658 & 1666. Boston: Priv.
Print., 1850. Pp. iii, 55.

9289   SNOW, ANNA MYRLE. Marshfield, a brief his-
        tory. [Marshfield]: Marshfield Historical
Commission, [1967?]. Pp. 7. M.

9290   THOMAS, MARCIA ABIAH. Memorials of Marsh-
        field and guide book to its localities at
Green Harbor. Boston: Dutton and Wentworth, 1854.
Pp. 108.
        Biographies.

MASHPEE

9291   APES, WILLIAM. Indian nullification of the
        unconstitutional laws of Massachusetts,
relative to the Marshpee tribe: or, the pretended
riot explained. Boston: J. Howe, 1835. Pp. 168.
        Joseph Sabin attributes authorship to
        William J. Snelling.

9292   BEATTY, JEROME, JR. "Mashpee stands alone."
        CCC, 23 (1970), 26-29.
        Centennial.

9293   BINGHAM, AMELIA G. Mashpee, 1870-1970.
        [Mashpee]: Mashpee Centennial Committee,
1970. Pp. 48.

9294   MASHPEE OLD INDIAN MEETING HOUSE AUTHORITY
        INC., BROCHURE COMMITTEE. Mashpee old Indian
meeting house, 1684-1961. [Mashpee, 1961?]. Unpaged. [MBaC].

9295   PHINNEY, LOUISE. "Squaw Island." Cape Cod
        Magazine, 3 (September, 1917), 20.

9296   SOPER, G. W. "Among the friendly Indians of
       Mashpee." NEM, New Ser., 2 (1890), 277-279.

MATTAPOISETT

9297   MATTAPOISETT, MASS. An account of the cele-
       bration of the fiftieth anniversary of the
incorporation of the town of Mattapoisett, Massachusetts, August 18-24, 1907. New Bedford: E.
Anthony & Sons, 1908. Pp. 74.

9298   ____. Town of Mattapoisett, Massachusetts,
       100th anniversary 1857-1957, souvenir book-
let [with] historical summary of Mattapoisett by
Charles S. Mendell, Jr. [New Bedford]: Reynolds-
DeWalt, [1957]. Unpaged.

9299   MENDELL, CHARLES S., JR. Shipbuilders of
       Mattapoisett. [New Bedford?, 1937?]. Un-
paged. MB.

9300   ROMAINE, LAWRENCE B. "William H. Tirrill,
       variety cobbler, 1836-1850." CEAIA, 4
(1951), 44.
       Account books.

9301   WOOD, EDWARD F. R. Sailing days at Matta-
       poisett, 1870-1960. [New Bedford?], 1961.
Pp. 107.

MAYNARD

9302   AALTONEN, FRANK. Maynard weavers, the story
       of the United Co-operative Society of May-
nard. Maynard: United Co-operative Society, 1941.
Pp. 72.

9303   GUTTERIDGE, WILLIAM H. A brief history of
       the town of Maynard, Massachusetts. Maynard:
The Town, 1921. Pp. 115.

9304   MAYNARD HISTORICAL COMMITTEE. History of
       Maynard, Massachusetts, 1871-1971. Acton:
Beacon Publishing, 1971. Pp. 234.

9305   "UNITED Cooperative Society of Maynard."
       Co-operation, 13 (1927), 62-64.

MEDFIELD

9306   GOULD, ELIZABETH PORTER. "An old town's
       school for good citizenship." NEM, New Ser.,
1 (1890), 672-674.
       Meetings for political study, 1798.

9307   HARWOOD, WILLARD. "The early homes of Jo-
       seph and Mary Baxter." DedHR, 8 (1897),
97-104.
       Biographical.

9308   HAYWARD, WILLIAM WILLIS. Address given at
       the commemoration of the one hundredth anni-
versary of the building of the First Congregational
Church, Medfield, Mass., Wednesday, Oct. 9, 1889....
[Medfield]: S. J. Spear, [1889]. Pp. 11.

9309   ____. "Remarks of Rev. W. W. Hayward."
       Worcester HSProc, (1891-1893), 107-110.
       Congregational ministers of the town.

9310   HEWINS, JAMES. "A few of the homes of Med-
       field, and what their names signify."
Worcester HSProc, (1891-1893), 97-105.

9311   LOVELL, ALBERT A. "Mr. Lovell's address."
       Worcester HSProc, (1891-1893), 79-89.
       History of the town.

9312   MEDFIELD, MASS. Exercises at the bi-centen-
       nial commemoration of the burning of Medfield
by Indians in King Philip's War, February 21, 1876.
Medfield: George H. Ellis, 1876. Pp. 56.

9313   ____. Medfield, Massachusetts: proceedings
       at the celebration of the two hundred and
fiftieth anniversary of the incorporation of the
town, June 6, 1901. Boston: G. H. Ellis, 1902.
Pp. 112.

9314   ____. Proceedings at the dedication of the
       town hall, Medfield, September 10, 1872:
with supplement containing an account of the exercises at the re-dedication, November 2d, 1874; brief
sketches of the churches of the town and the public
library; and a record of the soldiers furnished by
the town in the late War of the Rebellion. Medfield, 1875. Pp. 39, 63.

9315   MEDFIELD. Boston: Edison Electric Illumin-
       ating Co., 1909. Pp. 12. M.

9316   SANDERS, DANIEL CLARKE. A sermon preached in
       Medfield, 5th January 1817, near the 166th
anniversary of the incorporation of the town. Dedham: Abel D. Alleyne, 1817. Pp. 27. MB.

9317   TILDEN, WILLIAM SMITH. History...Baptist
       Church in Medfield...August 18, 1876. Bos-
ton: G. H. Ellis, 1877. Pp. 71. MBNEH.
       Centennial of the church.

9318   ____, ed. History of the town of Medfield.
       Massachusetts, 1650 [-] 1886; with genealo-
gies of the families that held real estate or made
any considerable stay in the town during the first
two centuries. Boston: G. H. Ellis, 1887. Pp. 556.

9319   ____. "Indians in Medfield." DedHR, 10
       (1899), 51-53.

9320   ____. "Medfield soldiers in the Revolu-
       tion." DedHR, 8 (1897), 70-76.

9321   ____. "Old Medfield superstitions." DedHR,
       9 (1898), 102-105.

9322   ____. 1651-1901; souvenir of Medfield: I.
       A visit to an early homestead. II. A Sunday
in the old meeting house. Boston: George H. Ellis,
1901. Pp. 22,23. MBNEH.

MEDFORD

9323 ACKERMAN, HERBERT N. "The Congregational Church of West Medford." MedHR, 13 (1910), 25-49.

9324 AMORY, THOMAS COFFIN. "The Cradock House at Medford." MHSP, 20 (1882-1883), 24-27.

9325 "THE ANDOVER Turnpike." MedHR, 23 (1920), 23-24.

9326 AYRES, ALICE C. "The Whitmores of Medford and some of their descendants." MedHR, 8 (1905), 64-74.

9327 BAKER, ABIJAH RICHARDSON. The ark, ships and ship-building, with a brief history of the art, and a register of vessels built in Medford. Boston: A. Forbes, 1847. Pp. 40.

9328 BARKER, ABNER H. "History of Wellington." MedHR, 30 (1927), 69-77. Area of the city.

9329 BARRETT, EDWARD W. Historical sketches, schools of Medford, and other topics. Medford, 1936. Pp. 81. MBNEH.

9330 _____, et al. "The later physicians of Medford." MedHr, 35 (1932), 21-33.

9331 _____. "The schoolhouses of Medford." MedHR, 37 (1934), 53-80.

9332 BRIGHAM, JENNIE PIERCE. "Mystic Hall Seminary." MedHR, 11 (1908), 49-63.

9333 BROOKS, MRS. ALFRED and MOSES WHITCHER MANN. "Colonial houses--old and new." MedHR, 15 (1912), 67-72.

9334 BROOKS, CHARLES. History of the town of Medford, Middlesex County, Massachusetts, from its first settlement in 1630 to 1855. (1855) Rev., enl., and brought down to 1885, by James M. Usher. Boston: Rand, Avery, 1886. Pp. 592.

9335 _____. "Indian necropolis in West Medford, Mass., discovered Oct. 21, 1862." MHSP, (1862-1863), 362-364.

9336 BULLOCK, M. L. "A short history of the Wellington Methodist Episcopal Church." MedHR, 31 (1928), 1-4.

9337 CAPEN, E. H. "Tufts College." NEM, 4 (1886), 99-112.

9338 CARMICHAEL, LEONARD. Tufts College, its science & technology; a centennial view (1852-1952). N.Y.: Newcomen Society in North America, 1952. Pp. 24.

9339 CONNORS, DANIEL W. "History of Medford's police." MedHR, 35 (1932), 61-66.

9340 COOKE, GEORGE. "Indian relics." Winchester Record, 1 (1885), 209-211.

9341 COOLIDGE, RICHARD B. "The Brooks estates in Medford from 1660 to 1927." MedHR, 30 (1927), 1-20.

9342 _____. "Medford and her minute men, April 19, 1775." MedHR, 28 (1925), 37-51.

9343 _____. "The Medford of Cradock and Winthrop." MedHR, 34 (1931), 2-20.

9344 _____. "Walnut Tree Hill." MedHR, 39 (1936), 21-36. Section of the city.

9345 COOLIDGE, RUTH DAME. "The 'Cradock' house, past and future." MedHR, 29 (1926), 37-56. Author maintains that it should be called Peter Tufts House.

9346 _____. "Indians of Medford." MedHR, 33 (1930), 26-28. Massachuset tribe.

9347 _____. and RICHARD B. COOLIDGE. "Medford and George Washington." MedHR, 34 (1931), 57-65.

9348 COOLIDGE, RUTH DAME. "The Medford High School under Lorin L. Dame." MedHR, 27 (1924), 65-81.

9349 CUMMINGS, ABBOTT LOWELL. "History in houses: the Royall House in Medford, Massachusetts." Antiques, 88 (1965), 506-510.

9350 CUMMINGS, CHARLES. "The days of hand engines." MedHR, 6 (1903), 63-65. Fire department.

9351 _____. "History of the Medford High School." MedHR, 27 (1924), 5-23.

9352 _____. "Medford in 1847." MedHR, 6 (1903), 39-47.

9353 _____. "The Second Congregational and Mystic churches." MedHR, 3 (1900), 49-71.

9354 _____. "A town meeting, 1847." MedHR, 7 (1904), 44-45.

9355 CURTIS, ELISHA B. "The old ship-building days." MedHR, 15 (1912), 77-80.

9356 CUSHING, FRED L. "Medford's water supply." MedHR, 13 (1910), 51-62.

9357 CUSHING, WALTER H. "Governor Cradock's plantation." MedHR, 1 (1898), 138-147.

9358 _____. "Slavery in Medford." MedHR, 3 (1900), 118-124.

9359 DAILEY, WILLIAM E. "History of St. James' Church, Wellington." MedHR, 30 (1927), 86-88.

9360 DELONG, HENRY C. "Early ministers of Medford." MedHR, 2 (1899), 95-118.

9361 _____. "The First Parish in Medford." MedHR, 12 (1909), 73-82.

9362 DENNISON, EDWARD B. "Medford railroad stations, notes and reminiscences." MedHR, 39 (1936), 1-19.

9363 DOLAND, HENRY B. "Union Congregational Church." MedHR, 15 (1912), 33-45.

9364 DRAKE, SAMUEL ADAMS. "The Cradock House, Medford." Appleton's Journal, 9 (1873), 495-497.

9365 [EWELL, WILLIAM GORHAM.] Medford Police Relief Association, grand concert and ball, Lawrence Light Guard Armory, Friday evening, Jan. 27, 1911. Cambridge: J. Frank Facey, [1911?]. Pp. 24. MBNEH.
A history of the Medford Police Department; author attribution by the New England Historic Genealogical Society.

9366 FARNUM, IRVING B. "Medford's postmasters." MedHR, 16 (1913), 33-39.

9367 "FIRSTS and lasts in Medford history." MedHR, 35 (1932), 17-18.

9368 FISKE, WILSON. "The state's oldest house." MedHR, 35 (1932), 43-44.
Blanchard House.

9369 FRANKLIN, JOHN SHADE. "The Fulton Heights Community Church." MedHR, 31 (1928), 36-39.
Baptist.

9370 FULLER, GEORGE S. T. "The history of the Royall House and its occupants." MedHR, 29 (1926), 1-11.

9371 GAFFEY, EDWARD J. "Ships of Medford." Med HR, 33 (1930), 24-25.

9372 GALLAGHER, MARK E. "The Lawrence Farm and farmhouse." MedHR, 36 (1933), 33-41.

9373 GILL, ELIZA M. "Distinguished guests and residents of Medford." MedHR, 16 (1913), 1-24.

9374 _____. "Lafayette's visit to Medford, people and incidents relating thereto reviewed." MedHR, 19 (1916), 1-12.

9375 _____. "A Medford garden and the gardener's notes." MedHR, 21 (1918), 69-73.
Martin Burridge as gardener for the Bigelow family.

9376 _____. "Medford horticulturists." MedHR, 21 (1918), 73-74.

9377 _____. "New Hampshire soldiers in Medford, 1775." MedHR, 8 (1905), 16-23.

9377A _____. "The pump in the market place; and other water supplies of Medford, old and modern." MedHR, 12 (1909), 25-41.

9378 _____. "Stage-coach days in Medford." Med HR, 13 (1910), 77-92.

9379 GLEASON, HALL. "Medford's part in American ship-building." MedHR, 37 (1934), 10-12.

9380 _____. Old ships and ship-building days of Medford, 1630-1873. West Medford: J. C. Miller, Jr., 1936. Pp. 84.

9381 GOLDING, THOMAS J. "The outline of St. Francis of Assisi Parish." MedHR, 31 (1928), 40-42.

9382 GREEN, CHARLES M. "The early physicians of Medford." MedHR, 1 (1898), 101-118.

9383 GREGG, PAUL A. "History of the Middlesex Fells Zoo." MedHR, 38 (1935), 74-78.

9384 GUILD, CLARA T. "The ministers and meeting-houses of the First Parish in Medford." MedHR, 33 (1930), 16-22.

9385 HAMMOND, STAFFORD. "High School Department, an early scourge in Medford." MedHR, 4 (1901), 17-20.
Smallpox.

9386 HARLOW, THOMAS S. "Some notes of the history of Medford from 1801 to 1851." MedHR, 1 (1898), 82-92.

9387 HERSEY, HARRY ADAMS. A history of music in Tufts College. Medford: Trustees of Tufts College, 1947. Pp. 369.

9388 HERVEY, JAMES A. "Reminiscences of earlier Medford: a familiar talk before the Medford Historical Society." MedHR, 4 (1901), 61-77.

9389 _____. "Ship-building in Medford." MedHR, 1 (1898), 65-81.

9390 HESSE, A. "Historical sketch of the Calvary Evangelical Church." MedHR, 31 (1928), 43-44.

9391 HOLLIS, BENJAMIN PRATT. "Grace Church, Medford." MedHR, 5 (1902), 25-43.

9392 _____. "Medford Young Men's Christian Association." MedHR, 13 (1910), 16-18.

9393 HOOPER, JOHN H. "About the old mill." Med HR, 17 (1914), 42-45.
Remains of a grist mill.

9394 _____. "Bridges in Medford." MedHR, 2 (1899), 1-25.

9395 _____. "The ford at Mistick." MedHR, 4 (1901), 1-5.

9396 _____. "Medford Turnpike Corporation." Med HR, 23 (1920), 1-10.

9397 _____. "More about the grist mill." MedHR, 23 (1920), 71-75.

9398 _____. "Nathan Wait's right of way." Med HR, 20 (1917), 74-77.
Along the Middlesex Canal.

9399 _____. "Pine and Pasture Hills and the part they have contributed to the development of Medford." MedHR, 18 (1915), 25-32.

9400 _____. "The roads of old Medford." MedHR, 2 (1899), 53-71.

9401 _____. The Royall House and Farm." MedHR, 3 (1900), 133-153.

9402 _____. "Sewage in Mystic River." MedHR, 23 (1920), 45-53.

9403 _____. "Some errors in Medford's histories." MedHR, 19 (1916), 25-43.

9404 _____. "The taverns of Medford." MedHR, 8 (1905), 1-12, 25-32.

9405 _____. "The Walnut Tree Hill Division of the Stinted Pasture." MedHR, 15 (1912), 46-53.

9406 "HOW a Medford ship was built." MedHR, 25 (1922), 15-18.
'Horsburg.'

9407 HUNT, LOUISE F. "The Roman Catholic Church in Medford." MedHR, 17 (1914), 1-8.

9408 HURD, CHARLES EDWIN. "Medford fifty-four years ago." MedHR, 11 (1908), 1-16.

9409 "IN earlier days." MedHR, 22 (1919), 59-62.
Temporary places of worship used by church groups.

9410 "THE ISAAC Royall House or the 'Plantation' in Medford." American Architect and Building News, 24 (1888), 171-172.

9411 JEPSON, SAMUEL G. "Incidents and reminiscences of the fire department of Medford." MedHR, 4 (1901), 6-16.

9412 LANE, ALFRED C. and ROBERT L. NICHOLS. "The early history of Medford." MedHR, 33 (1930), 11-16.
Geological development.

9413 LITCHFIELD, PARKER R. "First Universalist Society in Medford." MedHR, 4 (1901), 25-38.

9414 "LOCAL changes in Medford." MedHR, 23 (1920), 58-60.
Relocation and abolition of streets.

9415 "LOCAL history in a barber shop." MedHR, 24 (1921), 56-60.
First Methodist Episcopal Church.

9416 LOVERING, FRANK WOODS. "The Medford Co-operative Bank." MedHR, 34 (1931), 25-31.

9417 _____. "The Medford Home for Aged Men and Women." MedHR, 36 (1933), 17-29.

9418 _____. "The story of the West Medford Baptist Church." MedHR, 19 (1916), 73-78.

9419 MCCOLLOM, JAMES TOMB. Historical discourse, a sermon preached at the semi-centennial anniversary of the First Trinitarian Congregational Church of Medford. Medford: Medford Journal Pr., 1873. Pp. 24.

9420 "MAIN Street, 1835-1850." MedHR, 6 (1903), 92-95.

9421 MANN, MOSES WHITCHER. "The beginnings of a new village." MedHR, 28 (1925), 17-30.
Development of a part of Medford originally called the "Smith Estate."

9422 _____. "A bit of Medford archaeology." MedHR, 17 (1914), 15-18.
Grist mill.

9423 _____. "Changes along High Street." MedHR, 28 (1925), 71-75.

9424 _____. "Connecting links in Medford church history." MedHR, 21 (1918) 82-90.
West Medford Christian Union, a non-denominational church.

9425 _____. "Cradock Bridge--1637-1880." Med HR, 31 (1928), 83-87.

9426 _____. "Editorial comment." MedHR, 23 (1920), 75-78.
Grist mill.

9427 _____. "The 18-18 boys." MedHR, 15 (1912), 26-28.
Club.

9428 _____. "Fin de siècle." MedHR, 29 (1926), 21-32.
Development of an area of the city, 1829-1925.

9429 _____. "Forgotten industries and enterprises." MedHR, 5 (1902), 18-19.

9430 _____. "Governor Brooks Engine Company." MedHR, 17 (1914), 18-21.
Fire Department.

9431 _____. "High Street in 1870." MedHR, 18 (1915), 13-24.

9432 _____. "How did Medford get its name?" Med HR, 22 (1919), 21-25.

9433 _____. "How Medford began to grow." MedHR, 14 (1911), 9-14.
Population.

9434 _____. "In another corner of Medford." MedHR, 22 (1919), 25-37.

9435 ____. "The Jonathan Watson House." MedHR, 15 (1912), 59-63.

9436 ____. "Little walks and talks about Medford." MedHR, 32 (1929), 3-6, 17-32, 45-52.

9437 ____. "Medford artillery." MedHR, 17 (1914), 25-33.
Weapons.

9438 ____, and F. A. WAIT and CHARLES E. PRESTON. "Medford Branch Railroad." MedHR, 17 (1914), 34-39; 20 (1917), 37-43.

9439 MANN, MOSES WHITCHER. "The Medford grasshopper." MedHR, 16 (1913), 72-76.
A fire engine.

9440 ____. "Medford Hillside." MedHR, 20 (1916), 5-9.
Section of the city also known as College Hill.

9441 ____. "Medford journalism." MedHR, 26 (1923), 72-84.

9442 ____. "The Medford library building." MedHR, 22 (1919), 1-7.

9443 ____. "Medford mining matters." MedHR, 19 (1916), 65-67.
Silver and lead.

9444 ____. "Medford Square in the early days." MedHR, 28 (1925), 51-55, 63-71.

9445 ____. "Medford steamboat days." MedHR, 17 (1914), 92-98.

9446 ____. "A Medford town meeting." MedHR, 20 (1917), 31-34.
1857.

9447 ____. "Medford's bulky red rose." MedHR, 26 (1923), 45-55.
Pasture Hill area of the city.

9448 ____. "Medford's disused subway." MedHR, 20 (1917), 1-5.
A water conduit.

9449 ____. "Medford's municipal publications." MedHR, 25 (1922), 28-34.

9450 ____. "Medford's town farm." MedHR, 21 (1918), 37-46.

9451 ____. "The Meridian Monument." MedHR, 16 (1913), 45-48.
Cairn that bore the meridian mark of the observatory of Harvard College.

9452 ____. "More about the turnpike." MedHR, 23 (1920), 10-15.
Medford Turnpike Corporation.

9453 ____. "The Mystic Mansion." MedHR, 15 (1912), 80-88.

9454 ____. "Mystic River made over." MedHR, 20 (1917), 9-11.

9455 ____. "Mystic Valley Park." MedHR, 32 (1929), 41-44.

9456 ____. "The Mystic Water-Works." MedHR, 20 (1917), 21-30.

9457 ____. "North Medford." MedHR, 31 (1928), 21-34.

9458 ____. "The old Fountain Tavern." MedHR, 19 (1916), 68-70.

9459 ____. "The old powder house." MedHR, 29 (1926), 11-16, 35-36.
Ammunition storage; eighteenth century.

9460 ____. "On one side of Medford Square." MedHR, 21 (1918), 92-94.

9461 ____. "The passing of a Medford estate." MedHR, 15 (1912), 30-32.
Brooks family estate.

9462 ____. "A projected Medford railroad." MedHR, 16 (1913), 90-96.

9463 ____. "The renovation of Peter Tufts' House." MedHR, 29 (1926), 70-75.

9464 ____. "The road through the woods." MedHR, 30 (1927), 20-23.
Grove Street.

9465 ____. "South Medford one hundred and fifty years ago." MedHR, 16 (1913), 67-71.

9466 ____. "The Thatcher Magoun House." MedHR, 30 (1927), 61-65.

9467 ____. "Told on Winter Hill." MedHR, 17 (1914), 9-14.
Revolutionary battle.

9468 ____. "The tornado of 1851." MedHR, 29 (1926), 32-35.

9469 ____. "Trinity Methodist Episcopal Church." MedHR, 14 (1911), 25-50.

9470 ____. "Two Medford buildings of the fifties." MedHR, 19 (1916), 49-54.
The second Brooks Schoolhouse and Mystic Hall, built in 1852.

9471 ____, L. R. SYMMES, and DAVID YOUNGMAN. "Upper Medford." MedHR, 31 (1928), 49-70.

9472 MANN, MOSES WHITCHER. "Views of Medford." MedHR, 26 (1923), 1-12.

9473 ____. "The West End Schoolhouse." MedHR, 8 (1905), 75-77.

9474 ____. "West Medford in 1870." MedHR, 8 (1905), 81-97.

9475 _____. and WARREN E. WESCOTT. "The West Medford post office." MedHR, 29 (1926), 75-76.

9476 MANN, MOSES WHITCHER. "West Medford's schoolhouse evolution." MedHR, 35 (1932), 2-5.

9477 _____. "The western section of Medford." MedHR, 32 (1929), 66-68.

9478 _____. "What mean ye be these stones?" MedHR, 28 (1925), 4-7.
Indian monument in Sagamore Park and its inscription.

9479 _____. "The Withington Bakery." MedHR, 18 (1915), 49-53.

9480 _____. "Wood's Dam and the mill beyond the Mystic." MedHR, 12 (1909), 13-20.

9481 _____. "Ye old meting-house of Meadford." MedHR, 11 (1908), 25-42, 62-67.

9482 MEDFORD, MASS. Proceedings of the celebration of the two hundred and seventy-fifth anniversary of the settlement of Medford, Massachusetts, June, nineteen hundred and five, prefaced by a brief history of the town and city from the day of settlement, by John H. Hooper.... [Medford]: The Executive Committee, 1906. Pp. xii, 261.

9483 MEDFORD, MASS. FIRST CHURCH. Sermon and address delivered at the celebration of the two hundredth anniversary of the First Church in Medford.... Medford: J. C. Miller, Jr., 1913. Pp. 27. MWA.

9484 MEDFORD, MASS. MYSTIC CHURCH. Manual of the Mystic Church in Medford, 1848. Boston: C. C. P. Moody, 1848. Pp. 18. M.
Includes brief history.

9485 "MEDFORD a century ago--1819." MedHR, 22 (1919), 67-75.

9486 "MEDFORD Branch Canal." MedHR, 23 (1920), 25-30.
Middlesex Canal.

9487 "MEDFORD church anniversaries." MedHR, 25 (1922), 61-77.
First Methodist Episcopal Church, Trinity Methodist Episcopal Church, West Medford Congregational Church and Mystic Congregational Church.

9488 "MEDFORD, condita, 1628." MedHR, 23 (1920), 65-69.
Shipbuilding.

9489 "MEDFORD in 1837." MedHR, 25 (1922), 56-58.

9490 "MEDFORD in 1821." MedHR, 19 (1916), 80-83.

9491 "THE MEDFORD Indian Monument." MedHR, 25 (1922), 52-56.

9492 [MEDFORD PUBLISHING COMPANY]. Medford past and present; 275th anniversary of Medford, Massachusetts, June, 1905.... [Medford]: Medford Mercury, 1905. Pp. 170.

9493 "MEDFORD Saltmarsh Corporation." MedHR, 23 (1920), 30-34.

9494 "MEDFORD shipbuilding notes." MedHR, 25 (1922), 50-52.

9495 "MEDFORD sky-scrapers." MedHR, 31 (1928), 17-20.

9496 "MEDFORD Square, 1835 to 1850." MedHR, 5 (1902), 91-94.

9497 "THE MEDFORD 'Syren.'" MedHR, 22 (1919), 76-77.

9498 "THE MEDFORD Visiting Nurse Association." MedHR, 35 (1932), 37-40.

9499 "MEDFORD'S first gristmill." MedHR, 23 (1920), 53-58.

9500 "MEDFORD's home for the aged." MedHR, 18 (1915), 78-81.

9501 "MEDICAL work in the schools." MedHR, 35 (1932), 35-37.

9502 MILLER, RUSSELL E. Light on the hill: a history of Tufts College, 1852-1952. Boston: Beacon Pr., 1966. Pp. xviii, 734.

9503 "THE MILLS on the Medford Turnpike." MedHR, 23 (1920), 18-22.

9504 MORRISON, BENJAMIN F. "The schools and schoolmaster of colonial days in Medford." MedHR, 1 (1898), 1-10.

9505 MORSS, CHARLES H. "Development of the public schools of Medford." MedHR, 3 (1900), 1-41.

9506 "THE MYSTIC Church, Medford, Ms." CongQ, 2 (1860), 412-413.

9507 "MYSTIC River above the bridge, 1835-1850." MedHR, 6 (1903), 15-20.

9508 "THE OLD bob-tail car." MedHR, 21 (1918), 47-48.
Middlesex Street Railway line.

9509 "OUR autobiography." MedHR, 24 (1921), 45-50.
Medford Historical Society.

9510 PARADISE, SCOTT HURTT. "Some memories of an old house." MedHR, 31 (1928), 9-14.
Peter C. Brooks House; demolished.

9511 PERRY, PARKER W. "The vanished village of the Fells." MedHR, 38 (1935), 79-86.
Haywardville.

9512 PLUMMER, MRS. J. M. G. "The Baptist Church of Medford." MedHR, 6 (1903), 51-63.

9513 PRENDERGAST, FRANK M. "Library binding comes to industry." Industry, 21 (December, 1955), 20, 22-24.
F. J. Barnard & Co.

9514 ROLLINS, EDWIN B. "Country school expenses a century ago." MedHR, 35 (1932), 6-10.

9515 "THE ROUTE of Revere." MedHR, 24 (1921), 17-23.
Paul Revere.

9516 "THE ROYALL Towers." MedHR, 24 (1921), 14-17.
Royall House.

9517 SARGENT, GRACE L. "The loyalists of Medford." MedHR, 8 (1905), 49-61.

9518 SARGENT, LOUISE PEABODY. "Literary Medford." MedHR, 15 (1912), 1-22.

9519 SARGENT, MARY ELIZABETH FISKE. "The evolution of the Medford Public Library." MedHR, 2 (1899), 76-91.

9520 SAXE, ABBY DREW. "The First Methodist Episcopal Church of Medford." MedHR, 12 (1909), 1-12.

9521 SMITH, JOSEPH C. "Medford's zoning ordinance." MedHR, 35 (1932), 67-70.

9522 SONIER, ELIZABETH C. "A bit of a beam." MedHR, 31 (1928), 79-82.
Cradock Bridge.

9523 STETSON, CALEB. Two discourses preached before the First Congregational Society in Medford; one upon leaving the old church; and one at the dedication of the new. Boston: I. R. Butts, 1840. Pp. 59.

9524 STONE, KATHERINE H. "Thirty years' growth of Medford schools." MedHR, 35 (1932), 45-54.

9525 TOLLES, BRYANT FRANKLIN, JR. "Gridley F. J. Bryant and the first building at Tufts College." OTNE, 63 (1972-1973), 89-99.
Ballou Hall.

9526 "THE TOWERS of Medford." MedHR, 24 (1921), 1-14.

9527 TUFTS COLLEGE. Celebration of the semi-centennial of Tufts College, 1905. [Medford]: Tufts College Pr., 1905. Pp. 76.

9528 TUFTS COLLEGE. CLASS OF 1897. History of Tufts College. Alaric Bertrand Start, ed. [Medford], 1896. Pp. x, 382.

9529 WAIT, FRANCIS A. "Medford milkmen." MedHR, 14 (1911), 1-7.

9530 WAIT, WILLIAM CUSHING. "Maps of Medford at different periods." MedHR, 1 (1898), 119-137.

9531 "WASHINGTON and the Royall House." MedHR, 35 (1932), 56-58.

9532 "WASHINGTON Hook and Ladder Comapny." MedHR, 37 (1934), 13-14.

9533 WEITZ, HERBERT A. "Lawyers of Medford." MedHR, 5 (1902), 49-68.

9534 "WELLINGTON on the map." MedHR, 31 (1928), 6-8.
Area of the city.

9535 WHITNEY, ARTHUR EASTMAN. "Ancient legal contentions in upper Medford." MedHR, 13 (1910), 1-6.
Seventeenth century.

9536 WILD, HELEN TILDEN. "The building of the Town House." MedHR, 9 (1906), 40-43.
1832-1835.

9537 _____. "The Congregational Church in Medford." MedHR, 37 (1934), 1-10.

9538 _____. "Female Union Temperance Society." MedHR, 9 (1906), 90-92.

9539 _____. "High Street about 1820." MedHR, 8 (1905), 44-47.

9540 _____. "History told by names of streets." MedHR, 7 (1904), 22-24, 45-46; 21 (1918), 10-14.
Continuation is by Moses Whitcher Mann.

9541 _____. "The Lawrence Light Guard." MedHR, 5 (1902), 73-90; 6 (1903), 1-9.

9542 _____. Medford in the Revolution, military history of Medford, Massachusetts, 1765-1783; also list of soldiers and civil officers, with genealogical and biographical notes. Medford: J. C. Miller, Jr., 1903. Pp. 67.

9543 _____. "Medford in the War of the Revolution." MedHR, 2 (1899), 26-49.

9544 _____. "An old account book." MedHR, 4 (1901), 102-104.
Aaron Blanchard, tailor and church sexton; 1815-1848.

9545 _____. "The old Royall House." MassMag, 1 (1908), 168-173.

9546 _____. "Old Salem Street." MedHR, 16 (1913), (1913), 53-66.
Streets.

9547 _____. "Over the hill and to the poorhouse." MedHR, 6 (1903), 72-74.

9548 _____. "The Royall House loan exhibition, April 19 to April 29, 1899." MedHR, 2 (1899), 119-125.

9549 WOODS, AMY. "Tufts College." NEM, New Ser., 32 (1905), 415-430.

9550 WOOLLEY, FRED H. C. "Meeting House Brook and the Second Meeting House." MedHR, 7 (1904), 73-80.

9551 _____. "Old Ship Street, some of its houses, ships, and characters." MedHR, 4 (1901), 87-100.

MEDWAY

9552 BURR, JOHN EZRA. History of the Baptist Church in West Medway, Mass., and biographical sketches of its pastors, by Rev. Lyman Partridge, read at the fiftieth anniversary of the church, and re-dedication of the church office, November 15th, 1882. Mansfield: Pratt, 1853. Pp. 30.

9553 HIXON, HERBERT N. October 4th, 1750-- October 7-8th, 1950: historical address given at the bi-centennial of the Second Church of Christ in Medway, West Medway, Massachusetts. n.p., [1950?]. Unpaged.

9554 _____. "An old-time Sunday in the West Parish of Medway." OTNE, 19 (1928-1929), 141-144.

9555 JAMESON, EPHRAIM ORCUTT. The biographical sketches of prominent persons, and the genealogical records of many early and other families in Medway, Mass. 1713-1886.... Providence, R.I.: J. A. & R. A. Reid, 1886. Pp. 208.

9556 _____. Historical discourse preached on the one hundred and sixty-second anniversary of the First Church of Christ, Medway, Mass., first Sabbath in October, 1876. Boston: Alfred Mudge & Son, 1877. Pp. 86.

9557 _____, ed. The history of Medway, Mass., 1713 to 1885. Providence, R.I.: J. A. & R. A. Reid, 1886. Pp. 534.

9558 MASON, ORION THOMAS. The handbook of Medway history: a condensed history of the town of Medway, Massachusetts. [Medway]: G. M. Billings, 1913. Pp. 116.

9559 MEDWAY, MASS. VILLAGE CONGREGATIONAL CHURCH. Fiftieth anniversary of the organization of the Village Congregational Church, Medway, Mass., Friday, Sept. 7, 1888. Boston: Beacon Pr., 1888. Pp. 101. M.

9560 MEDWAY. Boston: Edison Electric Illuminating Co., 1909. Pp. 12. M.

9561 MEDWAY HISTORICAL SOCIETY, MEDWAY, MASS. Medway, Massachusetts, proceedings a the celebration of Old Home Day, Wednesday August third, nineteen hundred four, together with an account of the dedication of the Rev. Jacob Ide memorial in connection therewith. Rufus G. Fairbanks, ed. [Medway], 1904. Pp. 49.

9562 SWAN, MABEL MUNSON. "Some men from Medway." Antiques, 17 (1930), 417-421. Cabinetmakers.

9563 STATISTICS of the town of Medway and of the three Medways. Boston: Rockwell and Churchill, 1885. Pp. 15. MWA.

9564 WRIGHT, LUTHER, 1770-1858. A sermon, delivered at Medway, November 4, 1813, on the close of a century, since the incorporation of the town. Dedham: Gazette Office, 1814. Pp. 32.

MELROSE

9565 ADAMS, CHARLES H. Melrose, town and city: published on the occasion of the fiftieth anniversary of Melrose, Mass., May 1900. Melrose: Melrose Journal, 1900. Pp. 127. M.

9566 ATKINSON, BROOKS. "A Puritan boyhood." Massachusetts Review, 15 (1974), 339-380. Social life and customs.

9567 DEARBORN, GEORGE H. Historical sketch of the Unitarian Church of Melrose, Mass. [Melrose], 1900. Unpaged.

9568 _____. Historical sketch of the Unitarian Church of Melrose, Mass., 1867-1917, fiftieth anniversary June 3rd, nineteen hundred and seventeen. Melrose: Melrose Free Pr., 1917. Pp. 12.

9569 GOSS, ELBRIDGE HENRY. Bibliography of Melrose. L. F. Williams, 1889. Unpaged.

9570 _____. The centennial fourth, historical address delivered in Town Hall, Melrose, Mass., July 4, 1876. Melrose: Priv. Print., 1876. Pp. 46.
    Sketch of the town.

9571 _____. The history of Melrose, county of Middlesex, Massachusetts. Melrose: The City, 1902. Pp. xviii, 508.
    Supplemented by 'Melrose, Massachusetts, 1900-1950' by Edwin Carl Kemp.

9572 _____. The Melrose memorial, the annals of Melrose, county of Middlesex, Massachusetts, in the great rebellion of 1861-'65. Boston: A. Mudge & Son, 1868. Pp. xxix, 292.

9573 GOULD, LEVI SWANTON. "Reminiscences of North Malden (Melrose) and vicinity." MalHR, No. 4 (1915-1916), 65-84.

9574 KEMP, EDWIN CARL. Melrose, Massachusetts, 1900-1950; commemorating the one hundredth anniversary of the founding of the town of Melrose and the fiftieth anniversary of the incorporation of the city of Melrose. [Melrose]: Fiftieth Anniversary Committee, 1950. Pp. 183.
    Supplement to 'History of Melrose' by Elbridge Henry Goss.

9575 NORWELL, JOSHUA T. and HARRY A. BATCHELDER. Picturesque Melrose Highlands. Boston: C. W. Calkins, [1894?]. Pp. 56. MB.

9576 TAYLOR, JOHN G. Four historical sermons... origin and growth of the religious movement at Melrose Highlands, Massachusetts.... Boston: T. W. Ripley, 1887. Pp. 60. MB. Congregationalism.

9577 WALKER, CHARLES MONROE. The first hundred years: a history of the Melrose Unitarian Church from 1867 to 1967. Melrose: Melrose Unitarian Church, 1967. Pp. 30.

MENDON

9578 BLAKE, MORTIMER. A centurial history of the Mendon Association of Congregational Ministers, with the centennial address, delivered at Franklin, Mass., Nov. 19, 1851, and biographical sketches of the members and licentiates. Boston: Sewall Harding, 1853. Pp. vi, 348.

9579 CLARK, GEORGE FABER. "The early ministry of Mendon, Mass." Worcester HSProc, (1891-1893), 225-244. 1667-1751.

9580 _____. "Who was the first minister of Mendon?" NEHGR, 35 (1881), 157-159. Benjamin Eliot.

9581 HACKETT, PETER. Mendon, Massachusetts 1667-1967, mother of municipalities. n.p., [1967?]. Unpaged. MBNEH.

9582 KEELER, EDITH FLINT. Some Mendon families and their descendants. Mendon, [193-?]. Unpaged.

9583 MENDON, MASS. An address, by Rev. Carlton A. Staples, of Milwaukee, Wis.; a poem, by Hon. Henry Chapin, of Worcester, Mass., and other proceedings, in commemoration of the two hundredth anniversary of the incorporation of Mendon, Massachusetts. Worcester: Chas. Hamilton, 1868. Pp. 89 (i.e. 95). Paging irregular.

9584 METCALF, JOHN GEORGE, comp. Annals of the town of Mendon, from 1659 to 1880. Providence, R. I.: E. L. Freeman, 1880. Pp. vii, 723. Typescript index of names by Florence T. Allen is at MBNEH and MWA.

9585 A SHORT account of the state of Mendon Third Parish relative to the Rev. Benjamin Balch's settling there...September 14, 1768...and...his leaving them, March 27, 1773. By an inhabitant of said Parish. Boston, 1773. Pp. 16. MWA.

9586 STAPLES, CARLTON ALBERT. An address at Mendon, Mass., before the Worcester County Unitarian Conference, at the autumnal session, Sept. 10, 1873, on the history of the First Church in that town. Milford: George W. Stacy, 1873. Pp. 24.

MERRIMAC

9587 JUDKINS, J. B., COMPANY, MERRIMAC, MASS. Judkins; being the story of a New England handicraft and its honest expression in fine carriages and motor car bodies. Merrimac, [1930?]. Pp. 34.

METHUEN

9588 CARLETON, GEORGE E. Sketches of the town of Methuen: a lecture...February 9, 1863. Lawrence: C. A. Dockham, 1864. v.p. MSaE.

9589 CURRIER, LIZZIE B. "Music of other days in Methuen." Methuen Historical Society. Publication, No. 1 (1896), 11-19.

9590 HALL, KING S. Historical discourse, preached at the semi-centennial celebration, of the organization of the First Baptist Church, Methuen, Mass., October 18th, 1865, with an account of the celebration, and articles of faith. Lawrence: G. S. Merrill, 1865. Pp. 56.

9591 HAYWARD, FREDERICK D. A short history of the First Church and Parish of Methuen, Massachusetts, 1729-1929. [Methuen]: Methuen Pr., 1929. Pp. 67. MSaE.

9592 HOWE, JOSEPH SIDNEY. The growth of Methuen, a paper read before the Methuen Historical Society. [Methuen, 1898]. Pp. 15.

9593 _____. Historical sketch of the town of Methuen, from its settlement to the year 1876. Methuen: E. L. Houghton, 1876. Pp. 48.

9594 MANN, C. H. T. "The First Church in Methuen." ECHGR, 2 (1895), 84-86.

9595 MANN, CHARLES W. "The King's Highway, known as the Common Road from Swan's Ferry to Back River Mill." NEM, New Ser., 26 (1902), 525-535.

9596 METHUEN, MASS., FIRST CONGREGATIONAL CHURCH. Manual of the First Congregational Church, Methuen, Mass., adopted June 15, 1875. Lawrence: G. S. Merrill and Crocker, 1875. Pp. 128. M. Contains historical sketch of church.

9597 NOYES, MABEL F. and MINNA B. NOYES. West Methuen of long ago: chronicles. Bedford: Bedford Print Shop, 1929. Pp. 72.

9598 OLIPHANT, CHARLES R. "Methuen, Massachusetts." NEM, New Ser., 23 (1900-1901), 97-115.

9599 "SECOND Parish, Methuen, 1784-1846." ECHGR, 1 (1894), 49-52, 68-70, 101-103, 118-120, 130-133, 150, 152-169.

9600 TENNEY, DANIEL WOODBURY. Early manufacturers in Methuen: a paper read before the Methuen Historical Society. [Methuen, 1900?]. Pp. 12.

MIDDLEBOROUGH

9601 "ABORIGINAL history of Middleboro." Midd Antiq, 6 (June, 1964), 6-8.
Indians.

9602 BACKUS, ISAAC. "An historical account of Middleborough." MHSC, 3 (1794), 148-153.

9603 BEALS, AUSTEN L. "The horseless carriage comes to Middleboro." MiddAntiq, 5 (April, 1963), 1-2.

9604 BRACKETT, SUSAN B. "Old homes in South Middleborough." MiddAntiq, 4 (November, 1962), 5.

9605 BUTLER, LYMAN. "Changing scenes in Middleboro." MiddAntiq, 9 (October, 1967), 3-4.

9606 CLARK, CLINTON E. "Our architectural 'in-betweens.'" MiddAntiq, 7 (April, 1965), 8-9.
Houses.

9607 DEANE, ANNIE D. "History of the Middleborough High School." MiddAntiq, 6 (November, 1964), 4-5.
To 1895.

9608 DYER, ELIZABETH E. "Early history of the Sacred Heart Parish, Middleboro, Massachusetts." MiddAntiq, 11 (September, 1969), 6-8.

9609 EAYRS, FREDERICK E., JR. "An archaeological survey of Judge Oliver's ironworks." Midd Antiq, 6 (November, 1964), 1-3; 7 (February, 1965), 1-3.

9610 _____. "Judge Peter Oliver's ironworks." MiddAntiq, 5 (June, 1963), 6-7.

9611 EMERY, SAMUEL HOPKINS. The history of the Church of North Middleborough, Massachusetts, in six discourses.... Middleborough: Harlow & Thatcher, 1876. Pp. 106.

9612 "GLIMPSES of Middleboro in 1857." Midd Antiq, 7 (November, 1965), 1-4; 8 (February, 1966), 2-4.

9613 HALE, WILLIAM BAYARD. "A religious analysis of a New England town." Forum, 17 (1894), 71-80.

9614 HASKINS, ELMORE P. "Sampson's Tavern." ODHS, No. 51 (July, 1921), 26-34.

9615 JENNESS, JOYCE M. "A history of the American Revolution in the town of Middleborough, Massachusetts, 1765-1781." MiddAntiq, 13 (January, 1972), 2-3, (April, 1972), 4.

9616 LINDSAY, ALAN R. "A brief history of the men of '61, recruiting procedures and the establishment and deployment of Camp Joe Hooker." MiddAntiq, 10 (September, 1968), 2-4, (December, 1968), 3-6.

9617 MIDDLEBORO, MASS. Celebration of the two-hundredth anniversary of the incorporation of Middleborough, Massachusetts, October 13, 1869, including the oration of Hon. Thomas Russell, address by His Honor Mayor Shurtleff, of Boston, and other exercises of the occasion, with an appendix. Middleborough: Gazette Office, 1870. Pp. 51.

9618 MIDDLEBORO, MASS. FIRST CHURCH. Book of the First Church of Christ, in Middleborough, Plymouth County, Mass., with notices of other churches in that town. Boston: C. C. P. Moody, 1852 [i.e. 1854]. Pp. 124, 53.

9619 _____. Two hundredth anniversary of the First Congregational Church in Middleboro, Mass., historical discourse by George Warren Stearns, oration by Thomas Weston, with other addresses, portraits, descriptive catalog, etc. Middleboro, 1895. Pp. 136.

9620 MONTGOMERY, JOHN F. "Historical sketch of Middleborough and Taunton Precinct." Old Colony HSC, No. 5 (1895), 58-70.

9621 OLIVER, PETER. "Judge Oliver and the small Oliver House in Middleborough." CSMP, 38 (1947-1951), 292-305.

9622 PEIRCE ACADEMY. Semi-centennial jubilee of the Peirce Academy, Middleboro', Mass. August 6, 1858. Boston: J. M. Hewes, 1858. Pp. 48. MH.

9623 PENNIMAN, ETHEL RICHMOND. "Historical sketches of North Middleboro." MiddAntiq, 8 (April, 1966), 4-5, (June, 1966), 1-3.

9624 PRATT, ERNEST S. "Old saw mills of Middleboro as I remember them." MiddAntiq, 5 (November, 1963), 3-4.

9625 PRATT, ROSE E. S. "The LeBaron Foundry, 1855-1959." MiddAntiq, 1 (April, 1959), 5-6.

9626 _____. "Plymouth County's busy center of shoe manufactories." MiddAntiq, 9 (June, 1966), 5-7.
Signed: Mrs. Ernest S. Pratt.

9627 PUTNAM, ISRAEL WARBURTON. Two discourses on the divine faithfulness, as illustrated in the history of the First Church in Middleborough, Mass., during the period of one hundred and fifty years, preached January 5, 1845. Boston: C. C. P. Moody, 1852. Pp. 53.

9628 ROCKWELL, JOHN. "The birth and burial of Middleboro's trolley cars." MiddAntiq, 1 (June, 1959), 3.

9629 ROMAINE, LAWRENCE B. "A Yankee carpenter and his tools." CEAIA, 6 (1953), 33-34.
Amasa W. Thompson, 1830s.

9630 "SKETCHES of the early history of the town of Middleborough, in the county of Plymouth." NEHGR, 3 (1849), 213-220, 330-344.

9631 SKILLINGS, MAUDE B. "Middleborough's military record." MiddAntiq, 2 (June, 1960), 1-2.

9632 "SMALL Pox Cemetery, Brook Street, 1777." MiddAntiq, 13 (April, 1972), 5-6.

9633 STETSON, GEORGE WARD. "The Dr. Peter Oliver House of Middleborough." MiddAntiq, 14 (October, 1972), 2-3.

9634 _____. "Eddyville--1661-1969." MiddAntiq, 11 (September, 1969), 1-4. Section of the town.

9635 _____. "History of Middleborough churches." MiddAntiq, 11 (December, 1969), 2-4.

9636 _____. "Middleborough in the War of the Rebellion." MiddAntiq, 1 (April, 1959), 6-7.

9637 SWIFT, KARYL BENSON. "Three important women in the history of Middleborough." Midd Antiq, 6 (February, 1964), 1-3. Deborah Sampson, Lavinia Warren Stratton and Nina Louise Seymour.

9638 TAYLOR, WILLIAM B. "Indian artifacts of Titicut." MiddAntiq, 11 (December, 1969), 5-9; (May, 1970), 4-7; (July, 1970), 8-9; (October, 1970), 4-5; (December, 1970), 7-9; (April, 1971), 6-9.

9639 _____. "An Indian burial site in North Middleboro." MiddAntiq, 10 (April, 1969), 2-4.

9640 THACHER, PETER. Account of the great revival in Middleborough, Mass, 1741-42 during [his] ministry: with a notice of his character by Thomas Prince. Boston: T. R. Marvin, 1842. Pp. 34. MB.

9641 THOMAS, ERNEST E. "Three important men in the history of Middleborough." MiddAntiq, 6 (February, 1964), 5-6. Isaac Backus, Peter Peirce and Walter Sampson.

9642 THOMPSON, ISAAC. "Bills of mortality for Middleborough." MHSC, 8 (1802), 79; 9 (1804), 235; 10 (1809), 188; 2 Ser., 2 (1814), 261-263. 1779-1813.

9643 TRIPP, RICHARD S. "Early history of the Precinct Congregational Church." MiddAntiq, 9 (June, 1967), 3-4.

9644 "TWO famous artists: Cephas Thompson [and] Cephas Giovanni Thompson, native sons of Middleboro." MiddAntiq, 9 (February, 1968), 1-2.

9645 WASHBURN, ALBERT HENRY. Historical address delivered on the occasion of the two hundred and fiftieth anniversary of the town of Middleborough, Massachusetts, July 5, 1919. N.Y.: Appeal Printing, 1919. Pp. 30.

9646 WAUGH, WILLIAM L. "A sketch of Wappanucket." MiddAntiq, 10 (May, 1968), 4-5. Section of the town.

9647 _____. "Some history with reminiscences of Lakeside." MiddAntiq, 8 (November, 1966), 5-6. Summer community at Assawompsett Pond.

9648 WESTON, THOMAS. History of the town of Middleboro, Massachusetts. Boston: Houghton Mifflin, 1906-1969. 2v. Vol. 2 is by Mertie E. Romaine and has imprint: New Bedford: Reynolds-DeWalt Print.

9649 WHITCOMB, JOSEPH C. "Maxim's first fifty years." MiddAntiq, 6 (June, 1964), 1-4. Maxim Motor Co.; fire apparatus.

9650 WITBECK, MERTIE E. "Bay State Straw Works." MiddAntiq, 6 (April, 1964), 5-6. Straw hats.

9651 _____. "The Eaton Family School, 1863-1897." MiddAntiq, 8 (April, 1966), 1-2.

9652 _____. "Middleboro's famous 'little people.'" MiddAntiq, 5 (June, 1963), 1-3. Charles and Lavinia Stratton (Mr. and Mrs. Tom Thumb).

9653 _____. "St. Luke's Hospital--1920-1965." MiddAntiq, 8 (February, 1966), 7-8.

MIDDLEFIELD

9654 MIDDLEFIELD, MASS. A memorial of the one hundredth anniversary of the incorporation of the town of Middlefield, August 15, 1883, containing the historical discourse by Prof. Edward P. Smith of Worcester, with the addresses and letters. Middlefield, 1883. Pp. 96.

9655 _____. Sesquicentennial addresses and text of the pageant, Middlefield, Massachusetts, August 19th and 20th, 1933. [Middlefield]: The Town Committee, 1933. Pp. 65. MWA.

9656 SMITH, EDWARD CHURCH, PHILIP M. SMITH and THEODORE C. SMITH. A history of the town of Middlefield, Massachusetts. Menasha, Wis.: Priv. Print., 1924. Pp. xxv, 662.

MIDDLETON

9657 GIFFORD, GEORGE E. Biography of Charles L. Flint [and] history of Flint Public Library. n.p., [1952?]. Unpaged. MSaE.

9658 MIDDLETON, MASS. ANNIVERSARY COMMITTEE. 200th anniversary of the town of Middleton, June 20, 1928. Beverly: B. W. Ham, [1928?]. Pp. 28. MSaE.

9659   MIDDLETON, MASS. CHURCH OF CHRIST. The
         origin and history of the Church of Christ
in Middleton with the covenant, confession of faith,
&c., and list of members. Salem: Register Pr.,
1850. Pp. 22. MWA.

9660   MIDDLETON, MASS. EVANGELICAL CONGREGATIONAL
         CHURCH. Manual of the Evangelical Congrega-
tional Church in Middleton, Mass., containing an
historical sketch of the church.... Rev. ed.
Salem: Observer Steam Book and Job Print, 1889.
Pp. 36. MSaE.

9661   STILES, DAVID. "Historical notices of Mid-
         dleton." EIB, 4 (1872), 90-92.

9662   WATKINS, LURA WOODSIDE. "The district
         schoolhouses of Middleton, Massachusetts."
OTNE, 54 (1963-1964), 77-86.

9663   _____. History of the Middleton Congrega-
         tional Church, 225th anniversary. Boston:
Henry N. Sawyer, 1954. Pp. 24. MBNEH.

9664   _____. "The ironworks in Middleton, Massa-
         chusetts." OTNE, 49 (1958-1959), 72-78.

9665   _____. "Middleton buries its dead." EIHC,
         98 (1962), 26-34.
Funeral customs.

9666   _____. Middleton, Massachusetts: a cultur-
         al history. Salem: Essex Institute, 1970.
Pp. 341.

9667   _____. "Shoemaking and the small town."
         OTNE, 51 (1960-1961), 104-114.

9668   _____. "Water mills of Middleton." EIHC,
         99 (1963), 311-343.

9669   _____. "When they burned peat in Middleton."
         OTNE, 52 (1961-1962), 75-80.

9670   _____. "Where was the Indian Bridge over
         the Ipswich River?" OTNE, 16 (1955-1956),
68-71.

MILFORD

9671   [BACON, GEORGE FOX]. Leading business men
         of Milford, Hopkinton, and vicinity, embrac-
ing also Ashland, Holliston and Hopedale.... Boston: Mercantile Publishing Company, 1890. Pp. 64.

9672   BALLOU, ADIN. History of the town of Mil-
         ford, Worcester County, Massachusetts, from
its first settlement to 1881, in two parts, Part
I.--Strictly historical, Part II.--Biographico-
genealogical register. Boston: Rand, Avery, 1882.
Pp. xviii, 1154.

9673   BRAGG, ERNEST ATHERTON. Granite, its forma-
         tion, elevation, exposure and the develop-
ment of the granite industry in Milford, Massachusetts. Milford, 1941. Pp. 141.

9674   _____. History of Methodism in Milford,
         Mass., 1792-1948. n.p., [1948?]. Pp. 76.
MBNEH.

9675   CENEDELLA, ROBERT. "A lesson in civics."
         Am Heritage, 12 (December, 1960), 42-43,
100-102.
         Town meeting of 1925.

9676   DICKINSON, GIDEON. A hundred years; or, Mil-
         ford's first centennial.... Milford: Cook,
1880. Pp. 23.
         In verse.

9677   FREEMASONS. MILFORD, MASS. MONTGOMERY
         LODGE. Sesquicentennial history of Montgom-
ery Lodge A. F. & A. M., Milford, Massachusetts,
U. S. A., containing re-prints from the centennial
history, by Clarence A. Sumner and extracts from
the records of every meeting of the lodge, together
with a full list of all members from its institution
and of all officers serving in the last half century, by Ernest A. Bragg. Milford, 1947.
Pp. xxiii, 193.

9678   MILFORD, MASS. FIRST CONGREGATIONAL CHURCH.
         The confession of faith and covenant...with
a brief history of the church.... Milford: G. W.
Stacy, 1852. Pp. 22. MBNEH.

9679   O'DONNELL, WILLIAM G. "Race relations in a
         New England town." NEQ, 14 (1941), 235-242.
         Twentieth century foreign population.

9680   TILTON, CHARLES. A history of the Milford
         Methodist Episcopal Church with biographical
sketches and portraits of its pastors.... Cambridge: Riverside Pr., 1888. Pp. xi, 144. MB.

MILLBURY

9681   ADAMS, CHARLES F. A review of the vital sta-
         tistics of Millbury. [Worcester, 1882].
Pp. 10.
         Death rate: 1861-1881.

9682   BOTTY, KENNETH J. The town of Millbury 'A
         history of growth' 1913-1963...in cooperation
with the general and historical committees for Millbury's 150th anniversary.... Millbury, 1963.
Pp. 48. M.

9683   FREEMASONS. MILLBURY, MASS. OLIVE BRANCH
         LODGE. Centenary of Olive Branch Lodge,
A. F. & A. M., Millbury, Mass., September 12, 13,
and 14, 1897. [Millbury]: Millbury Journal,
[1897?]. Pp. 86.

9684   KEBABIAN, JOHN S. "Buck Brothers, Millbury,
         Mass." CEAIA, 25 (1972), 10-11.
         Chisels and planes.

9685   MILLBURY, MASS. Centennial history of the
         town of Millbury, Massachusetts, including
vital statistics, 1850-1899. Robert W. Dunbar, ed.
Millbury, 1915. Pp. 814.

9686   _____. Sesquicentennial souvenir program.
         n.p., 1963. Unpaged. M.

9687   "MILLBURY--our next door neighbor." Worces-
         ter Magazine, 16 (1913), 131-140.
         Centennial.

9688   PUTNAM, GEORGE A. The one hundred and fif-
       tieth anniversary of the First Congregation-
al Church in Millbury, Mass., a historical sermon.
n.p., [1897?]. Pp. 32. MWA.

MILLIS

9689   "THE CLICQUOT Club Company." Industry, 3
       (August, 1938), 7-9.
Soft drinks.

9690   MILLIS, MASS. Fiftieth anniversary of the
       incorporation of the town of Millis, Massa-
chusetts, May 30, 31, and June 1, 1935. Millis:
Millis Pr., 1935. Pp. 167. MB.

9691   MILLIS. Boston: Edison Electric Illuminat-
       ing Co., 1909. Pp. 8. M.

MILLVILLE

9692   CARROLL, MARGARET M. The town of Millville,
       1916-1966, 'the first 50 years.' Millville,
1966. Pp. 31. M.

MILTON

9693   CHANDLER, D. ELFLEDA. "Milton on the Nepon-
       set." NEM, New Ser., 41 (1909-1910), 291-
304.

9694   CHURCHILL, E. I. Brief sketch of the Gooch-
       Robbins-Churchill House, Milton, Mass.,
copied from the original manuscript by Gretchen
Gooch Troster. Yonkers, N.Y., 1958. Unpaged.
MBNEH.

9695   CUNNINGHAM, HENRY WINCHESTER. Brief sketch
       of the old Milton Church; its ministers and
meeting houses, 1678-1928. Milton, 1928. Pp. 10.

9696   DOUGLAS-LITHGOW, ROBERT ALEXANDER. "Gover-
       nor Hutchinson's house on Milton Hill."
MassMag, 3 (1910), 121-124.

9697   FROTHINGHAM, FREDERICK. A discourse occa-
       sioned by the two-hundredth anniversary of
the formation of the First Congregational Society
of Milton, Mass., delivered by Frederick Frothingham, associate pastor, in the meeting-house at Milton, Sunday, April 28, 1878.... Boston: T. W.
Ripley, 1878. Pp. 39.

9698   HALE, RICHARD WALDEN, b. 1909. Milton Acad-
       emy, 1798-1948. Milton: The Academy, 1948.
Pp. 185.

9699   HAMILTON, EDWARD PIERCE. "The diary of a
       colonial clergyman, Peter Thacher of Milton."
MHSP, 71 (1953-1957), 50-63.
       1678-1686.

9700   _____. A history of Milton. Milton: Milton
       Historical Society, 1957. Pp. xv, 275.

9701   HINCKLEY, MARY H. Sketches of early Milton.
       Milton: Milton Record, 1908. Pp. 37.
MBNEH.

9702   KIDDER, NATHANIEL THAYER. The first sixty
       years of the Milton Public Library, 1870-
1931. Norwood: Plimpton Pr., 1932. Pp. xii, 166.

9703   MILTON, MASS. Exercises at the 250th anni-
       versary of the incorporation of the town of
Milton, Massachusetts. Boston: Poole, 1912.
Pp. 46.

9704   _____. Milton records, births, marriages
       and deaths, 1662-1843, alphabetically and
chronologically arranged. Boston: A. Mudge &
Son, 1900. Pp. 4, 258.

9705   _____. Milton town records, 1662-1729,
       issued in observance of the tercentenary of
the founding of the Massachusetts Bay Colony.
Milton, 1930. Pp. xii, 385.

9706   MILTON, MASS. PUBLIC LIBRARY. One hundred
       years a-growing, 1871-1971. [Milton?],
1972. Unpaged. MB.

9707   MILTON, MASS. TERCENTENARY COMMITTEE. Three
       hundred years of Milton, 1662-1962. [Mil-
ton?, 1962?]. Pp. 35. MB.

9708   MILTON. Boston: Edison Electric Illuminat-
       ing Co., 1909. Pp. 16. M.

9709   MILTON HISTORICAL SOCIETY. A brief history
       of Milton, Massachusetts. James B. Ayer, ed.
[Milton], 1956. Pp. 43.

9710   _____. The Milton catechism: an outline of
       the history of Milton, Massachusetts, illus-
trated. [Milton], 1910. Pp. 88.

9711   _____. President's address and tenth anni-
       versary reports of Milton Historical Society;
a record of the society's first ten years. [Mil-
ton], 1915. Pp. 28.

9712   MILTON RECORD-TRANSCRIPT. Town of Milton
       celebrates its tercentenary, 1662-1962; a
commemorative review of 300 years of glorius heritage and tradition in honor of the historic town
of Milton. [Milton], 1962. Pp. 80.

9713   MORISON, JOHN HOPKINS. Two sermons preached
       in the First Congregational Church in Milton,
on the 15th and 22d of June, 1862, and suggested by
the centennial celebration, on the 11th of June,
1862. Boston: J. G. Torrey, 1862. Pp. 55.

9714   PIER, ARTHUR STANWOOD. Bits of Milton his-
       tory. Cambridge: Riverside Pr., 1930.
Pp. 25. MB.

9715   ROBBINS, JAMES MURRAY. Address delivered be-
       fore the inhabitants of the town of Milton,
on the 200th anniversary of the incorporation of the
town, June 11th, 1862. Boston: D. Clapp, 1862.
Pp. vi, 76.

9716 ROTCH, ABBOTT LAWRENCE. An account of the
foundation and work of the Blue Hill Meteorological Observatory. Boston: A. Mudge & Son,
1887. Pp. 29.

9717 SCAIFE, LAURISTON L. Milton and the Suffolk
resolves. [Milton]: Milton Historical Society, 1921. Pp. 39.

9718 TEELE, ALBERT KENDALL, ed. The history of
Milton, Mass., 1640 to 1887.... Boston:
Rockwell and Churchill, 1887. Pp. xiv, 668.

9719 ____. History of the Milton Academy,
Milton, Mass., 1798-1879. Boston: David
Clapp & Son, 1879. Pp. 29. M.

9720 ____. Noted men and historical narrations
of ancient Milton. Boston: David Clapp &
Son, 1900. Pp. 99. MB.

9721 TUCKER, JOHN ATHERTON. The first four
meeting houses of Milton, Mass., covering a
period of two and a half centuries. [Milton?],
1908. Pp. 5.

9722 ____. The meeting-house, the minister and
the parsonage of Milton, Mass., two hundred
years ago. Milton, 1905. Pp. 14.

9723 ____. A paper read at the 225th anniversa-
ry of the formation of the Milton Church...
Milton, Mass., November 15, 1903. Boston: David
Clapp & Son, 1903. Pp. 6. MBNEH.
First Congregational Church.

9724 ____. Tax rates of Milton 1674-1800.
[Milton]: Milton Record, 1908. Unpaged.

9725 WALLINGFORD, HOWARD. "Paper making on the
Neponset...from 1728 to 1951." New England
Printer, (February, 1951).

9726 WARE, HORACE EVERETT. The powder mill on
the Neponset; its importance to the colony
in Philip's War; read before the Milton Woman's
Club, May 6, 1901. n.p., n.d. Pp. 18. MBNEH.

9727 WEBSTER, MARY PHILLIPS. "The Suffolk Resolves." NEM, New Ser., 27 (1902-1903),
353-372.

MONROE

9728 SEE WORKS RELATING TO FRANKLIN COUNTY.

MONSON

9729 CARPENTER, CARLOS CLEMENT. The jubilee discourse delivered at the celebration of the
semi-centennial anniversary of the Linophilian Society in Monson Academy, June 29, 1869...to which is
appended a brief historical sketch of the society.
Springfield: S. Bowles, 1870. Pp. 24.
Literary society; historical sketch is by
Charles Hammond.

9730 HAMMOND, CHARLES. An address delivered at
the re-dedication of Monson Academy, July
12, 1864. Springfield: Samuel Bowles, 1865.
Pp. 32.

9731 HOWARD, R. H. History of Methodism in Monson, Massachusetts. Springfield: S. Bowles,
1869. Pp. 24. MB.

9732 MONSON, MASS. CONGREGATIONAL CHURCH. Congregational Church, Monson, Mass...one hundred and fiftieth anniversary, June 23-24, 1912.
n.p., [1912?]. Unpaged. MBNEH.

9733 MONSON ACADEMY. Discourses, and speeches,
delivered at the celebration of the semi-
centennial anniversary of Monson Academy, Monson,
Mass., July 18th and 19th, 1854. N.Y.: John A.
Gray, 1855. Pp. 90.

9734 ____. Seventy-ninth reunion of the stu-
dents, graduates, and teachers of Monson
Academy, June 20, 1883. Boston: Rand, Avery, 1884.
Pp. 64. MB.

9735 MONSON HISTORICAL SOCIETY. History of Monson, Massachusetts. [Monson], 1960.
Pp. 171.

9736 MOULTON, MIRA KEEP. A history of the First
Church of Monson. Monson: Blatchley's,
1962. Unpaged. MS.

MONTAGUE

9737 BUDINGTON, HENRY AARON. History of the New
England Spiritualist Campmeeting Association
at Lake Pleasant, Mass. Springfield: Star Publishing, 1907. Pp. 88.

9738 CRAWFORD, MARY CAROLINE. "A country church
industrial." Outlook, 73 (1903), 448-451.
Clairvaux Community.

9739 FOGG, FRANK PRESCOTT. "The Turners Falls
Company: one hundred and twenty years of
development, from 1792 to 1912." WNE, 2 (1912),
189-191.
Electric power.

9740 HAZELTON, CHARLES W. "The early days of
Turners Falls." PVMA, 7 (1921-1929), 424-
441.

9741 "NEW Clairvaux." Country Time and Tide, 6
(1904), 65-75.
Socialistic community; includes brief history
of the movement.

9742 PESKE-OMPSK-UT: or the Falls fight: a series
of random sketches showing a glimpse of the
early history of Turner Falls, which appeared in
the 'Turner Falls Reporter,' during the months of
January and February, 1875. Turner Falls: 'Reporter' Job Office, 1875. Pp. 21.

9743 PRESSEY, EDWARD PEARSON. History of Montague: a typical Puritan town...a history of Gunn family by Mrs. Lyman O. Gunn. Montague: New Clairvaux Pr., 1910. Pp. 264.

9744 ROBINSON, JULIUS B. "Industries of Turners Falls." WNE, 2 (1912), 245-252.

9745 ROLLINS, MARGARET. Carl Rollins at Montague, 1903-1918. [New Haven]: Yale Univ. Pr., [1963?]. Pp. 17. MDeeH.
New Clairvaux Press.

9746 "SETTLEMENT and early history of Montague." PVMA, 3 (1890-1898), 296-332.

MONTEREY

9747 FERGUSON, HARRY S. D., ed. 100th anniversary Monterey in the Berkshire hills of western Massachusetts, established 1735, incorporated and renamed 1847. n.p., 1947. Unpaged.

9748 MAKUC, ANNE MARIE, ed. Konkapoters, Monterey, 125th anniversary, 1847-1972. n.p., [1972?]. Unpaged. M.

9749 MINER, JULIUS and MARGERY MANSFIELD. New England's Monterey, stories of the town [and] its church. [Monterey]: Monterey Congregational Church, [1955?]. Pp. 70. MPB.

9750 MONTEREY, MASS. FIRST CONGREGATIONAL SOCIETY. History of the First Congregational Society in Monterey, Mass., with [a] brief history of the town and account of the anniversary exercises October 10 and 11, 1900. Great Barrington: Courier Book and Job Pr., 1900. Pp. 116. MB.

MONTGOMERY

9751 ALLYN, LEWIS BENAJAH. Ancient landmarks of Montgomery, Massachusetts. Westfield: J. D. Cadle, [1920?]. Pp. 13.

MOUNT WASHINGTON

9752 JELLIFFE, HELENA LEEMING. "The uplands among the farms." Outlook, 59 (1898), 287-294.

9753 KEITH, HERBERT F. History of Taconic and Mount Washington, Berkshire County, Massachusetts, its location, scenery, and history from 1692 to 1892. Great Barrington: Berkshire Courier Print, 1912. Pp. 28. MBNEH.

NAHANT

9754 BRANN, EUGENE H., comp. Sketches of Nahant, showing many points of interest...sketches of a few of the leading men. Boston: Atlantic Printing, 1911. Pp. 51.

9755 HAMMOND, MRS. SAMUEL. Nahant Church, 1832-1932. Boston: Thomas Todd, 1932. Pp. 12. M.

9756 LEWIS, ALONZO. Guide through Nahant with an account of the first inhabitants. Lynn, 1851. Pp. 14.

9757 LODGE, HENRY CABOT. An historical address delivered at the celebration of the fiftieth anniversary of the incorporation of the town of Nahant, July 14, 1903. [Nahant]: The Town, 1904. Pp. 22.

9758 NAHANT, MASS. Centennial celebration: Nahant, one hundred years a town. Nahant, 1953. Unpaged. MB.

9759 "NAHANT." Boston Monthly Magazine, 1 (1825), 76-80.

9760 NAHANT: A collection from sundry sources of some noteworthy descriptions of the town: Lynn: John MacFarlane, 1899. Pp. 50. MBNEH.

9761 ROGERS, REBECCA M. "Resort architecture at Nahant, 1815-1850." OTNE, 65 (1974-1975), 13-31.

9762 [WHEILDON, WILLIAM WILLDER]. Letters from Nahant, historical, descriptive and miscellaneous. Charlestown: Bunker-Hill Aurora, 1842. Pp. 48.

9763 WILSON, FRED ALLAN. "A glance at old Nahant." Lynn HSR, 23, Pt. 1 (1921-1923), 24-27.

9764 _____. Maolis Club history of Nahant, Massachusetts. Nahant: Maolis Club, 1914. Pp. 55. MBNEH.

9765 _____. The Nahant Public Library; containing a brief sketch of the public library movement; a history of the Nahant Public Library and a description of the new library building. Linn [sic]: Macfarlane Pr., 1895. Pp. 40.

9766 _____. Some annals of Nahant, Massachusetts. Boston: Old Corner Book Store, 1928. Pp. xiii, 412.

NANTUCKET

9767 ALLEN, MRS. G. MYRON. "The land of long ago." NHAP, (1921), 24-28. Quakers.

9768 ANDERSON, FLORENCE BENNETT. "A Nantucketer remembers." OTNE, 42 (1951-1952), 3-11.

9769 AUSTIN, JANE GOODWIN. Nantucket scraps: being the experiences of an off-islander, in season and out of season, among a passing people. Boston: J. R. Osgood, 1883. Pp. vi, 354.

9770 BACHMAN, MICHAEL. "Shipwrecks around Nantucket since 1940." HistNan, 6 (July, 1958), 34-38.

9771 BAIRD, HENRY M. "Nantucket." Scribner's Monthly, 6 (1873), 385-399.

9772 BARNES, MARGARET FAWCETT. "Nantucket's own, a short history of the U. S. Coast Guard on Nantucket Island." HistNan, 14 (January, 1967), 5-11.

9773 _____. "The Navy on Nantucket." HistNan, 11 (January, 1964), 5-9.

9774 BARTLETT, IRVING T. "History of the Nantucket Fire Department." HistNan, 6 (January, 1959), 44-46.

9775 BELOT, EMILE JOSEPH. "Nantucket: Étude sur les diverses sortes de propriétés primitives." Lyons. Université. Faculté des Lettres. Annuaire, 2 (1884), 91-180.
Real property.

9776 BENCHLEY, NATHANIEL. "The world & Nantucket." Am Heritage, 16 (June, 1965), 28-31, 109-111.

9777 BLANCHARD, DOROTHY C. A. Nantucket landfall. N.Y.: Dodd, Mead, 1956. Pp. 241.

9778 BLISS, WILLIAM ROOT. Quaint Nantucket. (1896) 2d. ed. Boston: Houghton Mifflin, 1897. Pp. xxi, 225.

9779 _____. September days on Nantucket. Boston: Houghton Mifflin, 1902. Pp. 145.

9780 BODFISH, ANNIE W. "A few facts relating to Main Street." NHAP, (1917), 36-38; (1918), 32-33; (1919), 25-27; (1920), 57-61.

9781 _____. "A sketch of a former Nantucket Historical Society." NHAP, (1899), 11-12.
1869-1870.

9782 BRIGGS, CHARLES F. "The island of Nantucket." Merchants' Magazine and Commercial Review, 17 (1847), 368-377.

9783 BROCK, MRS. ALBERT G. "The Pacific Bank." NHAP, (1904), 29-30.

9784 BROOKS, CHARLES FRANKLIN. "Island Nantucket." GeogRev, 4 (1917), 197-207.

9785 CAMPBELL, AMELIA DAY. "Nantucket-yesterday, today and tomorrow." Americana, 15 (1921), 305-324.

9786 CATALOGUE of Nantucket whalers and their voyages from 1815 to 1870. Nantucket, 1876. Pp. 54.

9787 CHADWICK, ALCON. "Reminiscences of old Podpis." NHAP, (1922), 54-61.
Section of the town.

9788 CHAMBERS, ARTHUR. "Typical Nantucket houses." HistNan, 10 (January, 1963), 24-26.

9788A CHASE, CHARLOTTE B. "Ordeal on Nantucket Sound." Steamboat Bill, (1952), 5-7.
Storm, 1871.

9789 CHASE, FREDERICK. "Historical Nantucket buildings." HistNan, 4 (July, 1956), 30-34.

9790 _____. "Nantucket history." HistNan, 5 (July, 1957), 26-32.

9791 CHASE, SIDNEY. "The story of golf." NHAP, (1921), 3-34.
Nantucket Golf Club, founded 1897.

9792 CHURCH, E. R. "A glimpse of Nantucket." Southern Magazine, 16 (1875), 389-396.

9793 CLEMENTS, ELIZABETH. "The birth and death of the Nantucket Railroad." HistNan, 10 (January, 1963), 21-24.

9794 COFFIN, ALLEN. "The courts of Nantucket-- the law and lawyers from an early period." NHAP, (1907), 30-42.

9795 COFFIN, H. ERROL. "The Jared Coffin House, formerly the Ocean House." HistNan, 9 (April, 1962), 41-57.

9796 _____. "Nantucket street lighting." Hist Nan 15, (October, 1957), 17-19.

9797 _____. "The Second Congregational Meeting House (Unitarian-Universalist)." HistNan, 12 (January, 1965), 5-19.

9798 _____. "65-67-69 Main Street." HistNan, 11 (April, 1964), 5-8.
Historic houses.

9799 [COFFIN, IDA GARDNER]. The oldest house on Nantucket Island, in two parts.... N.Y.: C. Francis, 1905. Pp. xii, 128.
Pt. 2: Echoes from Nantucket's oldest house is by Anna S. Jenks.

9800 COFFIN, KAREN. "A history of 'Sconset." HistNan, 17 (January, 1970), 13-19.

9801 COFFIN, MARIE M. The history of Nantucket Island: a bibliography of source material with index and inventory. Nantucket: Nantucket Historical Trust, 1970. Pp. viii, 63.

9802 COFFIN, PATRICIA. Nantucket. N.Y.: Viking Pr., 1971. Pp. 72.
Natural history.

9803 COFFIN, WILLIAM. A narrative of the robbery of the Nantucket Bank.... Nantucket: Henry Clapp, 1816. Pp. xviii, 69.
Robbery occurred in 1795.

9804 COLEMAN, M. FOLGER. "Nantucket in the early history of the country." JAmHist, 19 (1925), 187-188.

9805 COOK, R. H. Historical notes of the island of Nantucket, and tourist's guide. Nantucket, 1871. Pp. 23.

9806 CORNISH, CRAIG. "The cession and annexation of Nantucket." Green Bay, 11 (1899), 125-130.

9807 "THE CREATION of the island of Nantucket." United States Literary Gazette, 4 (1826), 357-361.

9808 CRÈVECOEUR, MICHEL GUILLAUME ST. JEAN DE, called SAINT JOHN DE CRÈVECOEUR. Letters from an American farmer. (1782) Warren Barton Blake, ed. N.Y.: E. P. Dutton, 1912. Pp. xxiii, 256.
Five of the twelve letters relate to Nantucket and Martha's Vineyard; has been translated into Dutch, French and German.

9809 CROSBY, A. MORRIS. "Gardner Street Hose Cart House." HistNan, 11 (October, 1963), 15-17.
Fire station.

9810 CROSBY, EVERETT UBERTO. Books and baskets, signs and silver of old-time Nantucket. Nantucket: Inquirer and Mirror Pr., 1940. Pp. 72.

9811 _____. "Coatue." HistNan, 7 (April, 1960), 45-61.
A peninsula of the island.

9812 _____. "Discoverers of Nantucket." NHAB, (1943), 35-39.

9813 _____. Nantucket in print. Nantucket: Tetaukimmo Pr., 1946. Pp. 225.

9814 _____. Ninety five per cent perfect. Nantucket's changing prosperity, future probabilities. The spoon primer. Silversmiths of old-time Nantucket. Nantucket's underground moon. Nantucket: Tetaukimmo Pr., 1953. Pp. 214.

9815 _____. Our gold mine: the dollars value of the remaining oldness of Nantucket town, a portion of the address by Everett U. Crosby to the Rotary Club at Nantucket, October 10, 1951. Nantucket: Tetaukimmo Pr., 1951. Pp. 32.

9816 _____. "Three men and three centuries." NHAP, (1944-1945), 17-19.
Peter Folger, Timothy Folger and Eastman Johnson.

9817 CROWLEY, JOHN W. "Eden off Nantucket: W. S. Bigelow and 'Tuckanuck.'" EIHC, 109 (1973), 3-8.

9818 DELL, BURNHAM N. "Quakerism on Nantucket." HistNan, 2 (January, 1955), 8-30.

9819 DOUGLAS-LITHGOW, ROBERT ALEXANDER. "Jethro Coffin's home, 'the oldest house' in Nantucket, 1686-1910." MassMag, 4 (1911), 23-28.

9820 _____. Nantucket: a history. N.Y.: G. P. Putnam's Sons, 1914. Pp. xiii, 389.

9821 DRAKE, THOMAS EDWARD. A scientific outpost: the first half century of the Nantucket Maria Mitchell Association. Nantucket: Nantucket Maria Mitchell Association, 1968. Pp. 32.

9822 DRAKE, W. B. "Nantucket." Lippincott's Magazine, 2 (1868), 283-292.

9823 DU BOCK, DEBORAH. "Glacial formation of Nantucket." HistNan, 16 (April, 1969), 22-27.

9824 DUCE, KENNETH. "Nantucket history." Hist Nan, 3 (October, 1955), 22-26.

9825 DUDLEY, MYRON SAMUEL. Churches and pastors of Nantucket, Mass., from the first settlement to the present time, 1659-1902. Boston: D. Clapp & Son, 1902. Pp. 21.

9826 _____, comp. Nantucket centennial celebration, 1695, 1795, 1895; historic sites and historic buildings. Nantucket: R. B. Hussey, 1895. Pp. 23.

9827 _____. "Silk industry in Nantucket." NHAP, (1898), 7-8.

9828 _____. "The site of the Peter Folger House." NHAP, (1898), 8-9.

9829 _____. "Two centuries of churches and pastors in Nantucket, Mass." NEHGR, 56 (1902), 17-26.

9830 DUPREY, KENNETH. Old houses on Nantucket. N.Y.: Architectural Book Publishing, 1959. Pp. xii, 242.

9831 EARLY, ELEANOR. An island patchwork. Boston: Houghton Mifflin, 1941. Pp. vii, 289.
Social life and customs.

9832 ELDRIDGE, GERALD E. "Nantucket lighthouses." HistNan, 4 (July, 1956), 25-29.

9833 FARNHAM, JOSEPH ELLIS COFFEE. Brief historical data and memories of my boyhood days in Nantucket. (1915) 2d. ed. Providence: Snow & Farnham, 1923. Pp. xii, 319.
Farnham family.

9834 FEE, SANDRA. "Railroads in Nantucket." Hist Nan, 5 (July, 1957), 21-25.

9835 FERNALD, SUSAN. "Nantucket lightship handbags and baskets." HistNan, 16 (January, 1969), 22-26.

9836 "THE FIRST Nantucket Yacht Club." HistNan, 19 (April, 1972), 8-9.

9837 FOLGER, EVA CELINE GREAR. The glacier's gift. New Haven: Tuttle, Morehouse & Taylor, 1911. Pp. 145.

9838 FOLGER, PAUL. "Ecclesiastical statistics of the First Congregational Church and Society in Nantucket." American Quarterly Register, 15 (1842-1843), 498-500.

9839 FOLGER, ISAAC H. Handbook of Nantucket, consisting of a brief historical sketch of the island, with notes of interest to summer visitors. Nantucket: Island Review Office, 1875. Pp. 97.

9840   FONDA, DOUGLASS C. Eighteenth-century Nan-
          tucket whaling; as compiled from the original
logs and journals of the Nantucket Atheneum and the
Nantucket Whaling Museum. Nantucket, 1969. Pp. 30.

9841   FORMAN, HENRY CHANDLEE. Early Nantucket and
          its whale houses. N.Y.: Hastings House,
1966. Pp. ix, 291.

9842   _____. "Swain's burnt-out Polpis lean-to."
HistNan, 9 (January, 1962), 5-16.
Historic houses.

9843   _____. "Vanished 'Sconset houses on Nantucket." HistNan, 6 (January), 1959, 34-43.

9844   "THE FORMATION of the Unitarian Society."
NHAP, (1910), 50-58.
1809.

9845   FOWLKES, GEORGE ALLEN. A mirror of Nantuck-
          et: an architectural history of the island,
1686-1850. [Plainfield?, N.J.], 1959. Pp. 136.

9846   GARDNER, ARTHUR H. "The Big Shop." NHAP,
(1916), 31-43.
Meeting hall.

9847   _____. "Nantucket." CCAPL, 6 (March, 1922),
5-9.

9848   _____. "Nantucket in the Revolution." NEM,
New Ser., 31 (1904-1905), 556-564.

9849   _____. Wrecks around Nantucket, since the
          settlement of the island, and the incidents
connected therewith, embracing over seven hundred
vessels. (1877) Rev. ed., with additional records
to 1954. New Bedford: Reynolds Print., 1954.
Pp. 176.

9850   GARDNER, ETHEL. "The Nantucket Indians."
NHAP, (1934), 25-27.

9851   GARDNER, HELEN A. "Cent schools." NHAP,
(1908), 41-45.

9852   GARDNER, WILL. "Events of 1659, four mind
          pictures." HistNan, 6 (January, 1959), 5-8.
Sale of Nantucket to Tristram Coffin.

9853   GARDNER, WILLIAM EDWARD. The Coffin saga:
          Nantucket's story, from settlement to summer
visitors. Cambridge: Riverside Pr., 1949. Pp. ix,
321.

9854   _____. The triumphant Captain John, and
          Gardners and Gardiners; twelve colonial
founders of families. Nantucket: Whaling Museum
Publications, 1958. Pp. 104.
          A Nantucket family; not a genealogy.

9855   GERSMAN, ELINOR MONDALE. "The significance
          of public schools in ante-bellum Nantucket."
HistNan, 20 (January, 1973), 8-18.

9856   GIBBONS, MARIANNA. "Old Nantucket." Lip-
          pincott's Magazine, 28 (1881), 303-310.

9857   GIFFIN, NORMAN P. "A twentieth century
          sketch of the island steamboat line." Hist
Nan, 7 (January, 1960), 30-34.

9858   GILBRETH, FRANK BUNKER. Innside Nantucket.
          N.Y.: Crowell, 1954. Pp. 231.
          Hotels and taverns.

9859   _____. Of whales and women: one man's view
          of Nantucket history. N.Y.: Crowell, 1956.
Pp. 242.

9860   GODFREY, EDWARD K. The island of Nantucket,
          what it was and what it is; being a complete
index and guide to this noted resort...including its
history, people, agriculture, botany, conchology and
geology.... Boston: Lee and Shepard, 1882.
Pp. vi, 365.

9861   GRAHAM, GERALD S. "The migrations of the
          Nantucket whale fishery: an episode in Brit-
ish colonial policy." NEQ, 8 (1935), 179-202.

9862   GUBA, EMIL FREDERICK. "Government of the
          fisheries of the great ponds of Nantucket
Island." HistNan, 12 (April, 1965), 12-15.
          Fish and game laws.

9863   _____. The Great Nantucket bank robbery con-
          spiracy and solemn aftermath, or the end of
old Nantucket. Waltham, 1973. Pp. 147. M.

9864   _____. Nantucket odyssey: a journey into
          the history of Nantucket. (1951) 2d. ed.,
rev. and enl. Waltham, 1965. Pp. ix, 438.

9865   _____. "Revolutionary War service roll."
HistNan, 11 (July, 1963), 5-17.
          Includes some detailed biographical sketches.

9866   _____. "The Sheep's Commons fight." Hist
Nan, 12 (July, 1964), 5-16.
          Division of common land.

9867   HAM, DAVID S. "Wrecks around Nantucket."
HistNan, 8 (October, 1960), 135-137.

9868   HANAFORD, PHEBE ANN COFFIN. The heart of
          Siasconset. New Haven: Hoggson & Robinson,
1890. Pp. viii, 180.

9869   HARDY, ELIZABETH. "The Nantucket tourist
          industry." HistNan, 11 (January, 1964),
19-20.

9870   HEFLIN, WILSON L. "Melville and Nantucket."
NHAP, (1951), 22-30.
          A visit in 1852.

9871   HINCHMAN, LYDIA SWAIN MITCHELL. Early set-
          tlers of Nantucket, their associates and
descendants. (1896) 4th ed. Philadelphia: Wellington Printing, 1934. Pp. 330.
          1659-1850.

9872   _____. "The Maria Mitchell House and Memori-
          al, Nantucket, Mass." OTNE, 16 (1925-1926),
105-117.

9873 _____. "William Rotch and the neutrality of Nantucket during the Revolutionary War." FHABull, 1 (1906), 49-55.

9874 HOADLEY, WILLIAM. "Nantucket newspapers, (1816-1955)." HistNan, 3 (October, 1955), 6-21.

9875 HOLDGATE, BRIAN. "Nantucket's railroads." HistNan, 14 (July, 1966), 10-11.

9876 HOSMER, SAMUEL DANA. "Indian churches on Nantucket." CongQ, 7 (1865), 31-34.

9877 _____. 'The sanctuary of our fathers,' a centennial discourse, preached Sabbath evening, October 15, 1865, in the lecture room of the First Congregational Church, Nantucket. Nantucket: Hussey & Robinson, 1865. Pp. 16. Centennial of the church.

9878 HOUGH, FRANKLIN BENJAMIN, comp. Papers relating to the island of Nantucket, with documents relating to the original settlement of that island, Martha's Vineyard, and other islands adjacent, known as Dukes County, while under the colony of New York. Albany: J. Munsell, 1856. Pp. xviii, 162. 1641-1692.

9879 HUSSEY, CHRISTOPHER COFFIN. Talks about old Nantucket. n.p., 1901. Pp. 70. The manuscript was left by the author in an unfinished state, and completed by Lydia Coffin Hussey.

9880 HUSSEY, ROLAND B. The evolution of Siasconset. [Nantucket?], 1954. Pp. 50.

9881 "INDIAN traditions, the creation of the island of Nantucket." United States Literary Gazette, 4 (1826), 357-361. Signed: J.

9882 JONES, BASSETT. "Was Nantucket ever forested?" NHAP, (1935), 19-27.

9883 JONES, CATHERINE. "Wharves of Nantucket." NHAP, (1931), 23-28.

9884 JONES, GEORGE W. "A brief account of whaleship building on Nantucket." HistNan, 13 (January, 1966), 5-12.

9885 _____. "Whalers and Quakers--historic Nantucket Island." Historic Preservation, 18 (1966), 157-159. Notes on structures built before 1860.

9886 KIMBALL, CHARLES P. "The Old North Burying Ground." NHAP, (1936), 28-30.

9887 KIMBALL, FISKE. "Moor's End, Nantucket." Architectural Record, 62 (1927), 190-200. Historic house.

9888 KING, CLARENCE. "What became of the first book of Nantucket town records, hidden in 1677." HistNan, 11 (October, 1963), 24-27.

9889 KYNETT, HAROLD HAVELOCK. Fountains of memory: Nantucket sprinkles quiet. Philadelphia: E. Stern Majestic Pr., 1972. Pp. 192. Social life and customs.

9890 _____. On-islanders and off-islanders: both look at Nantucket. Philadelphia: E. Stern Majestic Pr., 1971. Pp. 200.

9891 _____. Nantucket brevities: a glimpse of the environment. Philadelphia, 1966. Pp. 128.

9892 _____. The pervasive spirit: an off-islander views Nantucket. Philadelphia: E. Stern Majestic Pr., 1968. Pp. 161.

9893 _____. Quaker heritage: niceties of Nantucket. Philadelphia, 1967. Pp. 168.

9894 _____. Unforgettable intimacies: memories for comfort. Philadelphia, 1965. Pp. 158.

9895 _____. Why Nantucket? Questions and suggestions. Philadelphia: Edward Stern Majestic Pr., 1970. Pp. 192.

9896 LAMB, SALLY. "Mills on Nantucket." HistNan, 18 (October, 1970), 11-15. Windmills.

9897 LANCASTER, CLAY. The architecture of historic Nantucket. N.Y.: McGraw-Hill, 1972. Pp. xxxiii, 286.

9898 _____. The Far Out Railroad, 1879-1918, Nantucket's old summer narrow gauge. Nantucket: Pleasant Publications, 1972. Pp. 148. M.

9899 LARSEN, ALICE T. "Nantucket's great crisis." NHAP, (1929), 33-39. Revolutionary War.

9900 LATHROP, JOHN GARDNER. "Nantucket and the American Revolution." HistNan, 18 (January, 1971), 11-18, (April, 1971), 23-26.

9901 LEACH, ROBERT J. "The first two Quaker meeting houses on Nantucket." NHAP, (1950), 24-33.

9902 _____. "Nantucket-Vineyard relations." HistNan, 20 (October, 1972), 28-34. 'Continued,' but no more appeared.

9903 LOWENTHAL, DAVID. "The common and undivided lands of Nantucket." GeogRev, 46 (1956), 399-403.

9904 MACY, OBED. The history of Nantucket, being a compendious account of the first settlement of the island by the English, together with the rise and progress of the whale fishery; and other historical facts relative to said island and its inhabitants. In two parts, with a concise statement of prominent events from 1835 to 1880, by William C. Macy. (1835) 2d. ed. Mansfield: Macy & Pratt, 1880. Pp. xiv, 313.

9905 MACY, WILLIAM FRANCIS. "Migrations of Nantucketers to the south and west." NHAP, (1933), 24-27.

9906 _____, ed. The Nantucket scrap basket: being a collection of characteristic stories and sayings of the people of the town and island of Nantucket, Massachusetts. (1916) 2d. ed., rev., expanded, and rearranged. Boston: Houghton Mifflin, 1930. Pp. x, 163.

9907 _____. Nantucket's oldest house (1686) 'The Jethro Coffin House,' 'The Horseshoe House.' Nantucket: Inquirer and Mirror Pr., 1929. Pp. 35.

9908 _____. "The Sherburne Lyceum." NHAP, (1923), 53-61.
1870s and 1880s.

9909 _____. The story of old Nantucket: a brief history of the island and its people from its discovery down to the present day. (1915) 2d. ed., rev. and enl. Boston: Houghton Mifflin, 1928. Pp. xi, 190.

9910 _____. Ye old mill, 1746, Nantucket. Nantucket: Nantucket Historical Society, 1930. Unpaged. MB.

9911 MACY, ZACCHEUS. "Account of the settlement of Nantucket." MHSC, 3 (1794), 155-160.

9912 MARSHALL, ESTHER S. Polpis, past and present: Nantucket. [Nantucket?], 1962. Pp. 77. M.

9913 "THE MASSACHUSETTS Humane Society on Nantucket." HistNan, 13 (April, 1966), 14-16.
Life saving.

9914 MINTURN, R. R. "Nantucket." Lakeside Monthly, 10 (1873), 140-144.

9915 MITCHELL, MABEL G. "The Horseshoe (or Coffin) House, Nantucket." MagHist, 12 (1910), 275-276.

9916 MONAGHAN, JAMES. "Anti-slavery in Nantucket." NHAP, (1938), 23-26.
1769-1853.

9917 _____. "Audubon on Nantucket." NHAP, (1941), 26-30.
1840.

9918 _____. "Thoreau in Nantucket." NHAP, (1942), 24-30.
1854.

9919 MORGAN, ELEANOR W. "Old Nantucket gardens." NHAP, (1920), 41-46.

9920 MORRIS, PAUL C. "The island of lost ships." CCC, 19 (1966), 56-58, 60.
Shipwrecks off Nantucket.

9921 NANTUCKET, MASS. FIRST CONGREGATIONAL CHURCH. The confession of faith and covenant, of the First Congregational Church, in Nantucket, together with a historical sketch of the church, and a catalogue of members, from 1767 until the present time. Boston: Dutton and Wentworth, 1850. Pp. 36. M.

9922 "NANTUCKET Friends in 1799 and 1809." FHA Bull, 3 (1910), 139-143.

9923 NANTUCKET HISTORICAL ASSOCIATION. Centennial catalogue of the Nantucket Historical Association. Nantucket: Inquirer and Mirror Pr., 1895. Pp. 27.

9924 _____. The 1800 house: an exhibit of the Nantucket Historical Association. Nantucket, 1968. Pp. 25.

9925 NANTUCKET MARIA MITCHELL ASSOCIATION. History of the Memorial House. n.p., [not after 1927]. 2 leaves. M.

9926 NELSON, W. RIPLEY. "The Nantucket Whaling Museum." HistNan, 3 (July, 1955), 6-34.

9927 NORTHRUP, ANSEL JUDD. 'Sconset cottage life: a summer on Nantucket island.... (1881) 2d. ed. Syracuse: C. W. Bardeen, 1901. Pp. ix, 160.

9928 "THE OLD physical training classes." HistNan, 10 (January, 1963), 19-20.
In schools.

9929 O'NEILL, CHARLES. "Nantucket waterfront." HistNan, 13 (October, 1965), 21-22.

9930 PAGE, FRANCES. "The Great Hall." HistNan, 4 (April, 1957), 13-20.
Atheneum.

9931 PALMER, WILLIAM R. "Early American whaling." The Historian, 22 (1959-1960), 1-8.

9932 PARSONS, ROBERT. "The 'Telegraph' to the rescue." HistNan, 8 (October, 1960), 130-133.
Rescue of the 'Corinth,' 1851.

9933 PATTERSON, DAVID. "Saving ship 'Liverpool Packet' in 1881 [i.e. 1861]." HistNan, 21 (October, 1973), 8-10.
Rescue during a blizzard.

9934 PERKINS, W. D. "Education: Nantucket's schools from its settlement to the establishment of a public school system." HistNan, 7 (January, 1960), 11-19, (April, 1960), 63-74.

9935 QUINT, ALONZO H. "The church in Nantucket, Mass." CongQ, 14 (1872), 553-564.

9936 RANKE, MARY E. "The first decades of the Maria Mitchell Association." HistNan, 17 (October, 1969), 23-30.
Astronomy.

9937 RANNEY, H. FLINT. "Whaling and Nantucket." HistNan, 6 (April, 1959), 26-30.

9938 _____. "Whaling and Nantucket--the decline." HistNan, 8 (April, 1961), 56-67.

9939 REIS, MYLES, JR. "The oldest house." Hist Nan, 13 (October, 1965), 19-20.
Jethro Coffin House.

9940 ROTCH, WILLIAM. Memorandum written by William Rotch in the eightieth year of his age. Boston: Houghton Mifflin, 1916. Pp. xi, 88.

9941 "THE SAGA at Sankaty." NHAP, (1950), 34-42.
Lighthouse.

9942 SANSON, JOSEPH. "A description of Nantucket." Port Folio, 3 Ser., 5 (1811), 30-48.

9943 SCHWEINFURTH, JULIUS A. An architectural monograph on the early dwellings of Nantucket. St. Paul: White Pine Bureau, 1917. Pp. 16.

9944 SEABURG, ALVAN. "Universalism in Nantucket." HistNan, 14 (July, 1966), 5-9.

9945 SEELER, KATHERINE. "A short history of the summer Friends Meeting." HistNan, 19 (October, 1971), 16-17.

9946 ____. and EDGAR SEELER. Nantucket lightship baskets. Nantucket: Deermouse Pr., 1972. Pp. 116.

9947 SEVERANCE, MADELEINE FISH. "Streets Broad and Gay." NHAP, (1923), 39-45.

9948 SHARP, BENJAMIN. "Nantucket's representatives in national and state legislatures." NHAP, (1911), 29-33.
1780-1911.

9949 SMITH, SANDRA. "Quakerism in Nantucket." HistNan, 13 (July, 1965), 13-14.

9950 SNOW, MARGUERITE. "Nantucket lighthouses." NHAP, (1933), 20-22.

9951 STACKPOLE, EDOUARD A. "Angola Street and Arthur Cooper--a misplaced street and a rescued slave." NHAP, (1941), 31-35.
Arthur and Mary Cooper, fugitive slaves, 1822.

9952 ____. "First 150 years." HistNan, 17 (July, 1969), 6-11.
Newspapers.

9953 ____. "The 'great fire of 1846.'" NHAP, (1946), 35-45.

9954 ____. "Nantucket bar." NHAP, (1940), 33-60.
Sand bar as barrier to deeply laden ships.

9955 ____. "Nantucket's night of terror." CCC, 26 (1973), 48-49, 60-62, 64-65.
Fire of July 13-14, 1846.

9956 ____. "Nantucket's 'summer place.'" CCC, 22 (1969), 76-87.
Siasconset village.

9957 ____. "Nantucket's vanishing loaf." CCC, 25 (1972), 88-95.
Tuckernuck Island.

9958 ____. "The old mill." NHAP, (1946), 46-47.
Windmill built in 1746.

9959 ____. "Once along the waterfront." Hist Nan, 12 (April, 1965), 5-9.

9960 ____. "The path along the bluff." HistNan, 20 (April, 1973), 19-27.
History of a public way.

9961 ____. Rambling through the streets and lanes of Nantucket. New Bedford, 1969. Pp. 92. MB.

9962 ____. "Salvaging the sugar bark 'Mentor.'" NHAP, (1951), 19-21.
Norwegian vessel which ran aground in 1893.

9963 ____. "When Nantucket became part of Massachusetts and why." HistNan, 20 (October, 1972), 15-21.
1695.

9964 STARBUCK, ALEXANDER. A century of Free Masonry in Nantucket. [Nantucket]: Nantucket Historical Association, 1903. Pp. 44.

9965 ____. The history of Nantucket, county, island and town, including genealogies of first settlers. Boston: C. E. Goodspeed, 1924. Pp. 871.

9966 ____. "Nantucket in the Revolution." NEHGR, 28 (1874), 272-278, 436-442; 29 (1875), 48-53, 141-145.

9967 ____. "Nantucket's newspapers." NHAP, (1902), 11-20.

9968 ____. "A riotous town meeting." NHAP, (1911), 34-50.
1814.

9969 STARBUCK, MARY ELIZA. My house and I: a chronicle of Nantucket. Boston: Houghton Mifflin, 1929. Pp. 293.

9970 ____. "Our beginnings." NHAP, (1934), 14-20.
Nantucket Historical Association.

9971 ____. "Whale oil and spermaceti." NEM, New Ser., 26 (1902), 515-524.

9972 STARK, LOUISE. "Early Nantucket artists." HistNan, 6 (July, 1958), 12-24, (October, 1958), 28-39, (April, 1959), 8-17.

9973 SUTTON, RUTH HAVILAND. "The waterfront studios." HistNan, 5 (April, 1958), 6-10.
Art.

9974 STEVENS, WILLIAM OLIVER. Nantucket, the faraway island. N.Y.: Dodd, Mead, 1936. Pp. xi, 313.

9975 STOCKLEY, BERNARD H. "An introduction to the prehistory of Nantucket." HistNan, 15 (January, 1968), 5-15, (April, 1968), 6-10; 17 (October, 1969), 6-12.

9976 STROTHER, D. H. "A summer in New England: Nantucket." Harper's Magazine, 21 (1860), 745-763.

9977 STURDEVANT, LUCY HUSTON. "Two Quaker teachers." NHAP, (1922), 48-54.
John Boadle and Hepsibeth Hussey.

9978 SYLVIA, EILEEN. "Women and whales." Hist Nan, 10 (October, 1962), 26-29.
Lives of the whalers' wives.

9979 SYLVIA, ELIZABETH. "Notable old Nantucket buildings." NHAP, (1932), 12-16.

9980 TAYLOR, GEORGE ROGERS. "Currents of migration on Nantucket, 1760-1780." HistNan, 22 (July, 1974), 14-20.

9981 TITTLE, WALTER. The first Nantucket tea party. N.Y.: Doubleday, Page, [1907]. Pp. 82.
Social life and customs.

9982 TURNER, HARRY BAKER. Nantucket 'argument settlers': a complete history of Nantucket in a condensed form. Who? When? What? Where? (1917) Nantucket: The Inquirer and Mirror Pr., 1944. Pp. 115.

9983 ____. "Nantucket's early telegraph service." NHAP, (1917), 39-50.

9984 ____. The story of the island steamers, Nantucket freeze-ups, the story of the 'camels,' a few reminiscences.... Nantucket: Inquirer and Mirror Pr., 1910. Pp. 125.

9985 TURNER, MERLE. "The development of Nantucket." NHAP, (1926), 39-42.

9986 [UNDERHILL, EDWARD FITCH]. The credible chronicles of the patchwork village, 'Sconset by the sea. N.Y.: E. T. Underhill, 1886. Pp. 148.

9987 [____]. The old houses on 'Sconset Bank: the first history of Siasconset, Nantucket Island, America's most unique village. Henry Chandlee Forman, ed. Nantucket: Myacomet Pr., 1961. Pp. 37.

9988 ____. "Sconset by the sea. [N.Y.?], n.d. Pp. 32. MBNEH.
Siasconset is a section of the town.

9989 VAN ARSDALE, ROBERT. "Actors on the island during 'Sconset's heyday." HistNan, 10 (October, 1962), 29-30.

9990 WALLWORK, PHILIP C. "Nantucket's battle of the puff wagons." CCC, 23 (1970), 73, 82-83.
Automobile Exclusion Act, 1907.

9991 WEEKS, EMILY. "Development of schools in Nantucket." NHAP, (1903), 11-20.

9992 ____. "Women of Nantucket." NHAP, (1912), 31-47.
Nineteenth-century biographies.

9993 [WENTWORTH, RUTH STARBUCK]. An idyl from Nantucket, with a note by Rev. Robert Collyer. N.Y.: Thomas R. Knox, 1885. Pp. 23. MBNEH.
Nantucket's first tea party; author attribution by the New England Historic Genealogical Society.

9994 WILLSON, S. A. "Nantucket and the whalefishers." Magazine of Western History, 9 (1888-1889), 178-187, 537-544.

9995 WINSLOW, HELEN. "The Friends of Nantucket." NHAP, (1936), 31-33.
Quakers.

9996 WOOD, DAVID. "Nantucket's architectural heritage." NHAP, (1938), 19-21.

9997 WORTH, GEORGE F. "The duck factory." Hist Nan, 5 (April, 1958), 23-27.
Flax for sails.

9998 WORTH, HENRY BARNARD. "The colonial church and Nantucket." NHAP, (1906), 26-31.
Church and State.

9999 ____. "Early houses at Nantucket." NHAP, (1904), 19-24.

10000 ____. Nantucket lands and landowners. [Nantucket]: Nantucket Historical Association, 1901-1913. v.p.

10001 ____. Quakerism on Nantucket since 1800. [Nantucket]: Nantucket Historical Association, 1896. Pp. 38.

10002 ____. "William Gayer and his descendants." NHAP, (1922), 38-47.

10003 WYER, HENRY SHERMAN. "The Nantucket Historical Association: its origin and objects." NHAP, (1916), 31-34.

10004 ____, ed. Spun-yarn from old Nantucket; consisting mainly of extracts from books now out of print, with a few additions. Nantucket: Inquirer and Mirror Pr., 1914. Pp. 311.

NATICK

10005 BACON, AUSTIN. South Middlesex peculiar; or Natick view and review, containing the past history and present doings in and around said town.... Natick, 1869. v.p.

10006 BACON, HARRIET F. "Personal recollections of Natick." Historical Natural History and Library Society of South Natick. Historical Collections, 1 (1909), 34-42.

10007 BACON, JOHN WILLIAM. "Natick public libraries and their origins." Historical, Natural History and Library Society of South Natick. Historical Collections, 2 (1910), 41-45.

10008 BACON, OLIVER N. A history of Natick, from its first settlement in 1651 to the present time; with notices of the first white families, and also an account of the centennial celebration, Oct. 16, 1851, Rev. Mr. Hunt's address at the consecration of Dell Park Cemetery.... Boston: Damrell & Moore, 1856. Pp. 261.

10009 BIGLOW, WILLIAM. History of the town of Natick, Mass., from the days of the apostolic Eliot, MDCL, to the present time, MDCCCXXX. Boston: Marsh, Capen, & Lyon, 1830. Pp. 87.

10010 BOUTWELL & CO. Boutwell's ready reference book and pocket memoranda for Natick. Leominster, 1888. Pp. 64.

10011 CHADBOURNE, ROBERT A. "Town of Natick is rich in industrial and literary lore." Industry, 14 (May, 1949), 15-21, 50-51.

10012 CHENEY, AMOS P. "The first fourteen years of the Historical, Natural History and Library Society of South Natick." Historical, Natural History and Library Society of South Natick. Historical Collections, 2 (1910), 11-26.

10013 _____. Natick, Massachusetts, its advantages for residence, and as a place of business. Natick: Bulletin Steam Print, 1889. Pp. 32.

10014 CHENEY, O. AUGUSTA. "The first Irish settler in Natick." Historical, Natural History and Library Society of South Natick. Historical Collections, 1 (1909), 56-57.
          Thomas Lynch.

10015 _____. "How John Eliot laid out the town." Historical, Natural History and Library Society of South Natick. Historical Collections, 1 (1909), 4-8.

10016 CHILD, LUCIE M. WHITNEY. "West Central Street: its trees and residences." Historical, Natural History and Library Society of South Natick. Historical Collections, 2 (1910), 36-37.

10017 DANIELS, LEVERETT RICHMOND and ARTHUR BENEDICT. John Eliot's village of praying Indians, South Natick, Massachusetts, Mrs. Stowe's 'Oldtown.' Isabell R. Hernlein and Marie E. Boland, eds. [South Natick?, 1930]. Unpaged.

10018 ELIOT, NATHAN. "Natick, old and new towns." NEM, New Ser., 44 (1911), 91-105.

10019 "THE ELIOT Oak, under which John Eliot preached to the Indians at the old town, Natick." Historical, Natural History and Library Society of South Natick. Historical Collections, 1 (1909), 18-21.

10020 ESTY, MARY R. "The First Unitarian Church in Natick." Historical, Natural History and Library Society of South Natick. Historical Collections, 2 (1910), 3-8.

10021 _____. "The old Morse Tabern." Historical, Natural History and Library Society of South Natick. Historical Collections, 1 (1909), 64-65.

10022 FAIRBANKS, GEORGE C. "Natick parks and playgrounds." Historical, Natural History and Library Society of South Natick. Historical Collections, 2 (1910), 92-102.

10023 THE FIRST centennial celebration 1778-1881 of the incorporation of the town of Natick, Mass., June 1, 1881. Natick: H. L. Wells, 1881. Pp. 4.

10024 GALE, ABBY F. "Reminiscences of a quiet life." Historical, Natural History and Library Society of South Natick, Historical Collections, 1 (1909), 42-48.

10025 HARTWELL, ALFRED S. "A narration of old time incidents in South Natick." Historical, Natural History and Library Society of South Natick. Historical Collections, 2 (1910), 50-55.

10026 HISTORICAL, NATURAL HISTORY, AND LIBRARY SOCIETY OF SOUTH NATICK. Proceedings at the reunion of the descendants of John Eliot, 'the apostle to the Indians,' at Guilford, Conn., Sept. 15th, 1875; second meeting at South Natick, Mass. July 3d, 1901; and the two hundred and fiftieth anniversary of the founding of South Natick by John Eliot and his praying Indians, July 4th, 1901. South Natick, 1901. Pp. 114.

10027 _____. A review of the first fourteen years of the Historical, Natural History and Library Society of South Natick, Mass., with the field-day proceedings of 1881-1882-1883. South Natick, 1884. Pp. 126.

10028 HOSMER, SAMUEL DANA. An historical sermon preached in the John Eliot Church, South Natick, Mass., Nov. 15, 1874, on the fifteenth anniversary of the church. South Natick, 1875. Pp. 11.

10029 _____. "The Natick exiles of 1675." Historical, Natural History and Library Society of South Natick. Historical Collections, 2 (1910), 73-81.
          King Philip's War.

10030 JONES, JOHN. Book of minutes of Col. John Jones of Dedham, Massachusetts; with explanatory notes by his grandson, Amos Perry, of Providence, Rhode Island.... Boston: G. E. Littlefield, 1894. Pp. 42.

10031 MACEWEN, FLORENCE LOVELL. "Patriotic Natick." Historical, Natural History and Library Society of South Natick. Historical Collections, 1 (1909), 65-71.

10032 MCMANUS, JAMES. "Natick's Town Hall." Historical, Natural History and Library Society of South Natick. Historical Collections, 2 (1910), 59-64.

10033 MANN, JAMES BACON. "Cornwallis in Natick, 1833." Historical, Natural History and Library Society, Historical Collections, 2 (1910), 37-41.
    Account of reenactment of Cornwallis' surrender.

10034 MOORE, MARTIN. A sermon, delivered at Natick, January V, MDCCCXVII, containing a history of said town, from MDCLI to the day of delivery. Cambridge: Hilliard and Metcalf, 1817. Pp. 27.

10035 MORSE, IDA H. "The ministers of the four Indian meeting houses at South Natick." Historical, Natural History and Library Society of South Natick. Historical Collections, 1 (1909), 88-90.

10036 NATICK, MASS. FIRST BAPTIST CHURCH. Manual...[from] February 13, 1848 to January 1, 1880. So. Framingham: J. C. Clark, 1880. Pp. 40. MBNEH.

10037 NATICK, MASS. FIRST CONGREGATIONAL CHURCH. The confession of faith, covenant...with a historical sketch. Boston: Thomas Todd, 1877. Pp. 131. MB.
    Sketch is by Daniel Wight, Jr.

10038 NATICK. Boston: Edison Electric Illuminating Co., 1909. Pp. 20. M.

10039 NATICK FEDERAL SAVINGS AND LOAN ASSOCIATION. Story of Natick. Natick: Suburban Pr., 1948. Pp. 32. MB.

10040 NATICK FIVE CENTS SAVINGS BANK. Home of the Natick Five Cents Savings Bank for 100 years. Natick, 1959. Pp. 18. M.

10041 NOYES, S. B. "The old Eliakim Morrill Tavern." Historical, Natural History and Library Society of South Natick. Historical Collections, 1 (1909), 60-63.

10042 "OLD Natick farms." Historical, Natural History and Library Society of South Natick. Historical Collections, 1 (1909), 31-33.

10043 PERRY, ELIJAH. "Early white settlers, their homes on the route of the first field day excursion of the South Natick Historical Society." Historical, Natural History and Library Society of South Natick. Historical Collections, 1 (1909), 29-30.

10044 RICHARDS, MARY PERRY. "A tale of people and incidents in South Natick in the nineteenth century." Historical, Natural History and Library Society of South Natick. Historical Collections, 1 (1909), 72-79.

10045 SAWYER, EDITH A. "South Natick in fact and fiction." NEM, New Ser., 31 (1904-1905), 123-140.

10046 SHEAFE, J. P., JR. and HORATIO ALGER. Address delivered by Rev. J. P. Sheafe, Jr. and Rev. Horatio Alger at the semicentennial of the dedication of the First Unitarian Church, South Natick, November 20, 1878. Natick: Ryder & Morse, 1879. Pp. 41. MBNEH.

10047 SHEAFE, J. P., JR. "The Indian burying ground." Historical, Natural History and Library Society of South Natick. Historical Collections, 1 (1909), 79-82.

10048 _____. "Indian settlement and about 'old-town' Natick." Historical, Natural History and Library Society of South Natick. Historical Collections, 1 (1909), 25-28.

10049 _____. "The old meeting houses." Historical, Natural History and Library Society of South Natick. Historical Collections, 1 (1909), 58-60.

10050 SMITH, GUSTAVUS. "The old burying ground, where many of Natick's oldest families have been interred from 1731-1902." Historical, Natural History and Library Society of South Natick. Historical Collections, 1 (1909), 21-25.

10051 TOEPFER, LOUIS A., ed. Souvenir program of the 300th anniversary of the town of Natick June 10-17, 1951. [Boston]: Banker and Tradesman Pr., 1951. Pp. 40. M.

10052 TOOKER, WILLIAM WALLACE. The significance of John Eliot's Natick and the name Merrimac; with historical and ethnological notes. N.Y.: F. P. Harper, 1901. Pp. 56.

10053 TOWNSEND, LUCY M. "The centennial hob nob, how and why it was arranged." Historical, Natural History and Library Society of South Natick. Historical Collections, 1 (1909), 49-53.
    Historical pageant performed to raise money for expenses after fire of 1872.

10054 TRAVIS, ALONZO F. "Felchville: its past, present and future." Historical, Natural History and Library Society of South Natick. Historical Collections, 2 (1910), 86-91.
    Section of the town.

10055 WIGHT, LUCY ELLEN. "A brief history of the First Congregational Church." Historical, Natural History and Library Society of South Natick. Historical Collections, 1 (1909), 90-93.

10056 WORTHINGTON, ERASTUS. "John Eliot and the Indian village at Natick." HPHR, 4 (1904), 33-48.

NEEDHAM

10057 CLARKE, GEORGE KUHN. "Clerks of the First Parish in Needham." DedHR, 2 (1891), 95-96.

10058 _____. "The deacons of the First Church in Needham." DedHR, 3 (1892), 73-76.

10059 _____. "Needham: books, pamphlets, and newspapers that contain historical and genealogical matter relative to the town." NEHGR, 53 (1899), 33-34.

10060 _____. "Notes from the records of the First Parish in Needham." DedHR, 3 (1892), 35-37, 125-129; 4 (1893), 27-31, 122-125.

10061 _____. "The old Townsend House in Needham." DedHR, 1 (1890), 81-85; 10 (1899), 45-51.

10062 _____. "Schools and teachers in Needham." DedHR, 14 (1903), 11-18, 55-60, 94-98, 121-125.

10063 _____. "Schools in Needham, 1841-1859." DedHR, 11 (1900), 92-98, 137-144; 12 (1901), 30-33.

10064 HISTORY and directory of Needham, Massachusetts, for 1888/89, containing a complete resident, street and business directory... also a history of the town from the first settlement to the present time. Needham: A. E. Foss, 1888. Pp. 157.

10065 NEEDHAM, MASS. Needham's bicentennial celebration; a record of the exercises and a memorial of the celebration at Needham, Massachusetts, on the two hundredth anniversary of its incorporation. Thomas Sutton, comp. Needham: G. W. and W. M. Southworth, 1913. Pp. 232.

10066 NEEDHAM. Boston: Edison Electric Illuminating Co., 1909. Pp. 12. M.

10067 NEEDHAM COOPERATIVE BANK. A half century of community service in financing the building of Needham homes, 1892-1942.... Needham, 1942. Pp. 16. M.

10068 PALMER, STEPHEN. A sermon, delivered in Needham, November 16, 1811, on the termination of a century, since the incorporation of the town. Dedham: Herman Mann, 1811. Pp. 44.

10069 PRESTON, NEWELL T. New life for retired men. N.Y.: Exposition Pr., 1968. Pp. 96. Needham Retired Men's Club.

10070 SCHIRMER, J. WALTER. Needham, 1711-1944. Needham: Needham Historical Society, 1944. Unpaged. MBNEH.

10071 "THE WILLIAM Carter Company." Industry, 5 (August, 1940), 9-11. Clothing.

10072 "THE WILLIAM Carter Company--a century of 'sticking to its knitting.'" Industry, 31 (December, 1965), 13-14, 38. Clothing.

NEW ASHFORD

10073 SEE HISTORIES OF BERKSHIRE COUNTY.

NEW BEDFORD

10074 ALDRICH, HERBERT L. "New Bedford." NEM, 4 (1886), 423-441.

10075 ALLEN, EVERETT S. Children of the light: the rise and fall of New Bedford whaling and the death of the arctic fleet. Boston: Little, Brown, 1973. Pp. viii, 302.

10076 ALLEN, GEORGE H. H. New Bedford Five Cents Savings Bank, incorporated April 18, 1855, organized May 5, 1855, opened May 26, 1855.... New Bedford: Reynolds, 1923. Pp. 58.

10077 ANTHONY, JOSEPH R. Life in New Bedford a hundred years ago: a chronicle of the social, religious and commercial history of the period as recorded in a diary kept by Joseph R. Anthony. Zephaniah W. Pease, ed. [New Bedford]: G. H. Reynolds, 1922. Pp. 91.

10078 BRIGGS, JAMES F. Sails and sailmakers. [New Bedford?], 1937. Unpaged. MB.

10079 CAMPBELL, MARION H. "From the hilltop of grown-old." BJCH, (Winter, 1965), 4-14. Horticulture.

10080 "A CENTURY of expansion and success." Industry, 30 (December, 1964), 15, 41-42. Morse Twist Drill and Machine Co., metal cutting.

10081 "A CENTURY of Wamsutta." Industry, 11 (July, 1946), 11-14, 50. Cotton textiles.

10082 COGGESHALL, ROBERT C. P. Development of the New Bedford water supplies. [New Bedford?, 1915?]. Pp. 23. MB.

10083 CONGDON, JAMES BUNKER. An address delivered at the consecration of the Oak Grove Cemetery in New-Bedford, October 6th, 1843...with the regulations of the selectmen, for the government of the cemetery; and an appendix. New-Bedford: Lindsey, 1844. Pp. 35. Includes brief historical sketches of other New Bedford cemeteries.

10084 "CONTINENTAL Screw Company marks a fiftieth milestone." Industry, 20 (December, 1954), 13-16.

10085 CRAPO, HENRY HOWLAND. "Old buildings in New Bedford." ODHS, No. 23 (January, 1909), 17-29. Historic houses.

10086 _____. Story of cotton and its manufacture into cloth in New Bedford. [New Bedford?, 1937?]. Unpaged. MB.

10087 DENISON, FREDERIC. Illustrated New Bedford, Martha's Vineyard and Nantucket, sketches of discoveries, aborigines, settlers, wars, incidents, towns, hamlets, scenes, camp meetings, cottages and interesting localities.... (1879) 2d. and rev. ed. Providence, R.I.: J. A. & R. A. Reid, 1880. Pp. 78. M.

10088   ELLIS, LEONARD BOLLES. History of the fire
        department of the city of New Bedford, Mas-
sachusetts, 1772-1890. New Bedford: E. Anthony &
Sons, 1890. Pp. xi, 239.

10089   EMERY, WILLIAM MORRELL. New Bedford law-
        yers of the past. New Bedford: Dartmouth
Historical Society, [1944?]. Pp. 74.

10090   ____. One hundred years of the church:
        historical address, delivered at the exer-
cises commemorating the centenary of the dedication
of the meeting house of the First Congregational
Society (Unitarian), New Bedford, May 23, 1938.
New Bedford, 1938. Pp. 32, 7.

10091   FREEMASONS. NEW BEDFORD, MASS. ADONIRAM
        ROYAL ARCH CHAPTER. Celebration of the
centennial anniversary...October 8th and 9th,
1916. n.p., 1916. Pp. 53. MBNEH.

10092   FROTHINGHAM, PAUL REVERE. The First Con-
        gregational Society in New Bedford, 'Things
new and old', an anniversary sermon...October 8,
1899. New Bedford: E. Anthony & Sons, 1899.
Pp. 13.

10093   GARTLAND, EMMA LOUISE, ed. New Bedford's
        story, for New Bedford's children. New
Bedford: Reynolds Printing, 1930. Pp. 32.
        Not juvenile literature.

10094   [GAW, COOPER]. Capt. George Fred Tilton
        tablet dedication at the Seamen's Bethel,
Johnny Cake Hill, July 16, 1933; story of Tilton's
walk and whaling tradition. New Bedford: Reynolds Printing, 1933. Pp. 47.

10095   GIFFORD, PARDON B. The wing fleet...the
        stone fleet...loss of the arctic fleet, by
the late Wm. F. Williams. 2d. ed. New Bedford:
Reynolds Printing, 1939. Unpaged.

10096   GRIEVE, ROBERT, ed. New Bedford semi-cen-
        tennial souvenir, containing a review of
the history of the city, together with accounts of
the whale fishery, the early industries, the great
growth in the cotton manufacture and the social and
economic changes, also programme of the semi-centennial exercises.... Providence, R.I.: Journal
of Commerce, 1897. Pp. 90.

10097   HALL, CLARENCE JOSHUA. "From whales to cot-
        ton." CCAPL, 4 (June, 1920), 22-23.

10098   HASKINS, ELMORE P. "Some of the streets of
        the town of New Bedford." ODHS, No. 19
(1908), 7-13.

10099   ____. The story of Water Street. [New
        Bedford, 1906?]. Pp. 14.

10100   HEGARTY, REGINALD B. New Bedford's history.
        New Bedford: Reynolds Printing, 1959.
Pp. 24.

10101   HODGIN, EDWIN STANTON. One hundred years
        of Unitarianism in New Bedford, Massachu-
setts. New Bedford: Vining Pr., 1924. Pp. 57.

10102   HOLDEN, FRANK. "History of the New Bedford
        Institute of Technology." TextHR, 3 (1962),
205-217.

10103   HOLLISTER, PAUL. "The Kahila dig at Mount
        Washington." Antiques, 102 (1972), 455-459.
Mount Washington Glass Works.

10104   HOUGH, HENRY BEETLE. Wamsutta of New Bed-
        ford, 1846-1946; a story of New England en-
terprise. New Bedford: Wamsutta Mills, 1946.
Pp. 72.
        Cotton mill.

10105   HOW, MOSES. Diary of Rev. Moses How, pastor
        of the Middle Street Christian Church, New
Bedford, from 1819 to 1826 and from 1837 until 1844:
chaplain of the Seaman's Bethel from 1844 until
1859.... New Bedford: Reynolds Printing, 1932.
Pp. 29.
        Excerpts; complete diary in New Bedford
Public Library.

10106   HOWLAND, LLEWELLYN. The middle road. South
        Dartmouth: Concordia, 1961. Pp. 134.

10107   [KELLEY, JESSE FILLMORE and ADAM MACKIE].
        History of the churches of New Bedford: to
which are added notices of various other moral and
religious organizations, together with short memoirs
of Rev. Messrs. Wheelock Craig, John Girdwood, Timothy Stowe, Daniel Webb, and Rev. Messrs. Henniss
and Tallon, of St. Mary's Church. New Bedford:
E. Anthony & Sons, 1869. Pp. 148.
        History was published separately in 1854.

10108   [KELLEY, JAMES FILLMORE]. Sketches of the
        members in the municipal government, New
Bedford, for the year 1861. New Bedford: Office of
the 'Shipping List', 1861. Pp. 24.

10109   LEARY, FRANK J. "Industry's map of Massa-
        chusetts: New Bedford." Industry, 3
(October, 1937), 48, 69, 71.

10109A LITTLE, NINA FLETCHER. "New Bedford oil for
        Philadelphia Friends." BJCH, (Autumn, 1964,
4-15.
        Whale oil.

10110   MCAFEE, IDA A. "New Bedford one hundred
        and twenty years ago, as glimpsed through
the Medley." ODHS, No. 37 (January, 1913), 5-24.
        'The Medley or New Bedford Marine Journal'
was New Bedford's first newspaper.

10111   MATTOX, WILLIAM COURTNEY. "The copper in-
        dustry." Industry, 1 (February, 1936), 5-8.
Revere Copper and Brass, Inc.

10112   MOMENT, DAVID. "The business of whaling in
        America in the 1850s." BusHR, 31 (1957),
261-291.
        Centers on New Bedford.

10113   MORNING MERCURY, NEW BEDFORD, MASS. The
        story of the celebration of the semi-cen-
tennial of the incorporation of New Bedford as a
city. New Bedford, 1897. Pp. 20. MB.

10114   MOULTON, C. H., comp. New Bedford, Mass.,
        brief history, textile school, industries,
etc. [New Bedford]: Board of Trade, 1901. Pp. 124.
M.

10115   NATIONAL ARCHIVES PROJECT. Ship registers
        of New Bedford, Massachusetts. Boston,
1940. xvi, 411 leaves.
        1796-1850; index of owners and masters.

10116   NATIONAL COUNCIL OF JEWISH WOMEN. NEW BED-
        FORD SECTION. Twenty years with the coun-
cil. n.p., 1935. Unpaged. [MWalAJHi].

10117   NELSON, MAUD MENDALL. New Bedford fifty
        years ago. n.p., 1914. Pp. 28. MB.

10118   NEW BEDFORD, MASS. Centennial in New Bed-
        ford, historical address by Hon. William W.
Crapo, delivered on the occasion of the celebration
in New Bedford of the Fourth of July, 1876, to which
are added an account of the celebration, and an appendix. New Bedford: E. Anthony & Sons, 1876.
        Relates to the city.

10119   NEW BEDFORD, MASS. BOARD OF TRADE. New
        Bedford, Massachusetts: its history, in-
dustries, institutions and attractions. Writers --
Zeph[aniah] W. Pease, George A. Hough. William L.
Sayer, ed. [New Bedford]: Mercury Publishing,
1889. Pp. 318.

10120   NEW BEDFORD, MASS. CITIZENS. A plain
        statement of facts, or history of the dif-
ficulties existing in the Whig party of New Bedford,
for the past two years. New Bedford, 1848. Pp. 15.

10121   NEW BEDFORD, MASS. FIRST BAPTIST CHURCH.
        Articles of faith and covenant of the First
Baptist Church, William Street, New-Bedford, Mass.,
with a sketch of its history and a catalogue of its
members. Providence, R.I.: H. H. Brown, 1840.
Pp. 66. MBNEH.

10122   _____. Articles of faith and covenant of
        the First Baptist Church, William-Street,
New-Bedford, Mass., with a sketch of its history
and a catalogue of its members to August, 1842....
New-Bedford: Benjamin Lindsey, 1842. Pp. 60. MB.

10123   NEW BEDFORD, MASS. FIRST UNITARIAN CHURCH.
        A short history of the First Unitarian
Church in New Bedford, Massachusetts. New Bedford:
Board of Trustees, 1958. Pp. 20.

10124   NEW BEDFORD, MASS. FRIENDS ACADEMY. His-
        torical sketch of the Friends Academy, pre-
pared for the centennial year, to which is appended
a presentation of the course and methods of instruction at present pursued. New Bedford: Fessenden &
Baker, 1876. Pp. 73.

10125   NEW BEDFORD, MASS. TRINITARIAN CHURCH.
        Semicentennial anniversary of the Trinitari-
an Church of New Bedford, Mass., 1831-1881. n.p.,
[1881?]. Pp. 73. MB.

10126   NEW BEDFORD INSTITUTION FOR SAVINGS. Cen-
        tenary, 1825-1925.... New Bedford, 1925.
Pp. 28. MBNEH.

10127   THE NEW BEDFORD MERCURY. The New Bedford
        Mercury: one hundredth anniversary supple-
ment, Aug. 7, 1907. New Bedford, 1907. Pp. 80.
        Centennial of the newspaper.

10128   NEW BEDFORD PORT SOCIETY. One hundredth
        anniversary of the New Bedford Port Society
to be held on Sunday, May 18, [1930] at 7:30 P.M.
at the Seamen's Bethel, Johnny Cake Hill, New Bedford, Mass. New Bedford: Reynolds Printing, 1930.
Unpaged. MBNEH.
        Chapel for sailors.

10129   NEW BEDFORD TEXTILE INSTITUTE. ALUMNI ASSO-
        CIATION. New Bedford Textile Institute
golden jubilee. [New Bedford, 1948]. Unpaged.

10130   "NEW Bedford whaling fleet, 1790-1906."
        BBHS, 5 (December, 1931), 9-14.

10131   PEASE, ZEPHANIAH W. "The Arnold Mansion and
        its traditions." ODHS, No. 52 (June, 1924),
5-35.

10132   _____. "'The Blues'--a New Bedford social
        and literary organization." ODHS, No. 50
(December, [1920?]), 10-23.

10133   _____. "The brave industry of whaling."
        Americana, 12 (1918), 78-103.

10134   _____. Centenary of the Merchants National
        Bank. New Bedford: Reynolds Printing,
1925. Pp. 91. MBNEH.

10135   _____, ed. History of New Bedford. N.Y.:
        Lewis Historical Publishing, 1918. 3v.

10136   POTTER, WILLIAM JAMES. The First Congrega-
        tional Society in New Bedford, Massachu-
setts: its history as illustrative of ecclesiastical evolution. New Bedford, 1889. Pp. 151.

10137   [REED, BENJAMIN F. H.]. A hundred years
        ago: burning of Bedford village by the
British, September 5, 1778. [New Bedford]: Standard Office, 1878. Pp. 11. MB.
        Author attribution by Boston Public Library.

10138   REMINGTON, WALTER H. B. "Fourths of the
        past." ODHS, No. 40 (June, 1914), 4-11.
        Fourth of July celebrations.

10139   _____. "New Bedford." NEM, New Ser., 41
        (1909-1910), 819-831.

10140   RICKETSON, DANIEL. New Bedford of the past.
        Anna and Walton Ricketson, eds. Boston:
Houghton Mifflin, 1903. Pp. xiii, 196.

10141   RODMAN, SAMUEL. The diary of Samuel Rodman:
        a New Bedford chronicle of thirty-seven
years, 1821-1859. Zephaniah W. Pease, ed. New Bedford: Reynolds Printing, 1927. Pp. 349. MB.
        Lacks section for 1827 which was subsequent-
        ly published as 'New Bedford in 1827 as told
        in Samuel Rodman's diary.' See next entry.

10142   _____. New Bedford in 1827 as told in Sam-
        uel Rodman's diary. Bradford Swan, ed.
[New Bedford]: Reynolds Printing, 1935. Unpaged.
        The section missing from Rodman's diary,
        edited by Zephaniah W. Pease, which was
        published in 1927.

10143 ROMAINE, LAWRENCE B. "A New England town band, 1843-1860." OTNE, 43 (1952-1953), 80-83.

10144 SANFORD AND KELLEY, FIRM, NEW BEDFORD, MASS. New Bedford, Mass., interesting statistics relating to its location, history, government, banks, finances, cotton and other manufacturing industry, etc. New Bedford, 1893. Pp. 74. M.

10145 SHERMAN, FREDERIC FAIRCHILD. "An old American publisher." Literary Miscellany, 2 (1909), 73-79.
    Abraham Shearman; established 1798.

10146 SMITH, DAVID LOEFFLER. "New Bedford artists of the nineteenth century." Antiques, 92 (1967), 689-693.
    Albert Bierstadt, Albert Ryder, Albert Van Beest and William A. Wall.

10147 SOUTH BRISTOL FARMERS' CLUB, NEW BEDFORD, MASS. Souvenir history, South Bristol Farmers' Club. New Bedford: W. H. Collins, 1898. Pp. 70. M.

10148 STROTHER, D. H. "A summer in New England: New Bedford." Harper's Magazine, 21 (1860), 1-19.

10149 TRIPP, GEORGE HENRY. New Bedford libraries--then and now. [New Bedford, 1934]. Unpaged.

10150 TUCKER, GEORGE F. "New Bedford." NEM, New Ser., 15 (1896-1897), 97-116.

10151 "WAMSUTTA Mills." Industry, 7 (September, 1942), 21-24, 40.
    Cotton textiles.

10152 WHITNEY, SAMUEL WORCESTER. Address delivered at the anniversary of the New Bedford 'Ladies' Tract and Missionary Society,' Jan. 31, 1858. New Bedford: Standard Steam Pr., 1858. v.p. MB.

10153 WILSON, KENNETH M. "Documenting some Mt. Washington art glass." Antiques, 92 (1967), 367-372.

10154 WOLFBEIN, SEYMOUR LOUIS. The decline of a cotton textile city: a study of New Bedford. N.Y.: Columbia Univ. Pr., 1944. Pp. 179.

10155 WORTH, HENRY BARNARD. "Highways, post roads and public houses of New Bedford before the arrival of the train." ODHS, No. 51 (July, 1921), 17-22.

NEW BRAINTREE

10156 FISKE, JOHN, 1770-1855. Recollections and anticipations: a half-century and dedicatory discourse, delivered in New-Braintree, Mass., October 26, 1846. Greenfield: Merriam and Mirick, 1846. Pp. 34.
    Congregational Church.

10157 GREEN, SAMUEL ABBOTT. "Wheeler's defeat, 1675. Where? At Meminimesset Meadow." AASP, New Ser., 9 (1893-1894), 11-13.

10158 NEW BRAINTREE, MASS. Account of the observance of the one hundred and fiftieth anniversary of the incorporation of the town of New Braintree, Mass., June 19, 1901...historical address by George K. Tufts.... Worcester: Charles Hamilton, 1902. Pp. 105. MBNEH.

NEW MARLBOROUGH

10159 SOUTHFIELD, MASS. CONGREGATIONAL CHURCH. Articles of faith, covenant...Congregational Church in Southfield, Mass., organized April 25, 1794. North Adams: Mrs. W. B. Walden, 1887. Pp. 29. MPB.
    Includes historical sketch.

10160 TURNER, HADLEY K. History of New Marlborough, 1735-1943. Great Barrington: Berkshire Courier, 1944. Pp. 59. MBNEH.

NEW SALEM

10161 ADADOURIAN, HAIG. [New Salem pictures.]: This booklet, with the exception of the last four sketches, contains brief descriptions of a number of the residents of New Salem, Mass. Athol: Athol Transcript, 1913. 23 leaves.

10162 BULLARD, EUGENE. History of New Salem Academy. [New Salem?], 1913. Pp. 279.

10163 COOLIDGE, LILLIE PIERCE. The history of Prescott, Massachusetts, one of four townships in the Swift River Valley which was 'born, lived and died' to make way for Metropolitan Water Basin. [n.p., 1952]. Pp. 288.

10164 COX, FLORENCE COGSWELL. History of New Salem, Massachusetts, 1753-1953, prepared for the celebration of the 200th anniversary August 7, 8, 9, 1953. Amherst: H. I. Newell, 1953. Pp. 116.

10165 HOUSE, ALBERT VIRGIL. "Salem and New Salem." DanHC, 5 (1917), 90-109.
    Settlement of the town.

10166 NEW SALEM, MASS. The New Salem sesquicentennial; report of the addresses and proceedings of the celebration of the 150th anniversary of the incorporation of the town of New Salem, at New Salem on Thursday, Aug. 20th, 1903. Athol: Transcript Book and Job Print, 1904. Pp. 77.

NEWBURY

10167 CLEAVELAND, NEHEMIAH. The first century of Dummer Academy: a historical discourse, delivered at Newbury, Byfield Parish, August 12, 1863.... Boston: Nichols & Noyes, 1865. Pp. 71, xliii.

10168 _____. A history of Dummer Academy being the centennial discourse delivered by Nehemiah Cleaveland on August 12th, 1863 together with an account of the proceedings in commemmoration of the 150th anniversary of the school. Newburyport: Herald Pr., 1914. Pp. 103.

10169 CURRIER, JOHN JAMES. History of Newbury, Mass., 1635-1902. Boston: Damrell & Upham, 1902. Pp. 755.

10170 _____. 'Ould Newbury': historical and biographical sketches. Boston: Damrell and Upham, 1896. Pp. 729.

10171 DALTON, MARSHALL B. "The trustees of Governor Dummer Academy past and present." EIHC, 90 (1954), 217-228.

10172 DUMMER, JOSEPH N. A brief history of the Byfield Congregational Church and Parish, from 1702-1888. Salem: Observer Book and Job Print, 1888. Pp. 80.

10173 _____. "Newbury and its influence." Sons and Daughters of the First Settlement of Newbury, Massachusetts. Publications, No. 1 (1935), 17-30.

10174 _____. "The story of Byfield Parish." Mag Hist, 12 (1910), 27-35.

10175 ESTAVER, PAUL E. "The Tristam Coffin House, Newbury, Mass." The Shoreliner, 3 (November, 1952), 9-13.

10176 EWELL, JOHN LOUIS. The story of Byfield, a New England parish. Boston: G. E. Littlefield, 1904. Pp. xv, 344.

10177 FERRIS, S. HARRY. "Ancient houses of old Newbury." NEM, New Ser., 32 (1905), 73-78.

10178 FORBES, SUSAN E. P. "Eben Parsons and Fatherland Farm." NEHGR, 50 (1896), 59-64.

10179 GOVERNOR DUMMER ACADEMY, SOUTH BYFIELD, MASS. An account of Dummer Academy, together with a statement of the alterations and improvements, about to be made, by the trustees. Boston: Boston Courier, 1837. Pp. 12.

10180 _____. Exercises at the one hundred and twenty-fifth anniversary of Dummer Academy, at Newbury, Byfield Parish, Mass., June 19, 1888, address by Hon. William Dummer Northend. Salem: Salem Pr., 1888. Pp. 61.

10181 _____. The 175th anniversary of Governor Dummer Academy, South Byfield, Massachusetts, June ninth and tenth, 1938. Newburyport: Herald Pr., 1939. Pp. 14.
        Historical address by James Duncan Phillips.

10182 HISTORICAL SOCIETY OF OLD NEWBURY, NEWBURYPORT, MASS. Celebration of the two hundred and fiftieth anniversary of the settlement of Newbury, June 10, 1885. Newburyport, 1885. Pp. 150.

10183 ILSLEY, ELIZABETH HALE. Old homesteads. Salem: Newcomb & Gauss, 1948. Pp. 17. MBNEH.

10184 JACKSON, RUSSELL LEIGH. "The Jackman-Willett House." Sons and Daughters of the First Settlers of Newbury, Massachusetts. Publications, No. 1 (1935), 35-40.

10185 _____. "Kent's Island." EIHC, 80 (1944), 199-207.

10186 KINGSBURY, FELICIA DOUGHTY. "A roof-tree that grew--the Tristram Coffin House, Newbury." OTNE, 40 (1949-1950), 180-186.

10187 LITTLE, ELIZA ADAMS and LUCRETIA LITTLE ILSLEY, eds. The First Parish, Newbury, Massachusetts, 1635-1935. Newburyport: News Publishing, 1935. Pp. 104.

10188 LITTLE, NINA FLETCHER. "The house of Tristram Coffin Jr." Antiques, 77 (1960), 482-485.

10189 [LITTLE, WILLIAM]. A contribution to the history of Byfield Parish. Newburyport: C. B. Huse, 1893. Pp. 12.

10190 MOODY, ANNE COLMAN. "Story of the flag." Sons and Daughters of the First Settlers of Newbury, Massachusetts. Publications, No. 1 (1935), 41-42.
        Newbury flag.

10191 MORSE, GLENN TILLEY. Old Newbury initiatives. [Newburyport]: Historical Society of Old Newbury, 1935. Pp. 34. MSaE.
        Firsts.

10192 NEWBURY, MASS. Celebration of the 250th anniversary of the settlement of Newbury, June 10, 1885. Newbury: Historical Society of Old Newbury, 1885. Pp. 150. MB.

10193 NORTHEND, WILLIAM DUMMER. "Byfield and Dummer Academy." EIB, 7 (1875), 120-126.

10194 NOYES, BENJAMIN LAKE. "The Rev. James Noyes House in Newbury." MassMag, 2 (1909), 30-32.

10195 PARSONS, CLEMENTINE M. A colorful procession of the past. Newbury: Sons and Daughters of the First Settlers of Newbury, Massachusetts, 1937. Pp. 21. MBNEH.

10196 PHILLIPS, JAMES DUNCAN. "Governor Dummer's family and his school." EIHC. 81 (1945), 35-53.

10197 _____. "Harvard College and Governor Dummer's School." MHSP, 69 (1947-1950), 194-206.

10198 PLACES of historical interest within the limits of 'Ould Newbury.' Newburyport: City Improvement Society, 1897. Pp. 10. MBNEH.

10199   POPKIN, JOHN SNELLING. A sermon preached
          May 4, 1806, the last time of assembling in
the old meeting-house, in the First Parish in Newbury. Newburyport: A. March, 1806. Pp. 24. MB.

10200   RAGLE, JOHN WILLIAMS. Governor Dummer Acad-
          emy history, 1763-1963. South Byfield:
Governor Dummer Academy, 1963. Pp. xvi, 177.

10201   SPRAGUE, BLANCHE HAZARD. "Jacob Adams'
          shoemaking account." BBHS, 9 (1935), 86-
92.

10202   SPRING, JAMES WHEELOCK. "The Coffin House
          in Newbury, Massachusetts and those who
made it their home." OTNE, 20 (1929-1930), 3-29.

10203   NO ENTRY

10204   TOPPAN, ROBERT NOXON. Two hundred and fif-
          tieth anniversary of the settlement of New-
bury: brief biographical sketches. Newburyport:
The [Historical] Society [of old Newbury], 1885.
Pp. 134.

10205   TOWLE MANUFACTURING COMPANY. Newbury: a
          pattern of flatware made in sterling silver
by the Towle Mfg. Company; with some history of
Newbury: Massachusetts and its progenitor Newbury:
England. George P. Tilton, comp. Newburyport,
1907. Pp. 67.

10206   WATKINS, LURA WOODSIDE. "The Byfield
          stones--our earliest American sculpture?"
Antiques, 84 (1963), 420-423.

10207   _____. "The Dummer family and the Byfield
          carvings." EIHC, 105 (1969), 3-28.
          Carved stones.

10208   _____. "Highfields and its heritage."
          Antiques, 90 (1966), 204-207.
          Home of Abraham and Anne Adams.

10209   WILDES, GEORGE DUDLEY. Oration before the
          Historical and Antiquarian Society of New-
bury, Mass., September 11, 1878, commemorative of
the settlement of Newbury, 1635. N.Y.: T. Whit-
taker, 1878. Pp. 27. MB.

10210   WITHINGTON, LEONARD. A sermon for the two-
          hundredth anniversary of the standing of
the First Church in Newbury, on its present site,
October 20, 1846. Newburyport: E. Hale, Jr., 1846.
Pp. 18.

10211   WOODS, AMY. "Dummer Academy." NEM, New
          Ser., 32 (1905), 680-691.

NEWBURYPORT

10212   AN ACCOUNT of the great fire, which de-
          stroyed about 250 buildings in Newburyport,
on the night of the 31st of May, 1811. 2d. ed.,
improved. Newburyport: W. & J. Gilman, 1811.
Pp. 23.

10213   ADAMS, JOHN QUINCY. Life in a New England
          town: 1787, 1788; diary of John Quincy
Adams, while a student in the office of Theophilus
Parsons at Newburyport. Charles Francis Adams, ed.
Boston: Little, Brown, 1903. Pp. 204.

10214   ANDREWS, FRANCES E. A collection of recol-
          lections. Newburyport: Squire & Swan
[1904?]. Pp. 19.
          Reminiscences.

10215   ATKINSON, MINNIE. A history of the First
          Religious Society in Newburyport, Massachu-
setts. Newburyport: News Publishing, 1933.
Pp. 104.

10216   _____. Newburyport in the World War, with
          records of all the men and women who served
in the military and naval forces of the United
States and its allies. Newburyport: News Publishing, 1938. Pp. xx, 302.

10217   _____. "Old Newburyport ropewalks--a van-
          ished industry." EIHC, 82 (1946), 42-48.

10218   BAKER, ELEANOR J. "An eleemosynary institu-
          tion--the Institution for Savings in New-
buryport and its Vicinity." EIHC, 102 (1966), 311-
317.

10219   BARRISKILL, JAMES M. "Newburyport theatre
          in the early nineteenth century." EIHC,
93 (1957), 279-314.

10220. _____. "The Newburyport theatre in the 18th
          century." EIHC, 91 (1955), 211-245, 329-
352.

10221   _____. "Newburyport theatre in the federal-
          ist period." EIHC, 93 (1957), 1-35.

10222   BAYLEY, WILLIAM H. and OLIVER O. JONES,
          comps. History of the Marine Society of
Newburyport, Massachusetts, from its incorporation
in 1772 to the year 1906: together with a complete
roster and a narrative of important events in the
lives of its members. [Newburyport]: Daily News,
1906. Pp. 506.

10223   [BLAKE], EUPHEMIA VALE. History of Newbury-
          port; from the earliest settlement of the
country to the present time, with a biographical
appendix. By Mrs. E. Vale Smith. Newburyport,
1854. Pp. v, 414.

10224   BRADLEE, FRANCIS BOARDMAN CROWINSHIELD.
          "The 'Dreadnought' of Newburyport and some
account of the old trans-atlantic packet ships."
EIHC, 56 (1920), 1-23.

10225   BROWN, FRANK CHOUTEAU. "The spire of the
          First Religious Society in Newburyport,
Massachusetts." OTNE, 38 (1947-1948), 27-32.

10226   CAHILL, THOMAS PETER. The famous Tracys of
          Newburyport, Massachusetts. Somerville:
Captain Jeremiah O'Brien's Memorial Associates,
1942. Pp. 12.

10227   CHENEY, ROBERT K. "Industries allied to shipbuilding in Newburyport." AmNep, 17 (1957), 114-127.

10228   ____. Maritime history of the Merrimac, shipbuilding. Roland H. Woodwell, ed. [Newburyport], Newburyport Pr., 1964. Pp. xiv, 386.

10229   COOK, MOODY D. A genealogical address, giving a brief history of the parishioners and founders of the Federal Street Church, from 1745-6 to 1862, with the names of their descendants, now parishioners, delivered before the Ladies' and Gentlemen's Association of the parish, May 29, 1862. Newburyport: W. H. Huse, 1862. Pp. 35.

10230   CREASEY, GEORGE WILLIAM. The city of Newburyport in the Civil War from 1861 to 1865 with the individual records of the soldiers and sailors who served to its credit, also the war records of many natives and residents of the city, credited to other places. Boston: Griffith-Stillings Pr., 1903. Pp. 539.

10231   [____]. Historical sketch, by-laws and roster of A. W. Bartlett Post 49, G. A. R., Department of Massachusetts, Newburyport...also historical sketch and by-laws of the Newburyport Soldiers' and Sailors' Memorial Hall Association. Amesbury: G. T. Morrill, 1884. Pp. 41. MSaE.
        Author attribution by the editor.

10232   CUMMINGS, OSMOND RICHARD. Mass. Northeastern St. Ry. Vol. I, Newburyport Division. Forty Fort, Pa.: H. E. Cox, 1964. Pp. 58.

10233   CURRIER, JOHN JAMES. History of Newburyport, Mass., 1764-1909. Newburyport, 1906-1909. 2v.

10234   CUSHING, CALEB. The history and present state of the town of Newburyport. Newburyport: E. W. Allen, 1826. Pp. viii, 120.

10235   DAVIS, H. P. Exposé of Newburyport eccentricities, witches and witchcraft, the murdered boy, and apparition of the Charles-St. School-House. n.p., 1873. Pp. 24.

10236   DRIVER, JOSEPHINE P. "Newburyport and its business district." OTNE, 54 (1963-1964), 87-95.
        Nineteenth century.

10237   THE EARLY history of Newburyport, Massachusetts, which is intended to delineate and describe some quaint and historic places in Newburyport and vicinity. Newburyport: Fowle's News, 1926. Unpaged.

10238   "EDITOR'S fable." NEM, New Ser., 22 (1900), 614-627.
        Historical account of the city.

10239   ESSEX INSTITUTE, SALEM, MASS. Ship registers of the district of Newburyport, Massachusetts, 1789-1870: compiled from the Newburyport customs house records, now on deposit at the Essex Institute. Salem, 1937. Pp. 279.

10240   FISHER, RICHARD ARNOLD. An architectural monograph on old homes of Newburyport, Massachusetts. St. Paul: White Pine Bureau, 1917. Pp. 16.

10241   FISKE, DANIEL TAGGART. Historical discourse commemorative of the fiftieth anniversary of the organization of the Belleville Congregational Church, Newburyport, Mass. delivered on Thanksgiving Day, Nov. 25, 1858. Boston: E. P. Dutton, 1859. Pp. 48.

10242   FREEMASONS. NEWBURYPORT, MASS. ST. MARK'S LODGE. Centennial anniversary of St. Mark's Lodge, F. & A. M., Newburyport, Mass., September 28th, 1903. Newburyport: Newburyport Herald, 1911. Pp. 22. MSaE.

10243   GETCHELL, EMILY A. "An old home and its romance." Putnam's HM, 2 (1893-1894), 47-61.
        Pillsbury House.

10244   HALE, ALBERT, comp. Old Newburyport houses. Boston: W. B. Clarke, 1912. 68 leaves.

10245   HALL, ANNE G. A brief history of the Newburyport Society for the Relief of Aged Females.... Newburyport: William H. Huse, 1884. Pp. 58. MSaE.

10246   HARRIS, ELIZABETH J. and WILLIAM R. HARRIS. The Jackson-Dexter House: two centuries of life and legend. Newburyport: Historical Survey Associates, 1971. 17 leaves. MSaE.

10247   HISTORICAL SURVEY ASSOCIATES. The Brown Square House--Garrison Inn in Newburyport, Massachusetts. Newburyport, 1972. 16 leaves.

10248   "HOUSE of the month [Worthin House, Toppan's Lane, Newburyport]." The Shoreliner, 1 (December, 1950), 49-52.

10249   HOVEY, HORACE CARTER. The first century of the Merrimack Bible Society, its founders, workers, and early friends 1810-1910. Newburyport: Herald Publishing, 1910. Pp. 24.

10250   ____. 'The house of God': historical discourse on the sesqui-centennial of the Old South Meeting-House of Newburyport, Mass., December 16th, 1906. Newburyport: Herald, 1906. Pp. 27.

10251   INSTITUTION FOR SAVINGS IN NEWBURYPORT AND ITS VICINITY. A century of the Institution for Savings in Newburyport and its Vicinity, 1820-1920, printed in commemoration of the one hundredth anniversary of its opening. Newburyport, Massachusetts, April 5, 1920. [Newburyport, 1920]. Pp. 44.

10252   JACKSON, RUSSELL LEIGH. "History of Newburyport newspapers." EIHC, 88 (1952), 103-140.

10253   LABAREE, BENJAMIN WOODS and EDWARD M. RILEY. "Local history contributions and techniques in the study of two colonial cities." American Association for State and Local History. Bulletin, 2 (February, 1959), 227-250.
        Newburyport and Williamsburg, Virginia.

10254 _____. Patriots and partisans: the merchants of Newburyport, 1764-1815. Cambridge: Harvard Univ. Pr., 1962. Pp. 242.

10255 LUNT, GEORGE. Old New England traits. N.Y.: Hurd and Houghton, 1873. Pp. v, 244.

Limited to Newburyport.

10256 MCGINLEY, WILLIAM ANDERSON, ed. A record of the proceedings in the North Congregational Church, Newburyport, January 24, 1868, on the occasion of its one hundredth anniversary, consisting of a discourse, addresses, and letters. Newburyport: George W. Clark, 1868. Pp. 87. MB.

10257 MARQUAND, JOHN PHILLIPS. Federalist Newburyport; or, can historical fiction remove a fly from amber? N.Y.: Newcomen Society in North America, 1952. Pp. 24.

10258 _____. "My favorite town, Newburyport." Ford Times, 39 (October, 1947), 26-35.

10259 MERRIMAC SILVER MINING CO., NEWBURYPORT, MASS. History and condition.... Boston: Getchell Bros., 1876. Pp. 17. MSaE.

10260 MORSS, JAMES. An account of the origin, progress, and present state of the Episcopal Church in this town...January 6, 1811. Newburyport: E. Little, [1811]. Pp. 32. MBNEH.

10261 _____. Benefits of the gospel: a sermon in St. Paul's Church, December 25, 1837, added the substance of two discourses on the Sunday following, being the close of a century since the first church edifice was erected in Newburyport. [Newburyport]: Morss and Brewster, 1838. Pp. 44. MBNEH.

Episcopal Church in Newburyport and vicinity.

10262 NO ENTRY

10263 NEWBURYPORT, MASS. Celebration of the fiftieth anniversary of the city charter of Newburyport, Mass., June twenty-third, twenty-fourth, twenty-fifth, twenty-sixth, MCMI. Newburyport: News Publishing, 1901. Pp. 146.

10264 _____. A program of the celebration of the fiftieth anniversary of the incorporation of the city of Newburyport, 1851-1901, Monday, June twenty-fourth, Tuesday, June twenty-fifth, Wednesday, June twenty-sixth. Newburyport: Newburyport Daily News Pr., 1901. Pp. 96.

10265 NO ENTRY

10266 NEWBURYPORT, MASS. A report of the proceedings on the occasion of the reception of the sons of Newburyport resident abroad, July 4th, 1854, by the city authorities and the citizens of Newburyport. Joseph H. Bragdon, comp. Newburyport: M. H. Sargent, 1854. Pp. 116.

10267 NEWBURYPORT, MASS. BAPTIST CHURCH. Centennial celebration, one hundredth anniversary of the Baptist Church, Newburyport, Mass., May 7th and 9th, 1905. Newburyport, 1905. Pp. 55. MSaE.

10268 NEWBURYPORT, MASS. BELLEVILLE CONGREGATIONAL CHURCH. Souvenir volume of addresses and proceedings of the one hundredth anniversary of the Belleville Congregational Church, Newburyport, Mass., April 26-27, 1908. Newburyport: News Publishing, 1908. Pp. 151. MSaE.

10269 NEWBURYPORT, MASS. CHRISTIAN CHURCH. Brief history of the Christian Church in Newburyport. Newburyport: Nason, Bragdon, 1849. Pp. 13. MSaE.

10270 NEWBURYPORT, MASS. FIRST PRESBYTERIAN CHURCH. Origin and annals of the 'The Old South,' First Presbyterian Church and Parish, in Newburyport, Mass., 1746-1896. Horace C. Hovey, ed. Boston: Damrell & Upham, 1896. Pp. 223.

10271 _____. Presbyterian Church, 'Old South,' Newburyport, Massachusetts, April 7, 1946-April 14, 1946. Newburyport: News Printing, [1946?]. Pp. 40. MSaE.

10272 NEWBURYPORT, MASS. FIRST RELIGIOUS SOCIETY. Celebration of the one hundredth anniversary of the meeting house of the First Religious Society in Newburyport, October 31, 1901. Newburyport, 1902. Pp. 61.

10273 _____. The one hundred and fiftieth anniversary of the foundation of the First Religious Society of Newburyport, originally the Third Parish of Newbury, celebrated October 20th, 1875. Newburyport: William H. Huse, 1876. Pp. 72.

10274 NEWBURYPORT, MASS. FOURTH CHURCH. Record of the Independent Church (now Fourth Church) in Newburyport.... Newburyport: Hiram Tozer, 1835. Pp. 16. MB.

10275 NEWBURYPORT, MASS. NORTH CONGREGATIONAL CHURCH. Historical sketch, covenant, articles of faith and rules of the North Congregational Church in Newburyport, with a catalogue of its members, January 1, 1867. Boston: Alfred Mudge and Son, 1867. Pp. 35. M.

10276 NEWBURYPORT, MASS. PUBLIC LIBRARY. A statement of the proceedings resulting in the purchase of the Newburyport Public Library building, with a sketch of the history of the library. Newburyport: Wm. H. Huse, 1866. Pp. 43.

10277 NEWBURYPORT, MASS. ST. PAUL'S PARISH. Two hundredth anniversary, St. Paul's Parish, Newburyport, Mass., commemorative services with historical addresses. Newburyport, 1912. Pp. 64.

10278 NEWBURYPORT ARTILLERY COMPANY. Constitution of the Newburyport Artillery Company...to which is prefixed, a historical sketch of the corps, instituted, 1778. Newburyport: W. & J. Gilman, 1827. Pp. 15. MSaE.

10279 "A NEWBURYPORT wedding." EIHC, 87 (1951), 309-332.
Elizabeth Margaret Carter and William B. Reynolds, 1821.

10280 NEWBURYPORT WOMAN'S CLUB. A history of the first fifty years of the Newburyport Woman's Club, incorporated, 1896-1946. Sarah E. Mulliken, comp. [Newburyport, 1946]. Pp. 48.

10281 OAK HILL CEMETERY, NEWBURYPORT, MASS. Oak Hill Cemetery in Newburyport from its establishment and consecration to 1878. Newburyport: William H. Huse, 1878. Pp. 46. MBNEH.

10282 OSGOOD, GEORGE WESLEY, ed. Centennial anniversary of the Fourth Church, Newburyport, Mass., and the centennial anniversary of the Young People's Society of Christian Endeavor, Sunday, Nov. 19, 1893.... Newburyport: Daily News, 1893. Pp. 73. MSaE.

10283 PARSONS, JOHN D. Newburyport: its industries, business interests and attractions ...with interesting historical facts relating to the old town. Newburyport: William H. Huse, 1887. Pp. 100. MSaE.

10284 PARTON, ETHEL. "Newburyport." NEM, New Ser., 5 (1891-1892), 160-182.

10285 PILLSBURY, ALBERT ENOCH. Newburyport and city government; an address delivered at the celebration of the fiftieth anniversary of the incorporation of Newburyport as a city, June 24, 1901. [Newburyport, 1901]. Pp. 32.

10286 PUTNAM FREE SCHOOL, NEWBURYPORT, MASS. Exercises at the celebration of the fiftieth anniversary of the Putnam Free School, April 12, 1898. Newburyport: News Publishing, 1899. Pp. 78. MSaE.

10287 SNOW, FRANK WHIPPLE. "The history of medicine at the mouth of the Merrimack River, Newburyport, in relation to the Essex North District Medical Society." NEJMed, 204 (1931), 658-660.

10288 SPALDING, DEXTER EDWIN. "Abner Toppan, cabinetmaker." Antiques, 15 (1929), 493-495.
Late eighteenth century.

10289 SPOFFORD, HARRIET ELIZABETH PRESCOTT. "Newburyport and its neighborhood." Harper's Magazine, 51 (1875), 162-180.

10290 STEARNS, JONATHAN FRENCH. A historical discourse commemorative of the organization of the First Presbyterian Church, in Newburyport, delivered at the first centennial celebration, Jan. 7, 1846. Newburyport: John G. Tilton, 1846. Pp. 64.

10291 SWAN, MABEL MUNSON. "Newburyport furnituremakers." Antiques, 47 (1945), 222-225.

10292 _____. "Ship carvers of Newburyport." Antiques, 48 (1945), 78-81.
Biographies.

10293 THERNSTROM, STEPHAN. Poverty and progress: social mobility in a nineteenth century city. Cambridge: Harvard Univ. Pr., 1964. Pp. xii, 286.

10294 _____. "Yankee City revisited: the perils of historical naïveté." AmSocRev, 30 (1965), 234-242.

10295 TOWLE MANUFACTURING COMPANY. The colonial book...which is intended to delineate and describe some quaint and historic places in Newburyport and vicinity and show the origin and beauty of the colonial pattern of silverware. (1898) 5th ed. George P. Tilton, comp. Springfield: Springfield Printing and Binding, 1908. Pp. 74.

10296 "TOWLE Manufacturing Company." Industry, 1 (May, 1936), 7-10.
Silversmiths.

10297 "TOWLE silversmiths--275 years of sterling craftsmanship." Industry, 31 (December, 1965), 17, 43-44.

10298 VERMILYE, ASHBEL GREEN. A discourse delivered at Newburyport, Mass., November 28, 1856, on occasion of the one hundredth anniversary of the building of the First Presbyterian Church. Newburyport: Moulton & Clark, 1856. Pp. 74.
Relates to the church.

10299 WARNER, WILLIAM LLOYD. The living and the dead: a study of the symbolic life of Americans. New Haven: Yale Univ. Pr., 1959. Pp. xii, 528.
Last of the Yankee City series.

10300 _____ and PAUL SANBORN LUNT. The social life of a modern community. New Haven: Yale Univ. Pr., 1941. Pp. xx, 460.
First of the Yankee City series.

10301 _____. and JOSIAH ORNE LOW. The social system of the modern factory. The strike: a social analysis. New Haven: Yale Univ. Pr., 1947. Pp. xvi, 245.
In the Yankee City series.

10302 _____. and LEO SROLE. The social systems of American ethnic groups. New Haven: Yale Univ. Pr., 1945. Pp. xii, 318.
In the Yankee City series.

10303 _____. and PAUL SANBORN LUNT. The status system of a modern community. New Haven: Yale Univ. Pr., 1942. Pp. xx, 246.
In the Yankee City series.

10304 _____, et al. Yankee City. New Haven: Yale Univ. Pr., 1963. Pp. 432.
An abridgement of the five volume Yankee City series.

10305 WATKINS, C. MALCOLM. "Lord Timothy Dexter and the Earl of Chatham." Antiques, 82 (1962), 642-643.
> Wooden figures which adorned Dexter's estate.

10306 WILLIAMS, SAMUEL PORTER. Historical account of the First Presbyterian Church and Society in Newburyport, Massachusetts, addressed to the congregation, worshipping in Federal Street, July 9, 1826. Saratoga Springs: G. M. Davison, 1826. Pp. 67.

10307 WOODWELL, ROLAND H. "William Ashby of Newburyport and his Laurel parties." EIHC, 84 (1948), 15-28.

10308 WOODWELL, WILLIAM H. "The Woodwell Shipyard, 1759-1852." BBHS, 21 (1947), 58-74.

NEWTON

10309 ALLEN, LUCY ELLIS. West Newton half a century ago. Newton: Graphic Pr., 1917. Pp. 32.

10310 AUBURNDALE, MASS. EVANGELICAL CONGREGATIONAL CHURCH. 1850-1900, semi-centennial celebration of the Evangelical Congregational Church of Auburndale, Mass., November 4 to 16, 1900. Calvin Cutler, ed. Boston: Skinner, Kidder, [1900?]. Pp. 192. MBNEH.

10311 BATES, DOROTHY S. and RUTH E. CANNARD. Newton's older houses, Newton Lower Falls, Mass. Newton: Friends of the Jackson Homestead, Inc., 1974. Pp. 54. MNt.

10312 BATTISON, EDWIN A. "The Auburndale Watch Company, first American attempt toward the dollar watch." U. S. National Museum. Bulletin 218 (1959), 49-68.

10313 BAURY, ALFRED LOUIS. Historical sketch of St. Mary's Church, Newton Lower Falls, Massachusetts: a sermon, preached in St. Mary's Church, Newton Lower Falls, on the fourth Sunday after Easter, 1847, being the twenty-fifth anniversary of the incumbent's first officiating in that church. Boston: James B. Dow, 1847. Pp. 34.

10314 "BAXTER parsonage, West Newton, Mass." CongQ, 10 (1868), 38-42.

10315 BOSTON COLLEGE. Boston College, 1863-1938: a pictorial and historical review commemorating the seventy-fifth anniversary of the founding of the college. Chestnut Hill, [1938]. Pp. 41.

10316 BOSTON COLLEGE. COLLEGE OF BUSINESS ADMINISTRATION. 10 years of public service, Boston Citizen Seminars, 1954-1964. [Boston?, 1964?]. Unpaged. M.

10317 BRIMBLECOM, JOHN CLOON. Beautiful Newton: the Garden City of Massachusetts. Newton: Newton Graphic Publishing, [1916]. Pp. 316.

10318 BURROWS, F. W. "The Newtons." NEM, New Ser., 39 (1908-1909), 549-563.

10319 CHESTNUT HILL, MASS. TEMPLE EMETH. Twenty-fifth anniversary journal, 1939-1964. [Chestnut Hill, 1965]. Pp. 240.

10320 COLE, THOMAS CASILEAR. "Old Lower Falls and its church." NEM, New Ser., 41 (1909-1910), 349-354.
> St. Mary's Episcopal Church, Newton Lower Falls.

10321 CROKER, MARK F. "Progress in solving supply and distribution problems at Newton, Massachusetts." New England Waterworks Association. Journal, 66 (1952), 352-363.
> 1934-1952.

10322 CURTIS, AGNES BERYL. Glimpses of Newton's past told in history and drama. Boston: Geo. H. Ellis, 1918. Pp. 80.

10323 DAVIS, S. An appeal to the citizens of Newton, embracing a brief history of the town. [Newton?, 1847]. Pp. 25.

10324 EASTERBROOK, HORACE H., comp. History of the fire department of Newton, Mass.... [Boston]: Newton Veteran Firemen's Association, 1897. Pp. 240.

10325 FAMILY SERVICE BUREAU OF NEWTON, INC. Fiftieth anniversary of the Family Service Bureau of Newton, Inc. Newton, 1939. Pp. 14. MB.

10326 [FAY, EUGENE FRANCIS]. An illustrated biographical catalogue of the principals, teachers, and students of the West Newton English and Classical School, West Newton, Mass., 1854-1893, including an account of the re-unions November 15, 1871, and June 21, 1893. Boston: R. Avery, 1895. Pp. 176.
> Includes historical sketch.

10327 FROST, JOHN EDWARD. 'Ad majorem Dei gloriam,' ('For the greater glory of God'), the Church of Saint Ignatius of Loyola, Chestnut Hill, Massachusetts. [Chestnut Hill?, 1959?]. Unpaged.

10328 "THE GAMEWELL Company." Industry, 5 (April, 1940), 7-10, 28, 42.
> Fire alarms.

10329 GRAFTON, JOSEPH. A sermon, exhibiting the origin, progress and present state of the Baptist Church and Society in Newton, Mass., preached before them on the first Lord's day in January, 1830. Boston: W. R. Collier, 1830. Pp. 16.

10330 HERRICK, EVERETT CARLETON. Turns again home: Andover Newton Theological School and reminiscences from an unkept journal. Boston: Pilgrim Pr., 1949. Pp. 202.

10331 "HISTORICAL addresses delivered at the Newton centennial, June 1925." Institution Bulletin, 18 (1926), 3-63.
> Andover Newton Theological School.

10332 HOLLIS, WILLIAM H. Through the years with
       St. Mary's. n.p., [not after 1957].
Pp. 32. MBNEH.
       Episcopal Church.

10333 HOMER, JONATHAN. "Description and history
       of Newton." MHSC, [5] (1798), 253-280.

10334 _____. The succession of generations among
       mankind, illustrated and improved in a cen-
tury sermon, preached at Newton, on Lord's Day,
Dec. 25, 1791; being the commencement of a new century, from the incorporation of said town. Boston:
Belknap and Young, 1792. Pp. 27.

10335 HOVEY, ALVAH. Historical address delivered
       at the fiftieth anniversary of the Newton
Theological Institution, June 8, 1875. Boston:
Wright & Potter, 1875. Pp. 72.

10336 JACKSON, FRANCIS. Author's corrections to
       Francis Jackson's 'History of Newton.'
[Newton?], n.d. Pp. 12. MBNEH.

10337 _____. A history of the early settlement
       of Newton, county of Middlesex, Massachu-
setts, from 1639 to 1800, with a genealogical register of its inhabitants, prior to 1800. Boston:
Stacy and Richardson, 1854. Pp. iv, 555.

10338 KING, HENRY MELVILLE. Newton Theological
       Institution in the last fifty years: an
address delivered on the 50th anniversary of the
official service of President Alvah Hovey, June 7,
1899. n.p., [1899]. Pp. 14.

10339 LASELL JUNIOR COLLEGE, AUBURNDALE, MASS.
       History and description of the Lasell Sem-
inary for Young Women at Auburndale (near Boston)
Massachusetts. Boston: Frank Wood, 1876. Pp. 8.

10340 LEE, MARY. A history of the Chestnut Hill
       Chapel; being an address delivered at the
dinner held on October sixteenth, nineteen hundred
and thirty-six to celebrate the seventy-fifth anniversary of the founding of the chapel, compiled
chiefly from letters written by Francis L. Lee and
his wife, Sarah Wilson Lee. [Chestnut Hill]: The
History Committee of the First Church in Chestnut
Hill, 1937. Pp. 91.

10341 LORD, ARTHUR H. The Eliot Church of Newton,
       Newton, Massachusetts; the history of one
hundred years, 1845-1945, a century of service in
building a better world. Newton, 1945. Pp. 50.

10342 LOSSING, BENSON J. "The dwelling house of
       General William Hull." Potter's AmMo, 5
(1875), 561-568.

10343 MACINTIRE, JANE BACON, ed. Waban, early
       days, 1681-1918. Waban, 1944. Pp. xv,
294.

10344 MAYO, LAWRENCE SHAW. First Unitarian So-
       ciety in Newton, 1848-1923. n.p., [1923?].
Pp. 34. MBNEH.

10345 THE MIRROR of Newton, past and present.
       Newton: The Newton Federation of Women's
Clubs, 1907. Pp. 169.

10346 NEWTON, MASS. A brief notice of the settle-
       ment of the town of Newton, prepared by a
committee who were charged with the duty of erecting
a monument to the memory of its first settlers,
September, 1852. Boston: C. C. P. Moody, 1852.
Pp. 38.

10347 _____. Celebration of the two hundredth
       anniversary of the incorporation of the town
of Newton, Massachusetts, December 27, 1888. Boston: Avery L. Rand, 1891. Pp. 70.

10348 _____. The centennial celebrations of the
       city of Newton, on the seventeenth of June
and the Fourth of July, by and under the direction
of the city of Newton. Newton, 1876. Pp. 167.
       Relates to the city.

10349 NEWTON, MASS. CENTRAL CONGREGATIONAL
       CHURCH. Central Congregational Church.
[Newton]: Newton Graphic Print, [1889?]. Pp. 30.
M.
       Includes history.

10350 NEWTON, MASS. CHANNING CONGREGATIONAL
       CHURCH. 1851-1901, services in commemora-
tion of the fiftieth anniversary of the organization
of Channing Church, at Newton, Massachusetts, September 15, 1901. n.p., [1901?]. Pp. 39. MB.

10351 NEWTON, MASS. FIRST BAPTIST CHURCH. Manual
       of the Baptist Church at Newton Centre,
July 5, 1780 to February 2, 1885. Boston: Percival
T. Bartlett, 1885. Pp. 66. M.
       Includes history.

10352 NEWTON, MASS. FIRST CHURCH. A brief his-
       tory of the First Church, Newton (Newton
Centre) with articles of faith, covenant, standing
rules, and names of its members. Boston: Franklin
Pr., 1876. Pp. 46. MB.

10353 _____. The commemorative services of the
       First Church in Newton, Massachusetts, on
the occasion of the two hundred and fiftieth anniversary of its foundation, Friday, Sunday and Monday, Oct. 30, Nov. 1 and 2, 1914. [Newton], 1915.
Pp. 207.

10354 _____. The commemorative services of the
       First Church in Newton, Massachusetts, on
the occasion of the two hundred and twenty-fifth
anniversary of its foundation, Sunday and Monday,
Oct. 6 and 7, 1889. Boston: Rockwell and Churchill, 1890. Pp. 271.
       Historical discourse by Daniel L. Furber.

10355 NEWTON, MASS. FREE LIBRARY. Historical
       statement of [the] origin and growth,
adopted by the Board of Managers, Nov. 24, 1875.
Boston: Rockwell and Churchill, 1876. Pp. 8. MB.

10356   NEWTON, MASS. SABBATH SCHOOL UNION. Quar-
ter centennial celebration Eliot Church,
Newton, Oct. 16, 1863. Boston: Samuel Chism, 1863.
Pp. 35. M.
         Historical address by Marshall L. Rice.

10357   NEWTON CENTER, MASS. FIRST BAPTIST CHURCH.
Centennial anniversary of the Baptist
Church at Newton Centre, November 14, 1880. Boston:
G. J. Stiles, 1881. Pp. 105.

10358   NEWTON. Boston: Edison Electric Illuminating Company, 1909. Pp. 28. MBNEH.

10359   NEWTON ATHENAEUM, WEST NEWTON, MASS. Catalogue of books in the Newton Athenaeum
with a sketch of the origin and object of the institution. Boston: Bazin & Chandler, 1856.
Pp. 41. MB.

10360   NEWTON CENTRE IMPROVEMENT ASSOCIATION.
Comprehensive historical sketch of Crystal
Lake in Newton Centre, Massachusetts with incidental references to interesting events in the history
of Newton. Newton, 1911. Pp. 62. MBNEH.

10361   NEWTON GRAPHIC. Newton war memorial. John
C. Brimblecom, ed. Newton, 1930. v.p.
MB.

10362   NEWTON HIGHLANDS CONGREGATIONAL CHURCH.
Manual of the Newton Highlands Congregational Church in Newton, Mass. 1880, organized July
9, 1872. Boston: Alfred Mudge and Son, 1880.
Pp. 24. M.
         Includes historical sketch.

10363   NEWTON HOSPITAL. Silver anniversary report, 1881-1905, Newton, February 5, 1906.
n.p., [1906?]. v.p. MBNEH.

10364   NEWTON THEOLOGICAL INSTITUTION. Newton
Theological Institution: a sketch of its
history, and an account of the services at the dedication of the new building, September 10, 1866.
Boston: Gould and Lincoln, 1866. Pp. 54. MBNEH.

10365   "NEWTON Theological Institution." NEM, 6
(1887-1888), 358-362.

10366   "[125TH anniversary of the Newton Theological Institution]." Andover-Newton Bulletin, 43 (December, 1950), entire issue.

10367   PAIGE, LUCIUS ROBINSON. "Incorporation of
Newton." MHSP, (1873-1875), 111-113.

10368   PEHRSON, BENGT. "Printing business is in-
debted to centenarian for good impressions."
Industry, 19 (March, 1954), 21-24.
         Wild & Stevens, Inc.; rollers for ink.

10369   PELOUBET, LOUISE and CLARA A. WINSLOW, eds.
Early days in Auburn Dale: a village chronicle of two centuries, 1665-1870, containing reminiscences of early settlers, illustrations and
maps. [Auburndale]: Education Committee of the
Auburndale Woman's Club, 1917. Pp. 116.

10370   PRESCOTT, JOHN R. The story of Newton,
Massachusetts, its natural beauty, attrac-
tive homes and historical associations. (1936)
[Newton?, 1939]. Pp. 80.

10371   ROWE, HENRY KALLOCH. History of Andover
Theological Seminary. Newton, 1933.
Pp. vii, 208.

10372   ____. Tercentenary history of Newton,
1630-1930. [Newton]: City of Newton, 1930.
Pp. vii, 534.

10373   RUSSELL, RUTH WOODMAN. Pine Manor Junior
College: the first fifty years, 1911-1961.
Chestnut Hill: Pine Manor Pr., 1969. Pp. xvii,
221.

10374   "SERVING the marine field for 65 years."
Industry, 17 (July, 1952), 19-20, 36, 38,
40-41."
         L. W. Ferdinand & Co.; waterproof com-
pounds.

10375   SHINN, GEORGE WOLFE. Discourse commemorating the 25th anniversary of the organization
of the parish of Grace Church, Newton, Mass. Boston: David Clapp & Son, 1880. Pp. 26. MBNEH.

10376   SMITH, SAMUEL FRANCIS. History of Newton,
Massachusetts: town and city, from its
earliest settlement to the present time, 1630-1880.
Boston: American Logotype, 1880. Pp. xi, 851.

10377   ____. Life of the Rev. Joseph Grafton,
late pastor of the First Baptist Church,
Newton, Ms. with an appendix, embracing historical,
statistical, and ecclesiastical information pertaining to the town of Newton. Boston: J. Putnam,
1849. Pp. x, 213.

10378   SUB TURRI. Centennial history of Boston
College, published by the 1963 Sub Turri.
Stuart B. Meisenzahl, ed. [Boston, 1963].
Pp. 236.

10379   SWEETSER, MOSES FOSTER. King's handbook of
Newton, Massachusetts. Boston: Moses
King, 1889. Pp. 326.

10380   WELLMAN, JOSHUA WYMAN. The origin and
early history of the Eliot Church in Newton,
Massachusetts; an historical sermon preached...June
26, 1870. n.p., 1904. Pp. 35. M.

10381   WELLS, WILLIAM GOODHUE. St. Mary's Church,
Newton Lower Falls, sermon preached...cel-
ebration of the seventy-fifth anniversary of the
parish. Newton Lower Falls, 1889. Pp. 33. MB.

10382   WEST NEWTON, MASS. SECOND CHURCH. Celebration of the one hundredth anniversary of the
organization of the Second Church, Newton, Mass. at
West Newton, Tuesday, November 8, 1881. Boston:
Beacon Pr., 1882. Pp. 163. MBNEH.

10383   ____. History, standing rules.... Boston:
Damrell & Moore, 1852. Pp. 14. MB.

10384   _____. Manual of the Second Church in Newton, West Newton, Mass., including historical sketch...1760-1781-1910. Boston, 1910.
Pp. 72. M.

10385   _____. Manual of the Second Congregational
Church of Newton, Mass., including its confession of faith, covenant and standing rules, with
a brief historical sketch. Boston: Wright and
Potter, 1868. Pp. 45. M.

10386   _____. Our church: its history, its
buildings, its spirit. West Newton, 1926.
Pp. 106. MB.

10387   _____. The story of the Second Church in
Newton [by] the 175th Anniversary Committee.
West Newton, [1956]. Pp. 47.

10388   WEST NEWTON SAVINGS BANK. Fiftieth anniversary of the founding...1887-1937. n.p.,
[1937?]. Pp. 19. MBNEH.

10389   WISWALL, CLARENCE AUGUSTUS and ELEANOR BOIT
CRAFTS. One hundred years of paper making;
a history of the industry on the Charles River at
Newton Lower Falls, Massachusetts. [Reading]:
Reading Chronicle Pr., 1938. Pp. 115.

NORFOLK

10390   DOERING, CARL RUPP, ed. A report on the
development of penological treatment at
Norfolk prison colony in Massachusetts: official
manual of the State prison colony [by] Walter H.
Commons; a history of the State prison colony [by]
Thomas Yahkub; individualization of treatment as
illustrated by studies of fifty cases [by] Edwin
Powers. N.Y.: Bureau of Social Hygiene, 1940.
Pp. xxi, 274.

10391   NORFOLK. Boston: Edison Electric Illuminating Co., 1909. Pp. 8. M.

NORTH ADAMS

10392   "THE ARNOLDS of North Adams, their notable
manufacturing career." Berkshire Hills, 4
(1903-1904), 271-272.
          Oliver, Harvey, and John F. Arnold; cotton
manufacture and textile printing.

10393   BASCOM, JOHN. "Greylock Reservation."
BHSSC, 3 (1899-1913), 251-274.

10394   "A BERKSHIRE circus." Berkshire Hills, 1
(March 1, 1901), [6].

10395   "EARLIEST North Adams fire apparatus."
Berkshire Hills, 4 (1903-1904), 218.
          1844.

10396   "THE FATE of a northern Berkshire inven-
tion." Berkshire Hills, New Ser., 1
(1904-1905), 40.
          Sewing machine.

10397   "FIRST Baptist Church in North Adams."
Berkshire Hills, New Ser., 1 (1904-1905),
71-75.

10398   "THE FIRST butcher and meat market in North
Adams." Berkshire Hills, 1 (April 1,
1901), [12].
          Tom Baker, 1850.

10399   "A GREAT Berkshire industry: pioneer shoe
manufacturers of North Adams." Berkshire
Hills, 3 (1902-1903), 61-65.

10400   "GREYLOCK Mountain, the glory of the Berkshire Hills and a Massachusetts state
park." Berkshire Hills, 2 (Jan. 1, 1902), [1-5].

10401   GRIFFIN, THOMAS A. Historical discourse;
origin and progress of Methodism in North
Adams, delivered...April 21st, 1872. North Adams:
James T. Robinson & Son, 1872. Pp. 24. M.

10402   "THE HOME of calico printing in Berkshire,
the keystone to manufacturing prosperity in
North Adams from 1828 to 1903." Berkshire Hills, 3
(1902-1903), 141-142.

10403   JAMES HUNTER MACHINE COMPANY, NORTH ADAMS,
MASS. Heritage of dependability, James
Hunter Machine Company, North Adams, Massachusetts,
1847-1947. North Adams: Excelsior Printing,
[1947?]. Unpaged. MPB.

10404   "NINE North Adams postmasters." Berkshire
Hills, New Ser., 2 (1905-1906), 156.

10405   NORTH ADAMS, MASS. Official souvenir book,
Old Home Week, Sept. 5 to 11, 1909. North
Adams: Publicity Committee, [1909?]. Unpaged.
MBNEH.
          Historical.

10406   NORTH ADAMS, MASS. FIRST BAPTIST CHURCH.
History of the First Baptist Church, North
Adams, with an historical sketch of Baptists in
Northern Berkshire. North Adams, 1908. Pp. 19.
MB.

10407   NORTH ADAMS, MASS. FIRST CONGREGATIONAL
CHURCH. Addresses and papers presented at
the diamond jubilee, 1827-1902, May 11-14....
William Lawrence Tenney, ed. North Adams: Advance
Pr., [1903?]. v.p.

10408   _____. First Congregational Church, North
Adams, Massachusetts, an historical address delivered at the observance of the seventy-
fifth anniversary of the present building, October
6, 1940. North Adams: Byam, [1940?]. Unpaged.
MPB.

10409   "NORTH Adams, a city in the hills." National Magazine, 16 (1902), 625-629.
          Signed: L. V. B.

10410   "NORTH Adams in 1850, illustrated sketch of
Main Street structures and localities for
125 years." Berkshire Hills, 3 (1902-1903), 109-
115.

10411 "NORTH Adams National Bank." Berkshire
Hills, New Ser., 1 (1904-1905), 76-77.
1832-1904.

10412 "THE NORTH Adams Public Library." Berkshire
Hills, 4 (1903-1904), 200-201.

10413 "NORTH Adams school memories." Berkshire
Hills, 3 (1902-1903), 39-41.

10414 "OLD Drury Academy." Berkshire Hills, 3
(1902-1903), 25-31.

10415 "AN OLD-fashioned fourth, how it was observed in North Adams in 1865." Berkshire
Hills, 4 (1903-1904), 291-292.

10416 "OLD meeting houses in the town of Adams,
the history of the First Congregational
Church of North Adams." Berkshire Hills, 2 (July
1, 1902), [1-6].

10417 OSBORN, A. C. History of the North Adams
Baptist Church from October 30, 1808 to
October 30, 1878. Columbia, S.C.: R. L. Bryan,
1908. Pp. 115. MPB.

10418 PERRY, BLISS. "Hawthorne at North Adams."
Atlantic, 71 (1893), 675-682.

10419 RUDOLPH, FREDERICK. "Chinamen in Yankee-
dom: anti-unionism in Massachusetts in
1870." AHR, 53 (1947-1948), 1-29.
Limited to North Adams.

10420 "SOFT soap and phrenology, Elder Daniel
Haynes of Willow Dell and his intelligent
dogs: a sketch of the first soap factory in the
old Adams township--transformation of the proprie-
tor into a phrenologist and his mysterious disappearance." Berkshire Hills, 2 (July 1, 1902),
[10-11].

10421 SPARGO, JOHN. The epic of Fort Massachusetts: an address delivered at the dedication of the replica of Fort Massachusetts, August 19, 1933. Rutland, Vt.: Tuttle, [1933?].
Pp. 19. MH.

10422 SPEAR, WILLIS F. History of North Adams,
Mass., 1749-1885: reminiscences of early
settlers, extracts from old town records, its public institutions, industries and prominent citizens,
together with a roster of commissioned officers in
the War of the Rebellion. North Adams: Hoosac
Valley News, 1885. Pp. 116.

10423 WHITAKER, V. A. History of the First Baptist Church, North Adams, with an historical sketch of the Baptists in Northern Berkshire.
n.p., 1908. Pp. 19. MB.

NORTH ANDOVER

10424 "ANDOVER Church." ECHGR, 2 (1895), 65-67.
North Church.

10425 BARNES, HENRY ELBERT. Memorial and historical discourse, Trinitarian Congregational
Church, North Andover, Sunday morning, October 20,
1895. n.p., [1895?]. Unpaged.

10426 CUMMINGS, ABBOTT LOWELL. "The Parson Barnard House." OTNE, 47 (1956-1957), 29-40.
Formerly the Bradstreet House.

10427 DAVIS & FURBER MACHINE CO., NORTH ANDOVER,
MASS. The Davis & Furber Machine Company
and the men who made it, 1832-1908. Boston: A.
Mugford, 1908. Unpaged.

10428 FERGUSON, LLOYD C. From family firm to corporate giant: J. P. Stevens and Company,
1813-1963. Braintree: D. H. Mark, 1970. Pp. vi,
33.

10429 LEAVITT, THOMAS W. "Creating the past: the
record of the Stevens family of North Andover." EIHC, 106 (1970), 65-87.

10430 NORTH ANDOVER, MASS. Town of North Andover,
Massachusetts centennial 1855-1955, obser-
vance June 5 to 12. [Lawrence]: Eagle Tribune
Printing, [1955]. Unpaged. MSaE.

10431 NORTH ANDOVER, MASS. ST. MICHAEL CHURCH.
St. Michael Church, North Andover, Mass.
South Hackensack, N.J., 1969. Pp. 28. MB.

10432 PIERCE, GEORGE WILLIAMS. "The Captain Timothy Johnson Homestead." MassMag, 3 (1910),
94-98.

10433 RODDY, E. G., JR. Merrimack College: genesis and growth, 1947-1972. North Andover,
1972. Pp. ix, 113.

10434 ROGERS, HORATIO. Early owners of the Par-
son Barnard House and their times. North
Andover: North Andover Historical Society, 1958.
Pp. 15. M.

10435 STEVENS, HORACE NATHANIEL. Nathaniel Stevens, 1786-1865; an account of his life and
the business he founded. North Andover, 1946.
Pp. xvi, 266.

10436 STEVENS, KATE HASTINGS. "The old burying
ground on Academy Road, North Andover."
OTNE, 41 (1950-1951), 13-15.

10437 STEVENS, NATHANIEL. A sketch of the early
days of the woolen industry in North Andover, Massachusetts, an address delivered before
the North Andover Historical Society, February 13,
1925. North Andover, 1925. Pp. 23. MH.

10438 WHITEHILL, WALTER MUIR. "The North Andover
hay scales." OTNE, 39 (1948-1949), 35-37.

NORTH ATTLEBOROUGH

10439   BARTLETT, ELIZABETH M. "Angle Tree Monument." OTNE, 15 (1924-1925), 128-131.
Boundary marker between North Attleborough and Plainville.

10440   DIX, MARJORIE ASHWORTH. That reminds me... of North Attleboro. [North Attleborough?]:
North Attleborough Historical Society, 1965.
Pp. 48. MBNEH.
Ellipsis appears on title page.

10441   LEWIS, GEORGE HENRY. A short history of the Cushman Union Church of Adamsdale,
Mass., including a sketch of the early history of Adamsdale. Adamsdale: Cushman Union Church, 1914.
Pp. 82. MBNEH.

10442   PETERSON, BERNARD. "100 years of specialization in emblems." Industry, 18 (December, 1952), 10.
V. H. Blackington & Company; military insignia.

NORTH BROOKFIELD

10443   BATCHELLER, ROBERT. The Quaboag Historical Society: a sketch of its organization and
work 1894 to 1899, delivered Dec. 19, 1899, at Brookfield, at a meeting of the society. Spencer:
E. E. Dickerman, 1900. Pp. 35.

10444   BATES, THEODORE C. Tenth anniversary of the opening of the North Brookfield Railroad, and freedom of the town from debt, or the
final payment of its railroad notes, together with its entire indebtedness, January 1, 1885.... North
Brookfield: H. J. Lawrence, 1885. Pp. 39.

10445   HILL, ELIZABETH R. TYLER. False imprisonment of Elizabeth R. Hill by Rev. Gabriel
H. De Bevoise, and the selectmen of North Brookfield, Mass., Jan. 5, 1878, and incidents resulting therefrom to Feb. 15, 1881. [New York?, 1881]. Pp. 83.

10446   _____. Incidents and appalling trials and treatment of Elizabeth R. Hill, from the
plotting citizen confederacies in Worcester County, Mass. [New York?, 1877]. Pp. 199.

10447   NORTH BROOKFIELD, MASS. A historical record of the soldiers and sailors of North
Brookfield, and of others who counted upon the quota of the town, in the war for the preservation
of the union, against the rebellion, 1861-1865, regimental histories, etc. North Brookfield, 1886.
Pp. 71.
Biographies.

10448   POWELL, F. W. "Two experiments in public ownership of steam railroads." QJEcon,
23 (1908), 137-150.
Troy, N.Y., 1840-1858 and North Brookfield, 1874-1886.

10449   SNELL, THOMAS. A discourse containing an historical sketch of the town of North
Brookfield...delivered May 28, 1850. West Brookfield: O. S. Cooke, 1854. Pp. 24. MBNEH.

10450   _____. A sermon delivered...on the last Sabbath in June, 1838, which completed the
fortieth year of his ministry; containing a brief history of the town, and especially of the church
and parish of North Brookfield, from 1798 to the present time. Brookfield: E. & L. Merriam, 1838.
Pp. 55. MB.

10451   TEMPLE, JOSIAH HOWARD. History of North Brookfield, Massachusetts, preceded by an
account of old Quabaug, Indian and English occupation, 1647-1676, Brookfield records, 1686-1783,
with a genealogical register. North Brookfield: The Town, 1887. Pp. 824.

NORTH READING

10452   LE PAGE, SAMUEL MAYNARD. A history of North Reading. Wakefield: Item Pr., 1944.
Pp. 132.

NORTHAMPTON

10453   ADDISON, HENRY D. and LOUISE A. ADDISON. One hundred years of brotherhood: a centennial history of the Florence Congregational
Church, of Northampton, Mass., 1861-1961. n.p., [1961?]. Pp. xiv, 68. MNF.

10454   ALLEN, WILLIAM. An address, delivered at Northampton, Mass., on the evening of Oct.
29, 1854, in commemoration of the close of the second century since the settlement of the town.
Northampton: Hopkins, Bridgman, 1855. Pp. 56.

10455   "AMERICA'S most famous tooth brush." Industry, 11 (July, 1946), 15-18.
Pro-phy-lac-tic brand.

10456   ATWOOD, WILLIAM T. "Northampton, the Meadow City and capital of Hampshire County."
NEM, New Ser., 43 (1910-1911), 301-315.

10457   BASSETT, JOHN SPENCER. "The Round Hill School." AASP, New Ser., 27 (1917), 18-62.

10458   BENNETT, BRUCE LANYON. "The making of Round Hill School." Quest: A Publication of the
National Association for Physical Education of College Women and the National College Physical Education Association for Men. Monograph IV, (April, 1965), 53-63.

10459   BESTOR, ARTHUR E., JR. "Fourierism in Northampton: a critical note." NEQ, 13 (1940),
110-122.
Northampton Association of Education and Industry.

10460   BRESSETT, KENNETH E. "The day Northampton
         had a mint." Whitman Numismatic Journal,
2 (1965), 501-505.

10461   BRIDGMAN, S. E. "Northampton." NEM, New
         Ser., 21 (1899-1900), 581-604.

10462   CARPENTER, ALBERT H. "Northampton, past and
         present." WNE, 1 (1910-1911), 297-318.

10463   CESTRE, GILBERT RENÉ JEAN. Northampton,
         Massachusetts: évolution urbaine. Paris:
Société d'Édition d'Enseignement Supérieur, 1963.
Pp. 376.

10464   CHANDLER, CHARLES HENRY. The attractions
         of Northampton, with sketches and descrip-
tions of the various objects of interest in its
vicinity.... Springfield: S. Bowles, 1871.
Pp. 28.

10465   CLARK, SOLOMON. Antiquities, historicals
         and graduates of Northampton. Northampton:
Gazette Printing, 1882. Pp. xii, 374.
         Biographies and historic houses.

10466   _____. Historical catalogue of the North-
         ampton First Church, 1661-1891. Northamp-
ton: Gazette Printing, 1891. Pp. 239.

10467   CLARKE SCHOOL FOR THE DEAF. Addresses de-
         livered at the twenty-fifth anniversary of
the Clarke Institution, Northampton, Mass. October
12, 1892. Northampton: Gazette Printing, 1893.
Pp. 65. MNF.

10468   CLARKE SCHOOL FOR THE DEAF. ALUMNI. Clarke
         School and its alumni 1867-1947. Alice
Manning Williams and John Blake, eds. [Northamp-
ton]: Clarke School Alumni Association, 1947.
Pp. 155.

10469   _____. Clarke School and its graduates: a
         memorial volume issued to commemorate the
fiftieth anniversary of the founding of the school,
1867-1917. Northampton, 1918. Pp. ix, 150.

10470   COBB, ELISHA G. Historical sketch of the
         Congregational Church, Florence, Mass.
Florence, 1902. Pp. 42.

10471   COCHRAN, EVE OWEN. A short history and
         handbook of the Lathrop Home for Aged and
Invalid Women in Northampton, Massachusetts, 1884-
1928. [Northampton]: Kingsbury Print, [1928?].
Pp. 26. MNF.

10472   COGSWELL, JOSEPH GREEN and GEORGE BANCROFT.
         Some account of the school for the liberal
education of boys, established on Round Hill,
Northampton, Massachusetts. Northampton, 1826.
Pp. 19.
         Round Hill School.

10473   "THE COOLEY Dickinson Hospital." Timely
         Topics, 5 (July, 1963), entire issue.
         Periodical is published by the hospital.

10474   COTE, RICHARD C. "Rethinking the Greek
         revival: the success of influences and the
failure of a builder." OTNE, 64 (1974), 61-76.
         Houses of Thomas Pratt.

10475   CUTTEN, GEORGE BARTON. Silversmiths of
         Northampton, Mass., and vicinity down to
1850. [Northampton, 1942?]. 2 leaves.

10476   DALEY, E. HARTWELL. One hundred years of
         Methodism in Northampton, 1842-1942. n.p.,
1942. Unpaged. MNF.

10477   DAUGHTERS OF THE AMERICAN REVOLUTION. MAS-
         SACHUSETTS. BETTY ALLEN CHAPTER, NORTHAMP-
TON. Early Northampton.... Northampton,
1914. Pp. 229.

10478   DWYER, MARGARET CLIFFORD. Centennial his-
         tory of St. Mary of the Assumption Church,
Northampton, Massachusetts, 1866-1966. South Hackensack, N.J. Custombook, 1966. Unpaged.

10479   EDWARDS, JONATHAN. 1703-1758. Edwards on
         revivals: containing a faithful narrative
of the surprising work of God in the conversion of
many hundred souls in Northampton, Massachusetts,
A. D. 1735, also, thoughts on the revival of religion in New England, 1742. N.Y.: Dunning & Spalding, 1832. Pp. xxix, 424.

10480   _____. An unpublished essay of Edwards on
         the Trinity, with remarks on Edwards and
his theology, by George P. Fisher.... N.Y.: C.
Scribner's Sons, 1903. Pp. xv, 142.
         Appendix relates to Edwards' dismissal from
         the church in Northampton.

10481   EDWARDS Church, Northampton, Mass., semi-
         centennial services, January 30, 1883.
Northampton: S. E. Bridgman, 1883. Pp. 50.
         Historical address by Isaac Clark.

10482   ELIOT, SAMUEL ATKINS, 1862-1950. "The muni-
         cipal theatre in Northampton." Theatre
Arts, 3 (1919), 248-254.

10483   ELKS, BENEVOLENT AND PROTECTIVE ORDER OF.
         NORTHAMPTON, MASS., LODGE NO. 997. Elks
40th Anniversary Souvenir Program, 1905-1945. n.p.,
[1945?]. Unpaged. MNF.
         Includes history of lodge.

10484   ELLIS, GEORGE EDWARD. "Recollections of
         Round Hill School." Educational Review, 1
(1891), 337-344.

10485   FLORENCE, MASS. NORTH CONGREGATIONAL
         CHURCH. The seventy-fifth anniversary of
the founding of the Congregational Church, Northampton, Mass....November 14th and 15th, nineteen hundred and thirty six. n.p., [1936?]. Unpaged. MNF.

10486   FLORENCE MANUFACTURING CO. Fifty years of
         brush making, 1866-1916. n.p., [1916?].
Unpaged. MNF.

10487 FLORENCE SAVINGS BANK. Fiftieth anniversary...1873-1923. n.p., [1923?]. Unpaged. MNF.

10488 FLOWER, DEAN. Henry James in Northampton: visions and revisions. Northampton: Friends of the Smith College Library, 1971. Pp. 24.

10489 FUESSLE, NEWTON. The health makers. n.p., n.d. Unpaged. MNF.
Reprint of 'An institutional story advertisement' from 'Outlook'; a twelve page history of the Florence Manufacturing Company, manufacturers of Pro-phy-lac-tic tooth brushes.

10490 FULLER, MARY BREESE. "The development of history and government at Smith College, 1875-1920." SCSH, 5 (1919-1920), 139-173.

10491 GERE, HENRY SHERWOOD. Reminiscences of old Northampton, sketches of the town as it appeared from 1840 to 1850. Northampton: Gazette Printing, 1902. Pp. 151.

10492 GILFILLAN, JAMES R. and HERBERT E. RILEY. Northampton in the Spanish-American War. Easthampton: Enterprise Printing, 1899. Pp. 115.

10493 GILLETT, E. H. "Jonathan Edwards, and the occasion and result of his dismission from Northampton." HistMag, 2 Ser., 1 (1867), 333-338.

10494 GILMORE, BARBARA. A Puritan town and its imprints: Northampton 1786-1845. Northampton: Hampshire Bookshop, 1942. Pp. xi, 104.

10495 GREENE, LOUISA DICKINSON. Foreshadowings of Smith College: selections from letters of Louisa Dickinson to John Morton Greene 1856-1857. Helen French Greene, ed. Portland, Me.: Southworth Pr., 1928. Pp. vii, 43.

10496 GROSVENOR, LILIAN. "Deaf children learn to talk at Clarke School." National Geographic, 107 (1955) 378-397.

10497 HALE, PHILIP. "Musical and theatrical life in a New England village in the sixties." MHSP, 56 (1922-1923), 335-343.

10498 HANSCOM, ELIZABETH DEERING and HELEN FRENCH GREENE. Sophia Smith and the beginnings of Smith College, based upon the narrative of John Morton Greene.... Northampton: Smith College, 1925. Pp. x, 120.

10499 HARRISON, JOSEPH LE ROY. Forbes Library, the half century, 1894-1944, with a sketch of Charles Edward Forbes. Northampton: The Print Shop, 1945. Pp. 55.

10500 HAZEN, CHARLES DOWNER. Old Northampton, an address delivered before the faculty and students of Smith College, June 7, 1904, on the occasion of the two hundred and fiftieth anniversary of the founding of Northampton. Cambridge: Univ. Pr., 1904. Pp. 34.

10501 HEMENWAY, H. D. "The People's Institute of Northampton, Mass." WNE, 2 (1912), 210-214.
Club.

10502 HISTORICAL register and general directory of Northampton: containing a map of the town, historical sketch of Northampton, churches, pastors, schools, courts, canal, railroads...etc., together with sketches of the public institutions of the town, as well as banking houses, &c. Northampton: Gazette Printing, 1875-1876. Pp. vi, 220.

10503 HOLDEN, ISABEL ANDERSON. Northampton National Bank, 125th anniversary, 1833-1958. n.p., [1958?]. Unpaged. MNF.

10504 HOWE, FLORENCE THOMPSON. "The brief career of Ansel Goodrich." Antiques, 18 (1930), 38-39.
Chairs.

10505 JORDAN, M. A. "Smith College." NEM, 5 (1886-1887), 207-220.

10506 [KNEELAND, FREDERICK NEWTON]. Northampton, the Meadow City; over two hundred and fifty illustrations. Northampton: F. N. Kneeland and L. P. Bryant, 1894. Pp. 107.

10507 _____. One hundredth anniversary of Edwards Church, Northampton, Massachusetts, 1833-1933. n.p., [1933?]. Unpaged. MNF.

10508 KNEELAND, HARRIET I. Some old Northampton homes.... Northampton, 1909. Pp. 27.

10509 LEAGUE OF WOMEN VOTERS OF NORTHAMPTON, MASSACHUSETTS. This is Northampton. [Northampton], 1962. Pp. 72.

10510 LYMAN, CLIFFORD H. Northampton in the days of Jonathan Edwards, 1727-1750. Northampton: Metcalf Printing and Publishing, 1937. Unpaged. MBNEH.

10511 MCBEE, ALICE EATON. From Utopia to Florence: the story of a transcendentalist community in Northampton, Mass., 1830-1852. Northampton, 1947. Pp. x, 77.
Northampton Association of Education and Industry.

10512 MARR, HARRIET WEBSTER. "The Round Hill School for Boys, 1823-1833." OTNE, 49 (1958-1959), 49-55.

10513 MAYNARD, C. EDGAR. "How the plastics industry got started here." Industry, 19 (June, 1954), 11-12.
Pro-phy-lac-tic Brush Co.

10514 MENSEL, ERNST HEINRICH. Northampton and the Northampton Institution for Savings, 1842-1942. [Northampton]: Northampton Institution for Savings, 1942. Unpaged.

10515   _____. Northampton Social and Literary
        Club, 1925-1935. Northampton: The Club,
1936. Pp. 16. MNF.

10516   MILLER, PERRY. "Jonathan Edwards' socio-
        logy of the Great Awakening." NEQ, 21
(1948), 50-77.

10517   MILNE, CAROLINE C. and ALEXANDER W. MILNE.
        Official program, tercentenary celebration,
Northampton, Massachusetts, June 13-20, 1954.
Florence: Printing Arts, [1954?]. Pp. 80. MNF.
        Includes history.

10518   NONOTUCK SAVINGS BANK. A quarter century of
        the Nonotuck Savings Bank, Northampton,
Mass. Philadelphia: Elliott, [1924?]. Unpaged.
MNF.

10519   NORTHAMPTON, MASS. The Meadow City's
        quarter-millennial book: a memorial of the
celebration of the two hundred and fiftieth anniversary of the settlement of the town of Northampton,
Massachusetts, June 5th, 6th and 7th, 1904....
Springfield: F. A. Bassette, [1904?]. Pp. xv, 531.

10520   NORTHAMPTON, MASS. CHAMBER OF COMMERCE.
        Northampton, Massachusetts, the Meadow City.
Northampton, [1930?]. Unpaged. M.
        Includes historical sketch and chronology
        of events.

10521   NORTHAMPTON, MASS. COMMITTEE ON HISTORICAL
        LOCALITIES. Historical localities in
Northampton. Compiled...for the celebration of the
250th anniversary of the settlement of the town,
June 5th, 6th, and 7th, 1904. Northampton: Gazette
Printing, 1904. Pp. 40.

10522   NORTHAMPTON, MASS. CONGREGATION B'NAI
        ISRAEL. B'nai Israel Synagogue of North-
ampton, 1905-1927. n.p., [1927?]. Unpaged. MNF.

10523   NORTHAMPTON, MASS. FIRST CHURCH OF CHRIST.
        Historical sketch of five church houses
erected on Meeting House Hill, 1655-1878. n.p.,
1954. Unpaged. MNF.

10524   NORTHAMPTON, MASS. FIRST PARISH. First
        Parish, Northampton; meeting houses and
ministers from 1653 to 1878, containing a description of the new meeting house, together with the
dedication sermon, delivered Sunday, May 5, 1878.
Northampton: Gazette Printing, [1878]. Pp. 76.

10525   NORTHAMPTON, MASS. TERCENTENARY HISTORY
        COMMITTEE. The Northampton book; chapters
from 300 years in the life of a New England town,
1654-1954. Lawrence E. Wikander, et al, comps.
Northampton, 1954. Pp. xiii, 426.

10526   "NORTHAMPTON community." Country Time and
        Tide, 5 (1903-1904), 37-43, 63-68.
        Northampton Association of Education and
        Industry.

10527   "NORTHAMPTON has a birthday." Telephone
        Topics, 48 (June, 1954), 2-5.
        300th anniversary.

10528   "NORTHAMPTON, Mass.--its fame is its peo-
        ple." Chronicle [Metropolitan Life Insur-
ance Company], 20 (May-June, 1956), 2-5.

10529   O'BRIEN, MICHAEL JOSEPH. "Cornelius Merry
        and Matthew Clesson, Pioneer Irishmen of
Northampton, Mass." AirHSJ, 17 (1918), 137-143.

10530   "OLD covenant and confession of the North-
        ampton Church." CongQ, 3 (1861), 168-179.

10531   O'SHEA, PETER F. "Famous industries of
        Northampton." WNE, 3 (1913), 429-434.

10532   PARSONS, JAMES M.. 100th anniversary, Flor-
        ence Savings Bank, Florence, Massachusetts,
1873-1973. [Florence: Florence Savings Bank,
1973]. Unpaged. MNF.

10533   THE PARSONS House of the Northampton Histor-
        ical Society, being two conflicting accounts
entitled: 'The House of Cornet Joseph Parsons,' by
Anna Catherine Bliss [and] 'Parsons Houses in North-
ampton; reminiscent notes of Chauncey Lyman Parson.'
Northampton: Northampton Historical Society, 1972.
Pp. 34. MNF.

10534   PORTER, DOROTHY B. "Anti-slavery movement
        in Northampton." Negro HistB, 24 (1960-
1961), 33-34, 41.

10535   POWELL, LYMAN PEIRSON. The Emmanuel Move-
        ment in a New England town: a systematic
account of experiments and reflections designed to
determine the proper relationship between the
minister and the doctor in the light of modern
needs. N.Y.: G. P. Putnam's Sons, 1909. Pp. xv,
194.

        St. John's Church.

10536   "THE Pro-phy-lac-tic Brush Company." Indus-
        try, 5 (December, 1939), 7-10.
        Toothbrushes.

10537   ROTARY CLUB, NORTHAMPTON, MASS. 25th anni-
        versary, presentation of charter of the Ro-
tary Club of Northampton, Mass., Monday, October
27, 1952.... n.p., [1952?]. Unpaged. MNF.
        Includes history by Arch Galbraith.

10538   RUMSEY, OLIVE. "The Northampton Association
        of Education and Industry." NEM, New Ser,
12 (1895), 22-32.

10539   SAMPSON, MYRA MELISSA. A history of the
        Watson family, eminent in Northampton, 1860-
1948. Northampton: Trustees of Forbes Library,
1969. Unpaged.

10540   SEELYE, LAURENUS CLARK. The early history
        of Smith College, 1871-1910. Boston:
Houghton Mifflin, 1923. Pp. ix, 242.

10541   SHATTUCK, GEORGE CHEEVER. "The centenary
        of Round Hill School." MHSP, 57 (1923-
1924), 205-209.

10542   SHEFFELD, CHARLES ARTHUR, ed. The history
        of Florence, Massachusetts, including a
complete account of the Northampton Association of
Education and Industry.... Florence, 1895.
Pp. 250.

10543   SMART, GEORGE K. "Fourierism in Northamp-
        ton: two documents." NEQ, 12 (1939), 370-
374.
        Northampton Association of Education and
        Industry.

10544   SMITH COLLEGE. Celebration of the quarter-
        centenary of Smith College, October second
and third, 1900. Cambridge: Riverside Pr., 1900.
Pp. vi, 192.

10545   _____. Historical handbook of Smith Col-
        lege.... Northampton, 1932. Pp. 32.

10546   "SMITH College centennial, 1875-1975."
        Smith Alumnae Quarterly, 66 (November,
1974), entire issue.

10547   "SOME souvenirs of Round-Hill School." Old
        and New, 6 (1872-1873), 27-41.
        Signed: T. G. A.

10548   SPONSELLER, EDWIN HUMMELBAUGH. Northampton
        and Jonathan Edwards. Shippensburg, Pa.:
Shippensburg State College, 1966. Pp. 32.

10549   STUART, ROBERT LEE. "'Mr. Stoddard's way:
        church and sacrements in Northampton."
AmQ, 24 (1972), 243-253.

10550   "THREE glimpses of a New England village."
        Blackwood's Magazine, 136 (1884), 646-656.

10551   "TOGETHER: Northampton community." County
        Time and Tide, 5 (1903-1904), 37-43, 63-68.
        Northampton Association of Education and
        Industry.

10552   TOMLINSON, JULIETTE. The Bowers House,
        Northampton, Massachusetts. Springfield:
Connecticut Valley Historical Museum, 1954. Unpaged. MAJ.

10553   TRUMBULL, JAMES RUSSELL. History of North-
        ampton, Massachusetts, from its settlement
in 1654. Northampton: Gazette Printing, 1898-
1902. 2v.

10554   TYLER, HENRY MATHER. The beginnings of the
        Northampton Social and Literary Club.
Northampton: The Club, 1925. Pp. 17.

10555   U. S. VETERANS ADMINISTRATION HOSPITAL,
        NORTHAMPTON, MASS. Twenty-fifth anniversa-
ry, 1924-1949. [Northampton]: Manual Arts Therapy
Print Shop, [1949?]. Unpaged. MNF.

10556   WAITE, HELEN ELMIRA. "100 years of conquest
        of silence." Volta Review, 69 (1967), 118-
125.
        Clarke School for the Deaf.

10557   [WARNER, CHARLES FORBES], ed. Northampton
        of today: depicted by pen and camera.
Northampton: Picturesque Publishing, 1902. Pp. 96.

10558   _____. Representative families of Northamp-
        ton; a demonstration of what high character,
good ancestry and heredity have accomplished in a
New England town. Vol. I. Northampton: Picturesque Publishing, 1917. Pp. 411.
        No more published.

10559   WIKANDER, LAWRENCE EINAR. Completing a
        century: the Northampton Social and Lit-
erary Club, 1925-1962. Northampton: The Club,
1962. Pp. 11.

10560   _____. Disposed to learn: the first seven-
        ty-five years of the Forbes Library. North-
ampton: Trustees of the Forbes Library, 1972.
Pp. 97.

10561   WILLIAMS, SOLOMON. Historical sketch of
        Northampton, from its first settlement: in
a sermon, delivered on the national Thanksgiving,
April 13, 1815. Northampton: W. W. Clapp, 1815.
Pp. 24.

10562   YALE, CAROLINE ARDELIA. Years of building:
        memories of a pioneer in a special field of
education. N.Y.: Dial Pr., 1931. Pp. xi, 311.
        Clarke School for the Deaf.

NORTHBOROUGH

10563   ALLEN, JOSEPH. The day of small things:
        a centennial discourse, delivered in North-
borough, June 1, 1846, in commemoration of the organization of the First Congregational Church in
that place, and the ordination of their first minister, one hundred years ago.... Boston: Wm. Crosby
and H. P. Nichols, 1846. Pp. 64.

10564   _____. "Historical account of Northbor-
        ough." WMHJ, 2 (1826), 129-192.

10565   _____. Historical sketch of Northborough.
        [Boston, 1862?]. Pp. 10.

10566   _____. Topographical and historical
        sketches of the town of Northborough, with
the early history of Marlborough, in the Commonwealth of Massachusetts, furnished for the Worcester Magazine. Worcester: W. Lincoln & C. C. Baldwin, 1826. Pp. 66.

10567   HOUGHTON, WILLIAM ADDISON. Our fathers'
        altar: a centennial sermon, preached June
7, 1846, in commemoration of the founding of the
First Christian Church in Northborough, Mass.
Worcester: Henry J. Howland [184-?]. Pp. 26.

10568   _____. Semi-centennial of the Evangelical
        Congregational Church and Society in North-
borough, Dec. 19th, 1882, with commemorative notices
and historical address. Clinton: W. J. Coulter,
1883. Pp. 32.

10569 KENT, JOSIAH COLEMAN. Northborough history.
Newton: Garden City Pr., 1921. Pp. vi,
529.

10570 NORTHBOROUGH, MASS. The centennial celebra-
tion of the town of Northborough, Mass.,
August 22, 1866. [Northborough]: Printed for The
Committee, 1866. Pp. 47.
Address by Joseph Allen.

10571 NORTHBOROUGH, MASS. TOWN BICENTENNIAL COM-
MITTEE. Two hundredth anniversary, town of
Northborough, 1766-1966, official program. n.p.,
1966. Unpaged. M.

10572 SMALL, CORA. History of the Northborough
Free Library. Northborough: Northborough
Free Library, 1909. Pp. 39. MB.

10573 VALENTINE, THOMAS WESTON. Fifty years of
pilgrimage: a historical discourse delivered before the First Baptist Church in Northborough, Mass., on the first semi-centennial anniversary of its organization, July 2, 1877. Brooklyn, [N.Y.]: Brooklyn Daily Times, 1877. Pp. 44.
M.

NORTHBRIDGE

10574 BOTTS, ADELBERT K. "Northbridge, Massachusetts, a town that moved down hill."
Journal of Geography, 33 (1934), 249-260.

10575 CLARK, LEWIS FRANKLIN. A discourse delivered in Whitinsville, Northbridge, July 31,
1859, the twenty-fifth anniversary of the organization of the Congregational Church in that place....
Cambridge: Welch, Bigelow, 1861. Pp. 70.

10576 GIBBS, GEORGE L. Northbridge in the Rebellion: an address delivered before Jesse L.
Reno Post 167, G. A. R., Memorial Day, May 30,
1889, at Whitinsville, Mass., with an appendix
containing statistics concerning the town of Northbridge in the Rebellion. Uxbridge: L. H. Bal-
come, 1889. Pp. 40.

10577 GREGG, JAMES BARTLETT. Northbridge's part
in the Civil War; address, Memorial day,
May 30, 1912 [at] Whitinsville, Mass. Whitinsville:
Eagle Print, n.d. Unpaged.

10578 MITCHELL, EMILY M. Historical sketch of
the Congregational Church, Northbridge
Center...January 2, 1901. n.p., [1901?]. Unpaged.
MWA.

10579 NAVIN, THOMAS R. The Whitin Machine Works
since 1831: a textile machinery company in
an industrial village. Cambridge: Harvard Univ.
Pr., 1950. Pp. xxix, 654.

10580 "THE WHITIN Machine Works." Industry, 6
(March, 1941), 7-10, 52.

10581 WHITINSVILLE, MASS. ST. PATRICK'S CHURCH.
J. M. J. & St. P., Ad perpetuam Dei memori-
am, souvenir of the corner stone laying of the New
Saint Patrick's Church, May 15, 1898, containing a
retrospect by Peter S. O'Reilly, Rector, Whitinsville, Mass. Whitinsville: Eagle Printing, 1898.
Pp. 24. MB.

NORTHFIELD

10582 COMPTON, CARL C. The story of the North-
field Chateau. n.p., [1963?]. 14 leaves.
MDeeH.
Home of F. Robert Schell.

10583 COYLE, THOMAS, ed. The story of Mount Hermon. Mount Hermon: Mount Hermon Alumni
Association, 1906. Pp. 96.

10584 DICKINSON, RODOLPHUS. A description of
Northfield and Lexington, intended as an
exhibition of the plan of a contemplated gazetteer
of Massachusetts proper. Deerfield: C. J. Newcomb, 1818. Pp. 15. MDeeP.

10585 FITT, ARTHUR PERCY. All about Northfield:
a brief history and guide. Northfield:
Northfield Pr., 1910. Pp. 166.

10586 HUBBARD, JOHN. "An account of the town of
Northfield." MHSC, 2 (1793), 30-32.

10587 MABIE, JANET. The years beyond: the story
of Northfield, D. L. Moody, and the schools.
East Northfield: Northfield Bookstore, 1960.
Pp. 239.

10588 MITCHELL, ANN MARIA. Old days and new in
Northfield." NEM, New Ser., 16 (1897),
671-689.

10589 [MUNSELL, JOEL]. Reminiscences of men and
things in Northfield as I knew them from
1812 to 1825. Albany, 1876. Pp. 26.
Preface signed: J. M.

10590 NORTHFIELD, MASS. 250th anniversary cele-
bration of the town of Northfield, Mass....
June 22, 23 and 24, 1923. [Northfield?], 1923.
Pp. 118.

10591 NORTHFIELD, Mount Hermon, and Chicago, being
an account of four Bible schools. N.Y.:
Fleming H. Revell, 1892. Pp. 67. MB.

10592 NORTHFIELD SCHOOLS. The Northfield schools:
Northfield School for Girls, Mount Hermon
School. [East Northfield, 1956?]. Pp. 45.

10593 NORTHFIELD SEMINARY. Northfield Seminary,
thirtieth anniversary souvenir, 1879-1909.
East Northfield: The Bookstore, [1909?]. Pp. 48.
MNF.

10594 PARSONS, HERBERT COLLINS. A Puritan out-
post, a history of the town and people of
Northfield, Massachusetts. N.Y.: Macmillan, 1937.
Pp. xiii, 546.

10595 PIPER, GEORGE F. "Historical address."
PVMA 3 (1890-1898), 452-467.
Relates to the town.

10596 POLLEN, DOROTHY C., ed. Rivertown Review:
Northfield, Massachusetts, 1923-1973.
Orange: Enterprise and Journal Publishing, [1973].
Pp. ix, 262. M.

10597 STARK, STEPHEN. Fifty years of Mount Hermon. [Brattleboro, Vt.]: E. L. Hildreth,
1931. Unpaged. MB.
Preparatory school.

10598 TEMPLE, JOSIAH HOWARD and GEORGE SHELDON.
A history of the town of Northfield, Massachusetts, for 150 years, with an account of the
prior occupation of the territory by the Squakheags;
and with family genealogies. Albany: Joel Munsell,
1875. Pp. vi, 636.

10599 TEMPLE, JOSIAH HOWARD. "Settlement of
Northfield." PVMA, 1 (1870-1879), 114-140.

10600 WALKER, KENNETH H., ed. Northfield's 300th
anniversary, official souvenir tercentenary
program, Northfield, Massachusetts, May 26 through
June 3, 1973. n.p., [1973?]. Unpaged. MDeeP.

10601 WINCHESTER, MARY. "Fair Northfield, the
home of the evangelist Moody." NEM, 5
(1886-1887), 335-346.
Dwight L. Moody.

NORTON

10602 BUMSTED, JOHN M. "Religion, finance and
democracy in Massachusetts: the town of
Norton as a case study." JAH, 57 (1970-1971), 817-
831.

10603 CLARK, GEORGE FABER. A history of the town
of Norton, Bristol County, Massachusetts,
from 1669 to 1859. Boston: Crosby, Nichols, 1859.
Pp. xxv, 550.

10604 COPELAND, JENNIE FREEMAN. "The Rev. Pitt
Clarke House." OTNE, 41 (1950-1951), 7-10.

10605 HUBBARD, GEORGE H. "Wheaton Seminary,
Norton, Massachusetts." NEM, New Ser., 18
(1898), 102-115.

10606 LARCOM, LUCY. Wheaton Seminary: a semi-
centennial sketch. Cambridge: Riverside
Pr., 1885. Pp. 94.

10607 LEAGUE OF WOMEN VOTERS OF NORTON, MASS.
Norton, yesterday, today, tomorrow. Norton, 1954. Pp. 44. M.

10608 NORTON, MASS. Town of Norton Bicentennial,
1711-1911. n.p., 1911. Unpaged. M.

10609 SHEPARD, GRACE F. "Female education at
Wheaton College." NEQ, 6 (1933), 803-824.

10610 WHEATON COLLEGE, NORTON, MASS. Chronological catalogue of the trustees, principals,
teachers and graduates of Wheaton Female Seminary,
Norton, Mass., with a historical sketch of the institution from 1834 to 1869. Boston: Alfred Mudge
and Son, 1869. Pp. 19. M.

NORWELL

10611 "BOWKER Street and the Bowker Cemetery."
Historia, 1 (1898-1899), 41-43.

10612 DAMON, SUSAN C. "Happy and helpful memories." Historia, 1 (1898-1899), 33-36.

10613 ELLIS, RHODA BARKER. "The Quaker cemetery."
Historia, 1 (1898-1899), 17-19.

10614 MERRITT, JOSEPH FOSTER. A narrative history
of South Scituate-Norwell, Massachusetts.
Rockland: Rockland Standard Publishing, 1938.
Pp. 203.

10615 NORWELL, MASS. FIRST CHURCH. First Church
of Norwell, Massachusetts, two hundred and
seventy fifth anniversary, 1642-1917. n.p.,
[1917?]. Pp. 29. MBNEH.

10616 SOUTH SCITUATE SAVINGS BANK, NORWELL, MASS.
For 125 years...a friendly symbol of independence and security. Marshfield: J. D. Burgoyne,
1959. Unpaged. M.

10617 _____. One hundredth anniversary of the
South Scituate Savings Bank, 1835-1935.
Norwell, 1935. Pp. 24. M.

10618 TURNER, GEORGE C. "Ancestral pews." Historia, 1 (1898-1899), 1-8.
First Parish Church.

NORWOOD

10619 CHADBOURNE, ROBERT A. "Norwood is fountainhead as well as base of industrial century
plants." Industry, 14 (July, 1949), 7-12, 46-56.

10620 HISTORY and directory of Norwood, Mass. for
1890. Boston: Brown Bros., 1890. Pp. 122.
MBNEH.
History is by Francis Tinker.

10621 NORWOOD, MASS. PUBLIC LIBRARY. Catalogue
of the Norwood Public Library, together
with a brief history of the library.... Boston:
T. O. Metcalf, 1886. Pp. 183. M.

10622 NORWOOD COOPERATIVE BANK. Fifty years of
service 1889-1939, Norwood, 1939. Pp. 16.
M.

10623 ROCKWOOD, CHARLES M. "Norwood." NEM, New
Ser., 39 (1908-1909), 606-613.

10624 ST. CATHERINE OF SIENA CHURCH, NORWOOD,
MASS. Commemorating the 75th anniversary of
Saint Catherine of Siena Church. Norwood, 1965.
Pp. 134.

10625   TOLLES, BRYANT FRANKLIN, JR. Norwood: the
         centennial history of a Massachusetts town.
[Norwood]: Centennial Committee, Town of Norwood,
Massachusetts, 1973. Pp. xix, 242.

10626   WILLIAMS, ROY FOSTER. "Faith made its
         business grow." Industry, 22 (June, 1957),
34, 60-62.
         Plimpton Press, 75th anniversary.

OAK BLUFFS

10627   MCCULLOUGH, DAVID G. "Oak Bluffs." Am
         Heritage, 18 (October, 1967), 39-47.

10628   POOLE, DOROTHY COTTLE. "The Dukes County
         Historical Society, 1923-1973." DCI, 15
(1973-1974), 7-11.

10629   VINCENT, HEBRON. A history of the Wesleyan
         Grove, Martha's Vineyard, Camp Meeting,
from the first meeting held there in 1835 to that
of 1858, inclusive.... Boston: Geo. C. Rand &
Avery, 1858. Pp. 203. MB.

OAKHAM

10630   OAKHAM, MASS. BICENTENNIAL COMMITTEE. Bi-
         centennial anniversary, Oakham, Mass., 1762-
1962. Oakham, 1962. Pp. 25. M.

10631   PACKARD, CHARLES M. Oakham in my boyhood
         days...celebration of the one hundred and
fiftieth anniversary of the incorporation of the
town of Oakham, August 12, 1912. Oakham: Oakham
Historical Society, 1920. Pp. 28. MBNEH.

10632   WRIGHT, HENRY BURT and EDWIN D. HARVEY. The
         settlement and story of Oakham, Massachu-
setts. [New Haven?], 1947. 2v.

10633   WRIGHT, HENRY BURT. Soldiers of Oakham,
         Massachusetts in the Great War of 1914-1918.
[Oakham]: Oakham Historical Society, 1919. Pp. 31.
MB.

10634   WRIGHT, HENRY PARKS. Fobes Memorial Libra-
         ry, Oakham, Mass.... Oakham, 1909.
Pp. 121. MBNEH.

10635   _____. Independence Day in 1797 in Oak-
         ham, Massachusetts. [Oakham]: Oakham
Historical Society, 1911. Pp. 17.

10636   _____. Soldiers of Oakham, Massachusetts,
         in the Revolutionary War, the War of 1812
and the Civil War. New Haven: Tuttle, Morehouse &
Taylor, 1914. Pp. 325.

ORANGE

10637   "THE MINUTE Tapioca Company." Industry, 3
         (November, 1937), 7-10.

10638   NORTH ORANGE REUNION ASSOCIATION. History
         of North Orange, Mass., including leading
events from the first organization of Orange, 1781-
1924. North Orange, [1924?]. Pp. 60. MHi.

10639   ORANGE, MASS. PUBLIC LIBRARY. History of
         the Orange Public Library covering the
period from its inception in 1847 to 1933. Orange:
Enterprise and Journal, 1933. Unpaged. MBNEH.

10640   REEVES, RICHARD V. "Synonymous with Massa-
         chusetts quality." Industry, 26 (November,
1960), 37-40.
         Rodney Hunt Machine Co.; textile machinery,
water control equipment, industrial rolls.

ORLEANS

10641   BARNARD, RUTH L. History of the Congrega-
         tional Church, Orleans, Massachusetts.
Hyannis: Goss Print, 1947. Pp. 24. [MOHi].

10642   CROSBY, KATHARINE. "The little gray house
         on the Orleans Road." Cape Cod Magazine, 8
(June, 1926), 5-6.
         Kenrick Homestead.

10643   KIMBALL, RICHARD B. The story of a church:
         Church of the Holy Spirit, Orleans, Cape
Cod, Massachusetts. Orleans, 1953. Unpaged.
[MHy].

10644   KOEHLER, MARGARET. "The case of the Orleans
         French connection." CCC, 26 (1973), 27,
84-88, 90.
         French cable station.

10645   MURDOCH, RICHARD K. "The Battle of Orleans,
         Massachusetts (1814) and associated events."
AmNep, 24 (1964), 172-182.
         War of 1812.

10646   "THE OLD Kenrick House, South Orleans."
         CCB, 48 (Mid August, 1937), 19-29.

10647   OTIS, AMOS. "An account of the discovery
         of an ancient ship in the eastern shore of
Cape Cod." NEHGR, 18 (1864), 37-44.

10648   YE ANTIENT wrecke. --1626: loss of the
         Sparrow-Hawk in 1626: remarkable preser-
vation and recent discovery of the wreck. Boston:
Alfred Mudge & Son, 1865. Pp. 44.

OTIS

10649   OTIS, MASS. One hundred [and] fiftieth
         anniversary of the town of Otis, 1810-1960.
Becket: Helen D. Flynn, [1960?]. Unpaged. MPB.

10650   WILCOX, MARSHALL. "Hon. Marshall Wilcox,
         his reminiscent recollections of the town
of Otis." Berkshire Hills, 4 (1903-1904), 249-251.
         Nineteenth century.

OXFORD

10651 DANIELS, GEORGE FISHER. History of the town of Oxford, Massachusetts, with genealogies and notes on persons and estates. Oxford, 1892. Pp. vi, 856.

10652 _____. The Huguenots in the Nipmuck country or Oxford prior to 1713. Boston: Estes & Lauriat, 1880. Pp. xiv, 168.

10653 FREELAND, MARY DE WITT. The records of Oxford, Mass.; including chapters of Nipmuck, Huguenot and English history from the earliest date, 1630, with manners and fashions of the time. Albany: J. Munsell's Sons, 1894. Pp. 429.
     A typescript index by Avis G. Clarke is at the American Antiquarian Society.

10654 HOLMES, ABIEL. "Memoir of the French Protestants, who settled at Oxford, Massachusetts, A. D. 1686." MHSC, 3 Ser., 2 (1830), 1-83.

10655 HUGUENOT MEMORIAL SOCIETY OF OXFORD. Champions of freedom. Oxford, 1958. Pp. 96. Huguenots.

10656 JOSLIN, ADA L. "Oxford--its charms and its achievements." Worcester Magazine, 16 (1913), 172-181.

10657 OLNEY, PETER BUTLER. Historical address, delivered at the dedication of Memorial Hall, Oxford, Mass., Nov. 19, 1873. Worcester: Clark Jillson, 1884. Pp. 37.
     Huguenots.

10658 _____. "Huguenot settlement at Oxford." Huguenot Society of America. Proceedings, 1 (1889), 56-64.

10659 OXFORD, MASS. Official program of the celebration of the town of Oxford, Massachusetts, July 3, 4, 5, 6, 1913 in commemoration of the two hundredth anniversary of its settlement by the English. n.p., [1913?]. Pp. 64. MBNEH.

10660 OXFORD, MASS. FIRST CHURCH. The confession of faith and covenant of the First Church in Oxford, Mass...to which we prefixed some historical sketches of said church.... Worcester: Henry J. Howland, 1837. Pp. 15. MWA.

10661 OXFORD, MASS. FIRST CONGREGATIONAL CHURCH. Manual of the First Congregational Church of Oxford, Mass....with a historical sketch. Worcester: Charles E. Nye, 1873. Pp. 32. MWA.

10662 _____. Manual of the First Congregational Church, Oxford, Mass....with a historical sketch. Worcester: Charles Hamilton, 1888. Pp. 46. MWA.

10663 OXFORD, MASS. FREE PUBLIC LIBRARY. Souvenir of the Charles Larned Memorial and the Free Public Library, Oxford, Massachusetts, 1906. Boston: Geo. H. Ellis, 1906. Pp. 108.
     Includes history.

10664 "TWO centuries of community life." Worcester Magazine, 16 (1913), 169-172.

10665 WILKINS, MARIETTA B. "Birthplace of Clara Barton, North Oxford, Mass." OTNE, 20 (1929-1930), 87-90.

PALMER

10666 COTTON, SIMEON. "Palmer, Massachusetts." Historical Magazine, 16 (1869), 233-238. 282-284.

10667 [JENKINS, FRANK EDWIN and O. P. ALLEN]. History and manual of the Second Congregational Church and Society, of Palmer, Mass., 1847-1895. Palmer: C. B. Fiske, 1895. Pp. 61.

10668 PALMER, MASS. Palmer bicentennial. n.p., [1952?]. Unpaged. M. 1752-1952; includes a history of the town by C. Wesley Dingman.

10669 PALMER, MASS. ST. ANN'S CHURCH. Centennial of the first Catholic Church in the town of Palmer, Mass., 1855-1955. [Palmer?, 1955?]. Pp. 68. MB.

10670 ROCKWELL, E. F., ed. "Palmer, Massachusetts." HistMag, 2 Ser., 6 (1869), 233-238, 282-285.

10671 TEMPLE, JOSIAH HOWARD. History of the town of Palmer, Massachusetts, early known as the Elbow Tract: including records of the plantation, district and town, 1716-1889, with a genealogical register. [Palmer]: The Town, 1889. Pp. 602.

10672 WILSON, THOMAS. An historical address delivered at Palmer, Mass., July 5, 1852, in commemoration of the centennial anniversary of incorporation of the town. Lowell: S. J. Varney, 1855. Pp. 60.

PAXTON

10673 BILL, LEDYARD. The history of Paxton, Massachusetts. Worcester: Putnam, Davis, 1889. Pp. iv, 121.

10674 BUSH, ROXA HOWARD. Landmarks and memories of Paxton. Paxton, 1923. Pp. 61.

10675 CARMODY, JOAN. "Paper on the Nipmuck Indians: where was the last 'capitol' of the Nipmucks--could it have been Paxton?" Worcester HSPub, New Ser., 3 (1964), 37-45.

10676 "HISTORICAL sketch of Paxton." WMHJ, 2 (1826), 232-243.

10677 PAXTON, MASS. Centenary memorial of Paxton: or, the exercises of the hundredth anniversary of the incorporation of the town: including a historical address, by George W. Livermore...an

(PAXTON, MASS.)
oration, by Rev. John F. Bigelow...a poem, by Mr.
George Gardner Phipps...June 14, 1865. Worcester:
E. R. Fiske & Son, 1868. Pp. 78.

10678 _____. One hundred and fiftieth anniversary of the town of Paxton, Massachusetts,
celebrated June thirtieth, 1915. Worcester:
Davis Pr., 1917. Pp. 81. M.

PEABODY

10679 BUXTON, BESSIE RAYMOND. "History of the
South Church, Peabody." EIHC, 87 (1951),
41-64, 178-207, 341-372; 88 (1952), 167-198.

10680 [CARROLL, THOMAS]. "[Leather industry in
Peabody]." Hide and Leather, (January 18,
1902), Supplement.
Author attribution by Essex Institute.

10681 FREEMASONS. PEABODY, MASS. JORDAN LODGE.
One hundred years, Jordan Lodge, A. F. &
A. M., Peabody, Massachusetts. Peabody: Historical
Committee of the Lodge, 1908. Pp. 48. MSaE.

10682 GARDNER, FRANK A. "George Gardner House."
MassMag, 2 (1909), 230-233.

10683 GOODSPEED, H. C. "From hide to leather."
Industry, 1 (September, 1936), 9-11, 54-55.
A. C. Lawrence & Co.

10684 RAMSDELL, W. L. "Peabody, Mass. where
leather is supreme." Boot and Shoe Recorder, 47 (May 24, 1905), 73-96.

10685 SHEEHAN, JAMES J. History of the Peabody
Branch, American National Red Cross.
[Peabody]: Peabody Pr., 1919. Unpaged. MSaE.

10686 STIMPSON, SARAH E. Historical sketch of
the Ladies' Association of the South
Church, Peabody, read on the fiftieth anniversary
of the association, April nineteenth, 1893. Peabody: Peabody Pr., 1893. Pp. 25. MSaE.

10687 UNDERWOOD, MRS. GEORGE L. "The Derby-Osborn
Farm, Peabody, with its McIntire summer
house and barn." OTNE, 16 (1935-1926), 55-64.

10688 UPHAM, WILLIAM PHINEAS. House of John Proc-
ter, witchcraft martyr, 1692. Peabody:
C. H. Shepard, 1904. Pp. 17.
Relates to parcel of land.

10689 WELLS, JOHN A. The Peabody story: events
in Peabody's history, (1625-1972). Salem:
Essex Institute, 1972. Pp. 531.

PELHAM

10690 CONKEY, ITHAMAR. A centennial address, de-
livered at Pelham, Mass., January 16, 1843.
Amherst: J. S. & C. Adams, 1843. Pp. 24.
Historical review of the town.

10691 HAYNES, GEORGE HENRY. "The attempted suicide of a Massachusetts town." AASP, New
Ser., 16 (1903-1904), 180-191.

10692 "'LIFE' goes to a town meeting." Life, 8
(March 4, 1940), 90-93.

10693 LINEHAN, MARY LESSEY. "The Irish settlers
of Pelham, Mass." AIrHSJ, 3 (1900), 114-
117.

10694 PARMENTER, CHARLES OSCAR. History of Pelham, Mass., from 1738 to 1898, including the
early history of Prescott.... Amherst: Carpenter
& Morehouse, 1898. Pp. vi, 531.

10695 PELHAM, MASS. Pelham bicentennial celebra-
tion, 1743-1946. n.p., [1946?]. Unpaged.
MAJ.
Includes history by Elinor Genung Allen.

10696 PELHAM, MASS. TREASURES OF PELHAM COMMIT-
TEE. Treasures of Pelham. Pelham, 1968.
Pp. 44. MNF.

10697 "[PELHAM Historical Society, fiftieth anni-
versary]." Pelham Historical Society News,
1 (September 18, 1971), entire issue.

10698 ROMER, ALFRED S. Early Pelham: three
sketches. Pelham: Pelham Historical Commission, 1974. Pp. 18. MAJ.

10699 SEE, ANNA PHILLIPS. "Ancient Pelham and
the oldest town hall in New England."
Daughters of the American Revolution Magazine, 56
(1922), 286-292.

PEMBROKE

10700 ALLEN, MORRILL. Discourse delivered before
the Unitarian Church and Society in Pembroke, Sunday, June 15, 1862. Plymouth: Old Colony
Memorial Pr., 1862. Pp. 14.

10701 BUMSTED, JOHN M. "The report of the Pembroke (Massachusetts) town committee on the
currency, March 24, 1740/41." NEQ, 40 (1967), 551-
560.

10702 LITCHFIELD, HENRY WHEATLAND. Ancient landmarks of Pembroke. Pembroke: G. E. Lewis,
1909. Pp. 188.

10703 _____. The First Church in Pembroke 1708-
1908. Pembroke: George Edward Lewis,
1908. Unpaged.

10704 PEMBROKE'S oldest schoolhouse. n.p., n.d.
Unpaged. MBNEH.

PEPPERELL

10705 ANDREWS, DAVID. The sure and only foundation, with historical notices: centennial
discourse, delivered before the Church of Christ and
Second Parish, in Pepperell, Mass., January 29,
1847. Boston: Well-Spring Pr., 1847. Pp. 48.

10706 BABBIDGE, CHARLES. The claims of Congregational churches, a centennial address: being a plea in vindication of the rights of the
First Church of Christ in Pepperell, Mass., delivered Feb. 9, 1847. Boston: Wm. Crosby and H. P.
Nichols, 1847. Pp. 44.

10707 HARRINGTON, EMELINE. Address delivered on
the one hundred and fiftieth birthday of
the First Church of Christ in Pepperell, February
9, 1897. East Pepperell: Pepperell Printing, 1897.
Pp. 18.

10708 SHATTUCK, CHARLES P. Military record of
Pepperell, Mass.: historical address given
in Prescott Hall, June 18, 1877. Nashua, N.H.:
H. R. Wheeler, 1877. Pp. 38.

10709 SHATTUCK, MARY L. P. The story of Jewett's
Bridge. Ayer: H. S. Turner, 1912. Pp. 44.
M.
  Assembling of women in April, 1775 to pre-
  vent the British from entering the town.

PERU

10710 CLARK, E. L., ed. The building and dedica-
tion of the third meeting house of the Con-
gregational Church, Peru, Mass. Pittsfield: Sun
Printing, 1897. Pp. 23. MPB.
  Includes history of the church by Sarah
  Bowen.

10711 "RELIC of the seventeenth century, Indian
Sachem's grist mill." Berkshire Hills, 1
(November 1, 1900), [1-2].

PETERSHAM

10712 BLACK, JOHN DONALD and AYERS BRINSER. Plan-
ning one town: Petersham, a hill town in
Massachusetts. Cambridge: Harvard Univ. Pr., 1952.
Pp. x, 75.

10713 COOLIDGE, MABEL COOK. The history of Petersham, Massachusetts, incorporated April 20,
1754: Volunteerstown or Voluntown, 1730-1733,
Nichewaug, 1733-1754. [Petersham?, 1948].
Pp. 408.

10714 DANA, RICHARD HENRY, b. 1851. Address at
the one hundredth anniversary of the town
of Dana. n.p., 1901. Pp. 18.

10715 DANA, MASS. The Dana centennial; report of
the addresses and proceedings at the cele-
bration on Dana Common on the twenty-second day of
August, nineteen hundred one. Barre: Mrs. Jennie
C. Spooner, [1901?]. Pp. 103.
  Historical sketch by N. L. Johnson.

10716 DODS, AGNES M. "Nathan and Joseph Negus,
itinerant painters." Antiques, 76 (1959),
434-437.
  Nineteenth century.

10717 FENN, WILLIAM WALLACE. Historical address
delivered on June 23, 1919, the hundredth
anniversary of the installation of the Reverend
Luther Willson as minister of the Church of Christ
in Petersham. [Worcester?]: Worcester Unitarian
Conference and Petersham Centenary Committee,
[1919?]. Pp. 19.

10718 FISHER, RICHARD THORNTON. The management of
the Harvard Forest, 1909-19. Petersham:
Harvard Forest, 1921. Pp. 27.
  Administered by Harvard University.

10719 HOWE, JONAS BENJAMIN. Sketches of Petersham natives and adopted citizens. Charles
K. Wilder, comp. Athol: Athol Transcript Co.,
1915. Pp. 219.

10720 LUTZ, RUSSELL JAMES and ALBERT C. CLINE.
Results of the first thirty years of experimentation in silviculture in the Harvard Forest,
1908-1938. Petersham: Harvard Forest, 1947-1956.
2v.

10721 PETERSHAM, MASS. 1754-1904, one hundred and
fiftieth anniversary of the incorporation of
the town of Petersham, Massachusetts, Wednesday,
August the tenth, 1904. Boston: Everett Pr., 1904.
Pp. 60.

10722 _____. 200th anniversary celebration, town
of Petersham, Massachusetts July 4th and
5th, 1954; historical address by John Fiske. n.p.,
[1954?]. Unpaged. M.

10723 PETERSHAM, MASS. FIRST CHURCH. The First
Church in Petersham: the First Congregational Parish (Unitarian), founded 1738, centenary
of the installation of the Reverend Luther Willson.
n.p., [1919?]. Pp. 16. MH.

10724 PETERSHAM, MASS. FREE LIBRARY. Catalogue
of the Petersham Free Library. Athol:
Smith, Hill, 1880. Pp. 57. M.
  Includes brief history.

10725 PUTNAM, JOHN JAY. Petersham Lyceum, 1833-
1848. Worcester: Blanchard Pr., 1902.
Pp. 16. M.

10726 RAUP, HUGH MILLER and REYNOLD E. CARLSON.
The history of land use in the Harvard
Forest. Harvard Forest, 1941. Pp. 64.
  Administered by Harvard University.

10727 SHERMAN, JULIE. Old road through Pioneer
Valley. [Worcester: Commonwealth Pr.],
1931. Pp. 26. MWA.

10728 WILLSON, EDMUND BURKE. An address delivered
in Petersham, Massachusetts, July 4, 1854,
in commemoration of the one hundredth anniversary
of the incorporation of that town.... Boston:
Crosby, Nichols, 1855. Pp. iv, 133.

10729 WOOLSEY, JOHN MUNRO. Address delivered on
July 4, 1929, on the one hundred and seventy-fifth anniversary of the incorporation of the
town of Petersham, Worcester County, Massachusetts.
N.Y.: Pandick Pr., 1929. Pp. 55.

PHILLIPSTON

10730 ANDREWS, S. B. Historical address with a short account of the celebration of the centennial anniversary of the organization of the Congregational Church in Phillipston. Athol: Athol Transcript, 1886. Pp. 18. MWA.

10731 LORD, WILLIAM GARDINER. Historical address...at the celebration of the 150th anniversary of the incorporation of the town of Phillipston, Mass., Tuesday August 18th, 1936. Athol: Athol Printing, [1936?]. Pp. 67.

PITTSFIELD

10732 "A. H. Rice Company celebrates its 75th anniversary." Industry, 19 (October, 1953), 28, 30, 56, 58, 60.
Thread and braids.

10733 ADAMS, THOMAS BOYLSTON. "Adams, slavery, and western Massachusetts." Berkshire History, 1 (Winter, 1971), 3-15.
John Quincy Adams.

10734 AGRICULTURAL NATIONAL BANK, PITTSFIELD, MASS. A century of service; a brief account of the origin, growth, and present condition of the Agricultural National Bank, Pittsfield, Massachusetts, 1818-1918. Pittsfield: Franklin Pr., [1918?]. Unpaged.

10735 BALLARD, HARLAN H. "A forgotten fraternity." BHSSC, 3 (1899-1913), 279-298.
Washington Benevolent Society.

10736 _____. "The history, methods, and purposes of the Berkshire Athenaeum." BHSSC, 1, Pt. 4 (1891), 293-306.

10737 BARBRE, W. T. "Industry's map of Massachusetts: Pittsfield." Industry, 2 (August, 1937), 17-19.

10738 BARKER, JOHN, b. 1878. The first hundred years: BLICO. Pittsfield: Berkshire Life Insurance Co., 1951. Pp. 53.

10739 BARRETT, J. S. "Pittsfield reminiscences." Berkshire Hills, New Ser., 2 (1905-1906), 121-123.

10740 BATES, SHERRILL P. The first century of the South Congregational Church, 1850-1950. Pittsfield, 1950. Pp. 47. MPB.

10741 BERKSHIRE ATHENAEUM AND MUSEUM. The Berkshire Athenaeum and Museum; its history, charter, by-laws, rules and regulations. Pittsfield: Eagle Printing and Binding, 1922. Pp. 20.

10742 _____. 1872-1947: 75 years of library service. Pittsfield, 1947. Pp. 19.

10743 "THE BERKSHIRE County Savings Bank." Berkshire Hills, 3 (1902-1903), 119-120; New Ser., 1 (1904-1905), 77.

10744 "BLOWING up the powder house." Berkshire Hills, 1 (May 1, 1901), [11-12]. 1828.

10745 BOLTWOOD, EDWARD. The history of Pittsfield, Massachusetts, from the year 1876 to the year 1916. Pittsfield: The City, 1916. Pp. 387.

10746 BRAMAN, SIDNEY T. "Pittsfield's [150th] anniversary celebration." WNE, 1 (1910-1911), 234-237.

10747 BRISTOL, MARY A. The one hundred fiftieth anniversary of Methodism in Pittsfield, 1791-1941: an historical review...presented...in the First Methodist Church, Pittsfield, Massachusetts, Sunday, May the eighteenth, nineteen hundred forty-one. [Pittsfield, 1941]. Pp. 22.

10748 BROWN, BENJAMIN. Pittsfield fifty years ago as observed by Benjamin Brown.... Pittsfield, 1858. Pp. 32. MPB.

10749 CARLEY, GLENNA S. The one hundredth anniversary of the First United Methodist Church building, 55 Fenn Street, Pittsfield, Massachusetts, May 5, 1874-May 5, 1974. n.p., [1974?]. Unpaged. MPB.

10750 DAWES, ANNA LAURENS. Historical report of the Wednesday Morning Club of Pittsfield, Mass. Pittsfield: Sun Printing, 1885. Pp. 12. MB.

10751 "THE FAMOUS Berkshire Jubilee of 1844, the first celebration of Old Home Week in the Republic." Berkshire Hills, 3 (1902-1903), 118-119.

10752 FIELD, DAVID DUDLEY. A history of the town of Pittsfield, in Berkshire County, Mass, with a map of the county. Hartford: Case, Tiffany and Burnham, 1844. Pp. 80.

10753 "THE FIRST iron printing handpress in Berkshire County." Berkshire Hills, New Ser., 2 (1905-1906), 107.

10754 "THE FIRST town meeting in Pootoonsuck." Berkshire Hills, New Ser., 2 (1905-1906), 119.
1753.

10755 FREEMASONS. PITTSFIELD, MASS. MYSTIC LODGE. History of Mystic Lodge, A. F. & A. M....125th anniversary, June 16-17, 1935. Pittsfield, 1935. Pp. 41. MPB.

10756 _____. Mystic Lodge, F. & A. M., Pittsfield, Massachusetts, centennial celebration, Maplewood Hotel Friday evening, June tenth, nineteen hundred ten. Pittsfield: Sun Printing, 1910. Unpaged.

10757 FRIEDMAN, LEE MAX. "The phylacteries found at Pittsfield, Mass." AJHSP, 25 (1917), 81-85.

10758 "GATHERING places in Pittsfield from 1811 to 1903." Berkshire Hills, 3 (1902-1903), 105-106.

10759 GIBBONS, PETER D. "The Berkshire Medical Institution." BHistMed, 38 (1964), 45-64. Medical school, 1822-1867.

10760 HAMILTON, J. A. Methodism in Pittsfield: sermon preached...Methodist Episcopal Church...July 2, 1911. n.p., [1911?]. Pp. 19. MPB.

10761 HARRISON, SAMUEL. Pittsfield twenty-five years ago: a sermon delivered in the Second Congregational Church, Pittsfield, Mass., January 11th and 18th, 1874. Pittsfield: Chickering & Axtell, 1874. Pp. 34.

10762 HERBERG, THEODORE. History of the public schools of Pittsfield, Massachusetts, 1916-1954. Pittsfield, 1955. 84 leaves. MPB.

10763 "A HISTORIC illustration and sketch, upper North Street in Pittsfield in 1851." Berkshire Hills, 3 (1902-1903), 97-99.

10764 "A HISTORIC Pittsfield mansion, the home of the Golds, the Appletons and the Plunketts on East Street." Berkshire Hills, 4 (1903-1904), 174-175.

10765 HISTORY of playgrounds in Pittsfield, July the fifteenth, nineteen hundred and fourteen. n.p., [1914?]. Unpaged. MPB.

10766 JONES, DWIGHT E. The Jones story. Pittsfield: Jones Division, Beloit Corporation, 1966. Pp. 41. MPB.
Manufacturer of paper mill machinery.

10767 KAAN, FRANK W. "Historical sketch of Pittsfield." BSM, 2 (1884-1885), 193-210.

10768 KELLY, ERIC D. "Berkshire Athenaeum." Berkshire Athenaeum, 1 (Spring, 1971), 15-20.

10769 "LITERARY Pittsfield." Literary World, 24 (1893), 92-93.

10770 NEWMAN, ROBERT GEORGE. The history of Congragation Anshe Amonim. Pittsfield, 1961. Unpaged.

10771 "AN OLD Berkshire hat factory." Berkshire Hills, New Ser., 2 (1905-1906), 124.

10772 "THE OLD Pittsfield Elm, the most famous tree in Berkshire County." Berkshire Hills, 3 (1902-1903), 133-137.
1749-1864.

10773 "'THE OLD Pittsfield quartet,' five notable Pittsfield characters of the nineteenth century." Berkshire Hills, 2 (July 1, 1902), [12].
Edwin Clapp, George Brown, Robert Pomeroy, David Campbell and George H. Laflin.

10774 PETERSON, BERNARD and CLIFFORD S. FAHLSTROM. "Pittsfield bulges with business." Industry, 12 (September, 1947), 7-10, 30, 32, 34, 36, 38. Industry.

10775 PIERCE, DAVID S. "War at Finegan's section, and the Boston and Albany Railway." Berkshire Hills, 2 (October, 1901), [1-4]; 2 (November 1, 1901), [1-5].
Irish labor riot.

10776 PITTSFIELD, MASS. Mid-century review. Pittsfield, 1950. Pp. 32. M.

10777 _____. Pittsfield, Massachusetts, 1761-1911: 150th anniversary celebration July 2-4, 1911: official program and souvenir. Pittsfield: Eagle Printing and Binding, 1911. Pp. 116. M.

10778 PITTSFIELD, MASS. FIRST BAPTIST CHURCH. Centennial souvenir...in commemoration of the reorganization of the church, March 23rd, 1801. Pittsfield: Eagle Publishing, [1901?]. Pp. 39. MPB.

10779 PITTSFIELD, MASS. FIRST CHURCH OF CHRIST. First Church of Christ in Pittsfield; proceedings in commemoration of its one hundred and fiftieth anniversary...1914. Pittsfield: Sun Printing, 1914. Pp. 149. MPB.

10780 _____. Proceedings in commemoration of the organization in Pittsfield, February 7, 1764 of the First Church of Christ, February 7, 1889. Pittsfield: Sun Printing, 1889. Pp. 135.

10781 _____. Program of events and historical briefs...two hundredth anniversary. n.p., [1964?]. Pp. 28. MPB.
Includes biographies of past and present clergymen.

10782 PITTSFIELD, MASS. FIRST CONGREGATIONAL CHURCH. FREE WILL SOCIETY. An account of the celebration of the 75th anniversary of the founding of the Free Will Society of the First Congregational Church of Pittsfield, Mass. held January 24, 1895. Pittsfield: Sun Printing, 1895. Pp. 51. MPB.
Charity.

10783 PITTSFIELD, MASS. HOUSE OF MERCY. The celebration of the twenty-fifth anniversary of the establishment of the House of Mercy, containing an address on the development of hospitals, by Dr. J. F. A. Adams, and an historical sketch of the House of Mercy, by Mrs. H. M. Plunkett, and a financial statement, by Mrs. M. B. Root.... Pittsfield: Sun Printing, 1899. Pp. 39.

10784 PITTSFIELD, MASS. MORNINGSIDE BAPTIST
       CHURCH. Fifty years of Christian service,
Morningside Baptist Church, Pittsfield, Massachusetts. n.p., [1946?]. Pp. 97. MPB.

10785 PITTSFIELD, MASS. ST. CHARLES CHURCH. Gold-
       en jubilee, Saint Charles, 1893-1943,
Pittsfield, Massachusetts, October 17, 1943.
Pittsfield: Ben Franklin Pr., [1943?]. Pp. 48.
MPB.

10786 PITTSFIELD, MASS. ST. JOSEPH'S PARISH.
       Centennial celebration, St. Joseph's Par-
ish, 1844-1944. n.p., [1944?]. Unpaged. MPB.

10787 _____. St. Joseph's Parish, golden jubi-
       lee, 1849-1899, Pittsfield, Mass. [Pitts-
field]: Eagle Print, [1899?]. Unpaged. MPB.

10788 PITTSFIELD, MASS. SOUTH CONGREGATIONAL
       CHURCH. Jubilee of the South Congregation-
al Church, November the eleventh, twelfth, thirteenth and sixteenth, nineteen hundred. Pittsfield: Pittsfield Journal, 1900. Pp. 168. M.

10789 PITTSFIELD COOPERATIVE BANK. What happened
       then?: 50 years in the history of the na-
tion, the city of Pittsfield, and the Pittsfield
Cooperative Bank, 1889-1939. Pittsfield, 1939.
Unpaged. MPB.

10790 "PITTSFIELD Fire Department, sketch of its
       management, membership and machinery from
1844 to 1904." Berkshire Hills, 4 (1903-1904),
281-284, 296.

10791 "PITTSFIELD in 1846, a bird's-eye view from
       an ancient business corner." Berkshire
Hills, 2 (April 1, 1902), [9-11], (May 1, 1902),
[1-4].

10792 "PITTSFIELD schools in the early days."
       Berkshire Hills, New Ser., 2 (1905-1906),
135-136.
       1747-1845.

10793 "PITTSFIELD: The Electrical City of the
       Berkshires." WNE, 3 (1913), 462-465.

10794 "THE POMEROYS of Pittsfield: Lemuel, the
       pioneer manufacturer and Theodore and Rob-
ert, his notable sons and successors." Berkshire
Hills, 4 (1903-1904), 214-216.
       Woolen manufacture.

10795 PORTER, LEMUEL. History of the Baptist
       Church in Pittsfield from its organization
in 1772 to the present time, October 1, 1853.
Pittsfield: H. A. Marsh, 1853. Pp. 24, 21. MPB.

10796 "A PRINTING house with a history." Ameri-
       can Printer, 82 (January 26, 1926), 30.
       Phinehas Allen.

10797 REYNOLDS, GEORGE STODDARD. "The Berkshire
       Medical Institute." Surgery, Gynecology
and Obstetrics, 67 (1938), 700-703.

10798 ROYCE, J. A. "First fireworks in Pitts-
       field, a pyrotechnic remembrance." Berk-
shire Hills, 2 (December 1, 1901), [11].
       July 4, 1848.

10799 SALISBURY, MARY E. 1867-1898, a backward
       glance. Pittsfield: Miss Salisbury's
School, 1898. Pp. 30. M.
       History of Miss Salisbury's School.

10800 SCHUTT, KATE M. The first century of St.
       Stephen's Parish 1830-1930. Pittsfield,
1930. Pp. 80. MPB.

10801 "SKETCH [of the] history of Pittsfield as
       remembered in 1844." Berkshire Hills, 4
(1903-1904), 193-196.

10802 "SKETCH [of the] history of Pittsfield from
       1734 to 1844." Berkshire Hills, 4 (1903-
1904), 181-184.

10803 SMITH, JOSEPH EDWARD ADAMS, comp. The his-
       tory of Pittsfield, (Berkshire County,)
Massachusetts.... Boston: Lee and Shepard, 1869-
1876. 2v.
       1734-1876; volume 2 published in Spring-
       field by C. W. Bryan.

10804 _____. "Origin of the name of Pittsfield."
       BHSSC, 3 (1899-1913), 7-26.

10805 _____. Park Square, Pittsfield, Mass., an
       interesting history of the progress of the
town since 1760. n.p., [1889?]. Pp. 11. MPB.

10806 _____. The public school system of the
       town of Pittsfield, reviewed from 1761 to
1880. Pittsfield: Pittsfield Sun, 1880. Pp. 43.

10807 "SOME old Pittsfield taverns." Berkshire
       Hills, 4 (1903-1904), 261-265.

10808 SPALDING, C. H. Centennial sermon preached
       at the rededication of the house of worship
of the First Baptist Church, Pittsfield...April 6,
1873. Pittsfield: J. M. Durkee, 1873. Pp. 15.
MPB.

10809 SUN PRINTING CORPORATION, PITTSFIELD, MASS.
       The history of the Sun Printing Corporation,
1800-1954. Pittsfield, [1954?]. Pp. 36. MPB.

10810 STEVENSON AND COMPANY, PITTSFIELD, MASS.
       60th anniversary, May 2, 1927. n.p.,
[1927?]. Unpaged. MPB.
       Insurance agency; chronology.

10811 TAPPAN, GEORGE ARTHUR. "Pittsfield, Gem
       City of the Berkshires." National Magazine,
16 (1902), 358-361.

10812 "TWO pioneer Pittsfield doctors." Berkshire
       Hills, 2 (August 1, 1902), [6-7].
       H. H. Childs and Charles Bailey.

10813 "THE WAVING of the willow by the heavy-
       weights of Pittsfield in 1877." Berkshire
Hills, New Ser., 1 (1904-1905), 1-4.
       Baseball game organized by citizens in which
       all players had to be over 200 pounds.

10814 WEDNESDAY MORNING CLUB, PITTSFIELD, MASS.
        Wednesday Morning Club, 1879-1904. n.p.,
[1904?]. Pp. 50. MPB.

10815 ____. Wednesday Morning Club, 1879-1929.
        n.p., [1929?]. Pp. 56. MPB.

10816 WILLISON, GEORGE FINDLAY. The history of
        Pittsfield, Massachusetts, 1916-1955.
[Pittsfield]: The City, 1957. Pp. 519.

PLAINFIELD

10817 DYER, CHARLES NEWELL. History of the town
        of Plainfield, Hampshire County, Mass.,
from its settlement to 1891, including a genealogical history of twenty-three of the original settlers and their descendants, with anecdotes and
sketches. Northampton: Gazette Printing, 1891.
Pp. 187.

10818 HUDSON, CLARA ELIZABETH. Plain tales from
        Plainfield; or, the way things used to be.
Northampton: Metcalf Printing and Publishing Co.,
1962. Pp. 54.

10819 LAMB, MARTHA J. "Historic homes on golden
        hills." MagAmHist, 17 (1887), 217-232.
Town history; not about houses.

10820 PORTER, JACOB. Topographical description
        and historical sketch of Plainfield, in
Hampshire County, Massachusetts, May, 1834. Greenfield: Prince and Rogers, 1834, Pp. 44.

PLAINVILLE

10821 PLAINVILLE METHODIST CHURCH. Sixtieth an-
        niversary...October 19-26th, 1952. n.p.,
[1952?]. Unpaged. MBNEH.

PLYMOUTH

10822 ABBOT, ABIEL, 1770-1828. A discourse de-
        livered at Plymouth December 22, 1809, at
the celebration of the 188th anniversary of the
landing of our forefathers in that place. Boston:
Greenough and Stebbins, 1810. Pp. 28.

10823 ADADOURIAN, HAIG. 'Dying, and, behold, we
        live,' or, obituaries of some Manomet peo-
ple who entered into their rest between November 4,
1897, and January 9, 1899. Plymouth: Memorial
Pr., 1899. Pp. 50.

10824 ____. Historical address by Rev. Haig
        Adadourian on the occasion of the two-
hundredth anniversary celebration (1738-1938) of
the founding of Second Church of Plymouth, Mass.,
Congregational. Plymouth: Memorial Pr., 1938.
Pp. 10.

10825 ADAMS, HERBERT BAXTER. "Plymouth Rock re-
        stored." MagAmHist, 8 (1882), 789-806, 9
(1883), 31-52.

10826 ADAMS, JOHN QUINCY. An oration, delivered
        at Plymouth, December 22, 1802, at the an-
niversary commemoration of the first landing of our
ancestors, at that place. Boston: Russell and Cutler, 1802. Pp. 31.

10827 ADAMS, THOMAS BOYLSTON. "Of Plimoth Planta-
        tion." MHSP, 75 (1963), 3-9.

10828 BAILEY, RICHARD BRIGGS. "Pilgrim posses-
        sions 1620-1640." Antiques, 61 (1952),
236-239.

10829 BARKER, AMY H. A history of the Plymouth
        Antiquarian Society. Plymouth, 1959. Un-
paged.

10830 BARNES, HOWARD P. "Eel River and Plymouth
        Beach." PSN, No. 8 (August, 1958), 2-11.

10831 BARTLETT, ROBERT MERRILL. "The 1660 Bart-
        lett House." MayflowerQ, 33 (1967), 93-94.

10832 BELCHER, EDWARD R. "Notes on Cole's Hill."
        PSN, No. 1 (September, 1954), 1-12.

10833 BITTINGER, FREDERICK WILLIAM. The story of
        the Pilgrim tercentenary celebration at
Plymouth in the year 1921. Plymouth: Memorial Pr.,
1923. Pp. 155.

10834 BRADFORD, GERSHOM. "The 'Speedwell'--
        another look." AmNep, 22 (1962), 136-141.
Pilgrim ship.

10835 BREWSTER, ELLIS WETHRELL. 125 years of
        rope-making in Plymouth (1834-1949). N.Y.:
Newcomen Society in North America, 1949. Pp. 24.

10836 ____. Plymouth in my father's time. Plym-
        outh: Pilgrim Society, 1968. Pp. 98.

10837 ____. "Thrasherville, an old Plymouth set-
        tlement." PSN, No. 10 (June, 1960), 1-4.

10838 BRIGGS, HELEN T. and ROSE THORNTON BRIGGS.
        A guide to Plymouth and its history, com-
piled from inscriptions on tablets, monuments &
statues erected in honor of its founders, the Pilgrims, or given in prose or verse on occasions of
memorial celebrations. [Plymouth]: Pilgrim Society
and Plymouth Antiquarian Society, 1938. Pp. 54.

10839 BRIGGS, ROSE THORNTON. "The court houses of
        Plymouth." PSN, No. 17 (May, 1966), 1-9.

10840 ____. "Plymouth Rock." MayflowerQ, 34
        (1968), 85-87.

10841 ____. Plymouth Rock: history and signi-
        ficance (1953). Plymouth: Pilgrim Society,
1968. Pp. 20.

10842 _____. "The Pilgrim Society and Pilgrim Hall." NEHGR, 124 (1970), 113-115.

10843 BURBANK, ALFRED STEVENS. A souvenir of Plymouth parks containing a brief history of their acquisition by the town; views of some of the most attractive localities and a map of Morton Park. Plymouth: Burbank, 1901. Unpaged.

10844 BURRAGE, CHAMPLIN. "The earliest minor accounts of Plymouth Plantation." Harvard Theological Review, 13 (1920), 315-344.

10845 CARY, ALICE. "Plymouth, the Pilgrims, and Puritans." National Magazine, 5 (1854), 508-522; 6 (1855), 15-23.

10846 CHAMBERLAIN, DANIEL HENRY. The character and work of the Pilgrims of New England; speech at the annual dinner of the New England Society of Charleston, S.C., Dec. 23, 1889. Charleston, S.C.: E. Perry, 1890. Pp. 10.

10847 COFFIN, H. W. Historical sketch of the First Baptist Church of Christ, in Plymouth, Mass...delivered before the Old Colony Baptist Association, Middleboro', Mass., October 14th, 1885. Plymouth: Avery and Doten, 1885. Pp. 15.

10848 COGSWELL, WILLIAM. "History of the 'Pilgrim Society' with a brief account of the early settlement of Plymouth Colony." American Quarterly Register, 11 (1838-1839), 82-90.

10849 COTTON, JOHN. "An account of the Church of Christ in Plymouth." MHSC, [4], (1795), 107-14; 2 Ser., 3 (1815), 198-204.

10850 COUTER, E. LAWRENCE. "Plimoth Plantation." Mayflower Q, 35 (1969), 71-72. Condensed by Mrs. Robert M. Sherman.

10851 CRANDON, EDWIN SANFORD. Old Plymouth days and ways; eighteenth century celebrations of the landing of the Pilgrims [and] Red men in the Massachusetts colonies...addresses delivered before the Attleboro Community Fellowship, September 12, 1921.... Boston: Rosemary Pr., 1921. Pp. 26. 'Red men in the Massachusetts colonies' is by Charles Dana Burrage.

10852 CROSSMAN, CARL L. and CHARLES R. STRICKLAND. "Early depictions of the landing of the Pilgrims." Antiques, 98 (1970), 776-781.

10853 CUCKSON, JOHN. A brief history of the First Church in Plymouth, from 1606 to 1901. Boston: G. H. Ellis, 1902. Pp. xvi, 118.

10854 CULLEN, JOSEPH P. "Plimouth Plantation." AHI, 8 (July, 1973), 26-35.

10855 CUSHMAN, ROBERT WOODWARD. Plymouth's Rock: 'the rock whence we were hewn,' a discourse delivered in Plymouth at the Cushman festival, August 15th, 1855, on the CCXXXth anniversary of the embarkation of the Pilgrims for America. Boston: J. M. Hewes, 1855. Pp. 31.

10856 DAVIS, WILLIAM THOMAS. Ancient landmarks of Plymouth. Pt. I. Historical sketch and titles of estates. Pt. II. Genealogical register of Plymouth families. (1883) 2d. ed. Boston: Damrell & Upham, 1899. v.p.

10857 _____. Centennial memorial of the Plymouth Bank...June 23, 1803-June 23, 1903. Plymouth: Memorial Pr., 1903. Pp. 70. MB.

10858 _____. History of the town of Plymouth, with a sketch of the origin and growth of separatism. Philadelphia: J. W. Lewis, 1885. Pp. 188.

10859 _____. Plymouth memories of an octogenarian. Plymouth: Memorial Pr., 1906. Pp. 542.

10860 DE COSTA, BENJAMIN FRANKLIN. "Plymouth before the Pilgrims." MagAmHist, 8 (1882), 807-819.

10861 DEETZ, JAMES and JAY ANDERSON. "Ethnogastronomy of Thanksgiving." Saturday Review, 55 (November 25, 1972), 29-39.

10862 DEXTER, MORTON. "Alleged facts as to the Pilgrims." MHSP, 2 Ser., 10 (1895-1896), 257-263.

10863 DIAZ, ABBEY MORTON. "Antislavery times in Plymouth." NEM, New Ser., 20 (1899), 216-224.

10864 "THE DIVISION of Plymouth proposed in 1855 & 1856." PSN, No. 11 (October, 1962), 1-6.

10865 DREW, THOMAS BRADFORD. "The Pilgrim Society and the Monument." NEM, New Ser., 1 (1889-1890), 77-84.

10866 EATON, HOWARD F. "Plymouth's aid to transportation." SWJ, 9 (1911), 176-179.

10867 EATON, WALTER PRICHARD. Plymouth. [N.Y.]: New York, New Haven and Hartford Railroad Company, 1928. Pp. 46.

10868 ELLIOTT, C. WYLLYS. "The 'good old times' at Plymouth." Harper's Magazine, 54 (1877), 180-196.

10869 EVERETT, EDWARD. Remarks at the Plymouth festival, on the first of August, 1853, in commemoration of the embarkation of the Pilgrims. Boston: Crosby, Nichols, 1853. Pp. 18.

10870 FAIRFAX, GRACE BRADFORD. "Governor Bradford's manorial rights." MagAmHist, 26 (1891), 233-234. Land titles.

10871 FLINT, JAMES. A discourse delivered at Plymouth, December 22, 1815, at the anniversary commemoration of the first landing of our ancestors at that place.... Boston: Avery, 1816. Pp. 24.

10872 FRANCIS, CONVERS. A discourse delivered at Plymouth, Mass. Dec. 22, 1832, in commemoration of the landing of the fathers. Plymouth: A. Danforth, 1832. Pp. 56.

10873 GAY, S. H. "When did the Pilgrim Fathers land at Plymouth?" Atlantic, 48 (1881), 612-620.

10874 GOMES, PETER J. "Churches of the not-so-standing order." PSN, No. 18 (September, 1966), 1-14.

10875 GOODWIN, JOHN ABBOT. 'What new doctrines is this?'...'When did the Pilgrim Fathers land at Plymouth?' n.p., [1882]. Pp. 4.

10876 GOODWIN, WILLIAM W. "The landing of the Pilgrims." MHSP, 2 Ser., 17 (1903), 378-382.

10877 _____, ed. "Records of the Old Colony Club." MHSP, 2 Ser., 3 (1886-1887), 381-444.

10878 GOSS, ELBRIDGE HENRY. "The hungry Pilgrims." MagAmHist, 13 (1885), 477-481.

10879 GREAT BRITAIN. ORDNANCE BOARD. Notes regarding the guns of the Mayflower, prepared for the information of the Plymouth Plantation Foundation, Plymouth, Massachusetts, U. S. A. London: O. B. Pr., 1950. Pp. 7.

10880 GREEN, SAMUEL. A discourse, delivered at Plymouth, Dec. 20, 1828, on the two hundred and eighth anniversary of the landing of the Pilgrim Fathers. Boston: Pierce & Williams, 1829. Pp. 36.
    Date in title corrected in ms. to Dec. 22 in Library of Congress copy.

10881 [GREENE, RICHARD HENRY]. List of passengers who came to Plymouth in the 'Mayflower' on her first trip in 1620. New York, 1896. Unpaged.

10882 GREENWOOD, HELEN C. and GLORIA M. CHRISTENSEN. "The Jabez Howland House." MayflowerQ, 35 (1969), 93-94.

10883 GUERNSEY, JESSE. "The first year at Plymouth." Congregational Review, 10 (1870), 227-237.

10884 HALL, LEMUEL C. "The story of Plymouth." CCAPL, 5 (August, 1921), 7-10.

10885 HALL-QUEST, OLGA WILBOURNE. How the Pilgrims came to Plymouth. N.Y.: E. P. Dutton, 1946. Pp. 115.

10886 HANNAH, SAMUEL D. Plymouth Corporation, a trading company, located at Plymouth, a proprietary plantation.... Yarmouthport: C. W. Swift, 1928. Pp. 8.

10887 HARRIS, THADDEUS MASON. A discourse delivered at Plymouth, Dec. 22d., 1808, at the anniversary commemoration of the landing of our ancestors at that place. Boston: Belcher, 1808. Pp. 32.

10888 "HISTORICAL notes on schools in the town of Plymouth." MHSC, 2 Ser., 4 (1816), 86-96. 1670-1771.

10889 "HISTORY of the Pilgrim Society, with a brief account of the early settlement of Plymouth Colony." NEHGR, 1 (1847) 114-125.

10890 HITCHCOCK, GAD. A sermon preached at Plymouth, December 22d., 1774, being the anniversary thanksgiving, in commemoration of the first landing of our New-England ancestors in that place, Anno Dom. 1620. Boston: Edes and Gill, 1775. Pp. 44.

10891 HOAR, GEORGE FRISBIE. Oration delivered at Plymouth, December 21, 1895, at the celebration of the two hundred and seventy-fifth anniversary of the landing of the Pilgrims. Washington: R. H. Darby, 1895. Pp. 18.

10892 HOLISHER, DESIDER. Pilgrims path: the story of Plymouth in words and photographs. N.Y.: Stephen-Paul, 1947. Pp. 109.

10893 HOLMES, KNOWLTON B. "The Plymouth alms house." PSN, No. 2 (November, 1954), 1-3.

10894 HOWARD, ROBERT WEST. "Rope from Plymouth." Am Heritage, 5 (Spring, 1954), 16-19, 51-52.

10895 HOWE, HENRY FORBUSH. Early explorers of Plymouth Harbor, 1525-1619. Plymouth: Plimoth Plantation and the Pilgrim Society, 1953. Pp. 30.

10896 "THE HOWLAND House." MassMag, 4 (1911), 145-146.
    Also called the Carver House.

10897 HUNTINGTON, DANIEL. A discourse, delivered in the North Meeting-House in Bridgewater, on Friday, Dec. 22, 1820, being the second centurial anniversary of the landing of the Pilgrims at Plymouth. Boston: Lincoln, 1821. Pp. 24.

10898 HYDE, ALVAN. A sermon delivered at Lee, December 22nd, 1820, being the two hundredth anniversary of the landing of our ancestors at Plymouth.... Stockbridge: Charles Webster, 1821. Pp. 31.

10899 JAMES, SYDNEY VINCENT, ed. Three visitors to early Plymouth: letters about the Pilgrim settlement in New England during its first seven years, by John Pory, Emmanuel Altham and Isaack de Rasieres. [Plymouth]: Plimoth Plantation, 1963. Pp. xiii, 84.

10900 JENKS, FRED A. "The wharves of Plymouth." PSN, No. 3 (1955), 1-7.

10901 [KALER, JAMES OTIS]. Mary of Plymouth; a story of the Pilgrim settlement. By James Otis, pseud. N.Y.: American Book Co., 1910. Pp. 156.

10902 KINGMAN, BRADFORD. Epitaphs from Burial Hill, Plymouth, Massachusetts, from 1657 to 1892, with biographical and historical notes.... Brookline: New England Illustrated Historical Publishing, 1892. Pp. xv, 330.

10903 KINNICUTT, LINCOLN NEWTON. "The Plymouth settlement and Tisquantum." MHSP, 48 (1914-1915), 103-118.

10904 _____. "Plymouth's debt to the Indians." Harvard Theological Review, 13 (1920), 345-361.

10905 _____. "The settlement at Plymouth contemplated before 1620." American Historical Association. Annual Report, (1920), 209-221.

10906 KYLE, MARGARET. "Sociabilities, customs, and the welcoming door." PSN, No. 13 (August, 1963), 1-10.

10907 LABAREE, JOHN CODMAN. The Plymouth Pilgrims: a sermon preached in the First Church, Randolph, December 25, 1870. Randolph: Mrs. S. P. Brown, 1871. Pp. 20.

10908 LODGE, HENRY CABOT. The Pilgrims of Plymouth: an address at Plymouth, Massachusetts, December 21, 1920, on the three hundredth anniversary of their landing.... Washington: Govt. Print. Off., 1921. Pp. 35.

10909 LORD, ARTHUR. "The Pilgrim's church in Plymouth." NEM, New Ser., 7 (1892-1893), 777-788.
First Church.

10910 _____. Plymouth and the Pilgrims. Boston: Houghton Mifflin, 1920. Pp. 177.

10911 "MANOMET church celebrates century mark." Cape Cod Magazine, 9 (September 15, 1926), 18.
Second Congregational Church.

10912 MARSHALL, GEORGE N., ed. The church of the Pilgrim Fathers. Boston: Beacon Pr., 1950. Pp. xx, 143.

10913 MASSACHUSETTS. PILGRIM TERCENTENARY COMMISSION. Exercises on the three hundredth anniversary of the landing of the Pilgrims, held at Plymouth, Massachusetts, Tuesday, December 21, 1920. [Boston, 1921?]. Pp. 64.

10914 MEMORANDA, historical, chronological... Pilgrim memorials, and history. Boston: Todd, 1870. Pp. 39. M.

10915 MERRICK, DOROTHY D. "A framework for 17th-century Plymouth." PSN, No. 12 (May, 1963), 1-12.

10916 MORISON, SAMUEL ELIOT. "Plymouth Colony beachhead." United States Naval Institute. Proceedings, 80 (1954), 1344-1357.

10917 _____. The ropemakers of Plymouth: a history of the Plymouth Cordage Company, 1824-1949. Boston: Houghton Mifflin, 1950. Pp. vi, 177.

10918 NATIONAL ARCHIVES PROJECT. Ship registers of the district of Plymouth, Massachusetts, 1789-1908. Boston, 1939. Pp. ix, 209 leaves. Index of owners and masters.

10919 NEIL, E. D. "The Plymouth Company's patent." HistMag, 2 Ser., 3 (1868), 278-280.

10920 "NOTES on Plymouth, Massachusetts." MHSC, 2 Ser., 3 (1815), 162-197.

10921 PATTESON, MRS. NATHAN R. "Plymouth and the Mayflower Society house." MayflowerQ, 28 (November, 1962), 9-10.

10922 PERKINS, FRANK H. Handbook of old Burial Hill, Plymouth, Massachusetts: its history, its famous dead, and its quaint epitaphs. (1896) Plymouth: A. S. Burbank, 1902. Pp. 72.

10923 PHILLEO, CALVIN W. "A pilgrimage to Plymouth." Harper's Magazine, 8 (1853), 36-54.

10924 PIERCE, JOHN. "Two anniversaries at Plymouth." MHSP, 2 Ser., 10 (1895-1896), 392-403.
Edited by Charles C. Smith; celebrations of 1820 and 1845 of Pilgrim landing.

10925 PLYMOUTH, MASS. Records of the town of Plymouth. William T. Davis, ed. Plymouth: Avery & Doten, 1889-1903. 3v.
1636-1783; v. 3 published by Memorial Press in Plymouth.

10926 PLYMOUTH, MASS. CHURCH OF THE PILGRIMAGE. Manual of the Church of the Pilgrimage, Plymouth, Mass., 1884. Plymouth: Avery and Doten, 1884. Pp. 92. M.
Includes history.

10927 [PLYMOUTH, MASS. FIRST CHURCH]. Plymouth church records, 1620-1859. [Boston]: The [Colonial] Society [of Massachusetts], 1920-1923. 2v.

10928 _____. 1620-1893, the First Church in Plymouth. Boston: Sparrell Print, 1893. Pp. 12.

10929 PLYMOUTH, MASS. HISTORIC FESTIVAL COMMITTEE. Old Plymouth days and ways; handbook of the historic festival in Plymouth, Massachusetts, July 28, 29, 30, 31, August 2 and 3, MDCCCXCVII. Plymouth, 1897. Pp. 72.

10930 PLYMOUTH, MASS. SECOND CONGREGATIONAL CHURCH. Proceedings of the one hundred and sixtieth anniversary of the Second Congregational Church in Plymouth (Manomet) Mass., held on Nov. 9, 1898.... Haig Adadourian, comp. Plymouth, 1899. Pp. 67.

10931 PLYMOUTH CORDAGE COMPANY. Golden anniversary celebration by the Plymouth Cordage Company in honor of Gideon Francis Holmes, Plymouth, Massachusetts, March twenty-seventh, nineteen hundred and nine. Cambridge: Univ. Pr., 1909. Pp. 150.

10932 _____. One hundredth anniversary of the founding of the Plymouth Cordage Company, 1824-1924, celebration on Thursday, June 12, 1924, at Plymouth, Massachusetts. Cambridge: Univ. Pr., 1924. Pp. 27.

10933 _____. Pilgrim tercentenary: observances at Plymouth, December 21, 1920 and the summer of 1921. [Plymouth?, 1920]. Pp. 15.
Includes a bibliography.

10934 _____. Plymouth Cordage Company, one hundred years of service. Plymouth, 1924. Pp. 100. MBNEH.

10935 _____. Proceedings at its seventy-fifth anniversary, October seventh, MDCCCXCIX, 1824-1899. Cambridge: Univ. Pr., 1900. Pp. ii, 62.

10936 "PLYMOUTH Cordage Comapny." Industry, 1 (November, 1935), 3-5.

10937 PLYMOUTH NATIONAL BANK. Centennial memorial of the Plymouth Bank and the Plymouth National Bank of Plymouth, Mass., June 23, 1803-June 23, 1903. Plymouth: Memorial Pr., 1903. Pp. 71. M.

10938 _____. Plymouth, yesterday and today, 1803-1953.... Plymouth, 1953. Unpaged. M.

10939 _____. This book serves to commemorate the founding of the Plymouth Bank and Plymouth National Bank, one hundred and twenty five years ago, 1803-1928. Plymouth, 1928. Unpaged. M.

10940 PRATT, WALDO SELDEN. "The earliest New England music." UHSP, 1, Pt. 2 (1928), 28-47.

10941 _____. The music of the Pilgrims: a description of the psalm-book brought to Plymouth in 1620. Boston: Oliver Ditson, 1912. Pp. 80.

10942 PRATT, WALTER MERRIAM. The Mayflower Society house, being the story of the Edward Winslow House, the Mayflower Society [and] the Pilgrims. 2d. ed. Cambridge: Univ. Pr., 1950. Pp. 32.

10943 PRENDERGAST, FRANK M. "America's home town." Industry, 15 (September, 1950), 9-13.
Industry.

10944 PYLE, ARTHUR G. "Eel River Massacre at Plymouth--1676." PSN, No. 6 (March, 1956), 1-4.

10945 RAYMOND, PERCY E. "Latten spoons of the Pilgrims." Antiques, 61 (1952), 242-244.

10946 ROBBINS, CHANDLER, 1738-1799. Sermon preached at Plymouth, December 22, 1793; being the anniversary of the landing of our ancestors in that place, in 1620.... Printed at Boston--Stockbridge: Re-printed by Loring Andrews, 1796. Pp. 46.

10947 ROYAL, HENRY WASSON. The Pilgrims & early Plymouth, an address. Plymouth: Pilgrim Society, [19--]. Pp. 12.

10948 RUSSELL, ALLEN D. "America's oldest court house." MayflowerQ, 34 (1968), 59-60. Country House, 1686.

10949 _____. "Of ships and shoes and 'ceiling' wax: Plymouth, 1800-1850." PSN, No. 15 (March, 1965), 1-15.
General history.

10950 RUSSELL, FRANCIS. "The Pilgrims and the Rock." Am Heritage, 13 (October, 1962), 48-55.

10951 RUSSELL, WILLIAM SHAW. Guide to Plymouth, and recollections of the Pilgrims. Boston: G. Coolidge, 1846. v.p.

10952 RUTMAN, DARRETT BRUCE. Husbandmen of Plymouth: farms and villages in the Old Colony, 1620-1692. Boston: Beacon Pr., 1967. Pp. xi, 100.

10953 SACCO, NICOLA, DEFENDANT. The Sacco-Vanzetti case...supplemental volume, including Bridgewater case available material. (1929) Mamaroneck, N.Y.: P. P. Appel, 1969. Pp. 524.
Trial in Plymouth, June-July 1920 for attempted robbery in Bridgewater in December, 1919.

10954 SHERMAN, MRS. ROBERT M. "The Mayflower Society house." MayflowerQ, 34 (1968), 90-94. Edward Winslow House.

10955 _____. and MRS. HAROLD P. WILLIAMS. "The Mayflower Society house: owners and furnishings." MayflowerQ, 34, (1968), 124-127. Edward Winslow House.

10956 SHERRILL, E. PRESCOTT. The house of Edward Winslow.... Plymouth: Priv. Print., 1931. Pp. 28. MBSpnea.

10957 SHURTLEFF, NATHANIEL BRADSTREET. "The passengers of the Mayflower in 1620." NEHGR, 1 (1847), 47-53.

10958 SUMNER, CHARLES. A finger point from Plymouth Rock, remarks at the Plymouth Festival, on the 1st of August, 1853. Boston: Crosby, 1853. Pp. 11. MB.

10959 STODDARD, FRANCIS RUSSELL, JR. "The old Thomas House at Plymouth." MassMag, 3 (1910), 269-271.

10960 _____. "The old Warren House at Plymouth." MassMag, 4 (1911), 105-109.

10961 STRICKLAND, CHARLES RUTAN. "The first permanent dwellings at Plimoth Plantation." OTNE, 40 (1949-1950), 163-169.

10962 TAYLOR, SARAH WINGATE. Clark's in Plymouth Harbor: the Pilgrim Fathers' island, 1620-1690. Peterborough, N.H.: R. R. Smith, 1965. Pp. 37.
Narrative verse.

10963 THACHER, JAMES. History of the town of Plymouth, from its first settlement in 1620, to the present time: with a concise history of the aborigines of New England, and their wars with the English, &c. (1832), 2d. ed., enl. and corrected. Boston: Marsh, Capen & Lyon, 1835. Pp. iv, 401.

10964 THEY knew they were Pilgrims: essays in Plymouth history. Lawrence D. Geller, ed. N.Y.: Poseidon Books, c1971. Pp. 213.

10965 TIFFANY, NINA MOORE. Pilgrims and Puritans: the story of the planting of Plymouth and Boston. Boston: Ginn, 1888. Pp. 197.

10966 TITUS, ANSON. "The Howland House, Plymouth, Mass." MagHist, 13 (1911), 40-41.

10967 TRUMBULL, HENRY. History of the Indian wars; to which is prefixed a short account of the discovery of America by Columbus, and of the landing of our forefathers at Plymouth, with their most remarkable fngagements [sic] with the Indians in New England, from their first landing, in 1620, until the death of King Philip in 1679.... ([1802?]) Eleazer G. House, ed. New ed. Philadelphia: T. Cowperthwait, 1847. Pp. viii, 320.

10968 UPTON, D. T. "Prophesying at Plymouth." OPOCS, No. 3 (December, 1972), 12-22. Church history.

10969 VAN WYE, EUGENE. "Pilgrim chickens." MayflowerQ, 37 (1971), 54.

10970 WAKEFIELD, ROBERT S. "The 1623 Plymouth land division." MayflowerQ, 40 (1974), 7-13.

10971 WEST, SAMUEL. An anniversary sermon preached at Plymouth, December 22d, 1777, in grateful memory of the first landing of our pious New-England ancestors in that place, A. D. 1620. Boston: Draper and Folsom, 1778. Pp. 79.

10972 "WHAT 125 years have wrought in Plymouth." Industry, 14 (August, 1949), 21-23, 38-39. Plymouth Cordage Co.

10973 WILLIAMS, ELSIE B. "The Pilgrim women." MayflowerQ, 39 (1973), 47-51.

10974 "THE WINSLOW House." MassMag, 5 (1912), 102-104.

10975 WINTHROP, ROBERT CHARLES. Oration on the two hundred and fiftieth anniversary of the landing of the Pilgrim fathers at Plymouth, 21 December, 1870. Boston: J. Wilson and Son, 1871. Pp. 93.
Another printing, dated the same year, has 87 pages.

10976 "WINTHROP and Emerson on Forefathers Day." New Englander, 30 (1871), 175-202. Robert C. Winthrop and Ralph Waldo Emerson.

10977 WOOD, JOHN SUMNER. Cupid's path in ancient Plymouth: the last Pilgrim houses. [Rockville, Md., 1957]. Pp. xvi, 112.

PLYMPTON

10978 "HISTORY and description of Plympton, 1815." MHSC, 2 Ser., 4 (1816), 267-271.

10979 LORIMER, JOHN G. History of Plympton, county of Plymouth, state of Massachusetts, a concise and authentic narrative from its earliest settlement to the present time. Boston: Addison H. Getchell, 1896. Pp. 55. MBNEH.

10980 SHERMAN, JOHN. Historical address read at the 200th anniversary of the town of Plympton, August 8, 1907. Plymouth: Bittinger Bros., 1907. Pp. 14.

PRINCETON

10981 BLAKE, FRANCIS EVERETT. History of the town of Princeton, in the county of Worcester and Commonwealth of Massachusetts, 1759-1915. Princeton: The Town, 1915. 2v.
Includes a bibliography.

10982 HANAFORD, JEREMIAH LYFORD. History of Princton, Worcester County, Massachusetts, civil and ecclesiastical, from its first settlement in 1739, to April 1852. Worcester: C. Buckingham Webb, 1852. Pp. viii, 204.

10983 HITCHCOCK, JOHN H. "Wachusett Mountain, landmark of the past, challenge for the future." Appalachia, New Ser., 37 (June 15, 1971), 5-33.

10984 JACKSON, HELEN MARIA FISKE HUNT. "Hide and seek town." Scribner's Monthly, 12 (1876), 449-461.

10985 MASON, ATHERTON P. "Wachusett Mountain and Princeton." BSM, 2 (1884-1885), 35-40.

10986 PRINCETON, MASS. Celebration of the one hundredth anniversary of the incorporation of the town of Princeton, Mass., October 20th, 1859, including the address of Hon. Charles Theodore Russell, the poem of Prof. Erastus Everett, and other exercises of the occasion.... Worcester: Wm. R. Hooper, 1860. Pp. 119.

10987   PRINCETON, MASS. FIRST CONGREGATIONAL
         CHURCH. The history, articles of faith,
covenant and standing rules of the First Congregational Church in Princeton, Mass.... Worcester:
Henry J. Howland, [1859]. Pp. 14. MWA.

10988   RUSSELL, CHARLES THEODORE. The history of
         Princeton, Worcester County, Mass. from its
first settlement, with a sketch of the present religious controversy in that place. Boston: Henry
P. Lewis, 1838. Pp. viii, 130.

PROVINCETOWN

10989   AIKEN, MARY HOOVER. "Provincetown: long
         ago and far away." CCC, 14 (1961), 3-5.
         Railroad.

10990   CARPENTER, EDMUND JANES. The Pilgrims and
         their monument. N.Y.: D. Appleton, 1911.
Pp. x, 309.

10991   ____. "Provincetown, the tip of the Cape."
         NEM, New Ser., 22 (1900), 533-548.

10992   CLARK, BARRETT HARPER. "An eventful month
         in the theatre: end of the Provincetown
Playhouse.". Drama, 20 (February, 1930), 137-138.

10993   CLARK-SMALL, CARRIE W. "Early private
         schools." CCAPL, 5 (Mid-July, 1921), 9-11.

10994   CLARKE, EVERETT LADD. "Provincetown."
         NEM, 47 (1912), 60-70.

10995   CROTTY, FRANK. Provincetown profiles and
         others on Cape Cod. Barre: Barre Gazette,
1958. Pp. 146.
         Biographies.

10996   DEUTSCH, HELEN and STELLA HANAU. The Prov-
         incetown: a story of the theatre. N.Y.:
Farrar & Rinehart, 1931. Pp. xvi, 313.

10997   DEUTSCH, HELEN. "When the Provincetown
         group began." Drama, 21 (June, 1931), 3-4,
6, 9-11.

10998   EAMES, THOMAS HARRISON. "The wreck of the
         steamer 'Portland.'" NEQ, 13 (1940), 191-
206.
         1898.

10999   [FULLER, CORA GRAY WEST]. Official program
         of the dedicatory exercises attendant upon
the laying of the cornerstone of the Pilgrim Monument at Provincetown, Massachusetts, on August 20,
1907. Provincetown: Provincetown Beacon Pr.,
1907. Pp. 61.
         Program occupies only a portion of the
         inside of the lower cover; includes chron-
         ology of the town and a 'Cape Cod handbook
         of history.'

11000   GROZIER, EDWIN ATKINS. The Pilgrim Monu-
         ment, marking the first landing place of
the Pilgrim Fathers at Provincetown, Mass., November 11, 1620.... [Provincetown?, 1920]. Pp. 7.

11001   HARE, MAUD C. "Portuguese folk-songs from
         Provincetown." Musical Quarterly, 14
(1928), 35-53.

11002   HAWTHORNE, ROGER. "The Provincetown Art
         Association." American Artist, 25 (June,
1961), 36-41, 82-83.

11003   HUNTINGTON, CATHARINE. "O'Neill and the
         playhouse in Provincetown." CCC, 9 (1954),
37-38.

11004   ____. "Tradition at the Provincetown
         theatre." CCC, 4 (1949), 25-27.

11005   JENNINGS, HERMAN ATWELL. Chequocket or Coa-
         tuit; the aboriginal name of Provincetown.
Yarmouthport: Cape Cod Item Job Print Office, 1885.
Pp. 72. MWA.

11006   ____. Provincetown: or, odds and ends
         from the tip end: a brief historical de-
scription of Provincetown, past and present....
Yarmouthport: F. Hallett, 1890. Pp. 212.

11007   MOFFETT, ROSS. Art in narrow streets, the
         first thirty-three years of the Provincetown
Art Association. Falmouth: Kendall Printing, 1964.
Pp. 110. [MBaC].

11008   PROVINCETOWN, MASS. The 200th anniversary
         celebration of Provincetown, 1727-1927.
n.p., [1927]. Pp. 16. M.
         Includes history by Nancy W. Paine Smith.

11009   PROVINCETOWN, MASS. CENTRE METHODIST EPIS-
         COPAL CHURCH. Manual of the Centre Meth-
odist Episcopal Church of Provincetown, Mass.,
April 4, 1883. Boston: Deland and Barta, 1883.
Pp. 46. M.
         Includes historical sketch.

11010   PROVINCETOWN, MASS. FIRST NATIONAL BANK.
         One hundred years of growing with Province-
town, 1854-1954. Provincetown, 1954. Pp. 31. MB.

11011   QUINN, DAVID B. "Martin Pring at Province-
         town in 1603?" NEQ, 40 (1967), 79-91.

11012   SHERMAN, HARRY B. "The first New England
         sabbath." MayflowerQ, 11 (April 15, 1946),
3-4.

11013   SMITH, NANCY W. PAINE. "Fanlighted doorways
         of Provincetown." Cape Cod Magazine, 9
(January, 1927), 12.

11014   ____. The Provincetown book. Brockton:
         Tolman Print, 1922. Pp. 260.

11015   SMITH, SIMEON C. Leaves from an old church
         record book. Boston: Universalist Pub-
lishing House, 1922. Pp. 48. MBNEH.
         Universalist Church.

11016   SMYTH, THOMAS. Who owns the province
         lands, the Commonwealth or its tenants?
[Boston?, 1890?]. Pp. 16.

11017 [SYLVESTER, HENRY HARLOW]. Provincetown. Provincetown, 1881. Pp. 24.

11018 VORSE, MARY MARVIN HEATON. Time and the town, a Provincetown chronicle. N.Y.: Dial Pr., 1942. Pp. vii, 372.

11019 WILSON, HAROLD C. "Gosnold at Provincetown, 1602?" DCI, 13 (1971-1972), 109-114.

QUINCY

11020 ADAMS, CHARLES FRANCIS, 1835-1915. Address of Charles Francis Adams, Jr., and proceedings at the dedication of the Crane Memorial Hall, at Quincy, Mass., May 30, 1882.... Cambridge: J. Wilson and Son, 1883. Pp. 48.

11021 _____. The centennial milestone: an address in commemoration of the one hundredth anniversary of the incorporation of Quincy, Mass., delivered July 4, 1892. Cambridge: J. Wilson and Son, 1892. Pp. 59.

11022 _____. "The may pole of Merrymount." Atlantic, 39 (1877), 557-567, 686-697.

11023 _____. "Municipal government: lessons from the experience of Quincy, Massachusetts." Forum, 14 (1892-1893), 282-292.

11024 ADAMS, HENRY, II. "The Adams Mansion: the home of Presidents John Adams and John Quincy Adams." OTNE, 19 (1928-1929), 3-17.

11025 _____. "The birthplaces of Presidents John and John Quincy Adams, Quincy, Massachusetts." OTNE, 26 (1935-1936), 79-99.

11026 ATWOOD, WILLIAM T. "Quincy, city of progress." NEM, New Ser., 43 (1910-1911), 163-170.

11027 BARTLETT, MARTHA MAUDE. Ancient and modern Germantown. [Miami?], 1949. Unpaged.

11028 BEALS, CARLETON. "The rebels of Merry Mount." Am Heritage, 6 (June, 1955), 56-59, 101.

11029 BLOOD, W. H., JR. "The first railway in America." SWJ, 42 (1928), 163-171. 1826.

11030 BONSALL, GEORGE HICKMAN. Quincy Savings Bank, Quincy, Massachusetts; a brief history of its one hundred years of existence, 1845-1945. [Quincy]: Colmar Pr., 1945. Pp. 39.

11031 BRETT, JOSEPH E. Fifty years of Elkdom in Quincy. [Quincy]: Quincy, Massachusetts Lodge 943 of the Benevolent and Protective Order of Elks of the United States of America, 1955. Pp. 117. M.

11032 CAMERON, JAMES REESE. Eastern Nazarene College: the first fifty years, 1900-1950. Kansas City, Mo.: Nazarene Publishing, 1968. Pp. 420.

11033 "CELEBRATION of America's first railway." RLHSB, No. 11 (1926), 6-9. Granite Railway Co.

11034 CLARKE, BRADLEY H. South Shore: Quincy-Boston. Rolling stock and early historical research by Francis J. Cheney. Cambridge: Boston Street Railway Association, 1972. Pp. 44.

11035 "THE COLONEL Josiah Quincy Homestead, Wollaston, Quincy, Mass." OTNE, 28 (1937-1938), 85-89.

11036 COYLE, EDITH WOODBURY. "The Quincy Homestead." OTNE, 19 (1928-1929), 147-158.

11037 CRANE, FRANK FESSENDEN. "Quincy's waterfront." NEM, New Ser., 43 (1910-1911), 171-175.

11038 CUSHING, ARTHUR BOARDMAN. "The Dorothy Quincy Homestead, Quincy, Mass." MassMag, 4 (1911), 96-98.

11039 CUTLER, BENJAMIN CLARKE. A sermon preached in Christ Church, Quincy, on completing a century since its formation, on Christmas Day, 1827. Cambridge: Hilliard, Metcalf, 1828. Pp. 28.

11040 DRAKE, SAMUEL ADAMS. "The Quincy Mansion." Appleton's Journal, 14 (1875), 161-162.

11041 EDWARDS, WILLIAM CHURCHILL and FREDERICK A. COATES. City of Quincy, Massachusetts, 1625-1940. Quincy: Golden Print, 1940. Unpaged.

11042 EDWARDS WILLIAM CHURCHILL. Historic Quincy, Massachusetts. (1946) 3d. ed. [Quincy]: The City, 1957. Pp. 415.

11043 ELKS, BENEVOLENT AND PROTECTIVE ORDER OF, QUINCY, MASS., LODGE NO. 943. Historical sketch of the city of Quincy (the Granite City). Illustrated souvenir...sixtieth annual convention of Grand Lodge, B.P.O.E., Boston, Mass. n.p., 1924. Pp. 104. M.

11044 FAXON, ANNIE E. A brief history of physicians of Quincy, Massachusetts, from 1700 to 1906. Quincy: Geo. W. Prescott & Sons, [1906?]. Pp. 54.

11045 _____. A brief record of the physicians of Quincy, Massachusetts, from the earliest times. Boston: Rockwell and Churchill, 1890. Pp. 31.

11046 GARRETT, WENDELL D. "History in houses: the Adams National Historic Site." Antiques, 80 (1961), 248-251.

11047 GRANITE RAILWAY COMPANY. The first railroad in America, a history of the origin and development of the Granite Railway at Quincy, Massachusetts. [Boston]: Priv. Print., 1926. Pp. 29.

11048 ____. History of the Granite Railway Company, including granite quarries at Quincy, Mass., and Concord, N.H., with the charter and by-laws of the company, and a list of its officers. Capital stock, 250,000.... Boston: A. Mudge & Son, 1870. Pp. 21.

11049 GREGORY, JOHN. Commemorative address to the young men of Quincy pronounced May 25, 1840 on the second centennial anniversary of the incorporation of the town. Quincy: John A. Green, 1840. Pp. 28. MB.

11050 HANCOCK, JOHN, 1702-1744. A memorial of God's goodness, being the substance of two sermons, preach'd in the First Church of Christ in Braintree, Sept. 16th, 1739, on compleating the first century since the gathering of it.... Boston: S. Kneeland & T. Green, 1739. Pp. ii, 37.

11051 HILL, L. DRAPER. The Crane Library. Quincy: Trustees of the Thomas Crane Public Library, 1962. Pp. 32.

11052 HOEHN, WILLIAM FREDERIC, et al. No-license in Quincy: being a review of the early agitation of temperance and a record of the work of the Citizens' No-License Committee from 1882 to 1899: also, 'A century of temperance', and a life of Henry Hardwick Faxon. Quincy: Eastern Printing and Engraving, 1899. Pp. xii, 137.

11053 HOGAN, J. H. Directory and history of Quincy, Mass.... Plymouth: Avery & Doten, 1888. Pp. 329.

11054 "THE JOHN Adams Homestead." MassMag, 1 (1908), 21-23.

11055 KATZ, MICHAEL B. "The 'new departure' in Quincy, 1873-1881: the nature of nineteenth-century educational reform." NEQ, 40 (1967), 3-30.

11056 KLEIN, FRANK A. "Vanguard masters." American-German Review, 9 (1943), 15-17, 37. Granite industry.

11057 KYPER, FRANK. "The Quincy Center disaster: the day they failed to remove the track jack." RLHSB, No. 123 (1970), 62-67. Train derailment, 1890.

11058 LAING, DOROTHY T. and RUTH H. WAINWRIGHT. Hough's Neck history: fact and fiction, character and characters and Atherton Hough, a Puritan's progress. [Quincy]: Atherton Hough Parent Teachers Association, 1958. Pp. 19. M.

11059 LUNT, WILLIAM PARSONS. Two discourses, delivered September 29, 1839, on occasion of the two hundredth anniversary of the gathering of the First Congregational Church, Quincy, with an appendix. Boston: James Munroe, 1840. Pp. 147.

11060 MCCAIN, REA. "Merry Mount: an American folk tale." English Journal, 26 (1937), 205-214. Seventeenth century.

11061 MACEWAN, E. J. "Industry's map of Massachusetts, Quincy." Industry, 3 (February, 1938), 17-18, 43-44.

11062 NORTHROP, BIRDSEY G. New departure. New Haven: Tuttle, Morehouse, & Taylor, 1881. Pp. 24. MB. Public schools.

11063 PARKER, FRANCIS W. "The Quincy method." AmJSoc, 6 (1900-1901), 114-120. Education.

11064 "PNEUMATIC Scale Corporation." Industry, 4 (December, 1938), 7-10, 44-45. Food packaging equipment.

11065 PRENDERGAST, FRANK M. "Built to endure." Industry, 17 (April, 1952), 17-20. Brooks-Skinner Co.; pre-fabricated housing.

11066 QUINCY, MASS. FIRST CHURCH OF CHRIST. The 'chappel of ease' and church of statesmen, commemorative services at the completion of two hundred and fifty years since the gathering of the First Church of Christ in Quincy.... Daniel Munro Wilson, comp. [Quincy], 1890. Pp. viii, 159.

11067 QUINCY HISTORICAL SOCIETY. The President John Adams and President John Quincy Adams birthplaces, Quincy, Massachusetts: their origin, early history, and changes down to the present time. Waldo Chamberlain Sprague, comp. (1954) Rev. ed. Quincy, 1964. Unpaged. M.

11068 ____. Quincy, Massachusetts: historical information.... [Quincy], 1921. Pp. 30.

11069 SAILORS' SNUG HARBOR, QUINCY. The sailors' snug harbor of Boston: its origin and condition. Boston: Hewes, 1860. Pp. 24. A home for retired sailors.

11070 "SPEAKING of symbols and cymbals." Industry, 32 (April, 1967), 34-36. Avedis Zildjian Co.

11071 "SUOMAILAISET Quincyssa, Mass." Jouluviesti, (1907), 18-23. Title: 'Finns of Quincy, Massachusetts.'

11072 THOMAS, WILLIAM R. A brief historical sketch of the city of Quincy, Mass. Boston: E. P. Whitcomb, [1903?]. Pp. 32. MBNEH.

11073 UNDERWOOD, E. W. Rebellion record of the town of Quincy, an alphabetically arranged record of each resident of Quincy who has served in the Army and Navy of the United States during the late rebellion.... Boston: J. E. Farwell, 1866. Pp. 57. MHi.

11074 WALKER, WILLISTON. "A study of a New England town." Yale Review, 1 (1893), 268-280.

11075 WHITNEY, ARTHUR BRYANT. "Quincy, 300 years of independence." UHSP, 6, Pt. 2 (1939), 13-20.

11076   WHITNEY, FREDERICK A.   "A church of the
        First Congregational (Unitarian) Society in
Quincy, Mass. built in 1732." NEHGR, 18 (1864),
117-131.

11077   WHITNEY, GEORGE.   A commemorative discourse
        pronounced at Quincy, Mass., 25 May, 1840,
on the second centennial anniversary of the ancient
incorporation of the town.... Boston: James Munroe, 1840. Pp. 71.

11078   _____. Some account of the early history
        and present state of the town of Quincy, in
the Commonwealth of Massachusetts. [Boston]:
Christian Register Office, 1827. Pp. 64.

11079   WILSON, DANIEL MUNRO. Quincy, old Brain-
        tree, and Merry-Mount: an illustrated
sketch. Boston: G. H. Ellis, 1906. Pp. 64.

11080   _____. Where American independence began:
        Quincy, its famous group of patriots, their
deeds, homes, and descendants (1902) 2d. ed.
Boston: Houghton Mifflin, 1904. Pp. xxix, 327.
MB.

RANDOLPH

11081   BEAL, JOHN V. Randolph's centennial cele-
        bration: an address in commemoration of
the 100th anniversary of the incorporation of Randolph, Mass., delivered July 19, 1893. Randolph:
Randolph Register and Holbrook News, 1897. Pp. 42.

11082   BUTMAN, HARRY R. History of Randolph, Mas-
        sachusetts from earliest settlement to the
present time. Brockton: Standard-Modern Printing,
[1953?]. Pp. 95. MBNEH.

11083   RANDOLPH, MASS. An account of the centen-
        nial celebration...July 19, 1893. Ran-
dolph: Randolph Register and Holbrook News, 1897.
Pp. 80. MBNEH.

11084   NO ENTRY

11085   RANDOLPH, MASS. FIRST CONGREGATIONAL
        CHURCH. Manual of the First Congregational
Church in Randolph, with historical sketches....
Randolph: Samuel P. Brown, 1862. Pp. 43. MBNEH.

11086   _____. Proceedings at the one hundred and
        fiftieth anniversary of the organization of
the First Congregational Church, Randolph, Mass.,
Wednesday, June 8th, 1881. Boston: Thomas Todd,
1881. Pp. 150.

11087   RANDOLPH, MASS. NORTH BAPTIST CHURCH.
        Memorial...semicentennial celebration,
November 7, 1869. Randolph: S. P. Brown, 1870.
Pp. 65, 21. MBNEH.

11088   RANDOLPH, MASS. 175TH ANNIVERSARY COMMIT-
        TEE. Randolph, Mass., 175th anniversary,
1793-1968. n.p., [1968]. Pp. 20. M.
        Includes history by James Reese Cameron.

RAYNHAM

11089   LINCOLN, MARY E. "Raynham recollections."
        MagHist, 10 (1909), 86-93.

11090   SANFORD, ENOCH. History of Raynham, Mass.,
        from the first settlement to the present
time. Providence: Hammond, Angell, 1870.
Pp. 51.

11091   _____. History of the First Church and
        Society in Raynham, in two discourses, de-
livered January 1, 1832.... Taunton: Edmund Anthony, 1832. Pp. 24. MB.

READING

11092   BANCROFT, EDITH. First Congregational
        Church in Reading, 1770-1945; its history
as found in ancient record and present memory.
Reading, 1945. Pp. 36. [MRead].

11093   BARCLAY, MIRIAM. "Daniel Pratt, Jr., Read-
        ing (Mass.) clockmaker." National Associa-
tion of Watch & Clock Collectors. Bulletin, No. 2
(Summer, 1964), Supplement. Pp. 23.

11094   BISHOP, CHARLES NELSON, ed. Reading reflec-
        tions. Reading: Reading Chronicle Pr.,
1960. Pp. 60. [MRead].

11094A   _____. and ELEANOR C. BISHOP. Reading's
         colonial rooftrees built before 1800. Read-
ing: [Reading Chronicle Pr.], 1944. Unpaged.
MBNEH.
        Historic houses.

11095   _____. and _____. Schoolhouse for 96 years:
        three R's at Hill End. Reading, 1949.
Pp. 14. MBNEH.
        Chestnut Hill School.

11096   BISHOP, ELEANOR C., CHARLES NELSON BISHOP,
        and VICTOR E. PITKIN. Vignettes of Reading
history. n.p., [1944]. Pp. 146. MBNEH.

11097   BURHOE, WINSLOW P. 300 years of Reading
        Baptists. Reading: Chronicle Pr., 1948.
Pp. 72. [MRead].

11098   DINAN, MARY KELEHER. The golden jubilee,
        souvenir booklet; fiftieth anniversary of
St. Agnes Parish, Reading, Mass., 1904-1954.
Reading: Chronicle Pr., 1954. Unpaged. [MRead].

11099   HALL, JOHN PHILIP. "The journal of James
        Weston, cordwainer, of Reading, Massachu-
setts, 1788-1793." EIHC, 92 (1956), 189-202.
        Account based on the journal.

11100   _____. "Shoemaking in the post-Revolution-
        ary period: the business records of three
cordwainers of Reading, Massachusetts." BBHS, 25
(1951), 169-187.
        James Weston, John Goodwin, Jr. and John
        Johnson.

11101 HOWARD, LOEA PARKER. Ancient Redding in Massachusetts Bay Colony: its planting as a Puritan village and sketches of its early settlers from 1639 to 1652. Boston: Thomas Todd, 1944. Pp. viii, 56.

11102 _____. The beginning of Reading and Lynnfield, Massachusetts. Reading: Reading Chronicle, 1937. Pp. 33.

11103 _____. Early homesteads on Washington--High--Grove Streets in Reading, Mass. Reading: Reading Chronicle Pr., 1946. Unpaged. [MRead].

11104 _____. The Parker Tavern: being an account of a most interesting house built by Abraham Bryant in 1694, together with some facts about early owners. Reading: Reading Antiquarian Society, 1930. Pp. 31.

11104 _____. The Parker Tavern: being an account of a most interesting house built by Abraham Bryant in 1694, together with some facts about early owners. Reading: Reading Antiquarian Society, 1930. Pp. 31.

11105 _____. Reading men in the early colonial wars. Reading: Reading Chronicle Pr., 1934. Pp. xii, 35.

11106 MUNSTERBERG, MARGARET. "Documents of a New England town." More Books, 5 (1930), 305-312.

11107 PITKIN, VICTOR E. Story of Reading government. Reading: Reading Chronicle Pr., 1940. Pp. vi, 118. [MRead].

11108 READING, MASS. Historical address and poem, delivered at the bi-centennial celebration of the incorporation of the old town of Reading May 29, 1844, with an appendix. Boston: Samuel N. Dickinson, 1844. Pp. 131.
      Address by James Flint, poem by Lilley Eaton.

11109 READING, MASS. OLD SOUTH CHURCH. Manual of the Old South Church, Reading, Mass., adopted by votes of the church, July, 1873. Boston: T. Todd, 1873. Pp. 34. M.
      Includes a brief history.

11110 WADLIN, HORACE GREELEY. Old Parker Tavern. Reading, 1916. Pp. 27. M.

REHOBOTH

11111 ARNOLD, JAMES NEWELL. Vital record of Rehoboth, 1642-1896: marriages, intentions, births, deaths, with supplement containing the record of 1896, colonial returns, lists of the early settlers, purchasers, freemen, inhabitants, the soldiers serving in Philip's War and the Revolution. Providence, R.I.: Narragansett Historical Publishing, 1897. Pp. xxxvii, 926.

11112 BOWEN, RICHARD LE BARON. Early Rehoboth, documented historical studies of families and events in this Plymouth Colony township. Rehoboth: Priv. Print., 1945-1950. 7v.

11113 GOODELL, AKNER CHENEY, JR. "The Continental Congress in Rehoboth." Old Colony HSC, No. 5 (1895), 46-58.
      1709.

11114 [PERRY, EDGAR]. Historic Rehoboth: record of the dedication of Goff Memorial Hall, May 10th, A. D. 1886.... Attleborough: Perry & Barnes, 1886. Pp. 130.

11115 REHOBOTH, MASS. Historical addresses, poem, and other exercises at the celebration of the two hundred and fiftieth anniversary of the settlement of Rehoboth, Mass., held October 3, 1894. Thomas W. Bicknell, ed. [n.p., 1894?]. Pp. 157.

11116 REHOBOTH, MASS. 325TH ANNIVERSARY CELEBRATION COMMITTEE. BROCHURE COMMITTEE. Rehoboth, 325th anniversary. n.p., [1968?]. Pp. 98. MB.

11117 THOMPSON, OTIS. A sermon, preached November 29, 1821, the day which completed one hundred years since the organization of the Congregational Church in Rehoboth, Mass. Taunton: A. Danforth, 1821. Pp. 23.

11118 TILTON, GEORGE HENRY. A history of Rehoboth, Massachusetts: its history for 275 years, 1643-1918, in which is incorporated the vital parts of the original history of the town, published in 1836, and written by Leonard Bliss, Jr. Boston: 1918. Pp. x, 417.

11119 TRIM, ANNAMAE SECOR. "Rehoboth and public education." MayflowerQ, 38 (1972), 52.

REVERE

11120 ADAMS, CHARLES FRANCIS, 1835-1915. "The Revere catastrophe, 1871." Atlantic, 37 (1876), 92-103.
      Train wreck.

11121 [FULLER, HENRY WELD]. The Woodlawn Cemetery in North Chelsea and Malden.... Boston: Higgins and Bradley, 1856. Pp. viii, 125.

11122 HOLBROOK, STEWART H. "The great rail wreck at Revere." Am Heritage, 8 (April, 1957), 26-29, 104-105.
      1871.

11123 MCKAY, ROBERT D. Battle of Chelsea Creek, an account of the second engagement of the American Revolution, May 27, 1775. Chelsea, 1925. Pp. 35. MBNEH.

11124 REVERE, MASS. FIRST CHURCH. Celebrating 200th anniversary of first church building in Revere, Chelsea, and Winthrop, originally known as the First Church of Christ in Rumney Marsh...now

(REVERE, MASS. FIRST CHURCH).
called the First Church in Revere and conducted by
the First Unitarian Society. n.p., [1910?].
Pp. 24. MBNEH.

11125   SHURTLEFF, BENJAMIN, comp. The history of
        the town of Revere. Boston: Beckler Pr.,
1938. Pp. 618.

11126   TUCKERMAN, JOSEPH. A sermon preached on
        the twentieth anniversary of his ordina-
tion, with history of the First Unitarian Church
in Revere, Mass. Boston: Phelps and Farnham,
1821. Pp. 18. M.

RICHMOND

11127   ANNIN, KATHARINE HUNTINGTON. Richmond,
        Massachusetts: the story of a Berkshire
town and its people, 1765-1965. [Richmond]:
Richmond Civic Association, 1964. Pp. xiii, 214.

11128   GIBBS, REBECCA WHITEHEAD. Richmond looks
        backward. Los Gatos, Calif.: Los Gatos
Print Shop, 1936. Pp. 75. MPB.

11129   HALLOCK, TERRY F. Early houses of Rich-
        mond, Massachusetts. [Richmond, 1960?].
Unpaged.

11130   RICHMOND, MASS. CONGREGATIONAL CHURCH.
        Manual of the Congregational Church in
Richmond 1751-1855-1886. Pittsfield: Berkshire
County Eagle Print, 1886. Pp. 52. M.
        Includes history.

ROCHESTER

11131   LEONARD, MARY HALL. "Revolutionary records
        of a country town." NEM, New Ser., 19
(1898-1899), 289-299.

11132   "TOPOGRAPHY and history of Rochester,
        Mass., 1815." MHSC, 2 Ser., 4 (1816), 250-
267.

ROCKLAND

11133   ROCKLAND, MASS. FIRST CONGREGATIONAL
        CHURCH. Historical addresses and papers:
one hundredth anniversary 1813-1913, First Congregational Church, Rockland, Massachusetts.
Rockland: Young People's Society of Christian Endeavor of the First Congregational Church, [1913?].
Pp. 31. MBNEH.

11134   ROCKLAND, MASS. ROCKLAND BOOKLET COMMITTEE.
        Rockland centennial, past, present, prom-
ise, 1874-1974. Rockland: Fairmount Pr., [1974].
Pp. 96. M.

11135   ROCKLAND SAVINGS BANK. Rockland Savings
        Bank...a mutual savings bank...a short his-
tory 1868-1951. Rockland, 1951. Unpaged. M.

11136   ROCKWOOD, CHARLES M. "Story of Rockland."
        NEM, New Ser., 41 (1909-1910), 455-466.

11137   SHAW, ELIJAH. History of the parish and
        church of the Third Congregational Society
in Abington, now the First Congregational Church in
Rockland, Mass. n.p., 1890. Pp. 68. MBNEH.

11138   STUDLEY, GIDEON. "Industries in an Old
        Colony village eighty years ago." NEQ, 14
(1941), 292-308.

ROCKPORT

11139   BABSON, HERMAN. "The building of a break-
        water." NEM, New Ser., 11 (1894), 163-173.

11140   "A BLACKSMITH shop grows up." Industry, 31
        (September, 1966), 40.
        Cape Ann Mfg. Co., 75th anniversary;
        forgings.

11141   CHAMBERLAIN, ALLEN. Pigeon Cove, its early
        settlers & farms, 1702-1840. Boston:
Thomas Todd, 1940. Pp. 93.

11142   COOLEY, JOHN L. Rockport sketch book; sto-
        ries of early art and artists. Rockport:
Rockport Art Association, 1965. Pp. 119.

11143   FELT, JOSEPH BARLOW. "Historical, statisti-
        cal and biographical notices of Rockport."
EIHC, 4 (1862), 162-167.

11144   "THE GREAT storm of 1635." Essex Antiq, 1
        (1897), 93-95.
        Wreck of Isaac Allerton's pinnace.

11145   HISTORY of the town of Rockport, as com-
        prised in the centennial address of Lemuel
Gott, M.D., extracts from the memoranda of Ebenezer
Pool, Esq., and interesting items from other
sources. John W. Marshall, et al., comps. Rockport: Rockport Review Office, 1888. Pp. 295.

11146   LEONARD, HENRY C. Pigeon Cove and vicinity.
        Boston: F. A. Searle, 1873. Pp. viii, 193.

11147   LORENZ, CLARISSA. "Anna, damn her!" Indus-
        try, 22 (June, 1957), 27-30.
        Anadama Baking Co.

11148   MORLEY, ARTHUR P. Rockport, a town of the
        sea. Cambridge: Murray Printing, 1924.
Pp. 52.

11149   ROCKPORT, MASS. FIRST CONGREGATIONAL
        CHURCH. Historical sketch, First Congrega-
tional Church, Rockport, Massachusetts. Rockport,
1949. Pp. 2. M.

11150   _____. Manual of the First Congregational
        Church in Rockport, Mass. Gloucester:
John S. E. Rogers, 1870. Pp. 43. M.
        Includes brief history.

11151 ROCKPORT ART ASSOCIATION. Artists of the Rockport Art Association; a pictorial record of Cape Ann's oldest art organization with historical sketches of Rockport and reproductions of works in the graphic arts by several artist members. (1940) 4th ed. [Rockport], 1964. Pp. 184, 19. M.

11152 SOLLEY, GEORGE WILLIS. Alluring Rockport, an unspoiled New England town on Cape Ann.... Rockport: G. Butman, 1925. Pp. 122.

11153 TARR, FRANK WHITCOMB. "Quaint speech and lore of Sandy Bay now Rockport." OTNE, 24 (1933-1934), 20-28.

11154 VILLAGE IMPROVEMENT SOCIETY OF PIGEON COVE, MASS. 75th anniversary, 1889-1964. n.p., [1964?]. Unpaged. M.

11155 YE headlands of Cape Anne, Rockport, Mass. n.p., [not after 1932]. Pp. 44. MWA.

ROWE

11156 BLACK, MARGARET REED. "My vacations at grandma's." Rowe HSB, 5 (Summer, 1968), 4-8.

Social life and customs.

11157 BRIGHAM, UNA PECK. "Reminiscences of West Rowe in the nineties." Rowe HSB, 5 (Summer, 1968), 11-15.

11158 BROWN, PERCY WHITING. "An historical sketch of Rowe." PVMA, 7 (1921-1929), 73-115.

11159 _____. History of Rowe, Massachusetts (1921) 2d. ed. Cleveland: A. D. Williams, 1935. Pp. 114.

11160 "CEMETERIES in Rowe." Rowe HSB, 4 (Summer, 1967), entire issue.

11161 COGGINS, ESTELLE PICKETT. "Teenager in the twenties in Rowe." Rowe HSB, 10 (Fall, 1973), 14-16.

11162 "THE EARLY church in Rowe." Rowe HSB, 9 (Summer, 1972), entire issue. 1787-1833.

11163 FARLEY, FREDERIKA. "Summer 1896 in Rowe." Rowe HSB, 8 (Winter, 1971), 10-16.

11164 HENRY, ANNA L. "Men and events in Rowe's past." Rowe HSB, 2 (Winter, 1965), [2-4].

11165 HICKS, C. O. "Reminiscences of Rowe, Massachusetts." Rowe HSB, 6 (Winter, 1969), 9-11.

11166 "INDUSTRIES along Pelham Brook." Rowe HSB, 3 (Summer, 1966), entire issue.

11167 "INDUSTRIES in Rowe." Rowe HSB, 11 (Fall, 1974), entire issue.

11168 "INDUSTRY of Rowe." Rowe HSB, 1 ([Spring], 1964, [1-5]. Soapstone.

11169 MCCARTHY, HELEN. The story of the Davis Mine, Rowe, Massachusetts, 1882-1911. [Rowe]: Rowe Historical Society, 1967. Pp. 29. MDeeH.

Iron ore.

11170 "MORE industries along Pelham Brook." Rowe HSB, 4 (Winter, 1967), entire issue; (Fall, 1967), entire issue.

11171 "THE OLD center." Rowe HSB, 8 (Winter, 1971), 6-10. Town center.

11172 "THE OLD grist mill." Rowe HSB, 2 (Fall, 1965), 6-8.

11173 "OLD schools of Rowe." Rowe HSB, 1 (Fall, 1964), entire issue.

11174 "ONE hundred years ago." Rowe HSB, 3 (Spring, 1965), 5-7. Music.

11175 PECK, LILIAN CRESSY. Centennial history of the Baptist Church in Rowe...given at a meeting of Franklin Baptist Association held in Rowe, September 14th and 15th, 1910. n.p., [1910?]. Pp. 11. M.

11176 REED, MAX. "My boyhood memories of Rowe." Rowe HSB, 10 (Fall, 1973), 5-8.

11177 RICHMOND, MARY L. "Personal observations of the Cummington Press." PAGA, 5 (1957), 9-11.

Formerly in Cummington, Massachusetts, and later in Iowa.

11178 "THE ROWE town library." Rowe HSB, 6 (Spring, 1969), 3-10.

11179 "ROWE'S 'Who's who.'" Rowe HSB, 7 (Winter, 1970), 8-14; (Spring, 1970), 3-11.

11180 SMITH, MRS. M. A. Amid Rowe hills, an historical sketch compiled from various sources. Montague: New Clairvaux Pr., 1904. Unpaged. MDeeP.

11181 STANFORD, ERNEST ELWOOD. "Memories of the village school." Rowe HSB, 6 (Fall, 1969), entire issue.

11182 "STORMY weather." Rowe HSB, 5 (Fall, 1968), entire issue. Storms of 1888, 1898, 1938 and 1948.

11183 "THEY lived in Rowe." Rowe HSB, 10 (Summer, 1973), entire issue; 11 (Spring, 1974), entire issue. Biography.

11184 TRUESDELL, ALICE. "Growing up in Rowe." Rowe HSB, 10 (Fall, 1973), 17-18.

11185   TUTTLE, LOUIS. "My home in Rowe." Rowe
         HSB, 5 (Summer, 1968), 9-10.

11186   "THE VILLAGE stores of Rowe." Rowe HSB,
         2 (Spring, 1965), entire issue.

ROWLEY

11187   BRADFORD, JAMES. An address, delivered at
         Rowley, Mass., September 5th, 1839, at the
celebration of the second centennial anniversary of
the settlement of the town, embracing its ecclesiastical history from the beginning. Boston: F. Andrews, 1840. Pp. 54.

11188   BRAMAN, ISAAC. A centennial discourse,
         delivered at the reopening of the Congrega-
tional Meeting-house in New Rowley, December 6th,
1832. Haverhill: C. P. Thayer, 1833. Pp. 16.

11189   "A CENTURY of shoemaking by the Foster
         family." Weekly Bulletin Leather and Shoe
News, (August 25, 1951), 86, 88-90.
         R. H. Foster Shoe Co.

11190   "THE CHAPLIN-Clarke-Williams House, Rowley,
         Massachusetts." OTNE, 16 (1925-1926), 98-
100.

11191   CHENEY, RUTH LAMBERT. "Back to old pine
         and brick ovens in the Rowley Historical
House." RowHSP, No. 2 (1928), 36-38.
         Restoration.

11192   EWELL, JOHN LOUIS. "Ezekiel Rogers, the
         first minister of Rowley." NEM, New Ser.,
21 (1899-1900), 3-22.

11193   EWELL, WILLIAM STICKNEY. "The Metcalf Rock
         Pasture Burial Ground." RowHSP, No. 3
(1948), 21-23.

11194   JEWETT, AMOS EVERETT. "The Acadians in
         Rowley." EIHC, 84 (1948), 367-388.

11195   _____. "The Bay Road from Ipswich line to
         Newbury upper green." RowHSP, No. 3
(1948), 13-20.

11196   _____. "Deacon John Pearson and his full-
         ing mill at Rowley. RowHSP, No. 3 (1948),
24-26.

11197   _____. "Deacon John Pearson and his full-
         ing mill in Rowley." EIHC, 83 (1947), 289-
292.

         Differs from previous entry.

11198   _____. "A New England shoemaker's shop."
         RowHSP, No. 3 (1948), 27-29.

11199   _____. "The Platts-Bradstreet House and
         some of those who lived in it." RowHSP,
No. 2 (1928), 7-35.

11200   _____. and EMILY MABEL ADAMS JEWETT. Row-
         ley, Massachusetts, 'Mr. Ezechi Rogers
Plantation,' 1639-1850. Rowley: Jewett Family of
America, 1946. Pp. x, 350.

11201   JEWETT, AMOS EVERETT. "The tidal marshes of
         Rowley and vicinity with an account of the
old-time methods of 'marshing.'" EIHC, 85 (1949),
272-291.

11202   KING, GEORGE E. "An historic town, past
         and present of Rowley, Massachusetts."
National Magazine, 22 (June, 1905), [3 unnumbered
pages at end of issue].

11203   HISTORY of the Congregational parsonage,
         Rowley, Mass., erected 1889. Salem: Essex
County Mercury, 1890. Pp. 14. MSaE.

11204   ROWLEY, MASS. The early records of the
         town of Rowley, Massachusetts, 1639-1672,
being vol. 1 of the printed records of the town.
Benjamin P. Mighill and George B. Blodgette, eds.
Rowley, 1894. Pp. xv, 255.
         No more published.

11205   _____. The tercentenary celebration of
         the town of Rowley, August 24-25-26-27,
1939. n.p., 1942. Pp. 206. MBNEH.

11206   ROWLEY, MASS. TERCENTENARY COMMITTEE. The
         tercentenary celebration of the town of
Rowley, August 24, 25, 26, 27, 1939. [Rowley,
1942]. Pp. 206.

ROYALSTON

11207   ADAMS, ROBERT WINTHROP. The story of a
         meeting-house: a narrative of the antece-
dents and career, to date, of the fourth meeting-
house of the First Congregational Church of Royalston, Massachusetts. Royalston, 1952. Unpaged.
MBNEH.

11208   BARTLETT, HUBERT CARLTON. Reflections on
         Royalston, Worcester County, Massachusetts,
U.S.A. Fitchburg: The Reflector, 1927. Pp. 332.

11209   BULLARD, EBENEZER WATERS. A historical
         discourse delivered Sabbath, Oct. 14, 1866,
in commemoration of the one hundredth anniversary
of the First Congregational Church in Royalston,
Mass. Worcester: A. B. Adams, 1866. Pp. 40.

11210   BULLOCK, ALEXANDER HAMILTON. A commemora-
         tive address, at Royalson [sic] August 23d,
1865: the hundredth anniversary of its incorporation.... Winchendon: Frank W. Ward, 1865.
Pp. iv, 207.

11211   CASWELL, LILLEY BREWER. The history of the
         town of Royalston, Massachusetts, including
Royalston's soldier record, written and comp. by
Hon. Fred W. Cross. [Royalston]: The Town, 1917.
Pp. xv, 566.

11212   GALE, AMORY. Centennial discourse,
        preached in Royalston, at the first centen-
nial anniversary of the Baptist Church...June 10,
1868. Worcester: E. R. Fiske & Son, 1868. Pp. 28.

RUSSELL

11213   RUSSELL, MASS. 175TH ANNIVERSARY COMMITTEE.
        175th anniversary of the town of Russell,
1792-1967. Westfield: New England Printing, 1967.
Pp. 28. M.

RUTLAND

11214   BARRY, ESTHER E. "Historic Rutland, the
        cradle of Ohio." NEM, New Ser., 8 (1893),
762-772.

11215   BLAKE, FRANCIS EVERETT. "Rutland and the
        Indian troubles, 1723-30." Worcester
HSProc, (1885), 30-79.

11216   CARROLL, CHARLES E. "Two centuries young."
        Worcester Magazine, 17 (1914), 198-199.

11217   EARLE, STEPHEN CARPENTER. The Rutland
        home of Major General Rufus Putnam.
Worcester: G. G. Davis, 1901. Pp. 20.

11218   MURPHY, TIMOTHY CORNELIUS. History of
        Rutland in Massachusetts, 1713-1968.
[Rutland]: Rutland Historical Society, 1970.
Pp. xiii, 201.

11219   NADEAU, GABRIEL. "A German military sur-
        geon in Rutland, Massachusetts, during the
Revolution: Julius Friedrich Wasmus." BHistMed,
18 (1945), 243-300.
        A substantial portion relates to the
        town.

11220   POTTER, BURTON WILLIS. "Col. John Murray
        and his family." Worcester HSProc, 24
(1908), 15-33.

11221   _____. Colonial life in Rutland: address
        of Burton W. Potter, Esq. in the Congrega-
tional Church in Rutland, Massachusetts, Tuesday
evening, August 14, 1894, summer lecture course.
Worcester: L. P. Goddard, 1894. Pp. 16.

11222   RANDALL, E. O. "Rutland--'the cradle of
        Ohio.'" Ohio Archaeological and Historical
Publications, 18 (1909), 54-78.

11223   REED, JONAS. A history of Rutland;
        Worcester County, Massachusetts, from its
earliest settlement, with a biography of its first
settlers. (1836) Worcester: Reprinted by Tyler &
Seagrove, 1879. Pp. viii, 195.
        This reprint includes supplement for 1836
        to 1879, by Daniel Bartlett.

11224   RUTLAND, MASS. Tercentenary observance and
        Old Home Day, Wednesday, August 6, 1930.
Rutland: Tercentenary Committee, [1930?]. Unpaged.
MH.

11225   RUTLAND, MASS. FIRE DEPT. Picturesque
        Rutland: containing views of buildings
and localities, and brief historical sketches of
the town of Rutland, Mass. Worcester: E. H.
Tripp, [1904?]. Pp. 64.

11226   RUTLAND, MASS. FIRST CONGREGATIONAL CHURCH.
        The history, articles of faith, covenant
and standing rules of the First Congregational
Church in Rutland, Mass.... Worcester: Edward R.
Fiske, 1858. Pp. 20. MWA.

11227   RUTLAND, MASS. 250TH ANNIVERSARY COMMITTEE.
        Celebration souvenir booklet: 250th anni-
versary of the town's incorporation with the programs of events and historical information, 1722-
1972. Rutland, 1972. Pp. 55. M.

SALEM

11228   ABBOT, LILLY S. Grace Church in Salem:
        the first one hundred years, 1858-1958.
Salem: Grace Church Centennial Committee, 1958.
Pp. 36. MSaE.

11229   "AN ACCOUNT of the commemoration by the
        Essex Institute, of the fifth half century
of the landing of Gov. John Endicott in Salem,
Massachusetts." EIHC, 15 (1878), 101-323.

11230   "AN ACCOUNT of the commemoration, by the
        Essex Institute of the two hundred and fif-
tieth anniversary of the arrival of John Winthrop,
at Salem, Massachusetts, which took place at the
Willows, Salem Neck, on Tuesday, June 22, 1880."
EIHC, 17 (1880), 193-256.

11231   "AN ACCOUNT of the first centennial of the
        settlement of Salem." EIHC, 28 (1891),
179-180.
        1729.

11232   ADAMS, HERBERT BAXTER. "Allotments of land
        in Salem to men, women and maids." EIHC,
19 (1882), 167-175.

11233   _____. "Common fields in Salem." EIHC, 19
        (1882), 241-253.

11234   _____. "The great pastures of Salem."
        EIHC, 20 (1883), 161-179.

11235   _____. "Origin of Salem Plantation."
        EIHC, 19 (1882), 153-166.

11236   _____. "Salem meadows, woodland, and town
        neck." EIHC, 20 (1883), 52-62.

11237   "THE AFFAIR at the North Bridge, Salem,
        February 26, 1775." EIHC, 38 (1902), 321-
352.

11238   ALMY, JAMES F.   "A history of Methodism in
          Salem." EIHC, 24 (1887), 275-301.

11239   ALMY, BIGELOW AND WASHBURN, SALEM, MASS.
          Fifty years, 1858 [to] 1908, Almy, Bigelow
& Washburn, Salem, Mass. n.p., [1908?]. Unpaged.
MSaE.

          Department store.

11240   ANDREWS, JOHN F.   "John F. Andrews' reminis-
          cences of Salem, written in 1884." EIHC,
82 (1946), 378-380.

11241   ANNABLE, IRVING KINSMAN.   "Historical notes
          of the Crombie Street Congregational Church,
Salem, Massachusetts." EIHC, 77 (1941), 203-217.

11242   ARVEDSON, GEORGE.   Walks to school 60 years
          ago in Salem. n.p., [1906?-not after 1909].
3v. MSaE.
          Recollections of places seen along the
          route.

11243   ASHTON, JOSEPH NICKERSON.   The Salem Athe-
          naeum, 1810-1910. Salem: Berkeley Pr.,
1917. Pp. 67.

11244   ASSOCIATION FOR THE RELIEF OF AGED AND DES-
          TITUTE WOMEN IN SALEM.   A record of the
first fifty years of the Old Ladies' Home at Salem,
with sketches of some of its principal promoters,
and an account of the estate it occupies.... Robert S. Rantoul, De Witt S. Clark, and George M.
Whipple, comps. Salem: Observer Pr., 1910.
Pp. 95.

11245   "AUCTION sales in Salem, of shipping and
          merchandise during the Revolution."
EIHC, 49 (1913), 97-124.

11246   BANVARD, JOSEPH.   "Rev. Joseph Banvard's
          reminiscences of Salem, written in 1884."
EIHC, 83 (1947), 247-248.

11247   BARNES, ERIC W.   "All the king's horses...
          and all the king's men." Am Heritage, 11
(October, 1960), 56-59, 86-87.
          Alexander Leslie at North Bridge.

11248   BARRY, THEA SONIA.   "How it all began."
          Yankee, 31 (March, 1967), 86-87, 134-137.
          Witchcraft.

11249   BATCHELOR, GEORGE.   "Salem in Hawthorne's
          day." Critic, New Ser., 8 (1887), 7-9.
          Comment on a sketch by Henry James.

11250   [BATES, HARRIET LEONORA VOSE].   Old Salem.
          By Eleanor Putnam, pseud. Arlo Bates, ed.
Boston: Houghton Mifflin 1886. Pp. 120.

11251   [_____].   "Old Salem shops." Atlantic,
          54 (1884), 309-313.
          Signed "Eleanor Putnam," a pseudonym.

11252   [_____].   "A Salem dame-school." Atlantic
          55 (1885), 53-57.
          The Misses Witherspoon's School; signed
          "Eleanor Putnam," a pseudonym.

11253   BATTIS, EDWARD C.   "Leslie's retreat." Mag
          Hist, 3 (1906), 87-89.
          Alexander Leslie, February 26, 1775.

11254   BEAMAN, C. C.   "The Branch or Howard St.
          Church." EIHC, 3 (1861), 272-283.

11255   _____.   "The closing history of the Branch
          or Howard Street Church in Salem." EIHC,
11 (1871-1872), 241-248.

11256   BEARD, GEORGE MILLER.   The psychology of
          the Salem witchcraft excitement of 1692,
and its practical application to our own times.
N.Y.: G. P. Putnam's Sons, 1882. Pp. xx, 112.

11257   BELKNAP, HENRY WYCKOFF.   "A check list of
          Salem privateers in the War of 1812."
EIHC, 78 (1942), 241-264, 348-374; 79 (1943), 19-46,
153-176, 256-274, 371-386; 80 (1944), 79-91, 158-
176.

11258   _____.   "Furniture exported by cabinet ma-
          kers of Salem with special reference to
the Sandersons." EIHC, 85 (1949), 335-359.
          Elijah and Jacob Sanderson.

11259   _____.   The seventeenth century house.
          Salem: Newcomb & Gauss, 1930. Pp. 8.
MBNEH.
          John Ward House.

11260   BENJAMIN, A. N.   "Salem: historic and pic-
          turesque features." Outlook, 57 (1897),
591-598.

11261   BENTLEY, WILLIAM.   "A description and his-
          tory of Salem." MHSC, 6 (1799), 212-277.

11262   _____.   The diary of William Bentley, D. D.,
          pastor of the East Church, Salem, Massachu-
setts.... Salem: Essex Institute, 1905-1914.
4v.

11263   BERMAN, EDWARD H.   "Salem and Zanzibar:
          1825-1850." EIHC, 105 (1969), 338-362.
          Commerce.

11264   BONFANTI, LEO.   The witchcraft hysteria of
          1692. Wakefield: Pride Publications, 1971.
Pp. 63. MSaE.

11265   BONGARTZ, ROY.   "Pass go and retire." Sat-
          urday Evening Post, 237, (April 11, 1964),
26-27.
          Parker Brothers, game manufacturers.

11266   BOUCHER, RONALD L.   "The colonial militia
          as a social institution: Salem, Massachu-
setts, 1764-1775." Military Affairs, 37 (1973),
125-130.

11267   BOWDITCH, HAROLD.   "The buildings associated
          with Nathaniel Bowditch (1773-1838)."
EIHC, 79 (1943), 205-221; 80 (1944), 92-93.
          Houses.

11268   BOYER, PAUL S. and STEPHEN NISSENBAUM.
        Salem possessed: the social origins of
witchcraft. Cambridge: Harvard Univ. Pr., 1974.
Pp. xxi, 231.

11269   _____ and _____, eds. Salem-village
        witchcraft; a documentary record of local
conflict in colonial New England. Belmont, Calif.:
Wadsworth Publishing, 1972. Pp. xxv, 416.

11270   BRADLEE, FRANCIS BOARDMAN CROWNINSHIELD.
        "The Salem Iron Factory." EIHC, 54 (1918),
97-114.

11271   BRADY, CYRUS TOWNSEND. Commerce and con-
        quest in East Africa, with particular ref-
erence to the Salem trade with Zanzibar. Salem:
Essex Institute, 1950. Pp. xxi, 245.

11272   BRAGDON, CLAUDE FAYETTE. "Six hours in
        Salem." American Architect and Building
News, 39 (1893), 41-43.

11273   BREBNER, WINSTON P. "Salem." Holiday, 15
        (March, 1954), 106-108, 110, 112, 114-116.

11274   BREWINGTON, M. V. "The backon on Back-
        er's." EIHC, 101 (1965), 50-55.
        History of beacon on Backer's Island
        erected by the Salem Marine Society.

11275   [BROADHEAD, ELEANOR]. A brief history of
        the Negro in Salem. n.p., [1969?]. Un-
paged. MSaE.
        Author attribution by Essex Institute.

11276   BROOKS, HENRY M. "Some localities about
        Salem." EIHC, 31 (1894-1895), 103-126.

11277   BROWNE, BENJAMIN F. "An account of Salem
        Common and the levelling of the same in
1802, with short notices of the subscribers."
EIHC, 4 (1862), 2-13, 76-88, 129-140, 263-267.

11278   _____. "Youthful recollections of Salem."
        EIHC, 49 (1913), 193-209, 289-304; 50
(1914), 6-16, 289-296; 51 (1915), 53-56, 297-305.

11279   BRYN, KATHERINE. "The sins of Salem."
        Science Digest, 69 (May, 1971), 29-31.
        Witchcraft.

11280   BUCK, JOHN H. "The early church plate of
        Salem." EIHC, 43 (1907), 97-114.

11281   BUCKHAM, JOHN WRIGHT. "Literary Salem."
        EIHC, 43 (1907), 193-198.

11282   [_____]. The Salem pilgrim: his book.
        Salem: D. Low, 1903. Pp. 22.

11283   _____. "Some architectural details as il-
        lustrated by the doorways of old Salem."
Country Life in America, 2 (July, 1902), 85-89.

11284   _____. "Some old-time Salem houses and
        celebrities." Book World, 7 (1901), 799-
804.

11285   BUFFUM, REBEKAH NORTHEY. "Reminiscences of
        Salem, written by Rebekah Northey Buffum in
1884." EIHC, 83 (1947), 83-87.

11286   BURR, GEORGE LINCOLN, ed. Narratives of
        the witchcraft cases, 1648-1706. N.Y.:
C. Scribner's Sons, 1914. Pp. xviii, 467.

11287   BURSTYN, HAROLD L. "The Salem Philosophi-
        cal Library: its history and importance
for American science." EIHC, 96 (1960), 169-206.

11288   BUTLER, KATHARINE. "Weathervanes and sea-
        chests: Salem, 1626-1926, a city of treas-
ures." House Beautiful, 60 (1926), 45, 82, 84, 86.

11289   CARROLL, THOMAS. "Bands and band music in
        Salem." EIHC, 36 (1900), 265-284.
        Nineteenth century.

11290   CAULFIELD, ERNEST. "Pediatric aspects of
        the Salem witchcraft tragedy, a lesson in
mental health." American Journal of Diseases of
Children, 65 (1943), 788-802.

11291   CHADBOURNE, ROBERT A. and BERNARD PETERSON.
        "From witchcraft to craftsmanship in Salem."
Industry, 12 (February, 1947), 24-28, 44, 46, 70-
72, (March, 1947), 32-38, 69-74.

11292   CHADWELL, PAULINE SOROKA. "The Richard
        Derby House." Antiques, 47 (1945), 282-
283.

11293   CHAMBERLAIN, SAMUEL. "Early recollections
        of Salem, written in 1886." EIHC, 80
(1944), 286-290.

11294   _____. Salem interiors; two centuries of
        New England taste and decoration. N.Y.:
Hastings House, 1950. Pp. 176.

11295   CHAPPLE, WILLIAM DISMORE. "Salem and the
        War of 1812." EIHC, 59 (1923), 289-304;
60 (1924), 49-74.

11296   CHASE, FRANCIS N. "A trial in the days of
        witchcraft." Lowell HSC, 1 (1907-1913),
344-355.
        Susanna Martin.

11297   CHEERFUL WORKERS, SALEM, MASS. Celebration
        of the twenty-fifth season, Feb. 22, 1895.
Salem: Arthur N. Webb, 1895. Pp. 26. MSaE.
        Club.

11298   CHEVER, GEORGE F. "The prosecution of Ann
        Pudeator for witchcraft in 1692." EIHC,
4 (1862), 37-42, 49-54.

11299   _____. "Prosecution of Philip English and
        his wife for witchcraft." EIHC, 2 (1860),
21-32, 73-85, 133-134, 185-204, 237-248, 261-272;
3 (1861), 17-28, 67-79, 111-120.

11300   _____. "Some remarks on the commerce of
        Salem from 1626 to 1740--with a sketch of
Philip English--a merchant in Salem from about 1670
to about 1733-4." EIHC, 1 (1859), 67-91, 117-143.

11301   CHISHOLM, J. B. "J. B. Chisholm's reminiscences of Salem, written in 1885." EIHC, 81 (1945), 182-186.

11302   CLARFIELD, GERARD H. "Salem's great inoculation controversy, 1773-1774." EIHC, 106 (1970), 277-296.

11303   CLEVELAND, H. W. S. "Reminiscences of Salem written by H. W. S. Cleveland in 1884." EIHC, 82 (1946), 375-377.

11304   THE CLUB, SALEM, MASS. Sketches about Salem people. Salem: Newcomb & Gauss, 1930. v.p.

11305   CODMAN, MARTHA. "Mrs. Martha Codman's reminiscences of Salem, written in 1885." EIHC, 82 (1946), 186-189.

11306   COMSTOCK, HELEN. "A Salem secretary attributed to William Appleton." Antiques, 89 (1966), 553-555.

11307   CONKLING, FRANK J. "Salem and the Conkling family." EIHC, 31 (1894-1895), 43-53.

11308   COPELAND, CHARLES HENRY POWERS. "To the farthest port of the rich East." Am Heritage, 6 (February, 1955), 10-19, 114-115. Commerce.

11309   CORWIN, GEORGE. An inventory of the contents of the shop and house of Captain George Corwin of Salem, Massachusetts Bay, who died January 3, 1684-5, with a short introductory note by George Francis Dow. Salem: The Press in City Hall Alley, 1910. Pp. 19.

11310   COUSINS, FRANK and PHIL M. RILEY. The colonial architecture of Salem. Boston: Little, Brown, 1919. Pp. xxiii, 282.

11311   _____ and _____. The wood-carver of Salem; Samuel McIntire, his life and work. Boston: Little, Brown, 1916. Pp. xx, 168.

11312   CUMMINGS, ABBOTT LOWELL. "History in houses: the Crowninshield-Bentley House in Salem, Massachusetts." Antiques, 76 (1959), 328-329.

11313   _____. "The house and its people." EIHC, 97 (1961), 81-97. Crowninshield-Bentley House.

11314   _____. "Nathaniel Hawthorne's birthplace: an architectural study." EIHC, 94 (1958), 196-204.

11315   CURTIS, CHARLES PELHAM. "A strange story about Marbury versus Madison in Salem, 1808." MHSP, 71 (1953-1957), 133-146.

11316   _____. "The young devils and Dan'l Webster." Am Heritage, 11 (June, 1960), 52-54, 101-103. 1830 murder of Joseph White.

11317   CURWEN, GEORGE R. "Notice of the Curwen House and its occupants." EIHC, 2 (1860), 228-230.

11318   CUVIER NATURAL HISTORY SOCIETY. Cuvier Natural History Society, March 5th, 1881-March 5th, 1891. n.p., [1891?]. Pp. 14. MSaE.

11319   DABNEY, J. P. "Graduates of Harvard, originating from Salem, Ms." American Quarterly Register, 15 (1842-1843), 185-193. Short biographical sketches.

11320   DABNEY, M. P. "Reminiscences of Salem, written by M. P. Dabney in 1885." EIHC, 83 (1947), 88.

11321   DAVENPORT, GEORGE F. Homes and hearths of Salem. Salem: Salem Observer Pr., 1891. Pp. 112. Social life and customs.

11322   DENNIS, ALBERT WOODBURY. The Merchants National Bank of Salem, Massachusetts; an historical sketch. [Salem]: Salem Pr., 1908. Pp. 65.

11323   DENNIS, WILLIAM D. "The fire clubs of Salem." EIHC, 39 (1903), 1-28.

11324   _____. "The Salem Charitable Mechanic Association." EIHC, 42 (1906), 1-35.

11325   DERBY, JOHN BARTON. A few reminiscences of Salem, Mass., embracing notices of its eminent men known to the author forty years ago. Boston, 1847. Pp. 15.

11326   DEXTER, RALPH W. "The Cuvier Natural History Society of Salem." EIHC, 96 (1960), 149-155. Since 1881.

11327   DICK, RUDOLPH C. Nathaniel Griffin, 1796-1876, of Salem and his Naumkeag Steam Cotton Company. N.Y.: Newcomen Society in North America, 1951. Pp. 28.

11328   _____. "Pequot Mills: the Naumkeag Steam Cotton Company of Salem, Massachusetts." CottHR, 1 (1960), 109-117.

11329   DODGE, ELLEN MARIA. State normal school at Salem, Massachusetts, historical sketch read at the dedication of the new building, January 26, 1897. n.p., n.d. Pp. 14.

11330   DODGE, ERNEST STANLEY. "Cleopatra's Barge sails again." Antiques, 66 (1954), 44-46. Yacht owned by George Crowninshield, Jr.; launched in 1816.

11331   _____. "Indians at Salem in the mid-nineteenth century." OTNE, 42 (1951-1952), 93-95.

11332   _____. Salem Five Cents Savings Bank, 1855-1955, the story of its first hundred years. Portland, Me.: Anthoensen Pr., 1955. Pp. 29.

11333   DOW, GEORGE FRANCIS. "Old Salem houses." Architectural Review, 15 (1908), 161-164.

11334   DOW, JOY WHEELER. "A Salem enchantment." House Beautiful, 12 (1902), 335-344.
Historic houses.

11335   DRAKE, SAMUEL ADAMS. "The old witch-house at Salem." Appleton's Journal, 10 (1873), 673-675.

11336   DRAKE, SAMUEL GARDNER. The witchcraft delusion in New England; its rise, progress, and termination, as exhibited by Dr. Cotton Mather, in 'The wonders of the invisible world,' and by Mr. Robert Calef, in his 'More wonders of the invisible world.' Roxbury: Printed for W. E. Woodward, 1866. 3v.

11337   DRONEY, JAMES F. "The witches of Salem." Boston, 55 (October, 1963), 42-46, 65, 92-93.

11338   DUNNE, GERALD T. "Joseph Story: the Salem years." EIHC, 101 (1965), 307-332.

11339   EMERSON, BROWN. Anniversary sermon, a sermon delivered in the South Church, Salem, on the thirty-eighth anniversary of his ordination. Salem: Chapman and Palfray, 1843. Pp. 31.
Brief sketch of city's history.

11340   EMMERTON, CAROLINE O. The chronicles of three old houses. Boston: Thomas Todd, 1935. Pp. 57.
Hathaway House, Retire Beckett House and the House of Seven Gables.

11341   ENDICOTT, CHARLES MOSES. "Leslie's retreat, or the resistance to British arms at the North Bridge in Salem on Sunday, P.M., February 28, 1775." EIP, 1 (1848-1856), 89-135.

11342   ENDICOTT, WILLIAM CROWNINSHIELD, 1860-1936. Captain Joseph Peabody; East India merchant of Salem (1757-1844), a record of his ships and of his family...with a sketch of Joseph Peabody's life. Walter Muir Whitehill, ed. Salem: Peabody Museum, 1962. Pp. xv, 358.

11343   ESSEX CONGREGATIONAL CLUB. [Handbook, historical review, etc]. Manchester: North Shore Pr., 1925. Pp. 65. MSaE.

11344   ESSEX HISTORICAL SOCIETY. Essex Historical Society, incorporated June 11, 1821. Salem, 1821. Pp. 8.

11345   ESSEX INSTITUTE. An account of the First Church built in Salem, Mass., 1634. (1871) 5th ed. Salem, 1890. Pp. 26.

11346   _____. Early coastwise and foreign shipping of Salem; a record of the entrances and clearances of the port of Salem, 1750-1769. Harriet Silvester Tapley, ed. Salem, 1934. Pp. x, 217.

11347   _____. The Essex Institute, treasure house of American beginnings. Salem, 1929. Pp. 29.
Historical society.

11348   _____. First Church in Salem, Mass., 1634. Salem, 1871. Pp. 32.

11349   _____. Note on the authenticity of the Roger Williams House, Essex Street, Salem. Salem: Salem Pr., 1889. Pp. 6. M.

11350   _____. Old time ships of Salem. (1917) 3d. ed. Salem, 1925. Pp. 99.

11351   _____. The story of the first meeting house built in 1634-5 by the First Church, gathered at Salem, July and August, 1629. Salem: Salem Pr., 1897. Pp. 31.

11352   FABENS, BESSIE D. "The Doyle Mansion--some memories and anecdotes." EIHC, 84 (1948), 1-14.

11353   FALES, DEAN A., JR. "The Crowninshield-Bentley House in Salem--a documentary restoration." Antiques, 88 (1965), 486-493.

11354   _____. "The furnishings of the [Crowninshield-Bentley] House." EIHC, 97 (1961), 98-128.

11355   FALES, MARTHA GANDY. "Dr. Prince's air pump." Antiques, 103 (1973), 499-501.
John Prince, 1785.

11356   FARBER, BERNARD. Guardians of virtue: Salem families in 1800. N.Y.: Basic Books, 1972. Pp. xiv, 228.

11357   FARNAM, ANNE. "Uncle Venner's farm: refuge or workhouse for Salem's poor?" EIHC, 109 (1973), 60-86.
Uncle Venner is a character in Hawthorne's 'House of seven gables.'

11358   FARRELL, HUGH F. E. "Salem, Massachusetts, the City of Peace." National Magazine, 17 (1902-1903), 248-252.

11359   FATHER MATHEW TOTAL ABSTINENCE SOCIETY, SALEM, MASS. Fiftieth anniversary, banquet and ball of the Father Mathew Total Abstinence Society, Salem, Mass., November sixteenth, nineteen twenty-five. Salem: Newcomb & Gauss, [1925?]. Pp. 12. MSaE.
Includes history.

11360   FELT, JOSEPH BARLOW. Annals of Salem. (1827) 2d. ed. Salem: W. & S. B. Ives, 1845-1849. 2v.

11361   _____. Did the First Church of Salem originally have a confession of faith distinct from their covenant? Boston: E. L. Balch, 1856. Pp. 28.

11362 _____. "Historical sketch of the forts on Salem Neck." EIHC, 5 (1863), 255-260.

11363 FELTON, WILLIAM S. Financial review of Salem, Mass., 1891-1911. n.p., [1911?]. Pp. 10. MSaE.

11364 FENWICK, THOMAS. "The new Salem: remarkable evolution of historic Massachusetts city from Puritanism to progressiveness." NEM, New Ser., 40 (1909), 47-57.

11365 _____. "Salem from Puritan to progressive." NEM, 51 (1914), 161-177.

11366 FERDINAND, THEODORE N. "Politics, the police, and arresting policies in Salem, Massachusetts since the Civil War." Social Problems, 19 (1972), 572-588.

11367 FERNALD, JOHN P. History of the Salem Oratorio Society, 1868-1891, prepared especially for the concerts, April 21-23, 1891. Salem: Barry & Lufkin, 1891. Pp. 40.

11368 "FIRE clubs in Salem." EIB, 1 (1869), 119-120.
Since 1744.

11369 "THE FIRST Church." EIHC, 27 (1890), 183-186.

11370 "THE FIRST half century of the Essex Institute." EIB, 30 (1898), 1-77.

11371 "FIRST home of the Essex Historical Society, which later became the Essex Institute." EIHC, 82 (1946), 383-384.

11372 FISKE, JOHN, 1842-1901. Witchcraft in Salem Village. Boston: Houghton Mifflin, 1923. Pp. 60.

11373 FLINT, JAMES. Two discourses, delivered on taking leave of the old church of the East Society in Salem, Dec. 28, 1845. Salem: Observer Office, 1846. Pp. 48.

11374 FOOTE, CALEB. "A sketch of the First Church in Salem, Massachusetts and its ministers." MNEH, 1 (1891), 28-37.

11375 FORD, WORTHINGTON CHAUNCEY. "The ensign incident at Salem, in 1634." MHSP, 42 (1908-1909), 266-280.

11376 FORMAN, BENNO M. "The Osborne family chest rediscovered." Historical New Hampshire, 26 (Spring, 1961), 26-30.

11377 _____. "Salem tradesmen and craftsmen circa 1762: a contemporary document." EIHC, 107 (1971), 62-81.

11378 FOSTER, WILLIAM H. "The Salem and Boston Stage Company." EIB, 3 (1871), 139-144.
Coaching.

11379 FOWLER, SAMUEL PAGE, 1800-1888. "Salem witchcraft." HistMag, 2 (1858), 11-12.

11380 _____, ed. Salem witchcraft: comprising 'More wonders of the invisible world,' collected by Robert Calef: and 'Wonders of the invisible world,' by Cotton Mather: together with notes and explanations. Salem: H. P. Ives and A. A. Smith, 1861. Pp. xxi, 450.

11381 FOWLER, SAMUEL PAGE, JR., b. 1838. "A historical sketch [of the Essex County Natural History Society]." EIB, 16 (1884), 141-145.

11382 FRANKLIN, M. S. "Recording the architecture of late colonial times in Salem, Massachusetts." Pencil Points, 13 (1932), 408-422.

11383 FRANKS, JAMES POTTER. A jubilee, fiftieth anniversary of the consecration of Grace Church, Sunday, June 6, 1909. Salem, [1909?]. Pp. 13. MSaE.

11384 FREEMASONS. SALEM, MASS. ESSEX LODGE. Centennial anniversary of the introduction of masonry in Salem, by the institution of Essex Lodge, together with exercises of commemoration, including an historical address, by Right Worshipful Tracy P. Cheever...and other incidents, June 24, 1879. Salem: T. J. Hutchinson & Son, 1880. Pp. 88.

11385 FREEMASONS. SALEM, MASS. SALEM COUNCIL OF ROYAL AND SELECT MASTERS. Salem Council of Royal and Select Masters, 1818, June third 1943. n.p., [1943?]. Unpaged. MBNEH.

11386 FUESS, CLAUDE MOORE. "Webster enters the case." Am Heritage, 11 (June, 1960), 55.
1830 murder of Joseph White.

11387 GALEY, JOHN H. "Salem's trade with Brazil, 1801-1870." EIHC, 107 (1971), 198-219.

11388 GANNON, FREDERIC AUGUSTUS. A brief history of Salem witchcraft as described by the guide. Salem: Salem Books, 1949. Pp. 24.

11389 _____. Corn chemistry, commerce, consumers and customs of 300 years in old Salem. Salem: J. N. Simard, [1957?]. Pp. 11.

11390 _____. Early education in old Salem and around the world. Salem: Salem Books, [1960?]. Pp. 9.

11391 _____. A few notes about men of science in Salem, 1776-1960. [Salem]: Salem Books, [1961?]. Pp. 7. MSaE.

11392 _____. Food & farms in old Salem. [Salem]: Salem Books, 1943. Pp. 58.

11393 _____. The guide's story of the witch house in Salem. Salem: Cassino Pr., 1948. Pp. 16. MSaE.

11394 _____. Joshua B. Grant, maker of tables and tools for tanners and the Salem Senate which met in his store, an old Salem story. [Salem]: Salem Books, [1944?]. Pp. 11. MSaE.

11395 _____. Joshua B. Grant's store and the Salem Senate. Salem: Newcomb & Gauss, [not after 1928]. Pp. 15. MSaE.
An organization of tanners.

11396 _____. Lafayette in Salem and Salem soldiers in France. [Salem]: Salem Books, [1957?]. Pp. 11. MSaE.
1784 and 1824.

11397 NO ENTRY

11398 _____. Nicknames and neighborhoods and album of pictures of old Salem. Salem: Salem Book, [1945?]. Pp. 32.

11399 _____. Notes of men and methods and of mechanics and chemists in tanning. Salem: Newcomb & Gauss, [1943?]. Pp. 10. MSaE.

11400 [_____]. The Old Leather Bucket Club. n.p., n.d. Unpaged. MSaE.
Author attribution by Essex Institute.

11401 _____. Old Salem scrap book. Salem: Salem Books, [1947?-1954?]. 15v. MSaE.
Social life and customs.

11402 _____. "Old Senate days and ways." Salem Senate, 1, No. 1 (1934), entire issue.
Leather industry.

11403 _____. "Optics in old Salem." Optical Journal-Review, 78 (October 1, 1941), 21.

11404 _____. Pioneer traffic laws, we've had them here 300 years. Salem: Cassino Pr., [1941?]. Unpaged. MSaE.

11405 _____. Salem Christmas customs of fifty years ago. Salem: Lavender Printing, 1938. Unpaged. MSaE.

11406 _____. Salem Christmas customs of twenty five years ago. [Salem?, 1939]. Unpaged. MSaE.

11407 _____. Signs and portents in old Salem of ships and seamen, trade and sentiment, flowers and fans, etc.... Salem: Salem Books, 1944. Pp. 28.

11408 _____. Some starts of industry and commerce in old Salem. Salem: Salem Books, n.d. Pp. 11. MSaE.

11409 _____. Some stories of adventure in old Salem's commerce. Salem: Salem Books, [194-?]. Pp. 19.

11410 _____. A story of the Arbella, of Pioneer Village, and of Lincoln's address. Salem: Cassino Pr., [1945]. Pp. 11.

11411 _____. Two merchants of Salem: Philip English (1651-1720), John Bertram (1796-1882). Salem: Salem Books, [1961?]. Pp. 8.

11412 _____. Witchcraft in old Salem: the delusion in 1692, the recovery, the war, the free press. [Salem]: Salem Books, 1944. Pp. 16.

11413 GARDNER, FRANK A. "The Higginson-Skelton migration to Salem in 1629." MassMag, 6 (1913), 1-19.
Led by Francis Higginson and Samuel Skelton.

11414 _____. "John Endicott and the men who came to Salem in the 'Abigail' in 1628." MassMag, 3 (1910), 163-177.

11415 _____. "The old planters at Salem." Genealogical Quarterly Magazine, 3 (1902), 3-18.

11416 "THE GARDNER-White-Pingree House, built in Salem, Massachusetts in 1804." Pencil Points, 21 (1940), 515-530.

11417 GAUSS, JOHN D. H. Some important events in the history of Salem, Mass. [Salem, 1926]. Pp. 11.

11418 GAVET, WILLIAM F. Historical sketch of Saint Peter's Church, Salem, Mass., read before a parish gathering at Hamilton Hall, Nov. 5, 1908, in commemoration of the 175th anniversary of the church. Salem, 1908. Pp. 22.

11419 GEMMILL, WILLIAM NELSON. The Salem witch trials, a chapter of New England history. Chicago: A. C. McClurg, 1924. Pp. iii, 240.

11420 GELMAN, ALFRED. "Lowell Island." ORHAL, 4 (1888-1891), 338-351.

11421 NO ENTRY

11422 GOODELL, ABNER CHENEY, JR. "The centennial anniversary of the meeting of the Provincial Legislature in Salem, Oct. 5, 1774." EIHC, 13 (1875), 1-52.

11423 _____. The first meeting house in Salem, Massachusetts; a reply to certain strictures made by Robert S. Rantoul, president of the Essex Institute, in his 'Powerful defence of the old Salem relic'.... n.p., [1900?]. Pp. 68.

11424 _____. "The witch-trials in Salem in 1692 further considered." MHSP, 2 Ser., 1 (1884-1885), 65-70.

11425 GOODMAN Pioneer's story of witchcraft in Salem Village in 1692. Salem: Cassino Pr., 1935. Unpaged. MSaE.

11426 GOODSPEED, CHARLES ELIOT. "Nathaniel Hawthorne and the museum of the East India Marine Society." AmNep, 5 (1945), 266-285.

11427   GOUGH, IDA FORD. "The Endecott spring and pear tree, a visit to the Orchard Farm in 1950." EIHC, 87 (1951), 1-8.

11428   "GRADUATES of Harvard originating from Salem." NEHGR, 5 (1851), 47-56, 153-162. 1642-1849; biographies.

11429   [GREBANIER, FRANCES VINCIGUERRA]. Puritan city; the story of Salem, by Frances Winwar, pseud. N.Y.: R. M. McBride, 1938. Pp. x, 307.

11430   HACKER SCHOOL. [Historical sketch]. n.p., n.d. Unpaged. MSaE. 1785-1870.

11431   HALL, DAVID D. "John Cotton's letter to Samuel Skelton." WMQ, 3 Ser., 22 (1965), 478-485.
    1630; attacks separatism of Skelton's Salem church.

11432   HANSEN, CHADWICK. "The metamorphosis of Tituba, or why American intellectuals can't tell an Indian witch from a Negro." NEQ, 47 (1974), 3-12.
    Witchcraft.

11433   _____. "Salem witchcraft and De Forest's 'Witching times.'" EIHC, 104 (1968), 89-108.

11434   _____. Witchcraft at Salem. N.Y.: G. Braziller, 1969. Pp. xvii, 252.

11435   HARASZTI, ZOLTÁN. "Cotton Mather and the witchcraft trials." More Books, 15 (1940), 179-184.

11436   HARMONY Grove Cemetery, Salem, Mass. Salem: G. M. Whipple and A. A. Smith, 1866. Pp. 80.

11437   HARRIS, A. B. "A day at Salem." Appleton's Journal, 14 (1875), 431-432.

11438   HARWOOD, REED. "The history of Misery Island." EIHC, 103 (1967), 201-222.

11439   _____. "The ill-fated Misery Islands." Yankee, 30 (August, 1966), 54-59, 136-139.

11440   HATCH, JOHN BERESFORD. Old witch jail and dungeon: a 1955 report on one of America's greatest tragedies, 1692 to 1693. Salem: Newcomb & Gauss, 1955. Pp. 15.

11441   _____. Salem witchcraft--fact or fiction? Salem, 1963. Pp. 45. MSaE.

11442   HAUNTS of Hawthorne in Salem, Massachusetts. [Salem]: Salem Five Cents Savings Bank, [not after 1926]. Pp. 16. M.

11443   HAWTHORNE, JULIAN. "The Salem of Hawthorne." Century, 28 (1884), 3-17.

11444   HAWTHORNE, NATHANIEL. The Custom House, and Main Street, with an introduction and notes. Boston· Houghton Mifflin, [1899]. Pp. v, 94.
    'The Custom House' is a reprint of the introduction to 'The Scarlet Letter'; 'Main Street,' one of the sketches in the 'Snow image.'

11445   HAYDEN, BARBARA E. "Central Street, Salem, and the Ingalls House." EIHC, 85 (1949), 58-91.

11446   HEAGNEY, JOHN A. "Old Salem." SWJ, 47 (1930), 190-197.
    Commerce.

11447   HEHR, MILTON G. "Concert life in Salem, 1783-1823." EIHC, 100 (1964), 98-138.

11448   _____. "Theatrical life in Salem, 1783-1823." EIHC, 100 (1964), 3-37.

11449   HIGGINSON, THOMAS WENTWORTH. "Old Salem sea-captains." Harper's Magazine, 73 (1886), 602-616.

11450   "HISTORY of St. Peter's Church, Salem, Mass." Gospel Advocate, 2 (1822), 340-343.

11451   "HISTORY of the Salem, Mass. Fire Department." Firemen's Standard, 42 (January 1, 1922), 1-2, 4, 6, 8, 10, 12.

11452   HOLYOKE MUTUAL FIRE INSURANCE COMPANY, SALEM, MASS. Name and history of the company. Salem: A. N. Webb, 1901. Pp. 35. MSaE.

11453   _____. One hundred years of the 'Holyoke Mutual Fire Insurance Company in Salem,' Massachusetts, chartered March 14, 1843, first policy issued May 23, 1843. [Salem], 1943. Pp. 44.

11454   HORSFORD, EBEN NORTON. John Cabot's landfall in 1497, and the site of Norumbega: a letter to Chief-Justice Daly, president of the American Geographical Society. Cambridge: J. Wilson and Son, 1886. Pp. 42.
    Author concludes that Salem was site of Cabot's landfall and that Norumbega was in present town of Weston.

11455   HORTON, NATHANIEL A. Leslie's retreat, 1775: an address...October 25, 1887, and other exercises in connection with the erection of a memorial tablet to commemorate Lieut. Col. Leslie's retreat at North Bridge, February 26, 1775. Salem: Gazette Office, 1888. Pp. 36.

11456   HOUSE OF SEVEN GABLES SETTLEMENT ASSOCIATION, SALEM, MASS. House of seven gables, 1668-1968, Salem, Massachusetts. [Salem?, 1968?]. Unpaged. MSaE.

11457   HUTCHINSON, THOMAS J. and RALPH CHILDS, comps. Patriots of Salem: roll of honor of the officers and enlisted men, during the late Civil War, from Salem, Mass., containing the rank, age,

(HUTCHINSON, THOMAS J. and RALPH CHILDS)
date of mustering in, date of discharge and cause
thereof, prisoners of war, together with a list of
wounded, killed and those who died in the service.
Salem: Salem Publishing, 1877. Pp. vi, 126.

11458 "THE HYGRADE Sylvania Corporation." Industry, 2 (April, 1937), 7-10.
Light bulbs.

11459 JACKSON, SHIRLEY. The witchcraft of Salem
Village. N.Y.: Random House, 1956.
Pp. 176.

11460 JARVIS, CLIVE. The story of Pequot.
[Salem]: Naumkeag Steam Cotton Co., 1929.
Pp. 31.
Cotton mill.

11461 JENKINS, LAWRENCE WATERS. "The Marine Society at Salem in New England, a brief
sketch of its history." EIHC, 76 (1940), 199-220.

11462 _____. The Peabody Museum of Salem, Massa-
chusetts; a paper read before the Rotary
Club of Salem. Salem: Newcomb & Gauss, 1924.
Pp. 8.

11463 JENKINS, OLIVER. "A disaster of the first
magnitude." Yankee, 28 (June, 1946), 74-77,
155.
Fire of June 25, 1914.

11464 JOHNSON, LUCY P. "Historical sketch of
the Salem Female Employment Society."
EIHC, 16 (1879), 166-171.
1861-1879; charity.

11465 JONES, ARTHUR BARNETT. The Salem fire.
Boston: Gorham Pr., 1914. Pp. 137.

11466 KANAI, MADOKA. "Salem and Nagasaki: their
encounter, 1797-1807." Contemporary Japan,
29 (1968), 82-102.

11467 KEYES, WILLIAM EMERSON. "'Cleopatra's
Barge.'" Antiques, 17 (1930), 29-33.
Yacht owned by George Crowninshield, Jr.

11468 KIMBALL, FISKE. "A chest-on-chest with
carvings by Samuel McIntire." OTNE, 21
(1930-1931), 87-89.

11469 _____. "The Elias Hasket Derby Mansion in
Salem." EIHC, 60 (1924), 273-292.

11470 _____. "The estimate of McIntire." An-
tiques, 21 (1932), 23-25.
Samuel McIntire and furnishings in the
Elias Hasket Derby House.

11471 _____. "Furniture carvings by Samuel
McIntire." Antiques, 18 (1930), 388-392,
498-502; 19 (1931), 30-32, 117-119, 207-210; 23
(1933), 56-58.

11472 _____. "Salem furniture makers." Antiques,
24 (1933), 90-91, 218-220; 25 (1934), 144-
146.
Nathaniel Appleton, Jr., William Hook, and
Nehemiah Adams.

11473 _____. "Salem secretaries and their makers." Antiques, 23 (1933), 168-170.

11474 KIMBALL, HENRIETTA D. Old and new Salem,
historical. Salem: Geo. A. Kimball, 1891.
Pp. 35. M.

11475 _____. Witchcraft illustrated: witchcraft
to be understood, facts, theories and incidents, with a glance at old and new Salem and its
historical resources. Boston: Geo. A. Kimball,
1892. Pp. 135.

11476 KING, CAROLINE HOWARD. "The golden age of
Salem." Atlantic Monthly, 160 (1937), 151-
161.
Social life and customs.

11477 _____. "Old Salem." Atlantic Monthly, 160
(1937), 329-338.
Recollections written from 1898 to 1905;
social life and customs.

11478 _____. When I lived in Salem, 1822-1866.
Brattleboro, Vt.: Stephen Daye Pr., 1937.
Pp. 222.

11479 KINGSLEY, JOHN STERLING. "Salem witchcraft." Nebraska State Historical Society.
Transactions and Reports, 3 (1892), 44-58.

11480 KOCH, DAVID WARNER. "Income distribution
and political structure in seventeenth-
century Salem, Massachusetts." EIHC, 105 (1969),
50-71.

11481 KUO, PING CHIA. "Canton and Salem: the
impact of Chinese culture upon New England
life during the post-Revolutionary era." NEQ, 3
(1930), 420-442.

11482 LANDER, LUCY A. Synopsis of the work of the
Woman's Friend Society, from the time of its
organization in 1876 to 1889. n.p., n.d. Pp. 8.
MSaE.
Charity.

11483 LEAVITT, WILLIAM. "An account of the private armed vessels belonging to Salem,
Mass., during the War of 1812." EIHC, 2 (1860),
57-64.

11484 _____. "History of the Essex Lodge of
Freemasons." EIHC, 3 (1861), 37-47, 84-95,
121-133, 174-186, 207-218, 253-272; 4 (1862), 255-
263.

11485 _____. "Materials for the history of ship
building in Salem." EIHC, 6 (1864), 136-
140, 171-175, 226-227, 252-255; 7 (1865), 207-213.

11486 LEMMON, FLORENCE EDWARDS. "Planted by the
Puritans." The Country Home, 57 (March,
1933), 18, 48-51.
Gardens.

11487 LEVIN, DAVID. "Salem witchcraft in recent
fiction and drama." NEQ, 28 (1955), 537-
546.

11488 _____, ed. What happened in Salem? Documents pertaining to the seventeenth-century witchcraft trials, 'Young Goodman Brown' [by] Nathaniel Hawthorne [and] 'A mirror for witches' [by] Esther Forbes. (1952) 2d. ed. N.Y.: Harcourt, Brace, 1960. Pp. xviii, 238.

11489 LEWIS, WALKER. "The murder of Captain Joseph White: Salem, Massachusetts, 1830." ABAJ, 54 (1968), 460-466.

11490 LITTLE, DAVID MASON. "Documentary history of the Salem Custom House." EIHC, 67 (1931), 1-26, 145-160, 265-280.

11491 LITTLE, NINA FLETCHER. "The Blyths of Salem: Benjamin, limner in crayons and oil, and Samuel, painter and cabinetmaker." EIHC, 108 (1972), 49-57.

11492 _____. "Cornè, McIntire, and the Hersey Derby farm." Antiques, 101 (1972), 226-229.
    Painting by Michel Cornè of Ezekiel Hersey Derby's estate.

11493 _____. "Painted wall paper in the Lindall-Barnard-Andrews House." EIHC, 94 (1958), 328-333.

11494 LOINES, ELMA, ed. "Hard cash; on a Salem housewife in the eighteen twenties." EIHC, 91 (1955), 246-265.
    Correspondence between Mary Porter Low and Seth Low, 1828-1829.

11495 LORING, GEORGE BAILEY, ed. "Some account of houses and other buildings in Salem, from a manuscript of the late Col. Benj. Pickman." EIHC, 6 (1864), 93-109.

11496 LOW, DANIEL & CO., SALEM, MASS. The story of a store. n.p., [1926]. Unpaged. MSaE.
    Jewelers.

11497 LOW, SETH. "Address at the centennial celebration of the Salem Light Infantry, September 10, 1905." EIHC, 42 (1906), 65-81.

11498 LYNCH, FRANCIS J. 50 years on Blubber Hollow with Salem Oil & Grease Co., Salem, Massachusetts. Salem: Salem Oil & Grease, 1960. Pp. 59.
    Leather.

11499 LYNDE, BENJAMIN. The diaries of Benjamin Lynde and of Benjamin Lynde, Jr., with an appendix. Fitch E. Oliver, ed. Boston: Priv. Print., 1880. Pp. xvi, 251.

11500 MCCORD, DAVID THOMPSON WATSON. "The heritage of Salem." Lincoln and Mercury Times, 8 (November-December, 1956), 16-20.

11501 MACDONALD, ALBERT J. Selected interiors of old houses in Salem and vicinity...furthering a wider knowledge of the beautiful forms of domestic architecture developed during the time of the colonies and the early days of the Republic. Boston: Rogers and Manson, 1916. Pp. 55.

11502 MCDONALD, EDITH WILLOUGHBY. "The woodcarver of Salem." SWJ, 46 (1930), 53-63.
    Samuel McIntire.

11503 MCKERN, SHARON S. "They're digging up witch lore in Salem." Science Digest, 69 (May, 1971), 27-28, 32-34.

11504 MACSWIGGAN, AMELIA ELIZABETH. "Brickmaking: report on manufacturing methods of early America in colonial Salem." Brick and Clay Record, 122 (April, 1953), 64-65, 90.

11505 MACY, CLINTON T. Brief history of St. Peter's Church, founded 1733, Salem, Massachusetts. 2d. ed. n.p., 1958. Pp. 16. MSaE.

11506 MASSACHUSETTS. STATE TEACHERS COLLEGE, SALEM. Proceedings...quarter centennial.... Salem, 1880. Pp. 60. MB.

11507 _____. Salem Teachers College at Salem, Massachusetts, 1854-1954, 100 years of progress in the training of teachers. [Salem?, 1954?]. Pp. 40. MSaE.

11508 MASSACHUSETTS. STATE TEACHERS COLLEGE, SALEM. ALUMNI ASSOCIATION. Salem State College, 1954-1969: the Meier years. [Salem, 1969?]. Unpaged. MSaE.
    Frederick A. Meier.

11509 MATHER, COTTON. The wonders of the invisible world: being an account of the tryals of several witches lately executed in New-England (1693) to which is added, 'A farther account of the tryals of the New-England witches,' by Increase Mather (1693). London: J. R. Smith, 1862. Pp. xvi, 291.

11510 MEMORIAL services at the centennial anniversary of Leslie's expedition to Salem, Sunday, February 26, 1775, on Friday, February 26, 1875, by the city authorities of Salem. Salem: Salem Observer, 1875. Pp. 91.

11511 MERCHANTS NATIONAL BANK, SALEM, MASS. Being some interesting facts since the year 1811. Salem, 1911. Unpaged. M.
    Relates to the bank.

11512 MERCHANTS--WARREN NATIONAL BANK, SALEM, MASS. 150 years of pride and progress, 1811-1961, the Merchants-Warren National Bank of Salem, Salem-Peabody, Mass. Salem, 1961. Pp. 39. M.

11513 MERRILL, WALTER MCINTOSH. New England treasury of American beginnings: Essex Institute. N.Y.: Newcomen Society in North America, 1957. Pp. 28.
    Historical society.

11514 MESSER, NELLIE STEARNS. Historical sketch of the Tabernacle Church, Salem, Mass.... n.p., 1930. Pp. 6. MSaE.

11515 _____. "The Ropes Memorial at Salem, Massachusetts." OTNE, 14 (1923-1924), 149-163.
    Nathaniel Ropes House.

11516 MILLS, ROBERT C. Historical discourse on the 50th anniversary of the formation of the First Baptist Church, Salem, Mass., December 24, 1854. Boston: Gould and Lincoln, 1855. Pp. 78. MB.

11517 "THE MISERY Islands, and what has happened there." EIHC, 38 (1902), 225-256.

11518 MORISON, JOHN HOPKINS. Sermon...installation of Rev. Geo. W. Briggs...First Church in Salem. Salem: Gazette Pr., 1853. Pp. 62. MB. Contains sketches of ministers, 1829-1853.

11519 [MORSE, EDWARD SYLVESTER]. A brief sketch of the Peabody Academy of Science, Salem, Mass. [Salem?], 1900. Unpaged. Now the Peabody Museum.

11520 _____. "Notes on the condition of zoology, fifty years ago and today: in connection with the growth of the Essex Institute." EIB, 16 (1884), 113-121.

11521 MUDGE, ZACHARIAH ATWELL. Witch Hill: a history of Salem witchcraft, including illustrative sketches of persons and places. N.Y.: Carlton & Lanahan, 1870. Pp. 322.

11522 "THE MUNICIPAL seal of Salem." EIHC, 8 (1866), 3-10.

11523 "THE NAUMKEAG Steam Cotton Company, Pequot Mills." Industry, 4 (April, 1939), 7-10. Centennial.

11524 NEVINS, WINFIELD SCOTT. "Salem's charter experiences." National Municipal Review, 5 (1916), 289-291. 1912-1916.

11525 _____. "Stories of Salem witchcraft." NEM, New Ser., 5 (1891-1892), 517-533, 664-680, 717-729; 6 (1892), 36-48, 217-230.

11526 _____. Witchcraft in Salem Village in 1692; together with a review of the opinions of modern writers and psychologists in regard to outbreak of the evil in America. (1892) 5th ed. Salem: Salem Pr., 1916. Pp. lix, 273.

11527 NEWCOMB & GAUSS, SALEM, MASS. One hundred years of printing service, Newcomb & Gauss. Salem, [1923?]. Unpaged. MSaE.

11528 NEWHALL, JAMES SILVER. "Old time Salem sea captains." Lynn HSR, No. 14 (1910), 208-228.

11529 NEWMARK, JOSEPH D. and ERNEST A. DIMATTIA, JR. A history of the Rotary Club of Salem, Massachusetts, 1918-1968. n.p., [1968?]. Pp. 20. MSaE.

11530 NICHOLS, ELLEN A. Grace Church, Salem, personal recollections. Salem: Grace House Lunch Room, 1925. Pp. 43. MSaE.

11531 NICHOLS, JOHN H. "John H. Nichols' reminiscences of Salem, written in 1884." EIHC, 81 (1945), 176-181.

11532 NOBLE, JOHN. "Some documentary fragments touching the witchcraft episode in 1692." CSMP, 10 (1904-1906), 11-26.

11533 NORTHEND, MARY HARROD. Historic doorways of old Salem. Boston: Houghton Mifflin, 1926. Pp. xv, 96.

11534 _____. "Historic Salem." NEM, New Ser., 31 (1904-1905), 507-523.

11535 _____. Memories of old Salem, drawn from the letters of a great-grandmother. N.Y.: Moffat, Yard, 1917. Pp. 341. Social life and customs.

11536 _____. "Salem of to-day." NEM, New Ser., 32 (1905), 95-113. Includes history.

11537 _____. "Salem porches: a study in architecture." Boston Cooking-School Magazine, 11 (1906), 164-169.

11538 NORTHEY, RICHARD PRICE. "A brief account of the whaling industry in Salem 1820-1860." EIHC, 75 (1939), 234-248.

11539 NOTER, RALPH, pseud? A new history of old Salem, and the towns adjacent--viz: Danvers, Beverly, Marblehead and Lynn. Salem: J. P. Jewett, 1842. Pp. 18. Limited to Salem; satirical style.

11540 "NOTES on old times in Salem." EIHC, 74 (1938), 365-372. 1820s.

11541 "NOTES on the history of horticulture in Salem." EIB, 2 (1870), 22-27.

11542 NYMAN, RICHMOND CARTER and ELLIOTT D. SMITH. Union-management cooperation in the 'stretch-out': labor extension at the Pequot Mills. New Haven: Yale Univ. Pr., 1934. Pp. xiii, 210.

11543 ODD FELLOWS. INDEPENDENT ORDER OF. SALEM, MASS. FRATERNITY LODGE, NO. 118. First fifty years of the Fraternity Lodge, No. 118 of the Independent Order of Odd Fellows, Salem, Mass. Salem: Salem Pr., 1897. Unpaged. MBNEH. Historical sketch by William L. Welch.

11544 O'KEEFE, JOSEPH A. "Salem's conflagration of 1914." The Fireman, 31 (June, 1964), 14-17.

11545 OLD houses of Salem.... Salem: The Office of "To-day," 1870. Pp. 15. A burlesque.

11546 OLIVER, HENRY K. "Henry K. Oliver's reminiscences of Federal Street, written in 1885." EIHC, 82 (1946), 179-185.

11547 OSGOOD, CHARLES STUART. "The court houses of Salem." The Visitor, 1 (1890-1891), 169-174.

11548 _____. and HENRY M. BATCHELDER. Historical sketch of Salem, 1626 [to] 1879. Salem: Essex Institute, 1879. Pp. viii, 280.

11549 "OUR new domain." EIHC, 24 (1887), 241-274.
History of a tract of land bounded by Essex, St. Peter and Brown Streets and Washington Square.

11550 PAINE, RALPH DELAHAYE. The ships and sailors of old Salem: the record of a brilliant era of American achievement. (1908-1909) Revised with a new and complete index. Boston: Charles E. Lauriat, 1923. Pp. xvii, 471.
First published as a serialized article in 'Outing,' January, 1908-April, 1909, with title: Old Salem ships and sailors.

11551 PARKER, MARY SALTONSTALL. At the Squire's in old Salem. Salem: I. K. Annable, 1897. Pp. 21.
Social life and customs.

11552 PARKER BROTHERS, INC. 75 years of fun: the story of Parker Brothers, Inc. Salem, [1958]. Pp. 48.
Game manufacturers.

11553 "PARTIAL history of the Salem Fire Department." Veteran Fireman, 1 (November, 1893), 1-8.
1644-1859.

11554 PEABODY, DAVID R. "Notice of the temperance organizations in Salem." EIB, 1 (1869), 113-119.
1840-1869.

11555 PEABODY, ROBERT EPHRAIM. "The Derbys of Salem, Mass." EIHC, 44 (1908), 193-219.
Eighteenth-century commerce.

11556 _____. Merchant venturers of old Salem: a history of the commercial voyages of a New England family to the Indies and elsewhere in the XVIII century. Boston: Houghton Mifflin, 1912. Pp. 168.

11557 PEABODY MUSEUM OF SALEM. One hundredth anniversary of the building of 'Cleopatra's Barge,' 1816-1916, catalog of the commemorative exhibition held at the Peabody Museum...July 17-September 30, 1916. Salem, 1916. Pp. 36.
Yacht.

11558 PENFIELD, RODERIC C. "The dark years of New England history." The Peterson Magazine, New Ser., 7 (1897), 426-432.
Witchcraft.

11559 PERLEY, MARTIN VAN BUREN. A short history of the Salem Village witchcraft trials, illustrated by a verbatim report of the trial of Mrs. Elizabeth Howe: a memorial of her.... Salem, 1911. Pp. 76.

11560 PERLEY, SIDNEY. "Brooksby, Salem, in 1700." EIHC, 50 (1914), 357-365.
Locality.

11561 _____. "Cedar Pond region, Salem, in 1700." EIHC, 51 (1915), 23-40.

11562 _____. "Commercial history of Salem." Essex Antiq, 1 (1897), 1-6.

11563 _____. "The court houses in Salem." EIHC, 47 (1911), 101-123.

11564 _____. "Evidence relative to the authenticity of the 'First Church' (so-called) in Salem." EIHC, 39 (1903), 229-293.

11565 _____. "'Groton,' Salem, in 1700." EIHC, 51 (1915), 257-270.

11566 _____. The history of Salem, Massachusetts. Salem, 1924-1928. 3v.
1626-1716.

11567 _____. "Northfields, Salem, in 1700." EIHC, 48 (1912), 173-184, 260-262; 49 (1913), 186-192, 356-367.

11568 _____. "Part of Salem in 1700." Essex Antiq, 2 (1898), 167-174; 3 (1899), 65-71; 4 (1900), 17-23, 97-102, 161-170; 5 (1901), 33-37, 145-149; 6 (1902), 97-101, 148-155; 7 (1903), 18-21, 67-74, 116-124, 160-171; 8 (1904), 20-37, 66-78, 113-120, 152-164; 9 (1905), 37-43, 72-86, 114-123, 162-171; 10 (1906), 21-31, 60-74, 114-130, 152-166; 11 (1907), 12-21, 66-75, 108-117, 158-168; 12 (1908), 31-33, 113-115, 177-178; 13 (1909), 35-37, 80-82.

11569 _____. "The plains: part of Salem in 1700." EIHC, 54 (1918), 289-316.

11570 _____. "The Read farm, Salem, in 1700." EIHC, 50 (1914), 241-244.

11571 _____. "Rial Side: part of Salem in 1700." EIHC, 55 (1919), 49-74.

11572 _____. "The West Field, Salem, in 1700." EIHC, 50 (1914), 163-168.

11573 _____. "Where Roger Williams lived in Salem." EIHC, 52 (1916), 97-111.
Corwin House.

11574 _____. "Where the Salem 'witches' were hanged." EIHC, 57 (1921), 1-18.

11575 _____. "The woods, Salem, in 1700." EIHC, 51 (1915), 177-196.

11576 PERRETT, ANTOINETTE. "Old China trade." Country Life, 66 (June, 1934), 35-39.

11577 PEW, WILLIAM ANDREWS. The merchant adventurers of England: a narrative of their settlement in Salem. Salem: Newcomb & Gauss, 1926. Pp. 34. M.

11578 PHILLIPS, EDWARD HAKE. "Salem, Timothy Pickering, and the American Revolution." EIHC, 111 (1975), 65-78.

11579 PHILLIPS, JAMES DUNCAN. "The attack on the 'Marquis.'" AmNep, 9 (1949), 239-248. 1806; pepper trade.

11580 [_____]. Chestnut Street 40 years ago and the people who lived in and around it; written by one of them. Boston: Thomas Todd, 1938. Pp. 30.

11581 _____. "Commuting to Salem and its summer resorts fifty years ago." EIHC, 80 (1944), 99-108.

11582 [_____]. Famous Salem entertainments of the nineties...by the author of "Salem in the nineties." [Boston]: Thomas Todd, 1939. Pp. 17.

11583 _____. "Hamilton Hall, the hall of the Federalists." EIHC, 83 (1947), 295-307.

11584 _____. Pepper and pirates: adventures in the Sumatra pepper trade of Salem. Boston: Houghton Mifflin, 1949. Pp. xii, 141.

11585 _____. "Political fights and local squabbles in Salem, 1800-1806." EIHC, 82 (1946), 1-11.

11586 _____. "The routine trade of Salem under the Confederation Congress, May 1783-October 1789." AmNep, 1 (1941), 345-351.

11587 _____. Salem and the Indies: the story of the great commercial era of the city. Boston: Houghton Mifflin, 1947. Pp. xx, 474.

11588 _____. Salem in the eighteenth century. Boston: Houghton Mifflin, 1937. Pp. xix, 533.

11589 _____. "Salem in the nineties." EIHC, 89 (1953), 295-328; 90 (1954), 17-57.

11590 [_____]. Salem in the nineties and some of the people who lived there; written by one of them. Boston: Thomas Todd, 1937. Pp. 33.

11591 _____. Salem in the seventeenth century. Boston: Houghton Mifflin, 1933. Pp. xxi, 426.

11592 _____. "Salem merchants of 1800 and their vessels." EIHC, 80 (1944), 261-269.

11593 _____. "Salem ocean-borne commerce, 1783-1789." EIHC, 75 (1939), 135-158, 249-274, 358-381; 76 (1940), 68-88.

11594 _____. "Salem opens American trade with Russia." NEQ, 14 (1941), 685-689. Eighteenth century.

11595 _____. "The Salem shipbuilding industry before 1812." AmNep, 2 (1942), 278-288.

11596 _____. "Salem's part in the naval war with France." NEQ, 16 (1943), 543-566. 1790s.

11597 _____. Town House Square in the nineties, and some of the people who crossed it. Boston: Thomas Todd, 1940. Pp. 19.

11598 _____. When Salem sailed the seven seas-- in the 1790's. N.Y.: The Newcomen Society of England, American Branch, 1946. Pp. 28.

11599 _____. "Who owned the Salem vessels in 1810." EIHC, 83 (1947), 1-13.

11600 _____. "Why Colonel Leslie came to Salem." EIHC, 90 (1954), 313-316. Alexander Leslie.

11601 PHIPPEN, GEORGE D. "The 'old planters' of Salem, who were settled here before the arrival of Governor Endicott, in 1628." EIHC, 1 (1859), 97-110, 145-153, 185-199.

11602 PHIPPEN, WALTER G. "From Charter Street to the lookout: the Salem Hospital--a brief history." EIHC, 102 (1966), 91-162.

11603 THE PICKERING House, Salem, Mass. n.p., [1961?]. Pp. 12. M.

11604 A PILGRIMAGE to Salem in 1838, by a Southern admirer of Nathaniel Hawthorne, with a foreword by Victor Hugo Paltsits, another view by John Robinson, and a rejoinder by Mr. Paltsits. Salem: Newcomb & Gauss, 1916. Pp. 28. Paltsits attributes to William Gilmore Simms; Essex Institute and Goodspeed's Book Shop attribute to Samuel Gilman.

11605 "PINGREE House." Interior Decorator, 99 (February, 1940), 11-17.

11606 PLUMMER Hall, Salem: its libraries, collections, historical associations. Salem: Salem Pr., 1882. Pp. iv, 58. MB.

11607 POLLOCK, MABLE. Old Salem gardens. Salem: Salem Garden Club, 1946. Pp. 71. MSaE.

11608 POOLE, WILLIAM FREDERICK. "Cotton Mather and Salem witchcraft." North American Review, 108 (1869), 337-397.

11609 [_____]. Cotton Mather & witchcraft: two notices of Mr. Upham, his reply. Boston: T. R. Marvin & Son, 1870. Pp. 30. Charles W. Upham.

11610 [_____]. The Mather papers: Cotton Mather and Salem witchcraft. Boston, 1868. Pp. 23.

11611 POOR, ROGER A. A brief history of the First Universalist Society in Salem, Massachusetts. n.p., [1955?]. Unpaged. MSaE.

11612 _____. "Industry's map of Massachusetts: Salem." Industry, 3 (July, 1938), 17-19.

11613 _____. "Reminiscences of Salem sixty or seventy years ago." EIHC, 91 (1955), 147-162.

11614 _____. "The Thirteen: a Salem organization." EIHC, 99 (1963), 147-151.
Club.

11615 "POPULATION of Salem in 1637." EIHC, 42 (1906), 379; 57 (1921), 149-150.

11616 POTTER, DOROTHY MARIE. Witchcraft delusion of 1692: where were the accused hanged in Salem? Salem: Historic Salem, Inc., 1964. Pp. 19.
MSaE.

11617 "PRESIDENTIAL visits to Salem." EIHC, 82 (1946), 343-360.
Washington, 1789; Monroe, 1817; Jackson, 1830; and Polk, 1847.

11618 "PRIVATE armed ships belonging to Salem, 1799." EIHC, 71 (1935), 120-127.

11619 PROPER, DAVID RALPH. "Joseph Smith and Salem." EIHC, 100 (1964), 88-97.
Mormons.

11620 _____. "Salem witchcraft, a brief history." EIHC, 102 (1966), 213-223.

11621 PULSIFER, SUSAN FARLEY NICHOLS. "The Peirce-Nichols garden: or the bond of soil." EIHC, 102 (1966), 241-247.

11622 _____. Witch's breed: the Peirce-Nichols family of Salem. Cambridge: Dresser, Chapman & Grimes, 1967. Pp. 448.

11623 _____. Witch's breed: the Peirce-Nichols family of Salem. Supplement. Cambridge: Dresser, Chapman, & Grimes, 1967. 179 leaves.

11624 PUTNAM, ALFRED W. 25th anniversary, the Putnam Club of Salem, Massachusetts, two papers. Salem: Putnam Club, 1941. Pp. 23.
MBNEH.

11625 PUTNAM, ALLEN. Witchcraft of New England explained by modern spiritualism. Boston: Colby and Rich, 1880. Pp. 482.

11626 PUTNAM, EBEN. "An inquiry into the authenticity of the so-called First Meeting House at Salem, Mass." Putnam's HM, New Ser., 7 (1899), 207-223.

11627 PUTNAM, GEORGE GRANVILLE. Salem vessels and their voyages: a history of the 'Astrea,' 'Mindoro,' 'Sooloo,' 'Panay,' 'Dragon,' 'Highlander,' 'Shirley,' and 'Formosa,' with some account of their masters, and other reminiscences of Salem shipmasters. Salem: Essex Institute, 1925.
Pp. iv, 164.

11628 _____. Salem vessels and their voyages: a history of the European, African, Australian and South Pacific islands trade as carried on by Salem merchants, particularly the firm of N. L. Rogers & Brothers. Salem: Essex Institute, 1930. Pp. 8, 175.

11629 _____. Salem vessels and their voyages: a history of the 'George,' 'Glide,' 'Taria Topan,' and 'St. Paul,' in trade with Calcutta, east coast of Africa, Madagascar, and the Phillipine Islands. Salem: Essex Institute, 1924. Pp. iv, 166.

11630 _____. Salem vessels and their voyages: a history of the pepper trade with the island of Sumatra. Salem: Essex Institute, 1922. Pp. vi, 171.

11631 PYNCHON, WILLIAM. The diary of William Pynchon of Salem: a picture of Salem life: social and political, a century ago. Fitch Edward Oliver, ed. Boston: Houghton Mifflin, 1890. Pp. ix, 349.
1776-1789.

11632 RANTOUL, ROBERT SAMUEL. "Ancient Salem." Education, 23 (1903), 401-409.

11633 _____. "The date of the founding of Salem." EIHC, 40 (1904), 201-211.

11634 _____. "A historic ball room." EIHC, 31 (1894-1895), 69-87.
Assembly House, 1766-1805.

11635 _____. "How many men had Leslie at North Bridge?" EIHC, 32 (1897), 22-27.
Alexander Leslie.

11636 _____. "A paper on the early quarantine arrangements of Salem." EIB, 14 (1882). 1-56.

11637 _____. "The port of Salem." EIHC, 10, Pt. 1 (1870), 52-72.

11638 NO ENTRY

11639 _____. "Remarks at the meeting in Salem commemorative of the witchcraft delusion of 1692." Salem Press Historical and Genealogical Record, 2 (1891-1892), 168-170.

11640 _____. "The seventy-fifth anniversary of the founding of the Essex Historical Society." EIHC, 32 (1897), 99-132.

11641 _____. "Some claims of Salem on the notice of the country." EIHC, 32 (1897), 1-22.
Role of Salem in American history.

11642 _____. "Some notes on Chipman Hill." EIHC, 8 (1866), 118-123.

11643 RAYMOND, EDWARD H. "The fur-seal fishery and Salem." EIHC, 72 (1936), 181-207.

11644 RECORDS of Salem witchcraft, copied from the original documents.... Roxbury: Priv. Print. for W. E. Woodward, 1864. 2v.

11645 REINOEHL, JOHN H. "Post-embargo trade and merchant prosperity: experiences of the Crowninshield family, 1809-1812." MVHR, 42 (1955-1956), 229-249.

11646 ROBBINS, FRED GIBSON. "Witchcraft." EIHC, 65 (1929), 209-239.

11647 ROBBINS, JAMES H. "The impact of the first American party system on Salem politics." EIHC, 107 (1971), 254-267.

11648 ROBBINS, PEGGY. "The devil in Salem." AHI, 16 (December, 1971), 4-9, 44-48. Witchcraft.

11649 ROBOTTI, FRANCES DIANE. Chronicles of old Salem: a history in miniature. Salem, 1948. Pp. xi, 129.

11650 _____. Whaling and old Salem; a chronicle of the sea. N.Y.: Fountainhead, 1962. Pp. 292.

11651 ROBSON, MATTHEW. "Blubber Hollow and its leather industry." Weekly Bulletin of Leather and Shoe News, 19 (March 29, 1915), 36-38, 45, 47, 50.

11652 ROPES, WILLIS HENRY. "The famous mansions and gardens of old Salem." Hobbies, (July, 1939), 15-17.

11653 RYAN, MARGARET. "The Assembly House at Salem; built in 1782 and now restored to its former glory." House Beautiful, 50 (1921), 89-92.

11654 RYAN, PAT M. "The old Salem Theatre." EIHC, 98 (1962), 287-293.

11655 SALEM, MASS. Celebration at North Bridge, Salem, July 4th, 1862, oration by Dr. George B. Loring. Boston: J. E. Farwell, 1862. Pp. 30.
   Relates to the city.

11656 _____. Memorial services at the centennial anniversary of Leslie's expedition to Salem, Sunday February 26, 1775 on Friday, February 26, 1875.... Salem, 1875. Pp. 91. MBNEH.
   Alexander Leslie.

11657 _____. Town records of Salem, Massachusetts, 1634-1691. Salem: Essex Institute, 1868-1934. 3v.

11658 SALEM, MASS. ATHENAEUM. A catalogue of the library of the Salem Athenaeum, in Salem, Massachusetts: to which is prefixed a brief historical account of the institution, with its charter and bylaws. Boston: J. Wilson and Son, 1858. Pp. xxi, 179.

11659 SALEM, MASS. CITY GOVERNMENT. Salem tercentenary July 4th to 10th, official program of the celebration and episodes in history, Salem, Massachusetts 1926. Salem, 1926. Pp. 47. M.

11660 SALEM, MASS. CLASSICAL AND HIGH SCHOOL. 'The Puritan city', historical album of Salem and vicinity: sketches written and photographs taken by the pupils of the Classical and High School, Salem, Massachusetts. Salem, [189-]. Unpaged. M.

11661 SALEM, MASS. CROMBIE STREET CONGREGATIONAL CHURCH. 1832-1907, 75th anniversary celebration. Salem, 1907. Unpaged. MB.

11662 _____. One hundredth anniversary of the gathering of the Crombie Street Congregational Church....Salem, Massachusetts, May 1-15, 1932. n.p., [1932?]. Unpaged. MSaE.

11663 SALEM, MASS. ENGLISH HIGH SCHOOL. Catalogue of members of the late English High School of Salem, Massachusetts from...July 7, 1827, to...January 28, 1857 inclusive, embracing an account of the school by each of the principal teachers.... Salem: George Creamer; H. P. Ives & A. A. Smith; Henry Whipple & Son, 1857. Pp. 56, 4. MSaE.

11664 SALEM, MASS. FIRST BAPTIST CHURCH. The First Baptist Church, 150th anniversary, 1804-1954, sesquicentennial observance, May 23-27, 1954, Salem, Massachusetts. Salem, 1954. Pp. 44. MSaE.

11665 SALEM, MASS. FIRST CHURCH. Exercises in commemoration of the three hundredth anniversary of the gathering of the First Church in Salem, Massachusetts, May 26-June 3, 1929. Cambridge: Riverside Pr., 1930. Pp. xxiii, 122.

11666 _____ The records of the First Church in Salem, Mass., 1629-1736. Richard D. Pierce, ed. Salem: Essex Institute, 1974. Pp. xxvi, 421.

11667 _____. 325th anniversary of the First Congregational Society in Salem (founded August 6, 1629) now the First Church, Unitarian.... n.p., [1954?]. Unpaged. MSaE.
   Includes brief history.

11668 SALEM, MASS. FIRST UNIVERSALIST CHURCH. Centennial anniversary of the dedication of the First Universalist Meeting House of Salem, Mass.... Salem, 1909. Pp. 53. MSaE.

11669 SALEM, MASS. NORTH CHURCH. The first centenary of the North Church and Society, in Salem, Massachusetts, commemorated July 19, 1872. Salem, 1873. Pp. vii, 222.

11670 SALEM, MASS. PUBLIC LIBRARY. Address of Hon. John M. Raymond, at the opening of the Salem Public Library, June 26, 1889, with...a brief historical sketch of the movement for the establishment of such library in Salem and a notice of the libraries now in existence in the city. Salem: Salem Pr., 1889. Pp. 61.

11671 SALEM, MASS. ST. JOSEPH PARISH. La Paroisse Saint-Joseph, Salem, Massachusetts, 1873-1948. [Salem]: L'Association Laurier, 1948. Pp. 110. MSaE.
   In French and English.

11672 _____. St. Joseph Parish, Salem, Mass.,
1873-1973. Salem: Compass Pr., 1973.
Pp. 116. MSaE.

11673 SALEM, MASS. TABERNACLE CHURCH. The claims
of the Tabernacle Church, to be considered
the Third Church in Salem: or, the Church of
1735.... [Salem]: Salem Observer, 1847. Pp. 56.

11674 _____. Manual of the Tabernacle Church in
Salem, Mass. Rev. ed. Andover: Warren F.
Draper, 1863. Pp. 28. M.
Includes historical sketch.

11675 "SALEM, a port of vanished fleets." Sea
Breeze, 26 (October, 1913), 7-12.

11676 "SALEM and her architecture." Brooklyn Institute of Arts and Sciences. Bulletin, 10
(1913), 171-176.

11677 "SALEM and her witchcraft period." NOHR,
3 (August 6, 1904), 2-4.

11678 SALEM BILLIARD CLUB. Sketch, by-laws and
list of members of the Salem Billiard Club,
1893-1914. Salem: Milo A. Newhall, 1915. Pp. 38.
MSaE.

11679 SALEM EAST INDIA MARINE SOCIETY. History
of the Salem East India Marine Society.
Salem: Newcomb & Gauss, 1916. Pp. 71. MB.

11680 SALEM ELECTRIC LIGHTING CO. History of the
Salem Electric Lighting Co. with a brief
sketch of the development of the science of electricity in Salem. Salem: Salem Pr., 1889. Pp. 17.
MSaE.

11681 SALEM EVENING NEWS. Fiftieth anniversary
of the establishment of 'The Salem Evening
News', 1880-1930. [Salem?, 1930?]. Unpaged.
MSaE.

11682 _____. Highlights in the history of Salem:
a brief sketch of Salem from its settlement. [Salem?, 1926?]. Pp. 18. MBNEH.

11683 SALEM FEMALE CHARITABLE SOCIETY. An account
of the Salem Female Charitable Society.
[Salem]: William Carlton, [1803]. Pp. 8. MB.

11684 SALEM FRATERNITY. First twelve years of
the Salem Fraternity, 1869-1881. Salem,
1881. Pp. 31. MB.
Charity.

11685 _____. The Salem Fraternity, the oldest
American boys'-club, 1869-1909, its history, its work. Salem, 1910. Pp. 25. MSaE.

11686 SALEM GARDEN CLUB. Old Salem gardens.
Salem: Salem Garden Club, 1946. Pp. 71.

11687 "SALEM Hospital." Modern Hospital, 58
(February, 1942), entire issue.

11688 SALEM LIGHT INFANTRY VETERAN ASSOCIATION.
One hundred and tenth anniversary of the
organization of the Salem Light Infantry and the
fifty-third anniversary of the Veterans Association,
Thursday, October 7th, 1915. Salem: Newcomb &
Gauss, [1915?]. Unpaged.
Includes brief history by John P. Reynolds.

11689 SALEM LYCEUM. Historical sketch of the
Salem Lyceum, with a list of the officers
and lecturers since its formation in 1830, and an
extract from the address of Gen. Henry K. Oliver,
delivered at the opening of the fiftieth annual
course of lectures, November 13th, 1878. Salem:
Salem Gazette, 1879. Pp. 74.

11690 SALEM MARINE SOCIETY. History of the Marine
Society at Salem.... Salem, 1966. Pp. 99.
MB.
History is by Philip Chadwick Foster Smith.

11691 _____. The Salem Marine Society of Salem,
Mass., minutes and events in the celebration
of the one hundred and fiftieth anniversary of the
founding of the Salem Marine Society. Salem: Newcomb & Gauss, 1922. Pp. 29. MSaE.

11692 "SALEM, Massachusetts." Harper's Weekly,
15 (1871), 729-735.

11693 "SALEM reminiscences." The Sailors' Magazine, 55 (1883), 291-296.
Signed: C. B. T.

11694 SALEM SAVINGS BANK. The one hundred years
of the Salem Savings Bank: glances at an
interesting and useful past, presented by the Salem
Savings Bank. Boston: Walton Advertising and
Printing, 1918. Pp. 44.

11695 "SALEM social life in the early nineteenth
century." EIHC, 36 (1900), 105-127, 233-
244.
1812-1831.

11696 "SALEM vessels out at the beginning of the
War of 1812." United States Naval Institute. Proceedings, 58 (1932), 30-32.

11697 SALEM WILLOWS YACHT CLUB. Salem Willows
Yacht Club, 1933-1958, twenty-fifth anniversary. Salem, 1958. Pp. 96. MSaE.

11698 "THE SALEM witchcraft." American Review,
3 (1846), 60-67.

11699 SALEM witchcraft or the adventures of Parson
Handy of Punkapoag Pond. 2d. ed. N.Y.:
Elam Bliss, 1827. Pp. 70. MB.
"The narrative now republished was printed
seven years ago in detached portions, in a
monthly journal...."

11700 "SALEM'S First Church is 300 years old."
Christian Register, 108 (1929), 525-527.

11701 SALTONSTALL, LEVERETT, 1783-1845. Address
to the City Council at the organization of
the city government in Salem, May 9, 1836. Salem:
Palfray and Chapman, 1836. Pp. 32. M.
Historical.

11702 SALTONSTALL, LEVERETT, 1825-1895. "Leverett Saltonstall's reminiscences of Salem, written in 1885." EIHC, 81 (1945), 55-65.

11703 SAUNDERS, JOSEPH B. "Salem and the royal charter." EIHC, 66 (1930), 25-34.

11704 _____. A short story of three centuries of Salem, 1626-1926. Salem: Deschamps Bros., 1926. Pp. 109.

11705 SAWYER, F. E. "A history of the Salem Electric Lighting Company." Tenney Service, 5 (1918), 153-163.

11706 "SEAMEN from Salem and vicinity impressed by British war vessels, 1800-1813." EIHC, 49 (1913), 321-346.

11707 SECOND CORPS CADETS, SALEM, MASS. The history of the Second Corps Cadets. n.p., [1965?]. 2 leaves. MSaE.

11708 SHARF, FREDERIC ALAN. "'A more bracing morning atmosphere', artistic life in Salem, 1850-1859." EIHC, 95 (1959), 149-164.

11709 SHERIDAN, MARTIN. "Fun incorporated." Coronet, 25 (January, 1949), 146-150. Parker Brothers, game manufacturers.

11710 SIBSBEE, B. H. "East India Marine Society of Salem." HistMag, 2 Ser., 6 (1869), 242-244.

11711 SILSBEE, MARIANNE CABOT DEVEREUX. A half century in Salem. Boston: Houghton Mifflin, 1887. Pp. 120.

11712 "SKETCH of Lowell Island." EIB, 12 (1880), 137-165. Formerly Cat Island.

11713 SMALL, EDWIN W. "The Derby House." OTNE, 47 (1956-1957), 101-107.

11714 _____. "A national historic site at Salem, Massachusetts." Planning and Civic Comment, 4 (October-December, 1938), 14-15. Derby Wharf and vicinity.

11715 _____. "Wharf building a century and more ago." Regional Review, 3 (December, 1939), 8-13.
   Periodical was issued by Region One, Richmond, Va., National Park Service.

11716 SMITH, ELIZABETH B. "Fashions of the 'fifties." EIHC, 95 (1959), 186-198. 1850s.

11717 SMITH, HARRIS. "The case of the two 17th-century houses in disguise." Yankee, 32 (October, 1968), 86-91, 145-146, 148. Pickman and Gedney Houses.

11718 SMITH, J. FOSTER. "Stage Point and thereabouts." EIHC, 66 (1930), 1-20.

11719 SMITH, PHILLIP CHADWICK FOSTER. The frigate Essex papers: building the Salem frigate, 1798-1799. Salem: Peabody Museum of Salem, 1974. Pp. xx, 334.

11720 _____. "The Salem Marine Society, 1766-1966." AmNep, 26 (1966), 272-279.

11721 SMITH, SARAH EDEN. Reminiscences of a New England Church and people. Salem: Salem Pr., 1907. Pp. 27. South Church.

11722 SOMERVILLE, JAMES K. "Family demography and the published records: an analysis of the vital statistics of Salem, Massachusetts." EIHC, 106 (1970), 243-251.

11723 SOUTHAM, DOROTHY, ed. History of Salem. Salem: Salem Public Schools, 1952. Pp. 141. MSaE.

11724 "THE SPIRITS in 1692, and what they did at Salem." Putnam's Monthly Magazine, 7 (1856), 505-511. Witchcraft.

11725 STARKEY, MARION LENA. The devil in Massachusetts, a modern inquiry into the Salem witch trials. N.Y.: A. A. Knopf, 1949. Pp. xviii, 310, vii.

11726 _____. The visionary girls: witchcraft in Salem Village. Boston: Little, Brown, 1973. Pp. ix, 176.

11727 "A STATELY pleasure-house." EIHC, 31 (1894-1895), 205-212. Home of William Browne.

11728 STERNBERG, STANLEY M. Seventy five years of progress [of the Salem Five Cents Savings Bank] 1855-1930.... Salem: Salem Five Cents Savings Bank, 1930. Pp. 26. M.

11729 STEWART, ALEXANDER A., comp. Salem historical calendar, for the year 1892. Salem, 1891. Unpaged. Events listed next to appropriate date.

11730 STONE, LINCOLN R. "An account of the trial of George Jacobs for witchcraft." EIHC, 2 (1860), 49-57. 1692.

11731 STORY, JOSEPH. A discourse pronounced at the request of the Essex Historical Society, on the 18th of September, 1828, in commemoration of the first settlement of Salem, in the state of Massachusetts. Boston: Hilliard, Gray, Little, and Wilkins, 1828. Pp. 90.

11732 STRACHAN, RUTH and HELEN COMSTOCK. "Renewed study of Salem secretaries." Antiques, 88 (1965), 502-505.

11733 STREETER, GILBERT LEWIS. "Account of the newspapers and other periodicals published in Salem, from 1768 to 1856." EIP, 1 (1848-1856), 157-187.

11734 _____. "[Building of the frigate 'Essex' at Salem]." EIP, 2 (1856-1859), 73-80.

11735 _____. "Historical notices of Salem scenery." EIHC, 2 (1860), 2-13.

11736 _____. A letter to Mr. Thomas Carroll, of Peabody, concerning the first meeting-house in Salem, Mass. Salem: Newcomb & Gauss, 1900. Pp. 13.

11737 _____. "Salem before the Revolution." EIHC, 32 (1897), 47-98.

11738 _____. "Some historic streets and colonial houses of Salem." EIHC, 36 (1900), 185-213.

11739 STUART, MOSES. A sermon, delivered by request of the Female Charitable Society in Salem, at their anniversary the first Wednesday in August, A. D. 1815. Andover: Flagg and Gould, 1815. Pp. 32.
Contains an account of the society, 1801-1815.

11740 STURGIS, ELIZABETH ORNE PAINE. "Recollections of the 'Old Tucker House,' 28 Chestnut Street, Salem." EIHC, 74 (1938), 109-141.

11741 SWAN, MABEL MUNSON and LOUISE KARR. "Early marine painters of Salem." Antiques, 38 (1940), 63-65.

11742 _____. "Elijah and Jacob Sanderson, early Salem cabinetmakers." EIHC, 70 (1934), 323-364.

11743 _____. "McIntire: check and countercheck." Antiques, 21 (1932), 86-87.
Furnishings in the Elias Hasket Derby House by Samuel McIntire.

11744 _____. "McIntire vindicated, fresh evidence of the furniture carvers of Salem." Antiques, 26 (1934), 130-132.
Samuel McIntire.

11745 _____. "A revised estimate of McIntire." Antiques, 20 (1931), 338-343.
Furnishings in the Elias Hasket Derby House by Samuel McIntire.

11746 _____. "Where Elias Hasket Derby bought his furniture." Antiques, 20 (1931), 280-282.

11747 SYMONDS, CHARLES E. An historical address...on the Park Act...December 22, 1892 in which reference is made to several parks...and special reference to Liberty Hill and Cold Spring, its traditions and associations. Salem: Salem Observer, 1893. Pp. 36. MSaE.

11748 SYMOND, EBEN B. Old Northfields: stories of that part of Salem, Massachusetts, known in the old days as Northfields, now as North Salem of Ward Six...[Salem]: Salem Observer, 1916. Unpaged. MSaE.

11749 TAPLEY, CHARLES SUTHERLAND. Rebecca Nurse, saint but witch victim. Boston: Marshall Jones Company, 1930. Pp. xiii, 105.

11750 TAPLEY, HARRIET SILVESTER. "St. Peter's Church in Salem before the Revolution." EIHC, 80 (1944), 229-260, 334-367; 81 (1945), 66-82.

11751 _____. Salem imprints, 1768-1825: a history of the first fifty years of printing in Salem, Massachusetts, with some account of the bookshops, booksellers, bookbinders and the private libraries. Salem: Essex Institute, 1927. Pp. x, 512.

11752 TERRY, HARRIET S. "Reminiscences of Salem, written in 1884." EIHC, 84 (1948), 91-93.

11753 THACHER, JAMES. An essay on demonology, ghosts and apparitions, and popular superstitions, also, an account of the witchcraft delusion at Salem, in 1692. Boston: Carter and Hendee, 1831. Pp. iv, 234.

11754 THARP, LOUISE HALL. The Peabody sisters of Salem. Boston: Little, Brown, 1950. Pp. x, 372.

11755 THAYER, ALICE MANSFIELD. "The Salem fire [1914]." EIHC, 100 (1964), 183-194. Edited by Albert Goodhue, Jr.

11756 THAYER, OLIVER. "Early recollections of the upper portion of Essex Street." EIHC, 21 (1884), 211-224.
Houses.

11757 THOMPSON, ROGER. "Salem revisited." JAS, 6 (1972), 317-336.
Witchcraft.

11758 THORNTON, JOHN WINGATE, ed. "Witchcraft papers,--1692." NEHGR, 27 (1873), 55.

11759 THOUGHT AND WORK CLUB, SALEM, MASS. A new book of proverbs of Salem, Mass. Salem: Hutchinson & Son, 1893. Pp. 39.
Includes club history; preface signed K. T. W. [Kate Tannatt Woods].

11760 TOWNE, ABBIE W. "William Towne, his daughters, and the witchcraft delusions." Top HC, 1 (1895), 12-14.

11761 TRASK, WILLIAM BLAKE. "Trask House in Salem." EIB, 3 (1871), 126-128.

11762 TROW, CHARLES EDWARD. The old shipmasters of Salem, with mention of eminent merchants. N.Y.: G. P. Putnam's Sons, 1905. Pp. xxvii, 337.

11763 "TWO Salem dame schools." EIHC, 42 (1906), 82-84.
Higginson School and Endicott School.

11764 UPHAM, CAROLINE E. Salem witchcraft in outline. (1891) 2d. ed. Salem: Salem Pr., 1891. Pp. xiii, 161.

11765 UPHAM, CHARLES WENTWORTH. Address at the re-dedication of the fourth meeting-house of the First Church in Salem, Mass., December 8, 1867. Salem: Salem Gazette, 1867. Pp. 74.

11766 _____. Lectures on witchcraft, comprising a history of the delusion in Salem, in 1692. (1831) 2d. ed. Boston: Carter and Hendee, 1832. Pp. v, 300.

11767 _____. Principles of Congregationalism, the second century lecture of the First Church. Salem: Foote & Brown, 1829. Pp. 72. MB. A church history.

11768 _____. "Salem witchcraft and Cotton Mather." HistMag, 2 Ser., 6 (1869), 129-219.

11769 _____. Salem witchcraft: with an account of Salem Village, and a history of opinions on witchcraft and kindred subjects. Boston: Wiggin and Lunt, 1867. 2v.

11770 UPHAM, WILLIAM PHINEAS. "An account of the dwelling houses of Francis Higginson, Samuel Skelton, Roger Williams and Hugh Peters." EIHC, 8 (1866), 250-259.

11771 _____. "First houses in Salem." EIB, 1 (1869), 37-41, 53-57, 73-81, 129-136, 145-150; 2 (1870), 33-39, 49-60.

11772 _____. "Notes on the report as to the authenticity of the First Meeting House in Salem." EIHC, 40 (1904), 17-32.

11773 _____. "Town records of Salem, 1634-1659." EIHC, 9 (1868), 5-233. Detailed subject and name indexes.

11774 VALENTINE, HERBERT E. "The Amphions." EIHC, 45 (1909), 283-285. Men's chorus, 1860-1862.

11775 WALSH, LOUIS S. Origin of the Catholic Church in Salem and its growth in St. Mary's Parish and the Parish of the Immaculate Conception. Boston: Cashman, Keating, 1890. Pp. xii, 151. MSaE.

11776 WARD, BARBARA M. and GERALD W. R. WARD. "The John Ward House: a social and architectural history." EIHC, 110 (1974), 3-32.

11777 WARD, G. A. "Account of the formation of the Essex Historical Society." EIHC, 6 (1864), 41-43. 1821, later merged with Essex Institute.

11778 WARD, GERALD W. R. "Additional notes on the Crowninshield-Bentley House." EIHC, 111 (1915), 1-11.

11779 WARRINER, HORACE A. "Salem and the 'discontinuers.'" Americana, 26 (1932), 12-17. Religious toleration.

11780 WATERS, EDWARD STANLEY. "Some old estates." EIHC, 16 (1879), 37-54. Real property.

11781 WEBBER, HARRY ENDICOTT. Greater Salem in the Spanish-American War. Lynn: Perry & Searle, 1901. Pp. 88. M.

11782 [_____]. Highlights in the history of Salem. [Salem]: Salem Evening News, [1926]. Pp. 18. MSaE. Author attribution by the Essex Institute.

11783 _____. Twenty five years of history, Now and Then Association.... n.p., 1911. Unpaged. MSaE.

11784 WEBBER, WILLIAM G. & CO., SALEM, MASS. The old corner. Salem: Newcomb & Gauss, [1912]. Pp. 16. MSaE. Webber Department Store.

11785 WELCH, WILLIAM LEWIS. "Salem Neck and Winter Island." EIHC, 33 (1898), 81-128.

11786 WENDELL, BARRETT. "Were the Salem witches guiltless?" EIHC, 29 (1892), 129-147.

11787 WERKING, RICHARD H. "'Reformation is our only preservation': Cotton Mather and Salem witchcraft." WMQ, 3 Ser., 29 (1972), 281-290.

11788 WETMORE, PAUL. "The Daniel Eppes or the so-called Governor Endicott House." The Visitor, 1 (1890-1891), 69-70.

11789 _____. "The real 'House of Seven Gables.'" The Visitor, 1 (1890-1891), 59-61.

11790 WHEATLAND, HENRY. "Historical sketch of the Philosophical Library at Salem, with notes." EIHC, 4 (1862), 175-181, 271-282.

11791 WHIPPLE, GEORGE MANTUM. "History of the Salem Light Infantry." EIHC, 26 (1889), 161-308.

11792 _____. "A sketch of the musical societies of Salem." EIHC, 23 (1886), 72-80, 113-133.

11793 WHIPPLE, HENRY. "A history of the Salem and Danvers Association for the Detection of Thieves and Robbers." EIHC, 8 (1866), 65-72.

11794 WHITAKER, NATHANIEL. A brief history of the settlement of the Third Church in Salem in 1769 and also the usurpation and tyranny of an ecclesiastical council in 1784. Salem: Samuel Hall, 1784. Pp. 32. MSaE.

11795 WHITE, ARTHUR O. "Salem's antebellum black community: seedbed of the school integration movement." EIHC, 108 (1972), 99-118.

11796 WHITE, DANIEL APPLETON. A brief memoir of the Plummer family with historical notices relative to the gift of Plummer Hall. Salem: Wm. Ives and Geo. W. Pease, 1858. Pp. 36. MSaE.

11797 [_____]. A brief sketch of a lecture delivered before the Essex Institute, May 12, 1856, respecting the founders of Salem and the First Church. Salem: W. Ives and G. W. Pease, 1856. Pp. 14.

11798 ____. "[The fathers of Salem and the First Church]." EIP, 1 (1848-1856), 256-262.

11799 ____. New England Congregationalism in its origin and purity, illustrated by the foundation and early records of the First Church in Salem, and various discussions pertaining to the subject. Salem: Salem Gazette Office, 1861. Pp. iv, 319. MB.

11800 WHITE, GEORGE MERWANJEE. Old houses of Salem. Salem: Salem Gazette, n.d. 9 leaves.

11801 WHITEHILL, WALTER MUIR. The East India Marine Society and the Peabody Museum of Salem: a sesquicentennial history. Salem: Peabody Museum, 1949. Pp. xvi, 243.

11802 WHITNEY, WILLIAM T., JR. "The Crowninshields of Salem, 1800-1808--a study in the politics of commercial growth." EIHC, 94 (1958), 1-36, 79-118.

11803 WIGGIN, CYNTHIA B. "History of the Salem Book Club." EIHC, 105 (1969), 137-141. 1848-1965; merged with Salem Athenaeum.

11804 ____. "Salem Athenaeum." JLibHist, 3 (1968), 257-260.

11805 ____. Salem Athenaeum: a short history. Salem: Salem Athenaeum, 1964. Pp. 12. MSaE.

11806 WILLIS, LEMUEL. A semi-centennial address delivered in the Universalist Church, Salem, Mass., August 4, 1859.... Salem: Charles W. Swasey, 1859. Pp. 84. MBNEH.

11807 WILSON, RUFUS ROCKWELL. "The Salem of Hawthorne." The Criterion, 5 (July, 1904), 5-9.

11808 WINCHESTER, ALICE. "Living with antiques, the Pickering House in Salem, Massachusetts." Antiques, 61 (1952), 429-432.

11809 ____. "The Pingree House in Salem." Antiques, 49 (1946), 174-177.

11810 WISE, DEWITT D. Now, then, Baker's Island. Salem: Baker's Island Association, 1964. Pp. 199.

11811 WISWALL, RICHARD HALL. "Notes on the building of Chestnut Street." EIHC, 75 (1939), 203-233.

11812 WITCHCRAFT in olde Salem Village. Salem: Pilgrim Motel, 1964. Unpaged. MSaE.

11813 WOOD, FRANK A. "A bit of old Salem exposed." Contact, 21 (September, 1940), 4. Bowker Dock.

11814 WOODBURY, BENJAMIN COLLINS. Salem: an epic of New England. Boston: Geo. H. Ellis, 1926. Pp. ix, 65.

11815 WOODMAN, A. G. "Historic Salem." Western Camera Notes, 2 (January, 1901), 1-3.

11816 WORCESTER, SAMUEL MELANCTHON. A discourse, delivered on the first centennial anniversary of the Tabernacle Church, Salem, Mass., April 26, 1835. Salem: Henry Whipple, 1835. Pp. 64. MB.

11817 ____. A memorial of the old and new Tabernacle, Salem, Mass., 1854-5. Boston: Crocker and Brewster, 1855. Pp. 84.

11818 ZIFF, LARZER. "The Salem Puritans in the 'free aire' of a new world." Huntington Library Quarterly, 20 (1956-1957), 373-384.

SALISBURY

11819 BYRAM, BOHAN PRENTISS. History of the First Baptist Church, Salisbury and Amesbury, four discourses by the pastor. Salisbury: W. H. B. Currier, 1880. Pp. 120.

11820 EVANS, JOHN Q. Salisbury's earliest settlers, a paper read at a meeting of the Town Improvement Society held at Salisbury, Mass., June 17, 1896. Amesbury: C. S. Morse, 1896. Pp. 12.

11821 PETTINGELL, CHARLES IRELAND. History of Union Evangelical Church being the historical address delivered...at the centennial of the Church, October 14, 1935. n.p., [1935?]. Unpaged. MSaE.

11822 SALISBURY, MASS. TERCENTENARY COMMITTEE. A brief history of the town of Salisbury, Massachusetts and the program of the celebration. n.p. [1938?]. Pp. 68. MBNEH.

11823 SALISBURY, MASS. WEST PARISH CHURCH. The West Parish Church, Salisbury, Mass.: one hundredth anniversary, June 17, 1885. Boston: Gunn Curtis, 1885. Pp. 43.
    Later became the Rocky Hill Church in Amesbury.

SANDISFIELD

11824 FIELD, AARON W. "Sandisfield: its past and present." BHSSC, 2, Pt. 1 (1884), 73-104.

11825 SANDISFIELD, MASS. BICENTENNIAL COMMITTEE. Sandisfield bicentennial 1762-1962. Winstead, Conn.: Dowd Printing, [1962?]. Pp. 68. M. History by Janet Waterman Gowell.

SANDWICH

11826 ASHLEY, ROBERT PAUL. "The romance of a Sandwich bell." The Cape, 2 (March, 1968), 6-8.
    The Peter Adolph bell.

11827 ____. The Sandwich Historical Society. Plymouth: Leyden Pr., 1967. Pp. 25.

11828 BARBOUR, HARRIOT BUXTON. Sandwich, the town that glass built. Boston: Houghton Mifflin, 1948. Pp. viii, 318.

11829 "BOSTON and Sandwich Glass Co., 1825-1888." The Cape Cod Magazine, (1961), 5.

11830 BURBANK, GEORGE EVERETT, comp. Highlights of Sandwich history covering over 300 years. [Sandwich], 1946. Pp. 39.

11831 BURGESS, BANGS. History of Sandwich glass, [and] the Deming Jarves book of designs. Yarmouthport: C. W. Swift, 1925. Pp. 16. 'The Deming Jarves book of designs' is by Charles Messer Stow.

11832 BOURGOIN, RAYMOND B. The Catholic Church in Sandwich, 1830-1930. Boston: E. L. Grimes, 1930. Pp. 78. [MBaC].

11833 CARRICK, ALICE VAN LEER. "Historical glass-cup-plates." Antiques, 1 (1922), 61-66. Flint Glass Manufactory; Deming Jarves.

11834 CHENEY, DAVID MACGREGOR. "Roadside tales from Sandwich." Cape Cod Magazine, 9 (February, 1927), 7-8, 16.

11835 CHIPMAN, FRANK W. The romance of old Sandwich glass, with dictionary of old Sandwich patterns. Sandwich: Sandwich Publishing, 1932. Pp. 158.

11836 CRANE, PRISCILLA C. "The Boston and Sandwich Glass Company." Antiques, 7 (1925), 183-190.

11837 CROCKER, ALFRED. "The oldest church bell in the United States." CCAPL, 6 (September, 1922), 40-41. First Congregational Church.

11838 CROSBY, KATHARINE. "The house with the salt-box roof." Cape Cod Magazine, 9 (September 1, 1926), 12-13. John Smith House.

11839 ____. "Old Sandwich." Cape Cod Magazine, 8 (May, 1926), 5-6, 27.

11840 DYER, WALTER A. "The pressed glassware of old Sandwich." Antiques, 1 (1922), 57-60.

11841 FAWSETT, MARISE. Sandwich, the oldest town on Cape Cod. [West Harwich]: Jack Viall, 1969. Pp. 25. [MBaC].

11842 "FIRST establishing of high schools, Sandwich." CCAPL, 6 (August, 1922), 9.

11843 GAUPP, POLLY and CHARLES GAUPP. A Sandwich sampler: an alphabet salmagundi of the sundry Sandwich glass. East Sandwich: House of the Clipper Ship, 1970. Unpaged.

11844 GIBBS, CATHERINE B. "Sandwich--an historical sketch." CCAPL, 4 (August, 1920), 12-13.

11845 GREEN, CHARLES W. "Little-known Sandwich." Antiques, 38 (1940), 68-71. Glass manufacture.

11846 ____. "A most important discovery at Sandwich." Antiques, 32 (1937), 58-59. Glassware.

11847 HALL, CLARENCE JOSHUA. "Sandwich glass." Cape Cod Magazine, 8 (November, 1924), 10-11, 14.

11848 HARLOW, HENRY J. "The shop of Samuel Wing, craftsman of Sandwich, Massachusetts." Antiques, 93 (1968), 372-377. Furniture; eighteenth century.

11849 HARRIS, AMANDA BARTLETT. "Down in Sandwich town." Wide Awake, 25 (June, 1887), 19-27. Sandwich glass.

11850 HOLWAY, MRS. JEROME R. The old cemetery, Sandwich, Massachusetts: being a paper read before the Sandwich Historical Society on Oct. 20, 1908. Hyannis: F. B. & F. P. Goss, 1908. Pp. 16.

11851 IRWIN, FREDERICK T. The story of Sandwich glass and glass workers. Manchester, N.H.: Granite State Pr., 1926. Pp. 99. Boston and Sandwich Glass Co.

11852 KEYES, HOMER EATON. "Sandwich models." Antiques, 11 (1927), 212-213. Glass molds.

11853 LEE, RUTH WEBB. "Sandwich glass." CCC, 5 (1950), 14-18.

11854 ____. Sandwich glass...history of the Boston and Sandwich Glass Company...(1939) 10th ed. Wellesley Hills: Lee Publications, 1966. Pp. xxvii, 590. MB.

11855 MACFARLANE, VIRGINIA. "The story of Sandwich glass." The Cape, 1 (September, 1967), 3-4.

11856 MCKEARIN, HELEN. "Blown three-mold fragments excavated at Sandwich." Antiques, 35 (1939), 240-243. Glassware.

11857 "MUSEUM examples of Sandwich glass." Antiques, 34 (1938), 20-22.

11858 NASH, FRANCES TUPPER. "Descendants of Thomas Tupper and their pilgrimage to Sandwich." Cape Cod Magazine, 2 (August, 1916), 23-26.

11859 ____. "The Tupper House and its historic heritage." Cape Cod Magazine, 1 (January, 1916), 33-34, 36-37.

11860   NYE, WILLIAM L. "Sandwich Academy."
         CCAPL, 6 (August, 1922), 7-8.

11861   "OLD Sandwich." CCAPL, 4 (November, 1920),
         15-16.

11862   "ORIGINS of the Quakers at Sandwich, Massa-
         chusetts." FHABull, 8 (1917-1918), 66-68.

11863   PETERSON, BERNARD. Nye House at Sandwich.
         Yarmouthport: C. W. Swift, 1925. Unpaged.
MB.

11864   NO ENTRY

11865   PRESTON, JOHN A. "A Quaker school." Cape
         Cod Magazine, 2 (January, 1917), 25-26.
         Joseph Wing's boarding school.

11866   RAYMOND, PHYLLIS STEVENS. "Richard Bourne
         and the town of Sandwich." Cape Cod Maga-
zine, 7 (August, 1923), 7.

11867   ROMAINE, LAWRENCE B. "Some notes about the
         Sandwich Glass Company." CEAIA, 2 (1937-
1944), 22.

11868   SANDWICH-by-the-Sea: historical sketch of
         the famous old town. [Sandwich]: Sand-
wich Historical Society, 1914. Unpaged. MBNEH.

11869   "SANDWICH glass." CCAPL, 5 (September,
         1921), 34-37.

11870   "SANDWICH Glass Centennial." Cape Cod
         Magazine, 8 (June, 1925), 7-9.

11871   SETZER, DOROTHEA. The Sandwich Historical
         Society and its glass (1935) Sandwich:
Sandwich Historical Society, 1951. Unpaged.

11872   STEVES, NANCY ELIZABETH. A history of the
         Sandwich Public Library. [Bourne]: Horace
C. Pearsons, 1969. Pp. 25. [MBaC].

11873   SWAN, MABEL MUNSON. "The closing of the
         Boston and Sandwich Glass Factory." An-
tiques, 40 (1941), 372-374.
         1888.

11874   _____. "Deming Jarves and his glass-facto-
         ry village." Antiques, 33 (1938), 24-27.

11875   TOWNE, SUMNER. "Sand, smoke and spark of
         genius." CCC, 23 (1970), 30-35.
         Sandwich glass.

11876   TUCKER, EDWARD TOBEY and JOHN HOAG DILLING-
         HAM. Addresses...at the exercises held in
the Friends Meeting House at Sandwich, Massachusetts, 10 mo. 10, 1907, on the 250th anniversary of
the establishment of a meeting of the Society of
Friends in Sandwich, the earliest meeting of that
denomination in America. New Bedford: New Bedford
Evening Standard, [1907?]. Pp. 19.

11877   WALSH, LAVINIA. "Old Boston and Sandwich
         Glassworks." Ceramic Age, 56 (December,
1950), 16-17, 34.

11878   _____. "The romance of Sandwich glass."
         Cape Cod Magazine, 8 (June, 1926), 9-10,
33, (July 1, 1926), 9, 26-27, (July 15, 1926), 13,
28-29, (August 1, 1926), 13-14, 30-31, (August 16,
1926), 13, 27-28; 9 (September 1, 1926), 11, 20-21,
(September 15, 1926), 17-20, (July 1, 1927), 13,
24-25, (July 15, 1927), 11, 24-25, (August 1, 1927),
11 24-25, 27, (August 15, 1927), 18-20.

11879   WATKINS, LURA WOODSIDE. "Cup-plate frag-
         ments excavated at Sandwich." Antiques,
34 (1938), 132-133.

11880   _____. "More Sandwich patterns." Antiques,
         35 (1939), 244-245.
         Glassware.

11881   _____. "Positively Sandwich." Antiques,
         27 (1935), 132-135.
         Glassware.

11882   WILLIAMS, LENORE WHEELER. Sandwich glass.
         Bridgeport, Conn.: Park City Engineering
Co., 1922. Pp. 102. MBSpnea.

11883   _____. "Sandwich glass and some other
         pressed glass." OTNE, 13 (1922-1923), 135-
138.

11884   WINCHESTER, ALICE. "Why Sandwich glass?"
         CCC, 8 (1953), 16-18.

11885   WING FAMILY OF AMERICA, INC. The old Fort
         House. n.p., 1947. Unpaged. MBNEH.

SAUGUS

11886   ATHERTON, HORACE H., JR. History of Saugus,
         Massachusetts. [Saugus]: Citizens Commit-
tee of the Saugus Board of Trade, 1916. Pp. 107.

11887   CLARKE, MARY STETSON. Pioneer iron works.
         Philadelphia: Chilton, 1968. Pp. 80.

11888   CORNING, HOWARD. The first iron works in
         American [sic]--1645. [N.Y?], 1928.
Pp. 11.

11889   _____. The Saugus, Massachusetts, and other
         early New England iron works, a Newcomen
address delivered...at the May 2, 1945 meeting, held
at Worcester, Massachusetts. n.p., [1945?]. 12
leaves.

11890   CUMMINGS, ABBOTT LOWELL. "The 'Scotch'-
         Boardman House, a fresh appraisal." OTNE,
43 (1952-1953), 57-73, 91-102.

11891   FIRST IRON WORKS ASSOCIATION. The Saugus
         ironworks restoration. N.Y.: American
Iron and Steel Institute, 1955. Pp. 30.

11892 HALEY, PAUL ALEXANDER. Saugus, cradle of
American industry. Saugus: Saugus Publishing, 1938. Pp. 55.

11893 HATCH, ELSIE E. "Saugus, Massachusetts."
NEM, New Ser., 35 (1906-1907), 480-488.

11894 HAWKES, M. LOUISE. A brief history of the
First Parish in Saugus.... Saugus: Park
Pr., 1942. Pp. 12. MSaE.

11895 HAWKES, NATHAN MORTIMER. "A chapter in
the story of the iron works." Lynn HSR,
(1902), 46-60.

11896 _____. "The first iron works in America."
MagAmHist, 22 (1889), 404-410.

11897 PRENDERGAST, FRANK M. "Restoration of
America's first iron works in Saugus to be
completed in 1953." Industry, 17 (May, 1952), 16-
19, 34.

11898 RANDALL, CHARLES EDGAR. "The house that
was kept at home." American Forests, 74
(February, 1968), 26-27, 54-57.
Iron works.

11899 ROBINSON, E. P. "A notice of Saugus Seminary." EIHC, 19 (1882), 77-80.
Saugus Female Seminary.

11900 _____. "Sketch of Saugus." BSM, 2 (1884-
1885), 140-152.

11901 _____. "Sketches of Saugus." EIHC, 18
(1881), 241-254.
Iron works; seventeenth century.

11902 ROBINSON, HERBERT L. History of the Cliftondale Methodist Church, Saugus, Mass.,
1856-1956. Saugus: Ernest Light, 1956. Pp. 65.
MSaE.

11903 SAUGUS, MASS. BOARD OF TRADE. Saugus centenary, one hundredth anniversary of the
incorporation of the town of Saugus, 1815-1915.
Lynn: Perry & Searle, 1915. Pp. 60. M.

11904 SAUGUS, MASS. CLIFTONDALE METHODIST CHURCH.
Cliftondale Methodist Church, anniversary
program, week of March 17 to 24, 1946. n.p.,
[1946?]. Pp. 12. MSaE.
Hicludes history.

11905 WINCHESTER, ALICE. "The iron works house
at Saugus, Massachusetts." Antiques, 55
(1949), 31-33.

11906 WOODBURY, CHARLES JEPTHA HILL. Saugus Iron
Works at Lynn, Mass.: addresses at the
presentation to the city of Lynn of the first cast-
ing made in America...November 21, 1892. Lynn:
Thomas P. Nichols, 1892. Pp. 16. MB.

SAVOY

11907 MILLER, HORACE ELMER. History of the town
of Savoy.... West Cummington, 1879.
Pp. 24.

11908 "SAVOY previous to 1855: its original settlement and pioneer citizenship--its religious history--its clergymen and physicians."
Berkshire Hills, 3 (1902-1903), 89-90.

SCITUATE

11909 BLACK, MILDRED and KATHLEEN LAIDLOW. "History of the Scituate Garden Club." Scituate
HSB, 15 (June, 1963), [3-4].

11910 BONNEY, MRS. ALLERTON L. and MRS. DAVID M.
MISNER. "The history of Lawson Park."
Scituate, 23 (June, 1971), 4-7.

11911 "A BRIEF history of our [Scituate Histori-
cal] Society." Scituate HSB, 17 (December,
1966), 5.

11912 BROWN, SALLY BAILEY. "Scituate High
School--1889-1893." Scituate HSB, 10 (December, 1958), 1-3.

11913 CLYNE, PAT. "The historical scintillation
of Scituate." Scituate HSB, 27 (June,
1974), 5-7.

11914 DAUGHTERS OF THE AMERICAN REVOLUTION. MAS-
SACHUSETTS. CHIEF JUSTICE CUSHING CHAPTER.
Old Scituate. [Scituate], 1921. Pp. 292.

11915 DEANE, SAMUEL. History of Scituate, Massachusetts, from its first settlement to
1831. Boston: J. Loring, 1831. Pp. 406.

11916 EATON, WILLIAM H. "The history of a country chapel." Scituate HSB, 14 (March, 19
1962), 3-4, (June, 1962), 2-4.

11917 "GREENBUSH--Scituate, Massachusetts."
Scituate HSB, 11 (March, 1959), 2-4.
Locality.

11918 HUNNEWELL, MARY B., ed. The Glades. Boston: E. O. Cockayne, [1914?].
Club.

11919 IRWIN, WILLIAM HENRY. Scituate, 1636-1936:
an illustrated historical account of an old
New England town wherein history and literature have
gone hand in hand and where an old oaken bucket has
played a famous part. [Scituate]: Scituate Tercentenary Committee, 1936. Pp. 45.

11920 JOHNSON, MILDRED VINTON. "Story of the Micmac Indians of Scituate." Scituate HSB, 16
(June, 1964), 4.

11921 LINCOLN, CHARLES C. "The old neck road."
Scituate HSB, 4 (December, 1952), 3.

11922   MCCARTHY, RALPH F. and FRANK M. PRENDERGAST.
        "A picturesque 150-year-old industry." In-
dustry, 12 (August, 1947), 9-12, 30, 32.
        Sea moss.

11923   PRATT, HARVEY HUNTER. The early planters
        of Scituate: a history of the town of
Scituate, Massachusetts, from its establishment to
the end of the Revolutionary War. [Scituate]:
Scituate Historical Society, 1929. Pp. 386.

11924   ROBBINS, HAYES. "An old town by the sea."
        NEM, New Ser., 30 (1904), 167-174.

11925   SCITUATE, MASS. CHAMBER OF COMMERCE. Sci-
        tuate 1636-1961: a delightful Old Colony
town...published to commemorate the 325th anniversary of its incorporation, and to supplement a simi-
lar book published in 1936. Scituate: Booklet
Committee, 1961. Pp. 24. M.

11926   SCITUATE, MASS. FIRST CHURCH. Church
        manual: or the history, standing rules,
discipline, articles of faith, and covenant, of the
First (Trinitarian Congregational) Church of Christ
in Scituate, Mass. Boston: W. S. Damrell, 1844.
Pp. 36. MB.

11927   SCITUATE HISTORICAL SOCIETY. Rehabilita-
        tion of the Steadman-Russell-Stockbridge
Grist Mill, at Greenbush, September the fifteenth
1923, under the auspices of the Scituate Historical
Society. n.p., [1923?]. Pp. 8. MBNEH.

11928   "SCITUATE'S first store." Scituate HSB, 13
        (June, 1961), 2.

11929   TORREY, JAMES. "History and description of
        Scituate, Mass., 1815." MHSC, 2 Ser., 4
(1816), 219-250.

11930   [TURNER, JOHN B.]. A second series of let-
        ters concerning the history of the First
Parish in Scituate. Boston: James Munroe, 1845.
Pp. 84. MB.
        Author attribution by Boston Public Library.

11931   WIGHT, DANIEL, JR. Document of the Pilgrim
        Conference of Churches, containing an his-
torical sketch of the First Trinitarian Congregational Church of Christ in Scituate, Mass. Boston:
C. C. P. Moody, [1853?]. Pp. 49. MBNEH.

11932   WILLS, LOIS BAILEY. "Sea-mossing." NEG,
        10 (Winter, 1969), 61-69.
        A marine alga used in food, fertilizer, and
        medicine.

SEEKONK

11933   SEE HISTORIES OF BRISTOL COUNTY.

SHARON

11934   COOKE, GEORGE WILLIS. Origin and early his-
        tory of the First Parish, Sharon, Massachu-
setts: a sermon, preached on the occasion of the
150th anniversary of the formation of the church,
July 6, 1890. Boston: H. M. Hight, 1903. Pp. 27.

11935   GOULD, JEREMIAH. "Annals of Sharon, Massa-
        chusetts." Sharon Historical Society.
Publications, No. 1 (1904), 3-21.

11936   "ORIGINS of the Sharon Historical Society."
        Sharon Historical Society. Publications,
No. 1 (1904), 24-27.

11937   PARTRIDGE, LYMAN. History of the Baptist
        Church in Sharon, Mass., a historical dis-
course, delivered March 26, 1882. Mansfield:
Pratt & White, 1882. Pp. 20. MBNEH.

11938   PRATT, AMY MORGAN RAFTER. The history of
        Sharon, Massachusetts to 1865. Bridgewater:
Dorr's Print Shop, 1966. Pp. 84. MBNEH.

11939   SHARON, MASS. Sharon bicentennial, 1765-
        1965. n.p., [1965?]. Pp. 83. MBNEH.

11940   SHARON, MASS. FIRST CONGREGATIONAL CHURCH.
        The church records of Rev. Philip Curtis of
Sharon, 1742-1797. John G. Phillips, ed. Boston:
Arakelyan Pr., 1908. Pp. 64.

11941   SHARON. Boston: Edison Electric Illuminat-
        ing Co., 1909. Pp. 12. M.

11942   STOUGHTONHAM INSTITUTE, SHARON, MASS. First
        anniversary celebration of the Stoughtonham
Institute, Sharon, Mass., August 10, 1864. Boston:
A. B. Morss, 1864. Pp. 19. MB.

11943   WICKES, WILLIAM B. Sharon, Massachusetts,
        the healthiest town in New England. (1882)
Sharon: Advocate, 1892. Pp. 50.

11944   _____. Wickes' hand book of Sharon, Mass.,
        the healthiest town in New England....
Sharon: Advocate, 1896. Pp. 60.

SHEFFIELD

11945   BARNARD, JOHN GROSS. Historical address at
        the Sheffield centennial commemoration,
June 18th, 1876. Sheffield, 1876. Pp. 29.

11946   BRIGHAM, HARRY HILLYER. Two hundredth anni-
        versary of the First Meeting House in Shef-
field, Massachusetts. Sheffield: Howden Printing
Shop, 1935. Pp. 14. MWA.

11947   LITTLE, LAURA JANE ROYS. A mother's peace
        offering to American houses: or, the mar-
tyr of the nineteenth century. N.Y.: J. A. Gray,
1861. Pp. 109.
        Slavery.

11948 SCOTT, FRANK ARTHUR. Sheffield in the
Berkshires. Sheffield: W. D. French,
1904. Pp. 52. MH.

11949 SHEFFIELD, MASS. Centennial celebration of
the town of Sheffield, Berkshire Co.,
Mass., June 18th and 19th, 1876. Sheffield, 1876.
Pp. 103.

11950 SWAN, MABEL MUNSON. "Living with antiques,
the Ashley House in Massachusetts." Antiques, 56 (1949), 46-47.

11951 WARNER, HENRY C. "Bow Wow Cemetery."
Berkshire Hills, 1 (July 1, 1907), [10].

SHELBURNE

11952 BARDWELL, LEILA S. Bardwell's Ferry, Fox-
town history. [Shelburne, 1959], Pp. 35.

11953 DAVENPORT, ELMER F. As you were Shelburne:
interesting episodes in the history of
Shelburne, Mass. Worcester: Krizik & Corrigan,
1972. Unpaged. MBNEH.

11954 PRATT, H. A. "History of Franklin Academy." PVMA, 3 (1890-1898), 29-42.

11955 PRENDERGAST, FRANK M. "The sharp knives
of Shelburne Falls." Industry, 13 (June,
1948), 23-25.
Lamson & Goodnow Mfg. Co.

11956 SHELBURNE, MASS. Town of Shelburne bicentennial, 1968. Greenfield: E. A. Hall,
[1968?]. Pp. 80. MDeeP.

11957 SHELBURNE, MASS. HISTORY AND TRADITION OF
SHELBURNE COMMITTEE. History and tradition
of Shelburne, Massachusetts. Mrs. Walter E. Burnham, et al., comps. Shelburne, 1958. Pp. 222.

SHERBORN

11958 ADAMS, CHARLES FRANCIS, 1835-1915. A record of the exercises in honor of Rev. Edmund Dowse, who completed his sixtieth year as pastor of Pilgrim Church, Sherborn, October tenth,
1898, also a brief history of Pilgrim Church....
Sherbirn: Adams, 1898. Pp. 51, xxii.

11959 BARROWS, ISABEL C. "Ellen Johnson and the
Sherborn Prison." NEM, New Ser., 21 (1899-
1900), 614-633.

11960 BIGLOW, WILLIAM. History of Sherburne,
Mass. from its incorporation, MDCLXXIV, to
the end of the year MDCCCXXX; including that of
Framingham and Holliston, so far as they were con-
stituent parts of that town. Milford: Ballou &
Stacy, 1830. Pp. 80.

11961 COOLIDGE, DEBORAH PERRY DOWSE. Story of
Sherborn, containing also a 'Basket of
eggs,' a true story of June 17, 1775. Sherborn,
1918. Pp. 54. MBNEH.

11962 LORING, GEORGE BAILEY, et al. 1674-1874:
second centennial of the town of Sherborn.
October 21st, 1844. Natick, 1875. Pp. 43. MWA.

11963 SHAUGHNESSY, ANN CARR. A guide to Sherborn.
Sherborn: 300th anniversary committee,
1974. Pp. vii, 184. M.

11964 _____. The history of Sherborn. Sherborn:
300th anniversary committee, 1974. Pp. xv,
262. M.

11965 SHERBORN, MASS. Second centennial of the
town of Sherborn, October 21st, 1874. Natick: Cook and Sons, 1875. Pp. 43. MB.

11966 SHERBORN, MASS. COMMITTEE OF FIFTY. 250th
anniversary, town of Sherborn, Massachusetts, October the eleventh, twelfth and thirteenth,
nineteen hundred and twenty-four. Natick: Natick
Bulletin, 1925. Pp. 86. M.

11967 SHERBORN. Boston: Edison Electric Illuminating Co., 1909. Pp. 8. M.

11968 SHERBORN HISTORICAL SOCIETY. Sherborn, past
and present, 1674-1924. Sherborn, 1924.
Pp. 78. MBNEH.

SHIRLEY

11969 BOLTON, ETHEL STANWOOD. Farm life a century ago: a paper read upon several occasions. n.p.: Priv. Print., 1909. Pp. 24.

11970 _____. "Sawtell's Tavern, Shirley, Massachusetts." OTNE, 35 (1944-1945), 39-43.
Demolished in 1941.

11971 _____. Shirley uplands and intervales:
annals of a border town of old Middlesex,
with some genealogical sketches. Boston: George
Emery Littlefield, 1914. Pp. x, 394.
Social life and customs.

11972 CHANDLER, SETH. History of the town of
Shirley, Massachusetts, from its early settlement to A. D. 1882. Shirley, 1883. Pp. vi,
744.

11973 SHIRLEY CENTRE, MASS. TRINITY CHAPEL.
Trinity Chapel, 1901-1904. Boston: Todd,
[1904?]. Pp. 8. MBNEH.

SHREWSBURY

11974 "GENERAL Artemas Ward Homestead, Shrewsbury,
Massachusetts." OTNE, 17 (1926-1927), 147-
155.

11975 PUTNAM, HARRINGTON. An address...at the
celebration of the bicentenary of Shrewsbury, Mass., on September 9th, 1927. n.p.,
[1927?]. Pp. 12. MWA.

11976 SHREWSBURY, MASS. Two hundredth anniversary celebration, town of Shrewsbury, Massachusetts, September 9, 10, 11, 1927. Worcester: Commonwealth Pr., [1927?]. Pp. 19. MBNEH.

11977 STONE, ALDEN C. Shrewsbury, the first hundred years, a short history. Hiram and Viola Harlow, eds. Shrewsbury, [1962?]. Pp. 16. M.

11978 THAYER, FREDERICK D. Historical sketch of the First Congregational Church, Shrewsbury, Mass. Worcester: Stobbs Pr., [1924?]. MBNEH.
        Bicentennial.

11979 WARD, ANDREW HENSHAW. "History of the town of Shrewsbury." WMHJ, 2 (1826), 1-36.

11980 _____. History of the town of Shrewsbury, Massachusetts, from its settlement in 1717 to 1829, with other matter relating thereto not before published, including an extensive family register. Boston: Samuel G. Drake, 1847. Pp. 508.
        A portion of this work was issued separately under title: Family register of the inhabitants of the town of Shrewsbury, Mass.... 1847.

11981 WARD, ELIZABETH. Old times in Shrewsbury, Massachusetts: gleanings from history and tradition. N.Y.: McGeorge Printing, 1892. Pp. 187.

11982 WILLIAMS, NATHAN WITTER. Church hand-book for the Congregational Church in Shrewsbury, Mass. Boston: Damrell and Moore, 1850. Pp. 48. M.
        Includes historical sketch.

SHUTESBURY

11983 COLESWORTHY, GEORGE E. Historical sketch of the Baptist Church in Shutesbury, Mass. N.Y.: McBride Bros., 1882. Pp. 25. MBNEH.

11984 SHUTESBURY, MASS. Shutesbury, 1737-1937, commemorating the 200th anniversary of the town. [Shutesbury?, 1937?]. Unpaged. MBNEH.

SOMERSET

11985 BRAYTON, ELIZABETH HITCHCOCK. The Brayton homestead, 1714-1914, a sketch. Fall River: Dover Pr., 1914. Pp. 58.

11986 HART, WILLIAM A. History of the town of Somerset, Massachusetts: Shawomet Purchase 1677, incorporated 1790. Fall River: C. J. Leary & Sons, 1940. Pp. 247.

11987 SLADE, AVERY P. Sketches of the early history of Somerset Village. Fall River: Daily News Pr., 1884. Pp. 16. MWA.

11988 SOMERSET, MASS. FIRST METHODIST EPISCOPAL CHURCH. Exercises at the centenary celebration of the First Methodist Episcopal Church of South Somerset, Massachusetts, March second, 1902. Fall River: Almy and Milne, 1902. Pp. 36. M.

SOMERVILLE

11989 [AMERICAN LEGION. MASSACHUSETTS. SOMERVILLE POST NO. 19]. Centennial history of Somerville, county of Middlesex, Massachusetts... 1842-1942. William J. Donovan, comp. and John D. Kelley, ed. Somerville: City Pr., [1942?]. Pp. 176.

11990 AYER, JOHN F. "Medford and Walnut Streets." Historic Leaves, 2 (1903-1904), 42-46.

11991 BENNETT, EDWIN C. "Somerville soldiers in the Rebellion." Historic Leaves, 1 (January, 1903), 22-31.

11992 BOOTH, EDWARD C. "The Tufts family in Somerville." Historic Leaves, 1 (April, 1902), 21-24, (October, 1902), 21-27.

11993 BROWN, FRANK CHOUTEAU. "The Joseph Barrell estate, Somerville, Massachusetts; Charles Bulfinch's first country house." OTNE, 38 (1947-1948), 53-62.

11994 CARR, FLORENCE E. "The Mallet Family." Historic Leaves, 2 (1903-1904), 10-15.

11995 EASTERBROOK, HORACE H. History of the Somerville Fire Department, from 1842 to 1892. Boston: Robinson Printing, 1893. Pp. 100.

11996 EASTMAN, LUCIUS, R., JR. "Somerville and its churches." CongQ, 10 (1868), 241-244.

11997 ELLIOT, CHARLES DARWIN. Somerville's history. Somerville, 1896. Pp. 66.

11998 _____. The stinted common, Somerville: being an account of the division into lots and streets, of the common lands of Charlestown (between 1635 and 1685) now embraced within the limits of Somerville, Mass. Somerville: Somerville Journal Print, 1902. Pp. 10. MBNEH.

11999 _____. "Union Square and its neighborhood about the year 1846." Historic Leaves, 6 (1907-1908), 5-16.

12000 _____. "Union Square before the war." Historic Leaves, 6 (1907-1908), 32-42.

12001 EVANS, GEORGE HILL. George Washington in Somerville. Somerville, 1933. Pp. 14. Revolutionary fortifications.

12002 THE FIFTIETH anniversary of the Somerville High School, 1852-1902. n.p., 1902. Pp. 193.

12003 FREEMASONS. SOMERVILLE, MASS. KING SOLO-
MON'S LODGE. One hundred and fifty years
of King Solonom's Lodge, A. F. & A. M., 1783-1933.
[Somerville?, 1933]. Pp. 78.

12004 FURBER, WILLIAM HENRY. Historical address
delivered...in the High School building,
Somerville, July 4, 1876. Boston: J. E. Farwell,
1876. Pp. 24.
Sketch of the city.

12005 GALPIN, BARBARA JOHNSON. History of Somerville journalism. Somerville: Somerville
Journal Print, 1901. 31 leaves.

12006 HALEY, MARY ALICE. The story of Somerville.
Boston: Writer Publishing, 1903. Pp. vi,
157.

12007 HAWES, FRANK MORTIMER. "Milk Row School to
1849." Historic Leaves, 7 (1908-1909), 25-
41.

12008 _____. "The Walnut Hill School." Historic
Leaves, 8 (1909-1910), 41-48.

12009 HAYES, JOHN S. Souvenir: our public library. Somerville, 1896. Pp. 12.
Historical.

12010 HILL, HERBERT E. Historic heights and
points of interest in Somerville, Mass.
Boston, 1885. Pp. 14.

12011 HODGES, RICHARD MANNING. Life and providence: a sermon preached on the third
Lord's day in March, 1869, before the First Congregational Society in Somerville, in commemoration of
the twenty-fifth anniversary of the gathering of
that society, with an historical appendix. Boston:
Little, Brown, 1869. Pp. 35.

12012 HOLMES, WILLIAM B. "A brief history of the
[Somerville Historical] Society." Historic
Leaves, 6 (1907-1908), 75-78.

12013 JACKSON, GEORGE RUSSELL. History of the
churches of Somerville with portraits of
the pastors. Somerville: Murray & Walsh, 1882.
Pp. 38. MB.

12014 JONES, WILLIAM PREBLE. Somerville fifty
years ago, boyhood memories of the early
'eighties. Somerville, 1933. Pp. 70.

12015 KNAPP, MRS. O. S. "Washington Street as
it was." Historic Leaves, 2 (1903-1904),
46-47.

12016 MAULSBY, DAVID LEE. "Literary men and
women of Somerville." Historic Leaves, 2
(1903-1904), 1-10, 25-32, 66-71.

12017 MAYO, LAWRENCE SHAW. "Colonel John Stark
at Winter Hill, 1775." MHSP, 57 (1923-
1924), 328-336.

12018 PETERSON, BERNARD. "H. P. Welch Company
spans life of the trucking industry." Industry, 19 (December, 1953), 23-25, 65.

12019 PORTER, EDWARD GRIFFIN. "Demolition of the
McLean Asylum." MHSP, 2 Ser., 10 (1895-
1896), 548-552.
Architecture.

12020 PUTNAM, ALFRED PORTER. "Israel Putnam and
Prospect Hill." Historic Leaves, 2 (1903-
1904), 85-99.

12021 SAMUELS, EDWARD AUGUSTUS and HENRY H. KIM-
BALL, eds. Somerville, past and present:
an illustrated historical souvenir commemorative of
the twenty-fifth anniversary of the establishment of
the city government of Somerville, Mass. Boston:
Samuels and Kimball, 1897. Pp. 671.

12022 SARGENT, AARON. "Land on Barberry Lane."
Historic Leaves, 7 (1908-1909), 73-77.

12023 _____. "Original English inhabitants and
early settlers in Somerville." Historic
Leaves, 6 (1907-1908), 25-31, 49-55.

12024 SOLLERS, ALIDA G. "Ten Hills Farm, with
anecdotes and reminiscences." Historic
Leaves, 1 (January, 1903), 9-21.

12025 SOMERVILLE, MASS. Fiftieth anniversary of
the city of Somerville...celebrated July 2,
3 and 4, 1922. Somerville: Somerville Journal
Print, 1922. Pp. 60.

12026 SOMERVILLE, MASS. ADVENT CHRISTIAN CHURCH.
Historical review, 50th anniversary of the
incorporation of the Advent Christian Church of
Somerville, Mass. n.p., [1937?]. Pp. 33. MBNEH.

12027 SOMERVILLE, MASS. BOARD OF TRADE. Somerville, Mass.: the beautiful city of seven
hills, its history and opportunities.... Somerville: A. Martin & Sons, 1912. Pp. 200.

12028 SOMERVILLE, MASS. FIRST ORTHODOX CONGREGA-
TIONAL CHURCH. Manual of the First Orthodox
Congregational Church, Franklin Street, Somerville,
Mass., May, 1883. Boston: Frank Wood, 1883.
Pp. 26. M.
Includes historical sketch.

12029 SOMERVILLE, MASS. PERKINS STREET BAPTIST
CHURCH. Brief history...with the declara-
tion of faith, church covenant.... Boston: L. F.
Lawrence, 1873. Pp. 52. MB.

12030 SOMERVILLE. Boston: Edison Electric Illuminating Co., 1909. Pp. 32. M.

12031 SOMERVILLE HISTORICAL SOCIETY. Ye olden
times at the foot of Prospect Hill: handbook of the historic festival in Somerville, Massachusetts, November 28, 29, 30, December 1, 2, and
3, MDCCCXCVIII.... Somerville: Somerville Journal,
1898. Pp. 96.

12032   SOMERVILLE: its representative business-
men and its points of interest. N.Y.:
Mercantile Publishing, 1892. Pp. 80.

12033   SOMERVILLE JOURNAL CO. The Somerville
Journal souvenir of the semi-centennial,
1842-1892. Somerville: Somerville Journal, 1892.
Pp. 44.

12034   STONE, SARA A. "Some old trees." Historic
Leaves, 5 (1906-1907), 53-64, 85-91.

12035   TURNER, WALTER FRYE, comp. Representative
men of Somerville, from the incorporation
of the city in 1872 to 1898, containing the last
board of selectmen, senators, representatives, mayors, aldermen, city solicitors, city treasurers,
city clerks, city engineers, city messenger, clerk
of committees. Boston: Robinson Pr., 1898.
Pp. 103.

12036   WATKINS, LURA WOODSIDE. "The Union Glass
Company." Antiques, 30 (1936), 222-225.
1854-1935.

12037   WENTWORTH, L. ROGER. "Land on Barberry
Lane." Historic Leaves, 7 (1908-1909), 77-
85.

12038   WHITAKER, GEORGE. Historical address at
the semicentennial anniversary of the First
Methodist Episcopal Church, Somerville, September
29-October 4, 1908. n.p., [1908?]. Pp. 29.
MBNEH.

12039   WOOD, AMELIA H. "Somerville as I have
known it." Historic Leaves, 1 (October,
1902), 15-18.

SOUTH HADLEY

12040   COLE, ARTHUR CHARLES. A hundred years of
Mount Holyoke College: the evolution of an
educational ideal. New Haven: Yale Univ. Pr.,
1940. Pp. iv, 426.

12041   EASTMAN, SOPHIE E. In old South Hadley.
Chicago: Blakely Printing, 1912. Pp. 221.

12042   GREENE, JOHN MORTON. Historical address
given in the meeting house of the First
Church in South Hadley, Mass. on the sesquicentennial anniversary of the establishment of the Sabbath school in that town. Northampton: Trumbull &
Gere, 1870. Pp. 32. MNF.

12043   HOOKER, HENRIETTA EDGECOMB. "Mount Holyoke
College." NEM, New Ser., 15 (1896-1897),
545-563.

12044   [JOHNSON, CLIFFORD C.] Mount Holyoke and
vicinity: historical and descriptive....
Northampton: Gazette Printing, 1887. Pp. 32.

12045   MCLEAN, SIDNEY R. "Emily Dickinson at
Mount Holyoke." NEQ, 7 (1934), 25-42.
1840s.

12046   MAGNUSSON, MARGARET L. "'Your affectionate
Mary': a Vermont girl at Mount Holyoke."
VtH, 31 (1963), 181-192.
Mary O. Nutting.

12047   MOUNT HOLYOKE COLLEGE. The centenary of
Mount Holyoke College, Friday and Saturday,
May seventh and eighth, nineteen hundred and thirty-
seven. South Hadley, 1937. Pp. 195.

12048   _____. Memorial: twenty-fifth anniversary
of the Mt. Holyoke Female Seminary. South
Hadley, 1862. Pp. 174.

12049   _____. Mount Holyoke College: the seventy-
fifth anniversary, South Hadley, Massachusetts, October eighth and ninth, nineteen hundred
and twelve. Springfield: Springfield Printing and
Binding, 1913. Pp. 222.

12050   _____. Semi-centennial celebration of
Mount Holyoke Seminary, South Hadley, Mass.,
1837-1887. Sarah [D.] Locke Stow, ed. [Spring-
field], 1888. Pp. 155.

12051   MOUNT HOLYOKE COLLEGE. DEPARTMENT OF ECO-
NOMICS AND SOCIOLOGY. South Hadley: a
study in community life by the students in Economics and Sociology 117, 1946-1947, under the direction of Elizabeth R. Brown, Harriet D. Hudson [and]
John Lobb. [South Hadley, 1947]. 55 leaves.

12052   NUTTING, MARY OLIVIA. Historical sketch of
Mount Holyoke Seminary, founded at South
Hadley, Mass., in 1837. Washington: Govt. Print.
Off., 1876. Pp. 24.
Also published the same year in Springfield,
Mass. by C. W. Bryan.

12053   SOUTH HADLEY, MASS. A history of the sesqui-centennial anniversary celebration of
the town of South Hadley, Mass., July 29-30, 1903.
n.p., 1906. Pp. 140. M.

12054   _____. South Hadley, Massachusetts, in the
World War. Holyoke: Anker Printing, 1932.
Pp. 132.

12055   _____. 200th anniversary celebration, town
of South Hadley Massachusetts, 1753-1953.
South Hadley Falls: Hadley Printing, [1953?]. Unpaged. MAJ.

12056   SOUTH HADLEY FALLS, MASS. FIRST CONGREGA-
TIONAL CHURCH. Historical address by the
Pastor George Elisha Fisher with addresses and
letters at the semicentennial celebration of the
Congregational Church in South Hadley Falls, Mass.,
Aug. 9, 1874. Holyoke: Transcript Book and Job
Printing House, 1874. Pp. 46. MNF.

12057   _____. Manual of the First Congregational
Church in South Hadley Falls, Mass., issued
August, 1874. Springfield: Clark W. Bryan, 1874.
Pp. 24. M.
Includes historical sketch.

12058   STOW, SARAH D. LOCKE. History of Mount
         Holyoke Seminary, South Hadley, Mass., dur-
ing its first half century, 1837-1887. Springfield:
Springfield Printing, 1887. Pp. xi, 372.

12059   THOMAS, LOUISE PORTER. Seminary militant:
         an account of the missionary movement at
Mount Holyoke Seminary and College. South Hadley:
Department of English, Mount Holyoke College, 1937.
Pp. ix, 117.

12060   WARNER, FRANCES LESTER. On a New England
         campus. Boston: Houghton Mifflin, 1937.
Pp. vi, 279.
         Mount Holyoke College.

SOUTHAMPTON

12061   EDWARDS, BELA BATES. Address delivered at
         Southampton, Mass., at the centennial cele-
bration of the incorporation of that town, July
23, 1841. Andover: Allen, Morrill and Wardwell,
1841. Pp. 54.

12062   HOWLAND, DOROTHY PARSONS. Country fare.
         [Southampton, 1969). Pp. 78. MNF.
         Collection of historical articles.

12063   LINCKS, G. FRED. "Revitalizing Loudville,
         Massachusetts lead mines." Rocks and Min-
erals, 42 (1967), 578-582.

12064   PARSONS, ATHERTON W. History of old houses.
         Southampton: Southampton Historical Soci-
ety, 1966. 77 leaves. MNF.

12065   POLER, MIRA. The pageant of Southampton,
         Southampton, Massachusetts, August 2nd,
1930. Westfield: W. F. Leitch, 1930. Unpaged.

12066   RICHARDSON, JOHN P. Sketches of Southamp-
         ton's sons in the ministry. New Haven:
Hoggson, 1891. Pp. 221. MNF.

SOUTHBOROUGH

12067   BENSON, ALBERT EMERSON. History of Saint
         Mark's School. [Norwood], 1925. Pp. x,
269.

12068   FAY, PETER. Historical sketches concerning
         the town of Southboro, Mass., and other
papers. Marlboro: Pratt Bros., 1889. Pp. 75.

12069   HALL, EDWARD TUCK. Saint Mark's School: a
         centennial history. Lunenburg, Vt.: Stine-
hour Pr., 1967. Pp. xiii, 290.

12070   HUBBARD, LESTER COE. Deerfoot Dairy, South-
         borough, Mass.: the story of a great Ameri-
can farm, and the causes of its success. Boston:
Mills, Knight, 1897. Pp. 25.

12071   PARKER, JEROBOAM. A sermon delivered at
         Southborough, July 17, 1827, the day which
completed a century from the incorporation of the
town. Boston: John Marsh, 1827. Pp. 39.

12072   SOUTHBOROUGH, MASS. A record of the sol-
         diers of Southborough, during the Rebellion
from 1861 to 1866, together with extracts from public documents, &c. Marlboro': Mirror Steam Job
Pr., 1867. Pp. 127.

12073   SOUTHBOROUGH, MASS. PILGRIM CHURCH. Semi-
         centennial of the Pilgrim Church. Marlboro:
Stillman B. Pratt, 1881. Pp. 16. MBNEH.

12074   WHITE, MARTHA E. D. "Southborough." NEM,
         New Ser., 27 (1902-1903), 67-87.

SOUTHBRIDGE

12075   "THE AMERICAN Optical Company." Industry,
         3 (January, 1938), 7-10.

12076   AMMIDOWN, LUCIUS E. "The Southbridge of
         our ancestors, its homes and its people."
QHSL, 1, No. 2-4, 13-57.

12077   CLEMENCE, J. EDWARD. "Clemence Box Shop."
         QHSL, 2, No. 20, 201-208.
         Wooden boxes.

12078   COCHRAN, JOHN M. "Sandersdale." QHSL, 2,
         No. 21, 209-216.
         Locality.

12079   COREY, GEORGE W. "Southbridge in the Civil
         War." QHSL, 1, No. 10, 121-130.

12080   GATINEAU, FÉLIX. Histoire des Franco-
         Américains de Southbridge, Massachusetts.
Framingham: Lakeview Pr., 1919. Pp. 253.

12081   GRANT, GEORGE. "Newspapers of Southbridge."
         QHSL, 3, No. 3, 25-35.

12082   HADLEY, WILLIS A. "Elm St. Congregational
         Church." QHSL, 3, No. 7, 77-92.

12083   HOAR, GEORGE FRISBIE. A New England town:
         speech...in the Senate of the United States,
June 12, 1894. Washington, 1894. Pp. 16.

12084   "KNIVES for a nation." Industry, 26 (Sep-
         tember, 1961), 20-21.
         Russell Harrington Cutlery Co.

12085   LITCHFIELD, WILFORD J. "Shuttleville,
         Southbridge, Mass. and the Litchfield Shut-
tle Company." QHSL, 2, No. 10-11, 75-90.

12086   _____. "Southbridge as a poll parish."
         QHSL, 1, No. 1, 1-12.

12087   "MARCY St. Grammar School." Sturbridge
         Amateur, 1 (1904), 25-26.

12088   MURRAY, BARBARA T., ed. Historical album
         of Southbridge...Massachusetts: 1816-1966
sesquicentennial celebration--May 20-29. Southbridge: Sesquicentennial Committee, 1966. Pp. 140.
M.

12089   "AN OLD blade at the cutlery art." Indus-
         try, 33 (September, 1968), 43, 68-69.
         Russell Harrington Cutlery Co.

12090   "125 years of American Optical Company."
         Industry, 23 (April, 1958), 11-14.

12091   PAIGE, MRS. C. D. "Dresser Manufacturing
         Co. and Central Mills." QHSL, 2, No. 15-
16, 139-152.
         Cotton.

12092   PAIGE, JOHN E. "Taverns and early hotels
         of Southbridge." QHSL, 3, No. 6, 65-75.

12093   PLIMPTON, MOSES. History of Southbridge,
         delivered before the Southbridge, Mass.,
Lyceum, or Literary Association in three lectures,
March, 1836. Southbridge: Journal Steam Book
Print, 1882. Pp. 48.

12094   RUSSELL, WILLIAM BLACK. "The Y.M.C.A."
         Sturbridge Amateur, 1 (1904), 9-12.

12095   "SEVENTY-FIVE years of accumulated know-
         how." Industry, 15 (August, 1950), 19-22.
         Hyde Manufacturing Co., cutlery.

12096   SOUTHBRIDGE, MASS. Reference book of
         Southbridge. [Southbridge]: Geo. Grant,
[1898?]. Pp. 78. MBNEH.
         Biographies and a history of the fire
         department.

12097   _____. Southbridge centennial...1816-1916,
         July 2-3-4, 1916. n.p., 1916. Pp. 23. M.

12098   SOUTHBRIDGE, MASS. FIRST BAPTIST CHURCH.
         History of the division of the First Bap-
tist Church in Southbridge, Mass., which took place
in September, 1842. Worcester: Henry J. Howland,
1843. Pp. 36. M.

12099   SOUTHBRIDGE NATIONAL BANK. The Southbridge
         National Bank through a hundred years.
Southbridge, 1938. Pp. 50. MH-BA.

12100   WELLS, GEORGE W. "American Optical Com-
         pany." QHSL, 2, No. 17-19, 153-200.

SOUTHWICK

12101   CHAMBERLAIN, ALLEN. "An unwritten chapter
         in Massachusetts geography." NEM, New
Ser., 16 (1897), 339-345.

12102   MERRILL, DAVID. "Isaac Damon and the South-
         wick column papers." OTNE, 54 (1963-1964),
48-58.
         Architecture of Congregational Church.

SPENCER

12103   SPENCER, MASS. FIRST CONGREGATIONAL CHURCH.
         Manual of the First Congregational Church
in Spencer, Massachusetts, containing the history of
the church, articles of faith, form of admission,
covenant, rules, list of officers and members.
Spencer: Leader Print, 1905. Pp. 40. MWA.

12104   SPENCER bicentennial, 1753-1953. Spencer:
         Bicentennial Committee, 1953. Unpaged. M.

12105   SPENCER NATIONAL BANK. The fiftieth anni-
         versary.... Spencer: Heffernan Pr.,
[1925?]. Unpaged. MBNEH.
         1875-1925.

12106   TOWER, HENRY MENDELL. Historical sketches
         relating to Spencer, Mass. Spencer: W. J.
Heffernan--Spencer Leader Print, 1901-1909. 4v.

SPRINGFIELD

12107   ABBOTT, JACOB. "The armory at Springfield."
         Harper's Magazine, 5 (1852), 145-161.

12108   ADAMS, WILLIAM FREDERICK. "Home of the
         Connecticut Valley Historical Society."
WNE, 2 (1912), 115-117.
         Wesson Mansion.

12109   "THE ALEXANDER House - Linden Hall, State
         Street, Springfield, Massachusetts." OTNE,
30 (1939-1940), 35-40.

12110   ALLABEN, FRANK. "Ancient Agawam--modern
         Springfield." National Magazine, 16 (1892),
561-585.

12111   AMERICAN INTERNATIONAL COLLEGE. A history
         of American International College: commemo-
rating the 75th anniversary, 1885-1960. Springfield, 1960. Pp. 66. MNF.

12112   BAGG, ERNEST NEWTON. "Springfield, model
         city of the Connecticut Valley." NEM,
New Ser., 38 (1908), 711-721.

12113   _____. 'Springfield old and new,' tercen-
         tenary souvenir, 1636-1936. Springfield:
Historical Souvenir Publishing, 1936. Unpaged.

12114   BAILEY, HENRY LINCOLN. "Snapshots at Long-
         meadow Precinct." CVHSP, 4 (1904-1907),
79-89.

12115   "THE BALDWIN-Duckworth Chain Corporation."
         Industry, 3 (October, 1937), 7-9.

12116   BARROWS, CHARLES HENRY. An historical ad-
         dress delivered before the citizens of
Springfield in Massachusetts at the public celebration, May 26, 1911, of the two hundred and seventy-
fifth anniversary of the settlement: with five appendices, viz: Meaning of Indian local names, The
cartography of Springfield, Old place names of
Springfield, Unrecorded deed of Nippumsuit, Unrecorded deed of Paupsunnuck. Springfield: Connectucut
Valley Historical Society, 1916. Pp. 100.

12117 _____. The history of Springfield in Massachusetts, for the young: being also in some
part the history of other towns and cities in the
county of Hampden. (1909). Springfield: Connecticut Valley Historical Society, 1921. Pp. 194.
Not juvenile literature.

12118 "THE BAY State Thread Works." Industry, 7
(April, 1942), 23-26.

12119 BEMIS, EDWARD W. "Old time answers to
present problems as illustrated by the early legislation of Springfield." New Englander and
Yale Review, 46 (1887), 117-139.

12120 BLAKE, CLARENCE E. "Springfield, Massachusetts." NEM, New Ser., 9 (1893-1894), 574-
599.

12121 _____. The story of the French Protestant
college, Springfield, Mass. Springfield:
Journal Printing, 1889. Pp. 16.
American International College.

12122 BLISS, GEORGE, 1764-1830. An address, delivered at the opening of the town-hall in
Springfield, March 24, 1828, containing sketches of
the early history of that town, and those in its
vicinity.... Springfield: Tannatt, 1828. Pp. 68.

12123 BLISS, GEORGE, 1793-1873. Historical memoir of the Springfield Cemetery, read to
the proprietors at their meeting, May 23, 1857,
accompanied by an address delivered at the consecration of the cemetery, September 5, 1841, by Rev.
Wm. B. O. Peabody. Springfield: Samuel Bowles,
1857. Pp. 23.

12124 BOOTH, HENRY A. "Springfield during the
Revolution." CVHSP, 2 (1882-1903), 285-
308.

12125 BRECK, ROBERT. Past dispensations of
Providence called to mind, in a sermon, delivered in the First Parish in Springfield, on the
16th of October 1775, just one hundred years from
the burning of the town by the Indians. Hartford:
Barlow & Babcock, 1784. Pp. 28.

12126 BRIGGS, ALBERT D. Historical memoir of the
Springfield Cemetery, read to the proprietors at their annual meeting, May 6th, 1878 by their
president, with by-laws adopted June 24th, 1878,
accompanied by an address delivered at the consecration of the cemetery, Sept. 5th, 1841, by Wm.
B. O. Peabody. Springfield: Atwood and Noyes,
1878. Pp. 48.

12127 BROWN, RICHARD D. Urbanization in Springfield, Massachusetts, 1790-1830. Springfield: Connecticut Valley Historical Museum,
1962. Pp. 35.

12128 BURT, HENRY M. "Springfield in olden
times." CVHSP, 2 (1882-1903), 112-130.
Seventeenth century.

12129 CARVALHO, JOSEPH III and ROBERT EVERETT.
"Statistical analysis of Springfield's
French-Canadians (1870)." HJWM, 3 (Spring, 1974),
59-63.

12130 CHAPIN, CHARLES WELLS. History of the 'old
high school' on School Street, Springfield,
Massachusetts, from 1828 to 1840, with a personal
history in part, with portraits, and a sketch of
the building. Springfield: Springfield Printing
and Binding, 1890. Pp. 129.

12131 _____. Sketches of the old inhabitants and
other citizens of old Springfield of the
present century, and its historic mansions of 'ye
olden tyme,' with one hundred and twenty four illustrations and sixty autographs. Springfield:
Springfield Printing and Binding, 1893. Pp. xi,
420.

12132 CHATTO, CLARENCE I. and ALICE L. HALLIGAN.
The story of the Springfield plan. N.Y.:
Barnes & Noble, 1945. Pp. xviii, 201.
Education.

12133 COMMERCE, manufactures and resources of
Springfield, Mass. and environs, a historical, statistical and descriptive review. Springfield: National Publishing Co., 1883. Pp. 172.
MWA.

12134 CONE, LUTHER HART. Ten years' review: a
sermon by...[the] pastor of Olivet Church,
Springfield, Mass., October 28, 1877. Springfield:
Weaver, Shipman, 1878. Pp. 20.

12135 DENNIS, ALBERT WOODBURY. "The 'Springfield
Republican' and the Bowles family." Mass
Mag, 8 (1915), 109-122.
Newspaper.

12136 DOWLING, ROBERT L. "Identifying our early
Springfield muskets." Antiques, 35 (1939),
184-185.

12137 _____. "The last black-powder rifles used
in the United States service." Antiques,
48 (1945), 214-215.
Made at Springfield Armory.

12138 _____. "The Springfield Rifle of the Civil
War." Antiques, 41 (1942), 52-53.

12139 DUNBAR COMMUNITY LEAGUE, SPRINGFIELD, MASS.
Sociological survey of the Negro population
of Springfield, Mass. William N. DeBerry, ed.
Springfield, [1940?]. Pp. 15.

12140 DVARECKA, C. L. Springfield Armory: point-
less sacrifice. Ludlow: Prolitho Publishing, 1968. Pp. 177.
Closed in 1968.

12141 ELLIS, THEODORE W. Manual of the First
Church of Christ and names of all the members from the year 1735 to Nov. 1, 1885. Springfield: Springfield Printing, 1885. Pp. 170. M.

12142 ESSLEN, RAINER. "Pioneer lithographing company nears 100-year mark." Industry, 25 (November, 1959), 33-34, 71.
　　　Milton Bradley Co.: founded 1860.

12143 EUSTIS, WILLIAM TAPPAN. Lest the cross of Christ should be made of none effect, the atonement not a dramatic representation, but the central truth of the gospel: a sermon preached to the Memorial Church, Springfield, Mass., December 9th, 1877.... Springfield: Atwood and Noyes, 1878. Pp. 32. M.
　　　Includes brief history of the church.

12144 _____. The possibilities and limitations of Christian unity in the local church: a sermon delivered to the Memorial Church, Springfield, Mass., January 10, 1875. Springfield: C. W. Bryan, 1875. Pp. 23.
　　　Includes history.

12145 FAIRMAN, CHARLES G. "College-trained immigrants, a study of Americans in the making." NEM, New Ser., 42 (1910), 577-584.
　　　American International College.

12146 FRISCH, MICHAEL H. Town into city: Springfield, Massachusetts, and the meaning of community, 1840-1880. Cambridge: Harvard Univ. Pr., 1972. Pp. ix, 301.

12147 FULLER, CLAUD E., comp. Springfield muzzle-loading shoulder arms: a description of the flint lock muskets, musketoons and carbines and the muskets, musketoons, rifles, carbines and special models from 1795 to 1865, with Ordnance Office reports, tables and correspondence and a sketch of Springfield Armory. N.Y.: F. Bannerman Sons, 1930. Pp. 176.

12148 GERBER, RICHARD A. "Liberal Republicanism, Reconstruction and social order: Samuel Bowles as a test case." NEQ, 45 (1972), 393-407.
　　　1860s and 1870s.

12149 "THE GILBERT & Barker Manufacturing Company." Industry, 5 (July, 1940), 7-10.
　　　Gasoline pumps and oil burners.

12150 GREEN, MASON ARNOLD. "The Breck controversy in the First Parish in Springfield in 1735." CVHSP, 1 (1876-1881), 8-16.

12151 _____. Springfield memories: odds and ends of anecdote and early doings, gathered from manuscripts, pamphlets, and aged residents. Springfield: Whitney & Adams, 1876. Pp. 110.

12152 _____. Springfield, 1636-1886: history of town and city, including an account of the quarter-millennial celebration at Springfield, Mass., May 25 and 26, 1886. [Springfield]: C. A. Nichols, 1888. Pp. 645.

12153 HALL, EDWARD A. "The Catholic lot on the Armory grounds." CVHSP, 4 (1904-1907), 217-226.

12154 HALL, NEWTON M. "When Washington came to Springfield." MagHist, 1 (1905), 232-238.
　　　1789.

12155 HAMPDEN COUNTY CHILDREN'S AID SOCIETY, SPRINGFIELD, MASS. Constitution and by-laws of the Hampden County Children's Aid Association with a statement of the origin and object of the society. Springfield: Weaver, Shipman, 1880. Pp. 12. MB.

12156 HARDWICK, ARTHUR F., ed. History of the Central Labor Union of Springfield, Mass.; with some of the pioneers [and] brief sketches of affiliated unions, 1887-1912. [Springfield, 1912]. Pp. 180.

12157 HAWKINS, NEHEMIAH. "Springfield in retrospect and in prospect." CVHSP, 4 (1904-1907), 108-123.

12158 HIGHLAND CO-OPERATIVE BANK. Highland Community, Springfield, Massachusetts: facts of interest concerning its early and more recent history, its phenomenal growth and development, its residential and commercial advantages, and its educational, religious & industrial institutions; a city within a city. Springfield, 1921. Pp. 64.

12159 "HISTORY of firearms industry preserved at Arsenal." Industry, 34 (June, 1969), 12-13, 43, 47.

12160 HOOKER, RICHARD. A century of service: the Massachusetts Mutual story. Springfield: Massachusetts Mutual Life Insurance Co., 1951. Pp. 191.

12161 _____. The story of an independent newspaper, one hundred years of the Springfield Republican, 1824-1924. N.Y.: Macmillan, 1924. Pp. xii, 237.

12162 HOWARD, THOMAS D. "The north end of Main Street." CVHSP, 4 (1904-1907), 203-212.

12163 HOWE, FLORENCE THOMPSON. "A communion service of Springfield, Massachusetts." Antiques, 21 (1932), 33-34.
　　　First Church.

12164 _____. "The decline and fall of William Lloyd." Antiques, 17 (1930), 117-121.
　　　Cabinetmaker.

12165 _____. "Some early New England church pewter." Antiques, 22 (1932), 92-94.
　　　First Church.

12166 HUMPHREYS, CHARLES ALFRED. A sketch of the history of the first half century of the Third Congregational Society of Springfield, Mass., address at the dedication of the Church of the Unity, sermon upon the character and ministry of Rev. William B. O. Peabody. Springfield: Samuel Bowles, 1869. Pp. 50.

12167 HUTCHINS, W. T. Historical discourse delivered at the Evangelical Church, Indian Orchard, Mass., March 8, 1896. [Springfield]: Clark W. Bryan, [1896?]. Pp. 33. M.
　　　Semicentennial of the church.

12168 "THE INDIAN Motorcycle Company." Industry, 3 (May, 1938), 7-10, 57.

12169 "INDUSTRY'S map of Massachusetts: Springfield." Industry, 2 (April, 1937), 37-39.

12170 "INDUSTRY'S map of Massachusetts: Springfield." Industry, 3 (April, 1938), 11-14, 60.
　　　　Differs from above article.

12171 "IRISH pioneers in Springfield, Mass." AIrHSJ, 9 (1910), 475-477.

12172 JAMES, GEORGE WHARTON. "Municipal art in American cities: Springfield, Massachusetts." Arena, 37 (1907), 16-30.
　　　　Civic improvement.

12173 JOHNSON, GRACE PETTIS. Historical sketch: Museum of Natural History, 1859-1909. Springfield: The [City Library] Association, 1910. Pp. 58.

12174 JOHNSON, SCOTT R. "The trolley car as a social factor: Springfield, Massachusetts." HJWM, 1 (Fall, 1972), 5-17.

12175 [JOHNSON, STANLEY]. Springfield, Mass.: her picturesque beauty and commercial enterprise.... [Springfield]: Springfield Printing and Binding, 1889. Pp. 29.

12176 KIMBALL, W. G. C. "Committee of Safety muskets." Antiques, 50 (1946), 322-323.
　　　　Made by Martin Ely during the Revolution.

12177 KING, MOSES, ed. King's handbook of Springfield, Massachusetts: a series of monographs, historical and descriptive, one hundred and fifty views and portraits. Springfield: James D. Gill, 1884. Pp. 394.
　　　　Includes bibliography by William Clogston.

12178 LANE, E. N. and R. G. MURRAY. "List of 190 notable facts in the history of Springfield from 1635 to date." Springfield City Library Bulletin, 19 (July, 1899), 3-6, (August, 1899), 3-4.

12179 LESHURE, A. P. "Fire department of the city of Springfield." CVHSP, 2 (1882-1903), 133-146.

12180 LEWIS, BERKELEY R. "Springfield, Massachusetts: center of early ammunition manufacture." Military Collector and Historian, 17 (1965), 110-114.

12181 LEWIS, ELLA MAY SWINT, comp. Baptisms, marriages, and deaths, 1736-1809, First Church, Springfield, Mass. Springfield, 1938. 103 leaves.
　　　　Includes a name index.

12182 MCINTYRE, RUTH A. Old First Church: the fourth meetinghouse (1819). Springfield, 1962. Unpaged.

12183 MCKNIGHT, GEORGE H. Anniversary sermon delivered in Christ Church, November 29, 1863. Springfield: Samuel Bowles, 1864. Pp. 24. M.
　　　　1817-1863.

12184 "MANUFACTURERS for children." WNE, 1 (1910-1911), 173-175.
　　　　Milton Bradley Co.; games.

12185 MERRIAM, G. & C., COMPANY, PUBLISHERS, SPRINGFIELD, MASS. 100th anniversary of the establishment of G. & C. Merriam Company, Springfield, Massachusetts 1831-1931, publishers of the Merriam-Webster dictionaries since 1843. [Springfield, 1931]. Unpaged.

12186 "MERRIAM'S 100th birthday." Publishers' Weekly, 119 (January 10, 1931), 211-214.

12187 MILTON BRADLEY CO., SPRINGFIELD, MASS. Milton Bradley, a successful man; a brief sketch of his career and the growth of the institution which he founded, published by Milton Bradley Co. in commemoration of their fiftieth anniversary, Springfield, Massachusetts, February, 1910. N.Y.: J. F. Tapley, 1910. Pp. viii, 89.

12188 MORRIS, HENRY. History of the First Church in Springfield: an address delivered June 22, 1875.... Springfield: Whitney & Adams, 1875. Pp. 60.

12189 _____. "The old Main Street jail and house of correction." CVHSP, 1 (1876-1881), 29-35.

12190 _____. "The old Pynchon Fort and its builders." CVHSP, 1 (1876-1881), 123-133.
　　　　Pynchon family mansion.

12191 _____. 1636-1675, early history of Springfield: an address delivered October 16, 1875, on the two hundredth anniversary of the burning of the town by the Indians, with an appendix. Springfield: F. W. Morris, 1876. Pp. vi, 85.
　　　　King Philip's War.

12192 "A NEW England publishing house of world-wide name and fame: the Phelps Publishing Company." Progressive Springfield, 2 (1891), 163-168.

12193 NEWDICK, EDWIN W. "Springfield's growth: its quantity and quality." WNE, 1 (1910-1911), 116-120.
　　　　Includes statistics.

12194 NEWELL, J. K. "Old Springfield Fire Department." CVHSP, 1 (1876-1881), 19-28.

12195 "NEWER Springfield." National Magazine, 17 (April, 1893), i-x.

12196 "100 years of Merriam-Webster dictionaries." Publishers' Weekly, 151 (January 11, 1947), 156-160.

12197 "ONE hundred years old." The Spur, 7 (May-June, 1927), 3-15.
Springfield Institution for Savings.

12198 ORR, WILLIAM. "An American holiday." Atlantic, 103 (1909), 782-789.
Fourth of July.

12199 PRENDERGAST, FRANK M. "Allure is their business." Industry, 22 (February, 1937), 23-26.
John H. Breck, Inc., hair and scalp preparations.

12200 PRESCOTT, G. B. "The United States Armory." Atlantic, 12 (1863), 436-451.

12201 RIPPEL, J. ALBERT. "Springfield, Massachusetts, a city of homes." National Magazine, 17 (1902-1903), 97-102.

12202 RYWELL, MARTIN. Smith & Wesson: the story of the revolver...and 100 years of gunmaking. Harriman, Tenn.: Pioneer Pr., 1953. Pp. 139.
'100 years of gunmaking' by Carl Reinhold Hellstrom.

12203 SCANLON, JOHN J. The passing of the Springfield Republican. Amherst: Amherst College, 1950. Pp. 82.
Newspaper.

12204 SENTER, ORAMEL S. "Springfield as it was and is." Potter's AmMo, 9 (1877), 241-256.

12205 SIMMONS, GEORGE FREDERICK. Public spirit and mobs: two sermons delivered at Springfield, Mass., on Sunday, February 23, 1851, after the Thompson Riot. Springfield: Merriam, Chapin, 1851. Pp. 31.

12206 SMITH, WILLIAM I. "Springfield in the insurrection of 1786 (Shays' Rebellion)." CVHSP, 1 (1876-1881), 72-90.

12207 SPRINGFIELD, MASS. An epitome of Baptist history in Springfield, Mass., from 1811-1889, consisting of brief sketches of First, State Street, Highland, Carew Street, Third and West Springfield Baptist Churches and their missions. Springfield: Springfield Printing and Bindery Co., 1889. Pp. 15. M.

12208 _____. The first century of the history of Springfield: the official records from 1636 to 1736, with an historical review and biographical mention of the founders, by Henry M. Burt.... Springfield: H. M. Burt, 1898-1899. 2v.

12209 _____. 250th anniversary of the settlement of Springfield, Massachusetts, 1636-1886. n.p.: French & McDonald, [1886?]. Pp. 80. MWA.

12210 NO ENTRY

12211 SPRINGFIELD, MASS. FIRE DEPARTMENT. Historical and illustrated memento [of the] fire department of Springfield, Mass., 1897.... Springfield, 1897. Pp. 108. M.

12212 SPRINGFIELD, MASS. FIRST CHURCH OF CHRIST. First Church of Christ in text and picture, 1637-1912. Springfield: Two Hundred and Seventy Fifth Anniversary Printing Committee, 1912. Unpaged.

12213 _____. The First Church, Springfield, 1637-1915: milestones through twenty-seven decades.... Springfield: F. A. Bassette, 1915. Pp. 32.

12214 _____. Manual catalog of the First Church of Christ in Springfield, Massachusetts, issued January, 1866. Albany: Charles Van Benthuysen's Steam Printing House, 1866. Pp. 40. M.
Brief historical sketch.

12215 SPRINGFIELD, MASS. MUSEUM OF NATURAL HISTORY. The Museum of Natural History, 1859 to 1934...opening of the new building and 75th anniversary. Springfield, 1934. Pp. 31. M.

12216 SPRINGFIELD, MASS. NORTH CONGREGATIONAL CHURCH. Fiftieth anniversary, October 25 to November 1, 1896, sermon by Rev. Frank Barrows Makepeace. [Springfield, 1897?]. Pp. 53. M.

12217 SPRINGFIELD, MASS. OLIVET CONGREGATIONAL CHURCH. Semi-centennial: historical sermon by the pastor, Rev. L. H. Cone; papers, letters, addresses by the former pastors and ministers. Springfield: Cyrus W. Atwood, 1883. Pp. 43. M.

12218 SPRINGFIELD, MASS. ST. JOHN'S CONGREGATIONAL CHURCH. The history of St. John's Congregational Church, Springfield, Massachusetts, 1844-1962. Springfield: History Committee, St. John's Congregational Church, 1962. Pp. 138.

12219 SPRINGFIELD, MASS. SOUTH CONGREGATIONAL CHURCH. Fortieth anniversary...sermon by Noah Porter, historical discourse by Samuel Giles Buckingham. Springfield: M. C. Stebbins, 1882. Pp. 91. MB.

12220 _____. The history of South Congregational Church, Springfield, Massachusetts, including numerous illustrations recording the growth of the church over one hundred years, 1842-1942. James Gordon Gilkey, comp. Springfield: Centennial Committee, 1941. Pp. ix, 134.

12221 SPRINGFIELD, MASS. STATE STREET BAPTIST CHURCH. Twenty-fifth anniversary, Sunday and Monday, May 19 and 20, 1889. [Springfield]: Springfield Printing and Binding, [1889?]. Pp. 16. M.

12222 "THE SPRINGFIELD Armory, 1794-1968." Massachusetts Division of Employment Security. Quarterly Statistical Bulletin, (March, 1968), entire issue.

12223 SPRINGFIELD FIRE AND MARINE INSURANCE COM-
PANY. A century of achievement, 1849-1949:
the story of a century of constant devotion to protection against loss by fire and other perils.
Springfield, 1949. Pp. 66.

12224 _____. Half century's history...1849-1899.
Springfield: F. A. Bassette, 1901. MB.

12225 _____. Seventy-five years of fire insurance: an account of the origin and development of the Springfield Fire and Marine Insurance
Company, presented by the Springfield Fire and Marine Insurance Company of Springfield, Massachusetts,
in commemoration of its seventy-fifth anniversary,
1924. [Springfield, 1924]. Pp. x, 122.

12226 SPRINGFIELD HOMESTEAD. Springfield, Massachusetts, for two hundred and seventy-five
years: from the Springfield Homestead, issues of
May 22, 24, 27, 1911, anniversary week of the
founding of our city. Springfield: Springfield,
[1911]. Pp. 88.

12227 SPRINGFIELD HORSE SHOWS. Details and proceedings of the exhibition of 1867, with a
history of the origin and progress of the celebrated Springfield Horse Shows as shown by former exhibitions in 1853, 1857, 1858, and 1860. Springfield: Samuel Bowles & Co., 1867. Pp. 28. MB.

12228 "THE 'SPRINGFIELD idea,' a safe and sane
fourth: a reform of the greatest national
holiday, its history, methods and results in the
city and section where it originated." WNE, 1
(1910-1911), 228-234.

12229 SPRINGFIELD POLICE RELIEF ASSOCIATION. History of the Department of Police Service of
Springfield, Mass., from 1636 to 1906, historical
and biographical, illustrating the equipment and
efficiency of the police force today, with reminiscences of the past containing authentic information
carefully gleaned from official sources. Springfield, 1906. Pp. 104, xiv. M.

12230 SPRINGFIELD SAFE DEPOSIT AND TRUST COMPANY.
65th anniversary Springfield Safe Deposit
and Trust Company, June first, 1886-1951. Springfield, 1951. Unpaged. M.

12231 SPRINGFIELD ZOOLOGICAL CLUB. The Spring-
field Zoological Club. Springfield: City
Library Association, 1900. Pp. 7.
Includes a history of the club.

12232 STEARNS, CHARLES. The national armories:
a review of the systems of superintendency,
civil and military, particularly with reference to
economy and general management at the Springfield
Armory (1852). 3d. ed. Springfield: George W.
Wilson's Steam Power Presses, 1853. Pp. 82. MB.

12233 "SUCCESSFUL subscription book publishers:
King, Richardson & Company." Progressive
Springfield, 1 (1891), 175-176.

12234 TOBEY, FRANK G. "Old State Street; its
residences and the people who lived in
them." CVHSP, 4 (1904-1907), 184-203.

12235 TOMLINSON, JULIETTE. "Christ Church,
Springfield, Massachusetts from parish
church to cathedral of the diocese." HMPEC, 43
(1974), 253-260.

12236 _____. An outsider looks at Springfield
history; address delivered before the Bay
State Historical League, May 7, 1955. n.p.,
[1955?]. Pp. 10. MBNEH.

12237 _____. "The Reuben Bliss House of Springfield." Antiques, 61 (1952), 346-347.

12238 _____. Ten famous houses of Springfield.
Springfield: Connecticut Valley Historical
Museum, [1952]. Unpaged.

12239 TOWER, JAMES EATON, ed. Springfield present
and prospective: the city of homes, the
sources of its charm, its advantages, achievements
and possibilities, portrayed in word and picture.
Springfield: Pond & Campbell, 1905. Pp. xviii,
214.

12240 UNDERWOOD, SARA A. "A forgotten industrial
experiment." NEM, New Ser., 18 (1898),
537-542.
Indian Orchard Co. a utopian experiment
for working girls, 1854-1861.

12241 U. S. CHILDREN'S BUREAU. Unemployment and
child welfare: a study made in a middle-
western and eastern city during the industrial depression of 1921 and 1922, by Emma Octavia Lundberg.... Washington: Gov't. Print. Off., 1923.
Pp. viii, 173.
Middle western city is Racine, Wisconsin.

12242 "THE UNITED States Envelope Company." Industry, 7 (May, 1942), 37-40.

12243 USELDING, PAUL J. "Technical progress at
the Springfield Armory, 1820-1850." EEH,
2 Ser., 9 (1971-1972), 291-316.

12244 "THE VAN Norman Machine Tool Company." Industry, 4 (November, 1938), 7-9, 64.

12245 WARNER, CHARLOTTE EDWARDS. A chronicle of
ancient Chestnut Street. Springfield:
Clark W. Bryan, [1897?]. Pp. 41.
Social life and customs.

12246 "WASHINGTON at Springfield." MagHist, 16
(1913), 278-279.
1775.

12247 WATERS, STANLEY. "Witchcraft in Springfield, Mass." NEHGR, 34 (1880), 152-153.

12248 "THE WESTINGHOUSE Electric & Mfg. Company."
Industry, 5 (January, 1940), 5-8, 55.

12249 WILLIAMS, ROY FOSTER. "Gardner-Brooks at
the 70th milestone." Industry, 24 (May,
1959), 23-25.
Color lithography.

12250   WILLIAMS, TALCOTT. "Brief object lesson in
          Springfield architecture." American Archi-
tecture." American Architect and Building News,
10 (1881), 227-231.

12251   WISE, JAMES WATERMAN. The Springfield
          Plan. N.Y.: Viking Pr., 1945. Pp. 136.
          Education.

12252   "WITH pride and thankfulness." City Li-
          brary Bulletin, 76 (1957), 146-168.
          The City Library, 1796-1957.

12253   WRIGHT, HARRY ANDREW. The genesis of
          Springfield: the development of the town.
Springfield: Johnson's Bookstore, 1936. Pp. 47.

12254   _____. Meeting houses of First Church of
          Christ, Springfield, Massachusetts.
[Springfield]: The Church, 1945. Pp. 15. MWA.

12255   WRITERS' PROGRAM. MASSACHUSETTS. Spring-
          field, Massachusetts. Springfield, 1941.
Pp. 84.

12256   WYLIE, MAUDE GEORGE. "Springfield's fine
          homes." WNE, 2 (1912), 127-143.

STERLING

12257   A BRIEF history of Sterling, Massachusetts,
          from its earliest days to the present,
1931. Sterling, 1931. Pp. 68.

12258   COOLIDGE, EDWIN H. "An old-time sawmill at
          Sterling, Massachusetts." OTNE, 29 (1938-
1939), 5-8.

12259   _____. "The pottery business in Sterling,
          Mass." OTNE, 23 (1932-1933), 17-21.
          Nineteenth century.

12260   GANNETT, WYLLYS. "New England reminiscen-
          ces of T. Prentiss Allen's academy, Ster-
ling, Mass." NEM, 50 (1913-1914), 20-25.

12261   MELLEN, JOHN. "An account of some effects
          of the great earthquake, in the year 1755."
MHSC, [4] (1795), 231-232.

12262   STERLING, MASS. One hundred fiftieth an-
          niversary of the incorporation of the town
of Sterling, Massachusetts: exercises in the First
Parish Church, June seventeen, nineteen thirty-one,
at ten forty-five A. M. [Sterling?]: Priv.
Print. by Mary E. Butterick, [1931?]. Pp. 60.

12263   STERLING, MASS. FIRST PARISH UNITARIAN.
          The First Parish Unitarian, Sterling,
Massachusetts. Sterling, 1942. Pp. 32. M.
          1742-1942.

12264   STERLING, MASS. PUBLIC LIBRARY. Origin
          and history, rules and regulations and ded-
icatory exercises of Elizabeth Anne Conant Memorial Building. Clinton: W. J. Coulter, 1888.
Pp. 20. M.

12265   "STERLING." WMHJ, 1 (1825-1826), 272-275,
          313-317, 377-383; 2 (1826), 37-52, 213-231.

12266   WEYGAND, JAMES LAMAR. "The Scarab Press."
          American Book Collector, 18 (December,
1967), 19-21.

12267   WILDER, KATHERINE A. "The Wachusett Pot-
          tery Company, an old time industry of West
Sterling, Massachusetts." NEG, 12 (Spring, 1971),
50-54.

STOCKBRIDGE

12268   BOWKER, RICHARD ROGERS. The Stockbridge
          Library: address by R. R. Bowker, presi-
dent of the association, at the annual meeting,
September 30, 1905. Pittsfield: Sun Printing,
1905. Pp. 11.

12269   _____. The Stockbridge Library, 1904-1928:
          address by R. R. Bowker, president of the
association, at the annual meeting September 29,
1928. Pittsfield: Sun Printing, 1928. Pp. 20.

12270   CANNING, E. W. B. "Indian land grants in
          Stockbridge." BHSSC, 2, Pt. 1 (1894), 47-
56.

12271   _____. "Indian land grants in western
          Massachusetts." MagAmHist, 18 (1887), 142-
149.

12272   _____. "The Indian mission in Stockbridge."
          BHSSC, 1, Pt. 3 (1890), 233-246.

12273   CANNING, JOSEPHINE. "The Shays' Rebellion
          in Stockbridge." American Historical Reg-
ister, 2 (1895), 1265-1267.

12274   CLOUGH, ARTHUR J. "Williams Academy,
          Stockbridge, Mass." BHSSC, 3 (1899-1913),
339-352.

12275   CRESSON, MARGARET FRENCH. The Laurel Hill
          Association 1853-1953. Pittsfield: Eagle
Printing and Binding Co., 1953. Pp. 76.
          A village improvement association.

12276   DAVIDSON, J. N. Muh-he-ka-ne-ok: a history
          of the Stockbridge nation. Milwaukee:
Silas Chapman, 1893. Pp. xxii, 66. MPB.

12277   EGLESTON, NATHANIEL HILLYER. "A New Eng-
          land village." Harper's Magazine, 43
(1871), 815-829.

12278   FIELD, DAVID DUDLEY. Addenda to church
          history. N.Y., [1868?]. Pp. 32, 13.
          First Congregational Church; pagination
          continued from original history; see next
          entry.

12279   _____. An historical sketch, Congregation-
          al, of the church in Stockbridge, Mass....
John A. Gray, 1853. Pp. 30.
          First Congregational Church.

12280 FIELD, ELIZABETH CAMPBELL. A Stockbridge childhood. Asheville, N.C.: Stephens Pr., 1947. Pp. 93.

12281 HOPKINS, SAMUEL. Historical memoirs, relating to the Housatunnuk Indians: or, an account of the methods used, and pains taken, for the propagation of the gospel among that heathenish-tribe, and the success thereof, under the ministry of the late Reverend Mr. John Sergeant: together with the character of that eminently worthy missionary; and an address to the people of this country, representing the very great importance of attaching the Indians to their interest, not only by treating them justly and kindly, but by using proper endeavours to settle Christianity among them. Boston: S. Kneeland, 1753. Pp. iv, 182.

12282 JALONACK, H. M. History of the Riggs Clinic, Inc., 1920-1955. n.p., 1955. v.p. MPB.
Mental health.

12283 JONES, ELECTA FIDELIA. Stockbridge, past and present: or, records of an old mission station. Springfield: S. Bowles, 1854. Pp. 275.

12284 LAWRENCE, ARTHUR. A sermon preached on the twenty first anniversary of the consecration of St. Paul's Church, Stockbridge. , November 12th, 1905. Pittsfield: Sun Printing, 1905. Pp. 15.

12285 LYDENBERG, HARRY MILLER. "The Berkshire Republican Library at Stockbridge, 1794-1818." AASP, 50 (1940), 111-162.

12286 PLUNKETT, HARRIET M. "The evolution of beautiful Stockbridge." NEM, New Ser., 25 (1901-1902), 205-219.

12287 SEDGWICK, SARAH CABOT and CHRISTINA SEDGWICK MARQUAND. Stockbridge, 1739-1974. Stockbridge: Berkshire Traveller Pr., 1974. Pp. xxvi, 364.

12288 SPRING, LEVERETT WILSON. "A case of church discipline in the Berkshires." MHSP, 49 (1915-1916), 96-99.
Excommunication of Lavina Deane, 1777-1779, from the Congregational Church.

12289 STOCKBRIDGE, MASS. FIRST CONGREGATIONAL CHURCH. Historical sketch of the Congregational Church, Stockbridge, with events concurrent in its formation, brief notices of the lives, labor and characters of its early pastors. Stockbridge, 1888. Pp. 73. M.

12290 ____. Manual of the First Congregational Church, Stockbridge, Massachusetts, with historical sketch.... Pittsfield: Sun Printing, 1921. Pp. 47. MPB.

12291 TREADWAY, ALLEN T. Stockbridge: its history and attractions. n.p., n.d. Unpaged. MBNEH.

STONEHAM

12292 DEAN, SILAS. A brief history of the town of Stoneham, Mass., from its first settlement to the present time, with an account of the murder of Jacob Gould, on the evening of Nov. 25, 1819. Boston: S. R. Hart's, 1843. Pp. 36.

12293 "THE E. L. Patch Company." Industry, 3 (September, 1938), 7-10, 44. Pharmaceuticals.

12294 STANDISH, LEMUEL W. Stoneham, Massachusetts, the friendly town. Salem: Deschamps Bros., 1937. Pp. 100. MBNEH.

12295 STEVENS, WILLIAM BURNHAM. History of Stoneham, Massachusetts, with biographical sketches of many of its pioneers and prominent men. Stoneham: F. L. & W. E. Whittier, 1891. Pp. 352.

12296 STONEHAM, MASS. ANNIVERSARY CELEBRATION COMMITTEE. Two hundredth anniversary of the town of Stoneham, 1725-1925. [Stoneham?, 1925?]. Pp. 35.
Historical sketch by William B. Stevens.

12297 STONEHAM, MASS. CONGREGATIONAL CHURCH. Manual of the Congregational Church, Stoneham, Mass., containing its history, articles of faith, covenant, rules, etc., with a list of members, revised.... Boston: C. C. P. Moody, 1853. Pp. 19. M.

12298 STONEHAM. Boston: Edison Electric Illuminating Co., 1909. Pp. 16. M.

12299 STONEHAM FIVE CENTS SAVINGS BANK. A brief history of the Stoneham Five Cents Savings Bank. Stoneham, [1928?]. Unpaged. M. 1855-1928.

12300 STONEHAM SAVINGS BANK. ...100th anniversary, Stoneham Savings Bank. Stoneham, 1955. Pp. 16. M.

STOUGHTON

12301 CANTON, MASS. The records of births, marriages and deaths and intentions of marriage, in the town of Stoughton from 1727 to 1800, and in the town of Canton from 1797-1845, preceded by the records of the South Precinct of Dorchester from 1715 to 1727. Frederic Endicott, ed. Canton: W. Bense, 1896. Pp. vii, 317.

12302 CHANDLER, D. ELFLEDA. "Another offspring of old Dorchester." NEM, New Ser., 42 (1910), 355-365.
Town of Stoughton.

12303 EWING, EDWARD HILTS, ed. Two hundredth anniversary in commemoration of the incorporation of the town of Stoughton, Massachusetts, celebration the entire week August 22-28, historical pageant August 24-25-26, nineteen hundred and twenty-six. Stoughton: Tolman-Davidson Advertising Pr., 1926. Unpaged.

12304   OLD STOUGHTON MUSICAL SOCIETY. The Old
         Stoughton Musical Society: an historical
and informative record of the oldest choral society
in America, together with interesting data of its
organization, meetings, reunions and outings, and
a complete list of past and present officers and
members. Lemuel W. Standish, ed. Stoughton:
Stoughton Printing, 1929. Pp. 188.

12305   REYNOLDS, FRANK WESLEY. Through the years
         to seventy. n.p., [1957]. Pp. 284.
         Social life and customs.

12306   STOUGHTON HISTORICAL SOCIETY. Proceedings
         of the Stoughton Historical Society, April
19, 1899, at the dedication of the memorial stone
marking the location of the first house built in
Stoughton. Stoughton: Record Job Print, 1900.
Pp. 31. MB.

12307   TALBOT, NEWTON. Dorchester New Grant: its
         location and boundaries. A paper read be-
fore the Stoughton Historical Society, April 1,
1901. n.p., 1901. Unpaged. MB.

12308   WOODWARD, DOROTHY M., DANIEL E. HUGHES and
         BARBARA CANAVAN. Stoughton Public Library,
100 years, 1874-1974. [Stoughton?: Stoughton Public Library?, 1974?]. Pp. 24. M.

STOW

12309   CLARK, GEORGE FABER. "Was John Kettell an
         early settler of Stow?" NEHGR, 52 (1898),
37-38.

12310   _____. "Was John Kettell killed by the In-
         dians?" NEHGR, 50 (1896), 483-485.

12311   COOK, PHILIP H. "The nameless grave and
         the headless skeleton: a Middlesex mys-
tery." Worcester HSPub, New Ser., 3 (April, 1950),
8-14.
         Grave of a Regicide, possibly William
         Goffe.

12312   CROWELL, OLIVIA STOCKTON MURRAY and PRESTON
         R. CROWELL. Stow, Massachusetts, 1633-1933,
compiled in honor of the two hundred fiftieth anniversary of the town. Stow, 1933. Pp. ix, 122.

12313   DAY, JOHN ALPHONSO. A brief history of the
         Methodist Episcopal Society of Rock Bottom
and vicinity...August, 1889. Fitchburg: Sentinel
Printing, 1889. Pp. 37. M.

12314   GARDNER, JOHN. "An account of the town of
         Stow (Mass.), March 9, 1767." MHSC, 10
(1809), 83-84.

12315   HALE, ABRAHAM G. R. "The first two settlers
         in Stow, Mass., and their fate." NEHGR, 51
(1897), 294-297.
         John Kettell and a "Mr. Boon."

12316   NEWELL, JONATHAN. An aged minister's review
         of the events and duties of fifty years: a
sermon preached at Stow, October 11, 1824. Concord:
Allen & Lamson, 1825. Pp. 20. MB.

12317   STOW, MASS. Bicentennial celebration of the
         town of Stow, Massachusetts, May 16, 1883.
Marlboro: Pratt Bros., 1883. Pp. 28. MB.

12318   STOW, MASS. FIRST PARISH UNITARIAN CHURCH.
         1702-1902, the two hundredth anniversary of
the First Parish Church of Stow, Massachusetts;
sermons by Rev. J. Sidney Moulton, pastor, and Samuel Collins Beane, D. D., July 27, 1902. [Stow?],
1902. Pp. 28.

STURBRIDGE

12319   "BLACK lead mine at Sturbridge." NEHGR, 10
         (1856), 160.

12320   BRACKETT, HAVEN D. "The Hyde Box Shop and
         vicinity." QHSL, 2, No. 6, 47-57.

12321   CHAMBERLAIN, ALVIN B. "Sturbridge in the
         Civil War." QHSL, 1, No. 25, 305-317.

12322   CHENEY, G. A. "A Massachusetts mine." New
         England Notes and Queries, 1 (1890), 97-
104.
         Lead.

12323   CLARK, JOSEPH SYLVESTER. An historical
         sketch of Sturbridge, Mass., from its set-
tlement to the present time. Brookfield: E. and
L. Merriam, 1838. Pp. 48.

12324   COREY, CHARLES V. "Old houses in Stur-
         bridge." QHSL, 1, No. 5, 59-68.

12325   _____. "Sturbridge and its industries."
         QHSL, 2, No. 23, 225-235.

12326   CURTIS, JOHN OBED. "An early well house,
         Sturbridge, Massachusetts." OTNE, 53
(1962-1963), 79-82.

12327   CUTTING, MARTHA. "Westville and its manu-
         facturers." QHSL, 2, No. 7, 59-72.

12328   FENNELLY, CATHERINE M. "History-as-actuali-
         ty, or a spurious sketch of old Sturbridge,
1756-1830." New England Social Studies Bulletin,
12 (1956), 2-6, 24.

12329   GREGSON, JOHN. "Fiskdale and its indus-
         tries." QHSL, 2, No. 3, 17-24.

12330   HAYNES, GEORGE HENRY. Historical sketch of
         the First Congregational Church, Sturbridge,
Massachusetts, read at the dedication of the new
church, May 11, 1910. Worcester: Davis Pr., 1910.
Pp. 68.

12331   _____. "'The tale of Tantiusques,' an early
         mining venture in Massachusetts." AASP,
New Ser., 14 (1900-1901), 471-497.
         This article and the two which follow differ
         from each other.

12332 ____. "'The tale of Tantiusques.'" NEM, New Ser., 29 (1903-1904), 340-356.

12333 ____. "The tale of the Tantiusques: the Sturbridge lead mine." QHSL, 1, No. 13, 159-181.

12334 HEBARD, JOHN F. "Snellville and its manufactures." QHSL, 2, No. 4, 25-34.

12335 HOLMES, PHILA P. "Old inns and taverns in Sturbridge." QHSL, 3, No. 4, 37-49.

12336 LEONARD, ANNA R. "The church on Fiske Hill and its longest-settled minister, Rev. Zenas L. Leonard." QHSL, 2, No. 5, 35-46. First Baptist Church.

12337 ROWLEY, FRED W. "Globe village and its industries." QHSL, 2, No. 12-14, 90-137.

12338 RUSSELL, WILLIAM BLACK. "Sturbridge Public Library." Sturbridge Amateur, 1 (1904), 5-6.

12339 STURBRIDGE, MASS. BICENTENNIAL CELEBRATION COMMITTEE. Sturbridge Bicentennial 1738-1938, June 18, 1938. n.p., [1938?]. Pp. 15. MWA.

12340 "STURBRIDGE Congregational Church." Sturbridge Amateur, 1 (1904), 17-19.

12341 "UNITARIAN Church, Sturbridge." Sturbridge Amateur, 2 (1905), 38.

12342 VAN RAVENSWAAY, CHARLES. The story of Old Sturbridge Village. N.Y.: Newcomen Society in North America, 1965. Pp. 24.

12343 WALL, ALEXANDER J. "A village anniversary." NEG, 8 (Winter, 1967), 53-56. Old Sturbridge Village, twentieth year.

SUDBURY

12344 BENT, SAMUEL ARTHUR. The Wayside Inn, its history and literature: an address delivered before the Society of Colonial Wars at the Wayside Inn, Sudbury, Massachusetts, June 17, 1897. Boston, 1897. Pp. 27.

12345 BOUTWELL, GEORGE S. "Wadsworth Monument--date of Sudbury fight." NEHGR, 20 (1866), 135-141. King Philip's War.

12346 DOWNES, WALLACE. "The Wayside Inn, at Sudbury." NEM, 5 (1886-1887), 19-27.

12347 FEDERAL WRITERS' PROJECT. MASSACHUSETTS. A brief history of the towne of Sudbury in Massachusetts, together with the programme of the exercises enacted in commemoration of its three hundredth anniversary, 1639-1939. [Sudbury?, 1939]. Pp. 64.

12348 HUDSON, ALFRED SERENO. The history of Sudbury, Massachusetts, 1638-1889. Boston: R. H. Blodgett, 1889. Pp. xxii, 660.

12349 KIDDER, FREDERIC and A. B. UNDERWOOD. "Report on the Sudbury fight, April, 1676." NEHGR, 20 (1866), 341-352. King Philip's War.

12350 LORING, ISRAEL. "Memoir of Sudbury, (Mass.), 1767." MHSC, 10 (1809), 86-88.

12351 MCGLENEN, EDWARD WEBSTER. The Sudbury fight, April 21, 1676: an address delivered before the Society of Colonial Wars at the battle ground, Sudbury, Massachusetts, June 17, 1897. Boston, 1898. Pp. 14.

12352 MEAD, EDWIN DOAK. "The Wayside Inn." NEM, New Ser., 1 (1889-1890), 318-329.

12353 MERRIAM, JOHN MCKINSTRY. Tercentenary address at Sudbury, April 17, 1930. Framingham, 1952. Pp. 15. Tercentenary of Massachusetts Bay Colony.

12354 PINKHAM PRESS, BOSTON. Old Sudbury: the second in a series of portrayals of old New England towns, illustrated with reproductions of pencil sketches from the original domiciles built in the seventeenth and eighteenth centuries. Boston: Pinkham Pr., 1929. Pp. 48.

12355 POWELL, SUMNER CHILTON. Puritan village: the formation of a New England town. Middletown, Conn.: Wesleyan Univ. Pr., 1963. Pp. xx, 215.

12356 ____. "Seventeenth-century Sudbury, Massachusetts." SocArchHistJ, 11 (March, 1952), 3-15.

12357 RICE, LYDIA M. The Sudbury pound. n.p., [1939?]. Pp. 6. MBNEH. Restraint of animals.

12358 RUSSELL, HOWARD S. "A Massachusetts town is founded." New England Homestead, 128 (March 12, 1955), 8, 30-31, 39, 43.

12359 SUDBURY, MASS. Bi-centennial celebration at Sudbury, Mass., April 18, 1876, full report of exercises, including the oration by Prof. Edward J. Young.... [Sudbury]: Trustees of the Goodnow Library, 1876. Pp. 44. Battle of Green Hill, King Philip's War.

12360 ____. Quarter millenial celebration... Sudbury, September 4, 1889. Lowell: Marden & Rowell, 1891. Pp. 42. MB.

12361 "A TOPOGRAPHICAL description and historical account of East Sudbury, in the county of Middlesex and the Commonwealth of Massachusetts, including its ecclesiastical history." MHSC, 2 Ser., 4 (1816), 60-63.

12362 "A TOPOGRAPHICAL description and historical
account of Sudbury, in the county of Middlesex and Commonwealth of Massachusetts, including its
ecclesiastical history." MHSC, 2 Ser., 4 (1816),
52-60.

12363 "WADSWORTH Monument." NEHGR, 7 (1853),
221-224.
Sudbury fight in King Philip's War.

SUNDERLAND

12364 DELANO, JESSE LEMUEL. A record of Sunderland in the Civil War of 1861 to 1865.
Amherst: J. E. Williams, 1882. Pp. 43.

12365 POLITELLA, DARIO. My Sunderland: quarter-
millenial souvenir. Sunderland: 250 Years
of Sunderland Committee, 1968. 2v.

12366 SMITH, JOHN MONTAGUE. History of the town
of Sunderland, Massachusetts, which originally embraced within its limits the present towns
of Montague and Leverett; with genealogies prepared
by Henry W. Taft and Abbie T. Montague. Greenfield:
E. A. Hall, 1899-[1954?]. 2v.
1673-1954; v.2 is by Arthur W. Hubbard,
R. C. Warner, and B. J. Toczydlowski.

12367 SUNDERLAND, MASS. CONGREGATIONAL CHURCH.
Manual of the Congregational Church of
Sunderland, Mass., 1891. Holyoke: Transcript Pub-
lishing, 1891. Pp. 93. M.
Includes historical sketch.

SUTTON

12368 DODGE, REUBEN RAWSON. List of teachers in
school districts nos. 9 and 10, Sutton,
Mass., from 1790 to 1897. Worcester: C. Hamilton,
1897. Pp. 24.

12369 DUDLEY, FLORA. History of St. John's
Church, 1825-1950, Wilkinsonville, Mass.
[Sutton, 1950?]. Pp. 16.

12370 SUTTON, MASS. Bi-centennial of the town
of Sutton, Massachusetts...official programme, May 15-16, 1904. [Sutton?, 1904]. Pp. 8.

12371 SUTTON, MASS. FIRST CONGREGATIONAL CHURCH.
The First Congregational Church, Sutton,
Massachusetts, memorial manual issued in connection
with the two hundredth anniversary of the town.
Worcester: Lucius P. Goddard, 1904. Pp. 50. MWA.

12372 _____. Manual of the First Congregational
Church in Sutton, Mass., containing a history of its formation, the articles of faith, covenant and by-laws, with a list of the pastors and
deacons, and of all the members, from its organization to June, 1871. Worcester: Goddard & Nye,
1871. Pp. 40.

12373 _____. Supplement to the manual of the
First Congregational Church, Sutton, Mass.
Worcester: C. Hamilton, 1891. Pp. 12.

12374 TRACY, HIRAM AVERILL. A brief history of
the First Church in Sutton, Mass. contained
in a sermon preached Jan. 2d, 1842. Worcester:
Lewis Metcalf, 1842. Pp. 28. MB.

SWAMPSCOTT

12375 ALBREE, JOHN. "The Swampscott beaches."
Lynn HSR, (1904), 9-14.

12376 GILBERT, GEORGE E. Uncle George's story.
Lynn: "Albermarle", 1936. Pp. 208.
Social life and customs.

12377 GRANT, JEANETTE A. "A glance at Swampscott,
past and present." North Shore Reminder,
6 (July 27, 1907), 3-7.

12378 JOHNSON, RICHARD BRIGHAM. "Swampscott,
Massachusetts in the seventeenth century."
EIHC, 109 (1973), 243-306.

12379 LUTZ, ALMA. Mary Baker Eddy historical
house, Swampscott, Massachusetts: the
birthplace of Christian Science. Brookline: Longyear Foundation, 1935. Pp. 15.

12380 MANSUR, FRANK L. "Fifty years of Swampscott
schools, 1852-1902." EIHC, 105 (1969),
265-292.

12381 _____. "Swampscott, Massachusetts: the
beginning of a town." EIHC, 108 (1972),
3-48.

12382 MURPHY, JOSEPH W. "Swampscott fishermen."
NOHR, 3 (July 23, 1904), 2-5.

12383 "OLD houses of Swampscott." NOHR, 5 (August 25, 1906), 3-7.

12384 SWAMPSCOTT, MASS. CENTENNIAL COMMITTEE.
Centennial celebration, Swampscott, one
hundred years a town: official centennial book
and program. Swampscott, 1952. Pp. 40. M.

12385 "SWAMPSCOTT churches." NOHR, 5 (August 4,
1906), 3-5.

12386 "THE TEDESCO Country Club." NOHR, 3 (September 3, 1904), 5-7.

12387 THOMPSON, WALDO. Swampscott: historical
sketches of the town. Lynn: T. P. Nichols,
1885. Pp. xi, 241.

SWANSEA

12388 BICKNELL, THOMAS WILLIAMS. "The First Baptist Church in Massachusetts." BSM, 1
(1884), 90-95.

12389   BRAYTON, ALICE. Trading in Scrabbletown. Newport, R.I.: Ward Printing, [1952?]. Pp. 68.

12390   SHUMWAY, HENRY L. "John Myles, Baptist." NEM, New Ser., 33 (1905-1906), 29-32. First Baptist Church in Massachusetts.

12391   SWANSEA, MASS. Book A: records of the town of Swansea, 1662 to 1705. Alverdo Hayward Mason, ed. East Braintree: A. H. Mason, 1900. Unpaged.

12392   ____. Swansea tercentenary, 1667-1967, chronicles of life in Swansea. n.p., [1967?]. Pp. 64. MBNEH.

12393   THATCHER, J. J. Historical sketch of the First Baptist Church, Swansea, Mass., from its organization in 1663 to 1863.... Fall River: Wm. S. Robertson, 1863. Pp. 17. M.

12394   WRIGHT, OTIS OLNEY, ed. History of Swansea, Massachusetts, 1667-1917. [Swansea]: The Town, 1917. Pp. 248.

TAUNTON

12395   ATWOOD, CHARLES R. Reminiscences of Taunton, in ye auld lang syne. Taunton: Republican Steam Printing Rooms, 1880. Pp. 266.

12396   BENNETT, EDMUND HATCH. Historical address on the occasion of the 250th anniversary of the founding of Taunton, June 4, 1889. Taunton: C. H. Buffington, 1890. Pp. 49.

12397   BENT, NATHANIEL TUCKER. A discourse, historical of St. Thomas' Church, Taunton, Mass., delivered on the afternoon of Easter-day, 1844. Taunton: Hack and Bradbury, 1844. Pp. 33.

12398   BLAKE, MORTIMER. The first quarter century of the Winslow Church: containing a historical discourse, preached January 12, 1862, and an appendix. Taunton: C. A. Hack, [1862?]. Pp. 67.

12399   ____. "Taunton North Purchase." Old Colony HSC, No. 3 (1885), 31-53.

12400   THE BOOK of Taunton.... Taunton: C. A. Hack & Son, 1907. Pp. 50. Introduction signed: Joel H. Metcalf.

12401   BRISTOL COUNTY SAVINGS BANK, TAUNTON, MASS. One hundred years safeguarding your savings. Taunton, 1946. Pp. 28.

12402   BISTOL COUNTY TRUST COMPANY, TAUNTON, MASS. Looking backward: one hundred and twenty-five years of progress. Taunton: C. W. Davol, [1937?]. Pp. 36.

12403   COLE, SAMUEL V. "Taunton--an Old Colony Town." NEM, New Ser., 14 (1896), 65-85.

12404   CUSHMAN, JAMES M. "Cohannet alewives and the ancient grist mill at the falls on Mill River." Old Colony HSC, No. 5 (1895), 70-93.

12405   DAVOL, RALPH. Two men of Taunton, in the course of human events, 1731-1829. Taunton: Davol Publishing, 1912. Pp. xiii, 406. Robert Treat Paine and Daniel Leonard.

12406   EMERY, SAMUEL HOPKINS. Historical sketch of the city of Taunton, Mass. [Boston?, 1881?]. 4 leaves.

12407   ____. "Historical sketch of the Old Colony Historical Society." Old Colony HSC, [No. 1] (1878), 5-12.

12408   ____. History of Taunton, Massachusetts, from its settlement to the present time. Syracuse: D. Mason, 1893. Pp. 768, 110. Typescript index of names by Florence T. Allen is at New England Historic Genealogical Society.

12409   ____. The ministry of Taunton, with incidental notices of other professions. Boston: J. P. Jewett, 1853. 2v.

12410   ____. Supplement to the history of Taunton, Massachusetts. Syracuse: D. Mason, 1894. Pp. 13.

12411   FELTON, CORNELIUS CONWAY. An address delivered at the dedication of the new building of Bristol Academy in Taunton, August 25, 1852, with an appendix, containing an historical sketch of the academy, an account of the festival, and a list of the trustees and preceptors. Cambridge: Metcalf, 1852. Pp. 54.

12412   "FIFTY years of Taunton Pearl Works." Industry, 14 (January, 1949), 25-28.

12413   FISHER, CHARLES EBEN. "Locomotive building at Taunton, Massachusetts." RLHSB, No. 15 (1927), 15-19.

12414   FRASER, ESTHER STEVENS. "The tantalizing chests of Taunton." Antiques, 23 (1933), 135-138.

12415   FREEMASONS. TAUNTON, MASS. KING DAVID LODGE. Historical sketch and centennial anniversary of King David Lodge A. F. & A. M., Taunton, Massachusetts, 1798-1898. [Taunton], 1902. Pp. vi, 231.

12416   ____. One hundred anniversary of the institution of King David Lodge, A. F. & A. M. ...Wednesday, June 15th, 1898, chartered June 12, A. L. 5798. Taunton, 1898. Unpaged.

12417   FULLER, WILLIAM EDDY. Historical address at a celebration (June 30th, 1892) of the one hundredth anniversary of the founding of Bristol Academy. [Taunton, 1907]. Pp. 49.

12418 GIBB, GEORGE SWEET. The whitesmiths of Taunton: a history of Reed & Barton 1824-1943. Cambridge: Harvard Univ. Pr., 1943. Pp. xxxiii, 419.
    Silverware.

12419 HALL, JOHN W. D. "Ancient iron works in Taunton." NEHGR, 41 (1887), 281.

12420 _____. "Ancient iron works in Taunton." Old Colony HSC, No. 3 (1885), 131-162.

12421 _____. "Taunton Green one hundred years ago." Old Colony HSC, No. 5 (1895), 154-162.

12422 HARRIS, SHELDON H. "Abraham Lincoln stumps for a Yankee audience." NEQ, 38 (1965), 227-233.
    1848; Lincoln's visit in support of the Whig ticket.

12423 HATHAWAY, MARY E. N. "The early Hathways of Taunton." Old Colony HSC, No. 6 (1899), 76-81.

12424 HUTT, FRANK WALCOTT. "Seventy-fifth anniversary of the Old Colony Historical Society." Americana, 23 (1929), 190-204.

12425 _____. Taunton's priorities in its own history, read at the meeting of the Old Colony Historical Society...February 20, 1936 by Miss Myrtle Johnson. [Taunton]: Charles W. Davol, [1936?]. Unpaged. MBNEH.

12426 KENNEDY, EDWARD F., JR. The city of Taunton, 1864-1964. Taunton: Old Colony Historical Society, 1968. Pp. 26. MBNEH.

12427 LEONARD, ELISHA CLARK. "Reminiscences of the ancient iron works, and Leonard mansions, of Taunton." Old Colony HSC, No. 4 (1889), 51-65.

12428 MACHINISTS' NATIONAL BANK, TAUNTON, MASS. Taunton and the Machinists' National Bank: high lights in the history of the city and a record of the bank...published in commemoration of over eighty years of banking, 1928. Boston: Walton Advertising & Printing, 1928. Pp. 33.

12429 MANN, B. STUART. Tales and trails of Taunton. Taunton: Davol Printing, n.d. Pp. 28. MBNEH.

12430 ORDRONAUX, JOHN. Celebration of the semicentennial anniversary of the founding of the Old Colony Historical Society of Massachusetts, May 4, 1903. Taunton: Old Colony Historical Society, 1903. Pp. 44.

12431 PEIRCE, EBENEZER WEAVER. "Indian massacres in Taunton." Old Colony HSC, No. 4 (1889), 67-78.

12432 "[REED and Barton 150th anniversary]." The Silver Lining, 31 (November, 1974), entire issue.
    Silverware; periodical is the firm's house organ.

12433 ROMAINE, LAWRENCE B. "Trials and tribulations of publishing in 1833." Hobbies, 50 (1945), 126-127.
    C. A. Hack.

12434 SEAVER, JAMES EDWARD. "The two settlements of Taunton, Massachusetts." Old Colony HSC, [No. 7] (1903), 106-141.

12435 STAFFORD, JAMES W. The bygone years of West Taunton. n.p., n.d. Pp. 23, 9. MBNEH.
    West Congregational Church.

12436 TAUNTON, MASS. Quarter millennial celebration of the city of Taunton, Massachusetts, Tuesday and Wednesday, June 4 and 5, 1889. Samuel H. Emery, William E. Fuller, and James H. Dean, comps. Taunton, 1889. Pp. 426.

12437 _____. 250th anniversary of ye anciente towne of Taunton...June 4 and 5, 1889. Worcester: F. S. Blanchard, 1889. Pp. 32.

12438 TAUNTON, MASS. TERCENTENARY COMMITTEE. Taunton celebration of the Massachusetts Bay tercentenary, 1630, 1930. [Taunton], 1930. Pp. 64.

12439 _____. Tercentenary of Taunton, Massachusetts, 1639-1939, June 4-10. Taunton, 1939. Pp. 110. MBNEH.

12440 TAUNTON, MASS. TRINITARIAN CONGREGATIONAL CHURCH. Manual of the Trinitarian Congregational Church of Taunton, Mass., 1881. Boston: Beacon Pr., 1881. Pp. 39. M.
    Includes historical sketch.

12441 _____. Semi-centennial of Trinitarian Congregational Church re-union of the Sabbath School: historical review by Reverend Erastus Maltby. Taunton: Republican Steam Printing Rooms, 1871. Pp. 90. M.

12442 TAUNTON, MASS. WINSLOW CHURCH. The first quarter century of the Winslow Church: containing a historical discourse preached January 12, 1862 and an appendix, by Mortimer Blake, Pastor. Taunton: C. A. Hack, 1862. Pp. 67. M.

12443 _____. Manual...containing its history, standing rules, confession of faith and covenant with a catalogue of its members. Boston: Franklin Printing House, 1856. Pp. 24. M.

12444 "TAUNTON Locomotive Works." BBHS, 8 (1934), 70-72.

12445   TUCKER, CARLTON E.   "Taunton Street Railway
           Company, Taunton Division, Old Colony
Street Railway Co. and the independent lines operat-
ing in Taunton, Massachusetts." Transportation
Bulletin, No. 68 (March-September, 1963).

12446   NO ENTRY

12447   WATKINS, WALTER KENDALL.   "The iron works
           at Taunton in Plymouth Colony." NEHGR,
41 (1887), 83-85.

12448   WILLIAMS, HENRY.   "Was Elizabeth Pool the
           first purchaser of the territory and the
foundress, of Taunton?" Old Colony HSC, No. 2
(1880), 37-113.

12449   WILLIAMS, ROY FOSTER.   "A.I.M. [Associated
           Industries of Massachusetts] salutes Reed &
Barton." Industry, 15 (December, 1949), 11-14,
44-45.
           Silverware.

TEMPLETON

12450   ADAMS, EDWIN G.   An historical discourse in
           commemoration of the one hundredth anniver-
sary of the formation of the First Congregational
Church in Templeton, Massachusetts, with an appendix, embracing a survey of the municipal affairs of
the town. Boston: Crosby, Nichols, 1857.
Pp. vi, 175.

12451   DEXTER, HENRY VAUGHAN.   History of the
           Baptist Church in Templeton, Mass., with
an account of the centennial celebration at Baldwinville, August 22, 1882. West Gardner: Gardner
Record Office, 1882. Pp. 34.

12452   GREENE, RANSOM A.   "Templeton colony."
           Massachusetts Department of Mental Diseases.
Bulletin, 14 (April, 1930), 30-39.

12453   GREENWOOD, LUCIUS.   Wright Tavern, Temple-
           ton, Massachusetts, 1763-1931. Templeton:
Narragansett Historical Society, [1931?]. Unpaged.
MBNEH.

12454   HOSPITAL COTTAGES FOR CHILDREN, BALDWIN-
           VILLE, MASS. Twentieth anniversary....
Baldwinville: James M. Gage, [1902]. Pp. 15.

12455   LORD, ELIZABETH WELLINGTON, comp. The sto-
           ry of Templeton. Ethel M. Eaton, ed.
[Templeton]: Narragansett Historical Society,
[1947?]. Pp. 285.

12456   TEMPLETON, MASS. BOARD OF SELECTMEN.
           Templeton, 1762-1965, 200 years, program
of the bicentennial celebration. Baldwinville:
Temple-Stuart, 1962. Pp. 48. M.

12457   TEMPLETON, MASS. HIGH SCHOOL. General cat-
           alogue of the Templeton High School 1856-
1881, also, report of proceedings at the celebration
of the twenty-fifth anniversary, July 14, 1881.
Gardner: A. G. Bushnell, 1881. Pp. 39. MBNEH.
           Includes historical sketch.

12458   WELLINGTON, CHARLES. A sermon preached
           Sept. 1, 1811, on leaving the old and first
house of worship, built in Templeton. Brookfield:
E. Merriam, 1812. Pp. 19. MBNEH.
           Relates to the town.

TEWKSBURY

12459   MASSACHUSETTS. STATE HOSPITAL, TEWKSBURY.
           The State Infirmary, Tewksbury, Massachu-
setts. n.p., [not after 1939]. Pp. 82. M.
           History, 1855-1920.

12460   PATTEN, HAROLD J., comp. Ask now of the
           days that are past: a history of the town
of Tewksbury, Massachusetts, 1734-1964. n.p.,
[1964?]. Pp. 312. M.

12461   PRIDE, EDWARD W. Tewksbury: a short his-
           tory. Cambridge: Riverside Pr., 1888.
Pp. 73.

12462   PROSPECTUS for a manufacturing establish-
           ment at Belvidere, on Merrimack River,
with a topographical account of the place, and incidental remarks. [Belvidere, 1822?]. Pp. 24.

12463   TEWKSBURY, MASS. Ye towne book, two hun-
           dredth anniversary, August 25, 26, 27,
1934. Lowell: Balfe, [1934?]. Pp. 77. MBNEH.

TISBURY

12464   ELDRIDGE, SYDNA.   "Glimpses of Vineyard
           Haven and Vineyard Haven Harbor." DCI, 7
(1965-1966), 231-236.

12465   HARRIMAN, SHEPHERD FISHER.   History of the
           Methodist Episcopal Church of Vineyard
Haven, Mass. Vineyard Haven: Manter, 1885.
Pp. 31.

12466   NORRIS, MRS. HOWES. Sketches of old homes
           in our village. Vineyard Haven: Sea Coast
Defence Chapter, D. A. R., 1921. Pp. 22.

12467   TISBURY, MASS. Records of the town of Tis-
           bury, Mass., beginning June 29, 1669, and
ending May 16, 1864. Charles Edward Banks, ed.
Boston: Wright & Potter, 1903. Pp. xii, 841.

12468   WIGHTMAN, IDA MAY. The Mayhew Manor of
           Tisbury: address prepared for the New York
Branch of the Order of Colonial Lords of Manors in
America. Baltimore, 1921. Pp. 36.

TOLLAND

12469   SEE HISTORIES OF HAMPDEN COUNTY.

TOPSFIELD

12470   BALCH, BANJAMIN J. "Topsfield Warren Blues, old time Massachusetts independent infantry." TopHC, 1 (1895), 19-29.
Organized in 1836.

12471   CLARKE, MARIETTA. "The Howlett Mills with some account of the Hobbs family in Topsfield." TopHC, 3 (1897), 165-173.
Gristmill, sawmill, and cornmill.

12472   CLEAVELAND, NEHEMIAH. An address, delivered at Topsfield in Massachusetts, August 28, 1850: the two hundredth anniversary of the incorporation of the town. N.Y.: Pudney & Russell, 1851. Pp. 74.

12473   DOW, ALICE G. A Topsfield quiz. Topsfield: Topsfield Historical Society, 1949. Pp. 21. MBNEH.

12474   DOW, GEORGE FRANCIS. "Early Topsfield school reports." TopHC, 16 (1911), 34-49.

12475   _____. The historical address delivered at the celebration of the 250th anniversary of the town of Topsfield, Mass., Aug. 16, 1900. Topsfield: Merrill Pr., 1900. Pp. 22.

12476   _____. History of Topsfield, Massachusetts. Topsfield: Topsfield Historical Society, 1940. Pp. 517.
Continued and edited after the death of the author in 1936 by Alice G. Dow with the assistance of a group of W. P. A. workers and Ruth H. Allen.

12477   _____. "The Israel Clarke account book." TopHC, 13 (1908), 143-147.
1740s.

12478   _____. "Newspaper items relating to Topsfield, copied from Boston newspapers, 1704-1780." TopHC, 25 (1920), 97-100.

12479   _____. comp. "Newspaper items relating to Topsfield, copied from the files of Salem newspapers." TopHC, 3 (1897), 1-23; 5 (1899), 132-142; 10 (1905), 98-136; 12 (1907), 109-148; 15 (1910), 125-156; 16 (1911), 65-144; 17 (1912), 88-192; 18 (1913), 97-119; 20 (1915), 1-48; 22 (1917), 1-79; 23 (1918), 97-140; 24 (1919), 113-126; 26 (1921), 128-140; 27 (1922), 97-140; 28 (1923), 24-64; 29 (1928), 99-140; 30 (1933), 1-64.
1770-1879.

12480   _____. "The printing press in Topsfield." TopHC, 23 (1918), 46-49.

12481   _____. "The settlement of Topsfield." TopHC, 1 (1895), 15-18.

12482   _____. "The Topsfield copper mines." MHSP, 65 (1932-1936), 570-580.

12483   _____. "Topsfield in the Civil War." Top HC, 30 (1933), 65-112.
Biographies.

12484   FITTS, JAMES HILL. "Topsfield in the American Revolution." TopHC, 28 (1923), 65-126.

12485   FORMAN, BENNO M. "The account book of John Gould, weaver, of Topsfield, Massachusetts, 1697-1724." EIHC, 105 (1969), 24-36.

12486   GLAZIER, CLARISSA. "A historical sketch of the Methodist Episcopal Church in Topsfield." TopHC, 3 (1897), 24-36.

12487   GOULD, J. PORTER. "Localities and place names in Topsfield." TopHC, 11 (1906), 81-99.

12488   HAVEN, THEODORE W. "The trial of Elizabeth Porter Bradstreet for the crime of arson." TopHC, 1 (1895), 30-35.

12489   HUNTINGTON, ASAHEL. "Reminiscences of Rev. Asahel Huntington." TopHC, 10 (1905), 78-80.
Reminiscences of the town.

12490   LEACH, CHARLES H. "The Congregational Church choir." TopHC, 30 (1933), 113-119.

12491   LEACH, T. K. "The burning of Rea Tavern, Topsfield, October, 1836." TopHC, 1 (1895), 7-9.

12492   LONG, HENRY FOLLANSBEE. "The bridges in Topsfield." TopHC, 16 (1911), 50-56.

12493   _____. "The physicians of Topsfield, with some account of early medical practice." EIHC, 47 (1911), 197-229.

12494   _____. "The post-office in Topsfield with some account of the postmasters." TopHC, 13 (1908), 5-21.

12495   _____. "Topsfield streets and ways." TopHC, 12 (1907), 48-96G.

12496   MACEWEN, JAMES FRISBIE. New Year's sermon, a sermon, at Topsfield, January 7, 1840. Salem: Gazette Office, 1840. Pp. 22. MB.
Contains history of the Congregational Church in the town.

12497   MILLAR, DONALD. "A seventeenth-century New England house." OTNE, 11(1920-1921), 3-8.
Parson Capen House.

12498   PEABODY, CHARLES JOEL. "The story of a Peabody house and its neighborhood." TopHC, 26 (1921), 113-120.

12499 PERLEY, MARTIN VAN BUREN. History of the
Topsfield Academy, the literary exercises
at the reunion of the teachers and students of the
academy, held Aug. 12, 1897. George Francis Dow,
ed. Topsfield: Merrill Pr., 1899. Pp. 119.

12500 PERLEY, SIDNEY. "Topsfield houses and
lands." TopHC, 29 (1928), 49-98.

12501 ____. "Topsfield in 1800." Essex Antiq,
5 (1901), 97-103.

12502 ____. "Topsfield Village in 1800." Top
HC, 7 (1901), 124-140.

12503 PHILLIPS, JAMES DUNCAN. Three centuries of
Topsfield history. Topsfield, 1951.
Pp. 19. MSaE.

12504 ROBINSON, JOHN. "The old oak at Topsfield."
TopHC, 7 (1901), 105-106.

12505 "THE SEATING in the meeting-house, 1762 and
1771." TopHC, 7 (1901), 90-104.

12506 "TINTYPE portraits of Topsfield people taken
about 1868." TopHC, 16 (1911), 61-64.
Biographies.

12507 TOPSFIELD, MASS. The celebration of the
two hundred and fiftieth anniversary of the
incorporation of the town of Topsfield, Massachusetts, August 16-17, 1900. Topsfield: The [Tops-
field Historical] Society, 1900. Pp. vi, 156.

12508 ____. Topsfield tercentenary, 1650-1950:
souvenir program, August, 1950. Boston:
Rapid Service Pr., [1950?]. Pp. 40. MBNEH.

12509 ____. Town records of Topsfield, Massachusetts...1659-1778. Topsfield: Topsfield Historical Society, 1917-1920. 2v.
Name and subject indexes.

12510 ____. The war activities of Topsfield,
Massachusetts, during the great war--1917-
1918...Public Safety Committee. Topsfield, 1919.
Pp. 26.

12511 TOPSFIELD, MASS. CONGREGATIONAL CHURCH.
The Congregational Church of Topsfield,
tercentenary, November 4, 1963. [Topsfield?],
1963. Pp. 14. MWA.

12512 ____. Historical manual of the Congregational Church of Topsfield, Massachusetts,
1663-1907. Topsfield, 1907. Pp. 60.

12513 TOWNE, ABBIE PETERSON and MARIETTA CLARKE.
"Topsfield in the witchcraft delusion."
TopHC, 13 (1908), 23-38.

12514 TOWNE, G. WARREN. "The Topsfield copper
mines." TopHC, 2 (1896), 73-81.

12515 TOWNE, JOHN H. "The Boyd-Peabody-Waters
House on Salem Street, Topsfield." TopHC,
10 (1905), 86-87.

12516 ____, comp. "Fires in Topsfield." TopHC,
8 (1902), 70-86.
1661-1900.

12517 ____. "Francis Peabody's grist mill."
TopHC, 1 (1895), 39-45.

12518 ____. "Old Peabody mills, Topsfield."
Essex Antiq, 1 (1897), 109-112.

12519 ____. "The Peabody-Batchelder-Young House
on North Street, Topsfield." TopHC, 10
(1905), 84-86.

12520 ____. "Topsfield houses and buildings."
TopHC, 8 (1902), 1-69.

12521 WELCH, LEONE PARKER. "The ministry of the
Methodist Episcopal Church in Topsfield."
TopHC, 19 (1914), 89-116.

TOWNSEND

12522 CHARLTON, EMMANUEL CARLSON. The Squanicook
Parish. Townsend: G. A. Wilder, 1917.
Pp. 96.
Methodist Church.

12523 MORSS, GEORGE HENRY. Historical discourse,
preached on the Sabbath, October 16th,
1870, being the one hundred thirty-sixth anniversary
of the organization of the Orthodox Congregational
Church of Christ, in Townsend, Mass. Boston: A. B.
Morss, 1870. Pp. 32.

12524 "NOON House at Townsend Center." AmHist
Record, 1 (1872), 69-70.

12525 SAWTELLE, ITHAMAR BARD. History of the
town of Townsend, Middlesex County, Massachusetts, from the grant of Hathorn's Farm, 1676-
1878. Fitchburg, 1878. Pp. 455.

12526 ____. Sketches of the college graduates
of Townsend, Mass., a lecture delivered at
the Congregational Orthodox Church in Townsend,
Jan. 26, 1875. Fitchburg: H. F. Piper, 1875.
Pp. 30. MB.

12527 TOWNSEND, MASS. PUBLIC LIBRARY. Townsend
Public Library 1858-1928. Evelyn L. Warren, comp. n.p., [1929?]. Unpaged. MB.

TRURO

12528 "BEACONS of Cape Cod, Highland Light." CCB,
48 (July 1, 1937), 13.

12529 DUGANNE, PHYLLIS. The South Truro meeting
house. Truro: Truro Neighborhood Association, 1928. Pp. 11. MBNEH.

12530 DUNBAR, HAROLD. "South Truro." CCB, 48
(Late August, 1937), 21-23.

12531   DYER, JOHN B.   "Truro on Cape Cod." CCAPL, 5 (December, 1921), 7-11.

12532   MARSHALL, ANTHONY L.   Truro, Cape Cod as I knew it. N.Y.: Vantage Pr., 1974.
Pp. 253. MBNEH.

12533   "THE OLD church at South Truro." CCB, 49 (January, 1938), 13-15.
Methodist Church.

12534   RICH, SHEBNAH.   Truro--Cape Cod: or, land marks and sea marks, (1883) 2d. ed., rev. and corrected. Boston: D. Lothrop, 1884.
Pp. 580.

TYNGSBOROUGH

12535   "THE ANDREWS House." VIAA, 16 (1911), 1-2.

12536   BANCROFT, EDNA HELEN.   "The Timothy Bancroft Homestead." VIAA, 42 (1939), 1, 6-7.

12537   _____.   "Tyngsborough, past and present." VIAA, 38 (1933), 1, 6-7.

12538   BANCROFT, J. FRANK.   "The Cummings House." VIAA, 17 (1912), 1-2.

12539   _____.   "First Parish, Tyngsboro, Mass." VIAA, 12 (1907), [2-5].

12540   _____.   "The Horseshoe Farm." VIAA, 20 (1914), 1-3.

12541   _____.   "Tyng's woods--lease lots." VIAA, 18 (1913), 1-4; 21 (1915), 13-15.

12542   BANCROFT, JONATHAN FRANKLIN.   "Brush factory village." VIAA, 55 (1950), 1, 12.

12543   _____.   "The old Butterfield Stage Tavern, Tyngsboro, Mass." VIAA, 27 (1922), 1, 6.

12544   "BRIEF resumé of the V.I.A." VIAA, 22 (1916), 3-4.
Village Improvement Association.

12545   CURTIS, LOUVILLE.   "Tyngsboro Bridge." VIAA, 18 (1913), 16-18.

12546   _____.   "The Winslow Schoolhouse, how it came to be built." VIAA, 21 (1915), 1-2.

12547   "THE EARLY homestead of Lt. Joseph Butterfield which stood near the site of the stone house built by Deacon Cyrus Butterfield." VIAA, 50 (1945), 13.

12548   HAMMOND, BARBARA and CATHERINE W. LAMBERT.   "The old William Sherburne House." VIAA, 44 (1939), 1-2.

12549   "HISTORY of the Evangelical Church in Tyngsborough." VIAA, 41 (1936), 1, 7-9.

12550   HUTCHINSON, FRED M., ELDEN T. STAPLES and ROBERT LAMBERT.   "Massapoag Pond in early days." VIAA, 60 (1955), 1, 4, 12.

12251   LAMBERT, CATHERINE W.   "The Brinley Mansion." VIAA, 62 (1957), 1, 5.

12552   _____.   "The early industries of Tyngsboro." VIAA, 59 (1954), 1, 3-5.

12553   _____.   "Some things accomplished by the V.I.A. in fifty years." VIAA, 50 (1945), 2.
Village Improvement Association.

12554   _____.   "The Tyng House." VIAA, 49 (1944), 1-2.

12555   LAWRENCE, NATHANIEL.   "Historical sketch of Tyngsborough, Middlesex, Massachusetts, October, 1815." MHSC, 2 Ser., 4 (1816), 192-198.

12556   "LITTLEHALES of early days." VIAA, 52 (1947), 1-5.

12557   "THE MILL and box shop." VIAA, 33 (1928), 1-2.
Grist and saw mills.

12558   "THE OLD Butterfield Mill." VIAA, 29 (1924), 1, 13.
Cider mills, saw mills, and grist mills.

12559   PERHAM, ALFRED.   "Alfred Perham [Homestead]." VIAA, 53 (1948), 1-2.

12560   PERHAM, E. A.   "The village store." VIAA, 32 (1927), 1, 8.

12561   QUEEN, M. A.   "The old Parham House." VIAA, 43 (1938), 1; 45 (1940), 1.

12562   "THE RICHARDSON House." VIAA, 34 (1929), 1.

12563   SHERBURNE, R. W.   "The old stone house." VIAA, 57 (1952), 1.

12564   SWALLOW, S. C.   "The Evangelical Church of Tyngsboro." VIAA, 13 (1908), 2-4.

12565   "THE TOWN farm." VIAA, 50 (1945), 1.
Simon Thompson's farm; poor farm, 1826.

12566   TURNER, BERTHA M.   "The First Parish." VIAA, 58 (1953), 4.

12567   _____.   "No. 2 West Middle School, Tyngsborough." VIAA, 46 (1941), 1-4.

12568   _____.   "Our library and how it grew." VIAA, 40 (1935), 1, 4-5.
Littlefield Library.

12569   TYNGSBORO' YOUNG PEOPLE'S LEAGUE.   Tyngsboro' centennial record, 1876.... Lowell: Weekly Journal, 1876. Pp. 24.

12570 TYNGSBOROUGH, MASS. Ye anciente and modern historie of Colonial Hall & Tyngsborough, that health giving and life prolonging locality. n.p., n.d. Pp. 21. MHi.

12571 "THE TYNGSBOROUGH Fire Department." VIAA, 36 (1931), 1, 3.

12572 "TYNGSBOROUGH sesquicentennial program." VIAA, 64 (1959), 1-84. Contains historical articles.

12573 "TYNGSBOROUGH Town Hall--Tyngsborough, Mass." VIAA, 63 (1958), 1, 5.

12574 "WICCASAUKEE Island: its suspension foot bridge--the longest in this country; the Vesper-Country Club." VIAA, 26 (1921), 1, 6, 7.

12575 "THE WILLIAM Adams House." VIAA, 56 (1951), 1, 12.

TYRINGHAM

12576 MYERS, ELOISE. A hinterland settlement: Tyringham, Massachusetts, and bordering lands. 2d. ed. Pittsfield: Eagle Printing and Binding, [between 1962 and 1965]. Pp. 95.

12577 "OLD Home Week, celebration in Tyringham, August, 1905." Berkshire Hills, New Ser., 2 (1905-1906), 85-92.

12578 "THE OLD Turkey Paper Mill at Tyringham." Berkshire Hills, 4 (1903-1904), 165-166.

12579 SCOTT, JOHN A. Tyringham: old and new. Pittsfield: Sun Printing, [1905?]. Pp. 43.

UPTON

12580 POOR, WILLIAM GEORGE, et al., comps. Upton, Massachusetts. Upton, 1935. Pp. 194. Biographies.

12581 POOR, WILLIAM GEORGE. Upton's first forty years. [Upton?, 1935]. Pp. 25.

12582 UPTON, MASS. 1735-June 25, 1935: Upton, Massachusetts. Upton, 1935. Pp. 194. MBNEH.

12583 _____. Souvenir program, 200th anniversary. n.p., [1935?]. Unpaged. M.

12584 UPTON, MASS. FIRST CONGREGATIONAL CHURCH. Addresses delivered at the celebration of the one hundred and seventy-fifth anniversary of the First Congregational Church, Upton, Massachusetts, November ten nineteen hundred and ten. Boston: Fort Hill Pr., [1910?]. Pp. 46. MWA.

12585 _____. Manual of the First Congregational Church, Upton, Mass. 1877. Worcester: Lucius P. Goddard, 1877. Pp. 32. M. Includes historical sketch.

12586 _____. Manual of the First Congregational Church, Upton, Massachusetts. n.p., 1899. Pp. 39. MWA. Includes historical sketch.

12587 WALKER, CHESTER W. "The Eli Warren Tavern, West Upton, Massachusetts." OTNE, 28 (1937-1938), 114-117.

12588 WOOD, BENJAMIN. A centennial address, delivered at Upton, Mass., June 25, 1835. Boston: William Peirce, 1835. Pp. 30. M.

UXBRIDGE

12589 BLACKSTONE NATIONAL BANK, UXBRIDGE, MASS. One hundred years of banking service issued by the Blackstone National Bank in commemoration of its one hundredth anniversary. Boston: Walton Advertising, 1925. Pp. 31.

12590 BRISTOL, FRANK LOUIS. One hundred and sixty-one years: or, a history of the First Evangelical Church otherwise known as the First Church of Christ in Uxbridge, Mass. Uxbridge: Compendium Steam Print, 1891. Pp. 127.

12591 CHAPIN, HENRY. Address delivered at the Unitarian Church, in Uxbridge, Mass., in 1864, with further statements, not made a part of the address, but included in the notes. Worcester: Press of Charles Hamilton, 1881. Pp. xvi, 214. In essence, a town history.

12592 DRUMMEY, JACK. "Five generations give Stanley Woolen a fine tradition." Industry, 21 (December, 1955), 15-16.

12593 MOWRY, WILLIAM AUGUSTUS. The influence of the academy upon the town of Uxbridge: a paper read at Uxbridge, September 24, 1908, during 'Old Home Week.' n.p., [1908?]. Pp. 7. Uxbridge Academy.

12594 _____. The Uxbridge Academy, a brief history; with a biographical sketch of J. Mason Macomber.... Boston: Everett Pr., 1897. Pp. xiv, 151.

12595 ROYS, CYRUS A. A sketch of the history of the First Congregational Society of Uxbridge, Mass. n.p., [1904]. Pp. 16.

12596 SPRAGUE, BEATRICE PUTNAM, comp. Uxbridge year by year, 1727-1927, in commemoration of the two hundredth anniversary of the incorporation of Uxbridge, Massachusetts. Woonsocket, R.I.: E. L. Freeman, 1927. Pp. 126.

12597 UXBRIDGE, MASS. Uxbridge bi-centennial,
       June 25th, 26th, 27th, 1927. Woonsocket,
R.I.: E. L. Freeman, 1927. Pp. 24.

12598 UXBRIDGE, MASS. FREE PUBLIC LIBRARY. The
       proceedings in commemoration of the fif-
tieth anniversary of the opening of the Uxbridge
Free Public Library, Uxbridge, Massachusetts, January 20, 1925. Uxbridge, 1925. Pp. 45.

12599 UXBRIDGE, MASS. OLD HOME WEEK COMMITTEE.
       Old Home Week souvenir of Uxbridge, Massa-
chusetts. Arthur E. Seagrave and Edward T. Mc-
Shane, eds. Uxbridge: Uxbridge and Whitinsville
Transcript, [1908]. Unpaged.

WAKEFIELD

12600 BLISS, CHARLES ROBINSON. Wakefield Con-
       gregational Church: a commemorative
sketch, 1644-1877. Wakefield: W. H. Twombly,
1877. Pp. 90.

12601 EATON, WILLIAM EVERETT. The history of the
       Hartshorne House in Wakefield, Massachu-
setts. Wakefield: Col. Hartshorne House Association, 1937. Pp. 41. MBNEH.

12602 _____. History of the Richardson Light
       Guard, of Wakefield, Mass., 1851-1901, pub-
lished on the occasion of the semi-centennial celebration of the company, October 11, 1901. Wakefield: Citizen and Banner Office, 1901. Pp. 216.

12603 EVERTS, N. R. History of the First Baptist
       Church in Wakefield, Mass., 1800-1900....
Malden: George E. Dunbar, 1901. Pp. 131.

12604 GOLDSMITH, PAUL H. "Gremar Manufacturing
       grows and grows." Industry, 23 (February,
1958), 33, 46, 48.
       Electronic components.

12605 HAMILTON, SAMUEL KING. Commemorative ad-
       dress delivered at the celebration by the
First Parish in Wakefield, Massachusetts, of the
completion of payment covering cost of the fifth
meeting-house of the Congregational Church, Friday
evening, February 21, 1919. Wakefield: Item Pr.,
1919. Pp. 65.

12606 INGRAM, ELIZABETH FRANCES. The Lucius
       Beebe Memorial Library, an historical
sketch. Wakefield: Item Pr., 1925. Pp. 39.

12607 WAKEFIELD, MASS. Inaugural exercises in
       Wakefield, Mass., including the historical
address and poem, delivered on the occasion of the
assumption of its new name, by the town formerly
known as South Reading, on Saturday, July 4th,
1868: also, the exercises at the dedication of
Wakefield Hall, Wednesday, February 22d, 1871. Boston: Warren Richardson, 1872. Pp. 100.

12608 _____. Wakefield Park. Boston, [189?].
       Pp. 24. MB.

12609 WAKEFIELD, MASS. TERCENTENARY COMMITTEE.
       History of Wakefield (Middlesex County)
Massachusetts. William E. Eaton, comp. [Wake-
field], 1944. Pp. 263.

12610 WAKEFIELD SAVINGS BANK. Wakefield Savings
       Bank, incorporated 1869, February 1, 1929.
Wakefield, 1929. Unpaged. M.
       Historical.

12611 YOUNG, FRED W. Wakefield: how the 1000-
       year old name came from over-seas to the
town on the Quannapowitt.... Wakefield: Item Pr.,
[1938?]. Pp. 39. MBNEH.

WALES

12612 GARDNER, ABSALOM. An address delivered in
       Wales, October 5, 1862: being the centen-
nial anniversary of the municipal organization of
the town with additions...to January 1, 1866, to
which is annexed a 'roll of honor,' being a catalogue of the names, etc., of soldiers from this
town who served...in the late Civil War. Springfield: Samuel Bowles, 1866. Pp. 44.

12613 GREEN, DOROTHY and ELSIE DAVIS. Wales bi-
       centennial celebration, 1762, 1962, town
of Wales, August 11, 1962 to August 26, 1962.
Wales, 1962. Pp. 36. MBNEH.

12614 WALES BAPTIST CHURCH. The history of the
       Wales Baptist Church. Wales, 1961.
Pp. 30. MS.

WALPOLE

12615 "BIRD & Son--a time honored trend setter."
       Industry, 35 (September, 1970), 56-58, 71-
72.

12616 "BIRD & Son, Inc." Industry, 2 (September,
       1937), 9-12, 47-48.

12617 DE LUE, WILLARD. The story of Walpole,
       1724-1924: a narrative history prepared
under authority of the town and direction of the
historical committee of bi-centennial. Norwood:
Ambrose Pr., 1925. v.p.

12618 KENDALL, HENRY P. "The Kendall Company:
       50 years of Yankee enterprise!" CottHR, 2
(1961), 85-91.
       Cotton.

12619 "THE KENDALL Company." Industry, 2 (Au-
       gust, 1937), 7-10.
       Cotton.

12620 LEWIS, ISAAC NEWTON. Addresses on Sir Rob-
       ert Walpole and Rev. Phillips Payson, men
prominent in the early history of Walpole, Mass.
[Walpole]: First Historical Society of Walpole,
Mass., 1905. Pp. 55.

12621 _____. A history of Walpole, Mass. from earliest times.... [Walpole]: First Historical Society of Walpole, Mass., 1905. Pp. ix, 217.

12622 _____. The minute men and other patriots of Walpole, Mass., in our long struggle for national independence, 1775-1783. [Walpole, Mass.]: First Walpole Historical Society, 1913. Pp. 59.

12623 MADDEN, JAMES LESTER. A history of Hollingsworth & Whitney Company, 1862-1954. n.p., 1954. Pp. 16. MH-BA.
Paper.

12624 SHUMWAY, HARRY IRVING. "A tavern as it used to be." American Cookery, 38 (1933), 139-146.
Fuller's Tavern, South Walpole, 1807.

12625 SHURROCKS, ALFRED F. "Fuller's Tavern, South Walpole, Mass." OTNE, 18 (1927-1928), 147-157.

12626 WALPOLE. Boston: Edison Electric Illuminating Co., 1909. Pp. 12. M.

12627 WALPOLE TOWN PLANNING COMMITTEE. Town planning for small communities.... N.Y.: D. Appleton, 1917. Pp. xvii, 492.

12628 WHEELWRIGHT, WILLIAM B. "Established 1795: a chronicle of Bird & Son, Inc." Paper Maker, 21 (1952), 37-46.

12629 WHITING, HARRY A. "Old Fuller's Tavern reopens." OTNE, 18 (1927-1928), 158-159.

WALTHAM

12630 ABELS, MARGARET HUTTON. From school to work: a study of children leaving school under 16 years of age to go to work in Waltham, Mass., an industrial community of about 30,000 inhabitants. Washington: Govt. Print. Off., 1917. Pp. 59.

12631 ALLEN, GORDON. "The Vale." OTNE, 42 (1951-1952), 81-87.
Theodore Lyman House.

12632 ARMSTRONG, THOMAS H. "Glimpses of Lower Main Street." WalHSP, 1, (1919), 21-30.

12633 _____. "Piety Corner and Pond End Schools: characteristics and teachers." WalHSP, 1 (1919), 46-50.
1730-1851.

12634 _____. Waltham Common, its ownership and history [and] Reminiscences of homes and people. Waltham, 1926. Pp. 33.
'Reminiscences of homes and people' is by Mrs. Sumner Milton.

12635 ARNOLD, EARL J. "Industry's map of Massachusetts: Waltham." Industry, 2 (June, 1937), 15-17, 47.

12636 BARRY, EPHRAIM L. The city of Waltham, Massachusetts, its advantages to manufacturers and as a place of residence.... Waltham: Waltham Board of Trade, 1887. Pp. 96.

12637 CAROSSO, VINCENT P. "The Waltham Watch Company: a case history." BBHS, 23 (1949), 165-187.

12638 COMPTON, ANN E. "The Lyman greenhouses." OTNE, 50 (1959-1960), 83 and iv.
Lyman House.

12639 EATON, PERCIVAL R. "Works of the Watch City." NEM, New Ser., 34 (1906), 360-374.

12640 FREEMASONS. WALTHAM, MASS. MONITOR LODGE. Centenary...1920...list of members from 1820. Waltham, 1921. Pp. 100. MBNEH.

12641 _____. Sesquicentennial, 1820-1970. Waltham, [1970?]. Pp. 39. MBNEH.

12642 GITELMAN, HOWARD M. "The labor force at Waltham Watch during the Civil War era." JEconHist, 25 (1965), 214-243.

12643 _____. "No Irish need apply: patterns of and responses to ethnic discrimination in the labor market." LabHist, 14 (1973), 56-68.

12644 _____. "The Waltham System and the coming of the Irish." LabHist, 8 (1967), 227-253.
Recruitment and treatment of labor at the Boston Manufacturing Co.

12645 _____. Workingmen of Waltham: mobility in American urban industrial development, 1850-1980. Baltimore: Johns Hopkins Univ. Pr., 1974. Pp. xvi, 192.

12646 GOLDSTEIN, ISRAEL. Brandeis University, chapter of its founding. N.Y.: Block Publishing, 1951. Pp. xi, 188.

12647 "GORE Place." Antiques, 47 (1945), 217-219.
Home of Christopher Gore.

12648 LANE, ELLEN E. "Seventy-five years ago." WalHSP, 1 (1919), 7-15.
Written in 1914.

12649 _____. "Weston Street and thereabouts." WalHSP, 1 (1919), 16-20.

12650 LITTLE, BERTRAM K. "A McIntire country house." Antiques, 63 (1953), 506-508.
The Vale.

12651 MAILLOUX, KENNETH F. "Boston Manufacturing Company: its origins." TextHR, 4 (1963), 157-163; 5 (1964), 3-29.

12652 _____. "The Boston Manufacturing Company: the end of an era." TextHR, 5 (1964), 158-165.

12653 _____. "The Boston Manufacturing Company: the factory and the town." TextHR, 5 (1964), 114-122.

12654 MAYALL, R. NEWTON. "Country seat of a gentleman." OTNE, 43 (1952-1953), 37-41.
The Vale, home of Theodore Lyman.

12655 MOORE, CHARLES WALDEN. "Some thoughts on the early labor policy of the Waltham Watch Co." BBHS, 13 (1939), 24-29.

12656 _____. Timing a century; history of the Waltham Watch Company. Cambridge: Harvard Univ. Pr., 1945. Pp. xxxiv, 362.

12657 NELSON, CHARLES ALEXANDER. Waltham, past and present, and its industries, with an historical sketch of Watertown from its settlement in 1630 to the incorporation of Waltham, January 15, 1738. Cambridge: Thomas Lewis, 1879. Pp. 152.

12658 O'CONNOR, THOMAS F., ed. The bleachery district of Waltham, past and present: a souvenir. [Waltham]: The Bleachery Old-Timers, 1957. Pp. 198.

12659 PORTER, KENNETH WIGGINS. "'Maroons' in Massachusetts." JNegroHist, 28 (1943), 51-53.
Slavery.

12660 [RIPLEY, SAMUEL]. "A topographical and historical description of Waltham." MHSC, 2 Ser., 3 (1815), 261-284.

12661 RUTTER, JOSIAH. Historical address delivered before the citizens of Waltham, July 4, 1876, with an account of the celebration of the day. Waltham: Waltham Free Press Office, 1877. Pp. 29.
Relates to the city.

12662 SANDERSON, EDMUND LINCOLN. Highlights in Waltham history. Waltham, 1930. Unpaged. MHi.
Copy at New England Historic Genealogical Society contains a typescript index of names.

12663 _____. History of Piety Corner and the Piety Corner Club. Waltham: Piety Corner Club, 1929. Pp. 10. MHi.

12664 _____. and ELIZABETH D. CASTNER. History of the First Parish in Waltham, 1696 to 1957. [Waltham?, 1958?]. Pp. 41.
Includes a bibliography.

12665 SANDERSON, EDMUND LINCOLN. "Piety Corner and Pond End schools: history and description." WalHSP, 1 (1919), 31-44.
1730-1851.

12666 _____. Waltham as a precinct of Watertown and as a town, 1630-1884. Waltham: Waltham Historical Society, Inc., 1936. Pp. 168.

12667 _____. Waltham industries; a collection of sketches of early firms and founders. Waltham Historical Society, 1957. Pp. 164.

12668 STARBUCK, WALTER F. Picturesque features of the history of Waltham. Waltham: Waltham Publishing, 1917. Pp. 47. MB.

12669 STEARNS, GEORGE A. The First Parish in Waltham: an historical sketch. Boston: Priv. Print., 1914. Pp. 53. MH.

12670 SWINTON, JOHN. A model factory in a model city. N.Y.: Brown, Green & Adams, 1887. Pp. 16. MB.
American Waltham Watch Co.

12671 VIETS, HENRY ROUSE. "Edward R. Cutler and the first 'clean' appendectomy." JHistMed, 12 (1957), 388-390.

12672 WALTHAM, MASS. Proceedings at the celebration of the sesqui-centennial of the town of Waltham, held in Music hall, on Monday, January 16th, 1888. Waltham: Ephraim L. Barry, 1893. Pp. 104.

12673 WALTHAM, MASS. SENIOR HIGH SCHOOL. The golden door. Waltham: Waltham Publishing, 1959. Pp. xxiv, 199.
Economic conditions.

12674 WALTHAM. Boston: Edison Electric Illuminating Co., 1909. Pp. 28. M.

12675 WALTHAM COOPERATIVE BANK. Waltham Co-operative Bank, fiftieth anniversary, 1880-1930. Waltham, 1930. Pp. 16. M.

12676 WALTHAM FARMERS CLUB. Historical sketch... Waltham Farmers Club.... Waltham: Hasting's "Sentinel" Office, 1876. Pp. 14. MB.

12677 WALTHAM SAVINGS BANK. The Waltham Savings Bank, 1853-1924, a short historical sketch, together with a list of past and present officers.... Waltham, 1924. Unpaged. M.

12678 WARREN, NATHAN. "Development of the south side." WalHSP, 1 (1919), 51-60.

WARE

12679 CHASE, ARTHUR. History of Ware, Massachusetts. Cambridge: Univ. Pr., 1911. Pp. viii, 294.

12680 COBURN, DAVID N. Historical discourse, delivered at Ware, 1851: being commemorative of the formation of the First Church in Ware, May 9th, 1751. West Brookfield: O. S. Cooke & Co., 1851. Pp. 40.

12681 CONKEY, JOHN HOUGHTON and DOROTHY D. CONKEY. History of Ware, Massachusetts, 1911-1960. Barre: Barre Gazette, 1961. Pp. xix, 353.

12682 GILBERT, EDWARD HOOKER. Early grants and incorporation of the town of Ware. N.Y.: Fords, Howard & Hulbert, 1891. Pp. iv, 58.

12683 HYDE, WILLIAM. An address, delivered at the opening of the new Town hall, Ware, Mass., March 31, 1847: containing sketches of the early history of that town, and its first settlers. Brookfield: Merriam and Cooke, 1847. Pp. 56.

12684 PAGE, ALFRED BAYLIES. The manor of peace, Ware, Massachusetts: Reverend Grindall Rawson and his ministry. [Boston?]: Priv. Print., 1907. Pp. 13.
    Title refers to early name of a parish.

12685 REED, AUGUSTUS BROWN. Historical sermon, delivered at Ware First Parish, on Thanksgiving day, Dec. 2d., 1830. [Ware]: J. H. G. Gilbert, 1889. Pp. 21.
    Relates to the parish.

12686 WARE, MASS. EAST CONGREGATIONAL CHURCH. Articles of faith and covenant and standing rules. Ware: C. W. Eddy, 1874. Pp. 81. M.
    Historical sketch.

12687 WARE, MASS. FIRST CONGREGATIONAL CHURCH. Historical sketch, confession of faith, covenant and rules...with a catalogue of members. Ware: R. L. Hathaway, 1869. Pp. 28. M.

12688 WARE SAVINGS BANK. 'White power', Ware Savings Bank, Ware, Massachusetts, 1850-1950. Boston: A. W. Ellis, [1950?]. Unpaged. MAJ.

12689 WOOD, W. T. "Beautiful Ware." NEM, New Ser., 43 (1910-1911), 231-237.

WAREHAM

12690 BATES, CHARLES L. A brief history of the town of Wareham. Wareham: Courier Print Shop, 1939. Pp. 36. MBNEH.

12691 BLISS, WILLIAM ROOT. "The Agawame Plantation." NEHGR, 41 (1887), 194-201.

12692 BURGESS, EBENEZER. Wareham--sixty years since: a discourse delivered at Wareham, Massachusetts, May 19, 1861. Boston: T. R. Marvin & Son, 1861. Pp. 24.

12693 GILBERT, RUSS H. The story of a wigwam. Onset, 1904.
    Spiritualist community known as 'Co-workers.'

12694 HALL, LEMUEL C. "Wareham--the 'gateway to Cape Cod.'" Cape Cod Magazine, 1 (May, 1915), 10-11.

12695 LOVELL, DAISY WASHBURN. Glimpses of early Wareham. Taunton: Wareham Historical Society, 1970. Pp. 139.

12696 "THE OLD Fearing House at Wareham." CCAPL, 6 (May, 1922), 18.

12697 SOME account of the vampires of Onset, past and present. Boston: New England News Company, 1892. Pp. 80.

12698 "TOPOGRAPHY and history of Wareham, 1815." MHSC, 2 Ser., 4 (1816), 285-296.

12699 VAUGHAN, C. B. "Onset, a famous camping ground." NEM, New Ser., 32 (1905), 617-625.

12700 WAREHAM, MASS. 200TH ANNIVERSARY COMMITTEE. Souvenir of the 200th anniversary of the incorporation of the town of Wareham, Massachusetts, July 8, 9, 10, 1939. Wareham: Courier Print Shop, 1939. Pp. 36. M.
    Brief history by Charles L. Bates.

12701 WIXON, SUSAN HELEN. Summer days at Onset. Boston: G. E. Crosby, 1887. Pp. 84. MB.

WARREN

12702 DARLING, OLNEY IRMAN. History of Warren, Massachusetts. West Brookfield: Thomas Morey, 1874. Pp. 24.

12703 HAMILTON, JOHN. "Sixty years young and still growing." Industry, 23 (April, 1958), 23-24, 52-53.
    Wm. E. Wright & Sons, sewing notions.

12704 STEBBINS, SOLOMON BLISS. Western 1741-1834, Warren 1834-1891, Massachusetts: an account of the one hundred and fiftieth anniversary of the town of Warren, September 7, 1891. Boston: Nathan Sawyer & Son, 1891. Pp. 72.

12705 WARREN, MASS. CONGREGATIONAL CHURCH. Declaration of faith, covenant and by-laws of the Congregational Church in Warren, Massachusetts, with an historical sketch and a catalogue of members from 1791 to 1878. Warren: Melville & Goodhue, 1878. Pp. 53. MBNEH.

12706 "WARREN Steam Pump Company observes fiftieth anniversary." Industry, 12 (July, 1947), 19-21, 38, 42.

12707   "WM. E. Wright & Sons to mark 50th anniver-
        sary." Industry, 12 (September, 1947), 30.
        Sewing notions.

WARWICK

12708   BLAKE, JONATHAN. History of the town of
        Warwick, Massachusetts, from its first
settlement to 1854, brought down to the present
time by others [John Goldsbury and Hervey Barber],
with an appendix. Boston: Noyes, Holmes, 1873.
Pp. 240.

12709   _____. "Warwick, Mass." NEHGR, 21 (1867),
        124-127.

12710   MAYO, AMORY DWIGHT. Twenty-five years in
        old Warwick: an address delivered on Mem-
orial Day, August 18, 1904, in Warwick, Mass.
Washington: R. Beresford, 1905. Pp. 35.

12711   MORSE, CHARLES A. Warwick, Massachusetts:
        biography of a town, 1763-1963. Cambridge:
Dresser, Chapman & Grimes, 1963. Pp. 279.

12712   SMITH, MARY PRUDENCE WELLS. An address de-
        livered on 'Old Home' day, August 15,
1907 in Warwick, Mass. n.p., [1907?]. Pp. 22.
MDeeP.
        Notable Warwick women.

12713   SNOW, JULIA D. SOPHRONIA. "The Franklin
        Glass Factory--Warwick's venture." An-
tiques, 12 (1927), 133-140.
        1812-1817.

12714   WARWICK, MASS. Warwick bicentennial, 1763-
        1963. Warwick, 1963. Unpaged. MB.

WASHINGTON

12715   SEE HISTORIES OF BERKSHIRE COUNTY

WATERTOWN

12716   AITKEN, HUGH G. J. Taylorism at Watertown
        Arsenal: scientific management in action,
1908-1915. Cambridge: Harvard Univ. Pr., 1960.
Pp. 269.

12717   BOND, HENRY. Genealogies of the families
        and descendants of the early settlers of
Watertown, Massachusetts, including Waltham and
Weston: to which is appended the early history of
the town.... (1855) 2d. ed. Boston: N. E. His-
toric-Genealogical Society, for the benefit of the
"Bond Fund," 1860. 2v. in 1.
        Includes sketch of the author by Horatio
Gates Jones.

12718   CREECH, MARGARET D. "Six colonial 'case
        histories.'" Social Service Review, 13
(1939), 246-262.
        Poverty.

12719   DAVENPORT, ANNIE E. "Watertown, Massachu-
        setts." Daughters of the American Revolu-
tion Magazine, 58 (1924), 549-554.

12720   DE COSTA, BENJAMIN FRANKLIN. "The lost city
        of New England." MagAmHist, 1 (1877), 14-
20.
        Norumbega.

12721   ELIOT, SAMUEL. "The Perkins Institution
        and Massachusetts School for the Blind."
NEM, New Ser., 15 (1896-1897), 673-688.

12722   FISH, ANNA GARDNER. Perkins Institution
        and its deaf-blind pupils, 1837-1933. Wa-
tertown: Perkins Institution and Massachusetts
School for the Blind, 1934. Pp. 54.

12723   FRANCIS, CONVERS. An historical sketch of
        Watertown, in Massachusetts, from the first
settlement of the town to the close of its second
century. Cambridge: E. W. Metcalf, 1830. Pp. 151.

12724   _____. Three discourses preached before
        the Congregational Society in Watertown:
two, upon leaving the old meeting-house; and one,
at the dedication of the new. Cambridge: Folsom,
Wells, and Thurston, 1836. Pp. 79.

12725   FULLER, ARTHUR BUCKMINSTER, comp. A record
        of the First Parish in Watertown, Massachu-
setts. Watertown: Mount Auburn, printed at the
Memorial Office, 1861. Pp. 16.

12726   HOME FOR FRIENDLESS AND UNFORTUNATE WOMEN
        AND GIRLS (THE PORTLAND STREET MISSION
        HOME), EAST WATERTOWN, MASS. Historical
sketch of the home. Boston, 1907. Pp. 18. MB.

12727   "HOOD Rubber Company." Industry, 2 (Octo-
        ber, 1936), 9-12.
        Rubber footwear.

12728   HORSFORD, EBEN NORTON. Remarks at the sec-
        ond anniversary of the Watertown Historical
Society, November 18, 1890, Watertown: the site of
the ancient city of Norumbega. [Watertown?, 1890?].
Pp. 42.

12729   INGRAHAM, WILLIAM H. Address of Wm. H.
        Ingraham, Esq., and oration by Rev. J. F.
Lovering, at the centennial celebration, White's
Hill Grove, Watertown, Mass., July 4th, 1876.
[Watertown, 1876]. Pp. 35.

12730   [LEATHE, FRANCIS]. A glimpse at Watertown.
        By a 'native'.... 2d. ed. Boston, 1851.
Pp. iv, 42.

12731   LEWIS, M. M. "Watertown, Massachusetts:
        colonial beehive." Americana, 26 (1932),
18-22.

12732 LOCKE, HENRY DYER. An ancient parish: an historical summary of the First Parish, Watertown, Massachusetts. [Watertown]: Tercentenary Committee of the Parish, 1930. Pp. 19.

12733 MIDDLETON, ELINORE HUSE. History of St. John's Methodist Episcopal Church in Watertown, 1836-1936. n.p., [1936?]. Pp. 136. MWA.

12734 NORCROSS, JAMES EDWARD. Memorial history of the First Baptist Church, Watertown, Massachusetts, 1830-1930. Cambridge: Hampshire Pr., 1930. Pp. 169. MBNEH.

12735 NORRIS, WILFRED A. "The old burying ground at Watertown, Mass." OTNE, 16 (1925-1926), 3-9.

12736 PIERCE, CATHARINE W. "The Brownes of Watertown and the date of the Abraham Browne House." OTNE, 30 (1939-1940), 67-72.

12737 ROBINSON, GEORGE FREDERICK and RUTH R. WHEELER. Great little Watertown: a tercentenary history. [Watertown], 1930. Pp. 150.

12738 ROBINSON, GEORGE FREDERICK. Greetings of the mother church in Watertown, Massachusetts to her daughter, the First Parish Church in Wayland, Massachusetts, on the occasion of her three hundredth anniversary, January twenty-fourth, nineteen hundred and forty. Watertown: Watertown Historical Society, 1940. Pp. 21. MBNEH.

12739 _____. and ALBERT H. HALL, comps. Watertown soldiers in the colonial wars and the American Revolution. Watertown: Historical Society of Watertown, 1939. Pp. 75.

12740 ROCKWOOD, CHARLES M. "In Boston's new suburban district, old Watertown, a modern suburb." NEM, New Ser., 41 (1909-1910), 549-559.

12741 SAVAGE, WILLIAM H. "Annals of an ancient parish." NEM, New Ser., 6 (1892), 237-255.

12742 SIMMONS, RICHARD C. "Freemanship in early Massachusetts: some suggestions and a case study." WMQ, 3 Ser., 19 (1962), 422-428.

12743 VAUGHAN, MOSETTA I. The meeting houses of the First Congregational Society of Watertown, Massachusetts, written for the centennial of the seventh house, September 20th, 1942. [Watertown]: Historical Society of Watertown, 1942. Pp. 14.

12744 WATERTOWN, MASS. Watertown records.... Watertown, 1894-1939. 8v. in 7. Name and subject indexes.

12745 _____. Watertown: the mother town, 1635-1955, 325 years. Watertown: Eaton Pr., 1955. Unpaged. MBNEH.

12746 _____. Watertown's military history. Boston: David Clapp & Son, 1907. Pp. xvii, 281.

12747 WATERTOWN, MASS. FIRST PARISH. Two hundred and fiftieth anniversary of the First Parish of Watertown, Mass., Sunday, November 28, 1880. Boston: George H. Ellis, 1881. Pp. 36. M.

12748 WATERTOWN, MASS. ST. PATRICK'S PARISH. One hundredth anniversary, 1847-1947, Saint Patrick's Parish, Watertown, Massachusetts. Boston: Alhambra Pr., [1947?]. Pp. 59. MAJ.

12749 WATERTOWN. Boston: Edison Electric Illuminating Co., 1909. Pp. 16. M.

12750 WHITNEY, SOLON FRANKLIN. Historical sketch of the town of Watertown, commemorating the two hundred and seventy-fifth anniversary of its settlement as an English colony, embracing a detailed account of the limits of the town and the history of the old mill and the great bridge. Boston: Murray and Emery, 1906. Pp. 24.

WAYLAND

12751 CUTTING, ALFRED WAYLAND. An historical address delivered in the First Parish Church, Wayland, Mass., Sunday, June 25, 1911.... Boston: Geo. H. Ellis, 1911. Pp. 35. Church history.

12752 _____. A hundred years of the old meeting house, an address delivered...in the First Parish Church...January 24, 1915.... n.p., [1915]. Pp. 17.

12753 _____. "An old house at Wayland." NEM, New Ser., 31 (1904-1905), 569-576. 'The Island' or Heard House.

12754 _____. Old-time Wayland. Boston: Thomas Todd, 1926. Pp. 51. MBNEH.

12755 HUDSON, ALFRED SERENO. "The home of Lydia Maria Child." NEM, New Ser., 2 (1890), 402-413.

12756 MERRILL, TRUMAN ALLEN. Jubilee shall that fiftieth year be unto you, sermon: commemorative of the formation of the Evangelical Trinitarian Church, Wayland, Mass., May 21, 1878, on its fiftieth anniversary. Boston: Frank Wood, 1878. Pp. 32. MB.

12757 "PIONEERS in precision potentiometers." Industry, 23 (July, 1958), 19-20, 32. Waters Manufacturing, Inc.; electronic components.

12758 WAYLAND, MASS. Proceedings at the dedication of the Town Hall, Wayland, December 24, 1878; with brief historical sketches of public buildings and libraries. Wayland, 1879. Pp. 79.

12759 _____. The town of Wayland in the Civil
War of 1861-1865, as represented in the
army and navy of the American union.... Wayland,
1871. Pp. 452.

12760 WAYLAND, MASS. CONGREGATIONAL CHURCH. A
sermon, a charge, and the fellowship of
churches, delivered at the ordination of Reverend
John Burt Wight, A. M., pastor of the Congregational
Church in East Sudbury (Wayland) XXV January
MDCCCXV. Cambridge: Hilliard and Metcalf, 1815.
Pp. 36. M.
Includes brief history.

12761 WAYLAND, MASS. FIRST PARISH. First Parish,
Wayland, Massachusetts, 1640-1940, the ter-
centenary program and an address by William Lee
Raymond. Cambridge: Cosmos Pr., 1940. Pp. 20.
MB.

12762 WAYLAND. Boston: Edison Electric Illuminating Co., 1909. Pp. 8. M.

WEBSTER

12763 CONLIN, JOHN F. Historical sketches: a
retrospect of fifty years of St. Louis'
Church, with preliminary chapters on the early days
of Webster and Dudley. Boston: Washington Pr.,
1901. Pp. 139.

12764 REDING, CHARLES WILLIAM. Historical discourse delivered on the fiftieth anniversary of the organization of the Baptist Church,
Webster, Mass., October 30, 1864. Webster: Weekly
Times Office, 1864. Pp. 40. MBNEH.

12765 SLATER, S., & SONS, INC. The Slater Mills
at Webster, founded, Pawtucket 1790; established, Webster 1812; centennial, Webster 1912.
Worcester, [1912?]. Pp. 37.

12766 WEBSTER, MASS. Souvenir programme, dedi-
cation of Soldiers' Monument, Webster,
Mass., July 4, 1907. n.p., [1907?]. Unpaged. MWA.
Includes sketch of Webster's part in the
Civil War by Alice L. Rusack.

12767 WEBSTER, MASS. FIRST CONGREGATIONAL CHURCH.
Manual of the First Congregational Church,
Webster, Mass.... n.p., [1928?]. Unpaged. MWA.
Includes historical sketch.

WELLESLEY

12768 BAKER, WILLIAM EMERSON. Guide to Ridge
Hill Farms, Wellesley, Mass. and social
science reform, September, 1877. Boston: Getchell
Bros., 1877. Pp. 152.
An estate.

12769 BATES, KATHARINE LEE. "The beginnings of
Dana Hall." Our Town, 2 (June, 1899), 3-4.
Private girls' school.

12770 BRADFORD, GAMALIEL, 1863-1932. Early days
in Wellesley: being casual recollections
of boyhood and later years--1867 to 1881. (1928)
Wellesley: Wellesley National Bank, 1929. Pp. 43.

12771 BRADFORD, HELEN FORD. History of the
Wellesley Hills Woman's Club. Natick:
Suburban Pr., 1928. Pp. 160.

12772 BROWN, HELEN MARGARET. "Wellesley College
Library: an historical sketch." Bay State
Librarian, 49 (Autumn, 1959), 1-5.

12773 "THE CENTENNIAL celebration of the Wellesley Congregational Church." Our Town, 1
(September, 1898), 3-6.

12774 CHANDLER, EDWARD HERRICK. The history of
the Wellesley Congregational Church, including 'The influence of the church in the making
of New England'; centennial oration by William Hayes
Ward.... Boston: Benj. H. Sanborn, 1898. Pp. 241.

12775 CONVERSE, FLORENCE. Wellesley College: a
chronicle of the years, 1875-1938. Wellesley: Hathaway House Bookshop, 1939. Pp. xiii, 311.
A revision and expansion of the author's
'The story of Wellesley', published in
1915.

12776 EDWARD, MARY N. "The Pencil and Brush
Club." Our Town, 6 (1903), 1-2.

12777 FISKE, JOSEPH EMERY. History of the town of
Wellesley, Massachusetts. Ellen Ware Fiske,
ed. Boston: Pilgrim Pr., 1917. Pp. xiii, 92.

12778 FULLER, F. L. "The Wellesley Water Works."
Our Town, 2 (August, 1899), 5-6.

12779 GILSON, F. H. "The Abbot cedar." Our Town,
5 (1902), 1-2.

12780 GUILD, MARION PELTON. "Wellesley College,
her story and her need." NEM, 52 (1914-
1915), 57-73.

12781 HACKETT, ALICE PAYNE. Wellesley, part of
the American story. N.Y.: E. P. Dutton,
1949. Pp. 320.
Wellesley College.

12782 HILL, MARY BRIGHAM and HELEN GERTRUDE EAGER,
eds. Wellesley, the college beautiful.
Boston, 1894. Pp. 50.

12783 HODGKINS, LOUISE MANNING. "Wellesley College." NEM, New Ser., 7 (1892-1893), 361-
380.

12784 NO ENTRY

12785 LAKE, FLAVIUS J. "Growth of Wellesley."
Our Town, 2 (November, 1899), 5.

12786 PIERCE, T. RAYMOND. "The Wellesley Club--
a sketch." Our Town, 6 (1903), 162-165.
Men's club--devoted to town interests.

12787 PLETCHER, DOROTHY E. "Wellesley, the college beautiful." National Magazine, 53 (1924-1925), 475-478, 486.

12788 PONDEXTER, JEAN and LOUISE SANDERS. The new Wellesley, with thirty illustrations of the new Wellesley College. Boston: Priv. Print., 1931. Pp. 45.

12789 ROBERTS, ETHEL DANE. Brief history of the Wellesley College Library. Wellesley, 1936. Pp. 46. MB.

12790 SWIFT, W. B. "Indian remains in our town." Our Town, 5 (1902), 103-106.

12791 WELLESLEY, MASS. Town of Wellesley, 1881: 1931, semicentennial and Massachusetts tercentenary celebration. Wellesley, 1931. Pp. 55. M.

WELLFLEET

12792 COLE, CHARLES F. History of Colonial Hall, Wellfleet, Mass. [Wellfleet]: Wellfleet Associates, 1941. Unpaged. MWA.

12793 DOOLEY, MARGARET T. History and lore of South Wellfleet. Boston: Angel Guardian Pr., 1938. Unpaged.

12794 EKHOLM, ERIK and JAMES DEETZ. "Wellfleet Tavern." Natural History, 80 (August-September, 1971), 49-56.

12795 HINSHAW, JOHN V. Marconi and his South Wellfleet wireless. Chatham: Chatham Pr., 1969. Pp. 30.

12795A HOLBROOK, ALBERT W. Historical address, delivered before the town of Wellfleet, July 4th, 1876. Provincetown: Advocate Printing, 1876. Pp. 13.
    Relates to the town.

12796 NYE, EVERETT I., comp. History of Wellfleet, from early days to present time. Hyannis: F. B. & F. P. Goss, 1920. Pp. 48.

12797 PALMER, ALBERT P. A brief history of the Methodist Episcopal Church in Wellfleet, Massachusetts. Boston: Rand, Avery, 1877. Pp. 84.

12798 STETSON, JUDY. Wellfleet, a pictorial history. [Wellfleet]: Wellfleet Historical Society, 1963. Pp. 95. M.

12799 _____. "Wellfleet's 200th anniversary." CCC, 16 (1963), 16-17.

12800 WELLFLEET, MASS. FIRST CONGREGATIONAL CHURCH. Manual of the First Congregational Church in Wellfleet, containing...[an] historical sketch.... Boston: D. F. Jones, 1877. Pp. 19. MBNEH.

WENDELL

12801 WENDELL, MASS. CONGREGATIONAL CHURCH. Centennial celebration of the Congregational Church, Wendell, Mass., Wednesday, December 2, 1874: address of welcome by B. B. Cutler, historical discourse by W. H. Beaman, poem by V. W. Leach. Amherst: Henry M. McCloud, 1875. Pp. 42. M.

WENHAM

12802 ALLEN, MYRON OLIVER. The history of Wenham, civil and ecclesiastical, from its settlement in 1639, to 1860. Boston: Bazin & Chandler, 1860. Pp. vi, 220.

12803 APPLETON, WILLIAM SUMNER. "A description of Robert McClaflin's house." OTNE, 16 (1925-1926), 157-167.
    Claflin-Richards House.

12804 COLE, ADELINE P. Notes on Wenham history, 1643-1943. Salem: Newcomb & Gauss, 1943. Pp. 157.

12805 COLE, MRS. E. B. "The Claflin-Richards House, Wenham, Mass." OTNE, 16 (1925-1926), 153-156.

12806 DODGE, LOUIS ABRAHAM. The homestead of Richard Dodge, successive owners of his 'pioneer home' together with a general idea as to the location of the boundary of the several parcels herein described. [Wenham]: Wenham Historical Society, 1947. Pp. 25. MSaE.

12807 _____. The rise of Little Jacob: an historical sketch of the Wenham Baptist Church, 1831-1931. n.p., [1931?]. Pp. 24. M.

12808 _____. Wenham as it used to be. n.p., [1963?]. Unpaged. MSaE.

12809 NO ENTRY

12810 FISKE, JOHN, 1601-1677. Notebook of the Rev. John Fiske 1644-1675. Robert G. Pope, ed. Boston: Colonial Society of Massachusetts, 1974. Pp. xxxix, 256.

12811 GORHAM, MRS. A. D. History of the Female Benevolent Society of the Baptist Church, Wenham from 1833 to 1883. [Salem]: Essex County Mercury Pr., 1883. Pp. 8. MSaE.

12812 MANSFIELD, DANIEL. Two sermons, delivered on the second centennial anniversary of the organization of the First Church, and the settlement of the first minister in Wenham. Andover: Allen, Morrill and Wardwell, 1845. Pp. 72.
    Congregational Church.

12813 PEABODY, ALLEN. Poems: a humorous and historical collection, giving the jokes, experiences, and characters of many citizens of Wenham 30 years ago, and people of the present time. Salem: E. H. Fletcher, 1868. Pp. 35.

12814   PHILLIPS, JAMES DUNCAN. Wenham's 300 years:
        being the tercentenary address delivered at
Wenham, Massachusetts on July 4, 1943. Salem: Newcomb & Gauss, 1943. Pp. 14. MHi.

12815   PHILLIPS, JOHN CHARLES. Wenham Great Pond.
        Salem: Peabody Museum, 1938. Pp. xii,
108.
        Ice industry and water supply.

12816   PUTNAM, ALFRED PORTER. "Wenham Lake and
        the ice trade." Ice and Refrigeration, 3
(1892), 14-17, 179-182.

12817   RANTOUL, ROBERT SAMUEL. "Some notes on
        Wenham Pond." EIHC, 6 (1864), 141-152.

12818   WENHAM, MASS. 325th anniversary of the
        town of Wenham, Massachusetts. n.p.,
[1968?]. Unpaged. M.

12819   _____. Wenham, commemorating Massachusetts
        Bay Colony Tercentenary. Salem: Newcomb &
Gauss, 1930. Pp. 12. MSaE.

12820   _____. Wenham town records, 1642-1810.
        [Wenham]: Wenham Historical Society, 1930-
1959. 5v.

12821   WENHAM, MASS. CONGREGATIONAL CHURCH. Man-
        ual of the Congregational Church in Wen-
ham, Mass., 1644-1879. Bristol, N.H.: R. W. Mus-
grove, 1879. Pp. 96. M.
        Includes history of the church.

12822   WENHAM HISTORICAL ASSOCIATION. Wenham in
        World War II; war service of Wenham men
and women and civilian services of Wenham people.
Comp. and ed. by the Historical Assn. [and] Wenham
Village Improvement Society, Inc. [Wenham], 1947.
Pp. 310.

12823   WOOD, NATHAN ROBINSON. A school of Christ.
        Boston: Halliday Lithograph, 1953.
Pp. 217. MSaE.
        Gordon College.

WEST BOYLSTON

12824   CROSBY, C. C. P. "History of West Boyls-
        ton." WMHJ, 2 (1826), 193-204.

12825   FITTS, JAMES HILL. Historical address de-
        livered at the re-dedication of the brick
meeting house, West Boylston, Mass., Jan. 1, 1890.
Exeter, N.H.: John Templeton, 1890. Pp. 26.

12826   GOODALE, LEON A. Proceedings in connection
        with the one hundredth anniversary of the
incorporation of the town of West Boylston, Massachusetts...January 30, 1908, and the centennial
celebration held Thursday, July 16th, 1908.
Worcester: Belisle Printing and Publishing, 1908.
Pp. 164. M.

12827   HUNTINGTON, MRS. RAYMOND S. History of the
        beginnings of Methodism in Oakdale 1851-
1857, and of the Oakdale Methodist Church, 1857-
1951. Worcester: Hoyle Pr., 1951. Pp. 51.
MBNEH.

12828   KEYES, BENJAMIN FRANKLIN. Historical memo-
        randum and genealogical register of the
town of West Boylston, Massachusetts, from its early settlement to 1858: together with miscellaneous
items and incidents. Worcester: Spy Printing
House, 1861. Pp. 84.

12829   WEST BOYLSTON, MASS. Sesquicentennial cel-
        ebration of West Boylston, Massachusetts,
1808-1958. West Boylston, 1958. Unpaged.

12830   WEST BOYLSTON, MASS. FIRST CONGREGATIONAL
        CHURCH. Commemorative exercises of the
semi-centennial anniversary of the Sabbath school
at West Boylston, Mass., June 16, 1868. Worcester:
Tyler & Seagrave, 1870. Pp. 31. MBNEH.

12831   _____. Manual of the Congregational Church
        in West Boylston, Mass., its organization,
principles, articles of faith.... Worcester: Tyler and Seagrave, 1876. Pp. 20. M.
        Includes brief historical sketch.

12832   WEST BOYLSTON, MASS. METHODIST EPISCOPAL
        CHURCH, OAKDALE. Report of the twenty-fifth
anniversary of the Methodist Episcopal Church, Oakdale, Feb. 8, 1884: historical essay...by Mrs.
A. E. Russell. Clinton: Coulter, 1884. Pp. 30.
M.

WEST BRIDGEWATER

12833   COPELAND, ALBERT. Historical lecture show-
        ing the causes which led to the formation
of Baptist churches in Massachusetts; and particularly that in Bridgewater, Mass. (now West Bridgewater), with the history of that church, from its
formation to its dissolution, also a history of
the present church.... [Bridgewater, 1877].
Pp. 24.

12834   ROMAINE, LAWRENCE B. "Pardon Keith, cooper
        of West Bridgewater, Massachusetts, accounts
1826-1835." CEAIA, 5 (1952), 18-19.

WEST BROOKFIELD

12835   CHAMBERLAIN, DANIEL HENRY. Historical
        sketch of West Brookfield. n.p., n.d.
Unpaged. MWA.

12836   SPRAGUE, HOMER BAXTER. Address at the dedi-
        cation of the town library building, erected
for the West Brookfield Free Library and Reading
Room, delivered Friday evening, November 12, 1880...
with an appendix, giving a description of the building, the origin, history and present condition of
the library, &c. Springfield: Weaver, Shipman,
1882. Pp. 38.

12837   WEST BROOKFIELD, MASS. CONGREGATIONAL
        CHURCH. Manual of the Congregational
Church, West Brookfield, Massachusetts, being a
sketch of its history.... West Brookfield: O. S.
Cooke, 1853. Pp. 24. MWA.

WEST NEWBURY

12838   MARION, FRIEDA. "Indian Hill Farm."
        Shoreliner, 3 (September, 1952), 13-24.

12839   WEST NEWBURY, MASS. 150TH ANNIVERSARY CEL-
        EBRATION COMMITTEE. West Newbury, Massa-
chusetts, 150th anniversary, August 22-24, 1969.
West Newbury, 1969. Pp. 36. M.

WEST SPRINGFIELD

12840   BAGG, ERNEST NEWTON. "Leaves from the rec-
        ords of an old parish." CVHSP, 2 (1882-
1903), 66-77.

12841   BAGG, WINTHROP SEARS. Brief history of the
        Day House. [West Springfield]: Ramapogue
Historical Society, [1905]. Pp. 16.

12842   _____. "West Springfield in the early
        days." WNE, 3 (1913), 22-25.

12843   BROOKS, ANGELINE. "New England in the
        making." WNE, 2 (1912), 354-357.
        Settlement of the town and separation of
Church and State in Massachusetts.

12844   _____. "Some gleanings from early West
        Springfield records." WNE, 3 (1913), 17-
21.

12845   EASTERN STATES EXPOSITION. A brief history
        of the Eastern States Exposition. [Spring-
field, 1930]. Pp. 16.

12846   _____. Storrowton, a New England village.
        Boston: Todd, 1930. Pp. 25. M.
        Storrowton is comprised of a group of
houses of the period 1767-1834 which were
moved to grounds of the Eastern States Exposition.

12847   GROUT, HENRY MARTYN. "The First Church in
        West Springfield." CongQ, 13 (1871), 532-
536.

12848   LATHROP, JOSEPH. Steadfastness in religion,
        explained and recommended in a sermon de-
livered, in the First Parish in West-Springfield,
by Joseph Lathrop, D. D., minister of said parish,
on the 25th day of August, in the year 1796, it being the day which closed the 40th year of his ministry, and the year, which completed a century
from the incorporation of said parish. West-Springfield: Edward Gray, 1797. Pp. 34.

12849   LITTLEFIELD, BEATRICE B. History of the
        First Parish and the First Congregational
Church of West Springfield, Massachusetts: including the Park Street Church records, compiled for
the two hundred fiftieth anniversary of the church.
West Springfield: Bordeaux, 1948. Pp. 21.

12850   SPRAGUE, WILLIAM BUELL. An historical dis-
        course, delivered at West Springfield,
December 2, 1824, the day of the annual thanksgiving. Hartford: Goodwin, 1825. Pp. 91.
        Relates to the town.

12851   STEBBINS, DANIEL. "Ancient houses."
        American Pioneer, 2 (1843), 339-343.

12852   "THE STRATHMORE Paper Company." Industry,
        5 (May, 1940), 27-30.

12853   SWIFT, ESTHER M. West Springfield, Massa-
        chusetts: a town history. [West Spring-
field]: West Springfield Heritage Association for
the town of West Springfield, Mass., 1969.
Pp. xii, 344.

12854   WEST SPRINGFIELD, MASS. Account of the
        centennial celebration of the town of West
Springfield, Mass., Wednesday, March 25th, 1874,
with the historical address of Thomas E. Vermilye...
the poem of Mrs. Ellen P. Champion, and other facts
and speeches. J. N. Bagg, comp. Springfield:
Clark W. Bryan, 1874. Pp. 144.

12855   WEST SPRINGFIELD, MASS. FIRST CONGREGA-
        TIONAL CHURCH. The church book of the
First Congregational Church in West Springfield,
Mass.... Springfield: Weaver, Shipman, 1884.
Pp. 54. MBNEH.
        Includes historical sketch.

12856   _____. Manual of the First Congregational
        Church, West Springfield, Mass. and a cata-
logue of members, September, 1858. Northampton:
Metcalf, 1858. Pp. 27. M.
        Includes historical record.

12857   "WEST Springfield." WNE, 3 (1913), 1-12.

WEST STOCKBRIDGE

12858   GARNETT, EDNA BAILEY. West Stockbridge,
        Massachusetts, 1774-1974, the history of an
Indian settlement, Queensborough or Qua-pau-kuk.
West Stockbridge: Queensborough Association, 1974.
Pp. 135. MPB.

WEST TISBURY

12859   ALLEY, LILLIAN MARIE. "Dukes County Acad-
        emy." CCAPL, 5 (February, 1922), 20, 22-23.

12860   DAGGETT, JOHN TOBEY. It began with a
        whale: memories of Cedar Tree Neck, Mar-
tha's Vineyard. Somerville: Fleming & Son, 1963.
Pp. 133.

12861 ELVIN, JOSEPH B. "The Lambert's Cove Cemetery." DCI, 5 (November, 1963), 39-47.

12862 GIFFORD, FLAVEL M. "The peddle cart." DCI, 3 (November, 1961), [1].
Delivery cart used by S. M. Mayhew Co., general store.

12863 MAYHEW, ELEANOR RANSOM. "The Christiantown story, 1659-1959." DCI, [1] (August, 1959), [3-11].
Christianizing of Indians.

12864 MILLS, ELDEN H. "'Sweep out the place when necessary.'" DCI, 9 (1967-1968), 47-59.
West Tisbury Congregational Church.

12865 RIGGS, DIONIS COFFIN. "Dukes County Academy." DCI, 6 (1964-1965), 181-195.

WESTBOROUGH

12866 ALLEN JOSEPH ADDISON. Westboro' state reform school reminiscences. Boston: Lockwood, Brooks, 1877. Pp. 94.
Author was a former superintendent.

12867 BRIANT, SAMUEL INGERSOLL. Twenty years of the Westborough Historical Society; an address by the president...October 27, 1909. Westborough: Chronotype Printing, 1909. Pp. 11.

12868 DE FOREST, HEMAN PACKARD and EDWARD C. BATES. The history of Westborough, Massachusetts. Pt. I. The early history, Pt. II. The later history. Westborough: The Town, 1891. Pp. xvi, 504.
Mr. Bates is the author of the second part.

12869 FORBES, HARRIETTE MERRIFIELD. The hundredth town, glimpses of life in Westborough, 1717-1817. Boston: Rockwell and Churchill, 1889. Pp. 209.

12870 _____. "Two Indian chiefs." Worcester HSProc, (1891-1893), 422-433.
Manteo (Jack Straw) and Timothy Rice.

12871 PARKMAN, EBENEZER. "An account of Westborough (Mass.), January 28, 1767." MHSC, 10 (1809), 84-86.

12872 _____. Diary of Ebenezer Parkman, 1703-1782. Francis G. Walett, ed. Worcester: American Antiquarian Society, 1974-.

12873 _____. The diary of Rev. Ebenezer Parkman, of Westborough, Mass., for the months of February, March, April, October, and November, 1737, November and December of 1778 and the years of 1779 and 1780.... Harriette M. Forbes, ed. [Westborough]: Westborough Historical Society, 1899. Pp. viii, 327.

12874 _____. The story of the Rice boys, captured by the Indians, August 8, 1704. [Westborough]: Westborough Historical Society, 1906. Pp. 6.
Asher, Adonijah, Silas and Timothy Rice.

12875 ROCKWOOD, ELISHA. A century sermon delivered in Westborough, on Thanksgiving Day, December 3, 1818. Boston: Parmenter and Balch, 1819. Pp. 22. MB.

12876 ROE, ALFRED SEELYE. "Creating character at the Lyman School for Boys, Westborough, Massachusetts." NEM, New Ser., 26 (1902), 399-416.
Reform school.

12877 WESTBOROUGH, MASS. EVANGELICAL CHURCH. The articles of faith and covenant of the Evangelical Church of Christ in Westborough, Ms.... Boston: T. R. Marvin, 1842. Pp. 23. M.
Includes historical sketch.

12878 WESTBOROUGH, MASS. 250TH ANNIVERSARY COMMITTEE. Commemorative booklet, Westborough, Massachusetts, 1717-1967. North Conway, N.H.: Reporter Pr., 1967. Pp. 176. M.

12879 WESTBOROUGH HISTORICAL SOCIETY. More old houses in Westborough, Mass., and vicinity, with their occupants. [Westborough], 1908. Pp. 58.

12880 _____. Some old houses in Westborough, Mass., and their occupants: with an account of the Parkman diaries. [Westborough], 1906. Pp. 70.
Name index.

WESTFIELD

12881 ALDEN, JOHN, 1806-1894. History of Westfield: a sermon, by Rev. John Alden, pastor of the Central Baptist Church, Westfield, Mass., delivered January 28, 1851, at the remodelling of their house of worship.... Springfield: George W. Wilson, 1851. Pp. 20.

12882 DAVIS, EMERSON. A historical sketch of Westfield. Westfield: J. Root, 1826. Pp. 36.

12883 _____. Memorial sermon: a sermon preached on the occasion of leaving the old meeting house, in Westfield, Dec. 9, 1860. Westfield: T. P. Collins, 1861. Pp. 15.

12884 _____. A thriving town: a sermon, preached at the annual fast, April 6, 1837, in Westfield, Mass. Springfield: Merriam, Wood, 1837. Pp. 16.

12885 DEWEY LOUIS MARINUS. [Chronological history of Westfield, Mass.] n.p., 1910. Unpaged.

12886 _____. "The Moseley Homestead, Westfield, Mass." MassMag, 4 (1911), 211-212.

12887 "A FAMILY affair." Industry, 25 (April, 1960), 23-25.
H. B. Smith Co., cast iron boilers.

12888 "50TH anniversary, Westfield State Sanatorium." Commonhealth, 8 (May/June, 1960), entire issue.

12889 GRANT, FRANK, comp. The history of the celebration of the two hundred and fiftieth anniversary of the incorporation of the town of Westfield, Massachusetts, August 31, September 1, 2, 3, 1919, and appendix with reminiscences of the last half-century. Concord, N.H.: Rumford Pr., 1919. Pp. xiv, 239.

12890 HALL, P. N. "Industry's map of Massachusetts: Westfield." Industry, 3 (March, 1938), 31-33, 55.

12891 LOCKWOOD, JOHN HOYT. A sermon commemorative of the two-hundredth anniversary of the First Congregational Church of Westfield, Mass., delivered...Sunday, October 5, 1879.... Westfield: Clark & Story, 1879. Pp. 55.

12892 _____. Westfield and its historic influences, 1669-1919: the life of an early town, with a survey of events in New England and bordering regions to which it was related in colonial and revolutionary times. [Westfield], 1922. 2v.

12893 JANES, EDWARD C. and ROSCOE S. SCOTT. Westfield, Massachusetts, 1669-1969: the first three hundred years. Westfield: Westfield Tri-Centennial Association, 1968. Pp. viii, 476.

12894 MASSACHUSETTS. STATE TEACHERS COLLEGE, WESTFIELD. Alma mater: twenty first triennial, June 1, 1907, State Normal School, Westfield, Mass., 1839-1907. Boston: Wright & Potter, 1907. Pp. 52.
Historical sketches by Clarence A. Brodeur and Adeline A. Knight.

12895 _____. Semi-centennial and other exercises...June 25, 1889. Boston: State Printers, 1889. Pp. 79. M.
Historical address by John W. Dickinson.

12896 NEWDICK, EDWIN W. "The Whip City of the world." WNE, 1 (1910-1911), 53-62.
Horse whips.

12897 PITONIAK, STEPHEN J. Western Massachusetts history: the Westfield area. Westfield, 1970. Pp. 87.

12898 PLUMMER, EDGAR HOLMES, ed. Westfield's quarter millennial anniversary official souvenir.... Westfield: Westfield's 250th Anniversary Association, 1919. Pp. 144.

12899 SALMOND, ELOISE FOWLER. Mundale, the West Parish of Westfield, Massachusetts, in the olden days. Springfield: Pond-Ekberg, 1934. Pp. 93.

12900 "SPORTING arms firm's 100th anniversary." Industry, 30 (December, 1964), 16, 43.
Savage Arms.

12901 STARR, PETER. Address delivered at Westfield, August 14, 1844 at a meeting of the present and former pupils of Westfield Academy. Northampton: John Metcalf, 1844. Pp. 16. MB.
Historical appendix.

12902 STILES, CHESTER D., comp. A history of the town of Westfield.... Westfield: J. D. Cadle, 1919. Pp. 50.

12903 WARNER, MADELINE. "The Westfield home front during the Civil War." HJWM, 3 (Spring, 1974), 24-39.

12904 WESTERN HAMPDEN HISTORICAL SOCIETY, WESTFIELD, MASS. Presenting the fifty year story of the Western Hampden Historical Society, 1901-1951, First Methodist Church, Westfield, Mass., June 14, 1951. n.p., [1951?]. Pp. 12. MBNEH.

12905 WESTFIELD, MASS. Town of Westfield, past and present, progress and prosperity, souvenir, 1906. Westfield: W. M. Alcorn Souvenir Association, 1906. Pp. 36. M.

12906 _____. The Westfield jubilee: a report of the celebration at Westfield, Mass., on the two hundredth anniversary of the incorporation of the town, October 6, 1869, with the historical address of the Hon. William G. Bates, and other speeches and poems of the occasion, with an appendix, containing historical documents of local interest. Westfield: Clark & Story, 1870. Pp. viii, 226.

12907 WESTFIELD, MASS. SECOND CONGREGATIONAL CHURCH. ...fiftieth anniversary of the Second Congregational Church, Westfield, Massachusetts, observed December twenty-seventh, twenty-eighth and twenty-ninth, nineteen hundred and six. n.p., [1907?]. Pp. 44. M.

12908 WESTFIELD, MASS. WELCOME HOME COMMITTEE. Westfield and the World War: United States declared war April 6, 1917, armistice signed November 11, 1918. Edward G. Clark, comp. Westfield: Westfield Times, 1919. Pp. 55.

12909 WESTFIELD historical calendar, 1669-1920. Mrs. H. N. Kingsbury and Mary S. Thayer, comps. Westfield: Westfield Times, 1919. 57 leaves.

12910 WRITERS' PROGRAM. MASSACHUSETTS. The State Teachers College at Westfield. Boston: Jerome Pr., 1941. Pp. 114.

WESTFORD

12911 FLETCHER LIBRARY, WESTFORD, MASS. Westford, Mass., souvenir of the dedication of the J. V. Fletcher Library, June 4th, 1896. [Lowell]: Lowell Mail Print, 1896. Pp. 93.

12912 HODGMAN, EDWIN RUTHVEN. History of the town of Westford, in the county of Middlesex, Massachusetts, 1659-1883. Lowell: Morning Mail Company, 1883. Pp. viii, 494.

12913 _____. Patriotism of Westford in 1775. n.p., [1879?]. Pp. 4.

12914 WESTFORD, MASS. FIRST PARISH. 1794-1894: centennial celebration of the building of the First Parish Meeting House at Westford, Mass. Lowell: Courier Citizen, 1894. Pp. 35. MBNEH.

12915 WESTFORD, MASS. UNION CONGREGATIONAL CHURCH. Centennial poem and historic paper read at the centennial exercises...August 18th and 19th, 1928. n.p., [1928?]. Unpaged. MBNEH.
Poem by Elizabeth Cushing Taylor and address by Leonard W. Wheeler.

WESTHAMPTON

12916 CLARKE, DORUS. The centennial discourse delivered in Westhampton, Mass., Sept. 3d, 1879, on the one hundredth anniversary of the formation of the church in that town.... Boston: Lee and Shepard, 1879. Pp. 60.

12917 _____. 'Saying the catechism' seventy-five years ago, and the historical results: an address delivered before the New England Historic-Genealogical Society, Dec. 4, 1878. Boston: Lee & Shepard, 1879. Pp. 46.
A sketch of the town.

12918 WESTHAMPTON, MASS. Memorial of the reunion of the natives of Westhampton, Mass., September 5, 1866. Waltham: Free Pr., 1866. Pp. 85.
Includes historical address by C. Parkman Judd.

12919 WESTHAMPTON, MASS. CONGREGATIONAL CHURCH. Centenary memorial of the Congregational Church of Westhampton, Mass., September 3, 1879. Easthampton: Easthampton News, 1880. Pp. 65. MNF.

12920 WESTHAMPTON sesquicentennial, August 18-19, 1928: church sesquicentennial, September 1, 1929. Northampton: F. M. Crittenden, [1929?]. Pp. 101.
Congregational church.

WESTMINSTER

12921 GOULD, JOHN. "Yankee institution thriving in modern age." Industry, 25 (July, 1960), 16, 20, 44-45.
Dawley and Shepard, crackers; founded 1828.

12922 HATHAWAY, SAMUEL. The history of Redemption Rock. Worcester: F. S. Blanchard, 1898. Pp. 14.
Site of redemption in 1676 of Mary Rowlandson, who had been captured by Indians.

12923 HEYWOOD, WILLIAM SWEETZER. History of Westminster, Massachusetts (first named Narragansett No. 2) from the date of the original grant of the township to the present time, 1728-1893: with a biographic-genealogical register of its principal families. Lowell: S. W. Huse, 1893. Pp. xvi, 963.

12924 HUDSON, CHARLES. A history of the town of Westminster, from its first settlement to the present time. Mendon: G. W. Stacy, 1832. Pp. 42.

12925 RICH, ADONIRAM JUDSON. Historical discourse delivered on occasion of the one hundred and twenty-fifth anniversary of the Congregational Church, and the fiftieth anniversary of the Sunday school, in Westminster, Mass., September 9, 1868.... Springfield: Samuel Bowles, 1869. Pp. 98.

12926 WESTMINSTER, MASS. Celebration of the one hundredth anniversary of the incorporation of Westminster, Mass., containing an address by Hon. Charles Hudson...a poem, by Mr. William S. Heywood...and the other proceedings and exercises connected with the occasion. Boston: T. R. Marvin & Son, 1859. Pp. 127.

12927 WESTMINSTER HISTORICAL SOCIETY. A history of Westminster, Massachusetts, 1893-1958. Newton F. Tolman, ed. Peterborough, N.H.: Richard R. Smith, 1961. Pp. xi, 347.

12928 WHITNEY, WILBUR F. An account of the exercises connected with the 150th anniversary celebration of the town of Westminster, Massachusetts, 1909: together with historical & legendary reminiscences connected with the town. Gardner: Meals Printing, [191-]. Pp. 200.

WESTON

12929 BERRY, A. B. "New England's lost city found." MagAmHist, 16 (1886), 290-292. Norumbega.

12930 DICKSON, BRENTON H. Once upon a pung. [Boston?], 1963. Pp. 84.

12931 FISKE, CHARLES HENRY. Oration delivered before the inhabitants of Weston, at the townhall, July 4, 1876. Weston, 1876. Pp. 38.
Relates to the town; copy at New England Historic Genealogical Society contains a tipped in printed 'note' dated September 1, 1876 correcting information on p. 18.

12932 HILL, CAROLINE ROGERS. "The old Rand House." MassMag, 2 (1909), 165-167.

12933   KENDAL, SAMUEL. A sermon, delivered at Weston, January 12, 1813, on the termination of a century since the incorporation of the town. Cambridge: Hilliard and Metcalf, 1813. Pp. 60.

12934   LAMSON, DANIEL S. History of the town of Weston, Massachusetts, 1630-1890. Boston: Geo. H. Ellis, 1913. Pp. vii, 214.

12935   _____. and JOHN N. MCCLINTOCK. "Weston." MassMag, 2 (1909), 129-140.

12936   PAINE, THOMAS M. "John Davenport's rock." OTNE, 58 (1967-1968), 20-22.

12937   RIPLEY, EMMA FRANCES. Weston, a Puritan town. Weston: Benevolent-Alliance of the First Parish, 1961. Pp. 270.

12938   _____. Weston Town Library history, 1857-1957. Weston, 1957. Pp. 16. MB.

12939   WESTON, MASS. Town of Weston: births, deaths and marriages, 1707-1850, 1703--gravestones--1900, church records, 1709-1825, appendix and addenda, Cent Society, gleanings from the town files, bits of genealogy, errors, indexes, &c. Mary Frances Peirce, ed. Boston: McIndoe Bros., 1901. Pp. vi, 649.

12940   _____. Town of Weston: records of the First Precinct, 1746-1754, and of the town, 1754-1803. Mary Frances Peirce, comp. Boston: Alfred Mudge & Son, 1893. Pp. iv, 558.
        Name and subject indexes.

12941   _____. Town of Weston: records of the town clerk, 1804-1826. Mary Frances Peirce, comp. Boston: Alfred Mudge & Son, 1894. Pp. iv, 437.
        Name and subject indexes.

12942   _____. Town of Weston: the tax lists 1757-1827. Mary Frances Peirce, comp. Boston: Alfred Mudge & Son, 1897. Pp. v, 438.

12943   WESTON, MASS. FIRST PARISH. An account of the celebration by the First Parish of Weston, Massachusetts of its two hundredth anniversary on Sunday, the nineteenth of June and Sunday, the twenty-sixth of June, MDCCCXCVIII, also sundry addresses and other papers therewith connected, 1698-1898. Weston, 1900. Pp. 251.

12944   WESTON, MASS. ST. JULIA'S PARISH. Historical notes, St. Julia's Parish, Weston, Mass., golden jubilee 1969. [Weston, 1970]. 11 leaves.

12945   WESTON, MASS. 250TH ANNIVERSARY COMMITTEE. Weston 250th anniversary, program for the anniversary observance of the incorporation in 1713 of the town of Weston, Massachusetts. Weston, [1963?]. Pp. 28. M.

WESTPORT

12946   HALL, KATHERINE STANLEY and MARY H. SOWLE. The village of Westport Point, Massachusetts. New Bedford: E. Anthony & Sons, 1914. Pp. 43.

12947   HARRIS, SHELDON H. "Paul Cuffe's white apprentice." AmNep, 23 (1963), 192-196. 1807-1808.

12948   HAWES, RICHARD KINGSLEY. The hurricane at Westport Harbor, September 21, 1938: personal observations. Fall River: Dover Pr., 1938. Pp. 18.

12949   WORTH, HENRY BARNARD. "Head of Westport and its founders." ODHS, No. 21 (June, 1908), 17-21.
        Section of the town.

WESTWOOD

12950   COOKE, GEORGE WILLIS. A history of the Clapboard Trees or Third Parish, Dedham, Mass. now the Unitarian Parish, West Dedham, 1736-1886. Boston: G. H. Ellis, 1887. Pp. 139.

12951   FENERTY, MARJORY R. The meeting house on a rock, a history of the First Parish of Westwood, United Church. n.p., 1959. Pp. 98. MBNEH.

12952   _____. Meeting house on a rock: supplement 1959-1969. n.p., 1969. Pp. 16. MBNEH.
        First parish.

12953   _____. West Dedham and Westwood, 300 years. Westwood: Westwood Historical Society, 1972. Pp. 100. MBNEH.

12954   _____. "West Dedham's sock firing cannon." NEG, 9 (Summer, 1967), 41-45.

12955   FISHER, BENJAMIN. "The new town of Westwood." DedHR, 8 (1897), 33-37.

12956   KARR, LOUISE. "Old Westwood murals." Antiques, 9 (1926), 231-237.

12957   WESTWOOD. Boston: Edison Electric Illuminating Co., 1909. Pp. 8. M.

WEYMOUTH

12958   ADAMS, CHARLES FRANCIS, 1835-1915. "Site of the Wessagusset settlement." MHSP, 2 Ser., 7 (1891-1892), 22-30.

12959 _____. Wessagusset and Weymouth, an historical address delivered at Weymouth, July 4, 1874, on the occasion of the celebration of the two hundred and fiftieth anniversary of the permanent settlement of the town. Weymouth in its first twenty years, a paper read before the society by Gilbert Nash, November 1, 1882. Weymouth thirty years later, a paper read by Charles Francis Adams, before the Weymouth Historical Society, September 23, 1904. [Weymouth]: Weymouth Historical Society, 1905. Pp. 163.

12960 ALLEN, EDWARD B. "Some old New England frescoes." OTNE, 25 (1934-1935), 79-85. Learned-Senigo House; paintings revealed upon removal of wallpaper.

12961 CHAMBERLAIN, GEORGE WALTER. "Weymouth, ancient and modern." NEM, New Ser., 34 (1906), 705-723.

12962 CLAPP, EDWIN & SON, INC., EAST WEYMOUTH, MASS. Three score years and ten: a romance in the history of footwear. East Weymouth, 1923. Pp. 63.

12963 CRESSEY, FRANK B. Semi-centennial, Baptist Church, Weymouth, Mass. [Weymouth, 1904]. Pp. 32.

12964 "DIARIES of Rev. William Smith and Dr. Cotton Tufts, 1738-1784." MHSP, 42 (1908-1909), 444-478.

12965 EAST WEYMOUTH, MASS. METHODIST EPISCOPAL CHURCH. Celebration of the semi-centennial of the Methodist Episcopal Church, East Weymouth, Mass., June 18, 1873. Walter Ela, ed. [Weymouth]: Weymouth Weekly Gazette Pr., 1874. Pp. 28.

12966 _____. Program of the one hundredth anniversary, First Methodist Episcopal Church, East Weymouth, Mass., May 13 to 20, 1923. East Weymouth: Franklin N. Pratt, [1923?]. Pp. 55.

12967 EMERY, JOSHUA, JR. A discourse delivered in the North Church, Weymouth, January 5, 1851. Boston: T. R. Marvin, 1851. Pp. 18. History of the church.

12968 FEARING, CLARENCE WHITE. Weymouth town government, its beginning and development. [South Weymouth]: Weymouth Historical Society, 1941. Pp. 36.

12969 HOGAN, J. H. Directory and history of Weymouth, Mass.... Plymouth: Avery & Doty, 1888. Pp. 307.

12970 HUNT, EDMUND SOPER. Weymouth ways and Weymouth people. Boston: Priv. Print., 1907. Pp. 307.

12971 KENDALL, R. R. "An old-time ministerial contract." NEM, New Ser., 24 (1901), 329-333. Rev. Thomas Paine of the First Congregational Church.

12972 NASH, GILBERT, comp. Historical sketch of the town of Weymouth, Massachusetts, from 1622 to 1884. Boston: A. Mudge & Son, 1885. Pp. x, 346.

12973 REED, SAMUEL W. "Weymouth, Mass., during King Philip's War." MNEH, 3 (1893), 196-200.

12974 SOUTH WEYMOUTH SAVINGS BANK. 100th anniversary. n.p., [1968?]. Unpaged. MBNEH. 1868-1968.

12975 "STETSON Shoe Company." Industry, 1 (July, 1936), 7-9.

12976 TORREY, BATES, comp. The shoe industry of Weymouth. [Weymouth]: Weymouth Historical Society, 1933. Pp. 126.

12977 WEYMOUTH, MASS. Civil War centennial commemoration, March 30-31, 1963. East Weymouth: Lincoln Pr., 1963. Pp. 45. MBNEH.

12978 _____. Proceedings on the two hundred and fiftieth anniversary of the permanent settlement of Weymouth, with an historical address by Charles Francis Adams, Jr., July 4th, 1874. Boston: Wright & Potter, 1874. Pp. 107.

12979 WEYMOUTH, MASS. BAPTIST CHURCH. Semicentennial...1854-1904. [Weymouth]: Gazette Publishing, [1904?]. Pp. 32, 4. MBNEH.

12980 WEYMOUTH, MASS. FIRST CHURCH. The First Church in Weymouth, the manual, containing a brief history.... Weymouth Heights, 1912. Pp. 48. MBNEH.

12981 WEYMOUTH, MASS. SECOND CHURCH OF CHRIST. The book of records of the Second Church of Christ in Weymouth, Massachusetts, baptism and marriages. John J. Loud, comp. Boston: Somerset Printing, 1900. Pp. 36. 1722-1818.

12982 WEYMOUTH, MASS. UNION CHURCH AND RELIGIOUS SOCIETY. Historical record of the Union Church and religious society of Weymouth and Braintree.... Boston: T. R. Marvin, 1857. Pp. 23. MBNEH.

12983 WEYMOUTH HISTORICAL SOCIETY. History of Weymouth, Massachusetts.... Boston: Wright & Potter, 1923. 4v. Volumes 3 and 4 are genealogies.

12984 WEYMOUTH 350TH ANNIVERSARY. Lawrence W. Cassese and Harry C. Belcher, comp. Weymouth: 350th Anniversary Committee, 1972. Pp. 64.

WHATELY

12985 CANE, ENA M. Whately, 1771-1971: a New England portrait. Northampton: Gazette Printing, 1972. Pp. xi, 356.

12986   CRAFTS, JAMES MONROE. History of the town
         of Whately, Mass., including a narrative
of leading events from the first planting of Hatfield: 1661-1899, as revised and enlarged by James
M. Crafts, with family genealogies. Orange: D. L.
Crandall, 1899. Pp. 628.
         Revised and enlarged from Josiah H.
         Temple's 'History of the town...1660-
         1871.'

12987   TEMPLE, JOSIAH HOWARD. Early ecclesiasti-
         cal history of Whateley, being the substance
of a discourse delivered January 7, 1849....
Northampton: J. & L. Metcalf, 1849. Pp. 40. MB.

WHITMAN

12988   WHITMAN, MASS. FIRST CONGREGATIONAL
         CHURCH. 150th anniversary, 1807-1957....
n.p., [1957?]. Pp. 28. MBNEH.

WILBRAHAM

12989   MERRICK, CHARLES L. and PHILIP B. FOSTER,
         eds. History of Wilbraham, U. S. A.,
1763-1963. [Wilbraham?, 1964]. Pp. ix, 309.

12990   PECK, CHAUNCEY EDWIN. The history of Wil-
         braham, Massachusetts, prepared in connec-
tion with the celebration of the one hundred and
fiftieth anniversary of the incorporation of the
town, June 15, 1913. [Wilbraham?, 1914]. Pp. x,
469.

12991   SHERMAN, DAVID. History of the Wesleyan
         Academy, in Wilbraham, Mass., 1817-1890.
Boston: McDonald & Gill, 1893. Pp. xxx, 500.

12992   STEBBINS, RUFUS PHINEAS. An historical
         address, delivered at the centennial cel-
ebration of the incorporation of the town of Wilbraham, June 15, 1863. Boston: George C. Rand &
Avery, 1864. Pp. 317.

12993   WILBRAHAM, MASS. BICENTENNIAL CELEBRATION
         COMMITTEES. Wilbraham, Massachusetts...
program...compiled by the citizens...as a part of
the town's observance of the 200th anniversary
of its incorporation, 1963. Wilbraham, 1963. Unpaged. M.

12994   WILBRAHAM, MASS. Historical Research Com-
         mittee. Concerning Wilbraham and the
American Revolution. Wilbraham: Wilbraham-USA Bicentennial Committee, 1975. Pp. 24. M.

12995   WOOD, JAMES PLAYSTED. New England academy:
         Wilbraham to Wilbraham & Monson. Brattle-
boro, Vt.: R. L. Dothard Associates, 1971.
Pp. viii, 152.

WILLIAMSBURG

12996   DEMING, PHYLLIS BAKER, comp. A history of
         Williamsburg in Massachusetts, 175th anni-
versary. Northampton: Hampshire Bookshop, 1946.
Pp. xvi, 416.
         A typescript index of names by Inez S.
         Lederer is at the New England Historic
         Genealogical Society.

12997   LUSK, WILLIAM. A discourse delivered at
         Williamsburgh, January 24, 1836, being the
Sabbath after his installation, prefixed is an his-
torical sketch of that church.... Northampton:
John Metcalf, 1836. Pp. 32.
         First Congregational Church.

12998   O'CONNOR, JAMES P. Williamsburg, Massa-
         chusetts, 1771-1971. Commemorating the
first two hundred years. Williamsburg: Williamsburg Historical Society, 1971. Pp. ix, 164. MNF.

12999   WILLIAMSBURG, MASS. FIRST CONGREGATIONAL
         CHURCH. Our 200th year, 1771-1971. Los
Angeles: Jeffreys, 1971. Unpaged. MNF.

WILLIAMSTOWN

13000   [ADAMS, THOMAS RANDOLPH]. A brief account
         of the origins and purpose of the Chapin
Library at Williams College. Williamstown, 1956.
Pp. 19.
         Author attribution by the editor.

13001   BOTSFORD, ELI HERBERT. Fifty years at Wil-
         liams, under the administrations of presi-
dents Chadbourne, Carter, Hewitt, Hopkins and Garfield. Pittsfield: Eagle Printing & Binding, 1928-
1940. 4v.

13002   BROOKS, ROBERT ROMANO RAVI, ed. Williams-
         town, the first two hundred years, 1753-
1953. Williamstown: McClelland Pr., 1953.
Pp. xv, 458.

13003   CARTER, JOHN FRANKLIN. The rectory family.
         N.Y.: Coward-McCann, 1937. Pp. 275.
         Social life and customs; author's father
         was rector of St. John's Church.

13004   DANFORTH, KEYES. Boyhood reminiscences;
         pictures of New England life in the olden
times in Williamstown. N.Y.: Gazlay Bros., 1895.
Pp. 177.

13005   DURFEE, CALVIN. A history of Williams Col-
         lege. Boston: A. Williams, 1860. Pp. x,
432.

13006   _____. Williams biographical annals. Bos-
         ton: Lee and Shepard, 1871. Pp. 665.

13007   EGLESTON, NATHANIEL HILLYER. "Williams College." NEM, 4 (1886), 487-502.

13008   _____. Williamstown and Williams College. Williamstown, 1884. Pp. 76.

13009   HOPKINS, MARK. A discourse delivered at Williamstown, June 29, 1886, on the fiftieth anniversary of his election as president of Williams College. N.Y.: C. Scribner's Sons, 1886. Pp. 43.

13010   KAPPA ALPHA. MASSACHUSETTS ALPHA, WILLIAMS COLLEGE. Exercises in commemoration of the original settlers of West Hoosac in the province of the Massachusetts-Bay at Williamstown, Massachusetts, with dedication of a memorial by the Kappa Alpha Society in Williams College, Monday, June nineteenth, nineteen hundred and sixteen...in perpetual honor of Colonel Ephraim Williams killed at the battle of Lake George, September 8, 1755.... Boston: McGrath-Sherrill Pr., 1916. 4 leaves.

13011   LOWE, JOHN ADAMS, comp. Williamsiana: a bibliography of pamphlets & books, relating to the history of Williams College, 1793-1911. Williamstown: The Trustees, 1911. Pp. 37.

13012   MILHAM, WILLIS ISBISTER. The history of astronomy in Williams College and the founding of the Hopkins Observatory. Williamstown: Williams College, 1937. Pp. 25.

13013   _____. The history of meteorology in Williams College, temperature, precipitation, and other data for Williamstown, Massachusetts. Williamstown: Williams College, 1936. Pp. v, 21.

13014   MOUNT Hope: a story of Williamstown during the Revolutionary War. Williamstown: Mount Hope Forum, 1928. Pp. 42. MB.

13015   NILES, GRACE.GREYLOCK. "Albert Hopkins and Williamstown." NEM, New Ser., 31 (1904-1905), 665-680.

13016   NOBLE, MASON. Centennial discourse, delivered in Williamstown, Mass., November 19, 1865. North Adams: James T. Robinson, 1865. Pp. 60.

13017   "OLD and new South Williamstown churches: a record of their history and the pioneers who worshiped therein." Berkshire Hills, 2 (June 1, 1902), [5-6].
        First and Second Congregational parishes.

13018   "OLD Williamstown memories: its main streets and college buildings a half century ago." Berkshire Hills, New Ser., 1 (1904-1905), 25-28.

13019   PALMER, RICHARD F. "Informal history of the Williamstown & Redfield Railroad." RLHSB, No. 114 (1966), 53-56.

13020   PERRY, ARTHUR LATHAM. Origins in Williamstown. 2d. ed. N.Y.: C. Scribner's Sons, 1896. Pp. viii, 650.

13021   _____. Williamstown and Williams College. N.Y.: C. Scribner's Sons, 1899. Pp. viii, 847.

13022   RUDOLPH, FREDERICK. Mark Hopkins and the log; Williams College, 1836-1872. New Haven: Yale Univ. Pr., 1956. Pp. ix, 267.

13023   SCUDDER, SAMUEL H. "Alpine Club of Williamstown, Mass." Appalachia, 4 (1884-1886), 45-54.

13024   SMALLWOOD, W. M. "The Williams Lyceum of Natural History, 1835-1888." NEQ, 10 (1937), 553-557.
        Williams College.

13025   SPRING, LEVERETT WILSON. A history of Williams College. Boston: Houghton Mifflin, 1917. Pp. 341.

13026   _____. "Williams College." NEM, New Ser., 9 (1893-1894), 161-179.

13027   WELLS, DAVID AMES and SAMUEL H. DAVIS. Sketches of Williams College, Williamstown, Mass. Springfield: H. S. Taylor, 1847. Pp. vi, 99.

13028   WESTON, KARL E. "American furniture at Williams College." Antiques, 45 (1944), 73-75.

13029   WILLIAMS COLLEGE. A record of the commemoration, October eighth to tenth, 1893, on the centennial anniversary of the founding of Williams College. Cambridge: J. Wilson and Son, 1894. Pp. vii, 330.

13030   _____. Williams College, Williamstown, Mass., historical sketch and views. Richard A. Rice and Leverett W. Spring, comps. Boston: G. H. Ellis, 1904. Pp. 28.

13031   WILLIAMSTOWN, MASS. FIRST CONGREGATIONAL CHURCH. Manual of the First Congregational Church, Williamstown, Mass. Revised January 1, 1879. Pittsfield: Chickering and Axtell, 1879. Pp. 52. M.
        Includes a brief history.

13032   WILLIAMSTOWN, MASS. FIRST CONGREGATIONAL CHURCH. Proceedings in commemoration of the one hundred and fiftieth anniversary of the First Congregational Church, Williamstown, Massachusetts, October 9th and 10th, 1915. Pittsfield: Sun Printing, 1916. Pp. 165. M.
        Historical review, 1765-1915, by John DePeu.

13033   WILLIAMSTOWN, the 'Berkshire Hills,' and thereabouts. Glens Falls, N.H.: Parsons, 1890. Pp. 60. MB.

WILMINGTON

13034   NOYES, DANIEL P. Wilmington, 1730-1880:
        historical addresses delivered in the meet-
ing-house of the Church of Christ in Wilmington,
Mass., Sept. 24, 1880, upon the one hundred and
fiftieth anniversary of the incorporation of the
town. Boston: Cochrane & Sampson, 1881. Pp. 55.

13035   STARBUCK, WALTER F. Wilmington and the
        Middlesex Canal. Waltham: Courier Pub-
lishing, 1926. Unpaged. MBNEH.

13036   WILMINGTON, MASS. Wilmington records of
        births, marriages and deaths, from 1730 to
1898. James E. Kelley, comp. Lowell: Thompson &
Hill, 1898. Pp. 255.

13037   WILMINGTON, MASS. FIRST CONGREGATIONAL
        CHURCH. History, year book and directo-
ry.... n.p., [1932?]. Unpaged. MBNEH.
        Historical sketch by Clara Olmstead
        Simmons.

13038   WILMINGTON, MASS. 200TH ANNIVERSARY COM-
        MITTEE. Wilmington, Massachusetts, its
growth and progress, 1730 to 1930. n.p., [1930?].
Unpaged. MBNEH.

WINCHENDON

13039   HYDE, EZRA. History of the town of Winch-
        endon, from the grant of the township by
the legislature of Massachusetts in 1735, to the
present time. Worcester: H. J. Howland, [1849].
Pp. viii, 136.

13040   MARVIN, ABIJAH PERKINS. History of the
        town of Winchendon (Worcester County,
Mass.) from the grant of Ipswich Canada, in 1735,
to the present time. Winchendon, 1868. Pp. 528.

13041   _____. and HENRY BARTON DAWSON. "The Win-
        chendon, Mass. slave case." HistMag, 2
Ser., 5 (1869), 319-323.
        1807.

13042   "MASON & Parker Manufacturing Co." Indus-
        try, 1 (December, 1935), 5-6.
        Toys.

WINCHESTER

13043   AYER, THOMAS PRENTISS. "Fords and water-
        ing-troughs." Winchester Record, 2
(1886), 495-496.

13044   _____. "History of the Winchester Savings
        Bank." Winchester Record, 1 (1885), 33-38.

13045   _____. "Mystic School." Winchester Rec-
        ord, 2 (1886), 69-72.

13046   _____. "Winchester Fire Department." Win-
        chester Record, 2 (1886), 344-346.

13047   BAILEY, WILLIAM HARRISON. "Knights of Hon-
        or, Winchester Lodge, No. 556, K. of H."
Winchester Record, 2 (1886), 172-174.

13048   BOLLES, JOHN AUGUSTUS. An oration, deliv-
        ered before the inhabitants of Winchester,
Mass., July 4, 1860. Boston: T. R. Marvin & Son,
1860. Pp. 19.
        Relates to the town.

13049   BROWN, GEORGE P. "The telegraph in Win-
        chester." Winchester Record, 1 (1885),
204.

13050   "BURGLARIES." Winchester Record, 2 (1886),
        368-370.
        1861.

13051   CHAPMAN, HENRY SMITH. History of Winches-
        ter, Massachusetts. [Winchester]: The
Town, 1936. Pp. x, 396.

13052   CLARK, OLIVER R. "Reminiscences of South
        Woburn, 1838-39." Winchester Record, 1
(1885), 125-129.

13053   _____. "Reminiscences of South Woburn,
        1834-36." Winchester Record, 1 (1885),
13-19.

13054   _____. "Reminiscences of South Woburn,
        1836-38." Winchester Record, 1 (1885), 52-
56.

13055   "THE CONGREGATIONAL Church burnt." Winches-
        ter Record, 1 (1885), 212-214.
        1853.

13056   COOKE, GEORGE. "The First Congregational
        Church in Winchester." Winchester Record,
2 (1886), 101-109, 472-482; 3 (1887), 60-63.

13057   _____. "School history: District No. 7,
        South Woburn." Winchester Record, 2
(1886), 465-469.

13058   _____. "Winchester in 1840." Winchester
        Record, 1 (1885), 60-63.

13059   _____. "Winchester Library Association."
        Winchester Record, 2 (1886), 483-487.

13060   _____. "Woburn South Congregational Par-
        ish." Winchester Record, 2 (1886), 83-99,
469-472; 3 (1887), 50-60.

13061   CUTTER, STEPHEN HALL. "The history of Cut-
        ter's Mill." Winchester Record, 2 (1886),
78-80.
        Grist mill.

13062   CUTTER, WILLIAM RICHARD. "Black Horse Tav-
        ern." Winchester Record, 2 (1886), 127.

13063   _____. "Mill privileges." Winchester Rec-
        ord, 2 (1886), 266-272.

13064 "FIRES." Winchester Record, 2 (1886), 371-373.
1853-1886.

13065 "FIRES in Winchester." Winchester Record, 2 (1886), 175-178.
1850s.

13066 "FIRST Congregational Church, Winchester, Ms." CongQ, 3 (1861), 337-340.

13067 FORBES, ALLAN. "Early Myopia at Winchester." EIHC, 78 (1942), 1-19.
Myopia Hunt Club.

13068 GRAMMER, WILLIAM T. "An early store in Black Horse Village." Winchester Record, 2 (1886), 81-83.

13069 "J. H. Winn, Inc. dials its 100th year." Industry, 33 (September, 1968), 47, 70-71.
Watch hands and instrument pointers.

13070 JOHNSON, JAMES C. "The history of the old choir of the Congregational Church." Winchester Record, 2 (1886), 251-253.

13071 LITTLEFIELD, GEORGE SHERMAN. "The Highland School." Winchester Record, 2 (1886), 325-326.

13072 MCCALL, SAMUEL WALKER. Oration delivered on the 250th anniversary of the first settlement [of Winchester], July 4, 1890. Boston: Barta Pr., 1890. Pp. 19. MHi.

13073 NOWELL, SARAH M. "The Fortnightly." Winchester Record, 1 (1885), 93-96.
Women's Club.

13074 PETERSON, BERNARD. "A manufacturer's manufacturer." Industry, 18 (March, 1953), 13-15.
J. H. Winn's Sons; watch hands and instrument pointers.

13075 "PIONEERS in the field of vibration control." Industry, 23 (October, 1957), 29-30, 52, 54, 56, 58.
Calidyne Company.

13076 RAND, MARTHA J. "The Winchester Village Improvement Association." Winchester Record, 2 (1886), 503-510.

13077 RICHARDSON, NATHANIEL A. "General Abijah and Benjamin F. Thompson." Winchester Record, 2 (1886), 384-386.

13078 "ROBBERIES and burglaries in Winchester." Winchester Record, 2 (1886), 178-180.
1850s and 1860s.

13079 SANDERSON, EDMUND. "An account of the express and grocery business in Winchester, 1842-1885." Winchester Record, 2 (1886), 123-126.

13080 SYMMES, LUTHER RICHARDSON. "The Brooks Farm, and who lived on it." Winchester Record, 2 (1886), 73-78.

13081 _____. History of the roads of Winchester previous to 1850." Winchester Record, 1 (1885), 277-280.

13082 TEELE, WARREN. "What I remember about the west side schools." Winchester Record, 2 (1886), 308-310.

13083 THOMPSON, ABIJAH. "Winchester in 1640." Winchester Record, 1 (1885), 47-52, 259-264.

13084 _____. "The Winchester Light Guard." Winchester Record, 2 (1886), 327-331.

13085 THOMPSON, LEANDER. "The three Richardsons." Winchester Record, 2 (1886), 199-208.
Ezekiel, Samuel and Thomas.

13086 THOMPSON, STEPHEN. "Sketch of Benjamin F. Thompson's tanning and currying establishment." Winchester Record, 2 (1886), 354-362.

13087 WADLEIGH, EDWIN AUGUSTUS. "Winchester incorporated." Winchester Record, 1 (1885), 90-91.

13088 _____. "Winchester Unitarian Society." Winchester Record, 2 (1886), 149-168.

13089 WHITE, SAMUEL B. "The South Woburn Social Lyceum." Winchester Record, 1 (1885), 281-287.

13090 WINCHESTER, MASS. July 4th, 1890, 250th anniversary of the first white settlement within the territory of Winchester.... Boston: Barta Pr., 1890. Pp. 32.

13091 _____. Winchester honors the tercentenary of the Massachusetts Bay Colony 1630-1930, souvenir program, October 13, 1930. n.p., [1930?]. Unpaged. M.

13092 WINCHESTER, MASS. FIRST CONGREGATIONAL CHURCH. History, articles of faith.... Cambridge: Riverside Pr., 1875. Pp. 58. MBNEH.

13093 _____. History, articles of faith, and covenant of the Congregational Church, with a catalogue of its officers and members. Boston: William A. Hall, 1855. Pp. 23. MB.

13094 WINCHESTER. Boston: Edison Electric Illuminating Co., 1909. Pp. 20. M.

13095 WINCHESTER'S war records: Civil, Spanish-American, World. [Andover]: Andover Pr., 1925. Pp. 184. M.

13096 YOUNGMAN, DAVID. "The Congregational Church choir, South Woburn, 1840-1853." Winchester Record, 1 (1885), 294-306.

13097   _____. "Hearses, hearse-houses and under-
         takers." Winchester Record, 3 (1887), 73-
74.

13098   _____. "Singing schools in South Woburn."
         Winchester Record, 3 (1887), 38-50.

13099   _____. "The Winchester Library." Winches-
         ter Record, 1 (1885), 200-202.

13100   _____. "The Wyman School." Winchester
         Record, 2 (1886), 315-325.

WINDSOR

13101   PHILLIPS, JOHN L. T. "Sketches of the
         early ministers of Windsor." BHSSC, 1,
Pt. 2, (1889), 53-59.
         David Avery, Elisha Fish, Jr., Gordon
         Dorrance, and Philetus Clark.

13102   WINDSOR, MASS. 200th anniversary, town of
         Windsor, incorporated July 4, 1771. Dal-
ton: Studley Pr., [1971?]. Pp. 128. MPB.

WINTHROP

13103   CLARK, WILLIAM HORACE. The history of
         Winthrop, Massachusetts, 1630-1952. Win-
throp: Winthrop Centennial Committee, 1952.
Pp. 313.

13104   COBB, ALBERT WINSLOW. "The town of Win-
         throp." NEM, New Ser., 6 (1892), 645-659.

13105   GRIFFIN, MARY PRISCILLA. Winthrop days,
         and a half century, with the trees, 1855-
1905. Winthrop: Thornton Pr., 1905. Pp. 36.

13106   HALL, CHARLES WINSLOW. Descriptive his-
         tory and real estate guide of the town of
Winthrop, containing full and accurate descriptions
of over six hundred building lots.... Boston:
Cochrane & Sampson, 1877. Pp. 16.

13107   _____. Historic Winthrop, 1630-1902: a
         concise history of Winthrop. Boston:
Winthrop Publishing, 1902. Pp. 43.

13108   HOWARD, CHANNING. Annals of the town of
         Winthrop, Massachusetts. n.p., [1930?].
Broadside. 10 7/8 x 17 inches. MBNEH.
         List of events, 1614-1930.

13109   _____. History of the Deane Winthrop
         House, Winthrop, Massachusetts.... [Win-
throp]: Winthrop Improvement and Historical Association, [1942?]. Pp. 12.

13110   _____. Our streets: how we got them and
         their names, Winthrop, Massachusetts. Win-
throp, 1950. Pp. 12. MBNEH.

13111   "AN INTERESTING old house, the Deane Win-
         throp House." NOHR, 5 (September 1, 1906),
8-9.

13112   WILLOUGHBY, CHARLES CLARK. Indian burial
         place at Winthrop, Massachusetts, with notes
on the skeletal remains by Earnest A. Hooton. Cambridge: [Peabody] Museum, 1924. Pp. 37.

13113   WINTHROP, MASS. Descriptive history....
         Boston: C. W. Hall, 1877. Pp. 16. MB.

WOBURN

13114   CHARITABLE READING SOCIETY, WOBURN, MASS.
         Proceedings at the semi-centennial celebra-
tion of the Charitable Reading Society, June 21,
1865. Woburn: E. Marchant, 1865. Pp. 32. MWA.

13115   CONVERSE, PARKER LINDALL. 1642-1892. Leg-
         ends of Woburn, now first written and pre-
served in collected form...to which is added a
chrono-indexical history of Woburn. Woburn, 1892-
1896. 2v.

13116   COWLEY, CHARLES. "Experiments in sericul-
         ture and in India-rubber manufacture."
ORHAL, 3 (1884-1887), 243-251.

13117   CUTTER, WILLIAM RICHARD. "Business in Wo-
         burn in 1800." Winchester Record, 1
(1885), 155-161.

13118   _____. "Long Bridge." Winchester Record,
         3 (1887), 16-24.

13119   _____. Woburn historic sites and old
         houses.... [Woburn, 1892]. Pp. 57, vii.

13120   "DYNAMISM and 100 years of growth." Indus-
         try, 28 (December, 1962), 17, 36-38.
         A. W. Chesterton Co., industrial packings.

13121   EVANS, GEORGE HILL. The seven against the
         wilderness: a brief account of the settle-
ment of Woburn, Massachusetts, and of its founder,
Captain Edward Johnson, an address before the Som-
ervill Historical Society, April 12, 1920. [Som-
erville, 1920]. Pp. 24.

13122   "FIREMEN." Winchester Record, 2 (1886),
         347-353.

13123   "FIRST Congregational Church in Woburn, Ms."
         CongQ, 4 (1862), 298-300.

13124   LORING, ARTHUR GREENE and WILLIAM R. CUTTER.
         Woburn men in the Indian and other wars pre-
vious to the year 1754; supplementary to the names
in Diary of Lieut. Samuel Thompson, and the appendix to that publication. Boston: D. Clapp & Son,
1897. Pp. 16.

13125   MIDDLESEX CO., MASS. REGISTRY OF DEEDS.
         Abstracts of early Woburn deeds recorded at
Middlesex County registry 1649-1700, by Edward Fran-
cis Johnson, with some explanatory notes. Woburn:
News Print, 1895. Pp. 78, xii.

13126   PETERSON, BERNARD. "Industrial reincarna-
          tion in Woburn." Industry, 17 (June,
1952), 7-16, 47-55, 57.

13127   RUMFORD HISTORICAL ASSOCIATION, WOBURN,
          MASS. Rumford Historical Association,
Woburn, Mass., incorporated, 1877. Boston: Mudge
& Son, 1892. Pp. 16.

13128   SEWALL, SAMUEL, 1785-1868. The history of
          Woburn, Middlesex County, Mass., from the
grant of its territory to Charlestown, in 1640, to
the year 1860, with a memorial sketch of the author, by Rev. Charles Sewall. Boston: Wiggin and
Lunt, 1868. Pp. vi, 657.
          A copy at the Library of Congress has an
          index by George M. Champney, (pages 659-
          677), added in 1881.

13129   THOMPSON, LEANDER. "Old Woburn homes."
Winchester Record, 1 (1885), 131-147.
          Biographies.

13130   WHITNEY, ARTHUR EASTMAN. "Longe Bridg."
Winchester Record, 2 (1886), 426-437.

13131   ____. "The old Converse Mill." Winchester
Record, 1 (1885), 249-259; 3 (1887), 24-38.

13132   WOBURN, MASS. Proceedings, October second
          to seventh, 1892, at the two hundred and
fiftieth anniversary of the incorporation of the
town of Woburn, Massachusetts. Woburn: News
Print, 1893. Pp. 233.

13133   ____. Souvenir Memorial, 250th anniver-
          sary of Woburn, Mass., 1642-1892, Frank E.
Wetherell, comp. [Woburn]: David F. Moreland
and M. J. McCormick, 1892. Pp. 103. MWA.

13134   ____. Woburn records of births, deaths,
          and marriages...alphabetically and chrono-
logically arranged by Edward Francis Johnson.
Woburn: Andrews, Cutler, 1890-1919. 10v.

13135   WOBURN, MASS. BOARD OF TRADE. Woburn, an
          historical and descriptive sketch of the
town, with an outline of its industrial interests.... Cambridge: Riverside Pr., 1885. Pp. 60.
M.

13136   WOBURN. Boston: Edison Electric Illu-
          minating Co., 1909. Pp. 24. M.

13137   "THE WOBURN military." Winchester Record,
          1 (1885), 338-343; 2 (1886), 331-335.

WORCESTER

13138   "ABSTRACTS of early Worcester land titles,
          from the records of Middlesex County."
Worcester HSProc, 22 (1906), 184-238; 24 (1908),
50-72, 114-168, 247-295.
          Includes index to title holders.

13139   ADAMS, HERBERT LINCOLN. "Worcester Contin-
          entals, 1876-1908: a partial history."
Worcester Magazine, 11 (1908), 322-328.
          Military organization.

13140   ____. Worcester Light Infantry, 1803-
          1922: a history. Worcester: Worcester
Light Infantry History Association, 1924. Pp. 608.

13141   [ADOMEIT, RUTH E.]. "A silver anniversary
          and a five-inch shelf." Miniature Book
Collector, 1 (December, 1960), 3-7.
          Press of Achille J. St. Onge; author at-
          tribution by G. Thomas Tanselle in his
          'Guide to the study of United States im-
          prints.'

13142   ALLEN, C. F. H. "Worcester salt specials."
RLHSB, No. 113 (1965), 79-82.
          Railroads.

13143   ALLEN, GEORGE. Historical remarks concern-
          ing the Mechanic Street Burial Ground, in
the city of Worcester, offered to the joint committee of the legislature of Massachusetts. March 14,
1878. Worcester: Tyler & Seagrave, 1878. Pp. 17.

13144   ALLEN, JOSEPH. The Worcester Association
          and its antecedents: a history of four
ministerial associations: the Marlborough, the
Worcester (old), the Lancaster, and the Worcester
(new) associations, with biographical notices of
the members, accompanied by portraits. Boston:
Nichols and Noyes, 1868. Pp. xi, 426.

13145   AMERICAN STEEL & WIRE COMPANY. Worcester
          units of the American Steel & Wire Company
of New Jersey, North Works--South Works--Central
Works: an outline history including biographical
data relating to pioneer builders of the Worcester
wire industry.... [Worcester]: Industrial Museum
of American Steel & Wire Co., 1929. Pp. 27.
          Preface signed: Arthur G. Warren.

13146   "THE AUTOMOBILE in Worcester." Worcester
          Magazine, 11 (1908), 91-99.

13147   BACON, LEONARD. A historical discourse de-
          livered at Worcester, in the Old South
Meeting House, September 22, 1863, the hundredth
anniversary of its erection.... Worcester: Edward
R. Fiske, 1863. Pp. 106.

13148   BALDWIN, CHRISTOPHER COLUMBUS. Diary of
          Christopher Columbus Baldwin, librarian of
the American Antiquarian Society 1829-1835. Nathaniel Parne, ed. Worcester: [American Antiquari-
an] Society, 1901. Pp. xx, 380.

13149   BANCROFT, AARON. The world passeth away,
          but the children of God abide forever: a
sermon, delivered before the Second Christian Church
and Society in Worcester, on the sixth day of January, 1811.... Worcester: Isaac Sturtevant, 1811.
Pp. 24.
          Includes 'Facts relating to the town of
          Worcester.'

13150 BANCROFT, JAMES H. "History of the Central Exchange from 1804 to 1896." Worcester HSProc, 17 (1900-1901), 324-362.
Worcester Bank.

13151 _____. "Manchester Street fire." Worcester HSProc, 18 (1902), 33-48.
1854.

13152 _____. "The Merrifield fire of 1854." Worcester HSProc, 17 (1900-1901), 142-161.

13153 _____. "Worcester Branch Railroad." Worcester HSProc, 17 (1900-1901), 642-650.

13154 BARNARD, FREDERICK J. "Central Church, Worcester, 1820-1903." Worcester HSProc, 21 (1905), 107-116.

13155 BELISLE, ALEXANDRE. Livre d'or des Franco-américains de Worcester, Massachusetts. Worcester: Compagnie de Publication Belisle, 1920. Pp. 363.

13156 BLAKE, FRANCIS EVERETT. "Incidents of the first and second settlements of Worcester." Worcester HSProc, (1884), 70-99.

13157 _____. "Some Worcester matters, 1689-1743." Worcester HSProc, (1885), 15-29.

13158 BOLAND, MARGARET MOORE. "Worcester a century ago." Worcester HSProc, (1897-1899), 440-450.

13159 BOYDEN, ELBRIDGE. "Mr. Boyden's reminiscences." Worcester HSPub, (1889), 65-75.

13160 BRIGHAM, CLARENCE SAUNDERS. Fifty years of collecting Americana for the library of the American Antiquarian Society, 1908-1958. Worcester, 1958. Pp. 185.

13161 BROOKS, GEORGE F. "Metal trades and growth of Worcester." Worcester Magazine, 10 (1907), 86-87.

13162 BRYANT, FREDERICK. "Red men in Worcester." Worcester Magazine, 17 (1914), 281-285.

13163 BULLOCK, CHANDLER. "Early Worcester cattle shows." Worcester HSPub, New Ser., 3 (October, 1946), 21-36.

13164 _____. "High points in early Worcester politics." Worcester HSPub, New Ser., 1 (1928-1935), 89-102.
1788 and 1848.

13165 _____. "More high points in early Worcester politics." Worcester HSPub, New Ser., 1 (1928-1935), 239-249.
Ratification of U. S. Constitution by Massachusetts in 1788.

13166 CENTRAL SOCIETY IN WORCESTER. Historical sketch of the Central Society in Worcester with its charter, by-laws, members, et cetera. Worcester: Lucius P. Goddard, 1880. Pp. 25.
Congregational Church.

13167 CHAMBERLAIN, HENRY H. "The trade of Worcester during the present century." Worcester HSProc, (1881), 27-38.

13168 _____. "Worcester Main Street sixty-three years ago." Worcester HSProc, (1885), 105-124.

13169 _____. "The Worcester Post Office and its occupants." Worcester HSProc, (1897-1899), 19-26.

13170 CHANDONNET, THOMAS AIMÉ. Notre-Dame-des Canadiens et les Canadiens aux États-Unis. Montréal: G. E. Desbarats, 1872. Pp. 171.
French Canadian church.

13171 "A CHAPTER in the history of the Worcester Society of Antiquity." Worcester HSProc, 22 (1906), 118-136.

13172 CHASE, CHARLES AUGUSTUS. "The Baldwin-Eaton Estate." Worcester HSProc, 21 (1905), 102-107.

13173 _____. "The Boston meetings of the American Antiquarian Society." AASP, New Ser., 13 (1889-1900), 31-39.
1812-1852.

13174 _____. "Land titles of the American Antiquarian Society." AASP, New Ser., 14 (1900-1901), 193-210, 381-388; 18 (1906-1907), 365-366: 19 (1908-1909), 253.

13175 _____. "The Nathan Patch House and north end of Main Street." Worcester HSProc, 18 (1902), 242-253.

13176 _____. "Nobility Hill." Worcester HSProc, 24 (1908), 231-246.
Section of the city.

13177 _____. "Old Lincoln Street--the Daniel Henchman Farm." Worcester HSProc, 18 (1902), 255-264.

13178 [_____]. Worcester Bank, Worcester National Bank: 1804-1904. Worcester: Davis Pr., 1904. Pp. 34.

13179 CHENOWETH, CAROLINE VAN DUSEN. The school history of Worcester. Worcester: Oliver B. Wood, 1899. Pp. 167.
A general history of the city.

13180 CLARK UNIVERSITY. The fiftieth anniversary of the founding of Clark University, 1887-1937: address. Worcester, [1937]. Pp. 55.

13181 _____. The first fifty years: an administrative report, by Wallace W. Atwood, Clark University, Worcester, Massachusetts. [Worcester], 1937. Pp. xiii, 120.

13182 _____. Twentieth anniversary, 1909. [Worcester, 1909]. Unpaged.

13183 _____. Twenty-fifth anniversary of Clark University, Worcester, Mass., 1889-1914. Worcester: Clark Univ. Pr., [1914]. Pp. 77.

13184 COBURN, FREDERICK WILLIAM. "Worcester's great opportunity." NEM, New Ser., 34 (1906), 35-42.
Worcester Art Museum.

13185 COFFIN, EDWARD FRANCIS. "The daguerreotype art and some of its early exponents in Worcester." Worcester HSPub, New Ser., 1 (1928-1935), 433-439.

13186 _____. "History of the Worcester postage stamp." Worcester HSProc, 23 (1907), 243-249.

13187 COGSWELL, MARY LOUISA TRUMBELL. "The Trumbell Mansion and its occupants." Worcester HSProc, 17 (1900-1901), 241-250.
Formerly the Second Court House.

13188 COHEN, MORRIS H. "Worcester ethnics." Holy Cross Quarterly, 5, Nos. 3-4 (1973), 42-47.

13189 COLEGROVE, FRANK. "Green Hill, Worcester, Massachusetts, 'the Greens of Green Hill." Worcester HSPub, New Ser., 2 (1936-1943), 315-328.

13190 _____. "The procession of the churches of Worcester." Worcester HSPub, New Ser., 1 (1928-1935), 363-375.

13191 _____. "Some Worcester contacts with the Washingtonian temperance movement." Worcester HSPub, New Ser., 1 (1928-1935), 103-117.

13192 _____. "Worcester and its newspapers." Worcester HSPub, New Ser., 1 (1928-1935), 5-15.

13193 _____. "Worcester's unique Centre School District: a discursive study." Worcester HSPub, New Ser., 1 (1928-1935), 440-457.

13194 COMMERCE, manufactures, and resources, Worcester, Mass., a historical, statistical and descriptive review. [Boston]: National Publishing, 1882. Pp. 140. M.

13195 CONANT, LEVI L. "The population of Worcester." Worcester Magazine, 8 (1905), 142-144.
1800-1900.

13196 COOK, PHILIP H. "First automobiles in Worcester." Worcester HSPub, New Ser., 3 (1964), 1-13.

13197 _____. "Medical feuds and quackery in Worcester." Worcester HSPub, New Ser., 3 (December, 1947), 17-29.

13198 _____. "Pearl Street fifty years ago." Worcester HSPub, New Ser., 3 (April, 1952), 35-44.

13199 COOMBS, ZELOTES WOOD. The Worcester Art Society, 1877-1914. Worcester: [Worcester Art Museum], 1945. Pp. 36.
Predecessor of Worcester Art Museum.

13200 CRANE, ELLERY BICKNELL. "Beginnings of the Second Parish." Worcester HSProc, (1897-1899), 466-488.

13201 _____. "[The extension of Foster Street]." Worcester HSProc, (1879), 90-103.
1860-1870.

13202 _____. Historical notes, on the early settlements of Worcester, Massachusetts, with notices of the settlers, from the year 1665 to 1704. Worcester: C. Hamilton, 1885. Pp. 27.

13203 _____. "History of the Jo Bill Road." Worcester HSProc, 18 (1902), 206-217
Name changed to Institute Road in 1890.

13204 _____. "The kidnapping of Samuel Leonard." Worcester HSProc, 25 (1909-1910), 291-302.
By Indians in 1695.

13205 _____. "The lumber business of Worcester." Worcester HSProc, (1878), 13-33.

13206 _____. "Origin and early history of the building now known as Davis Hall, then recognized as the New England Botanico-Medical College, Worcester, Massachusetts." Worcester HSProc, 23 (1907), 27-44.
Later called the Ladies Collegiate Institute.

13207 CROMPTON, GEORGE. The Crompton loom: William and George Crompton. Worcester, 1949. Pp. 101.
Crompton and Knowles Loom Works.

13208 _____. Mariemont. Worcester, 1952. Pp. 88.
Crompton family homestead.

13209 "THE CROMPTON & Knowles Loom Works." Industry, 5 (November, 1939), 7-10, 73.

13210 CUNNINGHAM, WILLIAM H. Protecting three generations, commemorating ninety years of life insurance service by the State Mutual Life Assurance Co. of Worcester, Massachusetts. [Worcester]: The Company, [1935]. Pp. 179.

13211 _____. State Mutual's first 100 years, 1844-1944. Worcester: State Mutual Life Assurance Co., 1944. Pp. 89, v.

13212 CUTLER, URIEL WALDO. "Fifty years of the Worcester Historical Society." Worcester HSPub, New Ser., 2 (1936-1943), 79-84.

13213 _____. "The Isaiah Thomas House, Worcester, Mass." OTNE, 18 (1927-1928), 133-140.
Demolished in 1923.

13214 _____. Jottings from Worcester's history. Worcester: Worcester Historical Society, 1932. Pp. viii, 142.

13215 _____. "Polytechnic Institute." Worcester Magazine, 2 (1901), 73-86.

13216 DAUGHTERS OF THE AMERICAN REVOLUTION. MASSACHUSETTS. COL. TIMOTHY BIGELOW CHAPTER, WORCESTER. The first school house in Worcester: dedicatory exercises at the unveiling of the tablet, May 23, 1903, upon the site of the school house where John Adams, second president of the United States, taught from 1755-1758. Worcester: Commonwealth Pr., [1903]. Pp. 39.

13217 _____. Report of the Committe on Historical Research and Marking Local Sites, of the Colonel Timothy Bigelow Chapter, Daughters of the American Revolution. Worcester: [Commonwealth Pr.], 1903. Pp. 19.
    Relates to school house where John Adams taught from 1755-1758.

13218 DAVIS, ISAAC. An historical discourse on the fiftieth anniversary of the First Baptist Church in Worcester, Mass., Dec. 9th, 1862. Worcester: Henry J. Howland, [1863]. Pp. iv, 52.

13219 _____. Sketches of fifteen members of Worcester Fire Society. Worcester: C. Hamilton, 1874. Pp. 17.

13220 DAVIS, JOHN, 1787-1854. An address delivered at the dedication of the Town Hall, in Worcester (Mass.) on the second day of May, 1825. Worcester: W. Manning, [1825]. Pp. 36.

13221 DODGE, MARY COCHRAN. A list of the soldiers in the war of the Revolution, from Worcester, Mass., with a record of their death and place of burial. Worcester: Col. Timothy Bigelow Chapter, Daughters of the American Revolution, [1902]. Pp. 28.

13222 DRAPER, JAMES. "The parks and playgrounds of Worcester." Worcester Magazine, 1 (1901), 231-243.

13223 DRUMMEY, JACK. "A durable company celebrates 75 years of making durable products." Industry, 21 (September, 1954), 18, 60-62. Warren Belting Co., leather products.

13224 EARLE, STEPHEN CARPENTER. "The architecture of the second court house." Worcester HSProc, 17 (1900-1901), 212-216.

13225 EDDY, HARRISON P. "Sewerage and sewage disposal of Worcester." Worcester Magazine, 1 (1901), 47-51, 111-124.

13226 EMERSON, WILLIAM ANDREW. Old landmarks in Worcester, Massachusetts. Worcester, 1913. Unpaged.

13227 _____, comp. Worcester legends: incidents, anecdotes, reminiscences, etc., connected with the early history of Worcester, Mass., and vicinity. Corrected by Franklin P. Rice.... [Worcester]: Denholm & McKay, 1905. Unpaged.

13228 FAHLSTROM, CLIFFORD I. "Industry's map of Massachusetts: Worcester." Industry, 2 (March, 1937), 25-27.

13229 _____. "Washburn completes 75 years on note of accomplishment and unity." Industry, 21 (February, 1956), 29-30, 57, 62. Washburn Co., wire and household utensils.

13230 THE FAREWELL to the old school-house, and dedication of the new, at New Worcester, July 26, and Aug. 30, 1858. Worcester: Henry J. Howland, [1858]. Pp. 30.

13231 FARNSWORTH, ALBERT. "The Lincoln Farm: present site of the Worcester State Teachers College." Worcester HSPub, New Ser., 2 (1936-1943), 329-337.

13232 _____. "Old Worcester gardens." Worcester HSPub, New Ser., 2 (1936-1943), 181-192.

13233 _____. and GEORGE B. O'FLYNN. The story of Worcester, Massachusetts. Worcester: Davis Pr., 1934. Pp. 214.

13234 "FIFTY years of inspiring history." Worcester Magazine, 17 (1914), 189-193. YMCA.

13235 "FIRST Norton grinding machine went into production 50 years ago." Industry, 15 (May, 1950), 46, 48. Abrasives.

13236 FLANAGAN, BERNARD J. "Worcester's Catholic origins." Holy Cross Quarterly, 5, Nos. 3-4, (1973), 50-54.

13237 FLETCHER, PARIS. "Of fire societies and churches." Worcester HSPub, New Ser., 3 (1964), 15-24.

13238 FORBES, HARRIETTE MERRIFIELD. "The Salisbury Mansion, Worcester, Mass." OTNE, 20 (1929-1930), 99-110.

13239 FREEMASONS. WORCESTER, MASS. KNIGHTS TEMPLARS. WORCESTER COMMANDERY. Heart of the Commonwealth, Worcester, Mass. Worcester: F. S. Blanchard, 1895. Unpaged.

13240 FROST, RUTH HALLINGSBY. Dickens reads in Worcester--random readings in Worcester history. [Worcester]: Worcester Free Public Library, 1962. Unpaged. M.

13241 FULLER, HOMER TAYLOR. The progress of technical education including a quarter-century review of the work of the Worcester Polytechnic Institute. Worcester: C. Hamilton, 1894. Pp. 30.

13242 GAGE, THOMAS HOVEY. The first five minis-
ters of the Second Parish of the town of
Worcester...address...March 17, 1935. n.p.,
[1935?]. Pp. 12. MBNEH.
Aaron Bancroft, Edward H. Hall, Alonzo
Hill, Austin S. Garver, and Edwin M.
Slocombe.

13243 _____. "A United States military hospital
in Worcester." Worcester HSProc, 23
(1907), 10-25.

13244 "THE GENESIS and growth of the Worcester
Historical Society." Worcester HSB, [New
Ser.], No. 1 (November, 1939), [2-4]; No. 2 (Jan-
uary, 1940), [3-4].

13245 GETCHELL, MARGARET C. "Worcester parks."
Worcester Magazine, 19 (1916), 10-12.

13246 GOODNESS, CHARLES E. "Sixty-five years of
service to the steel industry." Industry,
18 (February, 1953), 21-23.
Morgan Construction Co.; rolling mills
for steel industry.

13247 GREEN, SAMUEL SWETT. "Gleanings from the
sources of the history of the Second Parish, Worcester, Massachusetts." AASP, New Ser.,
2 (1882-1883), 301-320.

13248 _____. "The Second Parish in the second
court house." Worcester HSProc, 17 (1900-
1901), 237-240.
Worcester County Court House.

13249 _____. Worcester, England, and Worcester,
Massachusetts. Worcester: F. S. Blanchard, 1908. Pp. 40.

13250 GROB, GERALD N. The State and the mentally
ill: a history of Worcester State Hospital
in Massachusetts, 1830-1920. Chapel Hill: Univ.
of North Carolina Pr., 1966. Pp. xv, 399.

13251 HALL, GRANVILLE STANLEY. "The story of
Clark University." Worcester Magazine, 17
(1914), 132-137.

13252 HALL, J. BRAINERD. "The history of transportation in Worcester." Worcester Magazine, 12 (1909), 380-381.

13253 _____. "Looking down the vista of departed
years." Worcester Magazine, 14 (1911),
551-555.
Collective biography of Board of Trade.

13254 _____. "The story of our union stations."
Worcester Magazine, 13 (1910), 3-4.
Railroads.

13255 "HARVARD and Yale on Lake Quinsigamond."
Worcester Magazine, 4 (1902), 59-68.
Rowing.

13256 HATHAWAY, SAMUEL. History of the Worcester
Guards and the Worcester City Guards from
1840 to 1896. Worcester: F. S. Blanchard, 1896.
Pp. 67.

13257 [_____]. A sketch of historical reality
with the blendings of the romance of ide-
ality. Worcester: F. S. Blanchard, 1897. Pp. 38.
Reminiscences of Worcester.

13258 HAYNES, GEORGE HENRY. "A chapter from the
local history of Knownothingism." NEM, New
Ser., 15 (1896-1897), 82-96.
American Party.

13259 "THE HEALD Machine Company." Industry, 5
(June, 1940), 7-10.
Grinding machines.

13260 "THE HEYWOOD Boot & Shoe Company." Industry, 9 (May, 1944), 13-16.

13261 HIGGINS, ALDUS C. "A brief history of Norton Company." Worcester HSPub, New Ser.,
3 (October, 1946), 64-72.
Abrasives.

13262 HILL, BENJAMIN THOMAS. "The history of the
second court house and the early bar."
Worcester HSProc, 17 (1900-1901), 220-236.
Worcester County Court House.

13263 "HISTORY of the Worcester Music Festival."
Worcester Magazine, 10 (1907), 163-170.
Established in 1858.

13264 HOAR, GEORGE FRISBIE. Address delivered
before the city government and citizens,
on the two hundredth anniversary of Worcester, October 14, 1884. Worcester: C. Hamilton, 1885.
Pp. 43.

13265 "THE HOSPITALS of Worcester." Worcester
Magazine, 19 (1916), 79-86.

13266 "HOWARD Bros. Manufacturing Company." Industry, 6 (June, 1941), 13-16.
Card clothing.

13267 HOWLAND, GEORGE W. "The Usher lot or land
titles near Highland Street, Worcester,
Massachusetts." Worcester HSPub, New Ser., 1
(1928-1935), 312-325.

13268 HOWLAND, HENRY JENKINS. The heart of the
Commonwealth: or, Worcester as it is: being a correct guide to all the public buildings and
institutions, and to some of the principal manufactories and shops, and wholesale and retail
stores, in Worcester and vicinity, with many engravings, and a new map of the city. Worcester:
H. J. Howland, 1856. Pp. viii, 131.

13269 HUNT, FREEMAN. "The city of Worcester,
Massachusetts." Merchants' Magazine and
Commercial Review, 22 (1850), 54-65.

13270 ISHAM, NORMAN M. "The Stephen Salisbury
House in Worcester and its restoration."
OTNE, 20 (1929-1930), 111-120.

13271 JAMES, HORACE. One-man power, a biographical sketch of Joel C. Stratton: being the first of a series of temperance tracts, issued by the Worcester Temperance League. Worcester: Worcester Temperance League, 1861. Pp. 12.
Includes a sketch of the league.

13272 KING, DOROTHY. "Notes on the Gehenna Press." PAGA, 7 (1959), 33-48.
Worcester and Northampton.

13273 KINNICUTT, LINCOLN NEWTON. "Historical notes relating to the second settlement of Worcester." AASP, New Ser., 26 (1916), 273-289.

13274 KNOWLTON, JOHN STOCKER COFFIN and CLARENDON WHEELOCK. Carl's tour in Main Street.... (1855) 4th. ed. Worcester: Sanford and Davis, 1889. Pp. 246.

13275 KOOPMAN, HARRY LYMAN. "A pilgrimage to a typographic shrine." Printing Art, 15 (1910), 429-436.
American Antiquarian Society.

13276 LAMSON, CHARLES MARION. "The churches of Worcester." NEM, New Ser., 5 (1891-1892), 768-792, 820.

13277 _____. Sermon read at the 31st anniversary of the Salem Street Church, Worcester, Mass., with historical matter. Worcester: Charles Hamilton, 1879. Pp. 38.

13278 LANCASTER, WALTER MOODY. "The Worcester Music Festival." NEM, New Ser., 23 (1900-1901), 3-18.

13279 LAPOMARDA, VINCENT A. "Worcester families." Holy Cross Quarterly, 5, Nos. 3-4 (1973), 4-13.
Green, Lincoln, Salisbury and Stoddard.

13280 LEVENSON, MINNIE GOLDSTEIN. A generation of art education for children at the Worcester Art Museum, 1911-1946. Worcester, [1946]. Pp. 27.

13281 LINCOLN, CHARLES HENRY. "The antecedents of the Worcester Society of Friends." Worcester HSPub, New Ser., 1 (April, 1928), 24-39.

13282 LINCOLN, WALDO. "Mrs. Penelope S. Canfield's recollections of Worcester one hundred years ago." Worcester HSPub, New Ser., 1 (1928-1935), 147-160.

13283 _____. The Worcester County Institution for Savings, 1828-1928, privately printed for the Worcester County Institution for Savings at Worcester, Massachusetts, on the occasion of the one hundredth anniversary. Worcester: Davis Pr., 1928. Pp. 138.

13284 LINCOLN, WILLIAM. History of Worcester, Massachusetts, from its earliest settlement to September, 1836: with various notices relating to the history of Worcester County. Worcester: C. Hersey, 1862. 2v. in 1.
Vol. 2, by Charles Hersey, has title: 'History of Worcester, Massachusetts, from 1836 to 1861....'

13285 LIVINGSTON, LUTHER S. "An American publisher of 100 years ago." Bookman, 11 (1900), 530-534.
Isaiah Thomas.

13286 LOVELL, ALBERT A. Worcester in the war of the Revolution: embracing the acts of the town from 1765 to 1783 inclusive.... Worcester: Tyler & Seagrave, 1876. Pp. 128.

13287 LUCEY, WILLIAM A. "College life in Worcester: 1848-49." NEG, 10 (Winter, 1969), 54-60.
College of the Holy Cross.

13288 MCCOY, JOHN J. "Church of St. John's, Worcester: the story of the first Catholic parish in the Diocese of Springfield, its history, activities and achievements. Worcester Magazine, 13 (1910), 249-253.

13289 "THE MAKING of leather belting." Worcester Magazine, 6 (1903), 60-66.
Graton & Knight Manufacturing Co.

13290 "THE MAKING of wire." Worcester Magazine, 4 (1902), 169-180.
American Steel & Wire Co.

13291 MANGE, PAUL. Our inns from 1718 to 1918.... Worcester: Hurley Printing, [1918?]. Pp. 36. MWA.

13292 MARBLE, ARTHUR J. "The old Pine Meadow Road and its forgotten bridge." Worcester HSProc, 19 (1903), 118-128.

13293 MARVIN, ABIJAH PERKINS. History of Worcester in the War of the Rebellion. (1870) New ed. Worcester, 1880. Pp. iv, 606.

13294 "MASONRY in Worcester." Worcester Magazine, 12 (1909), 223-224.
Freemasons.

13295 "MASTERS in the field of forgings." Industry, 18 (December, 1952), 15-17, 42, 44.
Wyman-Gordon Co.

13296 MAYNARD, MANDER A. "A chapter in the history of the Worcester Academy." Worcester HSProc, 23 (1907), 45-57.

13297 MEARS, DAVID OTIS. Jubilee Sabbath of Piedmont Church: two discourses delivered on June 5, 1881. Worcester: Charles Hamilton, 1881. Pp. 26. MB.

13298 MERRIMAN, DANIEL. The Central Church: an historical discourse on leaving the old house, Sunday, October 4th, 1885. Worcester, 1885. Pp. 47. M.

13299   MOONEY, RICHARD H.   "College of the Holy
        Cross." Worcester Magazine, 2 (1901),
139-156.

13300   MORGAN, PHILIP M.   The Morgans of Worces-
        ter. N.Y.: Newcomen Society in North
America, 1951. Pp. 28.
        Morgan Construction Co.; rolling mills
        for steel industry.

13301   MORIN, RAYMOND.   The Worcester Music Fes-
        tival, its background and history, 1858-
1946. Worcester: Worcester County Musical Assn.,
1946. Pp. xv, 189.

13302   NELSON, JOHN.   "The old Worcester County
        gardens." Americana, 28 (1934), 359-370.

13303   NICHOLS, CHARLES LEMUEL.   Bibliography of
        Worcester: a list of books, pamphlets,
newspapers and broadsides, printed in the town of
Worcester, Massachusetts, from 1775 to 1848, with
historical and explanatory notes. (1899) 2d. ed.
Worcester: F. P. Rice, 1918. Pp. xi, 244.

13304   _____.   "Three old Worcester books."
        Worcester Magazine, 13 (1910), 269-275.
        Printed by Isaiah Thomas.

13305   "NORTON Company." Industry, 1 (October,
        1935), 3-5.
        Abrasives.

13306   "[NORTON Company 75th anniversary]."
        Grits and Grinds, 51, No. 3 (1960), entire
issue.
        Abrasives.

13307   NUTT, CHARLES.   "Beginnings of Worcester,
        Massachusetts." Americana, 13 (1919),
1-20.

13308   _____.   History of Worcester and its peo-
        ple. N.Y.: Lewis Historical Publishing,
1919. 4v.

13309   NUTT, MRS. CHARLES.   "The furniture of the
        olden time, especially that owned in
Worcester." Worcester HSProc, 24 (1908), 36-49.

13310   O'FLYNN, THOMAS FRANCIS.   The story of
        Worcester, Massachusetts. Boston: Little,
Brown, 1910. Pp. vii, 159.

13311   O'GORMAN, JAMES F.   "O. W. Norcross, Rich-
        ardson's 'master builder': a preliminary
report." SocArchHistJ, 32 (1973), 104-113.
        Norcross Brothers, contractors and builders.

13312   "THE OLD South bi-centennial." Worcester
        Magazine, 19 (1916), 123-128.
        Congregational Church.

13313   PAINE, NATHANIEL.   An account of the Ameri-
        can Antiquarian Society, with a list of its
publications, prepared for the International Exhibition of 1876. Worcester: C. Hamilton, 1876.
Pp. 30.

13314   _____.   An account of the Worcester Lyceum
        and Natural History Association, prepared
for the International Exhibition, 1876. Worcester:
Priv. Print., 1876. Pp. 12.

13315   _____.   "An episode of Worcester history."
        Worcester HSProc, (1884), 57-63.
        Anti-Catholic riot, 1854.

13316   _____.   Notes, historical and chronological
        on the town of Worcester, Massachusetts.
Worcester: Priv. Print., 1876. Pp. 50. MB.

13317   _____.   "Random recollections of Worcester,
        1839-1843." Worcester HSProc, 6 (1884),
101-141.

13318   _____.   "School-day reminiscences." Worces-
        ter HSProc, 19 (1903), 35-58.

13319   _____.   Worcester's old common: remarks
        made at the annual banquet of the Worcester
Board of Trade, April 19, 1901. Worcester: F. S.
Blanchard, 1901. Unpaged.

13320   "THE PASSING of the Baldwin House." Worces-
        ter Magazine, 6 (1903), 80-86.

13321   PEHRSON, BENGT.   "Heald Machine Company
        completes 125 years of meritorious service."
Industry, 17 (October, 1951), 19-20, 24.

13322   PERRY, CHARLES B.   "Odd fellowship: its
        early history and present greatness."
Worcester Magazine, 12 (1909), 370-379.
        Independent Order of Odd Fellows.

13323   PERRY, JOSEPH HARTSHORN.   The physical geog-
        raphy of Worcester, Massachusetts.
Worcester: Worcester Natural History Society, 1898.
Pp. 40.

13324   PETERSON, BERNARD.   "A new century plant
        in bloom in Massachusetts industry." In-
dustry, 19 (May, 1954), 23-25.
        Thomas Smith Co., nuts, bolts, screws,
        rivets and washers.

13325   _____.   "Outstanding quarter century record
        by Johnson Steel and Wire Company." Indus-
try, 17 (October, 1951), 13-15, 87.

13326   PHIFER, LUTHER CURTIS.   Men of Worcester in
        caricature. Worcester: L. C. Phifer,
1917. Pp. 281.

13327   PHILLIPS, GEORGE WHITEFIELD.   Decennial
        sermon, Plymouth Congregational Society,
Worcester, Mass., January 1, 1882. Worcester: Lucius P. Goddard, 1882. Pp. 28. MB.

13328   "PIONEERS in the field of metal stamping."
        Industry, 22 (October, 1956), 21-22, 66,
68.
        Worcester Pressed Steel Co.

13329 QUINSIGAMOND BOAT CLUB. The Quinsigamond
Boat Club of Worcester, Massachusetts,
1857-1917. Worcester, 1917. Pp. 65.

13330 "REBUILDING of the cradle." Worcester
Magazine, 8 (1905), 51-55.
Growth of industry.

13331 RICE, FRANKLIN PIERCE. "Charles Dickens
in Worcester." Worcester Magazine, 11
(1908), 74-77.
1842.

13332 _____. Dictionary of Worcester (Massachusetts) and its vicinity. (1889) 2d.
issue. Worcester: F. S. Blanchard, 1893.
Pp. 135.

13333 _____. "History of the seal." Worcester
HSProc, (1888), 79-85.
The Worcester Society of Antiquity.

13334 _____, ed. The new city hall in Worcester,
Massachusetts. Worcester: F. S. Blanchard,
1899. Pp. 146. MWA.

13335 [_____]. A souvenir of ye Old South Meet-
in' House, 1719, Worcester, Mass., 1887.
Worcester: F. S. Blanchard, 1887. Pp. 24.

13336 _____. A summary military history of
Worcester. Worcester: Putnam, Davis,
1895. Pp. 12.

13337 _____. The Worcester book: a diary of
noteworthy events in Worcester, Massachusetts, from 1657 to 1883. Worcester: Putnam,
Davis, 1884. Pp. 159.

13338 _____, ed. The Worcester of eighteen
hundred and ninety-eight, fifty years a
city: a graphic presentation of its institutions,
industries and leaders. Worcester: F. S. Blanchard, 1899. Pp. 809.

13339 RICE, NATHAN. "Dr. Paine's and other early
grist mills." Worcester HSPub, New Ser.,
2 (1936-1943), 247-254.
William Paine.

13340 RICE, BARTON & FALES, INCORPORATED. A line
of men one hundred years long. Worcester;
1937. Pp. 69
Paper manufacturer; introduction signed:
George Sumner Barton.

13341 RIPPEL, J. ALBERT. "Worcester, heart of
the Commonwealth." National Magazine, 16
(1902), 614-621.

13342 "ROCKWOOD Sprinkler Co." Industry, 7
(February, 1942), 33-36, 46.

13343 ROE, ALFRED SEELYE. "The beginnings of
Methodism in Worcester." Worcester
HSProc, (1888), 43-71.

13344 _____. "The city of Worcester." NEM, New
Ser., 23 (1900-1901), 543-567.

13345 _____. "Twenty years of Harvard Street."
Worcester HSProc, (1894-1896), 263-299.

13346 _____. Worcester Classical and English
High School: a record of forty-seven years.
Worcester, 1892. Pp. 167.

13347 _____. The Worcester Young Men's Christian
Association: an account of its founding,
development, progress, departments, objects and
aims. Worcester, 1901. Pp. 176.

13348 RYAN, WILL CARSON. Studies in early graduate education, the Johns Hopkins, Clark
University, the University of Chicago. N.Y.: Carnegie Foundation for the Advancement of Teaching,
1939. Pp. viii, 167.

13349 NILSSON, HJALMAR and ERIC KNUTSON.
Svenskarne i Worcester, 1868-1898: strödda
anteckningar, historiker och biografier om Svens-
karne, deras lif och verksamhet i staden Worcester,
Mass., under de senaste 30 åren.... Worcester:
Skandinavias Bok-och Tidningstrychkeri, 1898.
Pp. 181.

13350 ST. WULSTAN SOCIETY, WORCESTER, MASS. St.
Wulstan Society. (1891) Worcester: Davis
Pr., 1941. Pp. 80.
Club.

13351 [SANDROF, IVAN]. The story of the Worces-
ter Mutual Fire Insurance Company. Worces-
ter: Worcester Mutual Fire Insurance, 1955.
Pp. 31. MWA.
Author attribution by the American
Antiquarian Society.

13352 _____. Your Worcester street. Worcester:
Franklin Publishing, 1948. Pp. 157. MWA.

13353 SAWYER, HERBERT M. History of the department of police service of Worcester,
Mass., from 1674 to 1900, historical and biograph-
cal.... Worcester: Worcester Police Association,
1900. Pp. 76. MWA.

13354 SCOFIELD, WILLIAM BACON. Some account of
the Worcester Association of Mutual Aid in
Detecting Thieves, instituted November 16, 1795....
Worcester: Print., 1929. Pp. 21. MBNEH.

13355 SHAW, ROBERT K. "The Highland Military
Academy." Worcester HSPub, New Ser., 1
(1928-1935), 118-128.
1856-1912.

13356 SHERER, JOSEPH F. The Sherer store as run
by the Sherer family. Fall River: Dover
Pr., 1939. Pp. 44. MWA.
Department store.

13357 SMALLEY, ELAM. The Worcester pulpit: with
notices historical and biographical. Boston: Phillips, Sampson, 1851. Pp. 561. MB.

13358   SMITH, HENRY M. The city of Worcester,
        Massachusetts: its public buildings and
its business. [Worcester]: Sanford & Davis, 1886.
Pp. 63.

13359   SONS AND DAUGHTERS OF NEW HAMPSHIRE.
        WORCESTER, MASS. Memoirs of the Worcester
Association of the Sons and Daughters of New Hampshire including an account of its origin, organization, and proceedings...1880-1885. Ellery Bicknell Crane, comp. Worcester: Daniel Seagrave,
1885. Pp. 94. M.

13360   SOUTHWICK, JEANIE LEA. "The last fifty
        years of the art life of Worcester in the
nineteenth century." Worcester HSPub, New Ser., 2
(1936-1943), 85-96.

13361   SPEARS, JOHN PEARL. Old landmarks and his-
        toric spots of Worcester, Massachusetts.
Worcester: Commonwealth Pr., 1931. Pp. 164.

13362   STURGIS, ELIZABETH ORNE PAINE. "Concerning
        schools for girls in Worcester in former
days." Worcester HSProc, 19 (1903), 246-260.

13363   _____. "A description of the Dr. Paine
        House at Worcester, called 'The Oaks,' as
it was in his day." Worcester HSProc, 21 (1905),
24-33.

13364   _____. "Old Lincoln Street, by gone days
        in Worcester." Worcester HSProc, 17
(1900-1901), 123-134.

13365   _____. "Old Worcester." Worcester HSProc,
        17 (1900-1901), 402-419, 470-488; 18
(1902), 69-90.
        Early nineteenth century.

13366   _____. "A story of three old houses."
        Worcester HSProc, 17 (1900-1901), 134-141.
Hancock House, Nashua Hotel and King's
Arms.

13367   SUTHERLAND, JOHN H., comp. The city of
        Worcester and vicinity and their resources.
Worcester: Worcester Spy, 1901. Pp. 124.

13368   "THE STATE Normal anniversary." Worcester
        Magazine, 17 (1914), 308-310.
        Worcester Normal School.

13369   STEVENS, CHARLES EMERY. Worcester church-
        es, 1719-1889. Worcester: Lucius Paulinus
Goddard, 1890. Pp. 174. MB.

13370   STILES, FREDERICK GREEN. "Exchange Street
        sixty years ago." Worcester HSProc,
(1897-1899), 491-496.

13371   _____. "A full century of light infantry."
        Worcester Magazine, 6 (1903), 6-10.
        Worcester Light Infantry.

13372   _____. "Recollections of Central and Thom-
        as Streets in the thirties of 1800."
Worcester HSProc, (1897-1899), 542-554.

13373   _____. "Recollections of Front Street,
        Worcester, in the thirties." Worcester
HSProc, (1894-1896), 300-313.

13374   _____. "Recollections of Mechanic Street,
        from 1830 to 1840." Worcester HSProc,
(1897-1899), 60-73.

13375   _____. "Recollections of old Market Street
        sixty and more years ago." Worcester
HSProc, 17 (1900-1901), 101-106.

13376   _____. "Recollections of School Street in
        the thirties and early forties of 1800."
Worcester HSProc, 17 (1900-1901), 93-101.

13377   _____. "A sketch of the Worcester Light
        Infantry, 1803-1902." Worcester HSProc,
17 (1900-1901), 616-639.

13378   STOBBS, GEORGE R. "Worcester Historical
        Society, seventy-five years old." Worces-
ter HSPub, New Ser., 3 (April, 1952), 10-13.

13379   STODDARD, HARRY GALPIN. "Romance of
        Worcester industry." Worcester HSPub, New
Ser., 3 (September, 1945), 10-32.

13380   _____. The 70 year saga of a New England
        enterprise at industrial Worcester. N.Y.:
Newcomen Society in North America, 1952. Pp. 32.
Wyman-Gordon Company, machinery.

13381   STODDARD, ROBERT W. and RICHARD C. STEELE.
        The Evening Gazette: 100 years--a consist-
ent story. N.Y.: Newcomen Society in North America, 1966. Pp. 24.

13382   STORY, WILLIAM EDWARD and LOUIS N. WILSON,
        eds. Clark University, 1889-1899, decennial
celebration. Worcester, 1899. Pp. vi, 566.

13383   TAYLOR, HERBERT FOSTER. Seventy years of
        the Worcester Polytechnic Institute.
Worcester: Davis Pr., 1937. Pp. vii, 415.

13384   THOMAS, ISAIAH. The diary of Isaiah Thom-
        as, 1805-1828.... Benjamin Thomas Hill, ed.
Worcester: [American Antiquarian] Society, 1909.
2v.

13385   TIBBETTS, JAMES H. "Early bath tubs of
        Worcester." Worcester HSPub, New Ser., 3
(1964), 69-74.

13386   TINSLEY, JOHN FRANCIS. Looms for the
        world; Crompton & Knowles in textile machin-
ery manufacture, since 1837. N.Y.: Newcomen Society in North America, 1949. Pp. 36.

13387   TRUE, MICHAEL. Worcester poets, with notes
        toward a literary history. Worcester:
Worcester County Poetry Association, 1972. Pp. 44.
M.

13388   _____. "Worcester radicals." Holy Cross
        Quarterly, 5, Nos. 3-4, (1973), 14-21, 24.
        Isaiah Thomas, Elihu Burritt, Stephen Sym-
onds Foster, and Abigail Kelley Foster.

13389 TULLOCH, DONALD. Worcester, city of prosperity.... Worcester: Commonwealth Pr., 1914. Pp. 324.

13390 "TWENTY years of Clark University." Worcester Magazine, 12 (1909), 287-293.

13391 "250 years of Worcester." Holy Cross Quarterly, 5, Nos. 3-4 (1973), 25-27.
Chronology of events.

13392 "TWO sons of the American Revolution." Worcester Magazine, 6 (1903), 17-23.
Elbridge Boyden and John P. Marble.

13393 TYLER, ALBERT. "The banner." Worcester HSProc, (1897-1899), 52-59.
Role of the Washingtonian Engine Co. in temperance reform.

13394 _____. "The Butman riot." Worcester HSProc, (1878), 85-94.
Slavery, 1854.

13395 TYMESON, MILDRED MCCLARY. Men of metal. Worcester: Worcester Stamped Metal Co., 1954. Pp. 45.
A company history.

13396 _____. The Norton story. Worcester: Norton Co., 1953. Pp. 312.
Norton Co., machinery.

13397 _____. Rural retrospect; a parallel history of Worcester and its Rural Cemetery. Worcester: Commonwealth Pr., 1956. Pp. x, 264.

13398 _____. Two towers; the story of Worcester Tech., 1865-1965. Barre: Barre Publishers, 1965. Pp. 243.
Worcester Polytechnic Institute.

13399 _____. Worcester bankbook; from country barter to county bank, 1804-1966. Worcester: Worcester County National Bank, 1966. Pp. 183.

13400 _____. Worcester centennial, 1848-1948: historical sketches of the settlement, the town and the city, Worcester of 1948. Worcester: Worcester Centennial, 1948. Pp. 83.

13401 _____. The Wyman-Gordon way, 1883-1958. Worcester, 1959. Pp. 138.
Machinery manufacturing.

13402 UTLEY, SAMUEL. "An ancient instance of municipal ownership." AASP, New Ser., 17 (1905-1906), 125-131.

13403 "VOCAL music in Worcester public schools." Worcester Magazine, 6 (1903), 101-104.
1841-1902.

13404 WAITE, EMMA FORBES. "Old-time taverns of Worcester." Worcester HSProc, 19 (1903), 70-82.

13405 WALKER, HOWELL. "Cities like Worcester make America." National Geographic Magazine, 107 (1955), 189-214.

13406 WALL, CALEB ARNOLD. Eastern Worcester: its first settlers and their locations, historical and genealogical, in three chapters. Worcester, 1891. Pp. 52.

13407 _____. North Worcester: its first settlers and old farms, an historical address, delivered before the Chamberlain District Farmers' Club, at the residence of A. S. Lowell, North Worcester, Dec. 6, 1889. Worcester, 1890. Pp. 21.

13408 _____. Reminiscences of Worcester from the earliest period, historical and genealogical, with notices of early settlers and prominent citizens, and descriptions of old landmarks and ancient dwellings.... Worcester: Tyler & Seagrave, 1877. Pp. viii, 392.

13409 WALLACE, ANTHONY F. C. Tornado in Worcester: an exploratory study of individual and community behavior in an extreme situation. Washington: National Academy of Sciences, National Research Council, 1956. Pp. xi, 165.
Tornado of 1953.

13410 WARD, GEORGE OTIS. The first four principals of the Worcester Academy. Worcester: Davis Pr., 1917. Pp. 29. MB.
Silas Bailey, Samuel Swett Green, Eli Thayer and Norman Wheeler.

13411 _____. Worcester Academy: its locations and its principals, 1834-1882. Worcester: Davis Pr., 1918. Pp. 95. MB.

13412 WARING, FREDERICK E. "Telephone development in Worcester." Worcester HSProc, 25 (1909-1910), 257-270.

13413 WASHBURN, CHARLES GRENFILL. An address delivered at Worcester, October 16, 1912, before the American Antiquarian Society on the occasion of the one hundredth anniversary of its foundation. Boston: Merrymount Pr., 1912. Pp. 45.

13414 _____. Address upon the celebration of the two hundredth anniversary of the adoption by the General Court of a resolve vesting the inhabitants of Worcester with the powers and privileges of other towns within the province, Mechanics Hall, Worcester, Massachusetts, Wednesday, June 14, 1922. Worcester: Davis Pr., 1922. Pp. 35.

13415 _____. "The development of a world famed institution." Worcester Magazine, 15 (1912), 317-323.
American Antiquarian Society.

13416 _____. "Historical address." AASP, New Ser., 22 (1912), 257-287.
Centennial of American Antiquarian Society.

13417 _____. Industrial Worcester. Worcester: Davis Pr., 1917. Pp. 348.

13418 WASHBURN, ROBERT MORRIS. Smith's barn: 'a child's history' of the West Side, Worcester, 1880-1923. Worcester: Commonwealth Pr., 1923. Pp. 147.
Profiles of local personages.

13419 WEIS, FREDERICK LEWIS. "A list of officers and members of the American Antiquarian Society, 1812-1947." AASP, 56 (1946), 289-333.

13420 "WHAT the Worcester Board of Trade has done." Worcester Magazine, 16 (1913), 17-20.

13421 WHEELER, HENRY M. "Early roads in Worcester." Worcester HSProc, 20 (1904), 72-127.

13422 _____. "Interesting data relating to the estates bordering on Lincoln Square." Worcester HSProc, 21 (1905), 46-92.

13423 _____. "A New England house one hundred years ago." Worcester HSProc, 19 (1903), 358-394.
Joseph Wheeler House.

13424 _____. "Reminiscences of Thomas Street schools and school-house sixty years and more ago." Worcester HSProc, 19 (1903), 82-115.

13425 _____. "Worcester as seen over one hundred years ago." Worcester HSProc, 22 (1906), 96-105.

13426 WILLIAMSON, HIRAM R. Fire service of Worcester, a souvenir, ninth annual ball of Worcester Firemen's Relief Association, December ninth, 1887. Worcester: Worcester Firemen's Relief Association, 1887. Pp. 121. MB.
Historical.

13427 "WOODBURY and Company." Industry, 32 (June, 1967), 32.
Engraved letterheads, founded 1879.

13428 WOODWARD, SAMUEL B. "Early charitable organizations of Worcester." Worcester HSPub, New Ser., 1 (1928-1935), 391-402.

13429 WOODWARD, WILLIAM. "Firearms--their evolution and Worcester's part therein." Worcester HSPub, New Ser., 1 (1928-1935), 264-278.

13430 WORCESTER, MASS. Celebration by the inhabitants of Worcester, Mass., of the centennial anniversary of the Declaration of Independence, July 4, 1876, to which are added historical and chronological notes. Worcester, 1876. Pp. 146.
Relates to the city; oration by Benjamin Franklin Thomas.

13431 _____. Ceremonies at the laying of the corner-stone of the new city hall in Worcester, Sept. 12, 1896, and at the dedication of the building, April 28, 1898, with an account of the semi-centennial celebration of the incorporation of Worcester as a city, June 20-24, 1898. Worcester, 1898. Pp. 86.

13432 _____. 1684. 1884: celebration of the two hundredth anniversary of the naming of Worcester, October 14 and 15, 1884. Worcester, 1885. Pp. 176.
Contains bibliography by Nathaniel Paine of historical works relating to Worcester.

13433 _____. Tables showing the population, valuation, taxes, and other statistics, 1850-1876. Worcester, 1876. Pp. 16. MB.

13434 _____ Worcester births, marriages and deaths. Franklin P. Rice, comp. Worcester: Worcester Society of Antiquity, 1894. Pp. 527.
Births 1714-1848; marriages 1747-1848; deaths 1826-1848.

13435 _____. Worcester town records.... Franklin P. Rice, ed. Worcester: Worcester Society of Antiquity, 1879-1895. 7 v. in 6.
1722-1848.

13436 WORCESTER, MASS. ALL SAINTS CHURCH. All Saints Church, Worcester, Massachusetts; a centennial history, 1835-1935. Worcester: Commonwealth Pr., 1935. Pp. xvi, 142.

13437 WORCESTER, MASS. ALL SAINTS CHURCH. THE WEDNESDAY CLUB. Twentieth anniversary book, MDCCCLXXVI-MDCCCXCVI. Worcester, 1896. Pp. 64. MB.
Woman's club.

13438 WORCESTER, MASS. BOARD OF TRADE. Worcester, the city of varied industries, an old New England municipality rendered pre-eminent by inventive genius...; just a glimpse of its civic life and an epitome of its educational insurance and industrial eminence from 1658 to 1909. Worcester: Blanchard Pr., 1909. Unpaged.

13439 WORCESTER, MASS. CENTRAL CHURCH. Manual of the Central Church in Worcester, with a sketch of its history.... Worcester: Charles Hamilton, 1886. Pp. 93. M.

13440 WORCESTER, MASS. CITY SOLICITOR. Brief history of the grade crossing abolition in Worcester from 1890 to 1906, by Arthur P. Rugg, February 2, 1906. Worcester, 1906. Pp. 28.

13441 WORCESTER, MASS. COLLEGE OF THE HOLY CROSS. Historical sketch of the College of the Holy Cross. [Worcester?, 1876?]. Pp. 20. MB.

13442 _____. Historical sketch of the College of the Holy Cross, Worcester, Massachusetts, 1843-83. Worcester: Chas. Hamilton, 1883. Pp. 43. M.

13443 WORCESTER, MASS. FIRST BAPTIST CHURCH. A brief history of the First Baptist Church, Worcester, Massachusetts, with the declaration of faith.... Worcester: Lucius P. Goddard, 1883. Pp. 20. M.

13444   WORCESTER, MASS. FIRST CHURCH. First
        Church, Old South, of Worcester, Mass.
Worcester, 1916. Pp. 79. MB.

13445   _____. The history, articles of faith,
        covenant, and standing rules of the First
Church in Worcester, Mass., with a catalogue of
its officers and members, April 1, 1864. Worcester: Adams & Brown, [1864].

13446   WORCESTER, MASS. FIRST UNIVERSALIST SOCI-
        ETY. Services at the installation of Rev.
B. F. Bowles as pastor of the First Universalist
Society, Worcester, Massachusetts, and the twenty-
fifth anniversary exercises, Wednesday, October
10, 1866. Worcester: Tyler & Seagrave, [1866?].
Pp. 52. MBNEH.

13447   WORCESTER, MASS. FREE PUBLIC LIBRARY.
        The fiftieth anniversary of the founding
of the Worcester Free Public Library, Dec. 23,
1859, Dec. 23, 1909. Worcester: F. S. Blanchard,
1910. Pp. 40.

13448   _____. Special report of the Free Public
        Library of the city of Worcester, prepared
for use at the International Exhibition of 1876....
Worcester: Charles Hamilton, 1876. Pp. 14.

13449   WORCESTER, MASS. OLD HOME CARNIVAL COM-
        MITTEE. Worcester Old Home Carnival,
June 17-18-19-20, 1907. Worcester, [1907?].
Pp. 160. MBNEH.
        Text is an 'Historical sketch of Worces-
        ter.'

13450   WORCESTER, MASS. OLD SOUTH CHURCH. The
        First Church, Old South of Worcester,
Massachusetts, bi-centennial celebration, May twen-
ty-one to twenty-eight, nineteen hundred and sixteen. Worcester: Commonwealth Pr., 1916.
Pp. 79. MBNEH.

13451   WORCESTER, MASS. ORDINANCES, etc. Laws
        and ordinances, together with the act to
incorporate the town of Worcester, and other special acts of the legislature relating to the town
and city; also, the revised charter, of the city,
with an appendix containing a chronological view
of the town, a chronological and financial view of
the city.... Worcester: Tyler & Seagrave, 1867.
Pp. viii, 373.

13452   WORCESTER, MASS. PIEDMONT CONGREGATIONAL
        CHURCH. Manual...containing a brief his-
tory.... Worcester: Charles Hamilton, 1883.
Pp. 55. M.

13453   WORCESTER, MASS. PILGRIM CONGREGATIONAL
        CHURCH. History and manual.... Worcester:
Blanchard, 1894. Pp. 57. MB.

13454   WORCESTER, MASS. PLYMOUTH CONGREGATIONAL
        CHURCH. History and articles of faith and
covenant of the Plymouth Congregational Church,
Worcester, Mass...organized in 1869. Worcester:
Goddard and Nye, 1870. Pp. 20. M.

13455   _____. Manual...with list of members, 1876.
        Worcester: Charles Hamilton, 1876.
Pp. 32. M.
        Includes historical sketch.

13456   WORCESTER, MASS. PROPRIETORS. Records of
        the proprietors of Worcester, Massachusetts.
Franklin P. Rice, ed. Worcester: Worcester Society
of Antiquity, 1881. Pp. 336.
        1667-1788.

13457   WORCESTER, MASS. ST. GEORGE SYRIAN ANTI-
        OCHIAN ORTHODOX CHURCH. Golden jubilee,
1956, St. George Syrian Antiochian Orthodox Church,
Worcester. n.p., [1957]. Unpaged.

13458   WORCESTER, MASS. UNION CONGREGATIONAL
        CHURCH. Manual of the Union Congregational
Church in Worcester, Mass., containing the history
of the church. Worcester: Charles Hamilton, 1881.
Pp. 81. M.

13459   _____. Semi-centennial of the Union Church
        of Worcester. Worcester: Worcester Print-
ing and Publishing, 1886. Pp. 64. MBNEH.

13460   WORCESTER BANK & TRUST COMPANY. Historic
        events of Worcester; a brief account of
some of the most interesting events which have occurred in Worcester during the past two hundred
years, issued by the Worcester Bank & Trust Company
in commemoration of the two hundredth anniversary
of the incorporation of the town of Worcester.
[Worcester], 1922. Pp. vii, 63.

13461   _____. Some historic houses of Worcester;
        a brief account of the houses and taverns
that fill a prominent part in the history of Worcester, together with interesting reminiscences of
their occupants. [Worcester], 1919. Pp. vii, 71.

13462   WORCESTER bi-centennial. (1884) 2d. ed.
        Worcester: F. S. Blanchard, 1884. Pp. 12.

13463   WORCESTER CHORAL UNION. History of the
        Worcester Choral Union. Worcester: West
& Lee Game and Printing, 1875. Pp. 28. MWA.

13464   WORCESTER CITY GUARDS. A souvenir of the
        celebration of the fifty-fifth anniversary
of the Worcester City Guards, Sept. 19, 1895.
Worcester: F. S. Blanchard, 1895. Pp. 33.

13465   WORCESTER CONFERENCE OF CONGREGATIONAL (UNI-
        TARIAN) AND OTHER CHRISTIAN SOCIETIES.
Twenty-fifth anniversary of the Worcester Conference
of Congregational (Unitarian) and other Christian
Societies held with the Second Parish, Worcester,
Mass., January 27 and 28, 1892. Worcester: Charles
Hamilton, 1892. Pp. 48. M.

13466   WORCESTER CONTINENTALS. Company proceedings
        of the Worcester Continentals, 1876-1878.
George Herbert Harlow, comp. Worcester: Noyes,
Snow, 1878. Pp. 40.

13467 WORCESTER COUNTY INSTITUTION FOR SAVINGS.
Worcester County Institution for Savings....
Worcester, [1928?]. Pp. 138. M.
1828-1928.

13468 WORCESTER COUNTY MECHANICS ASSOCIATION,
WORCESTER, MASS. Historical sketch of the
Worcester County Mechanics Association: with the
charter and by-laws, a list of members and officers
to July, 1861.... Worcester: C. Hamilton, 1861.
Pp. 70. M.

13469 "WORCESTER Evening High School." Worcester Magazine, 11 (1908), 56-58.

13470 WORCESTER FIRE SOCIETY. One hundred and
fiftieth anniversary of the Worcester Fire
Society. Worcester, 1943. Pp. 43.

13471 _____. One hundredth anniversary of the
Worcester Fire Society, address by George
F. Hoar. Poem by John D. Washburn. Worcester:
C. Hamilton, 1893. Pp. 35.

13472 _____. Reminiscences and biographical notices of past members. Worcester, 1870-
1946. 7v. in 5.
Title varies.

13473 WORCESTER FIVE CENTS SAVINGS BANK. [Worces-
ter Five Cents Savings Bank], 1854-1954.
Worcester, 1954. Unpaged. M.

13474 WORCESTER HISTORICAL SOCIETY. Proceedings
at the tenth anniversary...January 27,
1885, address by C. A. Staples. Worcester, 1885.
Pp. 100.

13475 WORCESTER illustrated, 1875. James A. Ambler, comp. Worcester: J. A. Ambler, 1875.
Pp. 56.

13476 [WORCESTER in the International Exhibition
of 1876.] Worcester, 1876. v.p. MB.
Collection of accounts of principal educational institutions, associations, etc.
of Worcester.

13477 WORCESTER: its past and present: a brief
historical review of two hundred years,
with an exhibit of the industries and resources of
the city at the commencement of the third century
of her existence...with a description of points of
interest, views of public and private buildings,
biographical sketches and portraits.... Worcester:
O. B. Wood, 1888. Pp. 247.
Compilation begun by I. N. Metcalf and
completed by A. W. Hyde.

13478 "WORCESTER, Massachusetts." Worcester
Magazine, 18 (1915), 305-310.

13479 WORCESTER MECHANICS SAVINGS BANK. Good
things come from the money you put in the
bank, 1851-1951. Worcester, 1951. Pp. 8. M.

13480 WORCESTER MORRIS PLAN BANKING COMPANY.
25th anniversary of the Worcester Morris
Plan Banking Company, Incorporated April 30, 1915.
Worcester, 1940. Pp. 16. M.
1915-1940.

13481 WORCESTER 250TH ANNIVERSARY COMMITTEE.
Worcester celebration, 1722-1972. James E.
Mooney, ed. Worcester: Worcester 250th Anniversa-
ry, Inc., 1972. Pp. 159. M.

13482 WORCESTER WOMAN'S CLUB. Columbian souve-
nir...1880-1893. Worcester: Gilbert G.
Davis, 1893. Pp. 41. MB.
Club history.

13483 "WORCESTER'S clubs." Worcester Magazine,
2 (1901), 127-129.
Worcester and Hancock Clubs.

13484 "WORCESTER'S evening schools." Worcester
Magazine, 5 (1903), 109-117.

13485 WORCESTER'S 200th anniversary, 1684-1884.
Worcester: H. R. Cummings, 1884. Unpaged.

13486 WORKMAN, FANNY BULLOCK. "The city of
Worcester--the heart of the Commonwealth."
BSM, 3 (1885), 147-164.

13487 WRIGHT, MARTHA ELIZABETH BURT and ANNA M.
BANCROFT, eds. History of the Oread Collegiate Institute, Worcester, Mass. (1849-1881),
with biographical sketches. New Haven, Conn.:
Tuttle, Morehouse & Taylor, 1905. Pp. xii, 517.

13488 "A YANKEE city--Worcester, Massachusetts."
Hogg's Instructor, New Ser., 8 (1852),
49-51.

WORTHINGTON

13489 BARTLETT, ELSIE VENNER. Handbook of questions and answers relating to the history
of Worthington, Mass. n.p., [1952?]. Unpaged.
MNF.

13490 HISTORY of the town of Worthington, from
its first settlement to 1874. Springfield:
Clark W. Bryan, 1874. Pp. 123.

13491 MOODY, GEORGE REED. The South Worthington
Parish, 1899-1905. [South Worthington,
1905]. Pp. 103.

13492 NO ENTRY

13493 [RICE, JAMES CLAY]. Secular and ecclesiastical history of the town of Worthington,
from its first settlement to the present time. Albany: Weed, Parsons, 1853. Pp. 72.

13494 STEPHENSON, C. A brief history of the West
       Worthington tribe of Indians.... Dalton:
J. M. Stearns, 1881. Pp. 13. MHi.

13495 WORTHINGTON, MASS. Town of Worthington,
       Massachusetts, bicentennial, 1768-1968,
souvenir program and historical brochure. West
Springfield: Agawam Printing, 1968. Pp. 202. M.
       Preface signed: Carl S. Joslyn.

WRENTHAM

13496 BEAN, JOSEPH. A sermon delivered at
       Wrentham, October 26, 1773, on compleating
the first century since the town was incorporated.
Boston: John Boyle, 1774. Pp. 36.

13497 FIORE, JORDAN DOMENIC. Wrentham, 1673-
       1973: a history. [Wrentham]: The Town,
1973. Pp. 270.

13497A FISK, ELISHA. Anniversary sermons, de-
       livered in the First Congregational Church,
in Wrentham, June 14, 1846.... Boston: Haskell,
[1846?]. Pp. 25.

13498 _____. Wrentham jubilee: a sermon
       preached in Wrentham, Mass., June 12,
1849.... Boston: C. C. P. Moody, 1850. Pp. 64.

13499 KEBABIAN, JOHN S. "More on the 18th cen-
       tury plane makers of Wrentham, Mass."
CEAIA, 25 (1972), 15-16.

13500 MANN, JAMES. "Account of the surprise and
       defeat of a body of Indians near Wrentham."
MHSC, 10 (1809), 138-142.
       About 1675.

13501 SHAFER, MELVILLE ARTHUR. Historical ad-
       dress delivered at the two hundred and
twenty-fifth anniversary exercises of the original
Congregational Church, Wrentham, Massachusetts,
April 15, 1917. n.p., [1917?]. Pp. 53. MBNEH.

13502 WRENTHAM, MASS. FIRST CONGREGATIONAL
       CHURCH. Covenants and sketch of the his-
tory of the original Congregational Church, with
the names of the members, January 1, 1818. Dedham:
A. D. Alleyne, 1818. Pp. 16. MB.

13503 _____. Historical sketch, articles of
       faith and covenants, of the original Con-
gregational Church, with a catalog of its offices
and members, April 13, 1845. Boston: S. N. Dickinson, 1845. Pp. 24. MB.

YARMOUTH

13504 BAKER, FLORENCE WING. "Indian history."
       CCAPL, 4 (March, 1921), 18-19.

13505 _____, et al. Yesterday's tide. Clinton:
       Colonial Pr., 1941. Pp. x, 309.
       South Yarmouth.

13506 BANGS, ELLA MATTHEWS. "Yarmouth--a typical
       Cape Cod town." NEM, New Ser., 30 (1904),
674-685.

13507 BARNSTABLE COUNTY MUTUAL FIRE INSURANCE COM-
       PANY, YARMOUTH PORT, MASS. A century of
service, Barnstable County Mutual Fire Insurance....
Brockton: Nichols & Eldridge, 1933. Pp. 29.
[MChaHi].

13508 BRAY, ELLA W. Early days of Yarmouth in
       Plymouth Colony.... South Yarmouth: Way-
side Studio, 1939. Pp. 16.

13509 CASTONGUAY, HAROLD. Two men on a mill, the
       story of the restoration of Baxter's Mill.
South Yarmouth: Wayside Studio, 1962. Pp. 42.
[MBaC].

13510 "A CENTURY of service." Cape Cod Magazine,
       8 (August, 1925), 19, 25.
       First National Bank of Yarmouth.

13511 CORNELL, EDNA. "Tide-water harvest."
       OTNE, 32 (1941-1942), 81-83.
       Salt marshes.

13512 DODGE, JOHN WESLEY. The glory of the
       church: a sermon preached at the dedication
of the new edifice of the First Congregational
Church, Yarmouth, November 29, 1870, with the ad-
dresses at the laying of the corner stone. Yarmouth
Port: Register Job Printing Establishment, 1871.
Pp. 22.

13513 _____ A history of the First Congregation-
       al Church, Yarmouth, Mass., in a discourse
delivered Jan. 26th and Feb. 2d, 1873. Yarmouth
Port: Register Steam Job Printing Establishment,
1873. Pp. 59.

13514 JENKINS, ELISHA LAWRENCE. Old Quaker vil-
       lage, South Yarmouth, Massachusetts....
Yarmouthport: C. W. Swift, 1915. Pp. 51.

13515 ROGERS, FRED B. "Dr. James Hedge and the
       inoculation hospital at Yarmouth, Massachu-
setts, 1797-1801." JHistMed, 24 (1969), 336-338.

13516 SHIELDS, ELLEN H. Summer Street--Hawes
       Lane. Yarmouthport: Swift, 1928, Unpaged.
MB.

13517 WALSH, LAVINIA. "The oldest wind mill--a
       Cape treasure." Cape Cod Magazine, 10 (Jan-
uary, 1928), 3-4, 15-16.

13518 WARNER, MARJORIE, A. "Yarmouth." Cape Cod
       Magazine, 4 (June, 1918), 5-8.

13519 WING, DANIEL. West Yarmouth houses seventy-
       five years ago from Parker's River westward.
Yarmouthport: C. W. Swift, 1915. Pp. 21.

13520 YARMOUTH SOCIETY OF THE NEW JERUSALEM. Com-
       memorative exercises of the fiftieth anni-
versary of the Yarmouth Society of the New Jerusalem. Boston: Massachusetts New-Church Union Pr.,
1893. Pp. 133. [MY].

Supplementary Bibliographies and Guides

It is assumed that the user of this bibliography is familiar with such basic reference works as Constance M. Winchell's Guide to Reference Books. Bibliographies and guides relating to Massachusetts subjects and places appear in the text proper. Listed below are a few additional subject bibliographies and guides to related materials which are either partially or wholly excluded from the bibliography, and which have geographical access.

AMERICAN ANTIQUARIAN SOCIETY. Index of marriages in [the] Massachusetts Centinel and Columbian Centinel, 1784 to 1840. Boston: G. K. Hall, 1961. 4v.

_____. Index of obituaries in [the] Massachusetts Centinel and Columbian Centinel, 1784-1840. Boston: G. K. Hall, 1961. 5v.

_____. Index to obituary notices in the Boston Transcript, 1875-1930.... [Worcester, 1938?]-1940. 5v.

BOSTON. ENGINEERING DEPARTMENT. List of maps of Boston published between 1600 and 1903 copies of which are to be found in the possession of the city of Boston or other collectors of the same. Boston: Municipal Printing Office, 1903. Pp. 248.

_____. List of maps of Boston published subsequent to 1600, copies of which are to be found in the possession of the city of Boston or other collectors of the same. Boston: Municipal Printing Office, 1904. Pp. 97.

ARNDT, KARL JOHN RICHARD and MAY E. OLSON. German-American newspapers and periodicals, 1732-1955: history and bibliography. 2d rev. ed. N.Y.: Johnson Reprint Corp., 1965. Pp. 810.
    Reprint of 1961 edition with the addition of an appendix.

BRIGHAM, CLARENCE SAUNDERS. History and bibliography of American newspapers, 1690-1820. Worcester: American Antiquarian Society, 1947. 2v.

_____. Additions and corrections. In the Proceedings of the American Antiquarian Society for April 1961 and reprinted separately.

CODMAN, OGDEN. Index of obituaries in Boston newspapers, 1704-1800. Boston: G. K. Hall, 1968. 3v.

COMPREHENSIVE DISSERTATION INDEX, 1861-1972. Ann Arbor, Mich.: Xerox University Microfilms, 1973. 37v.
    Volume 28, "History," has access under Massachusetts locales.

_____. SUPPLEMENT. Ann Arbor, Mich.: Xerox University Microfilms, 1974-.

DICKINSON, ARTHUR TAYLOR. American historical fiction. 3d. ed. N.Y.: Scarecrow Pr., 1971. Pp. 380

DICTIONARY OF AMERICAN BIOGRAPHY. Allen Johnson and Dumas Malone, eds. N.Y.: Charles Scribner's Sons, 1928-1937. 20v and index.
    Includes birthplace index and subject access under "Massachusetts."

_____. SUPPLEMENTS 1-3. N.Y.: Charles Scribner's Sons, 1944-1973.
    Edited by Harris E. Starr, Robert L. Schuyler, and Edward T. James, respectively. Together, the entire set covers persons deceased as of December 1945.

DISSERTATION ABSTRACTS INTERNATIONAL. Ann Arbor, Mich.: University Microfilms, 1938-.
    Covers dissertations written since 1935. Volumes 1-11 have title "Microfilm Abstracts" and volumes 12-29 have title "Dissertation Abstracts." Indexes in each volume provide geographical access.

DORNBUSCH, CHARLES EMIL. Military bibliography of the Civil War. N.Y.: New York Public Library, 1971-1972. 3v.
> Volume one is a reprint of the 1961-1962 edition published as: Regimental publications and personal narratives of the Civil War.

DRAKE, MILTON. Almanacs of the United States. N.Y.: Scarecrow Pr., 1962. 2v.
> Covers 1639-1850.

EDWARDS, EVERETT EUGENE. A bibliography of the history of agriculture in the United States. Washington: Govt. Print. Off., 1930. Pp. iv, 307.

FORBES, HARRIETTE MERRIFIELD. New England diaries, 1602-1800: a descriptive catalog of diaries, orderly books, and journals. Topsfield, Mass.: Priv. Print., 1923. Pp. viii, 439.

GOHDES, CLARENCE H. Literature and theater of the United States and regions of the U. S. A.: an historical bibliography. Durham, N.C.: Duke Univ. Pr., 1967. Pp. ix, 275.

GREGORY, WINIFRED, ed. American newspapers, 1821-1936: a union list of files available in the United States and Canada. N.Y.: H. W. Wilson, 1937. Pp. 791

GRIFFIN, APPLETON PRENTISS CLARK. Bibliography of American historical societies. 2d. ed. rev. and enl. Washington: Govt. Print. Off., 1907. Pp. 1374.
> Issued as volume two of the annual report of the American Historical Association for 1905.

GUERRA, FRANCISCO. American medical bibliography, 1639-1783. N.Y.: Lathrop C. Harper, 1962. Pp. 885.

HAYWOOD, CHARLES. A bibliography of North American folklore and folksong. N.Y.: Greenberg, 1951. Pp. xxx, 1292.

KUEHL, WARREN F. Dissertations in history, and index to dissertations completed in history departments of United States and Canadian universities. Lexington: Univ. of Kentucky Pr., 1965-1972. 2v.
> Covers 1873-1970.

LARSON, HENRIETTA MELIA. Guide to business history: materials for the study of American business history.... Cambridge: Harvard Univ. Pr., 1948. Pp. 1181.

LE GEAR, CLARA EGLI. United States atlases: a list of national, state, county, city, and regional atlases in the Library of Congress. Washington: Govt Print. Off., 1950-1953. 2v.

LOVETT, ROBERT WOODBERRY. American economic and business history information sources: an annotated bibliography of recent works pertaining to economic, business, agricultural and labor history, and the history of science and technology for the United States and Canada. Detroit: Gale Research, 1971. Pp. 323.

MILLER, GENEVIEVE. Bibliography of the history of medicine in the United States and Canada, 1939-1960. Baltimore: Johns Hopkins Univ., 1964. Pp. xvi, 428.
> Includes a section on local history arranged geographically.

NATIONAL CYCLOPEDIA OF AMERICAN BIOGRAPHY. N.Y.: White, 1892-.
> Volume 55 is 1974.

_____. CURRENT SERIES. N.Y.: White, 1930-.
> Volumes A-L have appeared as of 1972.

_____. REVISED INDEX. H. A. Harvey and Raymond D. McGill, comps. N.Y.: James T. White, 1971. Pp. 537.
> Subject index to events and institutions under "Massachusetts."

ROOS, FRANK JOHN. Bibliography of early American architecture: writings on architecture constructed before 1860 in eastern and central United States. Urbana: Univ. of Illinois Pr., 1968. Pp. 389.

SCHLEBECKER, JOHN T. Bibliography of books and pamphlets on the history of agriculture in the United States, 1607-1907. Santa Barbara, Calif.: Clio Pr., 1969. Pp. 183.

SPEAR, DOROTHEA N. Bibliography of American directories through 1860. Worcester, Mass.: American Antiquarian Society, 1961. Pp. 389.
　　Business, city, and county directories arranged by place. Many large libraries have in microform the directories listed herein.

STRATMAN, CARL J. Bibliography of the American theater excluding New York City. Chicago: Loyola Univ. Pr., 1965. Pp. x, 397.

TANSELLE, GEORGE THOMAS. Guide to the study of United States imprints. Cambridge: Harvard Univ. Pr., 1971. 2v.

Index

Biography, collected (continued)
7464, 7509, 7527-7528, 7530, 7533, 7594, 7635,
7653, 7667, 7672, 7679, 7738, 7755, 7770, 7787,
7848, 7858, 7877, 7894, 7962, 8049, 8086, 8096,
8099, 8107, 8134, 8205, 8217, 8296, 8298-8299,
8300, 8320, 8331, 8382, 8385, 8422, 8519, 8539,
8559, 8624, 8630, 8655, 8721, 8837, 8870-8871,
8876, 8882, 8916, 8950, 8955, 8987, 8998, 9004,
9031, 9053, 9056, 9059, 9093, 9109, 9171, 9176,
9238, 9326, 9373, 9542, 9555, 9562, 9565, 9572,
9578, 9582, 9672, 9680, 9685, 9720, 9831, 9992,
10089, 10107-10108, 10135, 10161, 10204, 10216,
10223, 10230, 10291-10292, 10361, 10376, 10427,
10447, 10465-10466, 10524, 10542, 10558, 10589,
10514, 10633, 10636, 10719, 10781, 10823, 10902,
10995, 11044, 11073, 11104-11105, 11118, 11141-
11143, 11151, 11179, 11183, 11244, 11277, 11319,
11325, 11374, 11428, 11457, 11484, 11601, 11627,
11629-11630, 11669, 11762, 11850, 11923, 12032,
12035, 12054, 12066, 12072, 12096, 12131, 12208,
12295, 12364, 12387, 12409, 12483, 12506, 12526,
12580, 12599, 12634, 12667, 12712, 12739, 12759,
12822, 12825, 12911, 13006, 13095, 13129, 13140,
13144, 13155, 13202, 13219, 13253, 13293, 13308,
13326, 13338, 13349, 13353, 13357, 13418, 13472,
13477
Birch Meadow, locality in Merrimac
Birchard, William Metcalf, 2817
Birchville, locality in Huntington
Birckhead, Hugh, 147
Bird, Charles Sumner, 1584, 12627
Bird, Francis William, 2068-2069, 2637
Bird, Ivy Manning, 6799
Birdsall, Richard Davenport, 2070-2073
Births, see Vital records
Bisbee, locality in Chesterfield
Bisbee, Frederick Adelbert, 7902
Bisbee, John Hatch, 148, 8459, 13490
Bisbee's Corner, locality in Rochester
Biscoe, T. C., 8019
Bishop, Charles Nelson, 11094-11096
Bishop, Eleanor C., 11094A-11096
Bishop, Robert Roberts, 149
Bistrup, Frank V., 150
Bittinger, Frederick William, 10833
Black, Frank Swett, 151
Black, John Donald, 2713, 10712
Black, Margaret Reed, 11156
Black, Mildred, 11909
Black, S. Bruce, 152
Black Horse Village, former name of Winchester
Black Rock, locality in Cohasset
Blackburn, locality in Ashburnham
Blackinton, locality in North Adams and
    Williamstown
Blackman, Joab L., Jr., 153
Blackstone, William, 15, 5874
Blackstone, Mass., 3300
Blackstone National Bank. Uxbridge, Mass., 12589
Blackwater, locality in Kingston
Blackwell, Walter, 2193
Blagden, George Washington, 3482
Blake, Clarence E., 12120-12121
Blake, Euphemia Vale, 10223
Blake, Francis, 11315
Blake, Francis Everett, 2714, 3483-3484, 10981,
    11215, 13156-13157
Blake, George, 11315

Blake, Henry Augustus, 3033
Blake, James, 3485
Blake, John, 10468
Blake, John Ballard, 154, 3486-3491
Blake, John Bapst, 3555
Blake, Jonathan, 12708-12709
Blake, Maurice Cary, 3492-3494
Blake, Morison, 3495
Blake, Mortimer, 7858, 9578, 12398-12399, 12442
Blake, Warren Barton, 9808
Blanchard, Aaron, 9544
Blanchard, Dorothy C. A., 9777
Blanchard, Jonathan, 155
Blanchard, Thomas, 2742
Blanchardville, locality in Palmer
Blandford, Mass., 3301-3313
Blanding, Thomas, 6962
Blaneyville, locality in North Attleborough
Blasberg, Robert W., 3496
Blasphemy, 1013, 1016
Blatty, Jerome, Jr., 9292
Blaxland, George Cuthbert, 156
Blaxton, William, see Blackstone, William
Bleachery, 12658
Bleachery, locality in Peabody
Bleachery, locality in Somerville
Blelock, George H., 3497
Blenkin, G. B., 3498
Blessing of the Bay (ship), 541
Blind, 12721-12722
Blind Hole, 7223
Bliss, Alvin E., 9177
Bliss, Anna Catherine, 10533
Bliss, Charles Robinson, 12600
Bliss, Daniel, 7056
Bliss, Edward P., 8752
Bliss, George (1764-1830), 157, 12122
Bliss, George (1793-1873), 158, 12123
Bliss, Julia M., 8851
Bliss, Leonard, Jr., 11118
Bliss, Reuben, 12237
Bliss, William Root, 2660, 9778-9779, 12691
Bliss Corner, locality in Colrain
Bliss Corner, locality in Dartmouth
Blissville, locality in Orange
Blithewood, locality in Worcester
Bloch, Samuel, 216
Blodgett, Caleb, 4682
Blodgett, Geoffrey T., 159, 3499
Blodgett, Stephen H., 3500
Blodgette, George Brainard, 11204
Blood, W. H., Jr., 3501, 11029
Bloody Brook, Battle of, 7419, 7431
Bloomingdale, locality in Worcester
Blubber Hollow, Mass., 11498, 11651
Blue Hill, locality in Milton
Blue Hill Lands, extinct place in Braintree and
    Milton
Blue Meadow, locality in Belchertown
Bluffs, the, locality in Ipswich
Blyth, Benjamin, 11491
Blyth, Samuel, 11491
Boadle, John, 9977
Boardman, Waldo Elias, 160
Boardman's Farm, extinct place in Lunenburg
Boats and boating, 1025, 1589
Bobtown, locality in Pittsfield
Bochat, Kenneth P., 161
Bodfish, Annie W., 9780-9781

Clapp, Otis, 3964
Clapp, Robert Parker, 9743
Clapp, Thaddeus, III, 2112
Clapp, William Warland, 3965
Clarendon Hill, locality in Somerville
Clarendon Hills, locality in Boston
Clarfield, Gerard H., 11302
Clark, Admont G., 1929, 3084, 7502
Clark, Annie Marie Lawrence, 8210
Clark, Barrett Harper, 10992
Clark, Calvin M., 8279
Clark, Clinton E., 9606
Clark, Daniel Atkinson, 2847
Clark, DeWitt Scoville, 11244
Clark, E. L., 10710
Clark, E. S., Jr., 3966
Clark, Edward G., 12908
Clark, Edwin R., 8873
Clark, Eli Benedict, 6901
Clark, Francis E., 1930
Clark, Frank G. 7940
Clark, George Faber, 313, 9579-9580, 10603, 12309-
    12310
Clark, Henry Alden, 6739
Clark, Isaac, 10481
Clark, James Freeman, 4325
Clark, John, see Clarke, John
Clark, John Calvin Lawrence, 8567, 8570
Clark, Jonas, 2518-2519
Clark, Joseph Bourne, 3967
Clark, Joseph Sylvester, 314-316, 12323
Clark, Kate Upson, 6806
Clark, Lewis Franklin, 10575
Clark, Lyman, 3064
Clark, Marietta, see Clarke, Marietta
Clark, Mary 317-319
Clark, Oliver R., 13052-13054
Clark, Perkins K., 7405
Clark, Peter, 7131
Clark, Philetus, 13101
Clark, Sarah E., 7878
Clark, Solomon, 10465-10466
Clark, Sydney Aylmer, 3968, 5121, 6007
Clark, Thomas March, 3969
Clark, Walter E., 320
Clark, William Horace, 321, 2292, 3970, 13103
Clark, William Robinson, 9019
Clark-Small, Carrie W., 10993
Clark Point, locality in New Bedford
Clark University, 13180-13183
Clarke, Avis Gertrude, 10653
Clarke, Bradley H., 3971-3973, 11034
Clarke, Dorus, 12916-12917
Clarke, Everett Ladd, 10994
Clarke, George Kuhn, 2643, 10057-10063
Clarke, Hermann, 3975
Clarke, Jonas, see Clark, Jonas
Clarke, Israel, 12477
Clarke, John, 974, 3976
Clarke, Julius L., 322
Clarke, Lois, 3977
Clarke, Marietta, 12471, 12513
Clarke, Mary Stetson, 11887
Clarke, Olive Cleaveland, 2487
Clarke, Pitt, 10604
Clarke, Samuel Fulton, 3036
Clarke, Stephen J., 3978
Clarke School for the Deaf, 10467

Clarke School for the Deaf. Alumni, 10468-10469
Clarksburg, Mass., 6913
Clason, A. W., 323
Clayton, John Middleton, 7647
Clayton, locality in New Marlboro
Cleaveland, John, 8469
Cleaveland, Nehemiah, 10167-10168, 12472
Cleghorn, the, locality in Fitchburg
Clemence, J. Edward, 12077
Clemens, Samuel Langhorne, 5503
Clément, Antoine, 8874-8875
Clement, Edward H., 3979
Clements, Elizabeth, 9793
Cleopatra's Barge (yacht), 11330, 11467, 11557
Clergyman, a, see Donahoe, Patrick
Clergymen, 304, 341, 352, 504, 510, 717, 742, 1586,
    1618, 1872, 2006, 2055, 2180, 2205, 2327, 2435,
    2466, 2482, 2613, 2646, 2655, 2676, 2717, 2758,
    2993, 3209, 4144, 4528, 4956, 5046-5047, 5148,
    5431, 5618, 6287, 6916, 7131, 7237, 7679, 8341,
    8837, 8992, 9309, 9360, 9578-9579, 9680, 9825,
    9838, 10035, 10107, 10502, 10524, 10781, 11374,
    11518, 11908, 12066, 12409, 12521, 12751, 13144,
    13357
Clesson, Matthew, 10529
Cleveland, Grover, 6005, 6010, 6344
Cleveland, H. W. S., 11303
Cleveland, Jennie Warren, 12467
Cleveland Circle, locality in Boston
Clevelandtown, locality in Edgartown
Clifford, J. Nelson, 897
Clifford, locality in Freetown
Clifton, Mass., 9208
Clifton Heights, locality in Brockton
Cliftondale, Mass., 11902, 11904
Cline, Albert C., 10720
Clinton, Mass., 2768, 6914-6930, 7738
Clinton Savings Bank, 6921
Clintonville, Mass., 6923
Clock and watchmaking, 104-105, 2324, 3012, 3030
    3438, 3980-3981, 4008, 5194, 5480, 5576, 5641-
    5642, 5921, 6208, 7115, 7804, 8009, 8322, 8772,
    10312, 11093, 12637, 12642, 12655-12656, 12670,
    12819, 13069, 13074
Clogston, William, 12177
Closson, Elizabeth K., 3085
Clothing and dress, 923, 958, 1799, 11716
Clothing trade, 5697, 7965, 8719, 8734, 8868,
    10071-10072
Clough, Arthur J., 12274
Clover Club of Boston, 3982-3983
The Club, Salem, Mass., 11304
Club of Odd Volumes, Boston, 3984
Clubs, 459, 461, 591, 674, 1212, 1360, 1395, 2330,
    2559, 2649, 2755, 2863, 3292, 3334, 3674, 3708,
    3725, 3806, 3956, 3961, 3982-3984, 4039, 4116,
    4154, 4190, 4195, 4200, 4250, 4314-4315, 4336,
    4348, 4432, 4436, 4453, 4688, 4699, 4701, 4744,
    4775, 4859, 5041, 5155, 5241, 5379, 5387, 5393-
    5394, 5527, 5545, 5556, 5573, 5622, 5687, 5734-
    5735, 5778, 5788, 5834, 5846, 5885, 5922, 5964,
    5979, 5995, 6022, 6159, 6162, 6331, 6357-6358,
    6395, 6410, 6441, 6509, 6625, 6752, 6806, 7038-
    7042, 7215, 7684, 7997, 8068, 8184, 8292-8293,
    8332, 8515, 8635, 8641, 8874-8875, 9009, 9024,
    9097, 9107, 9427, 9791, 10069, 10132, 10280,
    10501, 10515, 10596, 10686, 10735, 10750, 10814-

Lowe, Alice Alberta, 7593, 7597
Lowe, Hamilton, 6108
Lowe, John Adams, 13011
Lowe, Richard G., 1047
Lowell, Charles, 3665
Lowell, Daniel Ozro Smith, 4924
Lowell, Francis Cabot, 384, 8925
Lowell, James Russell, 4872, 6498, 6551A, 6971
Lowell, John, 445
Lowell, John Amory, 8856
Lowell, John Nathaniel, 8290
Lowell, William D., 2379
Lowell family, 721, 5835
Lowell, Mass., 1552, 2509, 2556, 2558A, 2571, 2608, 2616, 3769, 4511, 7715, 8854-9001
Lowell, Mass. Board of Trade, 8929
Lowell, Mass. Eliot Church, 8930
Lowell, Mass. First Baptist Church, 8931
Lowell, Mass. First Congregational Church, 8932
Lowell, Mass. First Unitarian Society, 8933-8934
Lowell, Mass. First Universalist Church, 8935
Lowell, Mass. John Street Congregational Church, 8936-8937
Lowell, Mass. Trades and Labor Council, 8938
Lowell Bar Association, 8941
Lowell Hospital, 8943
Lowell Institution for Savings, 8944-8945
Lowenstam, Benjamin G., 1048
Lowenthal, David, 9903
Lower Barkersville, locality in Pittsfield
Lower Mills, locality in Boston
Lower Mills, locality in Milton
Lower Plain, locality in Hingham
Lower Village, locality in Stow
Lower Wire Village, locality in Spencer, also known as Proutyville
Lowry, Ann Gidley, 7255
Loyalists, American, 345, 412, 423, 944, 1353, 1387, 1539, 1651, 2152, 2319, 2690, 2764, 3080, 4754, 5944, 6542, 6544, 7451, 8583, 9517
Lucas, Paul R., 1049
Lucas, Rex A., 1050
Luccy, William A., 13287
Ludlow, Mass., 9002-9004
Ludlow, Mass. First Congregational Church, 9002
Ludlow City, locality in Granby
Ludlow Savings Bank, 9003
Lumber trade, 3687, 3986, 4731, 13205
Lummus, Henry Tilton, 1051-1052
Lumpkin, Katherine DuPre, 1053
Lundberg, Emma Octavia, 12241
Lund's Corner, locality in New Bedford
Lunenburg, Mass., 2738, 2769, 9005-9007
Lunenburg, Mass. Proprietors, 9006
Lunt, Dudley C., 2034
Lunt, George, 10255
Lunt, Paul, 4925
Lunt, Paul Sanborn, 10300, 10303
Lunt, William Parsons, 11059
Lurie, Reuben Levi, 4926
Lusk, William, 12997
Luther, Clair Franklin, 8168-8170
Lutheran churches, see Churches, Lutheran
Luthin, Reinhard H., 1054
Lutz, Alma, 12379
Lutz, Russell James, 10720
Lyceums, 296, 1821, 2299, 3895, 6186, 6977, 7015 7116, 7946, 9908, 10725, 11689, 13024, 13089, 13314
Lydenberg, Harry Miller, 12285

Lydia (ship), 4141
Lydon, James G., 2380
Lyle, Joseph, 9033, 9114
Lyman, Clifford H., 10510
Lyman, George Hinckley (1819-1890), 4927
Lyman, George Hinckley (b. 1850), 1055
Lyman, Joseph, 8237
Lyman, Payson Williston, 2498, 3149, 3158, 7607-7609, 7700-7701
Lyman, Theodore (1753-1839), 12631, 12638, 12654
Lyman, Theodore (1792-1849), 3942, 4928
Lyman, Theodore,(1833-1897), 4928
Lymanville, locality in North Attleborough
Lynch, Charles, 2162
Lynch, Francis J., 11498
Lynch, Frederick, 8710
Lynch, Thomas, 10014
Lynch, Thomas E., 7702
Lynde, Benjamin (1666-1745), 11499
Lynde, Benjamin (1700-1781), 11499
Lynde family, 11499
Lyndon, Barry, 4929
Lynn, Mass., 974, 2375, 2425, 9008-9119
Lynn, Mass. Boston Street Methodist Episcopal Church, 9061-9062
Lynn, Mass. Central Congregational Church, 9063
Lynn, Mass. Chamber of Commerce, 9064
Lynn, Mass. First Church of Christ, 9065-9066
Lynn, Mass. First Congregational Church, 9067
Lynn, Mass. First Methodist Eipiscopal Church, 9068
Lynn, Mass. First Universalist Parish, 9069-9070
Lynn, Mass. Public Library, 9071
Lynn, Mass. Second Congregational Society, 9072
Lynn Five Cent Savings Bank, 9074
Lynn Historical Society, 9071
Lynn Institution for Savings, 9075-9076
Lynn Temperance Reform Club, 9077
Lynn Typographical Union, No. 120, 9078
Lynn Yacht Club, 9079
Lynnde, Elmer, 7447
Lynnfield, Mass., 2375, 9120-9138, 11102
Lynnhurst, locality in Lynn
Lynnmere, Mass., 9047
Lyon, Charlotte, pseud. see Leonard, Clara
Lyon, Irving P., 8509
Lyon, Lemuel, 1711
Lyon, William Henry, 6183-6184
Lyons, Donald H., 4930
Lyons, Louis Martin, 4931
Lyons, Richard L., 4932
Lyons Village, locality in Monson
Lyonsville, locality in Colrain
Lyttle, Charles, 6552

Mabee, Carleton, 4933
Mabie, Hamilton Wright, 8302
Mabie, Henry C., 6145
Mabie, Janet, 10587
McAfee, Ida A., 10110
McAvoy, Mary C., 1056
McBee, Alice Eaton, 10511
McBratney, William H., 1057
MacBrayne, Lewis E., 8946
McBride, Marion A., 1058, 4934
McCaffrey, George Herbert, 3540
McCain, Rea, 11060
McCall, Samuel Walker, 13072
McCarry, Charles, 2115
McCarthy, Helen, 11169

Marstrand, Vilhelm, 6911
Marten, Catherine, 1096
Martha's Vineyard, see Dukes County and towns therein
Martin, Austin A., 1097
Martin, Edward S., 2116
Martin, Frances S., 8596
Martin, George Henry, 1098-1102, 4982, 9082-9087
Martin, Joseph Gregory, 3441, 4983
Martin, Lawrence, 4984
Martin, Margaret Elizabeth, 1103
Martin, Susanne, 11296
Martinez, José Augustin, 7369
Martin's Pond, locality in North Reading
Martula, Mrs. John T., 8171
Martula, Richard, 8171
Martula, Susan, 8171
Martyn, Carlos, 1104
Marvin, Abijah Perkins, 1226, 2741, 8578, 13040-13041, 13293
Marvin, John R., 6185
Maryland, 1679, 6604
Mashpee, Mass., 1968, 9291-9296
Mashpee Indians, 9291, 9294, 9296
Mashpee Old Indian Meeting House Authority, Inc., Brochure Committee, 9294
Mason, A. F., 8727
Mason, Albert, 1105
Mason, Alpheus Thomas, 1106
Mason, Alverdo Hayward, 12391
Mason, Amos Lawrence, 3555
Mason, Atherton P., 7791-7794, 10985
Mason, Daniel Gregory, 6568
Mason, Edward Sagendorph, 1107
Mason, John B., 7167
Mason, Jonathan, 4985
Mason, Orion Thomas, 9558
Mason family, 2771
Masons, see Freemasons
Massachuset Indians, 518, 1633, 7373, 9346
Massachuset language, 1863
Massachusetts, 333, 587, 1490; 1-1896
Massachusetts (Colony), 1108-1109
Massachusetts (Colony). County Court (Essex Co.), 2386
Massachusetts (Colony). County Court (Suffolk Co.), 2696
Massachusetts (Colony). Court of Assistants, 1110
Massachusetts (Colony). Court of General Sessions of the Peace. Worcester County, 2752
Massachusetts (Colony). Courts, (Hampshire County), 2500
Massachusetts (Colony). General Court. House of Representatives, 1111-1112
Massachusetts (Colony). Laws, statutes, etc., 1113
Massachusetts (Colony). Probate Court, (Essex Co.), 2387
Massachusetts (Colony). Provincial Congress, 1114
Massachusetts (Colony). Superior Court of Judicature, 1115
Massachusetts (ship), 6051
Massachusetts. Adjutant General's Office, 1116-1117
Massachusetts. Ancient and Honorable Artillery Company, 1118
Massachusetts. Board of Managers, World's Fair, Chicago, 4986

Massachusetts. Board of Railroad Commissioners, 1119-1120
Massachusetts. Board of State Charities, 1121
Massachusetts. Bureau of Statistics, 4987-4988
Massachusetts. Bureau of Statistics of Labor, 1122-1124
Massachusetts. Bureau of Transportation Planning and Development, 6019
Massachusetts. Civil Defense Agency, 1125-1126
Massachusetts. Civil War Centennial Commission, 1127
Massachusetts. Commission on Lunacy, 1854
Massachusetts. Commission on Massachusetts' Part in the World War, 1129
Massachusetts. Commission to Investigate and Study Transportation Service in Southeastern Massachusetts, 1130
Massachusetts. Convention, (1788), 1132
Massachusetts. Department of Commerce, 1133-1135
Massachusetts. Department of Commerce. Division of Research, 1136
Massachusetts. Department of Commerce and Development. Bureau of Area Planning, 1137
Massachusetts. Department of Correction, 1138
Massachusetts. Department of Education, 1139-1141
Massachusetts. Department of Education. Division of Elementary and Secondary Education and Normal Schools, 1142
Massachusetts. Department of Labor and Industries, 1143, 1996
Massachusetts. Department of Public Health, 1146, 8640
Massachusetts. Department of Public Welfare. Division of Child Guardianship, 1147
Massachusetts. Division of Employment Security, 1148-1150
Massachusetts. Executive Office of Administration and Finance, 1151
Massachusetts. Finance Commission of the City of Boston, 4989
Massachusetts. First Corps of Cadets, 1152
Massachusetts. Fusilier Veteran Association, 1153
Massachusetts. General Court, 204, 419, 763, 818, 894, 1140, 1154-1157, 1170, 1178, 1335, 1415, 1638, 4909, 4990, 5293
Massachusetts. General Court. House of Representatives, 598; 183, 1080, 1111-1112, 1159-1160, 1171, 1889, 3820, 4991, 5876
Massachusetts. General Court. House of Representatives. Committee on History of the Emblem of the Codfish, 4991
Massachusetts. General Court. Joint Special Research Committee on Contested Election Cases, 1160
Massachusetts. General Court. Senate, 149, 1160, 1171
Massachusetts. Governor, 1800-1807 (Caleb Strong), 1161
Massachusetts. Laws, statutes, etc., 1162-1163
Massachusetts. Metropolitan District Commission, 4992
Massachusetts. Metropolitan Park Commission, 4993
Massachusetts. National Guard, 1164
Massachusetts. Pilgrim Tercentenary Commission, 10913
Massachusetts. Probate Court (Middlesex Co.), 2587

Metcalf, locality in Holliston
Meteorology, see Weather
Methodism, 2100, 2289, 2454, 3999, 7094, 7844,
   9125, 9170, 9674, 9731, 10401, 10476, 10629,
   10747, 10760, 11238, 12827, 13343
Methodist churches, see Churches, Methodist
Methodist Episcopal churches, see Churches,
   Methodist Episcopal
Methuen, Mass., 2283, 9588-9600
Methuen, Mass. First Congregational Church, 9596
Mettineague, Mass., 2482
Meyer, Isidore S., 6582
Meyer, Jacob Conrad, 1246
Michigan, 588
Micmac Indians, 11920
Middleberry (Middlebery), see Middleborough
Middleboro, Mass. First Church, 9618-9619
Middleborough, Mass., 2671, 2673, 2678, 9601-9653
Middlefield, Mass., 6891, 9654-9656
Middlekauff, Robert, 1247
Middlesex County, 3, 75, 101, 222, 223, 719, 1002,
   1541, 2506-2632
Middlesex County, Mass. Registry of Deeds, 13125
Middlesex East District Medical Society, 2591
Middlesex Village, Mass., 8902, 8966
Middleton, Elinore Huse, 12733
Middleton, Mass., 2453, 9657-9670
Middleton, Mass. Anniversary Committee, 9658
Middleton, Mass. Church of Christ, 9659
Middleton, Mass. Evangelical Congregational
   Church, 9660
Middleton, locality in Yarmouth
Middletowne, former name of Tisbury
Mighill, Benjamin P., 11204
Midwinter, Edward, 1248
Mikal, Alan, 5049
Milbert, Jacques Gérard, 5455
Mile & Half of Land, extinct place in Attleboro
   and Rehoboth
Miles, Henry Adolphus, 8956-8957
Miles, James B., 5050
Miles, Pliny, 5051
Milford, Mass., 2775, 8388-8389, 9671-9680
Milford, Mass. First Congregational Church, 9678
Milham, Willis Isbister, 13012-13013
Military bases, 42, 3061-3062, 3068-3069, 4046,
   4225, 9616
Military supplies, 1429
Militia, 51, 172, 192, 266, 370, 394, 507, 582,
   635-646, 648, 747, 824, 833, 1000, 1020, 1045,
   1066, 1116-1118, 1127, 1152-1153, 1164, 1167,
   1317, 1326, 1478, 1486, 1507, 1591, 1613, 1698,
   1715, 1721, 1829, 2094, 2122, 2176, 2340-2342,
   2363, 2413, 2442, 2489, 2550-2552, 2665-2666,
   2705, 2737, 3444, 3728, 3936, 4437, 4481, 4556,
   4944, 5172, 5729, 5843, 5976, 6565, 7113, 7205,
   7351, 7728, 7778, 8116, 8529, 8756, 9199, 9214,
   9249, 9541, 10278, 11266, 11497, 11688, 11707,
   11791, 12470, 12602, 13084, 13137, 13139-13140,
   13256, 13371, 13377, 13464, 13466
Milk trade, 8811, 9529
Mill River, locality in Deerfield
Mill River, locality in New Marlborough
Mill Valley, locality in Amherst
Mill Village, Mass., 7353-7354
Mill Village, locality in Ashby
Mill Village, locality in Deerfield
Mill Village, locality in Sudbury

Millar, Bruce, 4447
Millar, Donald, 5052, 12497
Millard, George, 10399
Millbury, Mass., 2711, 2726, 2728, 9681-9688
Miller, Amelia Fuller, 7452-7454, 7467
Miller, G. W., 7795, 8734
Miller, Horace Elmer, 7077, 7082, 11907
Miller, J. W., 1997
Miller, John C., 1249, 5053
Miller, Margaret, 8236-8237
Miller, Moses, 8327
Miller, Perry, 1250, 10516
Miller, Stephen R., 8758
Miller, William, 8133
Miller, William Anthony, Jr., 1944
Millerites, 3818, 8133
Millers Falls, locality in Erving and Montague
Millerville, locality in Blackstone
Millicent Library, 7662
Millis, Mass., 9689-9691
Mills, Elden H., 12864
Mills, Robert C., 11516
Mills, 603, 2169, 2360, 6809, 6842, 7350, 7352,
   7699, 9393, 9397, 9422, 9426, 9480, 9499, 9503,
   9624, 9668, 9910, 10711, 11172, 11927, 12258,
   12404, 12471, 12517-12518, 12557-12558, 12750,
   13061, 13063, 13131, 13339, 13509
Millvale, locality in Haverhill
Millville, Mass., 9692
Milne, Alexander, 10517
Milne, Caroline C., 10517
Milton, Mrs. Sumner, 12634
Milton, Mass., 591, 932, 9693-9727
Milton, Mass. Public Library, 9706
Milton, Mass. Tercentenary Committee, 9707
Milton Bradley Co., Springfield, Mass., 12187
Milton Historical Society, 9709-9711
Milton Record-Transcript, 9712
Milward, locality in Charlton
Milwood, locality in Rowley
Miner, A. A., 3638
Miner, Henry B., 5054
Miner, Julius, 9749
Mines and mining, 947, 1552, 6028, 9443, 10259,
   11169, 12063, 12319, 12322, 12331-12333, 12482,
   12514
Ministerial associations, 148, 217, 389, 501, 517,
   1475, 1477, 1618, 1810, 1816, 1872, 2055, 2086,
   2286, 2435, 2466, 2499, 2695, 2937, 2983, 4229,
   5995, 6666, 9578, 13144
Ministers, see Clergymen
Minot, George R., 913, 1251-1252
Minot's Grant, extinct place in Cummington
Minturn, R. R., 9914
Mirick, Benjamin L., 8304
Misner, David M., 11910
Missions, 907, 1425, 3338, 4103, 4199
Mitchell, Ann Maria, 5055, 10588
Mitchell, Betty L., 1254
Mitchell, Dale, 8311
Mitchell, Edwin Valentine, 1998
Mitchell, Emily M., 10578
Mitchell, F., 1999
Mitchell, Helen, 10696
Mitchell, Henry, 6836-6837
Mitchell, Mabel G., 9915
Mitchell, Maria, 9821, 9872, 9925, 9936
Mitchell, Nahum, 6082

Pratt, Ernest S., 9624
Pratt, Mrs. Ernest S., see Pratt, Rose E. S.
Pratt, Frank Wright, 7462
Pratt, Grace Joy, 7358
Pratt, H. A., 11954
Pratt, Harvey Hunter, 1462, 11923
Pratt, Jane, 7463
Pratt, Phinehas, 1463
Pratt, Richard, 9104
Pratt, Robert Irving, 5249
Pratt, Rose E. S., 9625-9626
Pratt, Thomas, 10474
Pratt, Waldo Selden, 10940-10941
Pratt, Walter Merriam, 6874-6875, 8647, 10942
Pratt Town, locality in Bridgewater, also known as
    Paper Mill Village
Prattsville, locality in Bridgewater
Prattville, Mass., 6875
Prattville, locality in Raynham
Pray, Lewis Glover, 5250
Preble, George Henry, 1464
Precinct, locality in Lakeville
Prendergast, Frank M., 1465-1466, 3004, 5252, 6111,
    6659, 7965, 9513, 10943, 11065, 11897, 11922,
    11955, 12199
Prentice, Solomon, 8006
Presbyterian churches, see Churches, Presbyterian
Prescott, G. B., 12200
Prescott, John R., 10370
Prescott, Oliver Sherman, 4968
Prescott, Samuel, 8833
Prescott, Samuel Cate, 6660
Prescott, William, 2552, 4418, 4498, 5253, 8110
Prescott, Mass., 10163, 10694
Prescott's Grant, extinct place in Middlefield
Press, freedom of the, see Liberty of the press
Pressey, Edward Pearson, 1467, 2137, 9743
Pressey, Park, 5254
Preston, Charles E., 9438
Preston, John A., 11865
Preston, Newell T., 10069
Preston, T. Davis, 7589
Prices, 425, 1122-1123, 1874, 2301, 4054, 5521,
    11309
Pride, Edward W., 12461
Pride's Crossing, locality in Beverly
Priest, Frank Bigelow, 8849
Priest, George F., 7196-7198
Prime, Daniel Noyes, 2411
Prime family, 2411
Primogeniture, 143
Prince, John, 11355
Prince, John Tucker, 5255-5256
Prince, L. Bradford, 1468
Prince, Moses, 7199
Prince, Thomas, 1305, 2232, 5257, 9640
Princeton, Mass., 10981-10988
Princeton, Mass. First Congregational Church,
    10987
Prindle, Frances Weston Carruth, 5258
Pring, Martin, 11011
Pringeyville, locality in Ayer
Pringle, James Robert, 7966-7967
Print makers and print making, 3726, 3788, 5662
Printers, 250, 1028, 2891, 3362, 3461, 4194, 4562,
    4739, 5100-5101, 5278, 5324, 5454, 5469-5471,
    5549, 5936, 5938, 5989, 6235, 6370, 6470, 6608,
    6608, 6626, 6641, 6673, 6702, 6713, 6751, 6370,
    7774, 8358, 9078, 10796, 11527, 12266, 13304

Printing, 599, 1028, 1265, 1595-1596, 2888, 2970,
    4650, 4738, 4904, 5474, 5601, 5987, 6459, 6469-
    6470, 6523-6525, 6561, 6621, 6644, 6675, 6707-
    6708, 6720, 6724, 6729, 6737, 6757, 6764-6767,
    7080, 7426, 7824, 8358, 9738, 9745, 10368, 10494,
    10626, 10753, 10809, 11177, 11751, 12480, 13141,
    13272, 13275, 13304
Printing societies, 4357-4359, 5100-5101
Prisons, 138, 558, 632, 1430, 1835, 2746, 3452,
    3508, 3553, 4004, 4034, 4604, 4717, 4936, 5015,
    5532, 5850, 7391, 10390, 11959, 12189
Private schools, 1099, 1670, 1769, 2862, 2905, 2915-
    2916, 2938, 2942, 2947-2949, 2959-2960, 2962,
    2964-2965, 2967, 2971, 2972-2974, 3020, 3176,
    3221, 3470, 3701, 3803, 4002, 4088, 4130, 4454,
    4504, 4539, 5093, 5270, 5432-5433, 5550, 5619,
    6053, 6069, 6280, 6415, 6638, 6648, 7246, 7404,
    7408, 7411-7412, 7435, 7439, 7610, 7612-7615,
    7859, 8094, 8182-8132, 8143, 8149, 8162, 8173,
    8198, 8246, 8254, 8284, 8297, 8302-8303, 8306,
    8311, 8397, 8464, 8498, 8603, 8678, 8691, 8694,
    8698, 8708, 8716, 8805, 8994, 9084, 9209, 9332,
    9622, 9651, 9698, 9719, 9729, 9730, 9733-9734,
    10124, 10162, 10167-10168, 10171, 10179-10181,
    10193, 10196-10197, 10200, 10211, 10286, 10414,
    10457-10458, 10472, 10484, 10512, 10541, 10547,
    10583, 10587, 10591-10592, 10597, 10605, 10993,
    11860, 11900, 11942, 11954, 12067, 12069, 12260,
    12274, 12411, 12417, 12499, 12591, 12593-12594,
    12769, 12859, 12865, 12901, 12991, 12995, 13206,
    13296, 13355, 13410-13411, 13487
Privateering, 41, 10226, 11257, 11483, 11618
Privilege, locality in Blackstone
Probate records (see also Court records), 2387,
    2587, 2653, 2697, 2753, 8374
Probation, 675, 1606
Processions, 4640
Proclamations, 5859
Procter, George H., 7968-7969
Procter, John, 10688
Proctorville, locality in Athol
Proell, Rosalba, 6266
Profiteering, 3901
Progressive Party (founded 1912), 245, 1584-1585
Proper, David Ralph, 2412, 11619-11620
Prospect Union, Cambridge, Mass., 6661
Prospectville, locality in Waltham
Prostitution, 3474, 3941, 5211, 12726
Protestant Episcopal churches, see Churches,
    Episcopal
Prouty, Florence Newell, 8384
Proutyville, locality in Spencer, also known as
    Lower Wire Village
Provident Institution for Savings, Boston, 5259
Provincetown, Mass., 163, 1967, 10989-11019
Provincetown, Mass. Centre Methodist Episcopal
    Church, 11009
Provincetown, Mass. First National Bank, 11010
Psychiatry, 1391
Psychoanalysis, 4614
Psychologists, 1191
Psychology, forensic, 11256
Public health, see Hygiene, public
Public houses, see Hotels, taverns, etc.
Public speaking, 3635
Public transportation, see Transportation, public
Public utilities, 1824, 9165, 9739
Public works, 744, 1567
Publishers and publishing, 3343, 3354, 3387, 3390,

Sanborn, Frank Benjamin, 2609, 7033-7034
Sanborn, Frank Berry, 8648
Sanborn, Nathan Perkins, 9248-9249
Sanborn, Tracy Lewis, 9250
Sanchekantackett, 2206
Sand Hill, locality in Chicopee
Sand Hill, locality in Sandwich
Sandemanianism, 4220
Sanders, Daniel Clarke, 9316
Sanders, Louise, 12788
Sandersdale, Mass., 12078
Sanderson, Anna H., 3792
Sanderson, Edmund, 13079
Sanderson, Edmund Lincoln, 12662-12667
Sanderson, Elijah, 11258, 11742
Sanderson, George Augustus, 2610
Sanderson, George W., 8850
Sanderson, Howard Kendall, 9109
Sanderson, Jacob, 11258, 11742
Sandisfield, Mass., 11824-11825
Sandisfield, Mass. Bicentennial Committee, 11825
Sandrof, Ivan, 1544-1545, 13351-13352
Sandsprings, locality in Williamstown
Sandwich, Mass., 1926, 1944, 1968, 2017-2018, 6009,
    6750, 11826-11885
Sandy Bay, Mass., 11153
Sandy Pond, locality in Ayer
Sanford, Edwin G., 1546
Sanford, Enoch, 1547, 3209, 11090-11091
Sanford, William Howe, 6033
Sanford and Kelley (firm), New Bedford, Mass.,
    10144
Sanford's Bound, locality in Westport
Sanger, Chester F., 1548
Sanitation, 5948, 5978, 9402, 13225
Sankaty Bluff, locality in Nantucket
Sanson, Joseph, 9942
Santerre, Richard, 8977-8979
Santuit, locality in Barnstable
Saquis, locality in Plymouth
Sargent, Aaron, 2611, 5386, 12022-12023
Sargent, David W., Jr., 2897
Sargent, George Henry, 5387-5389, 8980
Sargent, Grace L., 9517
Sargent, Horace Binney, 5344
Sargent, John Turner, 5390-5391
Sargent, Louise Peabody, 9518
Sargent, Lucius Manlius, 5392
Sargent, Mary Elizabeth Fiske, 5393, 9519
Sargent, Paul Dudley, 642
Satucket, locality in East Bridgewater
Satuckett, former name of Harwich
Saturday Evening Girls, 5394
Saugus, Mass., 2375, 11886-11906
Saugus, Mass. Board of Trade, 11903
Saugus, Mass. Cliftondale Methodist Church, 11904
Saul, Norman E., 5395
Saunders, Edith St. Loe, 8649
Saunders, Joseph B., 11703-11704
Saunders, Richard, 8018
Saunders, William A., 1549
Saunderson, Henry Hallam, 6683
Saunderson, Laura Dudley, 6684-6685
Saundersville, locality in Grafton
Savage, Edward Hartwell, 5396-5397
Savage, Frederick Schillow, 8217
Savage, James, 1550, 6191
Savage, William H., 12741

Savaryville, locality in Groveland
Saville, Marshall Howard, 2428
Savin Hill, locality in Boston
Savings Bank Life Insurance Council, Boston, 1551
Savoy, Mass., 11907-11908
Sawitzky, William, 7035
Saws, 7797, 7800
Sawtelle, Ithamar Bard, 12525-12526
Sawyer, Alfred P., 1552
Sawyer, Charles Winthrop, 1553
Sawyer, Edith A., 10045
Sawyer, F. E., 11705
Sawyer, Herbert M., 13353
Sawyer, Joseph Dillaway, 1554, 5398
Sawyer, Joseph Henry, 7610
Sawyer, Samuel Elwell, 5399
Sawyer, Timothy Thompson, 5400
Saxe, Abby Drew, 9520
Saxonville, Mass., 2508, 7844
Saxton, F. Willard, 5401
Sayer, William Lawton, 10119
Sayles, Adelaide K. Burton, 5402
Sayward, William, 4386
Scaden, locality in Uxbridge
Scaglion, Richard, 7886
Scaife, Lauriston L., 9717
Scaife, Roger Livingston, 2019
Scales, John, 5403
Scales, 10438
Scalise, Victor F., Jr., 6193
Scanlan, Michael James, 5404, 6876
Scanlon, John J., 12203
Scantic, locality in Hampden
Scargo Hill, locality in Dennis
Scheide, John Hinsdale, 8804
Schell, F. Robert, 10582
Schindler, Solomon, 5406
Schirmer, J. Walter, 10070
Schlesinger, Arthur Meier, 5407
Schlesinger, Elizabeth Bancroft, 6686
Schmeckebier, L. F., 1555
Schofield, George A., 8490
Schofield, Mike, 5408
Schofield, William Greenough, 5409
Scholz, Robert F., 1556
Schools, 83-84, 93, 141, 166, 281, 337, 340, 377,
    460, 496, 505, 789, 851-852, 998, 1098-1102,
    1245, 1406, 1676, 1748, 1835, 2529, 2795, 3172,
    3175, 3183, 3237, 3259, 3283, 3331, 3345, 3369,
    3449, 3570, 3587, 3595, 3620, 3633-3634, 3702-
    3705, 3776, 3978, 4007, 4089, 4099, 4144, 4152,
    4173, 4207, 4234, 4270, 4503, 4541, 4590-4598,
    4661, 4773, 4884, 4933, 4938-4939, 4980, 4982,
    4989, 5039, 5080, 5161, 5188, 5196, 5280, 5299,
    5310, 5366, 5413, 5435, 5450, 5526, 5606, 5804,
    5844, 5850, 5870, 5918, 5941, 6039, 6091, 6166,
    6277, 6546, 6774, 6851, 6918, 6925, 7097, 7134,
    7146, 7158, 7190, 7193, 7198, 7203, 7214, 7251,
    7266, 7282, 7284, 7322, 7370-7372, 7666, 7732,
    7811, 7991, 8134, 8236, 8485, 8487, 8510, 8682,
    8789, 8814, 8839, 8896, 8924, 8952, 8960, 9127,
    9144, 9164, 9273, 9306, 9329, 9331, 9473, 9476,
    9504, 9514, 9524, 9662, 9701, 9851, 9855, 9934,
    9991, 10063, 10326, 10414, 10467-10469, 10477,
    10496, 10502, 10556, 10562, 10704, 10762, 10792,
    10799, 10806, 10888, 11062, 11095, 11173, 11181,
    11252, 11430, 11763, 11795, 11865, 12007-12008,
    12087, 12368, 12380, 12547, 12567, 12591, 12633,